READINGS ON THE SOVIET ECONOMY

READINGS ON THE

SOVIET ECONOMY

Edited by

FRANKLYN D. HOLZMAN
Tufts University

RAND M^cNALLY & COMPANY
CHICAGO

RAND McNALLY ECONOMICS SERIES

Walter W. Heller, *Advisory Editor*

Barger, *Money, Banking, and Public Policy*
Coons, *The Income of Nations and Persons*
Dewey, *Monopoly in Economics and Law*
Holzman, *Readings on the Soviet Economy*
Kurihara, *National Income and Economic Growth*
Spengler and Allen, *Essays in Economic Thought: Aristotle to Marshall*
Whittaker, *Schools and Streams of Economic Thought*

To My Parents

CONTENTS AND ACKNOWLEDGEMENTS

INTRODUCTION

THERE HAS BEEN widespread interest in the Soviet economy ever since the Bolshevik Revolution of November, 1917. The Soviet leaders radically changed the organization of Russian economic activity—introducing objectives, institutions, mechanisms of control, forms of organization, and the like, which, until the development of parallel organizations in eastern Europe and China after World War II, were different from those of all other nations. The opportunity to observe an alternative economic system in action was taken up eagerly by a few Western scholars and a number of interesting articles and monographs appeared during the interwar period.

Interest in the Soviet economy has, if anything, increased with the passage of time. The importance of studying the Soviet economy has also increased; for while it was before World War II an isolated island of complete planning and "socialism," today, as we noted above, the Soviet system has been extended, albeit with some variations, to the nations of eastern Europe and mainland China. Furthermore, because of its impressive record of industrial growth, the Soviet planning model is viewed today as a possible alternative by dozens of underdeveloped nations in Asia, Africa, and Latin America. As a result of the general increase in scholarly activity in recent years, heightened interest in Soviet-type economies has been matched by vastly increased research and publication in this area. Many times more relevant books and articles have been published every year since World War II than was true in the years of the prewar period. Interested persons can no longer obtain the most authoritative available information as they could in the thirties by reading the few general books and articles which had been published. Today the student is confronted with the problem of searching out and choosing among dozens of books and thousands of articles. Many of these are published in esoteric journals and deal with some specialized aspect of the Soviet economy. The relative merits of these sources must often remain conjectural to the nonspecialist.

The present volume is designed to meet these difficulties. Collected under one cover are 41 of the best and most representative articles and extracts from books on the major phases of the Soviet economy. The selections tend to vary in difficulty. A few will be accessible only to graduate students. Most of them, however, can be read with profit in junior and senior courses and by any intelligent person with an interest in how the Soviet economy functions.

For purposes of selection, work on the Soviet economy was subdivided into ten major problem areas, and at least three articles were chosen to illustrate the thinking and research of Western scholars in each area. These problem areas constitute the main subsections of the book as indicated in the Table of Contents. Needless to say, the selection of problem areas, as well as of articles, was necessarily subjective and to some extent arbitrary. From my consultations with experts in the field of Soviet economics, I am convinced that no two persons would ever agree completely on the format or substance of a book of essays of this nature. On the other hand, I am also quite confident that there would not be much disagreement on the choices presented below.

It should also be emphasized that the particular articles chosen do not necessarily represent, in the opinion of the editor, the most important published work in a particular area. Many landmark papers were left out because they either were not comprehensive or up to date, or because they overlapped with other papers included in a particular section.

Other arbitrary decisions had to be made. In confining the articles here reproduced to those written by Western scholars about the Soviet economy, I have excluded both the works of Soviet economists (with one exception) and those of Western scholars on the economies of Soviet bloc nations. The output of articles by Soviet economists has been so vast that even if difficulties had not been compounded by translation requirements, it was immediately obvious that a separate compendium of such essays was appropriate and justified. Furthermore, many of the articles included in this book serve, in effect, as "surveys" of Soviet work permitting economies of space and thereby the inclusion of a wider variety of thought. Considerations of space also dictated the decision to focus on the Soviet economy to the exclusion of other bloc nations.

Both the institutional framework of the Soviet economy and the scope of available information have changed rather dynamically over the past fifteen years. Since, with one exception, the essays contained in this book were photo-offset from the original sources in which they were published, it was not possible to make corrections for recent changes. Some of the authors whose papers are included below have been concerned over the fact that statements they made several years ago are no longer fully accurate. The reader, particularly the specialist, is asked to make due allowance for this fact. Those contributors who wished to indicate shortcomings of this nature, as well as important typographical errors in the originals, were encouraged to do so, and these notes are included in an Appendix at the end of the book. The sum total of such shortcomings, however, is small, and most of the articles included will provide a standard framework of analysis for many years to come.

Each of the ten sections below is preceded by an introduction. These are brief because there is little that the editor can say about each topic which has not already been said better in the reprinted selections. The introductions were nevertheless included for three reasons. First, it was deemed useful to establish the general frame of reference of each section and indicate briefly how the articles selected fit into this framework. Second, the material in many of the articles is relevant to more than one section and the introductions provide a convenient place for cross-referencing. Finally, for those who wish to do further reading, annotated references are made in the introductions to other important writings in each area. These other writings are all contained in a selective Bibliography placed at the end of the book and are identified in the introductions by name of author and year of publication. The Bibliography is subdivided into the same ten sections (plus two additional sections) as the book and contains many other references over and above those mentioned in the introductions.

In selecting the articles for these *Readings*, I consulted frequently with a number of my colleagues in the field of Soviet economics. I would like to take this opportunity to thank them collectively for their advice. I am particularly indebted on this account to Gregory Grossman and to Joseph Berliner, Holland Hunter, and Herbert Levine. I am also indebted, of course, to the authors whose contributions are republished here for promptly granting permission to reprint and to the original publishers who did likewise. Finally, I would like to express my gratitude to the Far Eastern and Russian Institute of the University of Washington for support during part of the period during which these *Readings* were being prepared.

FRANKLYN D. HOLZMAN

Seattle, Washington
June 25, 1961

STATISTICS AND

MEASUREMENT

ANY NATION which is attempting to "plan" its economy must perforce collect large amounts of data about all aspects of economic life in order to have a basis upon which to make decisions. There is no doubt that the Soviet planners have had, since the mid-1920's, such data available to them. While internal statistical reporting undoubtedly increased quantitatively as well as qualitatively over time, the amount of data made available to outsiders has fluctuated sharply with the political climate. Large volumes of statistics were published for public consumption in the late twenties and until 1936. The amount made available began to diminish thereafter, and virtually dried up after the publication in 1939 of the Third Five Year Plan and of a statistical abstract. Both of these volumes were much slimmer than their predecessors. The state of drought remained almost complete until Stalin's death in 1953. Naum Jasny put it very aptly in a talk given in 1951 when he observed that the only statistics in current Soviet economic publications were the page numbers. In 1954 and 1955 a trickle of data appeared. The trickle became a flood in 1956, when the first of literally hundreds of statistical handbooks on virtually every aspect of Soviet society (with a few obvious exceptions) appeared in print and were made generally available.[1] At this writing, there are no signs that the flood is abating.

Because of the absolute censorship exerted by the Soviet government and the relative absence of usual channels for checking reliability, most scholars who have worked on the Soviet economy have regarded Soviet data with considerable suspicion. Two basic issues are involved. First, do the Soviet authorities deliberately falsify data—do they say, for example, that they have produced 50 million tons of steel when they know

[1] These have been listed periodically in the Glasgow journal, *Soviet Studies*, thanks to the efforts of Michael Kaser.

4

that they have produced only 40 million or perhaps 60 million tons? If they do deliberately falsify published information, then the task of the non-Soviet investigator is almost hopeless, since he does not have a basis of fact from which to work. Second, if the data are based on "fact," what are the methodological hurdles, if any, to their use? This can be broken down further into two separate questions: (1) What improper (if any) procedures do the Russians use in collecting, aggregating, and presenting statistical material? (2) What genuine and general methodological problems must be considered in using and interpreting Soviet materials?

Abram Bergson's article summarizes the evidence and general concensus of Western scholars on the problem of deliberate falsification. For a somewhat different view, the reader is referred to Dr. Jasny's pioneering articles (1947, 1950). A recent and very intensive study of Soviet industrial (physical) output statistics is presented by Gregory Grossman (1960).

The second pair of questions are considered by Campbell and Nove (as well as by Professor Bergson). Dr. Nove's paper is concerned with both the improper and genuine methodological problems involved in evaluating the progress of the Soviet economy; Professor Campbell is more concerned with the genuine methodological pitfalls and the often insoluble problems involved in making international comparisons. The pioneering critical study of the Soviet industrial production index is that by Alexander Gerschenkron (1947), with follow-ups by Maurice Dobb (1948) and S. Kasdan (1952).[2] For an interesting theoretical and quantitative study of the inherent difficulties in measuring the rate of growth of industrializing nations, the reader is referred to Professor Gerschenkron's book on Soviet machinery output (1951). A recent and readable elucidation of the problem of international comparisons is the paper by A. S. Becker (1960). Warren Nutter's paper (1957) adds a new and important dimension to the problem of international comparisons of growth rates.

Finally, some of the problems of statistics and measurement are discussed in Section II on the price system and in Section IV, particularly in the papers by Professors Nove and Bornstein.

The Appendix contains a correction to Professor Campbell's article.

[2] The last word in the controversy is yet to be published. New light is shed on the problem in Richard Moorsteen's forthcoming monograph, *Prices and Production of Soviet Machinery, 1927/8–1958,* and in a forthcoming article by Raymond P. Powell on the Soviet industrial production index.

PROBLEMS OF UNITED STATES-SOVIET ECONOMIC COMPARISONS

(By Robert W. Campbell, Department of Economics, University of Southern California)

INTRODUCTION—STATEMENT OF FINDINGS

The purpose of the present paper is to explain in a general way and illustrate with examples some of the most important difficulties involved in making comparisons of the economies of the United States and the Soviet Union. The past decade and a half of research has greatly increased the amount of solid evidence we possess concerning the comparative performance of these two economies. At the same time, however, it has also added greatly to the sophistication of economists concerning the pitfalls that await those who seek to appraise the relative performance of two economies so different as these.

The authors of the substantive comparisons that follow are well aware of these problems and it is not unlikely that some of them will be touched on in the course of the comparisons made. The paper is in no way intended as a critique of their efforts. Nevertheless it seems worth while to give some explicit, prefatory attention to the obstacles that complicate such undertakings. The current world situation has led to widespread recognition by the American people of the need to know more about the relative status of these two economies. Intelligent action on our part in many areas of public policy requires that we know how big Soviet output is in comparison with our own, how effectively the Soviet Union uses its resources by our standards, how fast their output and productivity are increasing, and what allocations the Soviet leaders make of their output.

The following discussion is intended to remind those who ask such questions as these of the limitations on the certainty and precision with which they must content themselves in the answers, and to emphasize the sort of questions they should always raise in evaluating the statistical comparisons offered in answer. By giving separate attention to this subject, it will be possible to make some generalizations about the nature of the problems in a way that is not possible in the substantive comparisons, and to discuss how they can sometimes be dealt with.

The obstacles to United States-Soviet economic comparisons may be said to comprise several distinct orders. It will be helpful to discuss them under three main headings as follows:

    (1) The availability and interpretation of statistical data;
    (2) The index number problems;
    (3) The danger of comparing isolated indicators out of context.

The availability and interpretation of statistical data.—One of the most frustrating problems facing anyone who tries to make United States-Soviet comparisons is in securing the raw materials for his

14   COMPARISONS OF UNITED STATES AND SOVIET ECONOMIES

effort, namely the statistical data.   This difficulty is most often presented by the Soviet side of the comparison rather than the American,
although there are also instances where U.S. data make comparisons
difficult.   The deficiences of Soviet statistics have often been recited.
Although the Soviet system generates a huge volume of statistical
information, the amount actually released by the Government is
limited in amount, the meaning of data in terms of its coverage or
definition is often left unexplained, figures are presented in a misleading way with the aim of serving propaganda purposes or ideological
pretensions.   In many cases, particularly in the case of complex economic indicators, such as output indexes or aggregative magnitudes
the Soviet statements are completely unreliable.

The amount of economic data published by the Soviet Government has varied greatly over time.   In the years before the industrialization drive, and even for some time after the beginning of the 5-year
plans in the early thirties, statistical information was relatively
abundant.   Subsequently, however, it dwindled in amount until
by the end of the thirties only isolated scraps were published.   This
mania for secrecy continued until Stalin's death in 1953.   Since then
the publication policy for statistical information has changed
drastically, and the amount of information released has been greatly
increased.   There have now appeared a larger number of statistical
handbooks; the periodical economic literature has begun to include
some discussion of real problems based on real data.   One now even
finds serious monographs discussing individual aspects of the economy
which contain actual data that has not yet been blessed with the
official imprimatur of release in an official speech or document.   Of
course, the Soviet statistical output is still only a tiny trickle compared
to the mass of economic data that is available for the U.S. half of
economic comparisons.   A suggestive measure of this difference in
volume is found in the size of the major statistical sources concerning
the industry of the two countries.   The Soviet statistical handbook for
industry contains a little less than 35,000 bits of data.

Many of these, however, represent mere recapitulations of absolute
data in percentage form, so that the actual amount of information is
not much over 30,000 bits.[1]   Volume II of the U.S. census of manufactures, by contrast, contains something more of the order of half a
million numbers.   Moreover, the Soviet source completely ignores
a number of important categories of statistics.   As far as the handbook
is concerned, there is no such thing as an industrial labor force or a
nonferrous metals industry, although there are many pages of information on such uninteresting matters as the geographic distribution
of the production of gypsum, lime, brick, slate, tile, and timber.
The distorted perspective of the handbook means that much of the
information it contains is not very useful.   Of course, much additional
statistical information on Soviet industry can be culled from other
Soviet sources, though proportionately these are much less rich
sources than similar ones in the United States.   The example of
industrial statistics is representative of the whole gamut of information and suggests how asymmetrical are the sources of information
underlying comparisons.

A second aspect of the information problem has to do with the
interpretation of the data which the Soviet Government does vouch-

---

[1] "Tsentral'noe Statisticheskoe Upravlenie," Promyshlennost' SSSR, Moscow, 1957.

safe us.   The statistical sources for industry again provide a suggestive comparison.   All the text and explanatory notes in the Soviet handbook would not add up to more than about seven pages, whereas the census of manufactures contains several hundred pages of explanation.   Moreover, in the U.S. source the lavish use of detailed breakdowns helps greatly to clarify the composition and scope of the data.

The importance of clarity in statistical definitions warrants additional explanation.   The difficulty is that it is possible for a notion which appears on the surface to be perfectly straightforward to be defined in a number of different ways and hence ambiguous in meaning unless the scope is clearly stated.   Many of these apparently simple concepts actually have a number of dimensions that make alternative definitions conceivable.   When one sets out to embody even such a notion as the output of electric power in numbers drawn from the actual workings of an economy, decisions must be made as to what producers will be included, at what point output will be measured, and so forth.   This point can be illustrated with examples drawn from an actual exercise in comparison.   Suppose that it is desired to compare the total industrial output of the United States with that of the Soviet Union, and it is decided to approach this problem by determining the relative outputs for as exhaustive a list of commodities as we can manage.   The final step would be to weight these separate comparisons of output by some notion of the relative importance of each commodity (such as value added or employment) to obtain a single index expressing the overall relative output.   In table I a few of the commodities that would be included in such a comparison have been listed and columns (1) and (2) show the outputs of these commodities in each country as given in the Soviet industrial handbook, and the Statistical Abstract of the United States.   Column (3) shows the ratio of Soviet output to U.S. output.

TABLE I.—*Comparison of selected commodity outputs in the United States and Soviet Union*

	Year	Unit of measure	United States	U.S.S.R.	U.S.S.R. as percent of United States
Electric power	1957	Billion kilowatt-hours	716.0	209.5	29.3
Coal	1956	Million short tons	529.8	472.1	89.1
Cotton cloth	1957	Million linear yards	9,563.0	6,119.0	64.0
Oil	1956	Million metric tons	364.0	83.8	23.0
Natural gas	1956	Billion cubic feet	10,082.0	483.0	4.8
Lumber	1957	Million board-feet	37,698.0	32,204.0	85.4

The specialist on the Soviet economy will immediately suggest many corrections that will have to be made in these numbers before they can be used as the raw material for a comparison of industrial output.   For example, the first item on the list—electric power—is defined in the Soviet Union as the total output of power produced by the generators, gross of the amounts used or lost within the generating plant itself, whereas the U.S. figure is net of this amount.   Fortunately the Russians tell us how much of the power generated goes for the needs of the stations themselves, so that it is possible to correct the Soviet figure to U.S. terms in this dimension.   When the correction is made, it changes the comparison markedly, reducing Soviet output from 29.3 percent of U.S. output to 27.5 percent. There are uncertainties in some other dimensions as well, however. In both countries electric power is produced both by specialized utility plants, and by industrial plants for their own use. The output of most of these nonutility plants is included in the total for both countries, but the cutoff point is apparently not the same in both cases. For the United States the output of industrial plants covers only those with a capacity of 100 kilowatts and over, but it is clear from the statistics in Promyshlennost' SSSR, page 176, that the Soviet figure includes the production of plants much smaller than this. This difference again involves an appreciable fraction of output—namely, about 2.1 percent of total Soviet output in 1955.

For coal, the next item in the list, even cursory examination of the sources raises a suspicion that there may be an important difference in coverage. The U.S. figure is defined as mine shipments, mine sales, or marketable production, including consumption by producers. This seems to imply that it is measured after preparatory processes such as cleaning and sorting, and one breakdown in the Statistical Abstract of the United States gives a figure of 58.7 percent as the percentage of total production mechanically cleaned. The Soviet figure, on the other hand, may well involve measurement before these processes. Some 26 percent of Soviet coal output was sent to beneficiation plants in 1955, and in the process underwent a reduction in volume of 11.9 percent. So total output after processing was 3.08 percent less than the figure shown in table I. A second difference is that the U.S. figure for bituminous coal output covers mines with an annual output of 1,000 tons or more. It seems probable that the Soviet total would not make such an exclusion, though there are no data to indicate how important this difference in scope would be.

This possible divergence in the meaning of the coal figure also serves as a reminder that even though the output of many commodities is measured in physical units, comparison in these terms may be deceptive, since the commodity may not be at all homogenous with respect to quality or some other dimension. This problem becomes most important when one is dealing with highly fabricated products, but is also serious even with commodities which seem to have easily indentifiable physical measures, such as those in table I. For instance, the figures on output of cotton cloth, given in table I in lineal yards as commonly measured in the statistics of both countries, are not at all comparable, since the average width of cotton goods produced in the United States is slightly over 40 inches, whereas it is slightly under 30 inches in the Soviet Union.

In the case of coal and electric power, the explanations in Soviet statistical sources are clear enough to make one aware of the differences in concept, though for neither country are the data detailed enough to permit bringing both figures to a common concept. For many commodities, however, the degree of comparability cannot be so easily ascertained. Output figures for the next two items on the list, i.e., oil and natural gas, are easily found in Soviet sources, but when U.S. sources are consulted for comparable data, it turns out that the petroleum extraction industry has another important output, namely, natural gasoline and natural gas liquids, equal in volume to about 10 percent of the crude oil output. These products are undoubtedly much less important in Soviet operations but must surely exist. Since they are not mentioned in the statistical source, one wonders whether they are perhaps included somehow in the oil output figure.

The notion of lumber output appears superficially to be a fairly simple idea, and the fact that the figures for both the United States and the Soviet Union are expressed in terms of physical volume is comforting.   But even the briefest survey of U.S. statistical sources will disclose a number of alternative figures for lumber output differing slightly from each other in concept and accordingly in amount.   To which of these concepts does the Soviet figure correspond?   Moreover, if the breakdown given in the census of manufactures are examined a number of possible differences in concept immediately suggest themselves.   The U.S. output figures cover sawmills and planing mills, and includes both rough and finished lumber.   Since the U.S. figures are collected on an establishment basis, there is probably some double counting of lumber sawed in one plant and finished in another.   To what extent is this true of the Soviet total?   Furthermore, suppose a Soviet enterprise both rough-saws and finishes lumber; is its output measured in terms of the volume of the finished or unfinished wood? Careful study may succeed in unearthing answers to these questions, but the answers are not at all obvious from the statistical sources themselves, from handbooks on industrial statistical procedure or from the more generally available books dealing with the economics, planning, and administration of the lumber industry.

It should be admitted that definitions are not always presented along with statistics in the more general U.S. statistical publications. Nevertheless it is almost always possible to find in easily accessible sources detailed explanations of what a given statistic covers and how it has been derived.   The difficulty of doing this for the U.S.S.R. often introduces an air of uncertainty into comparisons such as those in table I.

The existence of differences between the concepts underlying Soviet and U.S. economic data should not be surprising.   Comparison of the statistics of any two countries will always reveal similar inconsistencies.   They flow out of differences in the organization of the economy, different statistical traditions, divergent preoccupations among those who collect statistics.   Statistics are often a byproduct of some concern other than economic analysis and their definition is controlled in part by competing objectives and expediencies.   What is peculiar to Soviet statistical practice, however, is the great premium which the Russians place on the propaganda use of economic indicators, and in the service of this end concepts are sometimes deliberately defined in a misleading way.   This propaganda objective is one of the explanations for their secretiveness concerning the actual definitions of the statistical material they publish.   The propaganda uses of Soviet economic statistics also mean that definitions are sometimes changed to mask failure or exaggerate gains.   The most infamous example of such a change is the shift from the "barn yield" concept to the "biological yield" concept of grain output in the thirties, adopted to make grain output appear larger than it actually was. Even though it was possible to find out from Soviet sources that this change in definition had been made, the appropriate correction to achieve comparability with a barn-yield concept remained unknown. Not until Khrushchev's speech to the plenary session of the Central Committee in December 1958, was it revealed precisely how great the difference was. The figures he cited for 1952, i.e., barn yield as 30 percent less than the biological yield, involved a bigger difference than had commonly been estimated. A more recent example of the subversion of intertemporal and international comparability to propaganda objectives is the change in the definitions of meat and milk output. Khrushchev has made catching up with the United States in meat and milk production one of the important goals of his agricultural program, and to make the fulfillment of this goal easier, the scope of the definitions of meat and milk output has been broadened beyond past definitions and beyond the American concepts.

The examples discussed so far all involve a very simple class of economic magnitudes, namely, physical outputs. The possible differences in concept that can confound comparison in such cases are multiplied many fold when one turns to more complex statistical indicators. Any attempt at qualification of such complicated concepts as gross national product accounts, labor force and employment statistics, or output indexes, offers so many conceivable alternatives in conceptualization, and involves so many expediencies in implementing the concept with data, that it may be impossible to make any reasonably accurate reconciliation of the actual numbers that the statistical systems of the two countries actually generate. The Soviet concept of national income is far different from that accepted in most capitalist countries, for instance. Although we know in a general way many of the differences between the United States and Soviet concepts in this case, there are still many unanswered questions concerning the Soviet definitions, such as how they make the division of total output into an "accumulation fund" and a "consumption fund," for example. For many of these complicated indicators, the differences in concept and the uncertainty of interpretation are so great that economists outside the Soviet Union have traditionally rejected Soviet data and resorted to independent calculations from basic data.

Deficiencies in the statistical raw materials on which comparisons are based are not confined to the Soviet Union. There are also cases where the U.S. side of a comparison may be obscure. Inventory statistics may be cited as a single illustration. Recent data on Soviet inventories have included a number of breakdowns that make it possible to ascertain fairly well the range of items that are included in the Soviet inventory concept, and our knowledge of Soviet accounting practices makes it possible to state more or less precisely how inventory values are calculated. In many ways the U.S. inventory figures [2] are more detailed than the Soviet ones, but variations in the accounting practices of individual firms makes it impossible to state with certainty just how comprehensive these figures are in terms of the items included and the basis of valuation. It may well be that there is a difference in the scope of the inventory concept and as a result comparisons using these data may be misleading.

Finally, it frequently happens that the concepts relevant to some comparison in which we are vitally interested are not well enough defined to be embodied very satisfactorily in actual statistical data in either country. The vagueness of what is being measured means that the definitions used in generating the data are chosen somewhat

[2] For an explanation of the uncertainties involved in the meaning of U.S. inventory statistics, see George M. Cobren, "The Nonfarm Business Inventory Component," in National Bureau of Economic Research Studies in Income and Wealth, vol. XII, pp. 381–400.

arbitrarily. For example, speculation about the relative efforts of the United States and the Soviet Union in science and in research has recently become a popular enterprise in economic comparison. As one of the main ingredients of technical progress both in military and civilian applications, the amount of research is supposed to be a powerful influence on our respective power and growth possibilities. The Russians, incidentally, are also interested in this comparison. In the United States, this aspect of national economic activity has been labeled research and development, and some statistics purporting to show how many dollars worth of research and development are being carried out have been published in recent years. These statistics have been strongly criticized, however, as arbitrary in definition and vague in meaning. After all, this is a very new concept and effort, and those who report such expenditures at the local level face many unsettled questions in deciding how much research and development their firm does.

The Russians call this activity science, and in the past few years Soviet leaders have quoted a figure showing a global total for this magnitude. This Soviet figure, however, represents more a reflection of certain budgetary and administrative conventions than any well-defined concept of effort devoted to the expansion of knowledge and improvement of technology. The uncertainty in any comparison of the Soviet and American research efforts, therefore, is not so much due to the fact that the specific content of the respective ruble and dollar amounts differs, as to the fact that neither of these amounts measures very exactly just what we would like to measure.

The discussion above has concentrated on the obstacles to obtaining comparable statistical raw materials as a basis for comparative studies of the United States and Soviet economies. To restore a balanced perspective, it should be added in concluding this section that most of these problems can be dealt with tolerably well. Finding data and establishing their meaning is the expected task of any economist who sets out to make comparisons of the two economies. Given experience and enough time he can usually settle such issues as those described with an acceptable margin of error. These are obstacles that will succumb to knowledge, and the recent increase in Soviet statistical output is beginning to clarify some former mysteries. So far, however, the problem has only been ameliorated, not eliminated. When a researcher is unable to deal with some data problem satisfactorily, he has a duty to present his figures with an appropriate statement of reservations. Similarly, those who make use of the comparative studies that are made must know that such problems exist, that they cannot always be settled completely satisfactorily, and that comparisons made in this situation are always subject to some qualifications. Hence, they should always ask for the qualifications and alternative interpretations along with the answers.

The index number problem.—The second order of obstacles to international economic comparisons comprises a number of variants of what is known as the index number problem. These obstacles differ from those discussed earlier by the fact that they do not result simply from ignorance but rather from a number of unanswered, and perhaps unanswerable questions of theory and conceptualization. They are therefore more intractable than those discussed in the previous section. The index number problem arises whenever one tries to compare relatively large aggregates either between countries or over time.   Most of the questions which international economic comparisons are designed to answer involve the comparative measurement of such large aggregates.   The question of relative American and Soviet economic strength, for example, is usually posed as the size of Soviet output relative to our own, as measured by some indicator such as gross national product.   Or people may ask for comparisons of smaller but still very heterogeneous components of this aggregate.   It is common, for example to ask how well off the average Soviet consumer or industrial worker is relative to his opposite number in the United States. Those who are responsible for making U.S. defense policy would like to know how the Soviet military effort compares with our own in terms of its overall size.   Making comparisons in these aggregative terms is the only way to escape getting lost in a host of contradictory details.

Economic aggregates such as those listed above can be measured only in value terms.   The diverse physical goods and services encompassed in American or Soviet gross national product can be expressed in a single figure only through using the common denominator of monetary value.   Hence, if it is desired to compare Soviet and American gross national product it is necessary to find some conversion factor, some exchange rate, that permits one to translate the rubles of one into the dollars of the other, or vice versa.   Unfortunately, however, it so happens that the value of a ruble, expressed in how many dollars worth of output can be bought with it, varies markedly depending on the kind of product or service that is being considered. The structure of relative prices in the two countries is very different, so that the value of a ruble compared to a dollar is far greater in the purchase of some items than of others.   This difference between the Soviet and American price structure is the result of many separate factors, including differences in the scarcities of the resources going into different commodities, the differential degree to which the Russians have caught up with American technology in different sectors of the economy, and the peculiarities of Soviet accounting, pricing, and fiscal practices.   Hence any even moderately aggregative magnitude contains components for which the appropriate dollar-ruble conversion ratios diverge widely.   The problem is to find an average ratio appropriate to the conversion of the aggregate we are interested in. The approach that springs immediately to mind is to average the individual conversion ratios, weighted by the relative importance of the various components of the aggregate.

The problem, however, is that the relative importance of the components is different in the two countries.   As a result, there is a choice of weighting patterns and a choice of conversion ratios.   The problem can be illustrated by the simple numerical example shown in the following table, in which the gross national product of two countries is compared.   This example outrages reality in assuming that all gross national product is directed either to consumption or to military purposes, but this oversimplification makes the nature of the problem easier to see.   We have called the two countries the United States and the Soviet Union, although the magnitudes shown for the gross national product and its components in each case are completely arbitrary.   The proportions between consumption and military uses, however, and the implied difference in the price structures of the two countries are plausible reflections of reality. Columns (1) and (2) show the composition of the gross national product in each country measured in its own prices. Column (3) shows the value of a ruble in dollars in the purchase of the goods included in the respective components of the gross national product. Using these figures as conversion ratios, it is possible to calculate the size of each country's gross national product in the currency of the other. The results are shown in columns (4) and (5). There are now enough totals so that the gross national product can be compared either in dollars or in rubles, but a glance at the figures shows that the result will not be the same for both comparisons. When the output of both countries is measured in United States prices, Soviet output appears to be one-third as large as that of the United States, but if a comparison is made in Soviet prices, Soviet output turns out to be only 28.5 percent of American.

TABLE II.—*Schematic illustration of the index number problem*

	U.S.S.R. (in billion rubles)	United States (in billion dollars)	Conversion rate (dollars per ruble)	U.S.S.R. (in billion dollars)	United States (in billion rubles)
	(1)	(2)	(3)	(4)	(5)
Consumption	100	40	.10	10	400
Military expenditure	20	5	.25	5	20
Total	120	45	------------	15	420

NOTE.—Soviet output as a percentage of United States output:
In rubles: 120÷420=28.6 percent.
In dollars: 15÷45=33.3 percent.

What is the reason for this difference in the two answers? A rigorous explanation would involve going into the complexities of index number construction, but the essence of the mechanism at work can be explained as follows. Pricing in rubles is equivalent to converting total gross national product at an exchange rate of 10.71 cents per ruble, 10.71 being the average of the separate ruble-dollar price ratios, weighted in proportion to the relative magnitudes of the components of U.S. gross national product as they would look to a Russian. Valuation in dollars, on the other hand, amounts to the use of a conversion ratio of 12.5 cents per ruble, 12.5 being the average of 10 and 25, weighted by the relative importance of consumption and military expenditures as they would look to one accustomed to American prices.

The same mechanism can also be explained in somewhat different terms though with equivalent meaning. In the U.S. price system, consumer goods are priced cheaper relative to military goods than in the Soviet price system. We have indicated this difference in price structure in table II in an approximate illustrative way by the exchange rates shown in column (3). These conversion rates imply that a dollar's worth of consumer goods would be worth 10 rubles in the Soviet Union, but a dollar's worth of military goods would be worth only 4 rubles. Ruble valuation of the output of either country will therefore magnify the significance of the consumption component of its gross national product and diminish the significance of the military component, compared with valuation in dollars. Since the composition of Soviet gross national product differs from the U.S. pattern by its relatively higher emphasis on military expenditure, it will look bigger relative to the U.S. total when both are seen in the light of a price system which prices military goods relatively high and consumption goods relatively low (i.e., the dollar price system) than in the light of one that has high prices for consumer goods and low prices for military goods (the ruble price system).

This ambiguity of answers in international comparisons is not uncommon. Whenever the price structures and the composition of aggregates vary between countries, different answers about the relative size of the aggregates will be obtained, depending on which country's prices are used. The greater the differences in price relationships and in composition, the greater will be the difference between the alternative answers. There are appreciable differences between the alternative measures of relative size of gross national product even when the U.S. is compared with countries with relatively high productivity and modern technologies such as Great Britain or Germany.[3] When comparisons are attempted between the United States and countries where allocation and price structures are more radically different, such as Italy or the Soviet Union, the degree of indeterminacy is even greater.

What guidance can be offered the person who finds that the answer to his simple question about the relative size of the United States and Soviet economies is given in the form of an indeterminate range? In terms of the example in table II, is the figure of 33.3 percent or 28.6 percent the "correct" figure for the size of the Soviet gross national product relative to our own? The answer to this puzzle turns on the fact that the two numbers represent answers to two different questions. The comparison made in rubles (i.e., the one showing the Soviet gross national product as 28.6 percent of American) answers the question "How big is Soviet output?" if it is assumed that it was as hard for them to produce a given collection of consumer goods relative to, say, a missile, as in the United States. The figure of 33.3 percent answers the question "How big was it?" if we assume that in the United States a given basket of consumer goods was priced as high relative to a missile as in the Soviet Union. One might argue that neither of these questions is "realistic." The relative prices of consumer goods and military goods are not the same in both countries. The questioner did not intend it should be pretended they were when he asked how big Soviet output was relative to ours. This is perhaps true enough, but the researcher is forced to such expediencies in trying to make the comparison at all. The problem is that what appeared on the face of it to be a straightforward question; namely, "How big is Soviet output relative to our own?" really begs important issues, issues which the statistician must settle explicitly when he gets down to the mechanics of formulating a numerical answer. And though one may object that the way the statisticians have traditionally settled these issues (i.e., by seeing Soviet output in the light of U.S. value relationships or U.S. output in terms of Soviet scarcity relationships), he will find it difficult to suggest any more satisfactory approach. In a fundamental sense the two aggregates are not directly comparable, and the traditional approach has

[3] See Milton Gilbert & Associates, "Comparative National Products and Price Levels," Paris, 1958, OEEC, for illustrations of the differences that alternative pricing makes in comparing U.S. output with some countries of Western Europe.

at least the virtue of marking out the limits that one might reasonably wish to set conceptually.

The above example is only one variant of the index number problem; even when comparisons involve much smaller aggregates than gross national product the same difficulty arises. In the numerical example of table II, for instance, it was assumed that a ruble is worth 10 cents in the purchase of consumption goods and 25 cents in buying the inputs of a military program. But how can a conversion ratio for such a component of gross national product be arrived at in the first place? Each of these aggregates (i.e., consumption and military expenditures) is itself a heterogeneous collection of goods and services, the composition of which varies between the two countries. Furthermore, the purchasing power of a ruble in terms of dollars is very different as between, say shelter and bread or between the maintenance of a soldier and the building of a missile. This means that one would have to choose among alternative weighting systems in order to compute conversion ratios for the separate components of gross national product before the problem of gross national product comparison could even be formulated as in table II. The existence of a range of possible values for the conversion ratio applicable to consumption or to military goods means that the range between the extremes of relative gross national product magnitudes would be even greater.

Another well-known variant of the index number problem arises in the calculation of rates of growth of various economic magnitudes such as industrial output, consumption levels, labor productivity, or others. In such problems it is necessary to determine the relative size of a given aggregate (e. g., consumption or industrial output) at two different points in time. Characteristically, the composition and the price structures for such aggregates change over time. (In the Soviet Union the changes in composition and price relationships have been exceptionally great.) The problem is formally identical with that of international comparisons of aggregates, and the same indeterminacy arises. In this case, however, there are good grounds for arguing that extremes at the ends of the range of possible answers flowing from different weighting systems can be ignored and something like the geometric mean of the extremes taken as an acceptable measure of the rate of growth. The sharp difference in weighting patterns chosen from points far distant in time is a function of how far apart the terminal dates of the comparison are. By looking at shorter periods, the changes in structure and price relationships are found to be less important, and the range of estimates of growth is greatly reduced.

What implications does the index number problem hold for those who seek to make reliable comparisons of the United States and Soviet economies? (1) First, the existence of this problem allows a certain degree of subjective latitude to the person making a comparison. In comparing aggregates, or in measuring rates of growth in each system he has a choice of many alternative weighting systems, with no clearly, defined theory to indicate that one of them is better than the other. Despite this uncertainty, however, it is more or less customary to present answers as if they could be expressed in a single number. This is what we are accustomed to in statistical measures of our own economic performance, and those who ask for economic comparisons in the first place expect exact answers. People who want to determine policy on the basis of comparative studies that are made should take a somewhat critical point of view toward whatever numbers they are offered, and must understand how certain decisions made in the course of the calculations are reflected in the results. A corollary implication is that they should not fix on any one extreme figure among the many that are presented, but be prepared to think in terms of a range.

(2) A second implication is that the vagueness which flows from the index number problem can often be reduced somewhat by greater purposiveness in the comparisons that are made. As the one who asks for a comparison makes his question more precise and defines its purpose more clearly, it will generally be possible to find a reasonable basis for choosing among alternatives in concept and in weighting systems. Global comparisons such as the relative size of United States and Soviet total output have their uses, and there are good and sufficient reasons why they will continue to be made.

However, it often turns out that such comparisons are only a prelude to some more specific comparisons that the questioner is really interested in. For instance one common objective is to determine the relative economic power of the two countries in some sense, say their ability to support military programs, or their capability to engage in foreign trade and extend foreign aid. To answer such a question, it is tempting to take a figure on Soviet GNP in dollars from somewhere, apply to it the percentage share going to military purposes, perhaps from some other study, and get two figures expressed in dollars. Such a procedure is treacherous. At best it can give a very indeterminate answer. Choosing from the extremes at either end of the figures available for GNP in dollars and the share devoted to military purposes, one can get an absurdly wide range of estimates of Soviet military spending in dollars. This approach is at its worst when the figure on the percentage of GNP devoted to military uses comes from a calculation different in concept from the one underlying the total accepted for GNP. If the question is about relative size of the military effort, then it is much more useful to make this comparison directly. This makes it possible to work with smaller aggregates, which are less heterogeneous as far as price relatives and composition are concerned than GNP as a whole. The degree of vagueness inherent in the index number problem is therefore reduced. The latter approach may also stimulate one to think out more clearly just how to measure the power created by a given military budget, and suggest principles for adding up Soviet men and hardware for comparison with American that are more reasonable than those implicit but not clearly understood in the roundabout method of applying a percentage to a GNP figure in dollars.

Another common exercise in these comparisons is to ask how soon the Russians will catch up with us in GNP or in some element of it such as industrial output. By estimating the relative size of the chosen economic indicator at the present time, and then projecting each of them forward at some rate of growth a date for the Russian catching up emerges. Because of the wide range of relative sizes that one can start with, and the wide choice of growth rates (reflecting in both cases the index number problem) it is possible to determine a period for the catching up process varying from a decade and a half to four or five decades. What is the purpose of a question that cannot be answered more definitely than that?   Part of the indeterminacy comes from the fact that it is not clear what the comparison is aimed to show.   If the question one ultimately wants to answer is something like "how soon will Soviet machinery output be great enough to cover a program of investment, trade, and military expenditure such as ours, then it might be more nearly answerable with an acceptable degree of exactness.

Dangers in comparing isolated indicators out of context.—The third order of obstacles to meaningful comparisons of the American and Soviet economies involves the possibility of misinterpreting fairly specific indicators through ignoring important features of the context. If the index number problem makes the comparison of large aggregates difficult, at the other extreme differences in organization, in technology, and in resource availabilities often make comparisons of very narrowly defined magnitudes or overly specific indicators misleading.   The Soviet and American economies differ from each other markedly in administrative structure, in the resource endowment within which each must operate, and in technology.   Consequently the significance of a given economic indicator often varies between them.

In their zeal to make some comparison appear better than it really is. the Russians are frequently guilty of overlooking such differences. For instance Khrushchev has worked hard to make expansion of Soviet per capita butter production to the U.S. level a symbol of catching up with the United States in general.   Apart from the question of differing attitudes of the two populations toward fats in their diets, this comparison overlooks the fact that butter production in the United States is supplemented by an output of margarine 3 percent greater than the production of butter itself, whereas in the Soviet Union the output of margarine is only 70 percent of butter output.[4]

Another such prestige output which they have elevated to the status of a symbol is the output of sugar.   Soviet propagandists are fond of comparing sugar output in the two countries.   For instance, in one of the standard statistical handbooks for agitators,[5] the production of sugar in the two countries is shown as 17 kilograms in the Soviet Union and 12 kilograms in the United States.   This figure appears to be accurate enough as far as it goes, but what it fails to mention is that while Soviet sugar output is augmented by imports only to the extent of about 2 percent, U.S. domestic output is far overshadowed by imports so that per capita consumption is more nearly 45 kilograms than 12.[6]

Another common example is the preoccupation with individual commodity outputs, such as steel or electric power output, as general indicators of "industrial base," which in turn is thought of as being some indicator of relative Soviet military potential, or ability to implement other strategic objectives such as foreign aid capital accumulation or growth.   What this comparison overlooks is the radically different pattern of consumption of these two products in the two countries.   Consumer goods, such as automobiles and home

[4] These figures are taken from Statistical Abstract of the United States, 1958 edition, pp. 674 and 681, and V. P. Zotov, Pishchevaia promyshlennost' Sovetskogo Soiuza, Moscow, 1958, pp. 169–170.
[5] I. A. Ioffe, Strany sotsializma i kapitalizma v. tsifrakh, (The Countries of Socialism and Capitalism in Figures) Moscow, 1957.
[6] These figures are from Statistical Abstract of the United States, p. 671, V. P. Zotov, Pishchevaia promyshlennost' SSSR, p. 170, and Ministerstvo Vneshnei torgovli SSSR, Vneshniaia torgovlia Soiuza SSR za 1957 god, Moscow, 1958, pp. 21 and 33.

appliances take a vastly higher proportion of United States, than of Soviet steel output. Similarly with electric power output; the Soviet output of 231 billion kilowatt-hours in 1957 compared to the American output of 716 billion kilowatt-hours seems to suggest that the productive capacity of the Soviet economy must be strongly restricted by the lack of this vital ingredient of productivity. Again, however, the pattern of utilization is very different. Only a tiny fraction of Soviet power output goes for such uses as household consumption, and municipal and commercial lighting, whereas a very large share of U.S. power output is devoted to these purposes. Hence it is erroneous to consider the relative outputs as a reliable indicator of industrial power.

One of the common areas of concern for people who are making these comparisons is the productivity of the Soviet economy, that is the amount of output they get per unit of the resources at their disposal. The rationale of such comparisons is a belief that productivity has something to do with the relative efficiency of the two economies. Here, however, a different context of technology and of resource endowments greatly beclouds the meaning of specific productivity comparisons. One of the most commonly studied indicators is labor productivity. Such studies always show that output per Soviet worker in any area of the economy is considerably below output per worker in the United States. The Russians themselves claim that output per worker in industry is about half the U.S. level, although this is the kind of comparison that is suspect because of the index number problem discussed earlier. The calculation presupposes some estimate of the relative size of United States and Soviet industrial output, and the great variety of possible weighting schemes means that such comparisons have to be examined very skeptically. In a number of individual branches of the economy, where it is possible to find more or less homogeneous physical measures of output, output per worker can be easily enough compared, however. The result of such comparisons is to show a great range of comparative labor productivity, but despite the variation from case to case, such comparisons show clearly that output per worker is far lower in the Soviet Union than in the United States.

It is but a short step from comparisons such as these to the conclusions that the Soviet economy is extremely wasteful and inefficient. This is a conclusion that is often drawn, but one that is by no means warranted on the evidence of comparative labor productivity. In general this low labor productivity is far less a reflection of inefficiency or waste than of the different resource situation confronting the Russian planners, a resource situation fundamentally different from ours. Soviet industrialization has taken place against the background of an abundance of manpower. The planners have faced a situation where it was never any problem to secure additional labor. The real difficulty was in finding the capital to create new capacity, new factories in which the labor could be employed. It was therefore economically sensible for them to use labor lavishly, substituting it whenever possible for capital goods, and bringing in more workers whenever it was possible by doing so to squeeze a bit more output out of existing enterprises. The result of such a policy was to make output per worker low, but it was still the correct thing to do in the light of the abundance of labor.

The low productivity of the Soviet industrial labor force can be explained alternatively as the low level of mechanical assistance which the Soviet worker has at his disposal. A good summary indicator of the amount of mechanical power which the worker has to assist him in doing his job is the amount of electrical power consumed per worker. Consumption of electric power per industrial worker in the Soviet Union is less than half the American level, and this factor alone goes a long way toward explaining why Soviet industrial labor productivity is so much below ours. It should be emphasized, again, however, that the failure of the Soviet planners to supply their workers with as much mechanical assistance as American workers enjoy does not necessarily imply a mistake in planning. Given the population situation and the amount of capital that could be accumulated, the Soviet planners have found that they could expand the industrial labor force much more easily than they could build more generating plants and other power facilities to increase the mechanical assistance provided for the worker.

The difference in resource endowments distorts other indicators in the opposite direction. Because of the intensive utilization of capacity the output per machine or per other unit of capital is much higher than in the United States. One of the best known examples is the high productivity of capital in Soviet railroad transportation. The Russians have a much higher output of freight turnover per mile of track and per freight car than we do in the United States—something over three times as much freight turnover per mile of track and almost three times as much freight turnover per ton of freight car capacity. Another industry in which Soviet equipment productivity is much higher is in blast furnace operation. Measuring the blast furnace capacity by the total internal volume of the blast furnace and output in tons, in turns out that the Russians get on the average 1.25 tons of pig iron per cubic meter of blast furnace capacity, whereas American producers get only 0.92 ton. It should be added that the productivity of blast furnaces is a function of their size, with larger furnaces being appreciably more productive per cubic meter of space than small furnaces are. Since American furnaces are rather larger on the average than Soviet furnaces, the higher productivity of Soviet furnaces is all the more notable.

Soviet economists are very fond of making such comparisons of capital productivity and concluding that they prove the greater efficiency of their economic system and the chaotic wastefulness of capitalism. This conclusion is as dubious as the reverse one that we sometimes make on the basis of labor productivity comparisons. The high rate of utilization of capital equipment makes sense for the Soviet Union but not for the United States. The relative abundance and cheapness of capital in this country makes it rational for a firm to provide itself generously with capacity.

The argument above should not be understood as implying that the American and Soviet systems are equally efficient in making use of the different resource endowments which each enjoy. The point is rather that the difference in relative scarcities of the basic factors of production makes productivity comparisons a very ambiguous kind of evidence on this score, though superficially they seem so suggestive of relative efficiencies. To what extent the difference in some productivity indicator is evidence of inefficiency and to what extent a reflection of different resource availabilities is a question that can be answered with certainty, if at all, only by a detailed scrutiny of many other aspects of the context.

Even when the influence of such radically different scarcity relationships is absent, more subtle differences in the parameters which confront decision makers and in technology may mean that technological indicators must be interpreted carefully. For instance in a comparative study of the electric power industry of the two countries, one question that would immediately draw attention to itself would be the expenditure of fuel per kilowatt-hour of electric power produced. The electric power industry is engaged essentially in the transformation of the heat energy of fuel into electric energy, and so this ratio is an important indicator of its technological perfection. There is no particular statistical problem to such a comparison—this is an important operating indicator used in the planning and administration of the electric power industry and it is a statistic the Russians collect and publish. Data of the same form can easily be calculated for the U.S. power industry. But as the comparison of the two industries went further, it would soon be found that one of the important differences between the United States and Soviet power industries is that Soviet generating equipment includes an appreciable proportion of installations in which some of the waste heat is captured and used for heating purposes. The generation of electric power inevitably involves the loss of some heat—it is impossible to convert all the energy in the fuel into electrical energy. The Russians use a considerable amount of this heat. Americans use it very little. In computing the fuel consumption per kilowatt-hour of electric power, the Russians assign a significant amount of the fuel burned in power stations (i.e., about 16 percent) to the heating operations.[7]

When it comes to choosing a fuel expenditure ratio for comparison with the American should one use the one cited by the Russians or one corrected to include all fuel burned in electric power stations? There are objections to either alternative. There would be little justification for basing the comparison on the total fuel burned since the Russians are correct in implying that this fuel is not one of the costs of power. It is true that most of this heat could not be converted to electric power even if they did not have the alternative use for it. Nevertheless they do have a use for it, and have made a choice of equipment which will permit them to capture it and avoid burning fuel in conventional installations for heating purposes. In the light of the alternatives open to them, then they are correct in saying that part of the fuel is really chargeable to heating rather than power generation. On the other hand we hesitate to use the Soviet fuel expenditure ratio as they present it because of doubts about the correctness of the amount of the fuel they assign to heating. The allocation between the two purposes is made on the basis of an engineering convention rather than on the basis of what a sophisticated economist would consider correct. What it comes down to is that the power industry in the two countries employs two slightly different technologies, and as a result fuel expenditure per kilowatt-hour of power is an indicator with a slightly different meaning in the two countries. Even apart from this difficulty, other qualifications would have to be considered before this indicator could be taken as a measure

---

[7] This percentage can be calculated from data given in Promyshlennost' S.S.S.R.

of the relative efficiency of the Soviet Union and American power industries. Fuel expenditure per kilowatt-hour is a function of various design parameters of the equipment, such as the temperature and pressure of the steam. Rational decisions on these parameters are very sensitive to the costs of fuel relative to costs of the other inputs that go into the original construction and the operation of generating stations. Hence relatively small differences in price structure might mean that rational or "efficient" decisions would result in a different fuel expenditure ratio in the two countries.

A final illustration of the treacheries of comparing economic indicators torn from different contexts is provided by investment in the two countries. It has been a commonplace to explain the rapid rate of growth of the Soviet economy as flowing in part from the high rate of investment in the Soviet Union. The Soviet planners have been able to keep down consumption levels and in consequence devote a larger share of current output to building new production capacity than the United States does. To embody this argument in statistics, one commonly resorts to a comparison of the share of GNP devoted to investment purposes. Once attention is focused on this mode of analysis, actual statistical comparisons of investment in absolute terms or as a share of GNP are productive of considerable confusion. Investment as a percentage of GNP turns out to be not so radically different in the two countries, and this bolsters the suspicion that maybe the Soviet economy is not growing as fast as we have been led to believe. It also prompts the comforting thought that if small reallocations of Soviet GNP away from investment should take place the Russians will lose whatever advantage relative to the U.S. economy they may have had in the past. This confusion comes from focusing attention on gross investment as an explanation of growth rather than net investment which is the concept that covers the net additions to productive capacity. We have traditionally emphasized gross rather than net investment in our national income accounting and analysis because of the difficulty of measuring net investment meaningfully, and indeed for some international comparisons gross investment might serve well enough. Because the Soviet and American economies are so different with respect to the size and age of their capital stock and the rate of growth, however, the share of gross investment that represents real net additions to productive capacity is much greater for the Soviet Union than for the United States.

Conclusion.—The task of this paper has been to discuss the problems involved in United States-Soviet economic comparisons. It would be a source of great chagrin to the author if this listing of obstacles should be taken as a justification for a belief that it is hopeless or pointless to undertake such comparisons. With respect to the first problem, data availability, the limitations of what can be accomplished has certainly not yet been reached. Indeed the rate of flow of data has increased recently much faster than our efforts to make use of it. Also the possible approaches for clearing up obscurities in the meaning of Soviet statistics are greater than may have been implied. The index number problem is not peculiar to United States-Soviet comparisons alone, but actually affects many measurement problems within our own economy. It is only that the attention of economists has been directed toward these difficulties in comparison and measurement most strongly in the comparative study of the

United States and Soviet economies because intertemporal and international differences in economic structure are more striking when we try to evaluate their performance relative to ours than in many other kinds of problems that economists deal with. Likewise our preoccupation with the interpretation of data comes from the fact that the Russians are particularly persistent in choosing concepts that complicate comparability of economic indicators.

In this connection a final important implication of the discussion should be pointed out. The Russians are truly compulsive in making comparisons of their economy with ours, and in the process they turn all the ambiguities discussed above to good account in exaggerating their achievements relative to ours. They ignore important differences in the concepts underlying comparisons, choose weighting systems that present their achievements in the best possible light, and emphasize indicators the comparability of which is violated by differences in the context. All these misinterpretations can, of course, also be employed by those who would underemphasize Soviet economic performance. With a greater respect for truth than the Russians we should take pains to point out the errors involved in the Soviet comparisons, and with perhaps greater sophistication about the pitfalls of international economic comparisons we should be able to avoid the dangers of accepting misleading evaluations of Soviet economic performance from either end of the spectrum.

RELIABILITY AND USABILITY OF SOVIET STATISTICS: A SUMMARY APPRAISAL

by ABRAM BERGSON
Columbia University

The topic of this panel is the reliability and usability of Soviet statistics. As a preliminary to summary comment on this theme, it may be in order to say a few words about a closely related aspect with which the Western student of Soviet economics is hardly less concerned. I am referring to the fact that the volume of statistical data available is systematically limited under the operation of the Soviet secrecy policy.

It sometimes is suggested that this policy is of recent origin. This is not the case. I have had only limited occasion to make use of Soviet statistics released in the twenties. My impression is that given the volume of data available to the Soviet authorities themselves, the volume released was relatively large.

This situation, however, did not long persist. In the fall of 1928 the Soviet government inaugurated its

19

First Five Year Plan, and with this it soon found it expedient to curtail the release of statistical data. One of the outstanding events of the period of the plan, for example, was the collectivization drive and the attendant loss of a major part of Soviet livestock herds. The Russians lost within the few years 1928 to 1932 30 million head of cattle, or over two-fifths of their total herds; 14 million hogs, or over half their total herds; and nearly 100 million sheep and goats, or two thirds of their total herds.[1] These losses were an overwhelming blow to Soviet aspirations to ameliorate their Eastern European living standards with larger supplies of animal products.

In 1933 the Soviet government published a volume heralding the successes of the First Five Year Plan.[2] The section on agriculture abounds in statistics on peasant households collectivized, on the number of tractors available, and the like. There are no data at all on the losses of livestock. These latter data the government released separately at later dates.

A notable feature of the period of the five year plans is the inflation in money wages. Over the twelve-year period 1928 to 1940 money wage rates on the average increased on the order of 500 per cent. This is according to Soviet data, for the government has not hesitated to release figures on this aspect. It has not hesitated, either, to cite these figures as one more evidence of Soviet economic progress. On the other hand, it is quite inhibited regarding the measure of living costs, which is indispensable if the meaning of the money wage increases is to be adequately appraised. Publication of the Soviet official series on the cost of living ceased under the First Five Year Plan.

The government has not hesitated to release money wage rates, I should have said, until recently. In the last few years it has omitted to publish systematic figures on this feature as well. Interestingly, there are many indications that this change in information policy has lately been associated with a change in money wage policy, in the direction of stabilization in place of the former inflation.

In the late twenties and early thirties the Soviet government published systematic data on wage differentials. The number of workers was recorded by industry and by earnings class. Publication of this sort of data largely ceased with the release of statistics for the year 1934.

On the degree of secrecy maintained just before the German attack, there is at hand a very interesting measure. In February 1941 the plan for 1941 was the subject of a speech delivered by N. Voznesenskii before the eighteenth All-Union Conference of the Com-munist Party. The text of the speech was subsequently published as a pamphlet of 48 pages.[3] This is the only public release the Soviet government has made on the annual plan for 1941. As a result of the war, there is now available in this country a version of this same plan that circulated as a classified document in the Soviet Union.[4] This is a volume of 734 pages, consisting exclusively of statistical tables. Even this classified version is not complete. Data on munitions production apparently were released only in a more restricted document.

I have said that the policy of secrecy is not new. Broadly speaking, however, it is true that the policy has become more restrictive in the course of time. An illuminating commentary is provided by the successive releases of the five year plans. The First Five Year Plan as published occupies four volumes; the Second occupies two. The Third was released in one volume of 238 pages. The Fourth Five Year Plan, the first postwar one, has the dimensions of six pages in *Pravda*. The new Fifth Five Year Plan occupies three pages in *Pravda*.

Given the general trend to secrecy, there have been diverse oscillations. Among other things, there was an extreme blackout during the War. Since the War, data have been released on some scale both with regard to the war and postwar years. The famous practice of releasing data on production showing only the percentage increase from year to year and not the absolute level dates mainly from the postwar years. This practice has not always been systematically applied, but still Malenkov's speech at the recent Nineteenth Congress of the Communist Party seems so far to represent something of a special case. Malenkov releases a good deal of data in absolute terms.[5]

The view occasionally is encountered that the policy of secrecy is limited to matters immediately connected with military activities. As is already implied, this is by no means the case. The Soviet government systematically withholds statistics not only on munitions production and the like but on a great variety of economic matters. It would be quite erroneous, too, to think that the criterion of secrecy in the economic sphere is purely defense-relatedness. Before the war the Russians released data on steel production; they withheld data on the cost of living and on income differentials.

What, then, are the guiding principles of the Soviet policy of secrecy? In any full account of this complex

---

[1] Harry Schwartz, *Russia's Soviet Economy*, New York, 1950, p. 321.

[2] *Gosudarstvennaia Planovaia Komissiia, Itogi vypolneniia pervogo piatiletnego plana razvitiia narodnogo khoziaistva Soiuza SSR*, Moscow, 1933.

[3] N. Voznesenskii (N. Voznesensky), *The Growing Prosperity of the Soviet Union*, New York, 1941.

[4] *Gosudarstvennyi plan razvitiia narodnogo khoziaistva SSSR na 1941 god*. The title page states that this is the appendix to a decree issued January 17, 1941 by the Council of Commissars and the Central Committee of the Communist Party. The volume has been published in this country by the American Council of Learned Societies.

[5] *The Current Digest of the Soviet Press*, November 1, 8, 15, 1952.

question, no doubt, it would be necessary to refer to two factors already implied: military security and effective propaganda to create favorable impressions. Reference probably would have to be made, too, to the interesting question of the need to release data for the operation of a nationwide planning system, including the training of personnel.

Coming now to our main theme, the quality of data that are released, an initial question concerns the quality of the statistical reporting to the center by lower administrative echelons: the reporting by the managerial staffs of the state enterprise and collective farms. Here it is necessary to reckon first with the fact of falsification. This is often charged, and the charge clearly is in order. On this point, we have the evidence of both DP interviews[6] and statements by the Russians themselves.[7] The falsification takes various forms, including outright misstatements and improper classification; for example, the misclassification of ordinary wage payments as repair costs. The motivation apparently is to conceal illicit activities as well as to create favorable impressions generally.

As to how extensive this falsification by lower echelons is, the Soviet statements on this subject make clear that the culprits may not always proceed with impunity. There must be on this account some limit to both the degree and the frequency of fabrication. On the other hand, given the intense pressures under which the Soviet managerial staff operates, one might suppose that it would be difficult for the government to make the limit severely restrictive. The specific evidence that has come available so far, including both DP interviews and Soviet statements, seems to corroborate this general impression.[8]

It may be hoped that in time we shall have more information on this question of the extent of falsification at the lower echelons. Doubts on this score inevitably lead to corresponding doubts as to the margin of error in Soviet data generally.

Still referring to the statistical reporting by the lower managerial staff, there must be uncertainties too as a result of limitations in managerial ability. One thinks especially here of the fact that the Russians have only recently emerged from widespread illiteracy. Very likely this was still an important factor affecting the quality of statistical reporting in the early years of the five year plans; in the case of agriculture it may still be operative on some scale.

The quality of the statistical data released by the Soviet government depends not only on the quality of the reporting to the center. It depends also on the quality of the work at the center in collecting, process-ing and publishing the data. What of these latter features?

In the course of time, Western students of Soviet economics have become aware of many serious deficiencies. The official national income statistics in terms of 1926-27 ruble prices, it is generally agreed, are subject to a systematic upward bias. This is on various accounts, including chiefly the practice of valuing new commodities produced for the first time after 1926-27 in terms of prices prevailing around the time of their introduction.[9] What is true of the official national income statistics in 1926-27 rubles, is true also of other official production statistics in these terms, including data on industrial and agricultural production.

Over a period of time the Russians have revised their methods of crop reporting, so that in the case of grain, for example, harvesting and threshing losses which were once excluded have now for some time been included in official figures on the gross harvest. The revision may have been motivated in part by the desire to gain more effective control over losses. Data for different years are published in statistical hand-books, however, without any explanation, as if they represented a homogeneous series. In Soviet writings they are usually discussed in just these terms. In effect, harvesting and threshing losses become an element in the Soviet portrait of the gains of collectivized agriculture.[10]

Figures on employment and the wage bill in Soviet statistical handbooks seemingly are comprehensive, but it has been found that they fail to cover a sizeable fraction of the labor force. Apparently the shortfall is partly intentional but it is also due partly to short-comings in Soviet statistical administration.[11]

The list might be lengthened, but it is already clear that in terms of the quality of the work of collection, processing and publication, Russian statistics fall far short of what might be desired. No doubt they fall far short of the statistics of many Western countries.

But in any full account of the quality of Soviet statistics reference must be made not only to these deficiencies but also to another aspect: contrary to a common supposition, the Russians seem generally not to resort to falsification in the sense of free invention

---

[6] Joseph S. Berliner, "The Informal Organization of the Soviet Firm," *Quarterly Journal of Economics*, August 1952, especially pp. 355-356.

[7] *The New York Times*, June 27, 1946.

[8] Berliner, *op. cit.*

[9] The nature and deficiencies of Soviet official national income statistics are by now the subject of a lengthy literature. For a bibliography, see Abram Bergson, *Soviet National Income and Product in 1937* (forthcoming), Ch. I. Recently the Russians apparently abandoned 1926-27 ruble prices in the valuation of national income and for the duration of the current five year plan are using instead the prices of January 1, 1952. See *The Current Digest of the Soviet Press*, April 12, 1952 and *The New York Times*, September 21, 1952, where it is reported that this change has occurred in the case of statistics on industrial pro-duction.

[10] On the change in Soviet methods of crop reporting, see N. Jasny, *The Socialized Agriculture of the USSR*, Stanford, 1949.

[11] Abram Bergson, "A Problem in Soviet Statistics," *Review of Economic Statistics*, November 1947.

and double bookkeeping. I have already explained that there is falsification of a local sort by the managerial staffs of the state enterprise and collective farms. I am now concerned primarily with falsification of a comprehensive character at the center. It will be evident that the distinction in mind here is important.

By implication, I am distinguishing here, too, between, on the one hand, the deficiencies of the sort just referred to in the official income statistics and the like, and, on the other, outright falsification in the sense of free invention under double bookkeeping. This latter distinction, I fear, is a fine one. Almost all the deficiencies that have been discovered lead to unduly favorable impressions of the Soviet economy. If the Russians do not wilfully introduce such deficiencies to create such impressions, they are at least notably tolerant of them.

But, granting the possible similarity in motivation, I venture to think that the distinction still is in order. For one thing, the deficiencies all appear to have a methodological character or to be due to administrative inefficiency. As such, they are conceptually distinct from falsification in the sense of free invention and double bookkeeping. In the case of the national income statistics, for example, the distortions arise because of improper weighting. In the case of crop statistics, data for different years reflecting changes in concepts are presented nevertheless as a homogeneous series. In the case of labor statistics, the coverage is incomplete, due partly to the inefficiency in statistical agencies, but this is not explained in the statistical handbooks.

For another, the distinction, I believe, is of vital importance for the study of the Soviet economy. Given falsification in the sense of free invention and double bookkeeping, research on the Soviet economy clearly is ruled out at once for all practical purposes. Given the methodological deficiencies, there is at least a core of fact from which to start and one may hope to detect and even correct for the deficiencies.

On what basis, then, may we suppose that falsification in the sense explained is not generally practiced? The question is rarely elaborated. In the briefest terms the main grounds for this view, as I see them, are six:

First, the data appear to withstand tolerably well checks as to their internal consistency. For example, in compiling a series of national economic accounts for the USSR, I have found that the amount of household money incomes indicated by Soviet data checks closely with the amount of household money outlays indicated by these data.[12] Consistency of this sort probably would be difficult of attainment under double bookkeeping, though no doubt it is not impossible.

Second, I believe a careful inquiry would reveal a

[12] Abram Bergson, *Soviet National Income and Product in 1937*, forthcoming.

broad consistency also between the statistical data and other Soviet information on the Soviet economy. For example, the release of data on the underfulfillment of the plan in a particular industry has been followed by a report of a change in personnel in the industry concerned. This sort of consistency, too, might be difficult to maintain under double bookkeeping.

Third, there appears to be a broad consistency with information of all sorts gathered by foreign observers in the USSR, as where Soviet reports of improvements in consumers' goods production accord with foreign observations on the state of consumers' goods markets.

Fourth, the Soviet war experience falls under previous headings but may deserve separate mention nevertheless. In terms of their own statistics, the Russians probably fought the war with an annual steel output averaging during the years 1942-45 little more than 10 million tons. Even taking account of Lend-Lease, one may at least rule out the likelihood of overstatement.

Fifth, the Soviet policy of withholding obviously is often calculated to mislead, but as so applied it appears to be more an alternative than a complement to a policy of falsification. Moreover, the Russians occasionally release adverse information. The withholding of data on livestock herds from the volume on the fulfillment of the First Five Year Plan and equally the subsequent release of these data would be difficult to understand if the Russians made a practice of falsification in any case.

Sixth, and last (but not least), I have mentioned already that we have in this country two versions of the annual plan for 1941, one unclassified and the other classified. The goals in these two versions, it has been ascertained, check closely, item by item.[13]

I have said that the published Soviet data appear to be consistent both internally and with other available information. It is necessary now to observe that there are important exceptions. But in those cases that have been carefully examined to date, it generally seems possible to understand the inconsistency simply in terms of methodological deficiencies of the sort previously referred to, and without assuming free invention under double bookkeeping. Thus, the official national income statistics in 1926-27 rubles show a rate of growth all out of proportion to rates shown by Soviet data on the production of different commodities in physical units. But this discrepancy is explained mainly in terms of the erroneous weighting on the

[13] L. Turgeon, "On the Reliability of Soviet Statistics," *Review of Economics and Statistics*, February 1952.

While it has seemed in order to distinguish in this essay between falsification by lower echelons and falsification at the center, it will be evident that a number of the grounds for thinking that the latter is not a general practice must apply also to the former. As a result, there is some upper limit to the margin of error introduced by falsification by lower echelons.

basis of which the national income statistics are calculated. Other inconsistencies have been explained similarly. There is no basis, then, to assume free invention and double bookkeeping.

Why don't the Russians falsify their statistics systematically? I take it that the question is entirely in order. In trying to answer it, my own inclination is to think partly in terms of the probable difficulties of operating a double bookkeeping system on a national scale without detection. No doubt, however, another factor is the possibility of achieving major propaganda aims in any case through withholding and also through methodological manipulation.

But having said so much, it is necessary to say more. The view that I have outlined on falsification necessarily has a more or less provisional character. In the case of Soviet Russia, the reliability of official statistics has to be tested and retested and then tested again. If some data seem trustworthy, there is no guarantee that all others are likewise.

The last caution seems especially in order today. While the Russians already were withholding much data before the war, they have been much more secretive since. Possibly, as I have suggested, the withholding is something of a testimonial to the reliability of what actually is published. But with the curtailment in releases, the opportunities for an independent appraisal have been greatly reduced. Limitations on foreign travel in the USSR have worked in the same direction. Under the circumstances, a heightened caution is in order in the use of current Soviet data.

The view which I have outlined on the question of falsification, I believe, is one which in its essentials would be accepted by most Western students of the Soviet economy. In this connection, however, it may be in order to caution members of this audience against misunderstandings arising from polemics and careless terminology. For example, one writer in the field of Soviet economics recently has championed vigorously a view that appears diametrically opposed to the one I have outlined.[14] But on closer examination it is seen at once that in this case the term "falsification" is being used, not as I have used it — that is, to refer to free invention under double bookkeeping — but to refer to what I have called methodological deficiencies. I have already made clear my belief that this usage has something to commend it. But almost inevitably it is at the price of some confusion. As the reader is nowhere clearly informed, the writer in question assumes just as do other students of the Soviet economy that there is a core of fact from which to start. Obviously the assumption is essential if one is to do any research at all in this field.

Senator Claude Pepper has published an account of an interview Stalin granted him in September 1945.[15] Stalin closed the interview with these words: "Just judge the Soviet Union objectively. Do not either praise us or scold us. Just know us and judge us as we are and base your estimate of us upon facts and not rumors." Obviously the Soviet government has itself found it expedient to erect a formidable barrier to anyone who seeks to base his estimate of Russia on facts. Along with most Western students of Soviet economics, I am bold enough to think that the barrier may not be altogether insuperable. This, however, is a notion that has constantly to be reviewed.

---

14 N. Jasny, *The Socialized Agriculture of the USSR*, Stanford, 1949, Ch. I; "Soviet Statistics," *Review of Economics and Statistics*, November 1947; "Results of the Five Year Plans," in W. Gurian, ed., *The Soviet Union*, Notre Dame, 1951; *The Soviet Economy in the Plan Era*, Stanford, 1951; *The Soviet Price System*, Stanford, 1951.

15 *The New York Times*, October 1, 1945.

'1926/7' AND ALL THAT

No apology is necessary for inflicting on the reader a fairly detailed analysis of the '1926/7' price series. The official figures of the rate of growth of the national income, of gross industrial output, of labour productivity, in the decisive years 1928-50, were *and are*[1] calculated in terms of these prices, and so the degree of reliability of this measuring-rod is obviously of the highest economic and political interest, especially as other under-developed countries are at times tempted to compare their own rate of progress with that of the USSR. Therefore, while growth since 1950 is not now measured on this basis, the whole question of '1926/7 prices' is not purely of historical interest.

These prices have naturally attracted the attention of many Western scholars. Yet few seem to have taken cognizance of all the factors involved. Dr. Jasny, while subjecting the official series to a devastating analysis,[2] tends to present the whole thing as a machiavellian plot to exaggerate Soviet achievements (there is more to it than that), and his own attempt to substitute 'real' for official 1926/7 prices as a measure of these achievements does not show how (or whether) he has overcome the *genuine* difficulties which faced Soviet statisticians of the period. In his admirable survey of '1926/7 prices' in the light of the 1941 plan, Seton (*Soviet Studies* April 1952) points to a number of defects, but confines his attention inevitably to manufacturing industry, and so does not mention major distortions in other sectors, on which the 1941 plan sheds little or no light. Some other commentators confine themselves to mentioning only one of the distorting factors at work.[3] It is therefore useful to re-examine the whole controversy with, one hopes, a fresh approach.

The following is a resume of the official version of the evolution of the Soviet national income, in milliards of '1926/7' rubles:

1928	..	..	25.0
1932	..	..	45.5
1935	..	..	66.5
1936	..	..	86.0
1937	..	..	96.0
1940	..	..	128.3
1948	..	..	143.0
1950	..	..	210.4

It was in 1928 that it was decided to use the prices of the year 1926/7[4] as a base for planning and time comparisons, replacing 1912 prices. The five-year plan was just being launched. It is worth emphasizing that there is not the slightest evidence for the view that these prices were chosen with an eye to future exaggerations and distortions. The actual upward bias was due to a variety of circumstances, each of which will now be examined in turn.

(a) The price-relationships of the base year

The USSR of 1926/7 was a predominantly agricultural country, with its small and inefficient industry protected from foreign competition by the state monopoly of foreign trade. Prices of industrial goods and construction were high—relative to agricultural products, in comparison either with the then existing price-relationships in Western countries or with those which later came into being in the USSR. The process of industrialization involved a great expansion of the high-priced sectors of the economy, and the use of 1926/7 prices thus inevitably produced a more rapid rate of growth than any index based either on, say, American or post-industrialization Russian prices. In a stimulating paper, Professor Gerschenkron has shown the vast difference which the choice of price-weights can make to indices.[5] Since no set of price-relationships are more 'true' in any absolute sense than another, no statistician can legitimately describe the Soviet series as 'wrong' merely because of the peculiarities of the 1926/7 price structure. Indeed, it is arguable that pre-industrialization weights are a more accurate basis on which to assess the sacrifices made; it is as a *consequence* of industrialization that prices of industrial goods fell relatively to primary produce. With the passing of the years, these weights became less and less relevant, and of course it may well be that the desirable propaganda effect of showing a rapid rate of growth was an important factor in postponing a change in the base-year, but all this does not add up to 'falsification'. Dr. Jasny, indeed, does not base his charges on this ground.

(b) Treatment of new products

It is obvious that the process of industrialization involves the manufacture of numerous articles which were not made in the pre-industrialization base-year, while others are so redesigned as to be treated as new for pricing purposes. This makes the question of the value to be given to new products of great importance. The '1926/7' price regulations laid it down that the price to be taken was that of the year in which production in quantity began (*v god osvoenia*). Since the first five-year plan envisaged an all-round fall in prices, and since '1926/7 prices' were used for many years not only as a measure of progress but also as the basis of financial and output plans of thousands of enterprises, it seems unlikely that the distortions which in fact occurred, and which did evident harm to planning, could have been intended.

In the event, as is known, the planners miscalculated. It is well said of men and of mice that their plans

> 'Gang aft agley,
> And leave us nocht but grief and pain
> For promis'd joy'.

Amid the strains and stresses of Stalin's 'revolution from above', all price expectations proved false; acute shortages of consumer goods of all kinds were accompanied by a wage and price spiral. Labour productivity was low, labour turnover was phenomenal. Costs rose, and with them rose the values attached to new products. It was here that 'managerial private enterprise' played a very important role. The higher the '1926/7' price attached to any given product, the easier it was to overfulfil planned targets set in these prices. Every manager thus had a powerful stimulus to describe any product as 'new' if he could, and to persuade the authorities to accept the highest possible 'base-year' price for it; (there was at this time no centralized price-list, and all kinds of '1926/7' prices existed for the same product). Very speedily, the allegedly unchanging '1926/7' prices lost contact with their base. In a remarkably frank book published in 1936, Rotshtein stated: 'The list of comparable products . . . is very small. In this connection, a very significant part of output is simply valued at current or the previous year's prices, and it is comparatively rare to encounter valuations in terms of prices of three or four years ago'.[6] The same critic pointed out that prices in the first year of production were, naturally, often higher than they later became (after elimination of 'growing-pains'), and that this caused distortion by exaggerating the value of new against established products, since the *first* year's price was used as the '1926/7' price.

The proportion of new production is inevitably high in the engineering industry; thus in 1953 it was estimated that over 25 per cent of the output of machinery consisted of items not 'comparable' with any produced by the given enterprise in the previous year.[7] However, it is possible that the gains from mass-production were such as to offset the rise in costs due to increases in money wages, and until 1936 the prices of basic materials were kept low by subsidies. Consequently, the effect of the general inflation on the valuation of new products of the engineering industry could well have been smaller than might have been expected, at least until 1936.

None the less, over the economy in general the 'new product' distortions were clearly of very real importance. No wonder Rotshtein wrote: 'As they relate to different periods of time . . . , the 'basic' prices lose the quality of interconnected base-period weights. Due to this, the entire index of the volume of production has a highly restricted, formal significance. It reflects the real dynamic of events in a very circumscribed manner, simply incorrect from a statistical point of view'.[8] One is not surprised to learn that in many cases 'the relationship between current and "basic" prices is totally unreal', and that there were many 'corrections' made to base-year prices with the object of 'lessening the unreality—from the point of view of the given moment— of the price-relationships brought into being by the valuation of products arising at different times'.[9]

These and other confusions led to a change in the regulations in 1936: a new all-Union price list replaced a multitude of local and inconsistent '1926/7 prices' for most products. In the case of new products, or those not clearly listed, current prices were to be used and these, in some cases, were to be converted into '1926/7 prices' by some unstated coefficient; in other cases, enterprises were to select from the list a conversion coefficient relating to some similar article, but this required central approval.

It has been argued[10] that these regulations eliminated the earlier distortions in the valuation of new products, but this was not the case. As Rotshtein pointed out, the conversion coefficient would depend on the date on which the similar article was first produced; thus 'if the "analogous" old product was first made in 1934 or 1935, then the new product is "converted" into 1934 or 1935 prices. In reality there occurs in this case a simplified variety of "inventing" a base-year price, already analysed above'.[11] This quotation shows, inter alia, that the changes of 1936 did not lead to any revision in the 'base-year' prices of new products introduced in the preceding few years. Indeed, as was correctly pointed out by Hodgman[12] and Seton[13], the 1936 changes appeared to have the overall effect of making the position worse; we have seen that prior to that date there were substantial irrational variations between products, regions and even enterprises, and no doubt some order was brought into chaos in 1936; however, the temptation must have been to bring prices into line by upward amendment of the 'laggards' rather than by pulling down the high prices to the level of the rest, for this would be the line of least resistance (and greatest popularity with all concerned). The changes came into operation in January 1936, and the actual behaviour of published data provides abundant evidence in support of this view. Not only did national income increase at an unusually rapid rate in 1936, but gross industrial output showed a quite fantastic leap of no less than 30 per cent in this one year according to official figures in 1926/7 prices, with labour productivity rising by 22 per cent, both rates being quite abnormal.[14] Seton, in his already-cited article, puts forward the sensible hypotheses that, over a large part of industry, the '1926/7 prices' had by 1941 become the actual prices of the mid-thirties. To establish 'real 1926/7 prices' for products not made in the base-year, in an inflationary and rapidly-changing situation, presented very real difficulty; with strong pressure from managers (and many bureaucrats in the economic Commissariats) for maximizing the plan price of any and every article which could be described as 'new', it is hardly surprising to find an upward trend in the allegedly constant 'unchanged prices of 1926/7'.

An example can be cited from a good Soviet source, which would seem to dispose once and for all of the argument that this species of distortion was unimportant or that it ceased in 1936. Here is the relevant passage:[15]

In certain cases, the use of 1926/7 prices distorted the plan fulfilment indicators, encouraged enterprises to produce less useful articles. The trouble was that, for new products, the prices of the first year of mass production were considered to be the 'unchanged' [base] prices, and these relatively higher than the [real] prices of 1926/7. This caused some enterprises to increase the relative weight of output of articles with a high [base] price. The following typical example relates to prices of bottles, taken from the accounts of 1947:

Type of bottle	Capacity (litres)	1926/7 price (or price of first year) (kopeks)
Wine	0.375	8.0
Lemonade	0.300	6.5
Wine, 'Limburg' type ..	0.250	10.0
Liqueur	0.250	10.0
Blood-plasma	0.250	17.0

The blood-plasma bottle, similar in size and quality to the 'limburg' and liqueur bottles, was valued 70 per cent higher. *This was because blood-plasma bottles were first produced much later than the others.* This bottle was 'profitable' to produce. *since its higher [1926/7] price facilitated the overfulfilment of the plan.* In 1947, the plan for the production of wine and other bottles with a relatively low ['1926/7'] price was not fulfilled, while 5.7 million more blood-plasma bottles were produced than was envisaged by the plan. Consequently, although the plan was not fulfilled in quantity terms in the basic lines, *it was overfulfilled in value terms* [i.e. in '1926/7 prices'], and the appropriate individuals received bonuses. Such facts emerged in one enterprise after another.

(c) Inclusion of harvest losses

As has been shown on another occasion (in *Soviet Studies* vol. VII no. 3, January 1956), agricultural statistics have been somewhat inflated in the course of the period under discussion by the inclusion of harvest losses in production data. This naturally inflates to some degree both the total of the national income and agriculture's contribution to it.

However, since agricultural products are easy to define, and tended to have clear and relatively low 1926/7 prices, none of the other distorting factors operate (except possibly in the other reverse direction), with the result that the share of agriculture in the national income fell rapidly. Thus in 1937 it was only 14.9 out of the total national income of 96.3 milliards. By 1950 the national income had reached 210.4 milliards in 1926/7 prices, but gross agricultural output at this date was at most 24 per cent above 1937 levels, taking figures that may be too rosy given in *Voprosy Ekonomiki*,[16] and net output could scarcely have risen by much more than this even after allowance for inclusion of more of the losses in the 'net'. This suggests that agriculture, which employed still close to half the entire population, contributed a mere 9 per cent of the national income in 1950, a conclusion which confirms that something must be wrong.[17]

(d) Trade and the national income

In 1937, the last year for which any breakdown of the total is available, trade's contribution to the national income was given as 11.8 out of the grand total of 96.3 milliards ruble, in '1926/7 prices'. This seems very high, both relatively and absolutely. This figure of 11.8 is five and a half times as large as in 1928 in allegedly constant prices. It is possible that the result was arrived at by multiplying the high trade margin of the mid-twenties by the increase in the volume of trade turnover, but this hypothesis is scarcely tenable. The volume of retail trade is said to have been 230 per cent of 1928 in 1940.[18] It must have less than trebled to 1937 especially if the disappearance of private trade is borne in mind. The picture begins to look absurd if one takes into consideration the actual magnitude, in 1937 prices, of the factor costs making up the net 'product' of trade in that year. The largest, beyond doubt, was wages; these came to only 5 milliard rubles in 1937,[19] and indeed the total expenses of all levels of the trade network (including transport, packaging materials and other operating expenses) was only 12.3 milliards,[20] in 1937 prices of course. How all this can be reconciled with 11.8 milliards of *net* product in '1926/7 prices' is beyond comprehension, especially bearing in mind that retail margins had been falling and all costs rising through inflation.

(e) Construction

According to the official claim for 1937, the net product of construction in that year was 12.5 milliard rubles. Even at current prices it seems remarkably high. If one were to take the official figure of state fixed investment (30 milliards), add to it the probable value of other investment (e.g. by kolkhozy) and a reasonable sum for such capital repairs as may be deemed to be the product of building labour, the very highest possible total would be 40 milliard rubles. This includes the cost of machinery installed and other such 'non-construction' items; two thirds or so would represent construction and installation, which alone are relevant in this context.[21]

This reduces the figure to 27 milliards. We know that in 1936 over 55 per cent of expenditure on construction at current prices consisted of material expenses and amortization, i.e. items excluded from net product.[22] It follows that this figure of 12.5 roughly represents the net value of construction at current prices.[23] The rise in productivity from 1932 was almost exactly paralleled by rise in money wages[24] which does not leave room for any economy from this source to balance the undeniable and substantial increase in prices of nearly all materials which occurred in 1936. 1932, in its turn, was a year of extremely low productivity in the building industry. It is perhaps not surprising that no Soviet source, certainly not Chernomordik's symposium, explains just how the net product of construction at unchanged prices is supposed to be calculated.

One's suspicions are confirmed by the contradictory, partial data, which do appear in the symposium. Thus it is stated that the net value of construction in 1936 was 205 per cent of 1932, in 1926/7 prices; also that labour productivity rose by 83 per cent in unchanged prices; and finally that the number of workers in the building industry *fell* by 20 per cent.[25] This is obviously absurd. In any case, on grounds of common sense, one takes leave to doubt whether the *volume* of construction in 1936 could have been more than double that of 1932, which was a year in which vast construction projects laid down in the first five-year plan were being rushed to completion, the more so as an increase in volume of 46 per cent (!!) is claimed for the single year 1936, a year which saw a big rise in prices of building materials.[26]

One is driven to the conclusion that Construction's contribution to the total national income was not in '1926/7 prices' at all.

(f) Confusions and inconsistencies

Rotshtein's frank analysis includes several pages in which he describes the remarkable confusion which surrounded the determination of '1926/7 prices' at the time he was writing. One example will suffice: while the rules laid down that values of semi-manufactures and unfinished production were to be converted into 1926/7 prices by applying coefficients appropriate to the relevant completed articles, it was apparently very common to 'include the value of unfinished production and semi-manufactures in output expressed in unchanged prices in terms of their current cost, without any recalculation into 1926/7 prices'.[27] One result was that, in terms of these '1926/7 prices' the value of the partly-finished product sometimes exceeded that of the completed article. It should be noted that, while in other circumstances these various errors might have cancelled each other out, it so obviously paid the perpetrators to err on the side of picking a high '1926/7' valuation that the net effect must have been in that direction.

A minor distortion is due to one of a number of 'statistical stupidities' listed by Krasnolobov:[28] thus it appears that all postal services, including those rendered to productive enterprises, were omitted from national income calculations down to 1936, through the stupidity of some official.

Summary of Conclusions. The '1926/7 price' series may thus be described as open to the gravest objections. Although most of the detailed figures cited relate to the mid-thirties, it does not follow that the distorting factors ceased to operate in later years. The fact is that relevant data on the constituent parts of the national income are not available after 1937; it seems quite probable that '1926/7 prices' moved still further from their original base after 1937, though certainly not in the chaotic manner of the years prior to 1936 which Rotshtein so vividly described. As a measure of growth it seems evident that the published data in these prices are useless. It is a matter of semantics rather than economics whether the publication of aggregate data in such a changing and inconsistent set of 'unchanged prices' represents falsification, but the facts do suggest that here at least Soviet statistics are less reliable than is normally the case in other countries.

Granted that some degree of distortion is proved, what is its extent? In this connection, it is obviously necessary to differentiate between the effects of the choice of 1926/7 as a base (which is in no wise a 'distortion') and the other factors analysed above. This cannot be done by any analysis in terms of non-Soviet currencies (or of Soviet prices of later years), since in the nature of things the rate of growth would appear smaller than with the genuine Soviet prices of 1926/7. Dr. Jasny alone has attempted to measure the real amount of distortion, by recalculating national income in what he calls 'real 1926/7 prices'; however, while his methods are brave and his results fascinating, it is impossible to accept them without knowing more about how the results were arrived at, and in particular his treatment of new production. The verdict must be 'not proven'—and this without in any way denigrating Jasny's bold pioneering in the field of Soviet economic statistics.[29] The very valuable work of Hodgman[30] and Seton[31] on alternative measurements of individual output do not, of course, aim to reconstruct '1926/7' weights, and are concerned only with industry.

The use of 1926/7 prices virtually came to an end in 1949, except that, to express the results of the fourth five-year plan, certain calculations in those prices were continued into 1950. While it would seem broadly true to say that none of the distorting features of '1926/7 prices' were deliberately brought into being for propaganda purposes, the high rate of growth which their use produced was seized upon to demonstrate the superiority of the Soviet system. It may be true that this propaganda aspect contributed to keeping these prices in use longer than might otherwise have been the case. They were finally dropped when prices and costs showed a decidedly downward trend, and the cynic might say they were only dropped when their 'inflationary' effect on rates of growth was exhausted. However, it is true to say that the change of base-year was made as soon as the post-war price-structure was reorganized, a process which for various reasons was delayed until 1949-50.

What now?

Finally, a few paragraphs are called for on the subject of the situation since 1950. Is there now a more solid official statistical basis for the measurement of Soviet achievements in terms of aggregate indices? One of the difficulties in forming any definite view is simply lack of information. It seems that the prices of 1951 have been used during the fifth five-year plan period for measuring national income,[32] while gross industrial output was expressed in the prices of January 1st 1952, the volume of investment (and presumably construction) in the prices of July 1st 1950, the gross and/or net output of agriculture in some unknown price. In the sixth plan period, i.e. as from 1956, it would seem that the prices of July 1st 1955 are being used for national income, industry and construction, but it is still not clear whether this applies also to agriculture. There are no figures whatever, at the time of writing, about the *net* product of *any* economic sector, i.e. its contribution to the national income is unknown. Under the circumstances, one can only make a very partial comment.

Certain favourable indications can be cited: thus inflation is no longer a cause of exaggeration, because prices have shown a downward tendency since 1950. Then the use of a more recent price-base should have the result of correcting the obsolete pre-industrialization weights of '1926/7'. Also the abolition of biological yield as the basis of the measurement of farm output has eliminated the inclusion of harvest losses as a source of distortion—though some other problems connected with agricultural statistics remain obscure (for instance, the relative weight given to agriculture in the national income, and the possible

effect on net output of the big rise in the delivery prices of farm produce). However, there are certain general queries which must be raised.

Much the most important is the problem of the valuation of new
products, which continue to be of great significance in many major
sectors of industry. Firstly, there is the fact that a new product in its
first year of mass production is apt to cost more than subsequently, when
various growing-pains are overcome. The following example makes
the point clear: in 1953, the Belarus tractor was priced at 40,000 rubles
and was sold at a loss. In 1954, following a fall in costs, the price was
reduced to 24,000 rubles. Finally, in 1955 the price was fixed at 22,000
rubles, which gives the factory a 15 per cent profit margin over costs[32].
Question: find the base-year price. There is some evidence to show
that some downward adjustment is made, and certainly this was discussed, somewhat inconclusively, by Genin in an article on this whole
problem.[33] However, it is by no means clear whether *enough* allowance
is made.

Secondly, there is another aspect of this same matter: decisions about
comparability. Such decisions, everywhere and inevitably, contain an
element of arbitrariness. Let us take a simple example: an automobile
firm in 1952 made 100,000 units of model A, but in 1955 makes
105,000 units of model B. Let us imagine that model B differs from
model A by having a more modern shape, 6 cylinders instead of 4, 25
per cent more h.p., extra seating capacity, overdrive, built-in jacks,
and some other refinements. Then by how much has output increased?
Obviously, by more than 5 per cent, but there is no scientific, single
answer to the question. Several different solutions could be defended.
However, under Soviet conditions, the director and his accountant
will hardly adopt an attitude of statistical neutrality as between this or
that solution, because the valuation of their new output in base-year
prices often has a direct bearing on plan fulfilment, and so on their
bonuses and reputation. Therefore they will press for the variant
which shows the achievements of the enterprise to the best advantage
(since the assumption that most men are human most of the time is a
sound basis for forecasting behaviour-patterns). But as any statistician
would agree, the systematic choice of the upper point of a range of
possible solutions must, in the aggregate, result in an unreasonable
degree of exaggeration. This could be expected to be significant in the
machinery and vehicles sector, where there are many new products.

However, this is not evidence of anything approaching the statistical
peculiarities of the '1926/7' era.

A. Nove

London

After the above was written, there appeared a little statistical compendium, *Strany Sotsializma i Kapitalizma v Tsifrakh*, edited by the well-known economist Ya. A. Ioffe. It happens to contain, among much other interesting matter, a calculation relevant to the problem of measuring exaggeration of industrial output indices. It seems useful to devote some space to considering this new evidence. Ioffe's table 62 reads as follows:

				per cent of world industrial production			
				1913	1937	1950	1955
USSR	..	..	..	2.6	9.2	14.4	19.0
USA	..	..	..	38.2	37.8	44.8	39.8
UK	..	..	..	12.1	11.5	9.8	8.4
W. Germany	..	..	..	15.3*	8.4	5.8	7.4
France	..	..	..	6.6	5.5	3.4	3.3
All others	..	..	..	25.2	27.6	21.8	22.1

* all Germany

This is said to be 'calculated by the compiler', i.e. by Ioffe. In the same handbook, in Table 67, there is reproduced the official index of Soviet industrial production in all its uncorrected glory. Clearly, then, either the Soviet output index will be inconsistent with the above percentages, or the percentages must in some way be distorted in proportion to the exaggeration of the official index. (Since 'world output' indices are rather vague, the analysis can conveniently be confined to comparisons with USA.)

Let us first take the figures for 1955. They give the USSR 47.6 per cent of United States industrial production. While no such calculation can be 'true' or 'accurate' to the exclusion of others, it seems not unreasonable as an approximation. Thus goods transport is not a bad basis for a rough crosscheck, since nearly all industrial products involve movement, and both the USSR and USA are countries with long hauls (the same handbook, in Table 154, shows that the average length of railway haul was 766 kilometres in the USSR in 1955, and 727 kilometres in the USA in 1954). The grand total for the USSR for all forms of transport, including pipelines, was 1,163,600 million ton-kilometres in 1955. Ioffe quotes an analogous American figure of 2,137,700 for 1953. If, as is likely, the latter figure increased in the two years by about 8 per cent, then the US total would be a shade over double the Russian, which seems about right. This is not the place to pursue the complicated problem of US—Russian comparisons further. The object is merely to establish a *prima facie* case that an honest calculation was probably made for 1955. But the Soviet share for *earlier* years is consistent (with allowance for rounding) with the official Soviet output series. In other words, basing himself on a genuine 1955 calculation, Ioffe has worked backwards, using the official indices. Then we must expect the Soviet share in *past* years to be understated in conformity with the exaggeration in the official Soviet output index.

In seeking ways and means of pursuing the analysis further, one finds, not for the first time, that the essential pioneering work has been done by Dr. Jasny. He noticed that just the same method had been used in a similar Soviet handbook before the war (*SSSR i kapitalisticheskiye strany* 1939), and wrote about it in 1947 (in the *Journal of Political Economy*, Vol. LV pp. 307—309). He showed that the compilers had attempted a realistic calculation of the relation between Soviet and 'capitalist' output for 1937, and were compelled to understate the Soviet share in earlier years through using the official index. Thus Russia was alleged to produce only 6.9 per cent of US output in 1913, whereas the League of Nations had calculated a proportion of 12.3 per cent (*Industrialization and Foreign Trade*, Geneva 1945 p. 13). Equally striking was the fact that the 1934 edition of the same Soviet handbook claimed that the USSR's output in 1928 was 10.5 per cent of USA, whereas the 1939 edition reduced this to 6.7 per cent.[34]

Dr. Jasny rightly concludes that the exaggerations of the official index were to a substantial extent reflected in these curious disparities. There is really nothing one can usefully add to his argument, so far as the 1913-37 period is concerned, though more will be said about the validity of this species of comparison.

What of 1937-55? The pre-war handbook gives the USSR's 1937 proportion to US industrial production as 32.7 per cent. The latest version gives it as 24.3 per cent at the same date. It is curious that Ioffe was the author of the calculation on *both* occasions. If the official index were 'added' to 32.7 per cent, then Soviet output would now be 66.7 per cent of American, not 46.7 per cent. Conversely, if Soviet output were 32.7 per cent of American in 1937 and 47.6 per cent in 1955, then, since the American output index stands at 227 (1937=100), the Soviet index should be 330. But the official index is 463. This, *ceteris paribus*, suggests an exaggeration of close to 40 per cent, In fact, taking into account the fact that the pre-war calculations related to pre-war territory, the exaggeration would be slightly greater than this. It is still much smaller than the discrepancy noticed by Dr. Jasny in the 1913-37 period, and indeed this would conform with the generally-held view that Soviet indices became less fantastic after 1937.

But, it may be asked, how valid are such comparisons of percentages? They depend all too much on the weights chosen, on the prices in which they are calculated. Is it not possible that the difference between the two Ioffe figures for 1937 can be explained by a change in relative prices? It must be admitted that this is theoretically quite possible. One need only mention the terrifying example elaborated by Professor Gerschenkron in his paper on *A Dollar Index of Soviet Machinery*. We must certainly examine the price-bases. Unfortunately, the 1955 figure is quite unexplained; a short footnote tells us only that it is 'calculated by the compiler', but it tells us nothing else.

There is some support for the hypothesis that dollar or 'world' prices were in fact used. Dollar prices are known to Soviet statisticians in detail, if only because Soviet foreign trade data are expressed in these prices, converted into 'valuta' rubles at the official rate. The results of a calculation in dollar terms are likely to yield a more favourable result than in rubles, because of the relative cheapness (in rubles) of Soviet metallurgy, machinery and armaments output, and this too is an argument for using dollar values. Let it be said at once that *if* the prewar calculations were in dollars while this one based its comparison on *Soviet* prices, this would make a substantial difference; the fastest-growing sectors of Soviet industry (notably machinery) have relatively lower prices in 1955, and this may well depress the Soviet percentage in that year (and in any year derived 'backwards' from it) compared with a valuation in dollar prices (or, for that matter, 1937 ruble prices). However, this is unlikely. It is much more probably that world or dollar prices were used on both occasions.

If this hypothesis is correct, then Ioffe tells us this: Soviet output in 1937 *in the dollar prices of that year* was 32.7 per cent of the American. In 1955, it seems to have been 47.6 per cent of the American in the dollar prices of *that* year. Then, is there anything about the *American* price pattern of the two years which would cause the share of Soviet output to be seriously affected as between the two years? Or is the US output index, based on the prices of 1947-9, likely to affect matters one way or the other? It is, of course, not enough to point to the undoubted fact that American prices have changed. Of course they have. But has the change been one which would make the Russian total in 1955 prices relatively smaller than in 1937 prices? For example, it may well be that machinery and metalworking products have become relatively cheaper than textiles and bread. However, the proportion of machinery and metalworking in total industrial output has risen fairly rapidly in *both* the United States *and* the USSR, and so it might make little difference. Indeed, for all we know the effect of the relative price changes is to increase rather than reduce the gap to be explained.

In any case, the 1937 figure used by Ioffe in his new compilation is *not* calculated in 1955 dollars, or indeed at any price at all. It is just the arithmetical consequence of the official Soviet output index. It may therefore be concluded that the index which has been derived from the two Ioffe calculations, i.e. a Soviet industrial output index of 330 (1937=100), looks like a meaningful and useful approximation, perhaps more 'usable' than the official index of 463.[35] Of course, we do not know how much of this presumed exaggeration occurred after the abandonment in 1950 of '1926/7 prices'.

[1] Despite the changes in methods of calculation from 1950, the pre-1950 rates of growth are still expressed on the old '1926/7' basis, without any recalculation or amendment. The resulting indices are 'chained' onto those for the more recent years, expressed in the prices of 1952 (1951-5) · and July 1955 (1956 and on).

[2] See his *Soviet Price System* and *The Soviet Economy in the Plan Era* (Stanford 1951). In common with, I imagine, all other students of the subject, the writer learned a great deal from Dr. Jasny.

[3] For instance, even Colin Clark, in his pioneering *Critique of Russian Statistics*, was concerned primarily with base-year weights as a distorting factor.

[4] '1926/7' is not the average of two years; until 1930, economic accounting was based on the harvest year.

[5] *A Dollar Index of Soviet Machinery Output* (Rand Corp. 1951). The problem had not escaped the notice of serious Soviet writers—e.g. Krasnolobov, *Planirovaniye i uchet narodnovo dokhoda* (M. 1940) p. 78, mentions it in passing.

[6] *Problemy promyshlennoi statistiki SSSR* (M. 1936), p. 246.

[7] Stepanov: *Planirovaniye finansov mashinostroitelnovo zavoda* (M. 1953) pp. 20—22. Obviously the proportion was very much higher in, say, 1933.

[8] *Op. cit.*, p. 244-5.

[9] *Ibid.*

[10] For instance by Dobb in *Review of Economics and Statistics*, February 1948.

[11] Op. cit., p. 249. Savinsky, in the 1944 edition of his book, *Kurs promishlennoi statistiki* was even more forthright (p. 74), but, characteristically, the criticism is very much toned down in the 1949 edition of the same work.

[12] *Soviet Economic Growth*, p. 235.

[13] *Soviet Studies* April 1952.

[14] These figures are taken from *SSSR i kapitalisticheskiye strany* pp. 75 and 127. Part of the increase may have been due to the rise in the prices of certain basic materials which had been produced at a loss. The inadequate nature of the so-called correction coefficient was stressed by Ioffe (*Planirovanie promyshlennovo proizvodstva* M. 1948, p. 92), in a passage which is conclusive to all but Dobb; the latter even argues that the virtual identity of the value of machinery output in current and '1926/7' prices in the confidential *1941 Plan* constitutes supporting evidence for his (Dobb's) point of view—an astonishing interpretation (see *Soviet Studies* April 1952, p. 364).

[15] Kondrashev: *Tseno-obrazovaniye v promyshlennosti SSSR* (1956) p. 135. Emphasis mine.

[16] Article by Shabalin in no. 8 1953. This is not the place to discuss the accuracy or otherwise of the claim; it is not certain that it was weighted by 1926/7 prices.

[17] According to Kursky (*Planovoye Khozyaistvo* 1939 no. 3, p. 1) agriculture in 1937 contributed 12.5 per cent of national income in 1926/7 prices, and 25.7 per cent in current prices. It has been impossible to account for that 12.5 per cent, since the official data produces 15.45 per cent. Kursky does not explain how he arrives at the 25.7 per cent either.

[18] *Planovoye Khozyaistvo* 1955 no. 1, p. 83. In kindly drawing my attention to the data available on trade, Dr. Jasny pointed out that at one time it was customary to claim a volume increase of 4.6 times—e.g. Lifits: *Sovetskaya Torgovlya* (M 1949) p. 63. It is much to Dr. Jasny's credit that he always disputed this higher figure.

[19] Report on the fulfilment of the second five-year plan.

[20] *Planovoye Khozyaistvo* 1939 no. 6, p. 131.

[21] See Chernomordik (ed.), *Narodny Dokhod SSSR* (M. 1939), p. 159.

[22] *Ibid* p. 188. The 1937 figure could have differed little from this.

[23] It may be too high even in current prices, since the total wages bill in Construction was only 6.2 milliards; true, one must add some other labour items, including the building labour

of peasants, but neither they nor profits (a relatively small item in Construction) seem sufficient to make up the difference.

[24] Chernomordik, *Op. cit.*, p. 171.

[25] *Ibid.*, pp. 153, 155.

[26] *Ibid.*, p. 155.

[27] *Op. cit.*, pp. 255-6.

[28] *Op. cit.*, p. 58; the words are his.

[29] According to Jasny, national income in 1937 should have been 53.2 milliard '1926/7' rubles, against the official 96.3, and the disparity is even wider for 1948 (see *The Soviet Economy During The Plan Era*, p. 35.)

[30] *Soviet Industrial Production.*

[31] Especially his paper presented to the Manchester Statistical Society, January 1957.

[32] *Voprosy Ekonomiki* 1957 no. 2, p. 100.

[33] *Vestnik Statistiki* 1952 no. 2.

[34] Here is a minor statistical curiosity. Whereas the 1939 edition of Ioffe gives the USSR 6.9 per cent of US production in 1913, the 1957 booklet gives 6.8 per cent for that year. Logically the latter figure should be much lower than this, since Ioffe is working backwards from a later date and has a greater total amount of exaggeration to contend with. The explanation is this: in 1939, Ioffe had to use the official index for *large-scale* industry, which for 1937 was 816 (1913= 100). Since that time, it has become customary to use the less absurd index 588, relating to *total* industry.

[35] Seton, op. cit., arrives by an original calculation at 320 (all industry, variant A, 1937=100).

THE PRICE SYSTEM

THE SOVIET PRICE SYSTEM is quite different from and more complicated than those of capitalist nations. This is due to a number of factors,
the most important of which are: the Soviet economy is a planned economy which tends to rely very heavily on direct allocation as a substitute
for the price and market mechanism; Soviet adherence to a labor theory
of value which involves not including in their accounts either interest as
a cost of fixed capital or many forms of rent as a return to superior land
and resources; inadequate accounting for depreciation and, until recently,
no consideration at all of obsolescence; extensive use of enormous commodity taxes on consumers' goods on the one hand and, until 1948 at least,
extensive granting of subsidies to enterprises producing producers' goods
and raw materials on the other; and, finally, a particularly complicated
system of prices in agriculture, especially until 1958, which results from
the use of the collective farm method of agricultural organization, the
existence of collective farm markets or bazaars in which prices are freely
set by the interaction of supply and demand, and the special techniques
employed by the state to obtain produce from the farms.

We are indebted to Professor Bergson for having brought some order
out of all this chaos. His "adjusted factor cost standard" (AFCS) provides
a theoretical basis upon which to adjust Soviet prices so that they can be
used to aggregate outputs in a meaningful economic sense. The theory
is elaborated in the first reading below and its application is sketched in
the second reading (Professor Bergson and Mr. Heymann). The AFCS
is not without its critics, and for another view of the meaningfulness or
"rationality" of Soviet prices, the reader is referred to Peter Wiles's well-
known article (1955). As the bibliographical reference to his paper suggests, the AFCS has not gone undefended.

Professor Grossman's paper represents a first attempt to set up a
classification scheme for the various types of prices and "quasi-prices" in
the industrial sector of the economy. As such, it can be looked upon, in
theory, as a detailed supplement to the application of the AFCS in the

industrial sector as well as a useful supplementary framework for thinking about some problems of planning (Section V) and operation of enterprises (Section VI). Soviet economists have not been unconcerned over some of the shortcomings of their price system and for several years have been discussing possible reforms. These discussions are analyzed in Professor Dobb's paper. Another excellent survey of the Soviet discussions is that by R. Schlesinger (1957). The relationships between these discussions and the investment-choice controversy (Section V) are discussed in M. Dobb (1961).

Problems of Soviet pricing run through many other sections of this book. Professor Grossman's essay on the interest rate (Section V) should be read in direct conjunction with the material on prices. Similarly, F. D. Holzman's papers on inflation (Section VIII) and on foreign trade (Section X) provide, respectively, summary views of domestic price and wage trends (following the pioneering studies by Jasny [1951] and by Bergson, Bernaut and Turgeon [1956]), and of foreign trade prices and exchange rates. Consumers' goods price and wage trends can be found in the Nash and Turgeon essays (Section IX) and the role of differential wages in allocating labor in E. C. Brown's paper (Section IX). The reader should also reread A. Nove (Section I) on Soviet 1926–27 pricing, and Benjamin Ward (Section V) on the proposals of the Soviet mathematician Kantorovich for obtaining rational Soviet prices by the application of linear programming techniques.

See the Appendix for a qualification of his paper by Professor Dobb.

3 THE ADJUSTED FACTOR COST STANDARD OF NATIONAL INCOME VALUATION

The Adjusted Factor Cost Standard has the following features:

(i) All commodity prices resolve directly or indirectly into a series of charges for primary factors, particularly capital, land, and labor. Insofar as the prices may represent in part charges for materials, these resolve in turn into the charges for capital, land, and labor.

(ii) In the case of capital, there is a net charge and an "allowance for depreciation." The net charge, recorded either as a "cost" under the heading of "interest" or simply as a residual income, "profits," is at a uniform rate corresponding to the average productivity of capital in the economy generally. The average productivity of capital is understood to be an average of internal rates of return given by economies in costs realized through the introduction of capital in different branches. The allowance for depreciation supposedly is in accord with orthodox accounting principles.

(iii) The charge for land, "rent," corresponds on the average to the differential return to superior land.

(iv) The charge for labor, "wages," is at a uniform rate for any given occupation. At the same time, as between occupations, differences in wages correspond to the average difference in marginal productivities and also to differences in Disutility.[1]

(v) The principles in (iv) apply also to the relation of wages and farm incomes insofar as the latter represent the rewards of labor as distinct from capital or land.

(vi) Commodity prices are uniform within any market area.

I said I would comment here on the rationale and limitations of the Adjusted Factor Cost Standard as a norm for the measurement of "real" phenomena. This may best be brought out I believe by con-

---

[1] Here and elsewhere, Disutility is understood in the broadest sense, taking into account all factors influencing a worker's choice as between jobs, including not only arduousness, but also complexity, responsibility, etc. Those who are nevertheless averse to using this concept are free to think instead in terms of "competitive supply price," which is taken here to be its equivalent.

sidering the relation of this standard to certain ideal standards of national income valuation and certain applications of national income data which valuation in these terms permits. Let me first, then, explain briefly these ideal standards and applications. Readers familiar with recent theoretic writings on national income valuation will note that I do little more here than set forth in somewhat altered form the pertinent essentials of these studies.[2]

Welfare Standard. The different commodities entering into national income are valued proportionately to the Marginal Utilities of these commodities to consumers. In the case of investment goods, future returns are discounted at the prevailing Rate of Time Preference. In general the relative Marginal Utilities of different commodities might differ for different households; the Welfare Standard, however, presupposes an optimum disposition of consumers' goods among households in the familiar sense according to which this situation is excluded.[3]

Valuation in these terms, of course, is in order where the concern is to measure comparative Welfare. In principle, only if prices correspond to the Welfare Standard can national income data in "constant" prices be taken as they always are to measure differences in Welfare either for one country at different times or as between countries.[4] Although not usually thought of in the same connection, another familiar application, but one using data in "current" rather than "constant" prices, obviously also falls under this heading. I have in mind the case where data on the allocation of the national product as between alternative uses, e.g., consumption, investment, and the like, are taken as observations on the community's propensi-

---

[2] See especially J. R. Hicks, "The Valuation of Social Income," *Economica*, May, 1940; Simon Kuznets, "On the Valuation of Social Income," *Economica*, February, May, 1948; J. R. Hicks, "The Valuation of Social Income," *Economica*, August, 1948; P. A. Samuelson, "Evaluation of Real National Income," *Oxford Economic Papers*, January, 1950. I have also benefited from some privately circulated comments of Professor Samuelson on an earlier version of this study.

[3] Here and elsewhere where reference is to the question of the optimum resource allocation, the reader may find of value the brief survey in Abram Bergson, "Socialist Economics," in H. Ellis, ed., *A Survey of Contemporary Economics.*

[4] For a lucid exposition of the rationale of this application, see Hicks in *Economica*, May, 1940. Needless to say, there are also limitations, and on these reference is to be made again to this article of Hicks and also to the other writings cited above in note 2.

ties regarding income dispositions, e.g., the "propensity to save." [5]

By implication, I have referred here to a community in which "consumers' sovereignty" is a prevailing end and where accordingly Welfare is understood in terms of the Utilities of the individual households as they see them. In the present context it obviously is advisable to reckon also with the alternative case where resources are allocated in accord with a "collective preference scale" established by some political process or other, e.g., under socialism by decision of the Planning Board itself, and where accordingly Welfare is understood (at least by the Planning Board) in terms of these collective preferences and not necessarily in terms of consumers' Utilities.[6] In this case, of course, valuation is in terms of the planners' Marginal Rates of Substitution.

Efficiency Standard. The prices at which any pair of commodities is recorded in national income are inversely proportional to the relation of the Marginal Productivity of any given factor in the production of one of them to its Marginal Productivity in the production of the other. Insofar as the relative productivities of different factors vary as between industries, this principle leads to as many diverse results as there are factors. But according to familiar reasoning this awkward possibility is excluded if another optimum condition obtains, particularly the requirement that the community be operating on its Schedule of Alternative Production Possibilities, i.e., the alternative combinations of different products such that with the available resources the output of one cannot be increased without that of another being reduced. Valuation in terms of the Efficiency Standard presupposes this condition.

As appears only recently to have been clarified,[7] national income

---

[5] Insofar as the disposition of income in any particular period is supposed, as often is the case, to depend on "real" income, of course, this application too requires comparative data in "constant" prices. But although it is not always made explicit it generally is understood that the proportions in which income is distributed between different uses are given by data on the allocation of income in "current" rather than "constant" prices.

[6] In the case of communal consumption, of course, reference must be made in any case to a collective preference scale rather than to the utilities of individual households as such.

[7] Reference is to be made again to the writings of Hicks, Kuznets, and Samuelson.

data in "constant" prices measure not only comparative Welfare but also comparative Efficiency, understood in terms of shifts in the community's Schedule of Alternative Production Possibilities. But for this the pertinent valuation principle is not the Welfare Standard but the Efficiency Standard just described. A brief exposition is noted for a simple case.[8] Essentially, use is made of a schedule of Constant Dollar Output, i.e., for any given period the alternative combinations having in terms of prevailing prices a constant value. Given valuation in accord with the Efficiency Standard, this represents an upper limit to the community's production possibilities in the given period. And given this, one determines from the national income data in "constant" prices whether the actual output of one period is outside the range of the production possibilities of another.

I have spoken of the standard just described as *the* Efficiency Stand-

---

[8] Consider the simple community illustrated in the figure. The community produces only Butter and Guns, and in two periods considered in amounts designated by o and 1. The schedules of production possibilities for the two periods are shown as Q_0 and Q_1. Also shown are corresponding Schedules of Constant Dollar Output, P_0P_0 and P_1P_1. According to familiar reasoning, given that prices are in accord with the Efficiency Standard, these Schedules must be drawn as shown with the corresponding production

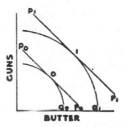

possibilities schedule either coinciding or lying to the left in each case. (Or rather this is so if there are Diminishing or Constant Returns; insofar as there are Increasing Returns, the production possibilities schedule might be to the right of the constant dollar output schedule. As the reader will readily see, the application is valid only in the former case.) From this it follows at once that alternative combinations of Butter and Guns which in terms of the prices of any given period have a greater dollar value than that actually produced at these prices, e.g., combination 1 compared with combination o at period o prices, necessarily lie beyond the production possibilities of the given period. Which is to say, of course, that a larger national income in one year in terms of the prices of another taken as base indicate the capacity to produce an output not previously feasible.

As will be seen, *decreases* in national income do not necessarily have a contrary implication. The reader will be aware that in this regard there is a parallel here to the application to Welfare, though interestingly as Samuelson has pointed out ("Evaluation of Real National Income," pp. 12 ff.), data which are decisive regarding changes in Efficiency cannot be at the same time decisive regarding changes in Welfare, and vice versa.

As with the measurement of Welfare, the measurement of Efficiency is subject to diverse limitations. One arising from Increasing Returns has been noted. On the limitations generally the reader may be referred to the theoretic writings already cited.

ard. Actually, Efficiency has been understood above in only one of several possible ways, and depending on the concept there are somewhat different standards. Insofar as it was required above that relative commodity prices correspond to factor Marginal Productivities for each and every factor, clearly reference was to Efficiency in a sense pertaining to the "long run" production possibilities schedule for which all factors, capital as well as labor and materials, are supposed to be allocable between different industries. Among the more interesting variants are these: (i) Reference is to Efficiency in terms of "short run" production possibilities, where labor and materials but not capital are supposed to be allocable between industries. In this case, the requirement concerning relative commodity prices may be somewhat relaxed. These prices must correspond to Marginal Productivity only for factors that are supposed to be allocable. (ii) Reference is to Efficiency in terms of "long run" production possibilities, but on the understanding not only that all factors are allocable but also that through retraining there may be shifts of workers as between occupations as well as between industries. In this case, the requirement concerning relative commodity prices has to be supplemented: for labor, commodity prices must reflect Disutility as well as Marginal Productivity.

As will be evident, there are corresponding differences in the conditions concerning resource allocation. In the case of the "short run" Efficiency Standard the community need be operating only on its "short run" production possibilities schedule while in the case of the two "long run" Efficiency Standards, the community must be operating on its "long run" schedule, with or without labor being shiftable between occupations, as the case may be.

The Efficiency Standard has been formulated so far in terms of factor Marginal Productivities and Disutilities. It is necessary to have in mind also another formulation. Given uniform factor prices, the correspondence of relative commodity prices to factor productivities evidently comes to the same thing as the equation of prices and Marginal Cost. At the same time, depending on what factors are supposed to be allocable, reference is either to "short run" Marginal Cost—which is to say Average Cost including rent to the "fixed factor"—or to "long run" Marginal Cost. Given constant returns to scale, the latter in turn comes to the same thing as "long run" Average Cost. In the case of such factors as are taken to be allocable, the factor prices in terms of which costs are calculated are supposed throughout to be proportional to factor Marginal Productivities in each and every industry. Finally, for the pertinent variant of the Efficiency Standard, wage differentials also correspond to Disutility.

In the case of the Welfare Standard, I referred to two kinds of applications, one the measurement of comparative Welfare, using global data in "constant" prices, the other concerning the community's propensities on income disposition, using data on the structure of the national product in "current" prices. Each of these has a counterpart in the case of the Efficiency Standard. On the one hand, given valuation according to this principle, national income data in "constant" prices, as has just been explained, provide a basis to measure comparative Efficiency. On the other hand, data in "current" prices on the allocation of the national product between investment, consumption, and the like provide a basis to calculate the alternative combinations of different kinds of output that the community is able to produce, e.g., taking the dollar value of the consumption sacrificed as an upper limit to the additional defense output made possible thereby, one calculates the community's defense production potential. This application is familiar, but it may not always be understood that it is in order only insofar as valuation is in accord with the Efficiency Standard. In the terms used here the application comes to the same thing as taking the Schedule of Constant Dollar Output as an upper limit of the Schedule of Alternative Production Possibilities. As was indicated earlier, this requires valuation in terms of the Efficiency Standard.

The theoretic standards of national income valuation have been formulated above in terms of rather abstract conditions on the price structure and without reference to the institutional arrangements under which the required price structure might be realized. For present purposes it is useful to have in mind also a few essentials on the latter aspect.

To refer first to a capitalist economy, the prevailing prices of course fully correspond at one and the same time to both the Welfare and the Efficiency Standard under "perfect competition" in the absence of distorting taxes. However, different features of "perfect competition" pertain to the different standards. For prices to correspond to the Welfare Standard it does not matter if there are sales taxes on consumers' goods or if monopoly power prevails in their production. But it would not do if there were consumers' goods rationing.[9] For prices to correspond to the Efficiency Standard, consumers' goods rationing is not necessarily of concern. But sales taxes and monopoly power at once cause deviations. Given a sales tax, for example, one can no longer suppose as is done in both the measurement of comparative Efficiency and the appraisal of alternative production possibilities that the dollar value of the Butter sacrificed is an upper limit to the dollar value of additional output of Guns made possible. If the tax is on Guns but not on Butter the increase in Guns may exceed the decrease in Butter, in dollar terms.

Strictly speaking the ideal is not "perfect competition" but the *equilibrium* of this system. Accordingly, one has to add to the list of causes of divergencies such aspects as windfall profits and rents which might occur under "perfect competition" itself. It will be evident, however, that in the case of the Efficiency Standard the situation in this regard differs depending on the variant.

For the socialist economy, one thinks at once of the familiar analogue of "perfect competition": the Competitive Solution of socialist planning.[10] As in the equilibrium of "perfect competition," so in the economic optimum of the Competitive Solution prices correspond completely to both standards.

The Competitive Solution, however, is only one of many possible planning schemes, and prices might possibly tend to correspond to the two standards under alternative arrangements. In the case of the Competitive Solution, the tendency of prices to correspond to these standards reflects the high degree of decentralization of decision-

[9] Actually a sales tax too appears to cause a deviation of prices from the Welfare Standard insofar as investment goods are valued in terms of discounted returns after taxes. In terms of consumers' Utilities the investment goods are undervalued in comparison with consumers' goods.

[10] See Abram Bergson, "Socialist Economics."

making, and together with this the fact that the Planning Board co-ordinates decisions only indirectly through "trial and error" price adjustments. Essentially, there is an open market for consumers' goods and labor, while the managers of socialist firms are allowed to determine for themselves their inputs and outputs subject to certain rules, i.e., cost economy and determination of the scale of output by the equation of Marginal Cost to price. The Planning Board manipulates prices in order to assure that Supply and Demand correspond throughout the system.

It sometimes is argued that the Planning Board might approach as closely if not more so to the optimum if in some measure it co-ordinates input and output decisions directly while still manipulating prices in some fashion to guide its own as well as its subordinate activities. The "trial and error" process is on paper rather than in the "real" world.[11] No doubt critics of planning generally will find this Centralist Scheme even more objectionable than the Competitive Solution, but it would seem that the administrative short cut envisaged is at least a logical possibility, and accordingly must be considered in any complete account of the subject being discussed.

It was said that under capitalism a sales tax causes a divergence between prices and the Efficiency Standard. This is not necessarily so. Conceivably the government might attempt through such a charge to compensate for the undervaluation of some productive factor and, insofar as this objective actually is achieved, evidently a correspondence of prices and the Efficiency Standard could be maintained. In effect, a sales tax, understood in the conventional sense of a charge based on the volume of sales and accruing as revenue to the government budget, does not represent as has been assumed a genuine addition to factor charges. Rather, it represents something of a factor charge itself.

Of course, a situation of this sort in actuality must be rare under capitalism, and a divergence between prices and the Efficiency Standard is a well-nigh universal result. On the other hand, such a situation seemingly might be of some importance under socialism, especially in a centralized type, where the government enjoys great

[11] *Ibid.*, pp. 410 ff.

discretion in deciding how to account for the different factors of production. Accordingly, while one might suppose that a divergence might be the usual result here too, the alternative is a real possibility. At the same time, what holds for the sales tax holds also for subsidies, understood as budgetary grants to cover accounting losses; and it is easy to see that there might be other elements in the socialist price system having different effects on the relation of prices to the theoretic standards, depending on the circumstances.

Actually, as will appear, these theoretic considerations have some application in the Soviet Union. On the other hand, it is only fair to say now that our appraisal of ruble prices in the chapter following attempts to proceed without any detailed inquiry into this aspect.[12]

To come finally to the relation of the Adjusted Factor Cost Standard to the theoretic standards, the essentials can now be readily set forth. If the reader will refer again to the definition of the Adjusted Factor Cost Standard he will see at once that this comes to the same thing as Average Cost, understood as not necessarily the cost actually recorded. Rather it is what would be recorded if factor prices were uniform as between industries and at the same time corresponded to

[12] It may be in order to comment briefly here on some special aspects of the problem of valuation discussed in the theoretic writings to which reference has been made at various points, particularly those of Hicks and Kuznets. First, while I am committed in this study to treat all of government as a final product (see above, Chapter 2, section on methodology), there is no reason to dissent here from the view of Hicks and Kuznets that in principle some of this category should be treated as intermediate. As to whether this is also a practicable procedure, as Kuznets affirms ("On the Valuation of Social Income," pp. 6 ff.) and Hicks has conceded (in his second essay in *Economica*, 1948, pp. 164 ff.), is a question which it may be just as well to pass by. Second, given direct taxes and free government services that affect factor supply prices, there seems to the writer to be no alternative but to recognize that there is no fully valid Efficiency Standard where the concern is with "long run" production possibilities taking into account workers' shifts between occupations as well as industries. Relative prices that correspond to factor productivities cannot at the same time correspond to Disutilities. This is to be contrasted with Kuznets' view (p. 123), apparently accepted by Hicks (pp. 165 ff.), that the valid Efficiency Standard in these circumstances is one for which factor incomes are included net of direct taxes and gross of free public services affecting factor supply prices. Third, the writer agrees with Hicks (p. 168) that contrary to the implied view of Kuznets (p. 123) free public services cannot be supposed generally to affect factor supply prices. Fourth and last, it seems necessary to follow Hicks in rejecting Kuznets' attempt to reconcile the Welfare and Efficiency Standards. Kuznets relies in this connection on the views to which the writer has just taken exception.

relative factor productivities *on the average* in the economy generally. In the case of labor there is an analogous relation of wages to
Disutility.[13]

Suppose now the community is on its production possibilities
schedule, and more particularly the "long run" one where there are
shifts of workers between occupations. In this case, relative factor
productivities are the same in each and every industry. Accordingly,
factor prices that correspond to relative factor productivities *on the
average* also correspond to these productivities in each industry. Also,
there is a similar extension of the relation of wages to Disutility. This
is to say, then, that the Adjusted Factor Cost Standard comes to the
same thing as the Efficiency Standard, given operation on the production possibilities schedule. The production possibilities schedule
is the "long run" one just referred to, and reference is particularly to
the variant of the Efficiency Standard pertaining to this schedule.[14]
But, of course, if the Adjusted Factor Cost Standard corresponds to
this variant it would also correspond to the others, which are less restrictive.

Suppose in addition the consumers' goods are disposed of among
households in an optimum manner, and furthermore there is an
optimum "bill of goods" in the familiar sense, in terms of consumers'
Utilities or planners' preferences as the case may be, i.e., if reference
is to consumers' Utilities, the ratio of the Marginal Utilities of any
two commodities corresponds to the rate at which one can be substituted for another through resource reallocation. In this case, it is self-

[13] In the case of materials which are at the same time a factor and a product, an
awkward possibility is that a price that corresponded on the average to the relative
productivity of this article in comparison with other factors would not at the same time
correspond to Average Cost in terms of the given prices of factors in general. It is a
familiar fact, however, that there are generally relatively limited possibilities of substitution between materials and other factors so one may be justified in assuming that
any of a wide range of prices might correspond equally well to relative factor productivities in the case of materials. On the other hand, where this is not the case, the
Adjusted Factor Cost Standard and Average Cost as understood are not the same
thing. I believe I am right in thinking that in the case of capital goods where there is
an additional degree of freedom to determine the value of the asset there is no
comparable problem.

[14] I am assuming of course constant returns to scale. Otherwise the Adjusted Factor
Cost Standard still diverges from the Efficiency Standard to the extent of the divergence
between "long run" Average and Marginal Cost.

evident that the Adjusted Factor Cost Standard corresponds also to the Welfare Standard.

On the other hand, if the bill of goods and their disposition are not optimal this is not the case. Furthermore, if the community is not on its "long run" production possibilities schedule the Adjusted Factor Cost Standard also diverges from the Efficiency Standard. Of course the community might still be on its "short run" production possibilities schedule but, even so, the Adjusted Factor Cost Standard diverges from the variant of the Efficiency Standard pertaining to this schedule. While valuation at Adjusted Factor Cost allows only an average return on capital, this variant of the Efficiency Standard requires the inclusion in prices of the entire "short run" profit to capital.

In the "real" world, of course, the optimum conditions are never fully met, so in actuality the Adjusted Factor Cost Standard never could correspond to either of the two theoretic standards. But clearly depending on the efficiency of resource allocation it approximates them more or less closely. Let me explain, then, that it is as such an approximation that the Adjusted Factor Cost Standard has been selected for study here. Given the inefficiency, the theoretic standards are themselves unattainable. There is no valuation for which national income data are theoretically valid measures of the "real" phenomena described. It may be hoped that with valuation at Adjusted Factor Cost the range of conjecture is less than it might be otherwise.[15]

But what of resource allocation in the USSR? To what extent is

[15] As is mentioned below and in any case is surely almost inevitable, resource allocation in the Soviet Union as in Western countries tends to approach more closely "short run" than "long run" production possibilities. Under the circumstances, the Adjusted Factor Cost Standard presumably approximates more nearly to the "long run" than to the "short run" variant of the Efficiency Standard. The approximate in neither case, however, could be especially close, and the possibility is suggested that, as an alternative, attention might be focused on an Adjusted Factor Cost Standard which would approximate more nearly the "short run" variant. Thus, an attempt would be made to allow for "short run" profits to capital rather than, as I have, merely to include an average return. Given the closer approach of resource allocation to "short run" production possibilities it might be hoped that the end result while still only an approximation would be more nearly valid theoretically. This alternative, I believe, is indeed an attractive one in principle; if I have not endeavored to apply it here it is simply because of the limitations of data which hardly permit a calculation of "short run" profits.

Of course, in Western countries, the tendency of resource allocation to approximate the optimum realized? From what is said in the chapter following on the relation of ruble values to Real Costs and from generally known facts, the reader will have some impression of Soviet economic efficiency. But it may be hoped that it will be understood, too, that no attempt can be made here to deal explicitly with this large question. Although it obviously is a major concern, the extent to which valuation at Adjusted Factor Cost approximates the ideal has to be left an open question here.

But obviously even in the best of circumstances the approximation could not be especially close; and it still remains to be seen to what extent the Adjusted Factor Cost Standard itself is realizable with available statistical data. Why not, then, do as Clark and Wyler do after all; that is, abandon the ruble standard altogether, and use instead non-Soviet prices? The writer does not deny that this alternative is tempting. But before renouncing calculations in terms of rubles once and for all, the reader should ponder, too, the limitations of non-Soviet prices.

Both Clark and Wyler resort to United States dollar prices: the former, the average dollar prices of the period 1925-34 (the calculations are in terms of "international units" having the average purchasing power of the dollar in this period); and the latter, dollar prices of 1940. But the dollar prices necessarily reflect the preferences, technology, and cost structure, not of the USSR at the time studied, but of the United States. Accordingly, the national income data might be used in comparisons of Welfare or Efficiency as between the United States and Russia, though obviously even here there is only a partial basis for an appraisal. But, except by chance, they could hardly be used to appraise the prevailing Soviet propensities on income disposition or alternative production possibilities; or for intertemporal

---

more to "short run" than to "long run" production possibilities is associated with a corresponding tendency of prices to approximate more to the "short run" than to the "long run" variant of the Efficiency Standard. Given this there is at once an impelling case for according priority to the former variant; and this is the general practice insofar as use usually is made of prevailing prices without any revaluation. But while there is a parallel to Western experience in the case of resource allocation there unfortunately is little basis to think there is one in the case of prices as well, so any arguments for the "short run" variant from this standpoint would be unfounded. As to this view on Soviet price formation, the information set forth in the next chapter may be illuminating but for present purposes it probably is best to consider it as a working hypothesis.

comparisons of Welfare or Efficiency for the USSR alone. For such purposes, the calculations almost inevitably are distorted. Thus, suppose as seems true that the United States technical superiority is more pronounced for highly fabricated than for little fabricated goods. One might expect United States dollar prices for investment goods, then, to be relatively low in comparison with consumers' goods. The reduction of investment in the USSR by one dollar in terms of United States prices might actually release resources sufficient to produce much more than a dollar's worth of consumers' goods in terms of the same prices, rather than less as is supposed in appraising alternative production possibilities.

Furthermore, it is self-evident that any limitations in our calculations arising from deviations of Soviet resource allocation from the optimum must inhere also in calculations in terms of dollar prices.

Finally the dollar price structure is something less than ideal even in reference to the appraisal of "real" phenomena in the United States. I have in mind, of course, such aspects as monopoly power, taxes and subsidies, and regulated prices.[16]

---

[16] Without attempting to outline an alternative, the writer has commented elsewhere on the limitations of the dollar valuation procedure. See Abram Bergson, "Comments" in "The Economy of the USSR," Papers and Proceedings of the Fifty-ninth Annual Meeting of the American Economic Association, *American Economic Review*, 1947, No. 2, pp. 643 ff. Maurice Dobb also discusses the problem in *Soviet Economy and the War*, pp. 37 ff.

The reader familiar with the earlier version of this study in the *Quarterly Journal of Economics* for May and August, 1950 ("Soviet National Income and Product in 1937, Part I: National Economic Accounts in Current Rubles; Part II: Ruble Prices and the Valuation Problem") will have noted that my treatment of the valuation question is now appreciably altered. Among other things, the Adjusted Factor Cost Standard as now understood represents a combination of a "real" cost standard, previously defined, together with another so-called "physical volume of resources used" standard that also was considered previously. The precise nature of and basis for this revision I believe are sufficiently evident, but it should be noted that the revision is intended in part to take account of illuminating comments on the earlier version in memoranda prepared for private circulation by Professor Paul A. Samuelson and Mr. Norman Kaplan. Also, I have taken the occasion now to discuss more explicitly than before the rationale of the standard adopted and in this connection acknowledgment is due again to these memoranda, especially Professor Samuelson's. Finally, mention should be made of a third memorandum by Professor Jacob Marschak. Among other things, this sets forth the interesting proposal that in view of the limited substitutability as between major categories of goods, e.g., food, plant construction, munitions, aggregation should be limited to summations within these categories and should not extend to summations of the categories themselves. The limited substitutability is from the standpoint of war potential.

To proceed first with the survey of the relation of ruble prices and Adjusted Factor Cost, we refer in turn to the more important features of the ruble price system in the years studied and ask in each case how this affects the relation of ruble prices to Adjusted Factor Cost.

Turnover tax. There appears to be no place in Adjusted Factor Cost for the famous turnover tax of the USSR. The tax is probably a more complex fiscal device than is generally supposed and among other things is calculated in very diverse ways, i.e., as a percentage of sales, as a fixed absolute charge per unit, as a residual charge to the distributor after allowance for a standard trade margin, etc.[1] But in all its manifestations the tax for all practical purposes comes to the same thing as a sales tax, this being understood as a charge against sales revenue based on the volume of sales and yielding a corresponding revenue to the government budget. As such, the tax represents a charge over and above the charges to factors. Accordingly, for all the years studied it must be reckoned as an initial source of divergence between ruble prices and Adjusted Factor Cost.

Such a divergence is of concern here of course only to the extent that it varies between different elements in our accounts, e.g., consumption and investment. Even a uniform sales tax would have this

---

[1] On the turnover tax, see *Soviet National Income*, pp. 56–57; also Appendix D, Section A, of the present study.

result, however, insofar as the tax would tend to pyramid in the process of the conversion of raw materials into finished goods. But in any case an outstanding feature of the turnover tax is the wide variation in rates. Throughout the period studied the rates have been practically nominal on basic industrial goods and notably high though still diverse on agricultural produce and consumers' goods. The rates in effect in the year 1940 are believed to be broadly illustrative of all the years considered. The tax was levied in 1940 at the rate of 1.0 percent on machinery and chemicals and .5 percent on coal, peat, and metal products. For men's leather shoes the rate was 10 to 40 percent; for salt, 70 to 80 percent; and for aluminum kitchenware, 50 to 60 percent.[2] Unlike practically all basic industrial goods, petroleum products were subject to a relatively high tax, e.g., in the case of fuel and motor oil, 60.5 percent; in the case of kerosene, 71.7 percent.[3] Under the circumstances, it turns out that the turnover tax is not only a cause of divergence between ruble prices and Adjusted Factor Cost but the most important one with which we have to deal.

Subsidies. Of a piece with a sales tax, though with opposite effects on the relation of prices to Adjusted Factor Cost, is a subsidy which permits operation at a price less than that corresponding to the charges for productive services. As is already clear, this is also a feature in the USSR, though one of varying importance in the different years studied.[4] Under a price reform of April, 1936, the government limited the previously extensive practice of granting subsidies to state enterprises, but such payments continued thereafter on some scale, and according to very rough calculations, which we have previously summarized in Table 4 (pp. 22 ff.), had again increased by 1940. During the war the government apparently was able to limit the total amount of subsidies to something like the 1940 level, but there was still another and notably large increase in the mid-forties. In 1948 subsidies had reached the impressive sum of over 50 billion rubles, or about 6.5 percent of

[2] See the sources cited in Appendix D, Section A. For machinery, chemicals, coal, peat, metal products, and salt the rates refer to the wholesale price gross of the tax. For leather shoes the rates refer to the retail price, and for aluminum kitchenware they refer to the retail price less an allowance for retail distribution costs.

[3] The rates refer to the wholesale price gross of the tax.

[4] On Soviet subsidies, see *Soviet National Income,* pp. 57–58, 114 ff., 128 ff., 139 ff.; also the present study, Appendix B, pp. 175 ff., Appendix D, Section B.

the gross national product. The government again curtailed subsidy payments, however, under a second major price reform of January, 1949.

As with the turnover tax, so with subsidies: what concerns us here is the relative incidence in different economic sectors. A major recipient of subsidies throughout was industry, especially the basic industrial branches. As subsidies mounted after the war this sector was by far the principal beneficiary. Because of the undervaluation of the income in kind of the MTS, however, this sector also had to be granted sizable subsidies, and at the low procurement prices paid state farms for their produce probably these too had to be subsidized continually. Varying sums were paid at different times to transport and other sectors.

To just what extent subsidies caused a relative divergence of ruble prices from Adjusted Factor Cost for different elements in our accounts is a matter for subsequent inquiry; but enough has been said to make clear that such an inquiry is much in order.

Interest and profits; depreciation. Under the *khozraschet* system, the Soviet enterprise obtains most of its capital without payment of interest. Interest is charged on short-term loans obtained from the State Bank for seasonal and other working-capital needs, and also on some long-term loans to agriculture and cooperatives; but for the rest capital is provided to the enterprise in the form of interest-free grants. On the other hand, except in the case of subsidized enterprises, prices generally are fixed to allow the enterprise a profit for operating in accord with the plan. At the same time, there necessarily are unplanned profits due to deviations from the plan.

Following the procedure of *Soviet National Income*,[5] we assume provisionally that planned profits are a more or less arbitrary category in Soviet accounts, and in any case not a bona fide charge for capital. Soviet sources have little to say about the determination of planned profits, and without a more detailed inquiry into the *khozraschet* system than can be undertaken here, we cannot exclude the possibility that the planned profits represent an indirect interest charge, but it is believed that the final upshot of our study is hardly affected by our assumption to the contrary. As to the extraplan profits, for present

[5] Pages 58–59.

purposes these must be considered as wages of management, insofar as they represent superior administrative ability or alternatively as a windfall gain of the type familiar under capitalism.

At this point, then, it is necessary to reckon with two divergencies between ruble prices and Adjusted Factor Cost: on the one hand, the omission of a systematic charge for interest in the case of most capital; on the other, the inclusion of a category "profits" which only in part represents a productive service rendered.[6]

Under the Soviet *khozraschet* system, ruble costs generally include a charge for depreciation, made at rates established by law. There are reasons to believe, however, that this charge is inadequate for purposes of this study. In the first place, it often is suggested that the charge, made at rates regulated by law, tends to overestimate the service life of fixed assets under the conditions of the five year plans. Whether and to what extent this is so in general must be left to a separate inquiry, but there clearly was such an overestimation, at least under wartime conditions of extreme use. Furthermore, depreciation is calculated in the USSR on the basis of original cost. In view of the price inflation under the five year plans, the corresponding allowance in terms of replacement cost undoubtedly would be much higher.

Beyond this, the *khozraschet* system does not apply to all branches of the economy; in particular it does not extend to the MTS or collective farms.[7] As will appear, the question of the relation of ruble prices to Adjusted Factor Cost for agricultural products revolves largely around the highly conjectural problem concerning the valuation of agricultural labor services; but in any wholly complete analysis one may also wish to take into account the omission from agricultural accounts of any systematic charge for depreciation.

Agricultural rent. In the USSR, there is no explicit charge for agricultural land comparable to the "rent" included in Adjusted Factor Cost. A concealed charge is made for this factor, however, under the

---

[6] Even in the case of short-term capital obtained in the form of loans from the State Bank a question is still in order as to whether the rate of interest charged is in accord with Adjusted Factor Cost. Furthermore, it will be evident that even unplanned profits cause a divergence from Adjusted Factor Cost insofar as they represent windfall gains rather than wages of management.

[7] In the case of the MTS, some type of depreciation charge is probably recorded in income accounts that are drawn up for individual stations. But no allowance is included

complex agricultural procurement system. More particularly, the obligatory deliveries at nominal prices tend to vary in accordance with differences in the quality and possibly also in the location of the land. At the same time, differences in procurement prices between obligatory and other deliveries are largely offset by differential turnover taxes. As a result, the farmers with better land are indirectly charged a higher tax than their fellows. Insofar as the turnover tax becomes in this way a form of agricultural rent, there is in effect an exception to the view expressed previously that the tax is a source of divergence between ruble prices and Adjusted Factor Cost.[8]

Wage differentials; collective farm incomes; military pay. According to *Soviet National Income,*[9] there probably was a very broad correspondence around the period considered, i.e., 1937, between wage differentials and productivity and possibly also between wage differentials and Disutility. This view was based on a variety of considerations, including chiefly the prevalence of the *khozraschet* system according to which state enterprises tended to economize money costs and consequently to limit their employment of different kinds of labor in the light of the relation of wages and productivity; the system of wage administration whereby wages tended to be differentiated on much the same basis as under capitalism; and the extensive reliance on an open market to recruit labor in accordance with the requirements of the plan.

The *khozraschet* system has continued to operate in the USSR in the period now studied, and in the light of the progress of Soviet planning as a whole the concern about money cost economy may well have grown in the course of time. The government similarly has continued to administer wages along the general lines marked out in the

---

in the comprehensive financial accounts that are used in the preparation of the government budget. See the comments on depreciation in Appendix B, pp. 189 ff.

[8] See *Soviet National Income,* pp. 59 ff. As was explained in the cited pages, there may be other instances of this sort where the turnover tax is a concealed factor charge. Also, in the case of subsidies, it is necessary to reckon with the analogous possibility that these are sometimes an offset to an excessive factor charge. For reasons that will become sufficiently clear, however, the end result of this study will be little affected if for the most part we pass by these special cases and proceed on the assumption made previously that the turnover tax and subsidies both represent to their full extent divergencies between ruble prices and Adjusted Factor Cost.

[9] *Ibid.,* pp. 63 ff.

thirties, though just how differentials have varied in the course of time has yet to be adequately explored.[10] On the other hand, as already has been explained,[11] the Russians, since 1940, have been relying to a significant extent on direct controls in recruiting labor. The change dates mainly from 1940, and in accordance with familiar economic reasoning this development, while perhaps not affecting the relation of wage differentials and productivity, would tend to impair the relation between wages and Disutility in the years of concern here. This relation has no doubt also been affected by the developments in the retail market in the years studied, including the growing deficiencies and the appearance of a spread in state and collective farm market prices before the war, the application of rationing after the outbreak of the war and until December, 1947, and the extremely high prices in the wartime collective farm market and "commercial shops." Under the circumstances, money wage differentials must have tended to lose significance to the Soviet worker, and the relation between wages and Disutility could only have been further impaired.

The precise relation between farm and city incomes that ought to prevail under Adjusted Factor Cost is conjectural, but it may be of interest here that the collective farmer's "real" income in 1937 probably was not much below that of the industrial worker. The average income of the Soviet collective farmer in 1937 was 1,760 rubles per full-time man-year.[12] This represents the sum of money earnings together with income in kind valued at realized farm prices. If allowance were made for the relative undervaluation of income in kind, the figure would be a good deal higher, and might approach the 3,005-ruble wage earned by the average industrial worker in the same year.

Because of gaps in information, trends in the relation of collective farm and industrial earnings over the years now studied have to be appraised from the following data (in percent of 1937), based in part on rule-of-thumb calculations:[13]

[10] See Schwartz, *Russia's Soviet Economy*, pp. 463 ff.

[11] See above, p. 14.

[12] *Soviet National Income*, pp. 68 ff.

[13] The figures on farm incomes are calculated from the data in Table 3, p. 20, on the total income of households from agriculture, and the following guesses as to the farm labor force: 1937, 35 million; 1940, 40 million; 1944, 30 million; 1948, 40 million. In contrast to the calculation of the 1937 study, the average farm income as now computed

YEAR	AVERAGE FARM INCOME	AVERAGE WAGE OF HIRED WORKERS	RELATIVE EARNINGS OF COLLECTIVE FARMERS AND HIRED WORKERS
1937	100	100	100
1940	159	134	119
1944	179	190	94
1948	194	234	83

Farm income in this tabulation represents farm income as it is recorded in our accounts, and changes in the relation of this to money wages do not necessarily measure changes in relative "real" income. Among other things, relative incomes as calculated might differ from relative "real" incomes because of the arbitrary valuation of farm income in kind in 1944 at 1940 farm prices. The wartime rationing obviously is a further source of divergence.

It is open to question, however, whether valuation at Adjusted Factor Cost necessarily involves valuing farm and nonfarm services in accordance with year-to-year changes in the relative "real" incomes accruing to them. What, for example, if the changes are only of a "windfall" character, due, say, to an abrupt shift in demand? In any event, we propose to adopt here an extremely simplified expedient: for purposes of appraising the relation of ruble prices to Adjusted Factor Cost, we arbitrarily take the relative values of farm and nonfarm services recorded in our accounts for 1937 as a norm, and we inquire as to the extent to which there have been divergencies in relative values from this norm in subsequent years. From this standpoint, then, the tabulation just set forth suggests a possible overvaluation of farm services in 1940 and an undervaluation of these services in 1948.[14]

relates to all farm workers and not merely to collective farmers. Also, the 1937 study took account of off-the-farm earnings together with off-the-farm working time, while in the present calculation we pass by both these aspects. For present purposes it will be evident that these divergencies in method are immaterial. In the case of the earnings of hired labor we start with a figure of 3,038 rubles representing the average earnings of all such workers in 1937. See Gosplan, *Tretii piatiletnii plan razvitiia narodnogo khoziaistva Soiuza SSR (1938–42 gg.) (prockt)*, p. 228. The figure of 3,005 rubles cited in the 1937 study refers to industrial workers alone. For the years 1940, 1944, and 1948 reference is made to the data on wages compiled in Appendix A, pp. 127 ff. These data again refer to the earnings of all hired labor.

[14] To come back to the valuation of income in kind in 1944, our national economic accounts and the tabulation given above, are based on valuation in terms of average realized farm prices of 1940, with the resultant magnitude of 33 billion rubles. If the

Military pay becomes an especially important item in one of the years studied; for this reason separate reference to this item is in order. In our accounts, we have sought to value military services at the prevailing military pay rates (for the remuneration in money) and at the costs of food and clothing to the government (for the remuneration in kind). The resulting earnings of military personnel averaged 2,286 rubles per man in 1937, 3,457 rubles in 1940, 3,767 rubles in 1944, and 8,250 rubles in 1948.[15] We tabulate, below, data on the relation of these earnings to the pay of hired civilian workers in the corresponding years:

YEAR	AVERAGE MILITARY EARNINGS AS PERCENT OF AVERAGE EARNINGS OF HIRED CIVILIAN WORKERS	RELATION OF AVERAGE MILITARY EARNINGS TO AVERAGE EARNINGS OF HIRED CIVILIAN WORKERS (1937 = 100)
1937	75	100
1940	85	113
1944	65	87
1948	116	154

As with collective farm services, so with the services of military personnel: the precise valuation called for by the Adjusted Factor Cost standard is open to diverse interpretations. If, as might be suggested, civilian earnings are taken as a norm, military services in our accounts are overvalued in 1948 and undervalued in all other years, especially 1944. On the other hand, we might instead adopt the expedient intro-

valuation had been made instead at the average realized farm prices of 1944, income in kind in that year would have come to some 83 billion rubles. With this revision, the average farm income in 1944 would be raised from 179 to 286 percent of that of 1937. The index of the relative earnings of collective farmers and hired wage earners (1937 = 100 percent) would be increased correspondingly from 94 to 150. In suggesting previously (p. 28) that valuation of 1944 income in kind at 1940 prices resulted in a more plausible figure for the value of farm services than did valuation at 1944 prices, we had in mind the foregoing relationships.

Regarding the problem of the valuation of farm services generally, evidently what is in question for present purposes is the relation to industrial wages of farm incomes qua returns to labor as distinct from land or capital. As is explained in *Soviet National Income*, p. 62, the farm earnings recorded in our accounts probably include elements of both rent to land and interest on capital in addition to the return to labor. In the context, however, any attempt to reckon with this aspect surely would represent an undue refinement.

[15] See Appendix A, pp. 136 ff.

duced with regard to agricultural services, i.e., take the 1937 relation to the earnings of civilian workers as a norm. In this case there is a limited overvaluation of military services in 1940, a comparable undervaluation in 1944, and a sizable overvaluation in 1948. In the subsequent attempt to appraise the effects on our accounts of divergencies between ruble prices and Adjusted Factor Cost, we shall be guided by the second of these two approaches to the valuation of military services.

Multiple prices. An outstanding case of multiple prices in the USSR has already been referred to. This is the case of agricultural procurement prices. But reference here is only to agricultural raw materials at the procurement stage. As a result of the imposition of turnover taxes, the prices charged to the processors of these materials are made more or less uniform. Accordingly, so far as the prices of processed goods are concerned, there is no major divergence of prices and Adjusted Factor Cost on this account.

But the use of taxes to equalize the prices of agricultural products, while the general rule, is not universal. For purposes of stockpiling and export, grain and possibly other unprocessed agricultural goods are turned over to the agencies concerned at the same low prices the government pays farmers for obligatory deliveries. At least this was the practice before the war and very likely it has continued.[16] To this extent, then, there is a divergence between prices and Adjusted Factor Cost which affects our accounts.

It was mentioned earlier that developments in the retail market in the period studied, particularly shortages, rationing, and multiple prices, would have tended to undermine the relation of money wages to Disutility and in this way cause a divergence of ruble prices from Adjusted Factor Cost. But insofar as there are multiple prices, this in itself constitutes a divergence from Adjusted Factor Cost, and one that was especially notable in the period considered. On the basis of diverse information, we think in terms of an average differential of 50 percent between collective farm market prices and state shop prices in 1940.[17] In 1944 collective farm market prices may have been of the order of eight times as high as state shop ration prices, while the differential

---

[16] *Soviet National Income,* p. 63.
[17] See Appendix D, Section C.

between the wartime "commercial shop" prices and the ration prices must have been similar. In 1948, after the abandonment of rationing, prices in the collective farm market probably were not substantially above the state shop level.

It is sometimes suggested that the ruble price system tends to "favor" the armed forces in the sense that prices are systematically differentiated so as to reduce the procurement costs to the military. Evidently, the prices of munitions "benefit" in at least the same manner as other nonconsumption goods from the uneven impact on different commodities of turnover taxes on the one hand and subsidies on the other. But the question that is raised here concerns the possibility that, over and above this, the armed forces and defense industries might be in a position to procure goods on uniquely favorable terms compared with other purchasers as a result of the extension to them of special exemptions from, or special low rates of, the turnover tax, of special subsidies, or of other discriminatory accounting arrangements. No evidence has been found in Soviet sources to support the suggestion that ruble prices are differentiated in this way. In fact, available information, including a price handbook issued by the Soviet air force procurement division, indicates important instances to the contrary. More particularly, in the case of grain, various other foods, and oil products, the armed forces apparently pay the same prices, inclusive of the turnover tax, as wholesale consumers generally.[18] The evidence on this matter is clearly insufficient to permit a definite conclusion, but in the absence of any

---

[18] According to A. K. Suchkov, *Gosudarstvennye dokhody, SSSR,* p. 81, the state grain procurement agency sells its grain at the same price, inclusive of the tax, to the military establishment as to other wholesale consumers. Elsewhere (p. 107) Suchkov informs us that the turnover tax is levied on aviation gasoline and lubricants; there is no suggestion that the armed forces are exempted from the tax. A 1944 compilation of turnover tax rates and regulations shows that various food products are sold to the military establishment at the same prices, inclusive of turnover tax, as are charged other consumers. See Narkomfin, SSSR, Upravlenie Gosdokhodov, *Spravochnik po stavkam naloga s oborota i biudzhetnoi raznitse po prodovol'stvennym tovaram,* 1944, e.g., pp. 21, 22, 25, 33, 44, 49, 53, 56, 60. The Soviet air force price handbook referred to is RKKA, Upravlenie Voennykh Vozdushnykh Sil, *Tsennik-spravochnik po material'noi chasti VVS RKKA, Chast' III,* pp. 69–71. A comparison of the petroleum prices quoted in this source with those cited in other price handbooks reveals that they are the prices which were established by a decree of the Economic Council under the Council of Commissars (No. 1,432 of August 19, 1940). These prices are inclusive of the turnover tax and evidently apply to all wholesale consumers.

positive indications we assume that special pricing arrangements of the sort mentioned do not constitute an important source of divergence between ruble prices and Adjusted Factor Cost.

During 1944 the Russians received about 3.5 billion dollars worth of imports on Lend-Lease account.[19] The Soviet government is believed to have transferred these imports to Soviet economic and military organizations for some 24 billion rubles, or at a ratio of about 7 rubles to a dollar.[20] If one adheres strictly to the view which has been the guiding one in this study, that customs and similar charges represent a form of national product domestically produced, there appears to be little basis to question this or any other valuation that the Soviet government might have placed on Lend-Lease goods. On the other hand, if these charges are included on the understanding that the end result is to be disposable national product, one might wish to value Lend-Lease imports more or less in accordance with ruble prices of similar domestic goods. Whether and to what extent the Soviet government's valuation approaches this result, however, must be left conjectural here. In terms of retail prices, a parity of 7 to 1 certainly overvalues the ruble; but it is not clear whether and to what extent this was also true of wartime wholesale prices. The fact that the arbitrary Soviet official exchange rate was 5.3 to 1 at the time considered is, of course, not especially pertinent to the appropriate valuation of the Lend-Lease goods.[21]

[19] Lend-Lease shipments from the United States alone amounted to 3.4 billion dollars. See United States Department of Commerce, *International Reference Service,* December, 1945, p. 3. In addition, a small amount of goods was shipped from Canada and the United Kingdom.

[20] See above, p. 43.

[21] In addition to the cases of multiple prices cited in the text, there have been various others in the USSR in the years studied, but it is believed that these are of relatively limited consequence for present purposes. Among the remaining cases, mention may be made of the limited premium above state shop prices which cooperatives were permitted to charge around 1948 on sales of goods procured locally as distinct from sales of goods obtained from central sources. See on this J. Chapman, *Retail Prices in the USSR, 1937–48,* pp. 42 ff.

TABLE 11

GROSS NATIONAL PRODUCT BY USE IN ESTABLISHED AND ADJUSTED PRICES, USSR, 1937, 1940, 1944, AND 1948[a]

A. BILLIONS OF RUBLES

ITEM	1937		1940		1944		1948	
	IN ESTAB-LISHED PRICES	IN AD-JUSTED PRICES	IN ESTAB-LISHED PRICES	IN AD-JUSTED PRICES	IN ESTAB-LISHED PRICES	IN AD-JUSTED PRICES	IN ESTAB-LISHED PRICES	IN AD-JUSTED PRICES
1. Consumption of households								
a. Civilian	181.0	122.9	280.3	195.8	217.9	137.5	451.8	265.9
b. Military subsistence	2.5	1.8	8.0	6.5	31.0	30.9	19.0	13.0
c. Total	183.5	124.7	288.3	202.3	248.9	168.4	470.8	278.9
2. Communal services	27.4	23.8	36.4	32.8	30.9	30.9	85.1	71.7
3. Government administration, including NKVD (MVD and MGB)	7.4	6.9	13.9	13.2	14.0	14.1	38.9	36.4
4. Defense (as recorded in budget)	17.5	17.3	56.7	57.1	137.7	139.9	66.3	72.0
5. Gross investment	56.1	51.2	62.7	60.6	55.9	55.2	150.1	157.8
6. Gross national product	291.8	223.9	458.0	366.1	487.4	408.5	811.2	616.7

B. IN PERCENT

ITEM	1937 IN ESTABLISHED PRICES	1937 IN ADJUSTED PRICES	1940 IN ESTABLISHED PRICES	1940 IN ADJUSTED PRICES	1944 IN ESTABLISHED PRICES	1944 IN ADJUSTED PRICES	1948 IN ESTABLISHED PRICES	1948 IN ADJUSTED PRICES
1. Consumption of households								
a. Civilian	62.0	54.9	61.2	53.5	44.7	33.7	55.7	43.1
b. Military subsistence	.9	.8	1.7	1.8	6.4	7.5	2.3	2.1
c. Total	62.9	55.7	62.9	55.3	51.1	41.2	58.0	45.2
2. Communal services	9.4	10.6	8.0	9.0	6.3	7.6	10.5	11.6
3. Government administration, including NKVD (MVD and MGB)	2.5	3.1	3.0	3.6	2.9	3.5	4.8	5.9
4. Defense (as recorded in budget)	6.0	7.7	12.4	15.6	28.3	34.2	8.2	11.7
5. Gross investment	19.2	22.9	13.7	16.6	11.5	13.5	18.5	25.6
6. Gross national product	100.0	100.0	100.0	100.0	100.0	100.0	100.0	100.0

* See Tables 6, 8, 9, 10. Minor discrepancies between calculated sums of items and indicated totals are due to rounding.

SOVIET ECONOMIC PLANNING

INDUSTRIAL PRICES IN THE USSR[1]

By GREGORY GROSSMAN
University of California

This brief paper inquires into the role of prices in the Soviet economy during the plan era, especially from the administrative and financial reforms of 1929-34 to the reorganization of industry and construction in 1957. My time is short, and I limit the scope of my attention equally severely. I am here concerned primarily with prices at the enterprise level, as contrasted with the planning level, and with only one of the four transaction areas of the Soviet economy; namely, that in which state entities deal with each other.

I

The transaction areas of the Soviet economy are defined by the four possible ways of pairing the two main categories of transactor—the state enterprise (or other state agency) and the household (in its capacity of petty private producer as well as consumer)—each of whom can be a buyer or a seller. Co-operative enterprises are assimilated into one or the other of the two categories as convenience dictates. The outside world is here ignored.

In our transaction area, which can also be spoken of as the state sector, the prices are chiefly those of intermediate and final products of industry, on which I shall concentrate here for the sake of simplicity, of the products of construction and transportation and of such primary factors of production as the state owns outright (land, mineral resources, investible capital, etc.).

But first I comment briefly on prices in the other three areas: (1) Since households deal with each other in an essentially free market (chiefly the so-called *kolkhoz* market, but also private leasing of dwelling space, "speculation," and so forth), prices in this area are defined by the simple interaction of supply and demand. Needless to say, because of its overwhelming role in the economy the state of course does influence these prices indirectly, whether incidentally or intentionally. (2) Prices charged by the state to households, primarily in the sale of consumers' goods to them, are so set—speaking generally but not very precisely—that the total value of sales will approximate the total disposable household income during the period and the retail price of an individual good roughly equates expected demand

---

[1] This and all other footnotes appear at the end of this paper.

and planned supply, for the whole country or a large zone of it. The chief financial instrument used to attain the aggregate and partial equilibria is the turnover tax. In normal times, formal rationing is avoided, except for housing space. This is not to say that the equilibria are usually achieved; prices probably tend to err on the low side for this. (3) Prices paid by the state to households are primarily for labor and for agricultural produce. Wages, based on complicated centrally-determined formulas, are roughly such as to deploy labor according to the needs of the production plan. This is not to overlook administrative direction, limitation of mobility, and coercion, applied to nearly all labor between 1940 and 1956 (or, effectively, 1951) and in varying measure to certain categories of labor throughout. The structure of prices paid for agricultural produce has been complicated in the extreme, especially prior to their reform of June, 1958. On the whole, these prices have been—and continue to be after the reform as well— so low as to be coupled with compulsory delivery quotas.

II

To return to the state sector, let us, perhaps at the risk of reciting the familiar, remind ourselves of some of the conditions that obtain in it.

There is of course state ownership of the means of production, and a hierarchical structure that administers this sector of the economy.

There is concentration of politico-economic power and authority at the center. Taken together, the central authorities[2] possess a common and strongly held set of goals and values and a will that they attempt to impose on the managers and other economic agents subordinated to them.

The goals and values of the latter, however, correspond only in part, in content and in ranking, to those of the central authorities. Thus there is a problem of enforcing compliance with the will of the central authorities—of what the Russians call "control"—a term that denotes a combination of supervision, surveillance, checking, and administrative prophylaxis.

The directing and co-ordinating principle is that of planning, which comprises the following main activities among others: specifying the direction of economic development (formulated in the prospective, i.e., multi-year, plans, and particularly in their investment and training programs; finding rational ways of utilizing the available resources, in the long run and in the short; specifying (chiefly in the one-year plans) the bill of goods to be produced; and assuring balance in the sense of compatibility between requirements and availabilities. The planning function is closely associated with, but is to be distinguished from:

The issuance of commands to enterprises (and their parent organizations) on the basis of which most production and much of the distribution take place. We may speak of the Soviet economy as a "command economy." (To my knowledge, the phrase "command economy" was first used in English by George N. Halm in his textbook, *Economic Systems*, 1951, page 310.) With regard to production, the commands lay down in varying degrees of detail minima for output (quantity, value, quality, assortment, timing) and maxima for input use. Commands flow down the economic-administrative hierarchy; information flows up the hierarchy. The information is essential for watching the progress of the current plan and initiating possible remedial measures, for drawing up plans for future periods, and for evaluating the performance of the managers. Responsibility for performance is attached to each assignment. There is continuous control over managers to ensure their compliance with the commands and regulations to which they are subject.

The plans and the commands are so drawn up as to fully commit, and even overcommit, the resources of the whole economy and of each enterprise. For this reason, as well as for others:

There is a persistent sellers' market,[3] by which I mean a condition wherein it takes generally more effort to buy (procure) than to sell. A result of this is dominance of the seller over the buyer in an actual or potential transaction, a fact that is of some importance in interpreting Soviet prices.

And of course, there is money, though as we shall see not all prices are expressed in money, or in the money that is the medium of exchange.

I have said enough to suggest that we may expect prices in this area of the Soviet economy to be called upon to perform a number of functions, some of which are not usually considered in Western value theory. In conjunction with the appropriate behavioral principles, prices in our area of the Soviet economy, as in a market economy, have the role of discouraging technological waste and of guiding the production and (productive) consumption of goods. One should note in this connection that the planners have much wider latitude of choice than do the managers, and that consequently the prices relevant to the former have much more of an allocative role to perform than the prices relevant to the latter. Further, Soviet prices have the most important function of facilitating control over the activities of managers (and other subordinates of the central authorities) in order to enhance compliance with the numerous commands and regulations and to ensure the conservation of state-owned material wealth, and, as a corollary, they also have the function of assessing managerial performance.

This double function of Soviet prices—and especially the evaluative aspect—is closely analogous to the function of intracompany prices in vertically extended companies in our own economy. Planning is a complicated and arduous process, and therefore Soviet prices must also in some measure respond to the necessity of simplifying its mechanics. The central setting of prices is in itself a drawn-out and laborious task, and even with all the will and competence in the world to produce a "correct" system of prices, there is a considerable cost involved in doing so. The Soviet price structure has been the poorer for having to reflect this cost. As anywhere else, prices in the Soviet economy perform the role of financing nonconsumption. And lastly, although their income-distributive function is much smaller than in private enterprise economies, their important success—and power-distributive functions—should not be overlooked.

The actual structure of Soviet prices in our area is of necessity a compromise between the many and often conflicting purposes that they are called upon to serve, the various interests affected, and the political forces involved.[4] Like any compromise—and especially a political one—it is complicated and untidy and can be expected to fail the test of rationality, at least of a rationality tied to a single desideratum. This is not to absolve Soviet price-setting from the charges of crudity and incompetence that have been leveled at it both at home and abroad.[5]

III

It is therefore hardly surprising that those of us who have been brought up on the logical and aesthetic qualities of the Walrasian and Marshallian price systems of our textbooks—I am leaving our capitalist reality aside—are easily struck by such characteristics of Soviet prices as multiplicity, asymmetry, compartmentalization, and discreteness. To illustrate multiplicity, let me list the main classes of price in our transaction area (that is, omitting the complex structure of prices in agriculture and in retail trade), thinking now of price in the general sense of terms on which alternatives are offered:

1. Transfer prices (at various times designated in Russian as *otpusknye, optovo-otpusknye,* and *optovye tseny*), at which goods actually change hands within the state sector. These can be net or gross of turnover tax. A variant of the transfer price is the so-called "settlement price" (*raschetnaia tsena*), differentiated as between firms, at which in some industries the marketing organization buys the article for resale to the user at the transfer price.

2. Index (constant, unchangeable) prices used for aggregating planned or actual output of the enterprise, of groups of enterprises, of branches of industry, and of industry as a whole. At some historical

point the index prices may be identical with the transfer prices but tend to diverge from them, in level and internal structure, as the two evolve separately (though the index prices are of course supposed to remain constant, allowing for the introduction of prices for new commodities at the appropriate level, until replaced by a new set of index prices).

3. What may be called "quasi-prices"; that is, money amounts per unit of commodity that do not have the usual outward form of price but nonetheless represent terms on which alternatives are offered to the enterprise. An example of a quasi-price is the bonus paid to management or a worker for saving a physical unit of a particular input or for increasing the output of a commodity by a physical unit.

4. What may be called "physical quasi-prices"; that is, the terms of exchange between two commodities at which substitution of one input for another, or transformation of one product into another, does not affect the physical indicator(s) of performance. Example: If the physical unit specified in the plan for, say, cloth is a linear meter, then a meter of one kind of cloth is equivalent to a meter of any other kind for purposes of meeting the production plan in physical terms.

5. Estimate prices (*smetnye tseny*) at which construction cost estimates are prepared, though not necessarily at which finished products of construction are transferred from builder to customer. Estimate prices may also serve as a sort of index price for the construction sector.

6. Planning prices; that is, prices at which calculations in the course of planning and project making (engineering design) are performed. These may be identical with some of the above-listed classes, or may differ by the application of "coefficients of deficitness" to the transfer prices of certain goods, or by elimination of the turnover tax where the transfer price includes it.

7. Price surrogates, where the use of prices in the conventional form is doctrinally repugnant. The best known of these are the minimum admissible recoupment (pay-off, pay-out) periods for additional investment in choosing between alternative technological variants of unequal capital intensity.

Besides, there are multiple prices within these classes; thus, transfer prices may vary at the same time and in the same place according to the type of producer (seller) and the type of buyer.

Asymmetry is indicated in that the class(es) of prices guiding the combination of inputs may not be the class(es) of pricing guiding output in the same enterprise, or the class(es) of prices guiding the producer's output need not be those which steer his customers in the use of the commodity. The price structure is compartmentalized in the sense that the attempts, if any, that are made to bring price ratios into approximate correspondence with marginal, or even average, rates of substitution, are limited to close substitutes, such as alternative sources of energy or nonferrous metals. And discreteness manifests itself in the large and abrupt changes over time and space.

IV

To draw attention to these characteristics is not to call the Soviet pot black. This would be unwise, not so much because our own kettle of actual prices is far from lustrous, but chiefly because the price system of our textbooks is not addressed to the problems of a command economy. In the extreme case of an absolute command economy —that is, a situation in which the product-mix, the input-mix, and all the technical coefficients are fully, consistently, and minutely prescribed from above and in which there consequently is no substitutive choice by managers to exercise—and of perfect compliance by managers, there would be no need for any prices at the operating level.[6] Commands flowing down and information flowing up could be entirely in physical terms, and because all managers are perfect by definition there is no need to evaluate their performance. If not realistic, the situation is at least conceivable.

While still disregarding choice on the enterprise level, let us take a step in the direction of reality by assuming that compliance by managers is imperfect. There is now need to control the firms' actions and to evaluate the performance of managers. This could be done by physical audits, but only laboriously and inconclusively for lack of common denominator for physical quantities. Hence the desirability of having prices—transfer prices or merely index prices—to aggregate outputs and inputs, and to compute unit costs. Further, to increase the alertness and sensitivity of control, it is desirable to keep enterprises on the brink of insolvency by planning their receipts to exceed their expenses by only a narrow margin; i.e., to exercise control by means of the budget constraint. Hence not only index prices but also transfer prices, and not only prices but also money and financial institutions. This adds up to the Soviet *khozraschet* ("business calculation") system. My point is that the control and evaluative functions of money and prices alone are sufficient to explain the need for *khorzraschet*. Delegation of some choice to the enterprise provides an additional but not a necessary reason for it. Note that in Russian parlance the *khozraschet* of the plan era is contrasted with *kommercheskii raschet* ("commercial calculation") which obtained during the NEP when the state-owned enterprises did have a good deal of choice with regard to outputs and inputs, and in some vague way were even expected to maximize profits.

A quick look at the early days of *khozraschet* may be instructive.

As I read it, the literature over the half-decade between Stalin's famous speech of June 23, 1931, and the (transfer) price reform of April, 1936, showed more concern with technological efficiency and managerial compliance than with ensuring the right choice by the enterprise. This is not very surprising as we recall the circumstances of those years: rapid introduction of new technologies, cocksureness by the central planners, a strong technocratic tinge, extension of physical norms and targets, and inexperienced or otherwise imperfectly reliable managers. In the speech, Stalin virtually identified *khozraschet* with the extirpation of *beskhoziaistvennost'* ("managementlessness"; i.e., avoidable waste), and, not surprisingly, the ensuing literature echoed him in this. Waste was to be avoided by attention to cost, but also, and more so, by manipulating physical "norms" and by controlling the allocation of producers' goods. Insofar as anything like a financial mechanism was invoked, it was largely the operation of the budget constraint; i.e., pricing the material in short supply out of wasteful use. If Soviet law (according to Harold Berman) has had a "parental" function, to ingrain habits while circumscribing action, so apparently has had *khozraschet*, especially in the early days of the plan era when economical habits were sorely lacking. Of course, as we know, certain parallel developments, such as those in the monetary and banking spheres, rendered the budget constraint highly elastic.

To illustrate that considerations other than allocative efficiency largely guided the thinking of price-planners, especially in the early years, we may refer to such an obvious principle as the differentiation of prices according to quality. It is interesting that Turetskii—a leading Soviet authority in this field—writing in 1932, subscribed to this principle specifically for reasons of facilitating control over and evaluation of management: poor quality of producers' goods should be reflected in the accounts of the producing and not of the consuming enterprise, so that responsibility can be readily ascertained. More generally, he favored invariable adherence to contract prices in transactions between enterprises to eliminate "the possibility of one enterprise taking advantage of the managerial [*khoziaistvennye*] attainments of another or the shifting onto the former of the managerial shortcomings of the latter."[7]

The logic of control over more or less decentralized units within heirarchical organizations reaches into quite different milieus: twenty-five years later an American authority on management accounting wrote, in almost the same words, that pricing for intracompany transfers should aim to avoid the situation where "production inefficiencies and efficiencies in plants [at the earlier stage of manufacture] would be passed on to the division [at the later state]," in which case "the profits of the latter would be determined in part by the performance in plants which are under another division's control."[8]

V

What we recognize today as the cardinal, though far from inviolable, Soviet principle of price formation in the state sector, namely, that the price (net of turnover tax) be equal to the anticipated industry-wide (or zone-wide) average cost of the good plus a small margin of profit, seems to have developed spontaneously during the early years of the plan era. The mystique of the law of value came considerably later, in the early forties.[9] It is not hard to see that in a thorough command economy, but with imperfect compliance by managers, such a conception of price has considerable merit from the point of view of the central authorities. First, the image of a price that is built up from cost elements—we may call it the "genetic" conception—corresponds to the main function of management under the postulated conditions, which is the building up of finished output from components (inputs) allotted to it for the task. Price is at once the weighted average cost for the industry (or zone) and the standard against which the individual plant's costs are measured. In accordance with the same conception, as Campbell has recently shown,[10] intrafirm accounting concerns itself primarily with providing average cost information to the enterprise's superiors and to the various control organs rather than with furnishing management with data for internal decisions. In other words, pricing and accounting have as a major purpose the exercising of control over and the evaluation of enterprise management. In this light, some of the seeming irrationalities of Soviet costing and pricing become more understandable. For example, an interest charge on fixed capital does not usually enter cost according to Soviet practice. This is irrational for allocative but not for control and evaluative reasons, because investible resources as such (contrasted with capital goods of which interest is not the price) are not among the inputs that are entrusted to the manager to be assembled into output. That the manager may hoard material wealth if he is freed from paying interest is a real problem, but it is a separate control problem (or at least has been so seen by the authorities).

Second, there is great convenience to the planners in this approach, both for price planning and for cost planning at later stages of production. *Ex post* unit costs of production are reported by enterprises; they can be converted into *ex ante* with the aid of some engineering data and by the mechanical application of what Berliner has called the "ratchet principle." Demand schedules are not in question. (Now there is talk of using matrices and electronic computers to solve simultaneously for the whole gamut of transfer prices.) What at first glance seems like a disadvantage—the need to define the scope of "industry," "zone," and "commodity"—is in fact an advantage because the economy is already partitioned this way for administrative and reporting purposes, and the existing organizational structure can therefore be utilized for both price computations and the control activities related to price. Lastly, uniform country-wide prices of producer goods are obviously of great convenience in planning costs at later stages of production.

A serious problem arises where average cost varies greatly from enterprise to enterprise, as in extractive industries or in industries containing plants of varying technological modernity. In the absence of rent and interest charges, in such cases price that is set at average industry-wide cost leads to large profits in some enterprises and to losses in others and it can be particularly deceptive as a basis for planning decisions. The Soviets have tried to solve this problem, not always successfully, by setting regional transfer prices, by paying subsidies out of the treasury, by special settlement prices (see above), and in other ways.

VI

Transfer price that is based on industry-wide average cost has also, in the eyes of Soviet theorists, the virtue of objectivity. It is not entirely clear what they mean by this, or that they all mean the same thing. At the least they seem to mean that the price represents a standard of value independent of the costs of an individual enterprise and against which these costs can be measured; that it is a useful yardstick for control and evaluation we have already seen. The vices of cost-plus pricing with reference to a single enterprise are at least as well recognized in the USSR as in this country. Yet objectivity that rests on a statistical basis alone is a frail reed on which to hang the price structure. It is manipulable as all statistically derived magnitudes are. It can be circumvented by redesigning, or merely redesignating, the product. And it has no doctrinal justification, or had none until, in reversal of the previous position, the Marxian law of value was declared to operate in the Soviet Union.

There is no space here to sketch out the evolution of the tenet that the law of value operates in the Soviet economy, or to attempt an adequate inquiry into its significance. The last would in any case be a painful task, for it is doubtful that an unambiguous meaning is to be distilled from the voluminous Soviet literature on the subject. The tenet is a curious one, not only because, as has been often observed, it introduces into a state-owned economy a category that Marx apparently did not regard applicable under socialist conditions,[11] but also because it does so on the shaky ground that since the state's relations with the peasants and the consumers are "commodity relations" all the trappings of "commodity production"—money, value, prices—must permeate the whole economy. This is surely one of very few instances where Soviet ideologists in effect assert that the private tail of the economy wags the socialist dog. Be that as it may, the law of value imparts the ultimate objectivity of historical necessity to price policy, elevates industry-wide average cost to the more exalted rank of "socially necessary production outlays," and thus legitimates in doctrinal terms the genetic approach to price formation. But the actual practice of Soviet price setting does little to sanctify the law, since industry-wide average cost has been apparently generally regarded as only the first bench mark in price formation and substantial deviations from it for various economic reasons have been widespread.[12]

VII

This brings us to the problem of choice, for the economic reasons in question involve attempts to steer decentralized decisions in the directions preferred by the central authorities. Choice by whom? Clearly the planners and project-makers have very much greater scope for choice than do the managers. But to stay with the managers: the Soviet command economy is clearly not an absolute one (in our sense). Some discretion must be exercised at the enterprise level, not necessarily because certain problems are better resolved on the spot (though the Soviet authorities do of course recognize this to a limited extent), but because it is impracticable for the central authorities to prescribe physically every product and input, or to prescribe some of them—indeed usually most of them—in completely disaggregated terms. Hence, we are told by Soviet sources, price policy aims (among other things) at inducing the production of the proper assortment of qualities, grades, and types of products, and steering industrial consumption by discouraging the use of materials in very short supply (in terms of the material balances), as well as by setting the prices of close substitutes in correct relation to each other.[13]

Though this may carry a familiar ring, we should be in error to conclude that the price mechanism is enthroned hereby. With regard to the steering of production, the product-mix in a broad sense—and to a great degree even in detail—is prescribed by physical commands. The mechanism of transfer prices plays the ancillary role of bolstering the assortment plan of the enterprise and of guiding what may be called "intracommodity assortment"; that is, the assortment within the bounds of a commodity as the latter is defined in the enterprise's plan. (Certain peripheral and on the whole insignificant spots in the state sector are indeed left to the joint operation of the profit incentive and the mechanism of transfer prices.)

While there is much empirical evidence to show that enterprises are guided by the relative profitability of products in fulfilling their assortment plans, the transfer price mechanism would seem to be unreliable in this respect. The degree to which substitution of one assortment for another is transfer-price-elastic depends on the management's outlook with regard to the success indicators expressed in terms of the other prices (gross value of production in index prices, physical volume of output, etc.), and, as we know, the other success indicators tend to outweigh profitability in the minds of Soviet managers.

Formally, there are as many price elasticities of transformation as there are classes of prices pertaining to the output of the enterprise. Because of the nature of managerial incentives, enterprises have tended to be more sensitive to changes in relative index prices and physical quasi-prices (insofar as the latter apply to the product) than to transfer prices. The central authorities have on many occasions altered physical quasi-prices (especially by changing the physical unit of measure specified in the plan) to guide the assortment, grade, and quality of the product. As we know, index prices, though nominally unchangeable, have also been manipulated, upward of course, though in this instance the chief pressure may well have come from the enterprises themselves. Upward revision of index prices may well have been a sort of bribe extracted by management for undertaking the production of new, or allegedly new, commodities and for the introduction of unfamiliar processes. In this regard, index prices may be functionally closer to prices in a market economy than are Soviet transfer prices.

Turning now to the guidance of industrial consumption by means of the transfer price policy, we find an even more complicated picture. The Soviet literature has much to say about setting prices correctly in order to discourage the use of "deficit" commodities and to bring the prices of substitutes into some sort of appropriate mutual relation. Where the substitutes have a common technological dimension, such as the caloric content of alternative sources of energy, this dimension is often invoked.[13] It is not always clear who is to be guided by such adjustments. The opportunities for input substitution in going industrial enterprises are generally limited, not only for technological reasons, but also because of the physical allocation of many materials and the earmarking of expense categories. The sensitivity of managers to prices of inputs cannot be high in view of the structure of incentives. Consequently, one is led to suppose that the policy regarding the prices of substitute materials is directed at least as much at the various intermediate-level and short-run planners as at the managers of enterprises.

The situation is different in construction, which has always been poorly amenable to direction by command due to its more flexible technology, unique conditions at each site, little standardization of finished products, and heavy reliance on local (and therefore usually noncentrally allocated) materials. For this reason, attempts to regulate the input-mix by transfer prices have always been of greater importance in construction than in industry proper. But these attempts have foundered on certain other characteristics of the industry, such as the weakness of financial incentives and poor financial discipline and the absence of a fixed price for the finished product. As a result, construction has combined greater reliance on regulation by price with some of the harshest physical controls, such as outright prohibitions against the use of certain materials (structural steel, roofing iron, etc.), and in this respect perhaps represents a valuable object lesson should there be a significant expansion in the role of the market mechanism in the Soviet economy.

It is interesting to note how Soviet price policy takes advantage of the power-distributive effect of the sellers' market by localizing the exercise of choice with the seller rather than with the buyer where this is practicable. To recall an earlier Russian phrase, the central authorities are "wagering on the strong" when they delegate these decisions by resort to the price mechanism. The classic example is the quoting of transfer prices on a delivered basis that has been lately introduced in a number of industries. This places the demand for transportation services with the seller, who is likely to be less under pressure to be wasteful of them than the buyer. (Of course this may lead to the opposite error, but it is characteristic of Soviet planners to be more concerned with breaking bottlenecks and eradicating major evils, such as unduly long hauls, than with optimization.)

In sum, to the extent that there is a (transfer) price mechanism in our transaction area of the Soviet economy, it is grafted onto the frame of physical planning and commands. Its operation is intentionally compartmentalized and contained by physical and financial devices. In a sense there are many separate price mechanisms inserted into the over-all framework of commands and controls. The mechanisms are not trusted to lead to results consonant with the goals and values of the central authorities; hence they are hemmed in by numerous prohibitions and directives. Nor are they regarded to be sensitive or dependable; hence the violent changes in relative prices (insofar as these are not simply blunders or reversals of blunders) and reliance on the budget constraint as well as on the substitution effect. For these reasons there is lack of confidence on the part of Soviet authorities and economists in the correctness of actual transfer prices, as manifested by continual checking against price ratios in the capitalist world. Stalin's famous observation that cotton has to be more expensive than grain in the USSR because this is the case on the world market[14] is only the best-known of such instances that can be found in the Soviet literature.

VIII

I have tried to show that there are several classes of price applicable to the Soviet enterprise, and further that, of these, transfer prices, which are the prices at which goods change hands in our transaction area, are called upon to perform a number of functions. For some of these functions—controls, evaluation of managerial performance—the genetic conception of pricing is not entirely illogical, and the more pervasive the command principle of economic organization, the more pressing the need for control (and perhaps for evaluation) and the more justification for the genetic approach to pricing at the enterprise level. If a significant degree of choice is entrusted to management, the imperative of economy-wide efficiency requires marginal productivity (or, more generally, opportunity-cost) pricing of producers' goods and of primary factors of production. For planning and project making, which I have not discussed here, clearly the opportunity-cost approach is called for. Should planning prices be more divorced from transfer prices than they are now? Should transfer prices in any case conform to opportunity costs? If so, how effectively can they perform the control and evaluative functions? But, we must remember, if transfer prices do approximate opportunity costs and the market is given considerable scope, then these functions of Soviet prices would, if not disappear, radically change in character. These are the kinds of questions that the current Soviet debate on price formation, proceeding as it does under the pall of the law of value, has hardly begun to adumbrate, but to which it may eventually have to turn, especially in view of the bothersome experimentation that is progressing west of the Soviet border.

Certainly the present structure of transfer prices for producers' goods does not aim to equate demand and supply on a broad front. An attempt to do so would bring about the threat of an indefinite inflation so long as the present institutional features of the Soviet economy obtain. The pressure of demand on available resources and the resulting sellers' market are due not only to what we might call price control, but also—and more fundamentally—to the system of planning that overcommits resources, the structure of managerial incentives that places quantity above cost, and the subordination of financial controls to the production program. So long as these features remain, the fear of inflation alone will inhibit a more liberal resort to the price mechanism at the expense of physical controls and commands. More liberal resort to the price mechanism runs into an even more basic dilemma: that of the place of money in a dictatorial society.[15] Money is power, even in the Soviet Union. Its exercise can divert activity away from approved channels and it can in general thwart the will of the central authorities. There is a striking parallel between workers' organizations and money in the Communist world. Both are sources of power that is potentially autonomous of the central authorities: the one enlarges the freedom of maneuver of management, the other of labor. Both exist nominally in the Soviet Union and both are subjected to numerous controls to limit the scope of action. This is especially so of workers' organizations, but the cash balances and the credit facilities of Soviet enterprises are likewise closely watched; their use is often earmarked and restricted in other ways lest they apply their power in undesired directions. It is interesting to note that Yugoslavia—the one Communist country that has radically reformed its institutional structure—has simultaneously given greater autonomy to both the market mechanism, in which money decides, and to workers' councils (although the increase in political freedom was not commensurate, as we know). The role of prices in the Soviet economy cannot be seen apart from the problem of power in the Soviet society.

FOOTNOTES:

[1] The theoretical and empirical literature on Soviet (and Soviet-type) prices is rapidly growing; there is no space here to list even the main works. I should like to acknowledge, however, my intellectual debt to the following recent works which, in various ways, approach the problem from a theoretical angle: K. Paul Hensel, *Einführung in die Theorie der Zentralverwaltungswirtschaft* (Stuttgart, 1954); various recent articles by Peter Wiles; John M. Montias, "Producers' Prices in a Centralized Economy: The Polish Experience" (Columbia Ph.D. dissertation, 1958) and his "Price Setting Problems in the Polish Economy," *J.P.E.*, Dec., 1957; David Granick, "An Organizational Model of Soviet Industrial Planning" (processed, n.d.); Benjamin N. Ward, "The Planners' Choice Variables" (processed, 1958); and Hans Hirsch, *Mengenplanung und Preisplanung in der Sowjetunion* (Tübingen, 1957). The last parallels my approach most closely, but came to my attention too late to be fully taken into account in this paper. It is my pleasure to mention that the present paper is being written while I am on leave under a grant from the SSRC and that it has had the benefit of comments from Andrew G. Frank and Benjamin N. Ward.

[2] The plural is to emphasize that they are neither monolithic in outlook nor perfectly co-ordinated in action.

[3] "Sellers' market" is an awkward term with reference to an economy that is not a market economy, but I defer to usage at the expense of precision.

[4] Conflicts over price fixing rarely come to the surface in the Soviet Union. It is therefore worth quoting the remark of the former Minister of the Construction Industry, USSR, before the 1954 conference on construction: "We have twice raised the question of reducing the prices on mineral building materials, but have not been allowed to do so due to the violent objections of the builders [who themselves produce these materials at much higher costs than the ministry] who expected to suffer great losses therefrom." *Vsesoiuznoe soveshchanie stroitelei . . . 30 noiabria—7 dekabria 1954 g.* (Moscow, 1955), p. 103.

[5] The strongest charges of this nature are to be found in Naum Jasny's two extensive surveys of actual Soviet prices: *The Soviet Price System* (Stanford, 1951) and *Soviet Prices of Producers' Goods* (Stanford, 1952).

[6] Prices in the other three transaction areas are not here in question, of course.

[7] Sh. Turetskii, "Tsena i khozraschet," *Planovoe khoziaistvo*, 1932, 4, pp. 127-28.

[8] I. Wayne Keller, *Management Accounting for Profit Control* (New York, 1957), p. 403.

[9] The acceptance of the law of value into the corpus of Soviet dogma was revealed in "Nekotorye voprosy prepodavaniia politicheskoi ekonomii," *Pod Znamenem Marksizma,* 1943, 7-8, pp. 70 ff. (English translation, this review, Sept., 1944, pp. 519 ff.).

[10] Robert W. Campbell, "Accounting for Cost Control in the Soviet Economy," *Rev. of Econ. and Statis.*, Feb., 1958, pp. 59-67.

[11] A Marxist critique of the Soviet position on the law of value may be found in Ronald L. Meek, *Studies in the Labour Theory of Value* (London, 1956), pp. 256 ff.

[12] This quite apart from extensive and heavy subsidization during periods of cost inflation and relative price stability. Nor am I here concerned with the position of some Soviet economists that the law of value requires inclusion in price of a proportionate share of the "surplus product" in addition to average cost.

[13] Two other "economic reasons" are often given: discouraging excessive use of transport facilities, and, specifically, unduly long hauls, and subsidizing the basic industries, and through them machine-building, in order to accelerate the introduction of new technology. I shall not inquire into these, except to comment that the latter looks very much like *post factum* rationalization of the large subsidies to heavy industry due to the cost-inflation of the early thirties.

[14] *Economic Problems of Socialism in the USSR* (Moscow, 1952), pp. 24 ff.

[15] With regard to the role of money in the Soviet economy, I have profited from the as yet unpublished paper by Donald R. Hodgman, "Soviet Monetary Controls Through the Banking System" (1958), who is not to be held responsible for the formulation herein. The remarks in the text of course do not directly apply to the role of money in the three other transaction areas of the Soviet economy.

A COMMENT ON THE DISCUSSION ABOUT
PRICE-POLICY

ANYONE acquainted with Marxist discussion of such questions will appreciate that 'the law of value' is regarded as applying essentially to a market- or exchange-economy; and the debate as to how far production is (or should be) 'influenced', or alternatively 'regulated', by the law of value is a debate about the degree of influence exerted by the market (and by prices as indices of exchange-relations) upon production. In the new debate (as was pointed out in the last number of *Soviet Studies*) the sufficiency of Stalin's formulation in *Economic Problems of Socialism in the USSR* is questioned, to the effect that the law of value continues to exercise an influence because of the survival of market-relations between the two main sectors of Soviet economy, state industry and the collective farm peasantry. Instead it is now maintained that it does so because of the persistence of exchange-relations between State industry and the consumer (i.e. of the retail market for consumer goods). Thus the influence of the law of value is made to depend, not upon an incidental (and in a sense 'external') feature, but on an essential feature of socialism (regarded as "the first or lower stage of communism"): namely, its wage-system, with the corollary that if wage-differentials continue to play a role as a production-incentive, wage-earners must be able to spend their wages freely on a retail market. Curiously enough, this is referred to in Stalin's booklet as a reason (p. 23: "consumer goods, which are needed to compensate the labour-power expended in the process of production, are produced and realized in our country as commodities coming under the operation of the law of value ... precisely here ... the law of value exercises its influence on production".) But subsequently this reason is forgotten apparently and is assigned no more than a quite secondary role.

It is of some interest to note that a similar discussion took place a year ago among Polish economists,[1] and also towards the end of the year among economists in East Germany.[2]

In this discussion it seems to me that three questions need to be clearly distinguished.

1. Should central planning of economic decisions be replaced by a mechanism whereby economic decisions are taken automatically by economically autonomous units ('enterprises') on the basis of market prices? In the Soviet discussion no proposal of this kind has

been canvassed (nor has it, to my knowledge, in the Polish and German discussions; although opponents of change have denounced tendencies to substitute 'market autonomism' for planning); but any decentralization must represent *some* move in this direction to the extent that it shifts more of the responsibility for economic decisions down to the level of the individual enterprise. In Yugoslavia in recent years a substantial degree of 'market autonomism' apparently applies to consumer goods industries.

2.   Granted that economic decisions are centrally planned, should such decisions, at least so far as they relate to the production of consumer goods, be guided by economic indices based on market prices? This applies particularly to decisions about investment designed to expand the output-capacities of different lines of production by various amounts. And is it a corollary of doing so that the prices of producer goods (machinery, fuel and power, raw materials) should be adjusted according to some consistent principle?

3.   The question of providing an inducement to managers of enterprises, in carrying out the targets assigned to them, to produce things in 'correct' amounts and proportions by fixing 'correct' prices both for their output and for all constituents of their input. This will be the more important the more discretion is left to managers. However centralized the planning may be, there is bound to be a considerable margin of discretion *de facto* about the precise assortment and detailed specification of products, as well as the methods of production; and the recent tendency of greater decentralization has evidently been to extend this discretion. It is noteworthy that a recurring complaint over a number of years has been the failure of industries to fulfil their so-called 'assortment plans', i.e. the range of variety assigned to them. (This was also a matter of complaint in the Polish discussion). Repeated attempts seem to have been made to correct this by administrative measures and stricter planning. If it persisted so long notwithstanding, this must have been presumably because the structure of relative prices was such as to provide a chronic inducement to produce the 'wrong' assortment (profitability to the enterprise being in conflict with the objectives of the plan).

With regard to this last point, it might seem that the problem was a purely empirical one and that no issue of principle was involved. In each particular case the planners can make prices what they need these to be in order to promote fulfilment of the plan. Prices (like taxes or subsidies) become an arbitrary planning instrument, and as such they have been used in the past. (This was denounced by one participant in the discussion as 'subjectivism' in price-policy and 'the rule of the arbitrary').[3] If too much of one constituent of input is being used (e.g. a scarce fuel or transport long-hauls), prices can be raised to encourage economy and substitution; if too little of some line of textile cloth is being produced, its selling price (*optovaya tsena*) and hence the profit-margin to be enjoyed on its production can be raised. If there is a tendency to hold unduly large stocks of materials or goods-in-process, then an interest-charge can be made for bank-credits with which enterprises hold stocks above the stipulated 'norma-tive'. This view of prices as arbitrary planning instruments, adapted *ad hoc* to meet particular supply-demand situations, clearly becomes inadequate the wider the area of discretion that is allowed to the management of enterprises (if, for instance, output targets for only one-third of the products and product-varieties are stipulated in the central plan, then for two-thirds of them no planned targets exist to the fulfilment of which prices can be geared). There are also more general objections that can be made to so empirical an attitude; chief of these being that it provides no answer to the question as to whether, when the price of a scarce input is raised to encourage economy in its use, this is to be regarded as the permanent solution, or whether alternatively efforts should be made in subsequent plans to expand the supply of the input that is in temporarily short-supply. If the latter answer is given, then it may well be preferable to ration the scarce supply temporarily instead of varying its price.

What the new discussion is concerned with is some principle that will define 'normal' price-relationships and enable some uniformity of treatment to be established in such cases.

A large part of the Soviet discussion has been occupied with the price-relationship between consumer goods (Sector B) and producer goods (Sector A)—this rather than the structure of relative prices *within* each group. (The Polish discussion, on the other hand, was concerned with both questions, and particularly stressed the need to adapt the pattern of output of consumer goods to the pattern of consumers' demand). In particular it is said that the prices of producer goods are 'too low' relatively to the prices of consumer goods and should be raised, e.g. by levying turnover tax on the former as well as on the latter, and at similar rates.

Under the existing system, as is well-known, turnover tax is levied as a rule (there are some exceptions)[4] only on consumer goods, and levied between the producer and the retail market. The wholesale (*optovye*) prices at which products leave the factory are based on 'planned costs' which include the cost of wages and salaries and raw material, *plus* an amortisation charge (but not an interest-charge)

B

on plant and equipment. Thus, the selling-price on which industrial enterprises operate, whether they belong to Sector A or Sector B, is based virtually on prime cost. The *rationale* of this system (which was defended in the discussion by Turetsky and Maisenberg) consists in the following very simple relationship. Ignoring for the moment what Strumilin calls 'social consumption' (incomes of non-productive workers in the health and education services and defence and salaries of administrative workers above the level of industrial enterprises), and remembering that in a 'closed system' prime costs are ultimately reducible to wages,[5] we can see that the ratio of final (retail) prices of consumer goods to their prime cost will depend upon the *rate of net investment*, measured by the proportion of the total wages-bill (and hence of personal incomes) that is represented by the cost of new construction and new capital goods. (If the reason is not immediately plain, reference may be made for an explanation of this relation to the present writer's *Political Economy and Capitalism*, London 1937, pp. 325-7, or his *Soviet Economic Development since 1917*, London 1948, pp. 361-3; or in its application also to a capitalist economy to Mrs. Joan Robinson's *Accumulation of Capital*, London 1956, pp. 74-5). If we reintroduce 'social consumption', then this ratio becomes dependent on the rate of new investment *plus* 'social consumption' as a proportion of national income (or rather of the total of personal incomes); further qualifications can be made in the relation if there is any substantial amount of individual saving out of personal incomes.[5a]

The reason for what Dr. Schlesinger calls 'the still current dogma'— the practice whereby this difference or gap between the level of retail prices and the level of industrial prices is siphoned off directly into the Budget, instead of being allowed to accrue initially as realized profits of State industry—was apparently an administrative one. The maximum incentive to cost reduction by the enterprise is evidently given when the whole (or a major proportion) of the results of such economy accrue in higher profit to enterprises. This is the case when the industrial selling-price which the enterprise receives for its output is fixed on the basis of 'planned cost' (*plus* a small profit-margin). If, however, the industrial selling price received by the enterprise were to be related, not to production-cost, but to the final price at the retail stage, both the initial profit and presumably the percentage rate at which that profit was taxed would be high; consequently the addition to *retained* profit as a result of any cost-reduction (as well as the proportionate addition to total profit that this represented) would be much smaller. No doubt some complicated grading of the rate of profit-taxation could be devised so as to leave a larger percentage of retained profit beyond a certain level. But the method of taking

100 per cent of the 'gap' between the two price-levels by a turnover tax has the advantage of simplicity. It has also the further advantage of providing an easy means whereby retail price can be adjusted to particular scarcities.

Academician Strumilin seems to imply that it is irrational for the turnover tax to be levied on consumer goods alone; and that, since a commodity's 'value' consists not only of wages expended but also of its appropriate share of the 'surplus product' of society, the prices of producer goods as well as of consumer goods should be raised by the amount of their respective shares of this 'surplus product' (representing, i.e., net investment plus 'social consumption'). This he suggests should be done by setting an 'accounting (*raschotny*) price' for each product, to include, in addition to prime costs or direct expenses, a proportional share of this 'surplus product'; this accounting price being paid to the enterprise, but the element of 'surplus product' being skimmed off in the form of two sets of taxes or deductions (a 'deduction' for the fund of social consumption and a profit-tax for the investment fund).[6] Whether made exactly according to the Strumilin-method or not, the upshot of the change would be to raise the prices of producer goods relatively to wages: i.e. to make all constituents of input *other* than labour more costly to industries using them. To judge from the statement of Kronrod (cited by Dr. Schlesinger), this change is prompted by the fact that the existing price-system encourages uneconomic use of capital goods and creates a bias towards saving labour at the expense of costly capital equipment, or alternatively of raw materials; in which case this discussion seems to be to some extent a direct sequel to the earlier one about calculating a coefficient of effectiveness of investment as a guide to choice between alternative technical variants.

But if this is the reason—the need to include a charge for scarce capital goods, any all-round increase in the supply of which would place a strain upon the limited current 'social investment fund'— the inadequacy of the remedy in the form in which it is proposed by Strumilin and Kronrod is at once obvious. (This proposal amounts to an equi-proportional mark-up all round on prime costs, since existing industrial prices, as we have seen, are based virtually on prime costs—Turetsky interprets it in the familiar Marxian notation as pricing at $c + v + (v \times \frac{s}{v})$, but of course c would itself have been marked up in similar degree at a previous stage of production).[7] It is inadequate, firstly because the conditions of production of producer goods (output of Sector A) are sufficiently various to make an equi-proportional addition to their existing prices a very crude expedient. Their conditions of production differ as regards both their composition of capital (or ratio of capital to labour) and the turnover period of various constituents of their capital; and what the logic of the Kronrod-Strumilin argument demands is some kind of general *agio* on capital—the all-round inclusion in the industrial selling price of a charge proportional to the capital used (so far as this can be measured). Secondly, if there is a tendency to over-use of scarce capital goods when their price contains no specific capital-charge (over and above amortization), then it follows, surely, that the prices of consumer goods should be adjusted according to the varying proportions in which capital (as compared with direct or 'living labour') is used in their production? (This should probably apply to the industrial selling price; but it should certainly apply to the 'normal' price, taken as the standard or accounting price with which current retail prices are compared when the planning authorities are considering the distribution of investment between different consumer goods industries.)

This is the *rationale* of those like Bachurin who claim that 'prices of production' and not the 'values' of vol. I of *Capital* should be adopted as the norm; and it seems to me that they have logic on their side. In other words, analogous reasons to those used by Strumilin in his *Promyshlenno-Ekonomicheskaia Gazeta* article for including in costs a charge for scarce natural resources[8] could be applied to the inclusion of a charge for scarce capital goods—or rather for things like buildings, plant and equipment in the degree to which they place a strain on the (limited) investible resources of society.

It is when one comes to determine the proper level of such a capital charge that the problem becomes difficult, even intractable; and it may be remembered that the earlier discussion about choice between alternative investment projects came to a stop precisely at this point. The fact is that (apart from the well-known difficulties about valuing 'capital' without getting involved in circular reasoning) there exists no generally agreed principle for determining a 'true', or socially optimum, level of interest-rate, either among Soviet or 'Western' economists (anyone inclined to doubt this statement may be referred to J. de V. Graaf, *Theoretical Welfare Economics*, pp. 99—105; also cf. the present writer in *Soviet Studies*, Vol. II, no. 3, p. 289 seq.). One can perhaps say that to include *some* interest-charge is better than to include none; though even this could be questioned—but probably one could safely say at least that to include some smallish capital charge is better than to include none.

To avoid misunderstanding, one should perhaps add this in parenthesis: the difficulty of which we have been speaking is *not* because of the absence in a socialist economy of a market for capital, as Mises and his school would maintain. It is a difficulty that applies just as much to a capitalist economy: here an interest-rate happens to emerge, but there is no valid ground for supposing it to be an optimum rate from the standpoint of society as a whole.

Nor would the difficulty be surmounted by taking the actual difference between the level of retail prices for consumer goods and the level of industrial (cost) prices, and averaging this out over industry as a whole in order to find an appropriate profit-rate on capital. That is to say, the difficulty is not surmounted if we are looking for some 'correct' relation between the price-level of capital goods and the level of wages—'correct' in the sense of yielding the optimum degree of substitution of capital goods for labour in production and no more. And this, it seems clear, is the preoccupation of much of the Soviet discussion.

However, if we are looking at the problem as being one of distributing a *given total* of investible resources, or a given total supply of capital goods, between various lines of production, then we have a different situation. The problem is then the purely relative one of comparing the social benefit to be derived from using those resources in one branch of consumer goods industry and in another—investing them in expanding, say, the productive capacity of the woollen industry or of the furniture industry or of the food industry. This is question no. 2 of the three questions that we distinguished above. For this purpose it would be both proper and sufficient to take the difference between the current (retail) price of the product and its direct cost (Strumilin's 'surplus product'), provided that this were expressed as a ratio to the total capital involved in its production (and not simply to its wage-cost). A comparison of such ratios would then give an order of priorities, on the assumption that the object was to satisfy consumers' demands in their market expression to the maximum extent (there might be, of course, numerous exceptions to this, where one wished to modify the resulting market order of priorities for various 'social reasons'). One method of doing this would be to calculate for each commodity a 'normal' or standard price, in which an average share of the 'surplus product' (= sum of the current investment fund and 'social consumption') was included, expressed as a ratio to the capital involved. If the actual retail price of a product was above this standard, it would be in the list for expansion of its supply in subsequent investment plans; if its actual price was below the standard price, the presumption would be that it had little need of expansion. The price to the enterprise (*optovaya tsena*) could remain unaffected; this being based on planned cost as at present, with the difference between it and the retail price (less distributive costs) being covered by turnover tax.

One could not, of course, stop at introducing such a principle for the consumer goods sector alone. One would have to work out analogous 'prices of production' for capital goods and all materials and components used by the former sector; with the difference that in this case these 'prices of production' would need to be, not merely planning-norms, but *actual* prices at which these producer goods were *bought* by enterprises and entered as constituents of cost in the industries using them in production. Again, these prices need not be the same as the prices *paid* to the supplying enterprise: the latter could be based on planned cost and the difference bridged by a turnover tax. But for consistency it would be necessary that the turnover tax should be so adjusted as to represent a uniform ratio to the capital employed in all cases—save for short-run departures from this uniform ratio to meet exceptional scarcities. It would be well, I suggest, to keep such departures from the rule rather exceptional in view of the well known advantages of stability in the prices of producer goods. (Since these goods enter into the cost of industries that use them and may affect their investment decisions, short-term fluctuations in their prices may cause decisions about technique, location, etc., to be made that from a long-term standpoint are wrong decisions).

Once the prices of capital goods have been regulated in this way, the choice of method of production by each enterprise, in so far as this concerns the type and amount of capital goods used, will evidently be decided—decided by what is profitable to the enterprises. For example, the choice between two alternative building materials, or between producing electricity from coal-burning plants or hydro-electric, will be governed by their comparative costs at existing prices (relative to their efficiencies); the least costly way of producing a given result being chosen. The price-level of capital goods relative to wages will also determine how far it is profitable for an enterprise to extend mechanization, i.e. to substitute capital for labour in its methods of production; and it will affect such decisions as the amount of 'manning' of productive equipment or the size of the repair-staff employed, which may be a crucial factor in the length of life of equipment. All such decisions will affect the demand for capital goods coming from all branches of industry—from the consumer goods sector (Sector B) and also from Sector A itself. Now, we have been assuming that the rate of investment (and hence, *ceteris paribus*, the total output of capital goods) is already given—that it has been determined in the Plan by an independent policy-decision. Accordingly, at any one time there must be one particular level of prices for capital goods (relative to the level of wages) that will make the aggregate demand for capital goods in any year equal to this supply. I can see

no reason why this price should be one that involves the inclusion
in it of the *same* rate of turnover rax (as a quasi-profit-rate) as is required
in the consumer goods sector. Of course, the demand for capital
goods will to a large extent be directly controlled by the investment
plan; and if the overall rate of investment is centrally decided there
are strong reasons for both the allocation between industries and the
technical forms of investment to be centrally planned as well. In so far,
however, as any of the decisions we have mentioned above are influenced by profitability to the enterprise, and hence by prices, it
would seem to be essential that the appropriate rate of turnover tax
(or profit mark-up) on capital goods should have the character of an
'arbitrary planning-price' (or, if you like, a 'trial-and-error price'),
fixed at whatever level will bring the total demand for capital goods
into equilibrium with the supply of them that the investment plan
has decided to make available.

On a first reading of the published summary of the Soviet discussion it looked as though the crucial issue as between the use of
'values' and the use of 'prices of production' as a basis for price-fixing—
the question of securing the most effective distribution of the current
investment fund—was not brought out clearly. A reading of two
contributions subsequently published *in extenso* in *Voprosi Ekonomiki*
(1957, no. 3) shows that this first impression was wrong. A. Malyshev,
maintaining that "in our conditions, it seems, the basis of price-for-
mation must be the more developed, enriched, concrete form of value
—price of production, with substantially another social content to
what it has in conditions of capitalism", suggests that the prices of all
goods, both means of production and means of consumption, should
be based on their prime cost (*sebestoimost*) *plus* a uniform rate of profit,
calculated in relation to all 'productive funds' (capital) employed in
the branch of industry in question. The reason he gives is that different
lines of production differ very greatly in the ratio of fixed capital
to labour, in the proportion of circulating capital embodied in raw
materials and in the length of their production-cycle (these he sums
up as "substantial differences in the relation of expenditure on stored-up
to living labour"); that since the available resources for investment
at any one time are insufficient to meet all the demands of technical
modernization and re-equipment, there must be some criterion
for "selecting the most advantageous variants" from among the
mass of competing claims; and that the most serviceable economic
criterion of the advantageousness of capital expenditure is a rate of
profit, "calculated in relation to all the basic and turnover funds
of the enterprise". "In face of given prices of output and on condition
that these prices are economically justified, any additional investment

in basic funds" (fixed capital), to be justifiable, "must raise or at least not lower the level of profit of the enterprise" below the given "normal level" (arrived at by expressing the aggregate surplus product as a ratio to the aggregate capital employed).[9]

The reason which his critic, M. Bor of Gosekonomkommissia, gives for not accepting this criterion is instructive. He takes an example of two branches of industry producing ferro-concrete constructions and timber for building respectively. To produce 'an equivalent mass of materials' it is necessary for society to expend 100 and 140 hours of labour respectively. But because the production of ferro-concrete is highly mechanized whereas woodworking is not, the proportions in which this labour consists of 'stored-up labour' and of 'living labour' are respectively 80:20 and 20:80. "Since prices of means of production, built according to Comrade Malyshev's scheme, are higher than their value, an hour of stored-up labour will be priced higher than an hour of living labour"; hence "in such a system of prices it may happen that it is economically more advantageous for society to produce timber than ferro-concrete constructions, although in actuality it is better to produce ferro-concrete constructions".[10] This certainly puts the issue in a nutshell. Ferro-concrete would indubitably be better than timber if we reckoned an hour of 'stored-up labour' on a par with an hour of 'living labour', currently employed. But it would only be reasonable to treat them as being on a par, for purposes of economic accountancy, if the amount of labour one could employ in current capital construction were unlimited, of if existing resources (stocks) of 'stored-up labour' were plentiful enough, as a result of quinquennia of past investment, to satisfy to the full all technical uses for it. Precisely because these conditions are not fulfilled, it is necessary that a rational system of economic accounting should place some premium on the use of 'stored-up labour' relatively to 'living labour' to ensure the most effective use of the former; and to this extent Malyshev was clearly right and Bor was wrong. But what exactly this premium should be is not easy, as we have seen, to determine (nor is it easy to find a quantitative measure for stored-up labour, which is not a simple but a complex entity compounded of labour and time). However, once the rate of investment is determined, it should be possible, as we have also seen, to find empirically a figure for this premium which will equate the demand for additional stored-up labour with the current supply of such additions that the Plan has decided to make available.

To close with a brief mention of two incidental points. Firstly, how much importance are we to attach to Kronrod's proposition about the so-called equality of the sum of values and the sum of prices? Various views were expressed in the discussion as to whether this was to be taken as applying *only* to consumer goods, or in some sense or other to total output of both sectors. In the original context in which it was used, this was a statement about the average value of commodities (*all* commodities, whether consumer goods or capital goods) and the value of money under a commodity-money system (gold).[11] It is questionable whether this can have any relevance to the quite different context of Soviet economy today. It could be said still to have a possible meaning as a postulate about monetary policy (that in conditions of constant labour-productivity the price-level of goods sold to the population should be constant; this price-level being reduced only in the degree to which labour-productivity rises). But in a planned economy monetary policy cannot be separated from wage-policy and investment-policy. The significant relation is that of the price-level of consumer goods to wages, and this we have seen is dependent, not only on the productivity of labour in the consumer goods industries, but also on investment policy (if the rate of investment rises, the price-level of consumer goods must rise, *ceteris paribus*, relatively to money wages). What significance then can be assigned to Kronrod's equality? At any rate it does not seem capable of sustaining any such corollary as that, if the prices of producer goods are raised, those of consumer goods must fall equivalently, or *vice versa*.

Finally one should perhaps remark that for Soviet economists to be discussing price policy at all is a considerable advance beyond what were previously regarded as the proper frontiers of Political Economy. So long as prices were regarded simply as arbitrary planning instruments, it was not unnatural that price-policy should be treated as part of the technology of planning. Stalin drew a sharp dividing line between "problems of the economic policy of the directing bodies" and "problems of political economy"; including economic planning among the former and defining the latter as follows: "Political economy investigates the laws of development of men's relations of production ... To foist upon political economy problems of economic policy is to kill it as a science."[12] It was scarcely surprising that economic writing thus divorced from policy-applications should confine itself either to description or to a few vague historical generalities. Now the dividing wall is down, and economists and economic discussion have a chance of generalizing the experience and problems of three decades of planning into a theory of the functioning of a socialist economy.

MAURICE DOBB

Trinity College, Cambridge

[1] See especially article by Professor W. Brus, 'On the role of the Law of Value in a Socialist Economy', and other papers at a Congress of Polish Economists and discussion of them, in *Ekonomista* 1956 no. 5; also articles in *Gospodarka Planowa*.

[2] See the special number of *Wirtschaftswissenschaft* devoted to 'Ökonomische Theorie und Politik in der Übergangsperiode', February 1957.

[3] I. Malyshev in *Voprosy Ekonomiki* 1957 no. 3 p. 97.

[4] Some examples of these are given by Sh. Turetsky in *Voprosy Ekonomiki* 1957 no. 5 p. 62. They include cases of materials in short supply and also products of extractive industries (e.g. fuels) where the tax is used to deal with the difference between 'average costs' and costs of the least favourably situated sources of supply (rather like the proposal of the Ridley Committee for the British Coal Industry).

[5] Amortization may be taken as roughly equivalent to current expenditures on capital maintenance or replacement.

[5a] It is of course this relationship which renders nugatory the "attempt to separate that part of net indirect tax paid by state enterprises which is properly factor income and that part which is truly tax", referred to in *Economic Bulletin for Europe*, UN Geneva, May 1957, p. 94: an attempt which is crucial to the 'adjusted factor cost' method of Professor Bergson and his school. Cf. the remarks of Professor F. D. Holzman in *Soviet Studies*, July 1957, pp. 35-6; and on the more general issue M. Kalecki, *Theory of Economic Dynamics* (London 1954), p. 62.

[6] It does not seem to be clear whether either or both of these are to have the form of the existing turnover tax or of a percentage tax on profit. One of the critics of the proposal at any rate suggests that it would be inferior to the present method since it would blur the distinction between 'net income of the enterprise' (profit) and 'centralized net income of the State' (turnover tax) and hence weaken the incentive to the enterprise to cost-reduction (M. Bor, in *Voprosy Ekonomiki* 1957 no. 3 p. 111). In an article in *Voprosy Ekonomiki* 1956 no. 12, however, Strumilin seems to suggest that these might have the form of a tax proportional to the wage bill (p. 99).

[7] Sh. Turetsky, *Voprosy Ekonomiki* 1957 no. 5 pp. 66-7.

[8] Cit. by Dr. Schlesinger in *Soviet Studies* July 1957 p. 95. It is true that Strumilin was here speaking of cost-*differences* in a diminishing returns industry. But (as Ricardo always recognized) there is an intensive as well as an extensive margin, and the rent-problem (depending on a difference between average cost and cost at the margin) derives essentially from scarcity of supply.

[9] I. Malyshev, *loc. cit.* pp. 99, 103, 104; also cf. *Voprosy Ekonomiki* 1957 no. 2 p. 73.

[10] M. Bor, *loc. cit.* pp. 112-3.

[11] In the classical context in which Marx used it, the statement implied that gold was produced under conditions of *average* composition of capital (and turnover of capital).

[12] *Economic Problems of Socialism in the USSR* (Moscow 1952) p. 81.

ASPECTS OF THE SOVIET

INDUSTRIALIZATION MODEL

THE SOVIET UNION launched its first Five Year Plan for rapid industrialization on October 1, 1928. The particular policies pursued in this
and subsequent plans were not arrived at easily. They were, in fact, the
end product of a five-year debate among political economists. The final
path chosen by Stalin by no means represented a democratic concensus;
differences of opinion on many crucial issues remained unresolved. The
major points of view presented by different schools of thought in this
historic debate and a chronology of Stalin's shifting position are presented
in Professor Erlich's paper below. It is interesting to note that many of
the issues discussed thirty-five years ago in the Soviet Union have been
resurrected in the Western postwar literature on economic development
of underdeveloped areas.

The forced collectivization of agriculture is an essential and distinctive feature of the Soviet industrialization model. The dramatic speed-up
of collectivization in 1930 is described and documented in the selection
reprinted below from Dr. Jasny's authoritative book on Soviet agriculture.

One of the major reasons for studying the Soviet industrialization
model is its relevance for the problems of the underdeveloped nations
today. This question is explored in Dr. Hoeffding's paper with particular
reference to the problems of the overpopulated nations like China and
India. An excellent exposition of the Soviet model and its relevance for
others nations today is contained in Dr. Seton's paper (1960) listed in the
Bibliography.

The Appendix contains a correction to Professor Erlich's article.

Stalin's Views on Soviet Economic Development

ALEXANDER ERLICH

I

On s'engage, et puis on voit: this phrase borrowed from Napoleon was used by Lenin more than once to describe the position of his party after November 1917.[1] With regard to the issues of economic policy the interval between getting involved and seeing, or even looking, was rather protracted. During the first few years the pressure of external events was so overwhelming as to leave virtually no room for choice. The spontaneous seizures of factories by the workers in early 1918 and the exigencies of the Civil War forced upon the reluctant Lenin and his collaborators the policy of "War Communism." With similar inevitability the swelling tide of popular unrest climaxed by the Kronstadt revolt and by the peasant uprisings of Central Russia imposed the retreat toward the NEP. And in both cases there was always the great expectation that the European revolution would link up before long with its Russian bridgehead and assist the Soviet republic with equipment, industrial consumers' goods, and organizing ability. In 1924 the situation was entirely different. Chances of a quick rescue from the West, which had already been declining at the time of the transition to the NEP, had now passed. The discontent of the peasants, moreover, was no longer restrained by the fear of the "White" counterrevolution: they had just forced the regime off the "War Communist" path, and they were grimly awaiting the results of this victory. Under such circumstances the policy could no longer consist of spasmodic responses to catastrophes and of fervent hopes for the future. Only positive action directed toward improvement in the wretched living standards of the population could stabilize the regime; only forceful economic development aimed at enlargement of the productive capacity of the country could provide a durable basis for such action and make the Soviet Union a viable state. But how could this be done, how could these two objectives be reconciled in conditions of a backward, war-

[1] The author acknowledges gratefully the support of the Russian Research Center of Harvard University in the preparation of this study. He is also indebted to Professor Alexander Gerschenkron and Dr. Joseph S. Berliner for valuable suggestions.

82

ravaged country in the thick of a great egalitarian upheaval? This was a question to which the "old books" provided no answer.[2]

Bukharin, who was at that time the leading economic theorist of the Party, felt that the solution was clearly at hand. It was contained, according to him, in continuing the NEP as conceived by Lenin and as elaborated on in his famous *O prodnaloge*. The vicious circle of idle industrial capacity in the cities and the supply strikes in the villages was to be broken by lifting restrictive measures which had hitherto inhibited the peasant's willingness to produce a surplus above his bare needs or at any rate to part with it. Transformation of the wholesale requisitioning into a limited "tax in kind"; opening the channels of trade through which the nontaxable part of peasant surplus could be profitably sold; denationalization and encouragement of small-scale industry which would not need, because of the nature of its plant, any protracted reconditioning in order to start producing goods demanded by the peasants — these were the key devices which were expected to unfreeze the productive energies of agriculture and make increased supplies of foodstuffs and raw materials flow into the nearly empty pipelines of the urban economy. The part of this flow which would reach the large-scale industrial sector would set some of its idle wheels turning and make possible a counterflow of manufactured products to the goods-starved village, thus providing the latter with an additional incentive to increase its marketings. A genuine process of cumulative growth would be set in motion hereby. The logic of the reasoning seemed compelling, and even more impressive was the

[2] It goes without saying that the men who faced this question approached it with some definite, preconceived ideas. All of them were emphatic in recognizing the need for rapid economic development and in taking the latter to be synonymous with industrialization; in this respect they were faithfully following the line of Russian Marxism of the prerevolutionary era. They sharply deviated from the traditional approach by accepting Lenin's view that a proletarian party which succeeded in rising to political power in a backward country had a clear duty not to leave the task of industrialization to the bourgeoisie but to put itself in charge after dislodging the propertied classes from their positions of control. But this amendment, which came in response to the massive *faits accomplis* of the first revolutionary years, could not by itself make the original doctrine grind out solutions which would provide a clear-cut directive for action. The Marxian theory, to be sure, helped to bring sharply into focus some phenomena and relationships which were of relevance for the impending decisions, like advantages of large-scale production, capital-consuming and labor-displacing effects of technological progress, importance of the relative size of investment and consumers'-goods industries. It was equally categorical in assigning to the transformation of property relationships the key role in the process of social change. But it provided no criterion for optimal solutions within each of these areas, or more particularly, for appropriate speed at which the transition from the existing state of affairs to a more satisfactory one should take place. Moreover, even determined efforts toward establishing such optimum conditions would not change the situation to any substantial extent. They could, at best, lead to a more clear-cut formulation of existing alternatives and, consequently, to elimination of some minor errors and inconsistencies from the judgments: but this would not eliminate the need for choosing nor reduce the formidable risks and uncertainties attendant upon the final decision and due to the nature of the problems involved.

impact of facts: between 1920 and 1924 the output of large-scale industry increased more than threefold.

Could this upward trend be relied upon to start off a process of long-range expansion and set the pattern for it? Lenin was never explicit about it: but his strong emphasis on the need of attracting foreign investment seemed to indicate some doubts whether the policy of "developing trade at all costs" would be sufficient to do the job. Bukharin, writing three years later, betrayed no such qualms. He enthusiastically proceeded to sharpen up Lenin's analysis by praising the high allocative efficiency of the market mechanism, denouncing the tendencies toward "monopolistic parasitism" in the nationalized industry, and sounding solemn warnings against "applied Tuganism" (*prikladnaia Tugan-Baranovshchina*), which postulated the possibility of expansion of productive capacity without proportionate increase in effective demand on the part of the final consumer. This disproportion, in his view, had been ultimately responsible for the downfall of tsarism as well as for the Soviet "scissor crisis" of 1923. In order to prevent this from happening again, a consistent policy of "small profit margins and large turnover" was called for. Nor was this all: Bukharin outlined an elaborate system of institutional arrangements serving the same purpose. Marketing and credit coöperation in agriculture were, in his opinion, the most desirable devices for enlarging the peasant demand for industrial goods. But he had some words of appreciation also for the village kulak whose relentless drive to raise his output and to expand his demand made him, like Goethe's Mephisto, *ein Teil von jener Kraft, die stets das Boese will und stets das Gute schafft*. In the long run, this stratum was expected to be gradually squeezed out under the joint pressure of the proletarian state and the growing coöperative movement among the peasants.

It was the last-mentioned aspect of Bukharin's conception that evoked particularly violent attacks. The conciliatory attitude toward the village rich could not but arouse most deeply the Left Wing of the Party, which had considered the compromise with the individualist peasantry a bitter, if temporarily unavoidable, sacrifice and which was pushing toward resumption of the offensive against propertied classes both on the domestic and on the international scene. But spokesmen of this group, with Preobrazhenskii as its leading economist, did not leave things at that; they penetrated to the core of Bukharin's reasoning and denounced his extrapolation of past experience into the future as a typical "psychology of the restoration period." They were explicit, if rather brief, in dealing with long-range issues like modernization of industry, opening up areas with untapped natural resources, absorption of agricultural surplus population, the importance of what we would call today "social overheads" like transportation and the power system (as well as of industrial development in general) for the efficiency

84

of peasant farming, and, last but not least, the requirements of national defense. They were equally specific in emphasizing some of the basic characteristics of modern productive technology which made its adoption a costly proposition. But the crux of their argument lay in pointing to definite short-term features of the situation of the Soviet economy which made it imperative to move toward these long-range objectives at a high speed in spite of the high cost involved. According to Preobrazhenskii and his friends, people who rejoiced in record-breaking rates of increase in industrial growth up to 1925 lived in a fool's paradise. The expansion at small cost was easy as long as the large reserves of unutilized capacity existed; but with every leap forward in industrial output the time at which future increases would require investment in additional productive facilities was drawing closer. To wait with such investment until that stage, however, would be dangerous. The replacement of a large part of equipment actually in service had been due, but not carried out, in the period of Civil War and in the early years of the NEP. Yet while such a life-extension was possible for a while, each passing year would increase the probability of breakdown of overaged equipment; and this would imply a shrinkage in the capital stock of the economy unless the replacement activities were drastically stepped up. Another powerful source of increased pressure for expansion of capacity lay in the redistribution of income along egalitarian lines which was brought about by the Revolution and which expressed itself in a steep increase in the share of consumption in income. At the same time the large-scale import of capital which had played an important role in the economic development of prerevolutionary Russia was now reduced to a trickle.

But the very circumstances which called for rapid expansion created a grave danger for the stability of the economy. The limitations of resources permitted the required increase in investment to develop only by keeping down the levels of current consumption, while the low real income and the egalitarian mode of its distribution made it more than unlikely that this restriction in consumers' spending would take place voluntarily. Such a situation, if left uncontrolled, would mean a "goods famine," more specifically, a shortage of industrial consumers' goods; and since the Russian peasant then enjoyed, in Preobrazhenskii's words, "a much greater freedom [than before the Revolution] in the choice of the time and of the terms at which to dispose of his own surpluses because of the decrease in 'forced sales,' " [3] he would be likely to respond to an unfavorable turn in the terms of trade by cutting down his marketable surplus and thus administering a crippling blow to the industrial economy. The way out of this deadlock was to be sought in compulsory saving, with monopoly of foreign trade and price manipulation

---

[3] "Ekonomicheskie zametki," *Pravda,* December 15, 1925. The notion of "forced sales" referred to the part of the produce sold by the peasant in order to meet such obligations as taxes or (in prerevolutionary Russia) payments to the landlords.

at home as its main tools; the first would secure high priority for capital goods in Russian imports, the second was expected to contain the pressure of consumers' demand at home against the existing industrial capacity by keeping the prices of industrial commodities higher than they would be under conditions of a free unrestricted market. As a result, the capital stock of the society would be permitted to increase up to a level at which the demand for high current output of consumers' goods and requirements of further expansion of productive capacity could be met simultaneously and not to the exclusion of each other. In the planning of this initial increase, moreover, particular care had to be exercised to keep its inflationary potentialities to a minimum: the largest volume of capital outlays would fall into the initial year of the Plan, when large reserves of the old capacity could provide a cushion for the unstabilizing effect of newly started construction projects, and then gradually taper off in the following years during which these reserves would approach exhaustion.

This last-mentioned point caused little interest at the time of its enunciation; it was, incidentally, brought up not in the actual debate but in a rather technical proposal of a committee of experts known by its initials as *OSVOK*.[4] But the proposals for compulsory saving (bracketed by Preobrazhenskii under the anxiety-provoking name of "primitive socialist accumulation") did call forth an immediate reaction; indeed, they proved an ideal target for attack. The representatives of the Bukharin group were quick to point out that a policy recommended by the Leftists would in its immediate effects greatly increase the tensions which its long-range consequences were expected to alleviate. The policy of monopolistic price manipulation would make the peasants worse off; they would be certain to resist this deterioration by using all the devices Preobrazhenskii and his friends had so eloquently described; and the possibility of steering through the economic and political trouble caused by such a policy toward the time at which the new investment would smooth the waves by starting to deliver the goods could be asserted merely as an act of faith.[5]

II

The assertion that Stalin's interventions in the debate of 1924–1927 did not break the impasse would be an understatement. Indeed, his pronouncements on controversial issues of economic policy in these years exhibit

---

[4] Abbreviation for *Osoboe soveshchanie po vosstanovleniiu osnovnogo kapitala promyshlennosti SSSR.*

[5] For a more detailed account of the controversy, see Maurice Dobb, *Soviet Economic Development Since 1917* (New York, 1948), ch. viii; my "Preobrazhenskii and the Economics of Soviet Industrialization," *Quarterly Journal of Economics,* LXIV (February 1950), 57–88; and my "The Soviet Industrialization Controversy" (unpublished Ph.D. dissertation on deposit at the New School for Social Research, New York, and the Russian Research Center, Harvard University, 1953).

such a definite tendency against sin and in favor of eating one's cake and having it too that it appears at first almost hopeless to distill out of them a clear view not only of the nature of the problems, but also of the attitude of the man. But after a closer examination of the record, there can be no doubt that Stalin's statement at the Fourteenth Party Congress: "We are, and we shall be, for Bukharin," [6] provides a substantially correct description of his position at that time. True, in certain respects he sounded a somewhat different note. He showed a strong inclination to indulge, on every propitious occasion, in exalting the glories of the coming industrialization; moreover, the aspect of the future developments which received the fondest attention on his part was the possibility of making Russia a self-contained unit, economically independent of the outside world — "a country which can produce by its own efforts the necessary equipment." [7] He started to emphasize the need for intensive reconstruction of Soviet industry earlier than Bukharin did; and in the same speech in which he dramatically refused to give "Bukharin's blood" to the opposition, he did not hesitate to disassociate himself from the "get rich" slogan.[8] But neither these nor similar instances could alter the fact that on issues which were relevant for actual policy the agreement was practically complete. When Stalin was applauding the removal of "administrative obstacles preventing the rise in the peasant welfare" as "an operation [which] undoubtedly facilitates any accumulation, private capitalist as well as socialist," [9] or when he denounced on an earlier occasion any attempt to fan the class struggle in the village as "empty chatter," while praising peasant coöperation as a road toward socialist transformation of agriculture,[10] he was talking like a Bukharinite pure and simple; his wailings about "get rich" sounded, in view of this, very much like the famous admonition given to Eduard Bernstein, the father of German "revisionism," by one of his senior friends: "Such things should be done but not said." The identity of position on the larger issue of relationships between industry and agriculture was equally evident. Although Stalin did not invoke the ghost of Tugan-Baranovskii (he was at that time somewhat chary of incursions into the field of theory), he believed firmly that "our industry, which provides the foundation of socialism and of our power, is based on the internal, on the peasant market." [11]

[6] *XIV s"ezd vsesoiuznoi kommunisticheskoi partii (b). Stenograficheskii otchët* (Moscow-Leningrad, 1926), p. 494. In Volume VII of Stalin's collected works containing the text of this speech the words "and we shall be" are omitted.

[7] I. V. Stalin, *Sochineniia* (Moscow, 1947), VII, 355.

[8] *Ibid.*, p. 382.

[9] *Ibid.*, p. 153.

[10] *Ibid.*, pp. 123, 125.

[11] *Ibid.*, p. 29. How seriously Stalin took this idea can be seen from the fact that in the immediately following sentence he expressed grave concern about the situation in which Russia would find itself after her industry had "outgrown" the internal market and had to compete for the foreign markets with the advanced capitalist countries.

The last point, to be sure, did not jibe very well with his other declared objectives: if industry had to be oriented primarily toward the satisfaction of peasant needs, it would be impossible to spare an adequate amount of resources for a large-scale effort toward reconstruction of industry, particularly if this should be done with a view to future self-sufficiency in the sphere of capital-goods production. But to proclaim long-term goals was one thing, and to rush toward them at a high speed was another. Stalin in these days showed no inclination toward the latter. In the same speech in which he extolled the virtues of economic independence, he readily admitted that large-scale imports of foreign machinery were, at least for the time being, indispensable for the development of the Soviet economy; and in his polemics against Trotsky at a somewhat later date, he went to considerable lengths in order to emphasize that the Soviet Union would not endanger her economic sovereignty by trading extensively with the capitalist world — first of all because the dependence involved would be a two-way affair and, secondly, because nationalization of large-scale industry and banking as well as state monopoly of foreign trade would provide powerful safeguards against any attempt at foreign encroachments.[12] His attitude toward the problem of the rate of industrial development was characterized by similar circumspection. At one point he would attempt to sidetrack the issue by injecting a larger one and by insisting that a reconstruction of fixed capital in industry would not solve the problem of building socialism in Russia as long as agriculture had not been transformed along collectivist lines.[13] On another occasion, he praised glowingly the rapid increase in output of the Soviet metal industry as proof that "the proletariat . . . can construct with its own efforts a new industry and a new society," [14] without mentioning the obvious fact that this increase had been so rapid precisely because it had been based on increased utilization of the old industrial capacity and *not* on the creation of the new. But when he actually came to grips with the problem in his report to the Fourteenth Congress, he left no doubts as to his real attitude:

[12] "Our country depends on other countries just as other countries depend on our national economy; but this does not mean yet that our country has lost, or is going to lose, its sovereignty [*samostoiatel'nost'*], . . . that it will become a little screw [sic] of the international capitalist economy" (*ibid.,* IX, 132–133). Contrary to what may be the first impression, this passage is not incompatible either with the above-quoted statements or with Stalin's well-known pronouncements of later years. It does, however, provide an additional indication that Stalin's real long-term goal was superiority and not insularity. Such a policy, and more particularly the high rate of economic growth implied in it, did in fact make it rational to develop the domestic capital goods industry on a substantial scale since the demand for the services of this industry was known to be large and sustained and a sizable initial stock was already in existence; but it would also call for making extensive use of the advantages of international division of labor. Still, in the middle twenties, all this sounded rather academic because, as will be shown presently, the decision in favor of the high rate of growth had not yet been made.

[13] *Ibid.,* VII, 200.

[14] *Ibid.,* p. 131.

In order to switch from maximal utilization of everything we had in industry to the policy of constructing a new industry on a new technological basis, on the basis of the construction of new plants, large capital outlays are needed. But since we are suffering from a considerable capital shortage, the further development of our industry will proceed, in all probability, not at such a fast rate as it has until now. The situation with regard to agriculture is different. It cannot be said that all the potentialities of agriculture are already exhausted. Agriculture, in distinction from industry, can move for some time at a fast rate also on its present technological basis. Even the simple rise in cultural level of the peasant, even such a simple thing as cleaning the seeds could raise the gross output of agriculture by 10 to 15 per cent . . . That's why the further development of agriculture does not yet face the technological obstacles our industry has to face . . .[15]

Stalin could not be more frank in formulating the basic problem which was, as we have seen, at the core of the whole discussion: the very same factors — limited productive capacity and low levels of income — that called for expansion in Soviet industry were putting obstacles in its way. In the paragraph quoted the emphasis was clearly on the obstacles. Still, when the arch-moderate Shanin applauded heartily, he must have done so with a twinkle in his eye: in fact the Fourteenth Party Congress did signalize the transition from "filling-in" to reconstruction — but reconstruction on a limited scale and in a cautious mood. Although the volume of capital outlays increased substantially in the years 1926 and 1927, the Leftists led by Preobrazhenskii and Trotsky immediately opened fire. The new investment program, they claimed, was neither here nor there; it was too limited to secure an increase in capacity large enough to stabilize the situation in a not too distant future, too ambitious not to cause inflationary disturbances now in view of the absence of drastic taxation measures.

In the face of these attacks, and of actual difficulties which did not fail to materialize, something more than a sober and judicious description of the two horns of the dilemma was called for. A characteristic division of labor developed at this point. Bukharin and Rykov, who were the guiding spirits of the new line, were wrestling with large, clear-cut issues — the relation between heavy and light industry, the limits for investment in time-consuming projects, the possibility of absorbing the surplus labor in production lines with low capital requirements — in a desperate search for solutions which would make the adopted policy work. Stalin followed a different procedure. He visibly tried to avoid sharply delineated problems; instead, he let his argument seesaw from bold statements of principles to sobering but comfortably loose observations on present-day realities, and he switched from obtuse mystique to gruff common sense. Rapid industrialization? Yes, indeed! More than that: it should be kept in mind that "not every development of industry constitutes industrialization" and that "the focal point of industrialization, its basis, consists of development of heavy industry (fuel, metals,

[15] *Ibid.*, pp. 315–316.

etc.) and of eventual development of production of the means of production, development of domestic machine-building." [16] But right on the heels
of such proclamations there would come a caustic remark about those who
"sometimes forget that it is impossible to make plans either for industry as
a whole or for some 'large and all-embracing' enterprise without a certain
minimum of means, without a certain minimum of reserves," [17] and a warning that "an industry which breaks itself away from the national economy
as a whole and loses its connection with it cannot be the guiding force of
the national economy." [18] Could the Soviet economy in its present shape
afford a rate of economic development which would exceed that of the
capitalist countries? Of course! The capitalist countries had based their
expansion on exploitation of colonies, military conquest, or foreign loans.
But the Soviet Union expropriated the capitalists and the landlords, nationalized strategic areas of the economy, and repudiated the tsarist foreign debts.
This circumstance enabled her to provide a sufficient volume of accumulation
without having recourse to any of these devices.[19] Furthermore, it permitted
this accumulation to unfold alongside of "a steady improvement in the
material conditions of the working masses, including the bulk of the peasantry . . . as contrasted with the capitalist methods of industrialization
based on the growing misery of millions of working people." [20] No specific
reasons for any of these assertions were given. However, the most elaborate
of such attempts at solution by definition concluded by admitting that the
socialist principles along which the Soviet economy was organized offered
merely a *possibility* of achieving the appropriate level of accumulation, but
no more than that; and the concrete proposals for policy which followed
were in their sum total excruciatingly modest not only in comparison with
the grandiloquent claims that preceded them but also, and more significantly,
with regard to the size of the investment programs they were supposed to
sustain.[21]

All this looked very much like trying to buy a second-hand Ford for the
price of a discarded piece of junk while pretending that a brand-new
Packard was being obtained. True, there was another line of defense: to

[16] *Ibid.*, VIII, 120.
[17] *Ibid.*, p. 131
[18] *Ibid.*, p. 132.
[19] *Ibid.*, pp. 122–125.
[20] *Ibid.*, p. 287.
[21] They include (1) improved incentives for peasant saving; (2) reduction in retail
prices of industrial goods; (3) orderly amortization policies; (4) building up export
reserves; (5) creation of budgetary surplus (*ibid.*, pp. 126–129). In other contexts
elimination of waste and inefficiency in economic and political administration receives
the top billing (*ibid.*, IX, 196 and joint declaration by Stalin, Rykov, and Kuibyshev
in *Pravda*, August 17, 1926). Some of these measures, while pointing in the right direction, could hardly be expected to have much effect in the immediate future, and others
involved putting the cart before the horse, e.g., price reductions not preceded by substantial expansion in productive capacity.

90   ALEXANDER ERLICH

play down the importance of recurrent spells of "goods famine" and to present them as transient phenomena. Although Stalin tried this device occasionally, it was obviously a tenuous argument to use, particularly since the assertion that "quick development of our industry is the surest way to eliminate the goods famine" [22] sounded too much like conceding a point to the Left opposition. It was therefore only logical for him to shift the battleground to the territory of the adversaries, to concentrate on the crucial weak spot in their position and to pound relentlessly upon it:

> The oppositionist bloc assumed a conflict between industry and agriculture and is headed toward breaking industry away from agriculture. It does not realize and it does not admit that it is impossible to develop industry while neglecting the interests of agriculture and hurting these interests in a rude fashion. It does not understand that if industry is the guiding force of the national economy, the agricultural economy represents in turn the basis on which our industry is able to develop . . .
>
> . . . The Party cannot and will not tolerate [a situation in which] the opposition continues to undermine the basis of the alliance of workers and peasants by spreading the idea of an increase in wholesale prices and in the burden of taxation upon the peasantry, by attempting to "construe" the relationships between proletariat and peasantry not as relationships of economic *coöperation* but as relationships of exploitation of the peasantry by the proletarian state. The Party cannot and will not tolerate this.[23]

At the Fifteenth Party Congress, which carried out this solemn vow by expelling the Left-wingers, Stalin was surveying the field once more. He displayed again the full array of the familiar arguments: praise for the growth of the Soviet industrial output at a rate which, while declining continuously since 1924–1925, was still showing "a record percentage which no large capitalist country in the world has ever shown";[24] reaffirmation of faith in the superiority which the Soviet system possessed with regard to capitalism in its ability to accumulate and which should make it possible to increase the industrial output by roughly 75 per cent during the coming five years in spite of the exhaustion of the capacity reserves; strong emphasis on the possibility of developing "in an atmosphere of constant *rapprochement* between city and village, between proletariat and peasantry," [25] as one of the greatest advantages of Soviet industry. His backhanded remarks about what he termed the "shadowy aspects" of the Soviet economy ("elements" of goods famine, lack of reserves, etc.) contained no specific proposals for remedy but carried a clear implication that if people on the spot would apply themselves to their tasks with more energy, all would be well. There was, however, no complacency in his remarks on agriculture, and here indeed something new was added: in view of the slowness of agricultural develop-

[22] Stalin, *Sochineniia*, IX, 120.
[23] *Ibid.*, pp. 288, 352–353.
[24] *Ibid.*, X, 300.
[25] *Ibid.*, pp. 301–302.

ment, Stalin declared, the task of the Party would now consist in bringing about "a gradual transition of pulverized peasant farms to the level of combined large-scale holdings, to the social collective cultivation of land on the basis of the intensification and mechanization of agriculture." [26] He was careful not to give any hint as to the anticipated speed of this movement, and, in an enunciation antedating by a few weeks his report to the Fifteenth Congress, he was explicit in emphasizing that it would take a long time to collectivize the bulk of the peasantry because such an undertaking would require "huge finances" which the Soviet state did not yet have.[27] Still, his statement was surprising: but events which were even then fast advancing were to provide *ex post* a clue to it.

III

The beginning of 1928 saw large consignments of the Leftist "super-industrializers" move toward places of exile in Siberia and Central Asia. But at the same time their dire predictions were coming true. For the first time since the "scissors crisis" of 1923 the peasant bolted the regime. By January 1928 the amount of collected grain fell by roughly one-third as compared with the same period of the preceding year. During the following few months it rose again only to drop in the spring; and the emergency methods by which the temporary increase was enforced stirred up once more the feelings of bitterness and resistance which had been dormant in the villages during the seven years of the NEP. The crisis of the system was there — the first crisis Stalin had to cope with as the undisputed leader of the Party and of the state. During the eighteen months that followed, Stalin was no longer arguing, as before, against opponents who had been isolated and out-maneuvered before they began to fight; he was reappraising a policy which had promoted his rise to power and which seemed now to explode in his face. It is therefore not surprising that his pronouncements of that period differ significantly from those of the earlier years. They certainly contain their due share of crudeness, obfuscation, and outright distortion; but at the same time they show flashes of astonishing frankness and incisiveness clearly due to realization that everything was at stake and that the time of muddling through was over.

The prime task consisted, understandably enough, in providing the explanation of the agricultural debacle. One can clearly distinguish several parallel lines of attack in Stalin's statements on the subject. The first of them was already indicated in his report to the Fifteenth Congress when he mentioned the low productivity of small-scale peasant agriculture and its low marketable surplus as a serious obstacle for the rapid industrial development of the country. This proposition was in itself neither new nor con-

[26] *Ibid.*, p. 309.
[27] *Ibid.*, p. 225.

troversial, provided that the "obstacle" was taken to be a retarding factor rather than an insuperable barrier. It was a breath-taking jump to conclusions, however, when Stalin went on to claim that "there is no other way out" except for collectivization. In the audience to which he was addressing himself there were, to be sure, no doubts as to the superiority of the large-size units in agricultural economy. But it was generally understood that there was still a wide range of opportunities for increases in the productivity of peasant farming which would not call for large-scale mechanized equipment and for drastic expansion in the size of the productive unit; and it was agreed that the extensive application of the latter category of improvements should be postponed, in view of the high capital requirements involved, until after the capital-goods industry had been sufficiently expanded. Consequently, while the idea of collectivization of agriculture as a long-range objective held a place of honor in the Party program of 1919 and was repeatedly invoked after that, particularly in the pronouncements of the Left, no one had thus far suggested putting it into effect on a large scale within the next few years in order to solve difficulties facing the Soviet economy at the end of the "restoration period." In fact, Stalin himself seemed to take quite an edge off his argument and to hark back to his earlier views when he admitted the existence of considerable reserves for improvement within the framework of the small-scale economy,[28] and as late as April 1929 he still kept insisting that "the individual farming of poor and middle peasants plays and will play the predominant role in supplying industry with food and raw material in the immediate future." [29] But, and most important, the whole point seemed to have no direct bearing on the concrete issue under consideration. By the end of 1927 and at the beginning of 1928 the Russian peasants had not less but more grain at their disposal than in the preceding years; still, they were willing to sell less of it than in the years of bad harvest. The reference to the low productivity of small-scale farming, even if reduced to sensible proportions, was definitely too "long run" to provide an explanation for this phenomenon.

The second line of argument was succinctly summed up in the phrase "as long as the kulak exists, the sabotage of grain collections will exist too." [30] This point, made in Stalin's speech in January 1928 and repeated by him with increasing vehemence ever after, was certainly straightforward enough; still it raised more questions than it answered. The fact of formidable kulak

[28] "There is every indication that we could increase the yield of the peasant farms by 15–20 per cent within a few years. We have now in use about 5 million hoes. The substitution of ploughs for them could alone result in a most substantial increase in the output of grain in the country, not to speak of supplying the peasant farms with a certain minimum of fertilizer, improved seeds, small machinery and the like" (*ibid.*, XI, 92).

[29] *Ibid.*, XII, 59.

[30] *Ibid.*, XI, 4–5.

Stalin on Economic Development

resistance did not fit very well, to begin with, into the rosy picture of the Soviet village Stalin had been unfolding before his listeners only slightly more than a year earlier when he proudly referred to the steadily increasing proportion of middle peasants in the agricultural population and asserted, with a long quotation from Lenin on hand to bear him out, that nobody but panic-stricken people could see a danger in the growth of "small private capital" in the villages because this growth "is being compensated and over-compensated by such decisive facts as the development of our industry, which strengthens the positions of the proletariat and of the socialist forms of the economy." [31] True, in this case also there were, at first, important qualifications which softened the impact of the shock: stern warning against any talk about "dekulakization" as "counterrevolutionary chatter," con-demnation of the excessive zeal in applying reprisals, and announcement of moderate increases in prices of agricultural products.[32] But after all this had been said and done, it was still to be explained why the kulak was so suc-cessful in his criminal endeavor — more particularly, why he was able, as Stalin reluctantly acknowledged, to carry along with him the "middle peasants" who were supplying the bulk of the marketable surplus at that time.[33]

Stalin had a clear answer to this as well as to all other questions the previous explanations had left unanswered; between the "low-productivity" argument and the cloak-and-dagger theory of the kulaks' plot he had a third line of reasoning which hit the nail straight on the head. It was less publicized than the former two and for good reasons: it amounted to a clear and unqualified admission of a complete impasse. Stalin no longer tried to play down the impact of the goods famine; he stressed instead that the shortage of industrial goods on the peasant market, aggravated by an in-crease in peasant earnings in the preceding period, had hit not merely the kulaks but the peasants as a whole and had made them strike back by cutting the grain deliveries.[34] He spelled out more fully than ever before the connection between the goods famine and the discontinuous increase in the volume of investment:

Industrial reconstruction means the transfer of resources from the field of pro-duction of articles of consumption to the field of production of means of produc-tion . . . But what does it mean? It means that money is being invested in the construction of new enterprises, that the number of new towns and new consumers is increasing while, on the other hand, the new enterprises will begin to turn out additional masses of commodities only in three or four years' time. It is obvious that this does not help to overcome the goods famine.[35]

[31] *Ibid.*, VIII, 291–292.
[32] *Ibid.*, XI, 15, 124–125.
[33] *Ibid.*, p. 12.
[34] *Ibid.*, p. 14.
[35] *Ibid.*, p. 267.

He rounded out the picture when he dropped his usual double talk and shocked his colleagues of the Central Committee by revealing his views on the true sources of accumulation in the Soviet economy:

The peasantry pays to the state not only the normal taxes, direct and indirect, but it *overpays,* first of all, on the relatively high prices of industrial goods, and is being more or less *underpaid* on the relatively low prices of agricultural products . . . This is something like a "tribute" [*nechto vrode "dani"*], something like a supertax we are temporarily compelled to impose in order to maintain and to develop further the present tempo of development of industry, to secure the industry for the whole country, to raise the well-being of the village still further, and to abolish entirely this supertax, these "scissors" between the city and the village.[36]

All this sounded very much like a somewhat awkward rephrasing of Preobrazhenskii's "law of primitive socialist accumulation." The crucial task at that time of the day, however, was not to restate an old diagnosis but to construe a "tribute"-collecting device that would work: and this was exactly what Stalin did. The collective farm, in which decisions about size and disposal of the marketable surplus were made not by individual farmers but by management carrying out the orders of the state, was to serve as a high-powered tool for enforcing the necessary rate of saving in the most literal sense of the standard Marxian definition: it could make the peasants "sell without purchasing" to a much greater extent than they would have done if left to themselves. Here was the decisive point. Still, Stalin was undoubtedly right in not being too ostentatious about it and in holding on firmly to the two other arguments referred to above in spite of their inadequacy. To proclaim in so many words that collectivization was needed in order to squeeze out the peasants in a most effective way would clearly be a poor tactic; it was much smarter to present the collective farm as an indispensable vehicle for modernizing Soviet agriculture and for drastically increasing its productivity. In view of everything Stalin had to say about the impact of the "goods famine" on the peasantry as a whole and about the inevitability of the "supertax," the diatribes against kulak sabotage could not be taken very seriously. They could, nevertheless, be of appreciable help in whipping up emotions against an alternative solution which was advanced at that time by Stalin's former comrades-in-arms. The representatives of the Bukharin-Rykov group did not propose to revise the investment plans below the fairly impressive levels set by the Party leadership at the end of 1927. They believed, however, that in order to carry out these plans it was not necessary to abandon support for individual peasant farming and to renounce the policy of no interference with the growth of large-scale kulak farms while curbing the nonproductive and exploitative activities of their

[36] *Ibid.,* p. 159 (italics in original). It may be worth noting that this speech, which led to the final break between Stalin and the Bukharin-Rykov group, was not published until 1949.

Stalin on Economic Development

owners. On the contrary, although by that time the controversy had already been quite muffled, and it was difficult to ascertain what exactly the leaders of the Right Wing were prepared to do, the general tenor of their pronouncements, as well as occasional statements of second-string representatives and "fellow travelers" of this group, indicated a willingness to go to greater lengths than ever before toward placating the peasants in general and the kulaks in particular, in order to provide them with incentives for increasing the marketable surplus and the volume of voluntary saving in an effort to contain the mounting inflationary pressures.

Stalin never earnestly tried to assail the economic logic of this position. He never attempted to prove that it was impossible for socialized industry and kulak farming to operate smoothly within one economic system, although he made a few obiter dicta to that effect. Neither did he care to show (which would be a more serious point) that an investment policy, sustained to a considerable extent by the peasants' free decision to restrict their consumption, would tend to be rather narrow in scope and susceptible to rude shocks as a result of such uncontrollable events as drought or changes in international terms of trade. Instead, he asked: "What is meant by not hindering kulak farming? It means setting the kulak free. And what is meant by setting the kulak free? It means giving him power." [37] Taken literally, this seemed to be one of the dubious syllogisms Stalin was notoriously fond of whenever a weak case was to be defended. It is quite conceivable, however, that in this particular instance he believed every word he said; and, what is vastly more important, there can be no doubt that the consistent application of the Rightist recipe would be fraught with gravest political dangers. The efforts to enlist voluntary support of the peasantry for the industrialization developing at considerable speed would require a veritable tightrope performance on the part of the Soviet rulers. In order to maintain the precarious balance and to steer clear of trouble at every sharper turning of the road, the regime would have to combine compulsory control measures with additional concessions; and since there was little room for compromise in the economic sphere, it could become well-nigh indispensable to explore a new line of approach and to attempt to earn the good will of the upper strata of the peasantry by opening up for them avenues of political influence even if confined, at first, to the level of local government. There was nothing either in the logic of things or, for that matter, in the tenets of the accepted doctrine to warrant the conclusion that such a situation, if permitted to endure, would inevitably result in "giving power to the kulaks" and in restoring capitalism. But it is quite probable that under the impact of initial concessions and of further maneuvering the system of authoritarian dictatorship would have become increasingly permeated by elements of political pluralism and of quasi-democratic give-and-take. The vacillating and

[37] *Ibid.*, p. 275.

conciliatory attitude which, judging by Stalin's own testimony,[38] was shown by the lower echelons of the Party hierarchy and governmental apparatus, during the critical months of 1928, underlined the gravity of the situation. The choice was clear: either a deep retreat and the gradual erosion of the dictatorial system or an all-out attack aimed at total destruction of the adversary's capability to resist.

Stalin's pronouncements since early 1928 showed beyond possibility of doubt that he had decided in favor of the second alternative. The transition from theory to action, however, was all but a masterminded advance toward a well-defined goal. Stalin evidently planned at first to move in the agricultural field by stages; his repeated declarations about the predominant role of individual farming for many years to come, as well as his condemnations of "dekulakization" and readiness to meet the restive peasantry part of the way by granting price increases, can be taken as a clear indication of this. And the impression of caution and groping for solution is still further reinforced when the position on issues of agricultural policy is viewed in a broader context. There was, undoubtedly, a perceptible change of emphasis in Stalin's declarations on questions of industrialization policy after January 1928. He no longer spoke about Soviet industry as "the most large scale and most concentrated in the world," as he had at the Fifteenth Party Congress.[39] Instead, he denounced its "terrible backwardness" and sounded a call for catching up with the West as a condition for survival: the old aim of "economic independence" was now transformed into "superiority" and further dramatized by the stress upon the element of tempo at which the catching up was to take place. And while all this talk was still couched in most general terms, the language of the drafts of the First Five-Year Plan, which were at that time being prepared by the official governmental agencies and which reflected in their successive versions the changes of the official policy, was much more outspoken: during the whole period between the Fifteenth Party Congress and adoption of the final draft of the First Five-Year Plan in the spring of 1929 there was a clear upward trend in all the crucial indicators of the "tempo" — rate of growth in industrial output, volume of investment and its increase over time, share of heavy industry in the total capital outlays. But at the same time there was strong evidence that the momentous implications of the new policy were not yet fully grasped. Stalin was, no doubt, most persistent in stressing that industry and agriculture were interdependent, the first constituting a "leading link," and the second being a "basis." Still, whenever he went beyond these generalities, he pointed out that industry would have to expand and to reëquip itself in order to start reëquipping agriculture; in fact this was, in his view, one of the strongest forces pushing for speedy industrialization.[40] The implication was clear: the

[38] *Ibid.*, pp. 3–4, 235.
[39] *Ibid.*, X, 301.
[40] *Ibid.*, XI, 252–253.

bulk of the reorganization of agriculture was to take place *after* the completion of a cycle of intensive industrial expansion and not *simultaneously* with it. Moreover, although Stalin kept extolling the superiority of *"smytchka through metal"* over *"smytchka* through textile," he could not refrain from remarking wistfully that it would be very fine indeed "to shower the village with all kinds of goods in order to extract from the village the maximum amount of agricultural products" and from leaving at least a strong implication that the attainment of such a happy state of affairs was one of the major objectives of the industrialization drive.[41] Stalin was merely hinting at these diverse points, but they were spelled out fully in the targets of the First Five-Year Plan: more than doubling of the fixed capital of the whole nonagricultural sector over the quinquennium, increase in output of industrial consumers' goods by 40 per cent, and no more than an 18 per cent share of the collective farms in the marketable output of agriculture.

No doubt, if the planned sizes of the first two items of the blueprint had been mutually consistent, the comparatively moderate targets for the third would be appropriate. But they were not; moreover, in view of Stalin's own statements about the causes of the "goods famine," the high target for consumers' goods could be to him only a pious wish, if not plain eyewash. As a result, there was an awkward dilemma. From the standpoint of reducing the pressures on the facilities of the capital goods industry, a postponement of full-dress collectivization seemed wise. But the function of collective farms consisted, first and foremost, in providing the technique for imposing the required volume of compulsory saving, and since the astronomic rate of planned expansion in fixed capital would inevitably entail, at the very least in the first years of the Plan, a drastic cut in consumption levels, such a technique was desperately needed from the very beginning of the process. How could the conflict be resolved? The answer was not slow in coming. Before the Plan was two months old the moderate targets in the agricultural field mentioned above went overboard, because Stalin had reversed himself; in response to the repeated and more dismal failure of the grain collections, all-out collectivization was sweeping the country.

Up to this point the whole development looked like some sort of cumulative process gone mad. To begin with, there was a "goods famine" generated by expanding industry and throwing agriculture into a crisis, with an incipient collectivization drive as a result. Then, there was the perspective of an extremely rapid transformation of agriculture imparting additional impetus to plans of industrial expansion and pushing them to lengths which would disbalance agriculture more than ever and, finally, the sudden burst of all-out collectivization spread disruption in the social fabric of the countryside and left in its wake the wholesale slaughter of livestock by rebellious peasants. But after reaching what seemed to be the stage of explosion, the

[41] *Ibid.,* p. 40.

fluctuations began to subside as the new device went to work. Collective farming pulled the Plan over the hump because it did what an agriculture based on individual ownership would never have done, even if confronted with an equally formidable display of terror and repression: amidst mass starvation, in the face of contracting agricultural output and an appalling shortage in industrial consumers' goods, the new set-up secured an iron ration of food sufficient to keep alive the workers of rapidly growing industry, and provided an export surplus big enough to finance record-breaking importations of foreign machinery. The feat was achieved to a large extent on the basis of old, decrepit equipment; the capital-goods industry was permitted to make huge forward strides in its own expansion before being called upon to supply the collective farms with technology which would correspond to their size. The moral of the story was clear: if a half-completed structure of collective farming and a capital-goods industry still in the throes of acute growing pains succeeded in making possible economic expansion at an unparalleled rate, there was every reason to maintain this pattern of development after these two key elements had been firmly established and to continue using up at a high rate the opportunities for investment in enlarged productive potential and increased power, with the satisfaction of consumers' needs firmly relegated to the rear.

Such was, in fact, the conclusion Stalin had drawn. But while the practical consequences of this decision were momentous, little would be gained by discussing his running comments on them in any detail. There is no doubt that after 1929 Stalin was more assertive than ever before in proclaiming his long-range goals and in exhorting to further efforts. All his earlier pronouncements on the need of catching up with the West look pallid in comparison with his famous "we-do-not-want-to-be-beaten" speech.[42] Although the successes of the five-year plans failed to improve the quality of their architect's theorizing, it was only natural that in the process of directing Soviet industrialization he sharpened some of his earlier notions of its distinctive features and made a few new observations: his remarks on short-term profit considerations as an inadequate guide for developing new areas of economy, and on Russia's advantage in not being weighted down in her attempts to adapt new technology by the massive stock of old-type equipment already in existence are cases in point.[43] And he displayed to the full his uncanny ability to change tactics and recast arguments in the face of unexpected difficulties.[44] For all these new touches and variations, however,

[42] *Ibid.*, XIII, 29–42, esp. 38–40.

[43] *Ibid.*, pp. 192–93 and *Voprosy leninizma,* 11th ed. (Moscow, 1947), p. 575.

[44] His "Golovokruzhenie ot uspekhov" (Stalin, *Sochineniia,* XII, 191–199), which put a temporary halt to the forced collectivization, is, to be sure, the best-known example of this. It may be worth while, however, to quote a similar instance from a different area. In 1930, with reports from industrial battlefields claiming big victories, Stalin allowed himself another brief spell of "dizziness with success": he called for raising the 1933 target

Stalin on Economic Development

there was no longer any real change either in the structure of the system or in the views of its builder. He summed up his ideas once more shortly after the war when he contrasted the "capitalist" pattern of industrialization, putting the development of consumers'-goods output first, and the "socialist" pattern starting with the expansion of heavy industries.[45] And he restated the same position in a more generalized way a few years later when he answered one of his last self-addressed questions: "What does it mean to give up the preponderance of the production of the means of production [over production of consumers' goods]? This means to destroy the possibility of the uninterrupted growth of the national economy." [46] Bukharin would have called it *prikladnaia Tugan-Baranovshchina*. Indeed, this it was: "applied Tuganism" harnessed to the service of a totalitarian state.

---

for steel from 10 to 15–17 million tons and used abusive language against the "Trotskyite theory of the leveling-off curve of growth" (*ibid.*, pp. 331, 349–352). In 1933, however, when the actual level of steel output fell far short of the initial target and the rate of over-all industrial expansion slumped heavily, he did not hesitate to move more than halfway toward this much-detested theory: he argued then that the rate of growth in output had shown a decline as a result of the transition from the "period of restoration" to the "period of reconstruction," and went on to say that there was nothing sinister about it (*ibid.*, 183–185). But in the following years the rate of increase went up again, if not quite to the level of the preceding period, and the unholy distinction between "restoration" and "reconstruction" disappeared from Stalin's vocabulary.

[45] Speech to the voters of the Stalin electoral district of Moscow, *Pravda,* February 10, 1946.

[46] I. Stalin, *Ekonomicheskie problemy sotsializma v SSSR* (Moscow, 1952), p. 24. It goes without saying that this is much too strong a condition. An "uninterrupted growth of the national economy" is secured whenever the volume of investment exceeds the amount needed to maintain the capital equipment at a level sufficient to keep the income per head of growing population constant. This requirement might indeed involve a "preponderance [for example, more rapid tempo of growth] of the production of the means of production" if at least one of the following assumptions could be taken to hold: (1) abnormally high rate of wear and tear due either to low durability of the average piece of machinery or to the unusually large share of old-vintage equipment in the existing capital stock; (2) necessity to provide productive facilities for a discontinuously large increase in the total labor force in order to offset the pressure of increasing population on the income-per-capita levels; (3) the capital-goods industry exposed to these pressures being adapted in its capacity to a very limited volume of net capital construction over and above the "normal" replacement levels. It would certainly be bold to argue that any of these assumptions actually prevailed in the Soviet economy of 1952. But it would be even more drastic to assume that when Stalin said "uninterrupted growth" he meant precisely this, and nothing else.

THE DRIVE

Between June 1, 1927 and June 1, 1928, the number of kolkhozy increased from 14,832 to 33,258, and their membership from 194,700 households to 416,700. The Gosplan touched upon this development as follows: "1927–28 was a year of rapid increase in collectivization. The collectives were being organized without plans, without serious organizational and agronomic help."[22] But these deficiencies were trifling compared with the chaos that followed.

The Gosplan's goal.—The Gosplan, whose appraisal of the activities of the kolkhozy was quite reserved, naturally displayed great reluctance in planning for a large expansion of collectivization during the 1st Plan Period. In spite of the urgent demands of the Party, individual peasant farming would have remained almost intact at the end of that period, with little more than the natural increase in rural population going into kolkhozy, had the 1st Plan been followed. Characteristically, the increase in collectivization planned for the sixth plan year was almost half as large as the increase planned for the first five years. The reluctance of the Gosplan to call for rapid collectivization is further indicated by the fact that, while the maximum variant of the Plan commonly had higher goals than the basic variant, the same rate of collectivization was specified in both.

Following are the highlights of the 1st Plan with reference to collectivization:[23]

Item	1927–28 actual	1932–33 Basic goal	1932–33 Maximum goal	1933–34 Basic goal	1933–34 Maximum goal
Rural population (millions)					
Collectivized	1.1	12.9	12.9	18.6	18.6
Non-collectivized	122.0	121.5	121.0	117.9	116.9
Cropped plowland (million hectares)					
Collectivized	1.1	14.5	14.5	20.6	20.6
Non-collectivized	113.3	120.7	122.4	118.5	120.5

---

[21] Prokopovicz, *op. cit.*, p. 82.   [22] *Control Figures* . . . . *for 1928–29*, p. 240.
[23] *1st Plan*, II, Part 1, pp. 328–29.

Item	1927–28 actual	1932–33		1933–34	
		Basic goal	Maximum goal	Basic goal	Maximum goal
Gross production (million 1926–27 rubles)					
Collectivized	88	2,005	2,480	3,000	3,800
Non-collectivized	13,722	17,180	18,459	17,780	19,298
Marketings (million 1926–27 rubles)					
Collectivized	24	796	1,060	Not stated	
Non-collectivized	2,774	4,107	4,754	Not stated	

Thus the individual sector of the peasantry in the last year of the five-year period (1932–33) would have declined, in number of population, by less than one percent. It would have retained almost 90 percent of the gross production of all peasants (i.e., of total production excluding that of state farms), and would have been responsible for 83.8 or 81.8 percent of the peasants' marketings. The share of the collectivized sector in gross production and marketings of all peasants at best (maximum variant) would have been 12.3 and 18.2 percent respectively.

The actual rate.—The provisions of the 1st Plan with reference to collectivization were discarded before the Plan as a whole was approved. The village peasantry, one hundred million strong, had to be—and were—collectivized practically overnight. On November 7, 1929, in an article in *Pravda* entitled "The Year of the Great Turn," Stalin enthusiastically proclaimed: "The peasants have been joining the kolkhozy, joining by whole villages, volosti, and raiony."[24] A more exact idea of the rate of increase in collectivization and the attitude toward it can be obtained from a leader in *Economic Review* by its editor, Svetlov:

To characterize the rate [of change in the social-economic structure of agriculture] it is sufficient to point out the rapidity with which the prospects of collectivization changed. Thus, in May 1929, in projections as to the rate of collectivization, we assumed the possibility of having, in the spring of 1932, 14.5 million hectares of cropped plowland collectivized. [This obviously refers to the 1st Plan, which was approved in May 1929.] In September 1929, however, it became possible to count on the fulfillment of that plan two years earlier, i.e., in the spring of 1930. [Plan for 1929–30 as given

[24] Joseph Stalin, *Problems of Leninism* (9th ed., Moscow, 1934), p. 439.

in *Control Figures . . . . for 1929–30* (Moscow, 1930), p. 124.] But even this "daring" plan also proved a great underestimate. As early as December 1929 a decision of the Council of People's Commissars ordered that a minimum of 32 million hectares of spring sowings, or one-third of the total, be collectivized the following spring. But events outran these projections as well.[25]

Svetlov finished by saying—and he was very enthusiastic over this prospect—that there would obviously be at least 40 million hectares of spring sowing collectivized in the spring of 1930. As to the expected rate of the collectivization of livestock, the following statement from the Livestock Plan of the Peoples' Commissariat for Agriculture of the USSR for 1930–31 is worth noting: "Considering that in 1930–31 not less than two-thirds of the livestock will be collectivized . . . ."—in other words, kolkhoznik holdings, at most, would be half those of the kolkhozy proper.[26] Since only a small proportion of the peasant livestock was kept specifically to produce products for sale, the plan clearly implied severe encroachment upon noncommercial and semicommercial holdings of the kolkhoz peasants. Later, the Party and government acted as if nothing like this had ever been contemplated, and as if the collectivization of peasant livestock that was not strictly commercial was attributable merely to excesses on the part of local officials.

The change from the torpor of the period 1921–27 to the furious increases in subsequent years, months, and even days, could not have been attained by persuasion. In his speech on December 29, 1929, Stalin branded reliance on the natural flow, "samotek,"[27] in socialist construction as an anti-Marxian idea. In plain language this meant that the peasants had to be whipped into the kolkhozy. In the crudest way, huge areas were designated for "complete" or "summary" collectivization by a certain date. "Raiony of entire collectivization" was indeed a legal term, if one can speak of legality in connection with all that violent lawlessness. The *History of the Communist Party* said clearly: "Complete collectivization meant that all land of the raion be-

[25] F. Svetlov, "A Bolshevist Sowing Campaign," *Economic Review*, January 1930, p. 3.
[26] *Laws on Collectivization of Agriculture . . . . ,* pp. 214–15.
[27] "Samotek" literally means natural flow of a liquid, but the word is frequently used figuratively in Russia.

came the property of the kolkhozy."[28] Each peasant in such a raion obviously had to join.[29] The kombedy were revived[30]— those disreputable organizations (well-remembered from the War-Communist period; see p. 158) of persons of the sort who have nothing to lose and easily become instruments of dictatorships.

To break any future resistance, it was important to eliminate those peasants who were about to lose most and were also most fit for leadership. An additional consideration in favor of liquidating these groups was the desire to use their property as a bait for the poorer peasants. Since collectivization had increased many-fold, the earlier system of inducements in the form of state credits and unreturnable donations could not have been maintained. The drive started at the end of 1927 with "limiting the exploitative tendencies of the kulaki." At the end of 1929, when the all-out struggle was decided, "liquidation of the kulaki as a class" became the battle cry.

In theory, only the kulaki and well-to-do were subject to liquidation as a class, but in practice—even in legislative practice—everyone unwilling to join was declared a kulak. The order of the Central Executive Committee of the USSR of January 25, 1930, concerning the new functions of the village soviets in connection with the widespread collectivization, stated: "A village soviet which does not revise its work to adjust it to the new functions in connection with the mass collectivization . . . . will be in fact a kulak-soviet."

What was going on is well described in the resolution of the Central Committee of the Party of March 15, 1930.[31] "In some raiony the percentage of *raskulachennyi*[32] reached 15, the percentage of those deprived of their suffrage rights, 15 to 20." "Marauding, dividing of property, arrests of average and even poor peasants . . . . ." "There were observed facts of com-

[28] *History of the Communist Party of the Soviet Union (Bolsheviks)*, ed. by a Commission of the Central Committee of the CPSU(B) (Moscow, 1946), p. 290.

[29] See also the vivid description of a participant on pp. 316–17.

[30] Orders of the Party of Dec. 24, 1929, and of the government of Feb. 25, 1930. See *Laws on Collectivization of Agriculture . . . .* , pp. 143–46 and 232–34, respectively.

[31] *Most Important Decisions on Agriculture* (2d ed.), pp. 417–19.

[32] *Raskulachennyi*, a term coined from kulak, means those deprived of their property that qualified them as kulaki.

pulsory collectivization of dwelling houses, small livestock [i.e., hogs, sheep, and goats], and milk cattle not producing for the market . . . . ."

The avalanche rolled on and on. When, in a few weeks, more than half of the peasantry was collectivized (about 60 percent in the RSFSR), a halt was called by Stalin's letter, "Dizziness from Successes," published in *Pravda*, March 2, 1930. This was followed by more detailed instructions, as in the decision of the Central Committee of the Party of March 15, 1930, "On Distortions of the Party Line with Reference to the Collectivization Movement," from which the quotations above were taken.

Stalin's letter and the various resolutions and orders reaffirmed the "voluntary" character of the joining of the kolkhozy. But the actual meaning of the call to halt had nothing to do with this. Otherwise the preceding planless herding of dozens of millions of peasants and practically all livestock into the kolkhozy would not have been proclaimed a "success," a "great achievement."[33] It was simply felt that the time was ripe to consolidate the successes by putting some restraint on the unbridled drive. The opportunity was also welcomed to transfer the responsibility for the ruthless compulsion to local officials.

The peasants were at first fooled by the reaffirmation of the principle of voluntariness. In two months the proportion of households collectivized in the RSFSR fell from 60 percent to 23.4 percent, i.e., over half of the households hastened to withdraw.[34] But the true situation was soon realized. Stalin's speech to the XVIth Party Congress on June 27, 1930, for example, left no doubt that the peasants *had* to accept collectivization. The VIth Congress of the Soviets in March 1931, having declared that "by that policy [collectivization] we have conquered hunger," continued: "The poor and average individual peasant who helps the kulak to combat the kolkhoz undermines the collectivization movement . . . . he is in fact an ally of

---

[33] The word "success" was in the title of Stalin's article. As to "great achievement," see Y. A. Yakovlev, *Red Villages, the 5-Year Plan in Russian Agriculture* (New York, 1931), pp. 22–26. Those interested in familiarizing themselves with the proceedings in those tragic days from an original source are advised to read this booklet by the Commissar of Agriculture of the USSR at that fateful time.

[34] L. E. Hubbard, *The Economics of Soviet Agriculture* (London, 1939), pp. 118–19.

the kulak," and finally, "The poor and average peasant has only one way . . . . joining the kolkhozy."

Those who had gladly rushed out were soon back. The official statistics indeed show 13.0 million households, or 52.7 percent of the total, collectivized by the middle of 1931. Measured in cropped plowland, collectivization exceeded two-thirds of the total at that time. Subsequent progress was necessarily slow because the steppe areas, considered to be particularly adapted to collectivization, were already largely collectivized. Still, in mid-1936, six and one-half years after the start of the full-scale drive, only 1.8 percent of peasant cropped plowland was outside of collectivization. In terms of collectivized households, the percentage was 90.5 in that year. The goal of the 2d Plan, to have no individual peasants by the end of 1937, was almost reached (see Chart 22, p. 314).

Regional and other variations in the rate of collectivization.— Steppe areas devoted mainly to grain growing were relatively best adapted or least unadapted to collectivization, since they were most suitable for the use of the tractor and, in general, to the combine as well. Least adapted were mountainous regions where farms or small groups of farms are frequently separated by hills. The many nations comprising the USSR and even the different groups of the same nations, such as the Cossacks, also differed considerably in their ability to resist collectivization.

The different adaptability of the various areas to collectivization was most strongly reflected in the rate of collectivization in the early period when joining was truly voluntary. But it was also apparent in the first years of the big drive. In its decision of January 5, 1930, the Central Committee of the Party declared that in the Lower Volga, Middle Volga, and North Caucasus regions collectivization could be "basically finished" in the fall of 1930 and in any case in the spring of 1931, while collectivization of the other grain areas was to be basically finished in the fall of 1931 or the spring of 1932 at the latest.[35] Using the scale

[35] See *Most Important Decisions on Agriculture* (2d ed.), pp. 411–12. Rather belatedly, when a great deal of irreparable damage had been done, the Central Committee of the Party in its decision of Aug. 2, 1931, specified that "basic accomplishment of collectivization" meant not an "obligatory collectivization of 100 percent of the poor and average peasants, but the joining of not less than 68 to 70 percent of the peasant households and not less than 75 to 80 percent of the peasants' cropped plowland." *Ibid.*, p. 427.

mentioned in the footnote, the Central Committee of the Party declared on August 2, 1931 that collectivization was basically accomplished in North Caucasus (without the so-called "national" raiony), Middle Volga, Lower Volga, steppe Ukraine, Ukraine east of the Dnepr, Crimea, and the grain areas of the Urals. In the remaining grain areas collectivization was to be basically finished in 1932; in other areas, including the grain-deficit areas, in 1932–33.

On July 1, 1934, when 71.4 percent of all peasant households were collectivized in the USSR as a whole, the percentage was over 80 in many level areas of European Russia devoted mainly to small-grain production. Representative of these were Saratov oblast (93.1 percent), Stalingrad oblast (81.0 percent), and Azov–Black Sea krai (81.8 percent). On the other hand, in mountainous South Caucasus with its non-Slavic population, and in even more mountainous Dagestan, only 44.7 and 23.0 percent of the respective households had been collectivized by that time. The level areas in Siberia devoted mainly to small grain lagged somewhat behind the all-Union average—the households of West Siberia were 66.9 percent collectivized and those of Krasnoyarsk 65.0 percent—simply owing to their greater distance from Moscow. In the sparsely inhabited Yakutsk oblast slightly less than 50 percent of all households were collectivized. The northern portion of European Russia, which is less adapted to mechanized crop production than the southern part, was also below the national average in collectivization. It is noteworthy that while the Western oblast had 68.8 percent of all households collectivized, the percentage was only 55.3 in the adjacent White Russia, the westernmost portion of the USSR.[36]

The regional differences became smaller as collectivization approached 100 percent, but remained clearly distinguishable. On July 1, 1938, the national average for collectivized households was 93.5 percent. But the Georgian Republic in South Caucasus had 78.7 percent collectivized, Chuvash Republic (a Tartar tribe not very far from Moscow) 74.8 percent, and Yakutsk 70.9 percent.[37]

[36] *Socialist Construction USSR, 1936*, Gosplan (Moscow, 1936), pp. 278–79.

[37] *Kolkhozy in the 2d Stalin Five-Year Period*, Gosplan (Moscow, 1939), pp. 4–5.

THE COST OF COLLECTIVIZATION

The results of the collectivization drive are officially measured in the proportions of households and cropped plowland that were collectivized. The use of proportions rather than of absolute figures conceals the disappearance of an unknown but very large number of households through deportation and outright deaths. The population of the USSR, where births exceeded deaths by over 20 per 1,000 before the drive, increased only 10.7 percent in the decade 1928–38; this fact cannot be talked away. The birth rate declined substantially during the period. Most of the decline was the direct result of the misery caused by the collectivization drive; abortions could have been only a minor factor among such backward, deeply religious people.[70]

Although the exact degree of the decline in birth rate is unknown,[70a] there can be no doubt that only part of the slow growth in population in 1929–38 was caused by the fall in the birth rate. Many millions died who would have lived under normal conditions. The excessive mortality extended over a number of years, but the peak of starvation deaths occurred in the winter and spring of 1932–33. Most of these were in the grain-surplus areas of European Russia.[71] Most outstanding, however, was the decline of the Kazakhi, a Mongol pastoral tribe inhabiting mainly Kazakhstan, whose numbers dropped from 3,968,289 on December 17, 1926 to 3,098,764 on January 17, 1939. Even at the slow rate of increase in all the USSR in 1926–38 the Kazakhi should have numbered 4.6 million in 1939; there was thus a swing of 1.5 million[72] caused simply by the annihilation of virtually all their livestock—their only livelihood—in connection with the collectivization drive.

Before the drive the peasants had about 18 billion 1926–27 rubles invested in means of production of the rural economy, of which over 5 were in buildings for productive purposes, around 3 in machinery, and about 9 in livestock (see p. 714). Much of this investment simply disappeared. The question of the magnitude of the loss could not of course be raised in the USSR.

Livestock is the only item in which the loss caused by the collectivization drive is obvious. As shown in Table 25, for each

[70] It is hardly correct in the matter of abortions to generalize from data pertaining primarily to Moscow, as Frank Lorimer does in *The Population of the Soviet Union: History and Prospects*, League of Nations (Geneva, 1946), pp. 172–78. Moreover, in Moscow and even more in the country as a whole, the jump in abortions in the early 'thirties may have been to a large extent the result of starvation or near-starvation, which lasted for years.

[70a] No data have been published since 1928; see p. 10.

[71] See the evidence quoted on p. 553, n. 27.

[72] See Lorimer, *op. cit.*, p. 140. The figure in the text may include some who migrated to China.

horse that was collectivized, almost two disappeared in the Union as a whole. Four cattle, 5.5 hogs, and 8.5 sheep and goats were lost for each animal brought into the kolkhozy. In the extreme case of Kazakhstan, the peasant livestock was almost wiped out,

TABLE 25.—LOSS OF LIVESTOCK DUE TO COLLECTIVIZATION*

(*Million head*)

Kind of livestock	Individual and kolkhoz peasants and kolkhozy		Kolkhozy 1933	Individual and kolkhoz peasants 1933	Loss 1928–33
	1928*a*	1933			
			Soviet Union		
Horses	33.4	14.9	10.1	4.8	18.5
Cattle	70.4	33.7	9.2	24.5	36.7
Hogs	25.9	8.9	3.0	5.9	17.0
Sheep and goats	145.9	41.8	12.2	29.6	104.1
			Kazakhstan*b*		
Horses	3.8	0.4	0.3	0.1	3.4
Cattle	7.7	0.9	0.5	0.4	6.8
Sheep and goats	26.6	1.2	0.9	0.3	25.4

* Official early-summer data from *Agriculture USSR, 1935*, pp. 517–19, 527–28, and 523–33; and *Statistical Handbook, USSR, 1928*, pp. 158–59.
a Total livestock less sovkhoz herds.
b The Kazakhi Mohammedans, do not raise hogs.

and the kolkhozy got practically none. The picture would be only slightly less gloomy even if the peasant stock obtained by the sovkhozy could be considered, but no data on these purchases have been published.

Through destruction of draft power and general disorganization, the output of the peasant-kolkhoz sector, i.e., excluding sovkhozy, declined by over 30 percent in the early 'thirties and negligibly exceeded the pre-collectivization level by 1938.[73]

The freedom and the remnants of the good will of nearly one hundred million people who survived the avalanche were lost in the drive.

[73] Total gross agricultural production was 23 percent below the 1928 level in 1932 and 12 percent above it in 1938 (pp. 673–74). The share of the sovkhozy in total output increased from less than 1 percent in 1928 to 10.6 percent in 1932 and about 9 percent in both 1937 and 1938, according to official data. Actually it was slightly over 10 percent in 1937 and 1938 (see p. 263).

State Planning and Forced Industrialization

By Oleg Hoeffding

THE AIM OF THIS ARTICLE is to inquire into the relevance of Soviet experience with centralized economic planning and forced industrialization to the specific problems faced by underdeveloped countries in Asia.

The area covered in the article excludes the Middle East as well as Soviet Central Asia; the generalizations which will be advanced, therefore, will refer to South and Southeast Asia, Communist and non-Communist alike. (This is not to say, of course, that some of the observations made will not apply to other countries on the Asian continent—or for that matter, to underdeveloped countries in other parts of the world.) Japan, although no longer in the "underdeveloped" category will figure in the discussion if only because her experience shows that for an underdeveloped Asian country there *are* alternatives to the Soviet path of industrialization, and because her current structural problems serve as a reminder that industrialization alone does not solve all the trouble of an economy developing in an Asian demographic setting.

Soviet "state planning" is a term capable of at least two definitions, a broad and a narrow one. In its narrow sense, the term stands for the technical paraphernalia of Soviet planning: the Gosplan, the mechanism

Mr. Hoeffding is a well-known economist currently on the staff of The RAND Corporation, Santa Monica, California.

of the Five-Year Plans, the economic controls used by the Soviet government in the implementation of its economic goals, *etc.*

In a broader sense—and as the term will be used here —"Soviet state planning" stands for a complex of political and economic institutions specifically evolved by the Soviet leadership for the purpose of pushing the Russian economy along the path of rapid industrialization. It was not, after all, either the *Gosplan* or the Five-Year Plans as such that provided the keys to success in the Soviet drive for industrialization. Rather, the plans and the planners functioned as effectively as they did because they were supported by (a) the system of property and production relationships established by the revolution, which gave the Soviet state almost exclusive control over economic activity and empowered it to enforce its goals on the whole population; and (b) a mechanism of executive controls, used forcefully and ruthlessly to move all resources in the "right" direction.

The "Soviet System"

Viewed in this light, "Soviet state planning" is virtually synonymous with the "Soviet system." Indeed, it would be fruitless to study the specific technical features of Soviet economic planning in isolation from its environment—that is, the "system"—for it is the latter that has lent the economic tools and techniques whatever effectiveness they have demonstrated. And what is true for the study of these techniques is even truer insofar as their piecemeal application in different social and political settings is concerned. Many an underdeveloped country, in Asia and elsewhere, has had a sad experience with shadowy Planning Boards and papery Five-Year Plans, all of which proved to be totally ineffective because they were backed neither by Soviet-type enforcement mechanisms, nor by any other workable alternatives.

The difficulty of separating the machinery of Soviet planning from the Soviet system as a whole—and particularly from the totalitarian features of the system — is directly related to the dilemma faced by non-Communist countries anxious to initiate or to accelerate economic development by extracting "lessons" from the Soviet "model." In reality, they either have to adopt the whole Soviet formula, with all its totalitarian ingredients, as China has done, or they have to seek different paths of development, as India is doing.

A word needs to be said here also about "forced industrialization." This term singles out that element of Soviet development in which the USSR was most conspicuously successful and which, understandably, attracts the greatest attention in Asia: the achievement, in forty years of Soviet rule and thirty years of comprehensive central planning, of a volume of industrial production second only to that of the United States, and exceeding that of any of the old industrial nations in Europe.

It should be clearly understood that industrialization is simply a special case of economic development, and that the Soviet Union committed itself not merely to a version of development which emphasized rapid industrialization above everything else, but to an economic policy specifically aimed at creating and operating a militarily powerful state. We owe a good description of Soviet development goals to a competent observer—certainly not suspect of rabid anti-communism—the Polish economist, Oscar Lange:

The Soviet economy was planned not for the harmony of its different branches, but for one single purpose, namely the most rapid industrialization and preparation of effective national defense. . . . Soviet economic planning did not serve the objectives of a harmonious socialist welfare economy, but served political and military objectives to which all other aspects of economic planning were sacrificed.[1]

---

[1] Oscar Lange, "The Working Principles of the Soviet Economy," in *USSR Economy and the War*, Russian Economic Institute, New York 1943, p. 43.

It is the central argument of this article that Asian countries cannot afford to commit themselves, as the USSR did, to a selective stress on rapid industrial growth with special emphasis on capital-heavy industries, and to neglect the growth of other branches of their economies—agriculture in particular.

The Prerevolutionary Russian Economy

The opinion has often been voiced that the state of the Russian economy before the revolution bears considerable resemblance to that of many Asian countries today—a comparison that is responsible for the great interest and attention paid in Asia to Soviet economic history.

Proponents of this view point out that Imperial Russia was an extremely backward and abjectly poor country. More than four-fifths of its population lived in the villages. Industry was in its infancy, and 75 percent of the working force was engaged in agriculture, even more than in present-day India. Farming methods were primitive and agricultural resources meager, and the Russian peasantry lived at a bare subsistence level. Nearly three-quarters of the population was illiterate. The birth rate, at 47 per thousand in 1913, was as high as anywhere in contemporary Asia, and although mortality was shockingly high, too, population was growing at more than 1.5 percent per annum.

If one contrasts the present Soviet economy with these unpropitious beginnings, it is easy to conclude that the USSR must indeed have possessed a uniquely promising and effective formula for overcoming all the obstacles which have frustrated economic progress in Asia. But how true is the view that in a mere forty years the Soviet Union pulled itself up by its own bootstraps from a *tabula rasa* of utter backwardness, resembling that of Asia today, to attain its present formidable industrial stature?

The data for a rigorous comparison of the level of economic development in Russia, say, in 1913, with that of the Asian countries in the mid-twentieth century, are hard to come by, and even harder to interpret. However, a quick survey shows persuasively that when the Soviets came to power, they took over an economy with much more favorable preconditions for rapid industrial growth than exist in Asia today. First, they were able to build on foundations laid during an extended period of prior capitalist development. Secondly, and more important, they disposed of a ratio of population to natural resources, land in particular, that compared very favorably to that of most Asian countries. In other words, when the

Soviets started, they already had the boots, and the straps to pull on, whereas contemporary Asia is, relatively speaking, still barefooted.

Capacity to Save

Let us first look at the Soviet starting point with regard to one crucial condition of economic progress: the portion of national income saved from consumption and applied to capital formation. It is a familiar proposition that to bring about an initial, and substantial, increase in the very low savings and investment ratio characteristic of poor and backward countries is to make the most important, and also the hardest, first step on the road from economic stagnation to progress. In one recent simple statement of this proposition, "communities in which the national income per head is not increasing invest 4 or 5 percent of their incomes per annum or less, whilst progressive economies invest 12 percent per annum or more." [2]

Data bearing directly on the rate of savings and investment in Tsarist Russia are woefully lacking, but what little information there is suggests that by 1913 Russia was well on the way from being a 5 percent saver to becoming a 12 percent saver. The eminent economist S. Prokopovich, in a discussion of this point, refers to estimates (by himself and others) which put the 1913 Russian "national savings" as high as 10 percent of "national income." [3]

Fortunately, there is better evidence to indicate that Imperial Russia had by then developed a "progressive economy," i.e., that real national income per head had been increasing over several decades prior to 1913. The increase was irregular and slow, since population was growing fairly fast while agriculture—the dominant economic sector—was growing haltingly (though still fast enough to allow per capita food output to rise). [4] Industry, however, although it contributed only one-fifth of national income by 1913, had been undergoing fairly rapid growth; according to one recent estimate, [5] the rate of growth was some 5 percent per annum over the long period 1860-1913.

---

[2] W. Arthur Lewis, *The Theory of Economic Growth*, London, Allen and Unwin, 1955, p. 225.

[3] S. N. Prokopovich, *Narodnoe Khoziaistvo SSSR*, (The Economy of the USSR) Chekhov Publishing House, New York, 1952, Vol. II, pp. 334-336.

[4] Cf., e.g., Colin Clark, *A Critique of Russian Statistics*, London, Macmillan and Co., Ltd., 1939, pp. 13-16.

[5] By Raymond Goldsmith, cited in G. Warren Nutter, "Industrial Growth in the Soviet Union," *American Economic Review*, May 1958, pp. 403-408.

This extended period of active industrial growth has important bearing on the question of pre-Soviet Russia's savings capacity, as the profits of nonfarm enterprise play an important role in augmenting the supply of savings in the early phases of economic development. That the stock of nonfarm capital accumulated in the capitalist phase of Russian history, and then inherited by the Soviet "public sector," was far from negligible is suggested by the volume of industrial production attained by 1913. The common view that pre-World War I Russia was extremely backward industrially is fully justified only if one compares her output levels with those of the advanced Western countries at that time. If the comparison is with contemporary Asia, however, a somewhat different picture emerges. In terms of total output of mining and manufacturing, Russia in 1913 was clearly ahead of both India and China at the outset of their respective first Five-Year Plans, and therefore very far ahead indeed of any other Asian country, save Japan. In terms of per capita output, Russia appears to have had a clear edge over India even as of 1956, when India passed from her first into her second Five-Year Plan, after a one-third expansion of industrial output in the preceding five years. This is shown by the following table of the ratios by which Russian per capita output of selected commodities exceeded India's or *vice versa:* [6]

Russia—1913 (India 1956 =1)		India—1956 (Russia 1913 =1)	
Steel	7	Electric power	2
Coal	2	Mineral fertilizers	2
Sulfuric acid	2	Bicycles	4
Soda ash	6	Cement	1
Caustic soda	4	Diesel motors	1
Cotton fabrics	1.4		
Paper	4		
Locomotives	8		
Sewing machines	6		

The evidence at hand is too flimsy to judge whether pre-Soviet Russia, in the currently fashionable phrase, had achieved a "take-off into self-sustaining growth." There are good reasons to believe, however, that even before the advent of the "Soviet model," the Russian economy had been well out of the phase of economic stagnation, and had embarked on a period of rising per capita national income, accompanied (and made possible) by an increasing supply of savings for capital formation.

---

[6] The reader is cautioned to accept this comparison for what it is worth. The criterion of selection of the commodities covered was the availability of comparable data.

This would imply that the "Soviet model" cannot take credit for breaking the impasse which still confronts so much of non-Communist Asia: *i.e.,* the problem of bringing about a rate of net investment that would permit capital formation on a scale sufficient to achieve the gains in productivity required to make growth of production exceed the rapid growth of population. The Soviet prototype must confine its claim to efficacy in raising the investment ratio from the respectable 1913 figure to the distinctively high levels (of 20 or more percent of national income) achieved in the USSR since the late 1920's.

For Asian countries still concerned with the problem of initial acceleration of savings (especially those which reject the coercive features of the Soviet model and which hope to raise per capita consumption while raising savings), such levels of investment are unattainable, save in some distant future. Fixing their sights on that future, they can well bear in mind the remarkable example of Japan, with its singularly high propensity to save and its capacity to submit to taxation and other less than "totalitarian" restraints on consumption.[7]

As far as Asia's more immediate tasks are concerned, India's progress, with all its ups and downs, provides a moderately heartening example that planning under democracy can put even a very poor country on the first hard stretch of the road to being a "12 percent saver." India has raised its rate of investment from 5 percent of national income in 1951 to 7.3 percent in 1956, and hopes to approach 11 percent by 1961, with relatively little foreign assistance: domestic savings, according to the Second Five-Year Plan will rise from 7.0 percent of national income in 1956 to 9.7 percent in 1961. India's hope is to combine these gains with modest increases in per capita consumption, by some 2 percent annually. Her actual progress since 1956 has been fairly consistent with the requirements of the Second Five-Year Plan, with investment doing somewhat better, and consumption a little worse, than the plan foretold.

The Quest for "Surplus Produce"

It would be premature to conclude, however, that India has won the race of output expansion against her rapid population growth and against what Myrdal conveniently calls pressures for "initial welfare."

---

[7] However, Asians should also bear in mind that neither the Japanese nor any other non-Soviet model provides a painless shortcut to development, and that any *Wirtschaftswunder* has to be dearly bought. For some sobering and well-stated reflections on this, see G. Myrdal, *An International Economy,* Harper & Bros., New York, 1956, pp. 160-166.

Other countries in non-Communist Asia have not, of course, even embarked upon this race. Indeed, little optimism is warranted on this score if one turns to another set of important dissimilarities between the points of departure of economic development in the USSR and in Asia—Communist and non-Communist countries alike.

To do this, it is necessary to consider primarily the problems of agriculture, for the industrialization potential of a poor and predominantly agricultural economy depends very heavily upon the excess of its food production over consumption by the farm population. When one-half or more of national income originates in agriculture, food withheld from consumption becomes a major component of national savings. Furthermore, industrialization and urbanization require the feeding and clothing of nonfarm labor and its dependents, and it is agriculture that supplies their wage goods. Adam Smith's words on this fundamental relationship still apply literally to contemporary Asia:

It is the surplus produce of the country only, or what is over and above the maintenance of the cultivators, that constitutes the subsistence of the town, that therefore increase only with the increase of the surplus produce.[8]

Precise comparisons on this point are difficult, but even a quick look at the pertinent data will show that Tsarist Russia could spare very much more "over and above the maintenance of cultivators" than most of Asia can today.

Russian grain production in 1913, a good crop year, was 82 million tons, or about 580 kilograms per capita. Even without the Soviet mechanisms of forced collection, nearly 21 million tons of grain was marketed outside the village. Of this, 9 million tons were exported, which still left something like 10 million tons for the "subsistence of the town," or roughly 400 kilograms per head of the urban population (not all of this, needless to say, for direct human consumption).

Russian peasant consumption of grain for food around 1913 has been estimated at 265 kilograms per capita.[9] This figure, of course, denoted acute rural poverty, but one should bear in mind the important fact that this poverty prevailed *after* Russian "cultivators" had relinquished a very sizeable margin of produce to "the town."

Let us now turn to Asia. India in 1956 (also a good crop year), with 250 million more mouths to feed than Russia had in 1913, produced a smaller grain crop, 72

---

[8] Adam Smith, *Wealth of Nations,* Book III, Chapter I.

[9] N. Jasny, *The Socialized Agriculture of the USSR,* Stanford, 1949, p. 183.

million tons,[10] or 190 kilograms per capita. Clearly, there is very little margin here for the "subsistence of the town." Yet proportionately India's urban population is just about the same as Russia's was in 1913, and in absolute terms it is more than double. Not surprisingly, even to maintain an "average intake of food . . . below accepted nutritional standards,"[11] India has been importing grain, and expects to go on importing at a rate which has recently been revised upward from previous estimates—namely, to between 2.5 and 3 million tons a year.[12]

Communist China, according to official statistics, is substantially better off than India in per capita grain output, with somewhat less than 300 kilograms in 1956. But again, this is just about half the Russian rate of 1913. Out of a total food grain output of 193 million tons in 1956-57, the Chinese government's net collection and purchase for sale to urban areas (and exports) totalled 21 million tons, exactly the volume marketed by Russian agriculture in 1913; in China's case, however, this volume is to be shared by an urban population of 88 million, compared with Russia's 25 million in 1913.[13]

It must be emphasized again that this picture is imprecise and rough, as there are smaller countries in Asia which are food exporters, while the food deficits of others reflect specialization in the export of agricultural raw materials. Yet, with regard to the ability of Asia to sustain industrialization and urbanization, it is an inauspicious fact that the region surveyed by the United Nations Economic Commission for Asia and the Far East (excluding mainland China) is a net importer of cereals—to the tune of 8 million tons in 1957 and on a rising scale in more recent years.

If one considers the task of the Asian countries to increase the "subsistence of the town" concomitantly with progress toward industrialization, and contrasts it with past Soviet experience with the very same problem, the long-term prospects for Asia seem even more disconcerting than the immediate future. Such a comparison also confirms that Asia—Communist and non-Communist alike—has little to learn from Soviet experience.

There is a remarkable disparity between the absolute population increase which the Soviet regime has had to provide for and the population increments which Asia as a whole, and its large countries individually, must expect in the future. Today, there are only 50 million more people living in the USSR than there were on the same territory in 1913, nearly a half-century ago. India, with a present population of close to 400 million, expects an increase by 50 million in the next ten years. China, with some 640 million people now, will in three or four years add 40 million. The various disasters which disrupted normal demographic trends in the USSR are well known. Paradoxically, their effect on Soviet population history was remarkably fortunate for the regime: the net population increase in the USSR during its industrialization period has been trifling compared to what is in store for Asia. In consequence, the increase which the Soviets have had to bring about in the total supply of food and other consumer goods has been relatively trifling, too.

Agricultural Resources

The Soviet task of providing for this comparatively modest rise in population was further eased by the fact that the agricultural resources per capita commanded by the USSR at its inception, however meager by comparison with more fortunate countries elsewhere, were vastly superior to those of less fortunate Asia. Russia in 1913 had a ratio of 0.75 hectares of cultivated land per inhabitant. For India, the same ratio in 1954-1955 was 0.37. Arable land in 1913 Russia amounted to 1.1 hectares per capita,[14] while China in 1956 had 0.2 hectares. Taiwan, Japan and South Korea are even worse off.[15]

Moreover—and this again in sharp and favorable contrast to Asia—the Soviet Union, judging by its record, disposed of considerable opportunities for *extensive* additions to agricultural output. Cultivated plowland per capita has kept up with the population increase, amounting to exactly 1.1 hectares both in 1913 and 1956,[16] an equality which largely reflects the plowing of the "virgin lands" in recent years. At the same time, there was some easy-to-come-by "intensification." More

---

[10] Total output of rice, wheat, barley, corn (maize) millet, and sorghum (*ECAFE, Economic Survey of Asia and the Far East 1957*, Bangkok, 1958 pp. 199-200). This aggregate, I believe, is more closely comparable to that for Russian grain output than the lower figures reported by India for "food grains" production, *e.g.*, 69 million tons for 1956/57 (Government of India, *Second Five Year Plan, Draft Outline*, p. 91.)

[11] *Second Five Year Plan, Draft Outline*, p. 5.

[12] ECAFE *1957 Survey*, op. cit., pp. 8, 85.

[13] Data on Communist China from ECAFE *1957 Survey*, pp. 95, 109.

---

[14] Strictly speaking, "plowed land" for Russia, which is less than "arable land." Data for Russia was taken from *Kommunist*, 1957, No. 12, pp. 64-65; for Asia, from ECAFE *1957 Survey*, and Government of India, *Second Five Year Plan*, 1956.

[15] On balance, climatic differences probably work in Asia's favor. That they may not be too important is suggested by the fact that Russia's average grain yield in 1913, at 0.85 tons/hectare, was the same as India's in 1956.

[16] *Kommunist, loc. cit.*

of the plowed land is now under crops, and cropped acreage has risen from 0.75 hectares per capita in 1913 to nearly one hectare in 1956. By contrast, "the scope for increasing the area under cultivation is extremely limited" in India.[17] China hopes, in the long run, to reclaim and add a maximum 33 million hectares to its present 112 million of arable land. Should it do so in ten years, it would, at the present rate of population growth, merely have maintained its present arable land per capita; in fact it would then possess *two-thirds* of the present arable acreage of the USSR, *for a population nearly four times as large.*

The problem of generating "surplus produce" to sustain urbanization is so very crucial to Asia's industrialization hopes, that a few more remarks on Soviet performance is this respect are in order. In the mid-1920's, the USSR went through its "grain crisis," when voluntary marketings by the peasantry were reduced to about half the 1913 volume. It was a mild crisis, as urban population had increased but slightly since 1913, and nearly one-half of 1913 marketings had been exported, whereas by 1927-28, grain exports had dwindled to a very small figure. Yet the expectation of a rapid growth of the urban population in the wake of accelerated industrialization, then under planning, was sufficient to prompt the authorities to enforce collectivization and thus to equip themselves with a mechanism for the forcible collection of "surplus produce." The devastating effects on farm production that followed are well-known.

Once the worst of these effects had been overcome, the Soviets centered their attention on perfecting the mechanism of *collection* of farm produce. The new institutions they had contrived for farm *production* were anything but perfect, and it was not until 1953 that the Soviets officially and publicly recognized that neglect of production had been carried too far—a recognition that reflected, inter alia, the urgent need finally to let "the countryside" share in the fruits of industrialization, by providing it with higher levels of real income. The effects of these incentives on the growth of agricultural output indicates the great expansion of opportunities that were, even·then, still inherent in Soviet agriculture.

Asia's main concern is, of course, production. It would be impossible to elaborate, within the confine of this article, on what the Asians are thinking—and, fortunately, doing—to keep their slender margin of "surplus produce" from diminishing or from disappearing altogether. Suffice it to say that the very real possibility that this margin will be eaten up by the swelling multitude of the "cultivators," rather than used to feed the growing urban population, should be seriously considered by those who are in charge of mapping the rate, scale, and structural pattern of their countries' economic progress. This is particularly true for the non-Communist countries, which are trying to prevent their very low consumption levels from falling—and are, in fact, even hopeful of seeing them rise without at the same time inhibiting the rate of savings and the process of industrialization as a whole.

Given this concern with consumer welfare, Asian leaders must surely not think in terms of "planning for the single purpose . . . of the most rapid industrialization," but rather for the "harmony of the different branches" of their economies. Since they will be haunted inexorably by the ghost of Malthus, and of Ricardo's Iron Law (which the Soviet leaders never were), they may well find better guidance for their development priorities in another passage from Adam Smith's classic, rather than in Lenin's work or in the current *Voprosy Ekonomiki:*

As subsistence is, in the nature of things, prior to conveniency and luxury, so the industry which procures the former, must necessarily be prior to that which ministers to the latter. The cultivation and improvement of the country, therefore, which affords subsistence, must necessarily be prior to the increase of the town, which furnishes only the means of conveniency and luxury.[18]

Rural Overpopulation and Unemployment

To emphasize that Asia's food situation and prospects are desperately precarious is but another way of saying that its poverty severely limits the supply of capital and wage goods which it can devote to industrialization, and thus also constricts the rate at which it can hope to expand industry. More particularly, Asia faces the formidably difficult problem of accelerating this expansion sufficiently to make full use of the one resource which it has in superabundance—labor. Most of its manpower is employed in agriculture which, as has been stressed before, is acutely overcrowded. Much of the farm labor force contributes less to food output than it does to food consumption. In some countries, excess supply of farm labor and rural misery have promoted an unhealthy kind of urbanization, with cities growing in advance of the increase in urban employment opportunities. The result is a backlog of urban unemployment, both open and disguised. Finally, as a function of generally high rates of population growth, the population of

---

[17] *Second Five Year Plan,* p. 260.

[18] *Wealth of Nations, loc. cit.* "Conveniency and luxury" may be interpreted here broadly enough to include H-bombs and missiles, as well as steel home-produced at any cost.

working age is growing rapidly; in China the labor force is currently increasing by five or six million annually, and in India by about two million.

Let us inquire again whether Soviet performance in dealing with the employment aspects of development holds any lessons for Asia. At first blush, the bald figures of Soviet net accomplishment in this respect suggest that the USSR has demonstrated the capability to find fast relief from rural overpopulation (if only in a mild form compared to Asia's) through rapid industrialization, and generally to combine economic development with full employment. From the start of the planning era to the outbreak of World War II, the Soviet Union achieved a remarkable shift in its employment structure. Non-farm employment trebled from 1928 to 1940, and the urban population more than doubled, from 26 million in 1926 to 56 million in 1939. In a single decade, 1928-1937, the share of agriculture in total employment declined dramatically from 80 to 56 per cent. Between 1926 and 1939, the rural population even declined absolutely, from 121 to 115 million. The trend towards industrialization and urbanization of the Soviet labor force resumed after World War II. Even though agriculture's share in total employment—43 per cent in 1956 —is still extremely high compared to North America or Northwest Europe, it has declined to nearly the level of present-day Japan.

One need not get involved in the difficult question of whether the USSR has actually eliminated excess labor in agriculture or has merely succeeded in hiding it in a system of farming well suited for masking underemployment, to conclude that it has at least achieved substantial relief from whatever problem of rural overcrowding it inherited. The rural population on present Soviet territory declined from 131 million in 1913 to 113 million in 1956. Compared to the spectacular reductions in rural population associated with the British and other Western industrial revolutions, this 14 per cent decline, spread over nearly half a century, was neither rapid, nor did it represent a smooth absorption of the labor supply into the expanding industrial sectors of the economy.

The transformation in the Soviet employment structure was in part the product of the coercive features of Soviet planning. Collectivization, as was noted earlier, had become an efficient device for collecting "surplus produce"; and a liberal definition of what constituted "surplus," reinforced by appropriate tax and price policies, depressed farm incomes and helped to drive peasants into industrial occupations. The severe controls on consumption, enforced on the urban side by rationing in the critical periods and by wage and price controls generally (non-farm real wages declined heavily from 1928 to 1940), allowed a high rate of capital formation, which in turn provided the factories and power projects for the growing industrial labor force.

But not even forced collectivization and the other repressive devices of economic control explain by themselves the decline in Soviet rural population. In perhaps equal measure, this result was brought about by famine and the deportations of the Stalin era—events which must have been reflected in the 1937 census clearly enough to cause its suppression. World War II carried on the decimation in a new form, and in inflicting a new population disaster upon the USSR, it too assisted the regime in combining industrialization with full employment.

Industrialization: Cure for Unemployment?

Assuming and hoping that the Asian countries will not be aided, as the USSR was, by self-inflicted or extraneously imposed catastrophies, it seems to this author that they cannot look to industrialization for more than partial and limited relief of their employment problems, whether they use coercive techniques or not. In other words, even if they succeed in increasing non-farm employment at a rapid rate, the increase will still be insufficient to prevent concurrent growth of the agricultural population and work force.

This much seems to be acknowledged by the Indian Second Plan, which warns against "the hope that full employment will be secured" by the end of the planning period, and which sets as its modest aim "that at least the deterioration in the unemployment situation should be arrested." Over the decade 1951-1961 India expects its urban population to increase by one-third, and hopes rather than expects to match this increase with new job opportunities. Even this rapid rate of urbanization, however, will bring no relief to the crowded countryside. On the contrary, over the same period the Indian rural population is expected to grow by 30 million.[19]

Similarly, in China, urban population has increased by 57 percent from 1949 to 1956, or by more than 30 million. Simultaneously, however, the rural population has grown by over 60 million. In spite of a phenomenally high growth rate of industrial output, Chinese authorities have in effect acknowledged that urbanization has been speeded not only by growing demand for labor but also by flight from rural poverty and famine. They have had to try to curb the "increase of the town," first by restricting migration from the villages, and since 1955 by expulsion of rural migrants from the overcrowded cities.

[19] *Second Five Year Plan*, pp. 109 ff.

The Chinese case shows that even when industrialization is spurred to the utmost by Soviet-style planning, its "employment content" (to use the Indian planners' graphic term) is insufficient to absorb more than a modest portion of the labor force increase. Even propagandistic statements which try to belittle the employment problem intimate that Chinese authorities expect industry to absorb only 800,000 to 900,000 workers annually over the next six years.[20]

One may note at this point that even Japan's relative success in industrialization has not yet brought a satisfactory solution of the employment problem. Although the share of agriculture in total employment has declined significantly since the postwar peak (to 41 per cent in 1956), that of manufacturing, mining and construction has risen only slightly, while the share of tertiary industries has sharply increased—particularly in what has been called the "vague, relatively unproductive types of service, which were often little more than a form of underemployment."[21]

All told, it seems clear that "industrialization" will have a different meaning in Asia from what it had in Europe or North America, and that in the foreseeable future there is no hope for the Asian countries to achieve even that incomplete shift in the farm/non-farm employment ratio which the USSR—aided, to stress the point again, by a relatively favorable initial position and by its abnormal demographic history—has brought about to date.

Conclusion

Economic progress in Asia is impeded by a variety of extremely difficult obstacles the majority of which the Soviet Union was lucky enough never to have to cope with. Among these are the following:

1). *The problem of initiating the first and hardest major increase in the ratio of savings to national income, which is the ineluctable prerequisite to economic advances.* It has been shown that the Soviet Union started building on economic foundations laid by an extended period of prior capitalist development which, like the Soviet ratio of population to natural resources, compared favorably to the current conditions in most of Asia. The "Soviet model" is thus hardly applicable to the long-range Asian problem of capital formation.

2). *The problem of expanding agricultural output sufficiently to overtake rapid population growth by the*

[20] Su Chung, "Facts About China's Population," *Peking Review,* July 1, 1958, p. 10.
[21] ECAFE *1957 Survey*, p. 51.

wide margin needed to sustain industrialization—starting from a most discouraging condition of rural overpopulation and land scarcity. All over Asia, including Communist China (despite the priority accorded heavy industry and transportation in the allocation of state-controlled investment), recognition has taken firm root that agricultural output is crucially important for the development of the economy as a whole; that contrary to the example of the earlier Soviet "model," emphasis must be put on production rather than collection of agricultural produce; and that, again in divergence from earlier Soviet practice, only intensification in cultivation can offer significant increases in Asian food production.

3). *The problem of finding reasonably productive employment for a labor force, rural and urban, inexorably destined to expand at a frighteningly rapid rate.* Again, even Communist China, after having followed in its first plan the Soviet preference for capital-intensive industrial techniques, embarked on its "small plants campaign" (a movement to set up smaller and much less elaborate enterprises in a wide range of industries), allowing for lower capital-labor ratios in production, enabling industry to spread to the countryside, and contributing to the immediate utilization of excess labor.[22] It is noteworthy that if China has looked to foreign models for this venture, they have been Asian and not Soviet, as the Soviet Union (until recently at least) has never shown much interest in capital-saving techniques. The Chinese Communists were preceded in this respect by the attention devoted to "cottage industry" and to

[22] The author is indebted here to Richard N. Moorsteen's article "Economic Prospects for Communist China," *World Politics,* January 1959. For a careful argument urging overpopulated countries to regard excess labor as a concealed potential for saving and capital formation, see Ragnar Nurkse, *Problems of Capital Formation in Underdeveloped Countries,* Basil Blackwell, Oxford, 1953, *passim.*

the entire "conflict between the competing claims of capital formation . . . and the provision of larger employment" in India's Second Plan,[23] and by Japan's spontaneous "small plants campaign."

4). *The problem of population control in a situation where the death rate is being rapidly reduced while lower birth rates remain slow and hard to achieve.* The Chinese Communists' recent willingness to abandon doctrinal rigidity in this field and to promote birth control represents another significant Asian departure from the Soviet prototype. It is another question, of course, whether even a determined and doctrinally uninhibited birth-control campaign would achieve the desired effect quickly enough, at a time when the art of death control is so much ahead of birth control. It is also doubtful that a totalitarian regime has any advantages over others in this sphere. It has recently been observed that even though the means of production have become public, the means of reproduction are still private.[24] One may note that, in this departure from the Soviet model also, Communist China was again preceded by non-Communist Asia. There is India's determined effort to confront the problem, and there is also the striking postwar decline in Japan's birth rate, a development which would indeed be worth copying, if only one knew how.

It may be observed in conclusion that, having never been compellingly challenged by these problems, the Soviet Government has failed to evolve any policies for dealing with the tasks that will make or break Asian economic development. Hence, quite apart from the coercive aspects of the Soviet model, the particular path of economic development taken by the Soviet Union can be of little practical interest to the countries of Asia.

[23] *Second Five Year Plan, op. cit.,* pp. 109 ff., 429 ff.
[24] Leopold Labedz, "Population Policies in China and Russia," *Soviet Survey,* No. 24, April-June 1958, p. 43.

ECONOMIC GROWTH

PROBABLY NO ASPECT of the Soviet economic system has received as much public attention and has had as much scholarly research devoted to it as its rapid economic growth. In fact, much of the discussion generated under the sections on statistics and measurement (I) and prices (II) were by-products of the problems of measuring the rate of Soviet economic growth.

The first paper by A. Nove provides a good summary statement not only of the rates of growth of different sectors of the economy, but also of the factors to which rapid growth may be attributed. While Professor Nove has been careful to point out that some of the statistical material he presents is now dated, the over-all picture remains essentially as he depicts it. For a sweeping view of Russian-Soviet growth over the past hundred years the reader is referred to Professor Gerschenkron's "Problems and Patterns of Russian Economic Development" (1960) which is shortly to be republished elsewhere.[1] Policy implications of the economic growth "race" are discussed by W. W. Rostow (1959) and Harry Schwartz (1959).

National income is represented by the papers by Professor Bornstein and Dr. Kaser. It should be noted that Professor Bergson's definitive study, *The Real National Income of Soviet Russia Since 1928*, is to be published shortly by the Harvard University Press.

More effort has gone into developing Soviet industrial production indices than any other aspect of growth. Following the pioneering work by Dr. Jasny (1951) and Professor Hodgman (1954), important studies have been published by Professors Gerschenkron, Nutter, Powell, Seton, Shimkin and Leedy, and others. The paper by Norman Kaplan and Richard Moorsteen (below) not only is the most comprehensive but has the additional value of comparing its results and methodology with those of earlier studies and with the Soviet official index. The reader is referred

---

[1] In a collection of his papers being published by the Harvard University Press. This book will include a number of other papers by Professor Gerschenkron listed in the attached Bibliography.

to another recent and comprehensive study by Francis Seton (1960) and to the forthcoming paper by Raymond Powell (see the introduction to Section I).

Agricultural growth is represented by the paper by Professors Johnson and Kahan and population and labor force by papers of Drs. Kantner and Eason. For further reading in these areas, the reader is referred to A. G. Frank (1959) and A. Kahan (1959) on labor requirements and productivity in agriculture, to Walter Galenson (1955) on industrial labor productivity, and to Warren Eason (July, 1959) on the implications for population and labor force of the recent Soviet Census.

The major gap in this collection of essays is the absence of original papers dealing with what might be called the "causes" of or "strategies" behind the rapid rate of Soviet economic development. I refer here to such factors as rate of investment, direction of investment, decisions regarding capital- and labor-intensity in production methods, technological borrowing, innovation, etc. Fortunately, the first paper in this section by Professor Nove performs a useful service in summarizing briefly much of the work in this field. In addition, rates of investment appear as by-products of the studies of Soviet national income by Professors Bornstein and Kaser. It should be noted, however, that rates of investment for the late twenties and thirties were probably much higher on the average than is suggested by published studies which concentrate almost exclusively on 1928 and 1937, years in which rates of investment were relatively very low (see F. D. Holzman, 1961). Probably the most important contribution in this area is that of Norman Kaplan (1953) on the rate and direction of capital investment. Unfortunately, too many of the estimates used by Mr. Kaplan are now out of date to warrant republication of the paper.[2]

Professor Grossman's article (1955) contains an important documentation of the tendency toward increasing capital-intensity of investment in the U.S.S.R. as well as an excellent discussion of the factors which may tend to slow down or speed up growth in the foreseeable future. The reader is also referred to the interesting attempts at constructing production functions for Soviet industry by Professors Berliner (1958), Frank (1958), and Seton (1959); to Professor Granick's valuable studies (both 1957) on how the Soviet institutional framework in industry affects decisions regarding technological-borrowing and capital-intensity; and to Professor Grossman (1960) on how institutional and organizational factors affect decisions regarding the introduction of new technology.

The Appendix contains a qualification to Professor Nove's article and some corrections to the article by Professors Johnson and Kahan.

[2] Mr. Kaplan is presently preparing a monograph on Soviet capital investment.

The Pace of Soviet Economic Development

By A. Nove

I T has been the comfortable belief of many thinking people in the West that the U.S.S.R., while certainly a military power worthy of respect, is not a serious economic competitor, that she is generations behind the more developed Western countries. The occasional appearance in the press of figures suggestive of impressive achievement did little to disturb the general air of complacency. It was thought that the figures were exaggerated, that the goods were probably defective anyway, or that the whole economy was more or less exclusively geared to arms production. The inefficiency of the economy was taken for granted. Such comforting thoughts were rudely disturbed by Peter Wiles's speech at the Milan Congress for Cultural Freedom last year. Wiles's case was not only that the U.S.S.R. was advancing extremely rapidly—far more rapidly than the Western world—but also that the Soviet economy was a peculiarly effective instrument for maximizing growth.

His views are in certain respects open to question, but his basic thesis was hardly a surprise to most serious students of the Soviet economy in Western countries. However, the work of these students has failed to penetrate far into the consciousness of informed public opinion, and so Wiles had anything but a calm reception. Some, indeed, considered his arguments in some way " pro-Soviet," as if the assertion that a given volume of goods is being produced is a political opinion. Others were dismayed by the implications of the pace of Soviet economic developments, but found some comfort in Colin Clark's counterarguments, which seemed to contradict Wiles's views. The object of the present paper is to consider the evidence. How rapid has been the pace of Soviet economic growth? How far has it been facilitated, or hindered, by the Soviet system? At what pace can we expect expansion to proceed in the future?

Mr. Nove is the author of numerous articles on the Soviet economy and visited the U.S.S.R. with the British agricultural delegation in 1955.

STATISTICAL DIGRESSION

I make no apology for starting with a discussion of apparent technicalities. Economic progress can only be measured by combining a large number of different figures into aggregate indices, and this at once raises two vital questions. First, are the figures published in the U.S.S.R. reasonably reliable? Secondly, on what basis and according to what principles should we measure growth?

(a) Soviet Statistics

First, then, a few words about the reliability of Soviet statistics. Some hold that the Soviet authorities just use statistics as a propaganda weapon and that we must consequently disbelieve them. If this be the case, then most research on the Russian economy is waste of time, since it consists in analysing false data. However, no serious scholar holds so extreme a view. Most would agree that it is not the practice of Soviet publicists to invent for purposes of deception. Thus, if it is declared that 200 million pairs of socks are produced, then it is reasonable to assume that this is the figure available to the authorities in Moscow. By selective suppression, indeed, a false impression can be created without actually telling any lies and the numerous gaps in statistical series are a serious handicap. Nevertheless, if it happens to be inconvenient to publish a figure, the normal course of action is to publish nothing, not to announce a falsehood.

To this there is one prominent exception: harvest statistics in the period 1933–53 were in varying degrees distorted by the inclusion of harvest losses or even unharvested crops (" biological yield "). Since 1953, harvest statistics have been based on barn yield, but no figures in quantity terms have been published, no doubt because they would be embarrassingly below the pre-1953 series, which had been inflated by the inclusion of losses.

But do the central authorities receive accurate information from their subordinates? They might *think* that 200 million pairs of socks are produced, whereas perhaps there are only 160 million pairs, the rest being the product of the imagination of bonus-seeking managers. This is quite a serious point, since large rewards await those who over-fulfil the plan, whereas the unsuccessful fear reprimands, demotion, and even, in " tough " years—worse. Falsification at local level can be substantial. Nevertheless, it is noteworthy that false returns are not always designed to exaggerate output: for example, socks might be pilfered by the workers, just as pigs on farms are sometimes " written off " and are in fact consumed by the management or local officials. In any case, one could legitimately invoke at this point the " law of equal cheating " : over the economy as a whole, there is no reason to suppose that Soviet managers and their accountants falsify more in one year than in another, and so the *rate of growth* is unlikely to be exaggerated on that account. Indeed, it is arguable that with the improvement of the statistical administration, and the reduction in penalties for non-fulfilment of plans, there may even have been some improvement in the quality of reporting.

Much greater caution is necessary in handling any indices of *total* output published in the U.S.S.R. Any output or national income series with a pre-1950 base is almost bound to be highly exaggerated, for reasons too complex to discuss here. These distorted pre-1950 figures have never been corrected, and the distortion remains present in any comparison currently being made with, for instance, 1940, 1928 or 1913. Generalizations about the real incomes of workers or peasants range from the merely doubtful to the fantastic ; thus it is repeatedly claimed that the real wages of workers are now six times what they were in 1913, which is pure nonsense. However, comparisons based on 1950 and later years contain relatively little in the way of exaggeration, though certain doubtful features of current series will be noted in due course.

(b) Problems of measurement

Economists are familiar with index number problems. Different price bases, different weights, produce different indices of growth, and no one of them is necessarily less " true " than another. All comparisons over time, or between countries, are affected by these inherent limitations, and particularly so when, as in the case of the U.S.S.R., change has been both rapid and uneven. Inevitably, therefore, the indices and comparisons cited in the present paper are, at best, rough approximations, and should be treated as such.

What is it we are attempting to measure ? A common approach is to analyse the evolution of the national income, or national product per head. Many scholars have done this.[1] But the results can be misleading. The normal Western

---

[1] E.g. Colin Clark, Julius Wyler, Naum Jasny. Their results are summarized and commented on by G. Grossman in the symposium *Soviet Economic Growth* (ed. Bergson ; Row, Peterson, 1953), with stimulating ideas of his own.

4

concept of national income includes services; these are conventionally valued at the incomes of the persons providing them. Thus the value of medical, educational and administrative services is valued by the incomes of doctors, teachers, civil servants, and so on. But suppose that, *as in Russia in 1928–37*, the real incomes of the above classes fall. Then, by the orthodox method, the " product " of these persons falls also, which has a downward influence on product per head. But can one meaningfully say that the " product " of a Russian teacher has fallen because he can buy less for his money? Or, conversely, are Russian doctors " producing " more medical services in 1956 than in 1955 because their salaries have just been increased? Also it is almost impossible meaningfully to convert the value of such services into another currency.

For all these reasons, it is intended here to concentrate on *material production*, and in particular on *industry*, though with some attention also (separately) to *agriculture*, i.e. we shall be dealing mainly with the most advanced and rapidly-developing sector of the Soviet economy, but also one which is rightly attracting most interest, and on which most data are available.

Various estimates have been made of Russian industrial output, of which the most thorough and impressive is that of Professor Hodgman.[1] Using as weights the relative wages bills of the various industries in 1934, he came to the conclusion that the output of *large-scale* industry in 1937 was 371 per cent. that of 1928. This compares with an official claim of 551 per cent. Making all due allowances (for instance, for the decline in the number of *small* workshops) there seems little doubt that industrial output must at least have trebled over this period, giving a growth rate of over 13 per cent. per annum. With this conclusion, at least, Colin Clark would scarcely disagree, since his own index for the period was 311.[2]

This relates, however, to an early stage in an industrial revolution, to a dramatic upsurge from small beginnings. Though it is probably an all-time record, other developing countries have sometimes been almost in the same class; for example, Japan's industrial output nearly trebled in the period 1905–20. A more recent period, when the U.S.S.R. was already largely industrialized, would be more relevant to the future. We must therefore look at the Soviet record in 1950–55.

---

[1] *Soviet Industrial Production, 1928–51* (Harvard, 1954). He describes the difficulties admirably. See also critique by F. Seton in *Soviet Studies* (Glasgow), October, 1955.

[2] *The Conditions of Economic Progress* (Macmillan, 2nd edition, 1951).

A glance at the output table[1] leaves one in no doubt that growth was very rapid indeed. The official Soviet index for 1955 is 185 (1950 = 100), and it seems to be free of the special distortions which destroy confidence in earlier Soviet indices. Can we then accept this one? Consideration of this point will end the " statistical digression," to the relief of some readers.

The Soviet index is very " gross " indeed ; it is built up by adding together the values of goods produced by each and every industrial enterprise[2], excluding only indirect taxes on the final product, corrected for price changes. There is no effort to eliminate double-counting, so that, for instance, the value of the automobile industry includes the steel in the automobiles, which has already appeared in the output of the steel industry. Such a procedure has the effect of relatively over-valuing finished products of all kinds, and under-weighting basic materials. This would inject an upward bias into the index if finished products had a tendency to grow faster than the average. It is hard to prove that this is so. Thus some products which show the most rapid rate of growth (coal, electric power, oil) are under-weighted.

On balance, it seems reasonable to conclude that the exaggeration, if any, is small. The official figures show an annual growth rate in 1951–55 of just under 13 per cent. ; it is unlikely to be below 12 per cent. per annum on a net basis. Unlike Colin Clark, I can see no reason why existing (or even 1937) Soviet price weights should cause any upward bias.

No such approximations are possible for agriculture, owing to almost complete lack of information on output of the basic farm products. In 1952, the gross output index was said to be 110 (1940 = 100), but nothing has been published which could explain how this official figure was calculated.

GROWTH AND EFFICIENCY IN THE SOVIET SYSTEM

It therefore seems that industrial output in the U.S.S.R. probably rose by upwards of 13 per cent. per annum in 1928–37 and perhaps 12 per cent. per annum in 1950–55. We will now seek to answer the following questions : How far were these achievements due to the Soviet system? How far were they due to " non-political " favourable circumstances? Can we expect such swift growth to continue? And if it does continue—the 1956–60 Plan envisages a continued growth of about $10\frac{1}{2}$ per cent. per annum—what would this mean for us?

---

[1] See page 21.　[2] Excluding building.

6

Wiles's assertion that the Soviet system is peculiarly efficient in fostering growth runs counter to the widely-held belief that the system is extremely inefficient. The following would seem to be the factors which bear on this complex and interesting problem.

In the first place, the Soviet political system facilitates the concentration of resources on capital goods, on investment. It is able to resist public pressure more effectively than any régime dependent on votes. No democratic government could have treated the peasants as they were treated in the decisive years of Soviet industrialization, yet the necessary accumulation was financed very largely at the peasants' expense. A more recent example is afforded by Stalin's policy in the period 1945–50 : whereas in Western countries attention was concentrated on the rapid recovery of living standards, in the U.S.S.R. there was actually a *larger* proportion of resources allocated to heavy industry than in pre-war years, and this despite the appalling conditions of life at the war's end.

The result of this policy was the extremely rapid recovery of heavy industry. It is, in fact, a matter of pride among Soviet economists that the U.S.S.R. accumulates a higher proportion of its national income than any Western country. It can hardly be denied that the burden of investment and of other non-consumption expenditures (including arms) is heavier in the U.S.S.R. than in the West, or that the political system has, shall we say, helped the government to persuade the people to bear this burden.

Not only has the Soviet government been able to devote large sums to investment, but, by its power of control over investment policy, it has directed these sums to those sectors which contribute most to rapid expansion : to steel mills and machine-tool works, rather than to housing and shops. A given quantity of basic materials tends to support a larger amount of investment—and so of growth—in the U.S.S.R. than in the West : a smaller proportion of Soviet steel output goes into making private cars, less of its chemical industry into the making of medicines and so on. This, of course, is another aspect of the *priority of growth*, which dominates all Soviet planning. This also shows itself in the direction into heavy industry of more than its " fair " share of scarce materials, skilled labour and managerial ability, giving capital goods priority on the railways and so on.

The entire system is geared to expansion. Incentives, for

workers and managers alike, tend to reward success disproportionately, and success is measured by the over-fulfilment of
plans, which themselves are always fixed higher and higher.
As a matter of routine, all production plans seem to be made up
on the principle : whatever it is, produce more of it. (Vodka
seems to be the one significant exception to this rule, its consumption on a large scale being considered, somewhat oddly,
as a survival of capitalism in the minds of men.) Financial
results, while important, have always tended to be subordinate
to the overriding aim of increasing production, and large losses
have at various times been covered by substantial budgetary
subsidies. The system of incentives has been used to encourage
growth-inducing sectors ; thus, over-fulfilment bonuses and
progressive piecework rates are much more " encouraging "
in metallurgy and coal-mining than, say, in the furniture and
clothing industries.

No resistance can be expected from trade unions, which in
the U.S.S.R. are agencies for the carrying out of State labour
policies, and which put all their strength behind schemes to
increase output. No thought of restrictive practices would be
countenanced by them, and in general there is a positive
approach to labour-saving devices. Wiles is fond of stressing
this, and he is right to do so. The general economic climate in
the U.S.S.R. is expansionist, and one of the Communist Party's
main functions in the Soviet State is to keep it that way, to
combat the natural tendency towards inertia, to kick and report
on the laggards. It may seem odd to think of that Party as a
principal substitute for the spur of competition and the fear of
bankruptcy, yet in an important sense it is so.

But, it may be objected, the word " arms " has hardly been
mentioned yet. Is not a high proportion of Soviet producers'
goods devoted to that most unproductive of activities, arms
manufacture ? Undoubtedly, the U.S.S.R. does produce
weapons of many kinds in impressive quantities, and it can be
shown that in certain periods—1938–41 and 1950–53, for
instance—arms formed a large part of the increase in industrial
production. However, we should not exaggerate the significance
of this point, which too often forms part of political wishful
thinking ; the blindly hostile critic, once convinced that Soviet
factories do produce a great deal, is apt to seek refuge in the
emotionally satisfying generalization : " Ah, it is mainly arms."
It is indeed possible, or even necessary, to view the whole
growth of Soviet industrial might from the standpoint of

8

military *potential*. But the mere fact that industrial growth has continued at a very high level is proof that arms as such are not the dominant product of Soviet industry; guns do not produce anything. Indeed, a by-product of the creation of new industries of *potential* military significance has been a sharp increase in the output of some types of consumers' goods : the electronics and optical glass industries help to produce large quantities of TV sets and cameras. The Soviet economy is geared to growth first and foremost; if it were crudely and directly geared to arms manufacture our problem would be crudely and directly military, which is not the case.

Now we must turn to the disadvantages and defects of the Soviet system, viewed from the standpoint of growth and efficiency. These are, perhaps, somewhat more formidable than Wiles's presentation suggests.

The first defect to be considered is to a great extent inherent in the system. It is the consequence of centralization of decision. This centralization need not be explained in terms of the " power-hunger of the men in the Kremlin," as our journalists might put it. An economy of the Soviet type must of its nature show very strong tendencies towards concentrating decisions in Moscow. The result is bureaucratic inflexibility, sometimes replaced by sweeping and ill-considered changes when at last the penny drops. In consequence, despite the lack of trade secrets, it often takes even longer to implement new ideas in the U.S.S.R. than to start building a road in England. The evil consequences of centralization are magnified by the constant tendency to overstrain resources, which in its turn leads to a system of centralized allocation of a large number of key or scarce commodities. Enterprises find that they cannot rely on supplies of materials and components. Either they incur losses through stoppages of work, or the enterprise itself has to produce or procure the missing items at high cost ; or perhaps the manager obtains the materials he needs by a mixture of cajolery, bribery and over-indenting, or retains unauthorized stocks.

However, the existing system of incentives to managers does not always have desirable results. Managerial bonuses and reputations depend on plan over-fulfilment. Suppose a new device or new design is proposed. It will generally require the approval of superior authority, which will grant it only if satisfied that output would increase. In other words, output plans would probably be revised upwards (or cost plans downwards). But new ideas generally involve a risk, and the Soviet system does lack reward for risk-bearing. The result is that the manager might well feel that it is not worth endangering his bonus or his reputation, and so the new project remains on the files. This defect is well known to the authorities, who are engaged in the task of enlarging the powers and responsibilities of managers, while retaining the necessary degree of centralization. Time alone will tell if a more satisfactory balance will be achieved.

Another of the manager's headaches arises from the number of checks and cross-checks to which he remains subject. Thus, the bank is under instructions to refuse to honour his cheques unless the payment is consistent with the given enterprise's plan or comes within narrowly-defined regulations. The department of the economic ministry within which the enterprise operates is always liable to interfere. Of at least equal importance is the Party. We have already noted that the Party plays a vital rôle in fighting inaction and complacency. But in doing so it interferes with managerial duties. The manager, who is generally a member of the Party himself, is liable to receive instructions from local and even factory officials of the Party, and it has certainly been Khrushchev's policy to increase rather than diminish the responsibility of Party officials for economic activity at all levels.

Nor is the labour position quite as favourable to growth and efficiency as might at first appear. Only on paper, and in the imaginations of some over-enthusiastic critics, are the workers docile recipients of whatever wage the State thinks good for them. (Forced labour is indeed a special case ; yet, apart from making workers go to remote areas into which they would not transfer voluntarily, forced labour has probably been no gain economically, owing to its extreme inefficiency.) Despite the existence at certain periods of laws forbidding a change of occupation by " free " labour without permission, labour turnover has been sufficient to allow the law of supply and demand greatly to modify the rules and orders of authority. The " wages fund " is commonly overspent, piecework norms are fixed well below the levels prescribed in the regulations, unskilled workers are upgraded for no better reason than their refusal to stay unless moved from the lowest grade. Branches of industry which pay badly, or where conditions of work are harsher than elsewhere, tend to lose labour. In recent years this has been particularly true of the timber and building

10

industries. In conditions of over-full employment, the worker is in a powerful bargaining position even if strikes are illegal and the right of combination non-existent. The unrepresentative nature of Soviet " trade unions " has been noted by many, but the corollary to this is less obvious : it is that the unions have little influence over the behaviour of their members, who are well aware that the union is not " theirs." Hence the recurrent reports that " socialist competition " obligations undertaken by the unions on behalf of their members are formal in character and not acted upon by the workers.

Another and more complex defect of the system is associated with the absence of a rational price pattern. By " rational " is meant a system which enables those who make economic decisions at all levels to compare the costs and advantages of alternative schemes and methods. In part, its absence is due to the refusal to place any value on land or to charge interest on the bu'k of capital investments, which tends to give an air of spurious profitability to capital-intensive projects located in big cities. But in any event a consistent price system has always been subordinated to other considerations. Thus Soviet politicians have always tried, in varying degrees, to make desirable activities look cheap. For instance, in 1955 the price of cement was reduced at a stroke by over 30 per cent., shortly after a decision was taken to use more cement and less bricks in building. Sudden changes are made, which upset relativities, and small adjustments are rare. The allocation of basic materials mitigates the practical consequences of the lack of order in the price system, but it remains an obstacle to rational planning decision.

Illogical price relationships are particularly noxious where one enterprise produces a number of different commodities or types. The classic example of this is a factory which makes nails. When the plan was established in *numbers*, only small nails were made ; so the basis of the plan was changed to weight, and then there were only *large* nails. If the plan is expressed in money, then only those which are cheapest to make will be produced, and probably all of the same size ; if each type of nail is to be separately specified in the plan, this would be a glaring case of bureaucratic over-centralization. If the price of nails reflected supply-and-demand conditions, of course, things would be different ; but this verges on heresy. Meanwhile, there are repeated appeals to the managers to provide a proper assortment of products.

No doubt some part of Soviet production includes avoidable waste. If, for example, the siting of an industry has been wrongly decided upon, consequent upon an irrational system of freight charges, more goods wagons and transport services are required. Of course, we must count them as part of the economic activity of the U.S.S.R., just as British railway passenger returns include the journey of the young man who went to meet his girl friend on the wrong day. In the last analysis there is a loss, avoidable waste, involved. But, just as we have no statistics of young men who get their appointments mixed, so we cannot even guess about *how much* Russian production is wasteful, though we can suspect it is substantial.

It is generally assumed that poor quality is a characteristic of Soviet production. This assertion has some truth in it, but needs to be carefully qualified. There is evidence that Soviet industry is capable of first-class precision workmanship, and also plenty of evidence of the contrary : of bathroom taps which do not run and textile dyes that do. One should beware of concluding that poor quality is an inherently " Soviet " characteristic. It would be wiser to bear in mind that these things are, at least in part, consequences of the sheer *pace* of Russia's industrial revolution. An industry staffed by half-trained ex-peasants is apt to produce a high proportion of spoiled work, under communism, fascism, feudalism or any other system known to man. With the passage of time, Russia has acquired a fairly large skilled-labour force, but there has not been enough of it to go round, and priority has been given to heavy industry. This, and the inevitable effect of a constant sellers' market, has certainly tended to depress the quality of consumers' goods and the standard (as well as the rate) of house building. Even so, this state of affairs cannot be assumed to last indefinitely, and the visitor who finds (as the author of these lines did) that door handles come off in hotels should not conclude that Soviet industry produces defective railway locomotives or machine tools. Door handles have no priority.

It is important not to be misled by the large number of criticisms of defects which appear often enough in the Soviet press. It is easy to catalogue these criticisms and derive from them a picture comforting for the complacent but fundamentally inaccurate. The system as a whole is not chaotic, even though examples of chaos can be properly cited ; it does work. The essential fact is that the U.S.S.R. is a vast country of contrasts, which has developed very unevenly, with the good and the bad existing still side by side. One should also remember that inefficiencies in Western countries would be better known if the private affairs of firms were liable to be released to the press. In the U.S.S.R., the authorities use publicity in a carefully selective way. Hence an outburst of criticism directed at some sector is not necessarily proof that it is peculiarly defective, or that its efficiency has declined ; the reason may be a decision to launch a campaign to improve it, or possibly even a desire to discredit the minister in charge.

* * *

While the facts certainly tend to show that industrial growth benefited from the régime's policies, which were designed to maximize it, *agriculture* has remained in a much less satisfactory state, for reasons which will now be briefly examined.

In part, the relative stagnation of farm output has been yet another consequence of the overriding priority of heavy industry. Agriculture was heavily taxed, by having to sell a proportion of its output to the State at very low prices, while receiving inadequate equipment, little fertilizer, few skilled men. Moreover, the situation was complicated by ideological-political considerations. The individual peasant has been regarded as an undesirable phenomenon, and industrialization coincided with compulsory collectivization. The State has ever since had to interfere to preserve the collective against the threat of the resurgence of private interests, which remain in the shape of the peasant's little plot of land and his right to sell surpluses in the free market.

The State found itself pursuing a contradictory policy : on the one hand, it wished to persuade the peasants to work hard for the collectives ; on the other, by taking much of the produce of the collectives at very low prices, the State made such work unremunerative and the collectives heartily unpopular. Efficiency and yields have remained low, and efforts to improve matters by central direction added the further evil of bureaucratic over-centralization, a disease particularly harmful under the conditions natural to farming.

The Soviet system as such, while reasonably well adapted to coping with problems of large-scale factory production, had nothing significant to contribute to the solution of the many problems of farm management. Indeed, it contributed " headaches " peculiar to itself : thus, the collective farms neither own nor control the machinery which serves them, this being held by State machine tractor stations, and there is plenty of evidence to show that this division of responsibility causes confusion and loss. To suggest the obvious way out, letting the collectives run their own machines, is heresy, for it would mean letting go a vital element of State control over peasants.

For all these reasons, Soviet agriculture in 1953 was relatively *further* behind advanced Western countries—in technique, productivity, yields—than, say, 25 years earlier. Apart from sugar-beet and cotton, there was very little progress to report even in absolute terms, and the *per capita* availability of animal products has never regained 1928 levels. It is true that agriculture had to recover from two disasters : collectivization, when peasants slaughtered the major part of the livestock population, and the war. It is also true that Soviet farming did manage to feed the growing towns with a slightly reduced rural labour force. One cannot, therefore, speak of complete failure. All the same, consumption standards and production efficiency alike remained deplorably low. A drive to improve matters is now in progress.

Two further negative features must be mentioned. The appallingly low standard of housing in the towns, reflected in most serious overcrowding, is notorious. Retail trade facilities have also been somewhat elementary, with queues and shortages fairly common even in quite normal years. This is connected with the strain on the transport system. With good roads still rare and lorries few, the overwhelming bulk of Russia's goods traffic is carried by rail. Yet there has been surprisingly little building of new lines : track mileage is only one-third that of the United States, although the volume of freight carried is larger. The absence of a professional trading class has been another factor contributing to poor distribution.

When all is said, the question remains : Is the Soviet system peculiarly suited to expansion ? On balance, surely, after giving due weight to the negative features, our answer must be " yes," even if the arguments put forward by Wiles in favour of this proposition are not wholly acceptable. Many of the defects are themselves due precisely to the speed of growth, to the concentration of limited resources into growth-inducing sectors.

OTHER FACTORS AFFECTING GROWTH

In the last few pages we have been considering the influence, for good or ill, of the Soviet *system* on the growth of the economy. However, it is also necessary to enumerate those features of the situation which, while independent of the political colouring of the Soviet régime, none the less had an important bearing on growth rates.

The first point, which needs to be briefly repeated, is simply the low starting point of the U.S.S.R. For example, Soviet output of cement in 1940 was over 300 per cent. of 1928 volume, but output in 1940 was still a third of U.S. production in 1913. This factor is of decreasing importance now that the U.S.S.R. is a major industrial power, but should not be overlooked. None the less, as has already been stated, Soviet industrial growth has been considerably more rapid than that of other countries in a comparable stage of industrialization.

Secondly, a most important factor has been the relative rural over-population of Russia. The transfer of labour from village to town was a clear gain to the economy, despite the inefficiency of most of this labour. Repeatedly, the labour productivity targets in industry were not reached, and production plans were fulfilled through the unplanned intake of men from the villages. Owing to a rate of natural increase high in relation to Western countries, this process was accompanied only by a surprisingly small diminution in the number of peasants.

The third point is a corollary of the second : the labour initially absorbed by industry was poor material, and there were big opportunities for improvements in productivity, as these recruits settled down, acquired elementary skills, became a working class instead of rootless ex-peasants. The resultant gains in productivity per head, though below optimistic expectations, were nevertheless substantial, and should continue.

The fourth point is frequently overlooked. The process of urbanization, when it takes place in a relatively primitive peasant economy, greatly increases the consumption of industrial goods and services. First, various formerly domestic processes find their way into industrial output statistics and influence the indices of the rate of growth. For instance, there was spectacular growth in the number of bakeries, meat-processing plant and much else besides, reflecting neither increased welfare nor increased consumption of these commodities, but simply urbanization. Then there is a marked increase in transport and other services required by the urban population : tramcars, laundries, a system of wholesale distribution of foodstuffs, etc. The process of urbanization calls for a much higher level of industrial production to sustain a given standard of consumer satisfaction. This is why, despite the grievously inadequate attention paid to consumer needs, the output of industrial consumers' goods has been rising by impressive percentages. It must be stressed that this is not a matter of statistical sleight-of-hand, nor is it in any way peculiar to Russia. All backward peasant countries experience the same thing when they industrialize. The relevant thing to bear in mind is that this factor has tended to expand measurable industrial growth and that the process tends to slow down with time.

A fifth factor has been the possibility of borrowing technical ideas from advanced countries. A large proportion of Russian machines and factory layouts are straight copies of Western models. This enabled the U.S.S.R. to make technical " leaps " impossible in countries where new ideas had first to be subject to trial and error. For example, the Soviet steel industry, virtually created in the last 25 years, could be based from the first on up-to-date German and American models, and so productivity per head in the steel industry compares very favourably with that in Western Europe.

Finally, there were and are ample supplies of most basic materials. Although inconvenient geographical location imposes a strain on transport, mineral deposits tend to be fairly easy to work. Coal and oil seem to be available in virtually unlimited quantities, iron ore is plentiful. Only certain non-ferrous metals constitute a bottleneck. To some extent, clearly, natural resources contribute to growth regardless of the political complexion of the rulers who make use of them. Thus the spectacular rise in production and national income recently recorded in Kuwait is not wholly due to the wisdom of its government.

FUTURE TRENDS AND PROSPECTS

We have discussed the influence of the Soviet system and of " non-political " factors on growth. We must now turn our eyes to the future and consider the following : Granted the declared desire of the Soviet leaders to reach and surpass the most advanced Western countries economically, what obstacles stand in the way of success and what are the chances of over-coming them?

One factor, while no doubt desirable in itself, will tend to hold back *industrial* growth. This is the much greater pro-portion of national resources (and of industrial production) now being devoted to agriculture. Since 1953, ambitious expansion programmes have been absorbing heavy invest-ments. The profit which the State draws from agriculture has been reduced by repeated increases in prices paid to pro-ducers, the last such increase having been announced as recently as February, 1956. The drive to provide modern equipment for agriculture may be measured by the fact that the number of grain combines to be delivered in 1956–60 significantly exceeds *all* the combines ever received by Soviet agriculture down to and including 1955. Few would doubt that some increases in production will result, despite the inefficiencies inherent in collectivized agriculture.

The sixth five-year-plan (1956–60) calls for an increase of 70 per cent. in gross output of the farms over 1955 levels, and for an even greater rise in output per peasant. This is probably fantasy, and 25 per cent. would be a worthy achieve-ment. Meanwhile the very scale of the effort means diversion of resources away from *industrial* expansion, and calls (in the short run, at any rate) for more labour on the land. After a few years, however, movement from village to town should be resumed, since there is much waste and inefficiency in Soviet farming and, consequently, ample scope for economies in manpower. Indeed, one of the objects of the great drive to extend mechanization is precisely to release labour from the farms.

The war-time dip in the birth-rate is now affecting the labour intake but this was, of course, only temporary. There has been a spectacular fall in the death-rate, and in the five years 1951–55 the population is stated to have risen by 16·3 millions. On the other hand, working hours—raised from seven to eight in 1940—are now to be gradually reduced again, until the standard working week falls to forty-one hours.

The labour intake will also be reduced by the raising of the school-leaving age : within five years nearly all Russian children will be receiving full-time education to the age of seventeen. But while this will for a time reduce the numbers available, it must have a profound effect on the efficiency of labour. There are ambitious plans to expand the already impressive output of specialists. Russia's educational progress is too pronounced to be explained away by comforting generalizations. While at first there were many instances of hasty half-training of technicians, present standards are high ; a Russian engineering degree, for example, demands higher qualifications than its British equivalent.

All this must surely have far-reaching consequences, and not only in raising the standards of skill. Thus, over-centralization of industrial administration may partly have been due to shortage of efficient subordinates ; the new generation of graduates may find much that is intolerable in a system largely designed for rule over ignoramuses. But the fact remains that, on balance, the annual intake of new labour into industry will tend to be somewhat slower than has been normal since 1928, and that this will of itself tend to slow down growth.

We must now turn to another " slowing " factor : this is the increasing pressure for improved living standards. We see this in the great agricultural drive, which, whatever its chances of success, is certainly *intended* to raise the output of foodstuffs. The doubling of the rate of house building in the sixth five-year-plan is also significant.

It is immaterial for our present purpose whether the Soviet leaders do these things willingly or not. They may wish to give their people the most that can be spared, or the least that will persuade them to work ; such fine distinctions can be left to philosophers. Social and economic pressures operate in the U.S.S.R., and only one totally blinded by the " totalitarian-state " generalization can deny it. Examples abound. For instance, efforts to persuade the peasants to produce more without adequate reward were repeatedly made, and as repeatedly failed ; to get results, Khrushchev must put more money into peasant pockets, whether he likes to do this or not. It follows that more goods must be produced for the peasants to buy. House building becomes a necessity to stimulate industrial recruitment, to avoid excessive labour turnover. Overtime rates in the building industry had to be improved (with effect from January, 1956), not necessarily for love of building workers but because of serious shortages of these workers. The progress of education will certainly stimulate a demand for higher standards, and nowhere more than in the villages, where amenities are generally poor in the extreme.

The Soviet government is thus being pushed all the time in the direction of devoting more resources to consumption, and many of its own higher officials must themselves be wishing for more security and comfort, less rush, fewer campaigns. Progress may at times be slow; in 1955, indeed, Khrushchev practically brought it to a halt, apparently with the object of eliminating bottlenecks in heavy industry. But pressures will accumulate, and should have the gradual effect of reducing the disproportionate share of the national income devoted to growth-inducing sectors of the economy.

The logic of events will also require increasingly heavy investments in transport. The rate of railway building has in fact been greatly increased, but the problem of roads has yet to be properly tackled.

Within industry itself, it is evident that those sectors in which Russian technique is furthest behind the West, i.e. where borrowing of Western ideas is likely to be most fruitful, are furniture, footwear, pottery, textiles, etc., i.e. precisely those sectors which are not themselves growth-inducing. Also, of the output of capital goods, a larger proportion must be devoted to replacements, i.e. to making good depreciation; as the average age of Soviet enterprises rises, so too must more of investment be devoted to keeping the existing capital stock intact. The difference between gross and net investment increases. In addition, an increasing proportion of capital goods is likely to be exported, and these exports may be paid for mainly in consumers' goods or in raw materials for consumers' goods. Clearly, if the Russians send steel-making plant to China, and receive in exchange pig-bristles and soya beans, housewives in Moscow might see more and better brushes and more and worse sausages, but the steel mill will make producers' goods for China and not Russia. So far, international trade has been of little relative importance to the Soviet economy, but it may not remain so.

All this means that there are forces which will tend to reduce the " growth-effectiveness " of each unit of industrial output. This development may not at first lead to any decline in the tempo of investment, but rather to a change in the *direction* of investment, which will exercise a slow damping-down effect on growth. A larger proportion of capital goods will be devoted to re-equipping light industry, building new blocks of flats, delivering more tractors to agriculture, relatively less to making " producers' goods to be used for the production of more producers' goods".

Lastly, one must mention one very important question-mark : as the U.S.S.R. climbs to higher economic levels, the need for greater efficiency and flexibility in economic administration becomes increasingly apparent. The Soviet authorities are well aware of the problem, which has been repeatedly discussed at conferences and in the press. Various remedies are being considered, including some devolution of control. Soviet economists, who have been in the habit of slavishly following and justifying whatever policy the government adopted, are being ordered to think, to make suggestions. There are signs of a serious effort to improve matters. The problem is : To what extent can one shed deficiencies hitherto associated with the Soviet economic system, while remaining within the essential framework of that system ? No doubt some improvements are possible, but it is only prudent to reserve judgement.

It may be considered certain that the annual rate of industrial growth will decline. Even the Soviet government says so : the sixth plan (1956–60) envisages increases of 10½ per cent. per annum, against the 13 per cent. claimed for the years 1951–55. Allowing for the labour stringencies which may be acute in the next few years, a small under-fulfilment seems likely, but a growth rate of 10 per cent. per annum until 1960 is quite possible, though probably at the cost of a good deal of overtime. Yet even 9 per cent. per annum means a doubling of output in eight years.

IMPLICATIONS FOR THE WEST

We are dealing with a country whose government has declared it to be its vital task to overtake the West, in total and in *per capita* output. Are we in fact in danger of being overtaken ?

Any attempt to answer this question lands one in a situation of acute methodological discomfort. Not only are we dealing with hypothetical situations, subject to many unforeseeable variations, but any comparisons between Soviet and Western growth rates or aggregate production raise a multitude of insoluble statistical problems.

First, a few words on industrial *productivity*. According to Galenson's excellent study,[1] Soviet labour productivity in industry in 1937–39 was about 40 per cent. of American, and a contemporary Soviet study reached the same conclusion. Galenson rightly argues that there was little relative change by 1950. If this be so, one may surmise that Soviet productivity is now half the American and possibly is somewhere about British output per head. If the difference between

---

[1] *Labour Productivity in Soviet and American Industry* (Columbia, 1955).

20

Soviet and American productivity growth remained 4 per cent. per annum for a decade (e.g. U.S.A. + 2 per cent., U.S.S.R. + 6 per cent.), Soviet labour productivity in industry would still be roughly 70 per cent. of American by 1965, though doubtless surpassing comfortably the West-European average. This probably is the uppermost point of the range of possibilities.

In turning from productivity to production, one should bear in mind that the Soviet industrial labour force will certainly expand faster than the American. It is not only a question of a higher rate of natural increase. Until recently, despite a much larger total working population, Russia has had fewer industrial workers than the United States. This was due primarily to having so many more persons employed in agriculture, and also to more manpower in the forces, in prison and on clerical and other unskilled tasks. The Soviet authorities thus have a potential labour reserve for industry to draw on, which the U.S. and West-European economies no longer possess to anything like the same extent.

How does Soviet industrial output compare with that of the United States? No precise answer is possible. With all due reservations, let us take the figure tentatively mentioned by Hodgman, which seems *very* roughly of the right order of magnitude : that in 1950 the Soviets were 35 per cent. of the United States. Purely for illustrative purposes, let us now make the following cautious assumptions : First, that U.S. industrial production continues to increase steadily at the same rate as in 1950–55, i.e. by 24 per cent. every five years. Let us take the Soviet growth figure for the same period at the conservative figure of 75 per cent., against their own claim of 85 per cent., even though this may do them an injustice. Let us further assume that Soviet growth rates fall, so that the increase from 1955 to 1960 is " only " 60 per cent. and that between 1960 and 1965 it falls further to 50 per cent. The result is as follows :

(U.S. industrial output 1950 = 100)			
	U.S.S.R.	U.S.A.	U.S.S.R. as percentage of U.S.A.
			%
1950	35	100	35
1955	61	124	49
1960	98	154	64
1965	147	191	77

The opposite table is based on assumptions which, on the whole, are favourable to the United States. Thus, it is possible that U.S. growth will not maintain for ten years the tempo applicable to the boom period 1950–55, whereas the Soviet rates indicated here cannot, on past performance and existing plans, be dismissed as unlikely. Yet it follows from the table that the U.S.S.R., though still well behind the United States, may have reached America's *present* industrial output by about 1963.

Industrial Output Statistics, U.S.S.R.

	1927/8 or 1928	1940	1950	1955	1960 Plan
Coal, including lignite (million tons)	36	166	261	390	593
Oil (million tons)	11·7	31	38	70	135
Electricity (billion kilowatt hours)	5	48	91	170	320
Pig iron (million tons)	3·3	15	19	33	53
Crude steel (million tons) ..	4·3	18	27	45	69
Rolled steel (million tons) ..	3·4	13	21	35	53
Timber (a) (million cubic metres)	54	119	160	197	264
Cement (million tons)	1·8	5·8	10	22	55
Mineral fertilizer (million tons gross)	0·2	2·6	5·5	9·6	19·6
Soda ash (million tons)	0·2	0·5	0·9	1·4	2·4
Machine tools (thousands) ..	n.a.	38	73	105	200
Automobiles, including lorries (thousands)	0·7	160 (c,d)	370 (c)	445	650
Tractors (thousands)	1·0	30 (c,d)	109	163	322
Grain combines (thousands) ..	0	13	46 (c)	48	140
Cotton fabrics (million metres) ..	2,703	3,836	3,899	5,904	7,270
Wool fabrics (million metres) ..	94	120	155	250	363
Silk and rayon fabrics (million metres)	10	70	125	526	1,074
Linen fabrics (million metres) ..	188	270	n.a.	305	556
Knitted garments (millions) ..	n.a.	150	n.a.	430	580
Footwear (b) (million pairs) ..	30	205	226	299	455
Clocks and watches (millions) ..	neg.	2·6	7·6	19·7	33·6
Radio and TV receivers (millions)	neg.	0·2	1·1	4·0	10·2
Bicycles (millions)	neg.	0·3	0·6	2·9	4·2
Sewing machines (millions) ..	neg.	0·2	0·5	1·6	3·8

NOTES.—The omission of small workshops seriously understates the production of certain consumers' goods, notably footwear and some homespun fabrics, in 1927/8. Figures for processed foodstuffs, though available, have been omitted because peasant processing is missing throughout the series.

(a) Haulage of timber, other than firewood. (b) Some of the later figures may refer to *all* types, though the series should be for *leather* footwear. The 1928 figure omits large numbers made by small craftsmen. (c) Approximations. (d) The 1940 output of tractors and automobiles was well below 1937 levels, owing to effects of war preparations.

n.a. Not available.   neg. Negligibly small.

22

The U.S.S.R., then, will be an industrial giant, *the* industrial giant of the Eurasian land mass. Her heavy industry should be capable of becoming a serious export competitor. British industry will look uncomfortably small by comparison. It is a sobering thought that the *increase* in Soviet steel production planned for the next five years exceeds *total* U.K. output and that for coal nearly equals it. But Russia has a long, long way to go to catch the United States, and, as Hodgman wisely remarks, she " may find the gap between Soviet and American industrial performance increasingly difficult to close the narrower it becomes." Percentages are apt to disguise the physical magnitude of the gap, and some comparisons of specific commodities does much to redress the mental balance.

A growth rate flattering to the United States can be arrived at by basing comparisons on 1938 (better still, 1932), when there was much unemployment of labour and resources. U.S. industrial production in 1938 was over 20 per cent. lower than in 1937, and steel output fell from 51·4 to 28·8 million tons. It makes a fairer comparison, with a country where resources tend to be over- rather than under-employed, to take the relatively good year 1937 as a pre-war basis.

It is not suggested that the sample below is representative. The Soviets would make a better relative showing in heavy

U.S. and Soviet Output of Certain Commodities

	UNITED STATES			SOVIET UNION		
	1937	1950	1955 (*y*)	1937	1950	1955
Coal, including lignite (million tons)	451	505	448	127	261	390
Oil (million tons)	179	287	346 (*a*)	30	38	70
Electricity (billion kilowatt hours)	146	388	625	36	91	170
Crude steel (million tons) ..	51	88	104	18	27	45
Cement (million tons)	20	39	46 (*b*)	5	10	22
Tractors (thousands) (*c*) ..	221	509	441 (*a*)	80	109	163
Cotton fabrics (million metres)	8,000	9,156	9,350 (*a*)	3,448	3,899	5,904
Radios and TV sets (thousands)	8,080	22,000	19,130	150	1,100	4,000
Private cars (thousands) ..	3,915	6,666	7,920	} 266	370	445
Lorries (thousands)	893	1,337	1,249			

NOTES.—(*y*) Provisional figures given where available. Otherwise, the higher of the figures for 1953 and 1954. (*a*) 1953. (*b*) 1954. (*c*) The U.S. tractor figures exclude small " garden tractors."

machinery and (say) bread-baking. But it is salutary to record that, for instance, American electric generation increased in the five years 1950–55 by more than the *entire* Soviet production of 1955. Soviet output of cement has roughly quadrupled since 1937, but the physical rate of increase in that period has been greater in the United States by a wide margin. Even in steel, in 1950–55 the United States has very nearly kept her lead in terms of tons. Of course, on a *per capita* basis, the gap is greater still.

The gap will be much wider if one concentrates only on consumers' goods, or on the non-industrial sector of the economy. The Soviet system is not well attuned to meet the variegated needs of personal taste ; quality, while it will improve, will surely remain well below Western standards. In housing, where present conditions are truly appalling, the gap cannot be bridged for generations under any conceivable circumstances. Finally, productivity in agriculture, and variety in diet, will certainly remain far below levels considered reasonable in England or America.

But these facts must be seen in perspective, before any valid political conclusions are drawn from them. Russian standards of living are no doubt well below the American and will remain so for an indefinite period, but they still make a favourable showing to " under-developed " peoples : Tashkent and Alma Ata are an impressive contrast to Tabriz, Kabul, Rangoon. To the inhabitants of these countries, Russia has the further attraction of a formerly backward country which has built a great industry with its own resources in record time. In Russia, consumer satisfaction must be measured by reference to the recent past of Russia itself, not to the unattainable standard of Iowa or Michigan. Compared with the recent past, there is a definite improvement, over low levels but still an improvement. A glance at the 1960 plan figures shows that it is to be continued.

The conclusion is inescapable : the West faces a really serious challenge on the economic front. The Russian leaders have given notice that they regard this front as vital in the world of " competitive co-existence," and it would be foolish indeed, through over-concentration on military dangers or through obstinate complacency, to disregard the facts.

London.   A. Nove.
 March, 1956.

A COMPARISON OF SOVIET AND UNITED STATES NATIONAL PRODUCT[1]

(By Morris Bornstein, University of Michigan)

INTRODUCTION

The purpose of this paper is to make selected comparisons of the structure, size, and growth of the national products of the U.S.S.R. and the United States.

Of all the respects in which the economies of these two countries may be compared, national product comparisons probably provide the broadest, most comprehensive view, because they embrace, for each country, the net output of all goods and services produced during the specified period. Furthermore, because national product data are obtained from detailed national accounts studies, they not only provide summary measures of total output but also furnish much information regarding the structure of the economy. Thus, the pattern of resource allocation may be illustrated by analysis of the distribution of national product by its major end-use components, such as consumption, investment, defense, and government administration. Likewise, the pattern of resource allocation may be analyzed in terms of the relative importance of the different sectors in which national income, generated in producing national product, originates, such as industry, agriculture, services and trade. Finally, these end-use and sector-of-origin breakdowns, together with other data, make possible international comparisons of relative size and estimates of growth trends.

However, because national product comparisons involve the aggregation of quite different items by value weights, the results obtained are very sensitive to the weighting systems employed. The usual weighting problems of intertemporal and interspatial comparisons are intensified in a Soviet-United States comparison because of uncertainties about the meaning of Soviet prices. Hence, it is desirable to consider national product comparisons in conjuncture with other comparisons which are less susceptible to weighting problems, such as selected physical output comparisons and labor force comparisons.

At the same time, it should be recognized that while national product provides a convenient measure of overall economic capability, this

---

[1] The author wishes to thank Janet Riddle, Florence Roof, and Harold Demsetz for their suggestions about various aspects of this paper.

378 COMPARISONS OF UNITED STATES AND SOVIET ECONOMIES

measure is not the most significant one for various economic, military, scientific, and political questions. For example, although Soviet national product may be only half the size of U.S. national product (by one measurement), the U.S.S.R. may, as a result of the particular composition and application of this smaller product, match or surpass the United States in military strength or in selected scientific programs. Thus, the usefulness of national product comparisons depends on the question at issue. For some questions, other measures are undoubtedly superior.

The national product comparisons in this paper concentrate on the period since 1950 because this period appears to be more representative of the conditions of economic competition between the two countries which may be anticipated in the future than would a longer historical period, such as that from 1913 or 1928 to the present. These longer periods span conditions of world war, the first rapid spurt of the Soviet industrialization drive, and a severe depression in the United States. In contrast, the period since 1950 has been more characteristic of likely future conditions in both countries. By 1950, the U.S.S.R. had largely recovered from the effects of World War II, while the United States had completed its reconversion from the war. In the conditions of internationl tension prevailing since 1950, both countries have endeavored to maintain a strong, up-to-date military posture while continuing to develop their civilian economies. So long as the international situation continues to be one of "cold war" and "competitive coexistence," analysis of the period since 1950 will be more useful for an appraisal of probable future trends and relationships than would reference to a longer period of significantly different political and economic conditions. Study of these longer, earlier periods does, of course, provide valuable insight into the dynamics of national product and is thus useful for an understanding of more recent developments and probable future trends. Some comparisons of Soviet and United States national product characteristics and trends before 1950 are available in various earlier studies.[2] For this reason, as well as for the reasons indicated above, attention will be focused on relationships and developments in Soviet and United States national product since 1950, with only limited reference to earlier periods.

The following sections of this paper are concerned, respectively, with (1) an analysis of the structure of Soviet and United States national product and income in 1955, (2) a comparison of their relative size in 1955, and (3) an estimate of trends in their gorwth since 1950. In each section, conceptual and statistical problems hampering such national product comparisons are discussed, and the approximate character of the estimates is stressed. Nevertheless, I believe the results provide a fairly reliable indication of the orders of magnitude involved.

---

[2] For national product comparisons for the period from 1928 to 1955, see Library of Congress, Legislative Reference Service, "Soviet Economic Growth : A Comparison With the United States," a study prepared for the Subcommittee on Foreign Economic Policy of the Joint Economic Committee, 85th Cong., 1st sess., Washington, Government Printing Office, 1957, ch. VI. References to other studies are given in this source.

STRUCTURE OF NATIONAL PRODUCT

In this section the structures of Soviet and United States national product are compared, first by analyzing the shares in the total product of each country of the principal end-use components, and second by analyzing the shares in the total national income of each country of the major sectors of origin in which income is generated. In both instances, reference is to each country's national product or income expressed in its own currency—rubles for the U.S.S.R. and dollars for the United States—with the resulting comparisons being only comparisons of the percentage shares of the specified uses or sectors in each country's total product or income. No comparison is made, at this point, of the relative size of the two economies. Rather only their resource allocation patterns are compared, without reference to the quantity of output produced in the two countries.

Before turning to these calculations, however, a few words are necessary regarding the serious conceptual and statistical problems encountered in such comparisons. Although these difficulties are not, in my judgment, so severe as to invalidate the basic conclusions to be drawn from such comparisons, they do qualify the precision which may be attributed to these figures, particularly the estimates for the U.S.S.R.

Two major conceptual problems are involved in such comparisons. First, output or productive activity in the two countries must be classified in comparable categories, which in some cases proves difficult because of the differences between the two countries in economic and political organization and objectives. Second, because of the different roles in the two countries of indirect taxes and subsidies, it is desirable to compare their economic structures not only in terms of established prices [3] but also in terms of adjusted prices, which allow for this difference and which, therefore, permit a somewhat more accurate comparison of real resource allocation.

The ability to make fairly precise comparisons of the structures of Soviet and United States national product is further hampered by a lack of necessary statistical data, chiefly for the U.S.S.R. The necessary basic national accounts are not published by the Soviet Government but must instead be compiled by a laborious and ingenious assembly of scattered Soviet data, supplemented by many estimates of varying precision. Likewise, Soviet data are lacking for many of the adjustments of basic accounts information which are needed to secure comparability with the figures for the United States. In contrast, most of the data needed for the U.S. side of such comparisons is readily available, primarily from the publications of the Department of Commerce. As a result, it ordinarily proves necessary to rearrange and adjust U.S. figures to match the categories used for the U.S.S.R., the opposite usually being impossible.

National product by end use

Table 1 shows the distribution of gross national product in the U.S.S.R. and United States in 1955 in terms of four end-use or

---

[3] The term "established prices" is used in this paper in preference to "market prices" in recognition of the fact that Soviet prices, with the exception of collective farm market prices, are determined by administrative decree rather than by market forces.

380 COMPARISONS OF UNITED STATES AND SOVIET ECONOMIES

purpose categories: Consumption, investment, defense, and government administration.[4]

The consumption category in table 1 includes both household expenditures on goods and services (including income-in-kind) and government current (i.e., noncapital) expenditures on health and education. This coverage is necessary to provide comparability, because in the U.S.S.R. virtually all outlays on health and education are made by the government, whereas in the United States a significant share of expenditures for these purposes is made by households.

TABLE 1.—*Gross national product by end use in the U.S.S.R. and the United States, at established prices and at adjusted prices, 1955* [1]

End use	U.S.S.R.[2]				United States			
	At established prices		At adjusted prices		At established prices		At adjusted prices	
	Billion rubles	Per-cent of total	Billion rubles	Per-cent of total	Billion dollars	Per-cent of total	Billion dollars	Per-cent of total
Consumption	840. 8	65. 4	566. 4	58. 9	269. 7	67. 8	240. 1	66. 3
Investment	263. 5	20. 5	241. 8	25. 2	77. 2	19. 4	73. 5	20. 3
Defense	144. 6	11. 2	125. 2	13. 0	38. 4	9. 7	36. 9	10. 2
Government administration	36. 9	2. 9	27. 6	2. 9	12. 1	3. 1	11. 7	3. 2
Gross national product	1, 285. 8	100. 0	961. 0	100. 0	397. 5	100. 0	362. 2	100. 0

[1] Gross national product (GNP) at adjusted prices=GNP at established prices—indirect taxes+subsidies. Components may not add to totals, because of rounding.
[2] Figures for the U.S.S.R. are for gross domestic product, exclusive of the net effect of transactions with foreign countries, rather than for GNP strictly defined, because of the lack of balance of payments information for the U.S.S.R. and even of merchandise trade data valued at internal prices. Published merchandise trade figures in rubles are expressed, essentially, at world market prices converted to rubles at the official exchange rate. This "valuta" or "foreign trade ruble" valuation differs from the value of these goods at their internal prices, which for most items exceeds their foreign trade ruble valuation. The effect of this omission on total product and its end-use distribution, however, is slight, because only net foreign sales or purchases of goods and services would be included in the calculation of GNP, and this net figure is undoubtedly a small fraction of Soviet GNP, much less than 1 percent. For data pertinent to this point, see A Nove and Alfred Zauberman, "A Dollar Valuation of Soviet National Income," Soviet Studies, vol. X, No. 2, October 1958, pp. 146–150. Similarly, for the United States, the difference between GNP and gross domestic product is insignificant.

SOURCES AND DERIVATION

U.S.S.R.—Morris Bornstein, "Soviet National Accounts for 1955," unpublished manuscript.
United States, established prices.—GNP data in Department of Commerce, Office of Business Economics, U.S. Income and Output, Washington, Government Printing Office, 1958, p. 119, were reclassified into the four categories shown in the table on the basis of information in that study and in other sources.
Consumption includes personal consumption expenditures plus current expenditures on health and education by Federal, State, and local governments. The latter represent purchases of goods and services

[4] Figures for the United States are derived from data of the Department of Commerce and other U.S. Government agencies, as explained in notes to the table. Figures for the U.S.S.R. are from an unpublished manuscript of the author, "Soviet National Accounts for 1955." This study follows the general approach of the pioneering studies of national accounts for the U.S.S.R. by Bergson, Heymann, and Hoeffding (Abram Bergson, "Soviet National Income and Product in 1937," New York, Columbia University Press, 1953; Abram Bergson and Hans Heymann, Jr., "Soviet National Income and Product, 1940–48," New York, Columbia University Press, 1954; and Oleg Hoeffding, "Soviet National Income and Product in 1928," New York, Columbia University Press, 1954). The results of the author's study correspond closely to those in two other recent studies of Soviet national accounts for 1955, one by the Economic Commission for Europe (ECE) ("An Estimate of the National Accounts of the Soviet Union for 1955, "Economic Bulletin for Europe, vol. 9, No. 1, May 1957, pp. 89–107), and one by Hoeffding and Nimitz (O. Hoeffding and N. Nimitz, "Soviet National Income and Product, 1949–55," RM–2101, Santa Monica, Calif., the Rand Corp., 1959). For the same aspects of Soviet national accounts in 1955, the results of these three studies differ relatively little, with the differences in results being fairly readily explained by conceptual differences, differences in data available at the time the studies were completed, and differences in estimating procedures. The major differences are those of coverage. The ECE study does not contain end-use or origin breakdowns or an adjustment of established prices for indirect taxes and subsidies. The Hoeffding-Nimitz study contains an end-use breakdown in established prices but not one in adjusted prices; it also lacks an origin breakdown. In the present writer's study, from which data for the U.S.S.R. in tables 1 and 2 are drawn, end-use and origin breakdowns and a price adjustment are included.

exclusive of investment in construction and equipment and were estimated from data in ibid., pp. 175 and 190.

Investment includes gross private domestic investment (ibid., p. 119); new public construction exclusive of military facilities (Economic Report of the President, January 1959, Washington, Government Printing Office, 1959, p. 176); an estimate of governmental purchases of producers' durables for non-defense purposes (based on data in Department of Commerce, Bureau of the Census, Summary of Governmental Finances in 1955, Washington, 1956, pp. 29–30); stockpiling and defense production expansion (U.S. Income and Output, p. 175); and net exports of goods and services (ibid., p. 182).

Defense includes expenditures on the military services, foreign military assistance, and atomic energy development. It excludes stockpiling and defense production expansion and expenditures on civil defense and selective service (ibid., p. 175).

Government administration includes government purchases of goods and services (ibid.) less expenditures for national defense, nonmilitary public construction, nondefense equipment purchases, and current expenditures on health and education; and plus civil defense and selective service expenditures.

United States, adjusted prices.—The distribution by end use of indirect business taxes was estimated by analyzing their composition and assigning to consumption Federal and State excise taxes on liquor and tobacco and most other Federal excise taxes, which are levied primarily on consumers' goods. Approximately half of all property taxes were estimated to be on residential property and therefore falling on consumption. The remaining indirect taxes were distributed among the end uses in the same proportion as the shares of the end uses in total GNP at established prices.

Both business transfer payments and subsidies were assigned to consumption. The statistical discrepancy was assigned to investment, in accordance with Department of Commerce practice (ibid., p. 116).

For both countries, the investment category comprises gross investment in construction and equipment and changes in inventories, including stockpiling and investment in defense production facilities, but excluding direct military construction and military equipment purchases. The U.S. figure includes net foreign investment, which is excluded from the figure for the U.S.S.R. for lack of data.

The defense category includes for the United States, and is believed to include for the U.S.S.R., the following: Pay, subsistence, and other current operational expenditures of the armed forces, military construction and equipment expenditures, military research and development expenditures, and atomic energy expenditures. For both countries, it excludes military pensions, which are considered transfer payments and accordingly excluded from gross national product. The figures for the U.S.S.R. include militarized internal security forces, such as border troops, for which there is no U.S. counterpart. The figures for the United States include, while those for the U.S.S.R. probably exclude, foreign military assistance and the cost of maintaining forces abroad. Soviet defense expenditures would, therefore, be understated relative to those of the United States. However, it should be noted that much of the cost of maintaining Soviet troops in Eastern Europe has been borne by the respective satellite countries, which have thus provided an offsetting form of reverse military assistance to the U.S.S.R.

The government administration category for both countries is essentially a residual of current government expenditures on goods and services not included in the other three categories. The figures for the U.S.S.R. exclude the cost of administering state-owned enterprises, as these overhead costs of enterprise management are included in product prices and appear, as in the U.S. figures, in the figures for the end uses to which these products correspond. However, the figures for the U.S.S.R. include expenditures of the Communist Party, which serves as a key arm of government administration and control in the U.S.S.R., and expenditures on nonmilitarized internal security activities, some of which have no counterpart in the United States.

Because the figures for the U.S.S.R. are derived from a national accounts study which (like all such studies for the U.S.S.R.) involves many estimates of varying reliability, they should be regarded as estimates intended to provide a fairly reliable, but by no means fully precise, indication of the pattern of resource allocation in the U.S.S.R. The consumption and investment figures may be considered

382 COMPARISONS OF UNITED STATES AND SOVIET ECONOMIES

to have a relatively high degree of reliability, because a substantial amount of data is available on these activities. On the other hand, the defense figure is necessarily more tenuous because of the need to make estimates for many items regarding which the Soviet Government discloses little or no information. The Government administration figure, being a residual of uncertain coverage, also is less reliable than the figures for consumption and investment, but its small size makes its deficiencies much less serious than in the case of the defense category.

In table 1, the distribution of Soviet and United States national product in 1955 among these four end-use categories is shown both at established prices and at adjusted prices. A comparison at established prices, however, does not adequately indicate the difference between Soviet and United States resource allocation patterns. A somewhat more accurate contrast is shown at adjusted prices, which attempt to exclude indirect taxes (which, although part of established prices, are not payments to factors of production) and to include subsidies (which are payments to factors of production not included in established prices). The resulting adjusted prices, intended to approach more closely a factor cost basis of valuation, depict more faithfully the distribution of resources among these end uses in the two countries.[5]

The effect of the adjustment is slight for the United States, where both indirect taxes and subsidies are of minor importance in the gross national product at established prices. For the U.S.S.R., however, the effect of the adjustment is striking, because indirect taxes account for over one-fourth of the gross national product at established prices and because they fall principally on the consumption end use, as a result of the heavy reliance of the Soviet budget on the turnover tax, an excise constituting about half of the value of state and cooperative retail sales. Subsidies, which were modest in 1955, also fell more heavily on consumption than on the other end uses in 1955, although this was not true in some earlier years, for example, 1948.[6] As a result of the importance and differential impact of indirect taxes, the share of consumption is much higher and the shares of investment and defense are significantly lower at established prices than at adjusted prices.

A comparison of resource allocation patterns at adjusted prices (cols. 4 and 8 of table 1) shows that in 1955 the U.S.S.R., in comparison with the United States, devoted a significantly greater share of its productive resources to investment (25 versus 20 percent) and defense (13 versus 10 percent) and a significantly smaller share to consumption (59 versus 66 percent). About the same share of resources went for general government administration in both countries.

[5] These adjustments follow the method developed in Bergson's "adjusted factor cost" approach; see Bergson, op. cit., ch. 4, and app. E, and Bergson and Heyman, op. cit., ch. III and app. D. Although these adjustments constitute only an approximation to a depiction of factor allocation in the U.S.S.R. because of many problems connected with the valuation of the services of land, capital, and enterprise in the Soviet setting, I believe they represent an improvement over the unadjusted established prices. For discussion of these problems, see the references just cited and also Peter Wiles, "Are Adjusted Rubles Rational?" Soviet Studies, vol. VII, No. 2, October 1955, pp. 143–160; Franklyn D. Holzman, "The Adjusted Factor Cost Method of Valuing National Income: Comment," Soviet Studies, vol. VIII, No. 1, July 1956, pp. 32–36; and ECE, op. cit., p. 94.
[6] See Bergson and Heymann, loc. cit.

National income by sector of origin

An alternative view of the difference in resource allocation patterns in the U.S.S.R. and the United States in 1955 is given in table 2. This table shows the distribution by sector of origin of factor incomes generated in the production of total national output in each country. The figures for the U.S.S.R., and the United States are, however, not strictly comparable, because of a difference in the national income concepts used for the two countries, which arises from the difficulties of valuing the return to property factors in the U.S.S.R.[7] A serious shortcoming of the calculation for the U.S.S.R. is the inadequate allowance for land rent and the consequent substantial understatement of the contribution of agriculture to Soviet national income. As a result, the percentage figures for the U.S.S.R. in table 2 understate the share of agriculture, and overstate the shares of the other sectors, in total Soviet national income.

With this caution in mind, one can nevertheless draw certain conclusions from table 2 regarding differences in the use of resources in the two countries in 1955. The most striking conclusion is the much greater share of total resources engaged in agriculture in the U.S.S.R. This conclusion is confirmed by the much greater share of the agricultural labor force in the total labor force in the U.S.S.R., as compared with the United States, and reflects the inefficiency of Soviet agriculture relative to U.S. agriculture. Another prominent difference between the two countries concerns the share in national income of services and trade. The much larger share in the United States reflects the orientation of the U.S. economy toward the satisfaction of household demand for goods and services. In the U.S.S.R., on the other hand, consumer services and retail trade facilities have been sacrificed in favor of investment and defense production. Finally, in 1955, the U.S.S.R. devoted a somewhat smaller share of its resources to industry and construction and to transportation and communications than did the United States.

TABLE 2.—*National income by sector of origin in the U.S.S.R. and the United States, 1955* [1]

Sector	U.S.S.R.[2]		United States [3]	
	Billion rubles	Percent of total	Billion dollars	Percent of total
Industry and construction	332. 0	36. 6	134. 5	40. 7
Agriculture	245. 7	27. 1	15. 2	4. 6
Transportation and communications	45. 5	5. 0	21. 2	6. 5
Services and trade	283. 3	31. 3	159. 2	48. 2
National income	906. 5	100. 0	330. 2	100. 0

[1] Components may not add to totals, because of rounding.
[2] National income includes wages, salaries, and other cash household income, income in kind, contributions for social insurance, and profits.
[3] National income includes wages and salaries and supplements to wages and salaries, proprietors' income of unincorporated businesses, rental income of persons, corporate profits, and net interest.

Sources: U.S.S.R.-Bornstein, "Soviet National Accounts for 1955." U.S. Department of Commerce, "U.S. Income and Output." p. 131.

[7] The calculation for the U.S.S.R. essentially follows the approach of Bergson, op. cit., app. C. Although the profits component in the present national income calculation for the U.S.S.R. contains some elements of rent and interest on capital, it clearly does not represent them adequately, either in total magnitude or in distribution by sector.

384 COMPARISONS OF UNITED STATES AND SOVIET ECONOMIES

COMPARATIVE SIZE OF NATIONAL PRODUCT

In order to compare the size of Soviet and U.S. national product, the national product figures calculated in native currencies must be expressed in a common currency, either dollars or rubles. In essence, the task is to price Soviet output at U.S. dollar prices and/or to price U.S. output at Soviet ruble prices. In practice, this is done by using international price deflators to convert the Soviet national product figures in rubles to dollars, and/or to convert the U.S. national product figures in dollars to rubles.

Foreign exchange rates are unsuitable as price deflators for such comparisons because they fail, for a number of well-known reasons, to measure the internal purchasing power of currencies, even in the case of market economies whose structure and pricing practices are broadly similar.[8] Because the official Soviet exchange rate is arbitrary and not intended to measure the relationship between foreign and domestic prices, it is particularly inappropriate for international comparisons of national product.

For a comparison of the size of Soviet and United States national products, it is necessary instead to use international price deflators which measure the internal purchasing power equivalents of the ruble and the dollar in purchasing the goods and services composing national product. The first step in obtaining these deflators is to derive ruble-dollar (or dollar-ruble) price ratios for individual products by comparing their internal prices in the U.S.S.R. and the United States. Then the ruble-dollar price ratios for individual items are aggregated into ruble-dollar ratios for categories of national product, such as consumption and investment. For this aggregation, it is possible to use as a basis for weighting individual items either their relative importance in Soviet national product or their relative importance in U.S. national product. In the former case, the aggregate ratios are said to be Soviet weighted; in the latter, United States weighted.

Table 3 presents the results of an effort to compare the size of Soviet and U.S. national product in 1955 by this method. It compares the national products both in rubles and in dollars. The ruble figures for the U.S.S.R. were taken from table 1, while the ruble figures for the United States were obtained by converting the dollar figures for the United States in table 1 to rubles by appropriate ruble-dollar ratios. Similarly, the dollar figures for the United States are from table 1, while the dollar figures for the U.S.S.R. were obtained by converting the ruble figures for the U.S.S.R. in table 1 into dollars by appropriate dollar-ruble ratios. In both cases, the comparisons involve the established price figures, rather than the adjusted price figures, in table 1 because their purpose is to compare the output of goods and services entering national product in the two countries, rather than the quantities of factor inputs devoted to the production of national product in the two countries. In the figures taken directly from table 1, output is valued at established prices in each country. Where ruble-dollar (or dollar-ruble) ratios have been applied to figures in table 1 to obtain those in table 3, these ratios were constructed

[8] See Milton Gilbert and Irving B. Kravis, "An International Comparison of National Products and the Purchasing Power of Currencies," Paris, Organization for European Economic Cooperation (OEEC), 1954, pp. 14–17; and Milton Gilbert and Associates, "Comparative National Products and Price Levels," Paris, OEEC, 1958, pp. 29–33.

by comparing established ruble and dollar prices for individual items and aggregating the results by using established price weights.[9]

TABLE 3.—*Comparison of gross national product of the U.S.S.R. and the United States, at established prices, in rubles and dollars, 1955* [1]

| End use | Ruble comparison | | | Dollar comparison | | | Geometric average of ruble and dollar comparisons |
	U.S.S.R. (billion rubles)	United States (billion rubles)	U.S.S.R. as percent of United States	U.S.S.R. (billion dollars)	United States (billion dollars)	U.S.S.R. as percent of United States	U.S.S.R. as percent of United States
Consumption	840.8	4,045.5	20.8	105.1	269.7	39.0	28.5
Investment	263.5	540.4	48.8	52.7	77.2	68.3	57.7
Defense	144.6	192.0	75.3	36.2	38.4	94.3	84.3
Government administration	36.9	24.2	152.5	18.4	12.1	152.1	152.3
Gross national product	1,285.8	4,802.1	26.8	212.4	397.5	53.4	37.8

[1] Components may not add to totals, because of rounding.

SOURCES AND DERIVATION

Ruble figures for U.S.S.R. and dollar figures for United States are from table 1.
Ruble figures for United States were obtained by multiplying dollar figures for United States in table 1 by a U.S.-weighted ruble-dollar ratio for each end use, computed as

$$\frac{\sum\left(\frac{Ps}{Pu} \cdot PuQu\right)}{\sum PuQu},$$

and dollar figures for the U.S.S.R. were obtained by multiplying ruble figures for the U.S.S.R. in table 1 by a Soviet-weighted dollar-ruble ratio for each end use, computed as

$$\frac{\sum\left(\frac{Pu}{Ps} \cdot PsQs\right)}{\sum PsQs},$$

where Ps and Pu represent Soviet and U.S. prices, respectively, and Qs and Qu represent Soviet and U.S. quantities, respectively.

The ruble total for the United States and the dollar total for the U.S.S.R. are the sum of their respective components.

Ruble-dollar ratios for consumption of 15 rubles per dollar with U.S. weights and 8 rubles per dollar with Soviet weights were estimated as follows. Aggregate ruble-dollar ratios in 1954 prices for household consumption of food products, nonfood consumers' goods, and services are available with 1950 U.S. weights in Norman M. Kaplan and Eleanor S. Wainstein, A comparison of Soviet and American Retail Prices in 1950, RM-1692-1, Santa Monica, Calif., The Rand Corp., 1950, p. 28, and with 1954 Soviet weights in idem, An Addendum to Previous U.S.S.R.-United States Retail Price Comparisons, RM-1906, Santa Monica, Calif., The Rand Corp., 1957, p. 3. The pertinent Soviet prices did not change from 1954 to 1955, according to Tsentral'noe Statisticheskoe Upravlenie, Sovetskaia torgovlia (Soviet Trade), Moscow, Gosstatizdat, 1956[,] p. 132. The ratios were adjusted, however, for U.S. price changes from 1954 to 1955, from data in Department of Commerce, U.S. Income and Output, p. 228. Two further calculations were made to take account of items in the consumption end use not covered by the Kaplan-Wainstein studies. First, their ruble-dollar ratios for food products, which consider for the U.S.S.R. only prices of state and cooperative retail outlet, were adjusted to take into account information regarding the higher prices prevailing on the collective farm market in the U.S.S.R. in TsSU, op. cit., pp. 133–134; and data on the relative importance of the former and latter marketing channels in total Soviet food purchases, in TsSU, Narodnoe khoziaistvo SSSR v 1956 godu (National Economy of the U.S.S.R. in 1956), Moscow, Gosstatizdat, 1957, p. 228. Second, ruble-dollar ratios for health and education expenditures in the consumption end use were estimated. Ruble-dollar ratios for the wage component of these outlays were estimated from data on Soviet health and education wages in Bornstein, Soviet National Accounts for 1955, and from data on U.S. health and education

[9] Thus, in this comparison no adjustment was made for indirect taxes and subsidies in either the national product figures or the ruble-dollar ratios. For a comparison of inputs, factor costs should be used both for value of product and for the construction of ruble-dollar ratios. To obtain such factor cost ruble-dollar ratios, individual established ruble and dollar prices should be adjusted to exclude indirect taxes and include subsidies. Cf. Gilbert and Kravis, op. cit., pp. 91–92. Although rough adjustments of this type can be made for the U.S.S.R. for broad categories of national product, as was done in connection with table 1, data are lacking for similar adjustments of individual ruble prices.

incomes in Department of Health, Education, and Welfare, Public Health Service, Health Manpower Chart Book, Public Health Service publication No. 511, Washington, 1957, pp. 11, 13, 57; Department of Commerce, Office of Business Economics, National Income, Washington, Government Printing Office, 1954, p. 201; Survey of Current Business, July 1957, pp. 19–21; and Journal of the American Dental Association, December 1956, p. 719. In addition to wage outlays, health and education expenditures in the consumption end use include outlays for materials inputs, such as supplies, food, heat, and electricity. In the absence of data on the specific composition of these materials inputs, the ruble-dollar ratios for household consumption of food products, nonfood consumers' goods, and services were used for health and education materials inputs. Finally, the ratios for the various components of the consumption end use were combined into aggregate U.S.-weighted and Soviet-weighted ratios for the category.

For the investment end-use category, very rough ruble-dollar ratios of 7 rubles per dollar with U.S. weights and 5 rubles per dollar with Soviet weights were estimated as follows. For producers' durables, a U.S.-weighted ratio of 6 rubles per dollar and a Soviet-weighted ratio of 4 rubles per dollar were taken, on the basis of the estimates of Abraham S. Becker, Prices of Producers' Durables in the United States and the USSR in 1955, Santa Monica, Calif., The Rand Corp., 1959, RM-2432, pp. 47–48. In the absence of a comparable ruble-dollar ratio study for construction, it was more or less arbitrarily estimated that the construction ratios would approximate 8 rubles per dollar with U.S. weights and 6 rubles per dollar with Soviet weights, on the basis of scattered evidence, such as a comparison of thermal electric plant construction in the U.S.S.R. and the United States (Soviet data in Elektricheskii Stantsii, No. 11, 1956, pp. 26–28; No. 2, 1958, pp. 46–53; No. 3, 1958, pp. 39–44; and U.S. data in Tennessee Valley Authority, Engineering Data, TVA Steam Plants, technical monograph No. 55, vol. 2, ch. 1, p. 8, and ch. 6, pp. 10–18). Because of the lack of data on the composition of inventories and because of the relatively small share of inventories in total investment in both countries, no effort was made to estimate ratios for this component of investment. The aggregate ratios for the investment end-use category therefore were obtained by combining the producers' durables and construction ratios according to each country's weights.

For the defense end use, rough aggregate ratios of 5 rubles per dollar with U.S. weights and 4 rubles per dollar with Soviet weights were obtained as follows. A ratio for military pay was calculated by comparing average annual Soviet military pay, in Bornstein, op. cit., with similar data for the United States, in Department of Commerce, Bureau of the Census, "Statistical Abstract of the United States, 1957," Washington, Government Printing Office, 1958, p. 241. Ratios for subsistence were estimated by adjusting downward the household consumption ratios, to take into account the greater relative importance in the military subsistence "basket" of items, such as food products, with lower ruble-dollar ratios. For the remaining components of this end use, such as procurement, operations, and research and development expenditures, the ratios for producers' durables were used, on the assumptions that weapons, with inputs rather similar to those of producers' durables, would have similar ratios and that higher ratios for some of the other items would be offset by lower ratios for others. Aggregate ratios were then derived with each country's weights.

For the Government administration end use, a ratio of 2 rubles per dollar was obtained by comparing the average wage of production and office employees in the U.S.S.R. (in Bornstein, op. cit.) with the average wage of Federal, State, and local government employees, excluding those in State and local education, in the United States (from data in "Survey of Current Business," July 1957, pp. 20–21). This ratio was used both to convert Soviet ruble figures to dollars and to convert U.S. dollar figures to rubles, in the absence of data from which to derive adequate weighted ratios based on each country's weights.

In examining the results shown in table 3, it should be remembered that they are offered only as approximate indications of the relative size of the two national products and their major end-use components. All of the problems and qualifications mentioned in connection with the derivation of the established price figures in table 1 of course apply also to table 3. In addition, the precision of the results in table 3 is limited by the rough character of the ruble-dollar ratio conversions, stemming from the problems encountered in obtaining price data, in matching Soviet and U.S. goods and services, and in deriving satisfactory weights.[10]

In the comparison of gross national product and its chief end-use components in table 3, the size of the U.S.S.R. relative to the United States differs considerably depending on whether the comparison is made in rubles (i.e., at Soviet prices) or in dollars (i.e., at U.S. prices). This difference is simply a manifestation of the fundamental index number problem encountered in both intertemporal and international comparisons and arising from the existence of alternative but equally appropriate weighting systems, corresponding to the Paasche and Laspeyres formulae.[11] Even the extent of the disparity

[10] The methodology and problems involved in ruble-dollar ratio calculations are discussed in Norman M. Kaplan and William L. White, "A Comparison of 1950 Wholesale Prices in Soviet and American Industry," RM-1443, Santa Monica, Calif., the Rand Corp., 1955; Norman M. Kaplan and Eleanor S. Wainstein, "A Comparison of Soviet and American Retail Prices in 1950," RM-1692-1, Santa Monica, Calif., the Rand Corp., 1956; and Abraham S. Becker, "Prices of Producers' Durables in the United States and the U.S.S.R. in 1955," Santa Monica, Calif., the Rand Corp., 1959, RM-2432. For an extensive discussion of the construction of similar price deflators for Western Europe and the United States, see Gilbert and Kravis, op. cit., and Gilbert & Associates, op. cit.

[11] Likewise, there are two sets of answers for the relative purchasing power of the ruble and the dollar in regard to national product, depending on whether the price relationships between the two countries are weighted by the relative quantities of goods and services in Soviet or in U.S. national product.

in results, attributable to differences in the two price structures, is not unexpected. A substantial, although not so great, spread was also found, as a result of differences in price structures, in a comparison of the national products of various Western European countries with that of the United States at their own prices and at U.S. prices.[12]

Likewise, it is not surprising that, for national product as a whole and for its components (except for Government administration),[13] the U.S.S.R. is smaller relative to the United States in the ruble comparison than in the dollar comparison. The explanation lies basically in a negative correlation between the relative prices and relative quantities; that is, goods which have lower relative prices tend to be produced in greater relative quantities in a country. Thus, goods and services with lower relative prices in the United States are, on the average, those which are relatively more abundant in the United States, as compared with the U.S.S.R.; an analogous situation prevails in the U.S.S.R. Consequently, when the two national products are valued at U.S. prices, a greater price weight is given to goods which are relatively more heavily produced in the U.S.S.R. than if Soviet prices are used. Similarly, when the two national products are valued at Soviet prices, a greater weight is given to items which are relatively more heavily produced in the United States, than if U.S. prices are used.[14] When one country's output structure is priced at the other country's price structure, the effect is to apply relatively high prices to relatively large quantities and relatively low prices to relatively small quantities. Thus, the comparison is more favorable to a country when the other country's prices are used for both.[15]

The existence of such a substantial disparity between the results of the ruble and dollar comparisons makes it inadvisable to use either one alone to depict the relative size of the two national products. Preferably, both comparisons should be used. However, because it is sometimes considered cumbersome to deal with two sets of compari-

---

[12] Gilbert & Associates, op. cit., pp. 97–106.

[13] Where separate U.S.-weighted and Soviet-weighted ratios were not used; see notes to table 3.

[14] See in this connection the results of Kaplan and Wainstein, op. cit., pp. 30–31, for the U.S.S.R. relative to the United States; and Gilbert and Kravis, op. cit., pp. 51–59, and Gilbert & Associates, op. cit., pp. 23–24, for several Western European countries relative to the United States.

[15] A quite different matter is involved when a calculation is made of the shares of the various end uses in a country's national product expressed in another country's currency. The results are likely to differ from the shares in a native currency calculation because of differences in the ratios at which the various end uses are converted from the native to the foreign currency (see notes to table 3). Thus, these shares of the several end uses in Soviet gross national product expressed in dollars in table 3 differ from their shares in Soviet gross national product expressed in rubles in the same table (and also from their shares in Soviet gross national product at adjusted rubles prices in table 1). The usual purpose of calculating the shares of end uses in total product is to measure resource allocation patterns in terms of the country's own price structure (at established or adjusted prices), as in table 1. The economic meaning of a calculation of end-use shares in terms of a foreign price structure is not clear. Under certain assumptions, however, the results may be of interest. For example, if U. S. prices were considered more "rational" (i.e., more indicative of scarcity relationships) for the U.S.S.R. than Soviet prices, then the shares of the end uses in Soviet gross national product in dollars would be regarded as more accurately reflecting their true relative importance. This is essentially the position of Colin Clark and Julius Wyler; see Clark, "The Conditions of Economic Progress," 2d ed., London, Macmillan, 1951, ch. IV, and 3d ed., London, Macmillan, 1957, ch. IV; and Wyler, "The National Income of Soviet Russia," Social Research, vol. 13, No. 4, December 1946, pp. 501–518, and "Die Schätzungen des sowjetrussischen Volkseinkommen," Schweizerische Zeitschrift für Volkswirtschaft und Statistik (Zurich), vol. 87, Nos. 5–6, 1951, pp. 1–35. While a dollar valuation of Soviet national product is of course of interest, and in fact necessary, for a comparison of the size of Soviet and United States national products, it is by no means clear that it provides a more reliable basis, than some (adjusted) ruble valuation, for measuring the resource allocation pattern at a given time or the real growth over time of Soviet national product. See Bergson, op. cit., pp. 53–54, and Abram Bergson, "National Income of the Soviet Union," Report No. A–5, Washington, Council for Economic and Industry Research, Inc., 1954, pp. 23–24.

sons, resort is sometimes made to an average of the results produced by the two sets of weights, such as the geometric averages in table 3. Such averages are convenient for various practical purposes, but it should be recognized that they have no unambiguous economic meaning. Where averages alone are presented, they may conceal a significant difference in results, corresponding to substantially different price structures, as in the case of Soviet-United States comparisons. Although the use of averages is often convenient for the sake of simplicity or brevity, a more precise discussion involves reference to both of the original comparisons.

The results in table 3 indicate that in 1955 Soviet gross national product was about one-fourth the U.S. level at Soviet ruble prices and about one-half the U.S. level at U.S. dollar prices. The geometric average of the ruble and dollar comparisons is about two-fifths. The relative size of the two economies (whether compared at Soviet or U.S. prices) differs, however, in regard to the several end-use components of national product.

Aggregate Soviet consumption was about one-fifth of the U.S. level at Soviet prices and about two-fifths at U.S. prices. If allowance is made for the 20 percent difference in population—about 200 million in the U.S.S.R. and 165 million in the United States in 1955—the respective per capita figures are even lower, approximately one-sixth and one-third. Such comparisons for consumption as a whole, however, conceal different relationships between the two countries regarding the various components of consumption, such as food, clothing, durable consumers' goods, etc. For example, Soviet per capita consumption levels are significantly closer to those of the United States in regard to food and basic types of clothing than they are in regard to durable consumers' goods, housing, and personal services.

In the case of investment, Soviet product was substantially larger relative to U.S. product than in the case of consumption; it was about half of the U.S. level at Soviet prices and about two-thirds at U.S. prices. The spread between the ruble and dollar results is not so great as for consumption, indicating less difference in the Soviet and U.S. price structures for investment goods than for consumption goods. As in the case of consumption, however, the aggregate nature of the investment comparison obscures important differences in the relationship between the two countries in regard to different types of investment. Because of the emphasis of the Soviet regime on economic growth, a much larger share of investment is devoted to industry, and a much smaller share to housing and consumer services, in the U.S.S.R. than in the United States. As a result, in 1955 Soviet investment in manufacturing, mining, and public utilities was larger, and Soviet investment in housing was smaller, relative to the U.S. level than the relationship for aggregate investment shown in table 3.

According to table 3, Soviet defense outlays in 1955 were about three-fourths of the U.S. level at Soviet prices and almost equal at U.S. prices. However, because of the especially crude nature of both the initial national accounts estimate for Soviet defense expenditures and the ruble-dollar ratios for this end use, it seems prudent to allow for some understatement of the Soviet level both in rubles and in dollars and to consider Soviet defense outlays as approximately equal to those of the United States. Even if aggregate Soviet and U.S.

outlays for defense are considered equal, however, it does not follow that the size, equipment, or effectiveness of the two military establishments is equal, for a number of reasons.

As in the case of the consumption and investment comparisons, the composition of the defense aggregate must be considered. Although total defense outlays may be equal in the two countries, the same relationship of equality obviously does not apply to all components of defense. The relationship of the two countries certainly differs in regard to troop strength and the various types of missiles, aircraft, ships, and other weapons. In a military contest, Soviet or U.S. superiority in one or more of these component categories of defense could be decisive, despite an accompanying inferiority in other categories. Other cautions must also be kept in mind in appraising national product comparisons of defense. For example, although Soviet and U.S. soldiers are, in this type of comparison, priced at the same pay rates, their productivity (i.e., combat effectiveness) may in fact not be the same. Also, because Soviet soldiers live more modestly than U.S. soldiers, Soviet subsistence outlays per man are less than U.S. outlays. Yet it should not be concluded from such a comparison that the effectiveness of Soviet soldiers is correspondingly below that of their U.S. counterparts. Instead, the U.S.S.R. may in fact support an equally effective soldier at less real cost in terms of resources devoted to his subsistence.

Comparisons of the relative size of the defense components of national product thus do not provide a sufficiently reliable index of the military strength of the two countries. For such an appraisal, other comparisons—of manpower, training, equipment, weapons technology, etcetera—are indispensable. The national product comparison does, however, furnish some corroborative evidence of the relative magnitude of the military programs of the two countries. The conclusion indicated by table 3, of an approximately equivalent military program in the two countries, seems consistent with other information on this question.

Little need be said about Government administration, the residual category in table 3. Outlays for the administrative apparatus concerned with planning, administration, and control in the U.S.S.R. far exceeded Government administration outlays in the United States, where some of the planning and control functions of the U.S.S.R. have no counterpart.

The general conclusions suggested by table 3 may now be summarized briefly in terms of the geometric average results. Although in 1955 the U.S.S.R. had a national product less than half that of the United States, the U.S.S.R. had an approximately equal defense effort and a level of investment about three-fifths that of the United States. In contrast, per capita consumption in the U.S.S.R. was only about one-fourth that in the United States. This performance reflects the desire of the Soviet regime for a strong and advanced military posture and a rapid rate of growth, and its willingness to pursue these objectives at the expense of the consumption level of the population.

GROWTH OF NATIONAL PRODUCT

In order to compare trends in the growth of national product in the U.S.S.R. and the United States, it is desirable to have for both

390 COMPARISONS OF UNITED STATES AND SOVIET ECONOMIES

countries data on national product and its components in constant prices for a series of years. Such data are published for the United States by the Department of Commerce, but comparable data are lacking for the U.S.S.R. Although national product accounts for the U.S.S.R. in current prices are now available for a number of years,[16] they have as yet not been deflated by appropriate price indexes to obtain a constant-price series.

In the absence of such a series, an effort was made for this paper to estimate the growth of Soviet national product from 1950 to 1958 by a sector-of-origin approach. Estimates of the growth of output in the principal sectors of the economy were combined into an aggregate index on the basis of the relative importance of the sectors in national product in 1955. This calculation must be regarded as very rough, because of the difficulties involved in establishing proper sector weights, the use of gross output rather than net output indicators, and the estimates necessary to obtain the indicators used.[17]

In table 4, these results are compared with an index for the United States derived from Department of Commerce data. In table 5, growth trends of Soviet and U.S. national product are shown in terms of average annual rates of growth, derived from table 4. In order to stress the approximate nature of the calculations for the U.S.S.R., the Soviet growth rates in table 5 are shown as ranges, within which the growth rates implicit in the estimated index in table 4 fall.

TABLE 4.—*Indexes of gross national product in the U.S.S.R. and the United States, selected years, 1950–58*

	U.S.S.R [1]	United States [2]
1950	100	100
1955	137	124
1958	170	125

[1] Index of gross national product (GNP) at factor cost. GNP at factor cost = GNP at established prices — indirect taxes + subsidies.
[2] Index of GNP at market prices.

SOURCES AND DERIVATION

U.S.S.R.: The index was constructed by aggregating sector indexes according to their weights in Soviet GNP at factor cost in 1955. The resulting index is shown in the table with 1950 as a base.

The sector weights were obtained by adding estimates of sector depreciation charges to figures for national income by sector of origin in Bornstein, op. cit., summarized in table 2. These charges were estimated by sector from data on amortization rates and capital stock and on the share of amortization charges in total production costs, in various Soviet sources.

For industry, the gross output index of Shimkin (Demetri B. Shimkin and Frederick A. Leedy, "Soviet Industrial Growth," Automotive Industries, vol. 18, No. 1, Jan. 1, 1958, p. 51) was used in preference to the Nutter index of all industrial output (G. Warren Nutter, "Industrial Growth in the Soviet Union," American Economic Review, vol. 48, No. 2, May 1958, p. 402) because the former includes and the latter excludes as estimate for military end items, which are an important component of Soviet industrial production. Although Shimkin uses 1934 value-added weights, based on Hodgman's work, these weights apparently do not yield much different results from 1955 price weights (see Joseph S. Berliner, "Capital Formation and Productivity in the U.S.S.R.," in The Economy of the U.S.S.R., National Academy of Economics and Political Science, Special Publications Series, No. 14, Washington, 1958, p. 6). The Shimkin index was

---

[16] See references in footnote 4.
[17] The construction of the index is discussed in the notes to table 4. The index is for gross national product at factor cost, rather than gross national product at established prices, because only an estimate for depreciation charges was added to the sector figures for national income to obtain sector weights, inasmuch as it was not possible to allocate indirect taxes and subsidies by sector of origin. If it is assumed that the sector weights in gross national product at established prices do not differ greatly from the respective sector weights in gross national product at factor cost, and that the net output indexes are similar to the gross output indexes, then the index for gross national product at established prices will not vary greatly from the present index for gross national product at factor cost. These assumptions do not appear implausible for the short period covered by this calculation.

extended from 1956 to 1958 on the basis of the results for 1956–58 of the official Soviet index and the relationship of the official Soviet index for 1950–56 and the Shimkin index for 1950–56.

For construction, the index used was based on the official Soviet series for state construction work (Vestnik statistiki, No. 4, 1959, p. 93) adjusted slightly to take into account collective farm construction.

The index used for agriculture is the index of Soviet agricultural output net of farm uses (such as seed and feed) based on 1958 prices prepared by Prof. D. Gale Johnson and Mr. Arcadius Kahan. This and alternative indexes prepared by them are presented in their contribution to the present Joint Economic Committee study. They kindly furnished me their results before publication.

For transportation, an index was constructed by weighting ton-kilometer data for the several types of transportation (in Vestnik statistiki, No. 4, 1959, p. 91) by their respective contributions to national income in 1955 (in Bornstein, op. cit.).

The trade index is a composite of a wage bill index, based on employment in state and cooperative trade, and a profits index, based on deflated state and cooperative retail sales. The former was estimated from data in TsSU, Sovetskaia torgovlia, pp. 113–114; TsSU, Narodnoe khoziaistvo SSSR v 1956 godu, pp. 204–205; and TsSU, SSSR v tsifrakh ("The U.S.S.R. in Figures"), Moscow, Gosstatizdat, 1958, p. 313. The latter was estimated from data in TsSU, Narodnoe khoziaistvo SSSR v 1956 godu, pp. 232–233; Sovetskaia torgovlia (magazine), No. 3, 1958, p. 4; Vestnik statistiki, No. 9, 1958, p. 88; and Pravda, Jan. 16, 1959.

For the services sector, indexes of employment were used for health and education (from data in TsSU, Narodnoe khoziaistvo SSSR v 1956 godu, pp. 204–205, and TsSU, SSSR v tsifrakh, p. 313), and a rough estimate of trends in armed forces manpower (based on scattered estimates of Western observers, such as Hanson W. Baldwin, "The Great Arms Race," New York, Praeger, 1958, pp. 37–38) was used for military services.

United States: Index calculated from series for GNP in 1954 dollars in Survey of Current Business, July 1959, pp. 6–7.

TABLE 5.—*Average annual rates of growth of gross national product in the U.S.S.R. and the United States, 1950–58*

	U.S.S.R.	United States
1950–55	6–7	4.3
1955–58	7–8	.5
1950–58	6.5–7.5	2.9

SOURCES AND DERIVATION

U.S.S.R.: Estimated on the basis of table 4, as explained in text.
United States: Computed from original figures, for the terminal years indicated, in the source cited for table 4.

The general conclusion indicated by the comparisons in these tables is striking. Even if allowance is made for the possibility of some overstatement of the Soviet growth rate, it is clear that Soviet national product has grown much more rapidly than U.S. national product in the periods indicated. Comparative growth trends shown for the 1955–58 period are particularly favorable to the U.S.S.R. and unfavorable to the United States, because in 1958 Soviet gross national product was exceptionally high as a result of an extraordinary harvest, while U.S. gross national product showed the full effects of the recent recession in business activity. The comparison for the 1950–55 period probably shows growth rates more representative of a high level of activity in both countries. The comparison for the 1950–58 period, on the other hand, understates the longer term U.S. growth rate somewhat, because it includes the recent recession but not the subsequent recovery from it. A rate of 3 to 4 percent is thus more representative of U.S. national product since 1950. Taking these various factors and qualifications into account, it nevertheless appears that since 1950 Soviet national product has been growing at approximately twice the U.S. rate—at an average annual rate of over 6 percent as compared with a rate of over 3 percent for the United States. These rates apparently represent a continuation of differential trends observed in the growth of Soviet and U.S. national product in the last three decades. A growth rate of 5 to 7 percent has been estimated for the U.S.S.R. during the "more normal" years of this period by various authors,[18] while the U.S. long-term growth rate since 1929 has been between 3 and 4 percent.[19]

As a result of its more rapid growth, Soviet national product has been increasing in size relative to U.S. national product. By combining the figures in table 4 with those in table 3, it is possible to derive an estimate of the change in the relative sizes of Soviet and U.S. national product from 1950 to 1958. In a ruble comparison, Soviet gross national product increased from about one-fifth the U.S. level in 1950 to about one-third in 1958. In a dollar comparison, it rose from a little less than half the U.S. level in 1950 to almost two-thirds in 1958. In terms of the geometric average of the two types of comparisons, Soviet gross national product grew from about one-third the U.S. level in 1950 to a little less than half the U.S. level in 1958. Inasmuch as Soviet gross national product was exceptionally high and U.S. gross national product was depressed in 1958, a 1958 comparison is particularly favorable to the U.S.S.R., as noted above. However, the increase in the relative size of Soviet national product compared to U.S. national product basically reflects the more rapid growth of the Soviet economy.

The reasons for the rapid growth of Soviet national product since 1950 have been analyzed in detail elsewhere and need only be summarized briefly here, as a basis for an estimate of future growth trends.[20] Primary among the factors responsible are the rate and composition of Soviet investment. Not only have the rates of Soviet gross and net investment been high, but, moreover, Soviet investment has been directed mainly toward heavy industry rather than toward consumers' goods industry, agriculture, housing, and consumer services.

Another factor of importance was the rapid growth of the nonagricultural labor force, chiefly from population increase, with little transfer from agriculture (in contrast to the prewar industrialization period and the postwar reconstruction period). In addition, there was continuing technological progress, in part through the adoption of Western technological progress and in part from Soviet technological achievements. Also significant was the increase in agricultural output after Stalin's death, as a result of the expansion of the crop area by more than 20 percent, greater investment in agriculture, and greater incentives to the peasants. Finally, explicit recognition should be given to the willingness of the Soviet leadership to restrain Soviet consumption levels in order to pursue the dual objectives of a rapid rate of growth and a strong military posture. In pursuit of these objectives, the Soviet leaders have used fully (though perhaps not always most efficiently) the resources at their disposal, maintaining a very high and steady rate of utilization of labor and capital, without the

---

[18] Estimates for the U.S.S.R. for 1928–37 and 1948–50 are examined in Gregory Grossman, "National Income," in Abram Bergson (editor) Soviet Economic Growth, Evanston, Ill., Row, Peterson, 1953, pp. 5–11.

[19] Survey of Current Business, July 1959, pp. 6–7.

[20] For a discussion of the factors responsible for past growth, as well as those influencing the future rate of growth, see, Bergson, "Soviet Economic Growth"; Library of Congress, Legislative Reference Service, op. cit.; Gregory Grossman, "Soviet Economy and Soviet World Power," ch. 2 in Columbia University, American Assembly, "International Stability and Progress," New York, 1957; and Grossman's statement in World Economic Growth and Competition, hearings before the Subcommittee on Foreign Economic Policy of the Joint Economic Committee, 84th Cong., 2d sess., Washington, Government Printing Office, 1957, pp. 29–33.

interruptions to production which occur in a market economy such as the United States as a result of business recessions and labor disputes.

It is difficult to estimate with precision what future trends in Soviet national product will be, even for comparatively short periods, such as 5 or 10 years. However, some idea of the probable trend of Soviet national product may be obtained by examining a number of factors in the economy which would tend to depress the rate of growth of national product in the future and, on the other hand, some which would tend to maintain or perhaps even accelerate it.

One set of retarding factors affects investment. The Khrushchev programs to improve the lot of the Soviet consumer by increasing per capita supplies of food and clothing and per capita housing space imply, if not a reduction in the overall rate of investment, a change in its composition which would reduce the share going to the producers' goods industries and increase the shares of agriculture, light industry, and housing. Although investment in the latter increases the output of goods and services, it does not, like investment in the former, provide the means for producing still more investment goods. In addition, as the age of the Soviet capital stock increases, a greater share of gross investment will probably be devoted to replacement of worn out and obsolescent facilities, leaving a smaller share for net investment. Also, investment costs associated with the exploitation of raw materials are likely to increase as it becomes necessary to use lowergrade or less accessible mineral deposits.

In addition, it does not appear likely that the nonagricultural labor force will grow as rapidly in the next few years as in the period since 1950. Annual increments to the labor force will drop sharply in the next 5 years, when the effects of the low birth rates during and shortly after World War II will be felt. In view of the continued emphasis of the Soviet regime on the expansion of agricultural output, no substantial transfer from agricultural to nonagricultural employment seems probable. Moreover, at the same time that annual increments to the nonagricultural labor force are declining, the Soviet regime has promised a reduction in the workweek from 45 to 40 hours by 1962. As a result, no significant increase in the number of man-hours of labor input in the nonagricultural sector appears likely. Thus almost all of the increase in output will have to come from the growth of productivity per man-hour. This will entail not only better job performance but also substantial investment in modernization and automation, intensifying the investment problem described above.

The agricultural sector likewise presents problems for the Soviet economy. A further expansion of the sown area comparable to that obtained during 1954–56 is not possible, because there is virtually no suitable additional land. Increased output will therefore depend on increased yields and on the growth of livestock and dairy production, through increased investment, more efficient management, and greater incentives. It is difficult to estimate how much agricultural output will be increased in the next few years by such measures.

Finally, greater Soviet economic aid to the European satellites, China, and underdeveloped countries outside the bloc may depress the rate of growth of national product, because this aid to a large degree involves the diversion of resources from domestic investment. On the other hand, the present level of Soviet foreign aid is sufficiently small relative to the level of Soviet investment that a substantial increase in the former could be made without a serious effect on the latter and thus on the rate of growth of Soviet national product.

The factors tending, in contrast, to sustain or accelerate the rate of growth can be listed more briefly, although they should not therefore be considered correspondingly less significant than the retarding factors. Of prime importance is the continued concern of the Soviet regime with economic growth, epitomized in the oft-stated Soviet objective of "catching up with and surpassing the United States in per capita output." In view of this objective, a substantial reduction in the rate of investment, or a drastic shift in its composition, in favor of increased consumption levels seems unlikely. Coupled with a continued high rate of investment will be greater emphasis on improvements in technology and on automation, which will tend to increase productivity and the rate of growth. The U.S.S.R. appears to have both the scientific and technical skills and the machine-bulding capacity to develop and produce advanced equipment and processes for modern, automated industry. Finally, allowance must be made for the possibility of greater efficiency in the planning and administration of the Soviet economy. There is ample evidence of Soviet concern with this element in economic growth in the changes in the past few years in planning methods, the reorganization of industry and agriculture, and the extensive discussions among Soviet economists about improvements in the price system. If these and similar measures are successful in increasing the efficiency of Soviet economic planning and management, they will help maintain or perhaps even raise the Soviet growth rate.

It is difficult to assess the likely future impact of the Soviet military program on the growth of national product. Clearly, the defense end use competes with the investment end use for resources, both in a general way and specifically for the output of such industries as machine-building, metal-working, chemicals, and electronics. If there were an across-the-board reduction in the Soviet military effort, say as a result of a disarmament agreement, the probable effect would be to reallocate resources from defense to investment (and possibly to a lesser degree to consumption and to foreign aid) and thereby to increase the rate of growth. However, if this reduction entailed primarily manpower, while emphasis on the development and production of aircraft, missiles, and atomic weapons continued, the favorable effect on the rates of investment and economic growth would be much less. Similarly, if the U.S.S.R. expanded its efforts in the missile and atomic weapon fields, this would tend to depress the rates of investment and economic growth. Hence, the classification of the Soviet military effort as a retarding or accelerating factor in regard to the future rate of growth of Soviet gross national product depends on which of many possible assumptions one makes about the future scale and nature of this effort.

Where does the balance lie between the factors tending to depress the rate of growth of Soviet national product in the next 5 or 10 years and those tending to maintain or accelerate it? To this writer, it appears that there may be some decline in the average annual rate of growth, say from 7 percent in the 1950–58 period to 6 or 6.5 percent in the next 5 or 10 years. Even with such a decline, however, the rate of Soviet economic growth would remain high, substantially exceeding a probable U.S. rate of, say, 4 percent.

One consequence of the higher Soviet rate, of course, would be an increase in the size of Soviet national product relative to that of the United States. For example, if it is assumed that Soviet gross national product grows at an average annual rate of 6 percent and U.S. gross national product at an average annual rate of 4 percent, Soviet gross national product would increase from about 46 percent of the U.S. level in 1958 to about 53 percent in 1965.[21]

Such an increase in the size of the Soviet economy compared with that of the United States need not in itself be considered alarming. More important is the significance of a rapid rate of economic growth for the world position of the U.S.S.R. A larger, and rapidly growing, national product will provide the U.S.S.R. a greater economic base for a strong military posture, for further scientific and technical progress, for greater foreign trade and foreign aid, and for an improvement in the living conditions of the Soviet population. Furthermore, an uninterrupted high rate of growth will be prominently cited in Soviet efforts to convince underdeveloped countries that they should emulate the Soviet "model" in their development programs. In all of these ways, a high rate of growth will strengthen the economic, military, and political position of the U.S.S.R. on the world scene. The consequences of this enhanced Soviet position will be of great importance to the United States and the rest of the free world.

---

[21] Both percentages are the geometric averages of the respective ruble and dollar comparisons.

ESTIMATING THE SOVIET NATIONAL INCOME [1]

IT is almost a century since the first estimate of the Russian national income was published in the *Journal of the Royal Statistical Society* of 1860, and fifty years since the appearance of the first estimates by a Russian economist. The Central Statistical Administration of the Soviet Union has prepared national accounts each year since the First World War; in addition, there are now nearly a score of estimates presented by scholars working in Britain or America, culminating in the recent appearance of Professor Bergson's comparative accounts for five selected years between 1928 and 1948.[2] It is thus an appropriate time to try to review the progress made in estimating the national income of the world's second industrial power and to compare the magnitudes, composition and methodologies of the computations.

The emergence of a considerable body of foreign academic work parallel-ing the data prepared by the national statistical office is unprecedented with respect to any other country and, although testimony to the natural interest the rest of the world shows in the Soviet economy, requires further explana-tion. Reference is made in the first section of the present study to certain statistical procedures of the official series which seriously affect intertemporal and interspatial comparisons, while the second and third sections consider the extent to which the foreign calculations seek to adjust Soviet data to different methodological and conceptual bases. As a measure of long-term change, the official Soviet figures suffer from the employment for nearly a quarter of a century of a constant-price structure at variance with actual factor rewards (and in the even longer term from improvements in accuracy); as a measure of short-term change and of sector contributions, they con-tinue to be influenced by a price valuation reflecting a highly discriminatory tax scale. The shorter answer, however, is that the Soviet official data are almost wholly unpublished. The last full account was published in 1929, and the last summary breakdown (by six main sectors) available is for 1937. In the twenty years since, the only data published have been totals [3]—

[1] The author is a member of the Secretariat of the United Nations Economic Commission for Europe at Geneva. The views expressed herein, however, are his personal views and should not be interpreted as those of the Organisation.

[2] Abram Bergson, *Soviet National Income and Product in 1937* (New York: Columbia University, 1953); Abram Bergson and Hans Heymann, Jr., *Soviet National Income and Product 1940–48*, and Oleg Hoeffding, *Soviet National Income and Product in 1928* (Both New York: Columbia University, 1954).

[3] Until 1950 the money aggregates (in 1926/27 prices) were published. Subsequently, only index numbers (measured in 1951 prices) have been released. The position has not been altered by the publication during 1956 of three Soviet statistical handbooks. The index numbers of national income are reproduced but no breakdowns are quoted. The handbooks nevertheless are of some use as sources for composing national accounts: they provided data directly for four (and indirectly, in conjunction with other information, for sixteen) entries in a set of accounts for the year 1955 prepared by the present writer (not yet published) and containing some seventy in-dependent entries.

at constant prices plus two isolated references (for 1940 and 1950) to the percentage breakdown (in current prices) between accumulation and consumption. The efforts of western scholars must primarily be viewed, therefore, as the provision of the statistical facts needed in a study of the Soviet economy rather than as an attempt to improve upon the work of Soviet statisticians, for it is clear that the official accounts must contain more accurate data than any outside estimate.

I

Sergei Prokopovicz published the first Russian estimate of the national income of his country exactly fifty years ago.[1] Inspired by Marxism,[2] he adopted that definition of the national income which excludes services not intimately associated with material production, a concept to which all estimates subsequently made in the Soviet Union adhered. Both statistical and territorial limitations inhibited Prokopovicz's computations, since the basic data, especially the agricultural, were collected by officials of a low level of literacy and covered only European Russia. He allowed for some shortcomings—e.g., for deliberate crop under-estimation by peasants by adding a sampled margin of 10%—but, faced with other inadequacies, he adopted very rough guesses with spurious accuracy. For example, he used the product of employment and per capita output in factory industry to the last kopek for urban handicrafts [3] and passenger carriage, non-housing construction and the retailing of excise goods: in aggregate the sectors thus estimated contributed one-tenth of the total and one-fifth of the non-agricultural income. For his study of gross national product in 1913,[4] Prokopovicz was able to use somewhat better basic statistics, in particular the 1916 census of livestock and Kevdin's survey of Russian fisheries (1915), but handicrafts, urban passenger carriage and trade in excise goods were no better treated than for 1900. His total of 11·8 billion (i.e., thousand million) roubles for European Russia (inflated, without detailed explanation, to 16·4 billions for the whole Empire) revalued in 1900 prices showed a 39% volume increase, within which industry had risen by 62%.[5]

[1] S. N. Prokopovicz, " Opyt ischislenia narodnago dokhoda v 1900 g." in Trudy Imp. Volnago Ekonomicheskago Obshchestva, 1906. Prokopovicz mentioned an earlier estimate of agricultural and industrial income by the Minister of Finance S. Yu. Vitte in 1897 (but this was so rough and inaccurate that it may be ignored) and another, published in St. Petersburg in 1896 and relating to 1894, by V. Pokrovsky incidental to a study on the Russian balance of trade (and whose income-per-head estimate was of the same order of magnitude as Prokopovicz's).

[2] He was deported from the Soviet Union in 1922, having formally broken with the orthodox Marxists in 1899, and is described by Soviet Marxists as a " bourgeois economist " (cf. A. Paltsev, Natsionalny dokhod pri kapitalizme (Moscow, 1954), p. 33). His estimates were accepted by Gosplan for 1900 and 1913 after deductions for depreciation and the reduced area of the country (cf. Gosplan, Kontrolnye tsifry narodnogo khozyaistva S.S.S.R. na 1928–1929 god (Moscow, 1929), p. 68).

[3] Nevertheless, he accepted for rural handicrafts an outside estimate of one-tenth this value.

[4] S. N. Prokopovicz, Opyt ischislenia narodnago dokhoda 50 gub. evropeiskoi Rossii v 1900–1915 gg. (Moscow, 1918).

[5] Prokopovicz also produced in the same study an approximate breakdown between incomes of the " working " and the " owning " classes.

The accuracy of Prokopovicz's estimate for 1913 [1] is of continuing significance to the extent that, only slightly adjusted by Gosplan, it is still frequently used by Soviet writers as the base year for national income index numbers. The official Soviet calculations have continued to use broadly the same coverage concept as Prokopovicz,[2] but this definition has not been without its critics in the Soviet Union. Thus N. Ya. Suzdaltsev [3] proposed to the Central Statistical Administration the inclusion of passenger transport; N. M. Krasnolobov [4] would also add private use of posts and telegraphs, and commercially-sold services; M. Bor [5] urged the inclusion of transport and communications used by individuals, and the exclusion of trading income not associated with a real appreciation of the worth of the traded goods (*e.g.*, retail profits and taxes, margin between cost of imports and receipts from exports); S. Turetsky [6] opposed the exclusion of education, public health and entertainment; while Kursky [7] strongly criticised on this score a text-book prepared by the Institute of Economics and argued for the inclusion of passenger transport, communal services, education, medicine and even Government administration.

Initially, official Soviet computations approached the national income from both the production and the expenditure aspects.[8] Computations on both methods were in fact made by Gosplan for only six years (1925–30), but they are of interest to the extent that their mutual relationship is precisely the opposite of that shown for the United Kingdom in not wholly dissimilar economic conditions: [9] the expenditure method showed a larger

[1] Two other estimates of the 1913 income (area and prices of that year) were 15 billion roubles (net of depreciation) by M. N. Sobolev, *Ekonomicheskoe Obrezenie*, No. 1, 1925, p. 48, who did not state his methods, and 17·6 billion roubles by A. Veinstein, *Sotsialisticheskoe Khozyaistvo*, No. 4, 1926, p. 8, who describes his figure as a revision of Prokopovicz's.

[2] " The national income of the U.S.S.R. is composed of the following branches of material production: industry, building, agriculture, transport (of freight), communications (serving the productive sector) and that part of trade which fulfils a productive function in circulation (packing, sorting, storage, movement) " (D. A. Allakhverdyan, *Natsionalny dokhod S.S.S.R.* (Moscow, 1952), p. 37). Other Soviet economists who defend this definition are V. Sobol, A. Petrov and A. Paltsev.

[3] *Vestnik Statistiki*, No. 1, 1954, p. 86.

[4] *Planirovanie i uchët narodnogo dokhoda* (Moscow and Leningrad, 1940), pp. 14–19.

[5] *Voprosy Ekonomiki*, No. 10, 1954, pp. 82–3.

[6] *Planovoe Khozyaistvo*, No. 1, 1940, p. 105.

[7] In a review of D. I. Chernomordik, *Narodny dokhod S.S.S.R.* (Moscow, 1939), in *Planovoe Khozyaistvo*, No. 10, 1939, pp. 92–3.

[8] " The study and computation of the national income make it impossible to give exclusive preference to one or other of these methods—we can approach the study of the size, structure and change of the U.S.S.R. national income only if we adopt and adapt both " (Gosplan, *Kontrolny tsifry, loc. cit.*).

[9] The comparison may be made with the United Kingdom from 1947 onwards, also both a post-war period and beginning with the re-attainment of the pre-war volume of national income. Although sector and factor proportions were widely different, the institutional structures (" productive relations " in Marxist usage) of the two countries were, at the time, both marked by predominant private enterprise co-existent with some recently-nationalised basic sectors. Roughly speaking, the price mechanism had a similar degree of operative significance at the beginning of each period, subsequently decreasing in the Soviet Union and increasing in the United Kingdom.

annual rate of increase in the Soviet Union when the growth of income was relatively large, whereas the converse was true of the United Kingdom.

During the twenties some national-income estimates using both approaches were published by private individuals,[1] but when subsequently the comprehensiveness of the State statistical services superseded the need for the collection of data by such independent workers,[2] the official estimates were confined to the production side. Krasnolobov mentions, only to reject, a further variant, summation by end-user: end-use aggregation, he explains,[3] would have no place for harvest losses or abandoned construction sites, and its price structure is very different from that used in national-product summation.[4]

Since the credit and tax reforms of 1930, the Soviet fiscal system has been such as to obscure its comparability with Western national-income estimates either at factor cost or at market prices. The official Soviet view is that in a socialist society factor cost and market-price valuations are identical, for the division of the margin between selling price and input costs in a State-owned establishment [5] ("turnover tax," "profit contribution to the budget," "retained profits," "Directors Fund," etc.) is guided by administrative convenience, not by explicit charges for capital or land. Some western commentators accept this contention,[6] others concede it in part,[7] while others regard it as outright catachresis.[8] An inversion of Hicks' postulate that a welfare appraisal requires market prices and a productivity appraisal factor cost [9] could, perhaps, be based on the predominance of the productivity motive. Although the Soviet Central Statistical Administration reports the national-income index under the head "Growth of the National Income and Improvement in the Material and Cultural Living Standards of the Nation," the definition used excludes a wide range of services obviously adding to welfare, and Soviet text-books always tend to stress the productivity implications.[10]

---

[1] L. N. Litoshenko, *Narodny dokhod* (Moscow, 1925), from the expenditure side; P. I. Popov (ed.) *Balans narodnogo khozyaistva Soyuza S.S.R. 1923/24 g.* (Moscow, 1926), from the production side. M. N. Sobolev, *op. cit.*, p. 53, and A. Veinstein, *op. cit.*, p. 9, produced production method index numbers, for 1923 and 1925/26 respectively, in constant prices on a 1913 base.

[2] Controversy on coverage or valuation procedure has nevertheless not resulted in the publication of estimates alternative to the official series.

[3] Krasnolobov, *op. cit.*, pp. 79–80.

[4] M. Bor, *op. cit.*, pp. 81–2, states that the production method is still the only method used, but argues for the computation of " utilised national income " (*i.e.*, excluding losses).

[5] If the majority of industrial co-operatives are eventually taken over by the State, as was suggested by the Chairman of the Council of Ministers (*Pravda*, July 17, 1955), State enterprises will control virtually the whole economy outside collective and private farming.

[6] Maurice Dobb, *Soviet Economic Development Since 1917* (London, 1948), p. 266.

[7] A. Bergson, *op. cit.*, p. 58.

[8] Alec Nove, *Soviet Studies*, January 1955, pp. 250–6.

[9] J. R. Hicks, " The Valuation of Social Income," *Economica*, May 1950, p. 124. For a proper measure of welfare Hicks was in fact prepared virtually to adopt the Soviet income definition and exclude public services (*ibid.*, p. 115).

[10] *E.g.*, T. Ryabushkin, *Ocherki po ekonomicheskoy statistike* (Moscow, 1950), Ch. 3.

Soviet practice is made the more acceptable to western statisticians by definitions offered by Nicholson and Kuznets. In a recent article the former reached the conclusion " that, except for any indirect taxes that may be imposed after the final stage of production, national expenditure at market prices is in fact equal to national expenditure at factor cost, if the latter is correctly defined." [1] Since Soviet indirect taxes are imposed during production, this identity may be established for the Soviet Union and the use of market prices vindicated for both welfare and productivity objectives of gross product estimation. Nicholson proceeds to the paradox that although total product should be valued at market prices, the relative contribution of each sector is correctly to be measured in factor rewards, *i.e.*, gross output exclusive of taxes *less* cost of inputs inclusive of taxes. The components of such a computation are, in fact, prepared by the Soviet Statistical Administration but are not so used. Each Soviet industrial enterprise (the procedure for other sectors differs radically only for agriculture) reports its output [2] in tax-free wholesale prices (monthly in constant prices and annually in current prices), as well as its expenditure subdivided by materials, fuel, energy, wages and amortisation. Summation of these enterprise outputs (including thereby outputs which are inputs of other enterprises) gives a tax-free gross output of industry used to measure the rate of growth of industrial output. [3] For the global value of industrial output, the Statistical Administration adds turnover taxes, [4] deducting duplicated inputs for the net contribution to national income. Although the concept used in the national accounts is thus value-added plus indirect tax, the Nicholson-type measure could be simply computed if the tax-free outputs were used instead of tax-inclusive outputs. The Statistical Administration has recognised that the levying of turnover tax almost exclusively upon consumer goods distorts the relative contribution of this sector [5] to global industrial output (without, however, admitting the same effect in the re-

---

[1] J. L. Nicholson, ECONOMIC JOURNAL, June 1955, p. 219. He points out that the " factor cost " of previous usage is better called " factor reward," since it will differ from the correctly defined " factor cost " if the price paid by the user incorporates a tax or subsidy.

[2] Net of intra-enterprise duplication. The turnover gross of intra-enterprise duplication was computed for industry as a whole until 1935, but the figure had, of course, no economic significance. Certain exceptions are made for vertically integrated enterprises, a list of which is given by A. I. Ezhov, *Promyshlennaya statistika* (Moscow, 1954), p. 80. Ezhov envisages a computation net of intra-industry duplication (" sometimes called the ' real ' method "), but does not imply that it is used in current Soviet practice.

[3] In constant prices: until 1927 prices of 1911 or 1912, from 1927 to 1950 in 1926/27 prices, from 1950 to 1955 in prices of January 1, 1952, and for 1955 to 1960 in prices of July 1, 1955.

[4] The use of different aggregates for the rate of growth and for global value appears to date from the reform of industrial index methodology whereby 1952 prices replaced the obsolete 1926/27 prices. The first mention of the new usage seems to be by M. S. Urinson in A. I. Petrov (ed.), *Kurs ekonomicheskoi statistiki* (Moscow, 1954), p. 178; and was clearly spelt out by S. Genin, *Voprosy Ekonomiki*, No. 8, 1955, p. 71. This change helps to explain why, since the index reform, only rates of change and not global output values have been published.

[5] And between consumer-good industries by imposition at one stage only (*e.g.*, baking and confectionery enterprises pay no tax because the levy is made on flour-milling and sugar-refining).

lative contributions of industry and agriculture to national product), and each industry's outputs and inputs [1] are computed free of turnover tax. At least one Sovier writer, Bor (*op. cit.*), has gone farther and has called for national accounts in which the relative sector contributions are free not only of turnover taxes but also of profits taxes (which are assessed on a scale similarly discriminating against consumer goods). In order not to alter the aggregate from its presently-defined magnitude, Bor would then treat taxes as payments for government services. This is tantamount to adopting a much decried definition proposed some years ago by Kuznets.[2] Sector contributions are further altered by the Soviet calculation of farm consumption at the " average realised price " of cash sales, since these are depressed by procurement prices. This practice, moreover, overstates the rate of income growth, for, as labour moves from agriculture to industry, some farm produce is transferred from valuation at levels heavily weighted by low procurement prices to valuation in prices incorporating (or, on farm markets influenced by) high rates of turnover tax. As a solution another Soviet author, Braginsky,[3] has suggested the computation of farm consumption at retail prices.

Valuation procedure has been a further cause of divergence between accounted and real contributions to national income to the extent that constant price bases have been unsatisfactory. Current-priced sector contributions are deflated to base year prices [4] (a combination of 1912 and 1913 prices until 1929, 1926/27 prices from 1926 to 1951, 1951 prices from 1951 to 1955 and 1955 prices for 1956 to 1960). The inflation of the rate of growth induced by the use of the 1926/27 price lists [5] still vitiates comparison

[1] This is made clear by Genin, *op. cit.*, p. 73. A less-explicit reference to the practice by A. I. Gozulov, *Ekonomicheskaya statistika* (Moscow, 1953), p. 183, led Nove (*op. cit.*, p. 256) to believe taxes on incorporated materials were not deducted. Nove saw the absence of corrections for taxes on materials and for subsidies as the sole obstacles to considering these tax-free totals as factor-cost elements for the national income. This is not the case, as the totals are not " value-added " but gross of duplication.

[2] " Total factor costs would equal total payments to all factors net of all taxes, plus direct services rendered by government to individuals and additions to capital under government auspices. This sum of returns to all factors in the economy would at the same time equal the value of net output at market prices " (S. Kuznets, *Review of Economics and Statistics*, August 1948, p. 159). He regarded this, however, as only a rough, first approximation.

[3] B. Braginsky, *Vestnik Statistiki*, No. 2, 1955, p. 20.

[4] The procedure, which varies from sector to sector, is critically described by Paul Studenski (*Studies in Income and Wealth*, VIII, 1946, and, with Julius Wyler, *American Economic Review*, May 1947) and by Nove (*op. cit.*, pp. 267–73); until 1951 construction seems to have been included at current prices without adjustment.

[5] Soviet and other criticisms of the 1926/27 prices are too well known for repetition here (see, in particular, Donald Hodgman, *Soviet Industrial Production, 1928–51* (Cambridge, Mass., 1954), pp. 8–17). Alexander Gerschenkron has shown (*Review of Economics and Statistics*, May 1955, pp. 127–8) from both American and Soviet data that very much higher rates of growth are shown by index numbers of engineering output when based on price structures pertaining to earlier periods of industrialisation. Ira Scott (*ibid.*, November 1952, pp. 386–7) had pointed out that this form of index-number bias was not uniform to all industry, and Gerschenkron shows the bias to be phenomenal only for machinery. The bias—as will be indicated below—seems generally to affect national product estimates.

between the official series before and after 1950, for the only retrospective repricing undertaken was for the link year needed to splice the two indexes. The 1951 base prices are in themselves more reflective of real factor rewards than their predecessors but still germinate, so far as industry and transport are concerned, two seeds of distortion. The less important is the evolution of production since 1951 (introduction of new goods not produced, and consequently not priced, in 1951 and changes in the pattern of cost relationships).[1] The more important is the temporary abandonment of the full-cost principle in 1950. Industrial wholesale prices and freight rates were raised in 1949 to allow for the elimination of subsidies by 1950 and were deliberately sighted slightly below current average full costs (*i.e.*, they were based on the planned costs for 1950). In 1950, however, although costs had not fallen to the extent required, two sets of price cuts were made—in January and July—embracing even goods whose average cost already exceeded price (*e.g.*, timber).[2] The price lists introduced on July 1, 1955, are officially reported not only correct for the first group of divergencies but will apparently make a return to the full cost principle.[3]

II

The estimates of Soviet income prepared abroad fall into two groups: those which use a rouble valuation (predominantly studies of static structure) and those which are valued in foreign currencies (and attempt primarily interspatial comparisons).

The rouble valuations are dominated by the work of Bergson and his two collaborators.[4] Bergson's aim was to extricate as many components of the national accounts as possible from Soviet sources, to estimate the others and to adapt these values at current transaction prices [5] to a theoretically conceived " adjusted factor cost standard." Bergson envisaged this standard as, under certain assumptions, satisfying both a welfare criterion (for which commodity values are proportionate to marginal utilities,[6] discounted

---

[1] As Genin, *op. cit.*, p. 74, makes specific references to these points, their effect cannot be wholly insignificant.

[2] The pricing policy changes of 1949 and 1950 were observed respectively by the present writer (ECONOMIC JOURNAL, March 1950, pp. 89–90) and by Nove (*op. cit.*, pp. 260–1).

[3] The scattered evidence for this view cannot be detailed in the present paper, but includes the price indexes (1955 over 1952) for certain products given in *Zasedanie Verkhovnogo Soveta S.S.S.R.* (Moscow, 1955), p. 242, and the evolution of costs as quoted in the annual plan reports and elsewhere.

[4] Of the three studies noted at the beginning of the present article, that for 1937 was originally published in the *Quarterly Journal of Economics*, May and August 1950. The revisions in the final monograph were mainly confined to a different treatment of subsidies.

[5] In 1928 most transactions responded to a freely functioning price mechanism, but for the later years studied this was probably true only of direct sales from farmer to consumer (now comprising about one-fifth of urban food supplies). Bergson has subsequently been elaborating price indexes to link these current-valued magnitudes: the first instalment of his study, written in collaboration with Roman Bernaut and Lynn Turgeon, on the prices of basic industrial products during 1928–50, was published in the *Journal of Political Economy*, August 1956.

[6] Interpreting this, if necessary, as the preference schedules of the planning authorities.

in the case of investment goods for time-preference) and an efficiency criterion (for which the price of any two commodities must vary inversely with the ratio of the marginal productivities of a given factor in each of them). On this standard, factor prices, on the one hand, reflect the resource allocation which would take place with a variation in the ratio between the marginal utilities of any commodities and, on the other hand, being uniform between users, correspond to relative factor productivities on the average in the economy. In application to the Soviet accounts Bergson concentrated upon the adjustments to Soviet market prices for meeting an efficiency criterion—viz., a net charge for capital (conventionally amortised), a rent corresponding to the differential returns on superior land, a wage to labour correlated with productivity and disutility, and non-discriminatory commodity pricing. Wiles [1] has demonstrated a defect in this procedure in that the Soviet wage structure significantly diverges from the pattern implied by existing scarcity relationships; in a comment on this criticism, Mrs. Robinson [2] has pointed out that there is no more rationality in the current capitalist solution of the attraction (expulsion) of labour by expanding (contracting) trades via wage inflation (depression), so that Bergson did not advance his case by equating Soviet with capitalist wage differentials. In fact, the Soviet wage and market-price systems are reasonably satisfactory measures of a Bergson welfare criterion; the other Bergson adjustments of factor remunerations reflect, however, an efficiency criterion.

This hybrid nature of the underlying criteria clouds the meaning of Bergson's final accounts, but the actual adaptations to Soviet-priced valuations other than those needed to reduce to conventional factor-cost (by eliminating the turnover tax,[3] and subsidies) are quantitatively small [4] and reduce to three. For the first adaptation, farm produce sold direct by the grower to the consumer is reduced to State prices free of tax, but the factor remuneration to the producer is maintained by raising agricultural procurement prices in the same amount.[5] Secondly, earnings in 1940, 1944 and 1948 in farm and military employment are raised to the parity with com-

---

[1] *Soviet Studies*, October 1955. He is less than just in claiming that neither established nor Bergson-adjusted prices allow anything for land and capital charges. The differential assessments of compulsory deliveries and planned profits may be inadequate payments for rent and interest, but they do form part of final price.

[2] *Ibid.*, January 1956.

[3] Only Hoeffding eliminated all indirect taxes. In the interests of accuracy (and Nove, *Review of Economics and Statistics*, May 1955, has criticised the spurious accuracy of some of their rougher computations carried to two decimals), the other studies could have done the same. Their exclusion in 1948 would reduce the share of civilian consumption in " adjusted " gross national product from 43·1 to 42·7%.

[4] George Jaszi (*American Economic Review*, March 1954) criticised Bergson for claiming to avoid the United States Department of Commerce's " national income at factor cost " when his accounts differ so little from this concept and when his computation, using the Department of Commerce concept, is in fact erroneous.

[5] This is the main adjustment made for multiple pricing. Bergson and Heymann (p. 62) have performed a signal service in proving from Soviet sources that purchases on military account are not—as is often suggested—made more cheaply than on civilian account.

parable work in other sectors believed to have existed in 1937; however, Hoeffding considered such a correction for 1928 as " altogether too speculative an undertaking " (p. 71). Finally, with some augmentation, recorded net profits and depreciation allowances [1] are used as the charge for capital and its amortisation.[2] When reporting that " regrettably Soviet sources have little to say on the principles according to which profits are fixed," Bergson does not refer to the presumption that a more efficient plant (which is usually more capital-intensive) is expected to earn more profits than its fellow producers or that profit margins in capital-intensive industries (*e.g.*, electricity generation) are set above the average for industry as a whole. This is far from implying a uniform ratio of profits to capital throughout the economy—which is not the case even after the reforms of 1949—but it is noteworthy that the sum of net profits amount to about 7% of the authors' estimate of fixed capital, and they take 8% as the appropriate standard.[3] The essence of the authors' adjustments is not, however, a correction to the average return on capital but to its distribution between sectors, since in the years studied some were absolved from profit (quasi-interest) charges, while others made disproportionately high payments.

The accounts are modelled on those prepared for the United States of America by the Department of Commerce, a choice justified by the interest of comparisons between the two major world powers. In one respect a case can be made out for slight divergence from the model, viz., in the treatment of counterpart funds derived from sale of Lease-Lend and reparations deliveries (significant in 1944 [4] and 1948 respectively) as customs revenue, and thus as domestic product. Bergson followed the Department of Commerce in its more recent accounts by abandoning depletion allowances, but the justification of this as being also Soviet practice is not quite accurate.[5]

In the case of the first three the choice of years is irreproachable—1928 was the first year of the First Five-year Plan, 1937 the first year of the Third (with its " New Deal " for the consumer and its reformed price structure) and 1940 the last pre-war year. Bergson and Heymann have incidentally

---

[1] Bergson and Heymann have not, however, observed that about half Soviet depreciation charges are in fact a savings device for paying repair bills. In consequence, the true depreciation charges recorded—currently little more than 1% of the stock of productive capital (including that against which no depreciation is charged)—were even further below their " correct depreciation charge " of 3·5% than they imagined.

[2] Interest payments as such by Soviet enterprises are virtually ignored, but interest-bearing loans at present cover about one-tenth of net investment.

[3] The difference is not significant, as the capital estimate was obtained by applying to a value in " 1945 prices " a capital-goods price index computed by Jasny (*Soviet Prices of Producers Goods* (Stanford, Calif., 1952)), which is not only perforce based on a narrow range of quotations but is of but partial relevance to the 1945 price lists (which were constructed by applying price, productivity and wage change-coefficients to the " 1936 prices " used for investment valuation in the Third Five-year Plan).

[4] Lease-Lend supplies are shown to have represented 5% of the 1944 gross national product.

[5] Enterprises working natural resources other than the commoner minerals are required, by charging scarcity-reflective prices, to earn a super-profit for the State; for timber-cutting the charge is in the form of a direct fee, but it was small until 1949, when it was tripled.

very usefully codified the territorial coverage of the data (both contemporary and post-war published) concerning 1940 [1]—the areas incorporated between September 1939 and August 1940 having added one-eighth to the Soviet population. The 1944 study is of small interest and was included " as a war year of high military output " (p. 17) presumably because the United States Air Force was among the sponsors of the research. Not only are data scanty for the year (though there are more for 1944 than for other war years), but the computations lead in some instances to unreal results. Thus the earnings of collective farmers, assessed as better on average than those of (mainly urban) wage-earners in 1940, are put at 6% below wage earnings in 1944: under conditions of stringent rationing of urban consumers (at one period the ration card for the lowest category of consumer was valid only for grits and matches) it would seem to be obvious that, at least in terms of the maintenance of a normal consumption pattern, the peasant is at an advantage. Similarly, 1944 military earnings (inclusive of subsistence) are held to have been below average civilian wages by very much more than the pre-war differential at a time when rations for the Armed Forces were the highest in the scale. Nor is the final year selected, 1948, an ideal post-war year for the purposes of the study, principally because it was the year of maximum divergence from the criteria required by Bergson's own " adjusted factor cost standard." The reforms which came into effect on January 1, 1949 proscribed the subsidy system (a few remaining exceptionally), fixed wholesale prices to cover costs and what could be termed capital charges (prices included an average profit of 2–5%, the more efficient firms to earn more than the mean) and initiated a downward trend in costs which has continued to the present. This downward trend, together with an overhaul of amortisation norms in 1950, brought depreciation charges nearer to the theoretical ideal (i.e., that, summed over the asset life, they should equal original cost).[2] Later reforms, from 1953 onwards, have done much to eliminate other factor-price disparities. Compulsory delivery quotas, supplementary State purchases and machine-tractor station fees have been transformed squarely into Ricardian rent, free of the previous tax on efficiency. Factor services in agriculture—undervalued in comparison with other sectors since the late twenties—were better remunerated by virtue of a series of laws and decrees, of which the first was promulgated in August 1953, and which have continued to the time of writing. Finally, work began in 1955 to bring labour remuneration more into line with efficiency and disutility criteria in industry,[3] construction and agriculture.

[1] Their evidence on the coverage of the agricultural data is slight, but better proof is to be found in the sown-area statistics for 1940 published in 1941, which may be shown to comprise the whole of the end-1940 territory, whereas those for the same year published after the war exclude the Bialystok region (incorporated in 1939 but retroceded to Poland in 1945).

[2] Bergson, p. 59, stresses the divergence from this ideal caused by inflation and overestimation of service life in the years studied.

[3] Official statements foreshadowing these reforms have shown that, contrary to the views expressed by Bergson and Heymann (p. 58) on post-war developments, the 1940 decree on labour

In as comprehensive a piece of research as these three studies, requiring the discovery [1] and interpretation of statistics covering the whole of the Soviet economy, it is inevitable that some small errors can be discovered, but they are very few indeed.   Bergson seems misinformed in stating (p. 113) that as premia from the Directors Fund are already included in wage bills, there is some double-counting in the computed gross national product, for Gozulov [2] makes it clear that these premia are excluded. Bergson refers (p. 117) to an inconsistency in Soviet sources between figures of working capital and attributes it " very likely " to a difference in coverage. It is more probable that one set of figures excludes and the other set includes the so-called " excess working capital," which has to be transferred to the budget at the end of the year.   Finally, he finds (p. 122) the scope of State expenditure on " forestry " unclear, since " lumbering generally is included under industry " :   the outlays are on forest services (fire prevention, re-afforestation, seedling nurseries, etc.).   Bergson and Heymann wrongly assume (p. 74) that Soviet statistics of fixed capital stock are net of depreciation, whereas the Statistical Administration, primarily concerned with assessing useful capacity, allows only for retirements.   They could have gone further in suggesting (p. 132) that rents may not much exceed operating expenses and depreciation, as Soviet text-books on housing administration show that rents do not always cover depreciation.   Moreover, they use the official scale relating rent to the tenant's wage to compute (p. 135) for 1944 and 1948 respectively rentals of 1.50 and 1.90 roubles per square metre, although the regulations set a maximum of 1.45 roubles.   It may also be recorded, though the information making the computation possible was not published until after the studies had appeared, that the 1948 urban housing stock was some 310 million square metres of living area,[3] compared with their figure (p. 132) of 261 million.   On the other hand, later information has shown the accuracy of their estimates of wages and retail turnover.[4] Subsequent official statements have also vindicated their assessment of the place of the budget surplus " as the counterpart of bank financed working capital and dishoarding by economic organizations and house-holds " (p. 215), although they were misled (p. 214), presumably by the pre-war decline of long-term bank credit (41% of bank loans in 1933, 13% in 1940, 15% in 1950), into concentrating attention on short-term credits.

A methodology similar to Bergson's had earlier been developed by Jasny.

direction had become a dead letter, and that the correlation of wages and productivity had been impaired in order to maintain wage/disutility relationships.

[1] Something like an official statistical abstract was available only for 1928 and 1937, and in the case of the latter year was restricted in scope.

[2] *Op. cit.*, pp. 282–3.

[3] Nor were they to know that, beginning with 1948, global housing data began to be quoted in terms of useful area: they assumed that the previous practice of measurement in living area (*i.e.*, excluding kitchens, bathrooms, etc.) was still in force.

[4] Cf. the present writer in *Soviet Studies*, July 1955, pp. 43 and 45.

He has computed [1] national product totals in terms of his " real 1926/27 prices," [2] goods not in production in that year being aligned with comparable goods for which a 1926/27 quotation is available. As Hoeffding has shown that the established price structure of 1928 diverged relatively little from the " adjusted factor cost standard," [3] the Jasny and Bergson criteria are reasonably close to each other. The resulting estimates of national product, both by origin and by use, are, however, at wide variance—compare, for example, their 1937 estimates of the share of agriculture (Table II) and consumption (Table III)—the principal reason being Jasny's wholesale rejection of many Soviet statistics which Bergson accepts. Thus Jasny claims that retail turnover declined in each successive year studied (admitting it a " startling result " when urban population increased 2·8 times during the period) and that the rates of growth of industrial production and construction were half those shown by the official statistics between 1928 and 1948. Much— though not all—of his deflation of the Soviet data in " 1926/27 prices " originates in the price indexes he computed. He was the pioneer in the field—official Soviet price series not having been published for a quarter of a century—and it must be recognised that three studies which have followed his agree remarkably with his findings. His retail-price index, although based on a mere sixteen goods and four services, shows precisely the same rise between 1928 and 1948 as one (based on 94 and 149 items in each decade respectively) compiled by Mrs. Chapman,[4] and his investment-goods price index is little different from those recently published by Wiles [5] and Bergson.[6] On the other hand, the industrial production index at which he arrived— showing a 220% increase between 1928 and 1948—is considerably below any alternative estimate. Thus Hodgman,[7] weighting 137 products with 1934 industrial wage-bills, showed a 364% rise (and there seems good evidence for considering this an understatement) [8]; Seton [9] computed an

---

[1] Naum Jasny, *The Soviet Economy during the Plan Era* (Stanford, Calif., 1951), for estimates to 1948 and in *Social Research*, Spring 1954, for 1948 to 1950.

[2] In *Journal of Political Economy*, August 1947, Jasny considers the main defects of the official series other than those of the 1926/27 prices to be the inclusion of unusable goods (*e.g.*, harvest losses or spoilt output); inadequate amortisation; the unrecorded decline in home processing; poor coverage of small-scale industry in the earlier years; and such miscellaneous faults as the inadequate allowance for seed.

[3] Apart from the exclusion of indirect taxes and subsidies normal to factor cost, Hoeffding's only quantitative adjustment is for differential profit incidence, involving no more than a 1% reduction in household consumption.

[4] Janet Chapman, *Review of Economics and Statistics*, May 1954.

[5] Peter Wiles, *Encounter*, November 1955, p. 66.

[6] A. Bergson, R. Bernaut, L. Turgeon, *op. cit.*, use considerably more refined methods and a much wider range of quotations: they show a 1949 index for basic industrial products (excluding tax) of 534 (1928 = 100) compared with Jasny's 500–600 (1926/27 = 100).

[7] D. Hodgman, *op. cit.*, p. 89.

[8] Cf. reviews of Hodgman's methods by Francis Seton, *Soviet Studies*, October 1955, and Richard Moorsteen, *American Slavic and East European Review*, February and April 1956.

[9] F. Seton, *The Tempo of Soviet Industrial Expansion* (a paper read to the Manchester Statistical Society on January 9, 1957).

increase of 414–421 % between those dates by applying regression equations relating the manufacturing indexes and energy and steel inputs of fourteen capitalist countries to Soviet energy and steel inputs; Clark [1] with, however, a mere twelve items to weight in his " international units," obtained a 1940 value of 3·4 times 1928 (1948 output is generally agreed to have regained the 1940 level); and Gerschenkron's dollar-priced index for heavy industry [2] summed with the Soviet series for light industry [3] showed a 3·5-fold increase on 1928 in as early as 1937. No such comparison can be made with his agricultural output estimates, in which his work stands alone, but the relationship he shows between farm and non-farm earnings seems better founded than those of Bergson and Hoeffding. In reproducing his figures (in Table III) no account is taken of his apparent error in deducting, as an alleged duplication, the labour remuneration component of public-service outlays.

Seton's study,[4] like Bergson's, is confined to structural analysis, in this instance for 1934: it is modelled on the form of national accounts developed by Stone and seeks maximum comparability with Bergson's accounts for 1937 in established prices. Although Seton is more detailed than Bergson, there seems only one difference in methodology, and that is minor; whereas the latter uses rentals for State-owned housing for the imputed rent of owner-occupied dwellings, Seton takes a Soviet estimate of depreciation on non-socialist property (i.e., including private farm capital) and provides no depreciation in the operational account of individual producers. This means that some outlay and income properly in the business ledger is entered in the household ledger. A similar, but even less significant, partial mis-entry is the attribution of Savings Banks deposits wholly to households, whereas some are made by institutions otherwise entered under business. Moreover, in confronting their estimates with the Soviet statistics of product distribution by use, Seton differs from Bergson in interpreting the division between " consumption " and " accumulation ": Seton includes defence in " consumption," while Bergson puts the munitions component in " accumulation " and pay and subsistence in " consumption." Both in fact seem wrong: [5] some share of munitions is included with pay and sub-sistence under " consumption," the remainder appears as " accumulation." Seton, while briefly discussing the effects of the established price structure, presents his accounts in current market prices, adopting the Soviet conven-tion of valuing farm income in kind at the average price realised for cash sales, but rejecting their convention of applying procurement taxes to in-

[1] Colin Clark, *The Conditions of Economic Progress*, 1951 edition, p. 186.
[2] Alexander Gerschenkron, *Review of Economics and Statistics*, May 1955.
[3] Very much less influenced than heavy industry by the inflation of " 1926/27 prices " as a result of the incorporation of new products.
[4] F. Seton, *Review of Economics and Statistics*, August 1954.
[5] Cf. D. A. Allakhverdyan, *Nekotorye voprosy teorii sovetskikh finansov* (Moscow, 1951), pp. 30 and 31, and M. Bor, *op. cit.*, p. 89.

dustrial value-added. The value of his accounts lies in the ingenious excavation of the figures which Soviet statisticians would have produced had they been asked to draw up a Stone-type matrix. Accounts for 1948 and 1953 drawn up by Nove [1] resemble those of Bergson rather than Seton but without any Bergson-type adjustment from current market prices. In quoting Nove's estimates, Wiles has applied sector-price indexes, calculated (except for consumption) by himself, to obtain growth rates in comparable prices. As would be expected for a period so short as 1948–53, the difference between base-year and end-year weighting is small—though even so, not insignificant, but the spread that he shows in applying his price indexes to compare Hoeffding's 1928 figure for gross national product with Bergson's datum for 1937 is a further vindication of Gerschenkron's hypothesis of inherent index number bias: on base-year weights the rise is 115% but on end-year weights only 58%. For his rate of growth Wiles uses the geometric mean of the two.

An impressive series of summary breakdowns of Soviet national product by use and by origin has been prepared by Block.[2] He has extended, with small modifications, Bergson's adjusted factor cost measures to 1953 but as yet only the results of his computations have been published.

Much less detailed accounts, also at current market prices, had earlier been prepared for 1940 by Baran,[3] Rosen[4] and Wyler.[5] Baran's object was not so much to prepare an account as to piece together items of national outlay for the sake of the total (used for comparison with United States magnitudes). Rosen's objective was more limited—to relate a breakdown by use, given by the then Chairman of the Soviet State Planning Commission,[6] to current price outlays, but he based his computation on an error (confusing State investment with total " accumulation ") and " proved it " by circular argument. A similar error was made in a computation by Laurat,[7] who made the further error of confounding national-income figures in 1926/27 prices with budget data in current prices. Wyler, whose dollar revaluation of the Soviet national product for four inter-war years is considered in the next section, confined himself to synthesising data computed by Jasny and Baran with Soviet budget statistics: the main subject-matter of his paper was a summary review of official and non-Soviet estimates published up to 1951. Prokopovicz, in his works written outside Russia, commented on the shortcomings of the official series, and made some corrections both to his

---

[1] Nove's accounts have been only privately circulated, but his use-breakdown has been reproduced by Peter Wiles, *loc. cit.*

[2] Herbert Block in *Trends in Economic Growth* (Washington, 1955, pp. 16, 57, 71 and 284), prepared for the Joint Committee of the United States Congress on the Economic Report.

[3] Paul Baran, *Review of Economic Statistics*, November 1947.

[4] Julius Rosen, *Schweitzerische Zeitschrift für Volkswirtschaft und Statistik*, No. 1, 1950.

[5] Julius Wyler, *ibid.*, Nos. 5 and 6, 1951.

[6] Nikolai Voznesensky, *Voyennaya ekonomika S.S.S.R.* (Moscow, 1947).

[7] Lucien Laurat, *Bilan de vingt-cinq ans de plans quinquennaux* (Paris, 1955).

own 1913 and to the later Soviet data.[1]   A rough calculation in the *Economist* of December 18, 1948, converted 1926/27 priced Soviet estimates into current roubles by applying an unexplained price index.

To the present writer's knowledge,[2] the only other rouble-priced estimates are those incidental to the rate-of-growth studies of Goldsmith and Grossman.   Goldsmith [3] constructed some income figures for pre-revolutionary years in an as yet unpublished study.   Grossman [4] suggested an approximation to an " ideal " measure of the rate of growth (the geometric mean of a chain index, each annual value of which is weighted according to the cost structure of that year) by taking the geometric mean of two indexes, the one using initial-year and the other final-year cost-weights, adapting Jasny's estimates for this purpose.

III

Of the estimates of Russian and Soviet national income translated into foreign values for international comparison,[5] the earliest are those of Levi,[6] now nearly a century old, and Mulhall,[7] both in terms of sterling.   Goldsmith (*op. cit.*) deprecates both as rough guesses because, despite a comparison of Levi's figure with Prokopovicz's, which shows a rate of growth similar to his own computation, he finds no supporting sources and methods. It is clear, however, that Levi used estimates of household incomes stratified

[1] In *Memorandum of the Birmingham Bureau of Research on Russian Economic Conditions*, No. 3, 1931, he deflated the Soviet figures to something like factor cost by excluding excise duties (but did not add in subsidies), revised agricultural income slightly upwards and added estimates for depreciation, and certain forms of transport, postal and restaurant services where these had been covered insufficiently (or not at all) by the Soviet data.   In his *Quarterly Bulletin of Soviet Russian Economics*, March 1941, and *Histoire économique de l'U.R.S.S.* (Paris, 1952), he indicated the direction (and sometimes the rough magnitude) of the corrections to the Soviet statistics which he found necessary in each producing sector; Chapter VI of his *Russlands Volkswirtschaft unter den Sowjets* (Zurich, 1944) develops a sector breakdown of national product for five years between 1913 and 1937 based on the official figures in 1926/27 prices.   Only his 1931 study presented a complete revision of the official accounts.

[2] He acknowledges with thanks the help of Professor Giorgio Fua and Drs. Lief Bjork, Eugène Zaleski and Theodor Zotschew for confirming the absence of other estimates in, respectively, the Italian, Scandinavian, French and German languages.   There is, however, a growing Continental literature on Soviet national-accounting methodology, cf. Jan Marczewski, *Income and Wealth*, IV (London, 1955) ; Stefano Somogyi, *Critica Economica*, No. 3, 1951, and there are, naturally enough, many studies in eastern European journals.

[3] Raymond Goldsmith, *The Economic Growth of Russia 1860–1913*, paper presented to the Fourth Conference of the International Association for Research in Income and Wealth, Hindsgavl, Denmark, 1955.   (Preliminary draft, privately circulated.)

[4] Gregory Grossman, " National Income " in A. Bergson (ed.), *Soviet Economic Growth* (Evanston, Ill., 1953) ; a Soviet notice of the book (*Planovoe Khozyaistvo*, No. 4, 1954, p. 79) observed with pleasure that " even using every device and slander to discredit Soviet statistics," the Soviet rate of growth was shown to exceed that of any capitalist country.

[5] Interspatial comparisons of the consumption sector of national income by household budget and price comparisons are excluded from the present study.

[6] Leone Levi, *Quarterly Journal of the Statistical Society*, March 1860, p. 42.

[7] Michael Mulhall, *The Dictionary of Statistics* (London, first edition 1884—fourth edition, 1909) ; reference here is to the fourth edition.

by class-group (his method for computing United Kingdom income in the same and later papers), and it was not much later that family budget studies were published in Russia.[1] Mulhall is clear enough on his methods, though less so on his sources, but the mystery in his figures is the inexplicable divergence between his breakdown by nine originating sectors for around 1890 (p. 320) and by eight mostly identical sectors for 1895 (p. 747): the rate of growth shown by the two estimates is, moreover, unrealistically small by reference to crop and industrial outputs of the time. No other valuation in sterling, or any other foreign money, appears to have been made until Polanyi's calculation [2] in the mid-thirties. On the consumption sector his method was reasonably sound (agricultural output valued at British wholesale prices and the annual wage-bill converted to sterling on a retail purchasing-power parity), but he confused investment with the gross value of producer goods. Clark improved upon this procedure, first in 1939 and in four subsequent revisions.[3] He avoided Polanyi's main error by valuing a sample of capital goods in sterling (in later revisions in dollars) and inflating to gross investment in the proportion shown by those goods within the United States gross investment; consumption of food and house-space was directly revalued, but for other services (including Government) he used rouble valuations converted at an estimated equivalent purchasing power. Brown [4] used Clark's 1934 and 1937 estimates, together with State budget data for rough estimates of war-time national income.

Soon after the war two dollar-valued estimates appeared. Wyler [5] adopted the technique of thorough-going revaluation: although he did not furnish details of his valuations (in 1940 dollars), he stated that:

> " the technique of conversion was adapted to the nature of the data available for each output or expenditure group. Where no measure of the quantity or quality of the output was possible, as in the case of civil servants and soldiers, an appropriate average value of the individual services was imputed. Farm operatives' income in kind was imputed at American retail prices " (p. 508).

The effect of this procedure was, in particular, to inflate, relative to Soviet values, services and farm consumption in kind. Baran (*op. cit.*), on the other hand, tried a short cut by employing a dollar–rouble conversion factor derived from a Soviet revaluation of the United States national income into

[1] Cf. A. A. Kaufman, *Statisticheskaya nauka v Rossii : teoria i metologia 1806–1917* (Moscow, 1922), pp. 70–9.

[2] Michael Polanyi, *The Manchester School*, No. 2, 1935.

[3] C. Clark, *A Critique of Russian Statistics* (London, 1939); in *Review of Economic Statistics*, November 1947, and in *The Conditions of Economic Progress* (London, 1940 and 1951); a third edition is in the press.

[4] A. J. B(rown), *Bulletin of International News*, March 4, 1944, for 1941 and 1943 estimates and A. J. Brown, *Applied Economics* (London, 1947), pp. 69 and 70, for 1941 (revised) and 1944 estimates.

[5] Julius Wyler, *Social Research*, December 1946.

roubles.[1]   Jasny [2] has demonstrated the errors Baran's route involved, but believes that so far as the 1940 factor-cost estimate is concerned the errors offset each other.   Baran's 1937 dollar valuation was less than it should have been because the " 1926/27 prices " used in the conversion factor with 1929 dollars was presumably the 1937 lists, and consequently included goods newly produced between 1929 and 1937 at inflated prices.   On the other hand, his 1937–40 link overstated the actual increase because Baran unreservedly used the official Soviet data in " 1926/27 prices."   Jasny also rightly points out that Baran's conversion of his dollar-priced national income at factor-cost into gross national product at market prices on the basis of established Soviet prices implies the same weight of indirect taxes in United States as in Soviet prices.   This procedure, however, commends itself to Dobb,[3] who calls Baran's factor-cost figure very nearly a measure at prime cost, since indirect taxes might be regarded as " that part of profit (and other property income) in a capitalist economy which is devoted to capital investment."   Baran's method was used in an estimate prepared by the United Nations Statistical Office for 1949,[4] primarily to assist the determination of contributions to the Organisation.   The main change from the methodology used by Baran was to apply " a statistical correction for the upward trend of the index of national income in constant prices ":   the magnitude of the correction was not stated.   There are, finally, two dollar-priced valuations for 1953 made by Harvey and Block in the United States Department of State,[5] which differ from each other by a margin of 28%. No computation details have been published for either figure, but one may hazard a guess (see Table IV) that Harvey's is in fact based upon the United Nations estimate for 1949.

IV

As the estimates described in the preceding sections are tabulated in comparable form in an Appendix, the only commentary needed is to draw attention to methodological or conceptual features which cause significant divergence between them.   In Table I the rate of growth shown by the Soviet estimates while the " 1926/27 prices " were in use (1928–50) is considerably higher than alternative estimates for the same period and for the period since the abandonment of that price valuation.   In fact, the 11% annual increase shown for 1950–55 is between the 12 and 13% hazarded by Jasny for 1948–50 and the 9% shown for 1948–55 by Wiles' adaptation of

---

[1] By M. Kolganov, *Problemy Ekonomiki*, No. 4, 1940, p. 111.   Kolganov has recently published (*Voprosy Ekonomiki*, No. 11, 1955) a reclassification of 1950 United States national income into Soviet concepts and presents it as a reply to the Bergson studies.

[2] *The Soviet Economy during the Plan Era*, pp. 38–9.

[3] *Review of Economics and Statistics*, February 1948, p. 37.

[4] United Nations, *National and Per Capita Incomes of Seventy Countries in 1949* (New York, 1950).

[5] Mose Harvey in *Industrial Russia* (Studies in Business Economics, No. 44, 1954), p. 7; H. Block, *op. cit.*, p. 16.

Nove's estimates. The rates of growth shown between the start of the First Five-year Plan and the war are greater in the rouble valuations (Grossman, Jasny and Wiles) than those in dollar prices (Clark and Wyler), since the latter are those of a more developed industrial structure.

An interesting feature of Table II is the quantitative difference between the Soviet and " bourgeois " concepts of the national product, *i.e.*, the value of " non-material services " excluded from the Soviet accounts. Seton and Bergson showed the addition to net material product to be almost one-fifth in 1934 and 1937 if measured in Soviet established prices, compared with 23·5% in Hoeffding's study of 1928. The differential is larger at factor cost because the incidence of indirect tax is heavier upon material production.[1] Jasny's computation of this margin is methodologically unsatisfactory. A recent recalculation of the 1950 United States national income to the Soviet concept by a well-known Soviet statistician [2] shows a difference of 27·5%, but it must be borne in mind that services occupy a larger place in the United States than in the Soviet economy. The variations between the origin breakdowns shown by the available estimates up to 1928 may be ascribed to relatively minor differences in accuracy and definition (*e.g.*, of transport), but the decline in the relative share of agriculture as collectivisation temporarily reduced output and as industry expanded after 1928 is very differently assessed. Jasny, using his " real 1926/27 prices," shows an even more rapid fall than the Gosplan estimates in the official " 1926/27 prices " and Bergson in established prices. Bergson's revaluation of farm consumption and elimination of turnover taxes from manufacturing considerably raises the agricultural at the expense of the industrial share.

Similarly the exclusion of turnover taxes sharply reduces the indicated share of consumption (Table III). The lowest share is shown by Jasny for 1948, computed in prices of a year when indirect taxes were very light, but Bergson and Heymann also indicate a low proportion, the main element in their adjusted factor cost being the deduction of turnover taxes: inclusion of these taxes (by them and by Nove) raises its share by 13 points. Clark's repricing in dollar values also diminishes consumption, since the tax element in those prices is relatively lower than in the Soviet Union, but not so much as by Wyler, despite his revaluation of food consumption on farms at retail prices.

The most uncertain set of estimates are those which try to situate the Soviet income magnitudes into international comparison. It has been shown that the size of a national product in relation to that of a more-industrialised economy is higher when valued in the prices of a more-industrialised economy (or in domestic prices of a later stage in industrialisation) than when valued in prices of a less-industrialised economy (or

---

[1] Bergson ignores the tax on " non-merchandise operations," which is the form of turnover tax levied on services, but the effect is insignificant.
[2] M. Kolganov, *Voprosy Ekonomiki, loc. cit.*

earlier stage).[1]   Both using United States prices Clark and Wyler nevertheless obtain for the inter-war period quite different magnitudes—the latter
exceeding the former in 1940 by more than one-third.   Wyler attributes the
discrepancy to different index-number usage and inaccuracies in the basic
statistics used by Clark.   Block [2] used Jasny's Soviet-priced and Clark's
American-priced estimates for a comparison of Soviet net national product
with that of the United States: for 1928 and 1937 respectively the Soviet-
priced set showed 15% and 25% while the American-priced set showed
30% and 37%.   For the post-war years rough estimates are available in
both Soviet and foreign prices and, if only an order of magnitude is required,
the Soviet national product at United States prices seems to be one-third
the size of the United States product, and at Soviet prices one-quarter the
size.

M. C. KASER

Geneva.

APPENDIX

The price bases of the computations of Soviet national income reproduced in
Tables II and III are indicated as follows: * denotes current prices, † denotes
prices of a different year and ‡ denotes valuation in a foreign currency.

TABLE I

Annual Average Rate of Growth of Net National Product % per annum

From: To:	1870 1885	1885 1900	1900 1913	1928 1937	1937 1940	1948 1950	1950 1955
Soviet official	—	—	2½	16	9	19	11
Clark, 1951 [a]	—	—	—	4½	8	—	—
Clark, 1951 [b]	—	—	—	2½	7	—	—
Grossman, 1954	—	—	—	7	—	7	—
Jasny, 1951 [c]	—	—	—	8	6½	—	—
Jasny, 1951, 1954 [d]	—	—	—	9	7	12½ [e]	—
Wyler, 1946 [f]	—	—	—	7	6	—	—
Wyler, 1951 [g]	—	—	—	5½	8	—	—
Block, 1955	—	—	—	—	—	10	6 [h]
Composite	3½ [i]	4½ [i]		7 [j]	—	9 [j]	

  [a] Valuation in United States dollar prices.
  [b] With Fisher-type allowance for valuation in rouble prices.
  [c] Distribution method.   [d] Production method.   [e] 12–13%.
  [f] National income.   [g] Social product.   [h] 1950–53.
  [i] Relationship of 1860 (Levi), 1895 (Mulhall) and 1913 (Clark) converted into dollars at
contemporary exchange-rates and inflated by United States price-index to a common year.
  [j] Relationship of 1928 (Hoeffding), 1937 (Bergson), 1948 and 1953 (both Nove) converted into
comparable prices by Wiles, 1955.

---

  [1] But the rate of growth is lower.   For a discussion of this problem with particular reference to
comparisons between the Soviet Union and the United States see *Trends in Economic Growth, op. cit.*,
pp. 54–9.
  [2] *Op. cit.*, p. 57.

TABLE II

Net National Product by Origin

Percentages of net material product [a]

Year and source.	Agri-culture.	Industry.[b]	Con-struction.	Transport and com-munica-tions.[c]	Trade.	Services.
At market prices :						
1895 (Mulhall, 1909) ‡ .	43·6	32·8		9·7	13·9	35·1
1900 (Prokopovicz, 1906) *	45·4	30·8	7·2	8·1	8·5	—
1913 (Prokopovicz, 1918) *	47·7	27·9	7·2	8·9	8·3	—
1925/26 (Gosplan, 1929) *	45·9	33·5	5·0	2·4	13·2	—
1928/29 (Gosplan, 1929) *	39·5	39·0	6·5	3·2	11·8	—
1928 [d] (Hoeffding, 1954) *.	40·7 [e]	45·1		5·7 [f]	8·5	23·5
1934 (Gosplan, 1936) † .	16·8	51·9	12·0	5·4	13·9	—
(Seton, 1954) * .	27·9	49·3	7·6	4·6	10·6	19·5
1937 [d] (Gosplan, 1939) † .	25·7	56·0	5·8	3·0	9·5	—
(Bergson, 1953) * .	26·2	58·1		4·7 [f]	11·0	19·6
(Jasny, 1951) † .	19·4	52·4	10·9	9·8	7·5	10·0
1940 (Jasny, 1951) † .	18·6	55·2	9·4	10·1	6·7	11·0
At adjusted factor cost [g] :						
1928 (Hoeffding, 1954) * .	45·3	41·5		6·0 [f]	7·2	25·2
1937 (Bergson, 1953) * .	39·8	47·1		6·8 [f]	6·3	27·7

[a] *I.e.*, Soviet definition of national product.

[b] Including forestry, fisheries and public utilities.

[c] Freight carriage; the distribution of communications between this head and " services " varies, but no adjustment has been attempted because exact data are lacking and the quantities involved are small.

[d] Clark, 1951, gives the following distribution of net national product:

	1928.	1938.
Agriculture, forestry and fisheries . .	36·7	25·9
Large-scale manufacture	9·4	20·0
Other manufacturing and services . .	53·9	54·1

[e] Forestry and fisheries (included with agriculture by Hoeffding) transferred to industry on the basis of Gosplan data for the same year.

[f] Use by individuals of transport and communications transferred to services, at an estimated one-third of total (as shown by Seton, *op. cit.*, for 1934).

[g] Block, 1955, uses this adjusted factor cost (with higher imputed land rent than Bergson) for the following distribution of net national product:

	1937.	1948.	1953.
Agriculture	36	28	23
Industry	34	36	46
Transport and communications .	7	8	10
Trade and services . . .	22	28	21

TABLE III

Gross National Product by Use

Percentages of net national product

Year and source.	Consumption.	Social services.	Administration.[a]	Defence.[b]	Net investment.	Depreciation.
At market prices :						
1928 (Hoeffding, 1954) *.	75·6	5·4	2·7	2·5	13·8	8·9
(Jasny, 1951) †	73·4	4·9	2·5 [c]	2·4	16·8	—
(Wyler, 1946) ‡	72·9	10·4		4·0	6·4	—
1934 (Wyler, 1946) ‡	62·2	18·3		6·1	13·4	—
(Clark, 1947) ‡	69·4	16·8			13·8	—
(Seton, 1954) *	65·9	6·4	1·5	3·7	22·5	5·5
1937 (Bergson, 1953) *	64·1	9·6	2·6	6·1	17·6	2·0
(Jasny, 1951) †	41·2	7·4	2·5 [c]	10·0	38·9	—
(Wyler, 1946) ‡	58·2	18·2		11·4	12·2	—
1938 (Clark, 1947) ‡	66·7	21·0			12·3	—
1940 (Bergson, Heymann, 1954) *	64·8	8·2	3·1	12·7	11·2	2·9
(Wyler, 1946) ‡	44·1	18·2		25·0	12·7	—
1941 (Brown, 1947) ‡	58·5		7·5	18·0 [d]	16·0	—
1943 (Brown, 1944) ‡	55·0		7·0	30·0 [d]	8·0	—
1944 (Brown, 1947) ‡	51·0		7·0	32·5 [d]	9·5	—
(Bergson, Heymann, 1954) *	52·2	6·5	2·9	28·9	9·4	2·3
1948 (Bergson, Heymann, 1954) *	59·0	10·7	4·9	8·3	17·1	1·8
(Jasny, 1951) †	30·7	7·4	3·3 [c]	19·2	39·4	—
(Nove, 1955) †	60·6	15·4		7·5	16·5	0·6 [e]
1953 (Nove, 1955) †	54·7	15·3		10·3	19·7	1·5 [e]
At adjusted factor cost :						
1928 (Hoeffding, 1954) *.	73·0	5·7	2·9	2·7	15·7	9·8
1937 (Bergson, 1953) *	57·2	10·9	3·2	7·9	20·8	2·7
1940 (Bergson, Heymann, 1954) *	57·3	9·3	3·7	16·2	13·5	3·7
1944 (Bergson, Heymann, 1954) *	42·4	7·8	3·5	35·2	11·1	2·8
1948 (Bergson, Heymann, 1954) *	46·3	11·9	6·0	11·9	23·9	2·3
(Block, 1955) ᶠ*	49	10	5	15	21	(2·3)
1953 (Block, 1955) ᶠ*	48	8	4	16	24	(2·3)

[a] Including internal security services.

[b] Outlays classified as defence in the State Budget, but excluding pay and subsistence.

[c] In the absence of a computation by Jasny, outlays on administration have been estimated as bearing the same relation to social services as they showed in current prices.

[d] Military pay and subsistence have been computed as the share of total defence outlay (in which they were included by Brown) shown by Bergson and Heymann and transferred to consumption.

[e] As recorded in the books of Soviet enterprises.

[f] Percentages of gross national product deflated to net by the Bergson, Heymann depreciation estimate for 1948.

TABLE IV

Valuation of National Income in United States Dollars of 1953 *Purchasing Power*

Billions of dollars

	Net national income.		Gross national product.	
	Soviet factor cost.	Foreign market prices.	Soviet market prices.	Foreign market prices.
1860	—	6 [a]	—	—
1895	—	18 [b]	—	—
1913	—	40 [c]	—	—
1928	—	41,[c] 46 [d]	—	—
1937	—	56,[c] 85 [d]	—	—
1940	70 [e]	75,[c] 102 [d]	100[e]	—
1944	—	76 [f]	—	—
1949	66 [g]	—	—	—
1953	86 [h]	—	—	110 [i]

Note. The price index used to inflate to 1953 prices is that of the United States Bureau of Labor Statistics; sterling valuations have been converted to dollars at the contemporary exchange-rate.

[a] Levi, 1860.

[b] Mulhall, 1909.

[c] Clark, 1951 (using only his values directly using United States dollar prices: his adjustment for rouble-price valuation was not suitable for inflation to 1953 United States prices).

[d] Wyler, 1946.

[e] Baran, 1947.

[f] Brown, 1947.

[g] United Nations, 1950.

[h] Harvey, 1954. This coincides exactly with an inflation of the United Nations, 1950, estimate for 1949, by an index in Soviet factor costs computed by Block, 1955.

[i] Block, 1955.

AN INDEX OF SOVIET INDUSTRIAL OUTPUT

By Norman M. Kaplan and Richard H. Moorsteen*

In this paper we present (a) the results of a calculation of an index of Soviet industrial output, and (b) some comments on, and applications of, these results. Underlying this paper are two studies: one on machinery prices and production [6] and another, which incorporates the relevant results of the machinery study, on the output of all industrial products [4]. This paper is a summary of the second of these studies and, as such, omits the detailed documentation and explanations which are available there or which, with respect to the machinery component, will be available when the machinery study is published. The results, shorn of important details, are presented here because the topic appears to be of some current interest. The results are, however, tentative for a variety of reasons; some of them are indicated below but others appear only in the underlying materials.

In Section I we present the index of industrial output and briefly discuss its nature and limitations. Section II is a miscellany in which we: (a) compare our index with others; (b) discuss some dynamic aspects of Soviet industrial growth; (c) explore the indications of future rates of growth; (d) present an index of the output of final products; and (e) estimate changes in productivity.

I. *The Index*

Table 1 presents the computed index for all industrial products and for major components thereof; the last column presents the weights employed in obtaining the index from the subindexes for the major components. The index is intended to measure the net product of industry, i.e., gross output less materials consumed in mining, manufacturing, and electric power production. At various stages in the aggregation, however, important compromises and approximations were neces-

---

* The authors are members of the economics staff of The Rand Corporation.

TABLE 1—AN INDEX OF SOVIET INDUSTRIAL OUTPUT
(1950=100)

	1927/28	1932	1937	1940	1945	1950	1951	1952	1953	1954	1955	1956	1957	1958	Weight for Commodity Group (percentage)
All Industrial Products	27.1	41.6	67.4	71.2	36.6	100.0	111.5	118.9	130.3	143.6	158.1	171.7	188.4	202.3	100.0
1. Machinery	6.8	19.5	40.9	34.3	13.6	100.0	98.5	100.2	111.4	120.7	136.2	150.6	175.1	185.0	19.4
2. Other producers' goods	21.4	41.1	66.5	71.5	43.1	100.0	112.7	121.5	131.2	145.0	160.1	173.2	189.8	206.8	54.8
a. Ferrous metals	15.7	24.5	66.1	68.0	43.3	100.0	114.2	127.5	140.5	153.2	167.9	179.9	189.7	202.7	9.5
b. Fuels	21.5	39.8	61.6	73.1	54.5	100.0	109.8	119.4	130.1	143.9	167.2	190.2	216.5	242.0	14.4
c. Electric power	5.5	14.8	39.7	53.0	47.5	100.0	114.0	130.6	147.4	165.1	186.6	210.2	229.9	255.9	1.5
d. Chemicals	6.9	17.8	52.6	56.5	25.4	100.0	110.6	119.5	130.1	146.0	165.3	182.2	198.6	214.3	3.3
e. Lumber, wood products and paper	28.7	56.8	72.9	78.7	42.5	100.0	113.1	116.5	120.5	132.7	139.1	143.8	153.2	161.8	19.9
f. Building materials	18.8	37.6	72.3	62.9	26.0	100.0	116.7	132.6	150.3	169.3	190.4	204.7	232.0	260.5	6.1
3. Consumers' goods	54.3	59.4	89.1	98.3	40.2	100.0	118.8	127.3	142.9	157.9	170.3	184.2	195.4	205.7	25.8
a. Foods	66.7	70.0	104.6	109.2	49.4	100.0	115.0	124.0	136.2	141.9	156.7	168.7	180.3	187.9	10.0
b. Nonfoods	46.4	52.7	79.4	91.4	34.4	100.0	121.2	129.5	147.1	167.9	178.9	194.0	204.9	217.0	15.8

Source: [4, Table 22].

sary: the index is computed by aggregating physical output series at various stages of fabrication, using 1950 price weights within certain groups of commodities and 1950 wage-bill weights among these commodity groups. Though limitations of space preclude a full account and appraisal,[1] we will describe, and comment briefly on, each aspect of the computation: (a) the underlying physical output series, (b) the first stages of aggregation, and (c) the higher levels of aggregation.

A. *The Physical Output Series*

Except with respect to machinery, no extensive survey of Soviet sources has been attempted and the present study relies primarily on the output data provided by the recent Soviet statistical handbooks—particularly by [15] and [16]. The most important but inevitable omission from our output sample is munitions and other military end-items. Probably the most important in the long list of other omissions are chemical equipment, nonferrous metals, refined petroleum products, sewn goods, nonalcoholic beverages, bread and bakery products, furniture.[2]

For a number of the important omissions other than munitions, we have attempted by imputation to employ surrogate commodities. That is to say, by appropriate choice of the weights, we let ferrous metals stand for nonferrous metals as well, textile fabrics for sewn goods as well, and similarly in other cases. Though each of these imputations undoubtedly gives rise to errors, the errors are believed to be less than those involved in no imputations, for the latter would imply a relative increase in output for the excluded commodities which is equal to that for all included commodities.

In addition to the omissions, there are a number of other difficulties with respect to the physical output series which we have been unable to allow for in the index computation. Probably the most important are the following: (1) The output data for the various periods refer to the

---

[1] For a detailed statement of sources and methods and for comments on the results, see [4, pp. 1-73 and Tables 1-22].

[2] All in all, the machinery index includes 210 physical output series; other producers' goods, 36 physical output series; and consumers' goods, 37 physical output series.

Not all the output series available from the statistical handbooks have been included in the index; some series do not extend over all years of interest and others were omitted because of the absence of appropriate weights. An alternative calculation was made incorporating the additional output series available for the 1950-1955 period and for which weights could be obtained; the result was a small but perceptible increase in the 1955 index with 1950 = 100 [4, Tables 14 and 15].

Also, many of the physical output series are themselves aggregates within which additional output data are available for some years. For example, the index includes pig iron output in tons and the statistical handbooks also provide data on six varieties of pig iron—cast iron for steel, foundry iron, spiegeleisen, etc. An alternative calculation for the 1950-1955 period, which incorporated the maximum detail available, yielded essentially no change in the index [4, Tables 10 and 11].

respective territorial boundaries of those periods. Hence, part of the 1927/28-1940 increment in output represents the 1939-1940 expansion in territory. (2) Some, though far from all, of the consumers' goods series exclude the 1927/28 output of small-scale industry. Hence, the 1927/28 value of the index is understated.

B. *The First Stages of Aggregation*

The weights by which the physical output series are combined into indexes for machinery and for the indicated commodity groups within other producers' goods are, or are intended to approximate, Jan. 1, 1950 wholesale prices. Prices of this date were chosen (a) because wholesale prices during the 1950's are believed to correspond at least roughly with production costs as reckoned in Soviet accounts, and (b) because previous studies of Soviet prices provide more abundant information for Jan. 1, 1950 than for any later date.

In the absence of wholesale price data for consumers' goods, the indexes for foods and nonfoods are obtained by weighting the relevant output relatives by the 1950 value of retail sales or approximations thereto. When these weights are multiplied by the corresponding output relatives, the results differ from the producers' goods values (price times output) in two ways: (a) the values are retail rather than wholesale;[3] and (b) they differ from a price-weighted output series to the extent that quantities *sold* differ from quantities *produced*.

Neither set of weights is available in sufficient detail or extent to correspond exactly with all the output series used. Hence, various approximations were often used: (a) estimates of average wholesale prices for output series more aggregative than the commodities for which price information exists; (b) the adjustment to Jan. 1, 1950 of prices of another date by the use of price index numbers; (c) the substitution of the product of a 1950 retail price and 1950 output for retail sales in cases where the latter are unavailable.

C. *The Higher Levels of Aggregation*

We regard an index of the net product of industry—i.e., of gross output less materials consumed—as an appropriate general-purpose measure of changes in the level of industrial activity. It is a measure which in principle (a) avoids the double-counting of gross outputs, (b) is in-

---

[3] However, as will be indicated below, we have used our weights to combine official Soviet indexes for branches of industry into indexes for foods and for nonfoods in the 1950-1955 period; the results are very close to the official indexes for foods and nonfoods. Since the official indexes use wholesale price weights, these results suggest that relative retail prices within foods and within nonfoods are not sufficiently different from wholesale prices to yield appreciable differences in the output indexes, at least in the 1950-1955 period. See [4, Table 26].

sensitive to changes in vertical integration, and (c) eliminates the contribution of nonindustrial sectors, in the form of materials supplied, to industrial output.

Unfortunately, we have not found it possible to construct such a measure directly for lack of adequate data. Instead, we have sought an approximate indirect measure—an index of output with value-added weights.[4] And even the latter is not properly constructed. We do not have value-added weights but must rely on wage-bill distributions as approximations. Furthermore, the wage-bill distributions cannot be applied at all levels of aggregation but are used only to obtain (a) the index for consumers' goods from the food and nonfood indexes, (b) the index for producers' goods other than machinery from the indicated subindexes, and (c) the index for all industrial products from the indexes for machinery, other producers' goods and consumers' goods.

The relevant wage-bill distributions, obtained from the 1950 distribution of wage-earners by industrial branches and estimates of 1950 average monthly earnings, are summarized in the last column of Table 1. The most important of the difficulties encountered in the derivation of the wage-bill distribution is the necessity to exclude from the data for the machine-building and metal-working industry that portion which represents payments to workers producing munitions. On the basis of somewhat ambiguous official data on the distribution of the gross value of output, we have taken the share of munitions workers in the machine-building and metal-working wage-bill to be 50 per cent. Though this is a rough calculation, substantially different alternative shares do not greatly affect the index for all industrial products: as against our index of 202 in 1958 and 27 in 1927/28, alternative shares of 25 and 75 per cent for munitions yield, respectively, indexes of 201 and 204 in 1958 and indexes of 25 and 29 in 1927/28.

Thus, the index in Table 1, conceived as a measure of the changes in the net product of civilian industry, is subject to errors which arise from various considerations: (1) ambiguities in, and exclusions from, the physical output series; (2) inaccuracies and imputations in the price, retail sales, and wage-bill weights; (3) the heterogeneity of the weighting system as a whole; and (4) the approximate nature of a value-added-weighted index.[5] In most cases, neither the magnitude nor

[4] Given complete commodity coverage, the direct and indirect measures will be identical if, for each commodity produced by industry, value added (gross value minus materials consumed, both at weight-year prices) varies over time in direct proportion to the output of that commodity. However, to the extent that real cost reductions (increases) have occurred in materials requirements, a value-added-weighted index will understate (overstate) the growth of net product.

[5] Also, for some of the years covered in Table 1, the indexes for some commodity groups are obtained by interpolations or extrapolations based on sets of commodities which are

the direction of error is known. In some cases, however, at least the direction of error is clear and these cases suggest that our index understates the 1950-1958 increase in output and overstates the 1927/28-1950 increase.

The overstatement arises from our exclusion of some small-scale industry output for 1927/28 and, in terms of growth rate comparisons, from our inclusion of the output in territories added in 1939-1940. The understatement of the 1950-1958 increase arises primarily from a deficiency in the post-1950 machinery index.[6] In the machinery index an attempt is made to allow for changes over time in the average quality of the products included within any single physical output series. Though precision in this aspect of the calculation is hardly possible, the problem of allowing for quality change in the 1927/28-1950 period is not so acute. Machinery output then was characterized by considerable standardization; and changes in quality, although large, tended to occur discretely and infrequently for most items. With the beginning of the 1950's, however, the level of technical sophistication in Soviet machine-building rose rapidly, the number of models produced proliferated, and the models changed frequently. Because of an insufficient allowance for post-1950 improvements in the quality of machinery output, the machinery index is believed to understate significantly the actual increase in output from about 1950 on.

II. *Some Implications and Applications of our Results*

A. *Comparisons of Our Indexes with Others*

Our index of industrial output, of course, is not the first computed by students of the Soviet economy: among others, D. R. Hodgman [1], N. Jasny [2], G. W. Nutter [7], F. Seton [12], and D. B. Shimkin

---

different from those underlying the indexes for other years. The indexes and commodity groups involved are the following: (a) the 1951, 1952, and 1954 indexes for foods and nonfoods and the 1958 index for nonfoods; and (b) the 1951-1954 and 1956-1958 indexes for chemicals and building materials and the 1951-1954 indexes for fuels. However, the errors involved in interpolation or extrapolation are relatively small. See [4, Section 3 and Tables 16, 17, 19, and 20].

[6] There is evidence that other factors also cause our index to understate the increase in output over the period as a whole and over the post-1950 period separately. Among them: (a) our omission of nonferrous metals output series; (b) our exclusion of output data available only for recent years; and (c) our use of wage-bill data rather than wage-bill plus capital consumption to represent value-added. See [4, pp. 71-73 and Table 15]. In each of these cases, the error appears to be relatively small, though taken together their effect may be appreciable.

The last of the factors listed above deserves an additional comment. In an effort to test the sensitivity of our results to inclusion of other factor payments, we have performed an alternative, illustrative calculation in which combined capital consumption and wage-bill weights replace the wage-bill weights used in Table 1. The result is an index which increases only slightly more than the index in Table 1 [4, pp. 33-36, 55-56].

and F. A. Leedy [13] have also made such computations. We add our estimates to those already in existence for the following reasons: (a) For various purposes, including the determination of changes in the annual rates of industrial growth, it is desirable to obtain annual indexes for the post-1950 period extending to the most recent years possible. The Hodgman index terminates in 1951, the Jasny index in 1950, and only the Shimkin-Leedy index goes beyond 1955 to 1956. Only the Seton and Shimkin-Leedy indexes provide annual 1950-1955 data. (b) The machinery component of our index, the most troublesome component of an index of industrial output, rests upon an independent and intensive study of machinery prices and production [6]. (c) While the indexes already available differ in results, little by way of published details, except for [1] and [12], are yet available to account for the differences.

Table 2 summarizes the results obtained in these other studies in comparison with ours. In some cases the results differ for more or less obvious reasons. The Hodgman indexes preceded the appearance of the recent Soviet statistical handbooks and hence rely on far fewer output series, particularly for the postwar years. The Seton index is not a

TABLE 2—COMPARISONS BETWEEN KAPLAN-MOORSTEEN INDEXES AND OTHERS
(All Indexes with 1950 = 100)

	1928	1937	1940	1955
All Industrial Products				
(i) Hodgman	15	57	67	—
(ii) Jasny	21	61	—	—
(iii) Nutter	29	68	66	146
(iv) Seton	14	52	63	165
(v) Shimkin-Leedy	23	63	68	165
(vi) Kaplan-Moorsteen	27	67	71	158
1. Machinery				
(i) Nutter	13	56	42	125
(ii) Shimkin-Leedy	7	38	32	147
(iii) Kaplan-Moorsteen	7	41	34	136
2. Other Producers' Goods				
(i) Nutter	24	65	68	154
(ii) Shimkin-Leedy	17	61	70	163
(iii) Kaplan-Moorsteen	21	67	72	160
3. Consumers' Goods				
(i) Hodgman	39	92	87	—
(ii) Nutter	56	86	93	161
(iii) Shimkin-Leedy	55	87	91	168
(iv) Kaplan-Moorsteen	54	89	98	170

Sources: Hodgman [1, pp. 89, 123, 134]; Jasny [2, p. 57]; Nutter [7, pp. 402, 404–5]; Seton [12, p. 30]; Shimkin-Leedy [13, p. 7]; Kaplan-Moorsteen: Table 1 above. We ignore here the difference between the calendar year 1928, and the fiscal year 1927/8 (Oct. 1, 1927–Sept. 30, 1928).

weighted aggregation of output series but is obtained from a few selected series, regarded as inputs, and a regression equation, relating such inputs and output from data for other countries.

In other cases, however, no ready explanation of the differences is available. The indexes do differ in weights: Shimkin-Leedy use a "modification" of Hodgman's 1934 wage-bill weights, Nutter a combination of 1955 prices and employment distributions, and Jasny "real 1926/27 prices." Though there are considerable areas of agreement among the Shimkin-Leedy indexes, the Nutter indexes, and ours, there are also appreciable and conspicuous differences. If the major differences among these indexes were differences in the *date* of the weights, two consequences would ensue: (a) our results and Nutter's should coincide quite closely, for the difference between 1950 and 1955 weights should yield insignificant differences in the results; and (b) our results should show substantially smaller increases than the Shimkin-Leedy indexes on the grounds that early-year weights (such as 1934) typically produce a more rapidly growing index than do late-year weights (such as 1950 or 1955). Yet our postwar results for all categories of output are closer to the Shimkin-Leedy than to the Nutter indexes, and in the 1927/28-1950 period our results for machinery are almost identical with the Shimkin-Leedy index but far different from the Nutter index.

It is clear that an explanation of the differences in results requires detailed comparisons of the individual output series, weights, and various adjustments employed. Both limitations of space and the absence of published details (including as yet those which underlie our machinery component) make such comparisons infeasible here. Until such comparisons are undertaken, our results and the subsequent applications we make of them should, for these reasons also, be regarded as tentative.

Let us turn now to the comparisons between our results and the official indexes in Table 3. For the 1928-1950 period and for all commodity groups, the official indexes and ours bear essentially no resemblance to each other beyond the fact that both record increases in output: the official indexes show increases from 1928 to 1950 which are from $2\frac{1}{2}$ to 6 times the increases shown by the corresponding Kaplan-Moorsteen indexes. These divergences are not surprising. In the 1928-1950 period, the official indexes are the 1926/27 ruble indexes which should yield increases substantially greater than ours for at least two reasons: (a) the official weights are, in principle, 1926/27 prices which, referring to an essentially "preindustrialization" economy, yield greater increases in output than an index constructed with weights of a recent year; and (b) in the 1928-1950 period, new products were often introduced into the index at essentially current prices—and, because of inflation, higher prices—rather than 1926/27 prices, thus imparting an upward bias to the official index. In addition, the official indexes for all industrial products and machinery include, and ours exclude, munitions; and the output of munitions in 1928 was negligible.

Though the divergences themselves are not surprising, three points perhaps deserve some emphasis. First, the divergences pervade all commodity groups in Table 3. Secondly, if the official and Kaplan-Moorsteen indexes for the 1928-1950 period are broken down into subperiod indexes—i.e., 1937 indexes with 1928 = 100, 1940 indexes with 1937 = 100, and 1950 indexes with 1940 = 100—the divergences pervade all commodity groups and all subperiods, except machinery in the 1940-

TABLE 3—COMPARISONS BETWEEN KAPLAN-MOORSTEEN AND OFFICIAL INDEXES[a]
(All Indexes with 1950=100)

	1928	1937	1940	1945	1950	1953	1955	1957	1958
All Industrial Products									
(i) Official (including munitions)[b]	9	40	58	53	100	145	185	225	247
(ii) Kaplan-Moorsteen (excluding munitions)	27	67	71	37	100	130	158	188	202
1. Machinery									
(i) Official (including munitions)[b]	2	27	47	60	100	159	217	279	318
(ii) Kaplan-Moorsteen (excluding munitions)	7	41	34	14	100	111	136	175	185
2. Other Producers' Goods									
(i) Official[e]	9	40	52	46	100	139	174	208	—
(ii) Kaplan-Moorsteen	21	67	72	43	100	131	160	190	207
3. Consumers' Goods									
(i) Official[b]	20	61	81	48	100	144	176	208	224
(ii) Kaplan-Moorsteen	54	89	98	40	100	143	170	195	206
a. Foods									
(i) Official[d]	25	78	104	52	100	138	160	192	202
(ii) Kaplan-Moorsteen	67	105	109	49	100	136	157	180	188
b. Nonfoods									
(i) Official[d]	26	67	89	55	100	143	178	200	218
(ii) Kaplan-Moorsteen	46	79	91	34	100	147	179	205	217

[a] The comparisons here, and others, for years through 1955 are found in [4, Table 27]. For further details see [4, notes to Table 27, and Section 4.3]. We ignore here the difference between the calendar year 1928 and the fiscal year 1927/8.

[b] For all industrial products, machinery, and consumers' goods, the official indexes for, respectively, gross industrial output, machine-building and metal-working output and group B output are used. They are found in [16, pp. 10, 32, and 37], and, for 1957 and 1958, in [15, p. 146].

[e] For other producers' goods, the official indexes are of two kinds. (a) In the 1928–1950 period the indexes are obtained by subtracting in each year the value of machine-building and metal-working output in 1926/27 rubles from the value of group A output in 1926/27 rubles. (b) In the 1950–1957 period, the indexes are obtained as averages of official indexes for relevant branches of industry, weighted by *our* wage-bill weights for those branches. The official branch indexes are found in [15, p. 140].

[d] The official indexes for foods and nonfoods are the official indexes for the food and light industries, respectively, from [15, p. 140] and [11, Jan. 16, 1959].

1950 period [4, Table 28]. Thirdly, the entire divergence observed should not be attributed to the "upward bias" of the official indexes if, by "bias," statistical malpractices such as the treatment of new commodities are meant. Part of the divergence, though a quantitatively unknown part, is explainable by differences between the official and Kaplan-Moorsteen indexes in weights and in coverage; nevertheless, a more detailed analysis of specific differences indicates that substantial "upward bias" exists, i.e., quantitatively important statistical malpractices are involved [4, pp. 97-102].

Contrary to their behavior in the 1928-1950 period, the official indexes and ours are, in general, not dissimilar in the 1950-1958 period. Only the machinery indexes exhibit a divergence which is reminiscent of the 1928-1950 behavior. Even so, appreciable divergences between the indexes persist in the 1950-1958 period; the official indexes tend to exceed ours; and the ratio of the official index to ours tends to increase over time.

Though in the 1950-1958 period the official indexes abandoned the use of 1926/27 price weights, the official indexes still differ from ours in several respects: (a) The official indexes for all industrial products and machinery include munitions. (b) The official indexes are price-weighted aggregates of gross output; in the 1950-1955 period, Jan. 1, 1952 prices are used, and in the 1955-1958 period, July 1, 1955 prices. (c) The official indexes are comprehensive in coverage, whereas ours refer only to a limited set of commodities. (d) The official indexes still appear to suffer from methodological shortcomings; for example, from official methodological statements it is quite possible to infer—though not with certainty—that the treatment of new products continues to impart an upward bias to the official index in the post-1950 period [12, pp. 4 ff.].

On the point of weight differences, two comments are necessary: First, for the post-1950 period, the differences in weight years are probably of limited significance, as the intervals between weight years are short and the changes in industrial price structure known to have occurred are limited. Secondly, the difference between the official set of price weights and our heterogeneous set of price, retail sales, and wage-bill weights also appears to be of limited significance at least for the 1950-1955 period. We have taken official indexes for branches of industry—ferrous metals, meats, cotton fabrics, etc.—and aggregated them by means of *our* weighting system into indexes for foods, consumers' goods, all industrial products, etc., and compared the results with official indexes for the more aggregative categories [4, Table 26]. Both our retail sales weights and our wage-bill weights yield results which are very close to the relevant official indexes. Hence it appears that we can compare the official indexes and ours for the post-1950 period without particular concern about the disturbing effects of differences in weights.

On the point of differences in coverage: First, our inadequate coverage of the proliferation of new machinery models in the post-1950 period and other evidence lead us to the belief that our machinery index significantly understates the actual increase in output. Secondly, it is not clear whether the commodities omitted by us increase, on balance, more or less rapidly than those included [4, Tables 4 and 25, pp. 107-10].

Finally, with respect to official statistical malpractices, we have compared the official indexes for branches of industry—e.g., ferrous metals, textiles, etc.—with corresponding aggregations of our physical output series [4, Table 29] [6, Ch. 7]. In a number of cases such comparisons could be made for branches which appear to be well covered by our physical output series and which are believed to include no munitions. In some of these cases, the output increases shown by the official branch indexes and by our aggregations correspond very closely or exactly. In many cases, however, the official branch indexes show appreciably larger increases which, in the absence of other information, suggests the existence of an upward bias in the official index.

Thus, there are a number of reasons to expect the official indexes and ours to diverge in the 1950-1958 period.[7] The official indexes for all industrial products and machinery should (a) differ from ours because of the inclusion of munitions in the former and (b) exceed ours because of our inadequate coverage of new machinery models.[8] All the official

[7] Also, the categories for which the comparisons in Table 3 are made do *not* have the same meaning in the official and in the Kaplan-Moorsteen indexes. In addition to the difference in coverage of munitions, the following differences are notable: (a) the official index for machinery includes consumers' durables and certain kinds of repairs, whereas our indexes exclude repairs entirely and include consumers' durables in nonfoods; (b) the official index for consumers' goods is the group B index and, hence, excludes a number of commodities which, with further fabrication, eventuate as consumers' goods—notably, textile fabrics—and which are included in our consumers' goods index; and (c) the official index for nonfoods is the light industry index which excludes consumers' durables. However, consumers' durables and repairs are relatively unimportant. And in our index textile fabrics stand for sewn goods output which is otherwise absent. Hence, on the assumption that textile fabrics are a reliable surrogate in this respect, the only significant difference among those enumerated is the difference in the treatment of munitions.

[8] These divergences may be explored in terms of employment and productivity increases in the 1950-1958 period. The increase in man-years of employment in machine-building and metal-working was about 36.7 per cent during 1950-1956 [4, Table 45] and about 8.7 per cent during 1956-1958 [15, p. 133]; i.e., the increase for 1950-1958 was roughly 48.6 per cent. Over the same interval, 1950-1958, the increase in output per man-year for workers in all industrial branches *other* than machinery and metal-working amounted to about 48.1 per cent (see Table 7 below). Thus, if the increase in productivity in machinery and metal-working was the same as in the other industrial branches, the 1958 output index (1950 = 100) would be 220 for machinery and metal-working and 210.9 for all industrial

indexes should (a) differ from ours because of differences in coverage, and (b) exceed ours because of the apparent existence of methodological shortcomings in the official indexes. Without additional information, however, it is impossible to assess the relative importance of the various reasons for divergence.

B. *Major Trends in the Annual Rates of Growth*

Table 4 presents the average annual rates of increase of industrial output, as implied by our indexes, over various periods from 1927/28 to 1958. The major trends in growth rates are as follows:

1. In the prewar years, the rates of increase for all industrial products decline slightly from 1927/28-1932 to 1932-1937, reflecting very substantial declines in the rate of increase for machinery and other producers' goods and a very substantial increase in the rate of increase of consumers' goods. In the 1937-1940 period, marked by intensive rearmament, the rate of increase for all industrial products is very modest, less than one-fifth the previous rates of increase; machinery output actually decreases over this period and the rates of increase for other producers' goods and consumers' goods are substantially below the 1927/28-1937 rates.

2. The war years, of course, saw a very large decline in civilian output—a decline of about 50 per cent from 1940 to 1945 in all industrial products, 60 per cent in machinery and consumers' goods, and 40 per cent in other producers' goods (see Table 1). Following these declines, the early postwar period shows unprecedentedly high rates of increase in all major categories of output. By 1948 the prewar levels of output were reattained for all industrial products, machinery and other producers' goods, though consumers' goods did not reach the 1940 level until 1950 and foods not until 1951 (Table 1).

3. In the 1950-1958 period, the rates of increase for all major categories of output decline sharply as against the immediately postwar rates. In comparison with the 1927/28-1940 rates, the 1950-1958 rates

products, including munitions. (The latter index is obtained by combining the machinery and munitions index just described with the Table 1 indexes for other producers' goods and consumers' goods, weighted by the wage-bill distributions *inclusive* of munitions in [4, Table 7].)

In other words, the assumption of equal productivity increases yields an index for all industrial output somewhat greater than ours (which stands at 202 in 1958) but substantially less than the official (which stands at 247 in 1958). On the other hand, the official machinery and metal-working output index, taken with the increase in employment indicated just above, implies a 1950-1958 productivity increase for the branch of over 10 per cent per year, double that for the rest of industrial output. While it seems possible for productivity in machinery and metal-working to have increased somewhat more rapidly than in the rest of industry, the rate of increase implied by the official index is so large as to suggest that differences with respect to munitions and new machinery models are not the sole explanation of divergences between the official machinery index and ours.

TABLE 4—AVERAGE ANNUAL RATES OF INCREASE OF INDUSTRIAL OUTPUT [a]

(Percentages)

	1927/28–1932	1932–1937	1937–1940	1945–1950	1950–1953	1953–1955	1955–1958	1927/28–1940	1940–1950	1950–1958	1927/28–1958
All Industrial Products	10.6	10.1	1.9	22.3	9.2	10.1	8.6	8.2	3.5	9.2	6.9
1. Machinery	28.2	16.0	Decrease	49.0	3.7	10.6	10.7	14.1	11.3	8.0	11.6
2. Other producers' goods	16.5	10.1	2.5	18.4	9.5	10.5	8.9	10.3	3.4	9.5	7.8
a. Ferrous metals	11.0	22.0	1.0	18.2	12.0	9.3	6.5	12.7	3.9	9.2	8.8
b. Fuels	15.6	9.1	5.8	12.9	9.2	13.4	13.1	10.5	3.2	11.7	8.3
c. Electric power	26.3	21.8	10.1	16.1	13.3	12.5	11.1	20.3	6.6	12.5	13.5
d. Chemicals	24.9	23.7	2.4	31.5	9.2	12.7	9.0	18.7	5.9	10.0	12.0
e. Lumber, wood products and paper	17.5	5.1	2.6	18.7	6.4	7.4	5.2	8.6	2.4	6.2	5.9
f. Building materials	17.7	14.0	Decrease	30.9	14.5	12.6	11.0	10.4	4.7	12.7	9.1
3. Consumers' goods	2.1	8.5	3.3	20.0	12.6	9.2	6.5	5.0	0.2	9.4	4.5
a. Foods	1.2	8.2	1.5	15.1	10.9	7.3	6.2	4.1	Decrease	8.2	3.5
b. Norfoods	3.0	8.6	4.8	23.8	13.7	10.3	6.6	5.7	0.9	10.2	5.2

[a] These are average annual rates of increase compounded annually over the indicated period. Calculated from the data underlying the indexes in Table 1, they may not quite coincide with the average annual rates of increase implied by these indexes which have been rounded to one decimal place.

are smaller for machinery and other producers' goods and larger for consumers' goods and all industrial products. In comparison with the 1927/28-1937 rates, the 1950-1958 rates are smaller for all industrial products, machinery, and other producers' goods and larger for consumers' goods; however, correction of the indicated understatement of the post-1950 growth of machinery output might be sufficient to remove or reverse the observed inequality in the 1927/28-1937 and 1950-1958 rates of increase for all industrial products.

4. Over the 1927/28-1958 period as a whole, by far the largest annual rate of increase among the major categories of output is that for machinery and by far the smallest is that for consumers' goods. This serves to place the 1950-1955 behavior of consumers' goods output in proper perspective: the increase in output for consumers' goods exceeded that for machinery and other producers' goods in the 1950-1955 period but *not* in the 1927/28-1940, 1940-1950, or 1955-1958 period.

5. Of some current interest is the question whether annual rates of increase have tended to decline since 1950. There is no evidence of retardation within the 1950-1955 period: the average annual rates of increase for all industrial products, machinery and other producers' goods are larger in 1953-1955 than in 1950-1953. There is, however, evidence of retardation in 1955-1958: (1) the 1955-1958 average annual rate of increase is less than the 1953-1955 rate for each of the commodity groups presented in Table 4 except machinery for which the rates are approximately the same; and (2) for all industrial products, producers' goods other than machinery, and consumers' goods, the 1955-1958 rates of increase are also less than the 1950-1953 rates. There is, however, considerable fluctuation in the annual increases for all industrial products and for the separate commodity groups. Calculated from the indexes in Table 1, the annual increases in all industrial products are (in percentages):

1953	1954	1955	1956	1957	1958
9.6	10.2	10.1	8.6	9.7	7.4

Thus, the observed decline in rates of increase within the 1953-1958 period is neither monotonic nor, except for 1958, substantial.[9]

[9] The official index for all industrial products (which includes munitions) exhibits the following annual rates of increase (in percentages):

1953	1954	1955	1956	1957	1958
11.8	13.3	12.4	10.6	10.0	9.7

[15, pp. 135, 137]. Thus, the official indexes also show a retardation in growth within the 1953-1958 period; but the marked decline in the 1958 annual increase fails to appear in the official data. One important factor which contributes to the 1958 retardation as measured by us is a very large decline in the 1958 machinery growth rate. Given the lack of information on the behavior of munitions output during this period and the limitations of our calculation for civilian machinery, one should not make much of this single year's variation in our index for all industrial products.

C. Indications of Future Rates of Growth

What does the seven-year plan, covering the 1959-1965 period, suggest with respect to future rates of growth in comparison with recent past rates of growth? Unfortunately, the physical output goals stated in the plan cover substantially fewer commodities than those underlying the indexes in Table 1. Hence, in order to discuss future versus past rates of growth, it is necessary to construct new indexes of output for 1950, 1955, 1958, and 1965(P),[10] which cover those commodities for which there are published 1965(P) goals and output series for the preceding years. The average annual rates of increase for 1950-1955, 1955-1958, and 1958-1965(P), which are implied by such indexes, are presented in Table 5. The underlying indexes require the following com-

TABLE 5—AVERAGE ANNUAL RATES OF INCREASE IMPLIED BY 1965(P) GOALS IN COMPARISON WITH RECENT RATES OF INCREASE[a]

(Percentages)

	1950–1955	1955–1958	1958–1965(P)	Percentage of 1950 Value of Commodities Included[b]
1. Machinery	7.0	8.2	9.2–10.7	34.3
2. Other producers' goods[c]	10.7	9.7	8.2– 8.8	85.3
3. Foods	8.8	12.1	8.6– 8.8	34.5
4. Nonfoods	11.9	6.3	6.4– 6.6	87.6

[a] The calculations underlying these results are summarized in [4, Table 37].

[b] The 1950 value of output or sales of the commodities included here divided by the 1950 value of output or sales of the commodities included in the corresponding indexes of Table 1.

[c] For other producers' goods, the aggregates are obtained as the sum of price times quantity data without the use of wage-bill weights for commodity groups within other producers' goods.

ments: (a) Their commodity coverage—particularly, in the cases of machinery and foods—is relatively small in comparison with the indexes in Table 1 (see last column of Table 5). (b) In the case of other producers' goods, commodity coverage is inadequate for lumber, wood products and paper, chemicals and building materials, though relatively high for ferrous metals, fuels and electric power [4, Table 36]. (c) Because of these coverage problems, the index for other producers' goods is a price-weighted aggregation of output series without any use of wage-bill weights. (d) Also because of these coverage problems, discussion is confined to foods, nonfoods, machinery, and other producers' goods separately. (e) Because the seven-year plan states a range of 1965(P) goals for many commodities, the indexes computed therefrom for 1965(P) and the implied 1958-1965(P) rates of increase also have a range.

[10] I.e., planned for 1965.

The average annual rates of increase in Table 5, taken as representative for the corresponding commodity groups, suggest the existence of a further decline in rates of growth in the seven-year plan as against the 1950-1958 period. Only for machinery is the 1958-1965(P) rate of increase substantially above the preceding rates. For other producers' goods and foods, the 1958-1965(P) rates are substantially below the 1955-1958 rates, and for nonfoods the rates are about equal. For other producers' goods and nonfoods, the 1958-1965(P) rates are substantially below the 1950-1955 rates; and for foods the rates are about equal.

The conclusion that future rates of growth will be less than those in the immediate past is subject, however, to at least two qualifications: First, the coverage of foods, machinery, and some commodity groups within other producers' goods is so inadequate as to cast doubt on the representativeness of the rates of growth calculated in Table 5; indeed, it is precisely in foods and machinery that the 1950-1958 rates of growth in Table 5 diverge markedly from those in Table 4 implied by our indexes with more comprehensive coverage. In support of retardation, however, are the official indexes which show 1958-1965(P) rates of growth less than both 1950-1955 and 1955-1958 rates of growth for all industrial output and for each of the major components thereof.[11]

Secondly, the conclusion assumes no overfulfillment of the output goals of the seven-year plan. There are, however, several indications of expectations to overfulfill. The Soviet press has reported "spontaneous" promises by individual plants and regions, frequently followed by Central Committee decrees of encouragement, to fulfill the 1965 goals in 1964 and, sometimes, in 1963.[12] Furthermore, some Soviet economists in analyzing the seven-year plan find substantial "reserves" towards overfulfillment.[13] Also, an October, 1959 decree called for increased

---

[11] The official annual rates of increase in percentages are:

	1950-1955	1955-1958	1958-1965(P)
All Industrial Output	13.1	10.2	8.8
1. Group A Industry	13.7	11.2	9.2–9.4
a. Machine-building and Metal-working	16.8	13.7	10.4
2. Group B Industry	12.0	8.2	7.1–7.4

The 1950-1955 rates are calculated from indexes in [16, pp. 10, 32, 37]. The 1955-1958 rates are calculated from indexes in [15, p. 146]. The 1958-1965(P) rates are calculated from indexes in [11, Feb. 8, 1959]. As before, all are average annual rates of increase, compounded annually over the indicated periods.

[12] E.g., see [11, June 11, June 18, June 23, 1959].

[13] For examples, see [14] and [5]. Also, in the last few years there has been a tendency for planned annual rates of increase of industrial output to be exceeded according to the official indexes [11, Feb. 6, 1957, Jan. 27, 1958, Dec. 20, 1957, Jan. 16, 1959, Dec. 23, 1958, Jan. 22, 1960]. Such claims are not always made [11, Dec. 27, 1955, and Jan. 31, 1957].

output of consumers' durables and items of household use over the 1959-1961 period and, thereby, fulfillment of the seven-year plan goals for these commodities before 1965.[14] Of course, these indications are too tenuous for predictive purposes. Nevertheless, if the 1965(P) goals are fulfilled a year earlier, the retardation inferred from Table 5 disappears. The 1958-1964 average annual rates of increase become: 10.1-10.3 per cent for foods, 7.5-7.7 for nonfoods, 10.9-12.6 for machinery, and 10.2-10.8 for other producers' goods. In the case of the official indexes, a similar conjecture yields 1958-1964 average annual rates of increase which are (a) on the average, equal to the 1955-1958 rates, but (b) less than the 1950-1955 rates.[15]

D. *An Index of Final Products*

In addition to the indexes in Table 1, we have computed an index of the output of final industrial products—i.e., products which are components of final demand.[16] We have done so because of possible interest in three aspects of the results: (a) they may be of use as interpolating or extrapolating indexes for national product components; (b) they may be of interest in relating changes in the level of industrial activity to changes in industrial deliveries of final products; and (c) the consumers' goods component, when related to population changes, serves as a measure of the changing contribution of industry to living standards.

The index (Table 6) includes the following commodity groups: machinery, building materials and consumers' goods. Of course building materials are not final products, strictly speaking, but are inputs to con-

[14] See [11, Oct. 16, 1959]. The decree calls for a 13 per cent average annual increase in 1958-1960 and a further 12 per cent increase in 1961 in the production of consumers' durables and housewares. Though our indexes do not cover all such commodities, we do have data on many. If we construct an output index for those items for which we have output series, the implied average annual rates of increase are 23 per cent in 1950-1953, 30 per cent in 1953-1955, and 6 per cent in 1955-1958. See [4, Table 3 and p. 130, fn. 1]. The index for consumers' durables and housewares increases much more rapidly than that for all nonfoods in the 1950-1955 period and somewhat less rapidly than that for all nonfoods in the 1955-1958 period. Thus, it appears that the decree in question is an attempt to improve a sector which in the 1955-1958 period failed by far to maintain the 1950-1955 annual rates of increase and that the original seven-year plan goals for this sector implied something much closer to the 1955-1958 rates of increase as against the 1950-1955 rates.

[15] Thus, the official rates of increase for 1958-1964 become (in percentages):

All Industrial Output	10.3
1. Group A Industry	10.8–11.1
a. Machine-building and Metal-working	12.2
2. Group B Industry	8.4–8.7

For the corresponding 1950-1958 rates of increase, see footnote 11 above.

[16] For the details of this calculation and for further discussion of the index, see [4, Section 4.5].

TABLE 6—INDEX OF OUTPUT OF FINAL PRODUCTS OF INDUSTRY[a]
(1950 = 100)

	1927/28	1932	1937	1940	1945	1950	1955	1958	Weight for Commodity Group[b] (Percentage)
All Final Products	37.3	45.9	74.0	75.6	31.5	100.0	158.6	200.8	100
1. Capital goods	9.3	23.3	47.4	40.2	16.2	100.0	147.5	200.6	42.0
a. Machinery	6.8	19.5	40.9	34.3	13.6	100.0	136.2	185.0	33.3
b. Building materials	18.8	37.6	72.3	62.9	26.0	100.0	190.4	260.5	8.7
2. Consumers' goods	57.6	62.2	93.2	101.2	42.6	100.0	166.7	201.0	58.0

[a] See [4, Table 40 and pp. 135–41] for the details of the calculation and for postwar annual values of the index of final products.

[b] Since an index of final products should have gross-value rather than value-added weights, we have reweighted the subindexes as follows: (1) The consumers' goods component is obtained by weighting the indexes of foods and nonfoods from Table 1 by the 1950 retail sales of each. (2) The machinery and building materials components are the indexes in Table 1— i.e., each with Jan. 1, 1950 wholesale price weights. To obtain the capital goods index the machinery and building materials indexes are weighted by the 1950 value of output for the two groups as computed in the present study—i.e., without imputations. (3) The resulting indexes for capital goods and consumers' goods are combined into an index of all final products by weights derived, with difficulties and uncertainties, from official gross value of output data.

struction activities whose outputs are final products. In the absence of direct measures of construction output at constant prices, others have used materials inputs as an indirect measure and it is in this sense that we include building materials as final products of industry.[17]

The index omits a number of important construction materials—notably, sawn wood and metals used in construction. If we substitute for our building materials index Raymond P. Powell's more comprehensive index of construction materials inputs and increase the weight assigned to construction materials accordingly [9], the index of all final products is essentially unchanged, while the capital goods index for the 1927/28-1950 period is changed substantially and shows a much smaller increase in output [4, pp. 142-43].

If we compare the index of final products with a similarly weighted index of all industrial products[18]—so that the only difference between

[17] For a materials inputs index of the volume of construction, see [10]. For a discussion of this type of index and of alternatives, see [3] and [8].

[18] I.e., an index of producers' goods other than machinery is obtained with Jan. 1, 1950 price weights throughout, and this index is combined with the consumers' goods and machinery indexes in Table 6 using the weights shown there. This gross-value weighted index differs only slightly from the value-added weighted index of all industrial products in Table 1 [4, pp. 144-45].

the two indexes is the inclusion of "intermediate products" in the latter —the two indexes move quite closely together in the 1950-1955 and 1955-1958 periods, but the final products index shows a much smaller increase over the 1927/28-1950 period than the index of all industrial products. Though these results suggest a more rapid increase for intermediate products than for final products in the 1927/28-1950 period and approximately proportionate increases in the 1950-1958 period, they should not necessarily be interpreted as indicative of changing structural relationships within Soviet industry. The results omit from consideration one additional commodity group—agricultural products consumed in industry, primarily in the production of consumers' goods —which (a) undoubtedly increased much less rapidly than intermediate products in the 1927/28-1950 period, and (b) increased very substantially in the 1950-1958 period.

Dividing the consumers' goods index in Table 6 by a population index [4, Table 41], we obtain the following index of per capita consumers' goods output:

1927/28	1932	1937	1940	1945	1950	1955	1958
69.9	70.8	102.9	93.7	45.4	100.0	153.6	177.4

This index shows essentially no change in the per capita output of consumers' goods between 1927/28 and 1932, a substantial increase between 1932 and 1937, an appreciable decline between 1937 and 1940, recovery beyond the 1940 level by 1950 but not yet to the 1937 level, and substantial increases between 1950 and 1955 and between 1955 and 1958. At best, however, this index measures not living standards but the contribution of industry to living standards. Omitted are a number of important elements of Soviet consumption: services, consumption in kind, direct sales by agriculture to households. If we confine our attention to the commodity component of living standards and examine the available data on consumption in kind and direct sales to households, both omissions appear to result in the same direction of error in the index of per capita consumers' goods output. On both counts, the "true" change in the commodity component of living standards between 1927/28 and later peacetime years appears to be either a smaller increase than our index indicates or a decrease [4, pp. 148-50].

E. Changes in Productivity

Table 7 presents estimates of changes in employment and in output per man-year for consumers' goods and producers' goods other than machinery.[19] The estimates require the following comments:

---

[19] Details of these calculations and a fuller statement of the underlying rationale and argument are found in [4, Sections 4.61 and 4.62].

TABLE 7—INDEXES OF EMPLOYMENT AND OUPTUT PER MAN-YEAR FOR PRODUCERS'
GOODS OTHER THAN MACHINERY AND CONSUMERS' GOODS
(1950 = 100)

	1927/28	1932	1937	1940	1955	1956	1958
Indexes of Employment							
1. Producers' goods other than machinery	31.7	56.8	59.6	69.0	124.4	127.3	—
2. Consumers' goods	62.6	66.2	90.2	97.5	129.3	131.9	—
3. Consumers' goods and producers' goods other than machinery	43.6	60.5	71.6	80.2	126.3	129.1	137.6
Indexes of Output per Man-Year							
4. Producers' goods other than machinery	68.7	74.1	112.5	103.8	127.5	134.1	—
5. Consumers' goods	86.7	89.6	98.8	100.8	131.7	139.6	—
6. Consumers' goods and producers' goods other than machinery	79.3	80.8	105.8	102.4	129.2	136.3	148.1

Source: The employment and productivity indexes are from [4, Tables 45 and 46, and p. 168].

1. The productivity indexes are the conventional kind: indexes of output divided by indexes of employment. For this measure, however, the output indexes used are not quite the same as those in Table 1. We have substituted employment for wage-bill weights wherever the latter are used in Table 1. This enables us to interpret the reweighted output indexes as indicators of labor requirements for the given year's output with base-year (1950) labor productivity. The ratio of this magnitude to the labor actually required—i.e., to the index of actual employment —is a measure of the change in labor productivity between the base and given years.

2. Our estimates refer only to consumers' goods and producers' goods other than machinery. They are limited in this manner because: (a) the employment data available for the machine-building industry include both civilian machinery and munitions employment, whereas the output data refer only to civilian machinery; and (b) productivity calculations for all industry are quite sensitive to this distinction. Although we are unable to distinguish with precision that portion of total employment in machine-building which is devoted to civilian output, we have attempted illustrative calculations based on alternative assumptions about the distribution of employment. These suggest: (a) that over the 1927/28-1937 period, the increase in output per man-year for *all* civilan output (i.e., including civilian machinery, other producers'

goods and consumers' goods) was about the same as that for other producers' goods and consumers' goods; and (b) that over the 1927/28-1950 period, the increase in output per man-year for all civilian output was considerably greater than that for other producers' goods and consumers' goods. We are unable to make similar calculations for the post-1950 period.

3. The employment series refers to man-years worked by direct production workers. Since, at least since 1932, *total* employment in industry —i.e., man-years worked by direct production workers, maintenance personnel and white-collar workers and technicians—appears to have increased less rapidly than employment of production workers [16, p. 23], our measures appear to understate the increase in productivity for the more comprehensive group of employed persons. Also, the number of hours worked per year has tended to decline over the 1927/28-1932 period, to increase over the 1932-1950 period, and to remain about constant thereafter; thus, for the pre-1950 period, output per man-hour changes somewhat differently from output per man-year.

4. The employment indexes are also subject to errors, the most important of which is the following: Employment in small-scale industry accounts for about 30 per cent of our estimated total in 1927/28 and about 18 per cent in 1932. The underlying data on small-scale industry employment are sufficiently ambiguous to yield the possibility of appreciable error in our employment and productivity estimates for those years.

With the foregoing qualifications in mind, let us turn to the productivity trends which emerge from Table 7: (1) During the prewar period, there were modest increases in productivity from 1927/28 to 1932, substantial increases from 1932 to 1937, and small changes in both directions from 1937 to 1940. For the prewar period as a whole, output per man-year increased much more rapidly for producers' goods than for consumers' goods. (2) The productivity indexes move uniformly upward in the post-1950 period, the increases for consumers' goods exceeding slightly those for producers' goods. In 1950, however, output per man-year was still below the peak prewar levels, and this in spite of a substantial increase in hours worked per year. (3) For the 1927/28-1958 period as a whole, output per man-year has increased by about 87 per cent, an increase compounded from a 33 per cent increase between 1927/28 and 1937 (the peak prewar year) and a 40 per cent increase between 1937 and 1958. Judging from the 1927/28-1956 data, the increase for producers' goods is substantially greater than that for consumers' goods.

The average annual growth rates in employment and output per man-

316   THE AMERICAN ECONOMIC REVIEW

year for producers' goods other than machinery and consumers' goods
are as follows (in percentages):

	1927/28–1932	1932–1937	1937–1940	1927/28–1940	1950–1955	1955–1958	1950–1958
Output per Man-Year	0.4	5.5	decrease	1.9	5.3	4.7	5.0
Employment	8.0	3.4	3.9	5.0	4.8	2.9	4.1

In the post-1950 period, the rate of productivity increase declines between 1950-1955 and 1955-1958, but only slightly, and is substantially
higher than that for the prewar period as a whole. In the post-1950 period, the rate of employment increase declines appreciably and is below that for the prewar period as a whole. Thus, our calculations show:
(1) no general trend toward retardation in the growth of productivity
within the prewar period or as between the prewar and postwar periods,
and (2) a slight, possibly insignificant, retardation within the postwar
period. They suggest as well that the productivity growth rates may
have been supported by a tendency toward decline over time in the rate
of increase of employment.

The seven-year plan implies a further decline in the future rate of
productivity increase. It suggests, without clearly indicating, that the
number of industrial workers is to increase by about 3.2 per cent per
year in the 1958-1965 period, as compared with the 3.3 per cent rate at
which employment in all branches of industry, including machine-building, grew during 1955-1958.[20] Since the seven-year plan output goals
imply a significant decline in 1958-1965 rates of increase relative to the
1955-1958 rates, they also imply a rate of increase of labor productivity
significantly below that realized during 1955-1958. Should the growth
of productivity continue at about the 1955-1958 rate, the plan would be
fulfilled ahead of schedule and the indicated retardation in the growth
of industrial output would not occur. Perhaps this is one of the "reserves" for overfulfillment mentioned above.

It would be desirable to accompany the foregoing discussion of trends
in labor productivity with a parallel discussion of trends in capital
productivity and to obtain measures of changes in capital-labor ratios.
Unfortunately, the only capital measures now available are the official
series about which little is presently known. Since we are unable to
vouch for the reliability of the capital series, about all we can do is
to make explicit the relationships implied by the official capital series
when compared with our employment and output indexes. Such com-

[20] For the seven-year plan data, see [11, Feb. 8, 1959], and also [4, pp. 175-76, fn. 1].
For 1955–1958, see [4, Table 45, and p. 168].

parisons for 1927/28, 1932, 1937, 1940, 1950, 1955, and 1957 yield the following highly tentative and provisional results:

1. The ratio of capital to labor has increased monotonically and substantially over the observed years from 1927/28 through 1957.[21]

2. The ratio of capital to output has increased (or capital productivity has decreased) monotonically and substantially over the observed years from 1927/28 through 1950, but the change is ambiguous from 1950 through 1957.[22]

[21] See [4, Table 49] for these comparisons through 1955. For the 1957 capital index, see [15, p. 59]. For the 1957 employment index see [4, Table 45]. Both the capital and employment indexes include factors engaged in munitions output; and hence, on this account, the observed changes in the capital-labor ratio are relatively reliable.

[22] See [4, Tables 22 and 49] and [15, p. 59]. Even if the official capital indexes are accepted as reliable, this comparison encounters a number of difficulties—especially, that the capital indexes include capital engaged in munitions output whereas the output indexes exclude munitions; and that the capital indexes appear to resemble chained rather than fixed-base index numbers. Thus to make the comparison more precise, one should include munitions in the output index and reweight the prewar output indexes with early-year weights. However, on examination of the resultant output increase which is necessary to yield a decrease in the capital-output ratio, it is still clear that the official capital series implies a substantial increase in the capital-output ratio from 1927/8 through 1950. In the post-1950 period, on the other hand, it is quite possible that inclusion of munitions output might have arrested or reversed the apparent increase in the capital-output ratio. For the underlying argument, see [4, Section 4.63].

A calculation of the change in the productivity of labor and capital combined over the 1927/8-1955 period, with hypothetical weights of ¾ for labor and ¼ for capital (and similarly for weights of ⅘ to ⅕ and ⅔ to ⅓), shows an increase in combined factor productivity from 1927/8 to 1940, from 1950 to 1955, and from 1927/8 to 1955. If, however, the weight of capital is increased to ½, then only the 1932-1937 and 1950-1955 periods emerge as periods with output increases clearly in excess of the increase in labor and capital combined. See [4, Table 50, and pp. 183-88].

REFERENCES

1. D. R. HODGMAN, *Soviet Industrial Production 1928-1951.* Cambridge 1954.

2. N. JASNY, *The Soviet 1956 Statistical Handbook: A Commentary.* East Lansing 1957.

3. N. M. KAPLAN, "Some Methodological Notes on the Deflation of Construction," *Jour. Am. Stat. Assoc.,* Sept. 1959, *54,* 535-55.

4. N. M. KAPLAN AND R. H. MOORSTEEN (with the assistance of E. S. Wainstein), *Indexes of Soviet Industrial Output,* RAND RM-2495. Santa Monica 1959.

5. V. KUROTCHENKO, "Mobilizovat' rezervy dosrochnogo vypolneniia semiletnego plana," *Planovoe khoziaistvo* ("Mobilize the Reserves for fulfillment of the Seven-Year Plan Before the Appointed Time," *Planned Economy*), 1959, No. 9, 3-14.

6. R. H. MOORSTEEN, *Prices and Production of Soviet Machinery, 1928-1958,* to be published.

7. G. W. NUTTER, "Industrial Growth in the Soviet Union," *Am. Econ. Rev.*, Proc., May 1958, *48*, 398-411.

8. R. P. POWELL, *A Materials-Input Index of Soviet Construction, 1927/28 to 1955: Part I*, RAND RM-1872. Santa Monica 1959.

9. ————, *A Materials-Input Index of Soviet Construction, Revised and Extended*, RAND RM-2454. Santa Monica 1959.

10. ————, "An Index of Soviet Construction, 1927/28 to 1955," *Rev. Econ. Stat.*, May 1959, *41*, 170-77.

11. *Pravda*. Various issues of the daily newspaper, specified by dates in the text.

12. F. SETON, "The Tempo of Soviet Industrial Expansion," *Manchester Stat. Soc.*, Jan. 9, 1957, 1-39.

13. D. B. SHIMKIN AND F. A. LEEDY, "Soviet Industrial Growth—Its Cost, Extent and Prospects," *Automotive Industries*, Jan. 1, 1958, *118*, 4-35.

14. S. STRUMILIN, "Dumy o semiletke," *Literaturnaia gazeta* ("Thoughts on the Seven-Year Plan," *Literary Gazette*), Dec. 2, 1958, 1-2.

15. Tsentral'noe statisticheskoe upravlenie, *Narodnoe khoziaistvo SSSR v 1958 godu.* (Central Statistical Administration, *National Economy of the USSR in 1958.*) Moscow 1959.

16. Tsentral'noe statisticheskoe upravlenie, *Promyshlennost' SSSR.* (Central Statistical Administration, *Industry of the USSR.*) Moscow 1957.

SOVIET AGRICULTURE: STRUCTURE AND GROWTH

(By D. Gale Johnson and Arcadius Kahan, University of Chicago)

During the past 3 years there has been a manyfold increase in the publication, and perhaps production, of official Soviet agricultural statistics. Many of these data were not available at the time of the preparation of the excellent publication, "Soviet Economic Growth: A Comparison With the United States," which was published by the Joint Economic Committee in 1957. The published data include detailed information on sown areas, on livestock numbers, on agricultural machinery and a large variety of miscellaneous information. In recent months long-term series have been published on the output of most major agricultural products, including, at long last, estimates that presume to reflect the actual harvest of grain for 1949 to date as well as for 1910–14 on present territory.

A. DATA PROBLEMS

Despite the very considerable increase in the volume of data available, it is not at all certain that our knowledge about and understanding of the agriculture of the Soviet Union have been significantly increased. Many of the data that have been released are of uncertain quality. Many other data that are vital to an understanding of the structure and growth of Soviet agriculture have not been made available. The pattern of release of agricultural data over the past several years has been consistent with the view that the selection of data to be made available is a part of a process designed to provide as favorable a picture as possible of developments in the Soviet Union. There are occasional exceptions to this, when the release of data is required to support an internal policy measure. But as a general rule, the agricultural data that have been made available have been timed to present a picture of achievement and progress. When the record is an unfavorable one, the data frequently have been withheld.

A brief résumé of the data that are still unavailable supports the view that statistics are used as a tool of the Communist state rather than as a means of providing a basis for analysis and understanding. While gross output data are available for most agricultural products, almost no information has been made available on the utilization of those products. How much of the milk is fed to calves? How much of the grain is available for human consumption? How many tons of potatoes are fed to livestock? Relatively few data are available on agricultural employment, apparently because the level of output per worker is so low compared to the United States and other western countries.

What of the quality of the data that are available? While generalization is not possible on the basis of present knowledge, brief comments concerning a few of the available series will indicate some of the difficulties involved in the use of these data.[1] The milk production estimates include the milk of goats, sheep, and other animals as well as cow milk.[2] The estimate of milk production apparently also includes the milk sucked by calves for recent years, though that does not seem to be the case for the period prior to 1940. Crude estimates indicate that the amount of milk sucked by calves may be as much as 6 or 7 million tons in recent years or more than 10 percent of total production. Separate estimates are not available for the amount of milk fed, by hand, to calves and this might amount to as much as 3 or 4 million more tons.

Furthermore, it is uncertain whether the estimate of total milk production is actual weight of milk produced or represents milk of standardzied butterfat content. The milk purchased from State farms is apparently paid for on the basis of milk of 3.2 percent fat content. If the average fat content is 3.8 percent, 5 million tons of milk may become almost 6 million tons in the reported data. And if the standardized fat content were changed or varied from period to period, the consistency of the series becomes very questionable. Finally, it is not at all clear that Soviet officials know the total output of milk with a reasonable degree of accuracy. Over half of the milk is produced by peasants and workers and employees. Several million different households are involved. Short of a carefully selected, large-scale sample with honest responses from the respondents, it is difficult to see how accurate estimates are possible. And such a sample does not exist.

The data on meat output, expressed both in slaughter and live weight, seem to provide a reasonably consistent series over time. At least comparisons with previously available data for the late twenties and the thirties indicate a consistent upward revision of the tonnage figures such as one would expect from the change in the concept of meat. One of the claims made for the American meatpacking industry has been that they make use of everything but the pig's squeal. The Soviet statisticians do the American industry one better; they weigh and count as meat everything but the pig's squeal. This is a slight exaggeration, but not by very much. The Soviet concept of meat includes offal products that are normally excluded in other nations, though there is little reason to believe that the Soviet utilization of offal products is much, if any, more extensive than elsewhere. The art of the sausage and bologna manufacture is well known throughout the world and the ability of the masters of that art to utilize any and every edible part of a slaughtered animal can hardly be questioned. Thus while the Soviet meat series may be internally consistent, the series cannot be compared to meat production or consumption figures for other nations.[3]

In the case of the grain production data, we are almost wholly in the dark concerning what concept of production is being used. Is it the weight of the grain as it comes from the combine? Or are adjustments made for loss of moisture and the trash and chaff included with the grain? Are postharvest losses excluded or included?

---

[1] More explicit comments appear as notes to some of the Appendix Tables.
[2] For an excellent discussion of the recent milk and meat statistics, see Nancy Nimitz, "Soviet Statistics of Meat and Milk Output: A Note on Their Comparability Over Time," RM–2326, the Rand Corp., 1959.
[3] The Soviet data on meat production should be discounted by at least 10 percent and perhaps as much as 20 percent to achieve comparability. See footnote C, table 12.

How accurately is the corn grain in the corn silage estimated? Khrushchev has accused previous holders of his office of deceiving the world about the level of Soviet grain production;[4] the level of production indicated by the recently released figures do not entirely persuade us that some degree of deceit is still not being practiced.

B. GROWTH OF AGRICULTURAL OUTPUT

Even if we ignore all questions of the accuracy of the available physical production data, there are a number of problems involved in the measurement of total agricultural output of the Soviet Union or any other country. One problem is that of the appropriate concept of output; another is that of the appropriate set of weights for aggregating the physical volume of the individual commodities to derive a single set of values or index numbers. In the particular case of the Soviet Union we have the difficulty arising out of the territorial expansion of the Soviet Union in 1939.

1. Measures of agricultural output

We have constructed two measures of total agricultural output. The first concept is that of gross agricultural farm output. In all reference to gross agricultural output we have used official Soviet data, when available, or have made estimates that we believe are consistent with the official estimating procedures and concepts.[5] Gross production figures are available for 11 groups of commodities. The data may be found in appendix table 3.

A legitimate objection to the concept of gross agricultural production, as a measure of total agricultural output, is that it involves duplication in the sense that a part of the output is required to produce the same or other agricultural products. The gross output of grain, for example, includes the grain that is used for seed and for feed for livestock as well as the amount that is available for direct human consumption, industrial use, export, or addition to stocks. For many reasons we are probably more interested in a concept of agricultural output that reflects the volume of production available for nonfarm use; in other words, we wish a concept which eliminates as much as possible the amount of double counting of agricultural output. In gross agricultural output, the grain that is used for feed is counted twice—first as a part of grain output and second as a part of livestock output. The concept that we have defined as net agricultural output is simply the gross agricultural output minus all farm uses of the various products. The farm uses are primarily feed and seed, though in some cases we have also subtracted a factor to represent waste.

We have used three different sets of price weights in the construction of the gross and net agricultural output indexes. The prices received by farmers in the 1926–27 production year are apparently those used by Soviet statisticians to measure agricultural output during the late twenties and the thirties. We have also used average prices received for 1925–29 in order to more fully reflect the under-

[4] Last December Khrushchev said: "Yet Malenkov, in defiance of the facts, declared before the Party Congress in 1952 that the country's gross grain harvest was 8 billion poods and that the grain problem had then, if you please, been solved once and for all. Malenkov acted dishonestly, manipulating by employing the data of the so-called biological yield. * * * In 1952, the best harvest year of the period. the collective and state farms harvested not 8 billion poods but only 5,600 million poods" (Pravda, Dec. 16, 1958).
[5] Our index of gross agricultural output is not directly comparable to the official Soviet index. The Soviet gross output index includes hay, straw, chaff, and manure as well as some minor commodities not included in our index because of lack of data.

lying conditions in the last years of peasant agriculture in the Soviet Union. The third set of price weights used is the official purchase prices announced in 1958.

2. *Indexes of agricultural output.*

As measures of the trend in agricultural output in the Soviet Union, it makes little difference which concept of output is used or which set of prices is used as weights. This is clear from inspection of the results presented in tables 1 and 2. The various indexes indicate that output in 1957 was approximately 64 to 67 percent greater than 1928.

TABLE 1.—*Indexes of gross agricultural output, Soviet Union* [1]

	1926–27 price weights (1926–29=100)	1926–27 price weights (1928=100)	1925–29 price weights (1928=100)	1958 price weights (1928=100)
1925	94.4	92.6		
1926	98.5	96.7		
1927	96.7	94.9		
1928	101.9	100.0	100.0	100.0
1929	102.9	101.0		
1930	106.2	104.2		
1931	94.1	92.4		
1932	83.2	81.7	80.3	79.3
1933	86.3	84.7		
1934	86.7	85.1		
1935	97.4	95.6		
1936	91.6	89.9		
1937	114.9	112.8	110.5	104.8
1938	100.4	98.5		
1940	122.5	120.3	120.3	118.0
1950	126.8	124.4	124.8	119.0
1951	115.2	113.1		
1952	131.1	128.6		
1953	131.0	128.6	128.8	125.7
1954	136.5	134.0	133.6	131.4
1955	154.6	151.8	149.9	148.2
1956	178.4	175.1	173.3	169.2
1957	170.4	167.2	167.3	166.8
1958 [2]	(195.6)	(192.0)		

[1] Indexes for each year are for the territory within the boundaries existing at the time; 1940 data refer to present territory. The prices used as weights in constructing the indexes are as follows (in rubles per ton, except as noted):

	1926–27	1925–29	1958
Grain	55.5	53.32	740
Potatoes	25.0	31.28	400
Vegetables	60.5	60.5	900
Sunflower seed	66.5	74.44	1,720
Sugar beets	11.6	12.08	235
Raw cotton	282.0	282.0	3,400
Flax fiber (scutched)	368.5	439.0	23,000
Wool (greasy weight)	1,079.0	1,126.8	
Wool, coarse			23,700
Wool, semicoarse			24,700
Wool, semifine			32,900
Wool, fine			41,000
Milk	59.8	68.5	1,150
Eggs (per 1,000)	30.47	32.864	600
Meat, dressed weight old concept	421.2	413.4	
Meat, dressed weight new concept	340.0		
Meat, live weight old concept	210.6		
Beef and veal live weight			6,190
Mutton, live weight			5,360
Pork			7,860
Poultry	725.0	772.5	
Hens and chickens			8,950
Ducks and geese			7,380

[2] A tentative estimate based on less complete data.

Sources: (1) Gossudarstvennaia Planovaia Komissia (Gosplan): Kontrolnye Tsifry Narodnogo Khoziaistva S.S.S.R. na 1929–30 god. Moscow 1930. pp. 581–583.
(2) V. K. Fedinin—Novaia Sistema Zagotovok Selskokhoziaistvennykh Produktovi Ekonomika Kolkhoznogo Proizvodstva. Moscow 1959. p. 12.

TABLE 2.—*Indexes of net agricultural output, Soviet Union* [1]

	1926–27 price weights (1926–29=100)	1926–27 price weights (1928=100)	1925–20 price weights (1928=100)	1958 price weights (1928=100)
1925	95.6	93.2		
1926	96.9	94.5		
1927	96.0	93.6		
1928	102.5	100.0	100.0	100.0
1929	104.7	102.1		
1930	110.2	107.5		
1931	97.1	94.8		
1932	83.6	81.6	79.6	77.3
1933	87.8	85.7		
1934	87.1	85.0		
1935	95.8	93.5		
1936	91.6	89.4		
1937	121.5	118.5	114.6	104.6
1938	103.3	100.8		
1940	123.9	120.3	120.5	115.1
1950	130.2	127.0	126.1	117.8
1951	122.4	119.4		
1952	132.6	129.3		
1953	134.4	131.1	130.1	125.2
1954	139.0	135.6	133.9	130.4
1955	156.1	152.3	149.0	146.1
1956	178.2	173.9	170.4	165.0
1957	170.5	166.3	165.7	164.1

[1] See appendix table 4.

However, one should not interpret all of the change in the index as a true increase in agricultural output. Some of the increase was the result of territorial change; on the basis of the available data it is not possible to determine with any precision the effect of territorial acquisition on the output index. As a rough estimate, if there had been no change in territory in the last three decades, the index of total agricultural output might have been 145 to 152 in 1957 instead of approximately 166. Put another way, approximately 12 to 14 percent of the net output on the present territory in 1940 was the output in the acquired territories.

A few comments may be pertinent concerning changes in the output indexes over time. There was a drastic fall in output following the collectivization of agriculture. Output in 1932 was about a fifth below that of 1928. While some of the decline was due to adverse weather, much of it was due to the resistance of the peasants, expressed in part through the slaughter of their livestock including over half of all the horses. Output gradually increased, reaching a peak in the favorable year weatherwise of 1937. Most of the increase in output between 1938 and 1940 was due to the acquisition of territory.

By 1950 the level of output was somewhat greater than in 1940, on the same territory. Output was relatively static through 1953. There was a small increase in 1954, but the gains in output through 1958 were very substantial indeed. At the present time it is not possible to determine how much of the recent increases in output have been due to favorable climatic developments. Of the 4 years, 1955 through 1958, one (1958) was an extremely favorable year, perhaps as far above average for the fifties as 1937 was for the thirties. Another year (1956) was also an exceptionally favorable one. In both 1955 and 1957 there were major areas of the Soviet Union that had adverse weather, but this is probably a normal or usual phenomenon and these 2 years were at least average in terms of the impact of climatic factors. It is probably true that a considerable fraction of the

206 COMPARISONS OF UNITED STATES AND SOVIET ECONOMIES

recent increase is the result of greater incentives, improved management and additional inputs, but at the present time it is not possible to indicate how large this fraction may be.

3. *Changes in output for major commodity groups*

The changes that have occurred in the output, both absolutely and relatively, of major commodity groups are of significance in indicating both the priorities of the planners and the productive possibilities that have existed. In table 3 we have divided total gross and net agricultural output into three broad groups. The first category includes the livestock products, for which the demand expands relatively rapidly as real income grows and which produce relatively few food nutrients per unit of land and labor. However, livestock do transform into food many agricultural products that cannot be directly consumed by the population—pasture, straw, chaff, certain byproducts of food preparation—and thus up to a certain level of output are not really competitive with the more economical sources of food. The second category is the major food crops and includes grain, potatoes, and vegetables. These crops provide a relatively high output of calories and other food nutrients per hectare of land and other inputs used in production. The third category includes the industrial crops.

The most striking change has been the rise in the level of output and the relative importance of the industrial crops in total output. The share in gross output has increased from less than 6 percent to almost 12 percent in recent years;[6] the output index increased from 100 in 1928 to 333 in 1957. This increase probably represents the priorities imposed by a policy of self-sufficiency. Recent levels of cotton output have been approximately five to six times the levels of the late twenties and have now reached approximately a half of the U.S. output which has been declining for the past three decades. The cotton area has more than doubled and yields have approximately doubled.

TABLE 3.—*Indexes of gross and net output of livestock products, technical crops, and food crops, Soviet Union* [1]

	Gross output			Net output		
	Livestock products	Food crops	Industrial crops	Livestock products	Food crops	Industrial crops
1928	100	100	100	100	100	100
1932	61	91	126	61	101	119
1937	71	131	218	71	161	213
1940 [2]	102	125	201	98	137	192
1950	107	124	240	100	140	240
1953	120	120	261	114	128	266
1954	127	125	267	120	131	266
1955	137	146	307	129	151	310
1956	149	176	342	142	183	343
1957	165	152	332	158	145	333

[1] 1926–27 prices used as weights; based on data in appendix tables 3 and 4.
[2] Present boundaries.

[6] The change in the share of net output has been 7.7 percent in 1928 to 15.5 percent in 1958.

4. Importance of private producers

Because of the basic differences in the relationship between the state and individual in the Soviet society from the relationships prevailing outside the Communist countries, it is pertinent to determine the relative shares of agricultural output produced by the private and socialized sectors in agriculture, as well as the relative shares of the prevailing institutions within the socialized sector, the collective farms (kolkhozy), the state farms (sovkhozy) and the auxiliary farms of various state institutions (podsobnyie khoziaistva). The distribution of gross output, valued in 1926–27 prices, is presented in the table below.

TABLE 4.—*Shares of producer groups in gross agricultural output*

[Percent]

| Years | Collective farms | Socialized sector | | Total social | Private sector |
		Sovkhozy	Total State farms		
1940	51.7	5.9	7.0	57.7	42.3
1950	54.2	5.7	6.8	61.0	39.0
1953	57.7	6.6	7.8	65.5	34.5
1955	61.1	7.4	8.3	69.4	30.6
1956	59.2	10.0	10.8	70.0	30.0

The distribution of output among the various sectors in 1940 especially the large share of the private sector, is partially explained by the territorial expansion of the boundaries of the Soviet Union in 1939–40, and the private farms of the acquired territories were not yet absorbed by the socialized sector. During the year 1937 for example the distribution was much more similar to the one observed in 1953. The 1950 distribution reflects the wartime and postwar expansion of private output in potatoes and vegetables, as well as the incomplete collectivization of the new territories.

The overall trends, however, are indicated by the table and may be summarized as the slow decline of the share of private output relative to the socialized share and within the socialized sector, the growth of the share of the state farms (sovkhozy). The available data for 1957 and 1958 indicate a substantial rise in the output of the state farms, in part due to the conversion of collective farms into state farms. How far and how rapid this process is intended to go on, is of course anyone's guess.

With respect to the distribution of livestock output we have more detailed data which permit estimates of the relative shares of private and socialized sectors for several consecutive years.

TABLE 5.—*Shares of socialized and private sectors in gross output of livestock products*

[Percent]

Year	Socialized	Private	Year	Socialized	Private
1940	24.9	75.1	1954	38.8	61.2
1950	29.3	70.7	1955	41.6	58.4
1951	33.3	66.7	1956	42.6	57.4
1952	37.0	63.0	1957	44.6	55.4
1953	39.9	60.1			

There is little question that the Soviet authorities have decided to assure the socialized sector with a dominant position in the output of livestock products.   Pressure is mounting upon all private producers— urban dwellers and state farm employees as well as collective farm members—to turn over their livestock to the collective and state farms.   But by and large this policy is more subtle and cautious than similar policies in the past.

5. Comparisons of agricultural output, U.S.S.R. and United States

The data presented in table 6 provide measures of the changes in the absolute levels of gross output, as officially reported, for the 11 major agricultural commodities for the Soviet Union and data that permit rough comparisons with the output of 9 of the groups in the United States.   The absolute level of output in the Soviet Union in 1955–58 exceeded that in the United States for potatoes, sugar, and wool. The Soviet output was substantially lower for grains, vegetables, cotton, meat, and eggs.   While the gross output of milk was only 10 percent less than in the United States, we believe that the amount of milk remaining for human consumption was more than a fourth less than in the United States.[7]

Because of the change in territory of the Soviet Union it is more difficult to make meaningful statements concerning output growth since 1925–29.   As noted above, Soviet agricultural output probably increased by about 12 to 14 percent in 1940 as a result of territorial expansion.   If one attempts to adjust for this in a crude fashion, it is clear that the Soviet output growth was significantly greater than ours for potatoes, sugar, cotton, and wool.   The increase in grain output was probably somewhat higher than in the United States, while the output growth of vegetables, meat, and eggs was less.   The case of milk is uncertain, though Soviet output on comparable territory may have increased slightly more than in the United States

Between 1925–29 and 1955–58 the index of farm output for the United States increased by 58 percent.[8]   This index is basically similar to the index of net agricultural output that we have calculated for the Soviet Union.   Based on a tentative estimate of the index of net agricultural output for 1958, the increase for the Soviet Union between 1925–29 and 1955–58 was approximately 70 percent.   This estimate is not adjusted for the change of territory.   If one makes the extreme assumption that there would have been no change in output on the acquired territories if they had remained independent of the Soviet Union, one arrives at an increase for the period for the 1928 territory of approximately 55 percent.

While this increase in total agricultural output is no larger than that achieved in the United States during a period of time when we have been trying to restrict agricultural output, there is no question that the increase in output is a very substantial one.   And output during 1958 was substantially above the average for 1955–58, though it may be noted that the same was true for the United States.   In both cases climatic conditions undoubtedly were in part responsible for the favorable outcome.

---

[7] See table 13 for a presentation of a net milk output series for the two countries.
[8] U.S. Department of Agriculture, "Agricultural Outlook Charts, 1959," p. 64.

TABLE 6.—*Gross output of major agricultural commodities, Soviet Union and United States* [1]

[Million tons]

	Grain	Potatoes	Vege-tables [2]	Sugar [3]	Seed cotton [4]
A. Soviet Union:					
1925–29	73.2	43.0	10.6	8.4	0.70
1950–54	84.1	72.8	10.5	22.0	3.85
1955–58	119.7	85.4	11.5	39.4	4.30
B. United States:					
1925–29	121.7	9.5	13.6	7.2	10.5
1950–54	140.7	10.1	19.0	14.2	9.7
1955–58	150.9	11.1	20.0	18.7	8.7
C. Ratio, Soviet Union to United States (percent):					
1925–29	60.1	452.6	77.9	116.7	16.7
1950–54	70.2	720.8	55.3	154.9	39.7
1955–58	74.8	769.3	57.5	210.7	49.4

	Flax-fiber	Sun-flower seed	Wool	Milk	Meat (dressed weight)	Eggs [5] (billions)
A. Soviet Union:						
1925–29	0.30	1.97	0.17	30.0	4.69	10.3
1950–54	.21	2.06	.21	36.4	5.36	14.5
1955–58	.45	3.01	.28	51.1	7.04	21.0
B. United States:						
1925–29			.15	43.0	9.8	37.6
1950–54			.12	53.9	14.4	58.4
1955–58			.12	56.7	16.6	59.5
C. Ratio, Soviet Union to United States (percent):						
1925–29			113.3	69.8	47.8	27.4
1950–54			175.0	67.5	37.2	24.8
1955–58			233.3	90.1	42.4	35.3

[1] Sources: Soviet data, see appendix table 3. U.S. data: U.S. Department of Agriculture, Agricultural Statistics, 1957; "Livestock and Meat Statistics, 1957," Stat. Bul. No. 230; "Consumption of Food in the United States, 1909–52," Agriculture Handbook No. 26, supplements for 1954 and 1957; "The National Food Situation," July 1959, "Major Statistical Series of the U.S. Department of Agriculture," vol. 5, Agriculture Handbook No. 118; Crop Production, 1958 Annual Summary," Dec. 17, 1958.
[2] Vegetables for United States excludes melons of all types.
[3] Sugar output for United States is in terms of sugar beet equivalent. Sugar refined from cane sugar converted into sugar beets assuming 14 percent sugar content.
[4] Cotton output for United States converted to seed cotton by assuming lint to seed cotton ratio of 0.33
[5] Egg production for United States is farm production only.

6. Per capita availability of farm products

Our general discussion of changes in agricultural output in the Soviet Union may be concluded by presentation of certain estimates on per capita availability of various agricultural products. The data presented in table 7 do not purport to represent per capita consumption; the data are estimates of net output which include industrial use, exports and changes in stocks, as well as consumption by the Soviet population. Nor has any attempt been made to include imports, but imports have generally been of little significance. The estimates are admittedly subject to error.

The situation with respect to per capita availability in 1950–53 compared to 1926–29 implies little or no improvement. The availability of grain was approximately the same; potatoes, sugar, and cotton had increased substantially. There was a small improvement in the case of eggs, but there were fewer vegetables, less meat and milk, less wool and flax fiber, and less sunflower seed, the major source of vegetable oil for human consumption. Roughly speaking, the index of net agricultural output on a per capita basis was slightly lower in 1950–53 than in 1928.

The data indicate a clear improvement in recent years, especially in grain, sugar, sunflowers, milk, eggs and flax fiber. The change in per capita meat availability has been rather modest, but an improvement has occurred.[9]

TABLE 7.—*Per capita net output of major agricultural products, Soviet Union* [1]

[Kilograms per annum]

	1926–29	1931–34	1935–38	1940	1950–53	1954–57	1955–58
Grains	241. 4	218. 9	247. 3	238. 4	247. 9	274. 6	297. 6
Potatoes	102. 1	133. 5	144. 1	194. 6	172. 8	164. 4	163. 2
Vegetables	49. 8	64. 6	57. 9	50. 1	41. 2	55. 0	56. 4
Sugar beets	52. 0	51. 7	104. 6	90. 5	118. 0	151. 5	187. 5
Sunflower seeds	12. 2	13. 4	10. 1	13. 0	10. 8	15. 2	18. 1
Milk	176. 2	111. 6	131. 6	144. 2	144. 8	182. 8	200. 9
Meat	32. 7	16. 7	19. 8	24. 5	27. 5	33. 5	34. 8
Eggs	64. 2	25. 7	41. 6	58. 9	68. 0	89. 7	95. 1
Cotton	4. 9	7. 5	13. 6	11. 7	19. 7	20. 8	20. 8
Wool	1. 12	. 4	. 6	. 81	1. 06	1. 25	1. 34
Flax-fiber	1. 86	2. 38	2. 33	1. 82	1. 18	1. 87	2. 09

[1] The population estimates used are as follows (in millions): 1926–29, 150.6; 1931–34, 165.6; 1935–38, 169.3; 1940, 191.7; 1950–53, 186.9; 1954–57, 198.3; and 1955–58, 202.3.

C. CHANGES IN IMPUTS AND AVERAGE PRODUCTIVITY

The increase in Soviet agricultural output has been associated with a large increase in the sown area, a small increase in the total labor input, a marked increase in machinery and equipment, and a substantial increase in fertilizer. While it would be desirable to have a measure of the total quantity of inputs used in agriculture for various periods of time, satisfactory estimates are not yet available for all inputs. At this time, we can only indicate the change in some of the major inputs and estimate average productivity or yield. It should be noted that changes in average productivity of labor or yield of crops is not an indication of change in efficiency since the quantities of other inputs have increased much more rapidly than either labor or land.

1. Sown area

By 1925 the total sown area had reached the same level as 1913, for comparable territory. By 1931 the total sown area had increased from 104.3 million hectares to 136.3 million. There was some retrenchment in sown area during the next few years, but by 1938 the sown area was again approximately the same as in 1931. The sown area increased by approximately 14 to 15 million hectares as a consequence of territorial expansion. The 1950 sown area of 146.3 million hectares was somewhat below the 1940 area on comparable terri-

[9] The very great change in the proportion of urban population in the Soviet Union since the late twenties creates certain problems in the interpretation of the per capita data. According to food consumption studies made during the late twenties, there were substantial differences in the food consumption patterns of urban and rural residents. As a result, one cannot interpret an increase in the per capita availability of meat, for example, as meaning that the per capita consumption of urban residents is now greater than during the late twenties. If the per capita consumption of urban and rural residents for the late twenties is weighted by the current population distribution, the weighted per capita availability of meat meat in 1955–53 was lower than in 1926–29. However, in the case of certain other foods, rural consumption rates were greater than urban rates and the weighted availability increased more than the per capita availability. This was true of grains, for example. The consumption data for the twenties were taken from Gossudarstvennaia Planovaia Komissia (Gosplan) S.S.S.R.: "Piatiletnii Plan Narodno—Khoziaistvennogo Stroitelstva S.S.S.R," vol. I, p. 106. vol. II, pt. 2, p. 305. Moscow 1930, 3d ed.

tory.   With the new lands program, which was inaugurated in 1954, the total sown area increased by 28 million hectares between 1953 and 1956 and has remained at roughly 195 million hectares in recent years.

While there is some cost in terms of alternative products foregone by increasing the sown area—the area of pastures and meadows is reduced—there can be no question that the expansion of the sown area has contributed to the increased output.   If the increase due to the acquisition of territory is included, the sown area increased by 88 percent between 1925 and 1958.

There has been a significant expansion of irrigation since 1913. At that time approximately 4.0 million hectares was irrigated while in 1955 the irrigable area was 11.1 million hectares,[10] though apparently a significant fraction of this area is not being cropped currently.

2. Crop yields

Annual estimates of crop yields are presented in appendix table 5, based on official gross production data.   In table 8 average yields for 4- or 5-year periods are presented.   Notable increases in yields were achieved for cotton, sugar beets, and sunflowers, while the increases for grain, potatoes, and flax-fiber were approximately 20 percent or less.   While we believe that the recent output data for grain are somewhat exaggerated, or at least may not be consistent with the earlier data, it should be noted that the eastward extension of the grain area would have resulted in a reduction in the average grain yields since the newer areas are intrinsically less productive than the areas sown to grain in earlier periods.

The increase in the yield of cotton is a striking one, but a major factor in the increase has been the virtual abandonment of the practice of growing cotton on unirrigated land in the Ukraine and the R.S.F.S.R. As late as 1952, about 35 percent of the cotton land was unirrigated, grown in climatically unsuited areas.   The yield of cotton on irrigated land has probably increased by about a third since 1935–38.

TABLE 8.—*Crop yields, Soviet Russia, 1925–58* [1]

[Centners per hectare]

	Grain	Cotton	Sugar beets	Sunflower	Potatoes	Flax fiber
1925–29	7.91	8.82	132.0	6.24	79.3	2.08
1930–34	6.77	6.28	95.3	5.31	80.0	1.76
1935–38	7.07	11.40	147.3	5.50	78.5	1.90
1950–54	7.85	16.50	150.8	5.47	86.2	1.32
1955–58	9.49	20.24	185.6	9.31	90.9	2.53

[1] Obtained by dividing gross physical output (appendix table 3) by sown area (appendix table 1), except that flax-fiber output is our estimate of net physical output.

TABLE 9.—*Crop yields, United States, 1925–58* [1]

	Centners per hectare			Cotton (bales per hectare)	
	Grain	Sugar beets	Potatoes	All	Irrigated [2]
1925–29	13.9	244	76.4	0.84	
1950–54	17.0	347	169.2	1.47	
1955–58	20.6	378	193.2	2.08	4.9

[1] USDA, Agricultural Statistics, 1957, and Crop Production, 1958 Annual Summary (Dec. 17, 1958).
[2] Average yields for the States of New Mexico, Arizona, and California.

[10] Central Statistical Board of the U.S.S.R. Council of Ministers, "Forty Years of Soviet Power," (English translation), Moscow, 1958, p. 165.

The increase in sugar beet and sunflower yields have been significant ones. The very substantial increase in sunflower yields between 1950–54 and 1955–58 raises the possibility that climatic factors may have played a significant role in the higher yields, though increased application of fertilizer and manure, improved seeds and better cultural practices have undoubtedly been important as well. It may be noted that the sugar beet yield for 1937 of 183.7 centners per hectare was not exceeded in recent years except in 1957 and 1958. The latter 2 years were favorable growing years in the Ukraine, where over half of the sugar beets are grown.

3. Yield comparisons, Soviet Union and United States

A comparison of average yields for the United States and the Soviet Union for the period 1955–58 may be of interest, though such comparisons may be more indicative of climatic and soil conditions than of differences due to management or incentives.[11] The average grain yield was 20.6 centners per hectare in the United States or more than double the 9.5 centner yield in the Soviet Union. The average yield of cotton in the Soviet Union, essentially all grown on irrigated land, was almost 3 bales of lint cotton per hectare. The average for the United States as a whole was a little more than 2 bales per hectare. However, the average yield in New Mexico, Arizona, and California, where all of the cotton is irrigated, was 4.9 bales per hectare. The average yield of potatoes in the United States was 193 centners per hectare or more than double the 91 centners in the Soviet Union. The U.S. sugar beet yield was 37.8 tons per hectare compared to 18.6 tons. A large proportion of the U.S. sugar beet area is irrigated while probably only a relatively small proportion of the Soviet area is.

4. Labor employment

The measurement of the amount of labor used in Soviet agriculture is beset with many difficulties. Even if one had access to all of the data that exists in the Soviet Union, which we do not, it is probable that any estimates that one could make would still be subject to significant error. An indication of the possible hiatus in the estimates may be seen from the following estimates found in or derived from Soviet publications:

[Millions]

	1928 or 1929	1940	1950	1955	1956
Number of workers [1]	53.2	31.7			33.5
Labor power in man-years [2]	27.4	31.0	24.7	33.4	33.5

[1] Derived from "Forty Years of Soviet Power," Moscow, 1958, pp. 136–137 on the basis of relation between total horsepower in agriculture and horsepower per worker. Data for 1940 and 1956 are said to refer only to socialized sector, but this is probably not correct.

[2] Estimates made by S. Strumilin ("Some Problems of the Further Development of the Kolkhoz Regime," Problems of Economics, November 1958, p. 18. Originally published in Voprosy Ekonomiki, May 1958.) Strumilin's estimates include private peasants for 1940 and later, but does not include the labor input on household plots. (See "Planovoye Khoziaistva," 1957, No. 2, p. 48.)

The close correspondence between the estimates for 1940 and 1956 is probably no accident; the estimate of the horsepower per worker, as published in "Forty Years of Soviet Power," was apparently obtained by dividing total horsepower in agriculture by Strumilin's estimate of

[11] The yield data for the United States are from USDA, Agricultural Statistics, 1957, and Crop Production, 1958 Annual Summary (Dec. 17, 1958). Yield data are not available for sunflower seed or flax fiber.

labor power measured in man-years. The small difference for 1940 is apparently due to a rounding error.[12]

According to Strumilin's data, the total labor input in agriculture increased a minimum of 22 percent; the increase was presumably more than this since his data include all of agricultural output in 1928, but entirely ignores the 30 percent of the gross output produced in 1956 by the private sector. If we were to add our estimate of the labor input required in the private sector for 1956, assuming 265 days of work per year, of 4.8 million man-years to Strumilin's total,[13] an estimate of 38.3 million years is obtained. This would imply an increase of 40 percent in total labor input in Soviet agriculture between 1928 and 1956. While such a large increase does not appear consistent with other data, such as the changes in agricultural population or the number of farm households, it cannot be completely ignored as a possible upper limit to the increase in the labor input.

It is clear that the 53.2 million workers indicated for 1928 or 1929 is not consistent with the other figures in the same series, since the data for 1940 and 1956 represent some concept of full-time employment, while the figure for 1928 refers to some particular group that performed some farm work during the year or perhaps to the total number of workers in the agricultural population aged 15–59 with an adjustment for the lower productivity of females.

Our own estimates imply that there was an increase in labor inputs between 1926–29 and 1956 of 10 to 16 percent.[14] The estimates indicate that the postwar low level of employment was reached in 1953 and that the labor input increased by about 13 percent between 1953 and 1956. Such an increase was due to the new-lands program, the corn program, and the expansion of livestock output. The latter two endeavors were highly labor intensive under Soviet conditions.

There was undoubtedly a decline in the total number of persons employed in agriculture over the past three decades. This was made possible by the lengthening of the work year per person at work from perhaps 120 days to about 185–190 days. The increased participation was made possible by a reduction in the importance of cottage industry in rural areas and an encroachment upon the time of the housewife. We believe that a reasonable estimate of the decline in farm employment is from about 53 million in 1928 to about 42 million in 1956, excluding the employment of children and workers 60 years or older.

5. Labor productivity and requirements

If we compare the change in net agricultural output (index weighted by 1958 purchase prices) with the change in the labor input measured by man-years worked, we find that the average product of labor increased by 36 to 43 percent between 1928 and 1955–57. The increase in average product per worker was 100 percent, which is a substantial increase. In the United States the increase in average product per man-hour, for the same period, was 142 percent. Since the length of the work year declined in the United States, rather than increased as

---

[12] Strumilin gives the average as 3.53, while in "Forty Years" the average was rounded to 3.5. For 1956 the average given by Strumilin is 3.50, which is given as 3.5 in "Forty Years."
[13] See the forthcoming article by Arcadius Kahan, "Changes in Labor Inputs in Soviet Agriculture," to be published in the Journal of Political Economy, October 1959, for the derivation of this estimate.
[14] A. Kahan, ibid.

214 COMPARISONS OF UNITED STATES AND SOVIET ECONOMIES

in the Soviet Union, the increase in average product per worker was 149 percent.[15]

In his speech before the December plenary session of the Party Central Committee, Khrushchev revealed the very large differences that existed between the amount of labor used to produce farm products in the U.S.S.R. and the United States. His data indicated that labor used per unit of output ranged from 160 percent of the U.S. level for cotton on state farms to 1,630 percent for production of hogs on collective farms.[16]

Two types of data on labor use by product are given. The first (table 10) is in terms of labor used per hectare. These data allow a comparison of labor use on the peasant farms for 1925–26 and on collective farms in 1937 and for 1954–55. These data indicate a very substantial decline in the use of labor for grain production following collectivization, though there was apparently no change between 1937 and 1954–55. The labor requirements for potatoes remained unchanged. The cotton data probably are not comparable because of the substantial increase in yield in the years just before 1956. The data for the other crops indicate a reduction in labor requirements of roughly 20 to 30 percent between 1937 and 1954–55.

The other table (table 11) presents somewhat more figures for 1956 and 1957 for the state farms than might seem to be appropriate. The reason for this is a remark made by Khrushchev in presenting the data for the United States:

One may assume that the bourgeois statistics make the situation look better than it is.

TABLE 10.—*Labor used per hectare of land by peasants and collective farms, U.S.S.R.*

[Man-days]

	Peasants		Collective farms	
	1925–26 [1]	1937 [2]	1954–55 [2]	1956 [3]
Grain	20. 8	10. 6	10. 0–12. 0	
Potatoes	61. 3	65. 2	60. 0–80. 0	
Cotton	117. 2	81. 8		145. 8
Flax		79. 2	66. 5	
Sunflower		13. 4	10. 6	
Sugar beets		131. 8	89. 6	

[1] See, Gosplan S.S.S.R., Perspektivnyi Plan Razvertyvania Narodnogo Khoziaistva S.S.R. na 1926/27–1930/31 gg. Edited by S. G. Strumilin, Moscow 1927, p. 15, and TsUNKhU Gosplana S.S.S.R., Sotsialisticheskoe Selskoe Khoziaistvo. Moscow-Leningrad, 1939, p. 47.

[2] See TsUNKhU Gosplana S.S.S.R., Proizvoditelnost' i Ispolzovanie Truda v Kolkhozakh vo Vtoroi Piatiletke. Edited by I. V. Sautin, Moscow, Leningrad, 1939, pp. IX, 12–16. Ekonomika Selskogo Khoziaistva #2, 1957. p. 96. Academia Nauk S.S.S.R., Voprosy Razmeschenia i Spetsializatsii Selskogo.

[3] Khlopkovodsvo, 1957, No. 11, p. 13. Khoziaistva, Moscow, 1957. pp. 65, 323.

[15] Based on U.S. Department of Agriculture, "Changes in Farm Production and Efficiency," Stat. Bull. No. 233, August 1958, pp. 6 and 27 and "Agricultural Statistics," 1957, p. 536.

[16] The data for the United States in table 10 are taken directly from Khrushchev's speech. We were not able to duplicate the result for cotton. The highest labor requirement obtained was 15.6 hours, while the requirement that seems most consistent with the Soviet data was 13.6 hours. For U.S. data, see USDA, "Agricultural Statistics," 1957, pp. 71, 139, and 589.

TABLE 11.—*Labor used per centner of output, U.S.S.R. and United States*

	State farms, U.S.S.R.						United States [3] 1956 (man-hours)
	Man-days		Man-hours				
	1956 [1]	1957 [2]	1956 [2]	1955 [2]	1954 [2]	1956–57 [3]	
Milk	1.76	14.5	14.0	15.9	15.6	9.9	4.7
Beef	10.0	64.0	76.0	79.0	82.0	52.0	7.9
Pork	8.0	57.6	65.9	73.4	73.0	43.0	6.3
Grain		2.9	2.0	3.5	3.6	1.8	1.0
Potatoes				8.0		4.2	1.0
Cotton	[4] 4.6					29.8	18.8
Sugar beets						2.1	.5

COLLECTIVE FARMS, U.S.S.R.

	1937 [5] (man-days)	1937 [6] (man-hours)	1956 [7] (man-days)	1956–57 [3] (man-hours)
Grain	(1.2–1.3)	(9–10)		7.3
Sunflower seed	1.97	16		
Potatoes	.67	5		5.1
Sugar beets	.73	6		3.1
Cotton	10.6	85		42.8
Flax	47.2	38		
Milk	4.6	37		14.7
Beef			2.9	112.0
Pork	23.6		21.0	103.0
			20.0	

[1] A.M. Brianskii, Voprosy Ekonomiki, 1957, No. 12, p. 118.

[2] I. Benediktov, Puti Snizhenia Sebestiomosti Produktsii Sovkhozov, Moscow, 1957 and "Sovkhoznoe Proizvodstvo," Nos. 6 and 8, 1958.

[3] N. Khrushchev, Pravda, Dec. 16, 1958.

[4] Figure is Uzbek S.S.R. only (V. Manyakhin, "Problems of Economics," November 1958, p. 29). Uzbek produces about ¾ of the total U.S.S.R. cotton. If one assumes an 8-hour day, the total man-hours would be 36.8 hours.

[5] See footnote [2], table 10. Grain estimate based on man-days per hectare, assuming a yield of 8 centners per hectare.

[6] Based on man-day data, assuming 8-hour day.

[7] Voprosy Ekonomiki, No. 12, 1957, p. 118.

Regardless of what the situation may be with "bourgeois statistics," Khrushchev must have made some adjustment in the data for the state farms to "make the situation look better than it is." It is a little difficult to average 14.5 and 14.0 and obtain 9.9, the average labor used to produce milk for 1956–57, or to average 64 and 76 and obtain 52.0 as the labor used for beef. The man-hour data for the years 1956 and 1957 were published by I. Benediktov, formerly Minister of State Farms, who would hardly have any reason to exaggerate the amount of labor used. While the evidence is not quite as clear for the collective farms, since we have data only for 1 year and expressed in days rather than hours, it appears that Khrushchev found it necessary to make a few adjustments in the data to prevent the ratio of labor used on collective farms from reaching a level of 20 to 25, instead of 16, times the U.S. level.

6. Mechanization and power

There can be no question that there has been a very considerable degree of mechanization in Soviet agriculture during the past three decades. But two points need to be remembered. First, the animal draft power situation in Russia, either before the revolution or just prior to the collectivization drive, was a relatively favorable one. In 1916, before either the United States or Russia had any significant number of tractors, there were roughly 50 percent more horses in

Russia than in the United States, even though the cultivated area was some 10 to 20 percent less. The much larger relative number of horses was in part a consequence of the much greater number of farms, but nonetheless the draft power was available for the performance of all farm operations.

Second, a very large fraction of the investment in tractors and tractor-drawn equipment, perhaps all the investment made through 1940, was required to offset the decline in the number of horses and to replace the horse-drawn equipment. The number of horses declined from 32.6 million in 1929 to 14.9 million in 1934; there was an increase to 17.7 million in 1940 and a further increase in 1941 due to the acquisition of territory. Approximately half of the horses were lost during World War II. The postwar peak in the number of horses was 15.3 million, reached in 1953 and 1954.

While the substitution of tractor and other means of mechanical power for horses and oxen made possible labor savings, it is quite likely that crop output suffered as a result of the substitution until very recently. This may have occurred because there simply was not enough of the large and cumbersome tractors and combines to perform the farm operations in a timely manner.

Tentative results indicate that an index, in constant prices, of farm machinery, equipment, and workstock declined by almost a third between 1928 and 1933 and then increased to about the 1928 level by the late thirties. By 1950 the index was perhaps 5 percent below the 1928 level and by 1956 had reached a level approximately 50 to 55 percent above 1928.[17] This index has undoubtedly increased since 1956. Roughly speaking, there has been a similar long-term movement of the index of machinery and power and of net output. If mechanization had been primarily labor saving instead of primarily displacing animal power, the index of machinery and power should have increased much more rapidly than the index of output.[18]

D. AN ATTEMPT AT EXPLANATION OF LONG-RUN CHANGES IN OUTPUT

The previous two parts of this paper have developed our estimates of changes in output of agricultural products, of the quantities of the major inputs used, and of the changes in the average productivity or yield of labor and land. Comparisons of the changes in the average product per unit of land and labor in the United States and the U.S.S.R. indicate rather clearly that the organizational structure of Soviet agriculture has not resulted in any production miracles or especially outstanding increases in resource productivity. Nevertheless, output did increase enough to approximately maintain per capita output at the levels of the late twenties during the early fifties and to increase per capita output substantially since 1953.

In this part we shall be primarily concerned with the longer run factors that have contributed to the higher level of output. One way of explaining changes in output is to accurately measure changes in the total quantity of inputs used, including in quantity a measure of changes in quality, and to determine whatever changes in efficiency

---

[17] We have not made a comparison of the levels of mechanization in the Soviet Union and the United States since there has been little change from the relative quantitative position discussed in "Soviet Economic Growth: A Comparison With the United States" (1957, pp. 70–72). There has been, however, some qualitative improvement in the kinds and types of equipment. More row crop tractors are available and hydraulically operated, tractor mounted implements are now being produced in quantity. In general, the trend has been toward lighter and less cumbersome machinery and the adoption of labor-saving attachments.

[18] If animal draft is excluded from the index, the index increases from 100 in 1928 to about 450 in 1956.

of utilization of the inputs, if any, may have occurred. While our research studies are moving in this direction, at this stage a much more mechanical approach is required. The mechanical approach does permit us to identify some of the specific changes that have been associated with the increased output.

1. Decline in the number of horses

The two most important factors in the increase of agricultural output for human consumption have been the substitution of mechanical for animal power and the increase in the sown area. Since 1928 the decline in the feed required for horses alone has been enough to account for about 60 percent of the feed required to produce the additional livestock output of 1958 compared to 1928, including the estimated change in livestock inventories in 1958.[19] Since horses were heavy users of grain and other concentrates, the contribution to the increase in livestock output for human use may be somewhat greater than that indicated.

2. Increase in sown area

Between 1928 and 1958 the total sown area increased from 113 to about 195 million hectares or by 82 million hectares (73 percent). Approximately 14 to 15 million hectares of the increase was due to the acquisition of new territories, thus the increase in sown area due to the agricultural activities of the Soviet Union comes to 68 million hectares or 60 percent. Even if the yields of the sown crops had remained constant as the sown area was extended into the drier areas, as was the case, this does not mean that agricultural output would have increased in the same proportion as the change in sown area. If one assumed that all of the increase in sown area had been devoted to grain or feed crops and that the sole objective were to increase the feed supply, the increase in feed supply due to increasing the sown area by 62 million hectares might have been from 40 to 50 million tons of feed units. This may be compared to the 35-million-ton reduction in estimated feed requirements for horses between 1928 and 1958 and a total estimated feed requirement of about 200 million tons in 1958. Of course, a large fraction of the additional sown area was used to produce grain for human consumption and to increase the area of industrial crops. The total increase in feed used between 1928 and 1958, including that derived from pasture and assuming constant feed requirements, was about 20 million tons of feed units.

3. Increase in crop yields

A factor, which was relatively unimportant prior to 1955, has been increased crop yields per hectare. Grain yields in the 4-year period 1926–29 may have averaged about 7.9 centners per hectare; the average yield for 1949–53 was 7.7 centners. During 1955–58, if we accept the official production data, the average yield was about 9.5 centners. The shift in the location of grain production should have reduced yields by a little more than a half centner, implying a real increase in the grain yield of about 20 to 25 percent since the late twenties. In the case of cotton and sugar beets yield increases have been greater than for grains.

---

[19] See sec. E below for estimates of feed requirements.

4. Increases in labor intensive crops

A fourth factor has been the increase in the relative importance of the labor intensive industrial crops, especially cotton and sugar beets. These crops normally have a relatively high value per unit of land. With the very great amount of labor available and the great emphasis that has been placed upon autarchy, the expansion of the industrial crops was not an unexpected development. As noted earlier, the share of the industrial crops in net agricultural output increased from 7.7 percent in 1928 to 15.5 percent in 1957. The percentage of the total sown area for the industrial crops for which we have made estimates of output actually declined from 7.7 to 6.1 percent between 1928 and 1957.[20]

The following tabulation presents data on changes in sown area for the crops included in our estimates of output and changes in the value of gross output (in 1926–27 prices) of the same crops, total and average per hectare, for 1928 and 1955–57:

	1928	1955–57
Total:		
Area of included crops (million hectares)	107.6	149.7
Total output of included crops (billion rubles)	6.5	11.3
Output per hectare (rubles)	60.3	75.3
Index, output per hectare	100.0	124.9
Grain, potatoes; and vegetables:		
Area (million hectares)	99.9	137.9
Output (billion rubles)	5.9	9.3
Output per hectare (rubles)	58.8	67.3
Index, output per hectare	100.0	114.4
Industrial crops:		
Area (million hectares)	7.71	11.8
Output (billion rubles)	.61	1.99
Output per hectare (rubles)	79.1	168.6
Index, output per hectare	100.0	213.1

The output per hectare of the crops included increased 24.9 percent between 1928 and 1955–57.[21] The increase in output per hectare for grains, potatoes and vegetables was only 14.4 percent, while the increase for the industrial crops was 113.1 percent. While a considerable part of the increase in the output of industrial crops per hectare has been due to the increased importance of irrigation, it is nevertheless true that a significant part of the increase in total output of crops was due to the greater emphasis given to industrial crops which use a relatively small part of the total sown area.

5. Increase in livestock output per unit of feed

While there has been some increase in output of livestock products per unit of feed, it is very difficult to say how important this factor has been. Undoubtedly livestock are better housed today than they were during the thirties or in the period after the last war. Whether they are better housed than during the twenties is a moot point. But milk represents one instance in which the ratio of output to feed intake must have increased. For a cow that produces only 1,000 kilograms

---

[20] This statement may be somewhat misleading in the sense that a much larger fraction of the industrial crops was grown on irrigated land in 1957 than in 1928.
[21] A similar measure for the United States indicates an increase in crop yields per acre of 56.4 percent for the same years. See U.S. Department of Agriculture, Major Statistical Series of the U.S. Department of Agriculture, vol. 2, Agriculture Handbook No. 118, 1957, p. 50, and Crop Production, 1958 Annual Summary (Dec. 17, 1958), p. 49. The index of yields per harvested acre for 18 field crops was used. The estimates for the Soviet Union are based on official Soviet data, which we believe are somewhat too high for the grain crops for 1955–57.

of milk per year, at least three-fourths of the feed is required for maintenance. But if the milk yield increases to 1,500 kilograms, only two-thirds of the feed is required for maintenance. On the basis of the net production of milk that we have assumed, the feed requirements per kilogram of milk declined from somewhat more than 1.9 feed units in 1928 to less than 1.5 in 1958. There is little reason to believe that there has been much change in feeding efficiency for other livestock products, except for pork. The increase in the availability of feed grains in the last 2 or 3 years may have resulted in some reduction in the amount of feed required per centner of pork.

6. The corn program and the feed supply

A final factor must be commented upon because of the great importance that Khrushchev has attached to it, namely the corn program. In 1955 it was announced that the corn area was to be expanded to 28 million hectares by 1960. This represented an increase of about 24 million hectares. The maximum area thus far realized was 23.9 million hectares in 1956. In 1958 the total corn area was 19.7 million hectares, of which 4.4 million hectares was harvested as dry grain, 3.7 million hectares in the milk-wax stage, and 9.6 million hectares of silage.[22] The remaining 5.9 million hectares was harvested as green feed. The total grain equivalent of corn was reported as 16.2 million tons, indicating an average yield of 20 centners of corn grain per hectare. Since the gross yield of all other grains was only 10.8 centners per hectare, it would appear that the expansion of the corn area had indeed been a considerable success. But it should be remembered that corn is grown for grain in precisely the areas where other grains give yields substantially above the national average. Approximately three-fourths of all the corn harvested for grain is in three areas—the Ukraine, Moldavia, and the Kuban. Data are available that allow us to estimate the official absolute yields for corn and for all wheat in the Ukraine for 1950–55 and 1958. The unweighted average yields for this 7-year period were 14.7 centners for corn and 12.9 for wheat.[23] This is a difference of 11 percent. In 1958 the corn yield was about 30 percent greater than the wheat yield, but in 1953 and 1954 corn yielded slightly less than wheat. One obvious advantage of corn should be noted; namely, that its seed requirement is at least 1.25 centners per hectare less than for wheat, oats, barley, and rye. Thus even if the harvested yield of corn were the same as for wheat, the amount of grain available for feed would be greater in the case of corn.

The major net contribution that corn has made to the feed supply has not been the grain, but the silage and the green feed. And even here the contribution has not been so much the increase in total quantity of feed, as conventionally measured, but through improvement in the quality of the available feed and a change in the seasonal distribution of feed. The available data indicate that the vast majority of the cattle in the Soviet Union receive very little grain. In 1956 the average grain fed in the collective farms to all cattle (converted to a basis of an adult milk cow) was 180 kilograms; in the

[22] N. Khrushchev, Pravda, Dec. 21, 1958. The 9.6 million hectares of silage includes the 3.7 million hectares of corn harvested in the milk-wax stage.
[23] Estimated from data given in Pravda, May 12, 1959, "Ekonomika Selskogo Khoziaistva," No. 2, 1959, pp. 25, 28, and 29, and "Narodne Gospodarstvo Ukrainskoi R.S.R. Statistichnii Sbornik," Kiev, 1957 pp. 101 and 116.

United States approximately 775 kilograms were fed.[24] The roughage available in the Soviet Union while reasonably adequate in amount, is of very poor quality. Over half consists of materials other than hay, primarily straw and chaff. And most of the hay is what we would call wild hay, which is relatively low in protein and has a relatively low net energy value. Silage has represented a valuable addition to a feed ration of so little intrinsic merit. Morrison reports experiments that indicate that corn silage added to a ration roughly comparable to that described above resulted in an increase in butterfat production per cow of about 50 percent.[25]

The other value of corn is as a source of green feed during the middle and late summer months when the pastures provide relatively little feed. Available data on the distribution of milk deliveries indicate that the production of milk declined rapidly after the flush pasture feeding period of spring and early summer. Once the milk flow is reduced, increased feeding at a period later does little to regain the original flow. The availability of immature corn, fed directly from the field, has undoubtedly maintained the milk flow at a relatively high rate for a longer period than was the case in the past.

The corn silage yields, as estimated from production and area data, are hardly spectacular. The average annual yields for the years 1955 through 1958 did not exceed the following amounts (tons per hectare): 6.6, 7.5, 8.1, and 11.2. The yields may have been a quarter or more less than this, since the stalks and leaves from the corn harvested in the milk-wax stage is also put in silos. Most of the corn that is put in silos has apparently not ripened to the milk-wax stage, which results in a considerably lower feed value per ton than would be true of silage prepared in the United States.

E. OVERTAKE THE UNITED STATES IN THE PER CAPITA OUTPUT OF BUTTER, MILK, AND MEAT

1. *The statement of the objective*

A little more than 2 years ago Nikita Khrushchev announced a campaign to overtake the United States in the per capita output of butter, milk, and meat. The goal was announced in the following manner:

> The successes achieved in agriculture and the excellent prospects for its development permit us to set and accomplish a task which is of great importance for the state: to catch up with the United States in the near future in per capita production of meat, butter, and milk.[26]

In the case of milk and meat, he defined what was meant by the "near future":

> In 1957 we will already have as much butter or even a little more than the United States had in 1956. This means that we will have a total amount of butter that is equal to or greater than the amount produced in the United States. But because our population is bigger than that of the United States we will have to make an effort. In per capita production of milk we cannot only catch up with the United States but even surpass it as early as 1958.

---

[24] Soviet Union data from "Selskoe Khozyaistvo v S.S.S.R." p. 327. Data for United States from R. D. Jennings, "Consumption of Feed by Livestock, 1909–56," USDA, Prod. Res. Rept. No. 21, pp. 95, 97–98 and 64. U.S. data relate only to dairy cattle, including heifers and calves.

[25] F. B. Morrison, "Feeds and Feeding" (Ithaca, 1943), 20th ed., pp. 547–548.

[26] Pravda, May 24, 1957.

With respect to meat:

> * * * we can surpass the United States in per capita meat production by 1960. But it will not be a tragedy by any means if for some reason we are not able to surpass America in meat production by 1960. We can permit some postponement. It would not be bad if we accomplished this task in 1961.

This particular propaganda drive has a number of interesting aspects. First, in announcing the goal of overtaking the United States, Khrushchev revealed to the Russian population the very great disparity between the per capita outputs of livestock products in the two nations, especially in the case of meat. The following figures on annual per capita production for 1956 were given: meat, U.S.S.R., 32.3, and United States, 102.3 kilograms; milk, U.S.S.R., 245. and United States, 343 kilograms; and factory butter, U.S.S.R., 2.8, and United States, 3.8 kilograms.[27]

Second, despite Khrushchev's great confidence, neither the milk nor butter goals were achieved in 1958. The per capita output of factory butter in 1958 was 3.2 kilograms and total production per capita was 3.8 kilograms.[28] The per capita production of milk accepting the official figures was less than 280 kilograms or significantly less than the U.S. level.[29]

Third, in announcing the program Khrushchev indicated that he had disregarded the advice of the economists who had said that it would not be possible to surpass the United States in per capita livestock production before 1975. In a most sarcastic fashion, Khrushchev said:[30]

> In connection with the task before us I want to tell you about one fact. After talking to the collective farmers and the state farm and machine and tractor station officials and getting to know their pledges, the idea of catching up with the United States in the near future in per capita production of meat, milk, and butter arose, and I asked the economists to present estimates of when we could catch up to America in the production of these items.
>
> I shall tell you a secret. They handed me a signed paper, as Mikhlkov writes in his verse fable in Pravda of May 22 and stamped it with a seal. On that piece of paper was written: We can increase meat production by 220 percent and catch up with the United States in 1975. Excuse me, comrade economists, if I rub a little salt in your wounds.

The evidence available to this point indicates that the economists he so strongly ridiculed are much more likely to be correct than Khrushchev.

2. Khrushchev's admission of inability to achieve meat goal

Finally, in announcing the goals of the new 7-year plan (1959–65), it has been admitted that there is no chance of catching up with the United States in meat production by 1960 or 1961. The meat production goal for 1965 has been set at 16 million tons, substantially less than the 20 or 21 million tons required for the 1956 population of 200 million. This admission of failure has had no apparent repercussions, which is perhaps not altogether unexpected since the agricultural output goals of the 5-year plans or other agricultural programs have seldom been met in the past. Yet this failure, which is so typical in the

---

[27] Pravda, May 24, 1957. If home production of butter is included, per capita production was 3.35 in the U.S.S.R. and 4.20 in the United States.
[28] "Vestnik Statistiki," 1959, No. 3, p. 94.
[29] Assuming a population of 206,500,000 for 1958 and total milk production of 57,800,000 tons. U.S. per capita production of milk declined 12 kilograms between 1956 and 1958. It may be noted that total and per capita production of butter has declined significantly during the past two decades. During 1935–39 per capita butter production was 7.7 kilograms. For U.S. data, see the National Food Situation, April 1959, pp. 4 and 22.
[30] Pravda, May 24, 1957.

agricultural area, should warn observers that the announcement and achievement of an agricultural output goal are not quite the same thing.[31]

3. Comparisons of livestock output and numbers, Soviet Union and United States

Before attempting to evaluate the possibilities of the Soviet Union eventually overtaking the United States in per capita output of meat and milk, we shall present certain information on the long-run relation between the meat and milk output of the two nations. What many people forget, and what Khrushchev certainly fails to remind us, is that Russia, prior to the revolution was a major livestock-producing nation, second only to the United States. If output on comparable territory is used for comparison, the output of meat in 1958 for the Soviet Union was a smaller percentage of the 1958 United States meat output than in 1913. In 1913, on present territory, meat output in the Soviet Union was 58.1 percent of the United States level; in 1958, 48.0 percent. Actually the present level of Soviet output compared to ours is at a lower level than that achieved by the millions of peasant farms in 1928. It was not until 1952 that the absolute level of meat output reached the 1928 output.

With respect to milk output, we are somewhat less certain concerning the long-term relationship between the output of the two countries. In table 13, we have presented two milk series, one defined as gross output and the other as net milk output. Net milk output excludes all milk fed to calves that has been included in the gross output series. This involves a relatively minor adjustment for the United States, but a substantial adjustment for the Soviet Union. Roughly speaking it would appear that the Soviet Union, by 1958, had roughly regained the same position relative to the United States that existed in 1913.

In table 14 data are presented on the size of the livestock herds of the Soviet Union and the United States. In 1916 there were substantially more sheep and goats and horses in Russia than in the United States. There were considerably more hogs in the United States, but the disparity in cattle was relatively small. By 1959 the number of hogs in the Soviet Union had risen significantly relative to the United States and the same is true for the number of sheep and goats. The total number of cattle declined from 87 percent of the U.S. level in 1916 to 73 percent in 1959. It may be noted that the number of cows milked was probably greater in the Soviet Union on all three dates, since almost all their cows are milked while a large proportion of cows in the United States are of beef breeds and are not milked.

---

[31] Khrushchev, in discussing the 1959–65 plan goals, did feel it desirable to explain the reasons for the discrepancy between the 1965 meat goal and the overtake the United States objective. His explanation was as follows:

"Now to turn to our plans and potentialities for increasing meat production. In 1958 the Soviet Union produced 38 kilograms of meat per capita; in the United States the anticipated figure was approximately 194 kilograms. In order to overtake the United States in per capita meat production we must increase gross meat products to 20 million to 21 million tons. Our country now produces about 8 million tons and 16 million tons are scheduled for production in 1965.

"From this it is clear that the meat production assignments laid down by the control figures are below the level required to catch up with the United States in this commodity. But this by no means signifies that our country has no chance of raising meat production to 20 million to 21 million tons."

"Thus, while not raising the state's planned assignment to 20 million to 21 million tons of meat, which would strain the plan, we must at the same time not inhibit but encourage the initiative of the leading individuals who launched the movement to catch up with the United States in a short time in per capita output of meat and other livestock products" (Pravda, Dec. 16, 1959).

TABLE 12.—*Meat production, Soviet Union and United States, 1913–58, selected years* [1]

	Million metric tons, slaughter weight		Soviet Union-United States (percent)		Million metric tons, slaughter weight		Soviet Union United States (percent)
	Soviet Union [2]	United States [3]			Soviet Union [2]	United States [3]	
1913 [4]	4.05	8.50	47.6	1952	5.17	14.37	36.0
1913	4.94	8.50	58.1	1953	5.82	15.00	38.8
1928 [4]	4.90	9.94	49.3	1954	6.28	15.38	40.8
1940 [4]	3.88	11.40	34.0	1955	6.32	16.24	38.9
1940	4.70	11.40	41.2	1956	6.60	17.22	38.3
1950	4.87	13.61	35.8	1957	7.37	16.70	44.1
1951	4.67	13.79	33.9	1958	7.85	16.34	48.0

[1] Sources: Soviet Union, appendix table 2, United States, U.S. Department of Agriculture, Livestock and Meat Statistics, 1957, Statistical Bulletin No. 230, July 1958, p. 140; Supplement for 1954 to Consumption of Food in the United States, 1909–52, Agriculture Handbook No. 62, October 1955, pp. 67, 171–172, National Food Situation, April 1959, p. 22; Agricultural Statistics, 1957, pp. 500 and 509, and The Livestock and Meat Situation, May 1959, p. 36.
[2] Includes all animal fats and offal. This series of slaughter weight is not directly comparable to the series for the United States.
[3] Includes lard and edible offal, but does not include tallow. In 1956 the United States produced 1,480,000 tons of tallow and inedible greases. These fats are apparently included in the Soviet data. All poultry meats are on a ready-to-cook basis, with a dressing percentage of 75; poultry meat in Soviet calculations probably based on 90 percent yield. If Soviet definitions and conventions were followed for the United States for 1956, for example, the U.S. meat output would have been at least 19,140,000 tons and perhaps as much as 20,620,000 tons. The percentage increase would have been at least 11 percent and perhaps 20 percent. The smaller increase reflects only the difference in percentage yield of offal products, the larger increase reflects the difference in offal and the inclusion of tallow and greases in the U.S. data.
[4] Territory as of boundaries prior to Sept. 17, 1939 all other data for present territory.

TABLE 13.—*Milk production, Soviet Union and United States, 1913, 1928, 1940, 1950–58* [1]

	Gross output [2]			Net output [3]		
	Soviet Union	United States	Soviet Union-United States	Soviet Union	United States	Soviet Union-United States
	Million metric tons	Million metric tons	Percent	Million metric tons	Million metric tons	Percent
1913 [4]	24.8	30.7	80.8	21.4	29.4	72.8
1913	29.4	30.7	95.8	25.5	29.4	86.7
1928 [4]	31.0	43.5	71.3	27.0	42.2	64.0
1940 [4]	26.6	49.6	53.6	23.3	48.2	48.3
1940	33.6	49.6	67.7	27.6	48.2	57.3
1950	35.3	52.9	66.7	26.5	51.4	51.6
1951	36.2	52.0	69.2	27.3	50.4	54.2
1952	35.7	52.0	68.6	26.8	50.5	53.1
1953	36.5	54.5	67.0	27.6	53.0	52.1
1954	38.2	55.4	69.0	28.9	53.9	53.6
1955	43.0	55.8	77.1	33.3	54.3	61.3
1956	49.1	57.0	86.1	38.9	55.5	70.1
1957	54.8	57.1	95.8	43.9	55.6	79.0
1958	57.8	56.8	101.8	46.5	55.3	84.1

[1] Sources: Soviet Union: appendix tables 2, 3, and 4. United States: D. R. Jennings, "Consumption of Feed by Livestock, 1909–56"; U.S. Department of Agriculture, Prod. Res. Rept. No. 21, p. 77; and the National Food Situation, April 1959, p. 22.
[2] Reported total milk production; Soviet Union data apparently include an estimate of amount of milk sucked by calves; U.S. data do not.
[3] Net output data represents total milk production minus quantity of whole milk fed to calves. United States data for 1913 and 1957 and 1958 estimated by writers. For Soviet Union data, see appendix table 4 except that 1913 estimated on basis of cow numbers for 1916.
[4] Territory as of boundaries prior to Sept. 17, 1939; all other data for present territory.

224 COMPARISONS OF UNITED STATES AND SOVIET ECONOMIES

TABLE 14.—*Livestock numbers, Soviet Union and United States, 1916, 1928, and 1959* [1]

[Millions of head]

	1916	1928	1959		1916	1928	1959
Soviet Union: [2]				United States:			
Cattle, all	58.4	66.8	70.8	Cattle, all	67.4	57.3	96.9
Cows	28.8	33.2	33.3	Cows, all	33.0	31.1	47.2
Hogs	23.0	27.7	48.5	Milk cows	21.2	22.2	21.6
Sheep and goats	96.3	114.6	138.6 [3]	Hogs	60.6	61.9	57.2
Horses	38.2	36.1	11.5 [4]	Sheep and goats	42.0	49.0	35.6
				Horses and mules	21.3	14.8	3.1

[1] Soviet Union data, see appendix table 2; U.S. data, U.S. Department of Agriculture, "Agricultural Statistics," 1957, pp. 388–389, 371–372, 403–404, 428–440, and "The Livestock and Meat Situation," March 1959, p. 5. Goat numbers estimated for 1959.
[2] All data refer to present territory.
[3] The number of sheep was 129,000,000; number of goats estimated to be 9,600,000. The number Jan. 1, 1958, was 9,900,000.
[4] The number of horses on Jan. 1, 1958, was 11,900,000; 1959 estimated.

NOTE.—Numbers are for Jan. 1 of each year.

4. Feed requirements

The major question concerning the feasibility of achieving either the objectives of the 1965 plan or of catching up with the United States in per capita production is that of the feed supply. While the labor inputs in livestock production are fantastically high compared to the United States, it is probably safe to assume that over a period of a decade that sufficient labor savings could be achieved to permit the production of the required output.

Data on the feed supply of the Soviet Union are extremely sketchy. While estimates for the late twenties have been published, no estimates covering all feed users for a more recent period have come to our attention. Khrushchev in his 1955 speech on livestock production provided estimates of the feed supply for 1953. However, these estimates were stated to pertain only to production in the socialized sector. While most of the feed is undoubtedly produced in the socialized sector, significant amounts of potatoes produced on private plots are apparently fed to livestock. While much of the feed for the private livestock owned by collective farm members and state farm workers come from the collective and state farms, we have little knowledge concerning the source of feed for the several million head of livestock owned by urban dwellers. One source was apparently the purchase of bread, but efforts have been made to stop such a use. Some of the relatively small amount of grain sold on the collective farm market is probably also used for privately owned livestock.

For present purposes, given the scanty and contradictory evidence on feed supplies, the most accurate indication of feed used may be estimates of the probable amount of feed required to produce the livestock output. At least this technique is accurate enough to give a reasonable indication of the magnitude of the necessary increase in feed availability if the Soviet Union is to overtake the United States in per capita production of meat and milk. The feed requirements used have been derived from Soviet sources. The results have been checked by the use of estimated feed requirements per unit of various kinds of livestock output in the United States. While there are differences for individual products, the total feed requirements are very similar. It is probable that the feed requirements used somewhat underestimate the actual feed consumed. The Soviet feed requirements have apparently been derived from experimental results and probably have not been duplicated under farm conditions.

The estimated feed requirements for specified years from 1928 through 1958 are of some interest since they indicate that until the past year there has been only a very small increase in the total feed supply. The increased output of livestock products for human consumption has primarily been due to the decline in the horse population. While the total feed requirements for 1928 and 1956 were almost identical, the amount required for livestock products increased from 122 to 158 million tons of feed units. There was an increase in feed of about 10 percent between 1956 and 1958. The 1958 feed supply was derived primarily from 1957 crop production; the feed supply available for 1959 is significantly greater than it was in 1958.

In estimating the feed requirements for the goal of overtaking the United States in per capita production, we have assumed a population of 230 million. At the current absolute rate of population increase, this level of population should be reached about 1964 or 1965. We have assumed the 1956 level of per capita consumption in the United States and in order to estimate total feed requirements, we have used the 1965 goal for egg production (37 billion eggs).[32]

The total feed requirements, including pasture, to overtake the United States amount to 385 million tons of feed units.[33] The estimated requirements for 1958 are 199 million tons. According to this method of estimation, it will require almost a doubling of the total feed supply from the 1958 level of utilization in order to reach the goal of overtaking the 1956 U.S. levels of per capita production of milk and meat.

TABLE 15.—*Estimated feed requirements, Soviet Union, selected years, 1928–58* [1]

| | Other (million tons of charge feed units) | | | | | Horses | Total |
	Hogs	Milk [2]	Live-stock	Inven-tory	Total		
1928	13.1	59.1	49.9	0	122.1	57.8	179.9
1950	12.4	50.8	51.7	.7	115.6	22.9	138.5
1953	19.8	50.9	54.0	6.3	131.0	27.5	158.5
1956	23.3	61.8	60.6	12.6	158.3	23.4	181.7
1958	28.8	71.2	67.8	10.5	178.3	21.4	199.7

[1] Method of estimation: Hogs, live weight produced multiplied by 6.3 feed units per unit of production; milk, beginning of year number of cows multiplied by 1,460 feed units plus net milk production multiplied by 0.5 feed units; other meat than pork, live weight produced multiplied by 7.7 feed units per unit of production; eggs, number produced multiplied by 0.36 feed units; inventory change, live weight multiplied by 7 feed units per unit of output; horses beginning of year numbers multiplied by 1,800 feed units. Sources of feed requirements: V. S. Nemchinov, "Economic Problems of Livestock Development," Voprosy ekonomiki, 1955, No. 2, p. 18, for beef, pork, poultry, eggs and mutton and I. S. Popov, Kormovye normyi Kormovye Tablitsy, Moscow, 1955, 13th ed., pp. 6 and 21.
[2] Milk production includes milk production from all sources; milk output differs from gross output in appendix table 2, due to subtraction of 250 kilograms per calf for the years 1950–58.

[32] This goal implies a per capita production of about 160 eggs compared to 391 in the United States in 1956.
[33] We have assumed that the horse population would decline from about 11 million in 1958 to 6 million. An estimate made in a Soviet publication indicates that the goal of catching up with the United States would require over 500 million tons of feed units. Of this amount, 125 to 150 million tons would come from concentrates, 100 to 125 million tons from hay and other coarse fodder, 85 to 100 million tons from silage, potatoes and melons, and 185 to 200 million from pasture and green feed. See "Selskoe Khoziaistvo S.S.S.R.," Moscow, 1958, p. 154.

5. Possibilities of increasing feed supply

Can this additional amount of feed be produced? Obviously no one knows for certain, but the magnitude of the task is an enormous one. Several points may be made, which taken together indicate that the Soviet Union is likely to fall considerably short of producing the required amount of feed. First, despite the large geographic area of the Soviet Union, the pasture resources are quite limited. The pasture area in farms is estimated at 212,434,100 hectares.[34] Excluding the tundra, the Botanical Institute of the Academy of Science estimates that there are about 300 million hectares of pastureland with an average yield, converted into hay equivalent, of 4.3 centners per hectare.[35] According to these estimates the total feed units produced by the pastures does not exceed 65 million tons.[36] Consequently almost all of the increase in feed supply must come from other sources.

Second, the productivity of the land now in meadows or wild hay can probably be increased substantially. In 1956 the yield of meadows harvested on the collective farms was estimated at 0.28 tons of feed units per hectare or perhaps 0.8 tons of actual hay per acre.[37] The Botanical Institute implies a hay yield from meadows of 1.27 tons per hectare, but this is apparently a potential rather than an actual yield.[38] Accepting it as a potential yield, a doubling of meadow hay is implied. This is probably not unreasonable, since the yield of meadow hay is now apparently substantially below the level obtained by peasants in the late twenties.[39] But a doubling of output per hectare would not add more than 15 million tons of feed units.

Third, at least 80 percent of the increased feed supply must come from additional concentrates, potatoes, and the output from the sown fodder area. In 1956 the sown fodder area, excepting grain and potatoes, was about 42 million hectares. This includes the silage crops, including corn grown for silage, the hay from sown grasses and the sown area used for green feed. Unless the meadows are plowed up, the sown fodder area is unlikely to increase significantly in the next few years. It could do so only at the expense of the grain area and the 1965 plan apparently implies no reduction in the grain area. In 1956, a very good year climatically, the average yield of fodder crops per hectare was estimated to be 0.93 ton of feed units.[40] Even if this yield is increased by more than 50 percent, to 1.5 tons of feed units per hectare, the total contribution to the feed supply would be about 25 million tons.

The above estimates indicate that increased or more effective utilization of meadows plus a substantial increase in the yield of sown fodder crops, other than grains or potatoes, might result in an increased output of 40 million tons of feed units. This is a substantial increase (about 20 percent of the estimated feed use for 1958), but it falls far short of a required increase compared to 1958 of about 185 million

---

[34] Ibid., p. 120.

[35] See I. V. Larin, "Osnovnye Voprosy Sozdania Ustoichivoi Kormovoi Bazy v S.S.S.R.," Moscow, 1958, p. 5.

[36] Excluding tundra pasture. We have assumed a feed unit value of the hay equivalent derived from pasture of 0.5 centners of feed units per centner of hay. Our estimates of the relation between feed requirements and feed availability for a number of years (1928, 1953, 1956, 1958) indicate a residual of about 60 to 70 million tons of feed units that must have come from pasture plus the pasturing of growing crops and harvested fieldsplus other sources not accounted for. Since not all of the pasture area is now being fully utilized, the two sets of estimates seem to be roughly consistent.

[37] "Ekonomika Selskogo Khozyiaistva," 1958, No. 6, p. 73.

[38] Larin, ibid.

[39] N. Jasny, "The Socialized Agriculture of the U.S.S.R.," Stanford, 1949, p. 615. Meadow hay yields of 13.4 and 11.3 centners per hectare were reported for 1928 and 1929, respectively.

[40] "Ekonomika Selskogo Khozyiaistva," 1958, No. 6, p. 73.

tons. The additional amount of 145 million tons must come from additional feeding of concentrates and potatoes, primarily from grains. The 1965 plan goals call for feeding 85 to 90 million tons of concentrates (out of a gross grain harvest of 164 to 180 million tons) and approximately double the amount of potatoes fed in 1957. Compared to the last 3 or 4 years, these goals imply an increase in feed units of about 70 million tons or only a half of the additional amount required.

There is admittedly a great deal of conjecture and speculation in the above appraisal of the possibilities of the U.S.S.R. overtaking the United States in the per capita production of meat and milk.[41] But even when fairly startling increases in yields are assumed, there remains a considerable short fall in the available feed supply. On the basis of our interpretation of the possible situation over the next few years, Khrushchev's economists had a more adequate understanding of the potentialities of socialist agriculture than did Khrushchev.

F. PROGRESS DURING SIXTH 5-YEAR PLAN

There can be no question that the growth of agricultural output in the Soviet Union has been at a rather rapid rate in recent years. The increases in production that have been achieved, however, generally fall substantially short of the increases that would have been required for the period 1956–60 if the agricultural goals of the sixth 5-year plan were to be achieved. In the past, there has generally been little correspondence between agricultural goals and achievement for any of the plan periods and we also noted that it was quite clear that the goals of the catching up with the U.S. program have not and will not be met on schedule, if at all. Nevertheless, it is instructive to compare the performance of Soviet agriculture for the period 1956–58 with the performance that would have been required to meet the 1960 plan goals. In the table below, we have simply compared the annual increase in output that would have been required between 1955 and 1960 if the output goal were to be met. For example, the annual increase in meat output required was 1.27 million tons (6.35 million tons divided by 5 years). The actual annual increase during the 3 years, 1956, 1957, and 1958 over 1955 was 0.51 million tons or only 40 percent of the required rate of annual increase. In other words, the annual increase in output envisaged in the plan was 250 percent greater than that actually achieved.

---

[41] The Soviet Union can equal or exceed the United States per capita level of milk output, and may well do so within the next 5 years.

TABLE 16.—*Comparison of average annual increase in production of agricultural products, 1956–58, with increases required to achieve goals of 6th 5-year plan*

Product	Output [1]		1960 goal	Average annual increase		Percent actual of required
	1955	1958		1956–58	Plan period	
	Million metric tons					
Meat	6.32	7.9	12.7	0.51	1.27	40
Milk	43.2	57.8	84.2	4.86	8.20	59
Grain	107.0	139.4	180.0	10.7	14.6	73
Cotton	3.98	4.4	6.2	.17	.44	38
Potatoes	68.4	86.1	126.5	5.9	11.6	51
Sugar beets	30.7	54.1	47.2	7.8	5.3	147
Vegetables	13.0	14.3	28.3	.5	3.1	16
Wool	.26	.32	.47	.02	.04	52
	Billion units					
Eggs	18.0	23.5	46.7	1.8	5.7	31

[1] All output data are official gross output data without adjustment; the 1960 goals based on percentage increases given in Pravda, Feb. 26, 1956, except that the grain goal was specifically stated to be 180,000,000 tons.

The relative degree of attainment of the goals ranges from 16 to 147 percent. The first is for vegetables; the latter is for sugar beets. The relatively high degree of attainment for grain—73 percent—was undoubtedly due to the very favorable growing conditions in 1958. The 1957 output of grain, as officially reported, was slightly less than the 1955 output. It should be noted that if inventory change in the livestock herds is included, the actual increase in meat output was about 50 percent of the increase required to achieve the 1960 goal.

APPENDIX TABLE 1.—*Area sown to crops, 1913–59, selected years, Soviet Union* [1]

[Million hectares]

	1913		1925	1926	1927	1928	1929	1930	1931
	Present boundaries	Pre-1939 boundaries							
Total	118.2	105.0	104.3	110.3	112.4	113.0	118.0	127.2	136.3
Grain total	104.6	94.4	87.3	93.7	94.7	92.2	96.0	101.8	104.4
Spring wheat	24.7	24.3	17.0	20.4	20.6	21.6	23.2	23.7	25.6
Winter wheat	8.3	7.8	7.9	9.6	10.7	6.2	6.6	10.1	11.3
Rye	28.2	25.8	28.8	28.5	27.3	24.6	24.9	28.9	27.6
Millet, buckwheat, and legumes	7.3	7.2	10.9	10.1	8.6	10.8	10.8	10.1	11.5
Oats	19.1	16.9	12.8	15.3	17.9	17.2	18.9	17.9	17.5
Barley	13.3	11.5	6.5	7.4	6.9	7.3	8.1	7.4	6.9
Corn	2.2	1.4	3.4	3.0	4.5	4.5	3.5	3.7	4.0
Industrial total	4.9	4.55	7.17	6.66	7.29	8.62	8.84	9.56	14.08
Sunflower seed	.98	.97	3.10	2.59	2.83	3.90	3.62	3.39	4.57
Sugar beet	.68	.65	.53	.54	.66	.77	.77	1.04	1.39
Cotton	.69	.69	.59	.65	.80	.97	1.06	1.58	2.14
Flax for fiber	1.25	1.01	1.27	1.27	1.20	1.36	1.63	1.75	2.39

See footnotes at end of table, p. 230.

COMPARISONS OF UNITED STATES AND SOVIET ECONOMIES **229**

APPENDIX TABLE 1.—*Area sown to crops, 1913–59, selected years, Soviet Union* [1]—
Continued

	1913		1925	1926	1927	1928	1929	1930	1931
	Present boundaries	Pre-1939 boundaries							
Total garden	5.1	3.82				7.68	7.64	7.97	9.06
Potatoes	4.2	3.06	5.02	5.21	5.46	5.68	5.69	5.73	6.17
Vegetables	.6	.49				.80⎱	1.95	1.18	1.99
Melons	.3	.26				1.21⎰		1.06	.90
Grasses	3.3	2.05				3.87			
Annual	.8	.60	.72	1.10	.91	1.16	1.47	2.02	3.28
Perennial	2.5	1.45	.85	1.05	1.78	2.40	3.15	3.94	4.13
Silage								.17	.76

	1932	1933	1934	1935	1936	1937	1938	1940	1950
Total	134.4	129.7	131.5	132.8	133.8	135.3	136.9	150.4	146.3
Grain total	99.7	101.6	104.7	103.4	102.4	104.4	102.4	110.5	102.9
Spring wheat	22.7	22.4	24.4	24.6	25.9	27.1	26.9	26.0	26.0
Winter wheat	11.8	10.8	10.8	12.4	13.1	14.3	14.6	14.3	12.5
Rye	26.2	25.4	24.0	23.5	21.8	23.0	21.4	23.1	23.6
Millet, buckwheat, and legumes	11.5	13.1	13.1	10.5	9.5	9.2	8.5	10.4	8.8
Oats	15.4	16.7	18.0	18.3	18.1	17.6	17.9	20.2	16.2
Barley	6.8	6.9	8.1	8.3	8.6	8.6	8.5	11.3	8.6
Corn	3.7	4.0	3.7	3.2	3.1	2.8	2.6	3.6	4.8
Industrial total	14.88	11.98	10.72	10.64	10.83	11.15	10.96	11.8	12.23
Sunflower seed	5.31	3.90	3.50	3.31	3.18	3.25	3.14	3.54	3.59
Sugar beet	1.54	1.21	1.18	1.23	1.26	1.19	1.18	1.23	1.31
Cotton	2.17	2.05	1.94	1.95	2.03	2.09	2.08	2.08	2.32
Flax for fiber	2.51	2.39	2.11	2.11	2.15	2.13	1.88	2.10	1.90
Total garden	9.22	8.68	8.84	9.94	9.80	9.00	9.39	10.0	10.45
Potatoes	6.11	5.66	6.13	7.38	7.58	6.87	7.37	7.7	8.53
Vegetables	2.24	2.32	2.13	1.90	1.50	1.39	1.32	1.5	1.32
Melons	.87	.70	.58	.66	.72	.74	.70	.8	.60
Grasses:									
Annual	4.46	3.09	3.03	4.26	4.72	3.55	4.46	4.2	7.05
Perennial	3.79	2.88	2.86	2.91	4.53	5.56	8.23	12.1	11.19
Silage	1.66	.62	.59			.67	.64	.8	1.30

	1951	1952	1953	1954	1955	1956	1957	1958	1959
Total	153.0	155.76	157.2	166.1	185.8	194.7	193.7	195.6	196.0
Grain total	106.4	107.34	106.7	112.1	126.4	128.3	124.6	125.2	
Spring wheat	27.4	29.1	30.5	33.6	42.2	49.1⎱	69.1	48.4⎱	
Winter wheat	15.6	17.2	17.8	15.7	18.3	12.9⎰		18.2	
Rye	23.9	22.8	20.3	20.5	19.1	18.4	18.2	17.7	
Millet, buckwheat, and legumes	7.7	7.6	8.3	10.1	11.9	10.4	8.0		
Oats	17.4	16.6	15.3	15.9	14.8	15.1	14.1	14.7	
Barley	8.1	8.6	9.6	10.7	9.9	11.9	9.2	9.6	
Corn	4.1	3.9	3.5	4.3	9.1	9.3	5.8	8.1	
Industrial total	12.61	12.74	11.47	11.78	12.29	13.15	11.8	12.31	
Sunflower seed	3.61	3.67	3.90	4.03	4.24	4.51	3.46	3.94	
Sugar beet	1.39	1.46	1.57	1.60	1.76	2.01	2.11	2.50	
Cotton	2.72	2.83	1.88	2.20	2.20	2.07	2.09	2.15	
Flax for fiber	1.60	1.53	1.24	1.11	1.48	1.92	1.69	1.60	

See footnotes at end of table, p. 230.

230 COMPARISONS OF UNITED STATES AND SOVIET ECONOMIES

APPENDIX TABLE 1.—*Area sown to crops, 1913–59, selected years, Soviet Union* [1]—
Continued

	1951 Present boundaries	1952 Pre-1939 boundaries	1953	1954	1955	1956	1957	1958	1959
Total garden	10.30	10.05	10.26	10.98	11.44	11.58	11.9	11.6	--------
Potatoes	8.45	8.21	8.31	8.71	9.09	9.20	9.80	9.50	--------
Vegetables	1.28	1.27	1.32	1.49	1.51	1.59	-------	-------	--------
Melons	.57	.57	.63	.78	.84	.79	-------	-------	--------
Grasses:									
Annual	7.47	7.05	7.84	9.43	14.77	20.83	------}	37.0	{-------
Perennial	12.85	14.82	16.85	16.10	13.69	12.28	------}		{-------
Silage	1.82	2.09	2.31	3.86	5.69	7.10	-------	8.1	--------

[1] The figures for each year are for the territory within the boundaries existing at that time, unless otherwise noted. For sources, see notes for appendix tables 1, 2, and 3.

APPENDIX TABLE 2.—*Total livestock numbers, Soviet Union* [1]

[Million head]

Year	Cows	Cattle (including cows)	Hogs	Sheep	Goats	Sheep and goats	Horses
January: [1]							
1916 [2]	28.8	58.4	23.0	89.7	6.6	96.3	38.2
1916 [3]	24.9	51.7	17.3	82.5	6.2	88.7	34.2
1928 [2]	33.2	66.8	27.7	104.2	10.4	114.6	36.1
1928 [3]	29.2	60.1	22.0	97.3	9.7	107.0	32.1
1929	29.2	58.2	19.4	97.4	9.7	107.1	32.6
1930	28.5	50.6	14.2	85.5	7.8	93.3	31.0
1931	24.5	42.5	11.7	62.5	5.6	68.1	27.0
1932	22.3	38.3	10.9	43.8	3.8	47.6	21.7
1933	19.4	33.5	9.9	34.0	3.3	37.3	17.3
1934	19.0	33.5	11.5	32.9	3.6	36.5	15.4
1935	19.0	38.9	17.1	36.4	4.4	40.8	14.9
1936	20.0	46.0	25.9	43.8	6.1	49.9	15.5
1937	20.9	47.5	20.0	46.6	7.2	53.8	15.9
1938	22.7	50.9	25.7	57.3	9.3	66.6	16.2
1939	24.0	53.5	25.2	------------	-----------	80.9	17.2
1940	22.8	47.8	22.5	66.6	10.1	76.7	17.7
1941	27.8	54.5	27.5	79.9	11.7	91.6	21.0
1945	21.6	44.2	8.8	57.9	12.3	70.2	9.9
1946	22.9	47.6	10.6	58.5	11.5	70.0	10.7
1947	23.0	47.0	8.7	57.7	11.6	69.3	10.9
1948	23.8	50.1	9.7	63.3	13.5	76.8	11.0
1949	24.2	54.8	15.2	70.4	15.2	85.6	11.8
1950	24.6	58.1	22.2	77.6	16.0	93.6	12.7
1951	24.3	57.1	24.4	82.6	16.4	99.0	13.8
1952	24.9	58.8	27.1	90.5	17.1	107.6	14.7
1953	24.3	56.6	28.5	94.3	15.6	109.9	15.3
1954	25.2	55.8	33.3	99.8	15.7	115.5	15.3
1955	26.4	56.7	30.7	98.9	14.0	112.9	14.2
1956	27.7	58.8	34.0	103.3	12.9	116.2	13.0
1957	29.0	61.4	40.8	108.2	11.6	119.8	12.4
1958	31.4	66.7	44.3	120.2	9.9	130.1	11.9
1959	33.3	70.8	48.5	129.6	-----------	-----------	-----------

[1] The figures for each year are for the territory within the boundaries existing at that time, unless otherwise noted. Data from official sources; see notes for appendix tables 1, 2, and 3.
[2] Present boundaries.
[3] Boundaries prior to Sept. 17, 1939.

APPENDIX TABLE 3.—*Gross physical output for 11 major commodity groups, Soviet Union*[1]

	Grain	Potatoes	Vegetables	Sunflower seed	Sugar beets	Seed cotton
	Million tons	*Million tons*	*Million tons*	*Million tons*	*Million tons*	*Million tons*
1913 [3]						
1913 [3]		31.6	5.5	0.747		
1925	72.7	38.6	12.7	2.230	9.070	0.567
1926	76.6	43.0	10.2	1.550	6.400	.550
1927	71.7	41.2	8.6	2.180	10.410	.720
1928	73.3	46.4	10.7	2.128	10.143	.821
1929	71.7	45.6	10.6	1.764	6.248	.864
1930	83.5	49.5	12.0	1.630	14.019	1.113
1931	66.0	44.8	14.6	2.506	12.052	1.290
1932	63.0	43.1	13.2	2.268	6.561	1.271
1933	67.1	49.2	16.5	2.354	8.989	1.315
1934	67.3	51.0	16.7	2.077	11.361	1.176
1935	69.3	69.7	19.8	1.850	16.200	1.729
1936	60.0	51.0	11.8	1.490	16.830	2.416
1937	91.9	65.6	15.5	2.080	21.860	2.576
1938	70.7	41.9	8.8	1.670	16.700	2.600
1939		51.3			16.900	2.682
1940 [3]					18.146	2.255
1940 [3]	83.0	75.9	13.7	2.578		2.255
1941						2.478
1942						1.329
1943						.726
1944						1.131
1945		58.3				1.161
1946						1.666
1947						1.703
1948						2.206
1949	69.7		10.4		15.565	2.547
1950	81.4	88.6	9.3	1.798	20.841	3.584
1951	78.9	59.6	9.0	1.744	23.760	3.763
1952	92.0	68.4	11.0	2.211	22.276	3.799
1953	82.5	72.6	11.4	2.630	23.176	3.871
1954	85.7	74.8	12.0	1.905	19.847	4.229
1955	107.0	71.8	14.1	3.808	31.049	3.976
1956	127.6	96.0	14.3	3.947	32.488	4.458
1957	105.0	87.8	14.8	2.800	39.672	4.371
1958	139.4	86.1	14.3	4.500	54.144	4.400

See footnotes at end of table, p. 232.

232 COMPARISONS OF UNITED STATES AND SOVIET ECONOMIES

APPENDIX TABLE 3.—*Gross physical output for 11 major commodity groups,* *Soviet Union* [1]—Continued

	Flax-fiber	Wool greasy weight	Milk	Meat live weight	Meat dressed weight	Eggs
	Million tons	*Million tons*	*Million tons*	*Million tons*	*Million tons*	*Billions*
1913 [3]	0.330	0.180	24.787	6,609	4.053	10.192
1913 [2]	.365	.192	29.430	7.933	4.954	11.919
1925	.300	.152	28.100	6.453	3.872	9.550
1926	.270	.164	30.500	7.183	4.310	10.470
1927	.240	.175	30.600	7.596	4.558	10.488
1928	.324	.182	30.978	8.047	4.900	10.770
1929	.361	.183	29.799	9.722	5.792	10.110
1930	.436	.141	26.955	7.835	4.301	8.000
1931	.553	.098	23.399	7.136	3.949	6.656
1932	.498	.069	20.558	4.949	2.762	4.432
1933	.548	.064	19.156	3.969	2.276	3.500
1934	.533	.065	20.800	3.463	2.049	4.200
1935	.550	.079	21.436	3.601	2.273	5.775
1936	.580	.099	23.507	5.910	3.749	7.449
1937	.570	.106	26.061	4.670	2.957	8.179
1938	.546	.137	28.955	6.933	4.457	10.475
1939 [3]	.500	.150	27.209	8.380	5.132	11.548
1940 [3]	....	.151	26.623	6.260	3.880	10.228
1940 [2]	.565	.161	33.640	7.502	4.695	12.214
1941	....	.161	25.495	7.044	4.087	9.261
1942	....	.125	15.762	3.405	1.841	4.513
1943	....	.100	16.391	3.288	1.767	3.469
1944	....	.103	22.044	3.632	1.953	3.588
1945	....	.111	26.428	4.690	2.559	4.883
1946	....	.119	27.663	5.620	3.082	5.248
1947	....	.125	30.204	4.536	2.508	4.917
1948	....	.146	33.426	5.419	3.060	6.568
1949	.312	.163	34.898	6.361	3.751	9.120
1950	.255	.180	35.311	8.125	4.867	11.697
1951	.194	.192	36.154	7.557	4.671	13.252
1952	.212	.219	35.702	8.526	5.170	14.399
1953	.163	.235	36.475	9.394	5.822	16.059
1954	.218	.230	38.197	10.007	6.281	17.179
1955	.381	.256	43.009	10.215	6.322	18.481
1956	.521	.261	49.111	10.653	6.598	19.532
1957	.439	.289	54.750	11.633	7.374	22.269
1958	.443	.321	57.786	....	7.851	23.451

[1] The figures for each year are for the territory within the boundaries existing at that time, unless otherwise noted. Data from official sources; see notes for appendix tables 1, 2, and 3.
[2] Present boundaries.
[3] Boundaries prior to Sept. 17, 1939.

SOURCES FOR APPENDIX TABLES 1, 2, AND 3

In compiling the table of the gross agricultural output reliance was placed primarily upon Soviet sources. The sources most frequently used were the following:

Gosudarstvennaia Planovaia Komissia (Gosplan) SSSR:
    Kontrolnye Tsifry Narodnogo Khoziaistva na 1925/26 god.   Moscow 1926.
    Kontrolnye Tsifry Narodnogo Khoziaistva na 1926/27 god.   Moscow 1927.
    Kontrolnye Tsifry Narodnogo Khoziaistva na 1928/29 god.   Moscow 1929.
    Perspektivy Razvertyvania Narodnogo Khoziaistva SSSR na 1926/27–1930/31 gg.   Moscow 1927.
    Piatiletnii Plan Razvitia Narodnogo Khoziaistva Soiuza SSR.   Moscow 1930.
    Narodno–Khoziaistvennyi Plan na 1935 god.   Moscow 1935.
    Narodno–Khoziaistvennyi Plan na 1936 god.   Moscow 1936.
Narodnyi Komissariat Zemledelia SSSR i Narodnyi Komissariat Sovkhozov SSSR:
    Selskoe Khoziaistvo SSSR, 1935.   Moscow 1936.
Tsentralnoe Statisticheskoe Upravlenie (TsSU) Gosplana SSSR:
    Slovar Spravochnik po Sotsialno Ekonomicheskoi Statistike.   Moscow 1944.
    Statisticheskii Spravochnik SSSR na 1927 god.   Moscow 1928.
    Statisticheskii Spravochnik SSSR na 1928 god.   Moscow 1928.
Tsentralnoe Statisticheskoe Upravlenie (TsSU) Sovieta Ministrov SSSR:
    Chislennost' Skota v SSSR, Statisticheskii Sbornik.   Moscow 1957.
    Narodnoe Khoziaistvo SSSR v 1956 godu.   Moscow 1957.
    Posevnye Ploshchadi v SSSR.   Statisticheskii Sbornik.   Moscow 1957.
    Promyshlennost' SSSR.   Statisticheskii Sbornik.   Moscow 1957.
    Zhivotnovodstvo SSSR.   Statisticheskii Sbornik.   Moscow 1959.

Tsentralnoe Upravlenie Narodno-Khoziaistvennogo Ucheta (TsUNKhU) Gosplana SSSR:
  Narodnoe Khoziaistvo SSSR, Statisticheskii Spravochnik 1932. Moscow 1932.
  Posevnye Ploshchadi SSSR, 1913–1938 gg. Moscow-Leningrad 1939.
  Proizvoditelnost' i Ispolzovanie Truda v Kolkhozakh vo Vtoroi Piatiletke. Moscow-Leningrad, 1939.
  Sotsialisticheskoe Selskoe Khoziaistvo, Statisticheskii Sbornik. Moscow-Leningrad, 1939.
  Sotsialisticheskoe Stroitelstvo SSSR, 1934. Moscow 1935.
  Sotsialisticheskoe Stroitelstvo SSSR. Moscow 1936.
  Sotsialisticheskoe Stroitelstvo Soiuza SSR (1933–38 gg.). Moscow-Leningrad 1939.
  Zhivotnovodstvo SSSR za 1916–1938 gg. Moscow-Leningrad 1940.

Extremely helpful among the books published outside of the Soviet Union were the books by Naum Jasny, Vladimir Timoshenko, and Lazar Volin, as well as some of the RAND publications.

Grain.—In 1932, in connection with the report of the first 5-year plan completion, a half-hearted attempt to "adjust" the grain output figure was made (although the official shift toward a reporting of "biological yield" took place in 1933). This has necessitated an estimate of the "adjustment" and a correction in terms of gross output or barn yield of grain. The biological yield data reported for the period 1933–38, were adjusted downward according to the estimates of the Soviet economist M. Kubanin.

The output for 1940 had to be estimated in view of the lack of published data. Although the practice of reporting the biological yield was supposedly discontinued and ridiculed since 1953 and the 1950–58 grain yields are claimed to represent barn yield, there is sufficient evidence to question whether they accurately reflect the amount of dry grain in a suitable storage place. The grain estimate probably reflects the weight of grain at the combine, thus include waste and excess moisture. Nor are subsequent losses or waste accounted for. In the gross output table the official grain output figures for 1950–58 are accepted, however.

Vegetables.—The vegetable output data for the first half of the 1930's possibly include the output of food melons, without making it explicit.

Cotton.—The output of cotton is reported in the Soviet Union in terms of seed cotton or raw cotton rather than lint, as in other parts of the world. No attempt to convert the data to their lint content was made in view of the lack of available coefficients for each of the years. On the average the ratio of lint to seed cotton is about 0.3 to 0.33.

Wool.—The wool output is reported in terms of greasy weight. Apart from sheep wool, mohair and camel wool are included, as well as wool taken from hides.

Flax fiber.—Output is reported for the whole period until 1950 in terms of the biological yield; no attempt was made to adjust for it in the table of gross output. The reported flax fiber is on a scutched base.

Milk.—The milk series represents the output of milk of cows, goats, sheep, and mares. In view of the changed concept of milk output (the broadening of the reported output by making it more inclusive) an adjustment was made for the years 1925–27 output for which only cow milk data were available. Sometime during the 1950's (possibly in 1955) another innovation in reporting the gross output was introduced, namely an unknown volume of milk sucked by calves was included in the gross output. How far back the output figures were adjusted is not known. The data prior to 1940—and possibly the year 1940—seem not to be affected by this change in the "inclusiveness" of the milk concept.

Meat.—The gross output series of meat have a history of their own. Originally, during the 1920's gross output included the three principal types of meat (beef and veal, pork, and mutton) and separately poultry. Gradually the definition of meat became more inclusive. At first fat was included in the meat, next various kinds of offal, and finally all edible offal and meat of horses, camels, reindeers, etc. A recent Soviet source (TsSU–Zhivotnovodstvo SSSR. Moscow 1959) presents a recalculation of the meat output for the years 1928–57. Apart from the impact of the recalculation upon the index of meat output in various years when compared with previous data for the same years and their relative position to the base year, the general level of output was substantially increased in terms of both live and dressed weight. We have for the purpose of this presentation accepted the official data and adjusted upward the previous data for 1925–27.

APPENDIX TABLE 4.—*Net physical output for 11 major commodity groups, Soviet Union* [1]

	Grain	Potatoes	Vegetables	Sunflower seed	Sugar beets	Seed cotton
	Million tons	*Million tons*	*Million tons*	*Million tons*	*Million tons*	*Million tons*
1913 [3]			4.400			
1913 [3]						
1925	38.7	14.4	9.525	2.178	8.418	0.549
1926	38.2	14.5	7.650	1.493	6.132	.538
1927	34.9	13.7	6.450	2.100	9.771	.690
1928	36.9	16.7	8.037	2.056	9.367	.788
1929	35.7	16.6	7.968	1.696	6.038	.825
1930	48.4	23.6	8.400	1.538	13.238	1.073
1931	37.0	18.9	10.220	2.400	10.435	1.273
1932	35.5	18.4	9.240	2.190	6.117	1.216
1933	40.2	24.7	11.550	2.284	8.198	1.291
1934	38.9	26.4	11.690	2.010	9.509	1.172
1935	38.9	33.0	13.860	1.786	15.723	1.706
1936	31.6	17.8	8.260	1.425	15.810	2.340
1937	59.1	33.1	10.850	2.018	21.449	2.576
1938	37.9	13.6	6.160	1.600	16.350	2.590
1939					16.500	2.650
1940 [3]						
1940 [3]	45.7	37.3	10.305	2.500	17.357	2.237
1941						
1942						
1943						
1944						
1945						
1946						
1947						
1948						
1949						2.688
1950	46.3	44.3	7.475	1.726	19.822	3.539
1951	45.2	23.6	7.200	1.670	23.400	3.670
1952	49.6	30.4	8.800	2.133	22.100	3.700
1953	44.2	30.7	9.110	2.550	22.891	3.853
1954	45.9	29.5	9.600	1.820	19.522	4.122
1955	55.9	27.2	11.280	3.718	30.664	3.881
1956	67.8	37.7	11.440	3.850	31.451	4.332
1957	48.2	36.0	11.480	2.680	38.535	4.200
1958	68.9	31.1	11.440	4.370	51.037	(4.300)

See footnotes at end of table, p. 235.

COMPARISONS OF UNITED STATES AND SOVIET ECONOMIES **235**

APPENDIX TABLE 4.—*Net physical output for 11 major commodity groups, Soviet Union* [1]—Continued

	Flax fiber	Wool	Milk	Meat (dressed weight)	Eggs
	Million tons	*Million tons*	*Million tons*	*Million tons*	*Billions*
1913 [3]	0. 314	0. 173	----------	4. 053	9. 377
1913 [2]	. 347	. 184	----------	4. 954	10. 965
1925	. 285	. 146	24. 517	3. 872	8. 786
1926	. 257	. 157	26. 610	4. 310	9. 632
1927	. 228	. 168	26. 595	4. 558	9. 649
1928	. 308	. 175	27. 029	4. 900	9. 908
1929	. 325	. 176	25. 904	5. 792	9. 301
1930	. 349	. 135	23. 418	4. 301	7. 200
1931	. 443	. 094	20. 416	3. 949	5. 990
1932	. 376	. 066	17. 900	2. 762	3. 989
1933	. 384	. 061	16. 708	2. 276	3. 150
1934	. 373	. 062	18. 378	2. 049	3. 780
1935	. 385	. 076	18. 950	2. 273	5. 198
1936	. 406	. 095	20. 900	3. 749	6. 704
1937	. 402	. 102	23. 281	2. 957	7. 361
1938	. 382	. 132	25. 978	4. 457	9. 428
1939	. 350	. 144	24. 225	5. 132	10. 393
1940 [3]	----------	. 145	23. 334	3. 880	9. 205
1940 [2]	. 349	. 155	27. 609	4. 695	10. 992
1941	----------	. 155	18. 219	4. 087	----------
1942	----------	. 120	10. 866	1. 841	----------
1943	----------	. 096	11. 240	1. 767	----------
1944	----------	. 099	15. 567	1. 953	----------
1945	----------	. 107	18. 863	2. 559	----------
1946	----------	. 114	19. 860	3. 082	----------
1947	----------	. 120	22. 248	2. 508	----------
1948	----------	. 140	25. 266	3. 060	----------
1949	. 280	. 157	26. 602	3. 751	----------
1950	. 230	. 173	26. 509	4. 867	10. 820
1951	. 175	. 184	27. 298	4. 671	12. 258
1952	. 191	. 210	26. 846	5. 170	13. 319
1953	. 154	. 226	27. 565	5. 822	14. 855
1954	. 207	. 221	28. 909	6. 281	15. 891
1955	. 362	. 246	33. 271	6. 322	17. 095
1956	. 495	. 251	38. 905	6. 598	18. 067
1057	. 417	. 277	43. 878	7. 374	20. 599
1958	. 421	. 308	46. 482	7. 851	21. 692

[1] See attached notes for derivation of estimates. The figures for each year are for the territory within the boundaries existing at that time, unless otherwise noted. Territorial coverage for 1940 is uncertain, probably refers to boundaries prior to Sept. 17, 1939. Data from official sources; see notes for appendix tables 1, 2, and 3.
[2] Present boundaries.
[3] Boundaries prior to Sept. 17, 1939.

DERIVATION OF ESTIMATES OF NET AGRICULTURAL OUTPUT FOR APPENDIX TABLE 4

The estimates of net agricultural output, by commodities, are derived by deducting from gross physical output that part of output used in the process of production (seed, feed, eggs for hatching, milk for cow feeding, etc.), as well as some losses which are not recognized in the Soviet measurement of gross output. Given the nature of the available data (the last published Soviet estimates of the distribution of output for different uses are for 1928), our estimates are crude having been derived from scattered sources, but in general, we believe, they reflect approximately the appropriate order of magnitudes.

The net agricultural output for each of the accounted crops or livestock products reflects the volume of each year's available supply for human consumption, industrial processing, Government stockpiling and exports. No estimates of changes in the yearly carryover were attempted, since the size of stocks is a state secret in the Soviet Union.

Grain.—In order to account for the losses during the period 1932–38, an adjustment for the gross output figure was included in the table on gross output. For the years 1940, 1950–55, 1957, 1958 a loss of 7 percent was assumed and for 1956 a 10 percent loss seems to be a reasonable assumption in view of the Soviet admission of the existence of heavy losses during this particular year. In addition, for the years 1956–58, we have excluded from the gross output 2.7 million tons for 1956 and 2.4 and 6.2 million tons for 1957 and 1958, respectively, which represents the estimate of silage corn converted into a dry-grain figure. In our opinion, such an elimination of losses and corn in silage provides a greater degree of uniformty for the whole period. In any case, the corn in the islage is fed to livestock and should be deducted to arrive at net output. The seed requirements were estimated on the basis of an average seeding rate of 1.5 quintals per hectare of next year's reported sowing area.

The utilization of grain for feeding of livestock was estimated according to a combination of factors: availability of feed grain, feeding norms of the peasants households during the 1920's, and meat and milk output. As a check against the results estimates of food consumption, industrial use of grain and additions to the Government's stockpile for various years were computed. Nevertheless, the feed estimates do not pretend to be highly accurate, since the year-to-year carryover could be indicated only vaguely.

Potatoes.—For potatoes a uniform loss of 10 percent of the reported gross output was assumed, which by and large seems to constitute an underestimate for the following reasons: (1) We believe the gross output figure to be very crude in view of the large share of private output in the total, considering the Soviet procedures of estimating the private output to be inadequate to derive an estimate with a high degree of accuracy; (2) scattered sources reported heavy losses of potatoes during the harvest and postharvest period in the socia.ized sector. The seeding rate was assumed to be 2 tons per hectare, which is below the collective farms' normative rate and was accepted on the assumption that the private producers make a more economical use of their seeding material. The seeding rate was multiplied by the next year's sown area to obtain the seed utilization out of each crop.

The feed utilization of potatoes was estimated on the basis of feeding norms prevailing in the peasant farms during the 1920's and by relating the feed to the meat output. Adjustment for certain years were made with respect to reasonable food use and with possible substitution of grain for feed.

Vegetables.—In order to arrive at an approximate estimate of actually available vegetables for the direct consumption by the population and for the processing industry, losses, waste, and spoilage were assumed to run about 25 percent of the reported gross output for the period 1925–29 and 1936–40. The estimated losses are 30 percent of the output for 1930–35 and 20 percent of gross output for 1950–58.

Sunflower seed.—The seeding rate of 20 kilograms per hectare of next year's sowing area was accepted for sunflower seed, which constitutes an unweighted average of various regional reported seeding rates. No attempt to arrive at a deduction for losses was made in view of the absence of data in this respect.

Sugar beets and cotton.—It was assumed that the officially reported marketed output for these two crops corresponds to the net output, since at least from 1928 the processing facilities were all in the possession of the State, and utilization in the household (especially in the case of cotton) was forbidden and heavy penalties imposed. An exception to our assumption might be the case of sugar beets in 1958, when some unspecified volume (negligible with respect to the total) was fed to livestock. But this is a possibility which has not been confirmed by official sources.

Flax fiber.—Deductions were applied to a series of gross output which was reported at least until 1950 in terms of a "biological crop" measurement. In fact, it was according to some official indication "very much biological." This made necessary the utilization of high deductions, which still may be on the low side. They are for the years 1925–28, 5 percent; for 1929, 10 percent; 1930–31, 20 percent; 1932, 25 percent; 1933–39, 30 percent; 1940, 38.2 percent (an officially used deduction for the year); for 1950–52, 10 percent; 1953, 57.5 percent.

Wool.—Since the reported gross wool output figure is given in terms of greasy wool, an estimated 4 percent of total output was assumed for waste, which for certain years may be an understatement.

Eggs.—The estimated percentage of eggs for hatching was assumed in the absence of yearly data pertaining to the size of the flock. For the 1920's, 8 percent; for the 1930's and 1940, 10 percent; and 7.5 percent for the 1950's.

Milk.—The deductions for milk pertain exclusively to estimated feeding of calves. For the period preceding 1940 the assumption was made that 150 kilograms of whole milk was fed per calf. For the period after 1940, 400 kilograms of milk per calf was assumed (since some time during the 1950's and estimate of milk supposedly sucked by calves was added to the gross output, and it is difficult to estimate how far back the output data were adjusted to include this "component"). For 1940 the average of 150 and 400 kilograms, or 275 kilograms was assumed; this is a purely arbitrary adjustment since three is some reason to believe that the 1940 output data on present territory is consistent with the older series for the 1930's. The yearly calf number was estimated as being 90 percent of the cow number for the 1920's, 85 percent for the 1930's and 1940, and 90 percent for the 1950's (the latest is an overestimate for the socialized sector, where the number of barren cows reported in various sources is still very large, but is probably offset by the lower percentage of barren cows in the private sector).

Meat.—Gross output series has been accepted as representing net output. Neither series includes changes in livestock inventories on farms, which have been substantial in recent years.

APPENDIX TABLE 5.—*Estimated annual yields of animal products and crops, Soviet Union* [1]

	Gross cow milk [2]	Net cow milk [2]	Gross sheep wool [4]	Net sheep wool [4]	Live pork weight [5]	Dead pork weight [5]
	Kilograms per cow	*Kilograms per cow*	*Kilograms per sheep*	*Kilograms per sheep*	*Kilograms per hog*	*Kilograms per hog*
1928	1,042	907	1.87	1.80	100	77
1929	1,017	882	1.88	1.80	115	88
1930	1,003	868	1.65	1.58	92	60
1931	925	797	1.57	1.51	110	68
1932	944	817	1.58	1.51	107	67
1933	1,000	873	1.88	1.81	87	56
1934	1,037	910	1.98	1.90	67	45
1935	1,069	942	2.17	2.08	62	45
1936	1,116	986	2.26	2.17	99	74
1937	1,195	1,068	2.27	2.18	65	50
1938	1,236	1,108	2.39	2.29	97	74
1939	1,163	1,035	2.15	2.06	90	69
1940	1,145	1,010	----	----	----	----
1940	1,180	[3] 946	2.27	2.18	07	52
1945	1,139	799	1.92	1.84	88	58
1946	1,154	814	2.03	1.95	105	72
1947	1,235	895	2.17	2.08	71	50
1948	1,330	990	2.31	2.21	74	54
1949	1,356	1,016	2.32	2.22	70	53
1950	1,365	1,005	2.32	2.23	84	63
1951	1,381	1,021	2.32	2.23	87	65
1952	1,373	1,013	2.42	2.32	89	65
1953	1,385	1,025	2.49	2.39	101	75
1954	1,403	1,043	2.30	2.21	115	85
1955	1,521	1,161	2.58	2.48	108	78
1956	1,674	1,314	2.53	2.43	99	71
1957	1,775	1,406	2.67	2.56	108	79
1958	----	----	2.67	2.56	----	----

	Gross flax fiber	Net flax fiber	Gross grain	Gross potatoes	Gross sugar beets	Gross seed cotton	Gross sunflower
	Centners per hectare	*Centners per hectare*	*Centners per hectare*	*Centners per hectare*	*Centners per hectare*	*Centners per hectare*	*Centners per hectare*
1925	2.4	2.2	8.30	76.9	171.1	9.61	7.19
1926	2.1	2.0	8.20	82.5	118.5	8.46	5.98
1927	2.0	1.9	7.63	75.5	157.7	9.00	7.70
1928	2.4	2.3	7.95	81.7	131.7	8.90	5.46
1929	2.2	2.0	7.47	80.1	81.1	8.15	4.87
1930	2.5	2.0	8.20	86.4	115.4	7.04	4.81
1931	2.3	1.9	6.32	72.6	105.0	6.03	5.48
1932	2.0	1.5	6.32	70.5	85.7	5.86	4.27
1933	2.3	1.6	6.60	87.0	74.3	6.41	6.04
1934	2.5	1.8	6.43	83.2	96.3	6.06	5.93
1935	2.6	1.8	6.70	94.4	131.7	8.87	5.58
1936	2.7	1.9	5.88	67.3	133.3	11.90	4.69
1937	2.7	1.9	8.80	95.5	183.7	12.32	6.40
1938	2.9	2.0	6.90	56.8	140.5	12.50	5.32
1940	2.7	1.7	7.51	99.8	153.8	10.84	7.28
1950	1.3	1.2	7.91	103.9	159.0	15.45	5.01
1951	1.2	1.1	7.42	70.5	170.9	13.83	4.83
1952	1.4	1.2	8.57	83.3	152.6	13.42	6.02
1953	1.3	1.2	7.73	87.3	147.6	20.59	6.74
1954	2.0	1.9	7.64	85.9	124.0	19.22	4.73
1955	2.6	2.4	8.46	78.9	176.4	18.07	8.98
1956	2.7	2.6	9.95	104.4	161.6	21.54	8.75
1957	----	----	8.43	89.6	188.0	20.91	8.09
1958	2.8	2.6	11.13	90.6	216.6	20.46	11.42

[1] Based on output data in appendix tables 3 and 4 and sown area (appendix table 1) or livestock numbers (appendix table 2).
[2] Average of cow numbers for beginning and end of year, except beginning year numbers for 1940 on prewar territory and end of year numbers for 1940 on postwar territory.
[3] An alternative estimate, based on 150 kilograms of milk per calf, is 1,052 kilograms.
[4] Sheep numbers for beginning of year.
[5] Average of hog numbers for beginning and end of year used.

THE POPULATION OF THE SOVIET UNION

(By John F. Kantner, Foreign Manpower Research Office, U.S. Bureau of the Census)

CHAPTER 1. GENERAL SUMMARY

The interrelationships between population and economic organization are numerous and complex. It scarcely exaggerates the matter to assert that for every population of a given size and structure there is a narrowly limited set of economic forms and arrangements which will work. Therefore, provided one has the information, treatments of the connections between demographic and economic phenomena can be as encyclopedic as time and inclination allow.

In seeking a basis for selection for this discussion, two problems of the current Soviet scene appeared to stand out as vitally related to the economic position of the U.S.S.R. now and in the future. These are the problem of labor supply and the growth prospects for the Soviet population over the next 15 years. Chapter 2 presents an analysis of the problem of labor supply and chapter 3 develops some of the implications of differing growth prospects and attempts to discern from very fragmentary evidence and trend in Soviet fertility. In discussing each of these topics comparisons with the United States are frequently made. To bring all comparative data together for convenient reference, a final chapter of basic U.S.-U.S.S.R. demographic comparisons has been added. An appendix is also included which provides some of the basic demographic information currently available on the Soviet Union.

Soviet economic development until recently has not been handicapped by a population surplus such as threatens to erase the economic gains of the underdeveloped countries of the present period. The Soviet Union presents a chronicle of catastrophic population losses which have kept the long-term growth rate (excluding population gains through annexation) below 1 percent per year. At the same time, however, the population in the age range considered, in Soviet usage, to cover the "able-bodied population" (16–59 years of age) has steadily increased in proportion to the total population.

The Second World War left the Soviet Union with a shortage of some 20 million men. For this and other reasons, a larger proportion of women are employed than in almost any other industrial country in the world and this proportion has declined only slightly since the end of the war. Having a delayed impact on the labor force is the enormous birth deficit of the war. Net additions to the working-age population currently run around 1 million persons annually or only about half the number 2 or 3 years earlier. Then those being added were persons born before the war. This number may drop to less than 100,000 per year in the near future, causing an even more critical manpower problem for the current 7-year plan (1959–65) than was faced by the abortive sixth 5-year plan (1956–60).

In years to come the numerical imbalance between men and women will be alleviated as more and more of the able-bodied population comes to consist of persons born since the end of the war. There will be also a sharp upturn in the number of annual additions to the population of working age after 1963. In spite of this, the growth of the population of working age during the period of the 7-year plan will amount to only about half of the 12 million increase in employment called for in the plan. The Soviet Government seems to be counting on three other principal sources to augment its labor supply: The household economy, the educational system, and the agricultural population. The prospects for obtaining additional labor force from each of these sources are to a large extent contingent upon the success of other parts of the Government's program. In particular, the extent to which the agricultural population can make up the greater part of the deficit will be determined, partially at least, by the success of efforts to modernize agricultural production, introduce substitutes for agricultural products, complete a vast urban housing program, consolidate the collective farms, and so on.

Expansion of the labor force by drawing upon the household economy and altering the school programs would increase the flow of people into production. The recent changes in the educational system will divert to the labor force most of those now enrolled in the last 2 years of general education. Generally these are children 15 and 16 years old. Recent surveys of persons entering the labor force from the household economy indicate that most of the men and about two-thirds of the women are under 20 years of age. The qualitative changes contemplated in Soviet education are designed to provide new members for the labor force whose training is more in keeping with the requirements of industry. The planned blending of study and productive work should also help to meet the planned labor force requirements. Soviet planners face a problem in giving proper direction to the rural to urban migration flow which is to be an important source of new industrial labor. Their efforts to move population to new industrial centers in the east have not been fully successful, and much of the limited success achieved is attributable to the forced evacuation of the population during the war years. The preference of migrants for the large old industrial towns has resulted in a substantial misallocation of labor since these places have not been favored in the allocation of new investment. The Soviet Union, therefore, faces a dual manpower problem, first the problem of size, and second the problem of efficient territorial distribution of labor. Its gigantic 7-year construction program may be of tremendous significance in the solution.

Looking beyond the 7-year plan, the outlook is for continued correction of the low ratio of men to women. The working-age population will also increase in proportion to the total population, but the rate at which this takes place will depend upon the trend of Soviet fertility. Since the proportion of persons over 60 years of age is increasing steadily, a substantial drop in fertility will be required if the population aged 16 to 59 years is to comprise as large a proportion of the total population in 1975 as it now does.

The nature of many other developments depends upon the trend in fertility. This is true even with respect to changes which are inherent in the present structure of the population.

The prospective trend in fertility is difficult to predict, however. since there are tendencies operating in both directions. Tentatively, the opinion is advanced that the combined effect of rural-urban migration, the diffusion of secular attitudes toward reproduction, and the spread of the practice of contraception will outweigh other tendencies toward an increase in average family size.

Among the more significant demographic comparisons which can be made between the U.S.S.R. and the United States, the following deserve to be noted:

1. Because of the enormous war losses sustained by the Soviet Union, its population now exceeds that of the United States by only 18 percent. whereas before the war, the margin was 46 percent.

2. The current natural increase of the Soviet Union is somewhat greater than that of the United States due principally to the lower Soviet death rate. The annual increase of the two countries is about equal because of immigration to this country.

3. The extent to which the two countries will differ in size in the future depends largely upon the trend in fertility. According to current projections, should the countries follow opposite courses the difference in size in 1975 might be as low as 4 million (Soviet fertility down; U.S. fertility up) or as high as 65 million (Soviet fertility up; U.S. fertility down).

4. The low Soviet death rate, which is currently below that of the U.S., is partly attributable to a favorable age composition and may increase somewhat in the future. It is clear, however, that the Soviet Union has participated substantially in the worldwide revolution in medicine and health.

5. The number of children in the ages to be attending elementary and secondary school, the group which will provide the coming generation of scientists and technicians, is nearly the same in the U.S.S.R. and the United States. In the United States, enrollment rates in higher education are mounting rapidly; in the U.S.S.R., the policy, at least for the short run, is to prevent expansion in higher education.

6. The number of Soviet men of military age (18–34) will remain relatively stationary over the next 15 years. The present numerical superiority which the U.S.S.R. has relative to the United States, will decline from about 11 million to about 3.5 million during that time.

7. By 1975 the United States will have nearly as many persons of university age (18–22) as the U.S.S.R. The U.S.S.R. now has some 22 million in this age group compared to 12 million in the United States.

8. During the period of the Soviet 7-year plan (1959–65), the population of working age (15–59) will increase by around 6.7 million in the U.S.S.R. and by more than 10 million (1958–65) in the United States.

9. The Soviet population 60 years of age and over will increase from 17 million to more than 30 million by 1975. In absolute terms this is a slightly larger group than the United States will have at that time. As a proportion of the total population, the U.S. figure is greater.

10. Expected changes in population composition among persons of the age to occupy the middle grade and senior positions in the economy suggest that by 1975 career advancement will be relatively easier in the U.S.S.R. than in the United States.

CHAPTER 2. POPULATION AND LABOR SUPPLY

THE ROLE OF DEMOGRAPHIC FACTORS DURING THE FIRST 40 YEARS OF SOVIET DEVELOPMENT

The Soviet Union, at least until World War II, never had a population problem in the sense that it lacked sufficient manpower or that its rate of population growth was greater than its rate of economic development.[1] It is true that prerevolutionary levels of economic activity were not regained until around 1926, by which time the population had increased (over 1914) by 4.7 percent, or nearly 7 million. But even during the post-World War I period, when both the economy and the population were recovering from its impact, the rate of economic development very likely exceeded the rate of population increase. The problems of the opening decade of Soviet rule are more accurately attributed to failures of economic and administrative organization than to the pressure of population on resources.

Since the institution of the 5-year plan in 1928, the rate of population increase has never threatened to overtake the rate of overall economic growth.[2] The fact is, rather, that to a considerable extent the Soviet Union's rapid industrialization was achieved by the profligate use of manpower. To achieve a sevenfold increase of industrial production between 1928 and 1956, the number of industrial-production workers in Soviet industry was increased nearly fivefold, or by 14,684,000 workers.[3] The United States, on the other hand, attained more than a sevenfold increase in the output of manufactured goods between 1935 and 1956 with less than a doubling of the number of production workers in manufacturing.[4] The concern in the U.S.S.R. with raising

---

[1] The Soviet Government is committed to the position that under communism there can be no such thing as a population problem. According to Marxian theory, the problem of too many people is an infirmity of capitalist societies which cannot occur under a Socialist allocation of resources. No one was worried in Marx's day about too few people.

[2] This conclusion is secure even though there is wide variation in measures of Soviet national product. Even the most conservative indexes increase at several times the rate of population increase. With respect to that part of the national product allocated to consumption by households, the situation is somewhat modified but the conclusion remains the same. During the first two 5-year plans, population growth just about kept pace with household consumption, although according to Chapman's calculations the real income of urban workers and employees actually fell during these years. However, consumption by civilian households during the last completed postwar 5-year plan—1951–55—increased at a rate about four times the rate of population increase. For discussions of Soviet national product see Gregory Grossman's article in Abram Bergson (ed.), "Soviet Economic Growth," Row, Peterson & Co., 1953, pp. 1–23; Oleg Hoeffding and N. Nimitz, "Soviet National Income and Product 1949–55," the Rand Corp., Santa Monica, Calif., Apr. 6, 1959; and Paul Studenski, "The Income of Nations," New York University Press, 1958, ch. 25; for estimates of changes in the real income of urban workers and employees, see Janet G. Chapman, "Real Wages in the Soviet Union, 1928–52," Review of Economics and Statistics, vol. XXXVI, No. 2, May 1954.

[3] Demitri B. Shimkin and Frederick A. Leedy, "Soviet Industrial Growth—Its Costs, Extent, and Prospects" in Automotive Industries, Jan. 1, 1958, p. 51, table 1; for the number of industrial-production personnel see Tsentral'noye statisticheskoye upravleniye pri sovete ministrov S.S.S.R., "Narodnoye khozyaystvo S.S.S.R. v 1956 godu (The National Economy of the U.S.S.R. in 1956)," Moscow, 1957, pp. 204–205.

[4] U.S. Department of Commerce, Bureau of the Census, "Statistical Abstract of the United States 1958," table No. 1020, p. 774.

labor productivity [5] through more efficient deployment of the labor force,[6] through plant specialization, increased mechanization and automation undoubtedly reflects a growing realization that the man-power pool is getting low and that new practices designed to improve labor utilization are in order.[7]

To insist that the Soviet Union has not encountered a population problem would be unrealistic from any point of view except that of economic development. The costs of development in human terms have been high. The human costs of the First World War, the revolution and famine during the early years of Soviet rule can be measured in terms of 12 million excess civilian deaths, 2 million refugees, and a birth deficit [8] of nearly 10 million. Direct military losses of some 2 million during World War I were thus only a minor part of the levy of those frightful years.[9]

The dozen years between the first and second national censuses in 1926 and 1939 encompassed the collectivization of agriculture and the liquidation of the wealthier or more independent peasants. The human costs of this period were also very large, running perhaps as high as 20 million. This figure includes the deaths of about 5 million persons who would have survived if more normal rates of mortality had prevailed and a birth deficit of about 15 million.[10] Births were limited through family separations and general interference with the process of family formation and also through abortions, which in 1934 and 1935 in some of the larger cities amounted to more than twice the number of live births. The Government responded in 1936 with a ban on nontherapeutic abortions, with the result that the number of certified abortions dropped by 97 percent between the first half of 1936 and the second half of 1937.[11] Following this action, and with the restoration of more settled conditions, the birth rate climbed rapidly toward its former level.

By far the most catastrophic period in the chronicle of Soviet demographic development was the period of World War II. Judging from estimates of the number of survivors of the prewar population in 1950, the loss of life between 1940 and 1950 among persons born before 1940 may be placed at somewhat more than 45 million. Had prewar

---

[5] Soviet levels of labor productivity are lower than the United States, the degree of difference varying greatly by economic sector. A recent article published in the U.S.S.R. on this subject makes the following comparison of Soviet and U.S. productivity for 1957:

	U.S.S.R. productivity as percent of U.S.
Branch:	
Industry	50
Construction	59
Transportation	33
Agriculture	20–25

See A. Aganbegyan, "Catching and Overtaking the U.S.A. in the Level of Labor Productivity," Sotsialisticheskyy trud (Socialist Labor), No. 4, April 1959, p. 19.

[6] Writing in Sovetskaya Rossiya, June 18, 1959, A. Abramov complained: "* * * it is well known to Gosplan that at times, and despite the objections of enterprises, young specialists are sent who were not requested. This can be explained simply. More of some specialists are trained than are needed and vice versa * * *. A precise, scientifically based method for determining the country's future needs for specialists is required. But neither Gosplan U.S.S.R., Gosplan R.S.F.S.R., nor the Ministry of Higher Education, U.S.S.R. is engaged in this complex problem."

[7] Undoubtedly it reflects also longstanding Soviet practice continually agitating on any point that may increase output.

[8] The term "birth deficit" is merely a handy reference for the difference between the actual number of births in a given period when fertility is low and the number which would have been expected under "normal" rates of reproduction.

[9] See Frank Lorimer, "The Population of the Soviet Union," League of Nations, Geneva, 1946, pp. 36–41.

[10] Lorimer, op. cit., pp. 112–137.

[11] Between 1922 and 1936, abortions were free and legal in the Soviet Union, so long as they were certified to have been performed under proper medical and sanitary conditions. For additional discussion, see Lorimer, op. cit., pp. 126–130.

death rates prevailed throughout the decade, only some 20 to 25 million deaths might have been expected.

The population under 10 years in 1950 was relatively small, partly because Soviet birth rates during the years 1940–49 were quite low, on the average, and partly because high infant and child mortality was characteristic throughout most of the nation during this period. The estimated number of children born during 1940–44 who survived to 1950 was about the same as the number of survivors of persons born during 1930–34, a period already noted to have been characterized by very low fertility.   Altogether some 9 to 15 million children would have been born had there been no war.[12]

From the viewpoint of economic development, the question can be raised whether the losses just outlined have not, in fact, been an important positive factor in Soviet economic growth.   To such a hypothetical question only a hypothetical answer can be given, since it is likely that with a different demographic past the course of social and economic change in the Soviet Union would have been altogether different.   Nevertheless, it is interesting to note that since the advent of the period of state planning in 1928, the rate of increase in GNP (gross national product) has been well ahead not only of the actual rate of population growth but ahead also of the rate of population growth which might have been expected under normal conditions.   A faster rate or population growth, however, would have called for greater diversion of the national product to household consumption and a reorganization of the whole matrix of economic activity.   This would have resulted in a dampening of the rate of increase in GNP so long as the greatly increased emphasis on armaments was maintained. A retarded rate of industrial growth, and a consequent reduction of economic opportunities in cities would have presented the Soviet Government with a host of new problems.

POPULATION COMPOSITION

The notion that in the past the Soviet Union has never been faced with a population problem can be examined further by looking at the age composition of the Soviet population.   Over the past 30 or more years—during most of which centralized state planning has been in effect—the population has been characterized by an increasing proportion of persons in the ages of maximum productivity [13] and a corresponding decline in young dependents (table 1).   The decline in the percentage under 15 years of age has more than offset the slow but steady increase in the percentage 60 years of age and over.   Even after the figures on the population 16 to 59 years old are reduced to allow for youths in school and in military service, the remaining population—that is the group potentially available for employment—comprised a higher proportion of the total population in 1959 than in 1926.[14]

---

[12] For a more extended discussion of changes in population during this period, see U.S. Department of Commerce, Bureau of the Census, "Estimates and Projections of the Population of the U.S.S.R.: 1950 to 1976" by Arthur A. Campbell and James W. Brackett, International Population Report Series P-95, No. 52, app. A.

[13] The age interval 16 to 59 is shown in table 1 since this is the range covered by the Soviet designation of the "able-bodied" population which includes men between the ages of 16 and 59 and women 16 to 54 years.

[14] In 1959 the combined total of persons in the final 3 grades of secondary school, in higher education, in tekhnikums, and in military service amounted to approximately 10,000,000.   The comparable figure for 1926 was slightly over 1,000,000

TABLE 1.—*Percent distribution of the population of the U.S.S.R. by age for selected years, 1926–1975*

(Figures for 1965–75 are projections by the U.S. Bureau of the Census)

Age	1926	1940	1950	1959	1965	1970	1975
All ages	100.0	100.0	100.0	100.0	100.0	100.0	100.0
Under 15 years	37.3	35.2	31.0	29.2	31.2	29.9	28.3
15 to 29 years	29.1	26.9	28.6	26.3	23.5	22.3	23.6
30 to 44 years	16.6	20.6	19.7	20.6	21.3	22.9	20.2
45 to 59 years	10.3	10.6	13.6	15.7	14.2	14.0	16.0
60 years and over	6.7	6.7	7.0	8.2	9.8	10.9	11.9
16 to 59 years	53.5	56.2	60.1	61.2	56.0 / 59.0	54.7 / 59.8	55.1 / 61.0

Source: 1926: Tsentral'noye statisticheskoye upravleniye SSSR. Vsesoyuznaya perepis' naseleniya, 1926 g. (All-Union Census of Population, 1926), Vol. 17, Moscow, 1929, pp. 46–48.
1940: U.S. Bureau of the Census. Estimates and Projections of the Population of the U.S.S.R.: 1950 to 1976 by Arthur A. Campbell and James W. Brackett. International Population Reports, Series P-95, No. 52.
1950–1965: Estimates prepared by Foreign Manpower Research Office. U.S. Bureau of the Census. These estimates are revisions of the Campbell-Brackett estimates taking account of the preliminary results of the 1959 Soviet census released in Izvestiya, May 10, 1959. The effect of the revision is to alter the balance between males and females. It has a negligible effect on the age distribution.
1970–1975: U.S. Bureau of the Census. Op. cit. The two figures given for each year represent a range resulting from the effect of differences in assumptions regarding fertility. The lower percentage is associated with a high fertility assumption; the high percentage figure assumes that Soviet fertility will decline within the next 10 years to a level similar to the low point reached by the United States in the 1930's. Age intervals represented by single figures rather than a range have been estimated on the basis of the assumption of a continuation of present estimated fertility rates.

In what sense, then, can it be said, as it sometimes is, that in the past several years the Soviet Union has been faced with a labor shortage? The answer lies in the fact that the term "labor shortage" is a many-faceted concept. Given demographic magnitudes in themselves do not necessarily cause or solve labor shortages. Relative to economic objectives, relative to prevailing levels of labor productivity, relative to traditional patterns of labor force participation and, too, relative to numbers, there may be a labor shortage. References to Russia's labor shortage began to be heard at the time of the abortive sixth 5-year plan (1956–60) which called for an increase over 5 years of 6.6 million in the State-employed labor force.[15] For this period, as table 2 shows, the estimated net increase in the population 16 to 59 years was approximately 7 million, or only slightly more than the number required by the plan. This slight margin is quite inadequate to take care of manpower drains of the educational system and the military establishment, of replacements for nonstate agriculture, and to allow for persons who either voluntarily or involuntarily do not take civilian employment. It is not easy to state this manpower drain in quantitative terms, although it is not difficult to demonstrate that the number is substantial. For example, in the 1956–57 school year there were approximately 1.5 million students enrolled in the 10th and 11th grades of the general schools.

[15] That is, the "workers and employees" (rabochiye i sluzhashchiye), Izvestiya, Jan. 15, 1956.

38   COMPARISONS OF UNITED STATES AND SOVIET ECONOMIES

TABLE 2.—*Estimated population of the U.S.S.R., 16 to 59 years of age: 1956–66*

(Figures for 1960–66 are projections by the U.S. Bureau of the Census)

[In thousands]

Year	Population 16 to 59 years	Population change during preceding year		Population 18 and 19 years	Population 16 and 17 years
1956	121,923	------		8,500	9,200
1957	124,094	2,171		9,300	8,500
1958	126,090	1,996		9,100	8,000
1959	127,709	1,619	7,160	8,400	7,600
1960	128,813	1,104		7,900	6,800
1961	129,083	270		7,600	5,700
1962	129,144	61		6,800	4,800
1963	129,386	242	5,633	5,700	4,900
1964	130,298	912		4,800	5,800
1965	131,914	1,616		4,800	7,300
1966	133,342	1,428		5,800	7,900

Source: Estimates prepared by the Foreign Manpower Research Office, U.S. Bureau of the Census.

Under normal matriculation and progression, most of these would be 16 years of age and therefore should not be counted among the available labor supply increment for that year. In addition, an undetermined number, perhaps a third or more, of the 1.2 million 2d, 3d, and 4th year tekhnikum students should also be regarded as unavailable. Most of these would enter the labor force in a year or two and some—over 200,000 in recent years—would enter institutions of higher education for periods up to 5 years. Even with the falling enrollments of the past few years, we would expect for the period as a whole a drain into educational channels alone of at least 2 million.[16] Diversions into other channels are impossible to estimate at present. In general we would anticipate that about three-fourths of the population of working age would participate in the labor force.[17] Thus, out of a net change of 7 million persons in the age group 16–59, a little more than 5 million would be found in the labor force. The planned increase of 6.6 million in state employment would have to be met in part therefore through transfers within the labor force, by cutting back on educational enrollment, by increasing the rate of military demobilization over the rate of recruitment and by general measures to reduce the number of persons of working age who were economically inactive. Without question, the sixth 5-year plan had to cope with a stringent labor supply situation.

Before following this problem of labor supply into the future, we should consider one other critical aspect of current demographic conditions in the U.S.S.R.—the shortage of males. A moderate deficit of males is characteristic of populations relatively closed to migration, which have attained high levels of longevity. In such populations the numerical superiority of males resulting from a greater number of male than female births is gradually dissipated with advancing age, since women tend to live longer than men. Thus, in the United States

[16] In considering the total Soviet labor balance the fact that these drains are offset to some extent by persons entering the labor force from the educational system, the military service, etc., is a relevant consideration. Here, however, we are comparing labor force requirements with the increments expected through natural increase of the population 16–59 years of age. Present information is not sufficient to permit a comparison of the flow in and out of the labor force of persons of working age.

[17] 1957 is the last year for which there is enough information to estimate the size of the civilian labor force. In that year there were 53,148,000 persons employed in State enterprises [see Tsentral'noye statisticheskoye upravlenive pri sovete ministrov SSSR, USSR v tsifrakh (The U.S.S.R. in Figures), Gosstatizdat, Moscow, 1958, p. 313]. Cooperative employment was 1,200,000 (ibid., p. 308) and collective farmers plus persons engaged in hunting and fishing is estimated at around 37 million. Thus, the sum of these amounts to nearly 75 percent of the estimated population between the ages of 16 and 59.

today, some 35 years after the last large wave of immigration, there are approximately 98 men for every 100 women. The sex ratio in the U.S.S.R. has been well below this level throughout the Soviet period, reaching a low point immediately after World War II. The ratio for 1950 shown in table 3 represents in absolute terms a shortage relative to females of 23.5 million males. By 1959, this male deficit had declined to 20.8 million—still an extremely high figure.

TABLE 3.—*Males per 100 females in the U.S.S.R., all ages and ages 15 to 59 years, selected years, 1926–75*

Year	All ages	Ages 15–59	Year	All ages	Ages 15–59
1926	93	90	1959	82	77
1940	92	91	1965	85	81
1950	77	68	1975	87	87

Source: Same as for table 1.

The relative size of the male deficit is even greater within the population 15 to 59 years of age. In absolute terms it amounted to 21 million males in 1950 and to 17 million males in 1959. As time passes, the trough in the male age distribution will move along the age scale so that the problem of a male deficit changes qualitatively as well as quantitatively. The problem in 1950 took its character from the fact that over 70 percent of the male deficit occurs in the age range 20 to 44 years. This had important qualitative implications not only for the labor supply but for the social structure generally—especially for the rates of family formation and reproduction. By 1959 the population having the heavy male deficit had grown older and had its greatest effect upon the ages between 30 and 54 years. Balance among the sexes had largely been restored below age 30, that is among those in the ages of maximum fertility and among those who for the first time enter the civilian labor force and the military forces.

The Soviet "solution" to its male deficit by way of extraordinarily high participation of women in the labor force is well known and is an interesting demonstration of the extent to which adaptable social organization can dull the edge of demographic forces. In 1957, the latest year for which there are full comparative data, we estimate that women composed 53 percent of the Soviet labor force whereas in the United States, which itself has experienced somewhat of a revolution in regard to the employment of women, 32 percent of the "experienced civilian labor force" consisted of women.[18] The differences are even more striking in individual branches of the economy as the comparisons in table 4 illustrate:

[18] U.S. Bureau of the Census, Annual Report on the Labor Force, 1957, series P-50, No. 86, p. 8. The concept "experienced civilian labor force" refers to persons who were employed or looking for work during the week of the employment survey, provided the latter had previously had a job. The estimate for women in the Soviet labor force is based upon participation rates reported for State employment which accounts for slightly more than half the labor force (see Tsentral'noye statisticheskoye upravleniye pri sovete ministrov SSSR, "SSSR v tsifrakh (The U.S.S.R. in Figures)," Moscow, 1958, pp. 336-337) and upon crude estimates for the cooperative and private spheres of employment. The estimate for total and for female labor on collective farms—which is the predominant female occupation—was based upon reports of the number of labor days earned by Soviet collective farmers and the assumption that the participation of men and women in this work would resemble the situation reported for the Ukraine where about one-fourth of the collective farmers are found.

40   COMPARISONS OF UNITED STATES AND SOVIET ECONOMIES

TABLE 4.—*Percent of total employment comprised of females, for selected economic branches, U.S.S.R. and United States, 1957*

Industry group	U.S.S.R.[1]	United States[2]
Industry [3]	45	26
Construction	31	3
Agriculture [4]	59	19
Transportation and communication	32	18
Trade and supply [5]	65	39
Government and administration [6]	51	27

[1] Tsentral'noye statisticheskoye upravleniye pri sovete ministrov, "SSSR v tsifrakh (The U.S.S.R. in Figures)," Moscow, 1958, pp. 336–337.
[2] U.S. Bureau of the Census, "Annual Report on the Labor Force, 1957," series p-50, No. 86, p. 8.
[3] In Soviet usage "Industry" includes forestry, fishing, and mining in addition to manufacturing. The figure for the United States given here refers to manufacturing only.
[4] Soviet agriculture includes collective and state farmers, personnel of machine tractor stations, and persons engaged in private subsidiary agriculture. The U.S. figure includes wage and salary workers in agriculture, self-employed workers and unpaid family workers.
[5] The U.S.S.R. figure covers persons employed in "trade, public catering, and material technical supply." The U.S. approximation to this is "wholesale and retail trade."
[6] The Soviet figure includes the administrative apparatus of the state, cooperative organizations and public organizations other than public health and education. The U.S. figure is for public administration.

Although the high labor force participation rates of Soviet women may be viewed as a response to both a war-produced shortage of males and more recently to a general shortage of manpower, it must be recognized that Russian women have traditionally been active in the economy. The evidence indicates, moreover, that during the past decade or so the Soviet Union has not solved its growing manpower needs by increased dependence on the employment of women. There appears, in fact, to have been a decline since the war in the degree to which women have participated in the labor force,[19] most likely as a result of an increase in proportion of women—especially urban women—who are married. Instead, the problem has been met by shifting manpower among different sectors of the economy, most significantly from collectivized and private agriculture to the state sector—to the accompaniment of a large rural to urban movement of population.

It would appear that between 1950 and 1959 rural to urban migration furnished at least half of the 16 or so million increase in state employment which, excluding state farm and machine tractor station employment, is mostly urban.[20] The still vast rural population of the U.S.S.R. will undoubtedly continue to be an important source of manpower as the net flow of new manpower slows to a trickle in the years immediately ahead.

It now appears that Russia's demographic past is beginning to have practical consequences. For almost 40 years nothing which could be called purely a population problem had slackened the pace of economic development unless it might be the postwar shortage of men. But even this shortage has not been wholly negative in effect since it has

[19] "SSSR v tsifrakh," op. cit., pp. 336–337.
[20] Urban increase from 1950 to 1959 amounted to about 28 million, of which 11 or 12 million would have resulted from a surplus of births over deaths (assuming an annual rate of natural increase of 17 per thousand). Thus, net urban migration (plus some administrative changes) would have added 16 or 17 million to the urban population of which perhaps 9 million would have entered the urban labor force. The net change in the urban labor supply (population 16–59) by very rough approximation might be placed at 8 or 9 million (the proportionate urban share of total net change in the population 16–59). The sharp increase in teenage school enrollment would cut into the number available to the labor force but there may have been a compensating return to the civilian labor force of demobilized servicemen. Whatever the resultant of these exchanges it seems that the combination of rural-urban migration and natural additions to the labor supply might have provided 17 or 18 million persons to fill the manpower demands of a growing urban economy. For state employment, which constitutes the bulk of urban employment, the increase between 1950 and 1959 is very likely close to 16 million.

built up a body of skills and work habits among a large part of the female population of the U.S.S.R. and at the same time, through its probable depressing effect on the birth rate, has kept the number of dependents and the consumption demands on the economy below the level they might otherwise have reached. As the birth cohorts of the war years have begun to enter the working ages—since 1956—the growth of the labor supply has slowed markedly and fallen behind the requirements set by Gosplan. The main solutions to a problem of this sort are to draw a larger proportion of the potential labor supply into the labor force or to obtain additional manpower for more favored sections of the economy by internal reorganization of the employed labor force.[21] The latter course has been followed by the Soviet Union since the war, notably so in the case of the diversion of labor from nonstate agriculture into urban state employment. There is no evidence up to the present of any substantial increase in the proportion of the potential labor supply which is active in the labor force, although, as we shall see, plans to this end are being actively considered in the Soviet Union.

THE PROBLEM AHEAD—SOLUTIONS

I. Contraction of the household and private economies

The manpower demands of the current Soviet 7-year plan (1959–65) are even greater than those of the defunct plan 6. At the same time, the estimated net additions to the overall labor supply are approaching a nadir (table 2). How are the Soviets to make ends meet? Both the question and the answer were given shortly after the plan was announced:

In the present 7-year plan the growth of production and the projected decrease in the length of work time requires an increase of 11.5 million persons in the number of workers and employees. What sources are available to us for increasing the army of working persons? Of course, the number of the population in able-bodied ages is increasing. But this is insufficient. It is necessary to enlist for work in production and in the area of cultural and personal services persons engaged in the household and private subsidiary economy.[22]

A more precise specification of this group which is to fill the manpower gap can be gained from the annual labor resource balance compiled by the Central Statistical Administration of the U.S.S.R. According to the balance, the group is a residual obtained by subtracting both students in the "able-bodied ages" and employed persons from total "labor resources," the latter consisting of physically fit, civilian men and women 16–59 and 16–54, respectively, plus older and younger persons who are regularly employed. Making up the residual, therefore, would be housewives, domestics, persons in various lines of private employment and the unemployed, including youths who have completed 7-year or 10-year school and are looking for work for the first time or are simply unemployed. M. Ya. Sonin, a prominent Soviet economist, maintains, perhaps with a touch of hyperbole, that there are millions of people in this group who can and should be drawn into employment in the socialized economy.[23]

---

[21] Other remedies, such as increased hours of work, increased work norms, the use of "volunteer" labor on weekends and holidays, etc., are available also. One of these measures, the increase in worktime, has apparently been discarded. Provided labor productivity is not adversely affected, it is planned to reduce the length of the workday from 8 to 7 hours in the course of the 7-year plan.

[22] B. Braginskiy: "The Achievements of October," Trud (Labor), Jan. 22, 1959, p. 2.

[23] M. Ya. Sonin, "On Actual Questions of the Multiplication of Labor Resources in the U.S.S.R.," Voprosy sotsialisticheskogo vosproizvodstva (Problems of Socialist Reproduction), ed. by Ya. A. Kronrod, Moscow, 1958, pp. 262–268.

Of this group, which we assume is the group earmarked in Trud, women without small children, who spend their time keeping house, would be among those most eligible for employment. It is not surprising, therefore, that the central statistical administration keeps close watch on this group by means of a special "female labor account" which separates women in the able-bodied age group by marital status and provides information on such items as the number with children of preschool age, the number who use Government crèches and nurseries, the number employed "only in housekeeping," etc.[24]

Information of this sort provides Government planners with a more accurate notion of the number of women who might be made available to the labor force with presumably the least discouraging consequences. It also furnishes some guidance as to the adequacy of the child-care facilities for working mothers, the shortage and poor quality of which appear to be current barriers to fuller labor force participation of Soviet women.[25]

Sonin, quoted above, describes a survey taken in February-March 1955, which revealed that there is also a significant number of youths who have completed their schooling and are looking for work for the first time. He concludes that labor recruitment methods must be improved to draw these youths into useful work more quickly since they have been well drained and would be valuable additions to the work force. The situation is becoming more and more critical, he warns, since the number of graduates from 10-year schools is increasing while the facilities in higher schools are not.

II. Draining the schools

The recent Soviet educational reforms are often mentioned in connection with the problem of supplying supplementary labor. One of the central provisions of the new educational program is a cutting back of full-time enrollment in the upper grades of the secondary level (formerly grades 8 to 10) and the diversion of students into production. Lenin is cited on the subject of the inseparability of work and study to give this unpalatable move the backing of orthodoxy. The old system of 7 years of compulsory schooling has been changed to require 8 years of schooling for all children. As before, there will be 3 additional years of noncompulsory secondary education (now grades 9 to 11 instead of 8 to 10) which students may complete either as evening or correspondence students in "schools for working and rural youth" or as full-time students of the new vocational schools which are to be substituted for the old general schools. Students in schools for working and rural youth will be full-time members of the labor force subject to the limitations put on their hours of work because of

[24] L. E. Minz, "Methodological Problems of Labor Balance Sheet Construction and the Importance of Investigating Levels and Factors Pertaining to Labor Input" in Reports Made by Soviet Scientists to the 31st Session of the International Statistical Institute, Academy of Sciences of the U.S.S.R., Moscow, 1958. The amount of information which Soviet planners have at their disposal for labor planning is impressive. In addition to overall labor balance sheets for the urban and rural population, there are balance sheets for each economic region and branch of industry, separate balance sheets of labor on collective and state farms and, as we have seen, a special balance sheet for female labor. Supplementing these are balance sheets of "free disposable time" developed from time-budget surveys conducted by the Central Statistical Administration. These time-budget surveys are conducted on a sample basis among workers, employees, collective farmers, and other groups of the population and indicate available free time (time not used in working, eating, or sleeping) according to sex, age, residence, occupation, length of workday, and social group subdivided into (a) time for household and other work, (b) attendance at schools, courses, lectures, (c) time used at home for studies and self-improvement, (d) sports, (e) visits to cinemas, theaters, houses of culture, and other cultural institutions, (f) time spent with children, including help in children's studies, (g) rest time spent in walks, conversations, entertainment of friends, etc., (h) other forms of time expenditure. Very little technical information is available relative to the representativeness, reliability, or precision of the sample.

[25] Significant in this regard is the planned expansion of boarding schools for elementary and secondary education. The planned enrollment in these schools for 1965 is 2.5 million. Some of these schools will provide 8 years, some 11 years, of instruction, depending upon local conditions.

age. Students in vocational schools will work 2 days a week in local enterprises or in school workshops if training facilities in local industry are inadequate. The time thus spent in productive labor does not count toward the "work experience" which most students are required to have for admission to higher education. A graduate of the proposed 8-year schools will be able to complete his secondary education also by enrolling in a tekhnikum either as a full-time day student, as an evening student, as a correspondence student, or as a working student carrying a reduced course load It is planned that 25 to 30 percent of tekhnikum students will be day students enrolled on a full time basis-In their final year (third or fourth) full-time tekhnikum students will be required to work a regular 46-hour week in their chosen trade or specialty.

During a transitional period of 3 to 5 years, the old system of secondary education will be retained in certain areas on a scale sufficient to insure the uninterrupted flow of candidates for higher education. After that the new system will be in operation. Under it preference in gaining admission to schools of higher education will be given to students who have completed their secondary education with a good competitive standing and who have accumulated 2 years of work experience (provided they are under 35 years of age and provided, doubtless, that they get the support of the Komsomol, trade union, party, and management representatives—all of whom have a hand in selecting the candidates).[26]

There is thus little doubt that, for the short run at least, the "reforms" will augment the flow to the labor force through a pruning back of enrollment at all levels beyond the first 8 years of schooling. The number to be gained is difficult to estimate, but most likely will be considerably less than the number of 9 and 10 graders currently enrolled. Excluding working youth and adults the number presently enrolled in grades 9 and 10 is thought to be around 2.5 million.[27] As the plan is set up for the transitional period, a certain minimum 9 to 10 grade enrollment will be maintained, thus putting the maximum estimate of the number to be added to the labor force at something less than $2\frac{1}{2}$ million. As an estimate of net additions to the civilian labor force, this figure should be further qualified in terms of the number who will be mobilized by the armed forces, the number who for various reasons remain out of the labor force, and the numbers of persons presently in the labor force who will leave it to enter school on the basis of their work experience. Finally, there is a large discount due to the fact that the man-hour contribution of persons in these ages is less than their contribution to the size of the payroll.

This scheme to inject more young people into the labor force may well be a short-run expedient. The new educational program worked out for the Russian Republic (RSFSR), which often takes the lead in implementing new policy lines, anticipates that by 1965 the enrollment in the upper grades of the new vocational schools will be roughly double the enrollment in the upper grades of the present secondary

[26] Eighty percent of the enrollment in institutions of higher education is to be reserved for students who have had at least 2 years of work experience. Izvestiya, June 4, 1958.

[27] This figure was obtained very crudely by subtracting an estimate for the number of students in eighth grade from the number enrolled in grades 8 to 10 in the 1957–58 school year (excluding working and rural youth and adult enrollees). General corroboration of such a figure is to be found in Khrushchev's address to the Presidium of the Central Committee of the party (published in Narodnoye obrazovaniye, No. 10, October 1958, p. IV), in which he explains that the plan to send youth to work after 8 years of education will add 2 to 3.5 million young people to the work force in the near future of which 40 percent will come from cities and the rest from rural areas.

system.[28] If this were to be the general pattern for the U.S.S.R., it would present a greater claim against the potential labor pool of persons 15–17 years of age than could be compensated for by the twice-weekly work contribution of vocational school students or by the moderate rise expected in the size of the age group.

The Soviet educational reforms, therefore, should not be interpreted solely as a device to solve the labor shortage of the 7-year plan in quantitative terms alone. Reports of young people unable to find employment suggest that there may be substance to the widely heard complaint that Soviet schools have been turning out an unacceptably high proportion of young people who are unprepared for the jobs available to them and disdainful of manual labor. Perhaps more important is the fact that managers of Soviet enterprises with their eye constantly on output and productivity are reportedly reluctant to hire these young people because of the short workday which is mandatory for personnel under 18 years of age.[29] Thus, the strong polytechnical emphasis and the combination of work and study in the new program are as much remedies for the qualitative deficiencies in the present system as they are devices for directly [30] infusing manpower into the labor force. A more direct explanation of the educational reforms than as a desperate quest for manpower is suggested by the facts shown in table 5 which indicate the nature of the logjam which has developed as enrollment and graduations from the high schools have increased many times more rapidly than admissions to universities and institutes of higher education.[31] To avoid tremendous waste of effort and frustration, either the higher educational facilities would have to be expanded, or else higher school education would have to be confined to a select few. In view of the heavy investment strain of the 7-year plan it is not surprising that for the short run the second alternative was chosen.

---

[28] Uchitel'skaya gazeta, April 1959, p. 1.

[29] "As is known, only a lesser part (of graduates from secondary schools) will be accepted into higher and secondary special educational institutions. The major part must be drawn into industry and agriculture. As a rule there is a reluctance to hire the young graduates in industrial plants and factories, regardless of specific instruction of the party and the Government. Young people who have not reached 18 years and who, according to law, have a right to a reduced workday, have special difficulties. Preference is also given to young boys; girls have more difficulty getting hired." (Editorial in Pravda, Sept. 25, 1957.)

[30] Several features of the reform, the effectiveness of which cannot be evaluated, seem designed to give the student a more productive role in the household economy and possibly, thereby, facilitate the release of some adult members.

[31] The downturn in enrollment (grades 8–10) and 10th grade graduations may be due to a combination of smaller age cohorts (children born during the war), an increased dropout rate attributable to discouragement over the possibility of admission to higher education (see Izvestiya, July 16, 1958, p. 2), and to the passing of persons whose education was delayed by the war.

TABLE 5.—*Enrollment in grades 8–10, graduates from the 10th grade, and 1st time enrollment in institutions of higher education, U.S.S.R.: Selected school years 1940–41—1958–59*

[In thousands]

School year	Enrollment in grades 8–10 [1]	Graduates from 10th grade [1]	First-time enrollment in institutions of higher education [2]
1940–41	2,558	(3)	162
1945–46	1,091	(3)	176
1949–50	1,151	276	210
1950–51	1,836	(3)	238
1951–52	2,789	394	256
1952–53	3,900	552	261
1953–54	5,220	972	282
1954–55	5,958	1,196	299
1955–56	6,159	1,400	286
1956–57	6,135	1,500	264
1957–58	5,570	1,600	(3)
1958–59	(3)	1,400	245

[1] As is customary, Soviet statistics for 10th grade students include the relatively small number who in a few areas attend an 11th grade.
[2] Excluding enrollment in correspondence courses.
[3] Not available.

Source: Enrollment in grades 8–10: 1945–46—1949–50 and 1951–52—1954–55 from Tsentral' noye statisticheskoye upravleniye pri sovete ministrov SSSR. Kul' turnoye stroitel'stvo SSSR (Cultural Construction of the U.S.S.R.), Moscow, 1956, p. 122 adjusted (except 1949–50) to include enrollment in schools for working youth and adults, ibid., pp. 156–157; 1940–41, 1950–51, 1955–56, and 1956–57 from Tsentral'noye statisticheskoye * * * Narodnoye khozyaystvo SSSR v 1956 godu (National Economy of the U.S.S.R. in 1956), Moscow: Gosstatizdat, 1957, p. 244. Enrollment in schools for working and rural youth and adults for 1945–46 from ibid., p. 248. 1957–58 from SSSR v tsifrakh (U.S.S.R. in Figures), Moscow: Gosstatizdat, 1958, p. 349.
Graduates from 10th grade: For 1956–59 figures reported in following sources:
    1955–56—Izvestiya, Aug. 2, 1956.
    1956–57—Pravda, Jan. 27, 1958.
    1957–58—Trud, Jan. 16, 1959.
    1958–59—Pravda, July 14, 1959.
For earlier years figures computed from linked percentages.
First-time enrollment in institutions of higher education:
Data exclude enrollment in correspondence courses and come from the following sources:
    1940–41—1955–56 from Kul'turnoye stroitel'stvo * * *, op. cit., p. 203.
    1956–57 from Narodnoye Khozyaystvo * * *, op. cit., p. 251.
    1958–59 from V. P. Yelyutin, U.S.S.R. Minister of Higher Education, statement released June 19, 1958.

III. Rural-urban migration

The 12 million additional workers which the Soviet Union needs to carry out its 7-year plan are largely nonagricultural workers. Although the plan contemplates that production on collective and state farms is to be 70 percent greater in 1965 than in 1958,[32] labor productivity in agriculture is supposed to nearly double.[33] Taken at face value these figures imply that approximately 5 million persons might be released from agriculture, the great majority, if not all, coming from collective farms. This group plus the 5.6 million expected from the growth of the able-bodied population (table 2) would take care of more than 90 percent of the planned growth of the state employment and would leave only a million or so to be gleaned from households, street corners, schoolyards, military posts, and the many unsocialized niches in the economy.

[32] "Kontrol'nyye tsifry razvitiya narodnogo khozyaystva SSSR na 1959–1965 godu (Control Figures for the Development of the National Economy of the U.S.S.R. From 1959 to 1965)," an address of N.S. Khrushchev to the XXI Congress of the C.P.S.U., Moscow: Gospolitizdat, 1958, p. 52.
[33] Kontrol'nyye tsifry * * *," op. cit., p. 59. The plan calls for a doubling of labor productivity on collective farms and a 55 to 60 percent increase for state farms. The mean increase, weighted by the present number of collective and state farmers, is around 95 percent.

However, since the rural-urban movement is to be largely voluntary [34] and since the increased productivity of farm labor depends upon the success of ambitious plans (i.e., nearly doubling the present tractor and combine park; [35] quadrupling the supply of electric power to agriculture; [36] tripling the output of chemical fertilizers; [37] changing the geographic pattern of crop production [38] and completing a prodigious housing and construction program,[39] it is apparent that the recruitment of labor from rural areas is not going to be an easy solution to the Soviet manpower shortage.

There is no doubt that great advances in labor productivity are possible for Soviet agriculture. From his studies of labor input in wheat production, V. S. Nemchinov has concluded that the 1952–53 level of mechanization in the North Caucasus achieved a two-third reduction in labor input required with the use of horse and manual power. According to his calculations, employment of the latest techniques in this area would reduce labor input requirements to less than 8 percent of the requirement under man-horse technology.[40] On his trip through the black earth belt of the Ukraine in the spring of 1959, Khrushchev deplored the great amount of hand labor still used on the farms and was particularly displeased at the sight of girls using shovels to winnow grain. He complained that "tens of thousands of young people are sent annually to harvest crops in the new lands in place of machines which would cut the labor force needed and the cost of production to a fraction." The problem then is not one of a lack of opportunities for increasing labor productivity, but one of the magnitude and cost of the effort which has been scheduled for the short space of 7 years.[41]

POPULATION REDISTRIBUTION

To achieve the ends of a plan for economic expansion, labor of the right kind must not only be found but also directed to its proper destination.

Economic change in the U.S.S.R. in the past has been associated with a massive movement of people to cities and a moderate but perceptible shift of population from west to east. Movement of population to the east—to the ore and coal deposits of the Urals and western Siberia, to the oilfields in the southeast—was a claimed accomplishment of the first 5-year plan and has been a feature of all Soviet plans since then as a means of rationalizing the distribution of productive forces in the country.

[34] This is not to say that a variety of pressures may not be applied to push population out of rural areas e.g., gradual liquidation of the collective farmer's private plots and livestock holdings, steps to increase the farmer's dependence on money wages, etc. Not to be overlooked either are the transfers of rural youth under the labor reserve program and the organized labor draft.

[35] SSSR v tsifrakh, op. cit., p. 179 and "Kontrol'nyye tsifry * * *," op. cit., p. 58.

[36] Ibid., p. 58.

[37] Ibid., p. 33.

[38] Ibid., p. 53. This shift in crop areas is premised on the reliability of output from the new grain areas in the submarginal steppe lands of Kazakhstan, the Urals and Western Siberia which, together in 1956 accounted for more than half of the area under grain crops in the U.S.S.R. See "sel'skoye khozyaystvo SSR (Agriculture in the U.S.S.R.)," sel'khozgiz, Moscow, 1958, p. 170.

[39] Because of the Soviet emphasis on industrial growth, we assume that the various plan targets which have been cited are felt to be necessary to achieve the planned level of productivity in agriculture and the consequent release of farm labor.

[40] Minz, op. cit., p. 47.

[41] Writing in the August 1959 issue of the propaganda magazine USSR published by the Soviet Embassy in Washington, Mark Postolovsky asserts that "the intensive farm mechanization called for by the plan" will ease the present situation on the collective and state farms which now "could use considerably more workers than they have." Thus he expects "that there will be some movement of workers to the cities to swell the industrial labor total."

The eastward movement has required continued prodding by the Government, which in some periods has had to resort to special incentives, appeals to patriotism, and to the imposition of quotas, to get the required number of migrants. Despite these measures there has always been a large backwash of migrants to their far more congenial communities in the west. Wartime evacuation to the Urals and to areas east of the Urals was responsible for important additions to both the population and the economic base of these regions. The population of the Urals region, of western and eastern Siberia, and of the Far East increased by nearly 10 million between 1939 and 1959. From an analysis of changes in the size of the employed population, Newth has concluded that "the greater part of the expansion of the eastern regions took place during and just after the war." [42] Newth was referring to the period from 1939 to 1956. Since 1956 the growth of the eastern regions has not been significantly greater than that of the rest of the country.

Consideration is now being given to overhauling the devices which the Soviet Government used before and since the war to provide pioneers for the territory beyond the Urals. According to the Soviet economist Sonin, the organized draft (nabor) of labor, the resettlement of families and entire villages by the Resettlement Administration, and the training program of the state labor reserves, no longer function effectively and new techniques are needed. Sonin endorses the recently innovated "public appeal" whereby the party and the Government "appeal" to organizations such as the Komsomol' and trade unions and to the public at large, to volunteer and to send "volunteers" for permanent migration to Siberia or Central Asia.[43]

The difficulty in attracting and holding migrants in the east is undoubtedly related to the inadequate provision of housing, transportation, consumer goods, and the entire range of municipal and cultural services. For years there have been appeals to local industrial organizations and cooperatives to aid in providing essential amenities, but the problem still remains. The higher level of nominal wages paid in the east is not sufficient to keep real wages on a par with those in the western part of the Union.[44]

The movement of population to cities poses a different problem for the Soviet Government. Partly for ideological considerations (the metropolis is an ugly manifestation of the unleashing of the profit motive), and partly to avoid the diversion of investment from direct production, Soviet planners have endeavored to check migration to the very large cities (Moscow, Leningrad, Kiyev, etc.), At the same time. they have tried to channel movement to the growing industrial cities and away from older urban centers which have not figured in Soviet plans for economic expansion. In both respects they have failed. Even within its unrealistically restricted boundaries, Moscow has now exceeded the limit of 5 million persons decreed for it when the plan for Greater Moscow was adopted in 1935. Movement to the older cities has also continued, and has resulted in a surplus of labor there and shortages elsewhere. More graphically, according to Sonin, there are millions of people who do not participate in the socialized economy [45] as a result of misdirected migration.

---

[42] J. A. Newth, "Some Trends in the Soviet Population, 1939 to 1956 (with particular reference to the RSFSR)," Soviet Studies, No. 3, January 1959.
[43] Sonin, op. cit., pp. 269–281.
[44] Ibid., p. 281.
[45] Ibid., p. 262.

48   COMPARISONS OF UNITED STATES AND SOVIET ECONOMIES

To meet its manpower objectives the Soviet Government must not
only release labor for transfer within the economy but must also
develop more efficient ways of transferring it to the places where it is
needed. Unless steps are taken to make the new industrial centers
more attractive to migrants, the ban on new construction and industrial expansion in the old industrial centers—seemingly preferred by
migrants—may result only in slowing the urban flow of rural migrants.
The solution to this problem, therefore, may lie in still one more
Gargantuan fact—the Soviet plan to increase the square meters of
urban housing during the 7-year plan period by an amount nearly
equal to that erected during all previous plans. This would represent a 60-percent increase over the 1958 housing inventory. If
actually accomplished, and if properly allocated, this effort could be
crucial in determining both the extent and direction of future rural-
urban movement.

SUMMARY AND CONCLUSIONS

There is ample evidence that after a long period of treating labor
as an abundant resource, the Soviet Union must now cope with an
acute shortage of replacements for its labor force. This problem is in
direct consequence of the drastically reduced birth rates of the war
years. Also a legacy of World War II is a large deficit of men in the
ages over 30. To achieve the mobilization of its labor resources
required by planned economic expansion, the U.S.S.R. must resort to
fuller utilization of its labor supply and to even more transfers of
labor between sectors of the economy.

Transfers between economic sectors are an inevitable concomitant
of economic expansion and involve the cityward migration of population as well as job mobility. In spite of efforts to channel this movement, the flow of rural to urban migration in the U.S.S.R. has not
coincided perfectly with the flow of capital investment. Migrants
have shown a preference for the older and larger cities, and have tended
to shun the new industrial complexes in the eastern regions of the
country. This has compounded the labor shortage in areas vitally
involved in the plan for economic growth.

Various expedients are being considered in the Soviet Union to deal
with these problems. In the short run the program of school reorganization will undoubtedly augment the labor force. The attempt to
obtain additional manpower from the household economy figures
prominently in Soviet discussions but its probable success is difficult
to assess. To a certain extent the success achieved in drawing people
from households into production depends upon the success of other
specific programs, e.g., the construction of nurseries, the effectiveness
of the home-chore features of the new educational program. It depends also on the trend in such unpredictable parameters as the
marriage rate, the level of real income, and so on. The single most
important source of added industrial labor is likely to be the collective
farm, provided the urban housing program is carried forward and provided the expected gains in agricultural labor productivity are
achieved.

This by no means exhausts the alternatives open to Soviet planners.
These are the "solutions" to the manpower problem which have been
discussed publicly and they have in common the fact that they

require minimum reliance on coercion.   Thus, it should not be over-looked that, as in the past, the U.S.S.R. may employ more direct, more forceful measures to assure the necessary labor input.   Hours of work could be increased (or not reduced as scheduled), work norms could be increased, "voluntary" labor contributions could harden its corvée exactments, pension rates could fail to respond to the push of inflation, etc.   A balanced consideration of the problem demands that we recognize alternatives of this sort, even though at the moment there is no evidence that the Soviet regime has any of these particular schemes in mind.[46]

There are other alternatives open to Soviet planners by which they might reach many of their economic goals in spite of a labor shortage. These consist of the whole complex apparatus of direct controls and priority systems, developed by modern nations for allocation of the factors of production.   Finally, of course, there is the alternative of general retrenchment and revision of economic objectives.   This course, under the concealment of spurious statistics, is one for which the observer of the Soviet economy must continually be alert.

COMPARISONS OF UNITED STATES AND SOVIET ECONOMIES   69

TABLE A.—*Population of the U.S.S.R., by urban-rural residence, selected years, 1913–59*

[Absolute figures in millions]

Year	Population			Percent urban
	Total	Urban	Rural	
1913				
Current boundaries_____	159. 2	28. 1	131. 1	18
Boundaries prior to Sept. 17, 1939_____	139. 3	24. 7	114. 6	18
1926				
Population census of Dec. 17, 1926 (boundaries prior to Sept. 17, 1939)_____	147. 0	26. 3	120. 7	18
1939				
Population census of Jan. 17, 1939 (boundaries prior to Sept. 17, 1939)_____	170. 6	56. 1	114. 5	331
Estimate, including western oblasts of the Ukraine and Byelorussia, plus Moldavia, Lithuania, Latvia, and Estonia [1]_____	190. 7	60. 4	130. 3	32
1956				
Estimate as of April 1956_____	200. 2	87. 0	113. 2	43
1959				
Population census of Jan. 15, 1959_____	⁹ 208. 8	99. 8	109. 0	48

[1] The expanded figure for 1939 (190.7) is treated in Soviet discussions as comparable to the 1959 census figure (208.8). This suggests that the former figure may therefore include the areas annexed after the war (Tannu-Tuva, Southern Sakhalin, and East Prussia).
² Of which 207,752,000 were originally enumerated, 285,000 added subsequently as a result of the post-enumeration control canvass, and 789,000 added following the checking of control sheets.

Source: The Central Statistical Administration's release of May 10, 1959, in Izvestiya; and Tsentral'noye statisticheskoye upravleniye. Narodnoye khozyaystvo S.S.S.R. v 1956 godu (National Economy of the U.S.S.R. in 1956). Moscow: Gosudarstvennoye Statisticheskoye Izdatel'stvo, 1957, p. 17.

[46] There are some very interesting recent developments in the Soviet Union which may be related in part to the labor shortage and which belong to the collection of inherent, semicoercive techniques: The decree prohibiting, as of Oct. 1, 1959, the keeping of privately owned cattle by residents of large cities (except in certain eastern areas) may well be designed, among other things, to force a large part of the 3 million or so urban dwellers who are engaged in the "private subsidiary economy" into the State labor force. Of interest also is the extensive formation of volunteer guard units for police duty during their free time, This may actually be, as it is claimed, an effective means of combating vandalism and delinquency. It is almost certainly a factor also in the recently announced 40 percent reduction in the regular constabulary forces.

PROBLEMS OF MANPOWER AND INDUSTRIALIZATION IN THE USSR

• • • WARREN W. EASON* • • •

IT IS generally acknowledged that the ultimate success of any industrializing economy depends largely on the solution of a wide range of problems with respect to the utilization of human resources.[1] At the earlier stages, ordinary manpower must be transformed from "primitive tillers of the soil into a disciplined industrial labor force," committed to a "drastically new way of life";[2] and at all stages, cadres of skilled and higher level manpower—in other words, "personnel with the skill necessary to formulate and execute developmental policies"[3]—must be generated to handle positions of management, planning and research.

This is not to say that the solution of "manpower problems" provides the key to economic development and progress. But it is nevertheless true that a significant number of countries today, otherwise possessed of the rudiments of industrialization, are experiencing singular difficulties in bringing about necessary changes in human direction and motivation.

So it is that the case of the Soviet Union has attracted increased attention and closer scrutiny in recent years. Starting with much the same general distribution of resources and conditions as many other underdeveloped countries—a large and unskilled labor force

---

* From the Department of Economics and Sociology, Princeton University.

[1] *Cf.* titles in Simpson K. and Benjamin, H. C.: MANPOWER PROBLEMS IN ECONOMIC DEVELOPMENT: A SELECTED BIBLIOGRAPHY, (Princeton: Industrial Relations Section, 1958. Kerr, C., Harbison, F. H., Dunlop, J. T., and Myers, C. A.: The Labour Problem in Economic Development: a Framework for a Reappraisal, *International Labour Review*, March, 1955, LXXI, No. 3, p. 4, presents a brief review of the literature on this point.

[2] Galenson, W., (ed.): LABOR AND ECONOMIC DEVELOPMENT (New York: John Wiley and Sons, 1959), p. 2.

[3] *Ibid.*, p. 15.

2   *Population Trends in Selected Countries*

relative to arable land; a small stock of capital; considerable untapped natural resources; a serious shortage of higher level technical and managerial manpower; and "an established economic
order [and] deeply engrained social habits of thought"[4] among the
population—the Soviet Union in the short space of thirty years has
been transformed into the world's second largest industrial power.

As an integral part of this transformation, the "organization of
men in the course of the productive process and of the ideas and
customs that drive this organization"[5]—to designate "manpower
problems" in their most general connotation—has been considerably affected. The purpose of this paper is to examine some of
these manpower problems as they appear in the Soviet context—
problems which are more or less universal to the industrialization
process wherever it appears, but in a context which is in many ways
unique.

I shall confine myself to some of the major problems arising
under four headings: (1) the overall supply of labor in quantitative terms; (2) the overall supply of labor in qualitative terms;
(3) the recruitment and allocation of labor; and (4) the management of labor in the enterprise and some problems of industrial
relations.

i. The Overall Supply of Labor in Quantitative Terms

As far as the overall supply of labor in quantitative terms is concerned, in a sense there has been to date no real "problem" in the
Soviet Union. To no significant degree, that is, has there been a
problem of either massive overpopulation or a critical shortage of
labor. At the beginning of the industrialization drive in 1928, it is
true, there was an admitted "surplus" of labor compared to other
resources, including arable land.[6] And the pattern of birth and
death rates (as we look at them now) was such as to give some

    [4] Dewar, M.: Labour and the Social Structure. *Soviet Studies,* October,
1957, p. 178, a review of Hofmann, W.: *Die Arbeitsver fassung der Sowjetunion*
(Berlin: Duncker and Humblot, 1956).

    [5] Kerr *et al.: loc. cit.,* p. 5.

    [6] *Cf.* Baster, N.: Agricultural Overpopulation in the USSR, unpublished
essay written for the Certificate of the Russian Institute, Columbia University.

expectation of a population "explosion" during the early stages of development, with its attendant complications.

In fact, however, the surplus was not particularly large by usual standards of measurements compared to some other countries, even in preplan years, and in any event it rather rapidly melted away, at least on the surface of things.[7] And instead of a population "explosion," the well-known demographic developments after 1928, including those due to World War II, tended to reduce the pressure of people on other resources.[8]

Within this general context, it is of interest to examine some of the conditions affecting the total number of persons in the Soviet labor force. Except for categories such as forced labor and the military service, by and large, individuals in the Soviet Union have been free to enter or leave the labor force, subject to economic incentives and the fact that there are virtually no non-labor possibilities for earning a livelihood. The position of the Government in this, speaking through various social and other indirect pressures, however, has been to encourage all able-bodied persons not in school or other acceptable non-labor force activity, to be in the labor force. This implies acknowledgment of the view that every man or woman added to the labor force, as long as there is a positive contribution to product, adds to the achievement of gross production goals.

What might thus be considered an "aim" to maximize the number of persons in the labor force, subject to the indicated exceptions, under conditions of industrialization, actually took place "naturally"

[7] According to several Soviet estimates reproduced in *ibid.*, especially Table 1, some 10 to 20 per cent of the agricultural labor force at the beginning of the Five-Year Plans could be considered "surplus" with respect to production at the then existing levels of technology, but assuming some full-time equivalent labor force as the number "necessary" for production. E. M. Kulischer in Long, C. D., (ed.): THE MEASUREMENT AND BEHAVIOR OF UNEMPLOYMENT, A CONFERENCE OF THE UNIVERSITIES–NATIONAL BUREAU COMMITTEE FOR ECONOMIC RESEARCH. Princeton: Princeton University Press, 1957, pp. 433–437, refers to Soviet estimates of a similar "surplus" in the later 1930's as well as discussion of its elimination by the post-war period.

[8] For demographic developments to World War II, *see* Eason, W. W.: Population Growth and Economic Development in the USSR. PROCEEDINGS OF THE WORLD POPULATION CONFERENCE, 1954. New York: United Nations, 1955, Vol. v, pp. 895–923; and for developments during and after World War II including long-run trends to 1959, *see* Eason, W. W.: The Soviet Population Today: an Analysis of the First Results of the 1959 Census. *Foreign Affairs*, July, 1959, 37, No. 4, pp. 598–606.

4 *Population Trends in Selected Countries*

in the earlier Soviet and pre-Soviet periods. In those years, when the overwhelming majority of the population was in agriculture, virtually every able-bodied person 10 years of age and older worked at least a few months of the year—albeit at low levels of productivity and therefore in the context that supported the aforementioned labor "surplus" or underemployment.

With economic development and a slowing down in the rate of population increase, and a consequent rise in labor productivity, under normal conditions, the proportion of the population in the labor force might be expected to decline. Together with the rising efficiency of labor utilization, these developments would tend to eliminate labor underemployment and even possibly unemployment. Under conditions of rapid economic growth, this could lead rather quickly even to a "shortage" of labor—defined as a persistent excess demand for labor over supply at going terms and conditions of work.

As a matter of fact, there was some talk of a labor "shortage" from the earliest years of Soviet industrialization. Its principal manifestation lay in the fact that state industrial enterprises were frequently portrayed as willing to take on virtually any number of additional workers, and collective farms as wanting to hold on to the ones they had. What this reflects is the preoccupation of these production units with the fulfillment and overfulfillment of real output goals. If one were to apply the rules of strict economic accountability to these enterprises, it is frequently argued, they might find it uneconomic to retain the indicated large numbers on the payrolls.[9] As an observation especially relevant for the early years of the plans (beginning with 1931), this represents what is frequently called "hidden unemployment"—a "surplus" of labor beneath the surface, while a "shortage" exists on top.[10]

However, the talk of a general labor "shortage" persists, and the efforts to get more persons into the labor force grows more apparent in recent years. With the manpower losses of World

[9] *Cf.* Oxenfeldt, A. R. and van den Haag, E.: Unemployment in Planned and Capitalist Economies. *Quarterly Journal of Economics,* February, 1954, LXVIII, No. 1, pp. 43–60.

[10] For some additional discussion of this period in Soviet development, *see* Eason, W. W.: Labor Force Materials for the Study of Unemployment in the USSR. In Long: *op. cit.,* pp. 414–415.

War II, now appearing particularly in the entry of war babies into the labor force, we are inclined to regard a labor "shortage" as a more real and serious proposition for Soviet authorities than it could have been in the 1930's.

Increasing labor productivity under conditions of economic development operates to raise in economic terms the real "cost" to the economy of someone who stays out of the labor force. In the 1930's the labor "shortage" on the surface concealed a hidden "surplus" of manpower underneath, and was to this extent not a "real" shortage. In recent years, the assumption seems to be that this "shortage" no longer conceals a "surplus"; that the "excess demand" for labor existing in the typical Soviet enterprise now represents real economic alternatives foregone.

In the typical state enterprise and collective farm this may very well be the case. However, state and collective farm and other co-operative enterprises do not even now account for all of the persons who might be estimated to be "in the labor force." There remains, in my opinion, a rather broader band of what is essentially private economic activity than is generally assumed, in the form of intermittent, partial and part-time work outside the socialized branches of the economy. Included here is the contribution of family members, principally females, but also the young and old of both sexes, to the private garden plot of collective farmers, and to the gardens of rural non-farm and urban residents, not to mention activity of a (loosely defined) handicraft type.

The collective farm families we can account for statistically, although very roughly, as well as the few individuals remaining who are privately occupied on a full-time basis as heads of households. But there is a substantial dearth of data and official commentary on the intermittent economic activity of the members of other households in the economy. I am suggesting that we may be dealing insufficiently with a relatively large number in this category.

If we were to apply the broad definition of the 1926 Soviet census to such people, many of them would be effectively counted as "having an occupation," even though they did little more than work a relatively small family garden plot for a relatively small amount of time each year. A 1926 census taken in 1959 might very well reveal a sizable number still so occupied. When I follow this procedure and estimate the total labor force as of 1959 from the population, on the assumption that such "fringe" elements of the labor force ought to be included—in other words, when I exclude from the labor force only urban youths presumably going full-time to school and to a camp or other non-labor force activity in the summer; but include most rural youths going to school, on the assumption that they would do some productive work on the farm in the summer, etc.,—I obtain a total labor force which represents a proportion of the population not far below that of 1926.

The total number of working persons that can be accounted for by available data by specific categories, i.e., state and co-operative enterprises, the military, etc., and the relatively few working solely in private economic activity as heads of households, falls considerably short of the above-estimated grand total—by some 10 million or 10 per cent. This may be a matter of bad statistics or inappropriate estimating procedures, although we may hope not; and it may also point to the presence of forced labor or other non-reported groups, but this seems less likely with each passing year. The persistence of this residual in such a calculation for as late as 1959 (it is also present in a similar calculation as of 1939[11]), therefore, tends to reinforce the possibility that a relatively broad band of "intermittent" labor force activity at relatively low levels of productivity continues to exist, despite the apparently brisk demand for labor on the part of state and co-operative enterprises.

It must be remembered that this is aside from the "intermittent" labor force contribution of members of families of collective farmers, presumably accounted for in the available statistics. What we are referring to are, for the most part, family members the head of which is in the nonagricultural labor force, in particular family members of wage and salary workers. The possible significance of this group is supported on two statistical grounds. First, it is reported that roughly 3 million *full-time equivalent* family members

11 For details on these estimates, *see* Eason, W. W.: Soviet Manpower: the Population and Labor Force of the U.S.S.R. Unpublished Ph.D. dissertation on deposit with Columbia University library.

of wage and salary workers are engaged in such "subsidiary economic activity."[12] The appropriate conversion coefficient, unfortunately, is not also given; but considering the nature of the work, it would not be surprising if 5 million or more persons in absolute number were included. Second, it is reported that these households of wage and salary workers account for anywhere from 5 to 35 per cent of the various types of livestock holdings in all agricultural units in the USSR.[13]

One would hesitate to call the subsidiary and secondary private economic activity of collective farmers and of the rural non-farm and urban families a continuation of the "surplus" labor of the earlier years, although these individuals do operate below the levels of productivity implied by the amount of capital and the organization of production in state and co-operative enterprises.

What may be suggested, however, is this: The overall labor "shortage" of the 1930's worked itself out partly by the absorption, through increased productivity and efficiency, of the "surplus" labor already in the plants. Similarly, it might be expected that the labor "shortage" of more recent years will have its effect partly through drawing into state and collective farm production a certain proportion of the fringe "surplus" elements of the labor force. At the same time, as real wages rise and the housing shortage abates, certain of these elements may be driven completely out of the labor force.

Soviet statistical procedures and analytical commentary also consider these to be "fringe" elements with respect to the labor force. This means that for certain purposes they are included in the labor force, but only on a full-time equivalent basis (as indicated above). For the problem of drawing people "into the labor force," however, or, more particularly, into state and co-operative employment, the activity of these elements is virtually synonymous with household activity. In one and the same context, for example, the

[12] TsSU: Narodnoe khoziaistvo SSSR v. 1958 godu: statisticheskii ezhegodnik. Moscow: 1959, p. 655. The report is actually that 3.7 *per cent* of the total "occupied population" is so engaged, and the latter can be estimated at something less than 100 million.

[13] *Ibid.*, pp. 447–448.

8 *Population Trends in Selected Countries*

problem may be expressed as that of drawing people from "household *and* subsidiary economic activity" (*domashnoe i podsobnoe khoziaistvo*) or, alternatively, from simply "household activity" (*domashnoe khoziaistvo*).[14]

In any event, only after these elements are drawn effectively into the principal categories of the labor force, or leave the labor force altogether, will it make sense to talk about a "real" labor shortage in the Soviet Union, if, indeed, this expression ought to be used at all to describe problems of *overall* labor demand and supply, as distinct from "shortages" in particular areas or skills, or in some short-run period. After all, an overall "shortage" of labor relative to capital is exactly what the process of economic development is supposed to bring about; and at all stages there is the problem of adjusting to changes in this relationship, in terms of methods and policies for manpower recruitment, allocation, and utilization.

II. THE OVERALL SUPPLY OF LABOR IN QUALITATIVE TERMS

The ability of the Soviet Union to supply its economy with the required number of persons having the skills appropriate to the demands for higher-level technical and managerial manpower under industrialization has been viewed with increasing concern by some Americans in recent years. If anything, however, the evidence suggests that they may have "over-supplied" themselves, in sheer numbers, at least—with too many chiefs and not enough Indians, if you will. I should like to examine this possibility and some of its implications.

We are experiencing in the United States, "the most advanced industrial country in the world," the situation where "managers, administrators, scientists, engineers, and skilled technicians [are increasing] as a percentage of total employment, while the proportion of manual workers and other less skilled employees [diminishes]."[15] This has a number of implications for our economy, more

[14] For example, Sonin, M. Ia: Ob aktual'nykh voprosakh vosproizvodstva trudovykh resursov SSSR. *In* Akademiya Nauk SSSR: Voprosy sotsialisticheskogo vosproizvodstva. Moscow: 1958, p. 264.

[15] Hill, S. E. and Harbison, F.: MANPOWER AND INNOVATION IN AMERICAN

(Continued on page 9)

narrowly in terms of recruiting and training higher level manpower; more broadly, in terms of the impact of the changing structure of the labor force in an "upward" direction on such things as the nature and vitality of the "labor movement" and the conduct of "labor relations."

It is a salient feature of the present stage of Soviet economic development that it is considerably below that of the United States in terms of its demand for "high-level manpower," even allowing for the presence of the Soviet administrative (ministerial) super-structure.[16] As a general rule in the economy, furthermore, eye-witness reports and other evidence seem to indicate, Soviet enter-prises are operating at considerably lower levels of technology and organization than comparable United States plants. Prospective plans for modernization in the near future, it would seem, will serve to modify the differential, but not eliminate it. Emphasis in production, moreover, is on a limited diversity of product, i.e., on the mass production of a relatively narrow selection of commodities.

The implication of these considerations for the demand for man-power, in terms of broad levels of skill and experience, is that the Soviet economy is still one based on the broad mass of manual and semiskilled labor—on the "proletariat," in a basic sense of the word. Consistent with this condition are the attempts of Soviet authorities to keep the administrative and technical superstructure of produc-tion enterprises within relatively narrow limits. It remains to be seen whether with the introduction of higher levels of technology and organization in the future there will be a shift away from demands for the mass of labor to a rapidly widening demand for persons with higher skills, such as is now taking place in the United States.

It is in these terms—of the distribution of the labor force by broad skill categories, taking into account developments in the rate

INDUSTRY. Princeton: Industrial Relations Section, Princeton University, 1959, p. 3.

[16] For data and further commentary on this subject, *see* Granick, D.: Soviet-American Management Comparisons. *In* United States Congress, Joint Eco-nomic Committee: COMPARISONS OF THE UNITED STATES AND SOVIET ECONO-MIES. Washington, D. C.: Government Printing Office, 1959, Part I, p. 146.

of growth of the labor force—that the primary reason given for the recent broad-scale reorganization of the whole educational system finds its principal defense, in my opinion. Two major aspects of the reorganization are the following: (1) If trends to last year had continued, in a relatively few years universal secondary education (through the equivalent of our 12th grade) would have been essentially established; but now, under the reorganization, the majority of students are effectively prevented from attending school full-time beyond the 8th grade. This is to say that a relatively small fraction of children of school age will complete their secondary education and go on to advanced training on a full-time basis throughout. (2) Preference in entrance to advanced training will now be given to persons with at least two-years of production-line experience, providing they have also completed their secondary education. For persons leaving school after the 8th grade and entering production, educational facilities are available for the completion of secondary training part-time.

The upshot of the reorganization is to direct a wider share of the training effort into preparing persons for the more ordinary production-line jobs,—a wider share, that is, than would have been the case if the reorganization had not taken place. Since this requires only a certain amount of formal education at best, the result is also to channel a substantial fraction of the population of school age into the ordinary work force. Widened opportunities will be available for these individuals to complete their secondary education on-the-job and to compete for entry at a later date into the higher educational institutions. Therefore, at *best* the reorganization postpones or lengthens the period of time required for persons now coming of age to acquire advanced training. At *worst* (from the standpoint of the personal ambitions of the school-age persons involved) it means that a higher proportion will never obtain advanced training.

The aims of the reorganization are couched in ideological terms —to bring the young people "closer to the facts of economic life." This should be thought of not so much as a return to the old faith, or as a renewal of the proletarian spirit for its own sake—although this is also involved—but more a reaction to the demands of economic efficiency and the effective use of manpower resources at present levels of technology and organization.

There was a relative shortage of skilled and higher level manpower in the 1930's and the rapidly expanding educational network operated to fill the need. But the expansion seems to have over-extended itself. What seems to have been developing in the Soviet Union up to the reorganization, in fact, is a relative shortage of manual and semi-skilled labor, and also a declining respect for ordinary work on the part of persons completing secondary training and looking forward to continuing their education. If the pre-reorganization trends had continued unabated; if universal education through the equivalent of our high school had been attained, considering the fairly respectable quality of Soviet secondary education, and if a widened number had gone on to advanced training, who would there have been to man the assembly lines, at least on the scale that the present levels of technique and economic organization imply? This question probably would have arisen, to one degree or another, in any event. But the evident note of urgency and the fairly drastic nature of the reorganization almost certainly also reflects the impact of the present substantial decline in the number of persons entering the workages, due to the lowered birth rate in World War II.

Formalized education and the accompanying aspirations to something better than the position of a worker in industry developed gradually in other industrialized countries; and the process of supplying the broad manpower base to the economy in the United States was supported by mass immigration. The spread of something approaching universal secondary education in the United States, perhaps not by chance, coincides with the widening demand for persons with more than rudimentary skills. The educational system of the Soviet Union, on the other hand, has grown more rapidly than some others. Perhaps it has succeeded "too well" in accomplishing its purpose, especially considering the recent changes in the rate of growth of the labor force. The present reorganization of the system serves to bring it into phase with the "realities of economic life"—to paraphrase the language of the reorganization itself—at the present stage of economic development.

III. THE RECRUITMENT AND ALLOCATION OF LABOR

One of the most important of the recent developments in Soviet labor policy with respect to the recruitment and allocation of labor has been the restoration of the freedom of labor to move from one job to another. With the exception of the period from about 1940 to the early 1950's, when labor was virtually tied to the job, and with the exception of graduates of advanced training institutions, who must still serve from 2–4 years at the pleasure of the government, the pattern of labor recruitment in the Soviet economy has been substantially based on the freedom of mobility. This is the freedom of the worker to respond to economic and other considerations, although within a highly institutionalized and structured framework, in deciding where he will work.

One question is the extent to which the freedom of mobility under Soviet conditions gives rise to actual movement between enterprises. Labor turnover in the early years of the plans took place on a relatively large scale, as peasants and other recruits to industry, unfamiliar with the industrial way of life, moved restlessly from one job to another in search of a better arrangement. As a matter of fact, the institution in 1940 of criminal punishment to tie workers effectively to their jobs has been attributed partly to the desire to reduce the general level of labor movement to manageable proportions, and partly to more specific considerations arising from war preparations.[17]

Unfortunately, the data are inadequate for a statistical presentation of labor turnover in recent years. Conversations with plant managers and economic administrators in a widely scattered number of Soviet cities, however, together with fragmentary evidence in the literature, suggest to me that overall labor turnover is on a considerably smaller scale than it was in the 1930's. In some of the older, more established urban areas, as a matter of fact, turnover

[17] *Cf.* Schwarz, S. M.: LABOR IN THE SOVIET UNION. New York: Praeger, 1952, especially Chapters 2 and 3.

appears to be very low, of an order of 1 or 2 per cent per month for all reasons. In the newer, more rapidly developing areas, on the other hand, labor turnover continues as a problem of considerable importance, and one which commands the attention of authorities responsible for recruiting labor to the outlying regions.

Nevertheless, in overall terms compared to the 1930's, Soviet labor seems to be reacting more and more to many of the same factors that lead the actual *movement* of labor in American industry to be relatively low despite the freedom to move. This is to say that even without overt controls on movement, there are "built-in" obstacles. In the Soviet Union, for example, housing in many cases is tied to the job, and certain social benefits are reduced for the first months on a new job. And in both cases there are the stabilizing influences involving one's friends and associations—the fact that differences between localities, in the mind of the worker, are frequently not worth the social cost of movement.

Up to a point, greater stability of the labor force, achieved "naturally," has positive implications for labor efficiency and productivity, although a certain amount of movement is entirely consistent with (and even required by) changing conditions of labor supply and demand in a dynamic economy. As a goal of Soviet labor policy, however, "stability" represents only one of a number of objectives involved in recent modifications of policy designed to increase the effectiveness of labor in the work place.

PLANNING

PLANNING IS PERHAPS the central topic in the study of the Soviet economy, for the major difference between capitalist and Soviet-type economies lies in differences in the basic mechanisms by which the economies are "directed": more reliance in the former on the market-price mechanism which both determines (in part) and reflects the independent decisions of myriads of consumers and producers; and more reliance in the latter on centralized decisions of political leaders and central planners, and upon direct controls as a substitute for the market-price mechanism in allocation and distribution.

Some of the earliest writings on Soviet planning in the twenties and thirties took the form of a controversy between Friedrich Hayek, Ludwig von Mises, and others (see F. Hayek, editor, 1935) on the one hand, and Oscar Lange, Fred Taylor (1938) and Abba Lerner (1946) on the other. The Hayek group argued that central planning could never work efficiently since it was impossible for a central planning board to comprehend and make the millions of allocational and distributional decisions which are handled quietly under capitalism by the invisible hand of the price-market system. The central planning board is faced, in effect, with the equivalent of having to solve a system with millions of equations and millions of unknowns, an impossible task. Professors Lange and Lerner, in reply, argued that it was not necessary for central planners to take on this enormous burden. Instead they proposed techniques for harnessing the price system to the wishes of the planners, thereby decentralizing most of the detailed decision-making and leaving the planners to deal with only major problems of policy. This is to be accomplished in theory by keeping the price and market system, and by substituting for the profit maximization motive some rules by which prices, outputs, and investment are to be determined. An exhaustive critique of the issues debated in this period is contained in Professor Bergson's article on "Socialist Economics" (1948).

The Russians have, in fact, used the price-market mechanism aux

Lange-Lerner to distribute consumers' goods and to allocate labor.[1] (The labor market is described in Emily Clark Brown's article reprinted in Section IX below. The consumers' goods market is not dealt with specifically in these *Readings,* and the reader is referred to Chapter XI of Harry Schwartz's textbook (1954), to Chapters 1 and 3 of F. D. Holzman (1955) listed in the Bibliography under Section VIII, and especially to the articles by Professor Goldman listed under Section IX.) On the other hand, the planners have been faced with the "Hayekian" problem of having to make thousands (at least) of micro-decisions in the intermediate product and producers' goods sector where direct controls rather than the free market are used to allocate important materials. At the macro level, it is necessary for the planners to insure that the total amount of each of these materials produced is just sufficient to meet planned requirements. Since there have been as many as 1,500 commodities allocated directly, and since a change in the supply of or demand for any of these affects the supply of and demand for many others, the coordination problem is very complex. For the past thirty years, the Soviets have employed a crude technique called the "method of balances" to achieve coordination. In the past few years, they have been working on the possibility of using input-output techniques and modern computers to solve the problem of coordination more quickly and accurately. All of these matters, which can be lumped under the heading of "short-run planning" are dealt with in Professor Levine's article reprinted below. On the use of input-output, the reader is also referred to J. M. Montias' (1959) excellent paper. Other aspects of short-run planning are discussed in each of the papers in Section VI.

The major feature of what might be called "long-run planning" is the problem of choosing among investment alternatives. Here, too, the Soviet planners have faced somewhat "Hayekian" problems. There is no capital market as such in the Soviet Union; capital is allocated free of charge to whichever plants or industries the political leaders or planners decide need expansion. The absence of a charge for capital, i.e., an interest rate, conforms, of course, to the strictures of Marxist economics in which labor is viewed as the only factor of production. The outlawing of the interest rate, as well as the many other inadequacies of the Soviet price system, have created grave investment-choice problems for the Soviets. The pre-

[1] Important exceptions should be noted: consumers' goods were rationed in 1918–21, 1929–36, 1941–47; in other years, the consumer market is better characterized by saying that the consumer has "choice" among goods produced but not too much "sovereignty" over what is to be produced; since 1921, the labor market has been relatively free with the exception of forced labor which has been "relatively" small numerically (see "Forced Labor in the Soviet Bloc," reprinted below) and a number of other minor restrictions in force primarily from 1939 through 1956.

cise nature of these problems and attempted solutions are traced in detail in the paper (below) by Professor Grossman. The reader is also referred to the excellent paper by N. Kaplan (1952) and to M. Dobb's attempt (1961) to relate the recent Soviet investment choice and price discussions (Section II). The gravity of the problem of making rational investment choices and consequences of Soviet failure to solve this problem have been sufficiently serious that various techniques devised as proxies for the rate of interest have finally been given official sanction despite Marxist ideological predilections to the contrary. The recommendations of a Soviet conference of June, 1958, on investment choice is reprinted as an accurate representation of the present Soviet position.

The essays by Professors Granick and Ward (below) deal with both short- and long-run planning. David Granick's paper presents the most comprehensive schema and evaluation of Soviet planning which has yet been published. While his "fundamental model," exemplified in Figure 1, may appear unfamiliar and discouraging, the reader is encouraged to push on, for the detailed application of the model is easily accessible and will prove very rewarding. Benjamin Ward's paper is a review article of a book by the Soviet mathematician L. V. Kantorovich, who is known in this country for having first developed linear programming. This book, published in 1959, represents the first attempt by a Soviet scholar to approach allocation problems in essentially "Western" terms. Kantorovich attempts to show how "special types of linear programs" can be used to get optimal solutions of both short- and long-run planning problems. His approach generates what amounts to scarcity prices (so-called shadow prices) of goods and factors, and these prices are essential to his optimal solutions. This approach to pricing is relevant to the recent Soviet discussions summarized in Section II by Professor Dobb.

AN ORGANIZATIONAL MODEL OF SOVIET INDUSTRIAL PLANNING[1]

DAVID GRANICK

Carnegie Institute of Technology

I

THIS is a period of ferment, with great possibilities for change, in the Soviet planning system. The decentralization movement of 1957; the multifaceted rationality controversy, offering the promise of a new and improved pricing system which for the first time would correspond with the planners' relative evaluation of physical alternatives; even the whiff, from elsewhere within the "socialist camp," of Lange-esque planning through price parameters—all these create possibilities for changes in planning operations that could be as significant as those of the first Five-Year Plan.

These are fascinating times for those of us interested in the origin of new ideas in economic organizations; in the frequent bottling-up of these ideas over a long period; in the search for release through minor individual innovations, unsuccessful because isolated; and in the culmination of the process by a breakthrough in a whole series of innovating measures. The Khrushchev decentralization scheme has its antecedents in the Regional Planning Committees of the 1930's, which were intended to exercise significant influence over all plants in their territories but which failed dismally in establishing any control whatever over firms within all-Union ministries.[2] The "rationality" movement is but a logical continuation of the economic accounting (*khozraschet*) development of the 1930's and 1940's, a movement which gained complete supremacy in Soviet economic

[1] The writing of this paper has been supported by a research grant from the Graduate School of Industrial Administration, Carnegie Institute of Technology. Some of the underlying research was done while on a fellowship from the John Simon Guggenheim Memorial Foundation. Criticisms of an earlier draft by Professor M. Anshen, J. Drèze, G. Grossman, O. Honkalehto, H. Hunter, M. Joseph, E. Mansfield, H. Simon, and H. White are gratefully acknowledged. Of course, I bear sole responsibility for all errors.

[2] D. Granick, "The Role of the Firm in Soviet Planning" (Columbia University Russian Institute Certificate Essay, 1949), pp. 21–29.

literature but which seems never to have attained a major role in determining the criteria used by operating administrative bodies in judging managerial efficiency.[3] Even planning through price parameters has its pygmy forerunners in decentralized production by local economic bodies and in the free sale of some producer goods and materials.

What forces have fostered these innovations in the Soviet system? What forces have blocked them? What indirect consequences of the present system may these innovations stultify? What consequences may they bring forth?

This paper will argue that these innovations have gathered strength not only from political occurrences but also from such developments as the technical advance of Soviet industry, the accumulation of capital resources, the creation of a skilled managerial group, and the changes in the characteristics of the labor force. It is my purpose to show the influence of such changes on Soviet industrial organization through the use of two conflicting models of Soviet industry. These models are posited as operating simultaneously in the economy, but with one completely dominating the other in its effects. As the underlying economic factors have altered with time, there has been a similar shift in the relative weight of functional and dysfunctional features of the dominant model. This shift has created great pressures for innovations in the economic system and is possibly leading to a greater role for the secondary model which up to now has been submerged.

[3] D. Granick, *Management of the Industrial Firm in the USSR* (New York: Columbia University Press, 1954), and J. Berliner, *Factory and Manager in the USSR* (Cambridge, Mass.: Harvard University Press, 1957).

II

I shall begin by presenting a fundamental model of Soviet industrial organization prior to the 1957 reorganization. Soviet industry is formally quite centralized, with elements of real autonomy appearing only in the interstices of the system. Yet problems of suboptimization by units of the over-all organization play a crucial role. A model of the type used in organization theory, rather than a traditional economic model intended to show interrelations between independent units within the economy, seems most appropriate to use here.[4]

This fundamental model brings into relief what I consider to be the key operating features of the Soviet industrial structure. Objectives (hereafter designated as $O_1, \ldots, O_n$) of Soviet planners are viewed as intermeshing with features of present-day Soviet environment (E) and with organizational theorems (OT) appropriate to Soviet society. From this network, there emerge secondary derived objectives (O_d). In order to achieve all these objectives, Soviet central authorities use both conscious, explicit mechanisms (M) and semilatent mechanisms (ML). Semilatent mechanisms are so designated because they are only partially accepted by central authorities and seem often to be perceived by them as only "emergency" or even "improper" mechanisms.

The M and ML mechanisms are carried on into only a few of their consequences. Those effects traced out in Figure 1 are, from the perspective of central authorities, negative unintended consequences (UC) and negative responses (R) by managements of plants and intermediate industrial bodies. Posi-

[4] Inspiration for this sort of model comes from J. G. March and H. A. Simon's *Organizations* (New York: John Wiley & Sons, 1958).

tive effects are not explicitly treated. The fundamental model is developed in order to analyze the roots of dysfunctional features of Soviet administrative behavior, and thus it is purposely left quite incomplete as an administrative model of Soviet industry.

Furthermore, the fundamental model is something of a hybrid. The mechanisms are viewed as implementations of the stated objectives, and the arguments linking objectives and mechanisms are my own and may well differ from those of Soviet planners. To this extent, it is a traditional type of theoretic model. Yet it is not constructed in the form of theorems following from premises. The mechanisms presented are not the only set which would implement the stated objectives, nor are they completely consistent with one another and with the objectives. Rather they are offered here as the key mechanisms which Soviet authorities in fact seem to have chosen in order to achieve their apparent objectives.

No effort will be made in this paper to present evidence as to the actual state of Soviet industrial organization and the degree of similarity between reality and my models. Space limitations prohibit this. However, I believe that this fundamental model, when modified by the market economy model presented later, gives a fair, although greatly simplified, picture of Soviet industrial administration.

These models are intended to apply to Soviet industry over the entire period since the early 1930's. During this quarter of a century many industrial conditions changed drastically. Some of the arguments linking objectives and mechanisms seem much stronger when applied to the 1930's than to the 1950's, and this fact is entirely consistent with the recent

movement of Soviet industry away from the structure outlined in the fundamental model. The assumption of some degree of cultural lag (in the form of maintenance of a mechanism when some of its original *raison d'être* has disappeared) is implicit in the application of the fundamental model to the mid-1950's.

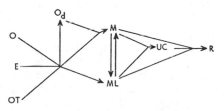

FIG. 1.—Fundamental model. Each feature of the model is dependent upon those elements which are inclosed in parentheses and follow it. Thus M_1 is dependent upon O_1, O_2, O_3.

Objectives
 O_1 Central planning
 O_2 Industrialization
 O_3 Revise production functions
 O_4 Motivate management
 O_5 Rational factor allocation

Objectives, derived
 O_{d1} (O_5, E_3, OT_2) Minimize transport
 O_{d2} (O_5, E_2, OT_2) Minimize inventories

Mechanisms, explicit
 M_1 (O_1, O_2, O_3) Physical planning
 M_2 ($M_1, O_{d1}, O_{d2}, ML_2$) Materials allocation
 M_3 (O_1, M_1, M_2, OT_3) Centralization of physical planning and allocation

Unintended consequences
 UC_1 (M_2, ML_1, ML_3) Supply uncertainty
 UC_2 (M_3, ML_1, ML_3) Systematic plan failures

Environment
 E_1 Uneven progress of firms
 E_2 Capital scarcity
 E_3 Capital intensity of transport

Organizational theorems
 OT_1 Firm's plan not geared to management ability
 OT_2 Engineering perfectionist bias
 OT_3 Continuous planning
 OT_4 Decentralization requirement

Mechanisms, semilatent
 ML_1 (O_4, E_1, OT_1) Target planning
 ML_2 (M_1, M_2) Success criterion is output
 ML_3 (M_3, OT_4) Decentralization through priorities

Responses
 R_1 (M_3, ML_2, UC_1) "Free goods" treatment
 R_2 "Search"

Figure 1 is the basic diagram for the fundamental model. One of the key mechanisms employed here is the prime reliance for industrial co-ordination upon *planning* the inputs and outputs of individual factories *in physical terms* (M_1). This mechanism is viewed as resulting from the interaction of three objectives. The first of these is the objective of central planning (O_1); but this, of course, might be realized without the setting of physical goals for individual production units. A second objective is that of radically altering the product composition both of total national product and of individual industrial sectors so as further to industrialize the economy and give an ever greater role to heavy industry (O_2). In a period when rapid structural change is desired, planning decisions are likely to be carried out more slowly and less effectively through indirect means such as the price system than through direct controls.[5] A third objective is that of drastic transformation of the production functions used in industry by means of the rapid diffusion of advanced technology throughout the economy (O_3). To the extent that the problem of improving production efficiency has been that of implanting known techniques into backward industries rather than that of developing new techniques, there is much to be said for centralized decisions as opposed to placing one's trust in the slower process of educating individual managers to the advantages of newer methods.

A second key mechanism is *"target planning"*; that is, the setting of extremely ambitious production goals for all organizational units, the realization of these plans being intended to strain the resources of the firms and higher organizational bodies to the limit (ML_1). This mechanism can be viewed as an implementation of the objective of motivating management personnel to achieve rapid industrial growth (O_4). In a society whose technology is being transformed and whose managerial staff is being totally renovated, a major problem is to cause a gap between past performance and management's aspiration

level sufficiently wide so that the new technological and managerial resources are fully used. In discussing American firms, Cyert and March have pointed to "organizational slack"—the gap between a firm's actual and potential performance—as a widespread and major feature of industry.[6] The danger that large amounts of "organizational slack" will be created in a period of rapid technological change is obvious, and an organizational system geared to eliminating it through raising managerial aspiration levels has equally obvious advantages.

However, target planning must inevitably have serious consequences for the co-ordination of production among firms. The rate of improvement will inevitably differ among firms (E_1), and thus a national plan that stretches the capacities of all plants will inevitably be underfulfilled by many. Not only does statistical variance enter here but also the fact that managerial capabilities are a major resource of any industrial organization. Yet it would scarcely be feasible for Soviet authorities to gear the level of the production plan of a firm to the efficiency of its management, for such a procedure would fatally sacrifice managerial aspiration levels (OT_1).[7] Thus it is scarcely surprising that, in any given year during the relatively stable period 1951–54, between 31 and 40 per cent of all industrial firms failed to fulfil their annual plans.[8]

To implement central planning through

[5] An obvious application of this line of thought is the virtually universal use of direct controls in wartime to achieve rapid structural production changes.

[6] R. M. Cyert and J. G. March, "Organizational Factors in the Theory of Oligopoly," *Quarterly Journal of Economics*, LXX (February, 1956), 44–64.

[7] Compare the discussion of target planning in Britain by Eli Devons, *Planning and Practice: Essays in Aircraft Planning in War-Time* (Cambridge: Cambridge University Press, 1950), pp. 35–41.

[8] *Pravda*, August 10, 1955, p. 1.

physical planning, co-ordination of the production goals of different segments of the economy is required. This seems to imply some sort of an input-output model—or a "system of balanced estimates" as the Russians call their form of this model. It might be possible to exercise such co-ordination without the physical allocation of materials and components to factories. "Balanced estimates" for the various materials and components might be formulated on the basis of average input requirements for the various final products to be produced, and the materials and components might be distributed to factories through a market system. In the best of circumstances this would present formidable administrative difficulties. Under conditions of target planning, particularly where this is extended into encouraging the overfulfilment of production goals by individual factories wherever possible, further controls would seem essential. Plants with excess capacity would have to be prevented from purchasing more than their share of materials and components and thus upsetting the materials balances.

American experience during World War II showed that this control could be accomplished essentially through the physical allocation of a handful of basic materials.[9] These materials acted as the bottleneck to excess production and, thus, to excess consumption of other materials in individual plants and industries. The restriction of physical allocation to only three or four basic materials would, of course, be highly convenient for Soviet authorities. But it would seem to be prevented by Soviet efforts to achieve rational factor allocation in the economy (O_6).

The Soviet economy has been characterized by extreme scarcity of capital relative to labor (E_2). Although Soviet authorities have by and large refused to give expression to this relative scarcity of capital through a high explicit discount rate, still they have taken account of their environment. Soviet policy seems to have been to achieve a desired final bill of goods with close to a minimum capital investment, particularly where this could be done through the substitution of labor for capital goods.[10] This general policy finds expression in minimizing demands on transport (O_{d1})[11] because of the highly capital-intensive character of this capacity (E_3) and in setting sharp restraints on the holding of inventories (O_{d2}).[12]

The minimization of both inventory holdings and of the use of transport tends to force a rigid planning pattern on the economy. If no more than a few national bottleneck items were allocated, then temporary and local shortages of other materials, components, and fuels would be constantly cropping up, accentuated by the element of "target" in output and input-coefficient goals. An averaging of shortages and of excesses in materials over a national market and over an extended time period would be prevented.

[9] These were supplemented both by inventory controls over the allocated materials (in order to prevent hoarding) and by production scheduling.

[10] See Granick, "Economic Development and Productivity Analysis: The Case of Soviet Metalworking," *Quarterly Journal of Economics*, LXXI (May, 1957), 205–33, for evidence supporting the assumption that this is Soviet policy.

[11] See H. Hunter, *Soviet Transportation Policy* (Cambridge, Mass.: Harvard University Press, 1957).

[12] It is, of course, not clear that O_{d1} and O_{d2} are in fact consistent with a minimal use of capital investment, since resulting inefficiencies may cause a waste of capacity greater than the saving. Thus the hypothesized Soviet conception of planning (OT_2), which is discussed below, is also relevant here.

Once shortages in non-allocated materials appeared, hoarding of these materials and components would appear inevitable, further accentuating the shortages. The few key commodities that were physically allocated would no longer be the sole materials bottlenecks of production. Thus the planners would have to find ways to guarantee enough non-allocated materials to individual firms to make possible the fulfilment of their production plans.[13] A widespread allocation system—of the sort now used in the Soviet Union—would reappear.

Moreover, allocation of only a few key materials requires that these be the production bottlenecks of the economy. In American experience during World War II, by and large the same materials—steel, copper, and aluminum—remained the bottlenecks throughout, and planning was based upon this stability.[14] But this was planning for a limited period. Soviet planning and allocation are considered to be a fairly permanent organizational system; with this time perspective, combined with a high rate of investment, it would make little sense to treat a few materials as semipermanent bottlenecks. (This would mean purposely

building and continuing to build excess capacity in the production of other materials, a crass violation of investment minimizing.) With the use of transport restrained, different regions would have different bottleneck materials, and these would change much more rapidly than would be the case in a fully national market. But if bottlenecks were to shift so that there was frequent movement of materials between the allocated and free-market list, there would be a great temptation for firms and higher organizations to hoard non-allocated materials.

Thus the interworking of the factors cited above leads to the *physical allocation of a wide range of materials and components* (M_2). Given the objective of central planning, and given the principle—clearly imbedded in Soviet theory and practice—that planning is a continuous operation and that the process of implementing the plans modifies the plans themselves (OT_3), the central planners must be in control of the allocation of materials and components (M_3). This further accentuates the planning burden of central authorities, tending to make the central allocation system a bureaucratic bottleneck of the planning system. The size of the burden may be seen by comparing the central allocation of hundreds of materials in the Soviet system with the detailed allocation of only steel, copper, aluminum, and minor subsidiary materials (such as industrial diamonds) by the American War Production Board during World War II.

The combination of detailed physical planning with detailed physical allocation of materials and capital equipment to plants make the *physical output criterion*[15] the natural one to be relied

[13] If they were to do this through the market mechanism, leaving price free to find its equilibrium, it would be necessary to make firm managements highly conscious of cost considerations. But if this were done, and if firm managements became as concerned with their costs as with their planned output targets, many managements would fail to produce their planned targets because of the cost of non-allocated goods rather than because of a shortage of the allocated items. In this approach, non-allocated materials might well become the production "bottlenecks" of the economy.

[14] This is somewhat of an exaggeration as to both the continuity of the particular bottlenecks and the reliance of allocation on only three materials in several forms. Some subsidiary materials were also involved, and, at the end of the war, labor was becoming a key bottleneck (cf. D. Novick, M. L. Anshen, and W. C. Truppner, *Wartime Production Controls* [New York: Columbia University Press, 1949]).

[15] The physical output criterion of success is here defined to include consideration of the quality and product-mix of output.

upon by higher authorities in *judging managerial performance* (ML_2). Dependence on financial criteria such as profit maximization would have the major disadvantage of frequently leading managements to pursue other goals than fulfilment of their production targets. This would mean that the production target for a firm would become little more than a planning parameter; prices would be set by higher authorities so as to try to motivate managements to fulfil their output plans, and allocations of materials would be related to the production targets, but plant managements would not be interested in the production targets per se. Nor, in an atmosphere of target planning, would it be meaningful to use a criterion of first meeting production targets and then of maximizing profits; the first goal alone is sufficiently difficult to achieve, so that success here would inevitably become the primary criterion of managerial performance.[16] Moreover, in this model, managements have few degrees of freedom left to them in the combination of production factors, and so relatively little attention need be paid to their skill in achieving optimum combinations of inputs.

Actually, the physical output criterion can be thought of as a crude profit criterion. With inputs allocated, managements try to minimize their input coefficients, even though they are uninterested in cost reductions. For only thus can they increase their production from a given allocation. Similarly, the management of a multiproduct factory will strive for a product-mix appropriate to the relative weights given to each

product in the determination of its total "output." This, of course, is similar to striving for a maximum gross sales from a given volume of inputs. The crudeness of the physical-output criterion stems from the existence of non-allocated factors—labor, in particular—and from the failure of central authorities to succeed in allocating to any given factory proportional amounts of all necessary materials, fuels, and components.

Up to this point our model is extremely centralized and rigid. We have highly centralized, detailed production programming, combined with reliance on target planning and detailed, centralized allocation of materials. Managerial incentives are geared directly into this centralized system through the use of an output criterion for judging managerial success. Yet we can set down as an organizational theorem that, in a large country with a complex economy, some organizational release is required if the work pressure on central authorities is not to become overwhelming (OT_4). Constant revisions of production targets and allocations are required, while the central authorities are unable to provide this flexibility no matter how large their staff becomes.

Soviet authorities have built in this organizational release partly through permitting operational revisions of plans and allocations by organizations intermediate between the factory and the center. But primarily they have tackled the adjustment problem through heavy reliance on the concept of *priorities* (ML_3); management at all levels is instructed to give preference to high-priority products within their product-mix and to high-priority purchasers among their customers. Thus a major task of any management is to apply national priorities correctly to its own particular problems and to make decisions

[16] This is not to argue that financial criteria are totally irrelevant. Clearly, it is possible to employ a multicriteria system of judging plant management. But, since financial criteria seem to be quite marginal in importance, and necessarily so given M_1 and M_2, they are relegated to our market economy model below.

similar to those which higher authorities would make in its position. When supply and demand (as expressed in central allocations) for a product do not match, balance may be achieved by means of informal priority choices by managements of subunits. Here we have a non-bureaucratic solution to the adjustment problem, filled with all the uncertainties and the opportunities for use of personal influence which bureaucratic structure is designed to avoid.

The combination of (1) target planning, which includes pressure on input coefficients; (2) detailed allocation of individual materials needed for production; and (3) ever continuing formal and informal changes both in allocations to individual plants and in their product-mix programs, the latter in turn creating new input requirements, causes firms to be constantly under pressure in their efforts to secure the materials inputs they require. Firms not of top priority are always uncertain about the volume and mix of materials they will actually receive, and even fairly high-priority firms can be victims of the fact that supplier plants operate in a seller's market with only loosely defined priorities as to their product-mix and the order in which to supply customers. This *supply uncertainty* is an unintended consequence (UC_1) of ML_1, M_2, and ML_3.

Another unintended consequence is a *systematic bias* among industries and economic sectors with regard to *plan failures* (UC_2). As we have seen, target planning inevitably leads to many plan failures by individual plants. These tend to be concentrated in the economic sectors of lesser priority, since formal materials allocations are in reality heavily modified by priority considerations (ML_3). Thus any original central "plan," as embodied in M_3, will in practice be

modified according to the relative priority of the various economic sectors. This conflict between centralization, as expressed in M_3, and decentralization through ML_3 can easily cause repercussions that affect central planning itself.

A major effect of supply uncertainty (UC_1) is that firms find themselves receiving an input mix of allocated materials which is unbalanced in terms of their production targets. This unbalance could arise simply from the process of bargaining implicit in any detailed physical allocation system, but, in addition, there are the uneven fulfilment of the original allocation orders and the changes in firms' production goals. Yet, in terms of the output criterion used for judging managerial success, there is no real incentive for management to economize on those allocated materials of which it receives a plentiful supply relative to other materials which become its bottleneck. How then should the firm management "maximize" in terms of its output criterion of success? Clearly, this is best done by *treating as "free goods" in a linear programming sense all except its bottleneck factor(s) (R_1)*. There is no incentive to expend managerial effort in economizing in the use of these "free goods," and any possible substitution of "free goods" for the bottleneck factor is justified.

But, while this response to M_2, ML_2, and UC_1 is quite rational from the point of view of Soviet plant managements, it is highly dysfunctional for the system as a whole. This is particularly true, since one firm may find certain materials plentiful relative to its production bottlenecks, while these same materials are bottlenecks for other firms. An informally organized priority system can scarcely avoid this difficulty.

It will be noted that the derived objectives (O_d) and the explicit mechanisms (M) of my model can be viewed as stemming from a particular concept of planning rather akin to a perfectionist, traditional engineering viewpoint. Central authorities co-ordinate a multitude of objectives and data into a detailed set of integrated planning decisions for the entire economy. Moreover, these decisions are based on the assumption that operating units will come close to getting the maximum physical output from the resources allotted to them. Thus, if only central authorities perform their function with the greatest possible efficiency, the system will mobilize maximum effort and will insure minimum waste. The factors considered are essentially physical: materials resources and work capabilities as judged by physiological and skill-level measures. Organizational and incentive problems are ignored in the establishment of the basic framework; for, while they are recognized as stubborn obstacles to plan realization at any given moment, they are treated as being of an order entirely different from physical "realities."[17] The apparent concept is that best results will be achieved through creating an administrative system designed for perfect operation in an economy which faces only physical problems and in which central authorities are able to design sufficiently ambitious but also perfectly realizable plans. Having established this sort of administrative system, all efforts should be mustered toward improving the economy in the direction of this efficiency utopia (OT_2).

At the same time it is recognized by Soviet planners that all sorts of individual problems will arise which are not dealt with in this formal structuring. To treat these, additional semilatent mechanisms (our ML) are used. These mechanisms are characterized by the fact that they have aspects that are in conflict with the basic objectives. Thus both target planning and decentralization through the priority mechanism conflict with the objective of co-ordination through central planning; the use of output as the prime criterion of success conflicts with the objective of rational factor allocation. These semilatent mechanisms are used by central authorities in an ambivalent fashion and are never given clear-cut, explicit recognition in Soviet administrative theory.

Pushing further in our fundamental model beyond the elements shown in Figure 1, we are led to a further basic aspect of the model. This is a key response made by managements to planning pressures, namely, stress on short-run results. Just like the "free goods" response of managements (R_1), it has negative connotations to Soviet planners and is deplored. The detailed treatment of this response given below seems justified both by its significance in the operations of Soviet industry and as an illustration of the type of approach which could be developed for other unintended consequences and managerial responses.

Great concern with, and struggle against, the formation of cliques is a widely observed feature of Soviet industry. Nor is this surprising. In an economy ruled by target planning and plagued by supply uncertainty, managements are

---

[17] A parallel may be drawn with inspection procedures in American manufacturing. The adoption of statistical procedures in inspection has in the past faced important psychological obstacles because of the built-in "failure" implicit in statistical methods: 100 per cent identification of acceptable and non-acceptable product is abandoned as a goal of the system. Resistance to statistical procedures can be interpreted as being of this same perfectionist type; even when statistical inspection procedures provide a higher proportion of correct identifications than 100 per cent inspection procedures did previously (because of greater alertness on the part of the inspectors), their "potential" is viewed as being lower.

strongly motivated to use personal relations to influence the determination of their plans, their allocations, and the judgment of their performance. Since intermediate control bodies, both ministry and Party, are in turn judged by the success of the operating bodies, the opportunities for building a "family relationship" (to use the Russian term) are considerable. With widespread modification of plans and allocations through informal and nebulous priority considerations, the possibilities for such influence are greatly expanded. Opportunities for exchange of favors between firms which supply each other with materials or investment goods, between firm managements and city administrations, and between a host of other organizations and individuals are legion. The existence of these opportunities and strong temptations create, in turn, a constant effort by higher authorities to prevent and break up cliques.

A simple and powerful means of forestalling the formation of cliques is the frequent transfer of personnel from one post to another. A second major factor contributing to a brief average job tenure of managerial personnel is the apparent readiness of Soviet authorities to exercise frequent judgment as to the success of individual managements, to apply high standards in such judgment, and to take resulting action with regard to promotion or demotion. Operating from a perfectionist concept of industrial achievement, the authorities seem reluctant to pick men carefully for management posts and to go along with them for a considerable time. On the contrary, a willingness to dismiss managers freely and to try someone else has characterized Soviet industrial policy. Such a policy, particularly when standards of evaluation are

based on target plans, naturally creates ever recurring openings, which must be filled by promotion. Thus there is frequent movement of managers upward as well as downward.

The particular historical setting of the 1930's and 1940's also contributed to rapid mobility in managerial ranks. With rapid industrial growth, the number of managerial posts mushroomed. Moreover, whole categories of management were periodically removed: tsarist-trained managers in the early 1930's, to make way for Party cadre; trusted Party members without technical training, to make room for those with engineering training; a broad sweep in the purges of 1936–38; and, finally, the widespread removal through military draft and war deaths during World War II.

Let us turn from this chain of causation for the *high mobility of managers* to the reasons for the observed pattern of *many overlapping control bodies*. One reason for this pattern is that it serves as an additional means of combating the formation of cliques. A second reason is that no one of these control bodies is strongly motivated toward the achievement of all the planners' objectives. Ministerial control groups, State Bank, trade unions, the Ministry of Finance, the Communist Party—each has its own ax to grind in the conflict for precedence among different goals of industrial activity, all of which are scheduled in target plans. In a situation when much activity is guided by informal priorities, it may be considered useful to bring a variety of control bodies into the picture so as to be sure that all interests are represented in some degree.

It can be hypothesized as an organizational principle that when a large-scale organization faces the need for frequently assessing the managements of subunits and for taking action on the basis of these assessments, when a number of control groups with different interests are concerned directly and indirectly in these judgments, and when target planning is used and thus not all explicit objectives set for management can generally be met, then there will be a strong tendency in making judgments to rely on *operational criteria of readily observable and measurable results*. This is the situation facing Soviet industry in our fundamental model.

The two chains of argument are now complete. High managerial mobility and the use of operational criteria in judging managerial performance combine to cause managements to lay primary stress on short-run results in their choices among different lines of activity for their plants. Immediate results of plant activity—especially output—are peculiarly observable and measurable and are thus in quite a different category from such achievements as good maintenance of equipment, the building of a strong labor force and managerial team, and research and development. Moreover, while the latter activities will have a major effect on production performance in the longer run, the chances are quite good that current managerial personnel will not then be in the plant to reap the benefits or ills flowing from the present policies.

The fundamental model of Soviet industrial organization which we have built is one geared to perfection both in planning and in the execution of plans. It is a high-pressure system, making demands on operating managements which cannot all be fulfilled. As such, it arouses an equally vigorous set of responses from these managements—in the form of a *search for slack* in the system. This search may take many paths: attempts to reduce plans by hiding resources and by developing good personal relations with the planners; schemes to simulate plan fulfilment through producing the desired volume but with poorer-quality goods and a product-mix easier to produce than that called for in the plan; or efforts to accumulate additional inventories, equipment, and manpower to meet the emergencies that constantly occur. Protection against supply uncertainties may be sought through vertical integration back into supply functions, with plants producing their own semifabricates and components and even doing their own repair and construction. As with tax evasion in Western countries, there are endless possibilities for plan evasion.[18]

The usefulness for the economic system of permitting some of this slack seems to be tacitly recognized by higher authorities. At least, this implication can be drawn from the fact that they do not attempt to close all these avenues of search. A comparison may be made with American income-tax law, where extremely severe marginal rates on high incomes are coupled with enough legal loopholes so as not totally to prevent the accumulation of wealth.

The "search process" of Soviet managements may be compared to the reaction to excessive psychological pressure by neurotics who find release in psychosomatic illness. If psychosomatic blindness is cured, psychosomatic paralysis may occur in the same patient. The search for escape may take many alternative forms, but it can be depended upon

---

[18] See Berliner (*op. cit.*), for an exhaustive account of the evasion methods of Soviet plant management. The "search" approach through vertical integration is treated in Granick, "Organization and Technology in Soviet Metalworking: Some Conditioning Factors," *American Economic Review, Papers and Proceedings*, XLVII (May, 1957), 633–40.

to occur unless the pressure is removed.

The particular expression taken by plant managements' search for slack cannot be predicted from our fundamental model. All the forms listed above have been historically important, but none is inevitable. Through rigid controls, higher authorities can close off some of these outlets—but only at the expense of strengthening the pressure behind the managerial push in other directions. Higher authorities are faced with the painful choice of deciding which methods of slack creation are least harmful to the economic system and of acting accordingly. As one would expect, their views on this subject—as indicated by their action in enforcing different regulations —have changed over time.

III

Looking at our model from the viewpoint of top planners, we can characterize it as a system of economic planning which fundamentally takes a linear programming approach to the national economy as a whole. Certain key end products are "shortage items" in terms of the planners' objectives: these are given all-out emphasis through the priority system. Although formal output targets are set for these products, above-plan production is considered highly desirable and is supported by allocations of materials beyond what was originally planned. Strategic intermediate products —whether raw materials, components, or capital goods—are in turn treated as shortage items and given similar priority. All other products and factors are considered to be "free goods." Since all inputs are endogenous to the system, they are all either "shortage" or "free" goods. There are no inputs entering the system from outside at a fixed market price, as there are for capitalist firms in a market economy.

This approach to planning can, of course, be followed only within broad limits. Some production of "free goods" is essential if these items are not to be transformed into shortage commodities; output greater than this is also desirable in terms of the secondary goals of the planners. Thus textile production in the 1930's could not be allowed to sink below a minimum level without jeopardizing key objectives of the regime through injury to the motivation and physical capability of the labor force. Production above this level was desirable but could be sacrificed to other priority considerations.

The administrative procedure for realizing this approach has been to set target output plans for all sectors, supporting them with paper allocations of necessary materials and capital investment. But when the inevitable inconsistencies in plans and the differences between planned and realized production appear, then the non-priority items bear the entire burden. The limit to this process of "plan revision" is reached when the production of non-priority items threatens to fall so low as to cause these items in turn to achieve priority.

Such an organization of an economy has many clearly dysfunctional characteristics. Production in different sectors of the economy tends to move upward in starts and jerks. "Free" factors and intermediate products are used wastefully[19] until they in turn become bottlenecks, and a crash program for

[19] The relationship between the railroads and the iron and steel industry in the early 1930's is a good example of this. Iron and steel facilities tended to be built in such a fashion as to minimize production costs in these plants, but without regard to the effect of such a policy on increasing transport requirements. With a shift in the relative shortage of steel and railroad transport in the mid-1930's, this policy was reversed (see M. Gardner Clark, *The Economics of Soviet Steel* [Cambridge, Mass.: Harvard University Press, 1957]).

their production is introduced. Structural deformations of industry occur as lower and intermediate organizations attempt to protect themselves against supply uncertainties. The "search" behavior described earlier occurs throughout the economy.

Two features of Soviet society have, until now, helped to make such an organization of the economy a viable one. One of these is the existence of surplus manpower relative to the available capital stock. Waste of unskilled and semiskilled manpower in industry has primarily led to a reduction of underemployment in agriculture rather than to a failure to achieve industrial potential.[20] The presence of this excess manpower in the economy has meant that plans for output per man-year of labor could be grossly underfulfilled without seriously affecting industrial production. Under these conditions labor-saving programs, absorbing investment resources and managerial talent, could be given up without doing much harm to industrial output. In addition, plant management could substitute labor for other factors in order to help make up shortfalls in their receipts of capital goods and proper materials. This has been a major source of sorely needed flexibility in the Soviet economy.

A second source of flexibility has emerged from the value system of Soviet planners. Consumer goods industries and agriculture have long been treated as secondary sectors of the economy, in which fulfilment of output plans was desirable but non-essential. Such treatment of huge portions of the economy has permitted a systematic priority treatment for heavy industry and transport and has helped to make possible the

satisfaction of input requirements for priority industries even when national plans went seriously astray. This has been a second important element in fulfilling the plan within priority sectors.

The organizational schema of our model has a number of aspects which in the past have been highly functional in terms of the goals of Soviet planners. First and foremost, it is a type of organization that makes relative output in different sectors of the economy highly responsive to the wishes of top planners; detailed decisions can be made by central authorities and, in particularly important segments, carried out by means of priority measures. In a period when planners' goals have been those of rapid industrial growth, mainly concentrated in only a portion of the economy, an organizational structure that helps to insure responsiveness of the economy to the central decisions made for this sector has been extremely useful.

It is true that this organizational schema might work quite unsatisfactorily if planners were equally concerned with the fulfilment of their stated targets in all sectors of the economy and if there were thus no "priority" segments. But this is a situation Soviet planners have not yet faced.

Second, a critical characteristic of the model is its stress on technical perfectionism and high pressure on managements at all levels. In a period of rapid technological change the value of eliminating "organizational slack" through raising managerial aspiration levels may considerably outweigh such disadvantages as the gearing of management effort to short-run results. These remarks seem particularly appropriate to Soviet industry of the 1930's and 1940's.

Finally, it is worth noting that some of the "negative" managerial responses to our model have until now had func-

---

[20] I am here ignoring side effects—such as those of inflationary pressure—which, while they are of considerable importance to the Russian economy, do not directly bear heavily on industrial potential.

tional aspects for the Soviet economy. To the extent that capital resources have been scarce in the U.S.S.R., a very high discount rate would have been appropriate.[21] In making investment decisions, however, the use of any formal discount rate whatever has at best been treated with deep suspicion and has at worst been absolutely banned.[22] Where Soviet organizations have used a discount rate, it seems to have fluctuated around the 10 per cent level—clearly quite low in terms of Soviet factor proportions. In this situation some additional mechanism has been needed to aid in the husbanding of capital.

A number of the unintended consequences of our model have helped to replace a formal discount rate by one built into the organizational structure of the economy. Management's emphasis on short-run results has meant the application of a high implicit discount rate to longer-range returns.[23] The simulation of output goals through lowering quality standards leads to an increased volume of goods available at the moment, although the goods have a shorter expected life-span than had been planned. Resistance by firms to product innovations has increased immediate output at the expense of the future.

Even a clearly dysfunctional consequence of the model—structural defor-

mation of industry—loses its importance if one applies an implicit discount rate that is sufficiently high. In a period of drastic capital shortage, structural deformation over time may rightly be of little concern to the planners.

This discussion may indicate why the organizational structure represented by our model has worked reasonably well in the Soviet Union and seems to have been considered fairly satisfactory despite all its obvious shortcomings.

IV

As stated previously, our fundamental model of Soviet industrial organization excludes very real elements found in the Russian system. To explain these other elements, let us posit a market economy model existing in a rudimentary form side by side with the fundamental model. The two models lead to different organizational behavior—and both types are found in the actual Soviet economy.

This approach to model-building can be viewed as an application of the concept that specific national economies, at any moment of time, are characterized by conflicting patterns of behavior and that social change can sometimes be usefully represented in terms of a shift in the relative importance of these patterns. The market economy model is perceived as one which in the past has satisfied enough needs of the Soviet economic system and of its planners to warrant the creation and maintenance of its main features but which at the same time has violated important principles of Soviet society and so has been kept in a decidedly secondary position. Future adminis-

---

[21] It is true that central planners' emphasis on the future relative to current consumption lowers the appropriate discount rate. But for any desired bill of goods in a particular time period, the appropriate discount rate should depend on existing factor proportions. Given the relative abundance of labor and scarcity of capital which has existed, this factor-proportions consideration would appear completely dominant. For the marginal efficiency of capital must in fact have been extremely high regardless of the planners' time preference.

[22] See G. Grossman, "Scarce Capital and Soviet Doctrine," *Quarterly Journal of Economics*, XLVII (August, 1953), 311–43.

[23] The implicitness of the "discount rate" makes it quite inflexible and should lead to variation from what would be "appropriate." It is the introduction of this "discount rate," rather than the appropriateness of its level, with which we are here concerned.

trative change in the Soviet Union may well take the form of giving greater importance to the market economy model and leaving less of a role to the fundamental model.

In the market economy model central planners continue to make key decisions for the economy; but these decisions are expressed through setting price parameters rather than through establishing physical output and input objectives for managements. It is expected that the centrally determined objectives will be achieved through profit-maximizing behavior by managements, operating within a framework of prices established by central authorities.

The *khozraschet* (economic accounting) system, omnipresent in Soviet industry for more than a quarter of a century, is the principal embodiment of this model. Soviet firms sell their products and are charged a price for their inputs; managements are instructed to operate so as to maximize profits within the constraints of prices over which they have no control. Managers are judged through a comparison of the profits earned by their plants with the profits expected from them by higher authorities. The volume of earned profits affects the bonuses given management, the premiums and awards distributed to workers in the plant, and the investment in social capital (clubs, housing) for the exclusive use of the plant personnel.

Here is a system which, on the face of it, would seem to have been fashioned with the purpose of making possible the decentralization of output and factor-combination decisions to the plant level. This, for example, is its function in

Lange's model of socialism.[24] But managers' efforts to maximize profits will generally lead to behavior at least somewhat different from what is demanded by the centralized physical plans. The *khozraschet* system stands in flat contradiction to what I have called the "fundamental model" of Soviet industrial organization. It seems fairly clear that, until the present, the dominant criterion in the evaluation of the performance of managers in Soviet industry has been that of the fundamental model rather than the profit test of the *khozraschet* system. The profit criterion seems to be used only as a minor, secondary indication of level of performance.

Can the *khozraschet* system be incorporated into the fundamental model? I think not. If target planning and priorities were not part of the fundamental model, then it might be possible for managers to be held to the two goals of, first, meeting production goals with allocated resources and, second, maximizing profits subject to this key constraint. But given target planning; given changing priorities as between overfulfilment of planned goals for one portion of a plant's output-mix and bare fulfilment of another portion of it; and, finally, given the priority concept as the basic means of evaluating the relative importance of reducing use coefficients for different inputs, the use of a common-denominator monetary criterion of managerial effectiveness flatly contradicts the many specific input and output criteria used in the fundamental model.[25]

---

[24] O. Lange, "On the Economic Theory of Socialism," in B. Lippincott (ed.), *On the Economic Theory of Socialism* (Minneapolis: University of Minnesota Press, 1938).

[25] It can be argued that the *khozraschet* system really does fit into the fundamental model as an important supplement to materials allocation. Some inputs—labor, in particular—are left either partially or entirely unallocated. Moreover, as indicated in Figure 1, those allocated materials that do not happen to be bottleneck items for a particular firm at a

If this contradiction exists, how can we explain the existence of the *khozraschet* system in Soviet industry? Primarily, it seems to me, it stems from an ambivalence in Soviet thinking. Recognition of the many dysfunctional features arising from the fundamental model, and particularly of the loss of resources stemming from management treatment of non-bottleneck factors as though they were "free goods," leads to efforts to use a pricing system both to spell out the degree of shortage of different factors and to avoid pure waste of any inputs. Development in this direction is particularly attractive in that the formal structure of annual plans and plan fulfilment is based on an input-output concept which contains no aspect of either target planning or of priorities; the *khozraschet* system is quite consistent with this formal system.

particular time will be treated by it as "free goods" (R_1) in the fundamental model. The *khozraschet* system causes firm managements to economize on both of these categories of inputs.

There are two difficulties with this view. The first is that a firm's profit position is very heavily influenced both by the level and composition of its gross output and by the quality and composition of the allocated bottleneck materials it actually receives. These factors affect the firm's average unit direct and indirect costs and also the gross sales against which its profit margin is calculated. Given the influence of these factors on the firm's profits, it would be very difficult for central authorities to use the profit tests as an indicator of management's frugality in the use of non-bottleneck inputs. If such an indicator were desired—rather than an overall common-denominator criterion of managerial effectiveness—surely some narrower and better measure could be devised.

Second, the greater the stress on the "target" aspect of central planning, the less is it feasible for firm managements to concern themselves with secondary criteria of success. But target planning is an integral part of the fundamental model.

The separation of *khozraschet* from the fundamental model should not be interpreted as a feeling on my part that *khozraschet* has no functional aspects for an economy primarily described by the fundamental model. A "mixed economy" may be logically untidy but quite workable.

Yet the raising of *khozraschet* considerations to real prominence in the evaluation of managerial effectiveness would threaten the fundamental organizational structure of the system. The great role of target planning, as well as of priorities as an adjustment mechanism, would be destroyed. Thus, while the *khozraschet* system has been promulgated, maintained, and given a great deal of attention, it has never become a real force in the economy. A symbol of its dwarf status is the extent to which relative prices for substitutable factors have been allowed to deviate from what they would be if they were truly to represent planners' preferences concerning the use pattern of these factors.[26]

Another primitive embodiment of the market economy model is the existence of a barter market for allocated materials. In the fundamental model I indicated that firms treat as free goods all except their bottleneck factor(s) and so use them extravagantly. This conclusion must be modified to the extent that firms can barter materials that are free goods for them but are bottleneck factors for their trading partners, receiving in turn materials with the converse properties. Such barter has been tacitly permitted by higher Soviet authorities, since it permits better use of these factors than would otherwise be possible.

Here we have a manifestation of the market model arising as an unintended consequence of the fundamental model itself. However, this barter not only has all the imperfections inherent in any barter but the further disadvantage that the

[26] This is best exemplified by the low money cost to firms of using capital goods as compared with labor. This low cost results from the artificially low price set on capital goods, the basing of depreciation on original cost despite the great inflation since the early 1930's, and the absence of an interest charge on fixed capital.

barter ratios cannot be set by the central planners. As an embodiment of the market model it is rudimentary in the extreme.

Three other elements of the market economy model have long existed. The first of these is a relatively free market for labor; workers to a large extent are at liberty to change jobs in response to primarily monetary incentives. This free market has been modified (1) by the existence of forced labor; (2) by various legal restraints (particularly since 1940), which have been enforced with varying degrees of stringency but which now seem largely to be lifted; and (3) by social pressures. But, despite these important limitations, it seems reasonable to consider the supply of labor as being far more responsive to market pulls than are the supply of materials and of capital goods.

The second element, symmetrical to the free labor market, is a free market for consumer goods. This market is free in the sense that goods are distributed through the pricing mechanism rather than by rationing, although not in the sense that demand affects supply through the medium of price changes. This free consumer market seems to be a precondition for successful reliance on monetary incentives to labor, as well as the means of avoiding the major administrative burdens of an extension of physical allocation to final consumer goods.

Finally, some production and distribution of materials takes place outside the central planning and allocation system. This production and source of supply—essentially for purposes of small, local markets—does not fit into the fundamental model at all but is a real embodiment of the market model. However, this is decidedly a fringe aspect of Soviet industry.

V

The state of the present Soviet economy—that is, the economy during the past few years—presents a challenge to Soviet administrators greater than any faced since the early 1930's. Fundamental aspects of Stalin's Russia have altered in such a way as to make an organizational system patterned on the fundamental model increasingly unsatisfactory. At the same time, other economic changes have tended to reduce the importance of some of the strong points of this model.

As mentioned earlier, Soviet administrators in the past have been able to count on two major sources of flexibility in the economy to help make their organizational system viable. First, there has been surplus manpower. But when one considers the present decline in growth of the total labor force resulting from the low wartime birth rate, the extent of past absorption of agricultural manpower into industry, and the new emphasis on agricultural output and thus on retaining manpower in the agricultural sector, it would appear that this source of flexibility has disappeared completely, or at least has been greatly weakened. The second element of flexibility in the past was the low priority given to the consumer goods economy and particularly to agriculture. A combination of changes in the political and value system in the Soviet Union appears to have considerably reduced the degree of flexibility present here. Production plans in housing, agriculture, and consumer industries can no longer be lightly brushed aside in order to make possible fulfilment of plans in the investment goods industries.

While these two major sources of flexibility in the economic system are disap-

126   DAVID GRANICK

pearing or, at least, being seriously weakened, the administrative burden is constantly increasing. As both total industrial production and the number of plants and shops in operation increase, the absolute magnitude of the planning problem facing central authorities also grows. This growth is greatly compounded by the increasing variety of final products, components, and materials. Not only is it more important for central decisions to be correct but there is a larger number of more complex decisions to be made.

An apparent political factor is also worthy of note. There are some indications that, together with the re-evaluation of the importance of consumer goods in the minds of middle management and Party personnel, there has been an upgrading of the goals of security in one's profession and of freedom from excessive pressure. Thus target planning, rapid turnover of managerial personnel, and pressure upon middle-management personnel to make priority decisions and accept judgment on the basis of them have all become increasingly unpopular. The presence of overlapping control bodies, each pursuing conflicting objectives, is no longer satisfactory. There is less acquiescence by managements in being forced into "search" behavior in which they must constantly violate laws and administrative regulations in order to survive. An organization based upon maximum stress and a high ulcer rate now faces political difficulties that were successfully repressed under Stalin.

Finally, some of the unintended consequences of the fundamental model, which in the past were quite functional, are now becoming dysfunctional. As we have seen, the organizational structure of Soviet industry generates a high informal time rate of discount. But now that capital goods have become increasingly plentiful relative to the labor supply, the marginal efficiency of capital seems to have declined, and a lower implicit discount rate would be appropriate. Since the high rate is imbedded deep in the current pattern of industrial organization, this is not something which can be changed by simple fiat. Furthermore, a process of structural deformation in industry, which could be brushed aside when discounted by a high implicit rate of interest, now becomes a major sore point in the system.

At the same time that the disadvantages implicit in the fundamental model have become serious as underlying features of the Soviet economy have changed, the strengths of the model have diminished. Since the quality of both the industrial labor force and management has been improved and made more homogeneous, the gains to be achieved by high pressure upon management have lost much of their value. No longer is there the old advantage in creating an enormous gap between a plant's past performance and its management's aspiration level for the future; in fact, too great a difference may now lead only to frustration and cynicism. Similarly, when lower- and middle-management personnel were poorly trained or wedded to traditional industrial practices, there were advantages to a high degree of centralization of decision-making. But these advantages have tended to disappear as the quality of management has become more uniform and as the minimum level of training and experience has been sharply raised. Finally, the importance of implementing known technology in Soviet industry has declined compared to the importance of developing new technology. This also makes for a shift in the relative advantage of centralized decision-making.

The concentration of decisions at a

high level in the industrial organization may be contrasted with their decentralization to those management levels where considerations of optimizing the production function through marginal choices can expediently be introduced into the decision-making process. The first of these alternatives is most functional in a society undergoing rapid structural transformation. In such an economy, projected changes are of such magnitude that marginal analysis may be quite inappropriate.[27] But as the Russian economy has matured, as the rate of change in the structure of the economy has been drastically reduced (whatever has happened to the rate of growth of total production), marginal considerations have become more important. Much more is to be gained than in the past from the decentralization of decisions and from the blossoming of the market economy model, which creates a reliable and trusted pricing system as a foundation for rational and orderly decentralized production decisions.

All these factors combine to force Soviet planners to think in terms of a change in industrial organization away from the pattern of the fundamental model. The post-Stalin intellectual ferment in Russia, as well as the ideas coming from Poland and Yugoslavia, undoubtedly plays an important role in making for changes at the present time. But the basic factor is the growing contradiction between the state of the economy and the state of its organization. It is the very real successes of Soviet industrial organization which have themselves made this same organizational pattern obsolete.

There are various alternative paths of

change open to the Russians. The one which would probably appear most obvious to Western economists would be shifting over to the market economy model. Central planning might be limited to investment planning and to the setting of prices as parameters for decentralized decisions. Alternatively, it might also include physical planning of the output of key products and the physical allocation of a few major materials (as in the American wartime system). In either case, the Soviet economic system would become one in which decisions decentralized to a plant level would predominate and would be made primarily on the basis of monetary considerations.

Some further steps have in fact been taken in the direction of applying the market model to industry. Efforts have been and are being made toward rationalizing the price system. The cost structure of industry, as it is affected by depreciation accounts, is scheduled to be improved through the re-evaluation of all existing fixed capital. Some investment apparently is now made simply because plant management and State Bank officials expect a short pay-off period. In agriculture, the shift to the market model seems to be going even further— at least on paper.

Yet, when all is said, only tentative and hesitant moves have yet been made toward expanding the influence of the market economy model. One may speculate that the fundamental cause of this hesitation—aside from conservatism—is the particular perfectionist, engineering bias of Soviet planners. The possibilities inherent in centralized decision-making are thought to be far greater than those of decentralization. Soviet planners may be reluctant to abandon an established organizational form for one whose theo-

[27] Cf. M. Dobb, *Soviet Economic Development since 1917* (London: Routledge & Kegan Paul, 1948), chap. i.

retic potential they consider to be less.[28]

An alternative approach would be for Soviet authorities to cease their apparent efforts at minimizing capital investment requirements for a given final bill of goods. With the change which has taken place in the relative scarcity of capital to labor (E_2), the pursuit of these efforts is no longer consonant with the objective of rational factor allocation (O_5).

If these efforts were given up, a new source of flexibility could be introduced into the system as a replacement for the disappearing features of excess labor and of the non-priority character of production for consumer needs. This source would be the creation of enough buffers to assure that industrial firms would always receive the materials and investment items allocated to them. These buffers would take the form of stocks; of planned excess capacity, which could be used in emergencies to expand the output of materials and investment goods; and of increases in transportation facilities, which would permit the rapid elimination of regional shortages.

What would happen if this "reform" were instituted? If desired, planning could be shifted reasonably easily from a "target" to a "realistic" basis, for plan failure by individual factories would not cause further failures elsewhere. In our

fundamental model ML_2 could be modified; for, with the abolition of target planning, managements of firms would be in a position to consider elements of "success" other than the single criterion of output. With the shift in criteria of success, the waste of resources involved in R_1 would disappear. As plans became realizable, and as uncertainty about receiving necessary supplies vanished (UC_1), the dysfunctional aspects of "search" by plant managements would also diminish. Priority considerations (ML_3) by managements of firms could be ended, since flexibility in the form of stocks and excess capacity would insure the needed supply to all industry. Overlapping control bodies and the central judgment of managements according to narrowly operational standards could be abandoned, and managerial stress on short-run results might well be sharply reduced.

This scheme would be much less expensive to initiate today than ever before in Soviet history. First, as indicated above, "target" planning now offers fewer advantages than it did earlier. Second, factor proportions have changed in the Soviet economy so that a policy involving increased capital expenditures in both stocks and capacity would be less damaging to economic growth than it would have been in the past. These considerations may well cause Soviet planners to move somewhat in this direction. But, clearly, any major development of this type would violate the sort of engineering perfectionist bias of Soviet planners I have hypothesized. In any event, there is no evidence to date of the adoption of this approach.

The 1957 Khrushchev policy of reorganizing the industrial structure seems to represent a third approach to this problem—a much more conservative one

[28] An interesting comparison from psychological literature is contained in J. S. Bruner, J. J. Goodnow, and G. A. Austin, *A Study of Thinking* (New York: John Wiley & Sons, 1956). In a series of experiments various approaches to individual problem-solving are compared. The least successful approach was that taken by a few subjects with mathematical training. This approach had the theoretic potential of solving the given problems more quickly than any other method, and so it was highly attractive to certain minds. But, since it implied the simultaneous processing of so many variables that it was quite impractical to apply, its practitioners were forced to allow it to degenerate into forms inferior to readily available alternatives.

than either of the others. In essence, it is a shift from a vertical (branch) to a horizontal (regional) organization of industry. To the extent that detailed decisions will really be decentralized to the level of the *sovnarkhozy* (economic councils) and their committees in the economic regions, and that the State Planning Commission will only set aggregative annual goals for the different economic regions and coordinate their activity, this decentralization should do much to reduce the workload of central authorities. The regional *sovnarkhozy* may be able to maintain sufficiently close contact with their firms so as to change plans as rapidly as conditions alter and thus end the need for priority decision-making as a means of flexibility. In the balancing of supply and demand, the frequent changing of plans will displace priority choices by plant managements as a balancing device.

A major explicit goal of the reorganization is to eliminate vertical integration by both plants and higher bodies back into supply functions, a "search" method that has been widely used in grappling with supply uncertainties. It is not at all clear that the reorganization will have much effect on the efforts by individual plants to continue this policy —for presumably they will still be plagued by all the old supply uncertainties.[29] But, to the extent that higher level bodies also have followed this policy, there now will be integration backward on a regional rather than on an industrial

[29] It is true that the elimination of priority decision-making by supplier firms will end one source of supply insecurity on the part of their customers. But frequent plan changes by the *sovnarkhozy*, needed in order to balance supply and demand, should make for an equal compensating insecurity. Furthermore, the probable autarkic development in supply (treated below) is likely to eliminate much of the washing-out of local supply difficulties which now takes place through "search" by firms for new suppliers in other regions.

branch basis. Not only should this improve the national transport situation but—at least for a time—it should be a healthy tendency in that it reverses the decades-long development of integration on an industry basis. In this latter sense it may be viewed as a continuation of an old Soviet policy of seeking "balance" through following opposite extreme programs in alternate time periods.

The Khrushchev decentralization approach can thus be viewed as one with quite limited objectives. It may be intended to ease the burden on the center, to eliminate the priority approach to plan fulfilment by individual factory managements, and to remove some of the structural deformations that have crept into Soviet industry. But it can scarcely be intended to improve the other malfunctionings of a system structured along the lines of our fundamental model.

Moreover, it seems likely that the price paid for these gains will be considerable. If planning is really decentralized, this will mean cutting down the national planning job into as many parts as there are economic regions. Exchange of products among regions may well take on the traditional characteristics of international trade among the countries of the Soviet bloc of nations: a drive for autarky and the organization of trade along the lines of bilateral arrangements. Khrushchev is keenly aware of the autarkic pressures, but it is hard to see— given a system based on what remains of our fundamental model—how he can really decentralize planning decisions to the regional level while still preventing autarky. For if the different regions are closely integrated, plan changes by any single *sovnarkhoz* will become a priority decision at this level, and so ML_3 will be reintroduced into the model. Moreover, past Soviet experience has shown that industrial organizations have striven for as much integration as possible in order to protect themselves against supply difficulties; it is questionable whether this situation will change simply because the relevant organizations are now horizontal instead of vertical.

VI

Briefly to sum up this paper, Soviet industrial organization structure is viewed as now being under a degree of pressure unparalleled since the early 1930's. For several decades Soviet industry has functioned along the lines of our fundamental model; but this procedure has always been sufficiently distasteful to warrant the creation and preservation of rudimentary and isolated forms of the antagonistic market economy model. Today, with changing economic and political values, the fundamental model is increasingly unsatisfactory for coping with the new problems. Moreover, it allows little scope for fulfilling potentialities of the Soviet economy that have only gradually been emerging.

In Soviet actions and writings of the recent period, one seems to find a recognition of this inadequacy. With ever increasing intensity, there is a groping for new approaches. Administrative innovation is in the air. Yet, while there is some movement toward the market economy model, such basic innovation is undertaken only with the greatest hesitation. More conservative paths of reform are preferred; thus we see the Khrushchev reorganization policy. Whether this will relieve the pressure, whether it will narrow the gap between Soviet planners' aspiration levels and the performance of their economy sufficiently to be psychologically satisfactory, only time can tell. But, in my view, it would be surprising if more fundamental reform were not pushed upon Soviet planners by the growing lack of relationship between economic forces and administrative procedures.

THE CENTRALIZED PLANNING OF SUPPLY IN SOVIET INDUSTRY*

(By Herbert S. Levine, Russian Research Center, Harvard University and University of Pennsylvania)

INTRODUCTION

Superficially, Soviet industrial supply methods do not appear to be much different from our own. A firm "buys" the input materials it requires, in most cases directly from the producer. Payment is made by transfers in bank accounts. Terms of the sale are stipulated in commercial contracts, and both buyer and seller are protected by the courts against violations, by the other party, of these contracts.

The similarities, however, end abruptly. First, the atmosphere in which the Soviet supply system operates is different from the one normally prevailing in the United States. The Soviet economy since its early days has been marked by a chronic sellers' market; i.e., the situation where demand is consistently pressing upon supply. This has been one of the major factors contributing toward the many negative characteristics of the supply system, which have been so well documented in both Russian and American writings. These writings center on the frequent inability of the system to satisfy the basic commandments of any supply system; namely, to get materials to consuming enterprises in the required quantity, of the required quality and at the required time, in the cheapest way possible. And they discuss what Soviet firms have had to do to counteract these deficiencies: padded orders, excess inventories, staffs of "expediters," vertical integration, etc.[1]

A second and more fundamental dissimilarity is the centralized nature of the planning and control of supply in the Soviet Union. The Soviet firm does not buy its major input materials on an open market where the ability to pay the price asked is the only requirement for acquisition of the material. Major materials in the Soviet Union are centrally allocated even though on the operating level of the firm; material transfers are accompanied by money payments. In order to acquire these major materials, a Soviet firm not only has to have the money, but it also has to have an authorization, in the form of a fund, from the government.[2]

---

*This is part of a study I am doing as a doctoral dissertation in the Department of Economics, Harvard University. I am happy to acknowledge my indebtedness to Prof. Abram Bergson for his advice and guidance, and the Russian Research Center and Ford Foundation for the assistance they have given me. I am also indebted to Profs. Alexander Gerschenkron, Robert Dorfman, and John M. Montias. I wish especially to thank the numerous Soviet economists who were kind and helpful to me on a trip I took to the Soviet Union during May and June 1959.

NOTE ON FOOTNOTES—Short titles are used throughout, author and date of publication. An alphabetical listing of sources is to be found at the end of the paper. All references to interviews in the Soviet Union are cited as: Personal interview with a Soviet economist.

[1] A good Russian source is "Gal'perin 57-1," Also any random sampling of Promyshlenno-Ekonomicheskaia Gazeta will pick up numerous examples of supply deficiencies. For American discussions see "Berliner 57," "Granick 57," and "Granick 59."

[2] In the American economy, also, something more than the mere ability to pay is sometimes required for the acquisition of certain materials. But we are here thinking of the capitalist process in its more generalized form, i.e. as an "ideal type," in the Weberian sense.

Many of the operating characteristics of the Soviet supply system have already been well described in the works of Professors Berliner and Granick.[3] In this paper I would like to focus on the planning of this supply system—the major element of dissimilarity between the Soviet and American supply systems. The planning of supply is differentiated from economic planning in general in that the fundamental question of the allocation of economic resources is not one of the primary problems. Supply planning begins from a set of given production targets, and its primary problem is achieve balance in the plan, i.e., to assure that if a certain number of tons of steel output is planned, then the necessary amounts of all the input materials into steel are also planned. It is this vitally important problem of achieving balance in the plan which will form the core of this paper: how is it done, how effectively is it done and what changes and improvements are in sight.

The operational plan in the Soviet Union is not the long-term plan, the 5- or 7-year plan, but the short-term plan, the annual plan. This paper will concentrate, therefore, on the problems of constructing the annual plan. The periods both before and after the recent reorganization of industrial administration will be covered. This is done because, first, as an aid in analyzing Soviet economic growth, both the present and the prereorganization systems are relevant; second, in order to understand and evaluate the reorganization, it is necessary to know what preceded it; and third, many of the essential features of the planning system have not changed, but they stand out more clearly in the prereorganization system than they do in the present system, which has by no means achieved any final form as yet. The coverage of the paper will be limited to the planning of supply within the industrial sector of the Soviet economy only.

The paper begins with a short description of the organizations involved in supply planning, as a sort of playbill to enable the reader to identify the performers. This is followed by a discussion of how the annual supply plan is constructed with special emphasis on the balancing methodology employed. Then comes a section on the major weaknesses of supply planning and the possibilities of correcting some of them through the use of modern mathematical methods and high-speed electronic computers. The paper ends with some brief conclusions. This is a lot of territory to cover within the delimited confines of this paper. As a result, many points have been brushed over quickly, often too quickly. For this, I apologize.

Those who are familiar with American handling of materials control problems during the war will see certain similarities in the description of Russian planning methods which follows.[4]

ORGANIZATIONS IN SUPPLY PLANNING

The basic impact of the reorganization of 1957 was to change the administration of Soviet industry from vertical, branch lines to horizontal, geographic lines. Prior to the reorganization, there were normally between 20 and 40 economic ministries (such as the Ministry of Ferrous Metallurgy), which administered firms throughout the country classified as being within a given sector.[5] Now almost all of

---

[3] See footnote No. 1.
[4] See "Novick 49."
[5] Actually the output of most ministries was fairly heterogeneous.

the ministries have been abolished and in their place there are more than 100 sovnarkhozy (councils of the national economy) each of which administers the firms lying within its economic-administrative region (a geographic area). The administration of the supply system has in a similar manner been changed from ministerial lines to regional lines.

At the top of the supply hierarchy, both before and after the reorganization, stands Gosplan S.S.S.R. (the State Planning Committee [6] of the Council of Ministers of the U.S.S.R.). This organization, since the end of World War II, has had a checkered career. At the end of the war, it was a "permanent commission" of the U.S.S.R. Council of People's Commissars (now Council of Ministers) responsible for the working out of long- and short-term plans, including the annual supply plan. Its primary mission, however, was not the initiating and formulating of major objectives, but the assuring of the feasibility and consistency of a plan, and the prevention and eradication of disproportions within the economy. Among its various departments, Gosplan had a set of branch departments and a set of summary departments (svodnye otdely) which were organized more or less parallel to the existing ministries. The former were concerned with the output and the latter with the distribution of the products which came under the planning jurisdiction of Gosplan. Soon after the war, control over supply planning was taken away from Gosplan, when in 1947, Gossnab (the State Committee of the U.S.S.R. Council of Ministers for the Supply of Materials to the National Economy) was formed. Gossnab took on the function of constructing the annual supply plan. In 1951, the planning of the distribution of consumers' goods was split off from Gossnab with the formation of Gosprodsnab (the State Committee of the U.S.S.R. Council of Ministers for the Supply of Food and Manufactured Consumer Goods). But in 1953, Gossnab and Gosprodsnab were put back into Gosplan and the top organizational level of supply planning returned to what it was 5 years earlier. However, this situation did not last very long. In 1955, not only supply planning was split off from Gosplan, but the entire function of short-term planning when a separate planning organ, Gosekonomkomissiia (the State Planning Commission of the U.S.S.R. Council of Ministers for the Current Planning of the National Economy) was formed. This arrangement lasted for 2 years. In 1957, under the reorganization of industrial management, current planning and, with it, supply planning were put back into Gosplan.

Even this short description of the repeated organizational changes at the top planning level is sufficient to give the flavor of the postwar developments. Change has been the rule rather than the exception.[7] There are several explanations for this, but one which is hard to avoid is that the political authorities have not been too happy with the organization of planning and within this of supply planning at the top level.

Before the reorganization, the hierarchy of supply planning below the top level ran as follows. Attached to the ministry, there was the glavsnab (main administration of supply) and the glavsbyt (main

---

[6] Gosplan keeps alternating between being a commission and a committee. At the end of the war it was a commission; in 1947 it became a committee; in 1955, a commission; and since 1957 it has again been a committee.

[7] This is also true at the ministerial level, where ministries were constantly being separated and consolidated.

administration of sales). In those cases where there were glavki (branch main administrations) between the ministry and a group of subordinate enterprises, each glavk had a supply department. Finally, at the lowest level, there was the supply department of the enterprise.

The reorganization led to a number of changes in the organizations involved in supply planning. The planning hierarchy is, of course, different. The various levels now are: Gosplan S.S.S.R., republican gosplan, sovnarkhoz, enterprise. At the top level, Gosplan acquired the former ministerial glavsbyty. Recently these were consolidated, reduced in number to between 10 and 14, and renamed, main administrations for interrepublican deliveries.[8] The gosplan of each union republic has increased in size and importance. The gosplan of the R.S.F.S.R. acquired the glavsnaby of the former ministries [9] and combined main administrations for supply and sales have been formed in every republican gosplan (one main administration for supply and sales for each broad category of product). Main supply and sales administrations have also been formed at the sovnarkhozy. In addition, the sovnarkhoz has a number of branch departments and each one of these branch departments has a supply section which is active and important in the planning of supply for the firms within that branch and subordinate to that sovnarkhoz. At the bottom level, remaining unchanged by the reorganization, are the supply departments of the individual enterprises.

II. CONSTRUCTION OF THE SUPPLY PLAN

THE SUPPLY PLAN AND WHAT IT COVERS

The planning of industrial supply is related more to short-term planning than to long term. There is no supply plan as such in the 5- or 7-year plan. But the annual plan for the development of the national economy contains, in addition to sections on targets for industrial output, agricultural output, capital construction, introduction of new technology, labor force, etc., a plan for the material-technical supply of the national economy. The main elements of this supply plan are (1) an introductory resolution of the U.S.S.R. Council of Ministers, which confirms the plan and contains its basic objectives, including some direct tasks to the individual ministries (now to the republics) for the economizing of materials; (2) material balances [10] compiled for all centrally allocated means of production; (3) distribution plans for each centrally allocated material, by user ministries (now by user republics); (4) norms for the input of materials, including fuels and electricity, in production and construction, and tasks for the lowering of these norms.[11]

The annual supply plan, confirmed by the U.S.S.R. Council of Ministers, does not cover the distribution of all materials used by industry, but only a selected group of them. Until recently, input materials were classified into three, sometimes four categories. First, there were the "funded" commodities. These were the commodities

8 " Gal'perin 58," p. 52 and "Koldomasov 59," p. 57.
9 "Gal'perin 58," p. 50. Thus, by preserving both the former glavsbyty and glavsnaby, a sharp break with the past was avoided and the transition from the old system to the new was made easier.
10 Material balances are balance sheets of the sources and uses of an individual product (see below, pp. 19ff).
11 "Lokshin 52," p. 65.

whose distribution was set in the state supply plan. The term "funded" meant they were products which could only be obtained if the consuming unit had a fund or an allotment for their acquisition. In other words, they were products centrally allotted by the Government. These included the most important producers' goods in the economy: ferrous and nonferrous metals, fuels, chemicals, etc. Also included were machinery and equipment, and in addition, the major materials used by the consumers' goods industries.[12] They were classified in varying degrees of specificity, but rarely as fine as an input material specification has to be at the level of actual use in production. For example, in 1946, there were 70 different classifications of "funded" rolled ferrous metal products, but the metallurgical industry produced several thousand different shapes, sizes, and qualities.[13] The number of "funded" commodities did not remain constant. It grew after the war, reaching a peak of 1,600 at the height of the centralization period just before the death of Stalin. In the early decentralization moves of 1953–54 they were reduced to about 800, and in 1958 they were reported to number 760.[14]

The second category was "centrally planned" commodities. The distribution of these goods was planned by the main administrations of sales of the producing ministries. They were either goods of lesser importance than the "funded" or they had a more restricted group of consumers. Also classified as "centrally planned" were those commodities whose distribution was planned by the republican gosplany.

The third category was "decentrally planned" commodities. The distribution of these was controlled by local governmental organs and by the local offices of the main administrations of sales of the producing ministries.

A fourth category was sometimes added: "decentralized and self procurement." This included those products a firm could procure by itself, such as sand, rocks, some types of lumber, etc.

After the reorganization, the classification into "funded" and "centrally planned" commodities lost much of its rationale. The main administrations of sales of the former ministries which distributed the "centrally planned" commodities were now part of Gosplan S.S.S.R. Therefore, Gosplan (or at least sections of it) was distributing both the 760 "funded" commodities and the approximately 5,000 "centrally planned" commodities. In addition, while the main administrations of sales at Gosplan were planning the distribution of "centrally planned" commodities, the republics were planning the output levels of these commodities.[15] The old classification system was clearly an anachronism. Soon the announcement came that "beginning in 1959, the notorious division of output into 'planned' and 'funded' will be abolished." [16]

Under the new classification system, Gosplan will plan the distribution of and issue fondy for the acquisition of those products which are the most important for the national economy, those which are in

---

[12] Classification as a "funded" commodity depended also on the degree of centralization of its production. In addition, I was told, in a personal interview with a Soviet economist, that the number of "funded" commodities in any 1 year was affected by how many Gosplan felt it could handle. For listings of "funded" and "nonfunded" commodities see "Shein 54," pp. 16–18, and "Demichev 57," pp. 29–32.

[13] "Kosiachenko 46," p. 14.

[14] "Lokshin 52," p. 76, "Glusker 54," p. 84, "Karpov 58," p. 18.

[15] "Gal'perin 58," p. 45.

[16] "Perov 58," p. 13. The use of the word "notorious" might reflect the Soviet proclivity for kicking fallen horses, but it also might be a reflection of some of the problems resulting from the classification system even before the reorganization, such as lack of coordination between the distribution of "funded" and "centrally planned" commodities.

the most serious short supply and those which are produced and used in several republics.   These commodities include almost all of the former "funded" and some of the former "centrally planned" commodities.   Estimates of the number to be planned by Gosplan vary from 800 to 1,500.[17]

The republics will plan the distribution of the commodities of lesser importance and those commodities produced either wholly or largely within one republic.   The individual sovnarkhozy will distribute those commodities of least importance and those commodities which are produced wholly within a single sovnarkhoz.

Our major interest, in this paper, is the centralized planning of supply.   Therefore, we will concentrate on the planning of the supply of those products which are under the jurisdiction of Gosplan S.S.S.R. and which appear in the annual state supply plan: formerly the "funded" commodities and presently those commodities in the first of the new three categories.

CHRONOLOGY OF PLAN CONSTRUCTION

In this section, we will outline the sequence of plan construction. The supply plan for the forthcoming year (the planned year) is constructed during the current year (the planning year).   The process is roughly one wherein general instructions flow down the planning hierarchy followed by a counterflow of fill-in information and suggestions from the bottom.   This is followed by coordination at the top and the issuance of a fairly detailed plan.   In the final stage the plan flows down again and is put into the thorough detail necessary for operational purposes.   The formal chronology which I have set out below is a generalized view of the process.   In reality, the stages are not always clear cut and practice often varies from one industry to another.   The prereorganization system is described first and then some of the changes introduced by the reorganization are discussed.[18]

The first stage of the planning process is a statistical analysis of the base period.   This is finished in the first half of the planning year. It includes a thorough statistical investigation of the previous year (that is 2 years before the planned year), preliminary data on the first 6 months of the planning year and some estimated data for the second 6 months of the planning year.   The purpose of this statistical work is primarily to aid in the construction of the control figures (stage two) by uncovering temporary "bottlenecks" which should be concentrated upon in the planned year and by uncovering possible supplementary sources of increased output.

The second stage is the drawing up of the control figures.   These are preliminary notes on the forthcoming economic plan.   They are a set of aggregate output targets for a dozen or so of the most important commodity groups.   They also contain some major investment targets.   Their purpose is to serve as guideposts to the lower economic units in the construction of the annual plan.   The control figures are worked out in Gosplan by the industrial and the summary departments, use being made of material balances to attain equality

---

[17] "Gal'perin 58," p. 45, "Karpov 58," pp. 18–19.   "Gal'perin 58," p. 45 gives a figure of 1,200 to 1,500; "Karpov 58," p. 19: 1,000.   But I was told in a personal interview with a Soviet economist that Gosplan was still planning the distribution of only about 800 commodities.

[18] This chronology has been put together from many sources, including: "Braginskii 54," pp. 331–345; "Lokshin 52," p. 27–37; "Gal'perin 57–1," passim, especially pp. 17–20, 32–34; "P. Kh. Editorial 58"; "Gal'perin 58"; "Koldomasov 59"; and a number of personal interviews with Soviet economists.

between the supply and demand for each of the commodity groups covered. According to the Soviet literature, these preliminary targets are based first of all on the economic-political tasks set by the party and the government, which in turn are determined by "the given stage of Socialist construction." [19]   They are also set in relation to the long-term plan then in force, relying heavily on the results of the statistical investigations carried out in the first stage.   The control figures are worked out in June and early July, and are confirmed by the Council of Ministers.

The third stage is the key stage.   It is the one in which the plan comes up the hierarchy, is coordinated on a national scale at the top, is confirmed by the government and becomes a law directing the operating units in the economy.   Actually, this stage begins before the completion of the second stage.   It appears that all the levels— ministries, glavki and enterprises—start to work on their plans prior to the publication of the control figures.   Sometime in May, Gosplan sends out forms for the ordering of materials.   These orders are called zaiavki.   (See chart No. 1.)   They contain data on materials required by the enterprise during the planned year, i.e., the year to come, and also data on materials used during the current year and the past year.   The materials required are calculated by the "direct method": output targets are multiplied by a set of input norms (from this product, above-norm stocks are subtracted).   Since work on the zaiavki begins before the release of the control figures, the enterprise puts together a set of tentative output targets, based on the enterprise's experience during the past year and the first part of the current year, and what directions it expects the forthcoming plan to take.   Once the control figures are released (end of June–beginning of July) and are broken down by the ministry and the glavk, the enterprise has a clearer idea of what its production targets will be, and it is able to introduce the necessary corrections in the plan calculations it has been making.

In addition to output targets, in order to complete the zaiavki, the firm has to know how much of each input it will need per unit of output. This information is supplied by the input norms.   The question, by whom and how these norms are set, is an extremely complicated one. For one thing, it depends upon the period.   In some periods there were many norms inspected and confirmed by the highest planning organ. For example, in preparing the supply plan for 1949, Gossnab inspected more than 1,800 material input norms, and this grew as the drive toward centralization increased until for the 1952 plan it was above 7,500.[20]   But then in the early decentralization moves of 1953–54, the ministries were given greatly increased power over norm setting and only the "most important norms" were to be inspected by the top planning organ.[21]   The importance of the input material being normed, thus, is another contributing factor.   The most important norms are established in the annual supply plan as obligatory direct tasks (adresnye zadaniia).   These are set either as an average for a branch, or, in the case of the most important firms in the country, by specific firm and by specific item produced.   In addition, the plan

---

[19] This is the phrase repeatedly used.   In Western terms it means "planners' preferences."   The planners look over the current stage of development and they (rather than the consumers) determine the major directions the economy will take in the coming year.   (In this sense "planners" means the political leaders, rather than the people at Gosplan.)
[20] "Lokshin 52," p. 125.
[21] "Braginskii 54," p. 222.

Chart #1

ZAIAVKA

For (Group of Materials) needed by the enterprise in 1960

Number	Designation of Materials	Unit of Measurement	1958			1959										Requirements in 1960 for main-temporary tenance stocks						Sources covering 1960 needs			By Quarter			
			Stocks on Jan. 1st	Delivered	Used	Stocks on Jan. 1st	Fund		Delivered		Used		Actual stocks on July 1, 1959	Expected stocks on Jan. 1, 1960	For output sold	Total	For capital repair	Quantity	In "days' needs"	TOTAL	Use of expected stocks	Mobilization of internal resources	Requested fondy	I	II	III	IV
							Confirmed	Including changes	Expected for year	Actual deliveries in first six months	Expected for year	Actually used in first six months															
1	2	3	4	5	6	7	8	9	10	11	12	13	14	15	16	17	18	19	20	21	22	23	24	25	26	27	28

This is a typical form of a *zaiavka*. It is illustrative of the documentation which constitutes the "paper pyramid" involved in centralized Soviet planning. (see Grossman 55, pp. 22-23) lists a number of targets for the general decrease in norms by industrial branch. The main mass of norms, however, are not listed in the plan, but are used for calculation purposes during the process of constructing the national economic plan. Some of these are confirmed directly at the enterprise and some at the glavk or ministry. Again there was much variation from year to year.[22]

The principle underlying the working out of input norms is that they must aid in the constant struggle to increase economic output by forcing the spread of technical progress and the economizing of material resources. To accomplish this, they must embody the achievements of the leading firms, but they must also be attainable by the average firm. The concept of an "average-progressive norm," which is a norm somewhere between the average and the best, was created to meet this need.[23] Norms are worked out originally by the firm and, depending upon the level at which they are confirmed, are inspected by technical bureaus up the bureaucratic line. As we will see below, norms are frequently changed by higher organs during the construction of the annual economic plan.

With its estimates of output targets and input norms, the enterprise fills out its zaiavki and sends these orders along with supporting documents up to the glavk. Thus begins what is in many ways a political process, something akin to our collective bargaining. The glavk checks the estimates and requests of the enterprise and tries to remove some of the slack the enterprise has put in. The "padding of orders" is one of the most common methods used by the Soviet firm to increase its chances of fulfilling its output plan, under the existing strains of tight plans and supply unreliability.[24] In its negotions with the glavk, the firm tries to defend the estimates and requests it has made. But since the glavk has administrative power over the firm, it can force its opinion to prevail (although a firm can appeal to the ministry).[25] The glavk then combines the zaiavki of the firms subordinate to it and sends the combined zaiavki up to the main administration of supply of the ministry. Here the bargaining process is repeated. The ministry then sends its aggregated plan and zaiavki up to Gosplan S.S.S.R. Usually this was to be done before September 1, or at the latest September 15.[26] The discussions which ensue between a ministry and the corresponding industrial department of Gosplan are a real analog of collective bargaining, for neither has administrative power over the other. In fact, there are at times unresolved disagreements which have to be settled by the Council of Ministers.[27]

[22] In 1952, at the height of centralization there were 2,230 norms established by Gossnab and the ministries for the use of rolled ferrous metal products, which covered 69 percent of its total use in the economy, and 1,145 centrally established norms for the use of lumber products, which covered 97 percent of their use ("Shein 54," p. 113).

[23] There are a number of different methods of calculating an average progressive norm. One is by the "analytical method," wherein the achievements of the leading firms are thoroughly analyzed and a realistic norm set as close to these achievements as possible. For more than 20 years this has been the only acceptable method and yet it would appear that in practice the more formal "statistical method" is still widely used. Under this method an average progressive norm is often just the average of all the above-average input relationships achieved in production. See, e.g., the December 1935 Plenum of the Central Committee of the Communist Party, "Direktivy II," pp. 485–6; "Shein 54," pp. 118–126; "Savkin 56," p. 67.

[24] "Berliner 57," ch. VII, and passim.

[25] The cutting away of fat is not carried to the limit because the plans of the glavki and of the ministries are (presumably) a summation of the plans of the enterprises, and thus their fulfillment depends upon the enterprise's ability to fulfill its own plan. (The appeal point is from a personal interview with a Soviet economist.)

[26] Personal interview with a Soviet economist. "Braginskii 54," pp. 337–338 states that the ministries in 1952 were supposed to have their drafts up by Aug. 15.

[27] "Strumilin 57," p. 39. It is also thought that the Central Committee of the Communist Party plays an important role in the settling of some of these disagreements.

During the period of September and early October, Gosplan is engaged in the crucial work of attempting to balance the supply and demand for each of the centrally allocated commodities. It does this by means of the material balances (this process will be discussed in some detail in the following section). Actually Gosplan, like the ministries and glavki, starts its work before the draft plans come up from below. In this way it has a forecast of what the material balances will be like when the ministries' plans do come up, and it is, therefore, prepared for the ensuing discussions. Gosplan sends a balanced draft of the plan to the Council of Ministers before the end of October.[28] The plan is discussed by the Council of Ministers and, if necessary, certain changes are made. The plan is then confirmed.

Stage 4, the final stage in the construction of the plan, is the bringing down of the plan to the enterprise and its transformation into detailed operational form. The final plan, the fondy for the centrally allocated commodities and the delivery orders for these commodities are sent to the ministries. The main administration of supply divides the fondy and the centrally established input norms among the subordinate glavki and the main administration of sales divides the delivery orders for the "funded" commodities produced by the ministry. The glavki in turn divide these among the enterprises.

A fund received by an enterprise entitles it to a certain amount of the "funded" commodity. But the "funded" commodity is defined in airly gross terms and thus the enterprise must specify exactly what shape, grade, and size it requires. The firm constructs a complete, specified list of the materials it needs within the limits of the fondy allotted to it and sends this list up to the glavk. The glavk checks the lists it receives, combines them, and sends the combined, specified lists to the ministry.[29] There, the main administration of supply combines the lists it receives and sends the specified orders to the main administrations of sales of the appropriate producing ministries. This is to be done 1 to $1\frac{1}{2}$ months before the beginning of the planned year.[30] The main administration of sales checks to see if the orders are within the limits of the fondy, and then it assigns specific orders to specific producing firms. Meanwhile, the aggregate delivery orders, which were sent down, have also been distributed to the glavki and the enterprises, so that the enterprises have already begun to work out their production and shipment schedules before receiving the specified orders from their main administration of sales.

As was the case with other stages, the fourth stage really begins before the end of the third. When Gosplan sends its draft of the plan to the Council of Ministers, it sends excerpts to each ministry so that the ministry can begin the arduous and labor-intensive job of specification and assignment of delivery orders. Then, when the plan is confirmed, the changes made by the Council of Ministers are incorporated by the ministries, glavki and enterprises into the work they have done up to that time.

---

[28] In 1952, Gosplan was to have this draft at the Council of Ministers by Oct. 10. "Braginskii 54," pp. 337-338.

[29] A census of inventories is taken in October, so that the glavk has a clearer idea of the stocks on hand at the enterprise and the expected stocks at the beginning of the planned year. It can take these into account in checking the specified orders of the enterprise.

[30] The specified orders cover only a 3-month period and thus the specification process is repeated before each quarter.

The planning process proper [31] concludes with the signing of contracts between producing units and consuming units, in which delivery schedules and other delivery details are stipulated.

Since the reorganization, the essential nature of the planning process has not changed, but some of its features have. The hierarchical line is now different: Gosplan S.S.S.R., republican gosplan, sovnarkhoz, enterprise.

The chronology also is somewhat different. Stage 2, the construction of the control figures, was omitted, but is now being reintroduced in altered form. Stage 3 now begins at the enterprise. No control figures containing output targets are issued, but rather each enterprise is to work out its own output targets on the basis of the yearly breakdowns of the 7-year plan. These yearly breakdowns have been worked out in much more detail and thus are more operational than were the yearly breakdowns of long-term plans in the past. As the middle and end years of the 7-year plan approach, the enterprise is expected to make corrections in these yearly breakdowns to take account of the accumulated divergences between experience and plan. The zaiavki are sent up to the sovnarkhoz, are reviewed, debated, and are combined and sent up to the republican gosplan. Here the bargaining process is repeated and then, for each centrally allocated product, the planned supply (including "imports" from other republics) and the planned demand (including "exports" to other republics) are balanced. For this purpose, regional material balances are used. A new procedure will be added starting in 1960. In order to give the gosplan of a union-republic some idea of how much of a given material it can expect to receive in the planned year, Gosplan S.S.S.R. will, at the beginning of June, issue a set of preliminary limits for the supply of somewhere between 50 to 200 of the most important input materials.[32] The gosplan of the republic is to send its output plan and zaiavki up to Gosplan by August 1. Gosplan then has until September 15 to work out a balanced all-union output and supply plan. The basic method is still the use of material balances. Fondy (now confirmed by Gosplan itself) are allocated to the republics; the republics distribute them among the sovnarkhozy; and the sovnarkhozy to the enterprises. The specified orders go up the line: sovnarkhoz, republican gosplan, Gosplan. This is supposed to be done 1½ to 2 months before the beginning of the planned year. In Gosplan S.S.S.R., the main administrations for interrepublican deliveries, which grew out of the main administrations of sales of the ministries, assign specified orders directly to individual producing enterprises. And the process again ends with the signing of delivery contracts between suppliers and users.

Summarizing the results of the reorganization, the following stand out as important new features of the process of supply planning: (1) the more detailed yearly subdivisions of the 7-year plan, which serve as a starting point for the planning process in place of the control figures which were formerly worked out each year by Gosplan; (2) the increased importance of the republican gosplany and of regional balancing; (3) also the increased importance of Gosplan S.S.S.R. with

---

[31] The other part of the planning process is the changing of the plan during the course of the year as the need for changes becomes apparent. Russian economists repeatedly claim this is an important part of the planning process, and indeed when one reads of the tremendous number of changes introduced during the year, it is hard to disagree. But a discussion of this falls outside of the restricted scope of this paper.
[32] Personal interview with a Soviet economist. See also Koldomasov 59, p. 60.

the addition to its staff of the former main administrations of sales of the ministries, now renamed, main administrations for inter-republican deliveries (this, however, may not be a permanent feature).

MATERIAL BALANCES

The key element in the planning of industrial supply is the material balance. Every Soviet writer on the subject pays homage to it:

> In the Socialist economy, the planned connection between the production and consumption of different types of products is guaranteed. Both the production and consumption of materials are determined by means of the material balances, which are an integral component of the plan for the supply of the national economy.
> By means of the material balances, the material needs of the national economy are determined, means for increasing the material resources of the economy are uncovered and the necessary proportionality in the growth of individual branches of the national economy in accordance with the demands of the law of the planned (proportional) development of the national economy is established.
> The material balances permit the planning organs to work out measures for the mobilization of production reserves, for the overcoming of "bottlenecks" in the development of individual branches and to uncover supplementary resources.[33]

A material balance is essentially a balance sheet of the supply and demand for a given product. At the Gosplan level a separate material balance is made out for each of the centrally allocated commodities (formerly the "funded" commodities.)[34] On the left side of the balance, are listed all the sources of the product and on the right side, its uses. (See chart No. 2.) Most of these categories are self-explanatory. On the sources side, the most important category is "Production." With most commodities it is often as high as 95 percent of the total supply. "Imports" is usually insignificant. "Other sources" is of varying importance. In some ferrous metals, for example, scrap metal ("other sources") is an important element of supply. "Stocks" includes only those at suppliers. This is done because they are the only stocks capable of being distributed.[35] Stocks at users (if they are above normed levels) are taken into account by being substracted from requirements when the zaiavki of an enterprise are made up.

The major categories on the distribution side are "production-operation needs" (which includes maintenance requirements) and "Construction." The "market fund" denotes that part of the output of the product which is distributed more or less without further processing to satisfy the consumption needs of the people. The two "reserves" are quite different from each other. The "state reserve" is a permanent one, built up as a protection against national disasters, natural or manmade. The "reserve of the Council of Ministers" is an operational reserve to be dispensed during the course of the years to firms which are overfulfilling their output targets and thus are in need of additional input materials, and to firms which did not get supplies which were allotted to them, because of supply failures.[36] The production categories on the sources and distribution sides, before the reorganization, were broken down by producing and consuming ministries.[37] They are now broken down by republics.

---

[33] Shein 54, p. 19.

[34] Material balances, in modified form, are also used by lower planning organs.

[35] Actually, the positive difference between stocks at suppliers at the beginning and end of the year is what comprises a source of distributable supply. A negative difference denotes an added demand for the product.

[36] The output targets of producers are set higher than the originally planned deliveries they have to make. This difference is what makes up the "reserves of the Council of Ministers." During the year the firms will receive orders telling them where to send this additional output. (Personal interview with a Soviet economist.)

[37] In most cases, there were a number of different ministries producing a given product.

Chart #2

MATERIAL BALANCE*

Product X

<table>
<tr><td>SOURCES</td><td>DISTRIBUTION</td></tr>
</table>

1. Production

    a) By major producing Ministries (now by Republics)

2. Imports

3. Other Sources

4. Stocks at suppliers, at beginning of period

    a) By major supplier Ministries (now by Republics)

1. Production-operation needs

    a) By major user Ministries (now by Republics)

2. Construction

    a) By major users

3. Market Fund

4. Export

5. Increase of State Reserves

6. Increase of Reserves of Council of Ministers

7. Stocks at suppliers, at end of period

    a) By major supplier Ministries (now by Republics)

This is a composite form. The categories often differ from product to product.

The material balances are used at two stages of Gosplan's work. First, they are used to assure consistency in the control figures (now the preliminary supply limits), and second, they are used in constructing the final draft of the annual economic plan. At the control figures stage, Gosplan uses its own estimates of sources and distribution, but in the final draft stage, the information which comes up from below is used. We will concentrate here on the final draft stage.

The crucial problem in material balance technology is how are the planned sources and distribution brought into balance when at first there is an imbalance? [38] Usually, the direction of an imbalance is that the demand for a product is greater than the originally planned supplies.[39] The procedure appears to be that the industrial departments of Gosplan (which are organized along product lines) work on the sources of each product, while the summary departments work on the distribution. The two work closely together in trying to achieve a balance, keeping each other constantly informed of the adjustments

[38] A subsidiary problem is: how is a change in the output target of one product reflected in the changes of other products?

[39] Personal interview with a Soviet economist. This can be logically deduced from the practice of padding orders by lower administrative organs.

each makes.[40] What steps do they take when it is found that the demand for a product is greater than the planned supply? [41]

The basic principle, it is claimed, is that a plan is not brought down to a "bottleneck," i.e., an output target of one branch is not reduced because of a "bottleneck" in the supply to it of a deficit commodity. This, one author states, would be the easiest way, but is sheer opportunism.[42]

What is done is that on the one hand the corresponding industrial department attempts to increase the supply of the deficit commodity. It sees if stocks at suppliers can be cut (further). Also, planned imports, in a few cases, may be increased. But the major effort is to increase current production. This is to be accomplished within the planned capacity, by better or more intensive use of equipment. Sometimes the planned introduction of new capacity may be speeded up so that more of the year is operated within the greater capacity.

At the same time that the industrial department is working on increasing the supply of the deficit commodity, the summary department is working on decreasing the demand for this commodity. The basic principle is to accomplish this without decreasing the output targets of the users of the deficit material. The method employed is to increase efficiency in the use of this material, to economize, to rationalize, to spread the advanced experience of the leading firms. In other words, pressure is applied to decrease (further) the input norms.[43] Another method is the substitution of nondeficit materials for the deficit. These are always described as "fully substitutable substitutes.[44] Throughout the balancing process, the priority principle is at work. Whenever possible, it is the sectors of secondary importance (usually the consumer oriented sectors) which have their allocations cut or are called upon to use substitutes. The emphasis is on guaranteeing the supply of the high priority sectors.

When a summary department makes changes which reduce the flow of the deficit commodity to other commodity sectors, it notifies the corresponding industrial departments. And when an industrial department increases the output of the deficit commodity in such a way as to call for an increase in required supplies, then it, in most cases, contacts the relevant summary departments.

To the extent that an imbalance is corrected by an increase in the output of a deficit commodity which is the type of increase that calls for an increase in the output of the materials used in its production, something similar to an iterative solution of the balancing problem might be envisaged. By an iterative solution, I mean one where the increase in the output of one commodity is followed by the increase in the output of all the inputs into that commodity, followed by the increase in the output of all the inputs into the inputs and so on down the line, all the time use being made of the set of input norms. Math-

---

[40] Personal interview with a Soviet economist.

[41] This is one of those clouded areas of administrative action, where a person would really have to be involved in the actual work before he could clearly analyze the method employed. The following "analysis" is based on personal interviews with Soviet economists and a number of written sources, including: *Zhukov 54*, pp. 103 ff.; *Braginskii 54*, pp. 292–294; *Strumilin 57*, pp. 54–56.

[42] *Strumilin 57*, p. 55. The phrase "deficit product" is used here to mean a product for which demand is greater than planned supply, during the process of plan construction.

[43] In a personal interview with a Soviet economist, the economist said that input norms could be decreased in two ways. One, he illustrated by tightening up his belt; the other was the method of increasing efficiency. He said they preferred to use the second method.

[44] It has also been suggested that the reserves of the Council of Ministers are originally set higher than required, so that, at the balancing stage, when the demand is greater than the supply, these reserves can be cut without any damage. But in a personal interview with a Soviet economist, it was strongly denied that such a method was used.

ematically, an infinite number of such steps will yield a perfectly consistent set of material balances.[45] But since the steps near the end become very small, the process may be stopped far short of infinity and an acceptably accurate solution derived.

It is frequently thought that the iterative approach is the basic method used by Soviet planners to achieve consistency in their plans. It do not think that this theory is correct. In order to see why, let us first look at the dimensions of the problem. How many steps, how many iterations would Gosplan have to perform in order to get a reasonably accurate approximation to a balanced plan? The number of iterations necessary, or in other words, the rate of convergence of the approximation procedure, depends on the structure of the economy—roughly speaking, on the degree of interrelatedness of the economy. The more interrelated an economy, the greater the number of iterations necessary. Unfortunately, data on the structure of the Soviet economy, in the detail necessary to give a precise answer to the question, are not available. But on the basis of *very crude* calculations, it might be said that somewhere between 6 and 13 iterations would be required.[46] It is inconceivable that Gosplan, under the conditions which prevailed, could have performed that number of iterations. First of all, Gosplan does not handle the problem in the formal way usually assumed in discussing iterative methods. It does not put together, into one list, all the imbalances which appear at the first

---

[45] This is so because, letting $[A]=$the matrix of input norms,

$$[I-A]^{-1}=[I+A+A^2+ \ldots A^n] \text{ (where } n \rightarrow \infty)$$

The iterative procedure, discussed in the text, concerns the total effects (direct and indirect) of changes in total output levels rather than the calculation of a vector of total outputs starting from a given vector of final outputs. Formally, however, the two problems are similar; both involve the $[I-A]^{-1}$ matrix. This can be shown in the following way:

At the first attempted balancing of the material balances, a number of discrepancies between the originally planned supplies and demanded outputs appear (let us say they are all shortfalls):

Let,

$\quad [A]=$matrix of input norms
$\quad X_s=$vector of originally planned supplies
$\quad Y=$vector of planned final outputs
$\quad X_d=$vector of the calculated demands

Then,

$$[A]X_s+Y=X_d, \text{ where } X_d \geqq X_s \tag{1}$$

Now let,
$\quad \Delta X=$the unknown vector of changes in X_s necessary to get a consistent set of material balances.

Set,

$$[I-A]\Delta X=(X_d-X_s)$$

$$\Delta X=[I-A]^{-1}(X_d-X_s) \tag{2}$$

Add ΔX to X_s to get a new level of planned supplies and the plan will be balanced:

$$[A](X_s+\Delta X)+Y=(X_s+\Delta X) \tag{3}$$

(Proof of (3) is relatively simple, once it is seen that: $[A][I-A]^{-1}=[I-A]^{-1}-[I])$

The iterative procedure discussed in this paper is the iterative approximation to $[I-A]^{-1}(X_d-X_s)$ from equation (2).

[46] The U.S. Bureau of Labor Statistics developed a method of approximating $[I-A]^{-1}[Y]$ through a series of iterations, followed by an extrapolation procedure. Using American data, they found that even with an extrapolation after the last iteration, in order to guarantee an acceptable level of precision, they would have to perform from 5–11 iterations ("Ritz 50," p. 4; "Evans 54," p. 78). The rate of convergence of $(I+A+A^2 \ldots)$ depends upon the dominant characteristic root of $[A]$, which is roughly related to the degree of interrelatedness of an economy ("Evans 54," p. 83). If the common assumption that the U.S. economy has a higher degree of interrelatedness than the Soviet economy is true, then it is possible that the rate of convergence of a Soviet matrix would be slightly faster than that of a U.S. matrix. Secondly, though Gosplan does not appear to use anything nearly as sophisticated as an extrapolation procedure, it most likely has developed some informal speed-up methods, such as increasing an output target more than the original shortfall called for. How much it does this and by how much it would speed up the convergence are hard to tell. Taking all these considerations into account, it would probably be safer to set the lower bound of the number of iterations required for a Soviet matrix somewhere toward the lower end of the number required for U.S. matrices by the BLS iteration and extrapolation method. Let us set it at 6.

The upper bound of 13 was calculated by means of an heroic adaptation of a method devised by Waugh. (See "Waugh 50.")

approximation, and then in an organized way apply the entire set of input norms to these imbalances. Rather, each product is handled by a separate section (indeed, by two separate sections), which keeps communicating its moves to the other sections. There does not appear to be any set order of communication such as first section A makes its changes, then section B, etc.; all sections work simultaneously.[47] Secondly, in the postwar period, Gosplan was trying to balance an extremely large number of material balances, ranging between the current 760 and a high of 1,600. The problem of working changes through that many different balances is a formidable one for any bureaucracy. Thirdly, all this was and is done without the aid of electronic computers. The method of material balances, in the form in which it exists, is not amenable to computer technology.

But we need not rely solely on deductive reasoning in this matter. In a recent book, the director of the Economic Research Institute of Gosplan stated, that it was rare for even three or four iterations to be performed in tracing the effects of a correction in an output target:

> Because of the great labor intensity of the calculation of changes in the materia balances and the insufficiency of time for the completion of such work in practice sometimes only those balances which are linked by first order relationships are changed. As regards relationships of the second order, and especially of the third and fourth order, changes in the balances are made only in those cases where the changes are conspicuous (zametnyi).[48]

This statement points out the additional fact that Gosplan's calculation of indirect effects is not uniform; it is limited to "conspicuous" changes. Another facet of the nonuniform approach is that a change need not be passed on in the increased output even of all direct inputs, but can be balanced out by decreases on the demand side of any of these inputs. These nonuniformities in handling the problem make it difficult to "count iterations" or to see an iterative process clearly.

I believe that more important in Gosplan's balancing methodology han iteration procedures is the use of techniques which avoid second-round effects. This is certainly true when changes are made on the distribution side of the material balance of a deficit commodity. Pressure is put on users of the deficit commodity to economize its use by producing more efficiently. The supply of the deficit input material is cut without any change in the output target of the product which uses it. In this way the original rebalancing change does not reverberate through the entire system of material balances; it has no second-round effects. It is less clear to what extent avoidance of second-round effects is important in the making of changes on the sources side. When stocks are reduced, there are no second-round effects, and when imports are increased there are little if any second-round effects. But when a production target is increased in an effort to close a balance, is this always passed on to other sectors in increased orders for input materials? I have heard and read contradictory answers to this question.[49] I think the safest thing to say is that

---

[47] Personal interview with a Soviet economist.

[48] "Efimov 57," p. 107. If there are "n" centrally allocated commodities, then to calculate the direct inputs into a single output change, you need "n" multiplications (ignoring zeros). But to calculate the inputs into the inputs, you need "n^2" multiplications and for each succeeding iteration, you need "n^2" multiplications. Since $760^2 = 577,600$ and $1600^2 = 2,560,000$, it is no wonder that Gosplan, operating without electronic computers, has had to limit itself to only "conspicuous" relationships.

[49] For example, in a personal interview with a Soviet economist, it was said that the practice was to back up increased output targets with increased supplies. On the other hand, an economist in an extremely good dissertation, wrote that when trying to close a balance, the attempt is made to increase the output of a deficit product "by means of internal reserves of production, such as better use of equipment and materials * * *" ("Zhukov 54," p. 103).

usually increased supplies are ordered, but at times, increased output targets of the deficit commodity are to be met by more efficient production methods without additional supplies, thus avoiding second-round effects.[50]

If the analysis offered here is correct, then we are led to the following hypothesis about the balancing methodology used by Soviet planners. By relying heavily on balancing methods which avoid second-round effects, through pressure on input norms, Gosplan contributes to the further tightening of the plan. That is to say, the very planning methodology used by Gosplan (the material balances and the ways in which they are balanced) itself adds an additional tightening to the plan as the balances in the final draft are hammered out at the top planning level.

WEAKNESSES OF SUPPLY PLANNING

In this section, we will discuss the problems connected specifically with the planning of supply, not supply problems in general (see "Introduction"). First the major planning problems as they existed before the reorganization will be described, and then one or two of the possible effects of the reorganization will be indicated.

Unrealistic balances

The first question which arises is: How good are the balances worked out in the national economic plan? Are they realistic balances, or are they to some extent mere "paper balances"? From speaking with Soviet economists, one gets the impression that most economists are quite proud of their method of material balances despite some admitted shortcomings. I am sure their feelings were accurately represented by a Polish economist who told me: "The method of material balances is a primitive method, but it works." On the other hand, the Soviet economy is constantly beset by shortages. Are these shortages, these "imbalances," caused by faulty, unrealistic balancing of plans on the part of Gosplan, or are they caused by other factors operating in the Soviet economy? (See below.) A number of recent official pronouncements and analyses by Soviet economists lead one to believe that unrealistic balances are, at least, partly to blame. Khrushchev, at the 20th Party Congress, claimed that sometimes imbalances arise which are caused not only by failures to meet the established plans, but also by the fact that the plans themselves are deficient.[51] The resolution of the December 1956 Plenum of the Communist Party stated that the top planning organs do not base their plans on the "real possibilities" of supplying the required materials to meet the established output targets. This leads to "excess tightness in the fulfillment of plans."[52] In the book by the director of Gosplan's Economic Research Institute, mentioned earlier, he claims that the balancing methodology used, its lack of a sufficient number of full iterations, leads to the accumulation of "a number of errors in various parts of the plan, which under certain conditions manifest themselves, giving rise to certain imbalances and tensions in various material resources."[53]

---

[50] There are also cases where an imbalance results from improper planning of types of products. For example, there may be enough steel planned, but it is in the wrong assortment (even at Gosplan allocated categories). Correction of such imbalances does not involve many second-round effects.
[51] Cited in "Koldomasov 56," p. 32.
[52] "Direktivy IV," p. 670.
[53] "Efimov 57," p. 107.

Thus there is some evidence that at times the balances achieved by Gosplan do contain elements of "paper consistency." This results, in large measure, from Gosplan's inability, in the material balances method, to cover enough of the indirect effects of a change in an output target, and its consequent reliance on pressure methods, which although having positive aspects from the point of view of forcing economic growth, at times introduce unrealistic relationships in the balances.

Lateness

A major problem of planning concerns the frequent failure of the planning organs to complete the annual supply plan before the beginning of the planned year. The Soviet literature is full of complaints about final plans not coming down to the enterprise until January, February, or March, and sometimes even later. This failure to complete the plan on time is not too difficult to understand when one thinks of what a tremendously involved job it is for a bureaucracy first to work up a balanced supply plan for an entire economy in a great number of aggregated indicators and then for subordinate levels to disaggregate the plan into the necessary operational detail. This problem was made even more difficult by the discontinuous nature of the annual plans before the reorganization: "* * * the planning system that developed was such that the annual plans broke off at the end of the calendar year and therefore had to be drawn up every year from scratch, as it were." [54]

Some of the methods adopted by Soviet planners to cope with this time problem are of interest. One is what might be called the "correction principle." In order to speed up the planning process, planning organs usually begin their own work before receiving information from the previous planning stage. When they do receive the information, they then make the necessary corrections in their preliminary estimates. [55] As we have seen, work on the zaiavki began before Gosplan released the control figures and then when the control figures came out, the zaiavki were corrected. Also the specification process began before the confirmation of the plan by the Council of Ministers, and then the changes it made were incorporated by correcting the specified orders. A second speedup method sometimes used was to begin the construction of the zaiavki and the working out of the input norms not at the enterprise, but at the glavk or even the ministry. [56] A third method was the practice of issuing "advance fondy." In order to allow an enterprise to operate during the first quarter in the absence of a supply plan, it was allotted "advance fondy" usually in the amount of 23 to 25 percent of its previous year's total allotment.

Lack of coordination

There is often a lack of coordination between the supply plan of an enterprise and its output and financial plans. [57] This is partly a result of poor planning originally, but probably it is more a result of the constant changes introduced in plans both before and after they are confirmed. Changes are frequently made in one set of plans (say,

---

[54] "P. Kh. Editorial 58" (translated in the "Current Digest of the Soviet Press," X : 33, p. 11).

[55] This correction process is not limited to the period of the construction of the plan, but continues during the year, while the plan is in operation.

[56] "Savkin 56," p. 61, and a personal interview with a Soviet economist.

[57] For example, see "Turetskii 57," p. 108 and "Kalinin 58," pp. 43–44.

output) without the necessary changes being made in the other set (say, supply).

Specification

One of the weakest parts of the entire planning process is the stage wherein the plan is brought down to the level of the enterprise and is put into operational form—the stage where the aggregate allotments are turned into contracts for specific goods. Remember, the system was: The fondy were distributed by the ministry to the glavk and by the glavk to the enterprise. The enterprise worked up a list of specified requirements within the limits of the fondy. The specified orders came up the hierarchy of the user ministry and a combined specified order was sent to the main administration of sales of each corresponding producer ministry. This ministerial main administration of sales then sent out specified production and delivery orders to the producing firms. The weaknesses of this process lay primarily within three major categories: Excessive centralization, the administrative objectives of sales administrations, and the time factor.

(i) Excessive centralization: The sales administration of the ministry assigned detailed orders directly to the producing firms. The frequent enormity of this job is indicated by the fact that every year the metals main administration of sales issued about 500,000 specified production and delivery orders.[58] This excessive centralization frequently led to the lack of coordination between different plans mentioned in the previous section. Producing firms were often given delivery assignments greater than their planned outputs.[59] The rational geographic distribution of orders was not sufficiently studied, resulting in excessively long transportation hauls. Contract details which should have been set in negotiations between producer and consumer firms were actually set by the producing ministry sales administration and the consuming ministry supply administration.[60] This meant that the real needs of consuming firms and the real production capabilities and specialties of producing firms were often not adequately perceived. It also meant that the efforts to inculcate cost minimization at the enterprise level were weakened, because the enterprise was deprived of the power to decide what materials to use.

(ii) Administrative objectives of sales administration: The sales administrations were concerned with the problems of the producing units rather than with those of the consuming units. Their objective, in the last stage of plan construction, was to achieve an efficient loading of the productive capacities of the firms within their own ministry. As a result of this one-sided concern, consuming firms often ended up with an irrational array of suppliers. Frequently, a firm was to be supplied by a large number of suppliers rather than having its orders concentrated in a few. In fact, as specifications were made out for each quarter, suppliers sometimes were changed from one quarter to the next.[61] These factors gave rise to serious scheduling and coordination problems. Another weakness was that the sales administrations did not put enough pressure on producing firms to adapt their detailed output assortments to the specific needs of the consuming firms, thus leading to imbalances in the detailed supplies and demands.[62] The

[58] "Gal'perin 57–1," p. 19.
[59] Ibid.
[60] Ibid., pp. 19–20.
[61] "Kalinin 58," p. 45.
[62] "Gal'perin 57," p. 85.

170 COMPARISONS OF UNITED STATES AND SOVIET ECONOMIES

supply administrations of the consuming ministries were forced to accede to these imbalances because of their inferior power in the prevailing sellers' market. Finally, the aim of spreading technical progress was weakened because the sales administrations had little motivation to force the production if new and more economical (in use) types of materials.[63]

(iii) Time factors: A firm was supposed to make out its specified input requirements 2 to 3 months before the beginning of the planned year, at a time when it did not know its detailed output plan. This created a number of difficulties in matching specific inputs and outputs. Due to the nature and timing of their planning process, Russian planners were forced to compress the planning of essentially successive problems into one time period. This was one of the factors which led to the great number of revisions in the plan while it was in operation.

All that has been said, here, about the weaknesses of supply planning should not be understood to imply that they were the sole cause of the general unreliability of the supply system. For there are two other major causal factors. One is the overall practice of tight planning; the other is the poor operation of supply organs. The supply plan could be perfectly constructed, perfectly balanced, but if the overall economic plan were very tight (marginal stocks of materials, tight construction schedules, little slack anywhere), then a few failures to meet some individual targets would create significant supply difficulties throughout the system. Also, plans could be moderately slack and well constructed, but if the supply bureaucracy operated in an inefficient manner, then supply difficulties would result. All three factors are important causes of supply deficiencies.

One of the primary aims of the reorganization was to improve the operation of the supply system and, along with this, the planning of supply.[64] It is still too early to evaluate the effects of the reorganization on supply planning, but some comments can be made. The changed role of the long-term plan, with its more detailed, operational yearly subdivisions, will probably help to speed up the planning process and to provide needed continuity in the annual plans.[65] On the other hand, specification procedures do not seem to have improved at all.[66] And it is hard to judge what effects the reorganization will have on the vital problem of achieving balances in the plan—the prime function of the material balances method.

But a new possibility now looms on the horizon, one which might have a profound effect on this balancing methodology. It is the possibility of adapting modern mathematical methods and computer technology to the planning of the supply system.

MATHEMATICAL METHODS AND ELECTRONIC COMPUTERS

Limitations of space do not permit a full discussion of the possible use by Soviet planners of mathematical methods. But let me here

[63] Ibid.
[64] The prime concern of the reorganization in the supply field was with the deficiencies in the operation of the system, rather than, necessarily, with the planning of it. The major operational deficiencies, which resulted primarily from the absence of cross-ministerial coordination, according to Soviet sources, were retardation of specialization and subcontracting for components; supply mainly within ministerial channels and thus often irrationally long transportation hauls; failure to develop diversified firms producing a range of byproducts from the given inputs; and duplication of staffs and organizations.
[65] In a personal interview with a Soviet economist, I was told that the plans for 1958 and 1959 were late. But this was because they were unfamiliar with the new system, they said.
[66] See the strongly critical comments in "Gal'perin 58," pp. 50–52.

just briefly outline what the Russians are saying and what they are doing about the possible use of one of these methods.

Input-Output (I–O) is a mathematical method, which analyzes the interrelationships existing in an economy.[67] Its great advantage over the material balances method is that it puts the technical intersector relationships among economic sectors into one unified scheme and allows them to be expressed mathematically in a very convenient and useful form—useful in the sense that vast numbers of equations can easily be handled through the use of electronic computers.[68] Soviet planners, by means of I–O techniques and electronic computers, after they had put together a realistic set of input norms, could rapidly construct a completely balanced output and supply plan.

Since 1956, Russian economists have been discussing the possibilities of adapting I–O techniques to their balancing methodology. Perhaps the first question which comes to mind is why were they so late. Professor Leontief's first book on I–O was published in 1941 and serious work on I–O problems began in the West soon after World War II. Among the reasons for the Russians' delay, I think, one can include bureaucratic inertia and opposition, low level of the necessary mathematical skills among economists, and the relative unavailability to economists of computers until recent years. But as important as any of these, is the fact that the use of mathematical methods in economics was, up to a few years ago, considered to be anti-Marxist. However, now I–O (also linear programing) has been separated from other econometric methods, and is considered not to be "negated by the Marxist theory of political economy."[69] In addition, in an attempt to add further legitimacy, it is now claimed, but not proved, that since Professor Loentief was born and educated in Russia, his ideas were developed on the basis of early Russian experiments with national economic balances. Yet the charge of unorthodoxy is still a potent weapon, and the supporters of I–O, it would appear, still have to tread carefully.[70]

The Soviet discussion of I–O has both its negative and positive camps. Members of both camps almost always begin with the statement that I–O cannot be used for prediction purposes in the capitalist economy, because the capitalist economy is completely unpredictable. Although some do say that it could be used for more limited problems, such as mobilization. The rest of the criticisms are not too different from those one hears in the West: assumption of constant coefficients, no substitution, no restraints, staticness, exclusion of capital equipment. It is common for a critic to end his article with an admission that I–O can perhaps play a small, restricted role in Soviet economics.

[67] In the I–O method, the output of each sector is divided into flows to each other producing sector and also to final demands (consumption, investment, government, and foreign trade). Starting from the intersector flows, a set of direct input coefficients is derived (direct input of one product per unit output of another product). Then by solving a set of equations, the direct and indirect input coefficients per unit of final output are found. These tell us, for example, not only how much coal is directly required to produce one automotibile for final use, but how much coal is needed for the steel which goes into the automobile and so on. Thus, the direct and indirect input coefficient of coal per automohile tells us that if we increase the output for final use of automobiles by one unit how much more coal will be required throughout the economy to support this change in output. In other words, with these total cost coefficients, if we have an estimate of final demand (be it forecast or plan), we can determine the total output of each sector required for the production of this final bill of goods. I–O makes use of electronic computers to solve, rapidly, large system of equations. Its development is associated with the name of Prof. Wassily Leontief of Harvard University.

[68] One weakness of the material balances is that they are similar to the rows of an I–O table, while the important technical relationships in an economy are to be found in the columns.

[69] "Nikitin 58," p. 103.

[70] It is a sobering irony that the U.S. Government's I–O program was discontinued in 1953 because of allegations that in some way it was a socialist scheme and a threat to private enterprise. (See Business Week, Aug. 29, 1953, p. 26.)

The supporters of I–O argue that it is a tool which could be used to utmost advantage in Soviet planning. It would assure a well-balanced plan. Through the use of total cost coefficients, the total effects of a change in any one output target could be calculated, and thus the necessary changes in all other outputs could be made.[71] And what is of extreme importance, all the required calculations could be done rapidly on electronic computers. One writer emphasized this point by showing that in the calculation of the total cost coefficients for a 44 sector I–O model (remember, at one point, Gasplan had to balance 1,600 "sectors") 2,500,000 arithmetic operations were necessary. Yet an electronic computer was able to complete this task within 8 hours.[72] Another advantage is that, after a balanced plan is derived, the calculation of the actual supply plan, i.e., the actual material flows from one sector to another, would be a simple matter—merely a multiplication of direct input coefficients times the levels of output of the corresponding products. Besides these basic points, supporters argue that changes during the operation of a short term or long term plan could more efficiently be made with the aid of total cost coefficients. The spreading of technical progress could be aided by using planned direct input coefficients rather than statistically derived ones as the basic data for I–O calculations. Under the new organization of industry, regional I–O balances could be made. On another level, I–O could be used for working out internally consistent prices. And finally, it could be used for some purely statistical purposes such as the calculation of certain economic proportions, comparisons of the labor and materials intensities of different products and certain statistical comparisons with the West.

If Russian planners were to adopt I–O methodology as it is practiced in the West, then among the many changes in planning techniques this would involve, there would be one of fundamental importance. This is the narrowing of the scope of politically determined basic plan goals from total outputs to final outputs (i.e., outputs for final uses: consumption, investment, etc.). In Western I–O practice, one starts with a given set of final demands and by means of a set of direct and indirect input coefficients, one solves for the levels of total outputs. Soviet planners, in the material balances method, start from a set of total output goals, which basically are determined by the political authorities in the society. That is the political authorities set targets, which include not only the amount of a product going to final uses, but also the amount, which is needed within the economy to produce other products.

Are Soviet economists advocating such a change? According to a number of leading economists, including the very highly placed Academician V. S. Nemchinov, they are not.[73] They intend to retain total outputs as the starting data for plan construction.[74] The primary use of I–O, according to these economists, will be to work out a number of different balanced variants of the plan. They say that

---

[71] Some articles point out that experiments have shown the total coefficients often to be many times larger than the direct. Thus, the ignoring of indirect effects leads to significant errors. (See "Tolkachev 58" and "Grebtsov 59," p. 61.)

[72] "Efimov 57," p. 11.

[73] Personal interview with Academician Nemchinov and other Soviet economists.

[74] The Soviet approach to the total output of steel and the total output of electricity as objectives in themselves is in part determined by the symbolic significance of these basic indexes as indicators of successful economic growth. But it is also a recognition of the fact that a high rate of growth of these basic industrial commodities is perhaps a safer assurance of economic growth than planning from a final bill of goods would be when foresight, knowledge, and techniques are still imperfect.

the material balances method enables them to work out only one balanced variant of the plan, but with I–O they will be able to work out many from which they will choose the "best." [75] In addition, they claim that the material balances approach will remain the dominant one and that I–O techniques will only be an auxiliary planning mechanism.

There are, however, a few Soviet economists who do favor planning from a set of final outputs:

* * * the starting point of planning must be the final bill of goods [investment and consumption]. It is not sufficient to produce much steel or cement, lumber, or cotton. The aim is to produce a sufficient amount of machines, buildings, furniture, cloth, etc.[76]

Another possibility is a mixed model, where some total output targets and some final outputs are given, and the remaining total outputs and final outputs are derived by solving the set of equations.[77]

Only time will tell how far Russian planning will go into I–O techniques, but it does appear probable that in the beginning at least, its use will be restricted to the calculation of a number of plan variants and the use of total cost coefficients to calculate the total effects of any change in the plan.

As regards actual experimentation, there have been reports so far of four models worked out, including 9, 15, 17, and 44 order systems.[78] These are all pilot models. For a system to have any operational significance it would have to be of the order of 500–1,000 sectors. There is also an experiment now in progress on a regional I–O study involving a single economic region (the Mordovskoi region). This is based on the method used in a U.S. study of the state of Utah.[79]

The new Laboratory for the Use of Statistics and Mathematical Methods in Economics, headed by Academician Nemchinov and the famous mathematician, L. V. Kantorovich, and possessing a staff of about 20, is working on I–O problems, mainly on problems of adapting statistical data to computer use.[80] It is scheduled to operate, in the near future, at the computing center, which is being erected in Novosibirsk. In addition, there are people working on I–O in the Economic Research Institute of Gosplan and in the Institute for Electronic Control Machines of the Academy of Sciences.

Thus Soviet economists are beginning to take notice of I–O and the possibilities of applying it to problems of planning. I–O in the Soviet Union has come a far way from the days when it was almost taboo to discuss it or work on it. Yet, on the other hand, it has by

[75] Any vector X would be a feasible plan as long as no element of Y were negative, where $Y=[I-A]\ X$. One of the problems involved here is, of course, how do you choose the "best." But this is a problem of a different order. A choice out of many is still better than no choice at all.
[76] "Belkin 57," p. 144.
[77] See "Grebtsov 59," p. 62. I was told in Warsaw, that Polish planners are working on a combined model of this type.
[78] See "Grebtsov 59," "Tolkachev 58" and "Belkin 57."
[79] Personal interview with a Soviet economist. For a description of the Utah study see Moore and Petersen, "Regional Analysis: An Interindustry Model of Utah," Review of Economics and Statistics, November 1955.
[80] Personal interview with a Soviet economist. This is a major problem. There have been numerous complaints that Soviet statistics are not adequate for use in I–O work. The main criticism is that they do not clearly show the technical relationships between sectors. For example, see "Tolkachev, 58," "Grebtsov 59," p. 57, and "Nemchinov 59," pp. 33–34. Nemchinov's apparent suggestion that some I–O research be treated as classified work, in the same way as atomic energy and rocket research, has been interpreted as an attempt to gain access to detailed statistical data.

174 COMPARISONS OF UNITED STATES AND SOVIET ECONOMIES

no means swept the field.[81] Much of the struggle still lies ahead. One bit of evidence of this is the extreme sensitivity, which supporters of I–O still retain, to questions of its origins and orthodoxy.

III. CONCLUSIONS

The general nature of Soviet supply planning can perhaps be best described as a combination of the central planning of aggregate categories with the successive setting of details down through the planning hierarchy and the application of constant pressure, from the center to tighten production methods and to economize materials. This is not a picture of finely calculated balances, but is a combination whose aim is to contribute to economic growth.

One of the important operating criteria in the Soviet economy is the priority principle. The possible negative effects on economic growth of imbalances in supply plans are lessened because there are low priority buffer sectors to absorb the shocks of these imbalances. The operation of the priority principle also lessens the negative effects of the interaction of imperfect supply planning, overall tight planning and a not overly efficient supply bureaucracy.

Even though overall tight planning prevails, it should not be thought that the Soviet economy is everywhere so taut that the slightest failure in any one place will cause the whole economy to burst. Some operational leeway does exist. There are usually some unemployed or underemployed labor and materials to be found, which can be pressed into service when the need arises. This leeway is, in large measure, a result of the "informal activities" of the Soviet firm. [82]

As an economy grows more developed, the number of interrelationships within it becomes larger. This intensifies the problems of supply planning. At the same time, however, the radical changes in the structure of the economy diminish, and thus supply relationships become more stable. This lessens the problems of supply planning. Yet it would appear that in recent years the increasing interrelationships have caused the Russians to become increasingly concerned with the deficiencies of their supply system.

One of the more promising means for counteracting these deficiencies is through the adoption of input-output techniques. The original flush of enthusiasm in the West for I–O may have diminished somewhat, and there are many perhaps who now feel that not too much should be expected of it. However, these criticisms apply to its use in the West. It should be kept in mind that under the type of economic organization that exists in the Soviet Union today, they have to plan their supply system. Thus, the appropriate question for them is not whether I–O is an ideal method, but whether it is better than the method Soviet planners use now—material balances. As far as assuring balance in the plan and speeding up the process of plan construction, there is no doubt of the superiority of I–O techniques. Yet the material balances method does have a significant organizational ad-

---

[81] In a personal interview with a Soviet economist, the economist complained that they could not get proper statistics for I–O work. When questioned on this, he said the data could be made available, but it would cost money to collect and process it and their problem now was to convince the higher-ups that I–O was a worthwhile project so that they could get the necessary budgetary allocations. He was told that this was a problem we could understand. See also the recent speech by L. V. Kantorovich in which he said, "The fear of mathematics has by no means been overcome" (Vestnik Akademii Nauk S.S.S.R., 1959:4, p. 61 and remarks by A. D. Kurskii, ibid., 1959:2, pp. 5–6).
[82] See "Berliner 57" and "Granick 59."

vantage. It allows for contact between planners and administrators and thus allows for the operation of certain pressure levers during the construction of the plan. What should perhaps be expected, therefore, is that the Russians will adopt I–O techniques in such a way as to combine it with these positive features of the material balances method.

If I–O techniques are adopted and thus the planning process speeded up, more time would be left for the troublesome specification stage. This would help, but an effective solution to the specification problem depends fundamentally on the creation of direct and stable relations between producers and users. It also depends on a diminution in the tightness of plans so as to lessen the degree of sellers' market and make the market power of buyers more equal to that of sellers.

This discussion has concentrated on centralized supply planning methods. It is theoretically possible, of course, for more decentralized methods to be used, ones that would give lower level units more freedom to make their own economic decisions. However, the efficacy of any meaningful decentralization would depend upon the significant improvement of the Soviet price system, which up to now has been incapable of playing an effective role in the Soviet industrial supply system.

SOURCES USED

Belkin 57: V. Belkin, "O primenenii elektronnykh vychislitel'nykh mashin v planirovanii i statistike narodnogo khoziaistva," Voprosy Ekonomiki, 1957 : 12.

Berliner 57: J. S. Berliner, "Factory and Manager in the U.S.S.R.," Cambridge, 1957.

Braginskii 54: B. I. Braginskii and N. S. Koval', "Organizatsiia planirovaniia narodnogo khoziaistva S.S.S.R." Moscow, 1954.

Demichev 57: G. M. Demichev, "Material'no-tekhnicheskoe snabzhenie na zheleznodorozhnom transporte," Moscow, 1957, (49 pp.).

Directivy: "Direktivy KPSS i sovetskogo pravitel'stva po khoziaistvennym voprosam, vols. I–IV," Moscow, 1957–58.

Efimov 57: A. N. Efimov, "Perestroika upravleniia promyshlennost'iu i stroitel'-stvom v S.S.S.R., Moscow, 1957.

Evans 54: W. Duane Evans, "Input-output Computations," from T. Barna (editor), "The Structural Interdependence of the Economy," (Proceedings of an International Conference on Input-output Analysis, Varenna, 1954) New York, N.Y.

Gal'perin 57: N. Gal'perin, "Sovremennye zadachi organizatsii material'notekhmicheskogo snabzheniia proizvodstva," Voprosy Ekonomiki, 1957 : 4.

Gal'perin 58: "Sovershenstvovanie material'no-tekhnicheskogo snabzheniia i bor'ba protiv mestnicheskikh tendentsii," "Voprosy Ekonomiki, 1958 : 7.

Gal'perin 57–1: "Novoe v organizatsii material'no-tekhnicheskogo snabzheniia, Gospolitizdat," Moscow, 1957.

Glusker 54: B. Glusker, P. Krylov, "O sisteme pokzatelei narodnokhoziaistvennogo plana," Planovoe Khoziaistvo, 1954, No. 5.

Granick 57: D. Granick, "Organization and Technology in Soviet Metalworking: Some Conditioning Factors," American Economic Review, XLVII : 2 (May 1957).

Granick 59: "An Organizational Model of Soviet Industrial Planning," Journal of Political Economy, LXVII:2 (April 1959).

Grebtsov 59: G. Grebtsov, "K voprosu o razrabotke svodnogo material'nogo balansa," Planovoe Khoziaistvo, 1959 : 6.

Grossman 55: G. Grossman, "In the Land of Paper Pyramids," "Problems of Communism," IV: 4 (July–August 1955).

Kalinin 58: I. Kalinin, "Sovershenstvovat' organizatsiiu material'no-tekhnicheskogo snabzheniia v promyshlennosti" Kommunist, 1958 : 18 (December 1958).

Karpov 58: P. Karpov, "Organizatsiia i planirovanie material'no-tekhnicheskogo snabzheniia v novykh usloviiakh upreavleniia promyshlennost'iu i stroitel' stvom," Planovoe Khoziaistvo, 1958: 7.

354

Koldomasov 56: Iu. Koldomasov, "Voprosy postroeniia material'nykh balansov v narodnokhoziaistvennom plane", Planovoe Khoziaistvo, 1956:4.

Koldomasov 59: _____, "Voprosy organizatsii i planirovaniia material'no-tekhnicheskogo snabzheniia," Planovoe Khoziaistvo, 1959:4.

Kosiachenko 46: G. Kosiachenko, "Preduprezhedenie disproportsii v narodnom khoziaistve—odna iz vazhneishikh zadach planirovaniia," Planovoe Khoziaistvo, 1946:4.

Lokshin 52: E. Iu. Lokshin, Planirovanie material'no-tekhnicheskogo snabzheniia narodnogo khoziaistva S.S.S.R., Moscow, 1952.

Nemchinov 59: V. S. Nemchinov, "Sovremennye problemy sovetskoi ekonomicheskoi nauki," Voprosy Ekonomiki, 1959:4.

Nikitin 58: S. Nikitin, "Ekonometrika v sovremennoi burzhuaznoi ekonomicheskoi nauke," Nauchnye doklady vysshei shkoly, ekonomicheskie nauki, 1958:2.

Novick 49: D. Novick, M. L. Anshen, W. C. Truppner, "Wartime Production Controls," New York, 1949.

Perov 58: G. V. Perov, "God raboty sovnarkhozov," Partiinaia zhizn', July 14, 1958.

Planovoe Khoziaistvo Editorial 58: "Planirovanie narodnogo khoziaistva—na uroven' vozrosshikh zadach," Planovoe Khoziaistvo, 1958:6.

Ritz 50: P. M. Ritz, Iterative Method for Applying a Bill of Goods to an Inter-industry Matrix," Technical Memorandum No. 1, Bureau of Labor Statistics, July 6, 1950, Washington, D.C.

Savkin 56: A. Savkin, "Zadachi uluchsheniia material'no-tekhnicheskogo snabzheniia promyshlennosti," Planovoe Khoziaistvo, 1956:1.

Shein 54: P. A. Shein, "Material'no-tekhnicheskoe snabzhenie sotsialisticheskogo promyshlennogo predpriiatiia," Moscow, 1954.

Strumilin 57: S. G. Strumilin, "Planirovanie v. S.S.S.R.," Moscow, 1957.

Tolkachev 58: A. Tolkachev, "Elektronnye mashiny i voprosy planirovaniia," Promyshlenno-ekonomicheskaia gazeta, Mar. 19, 1958, p. 2.

Turetskii 57: I. Turetskii, "Ob uluchshenii snabzheniia predpriatii i material' nykh zapasakh promyshlennosti," Voprosy Ekonomiki, 1957:4.

Waugh 50: F. V. Waugh, "Inversion of the Leontief Matrix by Power Series," Econometrica, 18:2 (April 1950).

Zhukov 54: V. N. Zhukov, "Voprosy raspredeleniia sredstov proizvodstva v promyshlennosti S.S.S.R.," Kandidatskaia dissertatsiia, Institut Ekonomiki an S.S.S.R., Moscow, 1954.   (Lenin Library, Moscow.)

SCARCE CAPITAL AND SOVIET DOCTRINE

By GREGORY GROSSMAN*

I. The Problem and Its Setting, 311. — II. *Exeunt* Economists — Enter Engineers, 315. — III. The Engineers' Theories, 320. — IV. Return of the Economists, 327. — V. The Economists' Attack and Its Aftermath, 333. — VI. Conclusion, 340.

The contest between doctrine and expediency among the "sources of Soviet conduct" awaits its judicious historian. The problem is as intricate as it is engaging, for expediency can wear the mask of ideology, while dogmatism may be transmuted into pragmatism by the felicitous touch of success. No doubt it will be in the major events of our time that the student will seek, and possibly find, his evidence. Yet, now and then, the true nature of things is tested in small matters as well as in large; especially if the matter, though minor in historical perspective, lies close to the core of socio-economic doctrine and at the same time bears directly on the actions of practical men. The episode in Soviet intellectual history to be presently described is of this sort. It remains to be seen whether the future historian of the mainsprings of Soviet behavior will find it of any relevance to his inquiry. In the meantime, the economist will recognize it as a fragment of *Dogmengeschichte* with regard to the theory of resource allocation in the Soviet Union.

I. THE PROBLEM AND ITS SETTING

The conflict examined here is that between the Marxian conception of value and the logic of the allocation of scarce resources to

*This article is based on my unpublished doctoral dissertation *Capital-Intensity: A Problem in Soviet Planning*, 1952 (on deposit at Widener Library and the Russian Research Center, Harvard University), to which the interested reader is referred for fuller exposition and documentation. It is a pleasure to acknowledge the Center's generous support of this study, and to thank Professor Alexander Gerschenkron, Mr. Edwin Kuh, and my colleagues at the Center for many valuable comments.

achieve posited goals; more precisely, between the absence of a value attached to capital *as such*, and the necessity for Soviet planners to husband their very scarce capital resources. Some comment on this specific problem has already appeared in western literature.[1]

It will be recalled that in the Marxian scheme of things exchange value is created by socially necessary labor alone. No other value-creating factors of production are recognized. It follows that no factor except labor is entitled to a functional remuneration, although (the theory holds) non-labor income does exist under capitalism thanks to the specific social relations making it possible. True, Marx recognized that under capitalism the tendency for profit rates to be equalized causes "prices of production" to deviate from "values" according to the relative amounts of capital invested, but there is no clear indication that he favored a similar deviation of prices from "values" in a socialist society. In any case, the Soviet authorities apparently understood him to mean that interest on capital is to have no important place in the cost structure of a socialist economy.

This interpretation found concrete legislative expression. After private enterprise was virtually eliminated and comprehensive planning installed, financial relationships and institutions were redefined by a series of laws issued during the years 1930 through 1932, collectively known as the Credit Reform.[2] The laws, amplified by executive orders, provided that a state-owned enterprise (the dominant type outside of agriculture) was to be endowed by the state with fixed and with much of working capital free of charge, although the enterprise remained responsible for the safeguarding of the principal value of the investment. A part of the working capital continues to be financed by short-term bank credit, but the interest charges are low and are levied chiefly for administrative reasons. Thus, with the exception of these relatively small charges, interest does not appear as a cost of

---

1. See especially: Holland Hunter, "The Planning of Investments in the Soviet Union," *Review of Economics and Statistics*, XXXI (Feb. 1949), 54–62; J. M., "Some Recent Developments in Soviet Economic Thought: Economic Choice Between Technological Alternatives," *Soviet Studies* (Glasgow), I (Oct. 1949), 119–27; A. Zauberman, "The Prospects for Soviet Investigations into Capital Efficiency," *ibid.*, I (Apr. 1950), 328–33; Charles Bettelheim, "The Discussion on the Problem of Alternative Investment Projects," *ibid.*, II (July 1950), 22–42; Maurice Dobb, "A Note on the Discussion of the Problem of Choice Between Alternative Investment Projects," *ibid.*, II (Jan. 1951), 289–95; and Norman Kaplan, "Investment Alternatives in Soviet Economic Theory," *Journal of Political Economy*, LX (Apr. 1952), 133–44.

2. A discussion of the Credit Reform in English may be found in Arthur Z. Arnold, *Banks, Credit, and Money in Soviet Russia* (New York, 1937), chaps. XII and XV.

production on the books of a Soviet state-owned enterprise, and no interest (with negligible exceptions, to be exact) is paid for the use of fixed capital.

These changes were accompanied by authoritative attacks in the literature against "bourgeois fetishism in science and technology" and the use of "capitalist methods of solving technical problems." The dominant attitude was perhaps summarized by an author writing in an engineering journal: " 'Interest charges' . . . artificially diminish the effectiveness of utilization of natural resources and capital investments. 'Interest charges' . . . retard the rise in the organic composition of 'fixed capital' and go counter to the technological policy of the party and the government."[3]

But although capital as such may appear as a free good to the Soviet accountant, it is hardly that to the Soviet economy. On the contrary, it is, and has constantly been, scarce in relation to the high production goals of the regime. Being scarce, its relative efficiency in alternative employments must be considered if maximum economic benefit is to be derived from a given amount of investible resources. Moreover, since an important range of investment decisions is actually made in a decentralized fashion — on this more presently — rational allocation of capital requires that a scarcity price, i.e., a rate of interest, be communicated to each decision-maker and he be required to abide by it. According to well-known maximization conditions, the rate of interest should be uniform throughout the economy and such as to equate the demand with the exogenous (i.e., politically determined) supply of investment funds.[4]

Very little is known about exactly how the *major* planning decisions are being made. But it is probably quite safe to assume that for the longer-range (say, five-year) plans, such crucial questions as the part of the national product to be devoted to investment over the prospective plan period, and the bill of final and key intermediate goods in its main outline, are resolved on the highest levels of the regime and are political decisions in the full sense of the phrase. The breakdown of total investment by ministries (roughly corresponding

3. L. M. Lezinov, "K voprosy o tekhniko-ekonomicheskikh raschetakh pri proektirovanii gidroelektrostantsii" ("On Technical-Economic Calculations in the Designing of Hydroelectric Stations"), *Gidrotekhnicheskoe stroitel'stvo* (*Hydrotechnical Construction*), 1935, No. 8, pp. 4–5; quotes in the original.

4. The uniformity condition presupposes that the other price parameters facing the decision-makers are meaningful for the purpose of maximization. Insofar as this is not the case, departures from a uniform interest rate may be warranted.

to branches of the economy) and their subdivisions, and the more detailed specification of the bill of final goods,[5] are probably also essentially political decisions and the results of intragovernmental bargaining.   The composition of the prospective bill of final *consumers'* goods may be affected by consumers' preferences, as they are vaguely transmitted to the central authorities, although a regimen of consumer sovereignty cannot be said to exist. Needless to say, even the highest political decisions are constrained by technological and economic considerations, but not uniquely determined by them. Moreover, there must be a certain reasonable, but again not unique, connection between the investment resources provided to a ministry and its production targets.

The ministry having received its longer-range production targets and having been informed of the approximate amount of investment funds at its future disposal, the actual production units necessary to realize these targets must be designed. This is the job of the highly specialized "project-making organizations" (*proektnye organizatsii*), of which there are usually several to an economic ministry. In time sequence, project-making falls between the preparation of the longer-range plan and the compilation of the annual plan. The project-maker, an engineer, is given the rough location of the future production unit, the desired annual output of the specific product or products, target dates for completion, and possibly a series of economic constraints (availability of material and equipment, labor problems) and noneconomic (strategic, sanitary, etc.) minimum requirements. On the basis of these data, and with the aid of the existing cost-price parameters, he is to transform the assignment into a set of blueprints for actual construction *plus* estimates of the cost of construction and the cost of operation of the plant. Note that the project-maker has no say as to whether the plant is to be built at all. However, he is typically faced with a number of *technological variants* (as the Russians put it), such as greater or lesser automaticity of equipment, alternative production systems, substitute materials and fuels, and so forth. Moreover, if the annual output of the production unit is expected to reach full capacity only after a number of years, e.g., traffic on a railroad, he may also have the choice of postponing a part of the capital outlays. In economic language, he must select the proper degree of *capital-intensity* of the project. But from the standpoint of the economy, the joint action of all project-makers, dis-

5. The term "final goods" should be understood to include those "key" intermediate goods, for which the output targets are subject to determination at high political levels. Coal, steel, petroleum, and other basic *materials* of similar importance probably belong in this group.

persed over the economy, has the effect of allocating a scarce means, currently investible capital, to achieve posited ends: the set of the "politically" determined production targets (and associated non-economic desiderata) at their lowest (i.e., most detailed) level. Analogously, from the standpoint of the smallest unit of "political" decision (in this sense), such as a ministry or subdivision thereof, the problem is one of rational allocation of investment funds within its own jurisdiction.

II. *Exeunt* ECONOMISTS — ENTER ENGINEERS

As indicated above, by the early thirties the ideological climate became hostile to any use of the concept of interest, and it was virtually "decreed out" of the Soviet cost structure. Nevertheless, one would search in vain in the Soviet *economic* literature after 1931, and until 1945, for any attempt to substitute new, "Marxian," principles of the allocation of capital among competing projects, from which a set of new criteria of capital-intensity of individual projects could be derived.[6] This silence, it must be remembered, coincided with the acceleration of economic expansion to unprecedented rates, extreme shortage of capital, and a leap from an obsolescent technology to a most modern one. Yet this silence was something entirely new in itself, for only a few years earlier, from 1927 through 1930, the then vibrant and often brilliant Soviet economic literature abounded with essays on this very range of problems.

The polemic over what then became known as the problem of the "effectiveness of capital investment" was a logical offshoot of the so-called industrialization debate, the great controversy of the twenties over the direction and speed of Russia's impending economic race with the capitalist world.[7] All of the participants ostensibly proceeded from Marxian premises and concepts, but their positions varied

6. To be sure, the literature of these years paid attention to the problem of balanced ("proportionate") development of the planned economy. But this refers to the question of what to produce and in what quantities, and not to precisely how much capital to devote to each line of production.

7. This debate, one of the great debates in the history of economics, has received little attention from western economists. Most of the original literature is unfortunately not available in English or other western languages. For some recent analyses in English see: Maurice Dobb, *Soviet Economic Development Since 1917* (New York, 1948), chap. 8; Alexander Erlich, "Preobrazhenskii and the Economics of Soviet Industrialization," this *Journal*, LXIV (Feb. 1950), 57–88; *idem*, "The Soviet Industrialization Controversy," 1953, an unpublished dissertation on deposit with the New School for Social Research, New York, and the Russian Research Center, Harvard University; Adam Kaufman, "The Origin of the 'Political Economy of Socialism,'" *Soviet Studies* (Glasgow) IV (Jan. 1953), 243–72.

widely. Some of them, at one extreme, readily placed their trust in the normative role of profitability and the rate of return on capital, though frequently qualified with regard to the development of "key" branches of the economy.[8] At the other extreme, even the very "commensurability" of capital outlays and current costs was denied, and decision was relegated entirely to the planner's arbitrary and eclectic judgment.[9] The product/capital ratio received much attention at that time as a measure of the "effectiveness of capital investment," frequently in a naive way, but sometimes with considerable sophistication.[1] The literature of this period is vast and varied; one cannot justly do more than mention it in this context.

The discussion ceased abruptly and without resolution of the differences. A plausible explanation of this sudden end is that the economic literature disappeared with the economists themselves. The years 1930 and 1931 saw a thorough purge of the economic staffs of government departments, especially those engaged in planning. Many, probably most, of the names vanished from the pages of economic journals forever. Both those who survived, physically or professionally, and newcomers refrained from disturbing a subject so eminently popular with their hapless colleagues. Economic literature turned from relatively free discussion of policy matters and their theoretical justifications to treatment of less controversial topics. The subject of investment choice was a chief victim.

But while the Soviet economist could, and for these or other reasons did, avoid raising the problem of the capital-intensity of a production process, the project-making engineer was forced by the very nature of his everyday work to take a stand on the issue. It is hardly surprising that under the institutional and ideological conditions already mentioned most Soviet project-makers from the early

8. See N. N. Shaposhnikov, "Ob osnovnykh printsipakh industrializatsii" ("On the Fundamental Principles of Industrialization"), *Ekonomicheskoe obozrenie (Economic Review)*, 1927, No. 1, pp. 42–53; A. I. Segal', "K voprosu ob effektivnosti kapital'nykh vlozhenii" ("On the Effectiveness of Capital Investment"), *Planovoe khoziaistvo (Planned Economy)*, 1927, No. 12, pp. 118–26; A. M. Ginzburg, "Nekotorye predposylki promyshlennoi piatiletki" ("Certain Premises of the Five-Year Plan for Industry"), *Ekonomicheskoe obozrenie*, 1927, No. 4, p. 29.

9. M. Barun, "Ob effektivnosti kapital'nogo stroitel'stva promyshlennosti" ("On the Effectiveness of Industrial Capital Construction"), *Puti industrializatsii (Ways of Industrialization)*, 1929, No. 3, p. 25.

1. E.g., the use of the Cobb-Douglas function by R. Gol'dberg in "O metodakh ischisleniia effektivnosti kapital'nykh vlozhenii" ("On the Methods of Computing the Effectiveness of Capital Investment"), *ibid.*, 1929, No. 11, pp. 10–24.

thirties on have apparently been omitting capital charges[2] in their calculations. That is, faced with a set of technological alternatives with which to produce a given bill of goods, they chose, as a rule, that variant which showed the lowest prospective operating cost, *excluding* interest on capital. In other words, they used an effective rate of zero and tended to select variants of correspondingly "high" capital-intensity.[3] Some engineers[4] approved of this procedure because it militated in favor of the relatively more "advanced" technical solutions — an important notion in the folklore of Soviet industrialization. However, since investment resources were clearly not so abundant in any sector of the economy as to warrant a zero rate, it must be inferred that the capital requirements of most projects were at some point curtailed by administrative decision.

But certain Soviet engineers, including some very outstanding ones, were soon to register disapproval of the omission of capital charges in the design of projects. They proceeded to develop various theories to justify the use of capital charges and to explain their nature, and frequently succeeded in incorporating these "heretical" methods in the official instructions of individual project-making organizations. What motivated these engineers to swim against the ideological and institutional tide of their day?[5]

There seem to have been two main considerations. (1) The

2. The term "capital charge" here refers to an interest rate or any other device having the effect of assigning a price to capital as such. It is not to be understood to include a depreciation allowance, which is not a fee for the use of *capital as such*, but the cost of using up a specific *capital good*.

3. A qualification must be entered here. There are scattered indications that some time *before* the Credit Reform, the Gosplan either directed or proposed that project-makers use a 6 per cent rate in their calculations. The rate was occasionally mentioned in the early thirties as though still in effect, but it is doubtful that it was much used after the Credit Reform. I do not know when the ruling was revoked; indeed, its very existence has been questioned by an opponent of the practice. (See my *Capital-Intensity* . . . , pp. 119 and 107.)

4. See, *e.g.*, the quotation on p. 313.

5. It must be stressed for the sake of correct appreciation of the history of the problem that these were engineers and *not* economists. It is unfortunate that Kaplan (*op. cit.*) lumps them with the economists who have entered the picture since 1945 under the common designation of "economists." Zauberman is perhaps closer to the mark when he speaks of " 'industrial' economists" (*op. cit.*, p. 328). Of the authors discussed by Kaplan, Aivazian, Gubin, Lur'e, Vedeneev, as well as others, are (or were) engineers by virtue of their primary training and occupation. Khachaturov is a borderline case: though a well-known transportation economist, and a corresponding-member of the Academy of Sciences of the USSR in this capacity, he has been apparently very close to the technical side of the industry. For instance, he has served as director of the All-Union Scientific Research Institute for Railroad Transportation, and as editor of the journal, *Tekhnika zheleznykh dorog (Railroad Engineering)*.

project-maker was prompted to develop criteria for the allocation of scarce capital among projects within the purview of his administrative unit (e.g., ministry), which would have a more rational basis than mere administrative fiat. For example, this seems to have been a compelling consideration in the railroad industry, which recognized it in an official document (the "TUM") as early as 1931.[6]

In this regard, the engineer was challenged by two special and immediate difficulties. One arose from the possibility of continuous variation in important technical (engineering) parameters, frequently leading to the existence of a continuous substitution function between capital outlays and current operating expenses. Thus, for example, the grades on railroads and highways can be varied almost continuously (within limits) by the designing engineer, and the lower the gradient, the lower will be the future operating expenses, though at the cost of higher initial outlay (i.e., higher capital-intensity). Similar possibilities of continuous variation arise with respect to the radius of curvature of roads and railways, location of tunnels, cross-section of flumes and canals at hydroelectric stations, diameter of transmission wire, and so forth. In the absence of discrete alternatives there are no "obvious" choices on which administrative decision can rest, and the Soviet project-maker very soon found himself in search of criteria for optimum capital-intensity in cases of this nature.[7]

The other challenge arose in connection with those projects where a part of the capital outlay is postponable, though at the disadvantage of incurring a larger nominal outlay in the future.

6. G. I. Chernomordik, "K konferentsii po peresmotru Tekhnicheskikh uslovii proektirovaniia zheleznykh dorog" ("Conference to Revise the Technical Specifications for Designing Railroads"), *Transportnoe stroitel'stvo* (*Transport Construction*), 1931, No. 6, p. 18; and *idem*, "O metodologii sravneniia variantov zhel. dorog" ("On the Methodology of Comparing Railroad Variants"), *ibid.*, 1932, No. 7, p. 19. "TUM" is abbreviation of the Russian equivalent of "technical specifications for the designing of mainline railroads"; the document itself was not available to me.

7. This type of problem has been of particular concern to Soviet electrical engineers. A controversy with regard to the optimum cross-section and gradient of canals at hydraulic stations began in 1933 and continued on the pages of *Gidrotekhnicheskoe stroitel'stvo* through most of the thirties. By 1940, Kukel'-Kraevskii gave a generalized solution with the aid of a capital charge (*Elektrichestvo* [*Electricity*], 1940, No. 8, pp. 30–40), which was soon substantially incorporated in an official instruction (see *Gidr. str.*, 1941, No. 1, pp. 4–8); but the instruction avoided Kukel's error of linking the capital charge to the durability of the equipment. In 1950, a controversy flared up on the pages of *Elektrichestvo* with regard to the applicability of interest to the determination of the optimum diameter of transmission wire, although the problem is identical in essence.

Clearly, a time-coefficient, such as an interest rate in the capitalist world, is indispensable for rational choice, unless one subscribes to the patently nonsensical position (particularly so under Soviet conditions of rapid accumulation) that, *ceteris paribus*, any nominally lower capital expense is to be preferred to a higher one *regardless* of time reference.[8] The classical example is perhaps the choice between building a double-track railroad initially, or double-tracking later at higher cost when the volume of traffic rises to require it.

(2) There was a desire to avoid absurdly capital-intensive solutions, such as might be brought about by a zero rate of interest in some cases. For instance, in railroad construction, unusually low grades, wide curves, long tunnels, and heavy bridges become appropriate if capital is free. In the power industry, where this reaction was particularly marked, every hydraulic plant becomes preferable to every thermal one, and of the former, the most grandiose projects become worthwhile.[9] To be sure, *a priori*, there is nothing absurd about such capital-intensive solutions, though they would have been unnecessarily capital-using under the specific Soviet conditions. The reaction which they provoked on the part of the Soviet engineers must be attributed to their doing violence to the common sense of the experienced professional man.

These considerations were buoyed by the strong current of enthusiasm for rationality which flowed through the professional literature of the time. Now that the old "chaotic" society had been superseded by a scientifically planned economy, decisions such as the choice between technological alternatives were to rest not on blind preferences but on conscious and rational calculation.

It must be emphasized that the engineers (and the economists who later joined them) were concerned with developing criteria of choice between technological alternatives of producing a given future output stream. They explicitly and clearly distinguished this problem from the determination of the *bill of goods* of the economy, and stressed that they were not concerned with the latter.[1] Where not

8. Conceptually, the "postponability" problem is identical with the problem of optimum capital-intensity; the essence of either case is choice between two or more time-patterns of outlays (on capital and current account). However, Soviet writers draw a sharp distinction between them; see, for example, Khachaturov's exposition as summarized by Hunter, *loc. cit.*

9. For these reasons, I. G. Aleksandrov, the author of the Dnieper hydroelectric project and an outstanding Soviet engineer of the time, came out squarely for interest charges. His unusual formula is discussed below (p. 324). See "Novyi transport" ("The New Transport"), *Sotsialisticheskaia rekonstruktsiia i nauka (Socialist Reconstruction and Science)*, 1933, No. 7, pp. 59–60.

1. For instance, see the distinction drawn by A. L. Lur'e in "Metody sopostavleniia eksploatatsionnykh raskhodov i kapitalovlozhenii pri ekonomi-

explicitly stated, the restriction is evident from the treatment itself. The problem was also frequently posed as one of commeasuring capital outlays and current costs. In effect, the criteria advanced were those of the capital-intensity of individual production units. Insofar as some form of return to capital was proposed as a guide to investment, it was only the return on incremental amounts of capital, realized as annual cost savings in the production of a *fixed* output. The test of the profitability of an enterprise as a whole was not invoked. Much less was return on capital advocated as a guide to the composition of the bill of goods (except in the trivial sense that any criterion of capital-intensity must perforce affect the demand for the output of preceding stages of production). One cannot agree with the conclusions drawn by Kaplan that "adoption of the proposals advanced [by some of the advocates of the use of capital charges] would serve to reverse the historical emphasis in Soviet investment policy" on producers' goods rather than consumers' goods,[2] or even that "the Soviet literature on investment choice . . . suggests, or perhaps forecasts, the possibility of wide disagreement over the future *course* of Soviet economic development."[3] While the authors in question might well have been harboring sentiments of doubt and opposition to the prevailing policy — one cannot tell — they were at least cautious enough not to advertise them.

III. The Engineers' Theories

As might be expected from what has been said so far, the theories advanced by the engineers varied greatly. With regard to the *rationale* for the use of capital charges in project-making at least three main lines of reasoning can be discerned.

(1) Reference to a more or less developed concept of opportunity cost was especially marked among those engineers who were seeking a rational method of allocating scarce investment funds. The railroad industry provides the best example. There, as we have seen, basic principles were officially expressed as early as 1931 in the "TUM," though the concept of opportunity *at the margin* took some time to develop. An approach toward marginalism was made by

cheskoi otsenke tekhnicheskikh meropriiatii" ("Methods of Collating Operating Costs and Capital Investment in Connection with Economic Appraisal of Technical Measures"), in E. D. Khanukov and V. I. Chernyshev, *Voprosy ekonomiki zheleznodorozhnogo transporta* (*Problems of the Economics of Railroad Transportation*) (Moscow, 1948), pp. 5 ff.

2. *Op. cit.*, p. 143.
3. *Ibid.:* my italics.

M. M. Protod'iakonov in 1934.[4]   The attempt apparently provoked
no significant criticism on doctrinal grounds at the time, although
marginalism always has been a serious ideological transgression.   It
was only in the forties that the theory of investment choice was
pushed close to its logical limits by Lur'e.[5]

Like his predecessors, Lur'e based the need for a capital charge
in project-making — he spoke outright of *protsentirovanie*, i.e., the
use of interest rates — on the ability of increments of capital to
substitute for future operating costs, and called the ratio of such
future annual savings to the incremental application of capital —
the "relative effectiveness of capital investment." Assuming a fixed
bill of goods and a definite investment fund for the economy as a
whole, he argued on grounds familiar to western economists that
capital should be allocated between lines of production so as to
equalize its marginal relative effectiveness in all uses.   The resulting
equilibrium rate, the *"norm* of relative effectiveness" or Δ, should
be assigned as a parameter to every project-maker, and should serve
as the criterion of the capital-intensity of each project.[6]   In this
manner, future current costs of production for the whole economy
would be minimized, given the production targets and the size of
the investment fund.   This was the purpose of Lur'e's model.

Lur'e stressed the desirability of a uniform capital charge (Δ)
over the whole economy, but lacking this, he accepted a single rate
for the railroad industry alone.[7]   This concession, plus his failure
to be concerned with the meaningfulness of the rest of the Soviet
price-cost structure, underscore the essential orientation of the whole
engineering literature on the subject: to achieve the best allocation
of appropriated capital funds within the limited purview of the
individual administrative unit.

It is interesting to note that Khachaturov, who (as we have

4. *Izyskaniia i proektirovanie zheleznykh dorog* (*Surveying and Designing
Railroads*) (Moscow, 1934), p. 127; the work was not available to me, and is here
cited after Lur'e, *op. cit.*, p. 52.   See also V. N. Orlov and V. V. Povorozhenko,
Tekhniko-ekonomicheskie raschety po organizatsii zheleznodorozhnykh perevozok
(*Technical-Economic Calculations in Railroad Traffic Management*) (Moscow, 1943),
p. 16; and T. S. Khachaturov, *Osnovy ekonomiki zheleznodorozhnogo transporta*
(*Economic Principles of Railroad Transportation*) (Moscow, 1946), I, 111.

5. *Op. cit.*   His dissertation for the degree of *kandidat* of engineering science,
in which the theory was first developed (see Khachaturov, *op. cit.*, p. 103), was
not available to me.

6. The relevant algebraic relationships are summarized by Kaplan, *op. cit.*,
p. 134.   Note that Δ is the marginal rate of substitution between current costs and
capital outlay for the isoquant representing the planned fixed bill of goods.

7. *Op. cit.*, p. 43.

seen)[8] straddles the borderline between the economic and engineering disciplines, espoused the theory and methodology of investment choice developed by the engineers, but firmly rejected the marginalist excursions.[9] Was his restraint derived from Marxian convictions or was it merely a step of prudence?

The continual search for a theory (or methodology) of capital allocation based on an opportunity cost concept in the railroad industry and elsewhere[1] went in numerous directions, thus underscoring the dispersed and *ad hoc* nature of the attempts, and the lack of theoretical economic background on the part of the authors. False leads were often persistently followed. For instance, in highway construction it became the usual and officially recommended method to accept that variant of a road improvement project which promises the *highest* ratio of annual savings in the cost of traffic and maintenance (as compared with costs on the unimproved road) to the one-time cost of improvement, rather than to push capital outlay until the marginal "return" on investment reaches a predetermined minimum admissible value.[2]

It has been usual in Soviet engineering literature on investment choice to define opportunity cost in terms of the *savings in current operating cost* which a certain amount of capital can achieve in alternative employment. The underlying assumption is one of a fixed and preassigned output program. In only a few known cases was opportunity cost visualized in terms of the *additional product* which the particular amount of capital might bring about if applied elsewhere.[3] Among them should be noted the unique contribution by N. M. Abramovich,[4] a production engineer, which is of some anti-

8. Note 5, p. 317.

9. *Op. cit.*, chap. III, esp. pp. 108–12; see also his debate with Lur'e and others summarized in *Tekhnika zheleznykh dorog*, 1947, No. 5, p. 29; as well as the discussion by Hunter (*op. cit.*) and Kaplan (*op. cit.*, p. 135).

1. E.g., in highway construction, electric power, machine shop operation, machine building, waterworks, industial transport.

2. The literature in this field is fairly extensive. E.g., see A. I. Anokhin (ed.), *Dorozhnoe delo (Roads)* (Moscow, 1935), pp. 48, 57, 209; *Spravochnik dorozhnika. Izyskaniia, proektirovanie, stroitel'-stvo, soderzhanie i remont dorog (Manual for Highway Personnel. Surveying, Designing, Construction, Maintenance, and Repair of Roads)* (Kiev, 1949), pp. 17 ff.

3. One such exception was the elaborate approach — more ingenious than successful — developed by V. G. Aivaz'ian in "Osnovnye polozheniia energo-ekonomicheskikh raschetov pri proektirovanii gidrostantsii" ("Basic Principles of Power-Economic Calculations in the Designing of Hydroelectric Stations"), *Gidr. str.*, 1945, Nos. 1–2, pp. 8–12; see also Kaplan, *loc. cit.*, and my *Capital-Intensity . . .* , pp. 250–53.

4. "Normirovanie razmerov nezavershennogo proizvodstva v mashino-stroenii" ("Determining the Proper Amount of Goods in Process in Machine-

quarian interest to western economists because of its striking formal similarities to the period analysis of the Keynesian models. His problem was to choose among production methods with varying requirements of goods in process, i.e., varying capital-intensities. Lacking a measure of capital scarcity, Abramovich proceeded to find one in the additional annual output foregone by virtue of the tying-down of one ruble's worth of capital in a specific use. In brief, he traced the capital needs at his and preceding stages of production, summed the convergent series in "multiplier" fashion to obtain a capital coefficient, and used the reciprocal of the coefficient (Domar's "sigma"!) as a rate of interest. Whatever the inherent merits of the method, Abramovich's attempt illustrates well the pains taken by some Soviet engineers to fill a void in their economic tool-box, a void which they sensed had to be filled if they were to proceed rationally.

(2) Another and fairly large group of engineers justified the use of interest and other capital charges on the basis of the economy's need to accumulate capital for new net investment. This approach, in one form or another, has been typical of the arguments advanced by Soviet power engineers in defense of the use of capital charges in project-making since at least the late twenties.[5] It has been advanced by engineers in other industries as well. The authors do not explain why capital has to bear a charge justified and determined on this basis; they present it as a self-evident proposition. Actually, of course, net investment can be just as well financed from other sources such as taxes, and in Soviet experience it has been in fact financed predominantly from indirect taxes. One gets the impression that the proposition is advanced not as a result of careful a priori reasoning, but as a rationalization of the "heretical" practice of employing interest in project-making, while the practice, in its turn, is followed in order to avoid "absurdly" capital-intensive solutions. The rationalization may, however, be reinforced by a misplaced analogy with capitalism, where the return on capital is at the same time (at least in Marxian conception) the financial source of new investment.

Building"), *Organizatsiia upravleniia* (*The Organization of Management*), 1935, No. 2, pp. 27–55.

5. E.g., see A. A. Gorev, "K voprosu o tom, chto takoe 'ekonomicheski naivygodneishee sooruzhenie'" ("What is the Economically Optimum Structure?"), *Planovoe khoziaistvo* (*Planned Economy*), 1929, No. 7, pp. 199–224; the views of Zakharov and Aivaz'ian as summarized in *Gidr. str.*, 1935, No. 1, p. 8; Vedeneev, Aivaz'ian, and Gubin in *Gidr. str.*, 1945, Nos. 1–2, pp. 5–16; F. F. Gubin, *Gidroelektricheskie stantsii* (*Hydroelectric Stations*) (Moscow-Leningrad, 1949), chap. 14. The last-named author would even burden capital with a charge for financing general government expenditures (pp. 661, 705).

The level of the interest rate in this case is usually equated with the annual rate of growth of some aggregative series, such as the fixed and variable capital of the economy, all industry or a specific industry, or the national product. Aleksandrov's formula falls into this category, and may be cited as a *curiosum*, also because of the importance and prestige of its author. Aleksandrov regarded the level of the interest rate as a function of the supply of capital and of the rate of growth of the economy. He therefore proposed that it be determined according to the following formula:[6]

$$\text{rate of interest} = r \left(\frac{n_0 - n}{n_0} \right)^2,$$

where r = annual rate of growth of output of the economy,

         n_0 = capital per person, in rubles, corresponding to the level of "sufficient saturation,"

         n = capital per person, in rubles, at the existing level.

No proof was given. Clearly, Aleksandrov was misguided in his belief that the appropriate rate of interest, i.e., the marginal opportunity cost of capital for any planning period, can be expressed by a simple mechanistic relationship. The proposal seems to have found virtually no response among Soviet engineers.

(3) A considerable number of Soviet engineers in several fields have advanced the criterion of the minimum sum of capital and current costs over an arbitrary period (T years).[7] Not infrequently this consideration is combined with the requirement of earning a return on capital for the purpose of financing new investment (see (2), *supra* p. 323).[8] The reasoning behind this approach is not entirely clear, but it seems to be a compromise between the need to take formal account of the size of capital investment, dictated by common sense considerations, and a reluctance to do so by means of explicit interest charges for reasons of doctrine or prudence. One might also mention the possible normative implications (in a Marxian

6. Aleksandrov, *loc. cit.* The equation in the original has n in the denominator; this is implausible, and the author's numerical example supports the formulation given above.

7. For instance, in electric power — the articles by Kukel'-Kraevskii, Vedeneev, Aivaz'ian, and Gubin, cited above; in general construction — S. V. Bashinskii, "Metod sravnitel'noi tekhniko-ekonomicheskoi otsenki stroitel'nykh konstruktsii" ("A Method of Comparative Technical-Economic Appraisal of Structures"), *Stroitel'naia promyshlennost'* (*The Construction Industry*), 1947, No. 1, pp. 18–20; in coal mining — L. D. Sheviakov, *Osnovy teorii proektirovaniia ugol'nykh shakht* (*Fundamentals of the Theory of Coal Mine Design*) (Moscow, 1950), pp. 296 ff.; in flood control — I. A. Lifanov, *Organizatsiia chashi vodokhranilishcha* (*Preparing the Reservoir Basin*) (Moscow-Leningrad), 1946, p. 183.

8. E.g., the articles in the field of electric power just cited.

framework) of minimum labor outlay, here represented by the sum of capital and current costs. However, the last explanation is weakened by the usual practice of taking current cost *inclusive of* depreciation allowances or actual replacement outlays. Thus, the labor on capital account is counted twice — once for depreciation or replacement, and once again as the initial capital outlay, i.e., in effect as a capital charge.

It can be easily discovered by dividing the sum in question by T (and assuming a uniform stream of annual current operating costs) that this procedure in effect is equivalent to applying an interest charge of $\dfrac{100}{T}$ per cent to the initial capital outlay. Its weakness lies in the arbitrary nature of T. In many instances the authors attempted to avoid arbitrariness by equating or otherwise relating T to the useful life of the equipment. Needless to say, such a procedure is fallacious, since the useful life of the capital good has no direct bearing on the scarcity of capital as such.[9]

The terminology and formal presentation of capital charges by their advocates underwent some change. Various aliases and euphemisms for the term "interest" (*protsenty*) appeared quite early. For instance, the railroad engineers associated with the "TUM" of 1931 spoke of the "effectiveness of investment," and represented its "norm" by the neutral symbol "Δ." Since the middle thirties, the term "interest" has been infrequently used, and such phrases as "the coefficient (or 'norm') of relative effectiveness of capital investment" have become current. Another favorite form, especially outside the railroads, has been the reciprocal of "relative effectiveness of capital investment" — the number of years in which the return on the additional investment (realized as savings in annual costs) is expected to attain the value of the initial capital outlay. This has been called the "period of recoupment" (*srok okupaemosti*), and is essentially the American businessman's "pay-off period." A maximum admissible pay-off period, instead of its reciprocal, the minimum admissible value of "relative effectiveness," then serves as a criterion of capital-intensity.[1] But the pay-off period is a clumsy device for most computations and its reciprocal, the interest rate (by this or any other name, or none), is sooner or later reverted to by nearly every author.

The engineers were careful to dissociate the capital charges advanced by them from the capitalist category of interest, even to

9. E.g., Kukel'-Kraevskii, *op. cit.*, pp. 33–34; Vedeneev, *op. cit.*, pp. 5–6; Bashinskii, *op. cit.*, p. 19; Sheviakov, *op. cit.*, p. 296.
1. See Kaplan, *op. cit.*, p. 134, for a summary of the algebraic relationships.

the extent of asserting that there is nothing in common between the two. The distinction was said to lie in the fact that the proposed capital charges are mere calculating devices, and are not a price paid for the use of capital or a form of personal income, as they are under capitalist conditions.[2] The case is not without a grain of validity, though greatly (and understandably) overstated. Like "capitalist" interest, the various devices proposed by the engineers aim at limiting or postponing the demand for capital in individual projects. (Whether a "price" for capital is established thereby is a question of semantics.) Some authors saw in these devices a means of approximating an optimum allocation of investment funds; others merely sought to avoid absurd solutions. Here the analogy ceases, for the capital charges are to have no other function commonly exercised by their "capitalist" counterpart. Indeed, their champions have been so modest in claiming a rightful place for capital charges as to fall into error. The engineers have in all cases (that is, since the early thirties) failed to require that the proposed "interest" enter into the accounting cost of the project, and thus become a price-forming element. Thus they remained true to Soviet *accounting* practice, at the expense of contradicting the logic of their own position. For if prices of intermediate goods do not incorporate the "cost" of capital, decisions with regard to capital-intensity at the subsequent stages of production are not independent of the degree of vertical integration in the industry.[3]

Strange as it may seem, a number of engineers were later criticized on doctrinal grounds for resorting to *compound* interest, that is, for merely employing a certain mathematical technique. Actually, compounding was resorted to very little, thanks to the usual assumption of instantaneous capital outlays and uniform annual operating costs. Where the central problem was the postponability of outlays, compounding was more difficult to avoid, though still attempted.[4]

2. See Orlov and Povorozhenko, *op. cit.*, p. 16; Khachaturov, *op. cit.*, pp. 104, 112; Gubin, *Hydroelectric Stations*, p. 705.

3. However, the project-maker was often cautioned, and sometimes ordered, to take note of the induced capital requirements elsewhere in the economy on a more or less *ad hoc* basis.

4. I. A. Romanenko, "Tekhniko-ekonomicheskoe proektirovanie dorozhnykh pokrytii" ("Technical-Economic Design of Highway Pavement"), *Stroitel'stvo dorog (Road Building)*, XII (1945), 2–4; and A. V. Gorinov, *Proektirovanie zheleznykh dorog (Designing Railroads)* (3d ed.; Moscow, 1948), II, 392 ff. An interesting case of disguising the use of compound interest appears in Bashinskii's article (*op. cit.*, p. 19), where a "durability coefficient" was introduced to compensate for differences in durability between two competing project variants. The nature of the concept was not explained, but a table of such coefficients was given. At first sight, the values appear arbitrary, and the author was indeed criticized

It must be remembered that these discussions on the propriety of capital charges under Soviet conditions went on in the darker corners of the all-encompassing ideological edifice, out of the direct line of vision of the guardians of doctrinal purity. The questions were debated by professional project-makers and other engineers, within the confines of drafting rooms or on the pages of narrowly specialized journals, in reference to specific constructional problems, and under the protective covering of mathematical symbols and esoteric terminology. These facts may explain why the "general" Soviet economist showed no signs of awareness of the engineering literature on investment choice until as late as the middle forties.

Even so, Marxian precepts were occasionally appealed to by the engineers, especially by the opponents of the use of capital charges.[5] The substitution of other terms for "interest"; the frequent resort to its reciprocal form, the "recoupment period"; and occasional heroic attempts to devise formal methods of allowing for the scarcity of capital without resort to any mathematical variant of the interest rate[6] — they all point to self-consciousness on the part of the advocates of capital charges in treading a path so uncomfortably near the abyss of ideological heresy.

IV. Return of the Economists

Not until 1946, after a decade and a half of silence, did Soviet economists return to the question of investment choice on the project-making level with the publication of two notable, though very dissimilar, articles by V. V. Novozhilov and S. G. Strumilin, respectively. Novozhilov's 1946 article[7] was actually the second of three. The first,[8] which appeared in 1939, confined itself to exploring the comparability of output streams and is not significant for this study, except insofar as it presented some of the author's fundamental

in Soviet literature on this score. Upon scrutiny, it appeared that the values are ratios of annuities (at a certain rate of interest, suggested by the author). This, of course, requires compounding.

5. See the summary of divergent views in the hydroelectric field reported in *Gidr. str.*, 1935, No. 1, pp. 7–18.

6. *E.g.*, see the two sources cited above, p. 326, note 4.

7. "Metody nakhozhdeniia minimuma zatrat v sotsialisticheskom khoziastve" ("Methods of Finding the Input Minimum in a Socialist Economy"), *Leningradskii politekhnicheskii institut imeni M. I. Kalinina-Trudy (The Leningrad Kalinin Polytechnic Institute — Papers)*, 1946, No. 1, pp. 322–27.

8. "Metody soizmereniia narodnokhoziaistvennoi effektivnosti planovykh i proektnykh variantov" ("Methods of Commeasuring the Economic Effectiveness of Variants in Planning and Project-making"), *Trudy Leningradskogo industrial'nogo instituta (Papers of the Leningrad Industrial Institute)*, 1939, No. 4.

postulates. The third article,[9] not available to me, apparently only expanded on the theory previously developed, with special emphasis on capital allocation.

Novozhilov seeks to determine the principles of allocating the available "means of production" so as to minimize the total labor input during the period, assuming a *fixed* bill of *final* goods[1] and a fixed amount of investment during the period. The *numéraire* is labor-time, and the investment fund is expressed in the same unit. His solution is closely analogous to the general equilibrium systems of Walras, Barone, Cassel, and other western economists, allowing for the two assumptions just mentioned. He resorts, in effect, to equilibrium prices for intermediate goods, scarcity rents, a rate of interest on capital as such — that is, precisely to those allocational devices which allegedly differentiate a capitalist market economy from the Soviet order. And yet, Novozhilov claims to proceed from the labor theory of value and to remain within the Soviet institutional framework! How does he accomplish the synthesis of Marx and Walras, if at all?

One must credit Novozhilov with a measure of success in his improbable task, a success based on an appropriate axiomatic premise and a clever use of concepts. The condition of a fixed and pre-determined bill of final goods is the key premise. It eliminates the problem of maximizing output (or utility), and therefore of imputing the relative prices of intermediate goods from the values of final goods. (Such imputation would, of course, be inconsistent with the labor theory of value.) But in the absence of a maximand, the system must at least have a minimand for a problem of optimum allocation to exist. By choosing labor input to be the minimand, Novozhilov determines the *numéraire* of his model, which must be, by the logic of imputation, the unit in which the minimand is expressed.[2] Thus Novozhilov is able to operate with values of "means of production" expressed in labor-time units throughout, and to achieve a formal

---

9. "Sposoby nakhozhdeniia maksimuma effekta kapitalovlozhenii v sotsialisticheskom khoziaistve" ("Methods of Finding the Maximum Effect of Capital Investments in a Socialist Economy"), *Trudy Leningradskogo finansovo-ekonomicheskogo instituta* (*Papers of the Leningrad Financial and Economic Institute*), Vol. III (1947). Critically reviewed by Mstislavskii in the first two articles cited in note 2, p. 333.

1. Final goods are defined as goods for individual and collective consumption and for investment.

2. Another way of looking at Novozhilov's model is that he seeks to *maximize leisure*. Since leisure is measured in the same units as labor input, the numéraire must be a unit of labor-time. Of course, he could have also measured labor input in "wage rubles," but did not choose to do so.

consistency with the labor theory of value. Note that this would have been impossible had he posed the aim of minimizing any input but labor, or of maximizing any final "product" but leisure.

Novozhilov attempts to justify his basic condition of a fixed bill of final goods by arguing that alternative collections of final goods are not commensurable, because they differ in their noneconomic effects (social, cultural, strategic) as well as in product composition. It follows (he holds) that the total effect of production cannot be quantified. Hence, also, products and inputs are incommensurable. But inputs, being in the last analysis always labor, are commensurable between themselves, and the minimization procedure is therefore feasible.[3] The argument is well devised to support Novozhilov's case, but is vulnerable with reference to actual Soviet conditions. For instance, it may be surmised (although it cannot be proved) that the task of the Soviet planning apparatus for a concrete planning period is essentially to maximize output (along some centrally established scale of values) rather than to minimize labor input.

Having thus expressed his system in labor-time units, Novozhilov proceeds to reconcile (what in effect are) scarcity rents and an interest rate with the labor value doctrine. He introduces the concept of "inverse relation" (*obratnaia sviaz'*) — the phenomenon that the *lower* (labor-time) costs achieved with the aid of "better"[4] means of production are necessarily accompanied by *higher* costs in those processes to which the "better" means of production are denied because of their scarcity. The additional labor input required in a certain process because a unit of a certain "better" means of production is *not* allocated to it, is called by Novozhilov an "inversely related input" (*zatrata obratnoi sviazi*), here abbreviated as i.r.i. An i.r.i. may be thought of as an opportunity cost of a unit of the means of production, although in terms of additional costs incurred rather than of output sacrificed. Novozhilov argues that investible capital *per se*, though not a "means of production" in the Marxian sense, also has its i.r.i.'s, because failure to apply it usually entails higher total (labor) cost in the given process.

Now, for each resource (means of production or capital), the i.r.i.'s corresponding to all its possible uses can be ranked in descending order and checked off until the supply of that resource is exhausted. The next highest i.r.i. of any resource (in western terminology, the first extra-marginal value when the whole supply of the given resource

3. "Methods of Commeasuring the Economic Effectiveness . . . ," pp. 3–5.
4. *I.e.*, more productive per unit of their straight labor-time cost than alternative ("worse") means of production.

has been allocated) is its "norm" of i.r.i. Novozhilov demonstrates algebraically that his minimization objective is attained if, for each final good, that technical production variant is adopted which has the lowest sum of actual labor-time inputs *plus* resource inputs valued at their respective "norms" of i.r.i. These "norms" are, of course, actually the interest rate on capital and the scarcity rents of physical resources. But by drawing attention not to the price which a resource could command in a competitive market, but to the extra (labor) costs entailed in foregoing a marginal employment of the resource (which would indeed determine its price in a competitive economy), Novozhilov is able to resolve all value of intermediate goods to labor.

Strumilin's essay, "The Time Factor in Investment Projects,"[5] has attracted more attention abroad than any other Soviet contribution to the theory of "capital effectiveness." This fact may be attributed to the author's novel (if not always tenable) approach, to his remaining true to Marxian concepts and categories, and possibly to the good fortune of the article's having appeared in a readily accessible journal. The work is rich in glittering veins awaiting the theoretician's careful assay, but only the more pertinent aspects of Strumilin's contribution can be commented upon here. For a fuller appreciation the reader is referred to the article itself and to the subsequent literature.[6]

Unlike Novozhilov, Strumilin did not develop a single and internally consistent method of variant selection, but merely advanced some principles for the project-maker's guidance, and mentioned a large number of criteria of investment choice. His inquiry was apparently provoked by the practice of some engineers (as discussed above) of resorting to interest rates, pay-off periods, and similar devices in choosing between technological alternatives — devices

---

5. "Faktor vremeni v proektirovkakh kapital'nykh vlozhenii," *Izvestiia Akademii nauk SSSR: Otdelenie ekonomiki i prava* (*Bulletin of the Academy of Sciences of the USSR: Division of Economics and Law*), 1946, No. 3, pp. 195–216; English translation in *International Economic Papers*, 1951, No. 1; English summary in the article by J. M. (*loc. cit.*). Academician Strumilin is one of the best known of present-day Soviet economists, and co-author and editor of the First Five-Year Plan and other early economic plans.

6. For comments in western literature see A. Zauberman, "Economic Thought in the Soviet Union: I. Economic Law and the Theory of Value," *Review of Economic Studies*, XVI, 7–10; *idem.*, "The Prospects for Soviet Investigations into Capital Efficiency," *Soviet Studies*, I (Apr. 1950), 328–33; Warren W. Eason, "On Strumilin's Model," *ibid.*, 334–42; Charles Bettelheim, "The Discussion on the Problem of Alternative Investment Projects," *ibid.*, II (July 1950), 22–42; Maurice Dobb, "A Note on the Discussion of the Problem of Choice Between Alternative Investment Projects," *ibid.*, II (Jan. 1951), 289–95; Kaplan, *op. cit.*, pp. 139–40. Also, my *Capital-Intensity: . . .* , chap. 11, sec. B.

which he considered without normative significance in the Soviet economy. But because of either a meager acquaintance with the engineering literature on the subject, or a failure to grasp its meaning, Strumilin's criticisms on this score are almost entirely irrelevant.

Strumilin also operates with a labor *numéraire*, but his Marxian orthodoxy goes further. For instance, he shuns marginalism (with some lapses); regards accumulation to be proportional to the input of living labor, though he actually deviates from this principle, as Eason[7] has shown; and avoids considerations of opportunity cost. It is the last doctrinal obstacle, above all, which keeps Strumilin from reaching a definite and cogent solution. He mentions at least eight widely different criteria of choice between technological variants,[8] such as, for example: the ratio of accumulation to value added, in any year; physical output per unit of direct labor input over the whole life of the equipment; and the ratio of cost to average value of a unit of product in the economy. The last is described as a "best measure," but none seems to be clearly preferred. No rationale is offered for any of the criteria; their normative qualities are taken to be immanent and self-evident. With one exception, they do not even take explicit account of the relative investments in the competing variants, much less the opportunity cost of capital in general.

It must be borne in mind that the economic categories which underlie the criteria are Marxian in definition, and it is in his attempt to refine them that Strumilin makes the more substantial contribution. There is no need to dwell long on his proposal that economic calculations take account of the "full labor input" in production, that is, as measured not merely by the actual remuneration of labor, but by this *plus* the "accumulation" (surplus product) created by labor. Marxian doctrine at once sanctions this refinement and deprives it of operational significance, since surplus product is assumed to bear a constant ratio to labor input throughout the economy, and labor cost is the only cost recognized in the final analysis. Thus, Strumilin's proposal would only cause all cost calculations to be multiplied by a constant factor, with no effect on the relative merits of alternative projects.

Much more significant is Strumilin's concept of "devaluation," which aims to take account of the prospective increase in labor productivity.[9] This problem is undoubtedly central to his conception

7. *Loc. cit.*
8. *Op. cit.*, pp. 206, 210, and 213.
9. Aivaz'ian (*op. cit.*, pp. 10 ff.) briefly anticipated Strumilin in taking the rise in labor productivity into account. See also Bashinskii, *loc. cit.*, for a somewhat different approach to the same problem.

of the impact of the "time factor" on economic calculations. He maintains that, in accordance with the labor theory of value, a rise in labor productivity causes a physical unit of a product, including existing capital goods, to be "devalued" proportionately. Thus he writes $C_t = C_0/(1 + p)^t$, where C is the value of a material good, p is the annual rate of growth of labor productivity over the whole economy, and the subscripts refer to the initial and the t-th years.

Strumilin employs the principle of "devaluation" in two ways. (a) He causes current production cost of a particular enterprise to fall over time because of the progressive devaluation of material inputs. (Labor costs remain constant, however, because labor-time is the *numéraire*.) (b) He includes in annual cost the value "lost" by fixed capital during the year, that is, about p per cent of its value at the beginning of the year. No rationale of this procedure is indicated. The amount so "written off" goes into a "compensation fund" to become a source of financing new investment. The charging of p per cent of capital value to current cost bears a formal resemblance to interest cost, but, as will be presently shown, there is no close analogy in substance.

He is partly correct with regard to (a), and in error with regard to (b). On (a): It is proper, of course, to allow for future changes in price-cost relationships, insofar as these can be foreseen. However, the estimates of prospective increases in labor productivity (i.e., declines in the prices of material inputs) should be specific to the production process. An economy-wide average is applicable only for want of more detailed data. With respect to (b): It is not clear why "the loss of . . . value of past labor embodied in our capital goods must be fully compensated for during the period of their operation" (p. 202), i.e., charged to current production expenses. This loss is not a real cost to the economy, directly or indirectly. (From the point of view of the individual firm aiming to preserve the real worth of its capital, only a "devaluation" of its own investment *in excess* of the average — p per cent — should be charged to current cost, while a lower than average "devaluation" would be a gain in real terms for the firm. But then Strumilin recognizes only an average rate of "devaluation.") Nor is it clear how the amounts so written off are available to finance new investment.

Thus, Strumilin's p is not an interest rate in any usual sense, though some authors have so identified it.[1] Rather, it is an annual rate of change in "value"; that is, say, in the price index with wages held stable. True, Strumilin does include it in current cost of pro-

---

1. E.g., Bettelheim, *op. cit.*, p. 29, and Kaplan *op. cit.*, pp. 139, 144.

duction, but erroneously so, as has been just shown.   Indeed p may move inversely with a capital charge based on the opportunity cost principle (such as that advocated by Lur'e or Novozhilov).   For instance, should the annual amount of investment be increased, the former would rise with the impetus to labor productivity, while the latter would fall, reflecting the lower marginal rate of substitution between capital and labor.

V. The Economists' Attack and Its Aftermath

Strumilin's critique of the use of capital charges in project-making was relatively mild compared with the attack against the practice launched a few years later, chiefly by "general" economists. The most outspoken critic has been P. S. Mstislavskii, a member of the editorial staff of *Voprosy ekonomiki* (*Problems of Economics*), the official organ of the Institute of Economics of the USSR Academy of Sciences.[2]   As might be expected, the main targets of the attack have been Lur'e and Novozhilov.   The strictures may be grouped under three headings: (1) contravention of Marxian doctrine and of Soviet planning principles; (2) harmful political implications and vicious intent; (3) errors in reasoning.

(1) Perhaps the most serious doctrinal failing attributed to the

2. The main works in this group are: P. Mstislavskii, "U trudakh Leningradskogo finansovo-ekonomicheskogo instituta" ("On the Papers of the Leningrad Financial and Economic Institute"), *Voprosy ekonomiki*, 1948, No. 7, pp. 131–35; *idem*, "O metodologicheskikh oshibkakh v literature promyshlennosti i transporta" ("On Methodological Errors in the Literature on Industry and Transportation"), *ibid.*, 1948, No. 10, pp. 34–48; *idem*, "Nekotorye voprosy effektivnosti kapitalovlozhenii v sovetskom khoziaistve" ("Certain Questions of the Effectiveness of Capital Investment in the Soviet Economy"), *ibid.*, 1949, No. 6, pp. 96–115 (condensed English translation in *Current Digest of the Soviet Press*, Mar. 4, 1950, and in *Soviet Studies*, I (Apr. 1950), 363–76); P. Milovanov and P. Petrov, "Vrednaia stateika v ekonomicheskom sbornike" ("A Harmful Article in an Economic Symposium"), *Gudok*, Mar. 25, 1949; P. Krylov, "Protiv burzhuaznoi metodologii v voprosakh ekonomiki transporta" ("Against Bourgeois Methodology in Transportation Economics"), *Planovoe khoziaistvo*, 1949, No. 4, pp. 85–91; D. I. Chernomordik, "Effektivnost' kapital'nykh vlozhenii i teoriia vosproizvodstva" ("The Effectiveness of Capital Investment and the Theory of Reproduction"), *Voprosy ekonomiki*, 1949, No. 6, pp. 78–95 (condensed English translation in *Current Digest of the Soviet Press*, Feb. 18, 1950, and *Soviet Studies*, I (Apr. 1950), 359–63); G. Levin, "Voprosy opredeleniia ekonomicheskoi tselesoobraznosti proektnykh reshenii" ("Problems of Determining the Economic Rationale of Project Solutions"), *Voprosy ekonomiki*, 1950, No. 4, pp. 72–85.

Milovanov and Petrov sign as engineers; Levin's status is not known; the rest are "general" economists.   Chernomordik (not to be confused with his namesake cited in note 6, p. 318, an engineer and a staunch advocate of capital charges) was, however, not unsympathetic to capital charges earlier (*Zheleznodorozhnyi transport* (*Railroad Transport*), 1946, Nos. 11–12, pp. 87–93), when he reviewed Khachaturov's book (*op. cit.*).

advocates of capital charges was that their method would subject
the composition of the bill of goods to the test of profitability, contrary to Soviet planning principles.   For instance, it would cause
light industry to expand faster than heavy industry, thus reversing
prevailing policy.   It has already been pointed out (p. 319) that this
criticism misrepresents the position of the proponents of capital
charges, who were not at all concerned with the determination of the
bill of goods, and invariably accepted it as a datum for their purposes.

The list of ideological transgressions further included: being under
the influence of bourgeois theories; resort to the bourgeois concepts
of scarcity and the economic margin; "idealism" (*i.e.*, reliance on
formal, especially mathematical, methodology allegedly divorced
from the laws and realities of the Soviet economy); and acceptance
of the "anti-scientific principle" of attaining the maximum effect with
minimum input.   (The last principle is allegedly too narrow a conception of the economic objectives of the Soviet state.)   Another
critique on doctrinal grounds referred to the use of *compound* interest
— a procedure that disregards Marx's view that compound interest
is (in the words of the Soviet critic) "an absurdity, mystification,
and nonsense."[3]

(2) The violence of the attack is evinced in the readiness with
which political opposition was inferred from methodological and
theoretical tenets.   Thus, Novozhilov was accused of questioning the
state's distribution of investment, and Lur'e's faith in the planned
order was challenged.[4]   The chief basis for these serious accusations
was the same false charge that it was intended to subject the determination of the bill of goods to the criterion of profitability.

(3) The errors in reasoning charged to the "heretics" need not
be examined here in detail.   These objections stem chiefly from
inability or unwillingness on the part of the critics to grasp the logic
of opportunity cost.   For instance, compounding was attacked also
on the ground that savings in current cost need not be wholly reinvested, but may be consumed, etc., and therefore there need not
actually be a geometric series. A similar argument was brought to
bear against the requirement of a uniform capital charge over the
whole economy.[5]

Having risen to the defense of ideological purity and political
loyalty, some of the critics felt moved to advance positive alternatives along theoretically acceptable lines.   Strumilin's proposals were

3. Mstislavskii, "On Methodological Errors . . . ," *op. cit.*, p. 41; reference
is to the sarcastic remarks on compound interest in Vol. III, chap. 24, of *Capital.*
4. *Ibid.*, pp. 40, 42.
5. *Ibid.*, p. 39.

too vague and dubious to fill the void. With one exception, to be taken up presently, the few positive solutions proffered by the economists were weak, and of little theoretical interest or practical import. Notably, there was no mention whatever of the rich economic literature on "the effectiveness of investment" of the late twenties.[6] The reader was given no hint that this was not exactly virgin ground in Soviet economic thought.

The exception is one of Mstislavskii's solutions, his "first case."[7] The striking (if not ironic) thing about it is that although its author has been the most outspoken critic of the use of capital charges, his solution in effect rests on the rate of substitution between capital and labor. Thus, without apparent awareness, he comes close to reproducing, though in a different and distinctive formal structure, the solutions of his arch-opponents, Lur'e and Novozhilov. Nor is there anything more "Marxian" about his model; if anything, he pays less respect than Novozhilov to the labor theory of value.

Mstislavskii's criterion of choice between technological alternatives is minimum total *capital* requirements, traced back through *all* stages of production. Capital requirements in the last analysis consist of capital outlays proper *plus* the "capitalized" equivalent of labor costs, the only ultimate current costs in his schema. The "capitalization" of labor costs is clearly the crux of the solution. Mstislavskii accomplishes it by arguing that, in the absence of unemployment, new enterprises can obtain the necessary labor only insofar as the rise in productivity in existing enterprises permits the latter to release workers.[8] Thus, the capital equivalent ("capital-intensity" in his terminology) of labor is the additional investment, per annual wage ruble, required to raise productivity in existing enterprises,

6. This circumstance can hardly be accounted for by the fact that none of the economists was familiar with it. First, it was too prominent a feature of the economics of its day; secondly, Strumilin himself participated ("K probleme effektivnosti kapital'nykh zatrat" ("On the Problem of the Effectiveness of Capital Outlays"), *Planovoe khoziaistvo*, 1929, No. 8, pp. 59–74); and thirdly, they were reminded of it by Lur'e (*op. cit.*, pp. 45 ff.).

7. "Certain Questions of the Effectiveness . . . ," *op. cit.*, pp. 106–13. The interested reader is referred to the economists' other positive contributions: Mstislavskii's second case, *ibid.*, pp. 113–15; D. I. Chernomordik, *loc. cit.*; A. Emel'ianov, "O metodakh opredeleniia ekonomicheskoi effektivnosti primeneniia mashin v sovetskom khoziaistve" ("On the Methods of Determining the Economic Effectiveness of the Use of Machinery in the Soviet Economy"), *Voprosy ekonomiki*, 1949, No. 11, pp. 104–14 (English summary in *Soviet Studies*, I (Apr. 1950), 376–82). For analysis and interpretation of these contributions see Kaplan, *loc. cit.*

8. He overlooks the natural accretion to the labor force, and seems to be thinking of intra-industry transfers, rather than rural-urban migration; the cost of urbanization is ignored.

plus the additional expenses of retraining and preparing labor for its new employment. He stresses that the relevant relationship is an *incremental* and not an average one. Thus, in effect, he converts current cost to capital cost by multiplying it by the marginal (incremental) rate of substitution of capital for labor. This coefficient (say, k) is closely akin in economic nature to the reciprocal of Lur'e's Δ, or of Novozhilov's "norm" of the i.r.i. of capital. The method is also very similar to the common "bourgeois" procedure of selecting the alternative with minimum capitalized cost.

However, Mstislavskii's coefficient (unlike Lur'e's and Novozhilov's) is not defined as an equilibrium magnitude, though one may well argue that a consistent application of the method in practice would tend to produce just that. Secondly, Mstislavskii operates with a "wider" margin than do his two antagonists, that is, with a "zone" representing the annual increments in a rapidly expanding economy. Thirdly, he does not assign scarcity rents to resources other than capital, while Novozhilov does (though Lur'e does not). But the distinction is not so significant as may appear at first glance. Novozhilov, it will be recalled, is concerned with the simultaneous allocation of *all* resources in the economy, both marginal and intra-marginal. Hence, he properly assigns rents to intra-marginal resources. Mstislavskii, however, is concerned only with the allocation of an incremental amount of capital and the reshuffling of other factors at the margin. And although his margin is quite "wide," he is perhaps not much at fault in treating resources implicitly as though they were all marginal, and not assigning rents to them (except the implicit charge on capital).

This solution has been criticized for being laborious in application and impracticable. Surely, it would be beyond the powers of an individual project-maker to determine the aggregate capital requirements of each input through several stages of production. The author tries to meet this objection by suggesting that the central statistical and planning authorities compute and establish parameter values of "capital-intensity" for each input. These would in effect constitute a list of values equal to current production costs within the marginal "zone" (including a capital charge of $1/k$ per annum), multiplied throughout by k. The capital charge coefficient would thus vanish into unity; all current input costs would be "capitalized" by the implicit interest rate of $1/k$. But a simpler procedure is available. One might just as well eschew "capitalizing," and operate more conveniently and conventionally with current prices-costs, including the interest rate of $1/k$ per annum. Thus Novozhilov's price system would be nearly reproduced in form as well as in essence. Apparently Mstislavskii was not aware of this close similarity. In any case, the "capitalization" procedure afforded a means of avoiding any formal resort to the interest rate.

Since the end of 1949, the controversy has remained smoldering, flaring up occasionally in isolated sectors, producing recantations and reaffirmations, rejoinders and retreats. At the time of this writing, the air is still full of uncertainty, with no discernible signs of resolution either by intellectual agreement or by authoritative dispensation. Lur'e and Novozhilov, the two extreme proponents of capital charges and outright marginalism, have not replied in print, to my knowledge. The grave allegations of political opposition and ideological deviation, based on false strictures as they were, remain unanswered. True, *Voprosy ekonomiki* did invite a full discussion of "capital effectiveness," but the consequences were meager and one-sided. The journal was chided for its failure on this score (among others) by an authoritative publication of the Central Committee of the Communist Party;[9] while Khachaturov publicly accused it of rejecting articles the content of which ran counter to the likes of individual members of the editorial staff (e.g., Mstislavskii?).

Khachaturov's own reactions serve to emphasize the prevailing ambivalence. His first response to criticism, if we can trust an unsympathetic secondary source,[1] was to recant fully. But his next article[2] is equivocal. Here he starts out by conceding that the criticisms of the use of capital charges in project-making have been "basically" justified; the "coefficient of effectiveness" has been "mechanistically" applied in disregard of the economic plan; it is not sufficiently confirmed on theoretical grounds. Moreover, experience has shown (he claims) that it is incorrect to apply a uniform coefficient (capital charge) over the whole economy, for it may lead to *technologically* inferior solutions in the case of highly durable structures.[3] And finally, compounding is rejected as "unjustified and incorrect." But when he turns to consider the guidelines for a new

9. *Kul'tura i zhizn'* (*Culture and Life*), Oct. 12, 1950.

1. P. Orlov and I. Romanov, "K voprosu o metodologii sravneniia variantov proektiruemogo stroitel 'stva" ("On the Methodology of Comparing Variants of Construction Projects"), *Voprosy ekonomiki*, 1951, No. 1, p. 104.

2. "Metody ekonomicheskogo sravneniia variantov kapitalovlozhenii" ("Methods of Economic Comparison of Investment Variants"), *Izvestiia Akademii nauk SSSR: Otdelenie ekonomiki i prava*, 1950, No. 4, pp. 235–52; English summary in *Soviet Studies*, II (Jan. 1951), 317–22.

3. *Ibid.*, p. 238. Needless to say, this argument begs the question of having an economic criterion to choose between technological alternatives

solution, Khachaturov goes through a chain of reasoning very similar to that underlying the usual advocacy of capital charges on the basis of an opportunity cost concept. His former views crop out especially in the discussion of postponable capital outlays, where he now stops just short of rehabilitating compound interest.[4] Following through his argument logically, one can only arrive at capital charges, compounding and all. The impression is inescapable that Khachaturov is torn between the logic of opportunity cost and the demands of doctrinal purity.

Unfortunately, there is no information whether Khachaturov's position (or lack of it!) reflects that of the railroad industry as a whole since 1949. Possibly not. In other areas, the data are somewhat less sparse. In the field of machine-design, where the problem arrived late and advocacy of capital charges reached a peak in 1948, all evidence points to a retreat. Later works by the same authors de-emphasize the usefulness and applicability of "pay-off periods" and similar devices, though they far from eliminate them entirely.[5] In the field of machine shop operation, with a longer history of "heresy," the retreat has been greater and more obvious, with denunciations of "bourgeois" thinking and "errors of bourgeois-objectivist character."[6] An indication of the official view in these two related fields may perhaps be gathered from the fifteenth volume of *Mashinostroenie* (Moscow, 1951), the encyclopedia of machine-building, which went to print in 1949. While containing sections on choice between technological variants, it either confines itself to platitudes or omits reference to capital charges. But curiously, it does cite works advocating their use in the bibliographies. No actual attack on capital charges appears, and again the total impression is one of ambivalence. In the highway construction industry, there are also signs of renunciation of pay-off periods and similar devices. It is not clear, however, whether the use of capital charges has been entirely discontinued in these three fields.

In the power industry, the reaction to criticism seems to have been quite different. It is perhaps significant that the only forceful defense of capital charges to have appeared in an economic journal

4. *Ibid.*, pp. 249–50.
5. See A. S. Konson, *Ekonomicheskie voprosy proektirovaniia mashin (Economic Problems in Machine Design)* (Moscow-Leningrad, 1951).
6. *E.g.*, G. V. Teplov in *Pravda*, Feb. 10, 1951; and T. D. Saksaganskii, "O kachestve literatury po ekonomike i organizatsii proizvodstva" ("On the Quality of the Literature on the Economics and Organization of Production"), *Vestnik mashinostroeniia (Herald of Machine-Building)*, 1951, No. 7, pp. 76, 81.

since 1948 was by an electrical engineer.[7] A vigorous debate on the applicability of interest for the choice of the optimum cross-section of transmission wire started in 1950, as has already been mentioned.[8] The technical literature still (through 1952) contains references to, and even defense of, pay-off periods and similar devices, and sometimes operates with concepts of cost *inclusive* of interest on capital, while the engineer's facility with differential calculus unwittingly pulls him down into the morass of marginalism.[9]

A recurring note in recent engineering literature has been the dissatisfaction with the ambiguous state of affairs with regard to the economic principles of investment choice, turning into an impatience for its resolution by competent bodies. The Institute of Economics, the economic journals, and the State Planning Commission are urged to hasten the solution. But theoretical solution or no, the engineers must design and build, and the following opinions are perhaps indicative of their mood.

''Since there is no theoretically grounded and generally accepted method of calculation [of capital-intensity] as yet, while calculations must take place, one is forced to look for an *arbitrary* method, *uniform* for all the computations.''[1]

"The discussion . . . conducted during 1949–1950 on the pages of . . . [economic journals] failed to give a satisfactory answer to the question at hand. Apparently it is necessary to turn to the solution of special problems peculiar to the various branches of industry, independent of the solution of the general problem [of investment choice].''[2]

To be sure, the Institute of Economics has carried the "problem of the effectiveness of capital investment" in its research plan since at least 1949, but no evidence of even partial progress has come forth. In fact, the opposite has been officially admitted, despite the problem's "great significance for the development of economic science as well as for the actual construction of communism."[3] The Institute's

7. A. I. Baumgol'ts, "K voprosu ob effektivnosti kapitalovlozhenii" ("On the Effectiveness of Capital Investment"), *Izvestiia Akademii nauk SSSR; Otdelenie ekonomiki i prava*, 1950, No. 6, pp. 440–52.

8. Note 7, p. 318.

9. E.g., T. L. Zolotarev, *Gidroenergetika (Hydraulic Power Engineering)*: Part I, *Osnovy ispol'zovaniia gidravlicheskoi energii (Fundamentals of Utilization of Hydraulic Power)* (Moscow-Leningrad, 1950), pp. 105–16. Incidentally, Zolotarev, a chief *opponent* of interest in the debate of the thirties, gradually shifted his position to the other side.

1. *Ibid.*, p. 113; italics in the original.

2. L. E. Zubrilov, "O primenenii analiticheskogo metoda v gornom dele" ("On the Application of the Analytic Method in Mining"), *Gornyi zhurnal (Mining Journal)*, 1952, No. 2, pp. 7–9.

3. *Izvestiia Akademii nauk: Otdelenie ekonomiki i prava*, 1952, No. 2, p. 119.

position is an unenviable one. Some of its specific difficulties will be touched upon in the next section. It has apparently not proved easy to find a solution which would meet the practical needs of the project-making engineer, and at the same time satisfy the scrupulous standards of ideological conformity. The concept of opportunity cost and the principle of demand-supply equilibrium are hard to refute, but they savor too much of "idealism," "formalism," marginalism, and other tabus. Furthermore, it does not seem likely that Soviet economists will find clear ideological guidance in Stalin's last theoretical work, "Economic Problems of Socialism in the USSR."[4] The passages on the operation of economic laws under socialism[5] are too vague to give unequivocal inspiration. True, he speaks of "paying-off" investment, but in a financial rather than an economic context, and not in a normative sense.[6] On the other hand, opponents of capital charges could point to his rejection of the test of profitability,[7] in support of their chief (and, as we have seen, irrelevant) objection. Nor are his remarks on the use of machinery in the USSR[8] likely to advance serious inquiry into problems of investment choice.

VI. Conclusion

The damage sustained by the Soviet economy due to the absence of an appropriate capital charge should not be exaggerated. On the one hand, even a uniform interest rate, faithfully expressing the marginal rate of substitution between capital and other factors, would be of questionable benefit while the rest of the Soviet price structure remained of doubtful meaningfulness for allocational purposes. It may be noted that Soviet project-making engineers have been not unaware of this consideration, and have occasionally introduced various "coefficients of deficitness," along with "norms of capital effectiveness," to correct for unduly low prices of rationed material inputs. And, as indicated above, Novozhilov's purpose was precisely to rationalize the *whole* price-cost structure. There is little doubt that the Soviet price system remains inefficient, in the strict allocational sense. Whether it is more so with reference to the ends posited by central authorities, than the price system of any other major

4. "Ekonomicheskie problemy sotsializma v SSSR," *Bol'shevik*, 1952, No. 18, pp. 1–50; also *Pravda*, Oct. 3 and 4, 1952. Reprinted and translated in *Current Digest of the Soviet Press*, Oct. 18, 1952, *Special Supplement*. Subsequent references are to *Bol'shevik*.

5. Pp. 1–5, 10–13, 20–22.

6. P. 48.

7. Pp. 12–13.

8. P. 23.

economy with reference to *its* ends, is a debatable issue, but perhaps not really pertinent here. It may be only noted in passing that an order claiming a monopoly of rationality in the economic sphere stands particularly vulnerable to failure on this score.

On the other hand, allocational inefficiency is overshadowed by the dominant and compelling characteristic of the Soviet economy — its rapid and determined growth. And yet, the two are not necessarily concomitant, even if frequently associated in argument as well as in fact. What has been recently said in relation to economic restrictionism in other societies may perhaps be applicable in the present context too:

" . . . economic growth and development are coming to figure in popular thinking as universal solvents or universal masks, dissolving and concealing the economic costs of other economic policies, however erroneous. The effects [of these mistaken policies] . . . float away and vanish down the stream of economic development, leaving no impress outside the diagrams and equations of static economics. Growth, for restrictionists, is like the earth for Molière's doctors of medicine. It covers their failures, while the sun shines on their successes."[9]

The mills and the dams stand in their glory, the more capital-intensive, the more impressive, but what might have been is not to be seen. One may venture the guess, and it cannot be more than that, that the penalties of inefficiency in the Soviet case are neither enormous nor negligible. Even if minor compared to the whole national product, they may loom large in relation to a particular sector to which the fruits of a better utilization of resources could conceivably be applied.

In the task of removing this inefficiency, Soviet economics, as a discipline, faces some serious obstacles. The chief of these is the axiom represented by the labor theory of value. Whatever its advantages for other purposes, and there may be such, the labor theory of value is a barrier to the development of a meaningful and cogent theory of resource allocation, and especially of the allocation of capital. Its fatal flaw is that it measures output in terms of input, and of only a certain kind of input at that. But the logic of rational allocation requires that alternative combinations of resources be measured in terms of the unit of the maximand (or minimand). Thus, inputs must usually be measured in output units. Only in the special case of labor input minimization (leisure maximization) with a *fixed* bill of goods, where the unit of the minimand happens to be a unit of labor-time, is rational resource allocation formally not

9. M. Bronfenbrenner, "The High Cost of Economic Development" (I), *Doshisha Daigaku Keizaigaku Ronso* (*Doshisha University Economic Review*) (Kyoto), IV, (Feb. 1953), 1–2.

inconsistent with the labor theory of value. This, of course, is the case so ingeniously presented by Novozhilov, and its practical limitations have been noted.[1]

Further, and also because of this, Soviet economics is today largely devoid of the concept of *economic* scarcity, and its corollary, the concept of opportunity cost, as well as of the principle of demand and supply equilibrium.[2] True, it must recognize that resources are limited in quantity, but it does so primarily in a physical sense, rather than in terms of the relationship between the productivity of resources and their cost. Similarly, the notion of equilibrium seems to be understood chiefly in an "arithmetic" sense. It is remarkable that, with the exception of Novozhilov (who stands apart in many respects), none of the Soviet "general" economists writing after 1931 premised their solutions to the problem of capital-intensity on the concept of opportunity cost. Almost invariably they have sought the key to the "effectiveness" of capital within the given process in which capital was to be invested, and not in its alternative uses. Strumilin's contribution is especially rich in examples illustrating this notion of an immanent effectiveness. Perhaps even more remarkable is the lack of concern (again, Novozhilov excepted) with the elementary precaution that the demand for capital, as determined by the proposed criteria of capital-intensity, equal its exogenous supply.[3]

Thus, the theoretical economist in the USSR finds himself in an anomalous position. He cannot question the ends of economic activity or the minutest policy of the regime. The domain left to his investigation is that of means to predetermined ends, and not even the full range of means. But stepping into this domain, he finds himself deprived by the prevailing ideology of some of the most powerful theoretical tools. Lacking them, he cannot construct a solution which will withstand logical scrutiny. If he reaches out for one beyond the bounds of established orthodoxy, as did Novozhilov, he is not only reprimanded for his audacity, but runs the grave danger of having ideological transgressions and political opposition imputed to him. The quality of present-day Soviet economic literature fully reflects this excruciating dilemma.

And yet the Institute of Economics is committed to search for

1. *Supra*, pp. 328, 329.
2. The existence of these gaps in the mental baggage of Soviet economists has also been confirmed by western economists through personal contact. See the interesting report of one such recent contact in P. Wiles, "Soviet Economics," *Soviet Studies*, IV (Oct. 1952), esp. 133–35.
3. Note the difficulty besetting Dobb in his interpretation of Strumilin's model ("A Note on the Discussion . . . ," *op. cit.*, pp. 294–95).

a solution to the problem of investment choice. It reached out to eradicate a heretical growth, but instead has grasped a nettle which it cannot quite let go. Zauberman's evaluation is probably in a sense correct: "The real issue in this discussion has not been: 'Is this or that Norm or index an adequate criterion of capital efficiency on the basis of Marxian teaching?' but: 'Is the economist to be allowed to offer any criterion at all to the Master Planner?' "[4] Perhaps the latter question ought to be repeated with the specific Soviet context in mind. That is, not only in relation to the conflict of ideology *versus* the logic of expediency, but also in the context of the struggles of institutions for recognition and authority, of the fates of individuals, and of manoeuvres of organizations and groups within the body of the regime. Having put forth a claim to authority in the matter, can the Institute, representing the profession, and the individual economists afford to have their claim challenged and overthrown? What constructive function will be left to the Soviet economist if this chance to re-establish competence in a pre-eminently economic matter is allowed to vanish? Such are perhaps the considerations which have kept the topic alive in the absence of a definitive ruling by high political authority, and which have so far stood in the way of a satisfactory solution.

GREGORY GROSSMAN.

RUSSIAN RESEARCH CENTER
HARVARD UNIVERSITY

4. "The Prospects for Soviet Investigations into Capital Efficiency," *op. cit.*, p. 332.

RECOMMENDATIONS OF THE ALL-UNION
SCIENTIFIC-TECHNICAL CONFERENCE
ON PROBLEMS OF DETERMINING THE
ECONOMIC EFFECTIVENESS OF CAPITAL
INVESTMENTS AND NEW TECHNIQUES IN
THE USSR NATIONAL ECONOMY

1. Problems of the economic effectiveness of capital investments and new techniques in the national economy are among the most important economic problems of communist construction. Capital investments of many billions are made every year aimed at expanding reproduction of basic funds in all branches of the national economy; the investments are directed at the comprehensive development of socialist production in all union republics and economic regions of the country and at ensuring the solution of vital tasks in the development of the USSR national economy on its way to communism.

The Soviet people are interested in the most effective utilization of capital investments because the rate of production development and the time needed for solving the basic economic problem of the USSR depends largely upon this.

The Communist Party and the Soviet Government pay great attention now (as they did in the past) to the proper utilization of the financial means used for capital construction and to the economizing of these means. The Party Congress, Plenum of the CC, CPSU and the USSR government, in their decisions repeatedly emphasized the necessity for widespread economy in spending state funds and for struggling to lower costs and increase social labor productivity.

The task of more effectively utilizing material resources and financial means was pointed out in the resolutions of the 20th Congress of the Party as one of the most pressing problems in the development of the socialist economy at its present stage.

Correct definition of the effectiveness of capital investments is of great importance for the preparation of long-range plans for the development of the USSR national economy.

2. Through the planning of capital investments by branches of the national economy, by types of production, by individual concerns, by individual republics and economic regions, the most important economic-political problems in the development of the socialist economy are solved, the direction, proportions and the rate of development of the national economy by branch cross sections and by territorial cross sections are determined.

In planning capital construction and in selecting the most effective volumes of capital investments for construction of new objects and the application of new techniques, it is necessary to utilize a scientific method for calculating capital investments.

The economic effectiveness of capital investments and new techniques is expressed in the increased productivity of social labor, that is, in the reduction of production costs.

Planning capital construction is a most complex and responsible type of work at center and lower echelons. Thus, calculating the effectiveness of capital investments should become a necessary part of planning for all echelons of planning organs — from the USSR State Planning Commission down to individual concerns.

3. The concerns and designing organizations and institutions have accumulated a great store of experience in calculating the economic effectiveness of capital investments in the course of their work. The usual method calls for capital investments to pay for themselves over a given period, accompanied by the use of a number of technical-economic indices of effectiveness. This method is also suggested in the "Provisional Standard Method of Determining the Effectiveness of New Techniques," published by the State Technical Commission in 1956, and in branch instructions based on this publication.

Utilization of the tremendous experience of the branch research and designing institutions, generalizations of theoretical studies and practical experiences make it possible to progress to the next step; how to determine the economic effectiveness of capital investments and new techniques.

Determination of the Economic Effectiveness of Capital Investments in the National Economy

4. For the expanded reproduction of individual branches of the socialist national economy capital investments are made on the basis of the economic laws of socialism which require the preferential development of the means of production and the achievement of the maximum rate of growth of production in general. The basic method of planning is the method of balances which ensures planned, proportional development of the branches of the national economy and removal of disproportions.

This method of balances allows a comparison of the needs for certain kinds of goods with available production facilities, and leads us to a conclusion about the volume of goods which should be produced during the planned period of new capital construction.

When tremendous growth of the national economy and an accelerated rate of growth of science and technique takes place, a combination of the method of balances with economic justification for the most advantageous direction of planned capital investments to ensure high social labor productivity and rentability of production acquires especially great importance.

5. Calculation of the effectiveness of capital investments and of new techniques should be based on value and "natural" indices which make it possible to compare expenditures of living labor of different qualities and of different branches of production with past labor.

At present the value of goods in the national economy is determined through the mechanism of prices. The expenditures of labor are registered according to cost, that is, without taking into consideration the expenditure of labor in the production of goods for the whole of society at a given concern. Prices are calculated at the established prices for materials, fuel, power, equipment, etc. Calculations of the effectiveness by cost do not give us a full and precise presentation of the effectiveness of capital investments just as calculations of the effectiveness according to rentability (that is, the difference between the price and cost multiplied by the annual amount of goods produced and divided by

the sum of capital investments). The method of determining indices of economic effectiveness of capital investments, in order to be practical, should be connected with the system of prices, cost accounting and production recording. In connection with this an improvement in price formation is of great importance.

6. To determine the amount of capital investments required, capital investments in the basic production funds and investments in circulation funds (in the form of stocks of raw and other materials, fuel, semimanufactured goods and other labor products) must be considered. Usually requirements of the operating concern for circulation funds increases after expansion and modernization.

Sometimes changes in production techniques results in a reduction of circulating funds (for example, in mining coal the usual method may be replaced with strip mining) after which the need for capital investments for new techniques will diminish proportionately.

7. Capital investments make it possible to arm workers with more advanced tools, to increase labor productivity, and attract new workers.

The main purpose of capital investments is a comprehensive development of production; thus, the effectiveness of capital investments, in the final account, is measured by the annual increase in the physical volume of national income obtained through these investments. This sum, divided by capital investments, is the coefficient of the effectiveness of capital investments in the national economy. Here we have to determine the ratio of total national income and its accumulated part to capital investments in the national economy. Total capital investments and, consequently, the rate of growth of production in the succeeding period are determined by the amount of accumulation.

8. Rational utilization of capital investments always requires finding the most effective (economically) variant of the solution of a particular economic problem so as to provide the greatest increase in social labor productivity. It is always necessary to determine the relative economic superiority of one solution over another (including a comparison of new techniques with old techniques).

The indices of the comparative effectiveness of capital investments and of new techniques are: changes in cost are compared to the additional capital investments (that is, the difference between the alternating solutions) and changes in cost expressed by the length of time during which capital investments pay for themselves. In a case when one solution results in lower costs and smaller capital investments, there is no need to calculate the length of the period during which the investments pay for themselves.

9. Relative capital investments — the volume of capital investments per unit of the product — is also an index of the effectiveness of capital investments. But this index does not give all the characteristics of the effectiveness of capital investments because it does not reflect the cost of the product.

10. Indices of value do not always give a complete picture of the actual effectiveness of capital investments. For example, a variant which would be acceptable on the basis of value indices may require labor power and materials which are in short supply etc. In such cases application of value indices alone may result in a wrong decision. Thus, selection of the most advantageous system of alternatives of capital investments requires indices expressed in physical units in addition to value indices, labor productivity (the number of units produced per worker per unit of time), expenditure of fuel, power, raw and other materials, utilization of equipment, of factory area, etc.

The final decision should be taken on the basis of an economic analysis of the value indices and indices expressed in physical units. A system of technical-economic indices, specifically for an individual branch, is to be established in the description of methods to be used in this particular branch.

11. To distribute capital investments among branches of the national economy and branches of industry, indices of effectiveness are applied mainly to determine the branches which should be developed to solve particular economic problems. (Example: Which branches of the fuel industry or which branches of the construction materials industry should be developed in order to ensure the necessary volume of fuel production and construction activity?)

Indices of effectiveness are of great importance for solution of the questions of geographic distribution of production, development of economic zones and regions, specialization and cooperation of industry, determination of the size of the concern, setting the time when operations should start, and selection of the proper equipment, technology, etc.

12. To calculate the effectiveness of capital investments in past years the data in the annual reports showing the growth of net production and national income should be compared with the size of the completed capital investments which determined this growth.

However the growth in production results not only from capital investments which equip the workers with new means of labor, but also results from an increase in the number of workers, improved quality of labor, better organization of labor and production, more rational utilization of the means of production, utilization of new natural resources and from carrying out other measures which require no capital investments.

In calculating the plans of effectiveness the planned increase in net production must be compared with the capital investments which were made according to the plan of the same period, provided these plans were put into action and brought about the increase. For these kinds of calculations the USSR State Planning Commission and the USSR CSA should introduce necessary improvements which would reflect the effectiveness of capital investments in the system of planned indices and indices of the annual reports. Capital investments and the product should be expressed in the same constant prices.

13. To find the best system of alternative solutions for calculating the effectiveness of capital investments the period during which the investments pay for themselves (or their reverse quantity — the coefficient of efficiency) should be compared with the standard magnitude of these indices. These standard indices may be established for the total national economy and for individual branches. This will show the maximal effect expected from capital investments throughout the national economy.

The maximal permissible (standard) period (the period in which capital investments pay for themselves) in the selection of the alternative solutions for capital investments and new technique must be determined by comparing old techniques with new, and an evaluation of the magnitude of capital investments appropriated for each individual branch.

Establishment of standard indices of economic effectiveness of capital investments in the form of periods during which capital investments pay for themselves does not mean that all objects which have smaller effectiveness should be automatically rejected.

Some projects with smaller effectiveness may be approved for construction because they accelerate the solution of basic economic problem, and are necessary for defense, political and other reasons.

14. The method of calculating the period (during which capital investments pay for themselves) in different variants consists of a comparison of capital investments which introduce new means of production with the saving of annual current expenditures obtained through this use. Determination of the period during which the capital investments pay for themselves or of the coefficient of comparative effectiveness of capital investments is determined through a comparison of the alternative solutions according to the formula $(K_1 - K_2)/(C_2 - C_1) = T$ or $(C_2 - C_1)/(K_1 - K_2) = 1/T$ where K_1 and K_2 are capital investments in the variants which are being compared, C_1 and C_2 — the cost of the product in each of these variants, T is the period during which the investment pays for itself and $1/T$ the coefficient of efficiency.

T, the period during which capital investments pay for themselves, or its coefficient $1/T$, must be compared with the standard period established for the individual branch, say T_s or the standard coefficient of efficiency $1/T_s$, and the results of this comparison determine the variant selected. The index of the period during which the capital investment pays for itself shows the period in which the investment will be paid out of savings from current production expenditures. These savings should be higher than the rentability of the production.

15. When two variants, with different periods of construction are compared, the economic consequences of delaying or accelerating production must be considered. This arises from the growth of national income connected with the production of additional products and from the reduction of the magnitude of uncompleted capital investments because of acceleration in construction of new projects.

Moreover, additional economic results may sometimes be obtained if the start of production in a concern contributes to the growth of national income in adjacent branches.

If a project is delayed, losses for the national economy result because of the failure to produce goods and an increase in the volume of uncompleted investments. These losses are calculated in a similar way.

The economic results of reductions or increases in the magnitude of uncompleted investments is determined on the basis of the established standard coefficients of effectiveness.

16. With the passing of time, the growth of labor productivity causes the value of the basic means to decrease and causes reductions in current expenditures for construction of projects. Thus, when alternative output schedules are compared, all value indices should be expressed in comparable prices.

When capital investments for new projects are compared with capital investments made earlier, they must be expressed in comparable prices, quoting capital investments of past years in comparable replacement prices.

17. If capital expenditures are made at different periods, comparison of the variants should take into account the sum of investments made and expenses of production, taking into consideration the length of time separating the investment from the present.

Expression of expenditures during past years in present terms is done according to the standards of the economic effectiveness of capital investments on the basis of the formula for compound interest.

18. If capital investments in one production scheme are connected with an increase in production, then the magnitude of capital investments, exploitation expenses and other indices of efficiency for both variants should be calculated on the basis of the same volume of production. When such a calculation is made difficult by the fact that, for example,

the designed capacity of the new project at the existing technological level becomes greater than the capacity of the existing project, then comparison by all indices should be done per unit of goods produced. The possibility of increasing production and satisfying additional needs by using new variants may be realized with capital investments which could achieve the same productivity without changes in equipment.

19. If utilization of the variant results in an improvement in the quality of the product, a corresponding increase in the price of the product must take place. If there is no change in price, then the effect of the improved product may be determined on the basis of savings in current expenditures of the concern which consumes this product.

20. In evaluating the effectiveness of a particular variant we must consider not only expenditures of building a project, but also the development of related branches of production. For example, if a thermopower station is to be built, we must consider capital investments not only in the power station, but also in the coal mines which are necessary to ensure the supply of coal for the station.

21. In determining the economic effectiveness of the geographic distribution, specialization, cooperation and combination we must make calculations of the capital investments and current expenditures by comparing these costs with the construction costs of an individual project. In analyzing the various variants of geographic distribution we must compare expenditures not only for production, but also for transporting products to the consumers. In calculating the effectiveness of specialization and cooperation we must compare capital investments and current expenditures for the whole chain of concerns connected with each other; the basic variant which does not foresee specialization and cooperation among concerns. We should also consider transportation costs which may arise in connection with the possible growth of the transport industry as a result of specialization and cooperation. In calculating the effectiveness of combines we should analyze the work of the combine as a whole and of all its parts as compared with concerns which are not combined, taking into consideration rises and falls in transport costs.

22. Besides calculating effectiveness by value and in kind — when it is possible to measure it — in comparing the variants of capital investments and the selection of the most effective among them we must also consider social factors: making labor easier and more healthful (this is of special importance in evaluating the effectiveness of mechanization and automation), increasing safety, and raising the cultural level and standard of living of the workers. In comparing variants we should also consider requirements for the defense of the Union.

Special Features of Determining the Economic Effectiveness of New Techniques

23. New techniques (new designs of machines, mechanisms, apparatus, new kinds of raw and other materials, new technological processes etc.) are techniques which are superior to techniques which have been applied.

24. The use of a new technique, as a rule, requires capital investments. In view of this the economic effectiveness of its application is determined with the help of value indices and natural (technical-economic) indices which allow comparison of the needed capital investments with savings of current expenditures of production.

25. New technical measures, introduced in one branch, may produce economic effects in the given branch or concern, or in adjacent branches (or concerns) which consume products or supply materials to the original branch (or concern).

The economic effectiveness of new technological processes and new means of production which do not change the character of a product is realized directly at the concern and is expressed in reduced production costs as compared with production costs under existing techniques. The economic effectiveness of new, superior products is realized in their places of use, and is expressed in reduced production costs in those branches of the national economy where they are used as means of production.

26. When selecting variants of new techniques the point of departure should be the available technique which ensures high technical and economic results when applied. Such an improved technique may be a) already available in blueprints or tested in practice; or, b) if such an improved technique is unavailable, the best Soviet or foreign technique already in application should be reviewed.

The economic effectiveness of blueprints approved for application must be determined by comparison with indices of the technique which is to be replaced. If designing, application and mastering of the new technique will take several years, it is necessary then to introduce corrections for the point of departure, to consider changes at the time it will be applied. In order to compare indices of the blueprinted technique and indices of existing production processes under various volumes of production corresponding corrections in the data on the point of departure on the basis of the volume of production according to the design connected with the corresponding capital expenditures, and changes in costs connected with changes in the volume of production should be introduced.

27. In determining the economic effectiveness of applying new kinds of products and complex new technological processes on the scale of whole plant sections (or other large plant subdivisions) it is necessary to compare the full costs of the product. If individual technical measures improve technological processes in some sections of production we should determine changes in cost only on those items of expenditures where the cost is increased or reduced by the new technical measures.

The basic problem is uninterrupted growth of labor productivity. Thus, in calculating cost reductions we should limit ourselves not only to the saving of living labor. In raising the technical level of production (especially in transition to automation) the importance of saving past labor is increasing. Thus, costs must be determined fully and precisely.

28. In order to determine savings in living labor we should compare the labor requirements of the designed production with the actual labor requirements under the existing technological process. If the design foresees the growth of production, the indices of labor requirements should be correspondingly changed. If the existing production is not yet fully mastered, certain corrections should be made in the indices.

Determination of production wages is made on the basis of the approved wage rates plus additional earnings for those who are paid according to piece work. Both these elements are taken as the basis of data for the concern where the new technology is introduced, and if it is introduced in several concerns, as the basis of averages for these concerns.

In order to determine correctly the wages needed for basic production workers we must consider, when a new technique is introduced (in particular in the case of complex mechanization and automation), the possibilities of a better organization of labor under the new conditions. For example, when introducing complex automation we must consider the necessity and possibility (as was done in some plants) of one worker combining the work of adjustment, operation and repair of mechanical and electrical equipment. Adjusters should be treated as basic workers.

Determining the quantity of basic materials and purchased goods to be saved by the new measure comes from comparison of the new standards with the standards used in the existing production and with actual expenditures, if they are lower than the standards. Materials are priced according to price lists. Transportation and purchasing expenses of the concern must be estimated on the basis of actual expenses for individual materials.

If the volume of shipments is changed, the savings (or additional expenses) are determined according to existing railroad rates.

29. The method of determining changes in section or overhead expenses proportionally to the basic production wages fund is wrong and should be given up. It is necessary to determine expenses on various items of overhead expenses (or section expenses) by a direct method.

In calculating expenses on power we must consider the existing rates for power in the regions where the new technique is applied. When we prepare standard designs for the whole country or region, average rates must be used.

In determining expenses for repairs we should make direct calculations by standards, taking into consideration the complexity of repairs.

Expenditures on instruments should also be fixed according to standards. One can use in this case the available standards of the designing institutes and the SKB.

When production rises as a result of the application of new technical measures we must calculate savings in the relatively constant part of the overhead expenses (this part of the overhead expenses as part of the cost per unit changes in inverse proportion to changes in the volume of production). When a considerable growth in production has taken place the relative savings in overhead expenses are determined through preparation of the estimate of the overhead expenditures by items (sectional and general plant overhead).

30. The sum of the year's savings on current expenditures when a technical change has been carried out must be determined in the estimates on the basis of the estimated cost and estimated volume of production. When a year's savings are determined after the technical change, they should be determined not for the first year after the change (as it was established by the Provisional Regulations), but as an average of several years after the change.

When new types of machines are introduced, it is necessary to calculate not only the year's savings, but savings for the whole life of these machines. In this case the determination of savings must reflect the whole period of the service of the machines until their replacement because of obsolescence.

The economic effectiveness of the new technique must be determined at each stage of designing and introduction. In the predesign and designing stages, one must learn the effectiveness of the new technique as compared with the best existing technique. The new technique should be compared with the best existing technique. In the predesigning stage we must decide, in general, whether it is worthwhile to introduce change.

31. In evaluating new, but already manufactured equip-

ment expenditures should be determined according to price lists. In evaluating new and not yet produced equipment we should take the estimated-standard cost of the plant and the number of the aggregates to be produced. In order to avoid pricing custom-built equipment too highly (and this is frequently a great obstacle to the introduction of new techniques) we must calculate standards ourselves in order to estimate expenditures on completely new equipment (on the basis of the models and corrections needed in order to take into consideration the complexity, weight, size of production etc.).*

The original expenditures on research and designing work as well as expenditures above standards in assembly and adjustment of new equipment models which can be used for designing other projects, should not be included in the cost of equipment when determining effectiveness. The cost of design and experimental work which went directly into the given project must be included in capital investments.

In determining the amount of needed equipment we must consider expenditure of time spent in its repair as well as replacement differences of the equipment work and the percentage of the capacity used.

In determining the size of expenditures which will not be repeated we have to determine the increase or decrease of the circulating means, which will result from the technical change introduced and which may require changes in production cycles or inventories.

These sums should be included when calculating expenditures which will not be repeated when determining the length of the period during which investments pay for themselves.

32. Unlike determining additional capital investments when two variants must be compared or when we compare one concern with some other concern, when we introduce new techniques at a functioning plant a question arises as to whether the old equipment should continue to be used. If this equipment can be used at some other section of the plant, no losses will take place when the old technique is replaced with the new one. If, however, the equipment after being replaced with the new will have to be scrapped, or if its next destination remains unknown, then a question arises as to what part of its original cost was not written off through depreciation and thus did not become a part of the cost of goods produced with its help. Such a situation may emerge when the actual length of service of the equipment does not coincide with the depreciation period. The new technique must be sufficiently effective not only to pay for all additional capital investments it requires but also to cover the loss to the economy of the value of the equipment which depreciation charges have not covered. The shorter the length of service of the equipment, the more effective must be the new technique replacing the existing technique.

What was said about equipment may be applied to all other basic means.

In evaluating old equipment so as to ensure its comparability with new, we must approximate its replacement cost.

***

In correspondence with these recommendations we must work out for each branch a method as to how to determine the economic effectiveness of capital investments and new techniques.

_____

* Evaluation of the structures and production areas is made according to estimates and standards per square meter of the area.

KANTOROVICH ON ECONOMIC CALCULATION[1]

BENJAMIN WARD

University of California

LAST year a book appeared which may take the decisive step in ending an era, a period of almost a century during which the vast majority of bourgeois and socialist economists were unable to communicate on matters relating to the allocation of resources. If so, it is appropriate that the step is the work not of a Soviet economist but of a distinguished mathematician, Professor L. V. Kantorovich, Corresponding Member of the Academy of Sciences U.S.S.R. and serious claimant to the title of "Developer of Linear Programing." This latter claim is based on a book published in 1939 and several papers that appeared, or were written, shortly thereafter, some of which are now available in English.[2]

The present work, though it may do both, was written neither to vindicate this claim nor to improve understanding among the world's economists. The aim rather is to explain how a number of problems which Soviet economists are frequently called upon to solve are presently done in an inadequate way and how substantial improvement can be made. The emphasis, as befits constructive criticism, is on the latter rather than the former. The method is the application of special types of linear programs. The general problem is that of choice of an optimal plan, the first two chapters covering problems of gradually increasing complexity in production and transportation planning, the final chapter dealing with investment choice. Numerical examples are used for the most part in the text, but two appendixes provide mathematical formulations of the various problems, discuss the properties of their solutions, and present algorithms. A fair amount of attention is de-

[1] A review of L. V. Kantorovich, *Ekonomicheskii raschët nailuchshego ispol'zovaniia resursov* ("Economic Calculation of the Best Use of Resources") (Moscow: Akademiia Nauk S.S.S.R., 1959). An English translation is in preparation. I am indebted to Gregory Grossman for bringing the book to my attention, for loaning me his copy, and for criticism of this review. In what follows, numbers in parentheses refer to pages in the text.

[2] L. V. Kantorovich, *Matematicheskie metody organizatsii i planirovaniia proizvodstva* (Leningrad, 1939). A translation by Robert W. Campbell, "Mathematical Methods of Organizing and Planning Production," will appear shortly in *Management Science*. See also the comments by T. Koopmans, *Three Essays on the State of Economic Science* (New York, 1957), p. 68.

voted to problems of doctrine, especially since shadow prices play an important role in most of the solutions. Among other things, linear programing solutions are related to the labor theory of value, and something more sophisticated than a payout period is recommended in investment choice. Finally, toward the end of each of the last two chapters a sort of vision is offered as to how a full panoply of mathematical programing techniques might be applied throughout the economy to provide an approximation to the optimal plan.

I

A typical formulation of a problem in production planning by Kantorovich is the following (pp. 272 f.). There are m economic entities (which may be anything from machines to economic regions), each capable of producing some or all of n different products. A matrix or table of coefficients lists the capacity of each entity in the production of each product in a given time period. The output of any good by an entity is a proportion of capacity output equal to the share, h, of total time available which is devoted to its production. In addition, this collection of economic entities is assigned a target, that is, a set k of outputs of each of the products. The problem then is to "fulfil and overfulfil" the plan as far as possible, but with the proviso that the assortment plan (the proportions of the various products produced) must also be preserved as far as possible. Algebraically, we are given a matrix

$$[a_{ij}] \qquad (i = 1, \ldots, m; \, j = 1, \ldots, n)$$

of non-negative numbers (capacities) with

$$\max_{1 \leq i \leq m} a_{ij} > 0 \qquad (j = 1, \ldots, n)$$

and a set of positive numbers (targets), $k_j > 0 \, (j = 1, \ldots, n)$. To be found is a plan

$$\pi = [h_{ij}] \, (i = 1, \ldots, m; \, j = i, \ldots, n),$$

also of non-negative numbers. In addition,

$$\Sigma_j h_{ij} \leq 1 \qquad (i = 1, \ldots, m).$$

Defining total output of a product in the plan,

$$x_j^{\pi} = \Sigma_i a_{ij} h_{ij} \qquad (j = 1, \ldots, n),$$

the problem is to find the maximum value of

$$\mu(\pi) = \min_{1 \leq j \leq n} \frac{x_j^{\pi}}{k_j}.$$

The ratios in the above expression represent relative degrees of fulfilment of the target (formally they may take any positive value; e.g., a target is not met if the ratio is less than 1). The task is thus viewed as that of finding a plan for which the minimum relative (percentage) fulfilment of any target of the plan has the highest possible value among all possible plans.

This problem was studied by Kantorovich in his 1939 book and probably arose out of his work at that time on the optimal assignment of tasks to machines (p. 12). For example, in producing on machines a number of parts for an assembly, alternative uses of the machines would often be available, and preservation of the product mix would be crucial. The extension of this formulation to strictly economic problems may at first sight seem a dubious enterprise, but under Soviet conditions it appears to make a good deal of sense. For example, at the level of the enterprise the manager is often confronted with just such a plan of physical output targets which he is instructed to overfulfil by as much as possible while preserving assortment.

Much use is made of shadow prices, called "objectively determined valuations" (*ob'ektivno obuslovlennye otsenki*)[3] in this work and "solution factors" (*razreshaiushchie mnozhiteli*) in his earlier writings. In our example the necessary and sufficient conditions for optimality of a plan are that there exists a vector of non-negative factors, $c = (c_1, \ldots, c_n)$, such that

1. $\max\limits_{1 \geq j \geq n} c_j > 0$,

2. $c_j a_{ij} = \max\limits_{1 \leq t \leq n} c_t a_{it} \equiv d_i$,

   for all i and j such that $h_{ij} \neq 0$,

3. $c_i = 0$ if $x_j^{\tau} > k_j \mu(\pi)$,

4. $\Sigma_j h_{ij} = 1$ if $d_i \neq 0$.

These c's are the shadow prices of the products. Condition 2 states that, for any given entity, the value in shadow prices of capacity production of each actually produced output will be equal and a maximum. Alternatively, the values in shadow prices of given equal proportions of production time devoted to each product will be the same and a maximum for all actually produced outputs of an entity. Condition 3 states that if the output of a product overfulfils relative to another in the same plan, its shadow price is zero (this is the reason for minimaxing the objective); condition 4 that if the value of the product of an entity is not zero, it will produce at capacity.

The usefulness of the shadow prices then lies in the fact that if you know them, you can tell whether or not a given plan is optimal. In addition, they may be employed to improve the non-optimal plan, using a solution procedure which Kantorovich applied to specific prob-

lems in 1939 (pp. 323–28). Further still, they may be used to obtain a new optimum when relatively small-scale changes are made in the conditions of the problem (pp. 54–55, 293–95). Kantorovich calls this an application of the property of stability (*ustoichivost'*) exhibited by the shadow prices: i.e., they tend to change not at all or at least not much under such minor alterations (pp. 50–54).

Kantorovich repeatedly emphasizes the "real, concrete" nature of shadow prices (pp. 50–54), by which he means apparently two things: first, that they are wholly determined by the conditions of the particular problem at hand and so are associated with a real situation and, second, that they measure something concrete: the opportunities foregone in the form of increments and decrements of goods. In the first example in the book (pp. 28 ff.) a numerical version of the above problem is considered with m equal to 5 and n to 2. The resulting relative shadow price (c_1/c_2) is, in our language, the equilibrium marginal rate of transformation between the two goods. Kantorovich then brings out in this context that the shadow price measures the amount of product 1 you must do without, in order to get more of product 2. In this sense it is real. The first and last of the above-mentioned uses of shadow prices are employed also in this example.

Of course, the problem is easily adapted to the introduction of variable (and limitational) inputs. When this is done, we have what Kantorovich calls the "fundamental problem of production planning" (p. 282). There is now a set of processes, each using in general both produced and primary inputs and producing intermediate and final products. The problem again is to minimax a target vector of products, that is, to maximize the minimum degree of fulfilment of the

[3] *Otsenka* is not the word used in Russian to designate the Marxian notion of value.

target outputs. Shadow prices can be applied in a new way in this situation. One of the conditions for optimality now is that the net value, in shadow prices, of production by means of a given process be zero if the process is used, and negative otherwise (p. 282). Kantorovich feels that this would be a very useful indicator of correct operation of a firm (the condition would apply equally of course to a group of processes) (pp. 153–57, 295–96).

The application of this criterion would require some departures from current Soviet practice, in Kantorovich's view. Of course, the condition applies only to shadow prices, not to existing prices (pp. 36–39). Second, economic rent (on machinery it is called "rental valuation," *prokatnaia otsenka*) would have to be calculated also in terms of shadow prices (pp. 99–128, 295–96). His general statements on rent are worth quoting:

Conclusion 19. In solving problems involving the use of equipment, one must take into account the fact that this type of equipment is being used in the production of the given product or for the given task, introducing into the calculation the rental valuation of the equipment. Its magnitude, equal to the saving of labor[4] which an additional unit of equipment yields in the optimal plan, is determined by *all the concrete conditions:* the volume and type of work to be carried out, the presence of this type of equipment and the like [pp. 108–9].

Conclusion 20. In solving problems involving the use of scarce [*nedostatochnykh*], more favorable natural resources, one must take account of their use by introducing differential rent into the calculation. The magnitude of the latter is determined by that saving of labor[4] which the use of these resources yields in the optimal plan. If rent is included in the valuation of costs, then the principle of minimum cost is observed in the optimal plan. The magnitude of rent must be taken into account in finding the objectively determined valuations of products [p. 121].[5]

⁴ See p. 550 below.

Rent arises because certain types of equipment or land are especially productive for certain tasks but, for the moment at least, are not available in sufficient quantities to be used wherever they are most productive. Since many types of capital are not given a scarcity value under the existing Soviet price system, this requires a fundamental reorganization and recalculation.

A number of particular problems closely related in form to the fundamental problem are discussed by Kantorovich in the first two chapters. A good deal of attention is also devoted to the transportation problem, including production on single-use locations and transport to centers of fixed demand at minimum total cost (pp. 129–42, 288–90). The presentation here is similar to Western treatments of the problem, but again it should be mentioned that Kantorovich was in the field at a very early date.[6]

II

In treating investment choice, Kantorovich divides the problem into two parts corresponding to the division in the Soviet Union of planning itself into short- and long-term components. The distinction is not sharply preserved, but it seems that the latter is a less partial context, one in which choice takes into account variation of relatively more factors, while, in the former, one may treat, in particular, the shadow prices as fixed

⁵ Italics throughout in text. Elsewhere, italics are in the original unless otherwise stated.

⁶ See L. V. Kantorovich, "O peremeshchenii mass," *Doklady AN S.S.S.R.*, XXXVII, No. 7/8 (1942), 227–29; English translation, "The Translocation of Masses," *Management Science*, V (January, 1958), 1–4. See also the work under review, p. 342, for a ten-item Bibliography, only two of which are non-Russian. These latter are the Koopmans volume on activity analysis and Kuhn and Tucker's *Linear Inequalities and Related Systems*.

over the time period to be considered (pp. 198–99).

In beginning the discussion, Kantorovich asks: "What is the criterion for the usefulness [*tselesoobraznost'*] of a given investment?" (p. 173). A necessary condition is that "the application of the machine during the whole period of its use must yield a saving of labor no less than the input of labor required for its manufacture" (p. 173). However, the number of machines having this property is very large, and the resources which could be devoted to their production limited. Consequently, it is necessary to choose only those machines which bring about the maximum saving of labor over the entire economy in carrying out given tasks. Since it has already been shown that the rental valuation of a machine measures precisely this saving, the solution to the problem is clear.

In the first example (pp. 174 ff.), a tool shop has been assigned the task of producing a number of various types of tools in one month, each of which is capable of realizing various amounts of savings (of rubles valued in already determined national economic shadow prices) in the next month (the savings being relative to the first month). In addition, the tools have a durability of one month, and the shop has limited resources (the limitation being expressed in the same kind of rubles). The problem then is to choose the best production schedule for the shop for the month. Those types of tools with the highest effectiveness or net saving ratio—i.e., saving next month minus costs this month divided by cost this month—are included in the program. The net saving ratio of the last tool adopted is called the "standard effectiveness" (*normal'naia effektivnost'*)[7] and can be used as a criterion for determining such things as

whether to introduce a new type of tool (with its own net saving ratio) into the program or what machine to introduce or exclude from the plan when small changes occur in availabilities or requirements.

The time factor is introduced in a rather artificial way in this example. However, further development of the notion of standard effectiveness leads Kantorovich to the following conclusion:

Conclusion 24. If the standard effectiveness and a system of objectively determined valuations are known for a given and for other intervals of time into which the period under consideration is divided, then, to judge the usefulness of a certain investment, it is necessary (1) to calculate the costs, according to o.d. valuations, entailed in producing the investment and also the effect achieved as a result of its application; (2) to reduce all these sums to a single time interval by means of the value of standard effectiveness; and (3) to compare total cost and effect, i.e., total saving [p. 184].

Later depreciation and the possible existence of different standard effectiveness ratios between different pairs of time periods are also considered (pp. 185–86).

For the most part, in chapter iii Kantorovich starts with shadow prices given. He justifies this in the case of such relatively small and short-term projects as that described above on the grounds that their introduction would have no significant effect on the already constructed plan and that shadow prices are stable over the period (p. 198). In the case of large-scale and relatively long-term investments these conditions would not hold, and it becomes desirable to work out distinct plans, each containing a significantly different variant of the project in order to be sure of optimality and also to introduce explicitly the varia-

[7] Kantorovich appears occasionally to use this term to designate the "own" effectiveness ratio of infra- or extra-marginal machines as well as the equilibrium value (see below, p. 551).

550   BENJAMIN WARD

tion of shadow prices over time (p. 199). No examples of the former calculation are offered, though it is discussed in general terms, and the "dynamic problem" posed in the Appendix really does no more than state that if you have a maximization or minimization problem, you can find a set of shadow prices from which can be derived the standard effectiveness. A number of examples of the latter problem are considered, however. Since the examples in the section on long-term planning are basically concerned not with programing but with further discussion of the role of the standard effectiveness, they will not be described here. Among other things, it is shown that, for a relatively small standard effectiveness, it may be desirable to replace even a new plant by another, much more capital-using one (pp. 204–5).

III

A good deal of attention is devoted by Kantorovich to problems of doctrine, i.e., to the relation between his new concepts and previous ones. In particular, one might wonder what has become of the labor theory of value. The answer is that it is still very much alive. The problem, of course, is how to deal with those relatively scarce products whose shadow prices appear to be raised well above those of the socially needed labor input. Kantorovich believes that "the structure of o.d. valuations related to the optimal plan is in full agreement with the labor theory of value; furthermore, the methods of finding these valuations provide an approach to the calculation of the full social expenditures of labor" (p. 296).

To bring the new doctrine into line with the old, several assumptions are needed:

(a) One must take into account the *full* social input of labor on a given product; (b) manu-facture of a given product must be considered *concretely* in terms of the given structure of productive forces; (c) the inputs *in the optimal plan* must be taken into account, i.e., inputs actually *necessary* for society; (d) the calculation must be made *in average labor*, i.e., labor corresponding to average social conditions [pp. 296–97].

Application of these principles includes a further reduction: various types of labor are reduced to simple labor "according to skill and intensiveness" (p. 297).[8] In addition, a distinct separation is made between factor and product. Then it is proposed to define the socially necessary labor in a unit of product by that number which bears the same ratio to total labor supply as does the shadow price of the product to total value (in shadow prices) of the social product (p. 298). This number is "in value form" (p. 300), but it "really corresponds" to average labor input in the sense that it is invariant under a small change in the plan involving a proportionate change in all factors, the increments all to be devoted to (withdrawn from) production of a specified output.

This is a labor theory of value in the small, i.e., over a range of variation in the plan or in inputs for which the shadow prices do not change. Essentially, it makes use of the substitution theorem. First, it reduces the number of scarce inputs to one by considering only proportionate changes in their availability; second, it considers only those small changes in the "assortment ray"[9] for which the optimal point does not move

[8] In the text (pp. 90–91)—the above discussion occurs in an Appendix—shadow prices of various types of labor are used to reduce each type to simple labor.

[9] The set of targets k_j determine a point in product space. The line from the origin through this point is the assortment ray, which denotes the set of points for which the proportions of the assortment plan are exactly fulfilled.

off the constraining facet on which it was originally located. Over a range of variation in which the particular effective constraint does not change, the linear programing problem is reduced to a problem in input-output analysis involving maximization of a linear combination of the bill of final goods. In such a problem the prices ("labor contents") do not change with a change in the structure of final demand. But this labor theory of value does not work when the optimal point does move off the original facet under a change in plan proportions.

Another question frequently discussed in the book is that of the relation of shadow prices to capitalist prices. Several important differences are found. Paretian rational economics, after all, has nothing to do with an economy in which large-scale unemployment is standard equipment (pp. 20, 303). The essential difference, however, is one of aims: the planned society consciously pointed toward important social goals versus the anarchic market society pointed in the thousand different directions indicated by the self-interest of the individual capitalists (pp. 15, 303–4). Rational calculation at the level of the national economy is simply not possible under capitalism (p. 303).

The business cycle and accompanying fluctuating prices is, of course, another demonstration of the inability of the capitalist system to obtain the shadow prices needed for planning. It is true that in the iterations of Kantorovich's solution procedure the shadow prices fluctuate at each step in the approach to the values of the optimal plan, but, since this occurs only in the calculation procedure, it does not involve those large losses which fluctuations in market prices entail for capitalism (p. 324).

Another comparison leads Kantoro-vich to formulate a theorem in comparative economics:

With an equal level of development of capitalist and socialist states in the economic relation, the profit rate in the capitalist regime is lower than the standard effectiveness in the socialist. This is related to the greater possibilities of development of productive forces in a socialist, than in a capitalist, society [pp. 224–45].

This is a peculiar theorem because, taken as an equilibrium condition, it implies, under the usual assumptions, more investment under capitalism than under socialism. He mentions that the absence of parasitic classes under socialism releases resources for investment projects, thereby tending to reduce the (equilibrium) standard effectiveness (p. 222).

It is possible that he is referring to the relative effectiveness of particular projects rather than to the national economic margin. Emphasis in the supporting text is placed on the failure of capitalist society to use its resources fully, so that any given project might be evaluated by a capitalist at a relatively lower net effectiveness. This could also occur as a result of the partial context in which such decisions are made under capitalism (p. 220) or the peculiarities of the market (see the example, pp. 214–16 in which a capitalist will not build a railroad which a socialist state would, because the capitalist must charge the same price per carload regardless of the cargo). As a result of these differences, it would be possible for Kantorovich's capitalist model to produce both less investment and less consumption than his socialist model, but it is not clear why this would always lead to an equilibrium profit rate lower than the socialist standard effectiveness.

Kantorovich offers an extended discussion of the relation between his proposals for investment choice criteria and those of his Soviet predecessors (pp. 246–67). These arguments are familiar ones, and the proposals against which he is arguing will not be discussed here in detail.[10] Kantorovich finds that V. V. Novozhilov[11] treats these problems more successfully than do the others, though tinkering with prices (applying "scarcity factors" and the like) as proposed by Novozhilov is no substitute for thoroughgoing substitution of shadow prices (pp. 260–61). Two lesser matters may also be noted. Kantorovich finds the use of classical analysis—in particular, the idea of continuous time in investment planning—unhelpful, and he rejects one solution on this ground (p. 259). Second, in calculations involving the standard effectiveness over several time intervals, "it is theoretically necessary to use compound interest (formulas), but practically one can limit one's self to simple interest" (p. 184). In one example, simple interest is justified on the ground that "considering the likelihood of some reduction of the standard effectiveness in the course of time, we would get approximately the same result" (p. 205) as would be given by compounding a decreasing standard effectiveness.

Kantorovich devotes brief attention to the "matrices of inputs and output of Leontief" (pp. 286–88). Deriving the open static system as a very special case of his fundamental problem, he remarks that "this model represents an unsatisfactory [maloudovletvoritel'noe] approximation to actual conditions of production." It does not take account of joint production of several products in a given

[10] See Gregory Grossman, "Scarce Capital and Soviet Doctrine," *Quarterly Journal of Economics*, LXVII (August, 1953), 311–43.

[11] Some of Novozhilov's work is available in English; see *International Economic Papers*, VI (1956), 66–87.

sector or of the existence of alternative processes for producing a given product, and it treats labor as the single scarce input, while, in fact, other factors of production will be available in limited amounts, and labor itself comes in different kinds. Finally, suggestions that the system may be used to generate values which would give "direct relations of equivalence" (i.e., be useful for pricing purposes in the socialist sector) are rejected on the same grounds, with an additional objection to the high degree of aggregation of the products.

IV

Kantorovich's new system of economic planning is designed to eliminate a number of defects in the existing organization. Some of his most interesting remarks deal with current planning practice, and a number of his numerical examples are designed to show that the use of shadow prices gives better results than some "arbitrary" or "fortuitous" determination which would be likely to be applied by Soviet planners at present. Perhaps most important among his criticisms are the following:

1. "Storming," or producing a large fraction of one's planned output in a small fraction of the time available (at the end of the plan period), is in considerable measure a consequence of improperly dovetailed plans so that shortages develop and hold up production all down the line. An increase of 25 per cent or more in output could be obtained if this practice were eliminated (p. 17).

2. There are tremendous losses in the economy which are hidden because they are indirect in their effects. This is a result of the interdependence of economic decision-making and the lack of flexibility in the distribution system (pp. 17, 19).

3. Present prices are not an adequate basis for making allocation decisions (pp. 36–39). To mention one example, steel making during the period of industrialization was not a "profitable" activity in terms of the existing price system, though it was obviously highly profitable in terms of social needs (p. 199). A major defect in the price system is the failure to value equipment at its rental valuation and fixed natural resources according to their economic rents (pp. 209–10). The inadequacy of present prices as a basis for various kinds of decisions is frequently mentioned (pp. 84–85, 200–201, 220).

4. Investment projects are often thought to be so obviously necessary that no economic accounting of the project is necessary for the decision. That this is an error can be seen from the example of electronic computers. At present they bring about such a tremendous saving of labor that their effectiveness might well be several thousand per cent. Thus almost any efforts to shorten construction time, however costly, would be desirable (pp. 197–98).

5. The limitational quality of equipment at the present stage of economic development is often not appreciated. This leads to that gigantomania which was so rightly criticized at the XVIII Party Congress in 1939 (pp. 213–14). Even when it *is* appreciated, only some sort of arbitrary and qualitative attention is given to the matter, a practice which makes the decision more difficult and often brings about no improvement (pp. 223–24).

6. There is currently a certain dichotomy in the construction of the plan by means of value and of (material) balancing approaches. Using shadow prices will provide an "organic union" of the two methods (p. 169).

Elimination of all these defects as a consequence of more rational planning would make it possible to increase efficiency by 30–50 per cent (p. 17).

Kantorovich does not pretend to have solved all problems of economic planning with his programing techniques. One particular difficulty will remain more or less permanently. This is the inability of the national planner, even if he could collect all the data, to solve the millions of equations which would be necessary to determine a national optimum (p. 233). This Hayekian defect in the planning system is by no means devastating in Kantorovich's view, and to provide the reader with some picture of the optimal functioning of a socialist society he sketches in briefly a picture of the rational planning machine in operation (pp. 166–69, 232–39). This is admittedly an idealized picture, and Kantorovich feels that, for good results in national planning, a great deal more work is necessary but that it provides a picture of the end toward which the work should be directed.

First and most important, the planner takes as given by "political and economic" authority and specified social needs the aims of society in the form of final demands. The shadow prices and standard effectiveness are not "regulators" of the economy but only means to the effective realization of goals (pp. 199 f.). On the other hand, certain of the goals may come to be altered as the planning process continues, but only because new possibilities may be uncovered as a result of planning, and this is not viewed as entailing any fundamental alterations of goals by the planners themselves (pp. 233, 237–38). In general, the planners start and end with the final demands determined outside the planning system, just as initial stocks of various resources are treated as data.

In the long-run plan, social aims will be specified for broad categories of goods, and, in its early stages, planning will be carried out in this aggregative form (pp. 240–41). Shadow prices and a standard effectiveness will be calculated and will provide a basis for assigning general goals farther down in the hierarchy.[12] These units—for example, *sovnarkhozy* and, eventually, firms—will be provided with their targets and will calculate their internal shadow prices, taking account of the objective conditions of their operation. These values can then be compared with others, say those of a neighboring *sovnarkhoz*. If they differ for a product or factor by more than the cost of transportation, then the plan is nonoptimal, and some reallocation of goals is required (p. 167). If the requirements for a particular factor turn out to be greater than its availability in a particular period, the planners will change the target, increasing its production and decreasing its use in those areas where net saving to the economy is maximized or net loss minimized. This in turn will lead to a rise in the shadow price(s) for the good (pp. 166–67).

Investment planning will be carried out in a similar manner. However, project makers will now have a national economic standard effectiveness to work with in choosing among projects whose value will truly reflect the usefulness of a given project to an economy possessing its particular configuration of needs and resources. For the larger projects, of course, interaction between the "labor savings" and the value of the standard effectiveness must be taken into account.

[12] The complications brought about by the existence of shadow prices for several levels of aggregation of goods are not discussed.

Thus, by a series of suboptimizations involving every level of the economic hierarchy, the planners will move toward the optimal plan. Taken into account will be the interdependence among successive current plans, the possibility of variation over time of the standard effectiveness, and, always, the fact that a decision with regard to one aspect of the economy has effects on the optimality of many other decisions. The standard format of decision-making at all levels appears to be that of the fundamental problem, though, of course, the central planners are perfectly free to alter these targets, provided that this involves no change in the general targets set for the planners themselves. Indeed, the central planners will presumably alter the targets of lower units whenever the shadow prices for the same good differ between two units by more than transport costs (pp. 166–67).

But it is unfair to Kantorovich's essentially pragmatic aims to overemphasize this vision of a sort of market socialism in reverse, a utopia at once controlled and decentralized. His primary aims are those of the "piecemeal social engineer," involving for the most part corrections of on-the-spot errors with techniques flexible enough to be adapted to the purpose at hand. The aim of the book is to popularize these techniques among economists, not to bring about fundamental changes in Soviet society. Issues of doctrine are raised only to prevent misunderstandings with regard to the meaning of the new concepts, and their "real" nature is emphasized in order to relate the concepts to *real* problems of a socialist economy and to distinguish them from the "subjective" formulations of bourgeois economists.

V

To what extent will Soviet economists be convinced by Kantorovich's arguments, and to what extent will the necessary institutional changes be approved? One bit of evidence on these questions is already in, for Academician V. S. Nemchinov has written a Foreword to the book which is in the form of a critical review.

In the first place, Nemchinov finds linear programing a very effective technique in various areas of economic planning. In particular, the idea that planning is an extremal problem appeals to him (p. 4). The proofs and illustrative examples developed by Kantorovich for the solution of particular problems are deemed the chief merit of the book.

The use of shadow prices as an aid in solving these problems is perfectly acceptable: "They represent unique technical indicators, characterizing the given task" (p. 6). Their application—and Nemchinov repeats this remark numerous times in his brief Foreword—results from the limitational nature of some resources. Under such conditions of scarcity their use helps one to find the maximum possible fulfilment of the plan with the given assortment.

However, Nemchinov believes that Kantorovich has made some serious errors: "The author pretends to the universality of the method of economic calculations proposed by him, which leads him to a number of non sequiturs and false conclusions" (p. 8). There are two related aspects of Nemchinov's criticism. The first is that, while, on the one hand, Kantorovich claims that shadow prices are determined by the particular needs of a particular problem, he nevertheless in other places claims that problems, to be solved correctly, must presuppose the existence of some universal shadow prices. (As noted above, most of the examples involving standard effectiveness in chap. iii are of this kind.) The general criticism of the Soviet price system which

this implies is rejected by Nemchinov, and this interconnection among sets of shadow prices used for different problems is denied.[13]

Second, Kantorovich's interpretation of shadow prices even within a particular problem is believed by Nemchinov to be wrong. Shadow prices "*are not indirect inputs*, as they are treated by the author (pp. 240, 270), but only constant elements of economic calculations of a special type, taking into account the limitational nature of resources" (p. 9). This criticism leads Nemchinov to reject the attempted reconstruction of the labor theory of value on the ground that Kantorovich's defined constant does not measure labor inputs. The attempt to avoid any economic interpretation of the shadow prices but to keep them simply as numbers useful in certain calculations appears to me to smack of that bourgeois idealist science which was once anathema in the Soviet Union. One consequence is that the equilibrium transformation interpretation, which appears to underlie Kantorovich's assertions as to the "reality" of shadow prices, is rejected.

Nemchinov's summary position on the book will perhaps serve as a prognosis for Soviet applications of linear programing, at least in the immediate future:

When the nature of the objectively determined valuations is correctly understood and when the unfounded pretensions of the author to the universality of the given method are dis-

[13] The reason that the need for an underlying set of values (i.e., coefficients of the objective function) only emerges with the investment problem is that Soviet institutions suggest a special form for the current planning problem. In Kantorovich's fundamental problem of production planning, the coefficients of the objective are the reciprocals of the plan targets, that is, the assortment proportions. These serve the same purpose as the set of *given* shadow prices in the investment choice problems: they help determine on the "demand" side the terms on which alternatives are offered. Values are being brought in through the back door.

556   BENJAMIN WARD

carded, then only can the method of economic calculations proposed by L. V. Kantorovich be applied usefully. In this area the author has no little merit, thus permitting publication of his work despite the incorrectness of a number of positions and the controversial character of certain conclusions [pp. 9–10].

The language is a bit harsh, but a large area of application of mathematical methods remains nonetheless. Later, when the machines are in place and the economists trained, the time may come to ask: What are the relations between various sets of shadow prices; or, how generally applicable is the criterion of profitability? And, who knows, maybe then some programer will offer a vision of an economy in which institutions and incentive systems are adapted to the application of these criteria. Whatever the more distant future may bring, it seems highly likely that in the immediate future we shall see a significantly improved orientation of Soviet economists toward problems of allocation of resources.[14]

[14] Nemchinov also edited in 1959 a volume entitled, *Primenenie matematiki v ekonomicheskikh issledovaniiakh* ("The Use of Mathematics in Economic Investigations") (Moscow, 1959). The tone he takes in his introductory article is rather similar to that in the volume under review. Among the more interesting features of this volume are the size of its printing—10,000 as opposed to 3,000 for Kantorovich—and the bibliographical essay and accompanying Bibliography. The latter contains some 150 items, primarily Western, devoted mostly to linear programing but including a number of items on game theory and a bit on stochastic models. Also listed are Wald's famous essay of the 1930's on general equilibrium systems and Neuman's dynamic model. A review of the Kantorovich book appeared in *Planovoe khoziaistvo*, XXXVII (January, 1960), 92–96. It is by A. Boiarskii and is generally critical in tone, emphasizing the un-Marxian nature of much of the work. Linear programing itself is praised, however.

ENTERPRISE AND THE

ORGANIZATION OF INDUSTRY

IT SEEMS quite obvious that both the theory of the firm and the organization of industry will differ between capitalist and "communist" nations. In the former, enterprise is privately owned and operates in a relatively free market milieu; in the latter, almost all enterprises are owned by the state and operated by managers in a context of central planning and direct allocation of factors and goods. This is not to deny, of course, that there are also many important similarities. The papers presented below bring out both the differences and similarities.

The pioneering study in this field is that by G. Bienstock, S. Schwartz and A. Yugow (1944). This study has since been superseded by the important monographs of D. Granick (1954) and J. Berliner (1957). The first paper by Dr. Berliner (below), which summarizes many of the essential ideas of his monograph, is the first to present a reasonably complete "theory" of the Soviet firm. Professor Granick, it should be noted, prefers to view the Soviet enterprise not as an independent decision-making unit but rather as the basic sub-unit in a larger organizational hierarchy (the industry or region). Some of the ideas from his monograph which reflect this approach are contained in his article in Section V. The similarities between these two approaches far outweigh their differences. Dr. Nove takes an approach which is similar to Professor Berliner's, and much of his paper can be viewed as an elaboration of Berliner's basic model. The same can be said for the latter's second paper which, however, stresses the comparative approach (U.S. versus U.S.S.R.).

Prior to 1957 Soviet enterprises were organized on an "industry" basis. That is to say, all ferrous metal plants were under the supervision of the Ministry of Ferrous Metals; similarly with fuel, transport, textiles, and so forth. All major Ministries were located in Moscow. This form of organization and control led to enough difficulties that a major reorganization of industry was undertaken in 1957 substituting for Ministries some 105 Regional Economic Councils or *Sovnarkhozy*. Dr. Hoeffding's article analyzes the causes and consequences of the reorganization. The reader is also referred to Professor Granick's article in Section V, the latter portions of which discuss the reorganization. Further papers on this subject are A. Nove's short and lucid analysis (1957), and M. Kaser's comprehensive and detailed study (1960).

THE INFORMAL ORGANIZATION
OF THE SOVIET FIRM

By Joseph S. Berliner[*]

I. Introduction

The defection of large numbers of former Soviet citizens as a consequence of the late war has provided Western students with a new source of information on the operation of the Soviet industrial enterprise. Formerly the only available sources were Soviet publications which deal, for the most part, with the formal and legal aspects of economic institutions and provide only occasional glimpses of those personal and *informal* relations which are the meat on the bones of a social system. In that literature it is often difficult to tell whether a writer means to describe things as they are or things as they should be according to ideology and law. Part of the literature, however, is a response to the system's need for frank criticism of certain practices, and by an astute reading of published materials Western students have been able to pierce the official façade and sketch out some of the informal features of the system.[1] Nevertheless, the exclusive reliance upon published sources and the absence of personal contact with the people who operate the enterprises have caused the methods of Soviet research to resemble the methods of economic history more than those of contemporary institutional research.

The new emigration from the Soviet Union has afforded an opportunity to talk freely with some of the people who actually managed the enterprises of that imperfectly understood system. Under the sponsorship of the Russian Research Center of Harvard University,

[*] The writer is indebted to the Russian Research Center of Harvard University, which sponsored this interview project under contract to the Human Resources Research Institute of the U. S. Air Force. He wishes to acknowledge his gratitude to Professor Gerschenkron who originally suggested this line of research, and to the many staff members of the Russian Research Center who have contributed the viewpoints of other disciplines to this work.

1. G. Bienstock, S. Schwarz, and A. Yugow, *Management in Russian Industry and Agriculture* (New York, 1946). A. Gerschenkron, "A Neglected Source of Economic Information on Soviet Russia," *The American Slavic and East European Review*, Vol. IX, February 1950, pp. 1–19. D. Granick, "Initiative and Independence of Soviet Plant Management," *The American Slavic and East European Review*, Vol. X, October 1951.

a group of social scientists traveled to Germany in the fall of 1950 to interview these people. A large volume of information on many aspects of Soviet life was collected, most of which is still in the process of analysis. The first results of the study of the management of the Soviet industrial enterprise are now available and are presented in this paper.

II. Sources and Reliability

The material on which this paper is based is a group of interviews conducted with twenty-six persons who had occupied positions at various levels in Soviet economic institutions. In view of the small number of people interviewed and of our lack of "feeling" for the day-to-day experiences and problems of Soviet management, it was decided not to attempt to test hypotheses formulated on the artificial basis of inferences from published sources, but rather to encourage the people interviewed to talk about what they considered important, what kinds of decisions had to be made, what they and their colleagues conceived to be their goals, what techniques were employed in the pursuit of these goals, and so forth. The persons selected were interviewed not as "average respondents" representing a parent statistical population, but as "expert informants" capable of stepping outside of their occupational roles and reporting objectively on what they had experienced and observed in others.[2] The informants were treated not as data themselves, but as sources of data. There are no calculable criteria for the number of persons to be interviewed in this type of study, but the number should be large enough to cover a wide range of industries and managerial positions.[3] The number of

2. The first approach is sometimes referred to as the "sociological" method, and is associated with quantitatively oriented studies such as public opinion measurement. The second, the "anthropological" method, is primarily used for qualitative studies. On the relatively few occasions when interviewing has been used as a method of economic research, the "sociological" approach has been adopted because the setting of the problem has been an economic system familiar to the experience of the researchers. The objectives have therefore been quantitative, as in Katona's consumer behavior studies, or the testing of hypotheses, as in the Oxford Research Group studies of entrepreneurial behavior. Although the Western student of the Soviet economic system is not quite in the position of the anthropologist approaching an entirely unfamiliar society, his "tactile" appreciation of that system is feeble enough to recommend strongly his use of the anthropologist's method.

Cf. (1) "Methods of the Survey of Consumer Finances," *Federal Reserve Bulletin,* July 1950. (2) *Oxford Economic Papers:* No. 1, October 1938, pp. 1–31; No. 2, May 1939, pp. 1–45; No. 3, March 1940, pp. 32–73.

3. The number of interviews was limited in order to reduce the scope of the study in line with the time allocated to the economics portion of the project, and manufacturing industry was made the focus of inquiry. However, qualified informants in related fields were also interviewed.

twenty-six is obviously too small for this purpose, but an effort was made to obtain as fair a spread as possible. The table on the opposite page gives the breakdown of types of industries and positions represented.

The interviews were based upon a prepared list of topics, covering such matters as planning, procurement, finance, investment and capital maintenance. The length of the interviews varied from two to twelve hours of interviewing time, depending upon the competence of the informant. Questions were posed as broadly as possible in order to encourage the informant to answer in his own terms and to stress those aspects of the question he considered important. Each interview was tailored to fit the experience of the particular informant: those who knew more about the enterprise's financial operations were urged to talk at great length on this subject and those who apparently knew little about them were led to talk on other matters about which they did have knowledge. The informants were interviewed only on positions held between the years 1938 and 1941, a compromise period which combined the advantages of recency and relative stability of industrial organization. This is the period to which this paper refers.[4] The interview protocols constitute a body of documents totalling 670 pages.

Space does not permit a discussion of all the methodological problems which the reader would rightly want to know about in order to evaluate these results. But one problem — that of the anti-Soviet bias of the informants — is so fundamental that something must be said about it. Although there is no doubt as to the anti-Soviet sentiments of the majority of these former Soviet citizens, it would be as idle to reject their testimony categorically as it would be to accept it uncritically. The following are some of the reasons for believing that the informants' discussions of their industrial experience provide valid information:

(1) Surprisingly enough, the overwhelming proportion of the non-returners, including those who are strongly anti-Soviet, are convinced socialists. What they point to as negative features of the Soviet economy are such things as excessive bureaucracy, the intensity of the production drive, and certain deficiencies in planning. But in principle they accept economic planning and government ownership of industry (especially the basic industries), and are quick to defend

4. For convenience of presentation the tense used in this paper is the historical present referring to the period 1938–1941. The names of administrative organs are those used in that period. Although most of the references to Soviet sources are taken from the postwar period, similar illustrations may be found in the prewar literature.

POSITIONS

Industries	Directors	Chief Engineers	Department Chiefs	Junior Managerial Personnel	Non-managerial Technical Personnel	Inspectors	Technical Planning, Research	Total
Heavy	2	1	4*	2	1	1*	3	14
Light (all-union)		1	2					3
Light (local and co-operative)		1	2*	1				4
Construction	1		2				1	4
Government Planning and Financial Organs					1	1		2
Trade, Law, Procurement	1		1		2		1	5
Total	4	3	11	3	4	2	5	32†

* One informant worked in a commissariat, not in an enterprise.
† Some informants were interviewed on more than one position which they had occupied during the later prewar years.

it against the claims of "capitalism" and "private property" which are semantically negative concepts to them. Therefore, in this rather technical, non-political interview on their industrial experience and attitudes the informants were inclined to take a much more objective position than, say, in a discussion of the secret police. It is one thing to talk with DP's about the injustices of the Soviet system, but quite another to talk about the socialist economy.

(2) Quite apart from anti-Soviet bias, most of the informants were professional engineers, economists, etc., with a natural sense of professional dignity. Most were proud of their technical education, their professional competence and, indeed, of their enterprises too. It was precisely on these subjects that the interviews were focused, not on political matters.

(3) The informants were carefully briefed on the nature of this research project, which was objective scholarly research on the Soviet enterprise. It was emphasized that people's judgments about the Soviet Union would be influenced by our findings, and that it was extremely important neither to underestimate nor to overestimate the efficiency of the economic system. A slight indication of the success of this approach is the fact that several informants asked about the views their compatriots had expressed on certain key issues, wanting to correct any anti-Soviet exaggerations which might have been made.

(4) Where conscious or unconscious bias did manifest itself, there is reason to feel that it did not operate in a single direction. Those who desired to magnify the danger of Soviet power would tend to depict it as an economically strong power, and those who desired to disparage the regime would tend to depict it as on the verge of economic collapse. Neither extreme was apparent in the interviews on the industrial enterprise.

(5) For a critical appraisal of the interviews, two types of evidence have been employed: the internal checks of consistency among the views of the different informants, and external checks against published sources. Where certain informants held views which were clearly extreme compared with the views of most informants (as on sensitive subjects such as the harshness of punishments for various economic offenses), the testimony of these informants was treated more critically. As for the check against published sources, almost all of the interview material can be documented by the literature. The contribution of the interviews is to fill some of the gaps in the existing body of knowledge.

(6) Finally, the judgment of the interviewer in the face-to-face

interview situation should be given some weight in appraising the integrity of the informants. The writer's opinion, which is shared by his colleagues who interviewed people on other specialized subjects, is that the great majority of informants sought to tell the truth as they saw it, and those who were inclined to exaggerate were rather easy to detect.

The interview material provides some interesting insights into the operation of the Soviet firm, but it cannot be taken to present a balanced picture. The number of informants is too small to provide a basis for any final conclusions. In particular, the quantitative importance of the aspects of management presented here must remain a matter of surmise and judgment. Unfortunately, the limitations of space do not permit a discussion of other aspects of management which undoubtedly exist in the system but for various reasons did not emerge from the interview material. Nor can more than a few illustrations from the interviews and published sources be given. The full documentation of the results presented here will be published in a forthcoming book. The reader should bear in mind that these results do not purport to present all of the incentives or all of the behavior principles of Soviet plant management, but only those which emerge from the analysis of the interviews.

III. GOALS OF MANAGERIAL BEHAVIOR

By reading the interview protocols with an eye for the reasons which the informants gave for doing the things they did, it is possible to make some statements about the goals of management.[5] It should be pointed out that a study of goals and incentives was not anticipated in the research plan and that informants were not asked directly about these matters. Therefore, virtually all the remarks indicative of incentives were uttered spontaneously by the informants in the context of a discussion of some other topic such as planning or procurement.

Premia

Soviet writers frequently point to monetary bonuses, alongside of certain social motivations, as an important incentive for plant management.[6] The great extent to which this incentive has actually penetrated into the decision-making processes of management is

5. By management we mean all levels from shop chief to director, and by the firm we refer to all manufacturing enterprises which engage in actual physical production. When a statement applies only to one group of management or to one type of firm, this will be specified.

6. E.g., P. Pavlov, *O planovykh khoziaistvennykh rychagakh sotsialisticheskogo gosudarstva* (The Economic Planning Levers of the Socialist State) (Leningradskoe gazetno-zhurnalnoe i knizhnoe izd-vo. 1950), p. 139.

testified to by the numerous references to "premia" in the interviews. In contrast to the basic salary, which is automatically forthcoming in return for a month's *work*, the premium is a bonus paid in return for *performance* equal to or better than planned. The basic salary was practically never mentioned in the interviews,[7] but the frequency of the references to premia indicates that it is the latter which are at the forefront of managerial decision-making. They operate at all levels of management in day-to-day decision-making, not in the analytical sense that a managerial official in an American factory seeks to "maximize profit," but in the concrete operational sense that the competitive business man tries to "make a buck."

There are three kinds of premia referred to by the informants. The main kind is that paid for successful fulfillment of the output plan. The second is paid in proportion to the overfulfillment of specific tasks, such as cost reduction, economy of fuels, economy of wages, etc. The third is paid for general performance and, unlike the first two, is not based on a fixed schedule of rates.[8]

These categories correspond more or less to the official classification of premia. For example, the rates of premia for overfulfillment of plan have been published for management of large automotive transport enterprises:

Size of Premia as a Percentage of the Basic Salary[9]

	For Plan Fulfillment	For Each 1% of Plan Overfulfillment
Senior Management (Director, Chief Engineer)	up to 30%	up to 4%
Intermediate Management (Chiefs of Departments)	up to 25%	up to 3%
Junior Management (Shop Chiefs, etc.)	up to 20%	up to 3%

7. Sometimes an informant may fail to mention something not because it is unimportant but because it is so important and self-evident that it does not occur to him to single it out. This may be true in the case of the basic salary, which undoubtedly is the main and ultimate monetary incentive. But the salary is fixed and only the premia vary with effort. Therefore in practical decision-making, the effective incentive which calls forth the extra effort is the variable portion of income, the premia.

8. This sort of premium is paid from the so-called "director's fund." The director's fund is formed out of the firm's profits, and is used for workers welfare, for housing, and to a limited extent for paying premia. But this type of premium does not have the same direct incentive effect as the first two because, as one informant expressed it, "The director's fund was less of an incentive to the technical personnel because the [premia] from the director's fund depended only on the director and you never knew who would get the benefit of it." The director's fund is therefore a second rate incentive compared to the direct premia.

9. L. Bronshtein and B. Budrin, *Planirovanie i uchet avtomobil'nogo transporta* (Planning and Accounting in Automotive Transport) (Gosplanizdat, 1948), p. 150.

Since a substantial proportion of management's earnings hinges upon plan fulfillment, there is little wonder that the informants frequently referred spontaneously to premia. It is also important to note that the difference between 99 per cent of plan fulfillment and 100 per cent means a difference of up to 30 per cent in income. This sharp discontinuity places a great strain upon the honesty of plant accounting[1] and also partially explains such phenomena as the safety factor (see below) and the typical breakneck pace of work toward the end of the month [*shturmovshchina*] in order to meet the monthly plan.

Since the striving for premia is uppermost in the minds of management, and since premia are paid according to certain formalized criteria, these criteria become effective determinants of managerial decisions. Soviet management thinks and works, as it were, on a piece-rate basis. In general, the consequence is the exertion of greater effort, which conforms to the interests of the State. However, there are certain conditions in which the premium incentive leads to behavior contrary to the State's interests. For example, the widespread tendency of management to submit plans which are below actual capacity is based largely on the fact that premia are paid in proportion to the ratio of actual output to planned output; therefore the lower the output plan which the firm succeeds in obtaining, the larger the premia paid for a given volume of actual output. Another example is the fact that the particular way in which premia are calculated may result in an assortment of products different from that planned. As a senior engineer of a production planning department said:

The director of the factory figures that if he puts out 100 machines with the proper quantity of spare parts, he does not get his premium. But if he puts out 102 machines and no spare parts then the chief engineer and all the technical personnel get premia. There is not enough stimulus to producing spare parts.

The tendency of plant managements to submit plans below capacity, and their failure to produce the required product-mix are perennial complaints in the Soviet press.

1. The calculation of plan fulfillment, on the basis of which premia are paid, is carried out by the planning department. A chief of a production planning department described how his management encouraged the planning personnel to manipulate their accounts in order to report plan fulfillment: "In our plant at one time the technical personnel in the planning department did not earn progressive premia. Therefore they were not interested in juggling the figures in order to increase plan fulfillment, so that the other people in the plant could earn progressive premia. Finally, the management itself went to the trust and asked that the planning department be permitted to earn progressive premia also. The trust had no right to do this, but it did."

Profits

Because of the unfortunate use of the word "profits" in Soviet economic terminology, Western students are wont to think of them as analogous in some sense to profits in a competitive economy. The interviews indicate quite clearly that profits play a rather secondary role as an incentive to Soviet plant management. The firm's plan contains a planned profit target, calculated as the residual between planned value of sales (net of the sales tax)[2] and planned cost of production. Fulfillment of the planned profit target is only one of the several criteria of the firm's success alongside of other "quantitative indices" (e.g., volume of output, total wage bill) and "qualitative indices" (e.g., reduction of cost of production, increase in labor productivity). But it is primarily for fulfillment of their output plans that managerial personnel earn premia,[3] and it is therefore significant that when the informants were asked why they desired *profits*, they usually reinterpreted the question and answered in terms of the benefits of *output plan* fulfillment, namely, premia. For example, the following discussion with a chief of a production-planning department:

Q   Were you interested in making profits?
A. Yes, if the plan were overfulfilled. Say we had a plan for 3,000 veneers and we produced 3,500. The chief administration[4] would automatically send funds as premia to our leading personnel. They might also send clothing as well as money. . . .   The director might get a premium of 5,000 rubles.   Also the commercial director and the shop chiefs.

Profits were desirable *"if* the [output] plan was fulfilled," and then the informant proceeded to list not the direct benefits of *profit* plan fulfillment, but the direct benefits of *output* plan fulfillment. In

2. The sales (or turnover) tax is a commodity tax levied almost exclusively upon consumers goods, and therefore plays a relatively minor role in inter-firm sales.
3. Officially, although premia are to be paid in proportion to output plan overfulfillment, they are not to be paid at all unless other planned indices are met, such as planned cost reduction, correct assortment of products, etc. (Bronshtein, *op. cit.*, p. 149).   However, it is clear from the interviews, and corroborated by long-standing complaints in the Soviet press that these side conditions are often overlooked.   For example, "The managers of individual plants think that it is enough to fulfill the plan for gross output alone, forgetting about qualitative indices." ("For Further Development of Socialist Competition," *Current Digest of the Soviet Press*, Vol. III, No. 2, p. 36.)   Then the article describes how a plant had won the challenge Red Banner (and therefore presumably had earned large premia) for the highest plan fulfillment, but the Banner had to be taken away from it later because it had failed to produce the correct assortment and to meet its labor productivity target.   Whether the premia were also withdrawn is not stated.
4. The department of the ministry responsible for a number of enterprises, to which the enterprises are directly accountable.

our interpretation, if the firm could fulfill either the profit plan or the output plan but not both,[5] it ordinarily would choose that alternative which provided premia, i.e., fulfillment of the output plan.[6]

It is true that a certain proportion of planned profits and a larger proportion of overplan profits are assigned to the "director's fund," the benefits of which go to the plant personnel in the form of housing, special bonuses, etc.[7] But, as indicated in footnote 8 on page 348, this fund does not have the direct day-to-day incentive quality of the striving for premia. As for that portion of overplan profits which does not go into the director's fund, the informants had no interest in this, because it was thought to be taken away automatically. As a chief engineer of a small rubber products plant said:

> If at the end of the year you have made a large supplementary profit, you do not keep it for the next year. The financial plan permits you to keep only a certain amount of working capital. . . . If the profit exceeds the legal amount of working capital, the excess is taken away next year.

Every Soviet firm has a maximum limit placed upon the volume of working capital which it is permitted to possess. Since overplan profits cause this limit to be exceeded, such profits are simply confiscated by the government financial organs. For example, a Soviet handbook for financial officials, after showing the procedure for analyzing the income statement of a chief administration, makes the following recommendation:

> Summarizing the foregoing, we come to the conclusion that the enterprises of the chief administration under examination had in their possession an excess of 14,618 thousand rubles in their working capital during this accounting period. This excess was formed as a result of the overfulfillment of the profit plan. . . .
> On the basis of the above considerations, we may raise the question of confiscating in the immediate future the surplus of 14,618 thousand rubles from the working capital of the chief administration.[8]

Soviet writers frequently refer to profits as an incentive for capital investment, implying that a large volume of profits strengthens

5. A situation which apparently sometimes occurred in the prewar period because output was measured in one set of prices (the so-called "constant prices of 1926/27") and profits in another set of prices (current prices).

6. The numerous complaints in the Soviet press about "narrow-minded" directors pursuing profits at the expense of the output plan usually refer to the distortion of the planned assortment and not to underfulfillment of the planned volume of output. They are therefore not contradictory to the above interpretation of managerial preference.

7. A firm may make overplan profits in various ways, such as producing at a lower cost than planned, producing a larger volume of output than planned, etc.

8. S. M. Kutyrev, *Analiz balansa dokhodov i raskhodov khoziaistvennoi organizatsii* (Analysis of the Income Statement of a Business Organization), (Gosfinizdat, 1948), p. 110.

the firm's case in a petition for new investment. For example, one writer showed an annual increase (1945–1949) in the proportion of new investment in working capital financed out of profits, as corroboration of his statement that "the business enterprise is given the right to increase its own working capital out of profits."[9] Although it is true that planned investment is *financed* out of planned profits, there is no reason to believe that, on the formal level, profits are taken into account in decisions governing new investment. On the informal level, however, a firm which has somehow gained possession of a substantial volume of funds has a good bargaining point in its petition for permission to undertake a small investment program, for then the chief administration has only to grant permission without having to worry about obtaining funds for the firm. As a chief engineer said:

> In order to undertake a small construction job it is necessary only to have the permission of the chief administration. . . . If we have our own funds it is easier to get permission than if you need a loan.

The main source of such funds is indeed profits, but profits which are concealed and not reported. Therefore, except for the small volume of investment financed out of the director's fund, management does not think of its legal profits as an incentive for investment.

The Quiet Life

In combing the interviews for statements of the motivations behind decisions, a concept which cropped up in a number of different interviews is "to live peacefully" [chtoby zhit' spokoino] or a variation of this. Actions are explained on the basis of the desire to "avoid trouble." But the interesting thing is that in most cases the desire "to live peacefully" was given as the motivation for an unlawful action. According to a construction materials testing engineer, who travelled widely among construction projects:

> In the exchange of materials people are not interested in prices.[1] They are mostly interested in getting materials, and it is all done in a friendly and co-operative way. People realize that they must help each other out so that all can live.

It is not quite clear whether the period referred to was after February 1941, when the exchange of materials was illegal, or before

9. P. Pavlov, *op. cit.*, p. 105.
1. It is a curious fact that when asked if the firm ever attempted to manipulate the official fixed prices, the informants almost unanimously denied it. Yet with equal unanimity they described widespread practices of giving gifts, favors and concessions of all sorts to the sellers of deficit commodities. Apparently on the formal level all transactions are carried out at the fixed prices, but there are informal ways of granting virtual price increases to sellers. This practice will give little comfort to our index-number colleagues.

that date when it was at best quasi-legal. In either case, the inference is that in order that "all can live" people must do unlawful things Ordinarily one would expect that people who are motivated to live peacefully would endeavor to stay on the right side of the law. It appears that the conditions of economic success in the Soviet system are such that even cautious people are often compelled to act contrary to certain State injunctions in order to comply with others. As a consequence, law must tend to lose some of its moral force,[2] and enforcement must rely more upon compulsion.

IV. Informal Behavior Principles of Management

Given the goals of management, what are the principles of economic behavior whereby the managers seek to attain these goals? The interviews bring out three modes of behavior which appear to be sufficiently widespread to warrant consideration as general principles. The development of these principles by management is a response not only to the nature of its goals but also to the specific conditions of the economic milieu within which the goals have to be achieved, namely, perennial commodity shortages, an irrational price system, and complex administrative controls over many detailed aspects of the firm's activity.[3]

The Safety Factor

An expression repeated again and again in the interviews is *strakhovka* (safety; insurance). This concept is related to the practice of measuring managerial performance by means of a series of numerical indices. For example, the index of production performance is the percentage fulfillment of the production plan; the index of efficient use of resources is the percentage fulfillment of the cost reduction plan; the index of labor management is the ratio of the final average wage to the planned average wage. It is an axiom of management that a measure of slack must be preserved, a factor of safety, in order that the planned target can be more easily achieved. The large number of specific techniques discussed in the interviews reflect the striving for a safety factor in every sphere of managerial activity. An example

2. Cf. Granick, *op. cit.*, pp. 196–97, for a description of the amoral attitude of Soviet managers toward economic laws.

3. The writer is indebted for this observation to Franklyn D. Holzman of the Russian Research Center. Indeed, changes in the economic milieu would cause changes in the behavior principles even if the goals of management remained the same. For example, a disappearance of commodity shortages as a consequence of a reduced rate of investment would undoubtedly weaken the desire for a "safety factor," although the goals of plant management might not be appreciably affected.

will be given from the area of industrial procurement, which the informants unanimously declare to be the source of more headaches to the Soviet firm than any other aspect of its activity.

The principal method of ensuring a safety factor in the procurement plan is to inflate the statements of material requirements (*zaiavki*)[4] which are approved by the superior organ and become the basis of the procurement plan. As an accountant in a procurement department said:

> We always submitted our materials plans "with a little bit of fat" and the superior organ always returned them "with the fat cut off."

In fact, the fat is not always "cut off," and enterprises frequently succeed in obtaining larger quantities of certain materials than the central planners would have permitted had they known. The device whereby the State seeks to restrain the efforts of plant management to build up a safety factor is the "norm" (*norma*) of materials utilization. This norm is essentially a coefficient of production which establishes the quantity of a factor which a firm may use for each unit of output. Thus, if the established norm is, say, one pound of cotton per yard of finished cloth, and if the firm's output plan has been confirmed at 10,000 yards of cloth, it may not order more than 10,000 pounds of cotton. Similarly, there are norms of labor productivity, norms of machinery utilization, inventory norms, working capital norms, and so forth, all of which set limits upon the freedom of management to make use of its material and financial resources in its own way. The frequent references to norms in the interviews indicate that much of management's energy goes into influencing and manipulating its norms so that it can build up its safety factor.

One consequence of the safety factor in the procurement program is the building up of material hoards, a subject of frequent criticism in the Soviet press. Although some of the informants denied that their firms attempted to hoard,[5] most supported the following statement of a chief engineer:

4. This is one of the key words repeated again and again by the informants which provide an insight into the way Soviet management thinks about the problems of the firm. Other frequently repeated words are the materials allocation order (*nariad*), the norm (*norma*), the report (*otchet*), the premium (*premiia*), overfulfillment of the plan (*perevypolnenie plana*). It would be interesting to compare a word-count of similar interviews with American and Soviet managers. One might guess that the American equivalents of the words listed above would be "taxes," "buyer," "price," etc.

5. When some informants denied and others affirmed the existence of a certain practice, consideration of the circumstances in each particular case provided a basis for differentiating the conditions in which the practice could take place from those in which it could not.

In planning you always try to order more than you need in case something happens. You often receive things you do not need. Every plant has some excessive materials which are not immediately necessary. They often lack things which other plants have in excess, but they do not know about it. They have no legal right to transfer these materials anyhow.[6] They are useless reserves which exist at the same time that other firms have a great need for them. Therefore this is a great loss and a brake on the turnover of goods. Great masses of goods lie in stockrooms and spoil. Sometimes they may lie around for fifteen years. If I order nuts and bolts of a particular size, I am often sent the wrong size, and the things which are sent lie around and rust, maybe for fifteen years. The money involved is insignificant, but you simply can't buy the materials. But in terms of over-all waste of materials, millions of rubles are lost in this way.

The other principal manifestation of the safety factor is the striving to have the firm's output plan set at a level well below capacity. Many of the specific forms of the safety factor have long been complained of in the Soviet press, and are well known to Western students.

Simulation

The Russian word, the frequent reiteration of which led the present writer to present it as a principle of managerial behavior, is *ochkovtiratel'stvo*. Literally it means "rubbing-in someone's eyeglasses," or in our idiom, "pulling the wool over someone's eyes." It refers to the practice of simulating successful performance by a variety of deceptive devices. Four principal techniques of simulation emerge from the interviews.

(1) Producing the wrong assortment of products. The firm's output plan consists of a target figure for total value of output and a series of individual sub-targets, expressed in real units, of the principal products. The firm is supposed to fulfill all of these targets, but in practice the total output target is considered most important, and fulfillment of it is usually enough for the earning of premia.[7] Because the prices at which value of output was computed (the so-called prices of 1926/27) did not reflect the current cost-price ratios of later years, it frequently happened that a given quantity of resources could produce a larger value of output of some products than of others. It was therefore a common practice for a firm to report a large overfulfillment of the value of output target (the main determinant of premia) by shifting factors of production away from the less advantageous

6. In fact, firms do have a legal obligation to sell these hoarded materials through their superior organizations, as this informant acknowledged later. But much of the hoarded material consists of relatively small quantities of a very large number of items, which makes the handling of it a great nuisance.

7. See footnote 3, page 350.

planned products into the overfulfillment of the targets for the more advantageous products. Thus the firm simulates plan overfulfillment by producing an unplanned product-mix.

(2) *Falsified accounting of goods in process.* Factories with relatively long periods of production carry over a large volume of goods in process from month to month. In reporting monthly plan fulfillment the net change in value of goods in process is added to or subtracted from the value of finished output in order to calculate gross value of output. The value of goods in process is extremely difficult to estimate, and the firm often exaggerates this figure in months in which its production has lagged. Related forms of simulation are treating incomplete output as if it were complete and ascribing the output of one period to another period.

(3) *Lowering the quality of output.* If the firm cannot meet its plan with the given quantity of resources, it simulates plan fulfillment by reducing the quality of production in ways that make the available resources stretch further. Sometimes this results in truly shoddy production (especially in consumers' goods production), but often quality reduction is of a less apparent kind, such as the use of fewer holding screws, or combining two bottle washes into a single operation.

(4) *Misappropriation of funds.* Since financial limits are placed upon various specific aspects of the firm's activity, the firm often simulates conformity to these limits by using funds for a purpose for which they were not earmarked. The most frequent manifestation of this is the payment of wages by means of funds earmarked and entered under repair, overhead costs, administrative expenditures, etc.

The specific techniques of simulation are often the subject of attack in Soviet writings. Although no quantitative statement can be made about the prevalence of these or indeed of any of the phenomena discussed in the interviews, the weight of the evidence supports the belief that they exist everywhere in tendencies, and are widespread as actual behavior forms. The evidence to date consists of the long-enduring condemnations of these practices in the official literature, the testimony of the informants, and the logical consistency of these behavior principles with the personal goals of management and the formal criteria of success.

"Blat"[8]

This untranslatable word stands for a widespread practice which seems to be a fundamental element of the informal management of industry. This practice is the use of personal influence, or "pull,"

8. Pronounced "blaht."

with particular reference to obtaining favors to which the person or firm is not *lawfully* entitled. Unlike the preceding behavior principles, this has received relatively little publicity in Soviet writings. But a good indication of the deep roots of *blat* in Soviet life is the rise of a number of widely quoted folk-sayings about it, such as "*blat* is higher than Stalin," or "you have to have *ZIS*." *ZIS* in this context is a play on words, for it is the brand name of a famous Soviet car, but here it represents the initial letters of the expression "acquaintanceship and connections" (*znakomstvo i sviazy*).

Like the other behavior principles, *blat* operates in all aspects of the firm's activity, but is most important in the area of the firm's greatest difficulties, industrial procurement. Most of the major industrial commodities are directly allocated, either by the State Planning Commission (in the prewar period) or by the commissariat whose firms produce them. The allocating organ issues an allocation order (*nariad*) to the consumer, which the latter must present to the producing firm before the producer has the legal right to sell the stated quantity of materials to the consumer. Much of the firm's energy is centered around the allocation order, as was indicated by the frequency with which this term appeared in the testimonies of the informants. The following are some typical situations in which firms are reported to have met their procurement problems by means of *blat*:

(1) If the firm has been unable to procure any allocation order at all through regular channels, it may still be able to obtain the order if it has good *blat* or personal connections with the responsible official in the allocating organ.

(2) If the allocation order specifies a quantity less than that asked by the firm in its statement of requirements, it may be able to repair the deficiency by means of *blat*.

(3) If the firm has been unable to obtain an allocation order by any means, it may still be able to obtain part or all of its requirements without the order if it has good *blat* in the producing enterprise or commissariat.

But even possession of an allocation order does not ensure delivery, for the producing enterprise may not have fulfilled its output plan, or may not be able to deliver on time. Hence the firm with the best *blat* will be able to get its order filled first, in the required quantity and quality. On certain occasions *blat* is used to arrange a mutually beneficial exchange of materials which would not have been possible if not for the personal connections between officials in the two firms.

Any of the officials of the firm who has a cousin or a good friend or a former colleague in the other firm or organ may effect the *blat* transaction. But the need for this sort of informal procedure is so great that it could not be entrusted to the haphazard personal influence of firm officials. Therefore, there has arisen the interesting penumbral occupation of the *tolkach*, or supply expediter.[9] The word means, literally, "pusher," which is also the term applied to the booster locomotive added to a long railroad train to increase its power. The supply expediter is sent out by the firm to "push" for its interests. Sometimes the term is applied to the regular supply officials of the firm when they are particularly skillful in procuring materials by informal means, but the most highly developed form of the supply expediter is a man who specializes in this sort of activity. Often he lives away from the firm, in Moscow or in some other large city where he has the best personal connections. He is usually carried on the books of one enterprise as a "representative," but he often works on a commission basis for several other firms as well. The informants had some very definite ideas about the prototype of the supply expediter. He is a nervous, energetic man, a master of high-pressure techniques, able to talk his way into enterprises and quickly establish a working friendship with the relevant officials. He is lavish with gifts and entertainment and "knows how to drink" with all people. His side earnings, based on special commissions and liberal expense accounts, are thought to be extremely large, but a good supply expediter is so important an asset to the firm that no one begrudges him his income. Furthermore his work is potentially quite dangerous, although he knows how to stay on the right side of the secret police by means of discreetly offered gifts.

Blat plays a role not only in procurement, but in obtaining easier production tasks, in facilitating financial operations, in inducing inspectors to be generous, etc. *Blat* plays an even greater role in the personal enrichment of people and in gaining private unlawful privileges than it does in the operation of the firm. It is an essential thread in the fabric of Soviet society.

V. Expectations Facilitating Informal Methods

The prominence of the principles of safety factor, simulation and *blat* testifies to a large degree of looseness and non-monolithic flexibility in the economic system. Management's ability to behave in these ways depends upon certain expectations of other people's behavior. That is, if large numbers of people engage in *blat*, it must

9. For an official condemnation of the activity of the *tolkach*, see "Ufa Expediters," *Current Digest of the Soviet Press*, Vol. III, No. 5, p. 37.

mean that they expect others to be receptive to propositions. The interviews provide some insight into these expectations.

An expression repeated several times is *krugovaia poruka*, which may be feebly rendered as "mutual support." As used by the informants it refers to the willingness of officials to neglect their official duties in order to help the firm in its unlawful manipulations or to line their own pockets. The chief accountant has to juggle his books in order to conceal certain heavy expenditures for the supply expediter, or the chief of the quality control department has to accept sub-quality production. Sometimes this support is given willingly, out of an awareness that all benefit from the firm's success. But sometimes an official has to be forced to do something illegal for the sake of the firm, by the director's threat that his premia will be cut off or that life will be made generally miserable for him. When people have worked together in a plant for a number of years, they have usually so compromised themselves that they are too dependent upon each other's confidence to resist further involvement. The following is a vivid description by a senior engineer of a production planning department of the forces making for mutual support:

> Sometimes the molds were badly made, and this resulted in a certain part being too heavy. Therefore, the final product will weigh 14 tons instead of 10 tons. I have to explain this error, but I cannot say that it was due to bad work. I must say that tests show that this added strength is necessary. The director will call in the chief design engineer to confirm this statement. He will have to confirm this or everybody will get into trouble, and he is too small a man to object. If he should refuse to do it, the chief engineer and the director will remember this and he will never get a premium again. If he ever gets into any minor trouble, they will make it very hard for him. The chief design engineer often gets into trouble, because his work is difficult and experimental, and he makes many mistakes. Therefore, he must be on good relations with the director, else they will "bury him" one day for one of his inevitable mistakes. . . . This mutual relationship is called *krugovaia proruka*. It is very hard to free yourself of it. You can get out of it only if the minister transfers you to another factory.

This involvement in mutual support may extend even to the secretary of the plant Communist party organization, or to the resident commissariat representative [*kurator*], for the performance of these officials also is measured by their superiors in terms of the success of the firms to which they are attached. Therefore, they are hardly inclined to report the manipulations of a shrewd and successful director or chief accountant. The expectation that numerous officials will countenance the informal manipulations of the firm encourages management to undertake these manipulations.

It is interesting that the commissariat, which is supposed to be the direct arm of State control and pressure upon the firm, was looked upon by many informants as involved in this web of mutual support, and therefore as a source of benevolent aid to the firm.[1] This is partly based on certain long enduring personal associations between plant and commissariat personnel as well as a certain amount of occupational fluidity between them. The commissariat is expected to be willing to help the firm out of difficulties with extra funds or materials, to ease the firm's plan if it can, to provide it with "secret funds" for premia,[2] and to overlook deliberately the unlawful operations of the firm. When the commissariat is referred to by the informants as a source of pressure, it is usually with an awareness that this is the reflection of pressure upon "our commissar" from above, and that basically, firm and commissariat are united by the need to fulfill the plan.

Wherever an official who is supposed to control the firm becomes involved in the web of mutual support, the control system is weakened at that point. It is the officials outside the firm, such as those in the Commissariat of Finance and to some extent the State Bank, who have no motivation to "look the other way" at the firm's transgressions. These officials are therefore more successful as controlling agents from the State's point of view, although *blat* and the generous gift can operate in these quarters too.[3]

1. A revealing article in *Izvestiia* describes how a ministry aided its firms in unlawful ways. The quality checkers of the Ministry of Agriculture had rejected some of the output of firms in the Ministry of Agricultural Machine Building. In response to the complaints of the agriculture people, the machine building ministry took the following actions "to eradicate sub-quality production": (a) firms were granted permission to sell to other ministries the machines rejected by the Ministry of Agriculture, and (b) the minimum standards of quality were lowered by special order. "Uluchshat' kachestvo selskokhoziaistvennykh mashin." (Improve the Quality of Agricultural Machinery), *Izvestiia*, January 6, 1951, p. 2.

2. Several informants, including a former director, referred to certain "secret funds" given to the director by the commissariat or the party, to be used for rewarding plant personnel. The director is accountable to no one for the use of these funds. They are reported to be quite substantial and, if true, must greatly strengthen the hand of the director. It is difficult to assess such statements. Possibly it is an occasional practice which became widely talked about and magnified in importance.

3. The reader will probably think in this connection of the scandals in the Bureau of Internal Revenue and the Reconstruction Finance Corporation and other current disclosures of unsavory practices in American business and government. Although the deification of the "almighty dollar" has undoubtedly succeeded in corrupting the morals of many Americans, public indignation at these disclosures indicates that there is still a moral resistance to these practices. In the case of the Soviet Union, however, the widespread acceptance of *blat* and favors as a normal means of attaining goals, and the glib way in which management breaks laws and regulations, makes the following hypothesis worth suggest-

VI. Characteristics of the Economic System

In considering the behavior of a specific firm it is necessary to know something about those characteristics of the economic system which form the background for decisions. For the free economy such characteristics are the degree of monopoly in the industry, the nature of the product, the point of the business cycle at which the decision is made, etc. The interviews bring out five such characteristics of the Soviet economy.

First is the relative priority of the firm. This is important not only in the firm's relations with the State, but in its relations with other firms. For the significant thing is that priority awareness is not confined to the highest decision-making organs, but has filtered down into the decision-making process of managerial personnel, and firms discriminate among each other according to relative priorities. Sellers take into account the relative priority of competing buyers in deciding who is to get the goods first. Insofar as allocative decisions have to be made on the firm level as well as the State level, the fact that firms actually operate on the basis of a priority scale more or less similar to that of the State means that these lower level decisions correspond to what the State itself would decide if it were able to make all decisions at all levels. Priority awareness becomes a sort of Lerner "Rule" for plant management.

In practice this means that there is a tendency for firms to fill the orders of military customers ahead of heavy industry customers, and of the latter ahead of light industry customers. While Western scholars may question the rationality of this "Rule" of allocation, it probably conforms to the desires of the State. It should be pointed out, however, that in informal inter-firm relations the priority scale used by the firm diverges from the official scale. For example, a textile firm will ordinarily favor an order placed by a military customer over one by another customer. But if the other customer happens to produce ball bearings which the textile firm desperately needs, an informal transaction may be arranged in which the ball bearing producer's order for textiles is quietly placed ahead of that

ing: people indicted for using their public office for illegal personal enrichment would be looked upon by the population with sympathy, as unfortunate victims, rather than with moral indignation.

Many of the things reported in this paper ring a familiar note of American practice. That a practice is not peculiar to the Soviet economy alone does not make it less relevant for the understanding of that system. It does draw attention, however, to the important truth that an industrial system has certain imperatives of its own which transcend the particular forms of social and economic organization. The glaring differences between the two economic systems should not blind us to the important similarities.

of the military customer. The ball bearing producer, of course, then accepts an unplanned order by the textile firm for the delivery of ball bearings.

The second characteristic is the relatively short tenure of office of plant directors. The informants seemed to think that a director who remains in the same plant more than two or three years is rare indeed. Such fluidity of directors must impair the efficiency of management, and directors must lose a considerable amount of time in getting used to new plants. On the other hand, there are certain beneficial consequences for the State, such as the disruption of a smoothly operating system of "mutual support" among officials who have worked together a long time in the same plant. But more interesting is the subjective significance of the short tenure of office, for if directors *expect* to be transferred soon, either as a reward or a punishment, their outlook will be more short-run than that of the more constant part of management. It is impossible to tell whether the general tendency for rapid turnover of directors is actually transformed into an expectation for individual directors, but there are indications of a more short-run outlook among directors. For example, several interviews report a struggle between the mechanical engineer, who is responsible for the long-run maintenance of equipment, and the director who would sacrifice maintenance for the immediate demands of plan fulfillment. If the director expected to remain in the plant for many years he would be more sympathetic to the claims of the mechanical engineer. This is an extremely complex question with ramifications into many other aspects of decision-making such as investment, the safety factor, and incentives.

A third consideration is the firm's recent record of performance. A firm with a record of successful operation can count on the continued informal support of controlling agents and on superficial checks by inspectors, which are necessary for the successful informal operations of the firm. But a firm which has begun to fail can no longer count on these things. The chief accountant will fear to break laws if he feels that an investigation of failure is imminent, the party secretary will prefer not to be implicated with an unsuccessful director and will begin to attack him, the Commissariat of Finance will check the firm's reports more closely, etc. The very fact of incipient failure deprives the firm of those expectations and supports which might have helped it to pull itself up, so that it is catapulted at an accelerating rate into failure. Success facilitates success and failure accelerates failure. Therefore in appraising the situation of a firm it is important to know at what point it is located in the spectrum of performance.

Fourth is the peculiar combination of informal and personal relations operating within the framework of a bureaucratic system. Many of the important decisions which affect the firm are made not on the basis of "arm's length" negotiation involving more or less objective parameters or universally applied criteria but on the basis of personal influence and cloakroom bargaining.   The firm's output plan depends to a large extent upon what the plant officials have been able to bargain out of "Moscow,"[4] the supply plan hinges upon how much can be haggled out of the functionary in the State Planning Commission, and the financial plan is based upon currying the favor of a minor official in the Commissariat of Finance. Informants gave illustrations of important investment decisions reflecting the caprice of an important party official.   The character of an influential commissar affects the conditions of operation of all firms in the commissariat.   The party prestige of the director affects the performance of the firm.   Therefore the personal influence which the firm enjoys in various quarters must be taken into account in explaining why, for example, firm A has less trouble procuring certain deficit materials, whereas firm B has less trouble obtaining funds for wages.

Finally, management does not feel that it has full control over all the operations of the firm. Movements may occur spontaneously inside the firm without the foreknowledge of the senior management, and may go a long way before they can be brought under control. The propaganda for *stakhanovism*[5] and "socialist competition" may set movements afoot in the shops which upset the plant work schedule and endanger some delicate equipment. Party activists and "climbers" may challenge the firm to accept higher production goals, a challenge

---

4. The frequency of the use of the term "Moscow," standing for generalized authority, reflects the degree of centralization of the system in the thinking of the informants. The trips to Moscow are great and important events in the lives of management, especially senior plant officials.   The months of December and January, when the new plans are approved and the annual reports are presented to the superior organs, appear to be a period of great activity and excitement in Moscow. One gets the impression that in these months the trains to and from Moscow are filled with directors, chief accountants, chiefs of planning department, and other officials coming for the annual bargaining over plans, reports, awards, etc. There appears to be a festive air about the occasion, and officials from far-off regions, who come to Moscow less frequently, are filled with the anticipation of renewing old friendships and having a good time on their expense accounts. Commissariats take advantage of the occasion to have business meetings with all their plant officials.   A great deal of money is spent in buying special foods and manufactures not available in smaller cities, to be brought home to eager families. The period seems to have much of the spirit of an annual convention of a trade association.

5. A movement to increase productivity by innovations suggested from below.

which it is difficult for management to ignore. Despite the principle of "one-man leadership," according to which only the direct superior may give orders to his juniors, functional officials in the party or commissariat bring direct pressure to bear on lower plant management. More important, perhaps, is the fact that organs such as the party and the secret police have pipelines of information out of the firm which do not pass over the desks of management, so that management may be confronted with data about the plant which it would have preferred not to have known outside the plant, or indeed, which it may not have known about its own plant. This absence of full control over the firm must also play a role in managerial behavior.

VII. Conclusion

The interviews are a window looking into the Soviet firm, but unfortunately the glass has the properties of a color filter. Only certain wave lengths of light pass through for us to observe. Undoubtedly a different glass would have admitted different kinds of light. It is the task of further research to relate those aspects of management presented here to the larger whole.

There can be little doubt that these results are part of that larger whole. The striking similarity in the independent testimonies of the various informants, and the neat dovetailing of these testimonies with candid hints found in the Soviet sources form too strong a body of evidence to be ignored. The two chief problems ahead are, first, to describe the elements of management which surely exist alongside of those presented here but which failed to emerge from the interviews, and second, to assess the quantitative importance of all of these elements.

For example, among the incentives of management not listed here are pride of work, devotion to the ideal of building for the future, making a successful career, and perhaps the need for recognition, medals, and "getting one's picture in the papers," as the Russians say. Our interviews do not reckon with directors such as Robert Magidoff's friend Golovenko, who did not care that his "bones will rot in the mines" as long as he could "bring to life the entire wealth of the land."[6] But although his incentives transcended the mere desire for premia, his "clever and unscrupulously 'capitalistic' " handling of the director's fund suggests that his behavior principles did not diverge much from those described above. It may be that the importance of the economic milieu in shaping behavior may exceed that of the incentives motivating management, so that managers with quite different motivations from those presented in this paper may nevertheless be forced to follow the behavior principles which the interviews bring out.

Another director whom our picture of management does not explain is John Scott's Zavenyagin, the director of Magnitostroi. The first quarter that his firm showed a profit, Zavenyagin, "with a quixotic gesture," declared that he would thenceforth get along without a subsidy.[7] For a director motivated by premia alone, such neglect of a safety factor would constitute quite irrational behavior. The full picture of Soviet management must account for the Golovenkos and Zavenyagins.

As for the quantitative importance of these results of the interviews, it would undoubtedly enhance our knowledge of the Soviet firm if we could make some statements about what proportion of Soviet managers do the things set forth in this paper and how often they do them. But to require that we measure the strength of the premium incentive or the extensiveness of *blat* is to require that we know more about the Soviet economy than we know about our own. The function of qualitative investigation is twofold; first, to indicate which questions should be asked and which phenomena should be measured when the data and methodology for quantitative research are available; and second, to deal with the kind of knowledge which does not depend upon size or frequency for its relevance but upon patterns and associations.[8] If it is true that the desire for premia is associated with a striving for a safety factor, this is important to know even if we cannot say what proportion of managers are primarily premium-oriented. At the present stage of our knowledge of the Soviet firm we must rely upon such statistical information as we are fortunate to have, and for the rest, continue to gather qualitative evidence in order to arrive at a more balanced judgement.

JOSEPH S. BERLINER.

HARVARD UNIVERSITY

6. Robert Magidoff, *In Anger and Pity* (New York, 1949), pp. 164–174.

7. John Scott, *Behind the Urals* (Cambridge, Mass., 1942), p. 162.

8. Cf. C. Kluckhohn, "An Anthropologist Looks at Psychology," *The American Psychologist*, Vol. 3, No. 10, October 1948, p. 440.

The Problem of "Success Indicators" in Soviet Industry

By A. Nove

Critical analyses of planned economies have tended to concentrate on such problems as rational investment choices, or the proper basis for planners' decisions. These are indeed matters of great importance, to which the experience of the Soviet Union is highly relevant, but it is not to them that the present paper is devoted. Let it be assumed that the decisions of the central planning authority about economic behaviour in all its aspects accord with ultimate wisdom, however this may be defined. There remains the problem of having these decisions implemented at the level at which production takes place, for it remains true, in Russia as elsewhere, that planning authorities produce only official documents. The actual work must be done within an enterprise or firm, under the authority of a director. The director is told from above what he should produce, and what he is told accords with the plan, so on the face of it there is no problem, so long as he does what he is told. However, the situation is much more complicated in reality, and it is my belief that much goes wrong precisely at this stage.

A director of a state enterprise in the Soviet Union owes his position to the ministry or regional authority which appoints him to manage state property, and he is bound by the orders he receives from his superiors. Failure to obey can result in dismissal. He is under orders to implement the plan. Many of the basic materials and components necessary for the productive process are allocated to the enterprise by decision of superior authority, and he must dispose of the product through official disposals agencies, at prices fixed from above. Yet despite all these things, the director is constantly presented with a range of alternative decisions. Let us briefly examine in what they consist.

In the first place, only the man on the spot is likely to know the precise possibilities of the plant under his control, and so he is bound to be involved in the elaboration of the production plan for the enterprise. The planning authority depends, therefore, on his positive collaboration at that stage.

Secondly, the large majority of commodities are not homogeneous. Listed or implied in the plan must be a variety of different types, models, sizes. Then, of course, many enterprises produce more than one commodity. The director is constantly involved in choices as to exactly what to produce, either because the plan does not itemise the variants in detail, or because it is found necessary or convenient to fulfil part of the plan at the expense of another.

1   A

Thirdly, it is vital to the central planning authority, and to the Soviet state, that enterprises produce goods with a minimum expenditure of resources. It is clear that economical operation must depend to a large extent on the management on the spot, and cannot just be prescribed from above—though efforts are made to lay down various " norms ", for instance for the utilisation of certain materials.

Fourthly, the development of new production methods, or of new variants and designs of the product, depend to a large extent on the initiative of those in charge of particular enterprises, or on their willingness to utilise positively the ideas and initiative of others.

Fifthly, despite the existence of central allocation schemes, for a number of materials, the director can, and does, exercise choice. He can, within fairly wide limits, decide what materials to indent for, he can take the initiative in seeking out suppliers and enter into contracts with them, he can try to use his own resources to make on the premises such components as he finds it difficult to obtain from outside sources.

The above list is by no means exhaustive, but should suggest to the reader that it is important for the Soviet economy that managers should use their powers in the desired direction. Mere orders, threats, " terror ", cannot do the job. This is not to say that straight coercion has not played an important role in Soviet economic history. Obviously, it has. However, coercion is not a means of ensuring efficiency, indeed, it is often directly destructive of efficiency. It is effective in ensuring that a few clearly defined priority objectives are met, *at any cost*. With the growing complexity of the economy, and with the emergence of more and more competing pressures for limited resources, the cruder methods of the thirties become less and less satisfactory. As the leaders strive after their basic objective—defined repeatedly as " catching up the most advanced capitalist power in the shortest possible time "—they are driven to consider more carefully the relative scarcity of resources. They are compelled more and more to make economic calculations, to count the cost. This has led to much discussion in print of how best to ensure the efficient operation of enterprises, especially in 1956–57, which has made possible a clearer view of the practical problems involved, and has contributed much of the raw material of the present paper.

The planners, then, must so stimulate the behaviour of plant managers as to achieve efficiency. This can only be done by rewarding " desirable " behaviour, either in cash or in increased esteem, improved chances of promotion, the issue of Orders of Lenin, or some other form of incentive. These rewards, in their turn, must be associated with some definable achievements. The management must know in advance what it must do to qualify for rewards. Therefore it becomes necessary to define what I have called " success indicators " (in Russian, *pokazateli*) under various desirable heads, such as volume of output, reduction in costs, labour productivity, and so on. In a number of respects, which may not be obvious at first sight, many of these indicators have operated in ways which cause managements to deviate from the pursuit of efficiency, and have largely defeated their own ends. The rest of this paper will be devoted to considering these difficulties.

The criterion of success most familiar to us is that of profit. Enterprises are encouraged to make profits in the USSR, and derive material advantages from so doing. A part of the planned profit, and a much larger proportion of any in excess of plan, is used to create a so-called " fund of the enterprise ", formerly known as the director's fund.[1] Part of this money may be devoted to expanding productive capacity over and above the authorised investment plan, part for housing and amenities, part for the payment of bonuses. There is thus an interest in increasing profits. Managers are also interested in avoiding losses, since these are likely to lead to difficulties with the State Bank and attract the unwelcome attention of inspectors from various supervisory agencies. However, profits have not served, so far, as a major criterion of success, and the reasons for this are not far to seek.

The basic difficulty has always been the absence of any objective criterion for price-fixing, and the lack of any logical relationship between prices, profits and the desired assortment of production. Indeed, one critic has rightly argued that this makes the present rules governing allocations to the " Fund of the enterprise " highly unfair, precisely because " it is clear that in the Soviet economy, profit is not the aim or the regulator of production ", so that a reward related to profits does not reflect real efficiency.[2] Another Soviet critic draws attention to the " enormous range of profit rates as between different sectors and between different products within the same sector ".[3] This is a consequence of arbitrary and centralised price-fixing. While it is no longer the normal practice of Soviet planners to fix prices below the prime cost of production, for many products they bare y cover average costs for the given industrial sector. This inevitably leaves a large number of enterprises working at a loss, and indeed their financial plans envisage a deficit. Even now, " in the extractive industries about 25 per cent. of enterprises make planned losses ", and 10 per cent. of engineering (" machine-building ") enterprises are in the same position.[4] The importance of the concept " profit " is necessarily affected by the existence of so many enterprises which make losses through no fault of their own. In any case, the measurement of profit under Soviet

---

[1] Usually from 1 to 6 per cent. of planned profits, plus 20–40 per cent. of any additional profits, subject to a maximum of 5 per cent. of the given enterprise's wages fund. The higher percentages apply to enterprises expected to make small profits. Those expected to make losses are rewarded by the transfer of part of any saving on cost of production to their Fund of the enterprise. Any profits remaining after allocations to this fund are transferred to the state budget, apart from amounts which are retained for purposes specifically authorised—e.g., an approved investment project.

[2] Kagaredov in *Finansy SSSR*, No. 6/1957, pp. 36–7.

[3] Kulikov in *Voprosy Ekonomiki*, No. 9/1957, p. 80.

[4] Kisman and Slavnyi: *Sovetskie Finansy v pyatoi pyatiletke* (Moscow, 1956), p. 63. The data relate to 1956. For a valuable survey of relationship of prices to costs in the last thirty years, see Lynn Turgeon in *Soviet Studies*, October 1957.

conditions is economically misleading, even if one leaves out of account the illogicalities of pricing. There is no interest payment on basic capital, and the depreciation allowances are much too low.[1] There is no land rent, with all the complications which must follow from its absence in the agricultural sector and elsewhere. Profits are expressed not in relation to capital but as a percentage of gross turnover. Under all these circumstances, profitability could not and cannot possibly be used as the basic criterion for economic decision. If managers were allowed to pursue maximum profits, it is clear that their choices between alternative inputs of materials and output of commodities would be highly irrational in relation to the requirements of the economy—unless and until there is a major overhaul of the theory and practice of pricing.

We will return to these problems later on. It is sufficient at this stage merely to note that profits have not been the dominant " success indicator " to which the operations of Soviet enterprises could be geared.

The primary, essential success indicator has been *plan fulfilment* in quantity terms. Other indicators of considerable importance have concerned labour productivity, costs per unit, economy of materials, economy of wages, and the list could be prolonged. In each case, achievement of the plan is rewarded, failure leads to loss of bonus and/or administrative reprimand. Rewards are often very substantial indeed. For example, a manager in the oil industry may receive a bonus of 42 per cent. of his salary for fulfilling the output plan, plus $4\frac{1}{2}$ per cent. for every 1 per cent. over-fulfilment.[2] There is abundant evidence that it is on plan fulfilment that the credit of a manager with his chiefs primarily depends. A whole complex range of problems and distortions arises in connection with the rewarding of plan fulfilment, and these must now be considered.

The first problem arises at the stage of deciding what the plan should be. The director knows that a large bonus awaits him if he exceeds 100 per cent., and the smaller the " 100 per cent." is, the easier it will be to exceed it. The more honest he is about production possibilities, the higher will be the target set him, the more difficult will it be to win the bonus on which, *inter alia*, his wife's promised fur coat may depend. As has been repeatedly pointed out by Soviet writers, honesty is thus penalised, and deceit rewarded.

Then, once the plan has been decided upon, it is often best to avoid overfulfilling it by too wide a margin, for fear of inciting the authorities to make an excessive upward adjustment in the year following. Several sources make this point: a wise director fulfils the plan 105 per cent., not 125 per cent.[3]

[1] Their extreme inadequacy is strikingly illustrated by Safrai in *Voprosy Ekonomiki*, No. 7/1957, and by many others.
[2] *Spravochnik po zarabotnoi plate v neftyanoi promyshlennosti* (Moscow, 1956), p. 192.
[3] For example, Nikolaeva in *Novyi Mir*, No. 7/1957, p. 74, and also *Kommunist*, No. 1/1957, p. 49, and so on.

However, a more serious problem is how to define what the plan is. In some industries, of course, this is not difficult. Thus, electrical energy can be conveniently defined in kilowatt hours. But most enterprises produce many varieties of articles, whether these be machine-tools or cloth, toys or building materials. Success, to be rewarded, requires a definition, a target figure of some kind. It can be in weight, length, numbers, money or some other suitable unit. In almost every case, distortions and illogicalities result in the course of plan fulfilment at the level of the enterprise. On these there is now quite an extensive literature in Soviet periodicals.

When the output target is in tons, then any shift to a less heavy variant will be avoided by the enterprise whenever possible. It does not " pay " to make lightweight rolling mill products, small cement blocks, and so forth. For example, a certain metal works increased its output of roofing iron in a five-year period by 20 per cent. in terms of tons, but by only 10 per cent. in square metres; the plan, of course, was expressed in tons, and the enterprise reached its output target by an economically and technically unnecessary increase in weight.[1] Needless to say, there would be an equally " logical " tendency to avoid making the heavier kinds of roofing iron if the plan were in square metres. A long catalogue of examples of this kind can readily be assembled from the Soviet specialised press.

More common, on the whole, is a measure of success in money terms, by the value of gross output. For many years this " success indicator " has discouraged the production of cheap clothing, since the cheaper is the material used, the harder—other things being equal —it must be to fulfil the plan. For the same reason there has been a marked reluctance to use any but the dearest kinds of steel in tool-making.[2] Again, examples can easily be multiplied, and there seems no doubt that substantial distortions have been introduced into the economy by what one critic has called " the cult of gross output " (kult vala).[3] Then, because gross output includes any increase in the carryover of uncompleted production, there is also a tendency for the management to aim at having an unnecessarily large amount of work in hand at the end of the plan period, exclusively to be able to score a " statistical " success.[4] A more serious, though less obvious, consequence of the use of gross output as an indicator of success is a shortage of spare parts, which for long has been a notorious source of weakness in the USSR. At first sight this may appear strange, since it seems that a sparking plug worth 10 roubles would " count " equally whether it is sold separately or placed in a completed tractor. However, in a tractor this sparking plug is combined with goods and services purchased from *outside* the given enterprise. Suppose, to take a simplified

[1] *Sotsialisticheskii Trud*, No. 1/1957, p. 50.   [2] *Ibid.*, p. 52.
[3] Kondrashev: *Tseno-obrazovanie v promyshlennosti* (Moscow, 1956), p. 32. This writer is among the more radical advocates of price reform.
[4] Antonov in *Planovoe Khozaistvo*, No. 5/1957, p. 83.

example, half of the completed tractor consists of components bought from other factories. Then its total value will be equal to twice the value of the parts which *are* made in the given enterprise. But then it follows that the sparking plug will be worth twice as much, in terms of plan fulfilment, if it is in a completed tractor than if it were sold separately.[1]

Of course, it has not escaped the notice of Soviet economists that gross output can be a misleading criterion of success, because of the effect on the end-result of purchases of goods and services. Some have argued for the use of value-added as a truer measure. Indeed, from 1957 the " cost of work done " in the enterprise, and not gross value, has become the basis for measuring plan fulfilment in the clothing industry.[2] However, the net output principle is also open to grave objection, in that it encourages maximising of work carried out within the enterprise, discourages rational forms of inter-enterprise co-operation and sub-contracting. These arguments were made in a vigorous discussion on this question, and the conclusions seemed on the whole not to favour a change to net output.[3]

Another weakness of plan fulfilment as a major success indicator is the influence of the calendar on economic activity. Targets have necessarily to relate to some date, and so the activities of the management inevitably concentrate on the task of recording the appropriate achievement by the date prescribed, which is by no means the same thing as acting in the most rational manner. This explains the marked tendency towards so-called " storming " (*shturmovshchina*); a mad rush occurs towards the end of every plan period, followed by a lull and then another mad rush. There is an extensive Soviet literature on " storming ", with many an official condemnation of the practice. Yet it goes on, which suggests that it is actively stimulated by the planning system.

The measurement of success over time also introduces the complication of deflating value figures for price changes, a process made difficult by the introduction of new products or variants. The attempt to express output in terms of " unchanged plan prices " has at times led to major distortions of both output and statistics, which it is impossible even to begin to discuss here.[4]

It has already been noted that the management is rewarded not solely for raising output, but also by reference to a whole number of other success indicators. However, far from correcting the deviations listed above, these other indicators either exercise a distorting pull in the same direction or introduce new distortions of their own. Some

[1] Similar cases are discussed by Antonov, *op. cit.*, and by Kontorovich in *Planovoe Khozaistvo*, No. 3/1957.

[2] *Vestnik Statistiki*, No. 3 /1957, pp. 74–75.

[3] Though in the discussion of measuring labour productivity, reported in *Vestnik Statistiki*, No. 3/1957, it was well argued that, for this purpose at least, net output is less misleading than gross.

[4] For a survey of the distorting effects of the use of so-called " unchanged prices of 1926–27 ", see Nove (" 1926–27 and all that ") in *Soviet Studies*, October, 1957.

of the clearest examples concern the rewarding of increases in labour productivity. Since this is calculated, in most cases, by dividing the labour force into the *gross output*, there is just the same interest in inflating the latter to any possible extent. Almost every example of the distorting effects of endeavours to fulfil the plan recurs repeatedly in discussions about the measurement of labour productivity. For instance, in one such discussion it was pointed out that output and productivity in the case of wool cloth are both measured in linear metres, with the consequence that its width averages 106 centimetres, against a technical optimum of 142 centimetres, as this is the easiest way to be rewarded for success under both these heads.[1] Indeed, many are the contrivances by which the management seems able to affect the statistical expression of productivity without any real gain in efficiency, and one wonders whether direct rewards for increases in output per head are a useful way of stimulating the rational use of labour.

Serious difficulties also stand in the way of finding some means of rewarding the management for reducing costs of production. These are mainly connected with changes, real or potential, in the assortment or type of product. Thus one Soviet critic has pointed out that such rewards can incite the management to reduce quality, a tendency which can also be encouraged by rewarding economy of materials.[2] Then there is the question of comparability. A Soviet economist has shown that " in order to provide effective checks on cost reduction, the greatest possible number of products are considered to be comparable ", even though the design may have been appreciably altered.[3] This affects not only the validity of aggregate output statistics, but also the pattern of production. The same economist added: " The question of comparability is often in conflict with the improvement of the quality and range of output of the enterprise, and sometimes acts as a direct obstacle in the path of introducing new and better types of products ", because the enterprise will tend to avoid making " those products which will be deemed ' comparable ' if the change in design involves increased costs per unit ". No one likes to lose their bonus. So here again the success indicator stimulates a departure from the path of economic common sense.

The " success indicator " system has a negative effect in two other ways. It fails to provide any encouragement for innovation, and it does not reward quality or, to put it another way, it does not provide the necessary link between the producer's behaviour and the user's requirements.

First, the question of innovation. The Soviet regime has devoted much effort to the encouragement of inventors, and whole sectors of its industry have certainly been equipped with excellent machinery. However, much of this occurs on the direct order or instigation of the

[1] *Sotsialisticheskii Trud*, No. 1/1957, p. 50.
[2] Kondrashev, *op. cit.*, p. 32.
[3] Vainshenker in *Vestnik Statistiki*, pp. 20–21.

central authorities.   Initiative at the level of the enterprise is, unintentionally, somewhat discouraged.   There is no disposition on the part of superior authority to tolerate a halt for retooling, which is involved in a change of production method or design, since it would affect the current output plan.   Nor is there any reward for risk-taking, though there is generally some risk if a manager takes it upon himself to try something new.   The difficulty has been well stated in a literary periodical: " The introduction of a new method involves risk and, as in all gambling, capital is needed.   Risk involves the possibility of loss, does it not ?   Yet even if a director is given the capital, just let him take a gamble and not win ! . . . No, it does not behove a director to take risks. . . . The trouble is not so much that a few millions might be lost but, God forbid, the quarterly output programme might be threatened.   Then the department concerned will appear in an unfavourable light in the statistical board's report ".[1]

Secondly, a few words about quality and the demand pattern.   Here the problem is intimately connected with the inadequacy of the price mechanism.   Clearly, so long as the primary object of the management is to strain to achieve plans expressed in quantitative terms, quality will suffer.   So long as the goods conform to some minimum standard, they will count for purposes of measuring gross output.   If the user's preferences—be that user a citizen or another factory—do not fit into the various success indicators, they tend to be disregarded.   Since prices are decided centrally, and cannot be varied (save in a very few instances) by agreement between supplier and recipient, an essential economic link is missing.   The consequences have been much commented upon in articles published recently in the USSR.   A Soviet technician argued that the managerial incentive system leads to failure to adapt civil aircraft to the needs of the *Aeroflot* line, and adversely affects the durability of such commodities as rubber tyres and electronic valves by providing no reward for quality.[2]   An economist pointed out that engineering factories are often " uninterested in improving their machines, as this might lead to a worsening of their economically-measurable activities " (i.e. would affect the success indicators).[3] Another economist criticised the repeated failure of the consumers' goods industries to respond to consumer demand.   Requests from the retail trade network are often rejected " because a change in output would lead to the non-fulfilment of the gross output plan " by the manufacturers.[4]

The tendency to distort the output assortment is, of course, limited by certain specifications in the plan itself.   One reason for the excessive centralisation and great detail of planning, which has been the subject of much criticism, has been precisely the need to combat the tendency to distortion inherent in the " success indicator " system.   However,

[1] Lebedev in *Zvezda*, No. 5/1957, p. 155.
[2] *Znamya*, No. 2/1957. This technician had no doubt that the " comrade economists " should devise a connecting link between use-value and profitability.
[3] Ganshtak in *Finansy SSSR*, No. 6/1957, p. 19.
[4] Lokshin in *Voprosy Ekonomiki*, No. 5/1957, p. 132.

there is ample evidence to show that those items which fit most easily into plan fulfilment indicators are produced in excess of the plan, while others remain relatively scarce. Nor can all variants be separately prescribed from above.

In theory, the supervisory organs are supposed to prevent the deviations which have been here described. Among them, the most important are the local Communist party organisations and the immediate superiors of the enterprise (i.e. a department of the economic ministry or, under the recent reform, the appropriate department of the regional economic council). Unfortunately, all these bodies are interested in just the same success indicators as the enterprise. Their credit depends in large part on the plan fulfilments in their area of responsibility. It is Khrushchev himself who has been urging the need to relate even the salaries of party officials with the economic success indicators of their areas. Therefore, far from checking these undesirable tendencies, the " supervisors " connive at, or even encourage them, judging from the indirect evidence available.

.   .   .   .   .

Before turning to a brief discussion of what can be, or is likely to be, done to correct these deficiencies, a few other remarks would be in order, if only to ensure a due sense of proportion. In the first place, it must be emphasised that the paper is concerned with an aspect of Soviet micro-economics—or should it be micro-planning—and not with the more general question of the relative strength and weakness of the Soviet economic system as a whole. This system grew up as part of an attempt by an authoritarian regime to maintain ultra-rapid tempos of industrialisation and to build up military might. To the extent to which these objectives were achieved, it would be foolish to speak of " failure ". Perhaps if the highest priority is maximum growth of heavy industry at almost any cost, in conditions of relative abundance of labour and a lavish supply of untapped natural resources, there is some logic in a system which provides the highest rewards for those who produce more. The student of the British war economy will have little difficulty in finding parallels for many, if not most, of the distortions listed in the preceding pages; the problem of how to stimulate and reward desirable activity by firms was a very real one. It is possible, therefore, that the harmful effects of " success indicators " are an inevitable part of the cost of running an economy dominated by a few priority objectives determined by politicians.

Then it should not be thought that, so far as the USSR is concerned, the distortions discussed here are in any sense new. There is ample evidence that they existed also in the thirties.[1] The new element in the

[1] See, for example, D. Granick's *Management of Industrial Firms in the USSR* (Columbia University Press, 1955). A new book by J. S. Berliner, *Factory and Manager in the USSR* (Harvard, 1957), also deals with these topics, using largely materials relating to the 'thirties, but this book was not to hand at the time of writing.

situation is the effort now being made to probe the sore as part of an attempt to find cures for the disease. For reasons too complex even to touch on here, there is now much less willingness to pay the price, in terms of waste of scarce resources, involved in the highly centralised system of " priority " planning of which the success indicators are a part.

Soviet economists have approached these problems on a number of different levels. Some have gone no further than pointing out ways of improving the existing success indicators—and it is certainly true that some indicators are less unsuitable than others. However, the more thoughtful members of the profession see this question as part of a more fundamental one: the role of the " law of value " (i.e. prices, profits, market forces, rationality) in the Soviet economy. Two national conferences, in December 1956 and May 1957, have been devoted to " the law of value ",[1] and the specialised press has been publishing articles on related topics throughout 1957.

A key element in any such discussion must be the relationship between the central plan and the actual operation of the economy. It must therefore be mentioned that, while the economists argued, the Soviet leaders introduced an important new element into the situation by a radical reorganisation of industrial planning and administration. By a new law, which came into operation on 1 July, 1957, the USSR has been divided into 105 economic regions. Most industrial ministries have been abolished. Each regional authority now plays an important role in directing the operations of industrial enterprises within it and for drawing up plans, subject to the authority of the centre. The reform has many aspects which cannot be discussed here, but in one respect it is most relevant to the problems with which we are concerned. A planning authority with *regional* responsibilities is in quite a different situation from that of the central planners. The latter can, at least in theory, estimate national need in quantitative terms. A planning chief located in Kursk or Archangel cannot do so, and indeed cannot even know the direct consequences of his decisions on enterprises located outside his own area of responsibility. No doubt each region will work to a plan prescribed from above, but there are bound to be decisions to be made at regional level—the more so as one object of the entire scheme is to ensure a much needed increase in local initiative. But what are to be the criteria underlying regional decisions? There are signs that the regions are being provided with success indicators of their own, and of course the obvious one, already in use in " inter-regional competitions ", is gross output in monetary terms. This suggests that all the distortions which have been noted at enterprise level will operate in the new regional structure, only on an even larger scale. Thus the creation of regional planning bodies, far from simplifying the relationship between planners and producers, has introduced

---

[1] Reported in *Voprosy Ekonomiki*, Nos. 2 and 9/1957. Also a similar discussion among statisticians is related in *Vestnik Statistiki*, No. 4/1957.

a new complication, and has made the search for more satisfactory economic criteria more urgent than ever.

These problems must lead to a reconsideration of the role of market forces, of profitability as the irreplaceable all-in criterion of success and of action. Once the economy grows too complex to be controlled effectively from the centre, it is increasingly difficult to avoid using the market mechanism, with a flexible price system responsive to supply and demand. There are signs that some Soviet economists see this clearly enough; thus I. Malyshev has argued for a recognition of the logical connection between rationality and profitability.[1] A leading " official " economist, Gatovski, has also spoken up in favour of a more logical price system and a more extensive role for the profit motive.[2] However, there are serious obstacles in the way of an explicit recognition of the needs of the situation.

One such obstacle is Marxist theory. It is not enough to advocate a more rational price system, it is also necessary to define some means of deciding what a rational price is. Turning to Marx, Soviet economists find themselves saddled with a definition of value in terms of " socially necessary labour power ". This has caused a number of them to criticise the existing price system by reference to the Marxist concept of value; values and prices should, they argue, equal wages of labour plus the " surplus product " created by the workers.[3] Certain exceptions are admitted, e.g. in the case of such interchangeable fuels as coal, oil and natural gas—but this approach involves basing prices on some version of factor *cost* (though there is disagreement about how cost should be defined for this purpose), while almost entirely disregarding use-value, demand. Under such a price system, at best the management will be *indifferent* on whether to produce article A or article B, even though the user would prefer A. Such a theoretical approach as this leaves no place for market forces. It is an interesting question whether Marxist modes of economic thought can be adapted to serve as a basis for necessary reform. The economist Kulikov, in his contribution to the discussion of December, 1956, brought up the point that an unsaleable commodity fails to achieve " social recognition ", i.e. that the labour used in its production is misapplied. Marx did, of course, recognise that a *useless* object has no value. Perhaps someone will have the sense to see that some commodities, though not useless, are

---

[1] *Voprosy Ekonomiki*, No. 3/1957, and again in *Planovoe Khozaistvo*, No. 7/1957. In the latter (p. 63) he urged the need for some objective basis for choice between alternatives at the level of the enterprise.

[2] *Kommunist*, No. 9/1957, and also his contribution to the discussion in *Voprosy Ekonomiki*, No. 9/1957.

[3] In pure form this somewhat scholastic approach may be found in Strumilin's contribution to *Planovoe Khozaistvo*, No. 2/1957. Variants of the same idea are put forward by Kondrashev and Kronrod, and even Malyshev is not free of it. In Strumilin's version the price of any one product should in principle be equal to wages paid out in its production, plus that fraction of society's total expenditure on accumulation and services which is represented by the enterprise's wages bill in relation to the total wages fund.

less useful than others. Then perhaps there will be forged the essential link between " value " and utility, by the recognition of " degrees of social necessity " or " degrees of social recognition ", thus bringing the operation of market forces within the verbal framework of Marxism (e.g., "A is more wanted than B, and therefore, *ceteris paribus*, the labour expended on A is socially more necessary. . . .").

However, there is little doubt that the principal obstacle is not theory, but rather the conviction of the political leaders and planners that *they*, and not any " law of value ", are the regulators of economic life. Their function, indeed, does to a large extent consist in replacing the operation of economic laws by political decision. This attitude is expressed by official economists by denying to the " law of value " a regulatory role under socialism. The contrary view is denounced as " revisionism ". Professor Ostrovityanov put the point this way: " The idea is widespread among foreign economists . . . that output should be regulated by the free fluctuation of market prices . . . under the influence of supply and demand. Such ideas involve the unleashing of elemental forces and would cause anarchy in production, contradicting the very essence of the socialist planned economy ".[1]

It is important to distinguish two strands in the debates now going on in Russia. One line of argument is primarily concerned with *criteria for planners at the centre*. It is admitted by everyone that the importance of economic calculation was underestimated, that planners' minds were confused by an illogical price system, and that in consequence expensive errors were made, particularly in the planning of investments. It may well be that, from the point of view of central planning, a system of values and prices based on some concept of factor cost could serve as a useful criterion. But this paper has been concerned with a rather different (though related) question; not with planners' decisions (be they sound or unsound), but with behaviour at lower hierarchical levels. It is on these levels that the success indicator system has so clearly shown its inadequacy, and official thinking has not yet advanced much nearer to the only possible solution. There is evidence that some Soviet economists have been advocating the " market " idea,[2] and many managers of Soviet enterprises must surely support it, since it is not only conducive to greater efficiency but also enhances their powers. However, it remains politically very difficult to pursue this line of argument.

---

[1] *Pravda*, 26 April, 1957. The " foreign economists " are, principally, Poles and Yugoslavs.

[2] Ostrovityanov, in *Kommunist*, No. 13/1957, p. 99, claimed that the heretical arguments of certain Poles, who had been advocating a free market, were rejected by " the overwhelming majority " of Soviet economists. This means there was a minority which accepted them. The tone of the articles against " revisionism " certainly suggests that Soviet economists have been straying from the path of orthodoxy in these matters. The logic of many of the arguments advanced by the more radical critics certainly leads towards the market solution, though the word " market " is still too " dirty " to appear in print in this connection.

The orthodox theoreticians, and also the Soviet leaders, face a dilemma. They need efficiency, they are in no mood to tolerate the irrationalities of the over centralised planning mechanism inherited from the Stalin period of industrialisation, they repeatedly stress the need for reform. Yet ideological principles and political interests cause them to shy away from a consistent approach to the problems they wish to solve. Marx has said nothing which can help them, but it must also be admitted that they would derive little aid from studies of planning by western economists, as these have dealt almost entirely with the behaviour of a central planning agency. Little has been done to consider the position of the productive units within a planned economy, in relation to the planners and to the incentives provided. It might be useful to compare the position of a Soviet enterprise to that of an autonomous division of a great western monopoly, where we also find the need to reconcile central control with initiative, the stimuli of market forces with the headquarters plan. British nationalised industries are another fruitful field of comparative study—though they mainly operate in sectors where the problem of choice between variants of output scarcely arises. (It might be said in passing that the price policies of our nationalised industries should remind us that irrational pricing is no monopoly of the Soviet world.) It would be useful to examine the experience of Yugoslavia, where market relations have to some extent been restored in recent years, and to consider the discussions which have raged in Poland. The " success indicator " problem is part of a neglected study—the micro-economics of planning. We could spare a sympathetic thought for the Soviet economists who, in not altogether favourable circumstances, are cautiously seeking ways and means of tackling it.

London.

MANAGERIAL INCENTIVES AND DECISIONMAKING: A COMPARISON OF THE UNITED STATES AND THE SOVIET UNION

(By Joseph S. Berliner, Syracuse University)

SUMMARY

The rewards in income and prestige in the United States and Soviet economies are such that a larger proportion of the best young people in the U.S.S.R. turn to careers in heavy industry, science, and higher education, whereas in the United States a larger proportion of the best talent flows into such fields as heavy or light (consumer goods) industry, finance, commerce and trade, law, medicine, etc. Higher education, particularly technical, is more of a prerequisite for the attainment of a top business career in the Soviet Union than in the United States.

The principal managerial incentive in Soviet industry is the bonus paid for overfulfillment of plan targets. The incentive system is successful in the sense that it elicits a high level of managerial effort and performance. But it has the unintended consequence of causing managers to engage in a wide variety of practices that are contrary to the interests of the state. Managers systematically conceal their true production capacity from the planners, produce unplanned types of products, and falsify the volume and quality of production. In the procurement of materials and supplies they tend to order larger quantities than they need, hoard scarce materials, and employ unauthorized special agents who use influence and gifts to ease management's procurement problems. The incentive system causes managers to shy away from innovations that upset the smooth working of the firm.

Since American managers operate in a different economic environment, their problems and therefore their practices differ from those of Soviet managers. But in those aspects of economic life in which the U.S. economy approximates the operating conditions of the Soviet economy, American managers develop forms of behavior similar to those of Soviet managers. The separation of management and ownership characteristic of the modern corporation leads to conflicts of interest between managers and stockholder-owners, and management's pursuit of its own interest leads to activities similar to those of the Soviet manager striving to defend his interests against those of the owner-state. The spread of legislation constricting the freedom of operation of the American firm leads to the evasion of laws and regulations characteristic of the Soviet economy, though on a larger scale there. Finally, under wartime conditions the burgeoning of Government controls and the dominant role of the Government as customer alters the operating conditions of the U.S. economy in such ways that it closely approximates some of the normal operating conditions of the Soviet economy. The change is accompanied by black-market opera-

350 COMPARISONS OF UNITED STATES AND SOVIET ECONOMIES

tions, hoarding, quality deterioration, and the use of influence, practices which are normal in the peacetime Soviet economy.

CHAPTER 1. MANAGERIAL INCENTIVES AND RECRUITMENT

The most important decision a manager has to make is made before he ever becomes a manager; namely, the decision to prepare for a managerial career. The factors influencing this decision are of vital importance for our industrial society. Imagine the consequences if no one aspired to become a manager, or if young people chose management only as a last resort, or if other careers were so attractive that management got only the last pickings of each year's crop of youngsters. It might therefore be appropriate to begin with some reflections on the incentives that the United States and the U.S.S.R. offer their young people to choose a managerial career rather than some other.

The factors motivating young people to choose one or another occupation are probably not vastly different in the two countries. Family tradition is often decisive; many a youngster chooses a career simply because he wishes to be like his father (or mother). Special talents such as those of the artist, or early conceived deep interests, like the boy who must be a scientist, account for the career choices of some others. But most teenagers have no clear idea of what they would like to be. It is with respect to these youths that it is most interesting to speculate upon the incentive-pulls that the two systems offer for the choice of one career or another.

EDUCATION AND CAREER CHOICE

The role of higher education in career choice is different in the two nations. Higher education is very much more of a prerequisite for the prestigeful and high income occupations in the U.S.S.R. than in the United States. To be sure, the person with a high school education or less has an increasingly difficult time entering the managerial ladder of the large American corporation. But in such fields as trade, commerce, construction and in small business in general, the opportunities are still vast for a financially successful career. College, and education in general, is not of decisive importance. And the brute fact is that a college diploma can always be obtained somewhere in the United States, with very little effort or ability, by just about anyone who can pay the tuition and write a semiliterate paragraph. Those who don't aspire to a managerial position or who fail to make the grade can, as workingmen, nevertheless enjoy a standard of living that is the the envy of the world. The point is that the young American who is not inclined toward academic work need not feel that he is out of the competition for our society's best rewards.

This is not true in the U.S.S.R. A number of conversations with young Soviet people have convinced me that to be "worker" is something devoutly to be shunned by most young people who have reached the high school level. There are at least two reasons for this attitude, which seems so anomalous in a "worker's state." The first is the enormously high prestige that Russian (and European) culture has always placed upon the "intelligent," the learned man, the man who works with his mind instead of his hands. The Soviet regime has striven hard to make manual labor respectable, and it undoubtedly has succeeded in endowing the worker with a social position relatively much higher than before the revolution. But the young person who has reached the educational level at which he can choose between being a worker or an "intelligent" would, other things being equal, choose the latter without question.

Other things are not equal, however. In particular, the income possibilities of a worker are far smaller than those of a college graduate, and this is the second reason for the desperate, and sometimes pathetic, drive for a higher education. Of course, a person must have reached the high school level before he can even begin to think about choosing between the career of a worker or an "intelligent." The steady annual expansion in the high school population has had the effect of presenting ever-increasing numbers of young people with the choice, and few of them would freely choose to be workers. If the expansion of the school population had continued, giving more and more young people the opportunity to avoid being workers, it would have raised serious problems for the recruitment of the labor force. The radical reform of the educational system by Khrushchev was undoubtedly motivated, in part, by the wish to avoid that problem.

Thus, the undesirability of a career as a worker has intensified the desire for higher education. Add to this the fact that there is no private enterprise, no small business in which a man could pull himself out of a worker's status and reach a position of prestige and income comparable to the self-made American businessman. I do not wish to state that the door is completely closed. By dint of hard work, ability, and certain other qualities, a Soviet citizen without the college diploma can from time to time rise to an important position in some economic hierarchy. But his chances are about as good as those of an equivalent person in a progressive American corporation. And the young person evaluating the importance of higher education understands this.

Finally, the Russian teenager who decides he has to get a college diploma has very few easy ways out. He can't buy his way into college, as the American student can if he has the money. There are no private colleges that can set whatever standards they wish. To be sure there are instances of bribery or influence, but they are certainly the exception. If the Soviet student wants a college diploma very badly, he has to work hard to gain admission and to be graduated. The very intensity of the drive for education, and the competition of many applicants for the limited number of admissions, permits the high schools and colleges to maintain high standards of performance. Moreover the colleges are financially independent of student tuitions: not only are there no tuitions but most of the students earn stipends. The consequence is that the typical Soviet student works harder and has to meet higher standards of performance than the typical American student. The standards are different in the two countries, of course, because of differences in the philosophy of education. But there is no doubt that study is a much more serious business for the young Soviet student than for the American.

One final note on education and incentives. The quality of the managerial (and technical) manpower of a nation depends on the proportion of the population comprising the pool from which the managers are drawn. That is, if half the population were for some reason excluded from the pool, the quality of the managers would be lower than if the whole population comprised the pool. Both nations suffer in this respect from the fact that rural educational facilities are poorer than urban, which reduces the pool of the potential college group. Since the Soviet rural population is larger percentagewise than that of the United States, and since their rural educational facilities are probably relatively worse than ours, they suffer more than we from this loss. But there are other ways in which our pool is curtailed more than the Soviet. First is the fact that the private cost of education keeps a substantial portion of our talented young people in the lower income groups out of college. I admit that this fact puzzles me. With our network of free State universities and with a fairly abundant scholarship program, I don't fully understand why any competent student who really desired it could not get a college education. It is my impression, however, that systematic studies generally show that we are losing an unfortunate number of young people to higher education for financial reasons. If this is so, we are worse off than the Soviets in this respect, for their education is absolutely free, and most students of any merit earn stipends besides. Lower income young Soviet people may nevertheless be unable to go off to college if the family needs their earnings. A young Soviet women told me, in reply to my question, that this was why she never went on to college. She is not a very good illustration of my point, however, for she went on to say that she really wasn't very smart anyhow.

The second group that is largely lost from America's pool of potential managerial manpower is the Negro and some other racial minorities. It may well be that the proportion of college graduates among some of the Soviet national minorities is smaller than for the Slavic nationalities; I have seen no data on this. But I would doubt that their loss from racial discrimination is as large as ours.

The third and largest group lost from our pool comprises exactly half our population—the female half. Sex discrimination certainly exists in the Soviet economy, probably more in management than in science and technology. But undoubtedly the female population enlarges the pool of technical and managerial manpower much more in the U.S.S.R. than in the United States. The difference in the role of women in the two countries must, I think enter into the balance I am trying to strike, but it is not a subject on which I would recommend that your committee consider writing corrective legislation. For one thing it is not perfectly clear which way sex discrimination works in the United States. Women discriminate against working about as much as jobs discriminate against women.

Let me summarize briefly this discussion of the relationship of education to career choice. Education, and particularly higher education, is more important in the U.S.S.R. than in the United States as the gateway to a prestigeful and highly remunerative career. Competition is keener for higher education, the cost of education to the individual is less, and the standards of admission and performance are higher in the U.S.S.R. Both nations lose part of the potential pool of managerial talent, the U.S.S.R. because of its large rural population, the United States because of financial burdens and racial and sex discrimination.

COMPETITION AMONG CAREERS

How does a managerial career compare with the attractiveness of other careers in the two nations? The young American not dedicated to some particular field, but motivated by a roughly equal desire for prestige and money, might select some field such as law, medicine, business, or engineering. He would decidedly not go into education or science. An equivalent young Soviet person would make a somewhat different choice. He would certainly not select law, which has been assigned a most humble role in Soviet society. Nor would he select medicine, for while the prestige is high, the income is low. On the other hand, higher education or science would be an excellent choice. The very title of "Professor" or "Scientific worker" would assure him one of the highest places of honor in the society. And an outstanding career in either of those fields would assure him an income ranking in the upper 10 percent or perhaps even 5 percent (data are hard to come by) of the population. The difference in the economic and social position of the scientist and teacher in the two countries is of fundamental importance in the matter of career recruitment.

The American who decides to choose a career in the business world has a much wider range of choice than his Soviet counterpart. A great variety of fields offer roughly equivalent rewards in prestige and incomes: advertising, accounting, finance, commerce, trade, sales, light manufacturing, heavy industry. Of all these fields, it is only the latter that would exert a great pull on the young Soviet person. For 40 years the Government and party have hammered home the central role of heavy industry, children are instilled with an admiration of technology, and heavy industry has been endowed with an aura of glamour that exceeds even our American fascination with technology. The ideological cards are stacked, in varying degree, against all other branches of the economy. In keeping with the ideology, the prestige and income possibilities in heavy industry are decidedly greater than in the other branches.

Not only will the student be attracted to heavy industry, but he is likely to choose engineering as his path of entry into whatever branch of heavy industry he selects. He would be attracted to engineering for the educational reasons discussed above. Engineering is, moreover, the most direct line of approach to a managerial career.

The Soviet engineering graduate will find his first job opportunities rather different from those of his American counterpart. If he is at the top of his class, the best offers will come from the research institutes, with top starting salaries and opportunities for graduate work. The poorer students will find lower paying jobs in industry. In the United States the situation is quite the reverse. The most successful students will be snapped up by recruiters from the large corporations, with the best starting salary offers. Some of the top students will, to be sure, spurn the attractive job offers and go on to further graduate work, but I suspect that many of those who go immediately into graduate work are the men who didn't get the good job offers. To be sure, many of the top American students who join the corporations are put immediately into research and development, but as many of them will be working on new passenger car or dishwasher design as will be working on electronic development and automation technique. The Soviet researcher is more likely to be working on the latter than the former.

The young Soviet engineer who goes into industry starts at the bottom of the managerial ladder, as chief of a production shop, or the design or maintenance departments of the enterprise. As new job opportunities develop, he faces the choice of continuing in direct production or taking one of the staff jobs in the enterprise, such as the planning department. If he stays in production proper, his career path may lead to chief engineer of an enterprise or to one of the higher economic agencies. If he moves into staff work, his career may lead to the directorship of an enterprise or of one of the higher organs. Either career leads to the pinnacle of Soviet management.

The paths that are least likely to lead to top management are finance or sales. I would guess the proportion of top management in the United States who started in such fields as finance and sales is much larger than in the U.S.S.R. There are no "colleges of business administration" in the Soviet Union. The ambitious youngster who wants to work for the top of the Soviet business world studies engineering, not personnel and marketing.

Summarizing, industry in the United States has to compete with a wide variety of other branches of economic activity for its share of the best potential managerial talent. In the U.S.S.R. the values and the rewards are concentrated in relatively fewer fields, and industry is far more attractive than most others. Science and higher education, which scarcely compete with industry in the United States, is a strong competitor of industry in the U.S.S.R. Among the various branches of industry, in the United States the light and consumer goods industries compete very effectively for both managerial and engineering talent. In the U.S.S.R. light and consumer goods industries are much less attractive than heavy industry. And finally the nature of industrial recruitment is such that technical education is much more important as part of the training of a would-be manager in the U.S.S.R. than in the United States.

My conclusion is that heavy industry, science and higher education attract, by and large, a better and more competent crop of young people in the U.S.S.R. than in the United States. Moreover, the competition for education is keener in the U.S.S.R., so that they get a more rigorously trained (trained in different ways, to be sure) corps of managerial, engineering, scientific and university personnel. On the other hand, such branches of the economy as sales, advertising, finance, trade and commerce, light industry, and law attract a much more competent group of people in the United States than in the U.S.S.R. Most of the outstanding people in these fields in the United States would, if they were Soviet citizens, have enjoyed successful careers in heavy industry, science, technology, or higher education, There is, after all, nothing startling in this conclusion. It is but another way of saying that each society gets what it pays for.

CHAPTER 2. MANAGERIAL INCENTIVES AND DECISIONMAKING

MATERIAL INCENTIVES

The incentives that attract people into management are not necessarily the same incentives that motivate managers to do their jobs and do them well. What are the goals of the manager? What are the considerations that impel him to make one decision rather than the other?

The moving force of our economic system is the pursuit of private gain. The worker chooses the higher paying job, the businessman accepts the more profitable contract, the investor buys the higher interest security. The usual exceptions must of course be made; the laws must be obeyed, public opinion may sometimes require that one decision be made rather than another, people make wrong decisions, a short-run loss may be accepted for a longer term gain. But by and large—"other things being equal," as the economist likes to say— it is private gain that determines economic decision.

The Soviets have at various times experimented with other forms of incentive, for it did not at first seem quite appropriate that a Socialist economy should stress private gain. But practicality won out over dogma, and private gain has for the last 25 years been the keystone of the managerial incentive system. To be sure, we still find references to various social incentives such as Communist enthusiasm. But we are also reminded that while enthusiasm is well and good, communism, as Lenin used to say, must be built "not directly on enthusiasm but with the aid of enthusiasm born out the great revolution; [communism must be built] on private interest, on personal incentive, on businesslike accounting." [1] Moreover, the incentive of private gain will be with us for a long time. According to the eminent labor economist E. Manevich, it will not disappear until the day of general overabundance arrives, until the differences between country and city are eliminated, and until the differences between mental and manual labor vanish.[2] We are safe in saying that for the next several decades at least, private gain will be the central economic inventive in both economic systems.

The form that material incentives take is of some importance. For the American businessman it is clearly profit. If you ask why did he take on this contract rather than that, why did he order this machine rather than that, why did he ship by truck rather than train, the answer would normally be, "because it's cheaper that way," or what comes to the same thing, "because he would make more money that way."

For the private businessman managing his own business, profit is clearly the guide to his actions. But most American business is not managed in this way. The men who actually run the firm are salaried managers, hired by the stockholders' representative body, the board of directors. The profit of the business does not belong to the manager but to the stockholder-owners. The fact is that the private interest of the manager need not necessarily coincide with that of the stockholder. In order to bring the manager's private interest into closer coincidence with that of the owners, most corporations have instituted some kind of bonus system, on the assumption that if the

[1] Voprosy ekonomiki, 1958, No. 6, p. 74.
[2] Voprosy ekonomiki, 1959, No. 1, p. 35.

manager has a direct stake in the profit of the enterprise, his decisions are more likely to be those that will earn more profit.

In fashioning an incentive system for its managers, the Soviet Government faced a problem similar to that of the American corporation. For all Soviet enterprises are run by salaried managers. If the Soviet manager's income consisted solely of his salary, it was conceivable that his private interest would not coincide at all points with the interest of the Government. Accordingly a considerable variety of supplementary bonuses are available to the managerial staff. The bonuses are designed to motivate managers to make those decisions that the Government considers to be in its own interest.

The amount of income earned in the form of bonuses is substantial. In 1947, the last year for which detailed data are available to me, the managerial personnel of the iron and steel industry earned bonuses averaging 51.4 percent of their basic income. In the food industry at the low end, the percentage was 21 percent.[3] Since these are averages, many individual managers earned considerably more than this. Bonuses of this magnitude must be a potent incentive indeed.

But incentive for what? This is surely the crucial question. For we can readily imagine an incentive which was extremely successful in motivating action, but action of an undesirable kind. The test of an incentive is therefore not only its motivating power, but the extent to which it leads to the desired kind of decision.

Before proceeding to the relationship of incentives to decision making, let me clarify the sense in which I use the term incentive. By incentive I mean that consideration which explains why one decision was made rather than another. If a young person decides to find employment in the electrical machinery industry rather than in the furniture industry, the difference in basic salaries in the two industries may well have been the decisive consideration. In this case salary is the effective incentive. But once in the job, the salary does not vary according to whether one operating decision is made rather than another. When the manager decides to put one order into production ahead of another, or to substitute one material for another, it is not his salary he is thinking about. It is usually the size of the month's bonus that will depend on the decision taken. It is in this sense that the bonus is the principal incentive in the operational decisions of the Soviet enterprise.

PRODUCTION DECISIONS

Two generations ago people debated the question of whether a Socialist economy could possibly work. History removed that question from the agenda. The last generation changed the question to whether the Soviet economy could work at all efficiently. That question has also been answered. These hearings would not otherwise be taking place. My discussion takes for granted that the Soviet economy is reasonably efficient, and that the question at issue is how efficient.

There is little doubt that the system of managerial incentives, broadly viewed, has created a corps of managers dedicated to their

[3] Documentation and further discussion of this chapter's argument may be found in the author's "Factory and Manager in the U.S.S.R." (Harvard University Press, 1957).

work and responsive to the production demands made upon them. Like their American counterparts, they are deeply involved in their work, they worry about production quotas, they demand results from their labor force. As hired managers, they are aware that if their performance is not satisfactory, there are always other persons spoiling for a chance at their jobs. I have no way of knowing whether the intensity of managerial life is greater in the U.S.S.R. than in the United States; in both countries there are variations from industry to industry. But there are two reasons why industrial life probably proceeds at a faster tempo in the U.S.S.R. than here. The first is that the absence of free trade unions makes it difficult for workers to resist pressure for intense operation. The second is that industry is under constant exhortation from Government and party for ever-increasing levels of production.

But the question as indicated above is not whether management is motivated to work hard. It is rather whether the incentive system motivates them to do what the state wishes them to do; whether, in other words, they get as much mileage out of their effort as they might get.

One of the most interesting conclusions of the study of Soviet managerial incentives is that the bonus system is directly responsible for motivating management to make a variety of decisions contrary to the intent and the interests of the state. The decisions to be described go far back in the history of the Soviet economy, and have resisted countless efforts by the Government to eliminate them. Most of them have survived the great organizational changes in industrial organization of the past several years. They are clearly deeply rooted in the soil of Soviet economic organization.

First, consider the matter of the reporting of information. In a planned economy it is vital that the central planners have as accurate information as possible about the productive capacity of enterprises. The bonus system, however, acts as a prevailing motivation for managers to understate their real production capacity. The reason is that the most important of the bonuses available to managers depends on the extent to which the production target of the enterprise is overfulfilled. If the manager honestly reports his full production capacity, and if for some reason something goes wrong in the course of the month, then he and his staff will lose that month's bonus. It is safer therefore to report a smaller capacity than really exists, in order that the production target will be kept low enough to allow for emergencies. The Russians call this "insurance" or "security." The consequence is that the planners can never be sure that their plans are based on accurate figures. The Government is aware of the problem: "This is fully understandable," writes a Soviet economist, "because the lower the plan, the greater the opportunity to fulfill and overfulfill it * * *."[4]

Because the higher state agencies cannot trust management's reporting of its productive capacity, various techniques have been fashioned for setting targets high enough to force the firms to operate as close as possible to capacity. One of these techniques is the arbitrary increase of targets over last year's production. As a prominent state planning commission economist put it, "they take as the base magnitude the level of production achieved during the pre-

---

[4] Voprosy ekonomiki. 1959, No. 3, p. 61, 67.

ceding period and raise it by some percentage or other." [5] Sometimes this technique helps flush out the manager's "hidden reserves," but in other cases the arbitrary increase in targets leads to impossibly high tasks. Indeed, the spirit of planning is reflected in the systematic use of high targets as a device for keeping managers working at as fast a tempo as possible. In the past targets have been set so high (deliberately, one suspects) that one-third of all enterprises failed to fulfill their annual plans. There is some evidence that in the last year or two this policy of deliberate overplanning has been modified, and we are told that in the first half of 1958 only 19 percent of all enterprises failed to fulfill their plans. [6] This still represents one out of five enterprises, and indicates that the high level of plan targets remains a dominant fact of life for the Soviet manager. The intense pace of plant operation has its distinct advantage from the state's point of view: it elicits from management a high level of effort that might not be forthcoming if the plans were set at a more modest level. But the price paid by the state is the manager's effort to defend his enterprise by concealing his full capacity.

When the target has been set, the manager's bonus depends on the success with which he fulfills it. Most of the firm's production does indeed follow the lines laid down in the plan. But when the end of the month rolls around and, as often happens, production is far short of meeting the month's target, then managers turn to a host of time-tested techniques of meeting—or seeming to meet—the targets. In certain types of production, such as metals, the target is expressed in tons; in such cases the manager might order his shops to curtail the production of relatively lightweight products (special and quality metals) and to throw more men and materials into the production of the heavier products. [7] In textile production we read that the practice of setting targets in "running meters" (that is, in measures of length, without regard to width) causes managers to overproduce narrow-width cloth and underproduce broad width. [8] In firms with a considerable variety of products, the production targets are expressed in value units—so many millions of rubles of production. In such cases managers tend to overproduce those products that have high fixed prices (all prices are fixed): they may deliberately use more expensive materials in order to drive up the value of production. [9] These are some of an endless variety of ways in which managers "violate the planned assortment of production"—to use the official expression of disapproval.

How widespread are these practices? We really don't know. From time to time individual managers are publicly excoriated for such practices, and figures are published to show how widely the planned assortment of production had been departed from. But these may well be extreme cases, and it would be unwise to generalize from them. Occasionally, however, the results of special studies are published, and they give us some idea of the magnitude of the problem. The State planning commission recently released the results of a survey of the production practices of 63 enterprises. Of the total production by these enterprises in excess of the plan targets,

[5] Voprosy ekonomiki, 1957, No. 4, p. 70.
[6] Planovoe khoziaistvo, 1958, No. 10, p. 5.
[7] Voprosy ekonomiki, 1958, No. 7. p. 51.
[8] Voprosy ekonomiki, 1959, No. 6, p. 19.
[9] Voprosy ekonomiki, 1958, No. 6, p. 129.

only 43 percent consisted of the basic products normally produced by them; 26.5 percent consisted of "products not included in the plan when it was originally confirmed," 20 percent consisted of "other production," and 7 percent consisted not of finished products but of an increase in semifabricated parts and good-in-process.[10] While these data are not precisely in the form in which we would want them, they do provide a good indication of managers' tendency to produce those products that are best from their own enterprises' point of view, rather than those products that the State would most wish to have produced.

Two other consequences of the bonus system (and the pressure of high targets) should be noted. One is the simple falsification of reported production. "Thus, for example," we read in a Soviet article, "if the plan is fulfilled 99 per cent, the managerial and engineering personnel receive no bonus. But if the enterprise fulfills the plan 100 percent, they receive bonuses of from 15 to 37 percent of their salary."[11] Quite a lot of money hinges on that last percentage of production, and it is no wonder that management may succumb to the temptation to "fudge" the report a bit in order to earn the bonus. Again, the techniques of covering up for falsely reported production are myriad. To cite only one, production is "borrowed" from next month. That is, production that is expected to occur next month is reported as having been produced this month. If things go well next month, the "borrowed" output is "repaid"; if not the manager may get into trouble.

More serious than falsification, however, is the deterioration of the quality of production. The poor quality of much of Soviet consumer goods production is well known. In other types of production the danger of detection is greater, and quality standards are less readily violated. But the explanation of management's tendency to shave on quality is the same: the high production targets are so often not attainable, and the manager wants to keep his job. Much of the quality shaving is of a kind that is not easily detected: fewer stitches in the garment, fewer screws in the piece, greener lumber in the building, more impurities in the metal. But if the pressure is keen enough, more extreme forms of quality deterioration will be adopted.

Summarizing, the bonus system is an effective device for eliciting a high level of managerial effort, but in the context of excessively high production targets, it induces management to make certain types of decisions that are contrary to the intent of the State. The production of unplanned products, the concealment of production capacity, the falsification of reports and the deterioration of quality are the unintended consequences of the system of managerial incentives.

PROCUREMENT DECISIONS

The high level of production targets is but half the problem facing the Soviet manager. The other half is the perpetual shortage of materials and supplies. In order to get the greatest possible production from the available stocks of materials and supplies, the State employs a variety of devices to minimize the use of materials in production and inventory. Undoubtedly these devices have served to

---

[10] Planovoe khoziaistvo, 1958, No. 10, pp. 5–6. The study deals only with that portion of the firm's production in excess of their planned targets.
[11] Voprosy ekonomiki, 1959, No. 3, p. 67.

360 COMPARISONS OF UNITED STATES AND SOVIET ECONOMIES

control wasteful use of resources, and they have also helped channel the flow of resources in the direction most desired by the State. But they have been self-defeating to some extent for they have forced managers to make certain kinds of decisions which frustrate the intent of the State.

The core of the matter is that managers simply don't trust the planning system to provide them with the supplies and materials they need in the right quantity and quality, and at the right time. The recent decentralization of industrial organization may have improved matters somewhat, but the evidence we have indicates that supply problems are still the most troublesome feature of managerial life. Moreover, the reasons are similar to those we used to read about before decentralization. For all important materials the manager must still obtain an allocation order from his home office (usually the Council of the National Economy of his district), which must in turn get the allocation order from the republican or all-union planning commission.

Thus, we still read of the "existing complicated system of obtaining allocation orders, under which every enterprise must submit detailed requisitions to Moscow a long time before the new planning quarter is to begin." [12] Because plans are not always finally set at the time the planning period is to begin, enterprises sometimes start with "advance allocations," that is, temporary allotments of resources designed to keep them operating until the final allocation orders are available. [13] Decentralization of the economy was supposed to have made it easier for neighboring enterprises to sell to each other without having to go through Moscow. But central purchasing agencies still exist, and agencies anywhere must find something to do. Thus the Chief Purchasing and Marketing Administration located in the republic capitals (Moscow, for example) still insist on being the middleman in purchase and sale contracts between enterprises, even when the latter are located in the same outlying city (such as Sverdlovsk). [14] Perhaps even more serious than the complex supply planning system is the large percentage of enterprise that regularly fail to fulfill their plans, or fulfill them by producing the wrong products or substandard products. Since the production of these enterprises constitute the planned supplies of other enterprises, the supplies of the latter are delayed or simply not available. Perhaps enough has been said to explain why "managers of enterprises did not have confidence in the possibility of getting their materials on time and having them delivered to the factory by the supply depot's trucks." [15]

What does the manager do to make sure he gets his supplies? Just as he "secures" his production plan by attempting to conceal the existence of some production capacity, so he "secures" the flow of supplies in various ways. He overorders, in the hope that if he doesn't get all he ordered, he may at least get as much as he needs. He also orders excessively large amounts of some supplies in order to be able to buy directly from the producer, instead of having to go through the maze of jobbing depots. A survey of 15 Moscow enterprises showed a 10.4 percent overordering of metals for just this reason. [16] Sometimes management's boldest efforts to obtain supplies

---

12 Planovoe khoziaistvo, 1959, No. 4, p. 58.
13 Ibid., p. 65.
14 Voprosy ekonomiki, 1959, No. 5, p. 75.
15 Planovoe khoziaistvo, 1959, No. 5, p. 85.
16 Planovoe khoziaistvo, 1959, No. 5, p. 84

are unsuccessful: "* * * over 300,000 construction workers undergo work stoppages daily because of the absence of materials at the workplace." [17] In other cases their padded requisitions are accepted and they receive more than they need of some materials. The consequence is the piling up of hoards of supplies of all kinds, one of the most enduring problems of Soviet industrial organization. The Government has waged a longstanding war against hoarding. One of the weapons by which it attempts to hold hoarding within bounds is through the use of quotas of working capital; that is, for its annual production program the enterprise is allowed to keep on hand at any one time no more than so many tons of coal, so many board feet of lumber, so many rubles worth of inventory. These quotas must be negotiated between enterprise and government, and the enterprise's interest demands that they be set as high as possible. The mutual attempt at outguessing the other leads to a familiar bureaucratic game: "* * * enterprises try to 'justify' and obtain as large quotas of working capital as possible. The financial agencies, aware of this, strive on the other hand to reduce the quotas of working capital." [18] This kind of planning is hardly calculated to lead to the establishment of the optimal quotas. It is more likely that some quotas will be too large and some too small.

The most interesting of the techniques used by managers to "secure" their supply of materials is the employment of special supply expediters called tolkachi, or "pushers." The table of organization does not provide for this occupation, yet so great is the need that firms manage somehow to employ these people. The chief job of the expediter is to make sure that his enterprise gets the materials it needs and when it needs them. Accordingly he spends most of his time on the road, visiting his enterprise's suppliers, handing out little gifts here and there to assure that his orders are well-handled, [19] picking up supplies of one kind or another that his firm may be able to use or trade for other goods. Much of their activity is associated with the black market, that is, obtaining materials for which no allocation order has been issued. This may be done either by wrangling an allocation order out of a reluctant government official by one means or another, or persuading an approachable enterprise official to sell him the things he needs without an allocation order.

Some tolkachi take up permanent residence in the city in which the chief suppliers are located, and only occasionally return to their home firms for consultations. To keep the record clean, they are carried on the books as "senior buyer," or "supply agent." If they are known to be particularly adept at their jobs, they may be asked by other firms to represent them. Nothing is known of their incomes, but there is no doubt that they earn many times their base pay. And they fully earn it, both because of the vital nature of their work, and because the risks they take make them vulnerable to prosecution.

How widespread is the use of these expediters? Again, we catch only occasional hints of their prevalence. The most recent outburst against them reports that the number of tolkachi who annually visit the typical large enterprise runs into the thousands of rubles.

[17] Voprosy ekonomiki, 1957, No. 8, p. 50.
[18] Voprosy ekonomiki, 1958, No. 7, p. 120.
[19] The gifts are not always very little. An expediter sent out recently to get tires for his trucking firm, was given 62,000 rubles in cash for the trip. He spent 42,000 rubles for gifts. He is now in prison. Izvestiia, Apr. 4, 1959, p. 2.

These, however, are only the reported expenses. More often than not their expenses are not reported as such but are concealed under such rubics as "exchange of technical information," or "contract negotiations." Our latest informant, who is a senior investigator for the state control commission of the U.S.S.R., is of the opinion that despite continued official criticisms of the use of expediters, their number has actually been increasing. One of the reasons he adduces is interesting. In 1956, along with a wave of measures designed to give more freedom to plant managers, an order was issued relieving managers of the need to report in detail on all minor expenditures. Travel expenditures were among the items exempted. The measure had the unintended effect of encouraging the increased use of expediters.[20]

The economic effect of the use of expediters is difficult to assess. There is no doubt that they are of vital importance to individual enterprises, but from the national point of view much of their activity involves merely the transfer to one fortunate enterprise of resources that otherwise would have gone to another. Since the higher priority enterprises have less need for expediters, the chances are that the net effect of their activity is to cause more resources to flow to lower priority enterprises at the expense of higher priority ones. On the credit side, however, their wide knowledge of sources of supply, of who has what to sell, is of some importance, and they do arrange for the movement of supplies that otherwise would have lain idle in one plant while another had need for it. In short the expediter possesses a certain kind of knowledge that may be as important to economic organization as the knowledge of the engineer or the machinist. The planning system is able to direct the bulk of the nation's resources with reasonable effectiveness, but substantial quantities of materials and equipment elude the main stream of planning. How to get these resources back into the system is a problem that has exercised Soviet economists for a long time.[21]

In summary, the incentives that motivate managers to strive for the fulfillment of their production targets are the same incentives that motivate them to evade the regulations of the planning system. Because of the tightness of the supply system, which is deliberately engineered by the state, managers are compelled to defend their enterprises' position by overordering supplies, by hoarding materials and equipment, and by employing expediters whose function it is to keep the enterprise supplied with materials at all costs, legal or otherwise. The very planning system that serves to channel most of the nation's resources in directions desired by the state, serves also to misdirect a substantial volume of resources toward uses that are contrary to the wishes of the state.

INVESTMENT DECISIONS

If one were to ask what feature of the Soviet economic system accounts most of all for the rapid rate of growth, the answer would undoubtedly be the high rate of capital formation. The question at issue is whether it is as high as it might be, other things being equal. An

---

[20] Izvestiia, Apr. 4, 1959, p. 2.
[21] Recently there have been numerous suggestions that enterprises and economic region publish catalogs of the commodities they produce and the surplus materials and equipment they would like to sell. The expediters are rather like walking catalogs. Planovoe khoziaistvo, 1959, No. 4, pp. 64, 96.

examination of the system of managerial incentives will provide part, though by no means all, of the answer to this central question.

Management has a direct interest in obtaining new capital. It adds to productive capacity, and it is good for the record to show steady increases in production. Moreover fixed capital is provided to the enterprise as a free grant by the state, with no interest charge. The problem, therefore, has not been one of inducing management to accept more machines; it has rather been one of dissuading management from ordering too many machines. Far back in Soviet economic history one can find expressions of the problem similar to that recently uttered by Khrushchev in connection with the dissolution of the agricultural machine-tractor stations:

> The machine-tractor stations accept any machine whether they need it or not. They don't grow flax, but they take flax-growing equipment. They don't grow cabbage, but they take cabbage-planting machines. Consequently many machines are not used for years and hundreds of millions of rubles worth of state resources are frozen.[22]

The reason enterprises accept any piece of equipment they can get their hands on is similar to that discussed above in connection with materials hoarding. One can never tell when he may need just that kind of machine and not be able to obtain it. If one has a chance to get it now, order it by all means. It may come in handy some day for trading in return for something one might be able to use more readily. And above all, there is no charge for holding the equipment; there is no interest payment, and if the machine is not used there is no depreciation charge either. Hence there is everything to gain and nothing to lose by holding on to as much machinery and equipment as one can obtain.

How to induce managers to take a less cavalier view of capital has been a longstanding concern of economists. They look with some nostalgia at the effectiveness of the profit motive under capitalism in this respect. An eminent Soviet economist put it this way recently:

> In order to increase his profit as much as possible, the capitalist strives to use his equipment to the fullest extent possible, and in no case will he buy a machine that he doesn't need at the moment, since every surplus machine slows down the turnover of his capital and reduces his profit. For the same reason he strives to keep his inventories down to the very minimum and to market his finished products as quickly as possible.[23]

Recent economic literature contains a number of suggestions of ways in which Soviet managers might be induced to order only that amount of capital needed for production purposes. One of the more interesting is a proposal advanced by the author quoted above. He suggests that profit be calculated not as a ratio to total production cost (as has always been done), but as a ratio to value of invested capital. In this way the enterprise with too much idle capital will show a lower rate of profit, and profit is one of the principal indicators of overall performance. The suggestion is interesting because it proposes that return on capital be used as a criterion of performance, a rather "bourgeois" notion. It should not, however, be thought that the proposal envisages reliance on the "profit motive" as we know it. Profit is an important indicator of the efficiency of plant operation, but the firm does not "own" its profit, although it shares in the profit

---

[22] Planovoe khoziaistvo, 1958, No. 7, p. 121.
[23] Ibid., p. 122.

in a minor way.   As a personal incentive, profit is relatively unimportant in Soviet industry, certainly by comparison with the bonus.

If the incentive system motivates managers to overorder and hoard equipment, the situation is quite the reverse with respect to technological innovation.   Concern over managerial resistance to innovation is of long standing, but it has come to the fore in recent years in connection with increased emphasis on automation and modernization of plant and equipment.   The reasons for managers' tendency to drag their feet in introducing new products or production techniques are well understood by Soviet economists:

> The explanation is, first of all, that the introduction of new technology involves certain risks and requires a considerable expenditure of time; secondly, after new technology has been introduced, more difficult plan targets are set and consequently there is less opportunity for fulfilling them and receiving bonuses.[24]

When a manager has a well-running plant, when the workers have learned their jobs and have become experienced in using the existing equipment, he is reluctant to upset the cart by trying something new. A new production line means trouble.   Production bugs have to be eliminated, workers have to be retrained, time is lost, and spoilage is high.   The chances are that plans will be underfulfilled and the precious bonuses lost, particularly in view of the tendency for plan targets to be raised to the rated capacity of the new equipment.   It is courting disaster to try new things.   If the old machines are wearing out, it is safer to repair or even rebuild them rather than introduce the more complicated new models.   Outlays on the rebuilding of old machines often exceed the price of a new modern machine.[25]

There is another reason why managers shy away from innovation. Even if the potential gains from new technology are great, it usually takes a number of years before they are realized.   But it is Soviet policy to shift managers around from plant to plant every few years. Therefore managers have a strictly short-run point of view.   Why take on all the headaches of introducing a new line when one is not likely to be around to enjoy whatever benefits may eventually accrue? Capital investment policy is by its very nature a matter of long-term planning, and therefore does not commend itself to the short-run horizon of management.

How does the state combat managerial resistance to innovation? One technique is direct pressure.   Pressure exerted on and by their own superiors explains much of the innovation that does occur. Enterprise managers may drag their feet for a long time, but when the direct order comes down that the new automatic line must be installed in the next 6 months, it is eventually acted upon.   Pressure is also exerted through the Communist Party; if the party officials in the enterprise are under direct orders from Moscow that automation must be accelerated, they are in a position to force the manager to move faster than he otherwise might.   Such pressures are important, although it must be noted in passing that both the manager's bosses and the local party people often try to shield the enterprise from such pressures.   They are as dependent for their careers upon successful plan fulfillment as are the plant managers themselves.

Direct orders from above are one way of getting management to innovate.   But innovation would proceed more rapidly if managers

[24] Voprosy ekonomiki, 1959, No. 1, pp. 44, 45.
[25] Voprosy eKonomiki, 1957, No. 4, p. 69.

could be made to wish to innovate, instead of waiting until they are forced into it   The literature of the past few years is full of suggestions on how this can be accomplished.   It is suggested, for example, that attractively high prices be set on new machines, in order to stimulate the producers of those machines to put them into production more rapidly.[26]   While this measures might ease the financial strain on the innovating firm, it will not remove the risk that the production plan may be sacrificed.   And production is much more vital to the success of the enterprise than finance.

More to the point are the suggestions that the bonus system be employed as an incentive for innovation.   Soviet economists seem to have enormous confidence in bonuses as a device for getting management to wish to do what the State wishes them to do.   But how to adapt the bonus system to this purpose is more difficult.   In the course of years a variety of special bonuses have been introduced for one purpose or another, in addition to the major bonus that comes from fulfillment of the production plan.   There are special bonuses available for economizing certain critical materials, for reducing the volume of goods in process, for conserving fuel, for increasing labor productivity, for keeping the plant clean, for reducing the volume of spoilage, for operating the plant without stoppages, for winning Socialist competitions, and many others.[27]

This dilution of the bonus system may actually weaken its power as an incentive.   If the special bonuses are small, they will not be very effective.   If they are large they may detract effort from what is, after all, the main objective of the state: fulfillment of the production plan.   For it is interesting to note the evidence that the relative size of the bonus for this or that special purpose often determines the manager's decision to concentrate on this or that objective. There are two types of innovation: relatively small measures such as organizational improvements or inexpensive alterations, and the more dramatic large-scale changes in production techniques.   The former are included in the overall enterprise plan each year, under the name of the plan or organizational and technical measures (Orgtekhplan).   It happens that there are certain bonuses available for the design and introduction of the large-scale innovations, but none for the fulfillment of the Orgtekhplan.   The consequence is that research and managerial personnel concentrate on the large items, and pay little attention to the small ones, even though the latter could result in great savings with relatively little cost and effort.[28]   Thus the very potency of the bonus as an incentive militates against its use for too many special purposes which may compete with each other.

To conclude this discussion, the unreliability of the supply system and the absence of a charge for the use of capital motivates management to order more fixed capital than they need and to hoard machines and equipment.   This tendency deflects a certain amount of currently produced capital goods from being put directly into production in their best uses.   On the other hand, the incentive system discourages management from taking the risks associate with innovation.   Direct orders from above lead to a substantial volume of

[26] Voprosy ekonomiki, 1959, No. 6, p. 16.
[27] Voprosy ekonomiki, 1959, No. 3, p. 66.   Not all these types of bonus are available to the director himself, but they are available to different groups of managerial personnel.
[28] Voprosy ekonomiki, 1958, No. 2, p. 136.

innovation, and in many cases management may consider certain forms of innovation to be to their interest. The provision of special bonuses for innovation, if they were large enough to compete with the production plan bonus, might help provide an incentive for innovation, and much of the current discussion in the Soviet Union seems to point to this as the next phase.

CHAPTER 3. SOME COMPARATIVE OBSERVATIONS

The preceding chapter has shown that Soviet managers are motivated to make a variety of decisions that are contrary to the interest of the state. Since the state's interest is paramount in the Soviet scheme of things, we may properly conclude that the incentive and decision making system is "relatively inefficient," or "less than perfectly efficient." Let me caution the reader once more against inferring from this that Soviet managers do not do a good job. They do. There is no doubt that their system works well. If I have chosen to concentrate on the "pathology" of Soviet management, the purpose was not to create the impression of ineffectiveness, but to illuminate the gap that every economy shows between the actual and the ideal.

A comparison of Soviet and American management will help drive the point home. No one doubts that American management does a good job. But it would be fatuous to allege that it operates with perfect efficiency. An exploration of the inevitable gap between the actual and the ideal in the case of American management will help to place the corresponding gap in the U.S.S.R. in proper perspective.

A comparison of Soviet and American management is difficult for a curious reason; namely, we don't know enough about the more intimate aspects of American managerial practice. A moment's thought will make the reason clear. The American firm is a private enterprise in the full sense of the word. Its internal affairs are no one's business but its own. No one has the right to pry except with special cause. To be sure, the laws of the land have, over the years, required enterprises to disclose more and more of their private affairs to public and governmental perusal. But large sectors of the enterprise's internal operations are protected from the eyes of curious outsiders.

One of the most striking differences in the conduct of American and Soviet management is precisely in this matter of privacy. The Soviet enterprise is a public enterprise in the fullest sense of the word. It has no right to conceal its operations from any officially recognized agent of the state. And a great range of such agents have been deliberately endowed by the state with the obligation of keeping close watch on management and disclosing any irregularities or sources of inefficiency that come to their attention. These agents include the "home office" of the firm (the regional economic council, or formerly the ministry), the state bank, the local governmental body, the central government's State Control Commission, the Finance Department (the tax collector), the local Communist Party boss and his staff, the party secretary of the enterprise itself, and indeed just about anyone in the enterprise who enjoys the extracurricular activity of attending meetings to discuss the affairs of the enterprise (the aktiv).

If we can imagine an American business executive suddenly placed in charge of a Soviet firm, it is this public character of the enterprise which above all would drive him to distraction. It means that any government official can at any time demand to examine any aspect of the firm's operations he wishes to, that at any time he can be called on the carpet by the local party boss to explain a charge made by an irate customer, that any member of his staff (perhaps bucking for his job) can write a letter to Pravda exposing him for having made an irregular deal on some supplies, that any scatterbrained worker who wants to "get his picture in the papers" can rise at a public meeting that the director is obliged to attend, and compel the director to explain why he hasn't yet installed the new assembly line. The point is that the results of this authorized prying often finds its way into the published Soviet economic and political literature, which gives us an insight into the more intimate operations of the Soviet firm that we cannot have in the case of the American firm. But in view of this committee's expressed interest in comparisons of the United States and Soviet economies, I have attempted certain comparisons below which appear to be highly suggestive.

MANAGERS AND OWNERS

The original form of modern business organization was the small firm in which the owner was also the manager. The owner-manager was responsible to no one but himself for his business decisions, and his interest as manager could not conflict with his interest as owner. The development of the modern giant corporation, however, had led to that separation of management and ownership first elaborated in the work of Berle and Means.[29] Under the new conditions the private interests of the hired managers (and the controlling group) need no longer coincide at all points with the interests of the stockholder-owners. This is precisely the relationship between the hired Soviet manager and the owner-state.

Berle and Means concluded from their study that "the controlling group, even if they own a large block of stock, can serve their own pockets better by profiting at the expense of the company than by making profits for it." [30] This is precisely what Soviet managers do when they produce unplanned commodities that are advantageous to their firms but not to the State, when they overorder and hoard commodities, and when they resist innovation. Because of the differences between the two economic systems, we should expect that the precise forms that the owner-manager conflict takes would be different in the U.S.S.R. and the United States. In the United States they are to be found in such decisions as the awarding of subcontracts, the accounting of profit in such way as to benefit the claims of the controlling group, the awarding of bonuses and other benefits to management, and in dividend payment policy. As in the Soviet enterprise, the accountant is of crucial importance in handling the books of the enterprise in such way as make the best possible case for the manager; it is he, for example, who figures out the best way to distract the state's attention from the large expenditures on talkachi.

---

[29] Berle, Adolph A., Jr., and Gardiner C. Means, "The Modern Corporation and Private Property" (New York: Macmillan) 1945.
[30] Ibid., p. 122.

The accounting techniques are, of course, different in the United States; they involve "the charging or the failure to deduct depreciation; charging to capital expenses which properly should be charged against income account; including nonrecurrent profits as income though their real place is in surplus; and the creation of 'hidden reserves.' "[31]

A major difference between the Soviet firm and the American firm is that in the last analysis profit remains the criterion of managerial performance in the latter, whereas the Soviet manager is evaluated by a number of criteria that are sometimes mutually exclusive. Both systems have attempted to bring managerial interests into harmony with owner interests by some sort of profit-sharing system. In the Soviet case, it is clear that profit plays a very minor role, compared with bonuses, as a managerial incentive. In the United States the manager shares directly in profit to a very limited extent, and often follows other goals in his decisions. "The executive not infrequently tends to look upon the stockholders as outsiders whose complaints and demand for dividends are necessary evils * * *" concluded one American student of management.[32] In like fashion the Soviet manager often begins to feel like the "boss" and resents the intrusion into "his" affairs of the state, which after all is the owner. I have described above some of the ways in which the Soviet manager promotes the interest of "his" enterprise by means contrary to the interests of the owner-state. In the American corporation the forms are somewhat different. "* * * profits are reinvested in the business for the sake of bigness and to protect the company, and the interests of the stockholders may be given second place to the business leader's conception of what is best for the firm itself." Executives manifest a "general unwillingness to liquidate unsuccessful enterprises" and thus put themselves out of jobs, however consistent liquidation might be with the interests of the stockholders.[33] The dramatic growth of corporate self-financing in recent years has strengthened the power of management to expand their own enterprises without having to go through the "test of the marketplace" for capital.

It was observed earlier that the desire for "security" and for what the Russians call a "quiet life" motivates a wide variety of managerial decisions such as concealing production capacity and resisting technological innovation that might rock the boat. Students of American management have also noted the change from the adventurous business tycoons of earlier days to a more professionalized managerial climate in which "greater emphasis is placed on education, training, and a scientific approach, and less on rugged, venturesome, and frequently heedless individualism. The desire for security seems to have increased, and the concomitant of a growing emphasis on security is a diminishing desire for adventure for its own sake."[34] There is indeed a remarkable parallel to this development in the change in the character of Soviet managers. There would have been a great affinity between the industrial empire builders of 19th century America and the Soviet directors of the first two decades of the Soviet regime.

[31] Ibid., pp. 202–203, 335.
[32] Gordon, Robert A., "Business Leadership in the Large Corporation" (Washington: Brookings) 1945 p. 309.
[33] Ibid., p. 309.
[34] Ibid., p. 311.

Those directors were often men of little education who came out of the romantic conflict of revolution, who dreamed great dreams of building an industrial nation and who created an ethos of bold plans and adventurous undertakings. The old Commissar of Heavy Industry, Sergei Ordzhonikidze, would have understood the spirit of the ironmonger, Andrew Carnegie, and the man who built the great ZIL automotive works (now named after him) had the drives and the dreams of the bicycle mechanic Henry Ford.

Time, and Stalin's purges, removed most of those oldtimers and their place has now been taken by Soviet-educated young men born not of revolution but of bureaucracy. Organizations seem to develop "organization men" types, whether the organization happen to be communist or capitalist. An American reporter visiting with a group of Communist intellectuals reports that one of them had badgered him with questions about David Reisman's book, "The Lonely Crowd." "The Communist had read Reisman's book and had been fascinated by it—not, he said, because of its application to life in the United States but because of what he maintained was its extraordinary relevance to the present conditions of life in the Soviet Union." [35] It is not, on reflection, very surprising that the job of running an industrial bureaucracy should place a common stamp on men of otherwise different backgrounds. The same would probably apply to the running of a large city or a large university.

MANAGERS AND THE LAWS

We have found that the Soviet manager is often compelled to evade regulations or even break laws. Part of the explanation is simply that there are so many laws. If a Chicago manufacturer fails to ship an order to a New York firm, and ships it instead to another Chicago firm, he has nothing to fear but the ire of the New York firm. But if a Kiev manufacturer fails to ship an order to a Moscow firm and ships it instead to another Kiev firm, he has injured a state enterprise and is subject to administrative action, a fine, or even criminal prosecution. If an American firm sells a substandard generator, he may lose money or his business. But if a Soviet firm sells a substandard generator, the director may go to prison. Thus, even if Soviet managers acted exactly as American managers do, we should expect to find more illegal or evasive activity in the Soviet Union than in the United States.

With the growing complexity of our society, more and more legislation is enacted to protect the public from potential abuses. With the growth of such legislation, managers find their activities more and more circumscribed by laws and regulations. The Soviet manager apparently treats such legislation rather lightly when it conflicts with the interests of his firm (and his career and pocketbook). How does American management react when confronted by a spreading web of restrictive legislation?

It is not easy to find out very much about American managerial practice in this respect. Unlike the Soviet press, which throws its pages open to reports of the irregular activities of managers in order to warn others, the American press is likely to shy away from this kind

---

[35] The New Yorker, April 6, 1955, p. 52.

of reporting. Moreover the private nature of American business keeps this sort of activity from coming to light as easily as it might in Soviet industry. Nor is it the sort of thing that businessmen are inclined to talk about very readily. If it is true that a businessman would more readily be interviewed on his private sex life than on his private business activity, then we should require the late Dr. Kinsey to help provide the answers to the extent of unlawful or quasi-lawful business activity.

Prof. E. H. Sutherland, the eminent American criminologist and sociologist, made a bold attempt to investigate the phenomenon he refers to as "white collar crime." His study is based on the decisions of a limited number of courts and administrative commissions against the 70 largest industrial-type corporations in the country. In the period 1935 to 1944 these 70 corporations were convicted 585 times for such practices as restraint of trade, misrepresentation in advertising, patent and copyright infringements, unfair labor practices, granting of rebates, and a few others.[36] The average was 8.5 convictions per corporation. These data provide some idea of the extensiveness of such practices but they clearly understate the magnitude for a variety of technical reasons. Sutherland's conclusion is that "a great deal of scattered and unorganized material indicates that white collar crimes are very prevalent." [37]

The point I wish to make is that when American management finds itself in a position approximating that of Soviet management they tend to react in ways similar to those of their Soviet counterparts. Sutherland's unique study notes many aspects of American managerial practice that are astonishingly similar to those one might find in the literature on Soviet management. "These crimes are not discreet and inadvertent violations of technical regulations. They are deliberate and have a relatively consistent unity." [38] It is in precisely this way that the Soviet manager deliberately misappropriates earmarked funds or decides to shave on the quality of production. There is evidence that the Soviet manager, aware of the fact that "everybody does it" and that the investigating agencies have restricted budgets, counts on the law of averages (and his own superior shrewdness) to get away with it. So a member of Federal Trade Commission wrote that "about the only thing that keeps a businessman off the wrong end of a Federal indictment or administrative agency's complaint is the fact that, under the hit-or-miss methods of prosecution, the law of averages hasn't made him a partner to a suit," and "Samuel Insull is reported to have remarked during his trial that he had only done what all other businessmen were doing." [39]

Similarities in managerial practice are paralleled by similarities in attitude to such violations, and toward the administrative agencies enforcing the laws and regulations. The Soviet manager does not think it is "wrong" to use influence to obtain materials unlawfully, or to fudge his reports to the Government. Success is the important thing, and if you are successful you can get away with all sorts of violations. There is evidence that the Soviet manager feels contemptuous of government planners and of party hacks who try to tell him how to run his business but who themselves had "never met a payroll."

[36] Sutherland, Edwin H., "White Collar Crime," (New York: Dryden) 1949, p. 26;
[37] Ibid., p. 10.
[38] Ibid., p. 217.
[39] Ibid., p. 218.

Sutherland's picture of American management's attitudes contains strains of the same kind.

The businessman who violates the laws which are designed to regulate business does not customarily lose status among his business associates. Although a few members of the industry may think less of him, others admire him * * *. Businessmen customarily regard government personnel as politicians and bureaucrats, and the persons authorized to investigate business practices as "snoopers." [40]

In the first chapter of this paper, it was pointed out that a managerial career carries a great deal of prestige in the Soviet Union and attracts a large number of the better students. These youngsters have been raised in Soviet schools and have absorbed the incessant propaganda of the Communist regime. Many of them enter industry as green novices fresh from school, filled with high ideals about building the socialist fatherland and working for the common welfare. One wonders about the process by which the naive, idealistic young Komsomol member is transformed into the hard-headed manager who knows all the angles for survival in the Soviet business world. Numerous incidents such as the following provide a key to the answer. A young Soviet chemist had been assigned to the quality control department of his enterprise. He was quite pleased with himself when his test showed that a sample of production, which had previously been declared acceptable by his laboratory chief, turned out to contain an excess of phosphorus. He reported the "error" and expected to get a bonus for it. Instead, his boss obtained a new sample, gave it to an outside chemist for analysis, and submitted a report showing that the batch of production was acceptable after all. The young chemist protested, was transferred to another shop, and was finally fired on trumped-up charges.[41]

What happens to such young people? Some never quite get the point and remain ordinary engineers in the plants. Others learn to adapt themselves after a few buffetings and when they decide to play the game according to the real ground-rules, begin to rise in the managerial hierarchy.

It is interesting to note that Sutherland's interviews with American businessmen turned up accounts rather similar to that narrated above. His explanation of the process by which the naive American youngster is initiated into the business of selling used cars, settling insurance claims, covering up irregularities in clients' accounts—indeed, toning down the results of chemical analysis—helps explain the process of transformation of the young Komsomol member:

In many cases he is ordered by the manager to do things which he regards as unethical or illegal, while in other cases he learns from others who have the same rank as his own how they make a success. He learns specific techniques of violating the law, together with definitions of situations in which those techniques may be used. Also he develops a general ideology. This ideology grows in part out of the specific practices and is in the nature of generalization from concrete experiences, but in part it is transmitted as a generalization by phrases such as "we are not in business for our health," "business is business," and "no business was ever built on the beatitudes." These generalizations * * * assist the neophyte in business to accept the illegal practices and provide rationalizations for them.[42]

Summarizing, the economic world in which the Soviet manager operates compels him to engage in a variety of illegal or evasive practices. Since the Soviet business world is enmeshed in a much greater

---

[40] Ibid., p. 220.
[41] Mashinostroenie, Feb. 17, 1939, p. 3.
[42] Ibid., p. 240.

web of laws and regulations than the American, the Soviet manager finds his interest in conflict with the laws and regulations more often than his American counterpart. But when American managers' interests conflict with the laws, they too are prepared to take the chance of violating them. Both American and Soviet managers justify their actions by an attitude of contempt for governmental controls and investigating personnel, and by a hardheaded view that "business is business" and "everybody does it." Young people in both systems who wish to achieve managerial prominence have to learn to play the game according to the rules, or disqualify themselves from the tough competition for the top.

MANAGERS AND OVERFULL EMPLOYMENT

Many of the peculiarities of Soviet management spring from the fact that the economic system works under conditions of perpetual overfull employment. By "overfull" employment I mean a condition in which there are not merely as many jobs as employables (as under full employment), but the demand for labor far exceeds the available supply. The same applies to other factors of production: materials, equipment, and commodities in general are demanded in far greater volume than the current rates of production. The ability of the Soviet Government to maintain, through the planning system, a condition of permanent overfull employment is one of the greatest economic assets of the regime. We err when we interpret evidence of shortages in the Soviet economy as signs of economic weakness; they are rather indications that the economic engine is racing with the throttle wide open.

But just as an engine does not work at its maximum efficiency when it is working at its maximum capacity, so the Soviet economy pays a certain price for the advantages of overfull employment. It is the perpetual shortages of supplies that account in large measure for the losses due to overordering and hoarding. The hunger for goods by both firms and consumers encourages the deterioration of quality. The "sea of ink" associated with materials allocations, price fixing, priorities, and all the rigamarole of a controlled economy nurtures the spread of the tolkach and the use of influence for personal gain.

The normally functioning American economy does not confront our managers with this kind of problem. Hoarding makes no sense when materials are in adequate supply. Competition and consumer resistance force the quality of production up to standard. The role of influence is narrowly circumscribed when the bureaucratic machinery of Government controls is removed. The biggest problem of American managers under normal conditions is marketing, not purchasing. The energy spent by the Soviet firm on obtaining materials is spent by the American firm on selling and advertising.

Thus, the major differences between the practice of American and Soviet management are to be ascribed to the differences in the economic environment. The interesting question is, How do American managers behave when placed in an environment that approximates that of the Soviet manager? The obvious test case is war. During World War II the national emergency forced us into a state of overfull employment. Along with this came the total immersion of Government into economic life, with a great burgeoning of materials allocation, price fixing, cost-plus contracting, and a prevailing shortage of supplies.

It is interesting to note that the rate of growth of production during the war rose to levels rivaling the current rates of Soviet economic growth. The implication of this fact is important; it means that there is no magic in the Soviet economic system. Our economy could grow as rapidly as the Soviet economy does if our people would consent to being pushed around as totally as the Soviet people are.

But like the Soviet economy, we paid for our high rate of production in various forms of waste. One of the first consequences of the introduction of materials controls was the rise of the black market. The only full-scale study of the black market, to my knowledge, confirmed what many people felt to be the case at the time:

> During the war at least a million cases of black market violations were dealt with by the Government. Illegal profits ran into billions of dollars. Business interests and Government vied with one another in estimating the seriousness of the black market; business estimates, curiously, often being higher than those of the Government. Such extensive conniving in the black market in illegal prices and rationed commodities took place among so many businessmen, ordinary criminals, and even the average citizen that serious questions might be raised as to the moral fiber of the American people.[43]

To understand the position of the Soviet manager, we must realize that the American black market flourished at a time when the Nation was fighting for its life and public indignation acted as a restraint. But if the economic controls that led to violations could not be justified by a national emergency, they would be thought of as just irritating obstacles, as so many hurdles that the resourceful manager must overcome as part of the risks of the game. There is good evidence that the Soviet manager takes just this amoral attitude toward economic controls, and it is therefore quite understandable that the evasion of controls would be more widespread.

The high quality of American production in normal times is a byword in international markets. But the effect of the economy of shortages was similar to that in the Soviet economy. One of the techniques used by Soviet managers is to represent lower quality merchandise as of higher quality, and to sell it at the higher price. In the United States during the war—

> upgrading was one of the most difficult violations to detect, particularly where no professional investigator was available who could appraise the grade or where there were no State or Federal grades stamped on the commodity.[44]

The reports of Government investigators read like some of the indignant letters of complaint we read in the Soviet press; men's shorts made of cheesecloth, water-resistant baby's pants which permit a third of glass of water to leak through after one laundering—

> if you pick up a board by both ends without breaking it in the middle, it's No. 1 Select—

testified an American businessman.[45]

One of the features of Soviet managerial life which helps protect the manager is the feeling of "mutual support" among various officials whose fortunes depend on the success of the enterprise. The Communist Party secretary doesn't report the manipulations of a success-

[43] Clinard, Marshall B. " The Black Market" (New York: Rinehart), 1952, vii.
[44] Ibid., p. 224.
[45] Ibid., p. 45.

ful director because the party benefits from the success of the enterprise; the people in the "home office" (the Ministry or the Council of the National Economy) are reluctant to fire a director who violates the laws in order to get the materials his plant needs, for while the next director may be more lawabiding, he may not succeed in fulfilling his plan. This tendency to maintain a solid front against authority is a source of great irritation to the Government, which periodically inveighs against it but has not been able to eradicate it. A similar sense of common front prevailed among groups of businessmen.

Nothing better illustrates the degree of organization and consensus among businessmen then their reluctance to testify against each other * * *. Some businessmen felt that the trade would disapprove of behavior that might undermine the solid front against the Government as well as interfere with supplies.[46]

One of the major differences in the position of management in the two countries is the nature of the penalty for failure. Under ordinary conditions the unsuccessful manager loses his job. But the Soviet manager faces many more situations in which the action necessary to get the job done carries with it the threat of criminal action. Indeed, whenever the Soviet Government has found some managerial practice too damaging to its interests and too intractable to the normal sanctions, it has turned to the criminal courts. Immediately after the death of Stalin the punishment for economic transgressions was relaxed, but the new regime has not been able to continue operating without the courts. One of the severest economic problems following the decentralization of industry was the tendency toward "localism": that is, each economic region tended to favor the plants in its "own" region, and would discriminate against plants in other regions. When all exhortation failed, the Government had to turn to the law. Today, a manager who fails to honor the orders of plants outside his own region is subject to "administrative action, fines, or even criminal punishment." [47]

Financial penalties, such as fines, have rarely proved successful as restraints on Soviet managerial behavior. American managers seem to have reacted the same way to the fines imposed for black-market violations. "They don't hurt anybody." "It just comes out of profits, like a tax." "They make so much money on the black market they can afford to pay steep fines." But imprisonment was another matter. "Jail is the only way; nobody wants to go to jail." "A jail sentence is dishonorable; it jeopardizes the reputation." [48] This would not be quite the same in the case of the Soviet manager. At least during Stalin's lifetime some of the best people served their time in jail, and it definitely did not destroy their reputation among their neighbors; although the neighbors might be wary of associating with them. One has the impression that large numbers of Soviet managers feel the chances are fair that some day they will do their stretch, hopefully for a minor transgression.

The wartime economy of shortages injects the government into business life not only as an agency of control but also as the largest customer of many firms. In the Soviet case we have noted the importance of the tolkach, the expediter, the peddler of influence. We might note in passing that the economic system of Nazi Germany, in

[46] Ibid., pp. 306–307.
[47] "Planovoe khoziaistvo," 1958, No. 7, p. 14.
[48] Ibid., p. 244.

which government had also assumed a dominant role, also gave rise to this chap. The Germans called him the "contact man." As described by an American student of the German economy:

> To influence the powerful agencies of control, however, he [the German business-man] has good use for what might suitably be called a private relations department. Under the Nazi system of control of business by an absolute government, the contact man, or graft, or both, take the place of the public relations executive.
>
> The contact man is primarily a political figure. His job is to pull wires. He knows the influential members of the all-pervading Nazi Party in a position to bring pressure successfully to bear upon the men in charge of controlling agencies. * * * Two types of contact man are known to be used: one is an independent agent whom the businessman hires, or attempts to hire, whenever necessary; the other is carried on the payroll of the business in a more or less permanent capacity.[49]

The words might well have been written about the Soviet economy. In that sector of the U.S. economy in which Government plays a dominant role as customer, the symbols of the mink coat or Dixon-Yates, depending upon one's political persuasion, come to mind. "Washington," wrote Senator Paul Douglas, "is indeed full of lawyers and 'representatives' whose primary commodity is 'influence'."[50] The techniques of the American influence-peddler differ little from those of his colleagues in the Soviet or Nazi economy. Gifts and quid pro quo favors are standard among Soviet tolkachi. Another way in which Soviet enterprises manage to exert influence is to have one of "their" men placed in other organizations that can be of use, rather like the unusually high employability in industry of retired military personnel. During the war the problem was particularly acute because of our Government's desperate need for skilled managerial personnel, many of whom were on loan from corporations with which the Government placed contracts. But the use of influence is not confined to Government-business relations, as Senator Douglas pointed out in his critical defense of the ethics of Government personnel:

> As a matter of fact, the abuses which have been exposed and properly denounced in the field of Government are quite widespread practices in private business. Thus the "padding" of expense accounts is so common that they are often referred to as "swindle sheets." Purchasing agents and buyers frequently exact toll from those who seek to sell to them, and their Christmas presents and other perquisites appreciably increase their income. Business managers and directors think nothing of awarding contracts, insurance, and underwriting privileges on the basis of friendship and relationship rather than the quality and prices of the goods and services supplied. All this is taken as a matter of course in private business, although it obviously increases costs and intercepts gains which should go to stockholders and consumers.[51]

While gifts, payoffs, and bribery play their role in the Soviet scheme of things, the subtler and much more pervasive technique of influence is known as "blat". To have good blat with someone means that one has an "in"; one can always count on him for a favor because of friendship or family ties or some other relationship of confidence. Blat may be used to obtain everything from a new apartment to a carload of coal. The prominent British observer, Edward Crankshaw, has called blat the most significant word in contemporary

---

[49] Hamburger, L. "How Nazi Germany Has Controlled Business" (Washington: Brookings), 1943, pp. 94–95.
[50] Douglas, Paul H. "Ethics in Government" (Cambridge: Harvard Press), 1952, p. 56.
[51] Ibid., p. 25.

376 COMPARISONS OF UNITED STATES AND SOVIET ECONOMIES

Russia.[52] The way in which the American equivalent of blat is cultivated is described in one final quotation from Senator Douglas:

Today the corruption of public officials by private interests takes a more subtle form. The enticer does not generally pay money directly to the public representative. He tries instead by a series of favors to put the public official under such feeling of personal obligation that the latter gradually loses his sense of mission to the public and comes to feel that his first loyalties are to his private benefactors and patrons. What happens is a gradual shifting of a man's loyalties from the community to those who have been doing him favors. His final decisions are, therefore, made in response to private friendships and loyalties rather than to the public good.[53]

Summarizing, many of the differences between Soviet and United States managerial behavior spring from differences in the economic climate in which they operate. The stress on quality and appearance, the drive for innovation and technological development, and the interest in cost reduction reflect the force of competition and the buyer's market. Such similarities as have been observed in managerial behavior, spring from features of the economic environment that are common to the two systems, such as large-scale organization and the intrusion of Government into the economy. Under wartime conditions our economy takes on more of the features of normal Soviet economic life, and the consequence is that our managers adopt more of the normal practices of Soviet management.

[52] New York Times Magazine, June 3, 1951, p. 35.
[53] Douglas, p. 44.

THE SOVIET INDUSTRIAL REORGANIZATION OF 1957

By OLEG HOEFFDING

The RAND Corporation

I

The thoroughgoing reorganization of industrial administration and planning carried out in the Soviet Union in 1957 is too large a topic to discuss comprehensively and systematically in the time at my disposal. I will confine myself to a commentary on some selected aspects of these measures, to the neglect of many other aspects at least equally important. Let me also emphasize that I am taking the 1957 measures, so to speak, at their official face value: as an effort to make industry more efficient, and economic policy more effective, by better planning and administration. In other words, I will ignore the political background of the 1957 reforms, important and intriguing as it may be, because my Kremlinological competence is as limited as my time.

To indicate the drift of my argument, I want to submit that the 1957 reform was a radical measure only in an administrative sense. It introduced a concept of direction of industry, an execution of industrial policy, practiced on a very limited scale only in recent Soviet history— a concept officially styled "administration according to the territorial principle." Under this concept, centrally determined (or at least approved) plans and policies are implemented by regional executive agencies, placed in general charge of their region's industry, regardless of branch affiliation. Even though the new administrative regime stops far short of establishing the "territorial principle" fully and purely, it differs sharply from the old system. This was based on the "branch principle" of vertical control of industry, regardless of location, by central agencies which, in name at least, were differentiated by industry branch. The radicalism of the 1957 reform derives mainly from the very substantial modifications which this changing of "principles" has wrought in the administrative environment of Soviet industrial and construction enterprises. At the risk of repeating what others have said before me, I am going to emphasize that "decentralization" is an inaccurate and misleading summary description of these changes.

Its administrative aspects apart, the 1957 reform impresses me not as a radical but as an eminently conservative measure, in the sense that it tries to correct various faults in the operation of industry and its structural and locational patterns, not by amending any of the basic institutions and operating principles of the Soviet economic system, as

65

it applies to industry, but by organizational and procedural improvements within that system.

II

Let me first explain my contention that the 1957 measures were essentially conservative and why this aspect merits some emphasis. The reorganization followed upon a period, dating roughly from Stalin's death, of sustained and critical public discussion of shortcomings in the planning and direction of industry and their ill effects on industry's performance and its structural, locational, and technological evolution. These discussions indicated profound dissatisfaction with the state and trend of affairs on the part of party and government leaders, industrial executives, and Soviet economists. Dissatisfaction among the leadership was also reflected in the frequent, if nonradical, organizational and jurisdictional reshuffles at the top levels of planning and administration. Some of these moved cautiously in the general direction of the 1957 reform, as the selective transfer of some industries to Union Republic jurisdiction, or the reduction in numbers of commodities subject to centralized planning and allocation. Other changes were reversed in 1957—like the 1955 bifurcation of *Gosplan* into long-term and short-term planning commissions. But they all had a distinctive feature in common with the 1957 reform: They sought to remedy the failings of industry by improving its environment of administration and planning without changing any essential characteristics of the centrally planned and administered "command economy."[1]

In other words, the main remedial actions of the period were confined to only a narrow range of the wide spectrum of remedial possibilities that were being proposed or academically explored. Some of these proposals and explorations were along lines that might have led to modifications of the very operating principles of Soviet industry if given institutional implementation. More specifically, there was an interesting concern with what were, at least, the prerequisites of economic decentralization. Among the men of affairs in industry there were pressures for greater scope for managerial decision making. Among Soviet economists, there was the well-known concern over the lack in their economy of valid criteria and incentives for rational economic choice, and their tendency to question and challenge, however guardedly and obliquely, the doctrinal and institutional constraints that tended to perpetuate these deficiencies. This was primarily an intellectual and academic trend, and there was certainly nothing to suggest that the Soviet Union was headed for some version of "market socialism." Yet, several Western observers—writing before the 1957 reform—had noted

[1] This and all other footnotes appear at the end of this paper.

that various minor policy adjustments of the period and contributions by Soviet leaders to the industrial discussions suggested that the leadership showed signs of being infected with this quest for "rationality."[2]

There were other developments in the Soviet sphere prior to 1957 which seemed to raise at least the glimmer of an intriguing possibility that an industrial reform, when it came, might bring innovations more radical than an overhaul, however drastic, of the organizational structure of the command economy. In Eastern Europe, by 1956, there had been some important departures from extreme economic centralism. In the USSR, even by 1956, Khrushchev had shown himself a bold and far from conservative innovator in his agricultural policies.

My emphasis on the various pre-1957 trends that were the possible portents of more fundamental changes in industry than actually occurred may be merely a confession of my own fallibility. Yet, if anybody else had his expectations heightened by preoccupation with these trends, there may be some point in stressing that none of them found any formal reflection in the 1957 measures.

At least one of them, in fact, suffered a distinct setback. This was the movement for greater "directors' rights," which had been of some interest as a possible portent of a move towards decentralizing economic decision making, by extending the authority of enterprise managers, and freeing them of "petty guardianship" by planners and administrators. The managers' demands had been particularly insistent in 1955,[3] when they actually won some very modest concessions from the government.[4] On the eve of the reform, the Party's Central Committee still expressed an intention to "extend the rights" of (inter alia) "enterprises."[5] The theme, however, was conspicuously absent from Khrushchev's reorganization "Theses" of March, 1957.[6] Nonetheless, there was considerable advocacy of greater directors' rights in the public debate of the theses. This was acknowledged by Khrushchev when he was introducing the reorganization law in the Supreme Soviet, but only to observe that "we must give serious thought to this matter so as to make the proper decisions."[7] No decisions appear to have been made to date. Published legislation on the reform is entirely concerned with the administrative environment of enterprises and makes no de jure changes in their status.[8] The drastic remodelling of this environment does, of course, introduce a variety of de facto changes. It is hard to judge how they affect, on balance, the manager's elbowroom for decision making, but it may well have been restricted and not widened. He has been placed under, possibly, more immediate and intimate supervision by the regional Economic Councils than the more remote ministries and their glavki could provide. He may have been subjected to greater influence and interference by regional Party authorities and now lacks recourse to countervailing ministerial authority. More extraneous interference may result from the emphasis placed on "mass participation" in making the new system effective; e.g., through greater activity of trade union committees, or the counsel tendered by the new "permanent production conferences."

In fact, it would have been illogical to combine the 1957 reform with an extension of managerial authority, since some major benefits expected from the reorganization will only be reaped if the Economic Councils can, and do, interfere rather drastically with the existing enterprise structure and enterprise production programs in their regions. Their main initial assignment is to tidy up an, allegedly, very messy industrial structure inherited from the ministerial era and to reorganize it for more efficient use of regional resources. The Councils are instructed, for instance, to promote vertical integration, where appropriate, by merging enterprises previously severed by departmental barriers, or else they are supposed to promote cleaner specialization of enterprise production programs, by making enterprises stop inefficient subsidiary activities, and rely instead on outside purchase of semimanufactures and components from specialized suppliers who, in their turn, will often have to be newly created out of the existing enterprise structure. At least for this transitional period of the restructuring of industry, then, the reform evidently had to be more concerned with giving the Economic Councils adequate power over enterprises, and their managers, than with giving more power to managers.[9]

Apart from the possibility of infringements of directors' rights originating at the new regional level, managers remain subject to essentially the same constraints from production and other plans prescribed for their enterprises. Soviet comments on the new planning procedures emphasize that plans, from now on, will be initiated by the enterprises themselves. One doubts, however, that this will enable the manager to exert more influence than before on his production program, as, in many branches of industry, his initial proposals are now subject to amendment at about as many stages as under the old system (Economic Council, Republican government and *Gosplan*, Central government and *Gosplan*, not to mention the Party hierarchy). Once his plan has been prescribed, the manager will be under the old pressures to abide by it, plus the new pressure (carried to him via the Economic Council) to be meticulous in living up to his extraregional production and delivery obligations, on which so much stress has been placed since the reform.

In brief, whatever the reform may have done to make the manager's life easier in various ways (as it probably has), it has transferred no powers to him from the planning and administrative bureaucracy and certainly has done nothing to increase his resemblance to the manager of a capitalist firm.

At the same time, the theme of directors' rights seems to have pretty well disappeared from public discussion since May, 1957. Otherwise, however, there has been no silencing of public exploration of additional remedies for the problems of industry. Soviet economists have been warned against the pitfalls of revisionism, but their quest for rationality continues actively. Also, one probably should not read too much conservatism into the lack of action on, say, the economists' counsel (which is divided counsel, anyway) on the need for a more sensible and more operationally influential price system for industry. Whatever the leaders' further intentions may be, they may have had strong pragmatic reasons for not changing too many horses in the midstream of industry's adaptation to its new administrative way of life and of preparing the new long-term plan. In any event, if Soviet agriculture has been the main sinner against rationality,[10] it seems but sensible to have beamed some of the light of reason into the darkest corner first, as Khrushchev has done in 1958, again in quite a nonconservative spirit. One prominent advocate of industrial price reform among Soviet economists, D. Kondrashev, was cheered by the June, 1958, reform of farm prices and marketings into observing that these measures "directly concern agriculture but are relevant to the entire system of price formation in the Soviet economy."[11]

Concessions to the forces of rationality, moreover, need not be cast into formal institutional changes to be important and influential, and Soviet economists would seem to have reason to be cheered by continued signs that some of their arguments are influencing the decision processes of economic policy-makers. Improved criteria of economic choice could be just as beneficial to the quality of planners' decisions in a command economy as they would be essential prerequisites to any extension of managerial decision making. Failure to grant such extension has not stopped the Soviet leadership from relying on some of the tools of rational decision advocated by Soviet economists—for instance, in the important area of investment allocation choices, an area in which some of the crucial decisions of economic policy have had to be made in recent years. Even in 1956 (as R. W. Campbell noted at the time), some of the leaders, including Khrushchev, had justified capital allocation choices in terms of the "pay-off period approach"—an approach which then was allowed only "a sort of *sub rosa* existence" in Soviet economic doctrine.[12] Recently, Khrushchev relied on this approach quite explicitly, and in some detail, to argue the economic merits of thermal-electric over hydroelectric power investment in the present phase of Soviet development (which he did on the awkward occasion of opening the world's biggest hydroelectric plant, thus dedicating it, it seems, as a big monument to irrationality).[13]

Other indications could be cited of an apparently increased awareness among the leadership of the need to have its command decisions in economic policy significantly and systematically influenced by prior economic calculation. It would be surprising, in fact, if the leadership had not learned some lessons from recent experiences that should have brought home the dangers of economic policy made by command decisions unrelated, and perhaps even contrary, to economic calculation. Although in public the need for administrative reform was justified mainly in terms of shortcomings of the old chain of command, there has been ample implicit admission that the quality of the high-level decisions and orders passing down this chain had often been defective. The outstanding and grossest case (and the most poorly documented one) was the Party Directives for the Sixth Five Year Plan, which evidently had badly failed to match the planners' targets with the real production possibilities of the economy. There have been more candid confessions on less comprehensive, but still very important, decisions of past industrial strategy which are now deemed to have been gross and expensive boners. The infatuation with hydroelectric power is one case in point. Another was the continued high-pressure expansion of coal mining, conducted, as is now claimed, against the better knowledge (at the staff levels of planning, presumably) of the superior economic advantages of developing the petroleum and natural gas industries.

This readiness of the policy-makers to let their command decisions benefit from economic calculation may be quite an important complement to the formal measures of reform in industry, and also an important qualification to my verdict on the conservativeness of that reform. In order to improve its strategic decisions and directives, the high command seems quite willing to draw on some of the heresies (or potential heresies) of yesterday, and thus to harness them to its conservative task of preserving the fundamentals of the command economy, while at the same time seeking to improve its functioning and structure.

III

On the administrative aspects of the reform, one may be flogging a dead horse by dwelling on the reasons why "decentralization" is not its essential feature and why this term is a misleading description of the whole thing. This has been pointed out by several Western observers.[14] In the Soviet Union, the term has been carefully avoided, and Khrushchev himself has praised the "shrewdness" of an unnamed American commentator who had suggested that the reform was not decentralization but "transfer of centralism nearer to the immediate production process,"[15] which is not a bad description for it. Yet, wrong labels hastily affixed are often hard to remove,[16] and a few words may be in order on why this label was picked, and why it is wrong. The label first appeared, I believe, because early interpretations of the 1957 measures fell prey to a sort of optical illusion. They focused their attention on the two most conspicuous features of the reform, which—viewed in isolation—did suggest that the center had divested itself of a significant portion of its authority over industry, and had dispersed it to an unexpectedly large number of regional bodies. These features were the disappearance of most of the central industrial ministries and the appearance instead of the hundred-odd Economic Councils.

Much less attention (and Soviet publicity) was given to other essential aspects of the reform, which limited very severely the element of administrative decentralization contained in it. These included: a thorough reorganization of the USSR Council of Ministers and the State Planning Commission, evidently designed to provide industry with a better informed and more effective central high command; and the narrow limitations placed on the authority vested in the new Economic Councils, and a system of checks and safeguards established to keep them within their limited bounds, and responsive to central direction.

The changes made in 1957 at the level of the USSR Council of Ministers and *Gosplan* may be discussed by comparing the nature of, so to speak, industrial representation on the Council, before and after the reform. Under the old system, industry was represented mainly by the thirty-odd ministers in charge of as many branches (in concept if not always in fact) of industry and construction. According to the official critique of this old system, each of these ministers was imbued with his particular departmental interests, had his vision and information restricted to his branch, and was heavily encumbered with routine administrative business. The old Council, on the other hand, provided relatively slight representation to central agencies concerned with, and informed on, broad interbranch and suprabranch aspects of industrial planning and policy, and not burdened by operating responsibilities. These were represented by the chiefs of the two Planning Commissions into which *Gosplan* had been split in 1955, those of the State Committees in charge of specific matters affecting industry as a whole (like promotion of new technology and co-ordination of wage policy), and the chief of the Central Statistical Administration.

Since we know so little about the internal operating processes at the top echelons of the Soviet State-Party hierarchy, there is little point in speculating on how the function of the Council of Ministers within its own decision-making sphere was affected by the prevalence of the spokesmen of industrial departmentalism over those of industry at large. However, since the top-level decisions of industrial policy, presumably, are made in the Party Presidium-Secretariat stratum, the Party leadership would probably assess the worth of the Council of

Ministers not so much by its efficacy as a decision-making body as by its quality as an executive agency for the transmission to industry of top-level directives. Here, it was probably important that the principal machinery for implementing industrial policy was provided by the branch oriented and highly self-contained vertical command structures of the industrial ministries. This system evidently had proved itself a very poor transmitter for the decisions of the high command to industry in the field, and rendered top-level industrial policy making rather ineffective. This much can be inferred, I believe, from the stubborn persistence of so many of the problems of industry, exposed in the years prior to 1957, in the face of repeated and insistent calls for corrective action in the resolutions and directives of the last two Party Congresses and several plenary sessions of the Party Central Committee.[17]

Also, the old system evidently suffered, not only from excessive branch differentiation, which allowed three dozen separate industrial chains of command to reach the "cabinet level," but even more gravely from dilution of the "branch principle," in practice and over time, by ministerial self-sufficiency, and empire-building tendencies. These are alleged to have turned what was intended to be direction of industry by branches into diffuse and somewhat chaotic "departmentalism." Two—possibly extreme—examples were provided by the Ministry of Tractor and Agricultural Machine Building, which accounted for only 16 per cent of agricultural machinery output, while such machinery was produced by enterprises of 24 ministries, and the Ministry of Machine Tool Production, which controlled only 55 out of a total of 171 plants primarily making machine tools, and scattered among 19 ministries.[18]

This administrative scrambling of industry (apart from its well-publicized effects on industrial structure, location, and performance) must have seriously degraded the effectiveness of the old system of central direction, both in the enforcement of policy decisions and in conveying information to the policy-makers. To the extent that it impaired their ability to oversee and foresee the sectoral development of industry, it must have been a source of special frustration for the high command at a time when its policy making was so prominently concerned with the correction of disproportions among, and within, industrial sectors.

These, I believe, were at least some of the defects of the old industrial center which were to be corrected by the simultaneous decimation and reconstitution of the Council of Ministers in May, 1957.

Abolition of most branch ministries was evidently intended to remove two of its faults: the fragmentation of the central chain of command into thirty-odd separate chains and the congestion of the system with administrative routine, which has now been delegated to the Union

Republic governments and the regional Economic Councils. The ministerial seats thus vacated were filled in a way that suggests two main objectives: to have the Council—and the Party policy-makers above it —better served with information relevant to the making of high-level industrial policy and to provide a simpler but more effective chain of command for transmitting directives to the new subordinate executive echelons.

The first objective was served by the allocation to the reunited *Gosplan* of no less than eight seats on the reconstituted Council. This decision to let the planners (with their, presumably, superior and more sophisticated insight into the affairs of industry at large) move in on the Cabinet may well be a formal manifestation of the tendency I had noted before to let central policy decisions be more directly influenced by economic calculation. In a military analogy, it looks as if the "senior staff" was asked to sit closer to the "commanders" to help guide them to better command decisions.[19]

Apart from its invasion of the Council of Ministers, *Gosplan* was also charged with new responsibilities which appear to go well beyond its traditional functions (and which I have not seen adequately explained in Soviet sources). It was directed by the reorganization law to help "implement" economic policies; e.g., a "unified centralized policy for the development of the most important branches of the national economy."[20]

The second objective—that of forging a simpler and more direct chain of command—was reflected, in part, in the appointment to the USSR Council of Ministers of the chairmen of the ministerial councils of the fifteen Union Republics, who are now charged with direction and supervision of the regional Economic Councils.

However, abolition of branch differentiation in the central direction of industry has not been complete by any means. Cabinet representation has been retained for several key sectors of industry (the defense production, electric power, and chemical industries). Enterprises in these sectors have been turned over to the Economic Councils for housekeeping purposes, but their ministries have either survived, or been transformed into State Committees. In both these forms, they evidently now serve as the planning staffs and supply close central supervision of these sectors. For other, publicly unspecified, sectors the same function is probably exercised by those major industrial divisions of *Gosplan* whose heads have been appointed to the Council of Ministers.

As to the other feature which heavily qualifies the "decentralizing" aspect of the reform—the careful and severe restrictions placed on the authority of the regional Economic Councils—I can do little more here than emphasize their existence and will not even try to summarize the catalogue of their rights and duties contained in the 138 articles of the *Sovnarkhoz* statute.[21] The Councils appear to have some scope for reorganizing industrial production in their regions, along the lines I have indicated above, but only to assure better fulfillment of prescribed plans. Also, their powers in this respect are acquired, to some extent, at the expense of the enterprises rather than by delegation of authority from above. Otherwise, their initiative seems largely confined to submitting proposals for review, change, and approval by higher authority— as in the planning process, where the Councils produce the first drafts of regional plans, with the benefit of the intimate knowledge of local conditions they are presumed to possess. The great stress placed since the reform on the Councils' duty to adhere faithfully to production, investment, and extraregional delivery plans seems to emphasize that the *Sovnarkhozy* are not intended to be autonomous regional authorities but rather are to serve as more effective agents than were previously available for executing plans centrally laid down.

Let me note that there is some inconsistency between the tight regimentation of the regional Councils and the official expectations of great gains in industrial efficiency to be derived from their vigorous exercise of local initiative. For the *Sovnarkhoz* chairman, the line between praiseworthy independent enterprise and blameworthy (or even criminal) infraction of "state discipline" may be finely enough drawn to discourage the former.

On the other hand, the tight reins placed on the Councils probably minimize the risk of unintended autonomy, in the form of promotion of regional autarky, or other manifestations of so-called "localism." The "localist" peccadillos of some *Sovnarkhozy* have been given much deterrent publicity in the Soviet press, but such tendencies (for which there may be some perverse incentive in the new method of planning by economic regions) seem detectable and controllable enough so as not to constitute a serious threat of unwanted decentralization.

It is my impression, in short, that what was done in 1957 at both the top and bottom levels of Soviet industrial administration was intended to remedy weaknesses in the system of central direction of industry and not in any sense to weaken central direction itself. Nor do I see any evidence that adoption of the "territorial principle" of industrial administration denotes any shift in the center's approach to industrial policy, towards a significantly increased concern with regional economics or some kind of "balanced regional development." It is true that in the twenties Soviet industrial policy and industrial organization reflected such concerns. It is also true that since the "branch principle" came into its own in the early thirties, there has been continuous—if rather academic and operationally noninfluential—interest in so-called "economic regionalization"; i.e., the identification of major "organic" economic regions which, nominally, were taken into account in long-range economic planning.[22] I do not think, however, that it is legitimate to regard the *Sovnarkhoz* system as a revival of the administrative concepts tried out in the twenties (as Soviet writers have done, in pursuit of the current Leninist myth),[23] or to interpret the 1957 reform as an implementation of economic regionalization. Some contributors to the Soviet debate on the 1957 theses seemed to expect that something like the latter was intended. *Gosplan* itself may have shared in this misapprehension, as in 1956 it appointed a commission to redistrict the USSR into a new network of major economic regions, only to have its proposals rejected in 1957.[24]

The territorial scheme adopted in 1957, however, was clearly selected by administrative and not economic criteria. All the new "economic-administrative regions" (to give them their full, and significant, title) conform to, or combine, existing divisions of local government and, at least equally important, the Party organization. The intention is evidently to utilize their apparatus to co-operate with, and supervise, the Economic Councils. To the extent that the 1957 reform was concerned with the spatial arrangement of industry, I believe its concern was confined to remedying the ill effects of ministerial departmentalism on industrial location and interenterprise relations, and to prevent recurrence of the locational absurdities alleged to have been frequent under the old system.

In fact, despite all the emphasis on the territorial principle of administration, many aspects of the reform acknowledge the paramount concern of present Soviet industrial policy with guiding the structural development of industry, on a national scale, in accordance with the leadership's preferences and priorities as to the relative pace of sectoral expansion, and with correction of the sectoral disproportions that have developed in the past. This concern is brought out in the retention of central policy direction of the key sectors by the USSR Council of Ministers, the directives to *Gosplan* which I quoted above, and the stress in the reorganization law that direction of enterprises by the territorial principle must "preserve their branch specialization."

These initial qualifications of the territorial principle have since been supplemented by indications of some reassertion by the center of authority delegated to Union Republics and Economic Councils in 1957, again for the sake of stronger enforcement of central preferences on the sectoral structuring of industry. Thus, any reallocation of investment funds assigned to numerous branches of heavy industry now requires special permission by the USSR Council of Ministers.[25] There is also a great deal of verbal stress in authoritative organs on the need for firm central controls. In September, 1958, *Pravda* declared that "centralized direction of economic activity is indispensable" for the "task of realizing radical changes in the structure of some branches of industry."[26]

All this may suggest that some conflict has emerged between the intent of the 1957 reform largely to do away with detailed, vertical control of industry by the branch principle and the center's concern with policy making, in effect, according to the same principle. This makes one wonder whether the next version of the organization chart of Soviet industry might not show some reappearance of branch-differentiated verticalism, at the expense of generalized territorialism. At the same time, the center's evident desire to keep a very watchful eye, even in detail, on the rather numerous "key sectors" makes one wonder whether the Soviet industrial high command has actually realized the perennial dream of all high commands: to be relieved of tedious minutiae and free to make its decisions on the lofty strategic level.

FOOTNOTES:

[1] A shorthand term borrowed from G. Grossman, "Economic Rationalism and Political 'Thaw,' " *Problems of Communism,* Vol. VI, No. 2, pp. 22-26.

[2] Cf., e.g., Robert W. Campbell, "Some Recent Changes in Soviet Economic Policy," *World Politics,* Oct., 1956, pp. 1-4; Gregory Grossman, *op. cit.;* R. W. Davies, "The Reappraisal of Industry," *Soviet Studies,* Jan., 1956, pp. 308-331.

[3] R. W. Davies, *op. cit.,* p. 318.

[4] In a decree of the USSR Council of Ministers, "On the Extension of the Rights of Enterprise Directors," *Direktivy KPSS i sovetskogo pravitel'stva po khoziaistvennym voprosam,* Vol. 4 (Moscow, 1958), pp. 451-459.

[5] Dec., 1956, resolution of Central Committee, *Pravda,* Dec. 25, 1956.

[6] N. S. Khrushchev, Theses of report "On the further perfection of the organization of administration of industry and construction," *Pravda,* Mar. 30, 1957.

[7] Report to VII Session of Supreme Soviet, *Pravda,* May 8, 1957.

[8] Reorganization Law, May 10, 1957, *Pravda,* May 11, 1957; and Statute of Economic Council, cited in footnote 21.

[9] More thorough inquiry than I have addressed to this point, and the progress of more time, might also show that the *de facto* effects of the reform may include an element of centralization, on the regional level, of what had been managerial functions in the hands of the Economic Councils and their Branch Administrations. Although conceived as supervisory administrative agencies, they seem to be intimately enough connected with their enterprises to be, in effect, quasi-managerial bodies. That some Economic Council officials feel that way is indicated by a suggestion that they (as well as enterprise directors) should receive bonuses for plan fulfillment and overfulfillment because (in contrast to the old ministerial officials) they are "in daily contact with the enterprises," and influence their operations (*Voprosy Ekonomiki,* 1958, No. 2, p. 135).

[10] Grossman, *op. cit.,* p. 23.

[11] D. Kondrashev in *Den'gi i kredit,* 1958, No. 9, p. 19.

[12] Campbell, *op. cit.,* pp. 8-9.

[13] *Pravda,* Aug. 11, 1958. The period-of-recoupment calculus also has gained a greater measure of doctrinal respectability. At any rate, there was nothing *sub rosa* about its recent endorsement as the preferred criterion of investment-project choice by the Institute of Economics of the Soviet Academy of Sciences. (*Voprosy Ekonomiki,* 1958, No. 9, pp. 154-162.)

[14] E.g., Philip E. Mosely, "Khrushchev's New Economic Gambit," *Foreign Affairs,* July, 1958, pp. 557 ff.; Michael Kaser, "The Reorganization of Soviet Industry and its Effects on Decision-making," paper presented at Berkeley Symposium on Economic Calculation and Organization in Eastern Europe, June 16-18, 1958.

[15] Speech to VII Session of Supreme Soviet, May 7, 1957.

[16] Cf. R. W. Davies, "The Decentralization of Industry: Some Notes on the Background," *Soviet Studies,* Apr., 1958, p. 1.

[17] For instance, the scrutiny of industrial problems by the Party Central Committee session of July, 1955, dealt with many of the same defects that were still being castigated early in 1957, in connection with the reorganization. Cf. Davies, *op. cit.,* in footnote 2 above.

[18] A. V. Efimov, *Perestroika upravleniia promyshlennost'iu i stroitel'stvom v SSSR* (Moscow, 1957), p. 22.

[19] Some of the changes made in the functions of the Central Statistical Administration (whose chief sits on the Council of Ministers, as before) probably are also part of the effort to improve information at the policy-making level. Industry statistics were previously channeled to this level through both the C.S.A. and the industrial ministries. C.S.A. has now become the sole channel; statistical reporting procedures have been simplified, and the frequency and detail of reports reaching high governmental levels has probably been reduced (*Vestnik Statistiki, 1958,* No. 7, pp. 75 ff.).

[20] For the first year of the new administrative regime, *Gosplan* was also entrusted with operating the very sensitive (and badly mismanaged) system of interenterprise "material-technical supply" left over from the disbanded ministries.

[21] *Polozhenie o sovete narodnogo khoziaistva ekonomicheskogo administrativnogo raiona,* Sept. 26, 1957. Published in *Sobranie postanovlenii pravitel'stva SSSR,* 1957, No. 12, pp. 409-429.

[22] Cf. R. W. Davies, *op. cit.,* footnote 16 above.

[23] E.g., V. Kostennikov, *Planovoe Khoziaistvo,* 1958, No. 5, pp. 25 ff.

[24] Efimov, *op. cit.,* p. 34.

[25] *Planovoe Khoziaistvo,* 1958, No. 10, p. 11. These branches include "ferrous and non-ferrous metallurgy, coal mining, the oil and gas, chemical and other principal branches of industry, as well as electric power generation."

[26] *Pravda* editorial, Sept. 19, 1958.

AGRICULTURAL ORGANIZATION

AND POLICIES

WHEN THE SOVIETS began their great drive for rapid industrialization in 1928, the nation was predominantly agricultural, with four-fifths of the people living on the land. Even today, after thirty years of industrialization, close to two-fifths of the labor force still works in agriculture. While agriculture is still very important in terms of labor force commitment, it has contributed very little directly to the rapid growth of the economy (though its indirect contribution through assistance to rapid industrialization was large). That this is the case is easily verified by comparing the Kaplan-Moorsteen industrial growth and Johnson-Kahan agricultural growth indices presented in Section IV.

There are a number of factors which explain the slow rate of Soviet agricultural growth and its relatively very low productivity in comparison with Soviet industry as well as with the agricultures of many other nations. First, the basic Soviet decision of the late 1920's to develop industry, and particularly heavy industry, at the expense of agriculture, so well described by Professor Erlich (Section III), has meant, in implementation, that the farm sector has received little more than the minimal amount of resources for new investment necessary to maintain output and to replace labor which has been siphoned off into the industrial labor force (see Lazar Volin's second article below). The reasons why the Soviets, in comparison with India and China, were able to consign agriculture to stepchild status are analyzed in Dr. Hoeffding's essay in Section III.

Second, despite (or perhaps because of!) its very great over-all size, only about one-sixth of the Soviet land mass has the proper combination of soil, temperature, and rainfall for successful crop cultivation (cf. V. P. Timoshenko [1953]; D. G. Johnson [1956]).

Third, the bulk of the Soviet peasants have been forced to work on collective farms, a form of economic organization not conducive, for a

488

number of reasons, to good work incentives. The nature of the collective farm and collateral institutions (such as the machine tractor stations) as well as recent institutional changes in agricultural organization are surveyed in the second of Lazar Volin's articles republished below. His first article compares the present collective farm (kolkhoz) system with its counterpart in the Czarist period, the mir, and points out the important similarities and differences between the two institutions. The abrupt and violent transition from private to collective farms in the Soviet Union in 1930 is described in Dr. Jasny's essay in Section III.

Finally, the essay by Drs. Nove and Laird (below) presents a study of comparative labor productivity on a Soviet collective farm and on a comparable Nebraska farm. The authors have some interesting hypotheses regarding the differences in productivity observed.

Considering its importance, Soviet agriculture has been relatively neglected by Western scholars. The outstanding study of the Soviet period is Dr. Jasny's thick monograph (1949). L. Volin's condensed *Survey* (1951) is also a very useful source. Sir John Maynard (1948) is excellent on the Czarist and early Soviet periods.

THE PEASANT HOUSEHOLD UNDER THE MIR AND THE KOLKHOZ IN MODERN RUSSIAN HISTORY

Lazar Volin

No OTHER institution of nineteenth-century Russian rural society was so much in the spotlight of public attention and controversy, scientific and political, as the Russian land commune—the "mir," or *obshchina*. No other institution was so much idealized or so much disparaged; none had so many friends and so many enemies in all political camps—conservative, liberal, and radical alike. Today the traditional Russian mir, which so recently pulsated with life, is dead, replaced by a more thoroughgoing collectivism.

As a result, while it was formerly an object of intense interest on the part of scholars in diverse fields, economists, sociologists, and students of law, as well as historians, the mir today is relegated entirely to the post mortems of historical research. Such research, however, not only can make a valuable contribution to general historical knowledge but can also contribute through comparative analysis to a better understanding of contemporary Soviet agrarian collectivism. I propose to attempt such a comparison in a tentative and necessarily sketchy fashion, from the standpoint of the peasant household as the social unit naturally closest to the individual. It should be borne in mind that I am not concerned here with an analysis of the theoretically possible or ideal forms of collectivism, but with institutions that actually existed or exist.

Now what were the essential characteristics of the Great Russian mir system as it existed in the nineteenth century? In the first place, the title to land was vested in the mir, which, as a type of rural organization, was carried over from serfdom by the emancipation legislation of the 1860's. The mir usually consisted of former serfs and their descendants settled in a single village, although sometimes a village included more than one mir and, conversely, several villages sometimes constituted a single mir.

In the second place, all members of the mir had a right to an allotment, on the same basis, of a separate family holding, which was separately cultivated. Moreover, the peasant household held, in addition, the home and kitchen garden in hereditary possession. Thus, except for common pasture and sometimes meadows and forests, there was no joint or coöperative farming of the mir land as a unit, but family peasant farming. In the third place, as a consequence of its collective tenure, the mir had the power to repartition the land from time to time among its constituent households on some uniform basis. Here we have the outstanding peculiarity of the Russian mir system.

The repartitional mir type of land tenure predominated among peasants of Great Russia and Siberia, while over a large part of the Ukraine and other western provinces the peasant family had its holding, as a rule, in hereditary possession and not in temporary possession at the discretion of the mir. Approximately three-fourths of all peasant households in the fifty provinces of European Russia (exclusive of Congress Poland and Finland) held more than four-fifths of the "allotted" [1] land in repartitional tenure and the rest was held in hereditary tenure, according to official data on land-holdings in 1905.

The basis on which land repartitions were made by the mir and their regularity or frequency varied from region to region. Not all mir communes repartitioned their land at regular intervals and some did not repartition at all, although the power to do so remained and was, in fact, increasingly wielded with the growing pressure of population on land. For instance, a study of data for 6,830 mir communes in 66 scattered districts of European Russia indicated that whereas during the 1880's, 65 percent had practically not repartitioned their land, during the period 1897–1902 only 12 percent failed to do so; 59 percent repartitioned largely on the basis of the number of males in a family, 8 percent on the basis

[1] Land held by peasants, whether in repartitional or in hereditary tenure, constituted a separate category of the so-called "allotted" (nadel'naia) land, i. e., land allotted to the peasants after the emancipation from serfdom in the middle of the nineteenth century and subject until 1907 to redemption payments. Such "allotted" land, even when held in hereditary tenure, was hedged by legal restrictions that distinguished it from land held as individual property in fee simple. The latter type was owned during the second half of the nineteenth century predominantly by the nobility and less so by business classes and corporations, but peasants were also purchasing such land. According to official data in 1905, there were in 50 provinces of European Russia about 275,000,000 acres of land owned in fee simple (of which peasants owned individually or coöperatively over 66,000,000 acres) and 375,000,000 acres of "allotted" peasant land.

of working adults, 19 percent on the basis of the total number in each family and its working power, and 2 percent resorted to partial repartitions.[2]

Blood relationship was not a basic factor in the modern Russian mir, as it is in the zadruga of the southern Slavs, although some students have traced its genesis to just such family association, while others have denied any historical affinity. However, the highly controversial problem of the origin of the mir, the question of how ancient it was, to what extent it was affected by the intervention of the state and landowners prior to the abolition of serfdom in the 1860's, are outside the scope of this paper.[3]

There were certain administrative and municipal functions of the mir that need not detain us, but one task assigned it was far too important to be left unnoted. This was tax assessment and collection, under the principle of joint unlimited liability of all members of the mir. The mir, therefore, was not only an institution of repartitional land tenure but equally an organ of fiscal administration.

The imprint left by the fiscal factor on Russian agrarian history, and especially on the emancipation reform that abolished serfdom

[2] P. Veniaminov, *Krestianskaia Obshchina (Peasant Commune)* (St. Petersburg, 1908), pp. 119–21. Based on material collected by K. P. Kocharovsky.

[3] The Russian literature on the subject of the mir is enormous. For valuable bibliographical material, consult E. I. Yakushkin, *Obychnoe Pravo (Customary Law)* (Iaroslav and Moscow), issues I, 1875; II, 1896; and III, 1908. See also a list of references given by the late Professor A. A. Kaufman in his article, "Sel'skaia Pozemel'naia Obshchina," in *Entsiklopedicheskii Slovar T-va, Br. A. i I. Granat i Ko.* 7th ed., Vol. XXXVIII. One work deserves special mention because of the part it played in the popularization of the mir among the Russian intelligentsia, August, Freiherr von Haxthausen, *Studien über die innern Zustände, das Volksleben und insbesondere die ländlichen Einrichtungen Russlands*, Vol. I–II, Hanover, 1847; Vol. III, Berlin, 1852. Translated as *The Russian Empire, Its People, Institutions and Resources*, 2 vols., London, 1856. Haxthausen performed a service for the Russian mir somewhat similar to that which Frederick Jackson Turner performed for the American frontier—he placed it definitely on the intellectual map. By a curious twist, not uncommon in the history of social thought, this treatise of a conservative Prussian scholar proved most helpful theoretically to the founders of Russian agrarian socialism (Narodnichestvo), Alexander Herzen and especially N. G. Chernyshevsky. Haxthausen and the Russian conservative proponents of the mir, such as the Slavophiles, for instance, valued this institution as a means of preventing the development of a propertyless proletariat in Russia and consequently as a bulwark against socialism. Herzen and Chernyshevsky, on the contrary, saw in the mir an embryo of socialism, which they believed could develop by skipping over the capitalistic stage of the Marxian evolutionary scheme. See Chernyshevsky's review of Haxthausen's *Studien* in *Sovremennik*, No. 7, 1857, republished in N. G. Chernyshevsky, *Polnoe Sobranie Sochinenii (Collected Works)*, III (St. Petersburg, 1906), 270–310.

in the middle of the nineteenth century, is well known. How the peasants were burdened with heavy redemption payments for the land allotted to them and how these payments, together with taxes, sometimes exceeded the income from the land is a story that has often been told.⁴ Now the primary task imposed on the mir by the government was to make the Russian peasantry bear this heavy fiscal burden; and from this fact stemmed much of the land-repartitioning and equalizing activity of the mir, as well as most of the fetters on the personal freedom of the peasant that remained after the emancipation and that legally set him apart from other more privileged classes of the community.

With land distribution and tax collection, the important functions of the mir came to an end. Not the mir but the peasant household was the actual farm unit. It owned or hired draft power and implements, performed all the farm operations on the land allotted to it, and disposed of its produce on a free market, without hindrance, if it had anything to dispose of. The peasant household was the actual unit of land allotment and had a voice through the head of the household in the governing body of the mir. The mir dealt with the household, not with the individual. We shall have to bear in mind this position of the peasant household vis-à-vis the mir when we discuss the *kolkhoz* (collective farm).

There were, of course, various limitations on the independence of the peasant farm unit under the mir. Thus the landholding could be changed both in size and in location by the mir, through either partial or general repartition. The allotted land could not be sold, mortgaged, or inherited by the peasant household. The latter, moreover, could not refuse to accept a holding allotted by the mir, as it was sometimes tempted to do when the income from the land was less than the various payments due. In other words, the right of the peasant household to be allotted a landholding entailed a correlative duty to accept an allotment.

There was also the very serious limitation on the independence of the peasant household arising from a compulsory cropping system, due to the unenclosed, scattered character of the holdings, consisting of a number of narrow strips, intermingled in each field with

⁴ For an excellent account of the Russian emancipation reform by an American scholar, see G. T. Robinson, *Rural Russia under the Old Regime, A History of the Landlord-Peasant World and a Prologue to the Peasant Revolution of 1917*, New York, 1932.

strips of other holdings. Such a system, coupled with the use of the stubble for common pasture, made the planting in any particular field of crops with a different growing season and maturity practically impossible. The division of fields into strips under the mir had the definite purpose of equalizing the holdings with respect to quality of the soil, topography, distance from the village, and so forth. The strip system, however, was characteristic not only of the mir but also of hereditary peasant tenure prevailing in certain sections of Russia. As a matter of fact, it was convincingly argued that under hereditary tenure the evil of scattered strip holdings was even less easily corrected than under the mir system, where excessive scattering of the strips usually led to a general repartitioning of land.[5]

As would be expected, arrears in the payment of taxes was responsible for most of the intervention on the part of the mir in the affairs of individual households. To insure payment, the mir could hire out a member of the defaulting household or could remove the head of the family, appointing in his place a different member of the household.[6]

Removal of an individual as head of a peasant household in practice occurred also for other reasons. Thus the head of the household was but an administrator, removable by the mir, though an administrator with easily and frequently abused autocratic powers while at the helm. This position of the head of the household demonstrates not only the power of the mir but also the tremendously important fact of the joint family ownership of the property of a peasant household.

The institution of family property among Russian peasants owes its origin to custom, which was recognized and preserved by the courts, and also to some extent by the emancipation legislation itself. It had disadvantages, as well as advantages, for the individual. For instance, all his earnings from whatever source, if he was not legally separated from the household, were supposed to go into the common pool [7]—a serious matter, considering the prevalence of

[5] George Pavlovsky, *Agricultural Russia on the Eve of the Revolution* (London, 1930), p. 83.

[6] A. A. Leontiev, *Krestianskoe Pravo* (Peasant Law) (St. Petersburg, 1909), p. 201.

[7] The earnings of women were excepted, but they were supposed to provide their own clothes and dowry for their daughters. This explains the paradoxical fact that peasant women, with their notoriously inferior status, had personal property rights

migratory work in the overpopulated Russian village. Even peasants who had long lived and worked away from the village were often forced to continue their contributions to the household of which they legally remained members. The weapon here was the famous Russian passport, which hung like the sword of Damocles over the head of any peasant who wanted to leave his native village. For to receive or to renew the much-coveted passport, he had to obtain the permission both of the head of the household and of the mir.

But the traditional Great Russian large peasant family, zealously guarded by the master for economic reasons during the period of serfdom, began to feel the disintegrating impact of individualism following the emancipation. This was manifested in numerous family divisions, in spite of the undisputed economic advantages possessed by a large peasant family. In the 1880's the government became so alarmed over the adverse effects of family divisions that it tried to restrict them by law. Such restriction, however, was unavailing and served only to provide an additional source of vexation to the peasant.

It is hardly surprising that the mir system, as it existed in reality, seemed to its critics an extension or projection of the old servile order, rather than an embryo of the future socialist commonwealth as envisaged by the earlier Russian non-Marxian socialists, the *Narodniki*. This view of the mir as a germ of socialist development was staunchly opposed by the younger school of Russian socialists, the Marxists (among them Lenin, the father of Bolshevism), who came to the fore in the 1890's and who accepted and applied to Russian conditions the orthodox Marxian dogma imported from Western Europe. The mir, according to the Marxists, retarded but did not prevent the evolutionary development that, in their view, doomed small peasant farming as small-scale production generally and that resulted in the splitting of the village, as of the town, into two antagonistic social classes: the bourgeoisie at the top and the proletariat at the bottom. On the other hand, the mir fell out of favor with conservatives, who had, prior to the revolution of 1905, looked upon it as the bulwark of law and order in the village. They blamed the mir for keeping alive the idea of general repartitioning

denied to men. For evidence from different sources on this point, see A. F. Meiendorf, *Krestianskii Dvor (Peasant Household)* (St. Petersburg, 1909), pp. 6–9.

of all land, the so-called *chernyi peredel,* which inspired the rising of the peasantry against the landlords and the state. Moreover, the opinion, not new in itself, that the mir with its repartitions and scattered-strip system was a serious obstacle to agricultural progress gained increasing adherence in conservative and official circles.

The government wanted to create a new class of peasant proprietors who would form a barrier against agrarian revolution and who could also utilize the advantages of an improved agricultural technique, for which the strongly fostered consolidation and segregation of scattered holdings paved the way. And finally, with the abandonment of the joint liability of the mir for taxes and the discontinuance of redemption payments, the mir was no longer needed as an organ of fiscal administration. Hence the famous Stolypin laws, with their slogan of the "wager on the strong," attacked the mir, and in the same sweep the institution of peasant family property. Some of the legal disabilities of the peasants were also removed. There is no space to deal here in detail with this legislation and the tendency toward the individualization of the Russian peasant agriculture that it ushered in.[8] Anyway, the victory of the individualistic system of land tenure, which the Stolypin laws promoted, was short-lived.

The revolution of 1917 gave the mir a fresh lease of life. The mir, in fact, was an active instrument of the revolution in the agrarian sphere, since it helped to carry out the partition of estate land among peasant cultivators. The ties that bound the individual to the peasant household, and both to the mir, as this emerged from the turmoil of the revolution and war communism into the brief breathing spell of the regime of so-called New Economic Policy (NEP), were looser than in the old mir. The sweeping away of the landlord, the partial restoration of the free market—which had been legally abolished during war communism—and the retention of various limitations on the development of capitalistic farming (such as the prohibition of the sale or mortgage of land, which legally remained nationalized, steep taxation, and the like) turned the period of the New Economic Policy into the heyday of very small peasant family agriculture. The number of peasant households, in fact, showed an extremely rapid growth from some 16,000,000 be-

[8] The subject has been admirably treated in G. T. Robinson, *Rural Russia under the Old Regime,* Chap. XI.

fore the revolution to over 24,000,000 in 1928.[9] However, just as the Stolypin laws were but an episode between the two revolutions of 1905 and 1917, so was the New Economic Policy but an interlude between the early Soviet war communism and the intensified collectivism of the five-year plan.

The process of collectivization of Russian peasant agriculture was not carried out by the Kremlin via the mir, as it might have been. On the contrary, by a government decree of July 30, 1930, the mir was to be liquidated in R.S.F.S.R. (the largest of the constituent republics of the Soviet Union), if not less than 75 percent of peasant households were collectivized. The rights and functions of the liquidated mir were to be transferred to the village soviets. By a subsequent decree, requirements for liquidation were lowered to 68–70 percent of collectivized poor and middle-class peasant households (i. e., exclusive of the "kulaki"), including not less than 75–80 percent of the peasant sown area.[10] In view of the speed with which collectivization was generally carried out,[11] the liquidation of the mir may be accepted as an accomplished fact. Thus the very demise of the mir, which had been sought by Stolypin and his friends in the name of individualism, was brought about a quarter of a century later by the Bolsheviks in the name of socialism. And yet it is at least open to doubt whether collectivization, involving as it did a profound agrarian revolution, could have been effected so speedily, even with the very liberal use of force, if the mir system had not hindered the crystallization of a concept of stable individual property rights in land among the Russian peasantry. There is good reason to believe, therefore, that in spite of the Bolsheviks' hostility and contempt for the mir, their agrarian collective system is indebted to it.[12]

[9] I treated this period in greater detail in "Agrarian Individualism in the Soviet Union: Its Rise and Decline," *Agricultural History*, Jan. and April, 1938.

[10] *Collection of Laws and Decrees of R.S.F.S.R.*, Part I, no. 51, Dec. 6, 1930, item 621; and no. 65, Nov. 10, 1931, item 465 (in Russian).

[11] In 1928 only a little over 400,000 peasant households out of an estimated total of 24,500,000 were collectivized; in 1932 the figures were respectively 14,900,000 and 24,200,000. By 1937, 18,500,000 peasant households, out of a diminished total of 19,900,000, were in 243,700 collective farms. I discussed the problem of collectivization in detail in "Agrarian Collectivism in the Soviet Union," *Journal of Political Economy*, XLV (Oct. and Dec., 1937), 606–33, 759–88.

[12] For an interesting defense of the mir under Soviet conditions by a well-known economist and publicist, N. I. Sukhanov, see his article, "Obshchina v Sovetskom Agrarnom Zakonodatel'stve" ("The Mir in Soviet Agrarian Legislation"), *Na Agrarnom Fronte*, no. 11–12, 1926. Also the reply by M. Kubanin in the same publication.

We saw that under the distributive collectivism of the mir organization the peasant household was the keystone of the farm system. Now what is its position in the integrated collectivism of the modern *kolkhoz?* First of all, the kolkhoz and not the peasant household is the basic farm unit, carrying on, often with the help and supervision of the state machine-tractor station, the actual farming operations. The peasant household plays a decidedly subordinate role in the kolkhoz, although by no means a negligible role in the economic life of the collectivized village.

Consequently the kolkhoz, unlike the mir, deals primarily not with the peasant household but with the individual peasant worker, man or woman, who is entirely independent of the family in his work relations with the collective. The worker is assigned to a brigade, or more recently, to the smaller unit, *zveno*, into which the labor force of a kolkhoz is subdivided. For his work on the collective farm the peasant is credited with the so-called *trudodni*, or "labor days," which are arbitrary units representing performance of specific tasks and used for calculating his eventual income in kind and in cash. This system of payment is based on results and is differentiated according to the skill required for various jobs, so that skilled workers are better paid than the unskilled.

In general, then, the relation of the peasant to the kolkhoz differs fundamentally from the relation of the peasant farmer to the mir and resembles that of a worker to a factory using a system of payment by results. It differs, however, from the position of the Soviet factory or state farm worker in that the latter, even though a pieceworker, receives a money wage at regular intervals, while the collective farmer is merely a residual claimant to the income of the kolkhoz after all the obligations to the state have been met and expenses defrayed.

Thus the collective farmer has neither the advantage of a specified income that the Soviet industrial worker possesses, nor has he the degree of independence of the small peasant farmer. Having said this, I must enter some exceptions. A young peasant, who may have been merely a cog in the family farm system, may be somewhat more independent on the collective farm. This is likely to be the case if he or she joins the ranks of skilled workers, tractor or truck drivers, combine operators, and the like. Such opportunities for skilled, better-paid occupations, formerly rare in Russian agriculture, have greatly increased with the collectivization and mechanization of farming and have continued to grow, as can be seen, for instance, from the increase in the number of tractor drivers and combine operators from 235,000 and 11,000 respectively on January 1, 1934, to 870,000 and 125,000 on June 1, 1938.[13]

This situation, however, has provided a new basis for economic stratification in the collectivized village, because of the higher earnings of the skilled workers. Whereas, for example, a large majority of collective farmers in 1936 and 1937 earned in cash less than one ruble (20 cents at the overvalued legal par of exchange) per "labor day" and many of them much less, tractor drivers were guaranteed a minimum of 2.5 rubles per "labor day." The same differentiation prevailed with respect to payments in kind. The introduction of the so-called Stakhanovist speed-up, or more intensive methods of work, often bringing large returns to the "shock" workers, has tended on the whole to accentuate economic inequality in the kolkhoz. And so, while much was made by Marxist critics of the failure of the old mir to prevent economic or class stratification in the Russian village, in the kolkhoz economic inequality has the official blessing so long as it is inequality in the distribution of income that stimulates productivity. Conversely, egalitarianism, *uranilovka* as it is contemptuously termed in Soviet parlance, is deemed to have an adverse effect on productive efficiency and therefore to be a petit bourgeois vice that has no place in the socialist economy of the kolkhoz.

Another exception to what was said concerning the loss of independence by the peasants is furnished by the poorest households of the precollective era, especially households that lacked livestock and implements. Such semiproletarian peasants, who constituted in some regions a third or more of all peasant families, had little to lose but their poverty on entering the kolkhoz. It is probably true, however, that for the mass of collectivized peasantry there was some real loss of independence, even remembering the limitations of the mir system.

How does the peasants' security of status and privilege of self-government in the kolkhoz compare with that in the mir? The history of collective farming is replete with evidence as to the in-

---

[13] *Pravda*, Aug. 13, 1939. These figures do not include state farms, or *sovkhozy*, which had 68,800 tractor drivers and 22,000 combine operators in 1938.

security of the peasant family. Expulsion from the kolkhoz, which often, as the Kremlin itself has publicly admitted, entails starvation,[14] always stares the collective farmer in the face. On occasions, as during the Great Purge of 1937–38, expulsions have assumed epidemic proportions. From time to time, and notably in 1935 when a new collective charter was adopted, legal safeguards have been erected against arbitrary expulsions; but, for the most part, they appear to have failed in their objective. In practice, then, the ties that bind the peasant to the kolkhoz are less stable than those that bound him to the old mir, and this lessened stability has not worked to his advantage.

In theory, the governance of the kolkhoz is more democratic than that of the mir, since the governing body consists not merely of the heads of the households but of the whole membership. Moreover, the mir was often, and rightly, criticized for being the tool of the well-to-do peasants ("kulaki") and the *chinovnik,* the government functionary; but the self-government of the kolkhoz appears to be, if anything, even more of a fiction. A new collective charter in 1935 aimed to insure the elective character and a degree of security of tenure of the officers of the kolkhoz, who were, in fact, frequently appointed and removed by the Soviet officials at will.

Yet the new law, which was hailed as the Magna Charta of collective democracy, has also been continually violated according to numerous reports in the Soviet sources; and the officers of the collectives have, on the whole, remained the tools of the Soviet bureaucrat, just as the officers of the mir were the tools of the Tsarist chinovnik.

Government interference in the affairs of the kolkhoz is, if anything, much more active and minute than it was in the mir. So long as the mir paid the taxes, the government as a rule was little concerned with its internal economic life. It is true, toward the end of the nineteenth century administrative regimentation increased and began to be extended even to such economic matters as household divisions, repartition of land, and the like. But even this was a far cry from the detailed control exercised over the working life of the

[14] See a Decree of the Council of Peoples Commissars of the U.S.S.R. and of the Central Committee of the Communist Party of April 19, 1938, entitled "Concerning the Prohibition of Expulsion of Collective Farmers from *Kolkhozy,*" published in *Izvestiia* and *Pravda,* April 20, 1938. I discussed this matter in "Effects of the Drought and Purge on the Agriculture of the Soviet Union," *Foreign Agriculture,* May, 1939.

kolkhoz. There is hardly a question within the whole gamut of farm management and practice, whether of crop rotation or cultural methods, of remuneration of labor or its most effective employment, that does not come within the range of government control and attention.

No problem, however, has attracted so much official attention as the division of the product of collective farming in which the state shares. The satisfaction of the claims of the state takes precedence over everything else and is, according to Stalin, the "first commandment" of the collective farmer, to which obedience has been ruthlessly exacted. As a result, the Soviet government, through the combined power of taxation, price fixing, the monopoly of ownership of tractors, and the direct control over collective farming, has been able to procure mounting quantities of farm products at low prices. For instance, it increased its vitally important grain collections from less than 12,000,000 short tons in 1928 to 32,000,000 tons in 1937, obtaining the great bulk of this quantity from the collectives. Thus the kolkhoz, no less than the mir, is in its own way a fiscal handmaid of the state.

However we view a kolkhoz—whether as a state-organized and controlled producers' coöperative, or as a form of collective sharetenancy with the state acting as the landlord—the fact remains that it must function within the framework of a planned state economy, to which it must be fully attuned. Here is another contrast with the mir, which, although sanctioned and long protected by the state, was nevertheless a precapitalist survival in an increasingly capitalistic world. Hence, when the government in the early years of the present century became seriously concerned with the improvement of agricultural technique, an added motive arose for destroying the mir, which was considered from a capitalistic standpoint an obstacle to progress. Technical, as well as social, revolution in agriculture, on the other hand, was at the root of Soviet collectivization, with its consolidation of the numerous scattered strip holdings into large fields, and its emphasis on mechanized, scientific farming.

The spearhead of this technical revolution was the tractor, in spite of much inefficiency in its utilization and operation. Furthermore, the tractor also greatly helped to strengthen Soviet control over collective farming, for the government owns all the tractors, combines, and other complicated machinery, concentrated in over 6,400 machine-tractor stations. These tractor stations not only service more than three fourths [15] of all collectives, but constitute the backbone of the local agricultural planning and administration and are a valuable source of revenue to the state. It is an interesting paradox that the peasants, by slaughtering their horses during the early years of collectivization, made the tractor more vitally necessary, thus unwittingly helping the cause of agrarian regimentation to which they were opposed. Thus it has come about that Lenin's prophecy twenty years ago of the vital role of the tractor in collectivization has been fulfilled.

The old mir knew no such powerful centralizing weapon as the tractor to transform its distributive collectivism into a more integrated large-scale type, as many of the Russian non-Marxian socialists hoped might be done. Interestingly enough, one of the earliest and ablest defenders of the mir, the famous Russian publicist Chernyshevsky, believed that machinery would facilitate the development of coöperative farming in the mir and pinned great hope on the steam plow.[16] But as it turned out, it was the internal-combustion engine of the tractor and not the steam engine that did the trick; in the meantime the mir was gone with the wind in the process.

Essentially, the kolkhoz is an economy of socialized production and individualism in consumption. While the kolkhoz performs certain welfare and cultural functions (libraries, theaters, clubs, child nurseries, and so forth) that come under the heading of communal consumption, still its present *artel* form is an institution primarily of production and not of consumption, which is left to the peasant household. In this respect the artel type of collective farm organization differs from a completely communistic form, the so-called commune.

The artel, moreover, unlike the commune, does not provide for complete socialization of production. As Stalin pointed out in the commission that drafted the model or standard charter of the kolkhoz in 1935: "If you do not have as yet in the *artel* an abundance of goods and you cannot give to the individual collective farmers and

[15] In 1937, 78 percent of all collectives comprising 91 percent of the total collective sown area were serviced by machine-tractor stations.
[16] Article on land tenure in the magazine *Sovremennik*, no. 9, 1857. Reproduced in N. C. Chernyshevsky, *Polnoe Sobranie Sochinenii* (Collected Works), III, 477–80.

their families all that they need . . . then it is best to admit openly and honestly that a collectivized peasant household must have its own small personal farming." [17] Hence, in addition to the collective farm, each collectivized peasant family is supposed to have a little plot of land and a few animals of its own. Any surplus beyond their own needs the collective farmers have a right to sell on the limited local market (from which the middleman is legally tabooed) or to the government. Thus the peasant household in the kolkhoz is not merely a consumption but also a farm-production unit of a sort and is recognized as such in the Soviet law.

In theory, of course, the personal farming of the collectivized peasants is supposed to have a strictly supplementary character, subsidiary to the basic economy of the collective farm. In practice this economic dualism in the kolkhoz may and does result in competition and conflict between the collectivist and the individualist elements which the artel organization of collective farming is supposed to reconcile.

Obviously, the smaller the return a peasant family receives from its work in a kolkhoz, the more it will tend to concentrate on its own personal farming, compensating for its small size by its highly intensive character. This is reflected especially clearly in such an intensive branch of agriculture as animal husbandry. According to official estimates in 1938, most of the livestock in the collectives, except horses, was in the individual possession of the collective farmers, although they planted only 13,000,000 acres to crops as against 290,000,000 acres of collective sowings. Personal farming of collectivized peasants, however, accounted for over a fifth of the officially estimated gross farm output of the Soviet Union in 1937.

The Kremlin's attitude, which since the promulgation of the new collective charter in 1935 had been favorable to such personal farming, shifted after the XVIII Communist Party Congress in the spring of 1939, on the ground that personal farming "in some places began to outgrow the collectivized economy and became the basic part, whereas collective farming, on the contrary, became secondary." [18]

In May, 1939, the Kremlin issued a decree which aimed to curb

[17] A. N. Nikitin, A. P. Pavlov, and A. A. Ruskol, editors, *Kolkhoznoe Pravo (Kolkhoz Law)* (Moscow, 1939), p. 342.
[18] Speech by A. A. Andreev at the XVIII Party Congress, *Pravda*, March 14, 1939.

the alleged illegal expansion of the personal farming of collective farmers.[19] It reiterated the requirement that the plots allotted to the farmers for their personal use should in no case exceed the limits specified in the 1935 charter—0.6 to 1.25 and in some regions 2.5 acres per household.

Accordingly a new land survey in the collectives was ordered during the summer of 1939, and all land found to be in excess of the prescribed limit was to be confiscated. Likewise land allotted to those who had not worked continuously in the collectives was to be forfeited and used for allotment to collective farmers having insufficient personal holdings. In general a careful demarcation of the common land of the kolkhoz from the area available for legitimate personal use of the collective farmers was decreed.

The common land of the kolkhoz could be increased, but under no circumstances reduced without the official permission of the government, and thus it was to be protected against the encroachment of personal (i. e., individual) farming. Where, as a result of these restrictive measures, a shortage of land available for allotment for the personal use of collective farmers might develop, emigration to sparsely settled regions was "recommended." Collective farmers who had farmsteads outside of the village (the so-called *khutor*), as was often the case in the Ukraine, Belorussia, and other western regions, were to be speedily moved into the village, where presumably they would be easier to control. Finally, a minimum of "labor days" to be earned by each able-bodied member of the collective (not by each family) was set up, and those who fell below the minimum were to be expelled.

These measures and the jeremiads that preceded and accompanied them serve to underline the fact that the peasant household, although shunted to an inferior place, still remains a serious rival of the kolkhoz in its present artel form of organization.

[19] Decree of the Central Committee of the All-Union Communist Party of May 27, 1939. "On Measures for Safeguarding Common Collective Farm Land against Squandering," published in *Pravda* and *Izvestiia*, May 28, 1939.

AGRICULTURAL POLICY OF THE SOVIET UNION

(By Lazar Volin, Foreign Agricultural Service, U.S. Department of Agriculture)

SUMMARY AND CONCLUSIONS

1. Agricultural policy has been a prominent question in the Soviet Union as it was in Czarist Russia. It has emerged at every critical juncture in the history of the country. The recent transition from the Stalin to the Khrushchev regime has been no exception.

Agriculture, with close to half the people depending upon it for a livelihood, continues to be a more important sector of Soviet national economy than it is in the more industrialized countries of the West—and this despite the industrial growth of the Soviet Union.

2. The Soviet Union, notwithstanding its huge crop acreage, has been bedeviled by agricultural underdevelopment, by the failure of its agriculture to meet increasing food and fiber requirements of a growing population that is becoming increasingly urbanized. Therefore, the principal objective of the Soviet Government has been expansion of agricultural production. A sharp upsurge in farm products output has become, for political and physical reasons, extremely urgent for the post-Stalin regime, which cannot afford to proceed at Stalin's pedestrian pace. Hence the flood of official reports, speeches, and decrees spotlighting the agricultural problem. This preoccupation of the Soviet Government with increased production sharply contrasts with the concern of the United States with farm surpluses and farm relief.

3. Climate is more of a limiting factor in agricultural production in the Soviet Union than in the United States. More important is the fact that other basic and closely related objectives of Soviet policy clashed with expansion of production, namely: the centrally controlled collectivization, ruthlessly forced in the 1930's on the small peasant family farming, which emerged victorious after the revolution, and (b) the acquisition by the Soviet state at a low cost to itself of large quantities of farm products, which left little incentive to the collectivized peasantry to work as diligently on the large collective farms as on their own little kitchen garden plots.

4. Solely from the standpoint of production, central direction and planning of collective agriculture permit the marshaling of all available resources to achieve a specific goal on a large scale. This has resulted both in improvements and in costly mistakes—and both often made with little regard to economy and efficiency. The impossibility of public criticism of a policy once it has been officially adopted and, often, inadequate critical discussion before it is adopted—coupled with reliance on pseudoscience of the Lysenko type, which promises spectacular "pie in the sky" results—make prevention or correction of such mistakes more difficult.

5. An early example of improvement was the consolidation into large fields, adopted for power farming, of the numerous noncontiguous

strips.   These strips, into which small holdings were formerly divided, meant waste of land (for boundaries) and of labor.   The plowing up and adding to the crop area of 90 million acres of virgin land within a period of 4 years (1954–57) is a more recent accomplishment; and it is a significant accomplishment even though much of this land must be considered marginal or even submarginal from a climatic standpoint.

Among the examples of costly mistakes committed by central authorities are: The great loss of livestock during the initial all-out collectivization drive; the indiscriminate adoption of many farm practices such as the universal use of perennial grasses in crop rotation without regard to regional differences; the equally indiscriminate adoption of certain types of farm equipment such as large tractors; the shift of crops into areas climatically or otherwise unsuitable for their production, such as the abortive extension of cotton growing from the irrigated regions of Soviet central Asia and Transcaucasia into the more northern dry farming regions of the Ukraine and north Caucasus; or the present extension of corn cultivation into regions in which it is either too cold or too dry for a successful corn culture.   Yet another manifestation of large scale policy errors is the persistent "giantism" which, despite recognition of mistakes committed in the early 1930's, led to the creation again in the 1950's of huge unwieldy farm units through widespread mergers of collectives and growth of state farms.

6. The efforts of the Khrushchev regime to remedy weakness on the agricultural front is being done without deviation from the basic principles of agrarian collectivism.   In fact, the grip of state and party rule over collective agriculture has been tightened, although a shift of authority from Moscow to the republics, provinces (oblasts), and districts (raions) and some decentralization of the rigid, highly centralized planning of Stalin's days has taken place.   However, decentralization is not permitted to interfere with national goals which are deemed of critical importance, such as the expansion of corn growing to bolster the lagging feed supply, the expansion of the crop acreage on the virgin lands east of the Volga and the Urals and the campaign to overtake the United States in per capita production of dairy products and meat.

7. The most important reform of the institutional structure of collective farming during the post-Stalin period was the liquidation of machine tractor stations and sale of the machines to the collective farms.   This move, stanchly opposed by Stalin during his lifetime, was made by the Khrushchev administration primarily to eliminate virtual dual management of collective farm operations or, as Khrushchev put it, the existence of "two bosses on the land."

8. The reform, undertaken to increase farm efficiency, tends to enhance the position of collectives, considerably enlarged by mergers, in the Soviet agrarian institutional scheme.   Nevertheless, the rapid expansion of state farming which now accounts for more than a fourth of the crop area instead of 12 percent in 1953, may point to the eventual takeover of collectives.   State farms had already absorbed many collectives and ideologically they have always been considered a superior type of economic organization, though this is at present officially minimized.   How long the coexistence of two organizational types of Soviet agriculture will continue may depend largely upon

whether the Soviet Government extends to collective farms the regular wage system now prevailing on state farms—a system which is similar to that in Soviet factories. The peasants or collective farms are residual sharers in the income after the state secures its share and current production expenses and capital outlays are met.

9. Although there has been no decollectivization recently in the Soviet Union such as took place, for instance, in Poland and Yugoslavia, limited concessions were made to peasants within the framework of Soviet agrarian collectivism. There was tax relief for the small allotment holdings of the peasants' and workers' families which plays such an important part in their income and in the national food supply, especially in animal products. Because this small "acre and a cow" type of farming competes with the collective farm economy for the labor and loyalty of the peasants, as well as for ideological reasons, the Stalin regime came to look upon it with a jaundiced eye and behaved accordingly. But the attitude of Stalin's successors, after the initial spurt of liberalism, also has been ambivalent—now relaxed, now restricted.

10. In general, Soviet policy toward peasants has always consisted of a combination of force, indoctrination, and economic incentives but the proportion varied from time to time. During the Stalin regime force predominated. After Stalin, Soviet policy shifted to a greater emphasis on economic incentives. The very low prices paid by the Government for the farm products which the collectives had to deliver were raised considerably. The whole system of deliveries was reorganized and simplified. Larger incomes of collectives as a result of higher prices and larger output permitted increased and often more regular distribution to peasants. But the stimulating effect of increased agricultural prices is to some extent lost when there is only a limited supply of consumer goods for farmers to buy because of the imbalance in Soviet industrialization. For the underemphasis on production of consumers goods has not been sufficiently redressed.

In any event, the visiting team of U.S. Department of Agriculture economists pointed out in its report.[1]

The system of collective and state-operated farms is not likely to provide production incentives for farm people that are equal to the incentives on family farms in this country. In other words, it may be difficult to substitute for the "magic of ownership which turns sand into gold." Also, the struggles incidental to establishment of collective farming may have left scars that will impede development of adequate production incentives.

11. The lagging capital investment in agriculture and inputs of agricultural machinery, commercial fertilizers and construction were increased. But capital investment is still inadequate to make possible an effective use of labor and land. Measures were also taken to increase or retain skilled labor on farms and to bring agricultural specialists nearer to grass roots. However, the problem of finding suitable managers for the large collective farms apparently has not been solved to the satisfaction of the government despite the large number trained and graduated from the agricultural colleges and vocational schools. Low labor productivity in agriculture, especially compared with the United States, has been giving considerable concern to the government which seems to lay increasing stress on cost

---

[1] "Economic Aspects of Soviet Agriculture. Report of a Technical Study Group," p. 54, Agricultural Research Service, U.S. Department of Agriculture, 1959.

reduction, economy of operation and greater incentive for individual effort in both work performance and management.

12. The changes in agricultural policy which have taken place during the post-Stalin period have had, for the most part, a beneficial effect on production. But some aspects, such as the persistent predilection for farm giantism and corn expansion on so large a scale, seem questionable. In the long run, even the program of expansion on the new lands in the eastern regions may prove unsound under the climatic conditions prevailing in those areas. During recent years, however, acreage expansion has been a highly important, if not the most important factor next to the weather in the rapid expansion of production. However, recent Soviet figures on grain, meat and milk outputs seem overoptimistic. Further progress in increasing farm output may be expected. But, inasmuch as the government plan (1959–65) relies primarily on improvement of yields rather than on increased crop acreage to achieve its targets of large farm output, the progress may be at a slower rate. For experience indicates that the Soviet system of centrally planned collective agriculture has been generally more successful in increasing acreage than in improvement of yields and most successful in extracting large quantities of farm products which the Soviet State requires.

INTRODUCTION

The problem of agricultural policy has long been in the foreground as a vital national issue in Soviet as in Czarist Russia. Following official revelation of weaknesses in Soviet agriculture after Stalin's death in 1953, agricultural policy aiming to remedy them has become the subject of many official decrees, lengthy reports, and speeches of Soviet leaders and officials. Prime Minister N. S. Khrushchev seldom fails to touch on agriculture in his numerous speeches and has made it one of his main preoccupations. The rapid industrial growth that began at the end of the past century and that was accelerated during the last 30 years, has not appreciably diminished the prominent role of agricultural policy. Even though the Soviet Union has lost its predominantly agrarian character, close to half of the population still depends on agriculture for a livelihood. The expanding food and fiber needs of the growing population and the strains and stresses of agrarian collectivization have combined to keep agriculture in the public eye.

CHAPTER 1. CONTRASTING OBJECTIVES OF AGRICULTURAL POLICY IN THE SOVIET UNION AND THE UNITED STATES

Agricultural policy, to be sure, has been a major problem in the United States as in Russia. But there the similarity ends. Actually the root causes and objectives of the agricultural problems and policies of the United States and the Soviet Union are diametrically opposite.

The United States, because of rapid technological development, has been steadily preoccupied with the problem of farm surpluses and excess capacity in agriculture, except during World War II and the years immediately thereafter, when maximum farm output was essential. Control of farm surpluses and other aspects of farm relief, therefore, have been the principal concern of U.S. policy.

The Soviet Union, on the other hand, has long been bedeviled by agricultural underproduction and agrarian overpopulation. Accordingly, not farm relief, but a rapid expansion of agricultural production in the face of considerable climatic obstacles,[2] to feed and clothe growing numbers and a reduction of the agricultural population has been the central objective of Soviet policy. In pursuit of that objective, considerable emphasis has been laid on modern technological development in Soviet agriculture, particularly on mechanization of farming, for which the United States has served as a model. Tractors and combines, for instance, were largely imported from the United States in the early 1930's until new Soviet factories could be built with the help of American engineering skill. However, expansion of agricultural production in the Soviet Union has been firmly bound up with another and, as it often proved, conflicting objective; namely, an all-embracing state control of agriculture. That led to the forced collectivization in the 1930's of small peasant farming, the horrors of which are only too well known.

In the collectivization process, the economic welfare of the Soviet farm population was sacrificed and subordinated to the ideological and economic objectives of the ruling Communist Party. Among these, a rapid and lopsided industrialization with an overriding emphasis on heavy industry acquired the highest priority. For Stalin was set on building socialism in a country where, ironically, it could not have been expected to develop according to the strict Marxian tenets, precisely because Russia was not an advanced industrial country. Accordingly, agriculture was forced to make a heavy contribution of farm products, little being given in return by the government to the collectivized peasantry. And, of course, the overpopulated and often starving Russian villages supplied in the 1930's most of the large labor force required by industrial expansion and inefficient factories. But a part of this increased manpower was labor of liquidated "kulaks" (the more prosperous small peasant farmers) and others forced off the land. The "colonial" role of agriculture was practically acknowledged by Stalin, when he said 30 years ago that agriculture provides the Soviet state, bent on industrialization, with "something like a tribute."[3] This idea strongly colored the Kremlin's attitude toward agriculture for many years, especially during the Stalin era.

In the United States, by way of contrast, agricultural policy has been aimed at protecting the independent family farm enterprise, based on private ownership of land and capital, from the adverse effects of depression, surpluses, and other economic maladjustments. This has been done through programs for "stabilizing, supporting, and protecting farm income and prices"[4] for reducing farm costs, and conserving soil resources. While there has been considerable divergence of opinion about the effectiveness and desirability of some of these programs, nevertheless, there has been widespread public agreement concerning the desirability of maintaining and improving the standard of living of the farm people and of protecting it and the family farm enterprise as far as possible, against the vicissitudes of the elements and sweeping economic changes.

[2] Harris, Chauncy D., "Soviet Agricultural Resources Reappraised," Journal of Farm Economics, 38: pp. 262-4, 1956; Volin, Lazar, "A Survey of Soviet Russian Agriculture." U.S. Department of Agriculture Monograph 5, pp. 5-9, 1951.
[3] J. V. Stalin's Collected Works (Russian) vol. 12, pp. 49-51.
[4] Sec. 2, Charter, Commodity Credit Corporation, 1933.

Another striking operational difference between agricultural policies of the Soviet Union and most non-Communist countries, including the United States, pertains to foreign trade. It is the field in which Government intervention on behalf of agriculture had early come on the scene and become especially active with the onset of the great depression. Tariffs, import quotas, and other forms of import restrictions to protect domestic producers from excessive imports and export subsidies and other export aids to help dispose of surpluses have become common practices of an active agricultural policy. (We are not concerned here with the merits or desirabilit of many of these devices, but merely with the hard facts of their existence.) In the Soviet Union, however, all foreign trading operations, exports as well as imports, are in the hands of the Government, which exercises a complete monopoly of foreign trade. There is no need, consequently, for the various restrictive and promotional devices employed in foreign trade policies of other nations. Those in authority decide how much and when and where to export or import farm products.

CHAPTER 2. COLLECTIVE AND STATE FARMS

In aiming at the expansion of agricultural production and, at the same time, at the establishment of a tight state control, Soviet agricultural policy was in a large measure devoted to making Russian agriculture conform to the Marxist-Leninist-Stalinist image. The transformation usually meant loss of efficiency, which became a problem in itself. It is still a problem of the Kremlin.

It was to the small family peasant farming that the weight of this collectivization policy was applied—and it was a crushing weight. Remember that small family peasant farming in Russia was important even before the revolution, when two-thirds of the private farmland in European Russia was owned by peasants who also leased a considerable proportion of the remainder. After the revolution and division of the larger land properties, small peasant farming became preponderant in the Soviet Union. (The collective sector, which came into being early in the Soviet regime, was insignificant.) Agriculture largely retained its individualistic character for a longer period than other branches of Soviet economic life, thanks to Lenin's new economic policy, or NEP, which replaced the regime of war communism in 1921. But toward the end of the 1920's this breathing spell came to an end, and it was the turn of agriculture to be ruthlessly collectivized. Thus the historic Russian trend toward small peasant agriculture, which began with the emancipation of peasants from serfdom in March 1861, was reversed by Soviet policy.

In developing agriculture along new collectivist lines, the Communist rulers were guided by the Marxist orthodox doctrine of the absolute superiority of large-scale production in agriculture as in industry. Lenin added to this doctrine the enthusiasm for that American invention, the tractor, as a vehicle for collectivist transformation of small peasant agriculture. As far back as 1918 he thought that if the Russian peasants were given 100,000 tractors and supplies needed to operate them, they would plump for communism, which he recognized was a mere fantasy in those days.[5] Stalin com-

---

[5] Lenin's Works, vol. 29, ed. 4, p. 190.

bined this ideological heritage with his notion of "building socialism in one country" through vigorous industrialization at the expense, initially at any rate, of agriculture. Resistance of peasants to such squeezing tactics of the Soviet state was only an additional argument from the Communist standpoint for speedy collectivization. For it is much easier, as experience proved, to make government-controlled collectives deliver grain and other required produce to the state at low fixed prices than to force a small individual farmer to do so. The latter is likely, under such conditions, to produce less, to consume more, in short to become more self-sufficient and turn away from commercial production.

This tough Soviet agrarian policy, which began in the late 1920's, was softened somewhat from time to time by concessions to the peasants in order to win their cooperation. Nevertheless, there has never been any tampering with the basic principles of agrarian collectivism. Except for a brief period at the very beginning of the collectivization campaign in 1930, there has been no move toward decollectivization in the Soviet Union—not even after Stalin's death as in other countries of the Soviet bloc, notably in Poland. It is, therefore, symptomatic that Khrushchev recently selected Poland as the place to make a speech extolling agrarian collectivism.

Two collectivist types of farm enterprise have emerged in the Soviet Union. One is the collective farm proper, commonly known as kolkhoz or artel (plural kolkhozy). The other type is the state farm or sovkhoz (plural sovkhozy). These units have often been described and only a few words need to be said here. The state farms are owned outright and managed by the state and are usually larger in size and more specialized than collective farms. The collective farm represents in theory a self-governing producer's cooperative consisting of the pooled holdings of the formerly independent small peasant farmers. The self-governing character of the collectives, however, has become a fiction. They are in reality subject to tight state control and their formally elected managers are actually selected and removed at will by Communist authorities.

What principally distinguishes the two kinds of farms is the position of the workers. On state farms, workers are paid wages as in Soviet factories. On collective farms, the rank and file members, both men and women, work in the fields and in livestock centers under the direction of managers and supervisors just as they do on state farms. But, as a rule, they are not paid wages. They are residual sharers in in the income of the collectives, after the state secures its share and provision is made for current production expenses and capital outlays. Thus, the workers have neither the certainty of income from their work on collective farms, which other Soviet workers possess, nor the control of farm operations exercised by independent farmers, (although, like the latter, collective farmers must bear the risks of weather, pests, and plant and animal diseases). Collective farmers are not covered by the national social security system as farmers are in the United States. Collectives are supposed to have their own individual pension funds.

The payments to collective farmers vary with their skill and the amount of work performed. The greater the skill required, the larger the remuneration. A cumbersome system of payment has developed, based on so-called workday units, in which the performance of specified tasks or norms is measured and which serve as a basis for distribution at the end of the year of cash, grain, and other products. These are prorated to the total number of "workday" units earned per year by membership, so that each "workday" unit is credited with the same amount of cash, grain, etc. But the number of "workday" units and consequently the earnings of individual workers vary.

The uncertainly, the irregularity, the long waiting and confusion engendered by this complicated system has led recently to efforts to simplify it and make payments more regularly, by means of so-called advances. There is also a tendency to substitute cash payments for the multiple distribution of various types of produce and cash, and dispense with the workday units. If was found that, in addition to its cumbersomeness, the workday system does not encourage reduction of labor expenditures and costs, since the greater the number of workdays earned by an individual or a group of workers the greater the payments.

To a considerable extent, the improvement in the methods of payment however depends upon the improved economic position and the larger incomes of collectives. As was stated by the official report on the fulfillment of the economic plan for the first half of 1959: "As a result of increased cash receipts from the sale of agricultural products to the state, the number of collectives making money advances to their members increased considerably * * *"

To complete the picture of a collective farm, it must be pointed out that the peasant families have continued to live in their rather primitive dwellings, grouped in farm villages as they did before collectivization. Even those peasant families in the western regions of the U.S.S.R, who lived on separate farmsteads (so-called khutors) similar to those in the United States, were, for the most part, forced by the Soviet Government to move into villages. Thus, collective farms, just as state farms, are essentially units of production. Consumption is of peripheral importance, and is left to the peasant household, except for the maintenance of such public welfare and educational institutions, as clubhouses, hospitals, schools, etc. It is true that Khrushchev has urged increased concentration by collectives on various forms of public consumption rather than continue augmenting the earnings of their members. He stressed especially such institutions as canteens, children's nurseries, school dormitories, etc., which tend to release woman labor that could be used in farm production. While some progress along these lines may be anticipated, for the present, there is no question, of any basic changes in the fundamental character of collective farms.

There is a question, however, whether the coexistence of collective and state farms, so unlike in many respects, will continue, or whether collectives will be supplanted by state farms. For ideologically, the state farm has always been considered a superior type of economic organization, or in Soviet parlance, a higher type of "Socialist property" than the so-called kolkhoz-cooperative property; though recently this theoretical distinction has been officially deemphasized. According to official slogans, state farms were supposed to serve as a model for the less advanced collective farming and, by inference, at any rate, could be considered the future Communist ideal goal of the institutional structure of Soviet agriculture. There was a wide gap, however, between theory and practice. State farming expanded considerably in the early 1930's when many giant farms were created, and then came a reversal. The unsatisfactory production results led to official condemnation of the giantism, subdivision of the huge units was ordered, and deflation of the state farm sector took place through transfer of land to the collective farm sector. In 1940 less than 10 percent of the total sown area was in state farms.

The limited role of state farming continued until the beginning of the Khrushchev program of expansion on uncultivated land beyond the Volga and Urals in 1954. In this area large mechanized state farms already were well established and, when the decision was again made to increase the grain area, several hundred new state farms were organized and many of the existing ones were enlarged. In the process, however, there was also a considerable absorption of collective farms. For instance, in the Kazakh Republic, where much of the expansion of the sown area on the so-called new lands took place, 833 collectives were merged into 188 state farms in 1957.[6]

Conversion of collectives into state farms, however, was not confined to the "new lands" regions of the eastern U.S.S.R., but spread to a number of other regions; among these were, for instance, the irrigated cotton-growing regions in Soviet Central Asia and areas in the former war zone, where collective farming disintegrated during the occupation and remained weak despite postwar rehabilitation. The need of new capital investment by the state has been, apparently, an important criterion in determining whether to convert collectives into state farms. As a result of the process of expansion on new lands and absorption of collectives, the share of state farms increased from 12 percent of the sown area in 1953, to more than one-fourth of the expanded acreage in 1957.

Another recent development also indicates greater reliance by the Soviet Government on state farms. It is the designation of a number of state farms, first near Moscow and subsequently near other large cities to specialize in growing cheaply potatoes and vegetables so as to lower their cost to the city consumer. Should this experiment prove successful it would operate to the disadvantage of those collectives which derive an important share of their income from selling potatoes and vegetables at high prices on the free market in the cities.

There are also other reasons why the revived dynamism of the state farming sector may portend a serious threat to collective farming. One is the considerably increased size of collective farms as a result of mergers and their acquisition of farm machinery from machine-tractor stations to be discussed in other sections. This further diminishes the difference between the two types of farming. Second is the revelation, by Khrushchev himself, of considerably lower labor productivity in collectives than on state farms (table 5).

Khrushchev's figures show that both state and collective farms in the U.S.S.R. have much higher labor requirements per unit of product than U.S. farms, but collective farms, have the highest of all, exceeding considerably even the state farm. Assuming similarity in the method of collecting these statistics on collective and state farms, some of the variations may be accounted for by differences in geographical location, in the quality of the labor force (age and sex distribution) in capital equipment or perhaps in some other aspect

[6] Kazakhstanskaya Pravda, Dec. 14, 1957.

of a sampling process. It is possible, too, that the system of regular wage payments on state farms, for which the authorities are responsible, as compared with the sharing principle in collectives, tends to induce a greater economy of labor on state farms. Since the Government is not responsible for the payment of labor in collectives, it could tolerate this inefficiency, so long as it was not required to raise the fixed low prices for farm products and there was an abundance of manpower in the villages. But the latter condition no longer prevails since the war. Also the Government raised agricultural prices during recent years. However, it aims at lowering such prices eventually in order to reduce the consumers' cost of living. If collectives are not to be economically injured by lower prices, increased efficiency and greater labor productivity is essential. Awareness of this need, and consciousness of a growing relative shortage of manpower, probably explains Khrushchev's emphasis on increased labor productivity even to the point of publishing comparisons with the United States, which are highly unfavorable to Soviet agriculture.

CHAPTER 3. FARM GIANTISM

Farm giantism has become a distinctive trait of Soviet agricultural organization. The cult of bigness, a feature of Soviet policy, has its ideological roots, as was pointed out earlier in the orthodox Marxist doctrine of economic concentration, which stresses the similarity, as far as large-scale methods of production are concerned, between agriculture and manufacturing. This doctrine, which makes no distinction between the large and the optimum size of an enterprise, was further reinforced by the unbounded enthusiasm of Lenin and his disciples for farm mechanization, modeled on the American pattern. It was one of the motivating forces in the collectivization of small peasant agriculture and establishment of huge state farms.

As already indicated, this cult of bigness miscarried in the case of huge state farms in the early 1930's and corrective steps were taken. As for collective farms, it was also found, in the mid-1930's, that a number of units in the southern and eastern regions were too large for efficiency and subdivision was not uncommon.[7] On the other hand, a "voluntary" merger of the usually small collective farms in the northern and north central regions was "recommended" by the decree of December 19, 1925, "Concerning the Economic and Organizational Strengthening of the Kolkhozy of the Non-Black Soil Area." In some regions then, before the war the average size of the collective farms was increasing, in other regions it was decreasing. In the country as a whole, however, the number of collective farms was slowly decreasing (after it reached a peak of 245,400 in 1935) to about 237,000 in 1940.

After collectivization in the annexed western regions after the war, the number of collectives in the U.S.S.R. increased to 252,000 at the beginning of 1950. In that year, however, a far-reaching change in the number and size of the collectives began. A mass campaign for merger and enlargment of farms was inaugurated, which resembled in its speed and relentlessness, and in the revival of gigantomania, the original mass collectivization drive of the early 1930's. This time, however, the pressure was exerted not on individual peasant farmers to join a collective, but on kolkhozy to merge "voluntarily" into super-

---

[7] Sautin, I. V., ed., Kolkhozy vo Btoroi Stalinskoi Pyatiletke, p. V, 1939.

collectives.   The merger drive which Stalin initiated in 1950, was spearheaded by no other person than N. S. Khrushchev, then one of Stalin's lieutenants, who was just transferred from the Ukraine to Moscow.   Khrushchev remains a dedicated believer in mergers on the ground of efficiency and economy, such as reduction of administrative expenses, etc.   A decree of the Council of Ministers of the U.S.S.R. of June 7, 1950, No. 2427, which was not published at the time in the daily Soviet press or in other sources available to western students of Soviet affairs, gave a formal blessing to the merger drive, which was then already in full swing.[8]

The mergers, ostensibly undertaken to increase farm efficiency, were not confined to small collectives or to specific geographic areas. Already—large collectives were also merged and the drive extended to regions with most diverse national and economic conditions.   Collectives with a large expanse of level farm land were merged with those whose terrain was criss-crossed by marshes, lakes, bushland and forests and, consequently, had small fields.   Neither sparsely nor densely settled regions escaped the merger drive.   Several collectives, whose members lived in one village, were merged with collectives whose members lived in several scattered villages.   In such cases, the peasants who became members of the new enlarged collectives continued, for the most part, to live in their separate villages which were connected, as a rule, by very poor roads, which often become no more than mud tracks in the early spring and fall.   However, Khrushchev's idea of speedy resettlement of villages into so-called agrotowns proposed by him in the spring of 1951, was quickly jettisoned by the Kremlin and has never been revived in its original form, even after its author came into power.

The irrationality of at least some farm mergers in the northern part of the country was acknowledged by an official report dealing with the Vologda Province.[9]

In a number of districts the enlargement of the collective farms was made without taking into account the natural economic and other peculiarities * * *. Many collectives consist of 25 to 30 and more inhabited points which are not only separated from each other by 5 to 7 kilometers, but often are also cut off by natural obstacles—lakes and rivers.

Even Khrushchev cautiously hinted in June 1955 at the desirability of breaking up some large units resulting from recent farm amalgamation in the Baltic Republics.

After only 1 year of the merger drive, the number of collectives decreased by more than one-half, from 252,000 at the beginning of 1950 to 121,000 at the end of that year.   By the end of 1953, there were only a little more than 91,000 collectives.[10]   Since 1954, a new factor—the absorption of collectives by state farms mentioned above enters the picture.   However, since the total figure of collectives absorbed by state farms has not been released, it is impossible to segregate the effects of such absorption from that of the mergers of farms into larger collectives.   The liquidation of machine-tractor stations as machine operating units in 1958, which will be discussed later, probably also contributed to the mergers.   It is significant that as late as the fall of 1958, Khrushchev urged the "model" collective in his native village, Kalinovka, with a tillable area of 3,200 acres, to

[8] Direktivy KPSS i Sovetskogo Pravitel'stva po Khozyaistvennym voprosam V. 4, pp. 726–727, 1958.
[9] Partiinaya Zhizn', No. 6, 1957, p. 50.
[10] "Norodnoye Khozyaistvo SSSR v 1956 Godu," p. 139, Moscow, 1957.

merge with a neighboring collective, as he did not consider it sufficiently large.[11]   At any rate, as a result of the two processes, mergers of collectives and their absorption by state farms, the total number of collective farms decreased to about 60,000 by July 1959 [12] or to less than one-fourth of the number at the beginning of the present decade.

The merger process resulted, of course, in a considerable enlargement of collectives.   In terms of sown area per farm, the average size of the collective increased nearly 3½ times, compared with the prewar period, and the average number of families per farm trebled. Collectives, however, vary considerably in size from region to region. Thus, in 1956, in the northwestern region of European Russia, for instance, 64 percent of all collectives had a sown area of 500 hectares and under (1,236 acres and under); whereas, in northern Caucasus, 23 percent of collectives and in western Siberia, only 5 percent had acreages that large.   On the other hand, no farms of more than 5,000 hectares (12,355 acres) were in the northwestern region, but more than one-third of the collectives in northern Caucasus, and nearly one-fourth in western Siberia had acreages of 5,000 hectares and over.

The large size of Soviet farms is particularly striking in comparison with U.S. units.   Although farm size in the United States in recent years has been trending upward, paralleling the growth in farm efficiency, yet only slightly over 2 percent of commercial farms in 1954 (not all the farms enumerated by the census, which includes a number of smaller units) had 500 acres or more of cropland harvested; many others had much less.

Yet collective farms despite their enlargement continue to be much smaller than state farms.   The latter also have become enlarged and in 1957 had on the average an area of more than 20,000 acres under crops per farm as compared with about 2,800 acres in 1940.   While a considerable number of new state farms were organized in recent years, some of the smaller farms were merged and others were transferred to various institutions or liquidated and a few were subdivided. The net result was first, a decrease in the number of state farms from 4,988 at the beginning of 1951 to 4,742 at the beginning of 1953, and subsequently an upward trend, which brought the number of farms to 5,905 at the beginning of 1958.[13]

The huge size of collective and state farms has made it necessary to decentralize operations into more manageable units.   The workers in collectives are organized into brigades, consisting of 40 to 60 workers, headed by a brigadier or a foreman.   Each brigade is assigned to a unit of cropland or to a livestock center.   Still smaller units, called zveno or squads are formed and these workers cultivate the more intensive crops such as sugar beets and cotton.   State farms also are subdivided into branches (otdelenie), each of which is a farm unit by itself.

The team of U.S. Department of Agriculture economists which visited the Soviet Union in the summer of 1958, states in its report that they—

inquired about the availability of studies analyzing the relation between the size of the farm unit and its efficiency, with a view to determining the optimum size in

---

[11] Sel'skoe Khozyaistvo, Oct. 21, 1953.

[12] Report of the Central Statistical Administration of the Council of Ministers of the U.S.S.R. on the "Fulfillment of the State Plan of Economic Development for the first half of 1959," Pravda and Izvestia July 14, 1959.

[13] "Narodnoye Khozyaistvo SSSR v 1956 Godu," p. 145: "SSSR v Tsifrakh, Statisticheskii Sbornik," p. 190.

different regions. We were told that such information was not available at the present time, although apparently some studies of this type are under way. We gained the impression that in striving for bigness, per se, farm efficiency was actually neglected. Even with brigade subdivisions, much time is consumed in going to and from places of work. Although Soviet agricultural authorities stress increasing efficiencies associated with larger sizes of operations in discussing desirable sizes of farms, their thinking is in terms of very large units by U.S. standards. They did state, however, that some of their largest farms, up to 150,000 hectares (about 375,000 acres), are considered to be too large. The present sizes probably are influenced by the greater ease of centralized management and control than by economics associated with size of operation. Large farms means fewer units of contact for state direction of planning and operation; also fewer managers will be needed to translate the overall plans into specific operations.[14]

In addition to the fact that it facilitates central control over collective farming, the Soviet predilection for farm giantism may perhaps be also explained by its tendency to widen the gulf between the rank and file peasant membership and the management of the big collective, now mostly in the hands of outsiders. This gap is useful in the context of Soviet rule for it tends to enhance the driving power of management over labor.

Chapter 4. Machine-Tractor Stations: Their Rise and Fall

The merger process was also extended to another type of farm unit, which was the handiwork of Soviet policy—the state machine-tractor stations or MTS. These were the special units into which tractors, combines, and other large machinery operating on collective farms were grouped, together with facilities for repairing machinery and operating and supervising personnel. For a long time, in fact, the collectives were not allowed to own such machinery. While originally the idea of MTS was associated with the advantages of pooling power and machinery for joint cultivation by small peasant farmers, too poor to own tractors individually, it was adopted since the early stages of collectivization as an important instrument of state ascendancy and control over collective agriculture.

It should be borne in mind that the very fact of a catastrophic reduction in the number of horses early in the collectivization greatly enhanced the importance of the tractor, which was thrown, so to speak, into the breach on the draft power front. It can, in fact, be truly said that the tractor in the Soviet Union did not displace the horse, as in the United States, but replaced it in an emergency. Thus, he who controlled the tractor—the new source of farm power—controlled agriculture. This helps to explain why the Soviet Government, which was anxious to extend a tight control over the amorphous structure of the peasant collective farming, was clinging to the possession of tractors and other farm machinery. Since MTS were paid for their services to the collectives in kind, they have also become significant revenue producers (in terms of farm products) to the state.

There was at first no change in the pivotal role of the MTS after Stalin. On the contrary, one of the first steps of the post-Stalin regime in the agrarian sphere was, in various ways, to still further enhance the supervisory powers and the importance of the MTS, as, for instance, by transferring collective farm personnel, seasonally employed by MTS, to their permanent staff. However, the advantage of pooling tractors and machinery in a central unit, like MTS, was offset, some-

---

[14] "Economic Aspects of Soviet Agriculture, " pp. 12–13.

298 COMPARISONS OF UNITED STATES AND SOVIET ECONOMIES

times seriously, by dual management of farm operations by the managers of the MTS and of the collectives. Khrushchev described this situation as having "two bosses on the land." There was often a conflict of interest between the management of the MTS and the collective. The former was interested primarily in performing those operations, like plowing, which brought the greatest financial returns, often at the expense of other necessary operations, like mowing hay. There were cases when plowing done by the MTS was superfluous or even harmful. Difficulties also often developed regarding the timeliness of MTS farm operations, which is so important in agriculture, especially in Russian agriculture with its short season. It was complained, on the other hand, that collectives tended to rely too much on the MTS, for even for the simplest type of work, such as carting feedstuff for livestock, which could have been done by farm horses.

The decreased number and the increased size of the collectives, as a result of the merger campaign, made the existence of separate MTS seem less essential even from the Soviet point of view. There were anomalous cases where one MTS serviced a single collective farm. At any rate, an abrupt about-face by the regime ended this dichotomy in the collective farm system. On January 22, 1958, following some limited public discussion, Khrushchev proposed that MTS were to sell most of the machinery, except highly specialized equipment to collective farms and, thus, be divested of the vital farm operating functions. They were to be converted into mere service and supply centers, so-called repair-technical stations or RTS. This radical reform was formally approved by the Supreme Soviet of U.S.S.R. on March 31, 1958, and was rapidly carried out. By July 1959, 94 percent of collectives bought farm machinery from the MTS on cash or credit. The magnitude of this transaction can be gaged from the fact that by July 1, 1959, there were purchased 512,000 tractors, 221,000 grain combines, and a large quantity of other machinery. In addition, collectives purchased also 100,000 new tractors, more than 25,000 grain combines and other new machinery. The total cost of the machinery purchased was 21.7 billion rubles, of which 17.2 billion rubles is the cost of the machinery acquired from the MTS. These expenditures may be compared with a total cash income of all collectives of around 95 billion rubles in 1956 and 1957 and a record of 130 billion in 1958.[15]

The liquidation or, as it is officially termed, reorganization of MTS encountered, judging from what Khrushchev said, some ideological opposition within the Communist ranks. It was apparently based on objection to the downgrading of what was regarded by the official Communist line as a higher type of property—the "state" property of the MTS to the lower level of so-called cooperative-kolkhoz property. It may be surmised that this opposition found support or was inspired by Stalin's adamant stand against liquidation of MTS, which was proposed during his lifetime by some economists. Khrushchev tried to meet this ideological opposition by arguments, which minimized the distinction formerly made by Soviet theoreticians between the two types of property. But in the main, in abandoning Stalin's legacy regarding MTS, Khrushchev was guided, to judge from his own utterances, less by ideological than by pragmatic considerations.

---

[15] Pravda, July 14, 1959.

First of all, reorganization of MTS eliminated dual farm management. Second, considerable strengthening of the party apparatus in
the countryside during the past 5 years made it feasible to dispense
with the control function of the MTS. Third, the importance of
MTS had diminished as an instrument of state acquisition of farm
products, Fourth, the leadership calculated that increased prices
and incomes and anticipated economies from more efficient management made it possible for the collectives to afford to purchase, maintain, and operate the MTS machinery. Indeed, its purchase may
be also desirable from the Soviet point of view as a proper channel
for investment of part of their increased income by collectives. For
otherwise, the opportunity for productive capital investment by
collectives is restricted if acquisition of machinery is barred, as it
largely had been heretofore. The alternative to capital investment
is, of course, a further increase of peasant earnings. But if this is
not to be inflationary, it would necessitate a considerably faster pace
for the Soviet consumers' goods industry and more efficient distribution of such goods in rural areas. There are, therefore, some implications in the sale of machinery by MTS to collectives of deflationary
or disinflationary character.

While the transition which the virtual merging of MTS with collectives involved seemed to be rapid, the very considerable readjust-
ment necessary was not always smooth, and it posed new problems.
Among the various problems of adjustment, are those of adequate
repair facilities and relations with the repair-technical stations, of
supplying farms adequately with proper machinery, and especially
with spare parts. A case for instance, was reported in the Soviet
press when, because of the impossibility of finding a wheel for a
tractor, a new tractor had to be purchased.[16] Repair technical stations were accused of selling defective machinery to collectives and
not being helpful with repairs.[17] But the elimination of "two bosses
on the land" should make it possible to pinpoint managerial responsibility. This should, in the long run, contribute to farm efficiency,
though the problem of finding suitable managers of collectives has,
apparently, also not been solved.

CHAPTER 5. HOUSEHOLD ALLOTMENT FARMING

While the dichotomy of the MTS and the collective farms was
eliminated by Khrushchev's 1958 reform, another dichotomy remains; namely, the coexistence side by side of the large collective
farm enterorise and the small household allotment farming (priusa-
debnoe khozyaistvo). The collectivist Leviathan has not swallowed
as yet the individualist dwarf.

At first, a few words about the nature of the allotment farming.
Peasant households in collectives as well as workers' families on state
farms and some others are allotted small plots of land on which they
grow potatoes, vegetables, sunflower seed, and other crops. These
plots are allotted to a whole family and not to an individual member
of the collective. This seems to be a survival of the old Russian institution of family property, though the plot, of course, is not legally
owned by the peasant family; it is merely set aside for the family's

---

[16] Sel'skoe Khozyaistvo, Aug. 9, 1959.
[17] Sel'skoe Khozyaistvo, July 18 and Aug. 7, 1959.

use at the discretion of the collective. Furthermore, all adult members of the household must do a certain amount of labor on collective farms or work in state enterprises to obtain the household allotment. The peasant households are also permitted to own a small number of livestock and an unlimited number of poultry. They can sell their produce direct to the consumers on the free, so-called kolkhoz market in the cities, but they cannot use middlemen.

Household allotment farms accounted for only 3 percent of the sown area in 1956 but for a much larger proportion of the livestock population, including almost half of all the cows. Such allotments were originally conceived as a subsistence, "an acre and a cow" farming, merely auxiliary to the collectives' farm economy at a time when they were not considered strong enough to take care fully of their members' needs. As so often happens, "the tail began to wag the dog". The household allotments not only helped greatly to feed the collectivized peasant population, but they frequently became the chief, or the only, sources of the peasants' cash earnings through sale at higher prices (not the low government fixed prices) on the free kolkhoz market.

How important the free market was as a source of peasants' cash earnings during the Stalin era can be gathered from the fact that, for some years, at any rate, the volume of sales on the kolkhoz market, mostly by members of the collectives, exceeded total cash income of collectives. This "acre and a cow" farming, however, is important, not only for the economic welfare and morale of the peasants, but also for the food supply, of the nonfarm population, especially the supply of livestock products—products sold not only through the kolkhoz market, but also through government controlled outlets. Even in 1957, when the share of allotment holdings in state acquisitions of agricultural products was considerably less than formerly, they.accounted for 19 percent of meat deliveries, 16 percent of milk and 11 percent of wool.[18]

Yet the household allotment became a thorn in the Kremlin's side, since it competed with the collective farm economy for the labor and loyalty of the peasants. The official view, therefore, has been that, as the collective farming becomes stronger and better able to satisfy the needs of its members and of the nation, the importance of household allotment farming should decline and eventually wither away. But, like the Soviet doctrine of the withering of the state—it is still in the future. Accordingly, the Soviet policy toward this kind of farming has been ambivalent, now restrictive, now relaxed—then again restrictive.

As during a short period in the mid-1930's under Stalin, so in 1953 after the late dictator, the "thaw" in agrarian policy began with a more encouraging or tolerant attitude toward allotment holdings. The cumbersome money tax on allotment holdings was simplified and taxes reduced in the fall of 1953. Acquisition of cows by peasant households was facilitated. Compulsory deliveries of farm products to the government were first reduced and since January 1958 were entirely abandoned.

This new liberal phase again did not last long. In 1956, legislation was passed ostensibly for the purpose of permitting collectives to set up their charters without modeling them on the general model char-

---

[18] Pravda, July 5, 1957. (Decree on abolition of compulsory deliveries by allotment holdings.)

ter of 1935. The really consequential provisions of this law was to enable each collective to set its own minimum of labor, the size of the household allotments and the number of privately owned livestock. This was accompanied by a declaration favoring, indirectly but not prescribing a reduction of the size of the plots. Subsequently there had been cases of reduction of plots, some apparently for purposes of equalization of such holdings between different families. But this has not assumed so far a mass character.

However, the government attitude toward private ownership of livestock, the most valuable component of household allotment farming, has become more restrictive in recent years, as was foreshadowed by Khrushchev in 1953 at the outset of the new post-Stalin course of agrarian policy. Khrushchev has been advocating during the last few years the sale of cattle by members to the collectives. He "recommended" to the peasants of his native Kalinovka to sell their cows to the model kolkhoz, and the "recommendation" was acted upon. But such liquidation is to be gradual with no definite time limit placed, depending upon when collectives are ready for the transition. Steps taken by authorities in some districts to hasten the process by pressuring the peasants were strongly rebuked. A much sterner attitude, however, has been adopted by the government toward private ownership of livestock by workers on state farms and by nonfarm population which is marked for elimination.

To sum up: household allotment farming is again being deflated. But, so deeply rooted is it in the rural fabric of the U.S.S.R., that it would be premature to conclude that its doom is near at hand.

Chapter 6. Government Procurements of Farm Products

Acquisition of farm products by the state is a fundamental problem of Soviet economics and politics. It runs like a red thread throughout the whole of Soviet history. It was at the root of both Lenin's new economic policy of 1921 and of Stalin's rural collectivization a decade later. It helped to kindle bitter intraparty strife in the 1920's and was a basic presupposition of the industrialization program under the 5-year plans. It is through government procurements and prices paid for them that economic incentives and disincentives to the farmers largely operate.

The procurement system, however, was characterized, with respect to the same commodity, by a considerable diversity of methods or types of delivery and by a corresponding multiplicity of prices. Basic to all were the compulsory delivery quotas, calculated as so much grain, potatoes, meat, etc., per unit of tillable or total land. The lowest fixed price was usually paid for this type of procurement. Next, there was the so-called contracting method used for industrial and intensive crops like cotton, sugar beets, etc. Though essentially similar to compulsory deliveries, this method involved a graduated price scale, depending upon the quantities delivered, and also provided an opportunity for the farmers to buy some commodities at concession prices. Then there were the extra-or-above-quota purchases by the state for which considerably higher prices were paid after 1953 than for the compulsory deliveries. In recent years the extra-quota purchases became increasingly important while lower priced compulsory deliveries declined. Finally, there were payments in kind for the work of machine-tractor stations, which, of course, are now being eliminated with the dissolution of the MTS.

The reform of 1958 unified the different types of procurements into a single system of state purchases. Compulsory deliveries as such were nominally abolished, but the new system retains quotas per unit of land which collectives are supposed to meet. Instead of multiple prices, single prices are now fixed by the state for each commodity within a region. Although price stability is one of the aims of the reform, provision is made for raising or lowering of prices to cope with sharp fluctuations in output, thus, some recognition is given to the law of supply and demand. Another important change is the abolition of the variable premium prices for larger deliveries used for some crops like cotton, under the so-called contract system, on a considerable scale. A sample study of three groups of cotton growing collectives in 1956 showed that the differential in the average price per unit of cotton between the highest and the lowest was 40 percent and between the highest and the middle group 20 percent.[19]

These changes simplified the cumbersome procurement and price system. There can exist now only two prices for a commodity in each locality, a government price and a free market price if a commodity is traded on the limited private market. This is still a far cry from a rational price system, the lack of which, as many western economists pointed out, greatly handicaps economic calculations and planning decisions in the Soviet Union. But the reform takes at least a small step towards such a goal.

The abolition of premium price payments, no doubt, hits collectives growing such crops as cotton, sugar beets, hemp, and others which received preferential price treatment. So much was openly admitted by Khrushchev, who contended that the more productive collectives should obtain higher income, not from price differentials but by lowering of production costs and increasing output. In any event the average prices paid by the state to such collectives will be lower and so will probably the gross money income. This may have an adverse effect upon the output of certain crops in these usually more productive farms, which may or may not be compensated by increased production of other farms. In general, the new prices appear to have been tailored to benefit the average or less prosperous collective farms. The guiding principle was stated by Khrushchev in 1958 as follows: "Although the total expenditures of the state for the purchase of agricultural products will remain approximately at the same level as last year, they will be distributed more fairly among the collective farms, thanks to the new prices."[20] Khrushchev indicated further that the total procuring expenditures include also the expenses formerly incurred by the state for the machine-tractor stations which are now borne by the collectives themselves.

As a matter of fact, the stated objective of Soviet price policy in the years to come is that of achieving lower prices, concomitant with a reduction of the production costs. This brings up a new important facet of the procuring policy, namely the projected concentration of procurements in areas of most economical production, instead of requiring every region from the Baltic to the Pacific and from the Arctic to the Black Sea to deliver identical products like grain, for

[19] Khrushchev's speech, Pravda, June 21, 1958.
[20] Ibid.

instance. This move is linked with what appears to be now more than a mere academic concern (as it had long been) with regional agricultural specialization. And regional specialization is to be based on production cost studies. This cost consciousness is itself a new phenomenon in the management of Soviet agriculture, heretofore preoccupied almost exclusively with fulfillment of physical targets. Khrushchev himself reflected the new cost consciousness when he said in his December 15, 1958 report: "It is impossible to carry on farming without a thorough analysis of the cost of commodities being produced, and without control by means of the ruble." [21]

Chapter 7. Economic Incentives and Farm Labor

Soviet policy in the agrarian as in other fields has always been a combination of coercion, indoctrination, and economic incentives. However, the proportions vary from time to time. There has been, for example, a special emphasis on economic incentives whenever a critical or difficult agricultural situation arose and appeasement of the peasantry was considered essential. It is only necessary to recall Lenin's celebrated NEP in 1921, which supplanted the harsh regime of war communism, with its requisitions of peasants' produce. Again, in the mid-1930's, Stalin relaxed his iron grip somewhat to secure a recovery of agriculture from the ravages of the initial collectivization drive.

But relaxation always was a short-lived luxury. Khrushchev himself showed in his famous "secret" de-Stalinization speech at the 20th Communist Party Congress, in February 1956, how harsh and unrealistic Stalin's policy toward the peasantry became in its latter stage. For instance, he proposed raising taxes on collective farms and their members by 40 billion rubles, when they received, in 1952, for instance, altogether only 26 billion rubles for the large quantity of products acquired by the state. This helps to explain the unsatisfactory agricultural production situation, particularly in the livestock sector, which Stalin's heirs inherited.

The contrast between agriculture and industry was especially glaring. According to Khrushchev, agricultural production in 1952 was only 10 percent higher than in 1940, when industrial production was more than twice as high.[22] Even the 10-percent increase may have been optimistic. During the Stalin era crop production estimates, especially the important grain figures, were inflated by the use of the so-called biological estimates which grossly exaggerated the picture. These were estimates of crops standing in the field prior to the harvest, which did not reflect the officially admitted large harvesting losses and, in general, lent themselves to manipulation. They were not comparable with crop figures for other countries, or, indeed, with Russian figures prior to the 1930's. Such a statistical malpractice brought down, after Stalin's death, even the official Soviet wrath. Malenkov, for instance, declared in August 1953 that: "it should not be forgotten that our country, our collective farms can prosper with a crop gathered in the barn and not with a crop standing in the field".[23] Khrushchev in December 1958, spoke even more harshly about biological estimates, which he called eyewash

[21] Pravda, Dec. 16, 1958.
[22] Ibid., Sept. 15, 1953.
[23] Ibid., Aug. 9, 1953.

(ochkovtiratel'stvo), accusing Malenkov himself of indulging in their use during Stalin's lifetime.[24] Incidentally, the U.S. Department of Agriculture and other agencies of the U.S. Government, as well as a number of other Western specialists, were long critical of these inflated biological figures and stressed the need of considerable downward adjustment if they were to be used at all.[25]

When it came to livestock figures, even Soviet official figures showed that cattle numbers at the beginning of 1953 were considerably below the precollectivization figures in 1928. No secret was made of the fact that livestock was greatly underfed. This, notwithstanding, the much publicized official policy to increase the output of livestock products and improve the monotonous starchy diet of the Russian people.

To remedy the difficult agricultural situation and increase production of food and feed, Stalin's heirs once more put in the forefront of their blueprint of agricultural policy, in 1953, increased economic incentives to stimulate the interest and cooperation of the peasants in expansion of production. Thus, with Stalin's exit, the big stick was again to be accompanied by a somewhat larger carrot.

Turning to the question of implementation, of economic incentives programs, it should be borne in mind that the collective farm system of payment for labor, described in an earlier section, was designed precisely to provide economic incentives to producers. For this reason equality of income, usually associated with socialism, has been rejected by the Communist rulers of Russia. They do not consider it applicable to the present economic stage of development of the U.S.S.R., which they call Socialist, as distinguished from a future, full-fledged Communist society. On the contrary, variation in earnings among members of collectives to provide incentives to workers has always been encouraged. In fact, the very method of payment, based on workday units, is patterned on a kind of incentive piecework wage. Attempts of collectives to introduce some sort of a uniform daily wage in terms of workday units has always been strongly disapproved by the authorities.

That is also why rural communes, in which not only production but also consumption is socialized on egalitarian lines, have been proscribed by the Soviets. There were, to be sure, some communes organized in the U.S.S.R. in the 1920's and during the initial collectivization drive in 1930, but they were converted to the present artel form of collective farming. It is significant, in view of the recent Red Chinese experiment with communes, that Khrushchev attacked this type of agrarian collectivism in his speech in a Polish collective in July 1959.[26]

Although the principle of economic incentives was thus recognized during the Stalin era, incentives failed to produce desired results because incomes of the collectives were very low, largely due to the low fixed prices paid by the Government, as admitted later by Khrushchev,[27] for the heavy quotas of grain and many other farm products which they were obligated to deliver. This resulted in very small earnings of the peasants from their labor on many collective farms.

[24] Ibid., Dec. 16, 1958.
[25] Jasny, Naum, The Socialized Agriculture of the U.S.S.R., pp. 659 and 728; Volin, Lazar, "Agricultural Statistics in Soviet Russia: Their Usability and Reliability," American Statistician VII, pp. 8–12, 1953.
[26] Pravda July 21, 1959.
[27] Ibid., June 21, 1958.

The effect was to make peasants less willing and less efficient workers and to encourage them to concentrate on their household allotment farming.

It is true that the delivery quotas of farm products were legally fixed quantities, which were not supposed to be increased, in order that the farmers should be interested in maximizing output. In practice, however, increased output often led to increased exactions. If some collectives in a district could not meet their quotas, other farms, which had already delivered theirs, were frequently called upon to supply additional quantities so that the plan for the district should be completed. Khrushchev called this pruning of the more prosperous or efficient collectives.[28] The disincentive effect of such exactions on the peasantry needs no elaborations and was reflected in the unsatisfactory agricultural situation during the Stalin regime described above.

The post-Stalin leadership adopted a policy of substantially raising the very low prices paid by the Government for farm products. Thus, in 1953 prices of livestock and poultry products were increased more than 5½ times; milk and butter 2 times; potatoes by 2½ times; and vegetables, on the average, by 25 to 40 percent. Prices of grain and other products also were raised later. As a result of the increased prices and larger quantities acquired, the payments of the Government to collective farms and small household allotment holders more than trebled between 1952 and 1957. See table 8. The total cash income of collectives more than doubled between 1952 and 1956-57, increasing from 43 billion to 95 billion rubles. This in turn made possible cash payments to peasants in many collectives in which such distribution had formerly been negligible. The cash payments, in fact, more than trebled between 1952 and 1956, increasing from 12 billion to 42 billion rubles.[29]

Yet, even the greatly increased volume of cash distributed in 1956 represents only an average cash income of something over 2,100 rubles per peasant family on the collective farms, a sum roughly equivalent to about $200 at a realistic rate of exchange. In 1952 the average was as little as 623 rubles, equivalent, with higher prices, to less than $60 per peasant household. Moreover, since distribution of cash in some areas of intense crop production (such as cotton, sugar beets, etc.) are considerably above the average rate, many peasant families in the less prosperous collectives received much less than the average. However, it is well to remember that cash distribution by collectives is not the only major source of peasants' money income. As was pointed out earlier, the anomaly persists of the small household allotments, playing not just the theoretically assigned minor role of a mere subsistence-farming appendage, but actually rivaling and often outstripping collective economy as a significant source of peasants' income. In this connection, as was pointed out earlier, sales on the free market in the cities are very important. However, receipts from private sales have become smaller in recent years and they no longer overshadow cash income from collective farms; though the situation varies widely from region to region and from farm to farm.

[28] Ibid., Sept. 15, 1953.
[29] Khrushchev's speech in Minsk, Pravda, Jan. 25, 1958, for figures of payments to collective farm members. S.S.S.R. v. Tsifrakh, p. 200 for total cash income of collectives.

Much less information is available concerning what is still the most important component of peasants' income from the collective farms— payments in kind. Without such information it is impossible to adequately assess the changed economic position of the peasantry. However, since in-kind payments are mostly in grain, and there were several large harvests in recent years, it can be assumed that more grain was distributed.

What of the effect of the post-Stalin policies of increased economic incentives on labor input? While helpful statistics on this point are by no means abundant, we do have some clue, however imperfect, from the reported total number of workday units earned annually by peasants in collectives. Between 1952 and 1956 the total number of workday units increased by 26 percent.[30] Incidentally, the figure for 1952 was still below prewar, but in 1956 it was 19 percent above. This improvement reflects both a larger number of workers and a greater contribution per worker. The latter is shown roughly by the claimed increase of the average number of workday units per able-bodied worker—from 295 in 1953 to 335 in 1957, or 14 percent.[31] The increased contribution per worker, however, does not signify anything like a corresponding rise in the efficiency of labor. For workday units do not measure uniformly labor input in different collectives. Moreover, Soviet sources often criticize the so-called waste of workdays, meaning simply the wasteful, inefficient employment of farm labor. Attention has already been called to Khrushchev's striking statistical comparison between labor requirements per unit of product in the United States and the U.S.S.R., thus confirming first-hand observations of western specialists regarding low labor productivity in Soviet agriculture.

Raising of labor productivity in agriculture has been a major concern of Khrushchev's administration. Considerable attention in this connection has been given to improved training of farm labor through the establishment of short-term courses and of special schools. Drives were also organized to return to the farms skilled workers who migrated to cities and to bring farm specialists closer to grassroots.

In 1954, a drive began to recruit several hundred thousand young men and women for agricultural development in the eastern virgin lands region. Since then, each summer additional thousands have been sent to those areas on temporary assignments. Their services, however, have not always been effectively utilized. There have been also many stories in the Soviet press of hardship suffered by the newcomers in those regions due to the housing shortages and other causes. Finally there must be mentioned the annual or perennial mobilizations of students and other city dwellers to assist in harvesting crops. However, Khrushchev, for some time, has been highly critical of this practice and called for its elimination.[32]

CHAPTER 8. CAPITAL INVESTMENT IN AGRICULTURE; FERTILIZER PROGRAM

Agricultural production in the Soviet Union has been handicapped by a shortage of capital, as well as by climatic obstacles, and inefficient

---

[30] Narodnoe Khozyaistvo v 1956 Godu, p. 140.
[31] S.S.S.R. v Tsifrakh, p. 198.
[32] Pravda, Dec. 16, 1958.

labor and management under the regimented system of a highly centralized agrarian collectivism.

For a long time agriculture served as an important source of capital accumulation for financing the Soviet industrial program. Reference has already been made to Stalin's statement in the late 1920's that agriculture contributed "something like a tribute" to the Soviet state. In addition, Russian agriculture suffered heavy capital losses during the all-out collectivization in the 1930's; as Jasny puts it: [33]

Instead of increasing by one-third, as planned, the investment in means of production in agriculture declined by considerably more, perhaps as much as one-half, during the first plan period, chiefly by livestock destruction in the collectivization drive. This decline was not fully made up until 1938.

During the post-Stalin period, however, belated recognition has been given to the capital needs of agriculture itself. Government capital investment in agriculture in 1956 was officially estimated (in July 1, 1955, prices) at 21 billion rubles, compared with a total of 63 billion during the preceding 5 years, and 25 billion during 1946–50.[34] The collectives also were spurred to increase their own capital accumulation out of increased income. Their officially estimated capital investments more than doubled between 1952 and 1957, increasing from less than 10 billion to more than 23 billion rubles.[35] The so-called indivisible funds, representing the capital assets of collectives, were estimated at 63 billion rubles at the end of 1952 and at 102 billion at the end of 1957, a rise of more than 60 percent.[36] Parenthetically, it may be noted that sizable collective farm investments acted as a brake on the rise of the peasant earnings. In addition to using their own resources for capital investment, there were also available to collectives increased long-term state credits in recent years. Whatever the faults or biases the above figures may have they are believed to be indicative of the trend.

Despite the marked improvement of the capital position of Russian agriculture during the post-Stalin era, the investment is still inadequate to use land and labor effectively. From this inadequacy stems, for instance, the imbalance in mechanization. Some operations, such as cutting the grain, are highly mechanized, while others, such as cleaning and drying of grain, are still to a large extent carried out inefficiently by hand labor.

Again Khrushchev stated in his June 29, 1959, speech that shortage of tractors hampered fall plowing in the new lands regions and consequently increased the load of fieldwork during the short spring season and affected adversely crop yields. As a matter of fact, Soviet farms have fewer tractors than the United States, even though the latter has a crop area of about 150 million acres less than the Soviet Union. At the beginning of 1957 there were 892,000 tractors on farms in the Soviet Union[37] compared with 4,975,000 in the United States.

Another example of a shortage of capital investment in agriculture is the paucity of irrigation development in the extensive subhumid zone plagued by frequent devastating droughts and low crop yields. It is doubtless because of the need of considerable capital investment that Stalin's large program of irrigation in the subhumid regions of

[33] Socialized Agriculture of the U.S.S.R., p. 61.
[34] Forty Years of Soviet Power in Facts and Figures, p. 193.
[35] Narodnoe Khozyaistvo v 1956 Godu, p. 173; S.S.S.R. v Tsifrakh, p. 254.
[36] Narodnoe Khozyaistvo S.S.S.R. v 1956 Godu, p. 140; S.S.S.R. v Tsifrakh, p. 198.
[37] Narodnoe Khozyaistvo S.S.S.R. v 1956 Godu, p. 155.

the European U.S.S.R. was deflated by his successors, though it would have paid off in stable and higher yields.

Still another type of deficiency in capital investment in Soviet agriculture is a qualitative one. It is characterized by wastefulness and decreased economic, and sometimes even physical, effectiveness of some forms of capital investment. There has been, for instance, a tendency in some collectives to build far too elaborate and costly shelters for livestock—so-called cow palaces. Then there were the tractors, produced uniformly much larger in size than needed in many regions. But this particular "gigantomania" is being corrected at present.

The utilization of capital equipment has also been often inefficient. The Soviet press, for instance, has been complaining year in year out about the idleness of tractors during the busy season because of poor repair work, shortage of spare parts, etc.

A field in which considerable investment of capital would be beneficial to agriculture is highways. As the report of the economists of the U.S. Department of Agriculture points out: [38]

> The lack of all-weather roads in much of the country no doubt explains in part the separation of cream for butter producton on most farms rather than the marketing of whole milk. The inadequate transportation system also probably hinders the development of such agricultural crops as fruits and vegetables. The relatively few trucks and automobiles (631,000 trucks and very few automobiles on farms in 1957, compared with nearly 3 million trucks and over 4 million automobiles on U.S. farms) makes for cultural as well as economic isolation for the rural villages and their inhabitants.

A new government program, which, if successful, is destined to have a significant effect on Soviet agricultural production is that of greatly stepped up output of commercial fertilizer. The importance of this program is accentuated by the fact that, following a large expansion of crop acreage during the years 1954–57, the new 7-year plan, 1959–65, relies for the achievement of its high farm output targets primarily on an increase of per acre yields. Certainly increased use of commercial fertilizer, especially in the humid regions, would contribute to this objective.

The gross supply of commercial fertilizer available to Soviet agriculture increased between 1953 and 1957 by nearly 60 percent.[39] But, on a plant nutrient basis of 2.7 million short tons, the 1957 supply was still only 40 percent of fertilizer consumption in the United States. Actually, commercial fertilizer in the Soviet Union so far has been used only in the growing of the most valuable crops, like cotton and sugar beets.

The 1957–59 plan calls for nearly trebling of the fertilizer supply. Whether this high goal will be achieved or not, it is reasonable to expect that a considerable increase of commercial fertilizer supply will take place during the next few years.

There is, however, great room for improvement in the handling, quality, and application of fertilizers. The Soviet press has been replete with complaints about the failure of collective farms to move fertilizer from warehouses. Even worse is the practice of dumping fertilizer in the open, near the railroad station, and allowing it to

[38] Economic Aspects of Soviet Agriculture, p. 32.
[39] S.S.S.R. v Tsifrakh, p. 182.

deteriorate. The U.S. soil and water use exchange group, which visited the Soviet Union in the summer of 1958 comments in its report:

The physical quality of mineral fertilizers in the U.S.S.R. is poor by our standards. The use of unmixed goods results in high expenditures of time on farms in handling, mixing, and application.

Fertilizer-application methods generally are crude, and there seems to be a lack of precision fertilizer-application machinery. On the other hand, airplanes are used extensively for broadcasting solid fertilizers, and the anhydrous ammonia applicators appear to be comparable to ours.

Decisions supplant extension education in obtaining widespread adoption of fertilizer practices on farms. This insures rapid adoption of practices but magnifies errors of judgment and prolongs poor practices that otherwise would soon be discontinued.

It should also be borne in mind that, while the use of commercial fertilizer has been increasing, Soviet authorities were seriously concerned in recent years about a decline, or inadequate use, of manure in the northern and central regions of the U.S.S.R. with their podzolic soils. The very low yields of grains and other crops in the podzolic soil area was attributed largely to the unsatisfactory manure situation.

CHAPTER 9. PLANNING AND MANAGEMENT

Not only in the case of state farms, machine-tractor stations, and repair-technical stations, but also with respect to collective peasant agriculture, the Soviet Government has largely taken over the function of planning and management, which formerly devolved on decisions of numerous independent farmers. The Government now makes many decisions on crops to be planted and livestock raised; assembling of seed; sowing and harvesting practices; supply and use of farm machinery; manure, and commercial fertilizer; crop rotation; capital investment; proper care of livestock; provision of adequate fodder; and other details of farming with which the Government formerly did not concern itself directly.

During the Stalin era, agricultural planning and direction were highly centralized. Plans and targets for many details of farm operations were laid down for different regions in Moscow and on their basis goals were established by local authorities for each collective farm. By 1955, however, the Kremlin finally became convinced that detailed rigid planning of agriculture from the top stifled initiative on the farm and was detrimental to efficiency. Khrushchev and other Soviet spokesmen now severely criticized the old planning methods. One practice particularly, aroused their ire; namely the widespread adoption of a crop rotations scheme in which perennial grasses played an important part. This crop rotation was recommended primarily as a soil improving practice, by a soil scientist named Williams who came to exercise a great deal of influence with the Communist Party leadership during the Stalin regime. It was adopted, not only in humid regions for which it was suitable and where it had been, in fact, long practiced, but also in subhumid regions where it only aggravated the difficult animal feed supply problem by displacement of other forage crops.

This incident highlights a striking peculiarity of Soviet agricultural policymaking and planning—the wholesale introduction by decree of innovations. It makes possible such accomplishments as expansion of the crop acreage in the course of 4 years by 90 million acres and rapid consolidation of the numerous noncontiguous strips of land into large fields adopted for modern power farming. But such planning from above also often leads to costly mistakes; sometimes, because the practice or measure introduced is based on unsound or obsolete principles and often, because of indiscriminate, general application of practices, suitable under certain conditions, but not under others. Since open criticism of principles is taboo in the U.S.S.R., once a certain line of policy is officially laid down, it often takes considerable time before such mistakes are corrected by an official reversal. Such was the case with crop rotation. A more recent example of indiscriminate application is the so-called double stage or windrowing method of grain harvesting, taken over from North America, which speeds the cutting of grain. It is very useful in regions with a short harvest season, like Siberia, often characterized at such times by inclement weather. But in the U.S.S.R. again all regions are urged to adopt this practice; those in which it is essential and those in which it is not necessary.

A good example of pushing a practice, which in the United States is considered largely obsolete, is checkrowing of crops. And for an illustration of the introduction of unsound pseudoscientific practices we must turn to the activity of the notorious opponent of Mendelian genetics and, for a time, under Stalin, a virtual dictator of Soviet biological and agricultural sciences, Lysenko. Although Lysenko's influence on research in biological and agricultural sciences declined considerably after Stalin's death, his star apparently is rising again. The Soviet Botanical Journal, which had vigorously criticized Lysenko and his methods, was curbed and had to change its tone.[40]

Khrushchev's dissatisfaction with highly centralized agricultural planning led to a move toward its decentralization. The decree of March 9, 1955, assigned responsibility for detailed production planning of crops and livestock to collective farms themselves. Central planning was to be confined to the setting of the delivery quotas for farm products and the volume of work to be performed by the MTS. With the liquidation of the latter, this task now also devolves on the collectives. However, the 1955 decree has given to local authorities (including then the MTS) certain responsibilities in farm planning supervision with the result that these agencies often usurped the planning functions of collectives.

National goals, or drives, like the corn growing drive or the campaign to "overtake the United States in per capita milk and meat output" often result also in intervention by authorities with collectives. It is inconceivable, for instance, that a collective in a cotton growing region could shift to raising other crops at the expense of cotton. Again a collective would probably have to give a very good reason for not growing corn (maize) in view of the strong advocacy of that crop by Khrushchev. In planning its livestock production the management of a collective is expected to set high targets of output per 100 hectares of land. For milk and all meat it is tillable land, meadows and pastures; but for pork a special target must be set per 100 hectares of tillable land only. The goal for the output of eggs is per 100 hectares of the sown area of all grain.

---

[40] Among some of the recent evidence of Lysenko's "comeback" is the appearance in Pravda of Dec. 14, 1958, of an unsigned lengthy article entitled "Concerning the Agrobiological Science and the False Position of the Botanical Journal," criticizing the Soviet and Western critics of Lysenko * * *. Subsequently considerable prominence was given to the attack of Lysenko himself on the Biological Department of the Academy of Science at the meeting of the Central Committee of the Communist Party (Pravda, Dec. 18, 1958).

It should also be remembered that for most agricultural products there exist two sets of prices: those fixed by the Government at which it buys farm products, and the usually higher free market prices. (Cotton is an example of a commodity for which there is no free market price since the whole output has to be sold to the Government.) Thus the managers of collectives are confronted by a multiciplity of yardsticks and pressures which makes proper planning difficult.

The pivotal role of the collective farm manager (chairman) and his assistants in the success of collectives, or lack of it, has been long recognized by the Soviet Government. The importance of the managerial function has been enhanced with the enlargement of the farm enterprise. But finding efficient and reliable managers poses a problem which the regime, apparently, has not been able to solve to its satisfaction, despite several campaigns to shift qualified and reliable party personnel and specialists from the cities to the farms, and notwithstanding the large number of agricultural specialists trained by colleges and vocational schools. In his speech at a meeting of the central committee of the Communist Party on June 29, 1959, Khrushchev again complained that party organs in a number of places, despite their large personnel—

cannot select good chairmen [managers] for the backward collectives. The result is as the proverb has it: "With 7 nurses in attendance—the child still manages to lose an eye." And what does it mean to select a good chairman of a collective, good brigadiers [foremen]? It means success of the enterprise * * * Why is it that collective and state farms do not organize their work as well as factory personnel? Because some collectives have been headed by poor chairmen for long stretches at a time; some have brought as many as three collectives to ruin and are looking toward a fourth * * * And the party organizations put up but a weak fight against such an evil * * *

On the other side, there had been complaints of frequent turnover and irresponsible removal of managers of collective farms. The managerial problem apparently continues to be a serious one.

CHAPTER 10. THE BATTLE FOR GRAIN; WHEAT AND CORN

Special Government programs, aiming at increasing the output of important commodities, have been characteristic of Soviet agricultural policy, both during the Stalin and post-Stalin periods. Such programs consist, as a rule, of a varying combination of increased economic incentives, higher targets for supply to collective and state farms of machinery, fertilizer, etc., and direct orders to local authorities and to collective and state farms, prescribing production targets and improvements in farm practices and management. Two of such programs, initiated by Khrushchev, have been of far-reaching significance; namely, the expansion of small-grain production, principally of wheat, and an increase in corngrowing. Together they constitute the latest phase in the "battle for grain" which the Soviet regime has waged throughout its history.

The importance of grain in the Russian economy cannot be exaggerated. It predominates in the caloric intake of the population, which is growing at the rate of over 3 million a year. Increasing quantities of grain are also needed as livestock feed, to assure the large increases in output of dairy products and meat called for by the Government.

Grain production during the postwar period, however, failed to keep pace with increased requirements. During the Stalin era this was obscured from public view, as was pointed out earlier, by the misleading huge "biological" estimates of the crops standing in the fields and not stored in the barn. A considerably larger production, of course, was desired by the Stalin administration (of which Khrushchev was an important member). It was one of the goals of the last Stalin 5-year plan, 1950–55. The total grain area, however, during the years 1951–53 of 263 to 265 million acres was below the prewar area of 273 million acres (1940), though the wheat acreage was above prewar and trending upward. Thus the steeply increased grain production target for 1955 was to be accomplished predominantly through increased yields per acre. The increase was expected to result from a combination of measures for a putative improvement of agricultural technique, such as soil-improving rotation with perennial grasses mentioned above, tree shelterbelts, irrigation of 15 million acres in the subhumid regions of European U.S.S.R., the whole array known as the great Stalin plan for reconstruction of nature.

The post-Stalin administration largely abandoned, or deflated, the great Stalin plan for reconstruction of nature, some aspects of which, like the universal crop-rotation scheme with grasses, appeared questionable, while others, like the irrigation program, were considered too costly. Under Khrushchev's leadership, the Kremlin returned to the traditional Russian pattern of increasing agricultural production extensively by expanding acreage. To pursue this the Soviet Government turned eastward, where there were still considerable tracts of long uncultivated, or virgin, lands.

Acreage extension, paralleling settlement of these eastern regions—which are to Russia what the West was to the United States in the last century—has been proceeding since the 1890's. But never before has the extension occurred at so rapid a rate. In the 3 years, 1954–56, 90 million acres were plowed up with the aid of tractor power and added to the Soviet crop area, mainly the spring wheat area. This acreage is almost equal to the combined arable land of France, Western Germany, and the United Kingdom—an achievement which should not be underestimated. However, most of this new acreage is in a zone of unfavorable climatic conditions. It is characterized by severe winters, a short growing season accompanied all too often by devastating droughts, and frequently a rainy and cold harvesting season. It is, therefore, a zone of hazardous agriculture, suited mainly to spring crops and characterized by sharply fluctuating yields. This is shown by data for Kazakhstan, one of the main areas where the new development took place. (See table 9.)

Even with low average yields, the multiplier of the large additional acreage is bound to result in a substantial increase of production, though one may be skeptical whether it is low-cost production as the Soviets claim. Since the eastern regions are relatively sparsely settled there is proportionately more grain available in good years above local requirements than in the older, more densely populated regions. This factor, and the prevalence of large state farms, facilitates the task of Government collections. Again, the extension of the acreage in the east provides a kind of insurance against mediocre crops in other regions of the country, as illustrated by the situation in 1959, when a considerable part of the new lands area was not affected by a drought or affected less seriously than most of the other important agricultural regions.

On the other side of the ledger is the fact of further considerable extension of Soviet agriculture into the precarious climatic zone of marginal or submarginal land. It is well recognized in Soviet agricultural circles that, in order to prevent dust bowl conditions and disastrous crop failures, a part of the acreage in these new land regions, perhaps a fifth or more should be annually rotated as summer fallow, a practice which has been little followed so far. To replace this acreage, additional new land must be brought under cultivation if the cropped acreage is to be maintained. Thus the maintenance of the acreage at its present level presents a problem. But so long as the huge wheat acreage is maintained, with correspondingly large harvests, especially in years of good weather, Soviet wheat exports pose the threat of increased competition on the world markets.[41]

The program for corn expansion is aimed directly at remedying the shortage of feed, which had been largely responsible for the weakness of the Soviet livestock sector. Khrushchev saw in corn a panacea for the unsatisfactory feed situation and he began to push strongly for a huge expansion of the corn acreage. In this he was admittedly influenced by the example of successful cultivation of corn as a major fodder crop in the United States.

Prior to 1955, corn acreage in the Soviet Union was small, varying between 9 and 12 million acres. By contrast there were planted 20 to 26 million acres of barley and 38 to 40 million acres of oats. Yields of corn per acre were about 14 to 17 bushels, or less than half of those in the United States. Climatic conditions in the Soviet Union do not favor corn growing beyond a limited southern area. In the rest of the country it is either too cold or too dry for successful corn culture. Nevertheless, the Khrushchev program in 1955 set a goal of not less than 70 million acres under corn by 1960, or nearly a sevenfold increase compared with 1954.[42] It was realized that this would involve considerable extension of corn cultivation into regions where the growing season was too short for the grain to mature. Consequently, a much larger proportion of corn was to be used as silage in the Soviet Union than in the United States.

This crash program was undertaken in the face of climatic obstacles and without adequate preparation, without proper varieties, machinery, fertilizer, and significant incentives to the farmers. It met only with limited success. It is true that the corn acreage increased from less than 11 million acres in 1954 to 59 million in 1956. But this was, so far, the high water mark and during the 2 succeeding years less than 50 million acres were planted to corn. This is still a fivefold increase and corn is now grown in many regions where it had not been known before. But Khrushchev himself was scornful of the results in 1958, a generally good crop year, with respect to more than half of this acreage from which corn was either harvested for

[41] For further discussion of this program, see: Volin, Lazar, "The New Battle for Grain in Soviet Russia," Foreign Agriculture, November 1954, pp. 194–199; Harris, Chauncey D., "Soviet Agricultural Resources Reappraised," Journal of Farm Economics, 38, pp. 258–273; W. A. D. Jackson, "The Virgin and Idle Lands of Western Siberia and Northern Kazakhstan: A Geographical Appraisal," Geographical Review, 46, pp. 1–19, 1956.
[42] Direktivy KPSS i Sovetskogo Pravitel'stva po Khozyaistvennym voprosam, vol. 4, p. 335.

silage before the ears were formed (30 percent of acreage) or was reported as having been used for green forage (29 percent of acreage). The latter is a euphemism, according to Khrushchev, for "the lost corn crop." Yet Khrushchev's enthusiasm for corn as "the queen of the fields" has remained unabated, despite some cautionary remarks, which he makes from time to time. Incidentally, he strongly recommended corngrowing to Polish farmers during his visit to Poland in the summer of 1959. However, the excessive concentration on corn has probably increased the Soviet feed supply to a lesser degree than it might have been with a more balanced program.

TABLE 1.—*Area sown to crops in selected years, Soviet Union* [1]

[Million acres]

Crop	1940 [2]	1945 [2]	1950	1951	1952	1953	1954	1955	1956	1957	1958 [3]
Wheat:											
Winter	35.34	22.24	30.89	38.55	42.50	43.98	38.79	45.22	31.88		
Spring	64.25	39.29	64.25	67.71	71.91	75.37	83.03	104.28	121.33		
Total	99.59	61.53	95.14	106.26	114.41	119.35	121.82	149.50	153.21	170.75	165.06
Rye, winter	57.08	50.16	58.32	69.06	56.34	50.16	50.66	47.20	45.47	44.73	43.74
Corn grown for grain [4]	8.9	10.38	11.86	10.13	9.04	8.65	10.63	22.49	22.98	14.33	20.02
Other [5]								21.74	36.08	30.89	28.66
Total	8.9	10.38	11.86	10.13	9.04	8.65	10.63	44.23	59.06	45.22	48.68
Barley	27.92	25.70	21.25	20.02	21.25	23.72	26.44	24.46	29.40	22.73	23.72
Oats	49.91	35.58	40.03	43.03	41.02	37.81	39.29	36.57	37.31	34.59	36.32
Rice	.49	.49	.25	.25	.25	.25	.25	.25	.25		
Buckwheat	4.94	4.45	7.41	6.67	6.18	6.42	6.92	6.92	6.67		
Millet	14.53	14.58	9.39	8.15	8.65	10.13	13.59	19.03	15.81		
Grain legumes	5.53	3.71	4.94	4.20	3.95	3.95	4.45	3.46	3.21		
Other grain	3.46	4.20	5.68	5.19	3.56	3.21	2.97	2.47	2.72		
Total grain	273.35	210.78	254.27	262.93	265.25	263.65	277.02	[6] 312.35	[6] 317.03	[6] 307.89	[6] 309.37
Potatoes	19.93	20.51	21.25	20.73	20.26	20.51	21.50	22.49	22.73	24.22	23.47
Vegetables	5.58	5.68	4.69	4.69	4.69	4.94	5.68	5.68	5.93	5.21	3.71
Sugar beets	3.44	2.05	3.24	3.43	3.61	3.88	3.95	4.35	4.97	5.21	6.23
Sunflowers	8.15	7.24	8.87	8.92	9.07	9.64	9.96	10.48	11.14	8.55	9.74
Cotton	5.24	2.99	5.73	6.72	6.99	4.65	5.44	5.44	5.11	5.16	5.29
Flax for fiber	5.39	2.47	4.69	3.95	3.78	3.06	2.74	3.66	4.74	4.18	3.95
Flax for seed	.47	.47	.89	.89	.94	1.14	1.09	1.04	1.16		
Hemp	1.86	.69	1.38	1.41	1.33	1.26	1.43	1.46	1.53	1.14	.99
Tobacco	.25	.20	.25	.27	.27	.27	.30	.27	.27		
Makhorka	.27	.27	.27	.27	.27	.27	.25	.22	.20		
Forage crops [7]	44.73	25.20	51.15	58.56	63.33	70.92	77.10	66.47	66.96	112.18	114.00
Other crops	4.13	2.64	4.82	5.36	5.09	4.25	4.00	3.48	3.24		
Total crops	371.65	281.19	361.50	378.07	384.88	388.44	410.46	459.13	481.09	478.63	483.08

[1] Data from official sources. Exclusive of winterkilled grain not resown in the spring.
[2] Figures for territory within the boundaries existing in that year.
[3] Preliminary.
[4] Includes some immature corn grown for silage and converted to dry-grain equivalent.
[5] Included with grain until 1955.
[6] Excludes corn not grown for grain.
[7] Includes some corn grown for silage and green fodder.

TABLE 2.—*Acreage and production of selected crops, United States and the Soviet Union, 1958*

| Crop | United States | | U.S.S.R. | |
	Acreage	Production	Acreage	Production
	Million acres	*Million bushels*	*Million acres*	*Million bushels*
Wheat	53.6	1,462.0	165.0	2,300.0
Rye	1.8	32.0	43.5	650.0
Barley	14.9	470.0	23.5	440.0
Oats	31.8	1,422.0	36.0	890.0
Corn	73.5	3,800.0	[1] 20.1	[2] 600.0
Grain sorghum	16.8	615.0	(3)	(3)
Soybeans	23.8	574.0	(3)	(3)
		Million bales		*Million bales*
Cotton	11.8	11.5	5.3	6.9
		Million short tons		*Million short tons*
Sugar beets	0.9	15.2	5.9	46.0
Sunflower seed	(3)	(3)	9.7	5.0
		Million hundred-weight		*Million hundred-weight*
Potatoes	1.5	266.0	23.5	1,898.0

[1] In addition nearly 29,000,000 acres of corn harvested for silage and fodder.
[2] Including some corn harvested in the milky stage for silage.
[3] Not available. USDA estimates and official figures.

TABLE 3.—*Livestock numbers in the United States and Soviet Union, selected years*

[In millions]

| Year January | All cattle | | Hogs | | Sheep | |
	United States	U.S.S.R.[1]	United States	U.S.S.R.[1]	United States	U.S.S.R.
1928	57.3	66.8	61.9	27.7	45.3	---------
1953	94.2	56.6	51.8	28.5	31.9	94.3
1958	93.4	66.8	51.0	44.3	31.3	120.2
1959	96.9	70.8	57.2	48.5	32.6	129.6

[1] Figures for the territory within present boundaries. Official sources.

TABLE 4.—*Livestock numbers in the Soviet Union by kinds of farms, Jan. 1, 1958*

[Million head]

Item	Collective farms	State farms	Other	Total
All cattle	29.2	8.0	29.5	66.7
Cows	10.7	2.8	17.9	31.4
Hogs	20.0	9.0	15.3	44.3
Sheep	70.0	24.0	26.1	120.1

Official sources.

TABLE 5.—*Labor requirements for crops and livestock products in the United States and the Soviet Union*

Item	U.S.S.R.[2] (Man-hours per centner)			Percent U.S.S.R. is of U.S.A.	
	U.S.A.[1]	State farms	Collective farms	State farms	Collective farms
Grain	1.0	1.8	7.3	180	730
Potatoes	1.0	4.2	5.1	420	510
Sugar beets	.5	2.1	3.1	420	620
Seed cotton	18.8	29.8	42.8	159	228
Milk	4.7	9.9	14.7	211	313
Cattle, liveweight gain	7.9	52.0	112.0	658	1,418
Hogs, liveweight gain	6.3	43.0	103.0	683	1,635

[1] In 1956.
[2] Average for 1956–57.

Source: Khrushchev's report of Dec. 15, 1958.

TABLE 6.—*Percentage distribution of collective farms by sown area, Soviet Union and selected regions, 1956* [1]

Sown area	All U.S.S.R.	North-western	Northern Caucasus	Western Siberia
500 hectares (1,236 acres) and under	17.8	64.2	22.6	5.4
501 to 1,000 hectares (1,238 to 2,471 acres)	24.7	25.9	6.7	5.8
1,001 to 2,000 hectares (2,473 to 4,942 acres)	29.0	9.3	7.5	17.9
2,001 to 5,000 hectares (4,944 to 12,355 acres)	22.5	.6	28.3	46.5
Over 5,000 hectares (12,355 acres)	6.0		34.9	24.4
Total	100.0	100.0	100.0	100.0

[1] Source: Narodnoe Khoziaistvo SSSR v 1956 Godu, p. 143.

TABLE 7.—*Percentage distribution of collective farms by number of households, U.S.S.R. and selected regions, 1956* [1]

Number of households	All U.S.S.R.	North-western	Northern Caucasus	Western Siberia
100 and under	19.0	61.6	9.2	17.3
101 to 200	34.3	33.2	24.4	44.4
201 to 300	20.7	4.4	20.6	25.0
301 to 500	17.6	.7	18.9	12.3
Over 500	8.4	.1	26.9	1.0
Total	100.0	100.0	100.0	100.0

[1] Source: Narodnoe Khoziaistvo SSSR v 1956 Godu, p. 142.

TABLE 8.—*Government payments to collective farms and individuals for farm products acquired, selected years* [1]

Year:

	Billion rubles
1952	31.3
1953	41.4
1955	64.0
1956	88.5
1957	96.7

[1] Including payments by government controlled cooperatives.

Source: SSSR v Tsifrakh, p. 187.

TABLE 9.—*Yields of all grains in Kazakhstan, selected years*

	Centners per hectare [1]	Bushels of 60 pounds per hectare
1954	9.1	13.5
1955	2.9	4.3
1956	10.6	15.8
1957	4.6	6.8
1958	(2)	(2)

[1] 1 centner= ⅒oth of a metric ton or 220.46 pounds.
[2] Reported as more than 9 centners, or more than 13.4 bushels.

Source: Plenum Tsentral'nogo Komiteta Kommunisticheskoi Partii Sovetskogo Soiuza 15–19 dekabrya 1959. Stenograficheskii otchet, p. 101.

A NOTE ON
LABOUR UTILIZATION IN THE KOLKHOZ

DURING the past two years several articles have appeared in the issues of *Soviet Studies*, which have presented different viewpoints as to the supply of kolkhoz labour. Although the authors of these articles have sometimes differed quite sharply in their interpretations of the materials available on the numbers of people engaged in collective farm work, they have been unanimous in agreeing that there is a considerable waste of kolkhoz labour. With this general consensus of opinion in mind, an exploration into specific farming operations should prove of value.

One of the primary arguments in favour of the amalgamated kolkhozy, which has been repeatedly emphasized in Soviet agricultural publications, has been that the enlarged collective would strengthen the kolkhoz economy by providing the most efficient usage of agricultural machinery and advanced farming techniques. Certainly, one of the basic goals involved in the efficient usage of agricultural machinery and advanced farming techniques would consist in the efficient employment of labour. The amalgamations have led to a crop of books and articles about the proper organization of production on the enlarged kolkhozy, and it is possible to get from these sources a glimpse of the kind of deployment of labour which various Soviet writers consider desirable. It is reasonable to assume that the examples they quote are better than was normal at the time at which they wrote. It may be worth examining a few of these examples, since they shed light on the general question of efficiency and productivity of Soviet agricultural labour and on the intensity of machinery utilization. Further since one of the authors of this article has had first-hand experience in farming in Nebraska (a flat prairie-land not unlike parts of the Russian wheat belt), it is possible to make certain significant comparisons with American practice.

We will take two operations, combine-harvesting and threshing, described in a symposium published by the state agricultural publishing house in Moscow in 1951.[1]

The first example concerns kolkhozy of the Deminsk area, in the Stalingrad region. Each brigade is allotted two combines, and this requires the simultaneous employment of the following numbers:[2]

---

[1] *Voprosy Organizatsii i Oplaty Truda v Kolkhozakh* (Questions of the organization and payment of labour in the Kolkhozy), Ed. by L. M. Furman.
[2] Ibid., p. 81.

(a) Servicing the combines:

Hauling grain on 12 carts	12 persons
Straw sheafing	4
Handling grain at conveyors (sacking)	2
Checkweighmen	2
Workers engaged in weighing	4
Sorting with 3 sorting and blowing machines	12
Drying grain	6
TOTAL	42
(b) Removal of straw from fields	2
(c) Straw stacking	4
(d) Workers on two horse-drawn rakes	2
(e) Transportation by truck of state grain deliveries	3
(f) Transport of grain to store (bins) in 3 carts	3

In addition each brigade provides 15 workers to form part of the tractor brigade.

In comparing this deployment of personnel with American practice, one should exclude: items (a) — second sub-item, 'straw sheafing', (b) (c) and (d) above, because in the United States the vast majority of the combining operations leave the straw in the fields — to return, in part, to the soil the fertile elements taken from it during the growth of the grain. This still leaves 59 men, or a total number of 29½ per combine, simultaneously employed. The brigade covers an area of some 1500-2000 hectares; no data are given about the time it takes to complete its work.

On a farm near Grand Island, Nebraska, during the current year's wheat harvest, five men (3 combine operators, 2 truck drivers) carried out the combining of 175 acres of wheat in approximately 15 hours with three self-propelled combines. Since the Soviet machines were apparently tractor-drawn another three men, representing tractor drivers, should be added to this Nebraska operation. Since, in Nebraska wheat areas, grain is generally hauled directly from the field to a neighbouring grain elevator where it is weighed and then unloaded, another man will be added to our Nebraska example to represent the scale attendant, although he actually serves many times the area represented by our example. This example, which is certainly typical of labour organization during Nebraska's small-grain harvest, represents a total of nine men for three combines, or three men per machine.[3]

If one were to grant that the Soviet combining operation was carried

---

[3] We should like to express our thanks to Mr. M. E. Olson of Grand Island, Nebraska, for his kind help in checking the specific data used in this paper, on Nebraska farm practices.

out at an equal rate of speed, per machine, as the one in Nebraska (which there is reason to doubt), and if the yield per acre was equal (which there is reason to believe) in the two sample areas — in this area of Nebraska the average is about 18 bushels (1 bushel equals 27 kgs.) per acre — then a simple calculation will reveal that in Nebraska the rate of work during the harvest can be represented as approximately 24 bu. per hr. per man, whereas in the Soviet example it would be of the order of 2.5 bu. per hr. per man.

A point by point comparison of the two harvesting operations should reveal the changes necessary to allow the Soviet system of grain harvesting to equal the efficiency in labour which is achieved in the Nebraska example.

SOVIET EXAMPLE (2 combines)

(1) Haulers: 12 men driving horse drawn carts; state grain deliveries, 3 truckers; handling the grain for storage in bins, 3 men. Total—18.

(2) Conveyors for handling the grain bags, 2 men.

(3) Weighers, 2; workers with scales, 4. Total—6.

(4) Sorting the grain, 12; drying, 6. Total—18.

NEBRASKA EXAMPLE (3 combines)

(1) Haulers: 2 truck drivers. When a truck is filled in the field it is driven to a local elevator where the grain leaves the farmer's hands. (The Nebr. farmers 'state grain delivery' is taken care of in his taxes.)

(2) The vast majority of American grain never touches a bag until after it is milled.

(3) This operation is generally handled by one scale man at the elevator.

(4) These tasks are accomplished in at least three ways: A—Most American combines require no additional sorting; B—Moisture content determines the price of a farmer's wheat and he usually manages to do his combining when his wheat is dry enough that he is not 'docked' for excess moisture; C—Any additional sorting or drying, which may be necessary, will be mechanically handled in huge quantities at the flour mills.

(5) Tractor and machine operators and servicing personnel, 15 men.	(5) 3 tractor drivers; 3 combine operators. The average Nebraska farmer, a fairly capable mechanic, makes his own minor repairs, and almost invariably hauls his fuel to the fields (in 50 gallon drums) in the empty grain trucks.

The above analysis would seem to reveal at least two considerable differences in the two systems of harvesting. First of all, the Nebraska farmer has more machines with which to carry out his work, and secondly that, at least to date, the communal system of Soviet agriculture has made several uneconomical demands upon the organization of work.[4]

To whatever extent one may be allowed to reason from the specific to the general, in this particular instance, the basic fact does appear to be that the average Soviet combining operation requires approximately ten men for every one man occupied in the Nebraska example.

It is fair to add that the newspaper *Sotsialisticheskoye Zemledeliye* of the 10th of September, 1952, in reviewing the book from which this example is taken, criticized this deployment of labour on the grounds that greater economies are possible. 'Can it really be normal to have six men involved in weighing grain?' However, it seems reasonably clear from the context that the newspaper critic was blaming the authors for not providing a more nearly model example, for there is little doubt that the example itself was above average.

Now for an example of threshing, taken from an outstanding kolkhoz in the Chernigov area.[5]

The norm for the standard threshing machine MK-1100 was 24-30 tons of grain in 24 hours. An outstanding innovator, Bredyuk by name, succeeded in increasing this to a maximum of 132 tons, and he did this partly by speeding up, and making some alterations in, the machine, and partly by increasing the labour force. This at first consisted of two 12-hour shifts with 40 in each shift. This was, finally, increased to a stage at which 70 persons were servicing the thresher, in each of two 12-hour shifts; it was soon found that work of this intensity for 12 hours tired the workers, and necessitated two one-hour meal breaks. This hold-up was liquidated by substituting a system of 4 hours on, 4 hours

---

[4] An example of this can be found in an explanation, which has been suggested, of why the kolkhozniki must sack the wheat in the fields. This is because there is too much apprehension on the part of the kolkhozniki, and the state, that too much of the grain would be lost (or stolen) if it were transported in open trucks and wagons, and that the kolkhoznik feels that he must be able to see the grain sacked while it is still in the field so that he may know just what remuneration he is entitled to.

[5] Op. cit., pp. 36ff.

off, for the two shifts all round the clock, which cut out meal breaks altogether. The thresher was thus able to work for 23 hours 20 minutes in 24 (the missing 40 minutes were used in oiling and overhauling the machine).

This is how the work was tackled. The wheat was piled into four stacks, in such a way that the threshing machine could be conveniently placed between two of them. On each of the two stacks on either side of the thresher were 8-10 women, i.e. 16-20 persons were passing sheaves (bundles) towards the machine. Two women on each side were engaged in cutting twine from the sheaves, two more passed the wheat into the machine:

> Therefore 24-28 persons ensured uninterrupted and regular feeding of wheat into the machine. The remaining kolkhozniki worked on raking, removal and stacking of straw; 8 women gathered straw from the machine and placed it into a net for removal for stacking; six juveniles hauled the straw away with horses in six nets and piled it into two stacks; 16 persons were engaged in stacking the straw; 5-6 persons removed and stacked the chaff. . . .

Four persons were also engaged in 'receiving grain under the thresher', but this is omitted from the comparison, as in the United States the analogous operation forms part of the process of transporting the threshed grain.

No less than 140 persons were engaged on this one machine during the 24 hours.

The task before this kolkhoz was accomplished in thirty days at an over-all average of 55 tons per 24 hours. The job was started at a rate far below the average, with 40 in each shift, and finished at a much higher rate, with 70 per shift. It cannot be said that this deployment of labour was the product of some quite exceptional circumstances, since it is being quoted as a model, as a great achievement (it was not criticized in the review to which we referred earlier).[6] Nor did this lavish use of labour lead to a fall in output per head. On the contrary, the author claims that whereas output per head per hour under the old methods (using 40 per shift) was 20.8 kilograms, the new method pushed this up to an average of 60 kilograms.

Although it is one of the principal wheat producing states of the United States, the threshing machine is almost a thing of the past in Nebraska. However, where the old type 'large' threshing machine (probably the most similar to the Soviet machine) is still used, the

---

[6] Indeed this same operation was praised in an editorial in the monthly *Sotsialisticheskoye Selskoye Khozyaistvo* 1950, no. 8, from which the average, 55, is taken. According to Anisimov, *Razvitiye selskovo khozyaistva v poslevoyennoi pyatiletke*, 1952, p. 76, Bredyuk won 'the high honour of Stalin prizewinner' for introducing this method of work.

following men comprising a crew furnishes the basis for a comparison to the Soviet example:[7] Two men to pitch the bundles (sheaves) from the stack directly into the machine, where the twine is automatically cut;[8] one separator man to watch the machinery, oil the separator, move the blower (which automatically forms the straw stack), watch the amount of grain in the straw, and generally oversee the entire operation, including tending the tractor which is used to power the thresher; three truck drivers who haul the grain, gravity loaded into the trucks, to the elevator. If run at normal speed this thresher handles approximately six acres of cut grain in an hour. With the Nebraska average yield at 18 bushels an acre this would be just under 2500 bushels in a 23 hour day, as compared with an average of nearly 2050 bushels (55 metric tons) represented in the Soviet example, where the yield per acre was roughly similar (the *maximum* achieved by the Soviet machine, 132 tons, substantially exceeds the U.S. figure). It seems reasonable to assume that the two machines are of nearly the same capacity. The Soviet example does not include workers engaged in receiving or transporting the threshed grain, therefore the three men in the Nebraska crew who are engaged in this task cannot be used in the comparison. Thus, for comparative purposes, the total number of men in the Nebraska crew is three.[9]

A point by point breakdown of the two threshing operations (similar to the one used for comparing the two systems of combining) should shed considerable light on a comparison of the utilization of manpower in the two systems.

SOVIET EXAMPLE (equivalent of one 12 hr. shift)

(1) 16-20 individuals passing sheaves towards the machine.

NEBRASKA EXAMPLE (one daylight shift)

(1) The average Nebraska operation would involve two men pitching bundles from the racks (or stack), into the machine, who can keep the thresher running at full capacity.

---

[7] The newer and now more popular U.S. machine is of a smaller size and of about one-half the capacity of the older machines.

[8] A U.S. threshing crew generally includes 8 additional men driving hayracks from the field where they are loaded, to the machine where two of the drivers, working together, can keep the machine filled. Since, however, the Soviet example starts from the stacks at the threshing site (it excludes labour used in transporting the bundles from the fields, or stacking them in the fields) the Nebraska example must include only the men involved in feeding the machine. Under certain circumstances the Nebraska farmer will stack his bundles in the same manner as do the kolkhozniki (at the threshing site), and when he does this only two men are required to work on the stacks pitching bundles into the machine.

[9] The MK 1100 thresher is run off a tractor, and so it is necessary to add a tractor driver to the Soviet example. It should be added that the MK 1100 is not the most modern machine in the USSR, though it seems to be the most common type.

(2) 4 women cutting twine.

(2) The American threshing machine automatically cuts the twine around the bundles.

(3) 4 women passing the wheat into the machine.

(3) This operation is included in (1).

(4) Some 35 individuals handling and stacking the straw and chaff.

(4) The Nebraska farmer locates the threshing machine at a spot where he wants his strawstacks. The machines are equipped with blowers which create the stacks with no assistance from the workers other than an occasional redirection of the blower's spout in order to assure the correct construction of the straw stack.

(5) Tractor driver, and presumably also supervising 'brigade-leader', possibly with an assistant.

(5) 1 man attending the thresher and the tractor.

After adjusting the Soviet and United States operations to make them reasonably comparable, it would seem that sixty kolkhozniki do the work of three American farm hands. However, these figures are in need of amendment, because the full deployment of so large a labour force made possible the threshing of considerably more than the average amount of grain. The 'top' figure of 132 tons a day looks like a 'once-only' record, but if one takes 100 tons as the average for the enlarged brigade, it would still mean an output of grain which is some 50 per cent higher than that of the average of the American machine. This would reduce the ratio of output per man from 20 : 1 to 14 : 1, in very rough figures.[10]

The evidence points to an even larger disproportion in the use of labour than the authors anticipated. A careful revision of the data produced no reason for supposing that the American labour output in these operations has been underrated. On the contrary, there are grounds for supposing that a good few could be added to the Russian figures, which do not appear to include either supervisory or auxiliary workers. Some guide to the numbers of these involved may be found in the following figures, quoted on page 82 of the symposium, of numbers *saved* by rolling two brigades into one (obviously, at least an equal number must still be employed in an enlarged brigade):

[10] It is worth noting that, at the recent party congress, Benediktov stated that the labour force in threshing might be reduced to one seventh or even one ninth of its present size (*Pravda*, October 11th, 1952). This is not so very different from the results of our analysis.

(a) *Saved by enlarging a Tractor Brigade.*

Brigade Leader 1
Assistant Brigade Leader ... 1
Checker 1
Refueller 1
Water-carrier 1
Food porter 1
Cook 1
Watchman 1

(b) *Saved by enlarging a Field Brigade.*

Brigade Leader 1
Checker.................... 1
Water-carrier 1
Food-porter 1
Herdsmen 2
Cook 1
Watchman 1

No account has been taken in the examples we have quoted of clerical labour involved in calculating the labour-day remuneration, with all the bookkeeping that it necessitates.

Clearly, a profound analysis of the whole problem of labour utilization in Soviet agriculture would require a lengthy book. We will therefore content ourselves with putting forward a few points which seem relevant to any comparison between American and Soviet practice:

(a) Perhaps the most important is that Russian agriculture has the organizational habits which spring from the fact of a large rural population, as against the long history of labour shortage in U.S. agriculture. It does not follow from this that there is a surplus of labour in Soviet agriculture relative to *Soviet* methods of utilizing labour. On the contrary, there is evidence that they consider themselves short of labour; certainly the hours of work suggest this.

(b) A good deal of the waste arises directly out of the nature of the kolkhoz system. Thus grain must be transported to two different destinations, to the elevators of the state procurement organization and to the kolkhoz store. It must be weighed to establish the exact piecework units involved. It must be safeguarded from theft. The low price paid by the state means low labour-day distributions, which lessen the peasants' response to incentives.

The emphasis which it has been found necessary to place on individual responsibility for clearly defined tasks leads to waste through excessive specialization, while a U.S. farmer is able to apply labour more flexibly to tasks as they arise.

(c) The harvest is computed 'on the root', without allowance for losses, and the kolkhoz is under pressure to minimize losses even at the cost of a quite uneconomic labour deployment. The pressure of the state is for more produce, and it has not the same interest in waste of labour, as this makes no difference to the price it pays for kolkhoz produce, nor indeed to the total 'wage bill' of the kolkhoz itself. This is a point of some importance. The Soviet factory manager, if he wastes labour, will exceed his wage fund, perhaps make a loss, probably involve himself in administrative reprimand and suffer a salary cut. The kolkhoz chairman, on the other hand, cannot 'overspend' his wage fund, for the total distribution to the kolkhozniki is in any event limited to what is left after all other commitments have been met. If labour-days are wasted, the only result is to reduce the payment per labour-day (one effect of this is that the management of the kolkhoz cannot measure in terms of rubles the degree of wastefulness of a given operation, and so must tend to adopt any measure which promises to increase total output, or the productivity of a given *machine*). The kolkhozniki have not the right to move to a kolkhoz where they would get more money.[11] Against this, it must be borne in mind that the kolkhoz chairman's own remuneration is in labour-days, and while he receives a big bonus for any overfulfilment of the quantity plans, the ruble value of each labour-day is reduced if, in overfulfilling the plan, he 'devalues' the labour-day.

A. NOVE
R. D. LAIRD

[11] He may, however, have the opportunity of volunteering to go into industry.

FINANCE

MANY PEOPLE have assumed that because the Soviet economy is a planned economy, money and monetary institutions are of no significance. This would be true if the Soviets relied exclusively on direct controls to allocate and distribute commodities and factors of production, and if money prices either did not exist or had no relevance at all for managers, planners, consumers, and workers. In fact, the consumers' goods and labor markets are relatively free markets, as I noted in the introduction to Section V. Furthermore, monetary incentives provide the major form of work-motivation in all areas of economic life, and money prices not only have relevance to consumers and workers but also have some relevance for the decisions of planners and managers (see Sections II and VI). It is important, therefore, to study the financial institutions of the Soviet Union and their role in the Soviet economy. The role of money in the Soviet economy is effectively analyzed in the paper by Professor Hodgman (below).

The two major Soviet financial institutions are the Unified Budget and the State Bank (Gosbank). The Unified Budget is comparable to a combination of the American federal, state, local budgets (see F. D. Holzman [1953]). Soviet taxes and other sources of finance are described briefly and analyzed in the first paper by Holzman below. For more detail, the reader is referred to R. W. Davies (1958) and F. D. Holzman (1955). The latter source (Chapter X) provides a statistical measurement of the enormous "burden" of Soviet taxation which has typically amounted to about one-half of total personal income. Budgetary expenditures are not explicitly described in any of the essays below. This is not an important omission, however, since for most expenditure categories the Budget does not provide a comprehensive account of state outlays. For these, the reader is referred to the national income accounts as provided in earlier essays (above) by Bergson and Heymann, Bornstein, and Kaser. The budget expenditure accounts are discussed explicitly in F. D. Holzman

(1953). Social welfare budgetary expenditures are provided by A. Nove's paper in Section IX.

The major economic functions and operations of the Soviet State Bank are outlined in the essays by Professors Hodgman and Powell. Neither of these papers describes the several minor features of the banking system such as the so-called long-term investment banks and the network of savings banks. The long-term investment banks, now in effect consolidated into a single bank, are better characterized as disbursing agents of the Budget than as true banks in the credit-creating sense; and the savings banks simply collect and turn the deposits of private individuals over to the Budget via the purchase of government bonds. These and other details can be found in any of the sources on banking listed in the Bibliography.

The success of a nation's combined fiscal and monetary policies is usually measured (in the absence of direct controls) by the stability of its price level. Soviet price history since 1928 can be divided into two phases: twenty years of rapidly rising prices, followed by twelve years of relatively stable or declining prices. What were the causes of the twenty year Soviet inflation? How was the inflation brought under control? To what extent are Soviet fiscal and/or monetary policies responsible for the present price stability? These important questions provide much of the focus of the papers by Professors Powell, Hodgman, and Holzman presented below. As the reader can verify for himself, the authors are not of one mind on these matters. A history of the inflation can be found in the second article by Dr. Holzman.

The Appendix contains a qualification of the first article by Dr. Holzman.

FINANCING
SOVIET ECONOMIC DEVELOPMENT

F. D. HOLZMAN

UNIVERSITY OF WASHINGTON

THE PURPOSE OF THIS PAPER is threefold: to explain Soviet choice among sources of finance, to present and analyze the relevant data, and to evaluate the fiscal and monetary policies pursued. It should be stated at the outset that the sum of amounts collected from the various sources of finance always substantially exceeds the value of gross national investment. This is because from the same pools of funds the Soviet government finances not only investment in fixed and working capital, but government stockpiles of strategic materials, expenditures of the Ministry of Armed Forces for defense, administrative activities of the various departments of the government, expenditures on health and education, transfer payments, subsidies to state enterprises which sell their output at below-cost prices, and gross expenditures of the machine tractor station complex.[1] Since budgetary receipts, the largest single source of funds, are not earmarked for specific expenditures, there is no way of determining how the one category of expenditures which is directly relevant to economic development, viz. gross investment, was financed. We are limited to discussing the sources of finance of the whole of the "nonconsumption" activities of the Soviet state, loosely defining "nonconsumption" as the sum of goods and services purchased by the state plus transfer payments to the household. Because of our interest in how the state planned its economic expansion, investment from private profits and private depreciation funds will not be considered; private investment expenditures were, however, insignificant in all but the first year or two of the period under review. Discussion will center around the first three Five-Year Plan periods, i.e. from 1928/1929, when the first Plan went into operation, until 1940, the third and last completed year of the Third Plan (which was truncated by World War II). This period is adequate

Part of the research for this paper was accomplished while I was attached to the Russian Research Center, Harvard University. The financial assistance of that organization is gratefully acknowledged, as are the critical comments of Mathilda Holzman and Gregory Grossman.

[1] Before 1930 the transportation and communications systems were included in the budget on a gross basis; this was true of almost all state enterprises during War Communism (1918-1921).

to illustrate the problems faced and policies adopted by Soviet planners.

Before turning to the sources of finance, a few words will be devoted to a consideration of the significance of money and finance for the functioning of the Soviet economy. Those unfamiliar with the Soviet economy may be misled by the emphasis on the words "planning" and "controls" into thinking that money is not important in the Soviet economy. While the Soviets rely more on direct economic controls than any other nation in the world today, and while such controls, where they are used, substitute for money and the market mechanism as the allocator of scarce resources, money has not been replaced by direct controls. There are no direct controls in large sectors of the Soviet economy. Consumer goods, for example, are distributed at present by the market mechanism; the amount of consumer goods which any household can purchase is determined by its current and accumulated earnings. The labor market, though less free than it was in the 1930's, still depends primarily on differential wage payments for the allocation of labor. Other markets (raw materials and producer goods), though on the whole more subject to direct controls, do nevertheless contain substantial areas in which free market forces are still allowed to operate. Even where allocation is accomplished directly, to the extent that prices provide the planners with a basis for allocation, money functions as a standard of value, if not as a medium of exchange.[2] Failure by the Soviets to keep their financial house in order will have a deleterious effect on the economy (through reduced incentives, misallocation of resources, etc.) so long as markets and prices are used by them to perform economic functions.

1. *Choice among Sources of Finance*

A listing of the major Soviet sources of finance has a conventional ring: direct taxation of the population, sales taxes, profits taxes, sales of government bonds to the population and to state institutions, retained profits of enterprises, depreciation reserves, bank credit, household savings. While there are many real similarities between the above categories and their Western counterparts, closer examination reveals substantial differences both of an institutional nature and in their relative importance. A cursory glance at Table 1 reveals

[2] Money continues to flow, of course, but the possessor of money has so little option as to its use that the role of money in the transaction must be considered trivial.

FINANCING SOVIET DEVELOPMENT

TABLE 1

Sources of Soviet Finance as Percentages
of Adjusted Total, 1937

Major indirect or commodity taxes	71.9
Direct taxes	3.8
Sales of government bonds to population	4.1
Miscellaneous budgetary receipts	7.3
Retained profits of state enterprises	4.6
Indivisible fund of collective farms	1.7
Depreciation reserves	5.4
Voluntary household savings	1.0
Increase of currency in circulation	1.4

Source: Taken from Tables 3 and 4 below. The above items total to more than 100 per cent for reasons discussed in the notes to Tables 3 and 4.

that the financial path followed by the Soviet Union differs in several significant respects from the paths followed by many Western nations.

FOREIGN BORROWING

Outstanding for its absence from Table 1 is foreign borrowing. I do not think it would be possible to single out over the past 150 years many nations which have industrialized, especially in the early stages, without some foreign aid. The Soviets industrialized without any significant foreign aid, not because they wanted to— they did not—but because the Western World was hostile to them[3] and they, in turn, were hostile to and distrustful of Western nations. This was not a climate in which international capital was likely to flow freely and abundantly. With some minor exceptions, the Soviets paid in gold, commodities, and in imperial crown jewels for all goods purchased from other nations in the interwar period. In recent years the situation has changed somewhat. During the war, of course, the Russians received considerable help from the United States in the form of lend-lease shipments; and since the war repara- tions have contributed, in some years, respectable sums to budget receipts.[4] Finally, there may be considerable capital flow between the Soviet Union and the countries within its political orbit, but on this there is very little reliable information as to either amount or direction.

[3] And not only for ideological reasons. Remember that Western investors took a heavy loss when the Bolsheviks refused to honor the very large foreign debts of the Russian imperial government.

[4] Amounting to as much as 3 to 4 per cent of total budget receipts.

VOLUNTARY SAVINGS

The Soviets have always encouraged voluntary saving by the population. A large network of banks in both urban and rural areas has been developed to foster the saving habit; the 5 per cent interest on time deposits (six months or more) is the highest obtainable in the Soviet Union;[5] the Currency Reform of December 1947 applied a much more favorable conversion rate to savings deposits than to either cash or government bonds. Nevertheless, understandably enough, savings have never amounted to much in the Soviet Union. The annual increment to savings deposits is only a fraction of 1 per cent of total household money income.[6] The average Soviet citizen is in much too great need of current goods and services to put aside large sums of money to meet future needs. And those future needs which induce the greatest amount of saving in Western nations (e.g. provision against sickness, accidents, old age, unemployment, etc.) are relatively well provided for in the Soviet Union by a comprehensive social security system. Furthermore, the incentive to save must certainly have been vitiated by twenty years of rapidly rising prices in the consumer goods markets, not ending until the currency reform of 1947.[7] Finally, of course, the state imposes upon the population such a high rate of compulsory saving that little is left to individual initiative.[8]

COMMODITY TAXES

Most of the compulsory savings of the economy are collected by the state in the form of taxes and are reflected in the budget accounts;[9] and indirect or commodity taxes are responsible for from two-thirds to three-fourths of budgetary receipts. The three principal commodity taxes are the turnover tax, deductions from the

[5] Demand deposits pay only 3 per cent.

[6] Cf. F. D. Holzman, "The Burden of Soviet Taxation," *American Economic Review*, September 1953, Table 1.

[7] Since the currency reform, consumer goods prices have declined steadily; this may eventually have a positive effect on the incentive to save. From 1928 to 1947, consumer goods prices increased, on the average, about twentyfold. Cf. Naum Jasny, *The Soviet Price System*, Stanford University Press, 1951, Chap. 2.

[8] Perhaps it should also be noted that the Soviet rural population appears to have the usual peasant distrust of banks and prefers to hold a large part of its savings in the form of cash.

[9] The Soviet state budget is a consolidated budget consisting of the all-Union, republican, and local budgets. It is equivalent to the sum of the federal, state, and local budgets in the United States.

profits of state enterprises (profits tax), and the social insurance markup. The turnover tax is essentially a sales tax levied, at present, exclusively on consumer goods—except for petroleum and petroleum products, where the tax substitutes for explicit rent payments. Before 1949 it was levied on producer goods as well, but for fiscal control of the tax-paying enterprises rather than for revenue. The rates on consumer goods are highly differentiated, varying from 1 per cent of the *selling price* on some commodities to as much as 90 per cent on others.[10]

The deduction from profits is correctly not called a tax on enterprise[11] by the Soviets because it applies to nationalized industries. The state does not tax the profits of its own industries; it simply transfers money from one state account to another. From a fiscal point of view the deduction from profits, as part of profits, adds to the price paid by the consumer; in this respect it does not differ from the turnover tax and can properly be considered a commodity tax on the household. Every enterprise pays a minimum 10 per cent tax on profits for purposes of fiscal control. The remaining profits are used as needed to finance investment planned for the enterprise and to make payments into the Directors' Fund.[12] Any surplus above these needs is *deducted* into the budget.

The social insurance markup is a form of payroll tax, and for our purposes can be looked upon as adding to the price of commodities bought by the household, just like the turnover and profits taxes. The receipts from this tax are derived as additions to the wage funds of enterprises, the percentage varying from 3.7 to 10.7, depending on conditions of employment and other factors in the separate branches of the economy. It is claimed that part of the receipts from this tax are earmarked for sickness and old age insurance.[13]

Why is commodity taxation the dominant method of extracting

[10] Looked upon as a markup over cost, as is customary in the West, the tax rates are much higher, of course. A 50 per cent tax becomes one of 100 per cent; a 90 per cent tax becomes one of 900 per cent.

[11] Although for convenience it will be referred to as a profits tax.

[12] For incentive reasons from 1 to 5 per cent of planned profits and 15 to 45 per cent of overplan profits are deducted into the Directors' Fund. These amounts are disbursed as bonuses to workers and managers, for workers' housing, for cultural projects, and for extra-plan investment in the enterprises.

[13] We might also have included in the category of taxes which enter the commodity price structure the incomes of economic organizations which are allocated "to the trade unions and special funds for workers' training and education" (cf. Abram Bergson, "Soviet National Income and Product," *Quarterly Journal of Economics*, May 1950, p. 288).

savings from the population in the Soviet Union? Conversely, why is little reliance placed upon income (direct) taxation, the form of levy preferred in the United States and in many other Western nations?[14] Soviet preference for commodity taxation is certainly not to be explained on ideological grounds. In fact, the predominance of the turnover tax among Soviet taxes has proved embarrassing to Soviet economists. Marxist writers consistently attacked indirect taxes as socially inequitable and regressive; bad associations also stem from the reliance of the tsars on highly regressive excise taxes (especially on alcoholic beverages) for the bulk of their revenue. That the Soviets rely on commodity taxation in spite of their "ideological" bias attests to its superiority for their purposes.[15]

Soviet preference for commodity taxation appears to rest primarily on three considerations. First, there is the "money illusion," which has it that workers are more conscious of the impact on their economic position of changes in wages than of the impact produced by changes in prices. A corollary to this is the hypothesis that workers are more sensitive to changes in direct taxes (and thus in take-home pay) than to changes in indirect taxes (reflected in commodity prices). The money illusion, therefore, would cause commodity and income taxes of equal size to have different impacts on work incentives. This is particularly important in the Soviet Union, where almost all income is earned income. Analytically, it is possible to separate the impact of taxes on incentives into at least two categories: the effect on the work-leisure ratio and the effect on differential wages as a factor in choosing between jobs. Most writers dealing with this subject concentrate on the work-leisure ratio, arguing that high taxes, and particularly high marginal rates of tax, reduce the incentive to work, and that indirect taxes, as a consequence of the

[14] The Soviet income tax on the urban population does not differ substantially from the income taxes in other countries except that different social and economic classes pay according to different rate schedules in application of Soviet "class policy." Thus workers, artists, professionals with private practices (e.g. lawyers and doctors), and private shopkeepers pay at rapidly ascending rates (on identical money incomes) from left to right. The rural population pays a very different sort of tax (called the agricultural tax) because the bulk of peasant income is in kind. This necessitates, among other things, fairly cumbersome methods of assessing personal income and estimating the amount of tax to be paid. The agricultural tax discriminates in favor of the collective farmer and against the private peasant.

[15] In fact, for about twenty years they have not referred to it as a tax on the population, but rather as "accumulation of socialized industry," implying that the amounts returned to the budget are a result solely of great increases in productivity.

illusion, minimize the disincentive effects of taxes. This line of reasoning ignores the income effect of taxation,[16] or at least assumes that the substitution effect between work and leisure is more important than the income effect. There is no empirical evidence, to my knowledge, to support this assumption, and, in fact, the income effect may actually be strong enough to induce Soviet workers to greater effort. If this were the case, it could not be argued that the Soviet choice of commodity taxation preserves work incentives.

It can be argued, without equivocation, that the Soviets took advantage of the money illusion effects of commodity taxation to preserve the effectiveness of their differential wage structure as an incentive mechanism for allocating labor. In order to attract workers, Soviet policy has been to pay higher wages to persons in jobs requiring greater skills, in expanding industries, and in jobs or areas where work conditions are undesirable. Up until the late 1920's or early 1930's this policy had not been implemented successfully, hampered to a considerable extent as it was by the hangovers of an earlier "equalitarian" philosophy regarding wage differentials.[17] An attempt was made to improve the situation; in 1931 Stalin intervened and, in a speech calling for greater wage differentials, set the new policy. He said: "In a number of our factories, wage scales are drawn up in such a way as to practically wipe out the difference between skilled labour and unskilled labour, between heavy work and light work. The consequence of wage equalization is that the unskilled worker lacks the incentive to become a skilled worker and is thus deprived of the prospect of advancement; . . . in order to get skilled workers we must give the unskilled worker a stimulus and prospect of advancement, of rising to a higher position. . . ."[18] Bergson's wage study indicates that wage differentials in the Soviet Union in 1934 were about as great as those in the United States at a comparable stage (1904) of economic development.[19]

In the late 1920's and early 1930's, at the same time that Soviet wage differentials were being increased for incentive reasons, taxes were also being increased. The average rate of taxation about doubled from 1926 to 1936, increasing by substantial amounts al-

[16] That persons having their incomes reduced by taxes would tend to work harder.

[17] Cf. Abram Bergson, *The Structure of Soviet Wages*, Harvard University Press, 1946, Chaps. 13 and 14.

[18] Joseph Stalin, *Problems of Leninism*, Moscow, Foreign Languages Publishing House, 1940, pp. 371-373.

[19] Bergson, *The Structure of Soviet Wages*, as cited.

most every year of the period;[20] by 1930 it amounted to about 50 per cent of household income.[21] Clearly, Soviet differential wage policy was in danger of being weakened by Soviet tax policy. Reliance upon income taxation under these circumstances would have had a much more adverse impact on the incentive-wage system than commodity taxation for at least two reasons. First, under the Soviet pay-as-you-earn system of income taxation, workers are as likely to base job decisions on differential take-home pay as on gross wage differentials. On the other hand, if no income tax were levied, gross wage differentials would probably retain much of their incentive effect, even with high levels of commodity taxation. Second, for political reasons income taxation would almost necessarily have to be progressive, or at least proportional, thereby reducing wage differentials relatively as well as absolutely; this would not necessarily be so for sales taxation, especially when the tax is hidden, and when it has a highly differentiated rate structure, as is the case in the Soviet Union.[22] This facet of the money illusion is undoubtedly an important reason for Soviet use of commodity taxation.

A second factor explaining Soviet reliance on commodity taxation is administrative in nature. The turnover tax, particularly in the early stages of its development, was levied on and collected from state industrial enterprises (procurement agencies in agriculture) and wholesale organizations. This provided the cheapest and least evadable method of collecting money taxes from the population since the number of industrial enterprises and wholesale organizations was not large and they maintained relatively good money accounts; it also provided a continuous source of funds—the larger enterprises made daily payments to the budget. These considerations were quite crucial in the late 1920's and the early 1930's, before the administrative apparatus of the state had achieved anything like its present-day efficiency. Reliance upon income taxation would have meant levying and collecting taxes from 30 to 40 million householders, many of whom were still illiterate. Furthermore, at that time a large segment of the peasant population still had not been herded into col-

---

[20] Cf. Holzman, *op. cit.*, Table 3.   [21] *Ibid.*, Table 3.

[22] The Soviet turnover tax appears to have had a somewhat regressive rate structure in the prewar period; the postwar structure seems to be considerably less regressive and may be roughly proportional. The rate structure is much too complex, and the information on income-expenditure patterns much too limited, for us to come to any but the most tentative conclusions on this matter, however. Cf. F. D. Holzman, *Soviet Taxation: The Fiscal and Monetary Problems of a Planned Economy*, Harvard University Press, 1955, Chap. 6.

FINANCING SOVIET DEVELOPMENT

lective farms, where it could be reached without excessive costs by tax collectors.

A third consideration, and one which is stressed by Soviet economists, is the use of the turnover tax to facilitate price planning. The Soviets have attempted to maintain a market for consumer goods in which free choice prevails. Prices are not set freely by decentralized agents as is usually the case in Western nations; rather, prices are centrally administered and the state is responsible for adjusting relative prices. Maintenance of appropriate price flexibility is, for obvious reasons, facilitated by the existence of a large element of tax in the cost-price structure. In fact, without either a commodity tax or a subsidy (which can be considered a negative commodity tax in this case) it would not be possible to alter relative prices much faster than relative changes in productivity would permit[23] (i.e. prices would approximate long-run cost).

INCOME TAXATION

In spite of the advantages and magnitude of Soviet commodity taxation, the population is also required to pay an income tax. The only significant function which this tax seems to serve is to discourage private practice by professionals[24] (e.g. doctors and lawyers) and other "nonworker" elements in the urban population. These groups pay a discriminatorily high tax, which reaches 55 and 65 per cent, respectively, on incomes in excess of 70,000 rubles; workers and salaried employees, who comprise 90 per cent or more of the nonagricultural labor force, pay according to a schedule which reaches a maximum rate of 13 per cent on all income over 12,000 rubles annually. While the "class policy" feature of the income tax may have been important twenty years ago, before the private sector of the economy had been thoroughly squelched, it can hardly be considered so any more. Moreover, the tax certainly has little fiscal importance.[25] It is difficult to understand why the Soviets continue to use direct levies on income when they could be replaced very easily by a small increase in commodity taxation. Perhaps they are continued through inertia, or because the Soviets wish to maintain intact the direct tax apparatus for possible future use.

[23] This is especially true since the Soviets have virtually no explicit rent payments but include them implicitly in the turnover tax.

[24] Also perhaps to extract the "economic rent" from such practices.

[25] What we have said of the urban income tax applies also to the agricultural tax. The agricultural tax discriminates against the private farmer and in favor of the collective farmer.

SALES OF GOVERNMENT BONDS

Sales of government bonds constitute, in effect, another form of direct levy on the Soviet population. Similarity of these bond sales to taxation rests on the following characteristics: considerable social pressure is brought to bear upon the population to subscribe from two to four weeks' wages a year; these amounts are deducted from workers' wages every month just as direct taxes are; most bonds are not redeemable until the full term has expired;[26] a series of conversions (1930, 1936, 1938) and the 1947 Currency Reform have together resulted in extended maturities, reduced interest rates, and a reduction by two-thirds, in 1947, of the value of all outstanding obligations; rapidly rising prices have steadily reduced the real value of these highly illiquid assets. The disadvantages of direct taxes, in general, seem to apply to sales of bonds also, although bond sales in the late 1920's may have been more "voluntary" in nature. To the extent that they were (are) voluntary, disincentive effects would, of course, have been (be) reduced.

Since the Currency Reform of 1947, consumer goods prices have declined steadily. If this trend should be continued, the usefulness of bonds as a form of taxation will have been substantially reduced. On the one hand, falling price levels will cause the real rate of interest on the bonds to exceed the nominal rate so that, in time, repayment may become a real burden on the current Soviet budget. Before 1947 the real rate of interest was undoubtedly negative due to continuous inflation—the burden of repayment was insignificant.[27] On the other hand, it seems doubtful that price levels will fall rapidly enough to increase voluntary savings, especially in the form of illiquid bonds, to the amount of the annual issue of bonds. Thus, as prices fall the disadvantage of larger "real" repayments would seem to more than offset the advantage of smaller disincentive effects as the bonds become a slightly less unattractive form of investment.

[26] Lottery winners have their bonds redeemed at the same time they receive their lottery prizes. At present, one-third of the subscribers to a bond issue eventually win lottery prizes.

[27] Of course, very few bonds were ever actually paid off: the conversions put off repayments in the 1930's and the currency reform of 1947 eliminated the need for repayment on two-thirds of all outstanding obligations. However, even if there had been no conversions, the real value of ten-year bonds at maturity could hardly ever have amounted to more than about one-quarter of original value, so rapid was the rise in consumer goods prices in the pre-1948 period. Cf. Naum Jasny, *The Soviet Economy during the Plan Era*, Stanford University Press, 1951, p. 58.

RETAINED PROFITS

Funds for investment are also available in the form of retained profits accumulated by both state enterprises and collective farms.[28] The annual plans usually call for a substantial part of the investment in the fixed and working capital of established state enterprises to come out of the retained profits of these enterprises. State enterprises also receive grants from the budget for the same purpose. It is difficult to understand what difference, if any, there is between these two methods of finance, and why the Soviets do not concentrate on either one or the other. It is frequently contended that managerial incentives are sharpened if managers are allowed to finance investment from retained profits rather than by budget subsidy. There is the implication in the case of retained profits that, if the manager is more (less) efficient, he may have more (less) funds to invest because profits will be larger (smaller). This implication does not square with the usual conception of an enterprise's fulfilling its investment plan from retained profits and then automatically transferring the remainder, after deductions into the Directors' Fund, into the budget.[29] Part of the Directors' Fund is, of course, used for extra-plan investment; but the incentive to increase profits by reducing costs and increasing output exists regardless of whether the enterprise has its own profits to begin with or receives a budget subsidy.[30] Soviet preference for budget-financed investment probably lies in the greater administrative flexibility which this method *may* confer; it is, undoubtedly, simpler to alter investment plans in the short run if funds are doled out from the budget than if they are accumulated by enterprises in which the investment is planned.

The collective farms (and other cooperatives) not nationalized and the property of the state (though under strict state control, of course) must meet the bulk of their investment requirements from their own resources. The farms are required by law to withhold

[28] This is also true of the consumer and producer cooperatives, but the amounts have never been significant.

[29] More often than not, the retained profit of a group of enterprises has been redistributed among them for investment purposes by the administrative head of the group (or *glavk*, translated "chief administration"). Recently, the power of the *glavk* to do this was reduced. Cf. *New York Times*, August 14, 1952, article by Harry Schwartz.

[30] This is because the bulk of the deduction into the Directors' Fund is based on overplan profits, and a firm which reduced planned losses by a certain amount would be considered to have exceeded the plan in the same direction as one which increased positive profits.

from 12 to 20 per cent of their total net money income (after meeting costs of production, excluding payments to labor) in a so-called "indivisible fund" which is to be used for capital investment.[31] Most of the current money income of the collectives is, of course, distributed among the collective farmers in payment for their labor. Investment by the collective farms (except in kind) has never amounted to much because most of their machinery requirements (tractors, combines, etc.) are met, for a price, by the state-owned machine tractor stations (MTS). The MTS have been since 1938 included in the budget on a gross basis; all of their expenditures, including new investment, are financed by budget subsidy. Collective farms with insufficient funds to finance their investment requirements can borrow small sums from the Agricultural Bank.

FUND FOR AMORTIZATION

Most economic organizations which use capital equipment are required to consider depreciation a cost of production and to maintain depreciation reserves. Western economists generally consider that these reserves understate depreciation in view of the extensive Soviet cost inflation, because of the fact that original rather than replacement cost is used in computing depreciation, and because inexpert handling of equipment appears to be widespread and may have had the effect of reducing the physical life of much equipment. Originally, the reserves were devoted exclusively to replacing old, and constructing new, equipment. Since 1938, part of these funds have been made available for capital repair.

MINOR SOURCES OF BUDGET RECEIPTS

The more important sources of budget revenue have already been noted: turnover tax, deductions from profits of state enterprises, the social insurance markup, direct taxes on the population, and sales of government bonds. The budget derives revenue from many other sources. Customs are, perhaps, the most important of these. In the prewar period they amounted to as much as 2 per cent of total budget receipts in some years. During the war, receipts from tariffs on regular imports were strongly supplemented by local currency resulting from lend-lease sales; since the war, regular receipts have

[31] Receipts from sale of surplus property or livestock are also deposited in the "indivisible fund." Initially, this fund is based on the value of the property and money payments of the collective farmers to the collective farm at the time the farm is organized.

been supplemented by reparations. Other sources are an inheritance tax which at present is simply a fee for the processing of legal documents, fees for commercial forestry and fishing, fines, licenses, the *gross* receipts of the machine tractor stations, and taxes on the profits of the collective farms and other cooperatives. Taken individually, these items do not generally provide much revenue; in the aggregate, however, their contribution is not insubstantial.

THE STATE BANK: CHANGES IN CURRENCY IN CIRCULATION

A substantial share of the working capital requirements of the economy are financed by the State Bank (Gosbank) in the form of short-term loans. In the early 1930's, when the basis of the present Soviet banking system was established, the Bank was given authority to extend short-term credit to finance goods in transit, seasonal production processes and expenses, and other temporary working capital needs connected with the production and turnover of goods.[32] Permanent working capital was to be furnished to new enterprises needing it by the budget in the form of interest-free grants; additions to permanent working capital were to be financed either by the budget or out of the retained profits of the enterprises. If the working capital needs of enterprises had been seasonally stable, there would have been no necessity, in the original Soviet scheme of things, for the short-term credit operations of the State Bank. "The function of short-term credit in the Soviet economy . . . [was], broadly speaking, to level out fluctuation in the flow of materials and goods."[33] The functions of the State Bank were extended in the mid-1930's, however, when it was authorized to finance a large percentage of the *permanent* working capital requirements of trade organizations; and again in 1939 when it was assigned the task of regularly financing part of the *permanent* working capital needs of heavy industry. This deviation from the original principle which guided the granting of short-term credit was introduced with the purpose of giving the State Bank control over the activities of enterprises in these sectors.[34] Apparently, these enterprises "experi-

[32] Cf. Alexander Baykov, *The Development of the Soviet Economic System*, London, Cambridge University Press, 1946, p. 404.

[33] L. E. Hubbard, *Soviet Money and Finance*, London, Macmillan, 1936, p. 228.

[34] This refers to the well-known "control by the ruble." That is to say, by making state enterprises dependent upon the State Bank for funds, the Bank is placed in a position in which it can supervise and check the progress of enterprises, and put pressure on enterprises which are not operating satisfactorily or according to plan.

enced little variation in working capital requirements, and thus were able to escape the control and supervisory functions of the Gosbank."[35] This is the situation at present; it should be noted, however, that during the war the Bank was authorized to advance large credits for the reconstruction of enterprises in liberated areas, to make payments to military personnel under certain special conditions, to facilitate the evacuation of industries eastward during the German advance, and to meet other extraordinary needs. Presumably, credit is no longer granted for these special purposes.

It is important to note that the State Bank is, in normal times, the *only* source of currency issue in the U.S.S.R. With the exception of the years 1941-1943—years of great internal disruption, when the budget ran deficits which were financed by currency issue—short-term loans to finance the above-noted working capital needs of enterprise have been the sole source of new currency in circulation. The extension of new short-term loans does not always, or usually, lead to a currency increment, however. New currency is issued to finance short-term loans only if no currency is returned by the population from other sources. Other sources of funds are excesses of budget receipts over budget expenditures, of retained profits over investment financed from retained profits, of depreciation reserves over expenditures from depreciation reserves, etc. These funds and others mentioned above are all reflected in the accounts of the State Bank either by direct deposit or indirectly through the deposit in the State Bank of the reserves of the special banks for long-term investment (see below). To the extent that currency receipts in the State Bank are greater than expenditures (including long-term loans) from these receipts, new short-term credit can be extended without the issuance of currency; in fact, if there should be a surplus of deposits over expenditures, including short-term loans, currency will be withdrawn from circulation. If, on the other hand, expenditures, including short-term loans, exceed receipts, new currency is circulated. If, therefore, we were interested in measuring the amount of Soviet nonconsumption expenditures (as we are below) from sources of finance, we would not include gross changes in the amount of short-term credit outstanding; this would involve a double count because bank loans are an expenditure item in the national financial accounts. We simply add (subtract) increases (decreases) in cur-

[35] Gregory Grossman, "The Union of Soviet Socialist Republics," in *Comparative Banking Systems*, B. H. Beckhart, editor, Columbia University Press, 1954, pp. 733-768.

FINANCING SOVIET DEVELOPMENT

rency in circulation. To clarify this point, an estimate of Soviet financial accounts for 1936 is presented in Table 2.

TABLE 2

Estimate of Soviet National Financial Accounts, 1936
(*billions of rubles*)

Receipts		*Expenditures*	
1. Budget receipts (including bonds)	94.4	1. Budget expenditures	92.5[a]
2. Retained profits		2. Investment and other expenditures financed outside budget	
a. State enterprises	8.9	a. From retained profits	
b. Collective farms	1.5	i. State enterprises	8.9[b]
c. Others	?	ii. Others	2.6[c]
3. Depreciation reserves	4.9	b. Depreciation	?
		c. Net increase in short-term credit (State Bank)	8.1
		d. Long-term loans to collective farms and farmers	1.5[d]
Subtotal	109.7		
4. Currency issue	1.6	Subtotal	113.6
5. Discrepancy	2.3	3. Currency withdrawal	0
Total	113.6	Total	113.6

Figures for which sources are not cited were taken from tables later in this chapter.

[a] Same source as budget receipts.

[b] Planned investment in fixed capital from S. N. Prokopovich, *Biulleten'*, March 1936, No. 127, p. 30. Planned investment in working capital from G. F. Grinko, *Financial Program of the U.S.S.R. for 1936*, Moscow, Foreign Languages Publishing House, 1936, p. 15.

[c] At least 2.6 billion rubles of other investment from profits can be estimated from A. Smilga, "Finansy sotsialisticheskogo gosudarstvo" ("Finances of Socialist State"), *Problemy ekonomiki* (*Problems of Economics*), 1937, No. 2, p. 115.

[d] K. Plotnikov, *Biudzhet sotsialisticheskogo gosudarstva* (*Budget of the Socialist States*), Moscow, p. 140.

It would hardly be necessary to discuss the special banks for long-term investment had they not been misnamed banks. Their primary function is to disburse and supervise the use of funds previously collected rather than to create new credit. The bulk of these funds are budgetary grants to enterprises in the national economy for investment in plant and equipment and working capital. Other funds held and disbursed by these banks are retained profits of state enterprises, the indivisible fund, retained profits of other cooperatives, and that part of the reserves for depreciation used to finance new investment.[36] Apparently, the special banks "lend" to both individuals and enterprises, but the amounts involved are

[36] The part used for capital repair is deposited in the State Bank.

not significant and will be ignored here except for long-term loans by the Agriculture Bank to collective farms. The special banks keep their excess funds on deposit with the State Bank; thus the State Bank is seen to be the custodian of excess investment funds for virtually the whole Soviet economy. Long-term loans of the special banks, like short-term loans, are expenditure, not receipt, items in Soviet financial accounts; they are reflected in "sources of finance" only insofar as they affect the amount of currency which has to be circulated by the State Bank to finance its short-term credit operations.

TAXATION IN KIND

No mention has been made so far of taxation in kind of agriculture because it does not *directly* provide the state with monetary reserves for financing nonconsumption expenditures; indirectly, however, it does. The tax in kind takes the form of compulsory deliveries of agricultural products by collective farms and peasant farmers to state and cooperative procurement agencies. While the farms and peasants are not uncompensated for their deliveries, the price paid by the state (called procurement price) is usually far from sufficient to cover costs of production; and, of course, it is only a fraction of the retail price (minus processing and distribution costs) at which the state resells these items to the population. The high retail price is achieved by superimposing a turnover tax on procurement price plus costs of processing and distribution. The portion of the turnover tax collected by virtue of the below-cost procurement price is the monetary equivalent of the tax in kind on that part of the compulsory deliveries sold to the household.[37] Delivered produce not sold back to the household (e.g. stockpiled or used in the production of final products not sold to the household) is not reflected in the budget and may be classified as "investment in kind" by the state.

This classification holds in all circumstances in which producing agents are directly paid less than cost of production or less than the value of their product (or not at all). A major case in point is, of course, that of unfree labor in the Soviet Union. The evidence indicates that workers in this category are remunerated at less than

[37] If the procurement price of a bushel of grain which cost 40 rubles to produce were only 20 rubles and the state resold the grain (as bread) for 100 rubles, the turnover tax on a bushel would be 80 rubles, of which it could be said that 20 rubles (40 minus 20) was paid by the producer and 60 (100 minus 40) by the consumer.

the free market wage for comparable performance.[38] To the extent that the products of unfree labor are sold to the population at high prices and add to the receipts of the turnover tax, the tax in kind on unfree labor (in the form of below-market wage payments) is reflected in budgetary receipts. To the extent that the services of these laborers are directed into nonconsumption activities such as gold mining, construction, irrigation projects, and the building of dams and roads (and these are the sorts of activities typically handled by the MVD), they may be classed as investment in kind by the state.

It should be noted that there is still another important source of investment in kind in the Soviet Union. We refer to that part of the income in kind of the agricultural sector of the economy which is neither taxed away by the state nor consumed by peasant households, but which is devoted to the following years' production (e.g. seed, feed, stockpiles, increasing livestock herds). Needless to say, none of the above categories of investment in kind are readily susceptible to measurement; nor can we, for that matter, even say what part of the turnover tax is a tax on the consumer and what part is a tax on the agricultural producer.[39]

How is Soviet preference for taxation in kind of agriculture to be explained? Basically, the difference between taxation of industrial income and taxation of agricultural income stems from the fact that industry and the output of industry are almost 100 per cent state-owned, while agriculture consists primarily of collective farms, which are not owned by the state, and of individual peasant farmers.[40] This form of organization of agriculture, rather than state-owned farms with the farmers receiving wages, creates two serious problems for the state. First, the state must secure by some means a substantial share of the output of the agricultural sector to be transferred to the city for personal and industrial consumption and for export. Taxation of the money incomes of agricultural producers would not necessarily secure this result: if the amount of the tax were calculated on the basis of actual money income, the peasants

[38] Bergson, in his famous study of Soviet wages, demonstrated that relative wages in the Soviet Union appear to reflect relative differences in productivity (cf. Bergson, *The Structure of Soviet Wages*, as cited, pp. 207-209). On this basis one can take the free-market wage for a particular job as a rough measure of the value of the job performance to the state.

[39] This separation is attempted for grains, on the basis of heroic assumptions, in Holzman, *Soviet Taxation*, as cited, Chap. 7.

[40] The *sovkhozy*, or state farms, are owned by the state but produce a very small percentage of total agricultural output.

could reduce their money income, hence tax payments, by cutting down sales of agricultural output; even if taxable income were based on production, the peasants could, by cutting back on their consumption of industrial consumer goods, still avoid the necessity of having to sell as much agricultural output as the state needed to meet its requirements. These are not idle possibilities in a country where adequately feeding the population has been—and will continue to be, barring unforeseen developments—a very serious economic problem. By means of money taxation, alone, it might prove impossible to reduce the food consumption of the peasants below a level consistent with the needs of the nation as a whole for food. Second, as we have seen, for incentive and other reasons the state collects most of its budget receipts in the form of indirect taxes. Since the bulk of the turnover tax, the major indirect tax, is collected in the form of a markup on agricultural products (because food is the principal item of personal consumption in the Soviet Union), the incidence of the turnover tax on the agricultural population considered as consumers is relatively small because a large part of its income takes the form of consumption of home-produced food. Another form of tax on the peasantry must be substituted for indirect money taxation if a high rate of saving for the economy as a whole is to be maintained. The tax in kind solves these two problems at once for the state: it insures state procurement of the required amount of agricultural produce, and it forces a high level of savings upon the agricultural population.

RECENT DEVELOPMENTS IN SOVIET MONETARY POLICY*

Raymond P. Powell

I had best preface my remarks by saying, what perhaps goes without saying, that I do not have sufficient information to discuss -- from a firm basis in fact -- the topic which I am supposed to discuss. While my predicament is scarcely unique, it is none the less awkward: the Soviet authorities have refused since the War, both before and after Stalin's death, to release anything more than fragments of monetary data. In particular, nothing like a complete balance sheet of the State Bank has been published in the postwar period, or, for that matter, since 1937. Some figures on total State Bank loans, for years since 1950, have been released, and there are a couple of figures on deposits of collective farms at the Bank. But there are no currency figures available and no figures on the deposit balances of the principal holders of such balances, state enterprises and the State Budget. Annual budget data have been released, but even these are incomplete and ambiguous at a number of points, one of which I shall describe shortly. In sum, while there is enough information to entice one into speculating, there is not enough information for well-founded speculation.

I shall put my comments -- my speculations -- in the form of a comparison of two periods, pre-war and postwar, where the data for the first period, though imperfect, are vastly better than for the second. [1] For brevity and simplicity, I shall take "pre-war" to mean only the period from 1932 to the outbreak of war and "postwar" to mean only the period from approximately 1948 on. By so restricting my time periods, I can disregard the rather special circumstances of the credit reforms of 1930-1931 and those of the war and immediate postwar periods, through the currency conversion of 1947. I address myself to the question: How far is any significant difference observable between pre-war monetary policy and institutions and those of the postwar period, especially the period since 1953? I turn first to banking policy.

In the 1930's, the State Bank, in accordance with its statutes, restricted its lending operations almost entirely to short-term loans against inventories held by enterprises and against bills outstanding on goods shipped, i.e., to loans intended to meet particular working capital needs. Initially, the purposes for which the Bank could lend were limited to seasonal and other temporary working capital requirements. In the course of the 1930's, the range of eligible assets was broadened to include a share of non-seasonal inventories, first in trade and subsequently in heavy industry. But at any given time, the purposes for which the Bank could lend were precisely specified, and neither the Bank nor its customers had any significant option in choosing the purposes for which, or the assets against which, bank loans could be made.

*This paper was presented at the Southern Economic Association Meetings in December 1957. Since its preparation, a considerable but by no means complete body of Soviet monetary statistics has become available. A number of the issues raised here have also come to be discussed, openly and quite revealingly, in Soviet publications.

At no time, so far as I can determine, did the Bank set for itself, or have set for it, any quantitative objective, apart from that implied by its qualitative criteria. Certainly interest rates were not varied to control the demand for loans. Certainly the Bank did not act, as it conceivably could have acted, as a residual source of funds, financing those capital needs, short-term or long, which could not be financed from budgetary sources or retained earnings. Certainly there is no hint of a suggestion that the volume of the Bank's loans was ever varied out of concern for the volume of its monetary liabilities.

The Bank, it is true, was supposed, in the course of its lending operations, to perform certain control functions which, if performed, could either alter the volume of eligible assets or could permit the Bank some discretion in observing the ordinary eligibility requirements. That is to say, the Bank did have some administrative control over the granting of particular loans and thus some control over the total quantity of loans outstanding. But the range of its discretionary authority was narrow; it appears to have been exceedingly slow to exert such authority as it had; and, in any case, there is no evidence that it exerted that authority with any deliberate intent to affect the total volume of bank loans. On the whole, the Bank automatically and mechanically issued loans to those enterprises which possessed the proper assets and refused loans to those enterprises which lacked the proper assets, regardless of the over-all financial position of the borrower and regardless of the consequences for the total volume of loans outstanding.

There is, of course, nothing novel in the lending policy I have described: this was a "real bills" or "commercial loan" or "Banking School" policy, defended, insofar as it was defended at all and not taken simply as the obvious and natural thing for any respectable bank to do, on grounds which would have been largely familiar to Adam Smith or the founders of the Federal Reserve System. If it was unusual, it was so solely in that the State Bank's adherence to the "commercial loan principle" was more rigid and thoroughgoing than that of banking systems elsewhere which have observed the same principle.

From such a lending policy, one would expect it to follow that the volume of bank loans would move passively with the value of working capital assets against which loans were made, and it is reasonably clear that this is what occurred in the Soviet economy in the 1930's. Changes in the prices of "bankable" assets were reflected, for example, in a doubling of bank loans in the course of 1935 and 1936, when both consumers' and producers' goods prices were adjusted sharply upward. The effect of changes in the physical volume of such assets is best illustrated by an incident lying outside of my chosen time period: from June of 1941 to the middle of 1943, bank loans fell absolutely, an event, incidentally, which Voznesenskii described as "an expression of the laws of reproduction, which forced the volume of credit to correspond to the material stocks of commodities in the country."[2] In general, loans seem to have followed quite closely changes in the value of total inventories; particular kinds of loans, presumably, followed more closely changes in the values of the particular kinds of inventories against which they were made.

One further proposition, which is substantially self-evident, follows from what I have said. Since loans constituted the bulk of the Bank's assets and money -- notes and deposits -- the bulk of its liabilities, the quantity of money generated by the Bank necessarily moved with the volume of its loans. This identity does not hold strictly, and in a less synoptic discussion it would be necessary to account for divergences between the two accounts,[3] but some imprecision may be permissible here. Roughly speaking, the quantity of money supplied to the Soviet economy by the State Bank was, like its loans, passively determined by the value of particular working capital assets held in the enterprise sector. That is to say, there was not, so far as the Bank was concerned, anything which we would recognize as a deliberate monetary policy.

So far as I can make out, no profound change has occurred in the pattern of the Bank's operations in the postwar period. In the middle of 1956, almost the whole of the Bank's loans were still on inventories and bills on goods shipped.[4] There is still no suggestion that any quantitative objectives have supplanted or modified the Bank's qualitative criteria. Though the statistics are sparse, those that are available do not controvert a continued dependence of the volume of loans on the volume of eligible assets in the system. No figures for bank loans prior to the beginning of 1951 have been released, but, from 1944, when loans were near the pre-war level,[5] to 1951, total loans approximately tripled,[6] a change which could plausibly be attributed to increases in physical inventories and to increases in prices over the 1944 level. From January 1951 to January 1957, loans increased by 50%, an increase which is exceptionally low in terms of past experience but which looks to be consistent with a presumed further increase in physical inventories together with a decline in commodity prices. Changes in total bank loans within the latter period -- a sharp rise from January 1951 to January 1953, a slight rise from 1953 to 1954, an absolute decline from 1954 to 1956, and a quite sharp rise, of 22%, from 1956 to 1957 -- appear rather erratic and, without more information on the behavior of inventories than is now at hand, are scarcely explainable in detail.

The most noteworthy changes in the Bank's operations that have occurred are associated with a decree dated August 21, 1954.[7] This decree contained two principal provisions relevant here: It authorized the Bank, at its own discretion, to issue loans to enterprises for periods of 2 to 3 years, for small-scale and unplanned fixed capital expenditures, connected with the introduction of new techniques and equipment. Secondly, it increased somewhat the authority of the Bank to discipline enterprises which were misbehaving -- in terms of costs, profits, or working capital -- and to treat with exceptional generosity enterprises which were performing exceptionally well. Both of these measures appear to me more significant for what they may portend than as accomplished facts.

By July of 1956, loans for so-called fixed capital purposes amounted to only slightly more than 1% of total bank loans outstanding.[8] Given the tightness of the central controls which have heretofore been applied to fixed capital outlays, it is hard to imagine circumstances under which such loans could become a large fraction either of total investment outlays or of total bank loans. On the other hand, the introduction of such loans represents a sharper break with the "commercial loan principle" than any that has been made in the past, and further changes in the same direction are not inconceivable.

The consequences of the increased discretion granted to the Bank as a control agency are not yet clear. The discussion which followed this decree and was reported in Soviet sources[9] is chiefly

of interest for the indications it contains that as late as 1954 the Bank
was still functioning in much the same automatic fashion as I have described for the 1930's. In view of the Bank's hesitancy to exert such
authority as it had, before the War, and, evidently, before 1954, one
might properly doubt that it is now likely to demonstrate any substantial initiative. On the other hand, between the increased discretion of
the Bank and the purported decentralization of industrial management
-- two measures which are presumably parts of a single policy change
-- it is conceivable, though I think not at all likely, that something more
like the kind of bank-customer relation with which we are familiar might
emerge in the Soviet economy.

Let me return to the pre-war period. While, as I have said,
there was nothing recognizable as a monetary policy pursued by the
Bank, there was at least the appearance of a monetary policy in the
operations of the State Budget. Throughout the 1930's, indeed from
1924 on, the Budget reported an annual surplus. While the accounting
of this surplus was peculiar in many ways and mysterious in others,
it appeared to represent approximately actual additions to the Budget's
deposit balances at the State Bank. [10] The Budget, in effect, absorbed
and immobilized a varying but often substantial share of the money
which the Bank pumped into the system.

Oddly enough, I know of no detailed rationalization of this Budget
policy in the pre-war literature, or, to anticipate, in the postwar literature either. In fact, it is not very often discussed at all. In the
1930's, there were suggestions in the literature of an assumed analogy
between public and personal finance. More recently, it has been argued that the surpluses "strengthen the monetary circulation,"[11] which
is probably reasonable if elliptic. But as recently as 1952, Peter Wiles
reported a conversation with Soviet economists in which they spoke of
the budget surplus "in pure Gladstonian terms."[12] And in no instance,
to my knowledge, has any Soviet official or academician argued that
there should be a deliberate and systematic tie between the Bank's creation of money and the Budget's absorption of money. [13]

Examined for year to year changes in the 1930's, the Bank's
and the Budget's operations in fact evidence no systematic tie, at least
of the sort one would expect. For the most part, budget surpluses
(planned and realized) were smallest when increases in bank loans
(planned and realized) were largest. But, over longer periods, especially if one looks back as far as 1928, there was an obvious tendency
of reported surpluses to rise relative to loans and to the total monetary liabilities of the Bank.

As I have already intimated, the Budget has continued in the
postwar period to report surpluses and, indeed, extraordinarily large
surpluses. [14] From 1951 through 1956, reported surpluses amounted
to 141 billion rubles, as against an increase in bank loans over the
same period of only 71 billion. From 1948 through 1950, for which
we do not have loan figures, surpluses amounted to an additional 74
billion rubles. As could be surmised from the figures themselves,
not all of the reported surpluses represented additions to the Budget's
account at the Bank. Of the surpluses of 1948 to 1950, it is reported
that "the greater part" -- and thus not the whole -- were added to the
Budget's deposit balances. [15] From 1951 through 1955, certain budgetary grants to finance the working capital of enterprises were charged
to accumulated surpluses, these transactions, evidently, being recorded
by writing up current budget revenues rather than by omitting the in-

dicated outlays from current budget expenditures. [16] From 1956, these expenditures were supposed to be charged to current revenues. [17] Though some positive relation between the Budget's deposit balances and its reported surpluses evidently still persists, the relation is obviously a rather loose one.

We do have some further information to the point. In 1951, it was reported that accumulated budget surpluses, together with the Bank's capital, "predominate" in the "resources" (i.e., liabilities and net worth) of the Bank. [18] Since capital accounts are small, this could be taken to mean that Budget balances at that time equaled something like one half of total bank assets. As of January 1, 1956, about 40% of State Bank loans were reported to be "on account of" accumulated budget surpluses, [19] a statement which could equally well mean that budget deposits were 40% of bank loans or 40% of total bank assets. In either case, these reports indicate a larger ratio of budget balances to bank loans than was attained in any pre-war year, and a much larger ratio than the pre-war average. [20]

Since we have no reported postwar data on the Bank's total monetary liabilities, and since it has by now become exceedingly hazardous to estimate those liabilities from the loan accounts alone, we cannot be sure what share of the total quantity of money created by the Bank is now immobilized by the Budget. It is certain that the Budget has continued, since the War as before, to sop up some part of the money poured into the system by the Bank; evidently, though less certainly, it has sopped up a larger share of the total since the War than before. [21]

My concern thus far has been with the money stock. Let me turn briefly to monetary variables of a different sort: money prices.

Throughout the 1930's, indeed throughout the entire period from the Revolution to the late 1940's, Soviet prices, with only momentary interruptions, rose. Wage rates, consumers' goods prices, and producers' goods prices, all trended sharply, if unequally and erratically, upward. It is worth noting, however, that from 1932 to 1940, and still more clearly from 1928 to 1940, the rate of inflation, as measured by the money wage rate, was markedly decelerating.

In the postwar period, the rate of increase in money wages appears to have been slowed to a very moderate 2-3% per year. [22] Since 1948, consumers' goods prices have been repeatedly reduced, though no general price cut has been made since 1954. [23] Since 1949, producers' goods prices have been reduced four times, the last general reduction occurring on July 1, 1955. [24] Clearly, the most spectacular postwar event in the realm of monetary phenomena has been the reversal of the pre-war price trend.

It would, of course, be pertinent to ask what accounts for this reversal, and, in particular, what, if any, connection exists between the observed behavior of prices and changes in the money stock. To undertake to answer these questions would require that I specify more about the Soviet economy than would be possible in the time available, or, perhaps, possible at all. It may be legitimate, nevertheless, to suggest some hypotheses without attempting here to substantiate them in detail.

I think a plausible case can be made for supposing that in the pre-war period the Bank and the Budget between them put or left in the hands of enterprises and households more money than those sectors were willing to hold at going prices. Each of those sectors had motive and opportunity to unload excess balances, and, in the process of doing so, they forced up wage rates and commodity prices. On wages, the monetary pressure operated directly; on commodity prices, it operated on administrative agencies who undertook, in the case of consumers' goods, to clear markets, and in the case of producers' goods, although at long intervals only, to cover costs. Whichever the mechanics of the process, prices did rise ultimately in response to excess monetary demand. And, since rises in prices increased the value of inventories which increased the value of bank loans, etc., the inflationary process, once commenced, tended to be cumulative.

It is altogether possible that the postwar decline in prices can be explained in the same way, the difference being solely that the Budget in this period absorbed not only a larger part of bank-created balances but a part sufficiently large that the remainder was <u>less</u> than enterprises and households were content to hold. If this was the case, the postwar reversal in price trends is less dramatic than it appears: in the pre-war period, the Budget increasingly offset the Bank's operations and the rate of inflation decreased; in the postwar period, the Budget further increased its offsets and the direction of the price change was finally reversed.

I am not at all confident that this is what has in fact happened, because of one important institutional difference between the two periods. In the pre-war period, at least until its very end, wage rates were almost certainly uncontrolled. This can be seen by comparing planned and realized increases in wage rates; it is substantiated by innumerable reports in Soviet sources. The market determination of wage rates was a crucial link in the pre-war inflationary mechanism. But from 1939-1940, wage controls were introduced which could conceivably have been effective. Obviously, if wage rates could be controlled, prices could be controlled. Therefore, what we may have witnessed in the postwar period is not a monetary "deflation" but a fully administered price decline.

Here we have two rival hypotheses. In the present state of our information, we certainly cannot choose between them. In view of the difficulty we have in distinguishing demand-induced inflation from administered-price inflation in our own economy, it may be that we could not choose between the two even with full information. If the demand hypothesis is right, then there would seem to be an essential continuity between pre-war and postwar monetary processes in the Soviet economy. If the administered-wage hypothesis is correct, then there is a discontinuity between the two periods, and one such that in the postwar period the money stock, and monetary demand, have ceased to have even that modest significance for the behavior of the system which they possessed in the pre-war period.

Though it has little connection with the rest of my remarks, I should perhaps add a footnote on the recent freezing of Soviet State bonds. The most convincing official explanation offered for the action, or, at least, for doing something or other about bond sales, was that current revenues from the sales were about to be outrun by current earnings and redemptions. [25] Why, given the need for some action, a 20 to 40 year freeze was decided upon, I cannot say. I would point out that the action was not without precedent, since conversions altering the yield rates, maturity, or face value, of outstanding bonds had been carried out in 1930, 1936, and 1947. While no previous conversion took the form of a complete freeze, no previous conversion was followed, as this one is supposed to be, by a complete cessation of compulsory bond sales. Needless to say, whether or not bond redemptions are postponed has little to do with how well or badly Soviet consumers in the aggregate fare, though there are doubtless some consequences for the distribution of consumption among individual households.

Footnotes

1. All material relating to the pre-war period is taken from my unpublished dissertation, Soviet Monetary Policy, University of California, 1952.

2. Voznesenskii, N. A., The Economy of the U. S. S. R. during World War II, English edition, Washington, 1948, p. 80.

3. In particular, note should be taken of the fact that both before and after the War some part of inventory gains and losses, resulting from price changes, were transferred to the Bank.

4. Cf., Dymshits, I. A., and others, Finansy i kredit SSSR, Moscow, 1956, p. 351.

5. Atlas, M., "Kreditnaia sistema SSSR v gody Velikoi otechestvennoi voiny." Sovetskie finansy, 1945: 6-7, p. 14.

6. State Bank loans, on January 1, in billion rubles, are reported as follows:

1951	:	162.9	1954	:	208
1953	:	203	1956	:	199.4
			1957	:	243.6

Sources:
1951 and 1956: Usoskin, M. M., Organizatsiia i planirovanie
    kratkosrochnogo kredita, Moscow, 1956, p. 100.
1953: Pravda, August 6, 1953.
1954: Usoskin, M. M., Kratkosrochnyi kredit v SSSR, Moscow,
    1955, p. 29.
1957: Den'gi i kredit, 1957: 2, p. 3.

7. See Kisman, N., and Slavnyi, I., Sovetskie finansy v piatoi piatiletke, Moscow, 1956, pp. 97 ff.; Kosygin, A., "Podniat' rabotu Gosbanka na uroven' otvechaiushchii vozrosshim trebovaniiam dal'-neishego ukrepleniia khoziaistvennogo rascheta," Den'gi i kredit, 1954: 3, pp. 5 ff.; and Dymshits, op. cit., pp. 346 ff.

8. Dymshits, op. cit., p. 351.

9. See sources cited in footnote 7; also, articles by V. Popov and V. Gerashchenko in Den'gi i kredit, 1954: 3.

10. Through 1936, there are some data on these balances, and changes in them correspond fairly well with reported budget surpluses. From 1937 through 1940, changes in these balances equal to reported surpluses would be consistent with the behavior of other components in the Bank's balance sheets, except in 1939 (where the inconsistency may be attributable to some account other than Budget balances), and except for a known reduction in the Budget's deposits, of 6 billion rubles in 1938, for the retirement of long-term bonds which had been issued in 1931 and which were held by the State Bank.

11. Cf. Zverev's budget messages, e.g., in Pravda, August 6, 1953. Zverev and others are given to asserting that the budget surpluses provide a basis for increased bank loans, but I think this must be taken merely as an illustration of the almost universal assumption among Soviet economists that the Bank lends out funds which have been deposited with it rather than creating deposits by its lending operations.

12. "Soviet Economics," Soviet Studies, October 1952, p. 137.

13. Something of the sort might be read out of a rather curious passage in Sitnin, V., and Slavnyi, I., "Nekotorye voprosy vzaimnootnoshenii biudzheta i kredita," Finansy SSSR, 1957: 2, pp. 25-26.

14. Surpluses are reported as follows (billion rubles):

1948	: 39.6	1952	: 37.5
1949	: 24.7	1953	: 25.1
1950	: 9.6	1954	: 4.7
1951	: 27.3	1955	: 24.8
		1956	: 22.0 (preliminary)

Sources:
1948-1953: Dymshits, op. cit., pp. 129 and 136.
1954-1956: Pravda, December 27, 1955 and February 6, 1957.

15. Kisman and Slavnyi, op. cit., p. 14.

16. Ibid., pp. 26 and 32.

17. Ibid., p. 26.

18. Usoskin, M. M., "Beznalichnyi denezhnyi oborot i bankovskii kredit," Den'gi i kredit, 1951: 4, p. 12.

19. Sitnin, V. K., Kontrol' rublem v sotsialisticheskom khoziaistve, Moscow, 1956, p. 56; see also Pravda, December 27, 1955.

20. On January 1, 1938, for which the data are fairly reliable, budget balances amounted to 31% of loans (including the 6 billion rubles of long-term loans) and 25% of total bank assets. By January 1, 1941, for which the data are less reliable and may overstate the Budget's accounts, budget balances amounted to 37% of bank loans and 31% of total bank assets. These two dates mark the apparent pre-war peaks in budget deposits relative to bank assets; they also, it may be noted, fall in periods of relatively slight inflationary pressures, as measured by wage-rate changes. Sitnin and Slavnyi, op. cit., p. 22, indicate that in the postwar period the ratio of the Budget's accounts to total bank assets has risen, but it is not clear in context that the rise is relative to pre-war levels.

21. I have here left out of account -- improperly but unavoidably -- some monetary institutions the operations of which are of considerable significance, notably the Savings Banks and a variety of clearing arrangements.

22. Cf., Yanowitch, Murray, "Changes in the Soviet Money Wage Level Since 1940," The American Slavic and East European Review, April 1955, pp. 217 ff.; and Kaser, M. C., "Soviet Statistics of Wages and Prices," Soviet Studies, July 1955, pp. 40 ff.

23. Cf., Chapman, Janet G., "Real Wages in the Soviet Union, 1928-1952," The Review of Economics and Statistics, May 1954, p. 142; and Tsentral'noe statisticheskoe upravlenie, Sovetskaia torgovlia: statisticheskii sbornik, Moscow, 1956, p. 131.

24. Kisman and Slavnyi, op. cit., p. 51.

25. See Pravda, April 20, 1957, and Zverev, A. G., Gosudarstvennyi zaimy i vklady v sberegatel'nye kassy, Leningrad, 1957, pp. 24 ff.

DONALD R. HODGMAN

•
•
•
•
•

Soviet Monetary Controls Through the Banking System

Anyone familiar with the problems of monetary analysis which currently occupy the attention of economists in the Western European tradition cannot fail to be impressed by the change in professional scenery that takes place as one enters upon the economies of Eastern Europe and especially that of the Soviet Union. In the West the problem of monetary stability is approached either in terms of stability of the general price level or steady growth of real national income and maintenance of high employment or of both, with price stability usually regarded as a subordinate objective. The Western student of money inquires concerning the effects of changes in money cost and availability upon aggregate income through their impact on the spending decisions of investors and consumers, debates the ability of the central bank to exert its influence on the commercial banks whose obligations constitute the predominant form of money, examines the forces which play on the money and capital market and by their joint action determine the level and structure of interest rates, and in general displays a concern with broad aggregates and hypotheses about their behavior. By contrast the East European and especially the Soviet monetary economist regards the determination of real national income and employment as none of his concern, thinks of monetary stability in terms of the prices of individual commodities and services as well as in terms of the general price level, studies the institu-

I am grateful to the Institute of International Studies of the University of California for financial support of the research for this paper and to Professor Gregory Grossman for helpful criticism of a late draft.

tional patterns of money flows, and addresses himself to a host of more or less practical problems such as how to speed up money circulation, how to enforce financial discipline on state enterprises, how to extend bank credit to enterprises, how to estimate and prepare the cash-and-credit plans of the State Bank and similar questions.

Doubtless both intellectual tradition and economic environment contribute to the differences of emphasis by Western and Soviet monetary economists. But it is the environmental forces to which I shall look for an intimation of why Soviet monetary economists devote so much of their attention to problems which may impress Western economists as having a closer affinity to bank operations than to economic analysis. Moreover, I shall explore the possibility that the principles of economic organization which prevail in the Soviet economy make it appropriate that Soviet monetary scholars concentrate on those problems which in fact they have selected for primary consideration.

THE ENVIRONMENT FOR MONETARY CONTROLS

The role of money in an economy and, therefore, the importance of monetary policies and institutions depend upon the power of monetary decisions (for example, the spending and saving decisions of households and firms) to influence those real processes by which income and wealth are created and distributed. This power of money to influence real processes is limited by the scope of direct administrative controls whether these are exercised by individual decision units or by some central authority. In all modern economies the decisions concerning real processes are implemented by some combination of monetary and administrative means.[1]

It is important to distinguish between the degree of control to which central authority in a society may aspire and the specific balance between monetary incentives and administrative controls by which this authority seeks to implement its decisions. Experience indicates that the comparative reliance of central authority on administrative as opposed to monetary measures has tended to increase with the degree of control over economic activity to which central authority has aspired. This observation may be supported by reference to wartime changes in Western economies and by comparisons between the centralized economies of Eastern Europe and those of Western Europe and the United States in peace time. Yet, logically, monetary incentives need not be replaced by direct administrative controls as the degree of centralization of economic decision increases. A central authority with complete control over wages, prices, and the financial system including the state budget theoretically can so design the structure of money incentives and obligations as to encourage or coerce households and firms to produce any bill of final products and services which lies within the productive capability of the economy. In practice, however, the precision of monetary and financial planning and the efficacy of the techniques for its implementation required to produce this result are beyond the power of any central authority yet known. Moreover, the increase in administrative controls which has accompanied increased centralization of economic decision suggests that the *extension* of controls to include additional economic variables (e. g., production allocation) may appear simpler than the *intensification* of controls over variables already subject to some degree of control (e. g., money supply, government taxes, and expenditures) given the existing level of control techniques with all this implies for supporting techniques of information flow and communication. However, the level of such techniques is not static, and as they improve it is possible that administrative controls over economic activity may be relaxed in favor of an increase in monetary controls without any decrease in the degree of effective centralization of control over the composition and allocation of national product. For example, increased reliance on market processes in the Polish economy need not imply any decentralization of effective control over real economic activity providing the authorities succeed in setting more appropriate prices and applying the tax and subsidy powers of the state budget with increased skill. Still less need the recent reorganization and geographic decentralization of administrative structure in the Soviet Union signify any decrease in the degree of centralization of effective control in that economy. Indeed, it may even increase it. An overcentralized administrative structure may do more to frustrate the will of central authority through inefficiency as a communication system than a less centralized but more efficient structure through its greater tolerance of autonomy on the part of subordinate decision units.

In the Soviet economy both monetary controls (including price setting) and administrative controls (planned production and allocation of goods) are used in concert. Neither system of controls is comprehensive. If either were the other would become superfluous. But the combination of the two sets of controls does not mean that they are equally weighted. The system of administrative controls is dominant in the sense that penalties for violation of administrative controls are greater than for violation of monetary controls: see for example the attitudes of industrial management toward fulfillment of the physical production plan versus preserving "financial discipline" as revealed in Joseph S. Berliner's *Factory and Management in the U.S.S.R.*[2] Yet it is also true that the effectiveness of the administrative controls can be seriously undermined by lack of effectiveness of the monetary controls. So long as the system of administrative controls is not fully comprehensive, money confers the power to influence economic decisions and thus for firms and households to frustrate the will of central authority in some degree. This point is illustrated by the problems which inflation, sometimes repressed sometimes open, has posed for the Soviet planners in the form of reduced work incentives, rationing, excessive labor turnover, reduced managerial efficiency, distortions in cost-price structure and like difficulties. These problems have been discussed at length by Franklyn D. Holzman and need not be elaborated here.[3]

To understand the nature of the Soviet monetary problem we need to view it within the context of the economic objectives of central authority and the existing structure of administrative controls which has been fashioned to support these objectives. It is not logically necessary to take the administrative controls as given because, as we have noted, monetary controls may be substituted for administrative controls and vice versa. However, I shall not venture into the broader problem of what changes in price and tax structure would be required to make such substitution of monetary for administrative controls possible and effective, but shall look at the problem of monetary controls in much the same manner that Soviet monetary economists and State Bank officials do, taking the economic objectives of central authority, the system of administrative controls, and the prices set by state authority as given.

Responsibility for monetary controls in the Soviet economy as in any economy is divided between the central bank and the government budget. It is my purpose in this contribution to examine primarily the area of responsibility of the State Bank, the problems which confront it, and the means by which it seeks to fulfill these responsibilities. Therefore, a first step is to distinguish between monetary functions of the State Bank and those of the government budget. The primary monetary responsibilities of the State Bank are control of the quantity of money and allocation of short-term credit. In addition it performs the customary banking functions of holding deposits and transferring funds from one economic entity to another. Derivative from these functions are others specific to the Soviet economy to which I shall come presently. The principal monetary function of the state budget is to assist in the preservation of monetary stability by reallocating money stocks which accumulate in the hands of the population and state enterprises in excess of their current needs as determined by government policy on prices and real output. Receipts collected through tax levies and sale of state bonds are utilized to make grants of fixed investment capital to enterprises and to pay for government services, social benefits, and other conventional categories of government expenditure. Given the price system and the composition of national product, the volume of money transfers which the budget must perform to maintain monetary stability is a function of the quantity of money supplied by the State Bank. The nature of this dependency will be explored more thoroughly below. Suffice it to say now that an over-issue of money by the State Bank can be neutralized by an appropriate withdrawal of money from the economy on the part of the state budget, that is, by a budget surplus.

HOW MUCH MONEY SHOULD THE STATE BANK SUPPLY?

Since the State Bank is responsible for controlling the supply of money in the Soviet economy, we are led to the question: "By what criterion or criteria are officials of the State Bank to decide what quantity of money is appropriate?" This is not an easy question to answer. Raymond Powell in his penetrating study, *Soviet Monetary Policy*,[4] has characterized Soviet bank lending as based on the "commercial bills doctrine" and has averred that automatic adjustment of the money supply to working-capital needs of enterprises provides no more satisfactory a guide to monetary equilibrium under Soviet conditions than in a market economy. Automatic adjustment of the money supply to the needs of the economy through the processes of the international gold standard has long since been discarded as a solution in the Western countries where the gold standard once held sway and, in any event, is irrelevant to the Soviet scene with its trade monopoly and centralized economic plan. Nor are the goals of a stable general price level and full employment appropriate

Donald R. Hodgman

as guides to regulation of the money supply in the Soviet economy. Employment and real national output are determined primarily by the administrative decisions of central authority. Stability of the general price level is inadequate since it is not price stability *per se* in which Soviet economic authorities are interested but price stability (or even a gradual, long-run price decline) accompanied by a particular volume and composition of national product. How then may the equilibrium quantity of money be defined in the Soviet setting?

The approach which appears to be most appropriate is for State Bank officials to attempt to adjust the money supply to the transactions requirements of the Soviet economy taking the price system (including wages), administrative controls, and the production and distribution plan as given. This is a counsel of perfection due to complications which arise in determining the transactions needs of the economy. Nevertheless, it is instructive to examine the problem of money supply from this viewpoint, because the difficulties encountered provide clues to the rationale of a number of actual practices and concerns of State Bank officials including their preoccupation with "economizing money means," "increasing the rate of turnover," innovations in clearing methods, and "enforcing financial discipline" on enterprises.

The problem, essentially, is to determine the minimum amount of money required to effect the planned real processes of the economy at established price levels.[5] In a money economy when real goods and services are transferred from one accounting-control unit[6] to another the real transfer is accompanied by a money transfer whose magnitude is determined by the prices of the real goods and services. The frequency with which real exchanges occur is a function of the organization of production and distribution of goods and services. This organization depends on administrative practice such as scope of activities included within a single accounting-control unit and the degree of accounting integration; these in turn may be influenced by underlying technological factors. Given the dimensions of the physical flows in the system and the administrative organization of the system, the volume of transfers of goods and services among the accounting-control units of the system is determined. The amount of money required (at given prices) to meet these transactions requirements of the system depends on the willingness of control units to accept the formal or informal debts of other control units in lieu of the standard money. Typically, debts between control units accumulate for a period and are then discharged in whole or in part by transfers of standard money. The intervals between like payments, such as wages or the settlement of interenterprise accounts, are set by law or custom. Given the payment intervals for different types of obligations, the minimum quantity of money required to carry out the physical transactions of the system at fixed prices will depend on the synchronization of receipts and expenditures; that is, the time sequence in which payments are made determines the volume of transactions balances and the period for which they must be held by individual control units to bridge gaps between expenditures and receipts. The sum of minimum transactions balances for individual accounting-control units constitutes the minimum quantity of money required for transactions purposes by the economy as a whole.

Obviously the task of forecasting minimum transactions balances even for a static economy where real plans are always fulfilled is tremendously complex. For an actual economy in which dynamic changes occur it becomes virtually impossible. When real flows depart from plan, money requirements likewise are altered. Even *planned* changes in the composition of real flows vary the relative importance of different payment circuits and thus total money requirements. In the unlikely event that minimum transactions balances could be calculated it would not necessarily follow that the financial system would achieve thereby a firm grip on real processes. To say that a given set of transactions cannot be accomplished with less than a specified sum of money does not imply that the same quantity of money may not support additional transactions if these are properly timed so as not to disturb the schedule of existing money flows. Nor does holding transactions balances to their minimum in relation to planned real transactions guarantee that firms and households will refrain from making payments other than those contemplated by central authority. Moreover, money balances are held for speculative and precautionary purposes as well as to meet definitely scheduled payments. Unless the monetary authority can control changes in speculative and precautionary balances it cannot regulate transactions balances simply by controlling the total money supply.

In the face of all these difficulties how is the State Bank to proceed in its task of regulating the money supply in the interests of preserving established prices and supporting the planned production and distribution of real national product? There are two components to the State

Bank's problem. The first is to prevent households and firms from using money in amounts and for purposes which will frustrate the decisions of central authorities while providing adequate funds to permit them to fulfill the purposes intended by these authorities. The second is to prevent both open and repressed inflation. Since the State Bank is unable, for reasons given, to determine in advance the proper size and distribution of the money supply to accomplish these objectives it must resort to a variety of practical measures whose combined effect may be expected to yield approximately the same results. These measures include direct surveillance of money transfers among economic entities,[7] close control of the amount and duration of short-term credit and the purposes for which it is provided, constant observation of general patterns of monetary behavior of the nonstate sector which lies outside its field of direct financial supervision, and development of methods for settling interenterprise indebtedness which avoid the expansion of the money supply in the form of deposit claims against the State Bank. Since many difficulties which arise in the monetary sphere during a planning period are initiated from the side of the real processes involved, the State Bank, itself, cannot correct these shortcomings. When these inevitable ruptures in the real relationships of the plan appear, the State Bank has the responsibility both to make the indicated monetary adjustments and to sound a warning so that corrective measures may be applied in the real sphere. This second function is not an integral part of the State Bank's primary function but stems from its strategic opportunity as an observer of the economic scene.

Paradoxically, there is a sense in which the importance of the State Bank's responsibility for *monetary* controls is measured by the imperfections in its system of direct surveillance of financial transactions which functions as an integral part of the whole Soviet system of direct orders and controls. To the extent that the legitimacy of any money transfer can be tested by comparing the underlying physical flows to planned magnitudes, the State Bank is not controlling physical flows by regulating money flows but more nearly the opposite, that is, the bank is controlling money flows by reference to *planned* physical flows. When the State Bank's actions are guided by the dictates of a detailed plan in real terms, the bank's role becomes that of an inspection agency for the provisions of the real plan. If both plans, the real and the financial, were fully comprehensive and detailed, the financial plan would be redundant as a control device. Such is not the case. The financial plan is more comprehensive and less detailed than the plan in real terms and is intended to maintain centralized control over classes of decisions whose details are left to the discretion of firms and households.

In the measure that financial controls replace direct controls, decisions are decentralized and the legitimacy of a transaction depends on whether a firm or other organization has adequate funds at its disposal for the intended purpose. But in these situations the effectiveness of the State Bank's efforts to detect and prevent unplanned and unlawful activities depends on the precision with which the money supply is adjusted to total planned transactions in a particular planning period. By accumulating working capital which, even temporarily, is in excess of planned needs, the enterprise gains elbow room and a measure of self-determination. In his *Factory and Management in the U.S.S.R.,* Berliner has noted the greater maneuverability that the availability of working capital gives to enterprise management "not because of the formal rights accorded to it but because of the informal and sometimes illegal uses to which working capital is often put."[8]

Thus the crucial issue for the State Bank in its attempt to exercise effective monetary control is its ability to adjust the money supply to the transactions requirements of the economy. It is this problem and the absence of any clearly discernible criterion for its solution *ex ante* which accounts for the State Bank's preoccupation with lending procedures, clearing arrangements, and the tasks of "speeding up money turnover" and "economizing money means": all of which have the simple objective of reducing free funds at the disposal of enterprises and through these of households. Both the administration of short-term credit and prevailing clearing arrangements help to determine the total supply of money required to effect a given schedule of payments and thus the size of enterprise bank accounts. Their effects are interdependent in a manner which will be made clear in the following discussion.

BANK CLEARINGS AND MONETARY CONTROLS

Under existing clearing arrangements enterprises are required to make all payments (with minor exceptions) to other enterprises through the State Bank. There are two prevailing procedures by which payment is made: the acceptance form and the accreditive form. The primary difference between them is that the latter involves advance earmarking or segregation of buyer's funds in the State Bank and thus assures the seller of payment upon satisfactory performance. The accreditive form is employed as a disciplinary measure for enterprises which are in financial difficulty or whose record for observing payment discipline is poor and in special situations which require that the buyer have an opportunity to receive and inspect goods before making payment. To obtain payment under either form the seller takes the initiative and submits his invoice with accompanying documents to the State Bank which in turn presents them to the purchaser for acceptance. Upon acceptance (which is usually based on the documents rather than physical inspection), or following a minimum delay established by regulation, the State Bank debits the account of the buyer and credits the account of the seller. Upon receipt of documents the buyer is required to settle promptly on a schedule which varies slightly with circumstances. The period is two days for intracity transactions, three days for intercity dealings, and the maximum is seven days for firms which are remote from a banking office.[9]

The passage of all enterprise financial transactions through the State Bank provides an opportunity for inspection to check actual against planned transactions. However, for monetary controls other aspects of the process are of greater interest. Typically the State Bank advances funds to the seller to bridge the gap between outlays and receipts implied by goods in transit. Thus the money supply is expanded by an amount and for a period which depends on the size of the transaction and on the time elapsed between shipment of the goods and receipt of payment by the seller. Any increase in the settlement interval tends to increase the money supply through bank loans and thus the volume of funds over which enterprises dispose. This fact dictates the unusually short settlement periods referred to above.

The relative importance of different clearing methods since 1940 is shown in Table 1. The significant development revealed in this table is the rapid expansion in the years since 1946 of clearing by means of the offset of mutual obligations. The formal procedure followed in offset clearing is that of the acceptance method, but there is one major distinction between offset clearing and regular acceptance clearing. In offset clearing enterprises carry accounts with a clearing bureau, and only *net* debits or credits are settled by transfer of deposits on the books of the State Bank. In effect, controlled "commercial credit" is substituted for

Monetary Controls 115

TABLE 1
Relative Importance of Different Clearing Methods
Used by the State Bank

(in per cent of total)

Method of Clearing	1940	1945	1950	1953	1955	1956
Acceptance without offset	77.9	73.5	58.8	50.5	50.9	50.1
Offset						
Continuous *(postoianno*						
deistvuiuschchie)	10.5	15.1	25.7	38.8	45.0	46.4
Occasional *(razovye)*	0.3	2.0	5.8	5.3	1.25	0.5
Other (including accredi-tive, special accounts, limited check books, and acceptance checks)	11.3	9.4	9.7	5.4	2.85	3.0
Total clearings (billion rubles)	555.6	561.0	1,537.7	1,896.1	2,195.2	2,368.6

source: V. F. Popov, ed., *Gosudarstvennyi bank SSSR* (Moscow: 1957), pp. 113 and 125.

bank deposits as a vehicle for interenterprise payments. By reducing the volume of payments which have to be made in the form of bank deposits this system reduces the amount of standard money and the volume of bank loans required to carry out any volume of payments. Unlike bank accounts, the claims of enterprises against mutual clearing offices do not constitute general-purpose money which can be withdrawn to pay wages or for other purposes which are difficult for the State Bank to observe in detail. Moreover, the method reduces the scope for enterprise initiative in diverting funds from their planned purpose to some other use. Under regular acceptance clearing when enterprises which are short of funds for this reason (or any other) are unable to pay debts to their suppliers, the State Bank normally makes loans to the suppliers and thus, indirectly, to the enterprises which have failed to observe financial discipline. Under offset clearing the debts of an enterprise are first paid by credits due it from other enterprises and only then are any excess funds credited to its bank account. Thus, the method restricts the maneuverability of enterprises by reducing the free funds over which they dispose.

State Bank officials are fully aware of these advantages of offset clearing. In a speech to financial and bank personnel at a seminar in Moscow V. F. Popov, chairman of the Board of Directors of the State Bank, remarked: "The offset of mutual obligations makes it possible to balance the payments between economic entities for a particular period. This speeds up money clearing in the economy, reduces the mutual indebtedness of economic entities, frees money from circulation, and as a consequence decreases the need for bank credit."[10] All of this, as we have seen, can equally well be interpreted as tightening monetary controls over enterprises.

SHORT-TERM CREDIT AND MONETARY CONTROLS

The principles which guide State Bank officials in their administration of short-term credit have the same objective. All capital funds of state enterprises in the Soviet economy are placed at their disposal by decisions of central authority. Funds are made available through nonreturnable grants from the state budget and through short-term loans from the State Bank. They are withdrawn by the imposition of taxes and the retirement of loans. Even retained earnings are determined by tax policy. The ultimate source of the funds in either case is the central authority. Thus, an explanation for the extent to which an enterprise is expected to rely on bank credit must be sought primarily in terms of convenience to central authority in the light of its purposes. In my view the central issue here is that of monetary controls and monetary stability.

The money investment represented by a firm's capital equipment, building, and inventories varies over time in response to such familiar factors as depreciation and replacement, the production and sales cycle, and the like. The importance of this for monetary controls is obvious. If the enterprise is endowed with enough money to meet its maximum needs it will ordinarily have surplus funds on hand as these accumulate in its amortization reserve, between settlement dates for material purchases and between payroll dates. In the interests of central control and monetary stability these free funds must be held to a minimum. This task is divided between the state budget and the State Bank.

Since all real capital is used up or wears out eventually and has to be replaced, the division between fixed and circulating capital is a matter of convention. Let us assume that this distinction has been made and that any capital which wears out or "turns over" in one year or less is circulating capital and the rest is fixed capital. Now let us assign to the budget the problem of monetary stability for fixed capital and concentrate on the State Bank's responsibility in relation to circulating capital (the budget will cope with its problem through a system of grants, taxes, and reallocation of amortization reserves).

The size and duration of "idle" transactions balances which an enterprise requires to carry out a volume of money transactions for a year depends on the synchronization of its receipts and expenditures. The less receipts and expenditures for a particular enterprise are synchronized, the larger will its minimum transactions balances become. Enterprises whose activity is seasonal typically have idle transactions balances which are large relative to total money payments. However, the difference between seasonal and nonseasonal enterprises in this regard is chiefly one of degree. The same lack of synchronization of receipts and expenditures may and does occur with a biweekly or monthly period for nonseasonal enterprises because of the periodic nature of payments for raw materials, wages, and other costs compared to the pattern of sales receipts. Idle transactions balances accumulate in both types of enterprise.

Bank credit provides a means for keeping temporarily free transactions balances of enterprises to a minimum. Ideally the banking system should supply the difference between the minimum and maximum transactions balances required by a particular enterprise. If this procedure is followed and the enterprise is required to repay bank loans as rapidly as it receives funds through the sale of its product, no surplus transactions balances will accumulate in its bank account. In my opinion it is primarily to this consideration rather than to the strengthening of the State Bank's surveillance function that we must look for an explanation of the post-1936 credit reforms in which the role of the State Bank in meeting the working-capital requirements of non-seasonal enterprises was greatly expanded.[11] In effect, even the nonseasonal enterprises have "seasonal" fluctuations in their working-capital requirements, and it is the task of the State Bank to absorb their temporary surpluses. Thus, Usoskin writes:[12]

> The regular turnover of working capital in nonseasonal enterprises does not preclude well-known fluctuations in turnover within each cycle. This makes it possible for bank credit to provide enterprises of heavy industry with a part of their circulating capital for the formation of normal inventories. . . . The participation of bank credit in the normal [*postoiannykh*] expenses of enterprises, that is, to meet their minimum needs, makes it possible to maneuver more flexibly the circulating capital of economic organizations, to provide them with circulating capital in the measure of their actual receipt of raw materials and supplies and the like and to exact repayment of the credit in close correspondence with the plan of completion of production according to the established production chart; this spurs the enterprise to plan fulfillment.

The criteria by which minimum requirements for transactions balances are established are more practical than theoretical. Presumably transactions balances could be held to an absolute minimum if all working capital requirements for enterprises were bank-financed and immediate repayment of credits upon receipt of funds was the rule. But too frequent resorting to bank credit may well occasion more clerical work than can be justified by the results achieved in terms of tightened monetary controls. It would appear, for example, that nonseasonal enterprises are not required to resort to bank credit for any portion of their normal biweekly payrolls.[13] Indeed, enterprises generally must be provided with adequate working capital to cover normal wage disbursements without resorting to bank credit, save as sale receipts fail to materialize on schedule. Table 2 taken from Usoskin classifies total bank loans on January 1, 1956, into the four categories: loans on raw materials, supplies and finished goods; loans for wages, unfinished production, technical improvements, capital repairs, and to facilitate the production of consumer goods; loans on goods in transit; and other loans including past-due credits. The small share of total loans made for the payment of wages and others items (type two) indicates that normally enterprises are provided with sufficient working capital to meet payrolls without resorting to bank credit.

TABLE 2

MAJOR TYPES OF BANK LOANS AS PERCENTAGES
OF TOTAL BANK LOANS

(January 1, 1956)

Loans on	Per cent
Raw materials, supplies, finished goods	64.9
Wages, unfinished production, technical improvements, etc.	1.8
Goods in transit	25.5
Other (including pastdue loans)	7.8
Total	100.0

SOURCE: M. M. Usoskin, *Organizatsiia i planirovanie kratkosrochnogo kredita* (Moscow: Gosfinizdat, 1956), p. 109.

Prewar statistics originally at my disposal cast some doubt on my thesis that there has been a systematic extension of the role of bank credit in financing the capital needs of state enterprises, because according to these the average share of State Bank Credit in enterprise working capital appeared to have been larger in the 1930's than in the 1950's. However, V. Gerashchenko, deputy chairman of the State Bank, Professor Usoskin, and others in a discussion in Moscow in July, 1958, confirmed my hypothesis that in general the share of bank credit in enterprise working capital has been deliberately extended to tighten the financial discipline of state enterprises. At this same meeting Professor Usoskin explained that his percentage data for the postwar period were gross of interenterprise indebtedness while those which I had obtained from Raymond P. Powell's *Soviet Monetary Policy* appeared to be on a net basis.[14] Professor Usoskin then referred me to his earlier study for comparable statistics for the prewar years.

Table 3 as now revised reveals the systematic expansion of the role of bank credit in enterprise working capital. In the twenty years from 1935 to 1955 the share of bank credit rose from 33.2 per cent to 42.3 per cent. Of course, such average statistics are somewhat ambiguous because the factors which influence the average ratio are many and diverse. For example, a change in the composition of industry will change the average ratio even if ratios for individual industries do not change. So presumably will changes in relative prices, but in ways too complex to attempt to trace. So also will the increase in the practice of mutual offset clearing, since this will economize on bank deposits and thus bank loans. However, the statement of State Bank officers was unequivocal, so that there is no question that bank financing of working capital has grown steadily in importance.

TABLE 3

Composition of Working Capital as of January 1

(in per cent)

Source of Working Capital	Entire Economy				Industry		Trade	
	1935	1938	1951	1955	1951	1955	1951	1955
Own working capital	41.3	40.4	34.5	33.6	45.7	43.3	10.8	14.2
Bank credit	33.2	34.5	39.9	42.3	32.7	35.5	56.7	59.3
Gross interenterprise debt	25.5	25.1	19.3	16.6	17.0	13.7	21.3	16.9
Other liabilities			6.3	7.5	4.6	7.5	11.2	9.6
Total	100.0	100.0	100.0	100.0	100.0	100.0	100.0	100.0

SOURCES: 1935 and 1938: M. M. Usoskin, *Osnovy kreditovaniia i raschetov* (Fundamentals of Credit and Clearing), (Moscow: Gosfinizdat, 1939), p. 84; 1951 and 1955 M. M. Usoskin, *Organizatsiia i planirovanie kratkosrochnogo kredita* (Organization and Planning of Short-Term Credit), (Moscow: Gosfinizdat, 1956), p. 27.

There is common agreement that Soviet monetary controls have been more effective in containing inflationary pressure in the period since the 1947 monetary reform than in earlier years. I am inclined to attribute this improvement in monetary controls in considerable degree to the success of the State Bank in restricting the transactions balances of enterprises through the increased use of mutual offset clearing and tighter administration of short-term loans. There is some evidence to support this view. According to Gregory Grossman before the war the clearing accounts of enterprises were, on the average, sufficient for only four days' expenses.[15] In a book published in 1957, A. Bachurin, a Soviet financial economist, claims: "In the majority of cases, temporarily free working balances of enterprises in accounts with the Gosbank do not exceed two days' expenses [turnover]."[16] A reduction of 50 per cent in transactions balances which are already very small by Western standards would appear to be a signal achievement by the State Bank in its efforts to establish more effective monetary controls. (With reference to the size of enterprise transactions balances Professor Usoskin remarked with evident satisfaction: "We have reached the technically feasible minimum.")

STATE BANK AND STATE BUDGET

No matter with what diligence and vigor the State Bank pursues its task of adjusting the money supply to the minimum transactions balances required by the economy, it is inevitable that its objective will not be fully achieved. Disruptions in the physical flow of goods and services are bound to occur, and when they do it may already be too late for the State Bank to undo the specific damage inflicted on the system of monetary controls: excess balances are already at large somewhere in the economic system. If the excess balances are in the hands of an enterprise which is unable to purchase needed supplies because of a production failure on the part of its supplier, it may be possible for the State Bank to siphon off the excess funds by requiring the repayment of a working-capital loan. Typically, however, state enterprises have succeeded in expending such surplus funds in the labor market and thus increasing the money incomes of the nonstate sector.[17] At this point the initiative for maintaining stability passes from the hands of the State Bank to the state budget. The State Bank can and does attempt to keep a careful account of the money income and expenditures of the population (the nonstate sector), but it is powerless to regain control of money balances once they flow into that sector.

By keeping a close watch on the money income of the population and the various purposes to which that income is allocated (purchase of consumer goods and services from the state, payment of taxes, transactions within the population through the kolkhoz market, purchase of bonds, bank deposits, and so on) the State Bank can estimate as a residual any increase in currency in the hands of the population. It is apparent from the emphasis placed on encouraging individuals to use savings deposits that the monetary authorities regard any unplanned increase in currency in circulation as suspect, whether it comes about because of overpayment of wages or because of a decision by the population to accumulate idle balances for precautionary or speculative purposes. The reasons for this difference in attitude toward savings deposits and currency hoards are not clear to me. In any event, from the viewpoint of maintaining a keen edge on work incentives, it is obvious that the amount of idle balances, regardless of form in which held, may become excessive. If both repressed and open inflation are to be avoided it then becomes the job of the budget through its tax powers to siphon off the excess purchasing power by running a surplus.

This problem and the failure of the state budget to solve it during the years before the 1947 monetary reform have been carefully studied by both Franklyn Holzman and Raymond P. Powell.[18] I am in general agreement with their analysis of the importance of budget surpluses as counterinflationary devices and with their conclusion that budget surpluses were not large enough to offset the inflationary expansion of bank credit before 1948. However, there is one important point in their analysis upon which I wish to comment to clarify what might otherwise appear to be a contradiction between their conclusions and my own.

Both Holzman and Powell maintain (following an analytical treatment developed by Sir Dennis Robertson) that Soviet financial policy in the prewar years erred in permitting the State Bank to finance too large a portion of the working-capital requirements of Soviet enterprises by bank loans and that the inflation would have been less had a larger share of these working-capital requirements been met by taxes and retained profits.[19] By contrast, earlier in this paper I have suggested that an *increase* in the share of bank credit in the working capital requirements of enterprises provides one means of keeping idle balances to a minimum and thus checking inflationary pressures. Space is lacking for a full discussion of this paradox, but I shall indicate briefly what I regard as a resolution of it.

Successful control of inflation is not just a question of the *proportion* of working-capital requirements which is bank financed but of whether the total money supply exceeds or equals the liquidity requirements of the economy. (In the Soviet setting we may identify liquidity requirements chiefly with transactions requirements.) Since the obligations of the State Bank, whether notes or deposits, constitute the money supply, there is a sense in which inflation is always due to excessive bank credit (in the Soviet economy bank credit is almost synonymous with loans). Thus, if there is inflation, we may say correctly that the bank has provided too large a proportion of the working-capital requirements of the economy. However, it is also true that had the budget made smaller or no nonreturnable (tax-financed) grants to enterprises for working capital purposes but instead sterilized a larger volume of tax receipts as idle deposits in the State Bank, inflationary pressures would have been reduced. But in this instance bank loans would have constituted an even larger proportion of the working-capital requirements of enterprises.

Given the setting within which monetary policy functions in the Soviet economy (especially the problems posed for monetary stability by inevitable dislocations from the real side of economic processes) I believe it is more appropriate to place the responsibility for the prewar inflation on an inadequate appreciation by Soviet monetary authorities of the counter-inflationary role of budget surpluses than on overexpansion of bank credit. Both are to blame. But for practical reasons the opportunity for improvement would appear to have been greater in the direction of budget policy than in that of bank policy.

There is some evidence in recent writings of Soviet monetary economists of their growing awareness of the importance of budget policy for inflation control. While they avoid saying directly that *realized* budget surpluses are necessary for inflation control they do assign this role to *planned* budget surpluses which can be used to cover unplanned expenditures and thus avoid deficit budgets. (In Soviet terms a budget is deficit only if it occasions an expansion of the money supply. Proceeds from the sale of state bonds are included under normal income and do not signify a deficit budget in Soviet usage.) Professor Z. V. Atlas in a recent discussion of the monetary system describes how an unwarranted increase in the money supply to cover budget outlays can disturb monetary stability and adds:[20]

> Consequently, there is an objective, regular relationship between the stability of the value of currency, the note issue, and the balancing of the state budget. The practical recognition of this regular relationship takes the form of a provision of a significant reserve sum for unforeseen expenditures when the state budget is approved each year. The budget reserve makes it possible to cover expenditures unforeseen in the plan without resort to currency emission.

A. Bachurin in a discussion of *The Economic Content of the Budget Under Socialism* goes even further to say: "The history of the development of Soviet finance shows that an excess of budget income over outlays is needed fundamentally in order to increase the credit resources of the State Bank."[21] He adds that more than 40 per cent of the credit which the State Bank currently supplies to the national economy is based on "reserves of the state budget accumulated in the course of a number of years as the result of an excess of income over outlays." Since the State Bank has a monopoly of commercial banking and, moreover, is the central bank of issue, I was at first somewhat incredulous that Bachurin really meant that the primary function of budget surpluses (deposited in the State Bank) is to provide the State Bank with lending power rather than to control inflation. However, several conversations with Bachurin and with officials of the State Bank of Moscow during July, 1958, confirmed that the official doctrine of the bank regards deposits as the source of the State Bank's lending power. It is curious to find this characteristic commercial banker's viewpoint tenaciously held by officers of the largest socialized bank of issue in the world.

In this contribution I have proposed that the goals and activities of Soviet monetary authorities may best be understood from the perspective of what might be termed an "inverted" version of the quantity theory of money with emphasis on the adjustment of the money supply to the transactions requirements of the economy taking prices and real flows as given. Viewed in this light the emphasis of State Bank officials on clearing arrangements and lending procedures appears both rational and relatively successful. Progress in banking procedures (possibly supported by increasing realization of the need for budget surpluses to neutralize the inevitable overexpansion of credit by the State Bank) may explain the improved record of inflation control which has been the outstanding achievement of Soviet postwar monetary policy. If this is so, the Soviet monetary authorities would appear to be prepared to make a substantial contribution to the maintenance of central controls by indirect rather than direct means should central authority come to regard this as desirable during the current experiments in reorganization of the system of economic administration. Needless to say, the system of prices within which monetary controls function will exercise a determining influence on the support which the monetary authorities are able to provide to the plans of the central economic authority. This subject, however, lies outside the scope of this discussion.

---

[1] For example, among the monetary means available to central authority are purchase of goods and services for money, taxation and subsidization, and price setting. Among administrative means are production and allocation orders, embargoes, drafting of manpower, licensing, and the like. Although prices may be set by administrative order I have included them under monetary means because, like taxation, they affect real processes of production and distribution by altering the immediate environment within which monetary decisions take place rather than by direct specification or prohibition of the real processes. Microdecision units, such as firms and households, use monetary means to affect real processes when they spend money for goods and services; administrative means usually control such matters as work assignment within the firm and the division of real income within the household.

[2] Joseph S. Berliner, *Factory and Management in the U.S.S.R.* (Cambridge, Mass.: Harvard University Press, 1957).

[3] Franklyn D. Holzman, *Soviet Taxation: The Fiscal and Monetary Problems of a Planned Economy* (Cambridge, Mass.: Harvard University Press, 1955), chaps. 1 and 2.

[4] Raymond P. Powell, *Soviet Monetary Policy,* an unpublished doctoral thesis (University of California, 1952), chap. 5.

[5] This problem has been given careful attention by Western economists at least as far back as Wicksell. Perhaps the most succinct treatment is that provided by Howard Ellis in his article, "Some Fundamentals in the Theory of Velocity," first published in *The Quarterly Journal of Economics,* LII:3 (May, 1938), and later reprinted in *Readings in Monetary Theory* (Philadelphia: Blakiston, 1951), pp. 89–127.

[6] By "accounting-control unit" is meant a decision unit, such as a firm or household, with some latitude of choice in its economic relations and for which financial bookkeeping is either explicit or implicit.

[7] Note that the bank's surveillance function is an instance of administrative (*not* monetary) controls.

[8] *Op. cit.,* p. 65. Berliner observes also that the prompt expropriation of excess working capital when it is detected (a proper action from the viewpoint of tightening central controls through the monetary system) is one of the reasons for the weakness of the profit incentive in Soviet industrial management (p. 59).

[9] M. M. Usoskin, *Organizatsiia i planirovanie kratkosrochnogo kredita* (Organization and Planning of Short-Term Credit), (Moscow: Gosfinizdat, 1956), p. 68.

[10] V. F. Popov, *Rol' gosudarstvennogo banka v narodnom khoziaistve SSSR* (Role of the State Bank in the Economy of the U.S.S.R.), (Moscow: Gosfinizdat, 1956), p. 22.

[11] In a conversation at the head office of the State Bank in Moscow Professor Usoskin stressed that the strengthening of the State Bank's surveillance function was an equally important consideration in the post-1936 credit reforms.

[12] Usoskin, *op. cit.,* p. 225.

[13] Usoskin, *ibid.,* p. 28.

[14] Powell estimates that bank loans averaged between 44 and 47 per cent of total working-capital stock in the years 1934–1941. *Op. cit.,* p. 319.

[15] Gregory Grossman, "Union of Soviet Socialist Republics," *in* B. H. Beckhart, *Banking Systems* (New York: Columbia University Press, 1954), p. 759.

[16] A. Bachurin, *Ekonomicheskoe soderzhanie biudzheta pri sotsializme* (The Economic Content of the Budget Under Socialism) (Leningrad: Gosfinizdat, 1957), p. 16.

[17] Note that the hand of the State Bank is strengthened if the disappointed purchaser has first to borrow from the bank to secure the funds in question. In this way tight lending procedures may help to control.

[18] Holzman, *op. cit.,* esp. chap. 2; Powell, *op. cit.,* pp. 294–295.

[19] Holzman, *ibid.,* chap. 2, esp. pp. 27, 45; Powell, *ibid.,* pp. 252–257, 262, 332.

[20] Z. V. Atlas, ed., *Denezhnoe obrashchenie i kredit SSSR* (Money Circulation and Credit in the U.S.S.R.), (Moscow: Gosfinizdat, 1957), pp. 168–169.

[21] A. Bachurin, *Ekonomicheskoe soderzhanie biudzheta pri sotsializme* (Economic Content of the Budget Under Socialism), (Moscow: Gosfinizdat, 1957), pp. 16–17.

SOVIET INFLATIONARY PRESSURES, 1928–1957: CAUSES AND CURES[*]

By Franklyn D. Holzman

I. Introduction

Discussions of postwar inflation have centered primarily on two classes of phenomena: the cost and price rises which are attributed to excess demand, otherwise known as "gap" inflation; and the inflation which is attributed to the ability of unions (or monopolistic enterprises) to push up costs or prices even against the downward pressure of inadequate demand.

It is not difficult to understand how either of these kinds of inflation might occur in Western capitalist nations. Demand inflation results when the sum of private investment and government expenditures exceeds the sum of private and corporate savings and taxes. This condition may occur for one of several reasons: the lack of an effective market mechanism for equating private savings and investment; the political and irreducible nature of most government expenditure goals; and the political impossibility of always being able to adjust taxes to eliminate whatever "gap" develops. Monetary policy may be of some aid but not where the gap is large. Cost-push inflation may develop because unions are strong enough to enforce wage increases upon reluctant employers who, because of inadequate demand, are unable to pass all of the wage increase into higher prices; or because employers, enjoying a monopolistic market, are willing to

[*] I am indebted to Gregory Grossman, Donald R. Hodgman, and Lynn Turgeon for helpful comments on the manuscript. I am also indebted to the Ford Foundation and the Russian Research Center at Harvard University, both of which provided financial support over the period in which this paper was written. Neither the above-mentioned organizations or persons are responsible for the views expressed below.

TABLE I

SOVIET PRICE TRENDS

(1928 = 100)

Year[1]	(1) Basic Industrial Goods Excluding Petroleum	(1) Including Petroleum	(2) Average Annual Wage[2] (Workers)	(3) Consumers' Goods Prices[3] State and Co-operative Stores	(4) Consumers' Goods Prices[3] Collective Farm Market	(5) Index of Ratio of (4) to (3)	(6) Partial Indicator of Suppressed Inflation[4]
1928	100	100	100	100	100+	100+	
1929	98	98	114				
1930	96	96	133		630		
1931	96	96	160				
1932	97	97	203	200	3,000 (max.)	1,500 (max.)	17.1[5]
1933	100	124	223	400	1,500–2,000	440 (aver.)	17.3
1934	101	149	264		1,200–1,680		
1935	103	152	323		900–1,470		
1936	157	200	406	700	700+	100+	
1937	175	220	432	700	700+	100+	
1938	180	226	493				
1939	201	240					
1939 July				840			
1940 January	231	266	579	1,000	1,780	178	
1940 July				1,400			7.7
1940 December					2,680	219	
1941 January	240	274		1,225			
1941					2,220		
1942	244	278			13,850		
1943	246	280			31,220		
1944	249	282	822		26,335		
1945	249	282		2,545	13,575	533	
1946	249	282		3,180			
1947	249	282	992				

Fourth Quarter							
1947				3,895	11,530	296	
1948	249	232		3,235	4,175	129	
1949	669	637		2,770	2,880	104	2.5
1950	556	533		2,215	2,770	125	3.4
1951	551	552	1,128	2,035	2,810	138	4.8
1952	523	519	1,140	1,925	3,100	161	3.5
1953	523	519	1,164	1,740	2,595	149	4.2
1954	523	519	1,190	1,640	2,855	174	4.1
1955	510	502	1,204	1,640	2,855	174	2.8
1956	497	484	1,240	1,640	2,610	159	
1957			1,290	1,640			
First Quarter 1957				1,640	2,412	<159	

Sources:

Prices of Basic Industrial Goods:

1928–50: A. Bergson, R. Bernaut, and L. Turgeon, "Prices of Basic Industrial Products in the U.S.S.R., 1928–50," *Journal of Political Economy,* LXIV (Aug. 1956).
1950–56: L. Turgeon and A. Bergson, "Prices of Basic Industrial Goods in the U.S.S.R., 1950–56," *RM 1919, RAND Corporation.*

Average Wage:

1928–40: Franklyn D. Holzman, *Soviet Taxation, op. cit.,* p. 39 (cited from Soviet sources).
1944: N. N. Voznesensky, *The Economy of the U.S.S.R. During World War II* (Washington: Public Affairs Press, 1948), p. 70. This figure was for industrial workers only.
1953: *Politicheskaia Ekonomiia: Uchebnik* (Moscow, 1954), p. 462 says 1953 = 201 per cent of 1940.
1952, 1954: Plan fulfillment for 1953 states that the 1953 average wage is 2 per cent above that for 1952. The 1954 estimate is obtained by assuming a 2 per cent increase over 1953.
1947, 1951, 1955–57: Based on a Soviet source cited by Lynn Turgeon in *Comparisons of the United States and Soviet Economies, Part I,* Joint Economic Committee, Congress of the United States (Washington, 1959), pp. 321–22.

Consumers' Goods Prices: State and Co-operative Stores:

1932: N. Jasny, *The Soviet Price System* (Stanford University Press, 1951), p. 154 (cites Prokopovich).
1933: *40 Let Sovetskoi torgovli* (Moscow, 1957), p. 112, states that 1933 is less than one-fifth of 1950.
1936: Assumes prices about the same as in 1937.
1937: Based crudely on Janet Chapman's cost of living index: cf. her "Real Wages in the Soviet Union, 1928–52," *Review of Economics and Statistics,* XXXVI (May 1954). Prokopovich's figure for 1937 is 335.
1939–41: Based on I. B. Kravis and J. Mintzes, "Food Prices in the Soviet Union, 1936–50, *Review of Economics and Statistics,* XXXII (May 1950)
1945, 1946: Estimated from retail trade turnover in current prices in *Sovetskaia torgovlia* (Moscow, 1956), p. 21 and in constant prices in the plan fulfillments of those years.
1947–56: Based on *Narodnoe khoziaistvo S.S.S.R. v 1956 goda* (Moscow, 1957), pp. 232, 233. The relationship between end-1940 and 1956 derived here is almost precisely confirmed by A. G. Zverev, *Voprosy natsional'nogo dokhoda i finansov S.S.S.R.* (Moscow, 1958), p. 216 who states that the prices in state and co-operative trade in 1956 were 34 per cent higher than at the end of 1940.
1957: Estimated as in 1945, 1946 from state and co-operative trade in current prices for 1956 and 1957 and the statement that the volume of trade in 1957 was 14 per cent greater than in 1956. Cf. *Vestnik Statistiki,* 1958: 2, p. 19 and 1958: 9, p. 92.

Consumers' Goods Prices: Collective Farm Markets

1931: I. Aizenberg, *Voprosy valiutnogo kursa rublia* (Moscow, 1958), p. 131. (Food prices only.) Aizenberg (p. 131) also says that collective farm market prices are 12–15 times state prices in 1933. This is a much higher ratio than that implied by the figures presented from other sources.

1932–35, 1939–40: *Soviet Taxation*, pp. 54–56 (citations from Soviet sources).

1936: According to *40 let Sovetskoi torgovli* (Moscow, 1957), p. 114, prices in state and co-operative stores and in collective farm markets were equal in 1936. I, personally, remain skeptical that collective farm prices were not, in fact, somewhat higher than state prices.

1937: Most observers agree that collective farm market prices in 1937 were little, if at all, above state prices. Cf. for example, A. Bergson, *Soviet National Income and Product in 1937* (New York, 1953), pp. 63–65.

1941–45: Averages of quarterly prices presented in *Finansy i sotsialisticheskoe stroitel'stvo* (Moscow, 1957), p. 39. These figures are very little different for 1943 and 1945 from those presented by Voznesensky, *op. cit.*, p. 76. The quarterly figures presented are (1940 average = 100).

	January	April	July	October
1941	103	95	88	112
1942	268	636	693	886
1943	1,440	1,602	1,467	1,077
1944	1,317	1,488	1,160	758
1945	754	737	590	417

1947–49: *40 let Sovetskoi torgovli*, p. 116 (representing prices in seventy-one large cities).

1950–55: *Sovetskaia torgovlia*, p. 179.

1956: *Narodnoe khoziaistvo S.S.S.R., 1956* (Moscow, 1957), p. 237.

1957–First Quarter: *40 let Sovetskoi torgovli*, p. 122.

Note: These prices correspond with Zverev's statement (*Voprosy*, p. 216) that 1956 prices in the collective farm markets were equal to the end-1940 level.

Note: Comparability between indexes of collective farm market prices and state and co-operative prices were obtained from data in *Sovetskaia torgovlia*, pp. 133–34. In this source, quarterly data are presented for 1954 and 1955 showing the relationships between (1) state prices and co-operative commission trade prices and (2) collective farm market prices and co-operative commission trade prices. From this it was possible to compute that collective farm market prices exceeded state prices on an average by 73.4 per cent in 1954 and 74.8 per cent in 1955. For purposes of getting the two indexes on the same base, it was assumed that collective farm market prices exceeded state prices by 74 per cent in both years.

1. Figures are averages for the year except where otherwise indicated.

2. Average annual wage comprises all forms of pay including overtime, bonuses, and premia.

3. For methodological qualifications see fn. 5, p. 173.

4. The amount by which prices in collective farm markets rise above state prices provides an indicator of the extent to which the state failed to siphon off excess purchasing power from households. A better measure, which takes into account the volume of sales in each market is presented in (6). This column presents the ratios of the excess money spent in the collective farm market due to higher prices to the sum of state sales plus collective farm market sales valued at state prices. In other words, letting P_s, P_k, Q_s, Q_k represent the prices and quantities on state and collective farm markets respectively, our ratio is:

$$100 \left(\frac{Q_k(P_k - P_s)}{P_s(Q_s + Q_k)} \right) \text{ or } 100 \left(\frac{C}{A+B} \right)$$

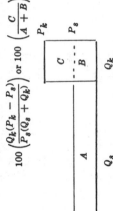

5. Understated as a result of understatement of value of collective farm market trade in 1932. Holzman, *Soviet Taxation, op. cit.*, p. 258.

raise prices above a level which for the economy as a whole is consistent with the existing level of employment.[1]   The government has no direct control over the wage bargain and, indirectly, is deterred

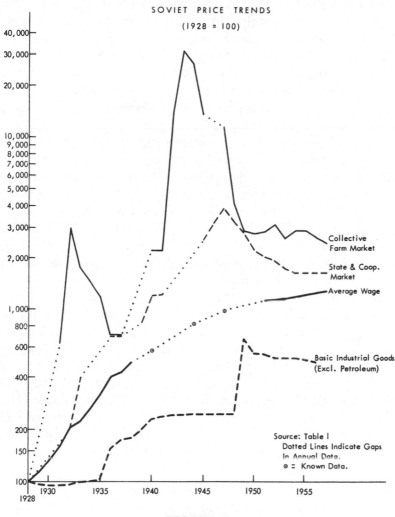

FIGURE I

from using fiscal or monetary policy to force resistance by employers to wage increases because of the unemployment which would result.

It might appear that the Soviet economy would not be subject to either of these types of inflation, or at least not to the same degree as capitalist nations.   With respect to demand inflation, although

1. Franklyn D. Holzman, "Inflation: Cost-Push and Demand-Pull," *American Economic Review*, L (Mar. 1960).

expenditure goals of the Soviet government are large and politically irreducible, the ability of the state to tax is almost unlimited. This is evident from the fact that the percentage of tax receipts to personal income doubled from 1926 to 1936 reaching a prewar peak of over 60 per cent. Indeed, right after World War II, taxes reached the unbelievable level of almost 70 per cent of personal income.[2] Cost-push inflation also seems unlikely in the U.S.S.R. Although there are unions with many members whom they serve in many useful ways, nevertheless these unions have no wage-determining functions. Wages are set by the state and workers have no organized method of affecting the level of their pay.

Despite the absence of obvious causes of inflation, a glance at Table I and Figure I conveys that the Soviet economy experienced rampant inflation from 1928 until 1947. By contrast, inflation appears to have been under control since 1948. One might argue that the Soviets could have avoided inflation in the earlier period, but chose it purposely as a means of financing their rapid industrialization. Examination of the prewar Five Year Plans indicates just the opposite. Each of the plans projected falling consumers' goods prices and stable or falling producers' goods prices. While increases in money wages were planned, the increases were always less than the projected increases in labor productivity. These facts are well known. It is also well known that the Soviets wanted no repressed inflation, were aware of the drawbacks of rationing, and strove for a consumers' goods market in which free choice without rationing could prevail.

In the sections which follow, we shall attempt briefly (1) to explain the peculiar price trends which developed in the 1928–47 period; (2) to present some hypotheses concerning the causal factors of the Soviet inflation; (3) and to consider the factors responsible for the end of price inflation in the postwar period.

II. THE PREWAR WAGE AND PRICE TRENDS[3]

The Soviet economy suffered from severe inflation in the prewar period. From 1928 to 1940, wage rates rose almost six-fold, consumers' goods prices in state and co-operative stores (hereafter state prices) about twelve-fold, consumers' goods prices in the collective

2. Franklyn D. Holzman, *Soviet Taxation: The Fiscal and Monetary Problems of a Planned Economy* (Cambridge: Harvard University Press, 1955), Chap. 10. These ratios of taxes to personal income, estimated in this source for 1926–40, 1947–53, are a rough indicator of trends in the ex-ante inflationary gap.

3. The peculiar price trends presented below were first roughed out by Jasny. Cf. Naum Jasny, *The Soviet Price System* (Stanford University Press, 1951).

farm markets[4] more than twenty-fold,[5] and prices of basic industrial goods about two-and-a-half-fold.

The twelve-fold rise in state consumers' goods prices may be ascribed primarily to two factors: the six-fold increase in wages (discussed in Section III) and the rapid relative rise in nonconsumption expenditures (investment, education, health, military) by the Soviet government. While the wage increase no doubt exerted upward pressure on the prices of industrial consumers' goods, this effect was not very important because about two-thirds of the commodities sold by the state to the population were food products. The cost to the state of food products was maintained fairly stable throughout the period under consideration by a system of procurement in which the collective farms were required to deliver to the state a large share of their crop at nominal prices.[6] Since personal savings were negligible, the rise in wages represented, in effect, an equal rise in demand (before taxes) for consumers' goods and was responsible for about half (i.e., six-fold) of the twelve-fold rise in consumers' goods prices.

The remainder of the price increase is to be attributed to the fact that the rate of nonconsumption expenditures of the state rose from 1928 to 1936, declined slightly in 1937 and 1938 and then rose again beginning in 1939 as the war clouds gathered. Had these expenditures been financed by direct taxes, state prices would still no more than have just paralleled the rise in wage rates. Direct taxes were not employed, however. Instead, for a number of reasons,[7] the Soviets chose to rely on sales taxes, primarily the so-called turnover tax on consumers' goods. The average rate of turnover tax, as a percentage of price, rose from 21.5 per cent in 1928–29 to 63.9 per cent in 1935, declined to 57.4 per cent in 1938, rose again to 60.5 per cent

4. The collective farm (*kolkhoz*) markets are bazaar-like markets throughout the Soviet Union where peasants and collective farms bring their surplus produce for sale or barter. Typically less than 10 per cent of retail sales takes place in these markets.

5. It should be pointed out that in deriving consumers' goods price indexes from Soviet sources, many discrepancies were encountered. Some of these have been noted in the Appendix. Some of these discrepancies may have resulted from use by Soviet statisticians (in constructing their own indexes) of different sets of weights, different baskets of goods, or different samples of collective farm markets. Western economists who have computed Soviet cost of living indexes have demonstrated that quite different price increases result from using different weighting systems. The consumer price series presented in Table I should therefore be taken to indicate general orders of magnitude rather than precision estimates. See also fn. 2, p. 184.

6. This amounted, in effect, to a tax in kind on the agricultural sector. Holzman, *Soviet Taxation, op. cit.*, Chap. 7.

7. *Ibid.*, Chap. 3.

in 1940.[8] To summarize, the rise in consumers' goods prices was the result of a demand inflation due, primarily, to the income (rather than cost) effects of rising wages, and, secondarily, to a rise in the percentage of resources devoted to state, as opposed to household, consumption.[9]

Collective farm market prices rose much faster than state prices from 1928 to 1932, declined from 1933 to 1936–37 to the level (approximately) of state prices, and then rose again faster than state prices. A spread between state and collective farm market prices indicates that the state has not been successful in closing its inflationary gap whether due to rising wages or rising percentage of nonconsumption expenditures. With low real income and faced with continually rising prices Soviet households have very little incentive to save or hoard. To the extent that they are unable to spend their income in state stores, it tends to spill over into the relatively narrow collective farm markets driving up prices. When the spread between the two sets of prices has been large, as was the case from 1928 to 1935 and during World War II, rationing has become necessary to prevent gross distributional inequities.[1] From the above trends, it is clear that despite the tremendous power of the Soviet state to levy high taxes, it has been unable to close the inflationary gap in periods when the level of consumption has declined sharply, such as from 1928 to 1932 and again from 1939 to 1943.

The roughly two-and-one-half-fold increase in producers' goods prices which occurred in the prewar period was mainly due to the cost effects of the six-fold rise in wages.[2] While (enterprise) demand certainly exceeded supply of these commodities, fairly rigid direct allocation and price control prevented this demand from having any impact at all on prices. Soviet policy was to maintain producers' goods prices stable. This policy was stubbornly pursued until 1935, despite the rapid rise in wage costs, by the granting of subsidies to enterprises which were forced to sell at below-cost prices. Mainly because of the bad effect of subsidies on management initiative, this policy was largely abandoned in 1936.[3] Subsidies were reduced or

8. *Ibid.*, p. 142.

9. The rising rate of nonconsumption expenditures was probably more important than rising wages in the 1940 price rise (below).

1. There is, in effect, repressed inflation in the state sector which is eventually partly relieved on the collective farm markets. However, the peasant sellers on these markets then accumulate the excess funds for which there is no further release.

2. By cost effects of rising wages we do not mean that there was an autonomous wage cost-push. As noted, wages rose because of excess demand in the labor market. See below.

3. Managers had little incentive to strive for "real" efficiency when (1)

eliminated and prices were raised to an extent warranted by higher costs.[4] Three reasons may be adduced to explain why industrial prices lagged behind wages after 1936. First, labor productivity in large-scale industry increased by 67 per cent from 1928 to 1940 according to one authoritative measure.[5] Second, the use of subsidies, especially until 1936, tended to lower the price of all nonlabor inputs by a factor of perhaps one and one-half to two throughout most of the thirties. Finally, subsidies, though reduced, were never wholly removed in the prewar period.

III. The Wage Inflation of the Thirties

Both the "monetary" and the "real" conditions necessary for wage inflation were present in the prewar period. On the "real" side, the Soviets practiced "overfull employment planning." Their plans, possibly realistic under the most favorable circumstances, typically projected larger increases in productivity than were achieved and greater availability of resources than materialized. The result was that in the first three Five Year Plans, planned targets were rarely achieved.[6]

In terms of the individual enterprise, overfull employment planning meant that managers were faced with targets which, on the average, were impossible to fulfill with the amounts of material and labor resources available. Had managerial incentives to meet targets been lacking, inflation might not have developed. This was not the case, however. Achieving production goals meant bonuses of as much as 30 per cent of basic salary to most managers.[7] Failure to achieve goals not only meant no bonus, but the possibility of demotion or worse — the stick certainly reinforced the carrot. So managers exercised all their ingenuity to get more coal, steel, labor, and all of the scarce commodities required for plan fulfullment.[8]

money costs were rising 15–20 per cent a year and (2) subsidies were being granted liberally to enterprises which suffered losses.

4. Subsidies were used to hold prices steady again from 1941 to 1949 (below).

5. Donald R. Hodgman, *Soviet Industrial Production, 1928–1951* (Cambridge: Harvard University Press, 1954), Chap. 7.

6. Naum Jasny, *The Soviet Economy During the Plan Era* (Stanford University Press, 1951), p. 20.

7. Joseph Berliner, *Factory and Manager in the U.S.S.R.* (Harvard University Press, 1957), Chap. 3.

8. It is worth pointing out that overfull employment planning is not the same thing as a high level of nonconsumption, nor is there a one to one relationship between the two. It is possible to devote all of a nation's resources to consumers' goods and still set plans for each enterprise which are impossible to fulfill. ("Overproduction" would develop, however, unless there were enough investments, or government spending, to absorb the voluntary savings of the economy.) It is, of course, unlikely that the planners will be as interested in

As already mentioned, nonlabor inputs were for the most part strictly rationed. While some illegal bartering and hoarding occurred, these were not on a large scale and prices of material inputs remained stable. The labor market, on the other hand, was free (with the exception of forced labor which, however, comprised only a small proportion *numerically* of industrial workers[9]) and managers raided each other for workers by bidding up wages. True, wages were set by the state; but these scales presented no obstacle to wage inflation because of the widespread upgrading, illegitimate use of bonus money, and other such devices.[1] The labor market was in such a turmoil that in 1930, for example, workers in large scale industry changed jobs, on the average, more than one and one-half times a year.[2]

The upward wage-drift which developed in the thirties provides abundant evidence of the excess demand in the labor market (see Table II). Soviet planners projected money wage increases in every year for which data are available. Part of the increase probably reflects shifts of workers to higher paying jobs as the technical composition and skill of the labor force improved, rather than increases in specific rates. The remainder probably is accounted for in the main by the Soviet practice of increasing wages in expanding industries and occupations in order to attract workers. But in each year for which data are available, actual rates exceeded planned rates; and in five of the seven years, the unplanned were much larger than the planned increases.

Needless to say, the rise in wages and prices described above could not have materialized as it did despite "real" pressures without a conducive monetary expansion. The remarks which follow should be prefaced by a brief explanation of the nature of Soviet money flows. In terms of money flows, the economy is segmented into cash and noncash sectors. Cash currency is used almost exclusively in transactions involving households. Enterprises and collective farms pay individuals wages in cash (the peasants receive some pay "in kind") and these individuals spend their cash buying back the products of enterprises. In addition, workers pay farmers cash in the

planning for such full use of resources if the targets are not of a sort to which they attach urgency such as those connected with rapid development and defense. It is also possible to have a large inflationary gap due to a high rate of nonconsumption and still not have overfull employment planning pressures in the factor markets if enterprise targets are set at attainable levels in terms of input availabilities.

9. Naum Jasny, "Labor and Output in Soviet Concentration Camps," *Journal of Political Economy*, LIX (Oct. 1951).

1. Holzman, *Soviet Taxation, op. cit.*, Chap. 2.

2. *Sotsialisticheskoe stroitel'stvo SSSR* (Moscow, 1936).

collective farm markets for surplus food which the latter sell. All interenterprise transactions are accompanied by money flows but these involve no circulating currency — the accounts of enterprises

TABLE II
THE SOVIET WAGE-DRIFT, 1928–42

		Average Annual Wage Rate (rubles)		Percentage Increment		
		Planned	Actual	Planned	Unplanned (drift)	Total
			Annual Plans			
	1928	690	703		2	
	1929		800			14
	1930		936			17
	1931	941	1,127	7	13	20
	1932		1,427			27
	1933	1,523	1,566	7	3	10
	1934	1,625	1,858	4	14	19
	1935	2,031	2,269	9	12	22
	1936	2,465	2,856	9	16	26
	1937	2,978	3,038	4	2	6
	1938		3,467			14
	1939			5	6[1]	11[2]
	1940		4,069			5[2]
			Five Year Plans			
First	1928	690				
	1932	934	1,427	35	71	107
Second	1933	1,523				
	1937	1,755	3,038	15	84	100
Third	1938	3,160[3]				
	1942	4,100	4,420[4]	30	10	40

Sources: Holzman, *Soviet Taxation, op. cit.,* pp. 39, 309–10 except as indicated.
1. V. F. Popov, ed., *Gosudarstvennyi bank S.S.S.R* (Moscow, 1957), p. 168.
2. No figure is available for 1939. Total payroll figures are available, however, in Holzman, p. 40. The payroll increase for 1939 was 21 per cent; the planned increase for 1940 was 11 per cent and the actual increase only 6 per cent. These data were used to allocate roughly the two year wage increase from 1938 to 1940 which amounted to 16 per cent.
3. Estimated as actual 1937 plus estimated 4 per cent planned increase.
4. Actual 1942 is not meant to represent the wage rate which existed in 1942 but the rate which would have existed had the 1938–40 trend continued. It is estimated for comparison with the 1942 plan figure (alternatively I could have interpolated the 1938–42 plan to 1940 and compared with actual 1940).

in the state bank are simply credited and debited respectively upon proof of delivery. Enterprises are allowed to draw upon their accounts for cash only to meet payrolls (with minor exceptions). All other payments are called "noncash" transactions.

The excessive monetary expansion which took place in the

prewar period was largely the unwitting result of Soviet reliance for stability on a "real bills" or "commercial loan" credit policy.[3] Following this doctrine, the Soviets grant short-term credit to state enterprises for various working capital needs such as: to tide them over while goods are in transit, for seasonal needs, and for part of any expansion in their permanent working capital requirements.[4] That such a policy does not guarantee monetary stability has been shown, in general, by D. H. Robertson and in the Soviet case by Raymond P. Powell.[5] The problem of achieving monetary stability under these circumstances is probably most easily explained in terms of the major items of a skeleton balance sheet of the state bank (Gosbank), the institution which is responsible for making short-term working capital loans to enterprises and for the issuance and management of cash currency:

Skeleton Balance Sheet of Soviet State Bank

Assets	Liabilities and Net Worth
1. Precious metals and foreign exchange	1. Cash in circulation (mainly bank notes)
2. Cash in vault	2. Deposits of enterprises, organizations and farms
3. Short-term loans to enterprises	3. Deposits of budget (Treasury account)
	4. Capital and surplus

The granting by the bank of a short-term loan to an enterprise is first reflected in the balance sheet as a rise in short-term loans on the asset side and an equal rise in the deposit account of the enterprise on the liability side.[6] The new currency can be spent in either of two ways. First, the enterprise may use its account to purchase goods or services from another enterprise. The bank's balance sheet will be unaffected by this transaction as the deposits of the second enterprise rise by an amount equal to the fall in the deposit account of the first. "Noncash" expenditures of loans are, of course, potentially inflationary. As we have seen, however, inflation in the producers' goods markets has been very successfully repressed and while swollen

3. Raymond P. Powell, "Soviet Monetary Policy," unpublished Ph.D. thesis, University of California, 1952.

4. Powell, *op. cit. Idem,* "Soviet Monetary Institutions and Policies," *The Economy of the U.S.S.R.,* National Academy of Economics and Political Science, Proceedings of October 1957 (Washington, D. C.). Most fixed capital and the remaining working capital is financed interest-free via budget grants (or their equivalent in the form of retained profits which would otherwise have been deducted into the budget).

5. D. H. Robertson, *Banking Policy and the Price Level* (London, 1926). Powell, "Soviet Monetary Policy," *op. cit.*

6. Assume that this loan is a net new loan in the system.

deposit accounts of enterprises probably facilitated inventory hoarding, and may have reduced managerial incentives to efficiency, noncash expenditures were not allowed to influence prices.

The new currency can also be spent in the form of "cash" for wage payments by the enterprise receiving the loan or by any other enterprise which has its deposit account enlarged as a result of noncash expenditures (receipts to it) based on the loan. In this case, the deposit account of the enterprise making the cash expenditure will decline and additional cash will enter circulation via a decline in cash in the vault or by the printing and circulating of new bank notes. These additions to cash in circulation, if excessive, have a directly inflationary effect and lead to rising wage rates and rising consumers' goods prices. Clearly it is these additions to cash in circulation which have made possible the inflation pictured in Table I and Figure I and which are therefore of interest to us.

It is important to note that the amount of cash in circulation will not increase on balance as a result of a loan if, at the same time the additional wage payments take place, an equal amount of additional cash is deposited in the Treasury's account in the bank as a result of a budgetary surplus.[7] Since the budgetary surplus is the major offset to the short-term credit operations of the state bank, the relationship between the surplus and the net granting of new short-term loans is the major indicator of the anti-inflationary policy of the government. This indicator is not very precise as a guide to the net increment to cash in circulation, however, since both the budget surplus and the increment to short-term credit reflect both cash and noncash transactions. There is no way of ascertaining (with the data available to us) either how much of the new short-term credit eventually is used to finance wage payments or what percentage of the budgetary surplus involves the withdrawal of cash from circulation.[8]

7. Directly, the cash is deposited to their accounts in the bank primarily by retail enterprises which sell consumers' goods to the population. (At this point these enterprises lose control of the cash and can only convert the balance in their accounts to cash for payroll purposes). Ultimately, the amount of cash drawn into the bank through retail sales depends primarily on the size of the sales taxes included in the price of consumers' goods. In the past, these taxes have been levied not only at the retail level but more often than not at earlier stages in the production-distribution process.

8. The usefulness of the surplus-bank loan relationship as an indicator of government policy is further reduced by the fact that there are other, albeit less important, items on the state bank balance sheet which must be taken into account. In addition, of course, any evaluation of financial policy must take into consideration the real growth of the economy and the financial requirements of such growth.

Despite these qualifications, there is little doubt that the combination of fiscal-monetary policy of the thirties was inflationary. The amount of short-term loans outstanding increased from 4.4 billion rubles on January 1, 1930 to 55 billion on January 1, 1941, for a total increase of 50.6 billion rubles. Over the same eleven year period, budget surpluses totalled only 26.4 billion rubles. One result was that it was possible for currency in circulation to increase from 2.86 billion rubles on January 1, 1930, to an estimated 16 billion rubles in 1940–41.[9] This was certainly a much greater increase than necessary to have financed at stable prices the real growth of the part of the economy serviced by cash flows: either the three-fold increase in the nonagricultural labor force[1] which took place over the first three Five Year Plans[2] or the small increase, if any, which took place in the volume of consumers' goods.[3]

From the literature of the thirties, it is clear that the Soviets were concerned with wage inflation (although the existence of inflation, as such, was never admitted by them). Their attempts, if any, to deal with the problem at its roots, were not successful. Overfull employment planning characterized the late thirties as it did the earlier period, though the gap between plan and availabilities seems to have been somewhat smaller,[4] and the increment in short-term loans continued to exceed the annual budget surpluses, though here

9. Sources for all these figures are provided in Holzman, *Soviet Taxation, op. cit.*, pp. 53, 229. It should also be noted that income velocity of circulation roughly doubled over the period under consideration (*ibid.*).

1. At least two-thirds of cash income payments were to workers and salaried employees.

2. *Narodnoe khoziaistvo SSR, 1956* (Moscow, 1957), p. 203.

3. In my opinion, wage inflation would have resulted even without the automatic mechanism of basing bank loans on working capital requirements which was responsible for the great liquidity of the thirties. This is because of the priority of output targets over financial targets in the eyes of the Soviet planners. In a sense, the planners were faced with the same dilemma as Western nations: price stability with unemployment *or* full employment with inflation. In their case it was: less than maximum output *or* inflation. Under the conditions which prevailed in the thirties, if there had not been sufficient liquidity for enterprises to bid for labor in the first instance, my guess is that loans for this purpose would have been made available. Enterprises were not supposed to spend more cash for wages than allocated to them in the plan and yet, until the War at least, their individual requests were usually granted because, without the cash, they could not fulfill plan. The fact that in the aggregate they could not fulfill plans anyway was no obstacle since the administration of the cash plan was decentralized to an enterprise (or group of enterprises) basis. Similarly, if loans for general working capital needs had not provided enterprises with surplus funds, I think that loans for payroll needs would have been forthcoming because of the high priority of output goals and the decentralized administration of loans.

4. Jasny, *The Soviet Economy During the Plan Era, op. cit.*, p. 20.

also to a smaller degree.[5] Faced with continuing real and monetary pressures in the labor market, the Soviets attempted to repress wage inflation by more stringent state bank controls over the conversion of enterprise deposits to cash for payroll purposes. Experiments along these lines were tried beginning in 1931,[6] but apparently without success until the passage of a decree on August 15, 1939, which forbid with some exceptions, overexpenditures on payroll (by industrial enterprises) which were not matched by an equal overfulfillment of output plan.[7] A steady decline in overexpenditures set in immediately after the decree went into force and one Soviet economist attributes to the decree the fact that overexpenditures, as a percentage of planned payroll, were "one and one-half times lower" in 1945 than in 1939. And the increase in the average wage rate was smaller in 1940 than in any previous year (Table II).

While bank control over wage-expenditures no doubt had an influence on the course of wages, bidding for workers must also have been hindered after 1938 by the introduction of a number of controls which reduced labor mobility. These included the introduction of labor books,[8] the establishment of labor reserve schools in 1940 into which hundreds of thousands of boys of ages fourteen to seventeen were drafted for training and then assignment to jobs, and a mobilization decree authorizing the state to control the movements of skilled workers when in the national interest.[9]

IV. WARTIME INFLATION

While inflationary pressures generated during World War II must have been much greater than those of the thirties, the wage and price indicators (Table I) with the exception of collective farm market prices, show a slower rate of growth. This indicates, of course, not a decline in pressures but an increase in direct controls. Apparently as a result of bank controls over payroll overexpenditures and of the immobility of labor during the war, average wage rates increased no

5. Holzman, *Soviet Taxation, op. cit.*, pp. 53, 229.
6. A history of these controls is contained in V. M. Batyrev, ed., *Kreditnoe i kassovoe planirovanie* (Moscow, 1947), pp. 61ff., and V. F. Popov, ed., *Gosudarstvennyi bank SSSR* (Moscow, 1957), pp. 165 ff. and summarized in Holzman, *Soviet Taxation, op. cit.*, pp. 35–38.
7. Enforcement of such a rule would not, of course, necessarily guarantee monetary stability. But where overexpenditures are large, it would serve to reduce them — as it did.
8. These books contained the occupational history of a worker and remained in the possession of his employer. Since a worker could not take another job without securing the book from his employer, the employer was often able to prevent competitors from bidding workers away.
9. Harry Schwartz, *Russia's Soviet Economy* (New York, 1954), Chap. 13.

182   *QUARTERLY JOURNAL OF ECONOMICS*

faster than in the last years of the thirties. Strict controls accompanied by subsidies kept the prices of basic industrial goods from rising despite the rise in wage costs.[1] The government also refused to allow state consumers' goods prices to rise to the full extent warranted by the inflationary gap. This, of course, explains the fifteenfold rise in collective farm market prices from 1941 to 1943. Closing the inflationary gap during the war was a well-nigh impossible job. The rate of nonconsumption must have risen very sharply — the value of goods offered in state stores fell from 175.1 billion rubles in 1940 to 77.8 billion rubles in 1942.[2] Since prices were rising, the drop in volume of goods sold must have been even greater.

In contrast with the situation in the prewar period, the high rate of nonconsumption appears to have been a more important cause of inflation during the war than the wage inflation. The latter, however, nevertheless contributed to the rise in demand. Also in contrast with the prewar situation, the budget played an inflationary rather than deflationary role. Over the years 1941–43, the budget ran its first and only deficits.[3] These totaled 39.2 billion rubles or more than the sum of all the surpluses of the 1928–40 period. Budget surpluses were achieved again beginning in 1944, and from 1944 to 1946, these totaled 26 billion rubles.[4] Short-term bank loans to enterprises increased by only 4.5 billion rubles from 1941 to 1946.[5] It is impossible to say exactly how much new currency entered circulation over this period but total currency in circulation must have amounted to more than 60 billion rubles in 1946 in comparison with an estimated 16 billion in 1941.[6] The state was simply not selling enough goods

1. This led to the following rise in subsidies (billions of rubles): 1943 — 4.6; 1944 — 8.1; 1945 — 13.9; 1946 — 25.8; 1947 — 34.1; 1948 — 41.2. After prices were raised in 1949, subsidies declined as follows: 1949 — 6.0; 1950 — 6.6. A. G. Zverev, *Voprosy Natsional'nogo dokhoda i finansov SSSR* (Moscow, 1958), pp. 212–13.

2. Because the bare necessities were so scarce, it was essential to have them relatively equally distributed and priced within the pocketbook of the poorest persons. This is why it would have been impossible to have raised prices to eliminate repressed inflation and to have done without rationing.

3. Budget deficits are defined by the Soviets as occurring when government expenditures exceed government receipts, the latter including sales of bonds to the population. This does little violence to the usual concept of a budget deficit since Soviet bond sales were largely compulsory and therefore contained a substantial tax element. Cf. Holzman, "An Estimate of the Tax Element in Soviet Bonds," *American Economic Review*, XLVII (June 1957), 390–96. The deficits of 1941–43 are reported to have been financed by currency issue and sales of state commodity reserves. Cf. Holzman, *Soviet Taxation, op. cit.*, p. 230.

4. Holzman, *Soviet Taxation, op. cit.*, p. 229.

5. Popov, *op. cit.*, p. 243.

6. Holzman, *Soviet Taxation, op. cit.*, pp. 235 ff.

nor levying high enough taxes to recapture the money put into circulation to finance rising wage rates and military expenditures.

Inflation reached a peak in 1943. From 1944 to 1946 the volume of goods sold by the state increased rapidly.[7] This enabled the state to work off part of the repressed inflation as evidenced by the decline in collective farm market prices after 1943 (Table I) and to achieve budget surpluses again.

Wartime inflation was finally wiped out by the Currency Reform of December 1947. The basic provision of the Reform was the calling in of all ruble notes outstanding and exchanging them for new rubles at an unfavorable 10 to 1 ratio.[8] Had cash holdings been evenly distributed among the various sectors of the population, the Soviet government might have attempted to "work off" the repressed inflation via higher prices and taxes. However, cash holdings were not evenly distributed. Most of the cash was held by peasants as a result of the very high prices received for food on the collective farm markets during the war. At going nonagricultural wage rates a policy of higher state prices designed to mop up cash in the hands of the peasants would have resulted in great hardship to wage earners. This consideration made a reform inevitable.

V. POSTWAR DEFLATION

Since the Reform, the planners have finally achieved some of the goals for which they strove unsuccessfully in the prewar period. Wages have been rising but more slowly than productivity has been increasing and, in consequence, the prices of basic industrial goods have been declining. The slow rise in wage rates and concomitant decline in the rate of nonconsumption expenditures[9] is responsible for the decline until 1954, and stability since 1954,[1] in the price index

7. The value of goods sold by the state (current prices) increased from 77.8 billion in 1942 to 160.1 billion in 1945 and 247.2 billion in 1946. *Sovetskaia torgovlia* (statisticheskii sbornik) (Moscow, 1956).

8. Savings bank deposits and population holdings of bonds were also exchanged but at more favorable rates. For description of the Reform see Holzman, *Soviet Taxation, op. cit.*, pp. 232 ff.

9. As the quantity of goods sold by the state to the population increased rapidly from wartime lows, there must have been a substantial increase in the share of the national output consumed by households. That this is the case is evidenced by the decline in the average rate of taxation at least until 1953. Holzman, *Soviet Taxation, op. cit.*, p. 253.

1. Real income increases probably would have continued to have been passed on to the population via declining prices had it not been for a number of extraordinary measures which served to increase household money income over and above the usual amount. Among these were: raising the money incomes of the peasants by paying much higher prices for agricultural produce; the big increase in pensions; the establishment of a minimum wage which affected

of consumers' goods sold by state and co-operative stores.[2] Only in the case of the collective farm markets have the Soviets failed to hold the line. While repressed inflation was all but eliminated in 1949,[3] it increased from 1950–52, declined in 1953, reached a peak in 1954–55, declining again in 1956 and the first quarter of 1957. It is difficult to understand why so much trouble has been experienced in closing the gap between prices in the state and collective farm markets.[4]

Obviously, the major factor responsible for the deflation of the postwar period (after the currency reform), in comparison with the inflation of the prewar is the relative stability of the wage level; and the interesting question is: have the Soviets succeeded in truly eliminating inflation from the factor (labor) markets or are they simply repressing it successfully? Unfortunately, the evidence does not permit a conclusive answer to this question.

several million wage earners; the abolition of compulsory bond sales to the population. In addition, much of the increase in the standard of living has been in housing services which are not reflected in our price indexes.

2. Table I and Figure I indicate that, since 1928, wages have not succeeded in overtaking state prices and, presumably, real wages are still below the 1928 level. This should not be taken at face value. While an attempt has been made to derive indexes which are as accurate as possible, the series presented are at best only crude indicators of wage and price trends. Over the thirty year period, index number problems, percentage of family at work, rising social services and other factors would invalidate attempts to make precise comparisons. The degree of repressed inflation also invalidates conclusions drawn from comparisons of state prices and wages. For example, the standard of living fell drastically from 1928 to 1932 but this does not show up because state prices were held at below equilibrium levels. It does show up, roughly, in the height of the collective farm market prices. Nevertheless, taking all things into consideration, it is unlikely, in light of the data presented in Table I, that the standard of living of workers rose about four-fold from 1928–56 as is claimed by Soviet writers. (This is about the amount implied in Zverev, *op. cit.*, p. 160.) Cf. also fn. 5, p. 173.

3. One would not expect complete equality of collective farm and state market prices since the quality of produce sold on the former tends to be somewhat higher. The collective farm market price figures for 1948 and 1949 dispose of the argument that the decline in prices on state markets after the Reform was a result of the fact that the Reform took more currency out of circulation than was necessary for stability. Cf. Alexander Gerschenkron, "Rebel in Russia," *Challenge*, Dec. 1957, pp. 58–62. Clearly there was still some repressed inflation after the Reform since bazaar prices were 29 per cent above state prices. In any case, the Reform took place at the end of a pay period so that only hoardings (of workers and peasants) were affected. The day after the Reform, all workers were paid their usual bi-weekly wages.

4. In private conversation in May 1958, Professor A. M. Aleksandrov of the Leningrad Financial-Economic Institute admitted that keeping the gap between state and collective farm market prices was a financial objective of the state, though I was not convinced from his discussion that it was a high priority objective. He laid much more stress on geographical equalization of the gap by shipment of goods from low to high gap regions.

As for the more fundamental causes of wage inflation, both the real and the monetary pressures appear to be less strong than before the war. There is less overfull employment planning than before the war. A glance at the results of any of the annual or quinquennial plans quickly reveals that the record of fulfillment and overfulfillment of plan is very high. Now it is the exception rather than the rule for an industry to fail to fulfill plan. Nevertheless there is still some reason to believe that the demand of managers for labor and other inputs is in excess of supply. First, despite the noteworthy success of plan fulfillment on an industry basis, from 1951 to 1954, "between 31 and 40 per cent of all industrial firms failed to fulfill their annual plans."[5] Failure to fulfill plan by firms is, of course, the significant variable. The general underfulfillment by industry during the pre-war period naturally indicated a much greater failure of individual plants to fulfill plan. Second, while the incentives to fulfill plan are much greater than those to overfulfill,[6] incentives to overfulfill do exist.[7]

The postwar financial picture is also, at first glance, less favorable to inflation than the prewar. While short-term loans increased by almost twice the amount of budget surpluses from 1930 to 1940, the

5. David Granick, "An Organizational Model of Soviet Industrial Planning," *Journal of Political Economy*, LXVII (April 1959), 112.

6. This is because (1) marginal bonus rates are much higher for 100 per cent fulfillment than for successive percentages of overfulfillment, (2) once the plan is fulfilled, punishments connected with "failure" no longer exist, (3) there is a tendency on the part of many managers not to overfulfill by much because of the possibility of having targets raised in the following year and in order to build up reserves to meet future contingencies which might otherwise cause failure to fulfill (Berliner's "safety factor"). Cf. Holzman, "Financing Soviet Economic Development" and "Rejoinder," *Capital Formation and Economic Growth*, National Bureau of Economic Research (Princeton, 1955), pp. 279–84.

7. In his speech to the Twenty-first Party Congress regarding the new Seven Year Plan Khrushchev as much as admitted that overfull employment planning was still being practiced. Quoting: "The Seven Year Plan is being drawn up in such a way that it can be carried out without overstrain. Why has this been done? Because, if we have a very strained plan, there is always the chance that some of its targets may not be reached, that some branches of the economy may not get all they require in the way of raw materials, supplies and equipment, and this is liable to cause interruptions in the work and, consequently, undercapacity operations of plants and factories, idle working time and all attendant consequences. This is what economists call disproportions. The SYP is being drawn up in such a way as to rule this out." Cited by Herbert Levine, "The Meaning of the Seven Year Plan," *New Leader*, May 25 and June 1, 1959.

One would expect a better "fulfillment" record at present than before the war not only because planning techniques have become more refined but because the planners no longer have to deal with problems of drastic structural change such as were faced in the first few five year plans.

reverse has been true in the postwar period. Total short-term loans outstanding increased from 59.5 billion rubles on January 1, 1946 to 243.6 billion on January 1, 1957, an increase of 184.1 billion rubles.[8] Over the same eleven year period, budget surpluses totalled 258.1 billion rubles.[9] There are several reasons why the excess of reported budget surpluses over the increment to bank loans cannot be taken at face value as the basic explanation of the end of wage and price inflation. First, as we have already demonstrated, there is no way of ascertaining what part of the excess of "budget surplus over increment to bank loans" represents a reduction (if at all) in cash in circulation and what part a reduction in the noncash (enterprise deposits) liabilities of the bank, respectively.[1] Secondly, as Powell has noted, not all of the surpluses recorded by the budget were deposited to the budget's balances at the bank in the postwar period.[2] Finally, it is not possible to say whether the budget surplus-bank loan relationship is independently responsible for stability of wage rates or whether it simply reflects a stability which has been achieved by other mechanisms.[3]

Turning to the labor market controls, it seems probable that the various measures which restricted labor mobility just before the war

8. Popov, *op. cit.*, p. 243.

9. Holzman, *Soviet Taxation, op. cit.*, p. 229; *Finansy i sotsialisticheskoe stroitel'stvo* (Moscow, 1957), p. 343.

1. The slack in the bank loan-budget surplus ratio as a controlling factor in wage and price inflation is highlighted by comparing the ratio for groups of years with the actual course of inflation. The figures (Powell, "Soviet Monetary Institutions and Policies," *op. cit.*, p. 11) are (billions of rubles):

	Increment to Loans	Budget Surplus	Increment to Loans — Budget Surplus (Annual Average)
1951–52	40	65	−12½
1953	5	25	−10
1954–55	−9	30	−19½
1956	44	22	+22

If the ratio between bank loans and budget surpluses were a controlling factor in wage and price inflation, then one would have expected the year 1956 to have been relatively inflationary and the years 1954–55 to have been relatively deflationary. In fact, there appears to have been little discernible difference between years during this period. In fact, some of the evidence points in the opposite direction. For example, overexpenditures on wages were relatively less in 1956 than in 1953 (see fn. 9, p. 187) and the collective farm: state price ratio was relatively high in 1954–55 (Table I).

2. Powell, "Soviet Monetary Institutions and Policies," *op. cit.*, p. 15.

3. Holzman, "Financing Soviet Economic Development" and "Rejoinder," *op. cit.*

Professor Donald R. Hodgman presents a sophisticated case for monetary stringency as the basic factor behind postwar stability. See his paper and my comment on it, "Soviet Monetary Controls through the Banking System," *Value and Plan: Economic Calculation and Organization in Eastern Europe*, ed. Gregory Grossman, to be published.

were even more stringent during the war and in the early postwar period. In 1956, however, the labor pass books were abolished thereby removing at least one hindrance to job-hopping. Furthermore, it seems doubtful that controls over mobility after, say, 1950, had any effect on wage inflation since they apparently had little effect on labor mobility. No less an authority than N. Bulganin[4] has stated that labor turnover in industry was 96 per cent in 1956.

As we have already indicated, state bank controls over payroll expenditures were strengthened in 1939, by tying overexpenditures in industry to higher than planned output, and were responsible, according to Soviet economists, for a reduction in overexpenditures. This measure was supplemented after the war by extending control to retail trading organizations, state farms, and other enterprises not covered in the 1939 decree. According to one source,[5] overexpenditures in industry had been reduced from 5.9 per cent of the planned wage fund in 1939 to 3.1 per cent in 1953.[6] A decree of August 21, 1954 apparently substantially strengthened bank controls in a number of ways,[7] including the requirement that enterprises which overspend their wage funds make good the overexpenditures during the subsequent three to five month period.[8] According to Soviet sources, this regulation cut overexpenditures roughly in half between 1953 and the first quarter of 1957.[9] There seems to be little doubt that bank controls deserve an important share of the credit for postwar wage stability.[1]

4. Cited in Leonard Kirsch, "Recent Changes in Soviet Wage Policy," unpublished manuscript.

5. Popov, *op. cit.*, p. 168.

6. This represents very little improvement over the "one-and-one-half-fold" reduction from 1939 to 1945, mentioned above.

7. Popov, *op. cit.*, p. 169.

8. As before, overexpenditures were allowed proportionally with overfulfillment of output, but with one now exception — workers not directly connected with the overfulfillment of output (administrative-overhead personnel) were excluded. Bank control was also to be administered more effectively under the new regulation.

9. Overexpenditures in nonagricultural enterprises declined from 4.3 per cent in 1953 to 3.1 in 1956 and 2.1 in the first quarter of 1957. For agricultural enterprises and organizations, the figures were: 5.9, 3.0, and 3.3 per cent. Popov, *op. cit.*, p. 170.

1. Apparently most of the rise in wage rates which has occurred since 1953 has been the result of unauthorized expenditures rather than planned increases. The actual increases in wage rates for 1953 and 1956 were 2 and 3 per cent respectively (see Sources to Table I). Overexpenditures on total payroll were 4.3 per cent and 3.1 per cent in the same years. Unless the overexpenditures are the result of substantial overfulfillment in the number of workers planned, then little or no increase in the average wage rate must have been projected in these years.

VI. CONCLUDING REMARKS

The Soviets experienced a serious price and wage inflation in the prewar period. The focal point of the inflation was the labor market in which excess demand for workers found full and free expression in rising wage rates as managers competed vigorously for their scarce services.[2] Rising wage rates plus a rising rate of nonconsumption expenditures resulted in demand inflation on the consumers' goods markets and to repressed inflation in some years as the state failed to match the rising "gap" with rising taxes.[3] Excess demand for nonlabor inputs was completely repressed and the rise in prices of basic industrial goods which was finally *administered* was the result of the upward pressure of rising wage costs.

Real inflationary pressures have declined since the war as planning has become more "realistic" and the tasks facing the planners more tractable. However, inflationary pressures from this source still seem to exist and the stable wage level since 1947 cannot be attributed to the end of overfull employment planning and to a real equality of supply and demand in the labor market. Nor can the absence of wage inflation be attributed to control over labor mobility since, as we have seen, mobility is still very high. Rather the evidence suggests either that the Soviets are successfully repressing wage inflation through direct bank controls over payroll expenditures or that the new regime of monetary stringency (deflationary fiscal-monetary policy) has prevented managers from bidding up wages. My personal predilection is to favor the former as the more important restraining factor since, if there were real monetary stringency, bank controls over wage expenditures would tend to "wither away" and Soviet economists would cease concentrating on the problem of controlling overexpenditures of the wage fund. In fact, this has not happened. Finally, while postwar repressed inflation is much milder than that during the prewar (excluding 1936–38) or wartime periods, the Soviets appear either unwilling or unable to eliminate the gap between state and collective farm market prices.

UNIVERSITY OF WASHINGTON

The decline in consumers' goods prices was the combined result of wage stability, rising productivity, and rapid increase in volume of consumers' goods made available.

2. The rise in wage rates cannot be attributed to cost-push — the unorganized Soviet workers would have had no power to "push" up wage rates in the absence of excess demand.

3. The fact that the bulk of Soviets taxes are price-increasing taxes gives the system very little built-in stability against wage inflation.

THE CONSUMER

AND WORKER

IN THIS SECTION, two distinct but related topics are considered: the household is viewed in its double role of consumer and of supplier of labor. The first three articles deal with the consumer and his standard of living, the remaining two with the labor market.

There are two aspects to the standard of living problem: changes in the Soviet standard of living over time; and comparisons of the Soviet standard of living with those in other countries. In either case, the measurement problem is fraught with methodological difficulties at least as intractable as those encountered in the construction of industrial production indices. These difficulties stem from differences over time and between nations in relative prices, tastes, quality of commodities, amount and valuation of leisure, number of working members per family, and so forth. Lynn Turgeon (below) discusses many of the difficulties of making international comparisons preparatory to his own comprehensive comparison of American and Soviet standards of living for the late 1950's. Dr. Nash's paper also deals with Soviet and American standards of living and for the year 1959. His technique, which is rather widely used and quoted, is to compare the working time required to earn the money to buy particular commodities in the Soviet Union and elsewhere (Moscow and New York in this case). This interesting approach is, of course, subject to some of the methodological limitations mentioned above. A standard of living comparison can also be derived from Professor Bornstein's estimate of the consumption "funds" in the U.S. and the U.S.S.R. in 1955 (his Table 3 above) by applying a population deflator. Needless to add, by any measurement the present Soviet standard of living is quite low relative to those in the more advanced Western nations. And as Marshall Goldman points out (*Foreign Affairs*, July, 1960), a further reduction in the relative position of the Soviet consumer would show in these measure-

625

ments if account were taken not only of current output of marketed consumers' goods and services, but also of the services of accumulated consumers' durables (automobiles, washing machines, etc.), stocks of which are relatively very low in the U.S.S.R.[1]

While a precise charting of the trends in the Soviet standard of living is impossible, certain general trends have been clearly discernible. From Mrs. Chapman's careful study (1954)[2] we know that workers' real wages declined sharply after 1928, had not regained the 1928 level by 1937, declined again during World War II, and were still below the 1928 level in 1952.[3] This is also indicated by the comparison of average money wages and consumers' goods prices in Table 1 and Chart 1 in the inflation paper by Dr. Holzman (Section VIII). Since the end of World War II the over-all standard of living has risen rapidly, however. As Professor Bornstein demonstrates, Soviet gross national product increased by 6.5–7.5 per cent per annum between 1950 and 1958. Unless the share in GNP of consumption has been declining, which appears unlikely, the volume of consumers' goods has been increasing at the same rate, and per capita income, therefore, by about 5–6 per cent per annum. Dr. Nash's paper (below) suggests a similar trend for the postwar period. Application of his "working time" technique to seven foods indicates a substantial real wage increase from 1953 to 1959. Dr. Nash also applies this technique to the entire 1928–59 period, indicating that real wages had declined. This result should not be generalized, however, because of the rapidly increasing importance of industrial commodities in the consumers' basket of goods. Certainly, real wages in terms of all consumers' goods rose over this period as the two-and-a-half-fold rise in the index of "industrial consumers' goods per capita output" of Professors Kaplan and Moorsteen (Section IV, p. 313) suggests.

A few final comments on the consumer. Professor Nove's paper presents a bird's-eye view of recent developments in what might be called

[1] In a still unpublished study, Janet Chapman has estimated that the Soviet per capita standard of living in 1958 was $480 (expressed in 1954 dollar prices). The corresponding United States 1958 figure was $1,423. This citation taken from *New York Times*, May 21, 1961, p. 26. The reference is contained in the Bibliography, Section XII, under Bergson and Kuznets.

[2] Mrs. Chapman's study of real wages, which originally covered the period 1928–52, has been revised and expanded and is to be published by Harvard University Press under the title *Real Wages in Soviet Russia Since 1928*. The revision includes updating to 1958.

[3] The trend in real wages of workers tends to understate the improvement in over-all standard of living. This is because the standard of living of the worker has always been higher than that of the peasant (see Jasny, 1960); and since there has been a substantial migration from rural to urban areas, the over-all standard of living might be rising even if those in both the rural and urban areas taken individually were falling.

social welfare. His discussion is supplemented by Dr. Nash. Soviet marketing and distribution systems are described in the several articles by Marshall Goldman listed in the Bibliography.

The labor market is described in two papers: Emily Clark Brown on the free labor market, and an extract on forced labor from a Joint Economic Committee study. A suggestive table on current differential earnings within the Soviet Union is contained in Dr. Nash's essay. More detailed studies of differential wages have been made by A. Bergson (1944) and M. Yanowitch (1960,1960). For an interesting attempt to get at Soviet income distribution, the reader is referred to J. A. Newth (1960). Trends in average money wages and their explanation are presented in F. D. Holzman (Section VIII).

The Appendix contains some corrections to the article by Lynn Turgeon and a summary of recent developments in the labor market by Emily Clark Brown.

LEVELS OF LIVING, WAGES AND PRICES IN THE SOVIET AND UNITED STATES ECONOMIES

(By Lynn Turgeon, Hofstra College)

INTRODUCTION

In the study of Soviet economic growth prepared for the Joint Economic Committee in 1957, a rather thorough evaluation was made of Soviet and United States levels of living in 1955, as well as changes in consumption between 1928 and 1955.[1] Since I find myself in general agreement with these earlier findings, I shall concentrate my attention on developments in Soviet levels of living since 1955, including projected changes in the current 7-year plan.

As the earlier report makes clear, the measurement and evaluation of international levels of living is a complex and difficult task, particularly when the consumption patterns of the nations involved differ significantly. It seems equally clear that recent and projected developments in the Soviet economy have tended to accentuate rather than reduce these methodological difficulties.

Generally speaking, the area of communal consumption—principally the free health and educational services, as well as the partially subsidized consumption of housing—seems to be expanding at a faster rate than the sector producing goods and services with price tags that more or less ration their supply. Direct taxes are being reduced and transfer payments (pensions and grants) are being liberalized. As a consequence, ordinary measures of real wage changes taking account of only the movements in price and money wage levels tend to understate the real improvement in Soviet levels of living.

To the degree that similar developments are not forthcoming in the United States, comparisons of price and wage levels in the two countries are also tilted in our favor. In an attempt to circumvent some of these difficulties, the major portion of this report will consist of an exercise designed to give greater meaning to Soviet prices relative to our own.

Finally, some consideration will be made of the potentialities for improving the Soviet level of living as well as the possibility that the Russians might achieve something comparable to our way of living.

RECENT AND PROJECTED DEVELOPMENTS IN SOVIET LEVELS OF LIVING

Each year a potential develops for raising levels of living in the Soviet Union. The two principal factors most directly responsible for this potential are the increase in the labor force employed in food processing and so-called light industries generally, and, coupled with

[1] Legislative Reference Service of the Library of Congress, "Soviet Economic Growth: A Comparison With the United States," U.S. Government Printing Office, Washington, 1957, pp. 107–123.

320 COMPARISONS OF UNITED STATES AND SOVIET ECONOMIES

this, the increase in output per worker in these branches. Indirectly, levels of living also depend on the ability of Soviet agriculture and other industries to supply the food processing and light industrial sectors with the capital plant and equipment, raw materials, fuel and power required. In addition, a number of relatively minor factors may also influence levels of living in the Soviet Union: Changes in the available produce on the collective farm markets; the impact of Soviet foreign trade on domestic supplies of consumer goods; and Government policies with regard to inventory accumulation or stock-piling of consumer goods.

Some recent, though incomplete, data on changes in the labor force and output per worker in industry generally, as well as in food processing and light industries, are presented in table I.[2] If we discount for a certain amount of possible unrepresentativeness in the Soviet labor force data divulged, as well as some possible upward bias in the Soviet labor productivity claims,[3] we might reasonably expect an average annual increase in the labor force of between 2 and 3 percent and a 4 to 5 percent increase in labor productivity in these sectors producing consumer goods. This would suggest that the potential average annual increment in the output of goods available for Soviet consumers might be expected to run roughly from 6 to 8 percent. All of these estimates are slightly below the rates of expansion for Soviet industry generally.

Taking population growth into account, it would seem that the potential per capita increase in consumption might be running around 5 percent annually. In recent years. there may have been a tendency for Soviet collective farmers to raise their much lower levels of living at a somewhat faster rate than urban inhabitants. As a consequence, urban consumption levels may be rising by slightly less than 5 percent annually.

TABLE I (revised).—*Series reflecting changes in levels of living in the U.S.S.R., 1955–65* [1]

Series	Year							
	1955	1956	1957	1958	1959	1960 annual plan	1960 plan VI target [2]	1965 plan[1]
(1)	(2)	(3)	(4)	(5)	(6)	(7)	(8)	(9)
1. Labor productivity (as percent of previous or indicated year):								
(a) All industry	108	107	[5] 106	106	108	105. 8	150	145–150
(b) Light industry	[4] 106	[5] 105	[5] 103	[5] 104	105	([6])	[7] 135	([6])
(c) Food processing	[4] 105	[5] 105	[5] 105	[5] 104	111	([6])	([6])	([6])
2. Labor force:								
(a) Workers and employees in industrial labor force by end of year (millions)	47. 9	50. 0	[5] 52. 7	[5] 54. 3	55. 3	([6])	55. 0	66. 5
(b) As percent of previous or indicated year	102. 4	104. 4	105. 4	103. 0	101. 9	([6])	114. 8	122. 5
(c) Workers in light industry (millions)	([6])	[8] 2. 349	[8] 2. 425	[5] 2. 475	([6])	([6])	([6])	([6])
(d) As percent of previous year	([6])	([6])	103. 2	102. 1	([6])	([6])	117. 0	([6])
(e) Workers in food processing (millions)	([6])	[8] 1. 563	[8] 1. 641	[5] 1. 643	([6])	([6])	([6])	([6])
(f) As percent of previous year	([6])	([6])	[5] 1. 629 105. 0	100. 9	([6])	([6])	([6])	([6])
3. Savings:								
(a) Total savings bank deposits (billion rubles)	[9] 53. 7	63. 7	80. 6	[5] 87. 2	97. 6	106. 0	([6])	([6])
(b) Increase in bank deposits (billion rubles)	5	10	16. 8	6. 6	10. 4	8. 4	([6])	([6])
4. Transfer payments and communal consumption:								
(a) Pensions (billion rubles)	[10] 30. 1	36. 5	57. 9	[11] 62. 9	[11] 67. 5	70. 0	([6])	([6])
(b) Total transfer payments and communal consumption (billion rubles)	[12] 154	169	[12] 202	[12] 215	232. 2	247. 4	210. 0	360. 0
(c) As percent of previous or indicated year	105	110	119	106	108	106	136	167
5. Average workweek (hours)	[13] 47. 2	[13] 47	[13] 45	[13] 44	([6])	[13] 42	([6])	−40
6. Money wages (as percent of previous or indicated year)	[14] 101. 2	103	[14] 104	[14] 104	([6])	([6])	([6])	126
7. Real income (as percent of previous or indicated year)	[14] 103	[14] 103. 6	107	105	([6])	105	130	140

See footnotes at end of table.

TABLE I (revised).—*Series reflecting changes in levels of living in the U.S.S.R., 1955–65* [1]—Continued

Series	Year							
	1955	1956	1957	1958	1959	1960 annual plan	1960 plan VI target [2]	1965 plan [3]
(1)	(2)	(3)	(4)	(5)	(6)	(7)	(8)	(9)
8. State and cooperative trade:								
(a) Total sales (billion rubles)_	502	547	[5] 625. 4	[5] 677	715	765	750	1,030
(b) As percent of previous or indicated year____ ____	104	109	114	108	106	107	149	157–162
9. Housing:								
(a) Total construction excluding collective farm housing (million square meters)_____	35	36	48	68	80	101	205	650–660
(b) As percent of previous year_____	108	103	133	142	118	115	_____	_____

[1] Unless otherwise indicated, the data for the following years are obtained from the sources listed below:

    1955: Pravda, Jan. 31, 1956.
    1956: Pravda, Jan. 31, 1957.
    1957: Pravda, Jan. 28, 1958.
    1958: Pravda, Jan. 16, 1959.
    1959: Pravda, July 14, 1959. Data are estimated on basis of achievement in first 6 months of the year compared with the first 6 months of 1958.
    1960: Pravda, Oct. 28, 1959. Data are annual plan goals.
    1960: Direktivy XX S"ezda KPSS po shestomu piatiletnemu planu razvitiia narodnogo khoziaistva S.S.S.R. na 1956–60 gody (Directives of the 20th Congress of the Communist Party of the Soviet Union on the 6th 5-year plan for the development of the national economy of the U.S.S.R. from 1956 to 1960), Izdatel'stvo Pravda, Moscow, 1956.
    1965: "Control Figures for the Economic Development of the U.S.S.R. 1959–65, Foreign Languages Publishing House, Moscow, 1958.

[2] 1955=100.

[3] 1958=100.

[4] Tsentral'noe statisticheskoe upravlenie pri sovete ministrov S.S.S.R., Promyshlennost' S.S.S.R.—statisticheskii sbornik (Industry of the U.S.S.R.—Statistical Handbook), Gosstatizdat, Moscow, 1957, p. 27.

[5] Tsentral'noe statisticheskoe upravlenie pri sovete ministrov S.S.S.R., Narodnoe khoziaistvo S.S.S.R. v 1958 godu—statisticheskii ezhegodnik (National Economy of the U.S.S.R. in 1958—Statistical Yearbook), Gosstatizdat, Moscow, 1959, pp. 101, 103, 108, 132, 154, 915.

[6] Not available.

[7] Editorial, "Proizvoditel' nost' truda v shestoi piatiletke" ("Labor Productivity in Plan VI"), Legkaia promyshlennost', No. 7, 1956, p. 1. The increase in the labor force is estimated from the planned increase in output and in labor productivity.

[8] Tsentral'noe statisticheskoe upravlenie pri sovete ministrov S.S.S.R., S.S.S.R. v tsifrakh—statisticheskii sbornik (The U.S.S.R. in Figures—Statistical Handbook), Gosstatizdat, Moscow, 1958, p. 59.

[9] Tsentral'noe statisticheskoe upravlenie pri sovete ministrov S.S.S.R., Narodnoe khoziaistvo S.S.S.R. v 1956 godu—statisticheskii ezhegodnik (National Economy of the U.S.S.R. in 1956—Statistical Yearbook), Gosstatizdat, Moscow, 1957, p. 282.

[10] V. Lavrov, "The Soviet Budget," Foreign Languages Publishing House, Moscow, 1959, p. 47.

[11] Pravda, Dec. 23, 1958, p. 3.

[12] Vestnik Statistiki: No. 5, 1959, p. 90.

[13] United Nations, "World Economic Survey, 1957," New York, 1958, p. 129; Economic Survey of Europe in 1958, Geneva, 1959, ch. I, pp. 6, 11. Although the increases for 1955, 1957, and 1958 are presented as increases in real wages, they are believed to refer to increases in real income.

[14] S. Figurnov, "Formy povysheniia real'noi zarabotnoi platy v S.S.S.R." (Forms of Real Wage Increases in the U.S.S.R.), Sotsialisticheskii Trud, No. 5, 1959, p. 52.

322 COMPARISONS OF UNITED STATES AND SOVIET ECONOMIES

Between 1947 and 1954 the Soviet Government pursued a somewhat unorthodox policy with respect to distributing the annual gains to consumers. The average annual increase in money wages amounted to a little over 2 percent per annum,[4] but substantial additional benefits were being provided to all consumers as a result of annual price reductions of considerable magnitude. By the time of the last of these annual price cuts in April 1954, the Russians claimed that the price index for all consumer goods stood at 43, taking the fourth quarter of 1947 as a base of 100. The corresponding food price index was 38; the index for other than food items stood at 53.

Since 1955 there seems to have been a definite change in the previous policy of passing on the gains to all consumers indiscriminately via the massive price cuts. Instead, selective corrections of existing wage and income inequities have been effected. The price level has been virtually stable, although a slight increase of about 2 percent in the consumer price index may have occurred in 1958 as the Government tood steps to reduce alcoholism and the black marketing of automobiles, which were being sold in Government outlets at prices which failed to ration effectively the existing relatively small supply.[5]

This does not mean that there have been no further price reductions since 1954, but rather that the cuts have been insignificant with respect to their effect on the general price level. In 1956 there were price reductions on clothing and other items for children, some fabrics, aluminum kitchenware, radios and radio equipment. In 1957 price reductions were made on medicines, watches, canned fish, fruits and vegetables, food concentrates, fat, pork, poultry, and smoked goods. Gains to consumers resulting from these reductions were said to be over 5 billion rubles.[6] More recently, on July 1, 1959, reductions of about 15 to 20 percent affected the prices of watches, bicycles, radios, cameras, nylons, wines, and children's toys. The Consumer savings involved were said to amount to over 6 billion rubles annually.[7]

Some idea of the relative magnitude of the price reductions which have occurred since 1954 can be obtained by comparing the above claimed savings to consumers with the savings announced in connection with the earlier massive price reductions. The previous aggregate annual savings to consumers supposedly ranged from a low of 20 billion rubles in 1954 to a high of 80 billion rubles in 1950.[8] The 20 billion rubles saving for consumers in 1954 corresponded with a 4 percent reduction in the general price level; the 80 billion rubles saving in 1950 coincided with nearly a 20-percent cut in retail prices.

The increases in money wages since 1955 have been somewhat greater than those taking place between 1948 and 1955. Although the average increase was 1.6 percent from 1951 to 1953, it averaged 3.6 percent from 1956 to 1958.[9] Part of the increase in average wages

---

[4] Between 1947 and 1954 average wages of workers and employees in industry grew by 22 percent; for the entire national economy, the increase was 20 percent. See S. Figurnov, "Formy povyshenila real'noi zarabotnoi platy v S.S.S.R." (Forms of Real Wage Increases in the U.S.S.R.), "Sotsialisticheskii Trud, No. 5, 1959, p. 52.

[5] See United Nations, "Economic Survey of Europe in 1958," Geneva, 1959, ch. I, p. 14. The losses to Soviet consumers as a result of the substantial increase in the prices of automobiles and motorcycles at the beginning of 1958 are difficult to estimate because the price hike may have resulted partly in a trasnfer of windfall gains from the hands of speculators into the Government treasury. Also, there were some concomitant price increases on machine-woven rugs, vodka and wines, as well as some price reductions on some models or types of TV sets, cameras, bread, jam, fish, and children's wear. See S. Figurnov, op. cit., p. 53.

[6] Pravda, Jan. 2, 1958, p. 1.

[7] Ibid., July 1, 1959, p. 2.

[8] A. G. Zverev, "Voprosy natsional'nogo dokhoda i finansy S.S.S.R." (Problems of National Income and Finance in the U.S.S.R.), Gosfinizdat, Moscow, 1958, pp. 214–215.

in 1957 occurred as a result of minimum wage legislation which raised the statutory minimum wage from 110 to 300 rubles per month and supposedly added 8 billion rubles to consumer incomes.   The revision of the wage structure in a number of industries beginning in 1956 has also meant that average wages in these sectors have increased rather sharply.[10]   In revising wage structures, it has apparently been much simpler as well as more palatable to raise wages selectively than it has been to lower some wages and raise others.

The great improvement in old age pensions meant approximately a doubling of pensions of all types between 1955 and 1958.   At present about 5 billion rubles is being added to disposable income annually from this source.   The elimination of the taxlike compulsory bond purchases in 1958 also gave many consumers the equivalent of 2 to 4 weeks of additional pay annually.   It is claimed that the increase in the minimum wages, the improvement in old age pensions, and the elimination of the compulsory bond sales were giving Soviet consumers in 1958 over 60 billion rubles more disposable income than they received in 1955.[11]

Transfer payments of all types and expenditures for communal consumption have been expanding at an especially rapid rate.   Judging by the data in table I, this is one of the few targets of the discarded plan VI which will be overfulfilled by a considerable margin.

There seems to have been some acceleration of the Government's housing program in the past few years.   During the last 3 years, more housing has been built than during the entire 5 years of plan V.[12] But despite the fact that the original 1960 target for housing construction seems likely to be overfulfilled by a substantial margin, housing undoubtedly still remains as the single weakest aspect of the Soviet level of living.

Not all of the increases in money income have been realized in current increases in consumption.   Net additions to savings bank deposits are currently running around 7 billion rubles annually.   But it is interesting to note in this connection that the planned increase of 13 billion rubles in 1958 was underfulfilled by a large margin, an increase of only 7 billion rubles having been realized.   This can be compared with an increase of around 17 billion rubles in 1957.   Quite possibly there is some connection between this lower rate of voluntary saving and the Government's announcement that no further massive price cuts can be expected in the coming 7 years.   The substantial increase in old-age pensions may have also tended to reduce the propensity to save.

Increases in personal savings may also reflect the nonavailability of desired consumer goods.   For this reason, great caution must be

---

[9] S. Figurnov, op. cit., p. 52.

[10] In this connection, see Nauchno-issledovatel'skii institut truda gosudarstvennogo komitet soveta ministrov. S.S.S.R. po voprosam truda i zarabotnoi platy, Iz opyta perekhoda promyshlennykh predpriiatii na semi- i shestichasovoi rabochii, den' v 1956–58 gg.   (From the Experience of the Transition of Industrial Enterprises to a 7- and 6-hour working day in 1956–58), Gospolitizdat, Moscow, 1959, pp. 23, 45, 63, 78, 93–94, and 105.   The increases in average wages associated with the transition in chemicals, coal, ferrous metallurgy, and machine-building have ranged from 0 to 25 percent.

[11] See Khrushchev's speech at the anniversary session of the Ukraine Republic's Supreme Soviet in Pravda, Dec. 25, 1957.   (Translated in Current Digest of the Soviet Press, vol. IX, No. 52, Feb. 5, 1958, p. 12.)   In addition, some minor taxes designed to encourage marriage and childbearing were greatly reduced in 1958, which supposedly gave bachelor women and small families 6 billion rubles in extra disposable income.

[12] A total of 156 million square meters were built compared with 151.7 million square meters during plan V. See Tsentral'noe statisticheskoe upravlenie pri sovete ministrov S.S.S.R., "S.S.S.R. v tsifrakh (The U.S.S.R. in Figures)," Gosstatizdat, Moscow, 1958, p. 447.   Although the quality of the recent housing constructed is very poor, this has also been true since the inception of planning, and there is apparently no recent qualitative deterioration involved.

exercised in interpreting movements in money wages and the price level as measures of real wage changes. The Soviet Government only imperfectly reflects equilibrium prices for consumer goods in their official price decrees. For example, it seems fairly clear that the 1954 consumer price reductions were too great, considering the available supplies of consumer goods. As a consequence, forced savings probably took place and personal savings accounts rose by 10 billion rubles. The following year, although the increase in average wages was only a little over 1 percent and the official consumer price level was stable, real wages probably rose to a greater extent due to the fact that a greater percentage of the money wage increase was realizable in current consumption. Consequently, the rise in savings accounts in 1955 amounted to only 5 billion rubles.

As near as one can judge, the current 7-year plan calls for something like a continuation of the policies of the past several years. Money wage increases are to be confined largely to the lower income groups, minimum monthly wages being scheduled to rise to between 400 and 450 rubles between now and 1962 and to between 500 and 600 rubles by 1965. Pensioners will also receive greater benefits, with the minimum monthly payment rising from the present 300 rubles to between 450 and 500 rubles by 1966.

Since wages on the average are to rise by only 26 percent during the 7-year period, and the wages of those in the lowest income brackets will rise by 70 to 80 percent, it seems evident that the wage increases for those in the upper income groups will be extremely modest. To compensate somewhat for the lack of increase in money wages at the medium and especially the upper income levels, the plan is to eliminate income taxes. Some price reductions in public catering establishments will also probably benefit, principally those in medium and upper income groups. The recent introduction of installment credit on items selling at prices exceeding 400 rubles will probably also tend to benefit more proportionately than those in medium and upper income brackets. Since real wages are scheduled to rise by approximately one-third on the average, some additional selective price reductions designed to reduce excess inventory accumulations may be planned along the same lines as those occurring since 1955.[13]

In addition, some of the potential for improving levels of living is being taken in the form of increased leisure. Two hours were lopped off the statutory workweek in 1956, and a number of industries have already been converted from a 46- to a 42-hour week.[14] Some difficulty may be experienced when the food and light industries convert to this shortened workweek, as they are scheduled to do by 1960. Although there has usually been an increase in man-hour productivity associated with the reduction of the workweek in the industries already affected, the rate of increase in man-year productivity has fallen substantially. This means that at the time when this reduction in the workweek takes place in the light and food processing industries, the improvement in living levels will depend heavily on any increase in the labor force in these sectors. Further reductions in the statutory minimum workweek are scheduled for the sixties, ones which, in the absence of any reduction in our workweek, are supposed to give

[13] Real incomes, including pensions and grants, will supposedly rise by 40 percent between 1958 and 1965.
[14] Coal miners are exceptional in that they are only required to work a 36-hour week at the present time

Soviet workers more voluntary leisure than any other workers in the world.

It seems clear that amny of the changes which are taking place, as well as those which are planned to improve the lot of the Soviet citizens, are not designed to affect materially the relationship between Soviet average wages and retail price levels. In general, the price level is apparently to be more or less stabilized; average wages are to be increased modestly; direct taxes are to be cut and perhaps eliminated; communal consumption and transfer payments will be systematically increased; and the statutory workweek is to be shortened. As a result of these new policies, international comparisons of wage and price levels involving the Soviet economy tend to become less meaningful.

INTERNATIONAL LEVEL OF LIVING COMPARISONS

The relationship between wage and price levels is clearly an appropriate object for study in a number of comparisons of relative well-being. In measuring real wage changes within any economy, for example, we must measure the relative changes in these two levels over a specified time period. If there has been no drastic change in the number of dependents per wage earner, the measure of real wage changes should ordinarily give us some indication of the change in the level of living. Likewise, a study of the relationship between wage and price levels in two economies as similar as those of the United States and Canada would also seem to produce meaningful results. But what happens when we attempt to compare price and wage levels for economies where the institutional differences are very considerable?

It is entirely conceivable that two economies might provide virtually identical levels of living, yet in one case the gap between the price and wage levels might be very great, while in the other the gap would necessarily be much smaller. The first of our hypothetical economies might have the following characteristics: a very high proportion of wage earners per household; heavy reliance on indirect or excise taxation; subsidization of the housing and transportation sectors; virtually free medical and dental services; and, in general, provisions for a smaller range of commodities from which consumers satisfy their other requirements. In the second hypothetical economy there might be higher dependency ratios; greater reliance on direct or income taxes; rental and transportation charges which include some substantial net income for property owners; price tags attached to the services of doctors and dentists; and a much larger range of commodities from which to choose.

With one exception—the number of breadwinners per family— Western European economies correspond more closely to the first model, while our own economy resembles the latter. The economy of the Soviet Union, as well as the economies of countries within the Soviet bloc, in addition to having all of the above institutional characteristics of many Western European economies, also has a very high proportion of households with more than one wage earner.

Most Western studies of comparative real wages or levels of living in the United States and the Soviet Union have been confined largely to a measurement of the relationship between wage and price levels in the two countries. We might first review briefly some typical approaches to the problem.

In the pioneer studies of our Bureau of Labor Statistics,[15] ruble and dollar prices for various consumer goods produced in the two economies were divided by the average hourly wage to obtain the working time required to enable the purchase of a unit of the same product in the two countries. As a hypothetical example of this type of calculation, we might assume that the average hourly wage in the two countries is 2 dollars and 4 rubles, respectively. With a loaf of bread selling for 20 cents in the United States and 80 kopeks in the Soviet Union, the working time required to buy a loaf of bread would be 6 minutes in the United States and 12 minutes in the Soviet Union.

Attempts have been made more recently to compute average ruble-dollar ratios for the principal commodities and services entering into American and Russian budgets.[16] Although the most ambitious of these calculations was undertaken primarily to provide "deflators" for various components of Soviet national income, tentative comparisons were made of relative real wages in the two countries. In this type of study, the Soviet retail prices expressed in rubles are divided by the dollar prices for the same unit of consumer good or service. The individual ruble-dollar ratios are then weighted in accordance with the relative importance of the different goods and services in either an American or Russian budget in a given year, resulting in an average ruble-dollar ratio with respect to consumer goods and services generally.[17] The ratio obtained is used to convert the average monthly ruble wage in the Soviet Union into a dollar-equivalent wage, which is then compared with our own average wage.

Presumably one could also reverse the above procedure by computing a ruble-dollar ratio for the average monthly industrial wages in the two countries (roughly 800 rubles and 320 dollars), and then proceed to convert the ruble prices of Soviet consumer goods and services into dollar-equivalent prices at this roughly 2.5:1 ratio.

The above-mentioned Western studies simply measure the relationship between the wage and price levels in the two countries, and not only tend to give an inflated picture of the height of Russian prices but also, to some extent, magnify the size of the gap between the levels of living in the United States and the U.S.S.R. Furthermore, these procedures which have ordinarily been employed extensively in the past will probably to an increasing degree tend to exaggerate the relative height of Russian prices as well as the gap between the two levels of living to an even greater extent in the future, as the Soviet area of communal consumption expands relative to our own.

[15] See, for example, Edmund Nash, "Purchasing Power of Soviet Workers, 1953," Monthly Labor Review, July 1953, pp. 705–708. Cf., also, the earlier studies of Irving B. Kravis in ibid., November 1949, and February 1951.

[16] See Norman M. Kaplan and Eleanor S. Wainstein, "A Comparison of Soviet and American Retail Prices in 1950," Journal of Political Economy, December 1956, pp. 470–491; also, "A Note on Ruble-Dollar Comparisons," ibid., December 1957. See also a similar ruble-pound sterling ratio computed by Alec Nove, "The Purchasing Power of the Soviet Ruble," Bulletin of the Oxford University Institute of Statistics, vol. 20, No. 2, 1958. To the extent that British institutions resemble to a greater extent those of the U.S.S.R., ruble-pound sterling ratios would seem to be more meaningful than those of Kaplan and Wainstein.

[17] Transportation and housing are included in the Kaplan-Wainstein computations. Although mention is made of such factors as the number of workers per family, taxation, and free health services, no precise evaluation is made of their impact on real wages or levels of living in the two countries.

A RUBLE-DOLLAR RATIO OF DISPOSABLE INCOME FOR FOOD, CLOTHING, DURABLE CONSUMER GOODS, PERSONAL CARE, AND RECREATION

The following calculations will focus on the relationship between disposable income and price levels rather than wage and price levels in the United States and the Soviet Union. A ruble-dollar ratio will be calculated for family disposable income available for the purchase of food, clothing, durable consumer goods, personal care, and recreation.[18] In other words, I believe that the meaningfulness of relative retail prices for Soviet and United States consumer goods and services can be ascertained more correctly in terms of the rubles and dollars available for these expenditures in the respective household budgets in the two economies.

In making such a comparison, we are handicapped to some extent by the relative lack of current Soviet budget data, but fortunately information is now available on budgeting in Eastern European households where the institutions affecting consumer expenditure patterns are virtually identical with those in the Soviet Union.[19]

Conceivably it might have sufficed to make this computation of family disposable income solely with respect to some sort of "average" worker or employee in the two countries. However, the computation of average family income in the Soviet Union is somewhat controversial, for reasons which will become evident presently. As a result, an additional ruble-dollar ratio for family disposable income will also be calculated with respect to subsistence workers at what we might label the "poverty level" in the two countries.

Gross family income

As a result of some comparatively recent Soviet legislation, roughly 8 million inhabitants of the Soviet Union, whose basic wages were formerly less than 300 rubles per month, had their basic wages raised to at least this legal minimum.[20] Some fairly recent labor legislation in the United States has established a minimum wage of $1 per hour for workers in industries engaged in interstate commerce.[21] On a yearly basis, this would amount to a little over $2,000. But it is well known that considerable numbers of American urban inhabitants, particularly among the nonwhite segment living in Southern States, still do not average even this minimum pay. We therefore take $2,000 as the annual subsistence wage for principal wage earners in the United States.

We assume that some chief breadwinners are included among the roughly 8 million Soviet workers whose earnings are near the subsistence basic wage. However, it seems fairly certain that no average family of four could subsist on these meager earnings. Supplementary

---

[18] In making my estimates of U.S. budgetary expenditures, I have relied very heavily on the advice of Prof. Doris Pullman, School of Home Economics, College of Agriculture, University of Wisconsin.

[19] See United Nations, "Economic Survey of Europe in 1958," Geneva, 1959, ch. IV.

[20] See Pravda, September 9, 1956, p. 1. The minimum wage now ranges from 300 to 350 rubles per month (in rural areas, it is as low as 270 rubles per month). The wages of these workers and employees were supposedly increased by one-third and the total cost of this increase to the Government budget in 1957 was put at about 8 billion rubles. It can be estimated that the wage increase amounted to about 1,000 rubles per subsistence worker per annum. The percentage of the labor force living at or near this subsistence level is surprisingly high. Occupations of those whose earnings are near this minimum amount might be the following: guards, maintenance personnel, firemen, messengers, domestic servants, street sweepers, and possibly some students on stipends. In addition to receiving the minimum wage, some of these individuals undoubtedly also share in bonuses distributed by the enterprise to which they are attached.

[21] It should be emphasized that the present calculation excludes those employed in agriculture. Levels of living for these persons in both countries are believed to be considerably lower than they are for urbanites. Rural inhabitants, of course, constitute a considerably lower percentage of our total population than they do in the Soviet Union.

earnings, therefore, either in the form of additional breadwinners or welfare payments from Soviet trade unions, would be required. Likewise, it seems doubtful that any U.S. urban family of four could subsist for any length of time on the assumed minimum for the principal wage earner.

In the Soviet Union, where women constitute about 45 percent of all workers and employees, and where a rather extensive system of preschool child care prevails, it seems certain that at least another member of the family would be working on a full-time basis.[22] Assuming that the additional worker also received the minimum basic wage, the subsistence level gross family income would be approximately 600 rubles per month.

In the United States, where less than one-third of the labor force are women, and where inexpensive preschool child care is to a great extent unavailable, it seems unlikely that a second full-time worker could possibly be maintained for long at the subsistence level. Instead, it is assumed that a second wage earner on the average brings in one-half of a full-time subsistence wage, as a result of part-time housework, sewing, paper routes, etc. In other words, gross family income at the margin in the United States is estimated to be $3,000 per annum, or $250 per month, compared with 600 rubles per month earned by the Soviet counterpart.[23]

The average monthly wage for urban workers and employees in the U.S.S.R. is taken to be 800 rubles.[24] Although this estimate is somewhat higher than the figure usually accepted for average wages, it should be borne in mind that rural workers are excluded, while higher paid engineers and professionals are included in this calculation. As was the case for subsistence workers, it is believed that a second full-time breadwinner would more often than not be essential for the Soviet family.

According to the findings of a recent Soviet budget study, in 1956 there were only 0.86 dependents per each worker, pensioner, or stipend recipient.[25] Between 1930 and 1935 the number of dependents per worker fell from 2.05 to 1.59 or a reduction of 22 percent; at the same time, the number of workers per family rose from 1.32 to 1.47 or by 11 percent.[26] We assume a continuation of the same inverse relationship between these variables; that is, a 1 percent increase in workers per family for each 2 percent decline in the number of dependents per worker or pensioner. Thus a 59 percent reduction in the number of dependents per worker or pensioner since 1935 would entail roughly a 30 percent increase in the number of wage earners per family. Our very tentative conclusion is that there were approximately 1.7 workers per Soviet family in 1956.[27]

---

[22] At present roughly 5 million children are accommodated in kindergartens, nurseries, and children's homes.

[23] We are aware that a fair number of urban families earn incomes of less than $3,000 in some years, but feel that welfare payments, dissaving, or gifts would bring total gross disposable income for all but a statistically insignificant minority up to this assumed subsistence level. In New York City, for example, one-sixth of the families on home relief in 1959 had a fully employed family head. A similar reservation would also be in order with respect to the assumed Soviet subsistence family income.

[24] See Leon M. Herman, "The Seven-Year Haul," Problems of Communism, volume VIII, No. 2, March-April 1959. Average workers' wages are scheduled to rise from 785 to 990 rubles per month between 1958 and 1965.

[25] Tsentral'noe statisticheskoe upravlenie pri sovete ministrov SSSR, Narodnoe khoziaistvo SSSR v 1956 godu—statisticheskii ezhegodnik (National Economy of the U.S.S.R. in 1956—statistical yearbook, Gosstatizdat), Moscow, 1957, p. 218.

[26] Tsentral'noe upravlenie narodno-khoziaistvennogo ucheta gosplana SSSR, Trud v SSSR-statisticheskii spravochnik (Labor in the U.S.S.R.—statistical handbook), Moscow, 1936, p. 342.

[27] In Czechoslovakia, where women constitute about 42 percent of the labor force, there were about 1.5 persons employed per household in 1956. See Statisticky obzor, No. 11, 1958, p. 503. The social and economic pressure driving women into the labor force in Czechoslovakia has probably been less due to generally higher Czech levels of living.

Because of lower skill composition, women's wages are on the average below those of men in the Soviet Union. But the average wage figure given above includes payments to both men and women. It is assumed that the typical principal wage earner on the average would earn more than 800 rubles per month; that his wife would earn less than this amount; but that their combined earnings would amount to roughly 1,400 rubles monthly.

For the average worker or employee family in the United States, a median yearly income of $5,200 was reported for nonfarm families in 1957.[28] It is possible that there may have been some decline in 1958 associated with the recession of that year, but our current median urban family income is taken to be roughly $5,200. No assumption concerning how this income was obtained need be made, but in many cases, additional income from supplementary wage earners is undoubtedly included. Gross family monthly income is thus taken to be 1,400 rubles in the Soviet Union and $435 in the United States at the level of the average worker or employee.

We now proceed to subtract from these gross family incomes some comparatively inflexible deductions and expenditures in the two budgets at both the subsistence and average income levels. These deductions and expenditures are summarized in table II.

Taxes

Our first deduction from gross family income will be direct taxes; that is, taxes other than those included in the retail prices of consumer goods. Some State and city sales taxes are levied in the United States, but principally we shall be considering income taxes withheld from pay envelopes in both countries. For the United States, we must also deduct social security taxes; in the Soviet Union, such deductions are paid out of enterprise funds as a cost of production.

TABLE-II.—*Estimate of family disposable income available for food, clothing, durable consumer goods, personal care, and recreation in the United States and the U.S.S.R., 1958* [1]

| | United States | | U.S.S.R. | |
	Subsistence family (dollars per month)	Average family (dollars per month)	Subsistence family (rubles per month)	Average family (rubles per month)
Gross family income before taxes	250	435	600	1,400
Family income after taxes	235	380	600	1,315
Less following expenditures for items other than food, clothing, durable consumer goods, personal care, and recreation:				
Shelter and household operations	70	100	40	100
Medical, dental, and child care	15	20	5	15
Transportation expenses	25	50	30	40
Insurance, contributions, savings, etc	10	30	5	40
Total deductions	120	200	80	195
Family disposable income remaining for food, clothing, durable consumer goods, personal care and recreation expenditures	115	180	520	1,120
Ruble-dollar ratio	1	1	4.5	6.2

[1] Estimates are explained in some detail in the text.

[28] Bureau of Census, U.S. Department of Commerce, Current Population Reports—Consumer Income Series, P-60, No. 30, December 1958.

330 COMPARISONS OF UNITED STATES AND SOVIET ECONOMIES

At the subsistence level, no income taxes have been levied in the Soviet Union since January 1, 1957. The U.S. subsistence family with two children would pay roughly $140 per annum in Federal income and FICA (social security) taxes. This sum is increased to $180 per annum to take account of various sales and State income taxes. After these deductions, monthly family income after taxes in the two countries amounts to 600 rubles and $235 at this poverty level.

In the case of average workers or employees in the U.S.S.R., the income of each member is taxed separately at slightly progressive rates resulting in deductions of approximately 50 rubles monthly on the average wage. For the average family with 1.7 wage earners, we deduct 85 rubles for Soviet income taxes, leaving monthly family income after taxes of 1,315 rubles. The average U.S. family would pay almost $600 per annum in Federal income and social security taxes. When sales and State income taxes are considered, total taxes might amount to $55 monthly, leaving a net monthly family disposable income of $380.

Shelter and household operations

Rent is ordinarily based on the income of the principal wage earner in the Soviet Union, and along with heat, electricity, and other utilities, accounts on the average for no more than 4 to 5 percent of the family budget.[29] At the subsistence level, these expenditures would amount to certainly no more than 25 rubles, while at the average income level, they might amount to 70 rubles monthly. There are probably great variations in the quality of housing obtainable for the same rent, but on the average, available shelter is considerably less adequate in the Soviet Union than it is in the United States. At the subsistence level, however, the difference may not be too great, particularly if one considers the quantity and quality of nonwhite and/or recent immigrant subsistence workers' housing in our large cities.

Shelter in the United States, in addition to being much more plentiful, is also more expensive. Rental income in the United States, unlike the U.S.S.R., considerably exceeds the expenses connected with the maintenance, repairs, taxation, and depreciation of the property. The Soviet Government, which is the landlord in most instances, makes no net income or rent on housing; that is, the rent charged is only designed to cover the upkeep of the state property. Judging by the accounts of the upkeep on Soviet housing, rent collections are probably inadequate for even these limited purposes. At our subsistence level, rent, including fuel, is assumed to account for about 20 percent of gross disposable income or about $50 monthly. The average family, on the other hand, is assumed to spend roughly 16 percent of its disposable income for rent, which would amount to about $70 monthly.

These U.S. estimates of shelter expenditures exclude gas, water, and light, as well as a rather large number of other miscellaneous items, all of which we might lump together and classify as "household operations." In the U.S.S.R., electrical appliances are far less prevalent, and consequently such things as repairs are probably relatively unimportant as compared with our family expenditures. Telephones, paper supplies, laundry, and drycleaning expenditures would also

[29] A. G. Zverev, op. cit., p. 152.

undoubtedly be of much less relative importance in Soviet budgets, especially at the level of the average worker or employee.

In the United States, these expenditures for household operations constitute roughly 8 percent of all outlays at both income levels, while in Soviet families, they probably do not run more than 2 percent of gross disposable income. At the Soviet subsistence level, these items are assumed to account for 15 rubles monthly; at the average level, 30 rubles are deducted. In the United States, $20 and $30 are deducted respectively at subsistence and average family income levels. Our remaining disposable incomes are now 560 and 1,215 rubles and $165 and $280.

Medical, dental, and child care

Although medical and dental services are provided free of charge to all Soviet workers and employees, drugs must still be paid for by outpatients. In addition, nominal charges for all but the indigent are made for child care by the nurseries. Some doctors evidently engage in private practice in addition to their employment by the Government health system, and these expenditures might figure in the outlays of Soviet citizens in upper income brackets. But in both subsistence and average budgets, it hardly seems likely that more than 1 percent of gross family income would be spent here. It is assumed that 5 and 15 rubles monthly would suffice for our subsistence and average Soviet families, respectively.

In the United States, medical, dental, and drug expenses (including medical insurance) are probably larger percentagewise at the subsistence level than they are at higher income levels, despite the existence of inexpensive clinics and some unpaid-for medical service. At the subsistence level, it is assumed that about 6 percent of income is spent for these items. while at the average income level, only about 5 percent is so allocated.[30] In absolute terms, $15 and $20 would be spent by subsistence and average families monthly. After these deductions, 555 and 1,200 rubles remain to be spent by Soviet families, while $150 and $260 are left for the U.S. counterparts.

Transportation

Workers and employees generally are believed to live in the same area as the factory or enterprise in which they work in the Soviet Union. A good deal of worker and employee housing is built and maintained by the factory and located in its environs. Nevertheless, it is assumed that one member of both families in the U.S.S.R. used public transportation at the rate of 50 kopeks per ride, or a ruble daily. In addition, some expenses connected with the operation of bicycles or motorcycles might figure in the transportation outlays at the level of the average Soviet family. We deduct 30 rubles from the gross family income at the subsistence level and 40 rubles at the level of the average family.

Transportation is much more important in the budget of U.S. citizens, even at the subsistence level where ownership of a "beat-up jalopy" might even be possible. Ten percent of gross family income of the subsistence family, or about $25 monthly, is deducted; at the average income level, 13 percent, or $50, is assumed. Remaining disposable income amounts to 525 and 1,160 rubles, $125 and $210 respectively.

[30] See U.S. Department of Labor, " ow American Buying Habits Change," U.S. Government Printing Office, Washington, 1959, p. 167.

332 COMPARISONS OF UNITED STATES AND SOVIET ECONOMIES

Insurance, contributions, savings, and other miscellaneous

Although life insurance is now being sold in increasing amounts in the Soviet Union, it is believed that persons in upper income brackets must be the principal purchasers. In the United States, personal insurance (mostly industrial life insurance) expenditures might amount to around $5 monthly at the subsistence level. At the level of the average family, $20 is deducted for life insurance.

Religious and other contributions including tipping are undoubtedly more significant in the budgets of Americans than they are for Russians. Trade union dues may figure in the budgets in both countries. In the Soviet Union, 1 percent of gross monthly wages is payable in initiation fees plus 50 kopecks per 100 rubles of monthly income. In the United States, union dues might average $3 to $4 monthly.

Personal savings may be of some minor consequence at average income levels in both countries. Some voluntary bond purchases may be taking place at average income levels in the two countries, but these outlays are probably not too representative of budgets at this level. Some savings may be taking place in personal savings accounts. In the Soviet Union, it is claimed that there are about 40 million depositors. Much of this saving may be taking place in anticipation of purchases of expensive durable consumer goods. In the United States, in contrast to the Soviet Union, some purchases of common stocks might be possible at average income levels, but here again these purchases are probably not too representative of family budgets at this level.

At most, it is believed that these various items could not account for more than 5 rubles monthly at the Russian subsistence level. But for the average family, as much as 40 rubles might be so allocated monthly. In the U.S. subsistence family, $10 is allocated for these items; at the average level, $30 is assumed.

Food, clothing, durable consumer goods, personal care and recreation

The balance of disposable income available for these purposes comes to 520 and 1,120 rubles for the two Soviet families; for the American counterparts, income available for these purchases amounts to $115 and $180. In other words, while U.S. families have already disposed of over 50 percent of their initial money earnings, the Russian family units have only been required to part with 15 to 20 percent of theirs.

In the case of the U.S. families, how realistic are the calculated residual amounts? We know that food and drink accounts for about 40 percent of income at subsistence levels which would amount to roughly $95 monthly for a family of four. Less than 10 percent of subsistence family income or about $20 would then be left for clothing, consumer durables, and other miscellaneous personal expenses. It is clear that hand-me-downs would have to be the principal source of apparel and consumer durables at this level.

For the average family in the United States, food and drink would constitute about 30 percent of all income or about $115 to $120 monthly. Clothing could easily comprise a further 10 percent of all expenditures or about $40 monthly. We would then have $20 to $25 monthly remaining for personal care and recreation, or a little over 5 percent of the initial family income. It seems fairly certain that the calculated disposable income for these items is not unreasonable in view of what we know about current U.S. budgets.[31]

Such data as are available for Soviet and Eastern European budgets are presented in table III. The data indicate that food and drink must account for about 50 percent of all expenditures in Soviet budgets. Although the scattered budgetary data published for Soviet families indicate that something less than 50 percent of all income is expended for food, beverages, tobacco, and housing, these surveys are believed to cover especially favored workers employed in industries where wages and salaries are above the national average. The Soviet level of living is probably somewhere between that of Czechoslovakia and Poland, which would imply food, beverage, and tobacco expenditures of somewhere between 48 and 54 percent of the family income; that is, approximately 700 rubles monthly. For the subsistence family at least 65 percent of all income would be allocated for food or approximately 400 rubles monthly.[32] At above-average income levels, food and drink expenditures undoubtedly absorb at least 1,000 rubles monthly.[33]

Clothing expenditures are undoubtedly very important for Soviet workers and employees, partly because of the climatic conditions, but also because of the general lack of personal clothing inventories. In 1956, total sales of clothing, including shoes, were equal to about 45 percent of the total sales of food in state and cooperative outlets.[34]

TABLE III.—*Composition of personal expenditures of workers in Eastern Europe and the Soviet Union, selected years (as percent of total)*

Country	Year	Food	Food, beverages, and tobacco	Rent, heat, and light	Clothing, including footwear	Household equipment	Transportation
(1)	(2)	(3)	(4)	(5)	(6)	(7)	(8)
Bulgaria [1]	1957	40.4	44.2	4.2	15.6	4.3	2.6
Czechoslovakia [1]	1957	44.1	48.5	4.3	10.6	5.7	1.9
Eastern Germany [1]	1955	42.0	49.8	8.9	16.7	3.4	2.3
Hungary [1]	1957	(2)	48.5	7.3	17.9	7.7	(2)
Poland [1]	1957	49.2	54.1	3.9	19.5	3.9	1.1
Rumania [1]	1956	42.2	46.9	(2)	17.1	(2)	2.1
Eastern Europe [3]	1956–57	(2)	(4)	6–9	13–24	(2)	(2)
U.S.S.R.[5]	1956	(2)	46.3–49.4	(2)	(2)	(2)	(2)

[1] United Nations, Economic Survey of Europe in 1958, Geneva, 1959, ch. IV, p. 18. The budgetary data for Hungary cover workers and employees. The data for Poland cover workers in coal mining, metallurgy, engineering, and textiles only.

[2] Not available.

[3] Voprosy Ekonomiki, No. 11, 1958, p. 127. The percentages for rent, heat, and light also include expenditures for furniture.

[4] About 50.

[5] Nauchno-issledovatel'skii institut truda gosudarstvennogo komiteta soveta ministrov S.S.S.R. po voprosam truda i zarabotnoi platy, Voprosy truda v S.S.S.R. (Problems of Labor in the U.S.S.R.), Gospolitizdat, Moscow, 1958, p. 393. Percentages include housing expenditures and cover workers in machine building, oil extraction, and textiles.

[31] Ibid., p. 232. Estimated 1956 expenditures for these items are about the same for food and clothing and somewhat higher for personal care and recreation.

[32] United Nations, op. cit., ch. IV, p. 22. In Poland, workers in the lowest income group spent 64.9 percent of their income for food and beverages.

[33] One recent traveler in the Soviet Union reports that a family with considerably above average income was spending 32 rubles daily for food.

[34] Tsentral'noe statisticheskoe upravlenie pri sovete ministrov S.S.S.R., Narodnoe khoziaistvo S.S.S.R. v 1956 godu—statisticheskii ezhegodnik (National Economy of the U.S.S.R. in 1956—Statistical Yearbook), Gosstatizdat, Moscow, 1957. p. 229.

Assuming that 10 percent of total food purchases were made on the collective farm markets, we can estimate that about 20 percent of total family income went for clothing, or about 275 rubles monthly at the average income level. At the subsistence level, a somewhat lower percentage might go for clothing or about 100 rubles monthly.

The average Soviet family would then have about 150 rubles remaining monthly for expenditures on durable consumer goods, personal care, or recreation.[35] Personal care and recreation services are priced fairly reasonably, so consumption of these items would probably be rather liberal. But the Soviet subsistence family would have virtually nothing left for such expenditures.

MEANINGFULNESS OF SOVIET RETAIL PRICES

Our findings indicate that for every dollar that the U.S. subsistence family has available for food, clothing, consumer durables, personal care, and recreation, the Soviet counterpart has about 4½ rubles; for every dollar the average American family has, the average Soviet family has around 6.2 rubles. One thing seems certain: inequality or the gap between subsistence and average income levels as far as the purchases of these day-to-day items is greater in the Soviet Union than it is in the United States. The average Soviet family's net disposable income for these purposes is about 2.1 times that of the subsistence family; the average American family's disposable income is only 1.6 times that of the family at the poverty level. On the other hand, the consumption of housing, medical and dental services, and transportation is more egalitarian in the Soviet Union than it is in the United States.

The meaningfulness of Russian prices for food, clothing, consumer durables, personal care, and recreation is now calculable at both income levels using the indicated ruble-dollar ratios of disposable income for these purposes: 4.5:1 for families at the subsistence level and 6.2:1 at the average income level. Obviously, the dollar-equivalent prices will be considerably lower than they would be were we to use the 2.5:1 conversion rate implicit in the calculations of Kaplan and Wainstein.

The conversion of ruble prices for representative goods and services into dollar-equivalent prices is presented in table IV. The resulting dollar-equivalent prices for different goods and services at each of the two income levels can then be compared with current prices prevailing in our markets giving U.S. families at subsistence and average income levels some idea of both the absolute and relative prices a person in their relative income position would face were he instead a Soviet citizen.[36]

It seems clear from the dollar-equivalent prices in columns (3) and (4) of table IV that the prices of practically all consumer goods and services are higher for Russians than they are for Americans. Except for rye bread, all food items are more expensive for Russian subsistence families. Potatoes, salt fish, and cabbage are only slightly higher

---

[35] Additional sources of income for purchasing durable consumer goods would come out of past savings referred to above.

[36] Occupational wage differentials might be somewhat different in the two economies. In both countries engineering and technical personnel would be paid above average, while unskilled workers would be found near the subsistence margin. Coal miners on the average are among the better paying industries in both economies.

and these items would undoubtedly constitute an important component of diets at this level. Fortunately, the noon meals at the factory are relatively inexpensive. A three-course meal can be obtained for the equivalent of a little over a dollar at this poverty level. Children also receive substantial meals in their nurseries.

TABLE IV.—*Conversion of Soviet prices for food, clothing, consumer durables, personal care, and recreation to dollar-equivalent prices at average and subsistence family income levels, 1958* [1]

Commodity	Official Soviet price (rubles per kilogram unless otherwise indicated for food)	Dollar-equivalent price, subsistence family level (dollar per pound or indicated unit) Soviet price ÷ 4.5		Dollar-equivalent price, average family level (dollar per pound or indicated unit) Soviet price ÷ 6.2	
(1)	(2)	(3)		(4)	
Food:					
Chicken		16.50		1.63		1.21
Beef (stewing)		12.00		1.20		.88
Mutton (moderate quality)		13.00		1.30		.95
Pork		19.50		1.95		1.42
Frankfurter sausage		16.50		1.63		1.21
Average fish		11.00		1.18		.80
Coarse salt fish		4.00		.40		.29
Butter		28.00		2.82		2.04
Margarine		14.00		1.41		1.02
Milk (liter or quart)		2.20		.46		.32
Eggs (10)		7.50		1.67		1.21
Sugar		10.00		1.01		.73
Ice cream cone		1.90		.42		.30
Tea		70.00		7.05		5.12
Rye bread		1.24		.12		.09
White bread		2.35		.24		.17
Potatoes		1.00		.10		.07
Cabbage	1.50–	2.00	.15–	.20	.11–	.15
Carrots		3.50		.35		.26
Onions	3.00–	4.00	.30–	.40	.22–	.29
Oranges	15.00–	20.00	1.51–	2.02	1.00–	1.46
Lemons (each)		3.50		.77		.56
Strawberries		15.00		1.51		1.09
Apples		20.00		2.02		1.46
Prunes		17.90		1.80		1.30
Cucumbers (each)		3.00		.66		.49
Beer (small bottle)	3.00–	3.50	.66–	.77	.49–	.56
Coffee		40.00		4.03		2.92
Cigarettes (box of 25)		2.20		.49		.36
Champagne (bottle)		30.00		6.67		4.89
Noon meal at work	5.00–	6.00	1.11–	1.33	.80–	.96
Clothing:					
Cheap cotton print (meter)		6.50		1.44		1.04
Wool-mixture blanket		100.00+		22.00		16.00
Silk dress fabric (meter)	110.00–	125.00	24.00–	28.00	17.00–	21.00
Rayon-crepe fabric (meter)	57.00–	62.00	13.00	14.00	9.00–	10.00
Cotton print dress		200.00		44.00		33.00
Wool dress		475.00		106.00		76.00
Man's overcoat		720.00		160.00		116.00
Man's all-wool suit		2,000.00		444.00		326.00
Man's wool mixture suit		700.00		156.00		112.00
Poplin shirt		50.00		11.00		8.00
Man's felt hat		69.00		15.00		11.00
Man's fur hat	63.00–	300.00	14.00–	67.00	10.00–	49.00
Wool sox		11.00		2.44		1.74
Kapron (nylon) hose	14.00–	30.00	3.11–	6.67	2.28–	4.89
Shoes (adequate)		200.00		44.00		33.00
Boy's leather shoes		85.00		19.00		14.00
Canvas shoes		27.00		6.00		4.35
Felt boots		140.00		31.00		23.00
Durable consumer goods:					
Aluminum frying pan	7.50–	8.50	1.67–	1.89	1.21–	1.30
Fountain pen		17.50		3.89		2.83

See footnotes at end of table, p. 336.

336 COMPARISONS OF UNITED STATES AND SOVIET ECONOMIES

TABLE IV.—*Conversion of Soviet prices for food, clothing, consumer durables, personal care, and recreation to dollar-equivalent prices at average and subsistence family income levels, 1958* [1]—Continued

Commodity	Official Soviet price (rubles per kilogram unless otherwise indicated for food)	Dollar-equivalent price, subsistence family level (dollar per pound or indicated unit) Soviet price÷4.5	Dollar-equivalent price, average family level (dollar per pound or indicated unit) Soviet price÷6.2
(1)	(2)	(3)	(4)
Durable consumer goods—Continued			
Bicycle	450.00– 600.00	100.00– 133.00	73.00– 97.00
Motorcycle	4,200.00	933.00	674.00
Radio receiver (good)	400.00	89.00	64.00
Pobeda or Volga auto	30,000.00	6,667.00	4,890.00
Washing machine	2,250.00	500.00	369.00
TV (14 inch)	2,400.00	533.00	381.00
Record player	250.00– 300.00	55.00– 67.00	40.00– 49.00
Refrigerator (Zil)	2,000.00	444.00	326.00
Vacuum cleaner	425.00	94.00	68.00
Alarm clock	30.00– 50.00	7.00– 11.00	5.00– 8.00
Popular wristwatch	500.00	111.00	80.00
Family divan	1,300.00	289.00	207.00
Hi-fi radio	2,100.00	467.00	337.00
Pillows	35.00	7.78	5.65
Personal care:			
Toilet soap (bar)	2.20	.49	.36
Real leather handbag	140.00	31.00	23.00
Lipstick	4.50– 6.00	1.00– 1.33	.73– .97
Haircut	.90– 1.50	.20– .33	.15– .25
Shoeshine	1.00	.22	.16
Recreation:			
Film (roll)	5.80	1.29	.93
Football	35.00	7.78	5.65
Balalaika	40.00	8.90	6.42
Accordion	300.00–1,000.00	67.00– 222.00	49.00– 161.00
Record (12-inch long play)	7.90	1.76	1.27
Gasoline (gallon)	3.00	.67	.49
Newspaper	.20	.04	.03
Movie admission	3.00– 5.00	.67– 1.11	.49– .80
Theater seats	5.00– 25.00	1.11– 5.56	.80– 4.00
Postage (domestic)	.60	.13	10.00

[1] All dollar-equivalent prices above $10 have been rounded to nearest dollar.

At the average family income level, the Soviet citizens are faced with a set of food prices which most Americans would consider to be high but within reason. At this income level, only the prices of pork, butter, sugar, fresh fruits and vegetables, and imported products (coffee, tea, lemons, and oranges) appear to be outlandish by our standards. The price of tea appears to be particularly high, but fortunately Russians have always preferred weak tea. By a process of substituting beef or fish for pork, margarine for butter, cabbage and carrots for other fresh fruits and vegetables, the average Soviet family—particularly the workers and students who eat their noon meal in the factory or school restaurant or cafeteria—probably eat reasonably well by American standards.

Clothing is relatively much more expensive than food, even for the average Soviet family. Furthermore, styles are very passé, again by our standards. The only bright note here is found in children's apparel which sometimes sells below cost.[37] Consumer durables are not as expensive as might be imagined. Since in most cases the established prices ration a fairly limited supply (at least compared to United States per capita supplies), it seems obvious that not a

[37] There seems to be some possibility that children's apparel may be among the first items to be distributed according to Communist principles, that is, according to need.

great deal of family disposable income remains after purchases of the more essential food and clothing.

Although no effort will be made to establish the level of living in Soviet upper income groups, the relative prices and other information given above provide us with clues as to the nature of conspicuous consumption in the Soviet Union. The Soviet family with above-average income probably pampers himself with pork, butter, imported foods, eating out in restaurants, a more stylish and diversified wardrobe, including perhaps imported fabrics, and a few extra consumer durables. At very high income levels, wives may even give up their jobs unless social pressure is too great. In addition, domestic servants, private medical attention, voluntary saving, and insurance might enter into their budgetary expenditures. For the elite, automobiles, travel abroad, and country homes become attainable.

Some mention should be made of the qualitative differences in the consumer goods sold in the two countries. In the United States, we most frequently have a situation which can perhaps be best described as a buyers' market, where sellers are ever searching for potential buyers; in the Soviet Union, the reverse situation prevails chronically. There is a sellers' market with potential buyers chasing frequently unavailable commodities. As a result, despite some long-run improvement in the quality of Soviet consumer goods, our products and retail services are undoubtedly generally superior qualitywise. The range of commodities, grades, and models from which Soviet consumers are able to select is also much narrower than is the case in the United States. To some extent, this is counterbalanced by the fact that many more consumer durables are purchased on time in the United States, so that a rather substantial interest charge should be added to some of our prices. Finally, a considerable amount of food must be purchased on the collective farm markets in the U.S.S.R., where prices are ordinarily considerably higher, especially in winter when food supplies are short.

A COMPARISON OF CONSUMPTION IN THE UNITED STATES AND SOVIET ECONOMIES

It is somewhat easier to gage the meaningfulness of retail prices in the Soviet Union than it is to estimate Soviet consumption relative to our own. Since the earlier report prepared for the Joint Economic Committee compared per capita availability, consumption, or stocks of various consumer goods in the two countries, I shall suggest a somewhat different approach to the problem.

The industrial labor forces of the two countries are of approximately the same overall magnitude. Actually, the Soviet industrial labor force may be slightly larger than ours. Consequently, the relative number of workers engaged in light industry (principally textiles, apparel, and footwear) and in food processing will also indicate approximately the absolute numbers of workers employed in these sectors in the two countries. According to a very detailed analysis of the labor forces of the two countries, about the same percentage of workers are engaged in food processing in both countries, while a slightly greater percentage of Soviet workers is engaged in light industry as compared with the corresponding U.S. sectors.[38]

[38] A. David Redding, "Nonagricultural Employment in the U.S.S.R., 1928-55," unpublished Ph. D. dissertation, Columbia University, New York, 1958, pp. 162, 165, and 166.

338 COMPARISONS OF UNITED STATES AND SOVIET ECONOMIES

Very roughly speaking then, the relative output per worker in the two economies will give us the relative output of these two sectors in the two countries. A recent Soviet study of comparative labor productivity in a good many sectors of both Soviet and United States industry has produced results which appear to be fairly consistent with the earlier findings of Galenson, and must therefore be taken seriously.[39] According to these Soviet claims, labor productivity in the U.S.S.R. as a percentage of the United States ranged from 17.1 percent in the production of margarine to 147.4 percent in bakery products, with an average level of labor productivity in food processing and light industry of between 50 and 65 percent of our own. According to these calculations, Soviet output per worker relative to our own is higher in the food processing and light industries, particularly the former, than it is in industry as a whole. This phenomenon is explained primarily by the fact that many U.S. consumer goods sectors are less concentrated as well as more backward technologically as compared with our heavy industry.

If we assume only the lower limit of the Soviet claims, it would seem that very roughly speaking the output of their light and food processing industries could hardly be much more than roughly half of our own. Still to be considered is the fact that the Russians have 30 million extra people to feed and clothe. On the other hand, a much larger percentage of the Soviet population—those living in rural areas and growing much of their own food—do not rely on state industry for a great deal of their food. Also the Soviet Union seems to be a net importer of consumer goods, while we tend to have an export surplus in this respect.[40] Taking all of these modifying factors into account, as a first approximation, we might estimate that Soviet per capita consumption of food might be slightly more than half of our own. On the other hand, Soviet per capita consumption of clothing might be somewhat less than half of our own. But the big advantage that American consumers have over their Soviet counterparts must surely be found in the area of durable consumer goods and services.

CAN THE SOVIETS ACHIEVE THE U.S. LEVEL OF LIVING?

In terms of food and clothing, the Soviets stand the best chance of overtaking our level of living. As consumers, we tend to have reached something of a plateau with respect to our per capita consumption of food.[41] As our incomes rise, we also tend to be increasing our purchases of durable consumer goods and services generally rather than clothing. More specifically, to a great extent, we tend to have substituted the automobile and travel for additional food and clothing. The ability of the Russians to close the gap with respect to food and clothing will therefore depend primarily on their own ability to augment the labor force employed in these branches as well as their success in increasing labor productivity in these sectors.[42]

[39] A. Kats, "Proizvoditel'nost' truda v SSSR i v kapitalisticheskikh stranakh" (Labor Productivity in the U.S.S.R. and in Capitalist Countries), Sotsialisticheskii Trud, No. 1, 1959, pp. 42–55. (For a translation of this article, see the Current Digest of the Soviet Press, vol. XI, No. 32, 1959, pp. 3–8.) Cf., also, A. Aganbegian, "Dognat' i peregnat' SSHA po urovniu proizvoditel'nosti truda" (To Catch Up With and Surpass the United States in the Level of Labor Productivity), ibid., No. 4, 1959, pp. 11–22, especially p. 15.
[40] In 1956, when imports and exports virtually balanced for the Soviet Union, 24.6 percent of all exports could be classified as consumer goods compared with 27.7 percent of all imports which could be so classified.
[41] According to the U.S. Department of Agriculture, Agricultural Statistics, U.S. Government Printing Office, 1958, p. 688, the index of per capita food consumption in the United States in 1956 was still slightly below the 1946 level and only 13 percent above the 1928 level.
[42] This assumes that there is no massive import program for consumer goods.

Until 1964 at least, there will undoubtedly be certain difficulties with respect to increasing the labor force employed in these branches due primarily to the lowering of the Soviet birthrate during World War II. By scraping the bottom of the barrel, they may be able to get more work from students, older persons, and housewives than they are currently, but the prospects for a greatly expanded labor force in food processing and light industries remain rather dim, at least until the latter half of the sixties. As far as increasing labor productivity is concerned, there seems to be no increase in the relative planned investments in light and food processing industries during the coming 7 years, although the absolute amounts invested will approximately double. Some improvement in the rate of increase in output per worker may possibly be expected since diminishing returns are probably less significant in light and food processing industries than they are in the extractive industries.[43] Even a below normal rate of growth due to the labor shortage would undoubtedly mean a closing of the gap with respect to the consumption of some food products or apparel; as a result, Soviet per capita consumption of a few items—fish, woolen fabrics, butter, etc.—may equal or even exceed ours by 1965.

For the period after 1965, there are a number of important variables which could potentially affect any closing of the gap in levels of living and which make predictions at this point seem especially hazardous. Nevertheless, we might mention a number of factors which may or may not affect the achievement of something approaching our level of living by the Soviets.

By the latter half of the sixties, the normal yearly influx of new, young workers into the Soviet labor force should be resumed. Presumably at least a proportionate share of this manpower would be available for the light and food processing industries. If there should be any shift in the pattern of investment favoring light and food processing industries after 1965, the growth in the labor force employed in these sectors might even be greater than the gains for industry as a whole. Any increase in the proportion of total capital investment allocated to consumer goods industries would also presumably show up in a more rapid increase in labor productivity in these sectors.

Any reduction or elimination of Soviet occupation forces in Eastern Germany, Poland, and Hungary would also release additional labor, part of which would possibly find its way into the consumer goods sectors. Reduction in domestic defense requirements might also have a similar beneficial impact on levels of living in the U.S.S.R.

On the other hand, any extension of the Soviet sphere of influence or program of economic assistance to the underdeveloped areas of the world would tend to retard the closing of the gap in levels of living. In this connection, it has also been made clear by Premier Khrushchev that all members of the Soviet bloc will approach communism or their version of the "affluent society" at approximately the same time.[44] As a result, the rise in levels of living in Czechoslovakia and the Soviet Union will be retarded to the extent that workers and employees in

[43] As mentioned above, the reduction in the statutory workweek to 42 hours will further interfere with the ability of the Soviets to increase annual output per worker.
[44] See Pravda, Jan. 28, 1959. (Translated in the Current Digest of the Soviet Press, Mar. 11, 1959, p. 13.)

340 COMPARISONS OF UNITED STATES AND SOVIET ECONOMIES

these economies are required to assist underdeveloped areas in the Soviet bloc in their industrialization and development programs.

It also seems reasonably clear that lack of effective demand should never be a retarding factor in raising the Soviet level of living, as it sometimes is in our own economy. Up until the present, the principal problem of Soviet planners has been one of restraining effective demand, and, as we have already noted, a permanent sellers market prevails. Furthermore, the Soviet Government, through its control over prices and the relationship between prices and costs, can virtually guarantee a continuation of these operating conditions if it so chooses.

TABLE 2.—*Levels of living: Per capita availability, consumption, or stocks of goods in 1955*

Commodity	U.S.S.R. Unit	1955 sales	1955 production	United States, 1955	Per capita Unit	Per capita 1955 U.S.S.R.	Per capita 1955 United States	Per capita ratios, 1955, U.S.S.R./United States
FOODS								
Meat	Million metric tons	(4.874)	4.0 (2.522)	12.050	Kilogram	20.2	72.9	0.28
Fish	do	1.990	2.498	0.744	do	10.1	4.5	2.24
Poultry meat	do	[1]	[1]	1.951	do	[1]	11.8	[1]
Eggs (number)	Billions	(2.281)	[1]	60.500	Number	[12]	366	
Milk fat solids	Million metric tons	[1]	29.8 (13.5)	44.118	Kilogram	130.7	266.9	0.35
Milk nonfat solids	do			26.398	do		159.7	
Fluid milk and cream	do				do			
Butter	do	0.439	(0.459)	0.661	do	2.2	4.0	0.55
Margarine	do	0.461	(1.156)	0.595	do	2.3	3.6	0.64
Other fats and oils	do	(1.998)		2.347	do	10.1	14.2	0.71
Fruits	do	[1]		11.240	do	[1]	68.0	[1]
Vegetables	do	[1]		14.348	do	[1]	86.8	[1]
Potatoes	do	[1]	67.000	12.844	do	338.7	51.2	6.62
Grain, dry pulses	do	[1]		8.463	do	290.0	77.7	2.96
Coffee	do	[1]		1.141	do	[1]	6.9	[1]
Tea	do	0.051		0.050	do	0.3	0.3	1.00
Cocoa beans	do	[1]		0.298	do	[1]	1.8	[1]
Peanuts	do	[1]		0.331	do	[1]	2.0	[1]
Confectionery items	do	1.706	1.382	[1]	do	8.6		[1]
Salt	do	4.467	6.200		do	22.6		
Sugar	do	(11.14.)	3.419	7.224	do	17.3	43.7	0.40
CLOTHING AND TEXTILES								
Cotton fabric	Billion linear meters	[1]	5.90	11.9	Linear meters	29.8	72.0	0.41
Wool fabric	do	[1]	0.25	0.4	do	1.5	2.4	0.63
Linen fabric	do	[1]	0.31	0.05	do	2.5	0.3	5.00
Silk fabric	do	[1]	0.53	0.05	do		0.3	8.33
Rayon, acetate fabric	do	[1]	0.11	2.2	do	0.5	13.3	0.03
Synthetic fabric	do			0.9	do		5.4	
Hosiery	Million pairs	[1]	772	1,811	Pairs	3.9	11.0	0.35
Knit underwear	Million pieces	[1]	345	940	Number	1.7	5.7	0.30
Shoes	Million pairs	[1]	275	639	Pairs	1.4	3.9	0.36

See footnote at end of table, p. 112.

TABLE 2.—*Levels of living: Per capita availability, consumption, or stocks of goods in 1955*—Continued

Commodity	U.S.S.R. Unit	1955 sales	1955 production	United States, 1955	Per capita, 1955 Unit	Per capita, 1955 U.S.S.R.	Per capita, 1955 United States	Per capita ratios, 1955, U.S.S.R./United States
DURABLE MANUFACTURES								
Automobiles	Thousands	64	108	7,763	Number	0.0003	0.047	0.006
Motorcycles	do	216	245	40	do	0.001	0.0002	5.00
Bicycles	do	2,801	2,884	2,900	do	0.014	0.018	0.78
Sewing machines	do	1,647	1,611	2,200	do	0.008	0.013	0.62
Electric irons	do	(1)	(1)	7,900	do	(1)	0.048	(1)
Washing machines	do	83	87	4,300	do	0.0004	0.026	0.02
Clothes dryers	do	(1)	(1)	1,400	do	(1)	0.008	(1)
Refrigerators	do	144	151	3,700	do	0.0007	0.022	0.03
Vacuum cleaners	do	121	(1)	3,400	do	0.0006	0.021	0.03
Clocks and watches	do	19,193	19,700	43,000	do	0.097	0.260	0.37
Cameras	do	971	1,023	5,900	do	0.005	0.036	0.14
Record players	do	846	848	(1)	do	0.004	(1)	(1)
Radios	do	3,474	} 4,024	14,100	do	0.018	0.085	0.21
Television sets	do	483		7,800	do	0.002	0.047	0.04
Electric shavers	do	(1)	(1)	4,600	do	(1)	0.028	(1)
Room air conditioners	do	(1)	(1)	1,200	do	(1)	0.007	(1)
Electric blankets	do	(1)	(1)	1,300	do	(1)	0.008	(1)
HOUSING								
Living space, total available					Square meters	4.8	32.0	0.15

1 Not available.

Purchasing Power of Workers in the U.S.S.R.

EDMUND NASH*

THE PURCHASING POWER of Soviet workers has been increasing steadily in recent years, mainly as the result of rising wages. However, real earnings of the average worker in the Soviet Union, in terms of food-buying power, are still below the high point in the Soviet level of living reached in 1928, when private enterprise was permitted to a minor extent under the then New Economic Policy (the "NEP") and the peasants had not yet been forced into collective farms. The level of living declined after the introduction in September 1928 of the Five Year Plans (which continued through 1958), with their emphasis on the expansion of heavy industry. This emphasis has continued up to the present. The most recent Soviet statistical yearbook [1] reported that by 1958 capital goods production had increased to 570 percent of its 1940 level, while consumer goods production had reached only 270 percent. The Seven Year Plan (1959–65) calls for an average annual increase of 9.4 percent in the production of capital goods, as against 7.4 percent for consumer goods.

Official Soviet price and wage data indicate that the average Soviet worker had to work about 8 percent longer in 1959 than he did in 1928 in order to buy for his family the same average weekly supply of seven essential foods—bread, potatoes, beef, butter, eggs, milk, and sugar. (See table 1 and chart 1.) In particular, he had to work about 18 percent longer for a pound of bread, about 10 percent longer for sugar, about 153 percent longer for milk, and 190 percent longer for eggs. Beef was just as "cheap" as in 1928, and potatoes and butter were slightly "cheaper." Comparable data

for 1928 are not available for other consumer goods; however, other data clearly indicate that prices for these goods, especially clothing, also rose after 1928 at a higher rate than money earnings.[2]

In 1959, a Soviet worker, if the sole supporter of a family of four, would have had to work 28.49 hours, or 62 percent of the legal 46-hour workweek of most workers, to buy enough of the seven foods listed for his family. An earlier study [3] showed that in 1953 the average Soviet worker had to work approximately 38.17 hours for the same amount of food, or 79.5 percent of the then prevailing legal 48-hour workweek of most workers. The relatively high cost of food in the Soviet Union helps explain the exceptionally high percentage of the labor force who are women (47 percent of the labor force in January 1960 were women, compared with 35 percent in the United States). To ease the homework of employed women with families, the Soviet Government has been encouraging factory and other restaurants (some created solely for this purpose) to prepare take-home meals and cooked foods, and encouraging grocery stores to extend home deliveries of milk, bread, potatoes, and vegetables. However, in Moscow, where the system of home deliveries was most highly developed in mid-1958, less than 1 percent of the bread sold was delivered to homes.

The seven foods given in table 1 do not include various other customary and important foods such as vegetables (especially cabbage), fruits (in season), and tea. In 1953, presumably to hold down their expenditures for food, about 40 percent of the Soviet wage and salary earners (18 million out of a total of 44.8 million) worked individual or collective gardening plots to produce their own potatoes, other vegetables, and fruit. Home production of food may become less important in the future: A joint Communist Party-Government decision published in Pravda on January 27, 1960, provided for supplying the Soviet people with various processed foodstuffs to be obtained from the scheduled increased

*Of the Division of Foreign Labor Conditions, Bureau of Labor Statistics.
[1] Narodnoe khozIaistvo SSSR v 1958 godu [The USSR National Economy in 1958] (Moscow, 1959), p. 142.
[2] For a discussion of the decline in real earnings in the Soviet Union between 1928 and 1952, see Janet G. Chapman, Real Wages in the Soviet Union, 1928-1952 (in Review of Economics and Statistics, Cambridge, Mass., May 1954, pp. 134-156).
[3] Purchasing Power of Soviet Workers, 1953 (in Monthly Labor Review, July 1953, pp. 705-708).

production by collective and State farms of potatoes, vegetables, and fruit. The expectation apparently is that the people's earnings will increase in the years to come to enable them to buy the new processed foodstuffs.

Soviet Wage-Price Policy

The present policy is to increase purchasing power (real earnings) especially of low and average earners by increasing money wages, mainly through the promotion of higher labor productivity; this indicates a change in the policy dominant in the period 1947–54, when the Government considered the annual across-the-board price cuts on essential consumer goods as the "most important means of raising real earnings." [4] Since 1954, there have been only occasional price cuts, mostly on luxury and semiluxury goods; for example, on July 1, 1959, prices were cut on bicycles, cameras, women's rayon stockings, wines, and children's toys, and on March 1, 1960, on electrical sewing machines, silk clothing, radios, motor scooters, accordions, safety razor blades, and certain other items. There have also been some price increases; for example, in 1958, for vodka, wines, automobiles, and machine-made carpets.

To encourage the purchase of certain high-priced consumer goods, the Soviet Government introduced installment buying in three Ukrainian cities in the spring of 1959, and in Moscow on October 1, 1959. In order to get credit, a buyer had to have a reference from his place of work, make a downpayment of 20 to 25 percent of the purchase price, and agree to pay the remainder within 6 to 12 months. By February 1960, installment buying had been expanded to about 2,000 stores in the Russian Republic, the largest of the 15 Republics in the Soviet Union. Radios and radio-phonographs constituted about one-third of the installment purchases. Other popular items among installment buyers were woolens, silks, watches, and furs.

The Soviet worker's purchasing power also is affected by the availability of consumer goods, many of which are still in short supply despite recent increases. Since 1953, sales of consumer goods in State and cooperative stores in the Soviet Union has been increasing at a faster rate than the growth of population (which has risen about 1.5 percent annually). For example, in 1957, the volume of sales had increased 14 percent over 1956; in 1958, 6 percent over 1957; and in 1959, 8 percent over 1958. Despite this continued increase, the Central Statistical Administration in its economic report for 1959, which was printed in the Moscow daily press on January 22, 1960,

[4] Pravda, April 3, 1953.

TABLE 1. APPROXIMATE WORKTIME REQUIRED TO BUY SELECTED FOODS AT STATE-FIXED PRICES IN MOSCOW, APRIL 1, 1928, APRIL 1, 1953, AND AUGUST 15, 1959

Food	Prices (in rubles)			Quantity consumed per week by a family of 4 [4]	Approximate worktime [5]			1953 [2] as percent of 1928	1959 as percent of 1928
	1928 [1]	1953 [2]	1959 [3]		In hours				
					1928	1953 [2]	1959		
Rye bread, 1 kilogram	0.080	1.35	1.30	9.84 kilogram	2.71	4.52	3.20	167	118
Potatoes, 1 kilogram	.085	.75	1.00	12.16 kilogram	3.56	3.10	3.04	87	85
Beef, 1 kilogram	.870	12.60	12.00	3.68 kilogram	11.04	15.77	11.04	143	100
Butter, 1 kilogram	2.430	26.75	27.00	.44 kilogram	3.69	4.00	2.97	108	80
Sugar, 1 kilogram	.620	9.09	9.40	1.80 kilogram	3.85	5.57	4.23	145	110
Milk, 1 liter	.063	2.20	2.20	4.96 liter	1.08	3.71	2.73	344	253
Eggs, per 10	.200	6.88	8.00	6.40 eggs	.44	1.50	1.28	341	290
All 7 foods					26.37	38.17	28.49	145	108

[1] Official Soviet prices from the People's Commissariat of Labor, as transmitted to the International Labor Office (see International Labor Review, Vol. 18, October–November 1928, pp. 657–660). These prices were lower than those in private trade which played a large role in workers' consumption, and their use may somewhat inflate the workers' real purchasing power at that time. On the other hand, it appears that Moscow food prices were noticeably higher than the national average in 1928; but Moscow goods were superior in quality. (See Naum Jasny, The Soviet Economy During the Plan Era, Stanford, Calif., Stanford University Press, 1951, p. 105.)
[2] Data from Purchasing Power of Soviet Workers, 1953 (in Monthly Labor Review, July 1953, pp. 705–708).
[3] Prices in Moscow State stores during August 1959, based on information appearing in the Soviet press.
[4] Weekly consumption figures per person in 1928 from International Labor

Review, ibid., p. 659; the average worker's family in 1928 consisted of 4 persons. (See Solomon Schwarz, Labor in the Soviet Union, New York, Praeger, 1952, p. 145.) The same percent relationship between 1928 and 1959 would be obtained if the quantities for 1 person were used instead of the quantities for a family of 4.
[5] Worktime is computed by multiplying quantity consumed by price and dividing the product by average hourly earnings. In 1928, official national average earnings were 703 rubles per year (figure given in Trud v SSSR [Labor in USSR], Moscow, 1936, p. 17), or 0.29 rubles per hour; in 1953, the estimated average earnings were about 600 rubles a month, or 2.94 rubles per hour; in 1959, the estimated average earnings were about 800 rubles a month, or approximately 4 rubles per hour, according to an analysis of scattered data appearing in the Soviet press.

Chart 1. Worktime Required to Buy Week's Supply [1] of Selected Foods in Moscow, 1959 as a Percent of 1928

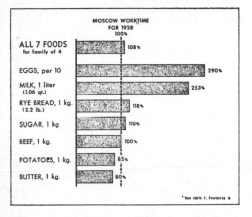

MOSCOW WORKTIME FOR 1928
100%

ALL 7 FOODS for family of 4	108%
EGGS, per 10	290%
MILK, 1 liter (1.06 qt.)	253%
RYE BREAD, 1 kg. (2.2 lb.)	118%
SUGAR, 1 kg	110%
BEEF, 1 kg.	100%
POTATOES, 1 kg.	85%
BUTTER, 1 kg.	80%

[1] See table 1, footnote 4

Average Earnings in the U.S.S.R.

Since the Soviet Government does not publish statistics on average money earnings in Moscow (or any other Soviet city), it has been necessary to estimate earnings from scattered data appearing in the Soviet press. The estimate arrived at is about 800 rubles (or $80 at the tourist rate of exchange of 10 rubles for US$1) a month, or approximately 4 rubles an hour. The prominent Soviet economist and member of the Academy of Sciences, S. Strumilin, in an article published in 1956,[5] assumed an average hourly wage of 4 rubles. This estimate was evidently a rounding up of the actual average, because there is evidence of some increase in earnings since that time.

Factors which have contributed to increase the average money wage in recent years (the BLS estimate in 1953 was 600 rubles a month) include the reclassification of millions of workers annually into higher wage categories reflecting their acquisition of new work qualifications, the increase as of January 1, 1957, of minimum

specifically mentioned a shortage of cotton fabrics, furniture, and home refrigerators, and stated that in general, there was an insufficient assortment of consumer goods and too many low quality goods.

Government and Party leader Nikita Khrushchev promised in a speech on March 14, 1958, that the scheduled production of clothing and footwear would meet the needs of the Soviet population by 1965. On March 20, 1958, an immediate increase in the production of children's clothing and footwear was decreed, and on May 7, 1958, the Central Committee of the Communist Party adopted a decision providing for speeding up production of synthetic materials to be used in the manufacture of fabrics, clothing, footwear, and other consumer goods. A joint Party-Government decree published on October 16, 1959, provided for sharply increased production in 1960 and 1961 of durable consumer goods such as refrigerators, television sets, washing machines, metal beds, electric irons, and kitchenware; automobiles, the cheapest of which costs about 25,000 rubles and which requires years of customer waiting, were not mentioned. The measures just enumerated indicate that for the Soviet people an adequate supply of consumer commodities is still a matter of the future.

[5] In Promyshlenno-ekonomicheskaya gazeta [Industrial-Economic Gazette], November 4, 1956.

Chart 2. Worktime Required to Buy Selected Commodities, Moscow as a Percent of New York City, 1959

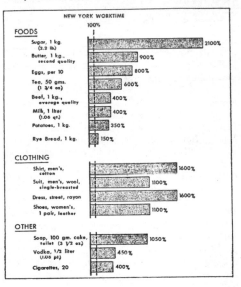

NEW YORK WORKTIME
100%

FOODS

Sugar, 1 kg. (2.2 lb.)	2100%
Butter, 1 kg., second quality	900%
Eggs, per 10	800%
Tea, 50 gms. (1 3/4 oz)	600%
Beef, 1 kg., average quality	400%
Milk, 1 liter (1.06 qt.)	400%
Potatoes, 1 kg.	350%
Rye Bread, 1 kg.	150%

CLOTHING

Shirt, men's, cotton	1600%
Suit, men's, wool, single-breasted	1100%
Dress, street, rayon	1600%
Shoes, women's, 1 pair, leather	1100%

OTHER

Soap, 100 gm. cake, toilet (3 1/2 oz.)	1050%
Vodka, 1/2 liter (1.06 pt)	450%
Cigarettes, 20	400%

TABLE 2. APPROXIMATE WORKTIME REQUIRED TO BUY SELECTED COMMODITIES AT STATE-FIXED PRICES[1] IN MOSCOW AND AT RETAIL STORE PRICES IN NEW YORK CITY, AUGUST 15, 1959

Commodity	Moscow price (in rubles)[2]	New York City price (in dollars)[3]	Approximate worktime[4]			Moscow worktime as a percent of New York City worktime
			Unit	Moscow	New York City	
Foods:						
Rye bread, 1 pound	[2] 0.59	[5] 0.215	Pound	9 min	6 min	
1 kilogram (2.2 lb.)	1.30	[5] .473	Kilogram	19.5 min	13 min	} 150
Potatoes, 1 pound	.45	.060	Pound	7 min	2 min	
1 kilogram	1.00	.132	Kilogram	15 min	4 min	} 350
Beef, rib roast, 1 pound	5.45	.757	Pound	82 min	21 min	
1 kilogram	12.00	1.665	Kilogram	180 min	46 min	} 400
Butter, salted, 1 pound	12.27	[6] .741	Pound	184 min	20.5 min	
1 kilogram	27.00	1.630	Kilogram	405 min	45 min	} 900
Sugar, 1 pound	4.27	.110	Pound	64 min	3 min	
1 kilogram	9.40	.242	Kilogram	141 min	7 min	} 2,100
Milk, at grocery, 1 quart	[2] 2.08	.273	Quart	31 min	7.5 min	
1 liter (1.06 qt.)	2.20	[5] .289	Liter	33 min	8 min	} 400
Eggs, 2d grade, per dozen	[2] 9.60	[7] .629	Dozen	144 min	17.4 min	
per 10	8.00	[5] .524	Per 10	120 min	14.5 min	} 800
Tea, 50 grams (1¾ ounces)	3.80	.200	Ounce / 50 grams	33 min / 57 min	5.5 min / 10 min	} 600
Men's clothing:						
Shirt, cotton[8]	60.00	2.03	Each	15 hr	56 min	} 1,600
Suit, wool, single-breasted, middle of price range	1,100.00	50.41	Each	275 hr	23 hr	} 1,100
Shoes, leather oxfords, pair	245.00	15.10	Pair	61 hr	7 hr	} 850
Women's clothing:						
Dress, street, rayon	294.00	10.00	Each	73 hr. 30 min	4 hr. 36 min	} 1,600
Shoes, leather oxfords, middle of price range	230.00	11.21	Pair	57 hr. 30 min	5 hr. 10 min	} 1,100
Stockings, nylon	32.00	1.35	Pair	8 hr	37 min	} 1,300
Other commodities:						
Soap, toilet, 100-gram cake (3½ ounces)	2.10	.105	Each	31.5 min	3 min	} 1,050
Cigarettes, package of 20	[9] 1.80	.25	Package	27 min	7 min	} 400
Vodka, pint	25.28	[10] 2.98	Pint	6 hr. 19 min	1 hr. 22 min	
½ liter (1.06 pt.)	26.80	3.16	½ liter	6 hr. 42 min	1 hr. 27 min	} 450

[1] Prices observed on the open market, where collective farmers sell their produce, were much higher in comparison with State store prices. For example, potatoes were 1.50 rubles per kilogram; beef, 25 rubles per kilogram; and eggs, 15 rubles for 10.

[2] Moscow prices in State stores, based on information appearing in the Soviet press, were calculated from Moscow prices for kilograms, liter, and 10 eggs, respectively.

[3] New York City prices in retail stores were collected by the Bureau of Labor Statistics; the prices for kilogram, liter, and 10 eggs were calculated from New York City prices for pound, quart, and dozen, respectively.

[4] Worktime figures for Moscow were computed on the basis of estimated average gross earnings of 4 rubles per hour of Moscow workers in manufacturing, a figure that is consistent with the Bureau of Labor Statistics' estimate of about 800 rubles a month. New York City worktime figures were computed from BLS retail prices and earnings in mid-August 1959 of $2.17 per hour of production workers in manufacturing in New York City.

[5] For white bread.

[6] First quality (92–93 score).

[7] Large eggs, grade A.

[8] Lowest priced shirt in Moscow.

[9] Brand name: Avtozavodskie.

[10] Spirit blended whiskey.

monthly basic pay rates, and the increase of lowest basic wage rates in connection with the new policy of narrowing the spread in wage rates (discussed later). Take-home pay has also been increased by the 1957 abolition of the special income tax on single persons and heads of small families, the 1957 exemption of additional low earners from income tax payment, and the abolition in 1957 of 50 percent of compulsory bond purchases and, as of January 1, 1958, of all such purchases (before 1957, bond purchases amounted to 3 or 4 weeks' pay annually).

Variations in Earnings. A wide variation in earnings exists in the Soviet Union not only between workers in different sectors of the national economy, as is illustrated in the following tabulation of selected salaries and wages in 1960, but also among production workers in particular industries.

Monthly earnings, 1960 (in rubles[1])

Scientist (academician)	8,000–15,000
Minister (head of Government ministry or department)	7,000
Opera star	[2] 5,000–20,000
Professor (science)	6,000–10,000
Professor (medicine)	4,000–6,000
Docent (assistant professor)	3,000–5,000
Plant manager	3,000–10,000
Engineer	1,000–3,000
Physician, head	950–1,800
Physician, staff	850–1,000
Teacher, high school	850–1,500
Teacher, primary school	600–900
Technician	800–2,000
Worker, skilled	1,000–2,500
Worker, semiskilled	600–900
Worker, unskilled	270–500

[1] The official rate of exchange, as fixed by the Soviet Government, is 4 rubles=US$1. The actual purchasing power of the ruble, however, is more accurately represented by the official tourist rate of exchange of 10 rubles for US$1.

[2] The top salary at the Bolshoi Theater has been reported as 5,000 rubles a month. Outside appearances increase the artist's income.

For example, factory or plant managers receive about 3,000 to 10,000 rubles ($300 to $1,000) a month, not counting such perquisites as the use of a car or a house, compared with the 270 to 500 rubles ($27 to $50) of the unskilled workers. The minimum pay of 270 rubles a month for workers in nonurban areas was fixed by decree, effective January 1, 1957.[6] The range in earnings for each type of position reflects the individual's initiative, his length of service, the amount of supervision and responsibility required of him, the type of industry, and other factors.

A Bureau of Labor Statistics study [7] showed that in 1951, there was a much wider spread in the basic hourly wage rates of production workers in the Soviet steel and construction industries (whose wage structures were typical of most Soviet industries) than in the same industries in the United States. In the Soviet Union, the highest basic wage rate for skilled workers in each of these industries was approximately 3.6 times that of the lowest for unskilled workers, while in the United States, it was found that the ratio was approximately 2.2 in each industry. Since that time, however, the Soviet Government has adopted a policy of decreasing the spread in basic wage rates. The chairman of the U.S.S.R. Council of Ministers' State Committee on Questions of Labor and Wages reported in 1958 [8] that the then prevailing system of 8, 10, and 12 wage grades in various industries would be reduced to a system of 6 or 7 grades where the basic wage rate for the top grade would not be, as a rule, more than twice the lowest wage rate. In implementation of this policy, a system of six basic wage rates was introduced in the construction industry, with a ratio of 2.1 to 1 between the

highest and the lowest basic wage rates. In the chemical industry, a system of seven basic wage rates was introduced, with a ratio of 2.3 to 1. Most recently (during the fourth quarter of 1959), a single system of six basic wage rates, with a ratio of 1.8 to 1, was introduced in cotton and linen mills in certain areas of the Soviet Union, and is to be extended to woolen, silk, and all other textile mills during 1960. In all cases, the new low ratios have been or are to be achieved by raising the lower basic wage rates.[9] However, Soviet sources indicate that in some industries, other than the textile industry, extremely high wage rates will be decreased and that take-home pay in some cases will drop as a result of the scheduled introduction of the 7-hour workday.[10]

Real Earnings, United States and U.S.S.R.

Chart 2 and table 2 show that the average Moscow worker has to work much longer than the New York City worker to buy basic consumer goods. For potatoes, he has to work about 3 times as long; for beef and milk, 4 times; for eggs, 8 times; for butter, 9 times; and for sugar, 21 times. The worktime required to buy clothing is 8 to 16 times more in Moscow than in New York City, and reflects a clothing shortage in the Soviet Union. However, as previously indicated, this shortage is not as great as it was in 1953, when the worktime required to buy clothing in Moscow was 10 to 20 times more than in New York City.

The Soviet press frequently boasts that, unlike workers in the United States, Soviet workers have the benefit of low rentals and free medical services. Soviet medical care, however, is free only in the sense that the Soviet population does not pay for it directly on a fee-for-service basis; it is paid for by part of the funds obtained through taxation in the form of increased prices of consumer goods.[11] This taxation constitutes roughly one-half the price of all consumer goods.[12] It is universally admitted in the Soviet Union that housing is the biggest problem in every city.[13] In 1957, the Government decreed a 12-year program to ease this situation.

The English-language newspaper Moscow News on September 16, 1958, reported that, under a 1926 decree still in force, Soviet workers expended only 4 to 6 percent of their monthly earnings for rent, the amount depending on the income of the

[6] Pravda, September 9, 1956.

[7] Wage Spread in the Steel and Construction Industries, U.S. and U.S.S.R. (in Notes on Labor Abroad, U.S. Department of Labor, August 1952).

[8] Pravda, November 25, 1958.

[9] Sotsialisticheskii trud [Socialist Labor] (Moscow, December 1959), p. 47.

[10] For discussion of the 7-hour workday decree, see Monthly Labor Review, January 1960, p. 44.

[11] For detailed discussion of medical services to workers, see Occupational Health Services in the Soviet Union (in Monthly Labor Review, November 1959, pp. 1218–1224). For discussion of the extent of private health insurance available to workers in the United States, see Supplementary Wage Provisions in Major Labor Markets, 1953–59 (in Monthly Labor Review, October 1959, p. 1131).

[12] For discussion, see Leon M. Herman, Taxes and the Soviet Citizen (in Problems of Communism, United States Information Agency, Washington, D.C., September–October, 1959, pp. 21–26).

[13] Adlai E. Stevenson, in reporting on his visit to the Soviet Union in the New York Times (November 19, 1958, p. 20), said, "In every city, the 'Mayor' told me housing was his biggest problem."

tenant, the building in which he lived, and other factors. However, it was not mentioned that in Moscow, most families lived in only one room [14] and had to share bathrooms and kitchens with other families, and that every family had to pay extra for such utilities as light and heat. One Soviet writer reported that in 1936 (it could be 1960 just as well, because of the Soviet unchanging rent rates), rent accounted for 5.4 percent of the worker's budget, and expenditures for heat, light, etc., accounted for an additional 4.9 percent, for a total of 10.3 percent.[15] In the United States in 1950, the comparable total figure for renters was about 15 percent,[16] but the average family lived in four or five rooms, with its own kitchen and bathroom.[17]

---

[14] According to data published in the newspaper Vechernaya Moskva [Evening Moscow], August 12, 1958, new housing in 1957 was allocated on a priority basis at the rate of about 6 square meters (about 65 square feet) per person; that is, a family of 4 received floor space equivalent to 2 rooms, each about 12 feet by 11 feet. In the new housing, each family has its own kitchen and bathroom.

[15] N. L. Filatov, Ocherki po ekonomike i finansam sotsialisticheskogo zhilishchnogo khozialstva [Articles on the Economics and Financing of Socialist Housing] (Moscow, 1947), p. 62.

[16] Study of Consumer Expenditures, Incomes, and Savings (Philadelphia, University of Pennsylvania, 1956–57), Vol. XVIII, table 6–4, p. 65.

[17] 1950 Census of Housing, U.S. Summary, General Characteristics (U.S. Bureau of the Census, 1953), Census Report H–A1, table 9, p, 1–7.

Social Welfare in the USSR

By Alec Nove

AS SOME CRITICS SEE IT, the Soviet state is exclusively an organ of oppression. The motivations of its leaders, they believe, are to be found solely in the pursuit of world revolution, of national aggrandizement, of personal power—or of all these at once. The attitude of the Soviet leaders toward their own people is often represented as if it were mainly inspired by the objective of keeping the mass of Soviet citizens on the lowest possible living standard consistent with the necessity of providing minimum work incentives.

Hence such critics are inclined to view all Soviet measures which seem to increase public welfare as "concessions" wrung from a reluctant regime by irresistible force of circumstance or popular pressure. It is but a short step from this view to the conclusion that such measures are, in themselves, proof of the regime's weakness or instability. If more was done to improve welfare in the first years after Stalin's death, these critics might argue, it was only because the struggle for power among Stalin's successors was undecided, and because the police apparatus had lost much of its capacity to intimidate. Inversely, now that Khrushchev has become unquestioned boss, they should logically expect a return to the old ways.

The purpose of the present article is to inquire into the validity of such interpretations of the "welfare" aspect of Soviet rule. But it is necessary first of all to define the area of discussion. To take a negative approach, the

1

author does not propose to discuss such matters as wage rates and consumer goods production. It is acknowledged fact that real wages in the Soviet Union have been rising slowly but steadily, that peasant incomes and retail trade turnover have gone up, and that the present Soviet leadership has declared its intention to continue this process through the period of the Seven-Year Plan (1958-65). It is also true that the upward trend in these areas is highly relevant to welfare in the general sense and should be duly noted. In the present paper, however, attention will be concentrated rather on activities of a more direct "public welfare" nature, *i.e.,* on the various social services (health, education, *etc.*), on housing and such other state measures as affect the everyday life of Soviet citizens.

A Look at the Record

Before inquiring into the question of motivation, it is also necessary to set forth a few facts showing what actually *has* been done, or is being done, by the Soviet Union in the area of welfare. Such a survey of the record may best begin with a look at budget allocations for social and cultural expenditures during the 1950-59 period, presented in the table on this page. Keeping the general trend toward increased outlays in mind, the in-

dividual categories of welfare listed are reviewed below with particular attention as to whether or not there has been any recent change of policy.

Health. There is no evidence that Soviet policy in this field has undergone any basic change in recent years. Vigorous efforts to expand medical and health services were already a feature of Stalin's reign, and the progress that was achieved is clearly indicated by the fact that the Soviet Union, as the following figures attest, has since 1951 boasted a larger number of doctors per thousand inhabitants than most Western countries:

USSR (1951) _____ 13.9
USSR (1957) _____ 16.9
United States (1954) _____ 12.7
United Kingdom (1951) _____ 8.8
West Germany (1955) _____ 13.5

(Source: *Dostizheniia sovetskoi vlasti za 40 let* [The achievements of the Soviet Government in 40 years], Moscow, 1957, p. 348).

Thus, while the 1957 and 1959 budget figures show relatively sharp increases in health expenditures, it is clear that these are not a new departure in Soviet policy, but rather a continuation of past trends.

It is true that the equipment of many Soviet hospitals is antiquated, that drugs are often scarce, and that the

USSR Social-Cultural Budget: 1950-59

(in billions of rubles)

	1950	1953	1957	1959
Total Health	21.4	24.2	38.3	44.0
(of which)				
Hospitals & clinics, urban	10.3	12.3	18.6	----
Hospitals & clinics, rural	2.6	3.1	4.6	----
Total Education	56.9	61.1	80.7	94.3
(of which)				
General schooling (a)	30.4	32.2	37.6	----
Higher and technical	18.3	19.3	24.2	----
Science and research (b)	5.4	6.2	13.6	23.1 (c)
Total Social Security	22.0	22.8	52.8	88.2
Total Social Insurance	12.7	16.2	23.5	----
Total Maternity Assistance	1.2	4.5	5.2	5.5
Total, Social-Cultural	116.7	128.8	200.5	232.0

Source: *Raskhody na sotsialno-kulturnye meropriiatia po gosudarstvennom byudzhetu SSSR* (Expenditures for Social-Cultural Measures in the State Budget of the USSR), Moscow, 1958; also Finance Minister Zverev's speech, reported in *Pravda,* December 23, 1958.

Notes: (a) Includes kindergarten and adult education. (b) As most all-Union expenditures for science and research are kept secret, no complete breakdown of this item is given in the budget, but nuclear research is doubtless a major element. The item as a whole has practically no relevance for "welfare" in any sense. (c) Part of the big increase in 1959 is accounted for by a change in definition hinted at in Zverev's budget speech.

2

general level of health facilities is not up to the best Western standards. Nevertheless, a great deal has certainly been done to spread hygiene, combat epidemics, and reduce infant mortality. The services of state doctors and hospitals are free, although most medicines have to be bought by the patient.

Education. Here again, recent Soviet policy has not basically altered Stalin's approach insofar as the latter aimed at a large-scale expansion of the educational system, but there have been important changes in emphasis and direction. Thus, the decision of the 20th CPSU Congress (February 1956) to extend full-time secondary education to all has since been modified in favor of part-time education after the age of 15, and Khrushchev's reform of higher education also seems likely to result in a reduction of the number of *full-time* university students. It is not, of course, within the scope of the present article to discuss the detailed causes and consequences of Khrushchev's reforms of Soviet education. Regardless of the effect they may have on academic standards, however, it can be stated that these reforms are unlikely to result in any modification of the upward trend in Soviet educational expenditures (except for a possible large saving in student stipends).

One notable reason for this assumption is the evident rise in the school building program, partly as a result of an overdue effort to remedy the overcrowding which at present necessitates a two-shift, and sometimes even three-shift, system of attendance, and partly to set up the new-type boarding schools in which Khrushchev plans to train the "new Soviet man." It is only fair to add that, in contrast to the continuing shortage of physical facilities, the situation of Soviet schools with regard to the ratio of teachers to pupils compares very favorably with that in many other countries including the United States, as evidenced by the following figures:

	Pupils Teachers *(in thousands)*		Pupils per Teacher
USSR (1956-57)	30,127	1,811	16.6
United States (1955)	30,531	1,135	26.9
United Kingdom (1956)	7,981	309	25.8

(Sources: For the USSR *Dostizheniia. . . .* p. 274; for the US and UK, *United Nations Statistical Yearbook, 1958.*)

Mention should also be made of the Khrushchev leadership's action in 1956 to abolish all fees in schools and universities, which reversed one of Stalin's counter-reforms. It will be recalled that free education had been a feature of the Soviet regime from the beginning and was explicitly guaranteed by the 1936 Stalin constitution. Despite the constitutional guarantee, however, educational charges were imposed in the top three grades of

secondary schools and in universities by a simple decree of the Council of Ministers in 1940. Although the action did not have such a serious effect on university students because of the fact that the large majority were receiving stipends from which the fees simply were deducted, its impact on children of poor families enrolled in secondary schools, where stipends were not payable, was much more severe. Without doubt the restoration of free education was a highly popular act.

Social insurance, social security, and pensions. Sick-pay benefits in the Soviet Union have long been on a relatively generous scale, and there have been no significant changes in rates of payment in recent years, although overall expenditures for this purpose have increased as a result of the upward trend in total numbers of employed and in the average wage. As part of the campaign launched in the 1930's to reduce the high rate of labor turnover, full rates of sick pay were made conditional upon a minimum period of work in the same enterprise or office, except in cases where workers had transferred under official orders. These rules remain in force, although with some modifications in favor of the worker.

Provided he is a trade-union member, a worker who falls ill is paid the following proportions of his actual earnings (non-members receive one-half these rates, subject to the minima referred to below):

Years of service	% of Earnings
Less than 3	50
3-5	60
5-8	70
8-12	80
More than 12	90

Present regulations provide for minimum monthly payments of 300 rubles in towns and 270 rubles in rural areas, and a maximum payment of 100 rubles per day.* Those who are injured at work or suffer from diseases

---

* To give the reader some idea of the purchasing power of the ruble, here are the official Soviet prices (in rubles) of a few representative commodities (per kilogram in the case of food, unless otherwise stated): chicken, 16.5; beef (stewing), 12; pork, 19.5; average fish, 11; butter, 28; milk, 2.2 per liter; eggs (10), 7.5; rye bread, 1.24; potatoes, 1; cabbage, 1.5-2; coffee, 40; wool-mixture blanket, 100+; cotton print dress, 200; wool dress, 475; man's overcoat, 720; man's all-wool suit, 2,000; shoes (adequate), 200; bicycle, 450-600; motorcycle, 4,200; radio, 400; washing machine, 2,250; family divan, 1,300; toilet soap, (bar) 2.2; lipstick, 4.5-6. Source: Lynn Turgeon, "Levels of Living, Wages and Prices in the Soviet and United States Economies," *Comparisons of the United States and Soviet Economies,* Joint Economic Committee of the US Congress, US Government Printing Office, Washington, 1959, pp. 335-36.—Ed.

caused by their work are entitled to sickness benefits at the rate of 100 percent of their earnings regardless of length of service. Where a worker leaves his job of his own volition, he is not entitled to sickness pay for ordinary illness until a period of six months has elapsed, but this limitation does not apply (since February 1957) to cases of accident or disease caused by a person's work.[1] Of course, the social insurance rates described here apply only to disability for a limited period of time, permanent disablement being dealt with under pension regulations.

The maternity benefit rate itself also has not been changed in recent years, but in 1956 the period of paid maternity leave was lengthened to 112 days.[2] This was, in effect, a return to the regulation which had been in force up until 1938, when the period of maternity leave was reduced from 112 to 70 days.

The biggest improvements in this general area recently have been in the field of old-age and permanent disability pensions. Their effect, according to Finance Minister Zverev, was to raise the average rate of all pensions by 81 percent,[3] but certain groups of workers who had fared relatively worse under the pre-1956 pension regulations secured much bigger gains than this, for the following reasons: The previous regulations nominally entitled a worker qualifying for an old-age pension by length of service to receive payments at the rate of two-thirds of his final wage. This looked extremely generous until one noticed the proviso, often omitted from propaganda statements, that the two-thirds was to be calculated on the basis of a *maximum* "reckonable" wage of 300 rubles per month, meaning an effective maximum pension of 200 rubles per month. This figure, when originally fixed some 25 years earlier, was quite legitimate, but wages and prices subsequently multiplied without any upward revision of the allowable maximum. The result was considerable hardship for ordinary workers, while on the other hand exceptional treatment was granted to certain categories including not only the professional and official classes but also workers in some priority occupations. For example, coal miners, steel workers, and those engaged in electricity generation were allotted a much higher reckonable maximum. Similar discriminatory rules applied also to pension benefits for surviving dependents and victims of industrial accidents and the like.

---

[1] These details are taken from S. A. Mitin (ed.), *Spravochnik po trudui zarabotnoi platy v stroiteltsve* (Reference Book on Labor and Earnings in Construction), Moscow, 1957, pp. 438-41.

[2] G. A. Prudenski (ed.), *Voprosy Truda v SSSR* (Problems of Labor in the USSR), Moscow, 1958, p. 66.

[3] In *Finansy SSSR* (Finances of the USSR), No. 10, 1957, p. 17.

The reform of 1956, while reducing certain very high pensions, established an all-round minimum old-age pension of 300 rubles per month for those qualified by length of service, an advance of great importance. In addition, it put into effect a new scale of payments benefiting lower-paid workers, so that those earning up to 350 rubles per month now receive pensions amounting to 100 percent of earnings, with progressively smaller percentages for those with higher earnings, and with a maximum overall ceiling of 1200 rubles per month. An average worker earning, say, 750 rubles per month qualifies for a pension of 487 rubles under the new rules, as against probably only 200 under the old.[4] One offsetting feature of the reform is that working pensioners are no longer permitted to receive full pensions on top of their wages.[5] (This provision, together with the better pension rates, has very probably encouraged many old people to retire.) On balance, however, the net gain to Soviet pensioners can readily be measured by the increase in pension expenditures shown in the following table (in billions of rubles):

	1950	1956	1957 (prelim.)	1958 (plan)
Total pensions	30.1	36.5	59.9	66.0
(of which)				
Non-working pensioners	8.7	12.6	27.6	34.2
Working pensioners	4.7	5.1	5.3	5.8
Ex-military & families	15.6	17.5	23.5	23.4

(Source: A. Zverev, in *Planovoe Khoziaistvo*, No. 12, 1957, p. 24.)

The improvement in old-age pension benefits was accompanied by substantial increases in pensions for those suffering permanent disability of varying degrees and for dependents, the increases reportedly amounting to 50-65 percent.[6] Further sizable increases in minimum pension rates have been also promised under the Seven-Year Plan, along with a raising of minimum wages. No doubt exists regarding the general popularity of these measures.

There has also been a good deal of talk about extending social insurance and pension rights to collective farmers, who have thus far never enjoyed them. Some farms are reported to have adopted a system of paying fixed amounts of money and produce to their sick and aged members, which represents a step forward from the normal collective farm practice of extending relief to

---

[4] Prudenski, *op. cit.*, p. 357.

[5] The normal payment to working pensioners is now only 150 rubles per month.

[6] See *Vedomosti Verkhovnovo Soveta* (Supreme Soviet Gazette), July 28, 1956.

such members out of a small fund set aside for this purpose. Cases where fixed payments have been instituted are still the exception since the vast majority of collective farms do not yet have sufficient revenues for this purpose, but it is a fact that the number of such exceptions is steadily growing, and the extensive publicity given to them in the Soviet press indicates that the new system is officially regarded as a desirable development. It must be noted that, at present, all such payments are made out of the resources of each farm, and that the state has no responsibility, financial or otherwise. However, as the regime's policy toward the peasants is, in principle, to reward regular collective work with regular pay, and to bring the status of the peasant gradually closer to that of the industrial worker, it seems to follow that the state eventually will have to accept some responsibility for at least ensuring that the collective farms are financially capable of providing social-insurance benefits. This is all the more necessary because the collective farms have now absorbed the workers of the disbanded Machine Tractor Stations, who were promised the continuation of the benefits they formerly enjoyed as state employed workers. It is too soon, however, to say how the problem will be tackled.

Other Welfare Benefits

Holidays. Turning to other kinds of social welfare benefits for state-employed persons, there appears to have been no appreciable change in the rules governing paid holidays, which already were on a fairly generous scale under Stalin. These regulations compare favorably with those of West European countries, especially for workers in what are deemed to be arduous or unhealthy occupations. For example, miners, steel workers, and bus drivers are allowed up to four weeks of paid vacation per year. Overall statistics showing the distribution of the total working force according to numbers of paid (working-day) holidays per year are as follows:

Days of vacation	% of Total Workers
12	43
15	12
18	11
21	3
24	19
Over 24	12
	100%

(Source: *Vestnik Statistiki*, No. 10, 1958, Statistical Supplement.)

A less desirable feature of the Soviet holiday system is the practice of spreading vacations over the whole year, so that many are on vacation when the weather is unfavorable. There is also a grave shortage of holiday accommodations: despite the existence of much-publicized trade-union rest homes charging low prices, these can accommodate only a small fraction of the workers.

Working Time. There has been significant improvement in respect of hours of labor, although here again the reform effected by the present leadership so far represents, in large part, a return to the more liberal regulations which prevailed prior to Stalin's oppressive labor legislation of 1938-40. A 1940 decree lengthened the standard workday from seven to eight hours, increasing total hours for the six-day work week to 48. This remained unchanged until 1956 when the Khrushchev leadership, implementing its promise at the 20th Party Congress to reduce working hours, took an initial step to cut down Saturday work to six hours, leaving most of the afternoon free and thus creating the beginnings of a Soviet "weekend."

During 1957-58 further reductions of working hours were made effective in certain industries, notably mining and metallurgy.[7] These were followed by still greater promises at the 21st Party Congress in January 1959, when the leadership explicitly pledged a standard 40-hour week (and a 35-hour week in unhealthy occupations) by no later than 1962, with further reductions to follow later in the decade. There was even talk of achieving "the shortest working week in the world" by 1967. The promises have been so definite and attended by such great publicity that it will be hard indeed for the leadership to go back on its word, except in the event of dire emergency. Reduced hours are in fact already being put into effect in several key industries. A statement jointly issued by the CPSU Central Committee, the Council of Ministers, and the central trade union organization, and published in the Soviet press on September 20, 1959, announced a detailed time schedule for the gradual extension of the seven-hour day to "all workers and employees in the national economy." (With six-hour Saturdays, this will reduce the standard working week to 41 hours.) The process began October 1, 1959, and is to be completed in the fourth quarter of 1960.

Some Western critics, pointing to the fact that planned productivity increases are greater than would be necessary to compensate for the reduction of working hours, conclude from this that the reform is in some way not genuine since there will have to be greater intensity of effort in the shortened work period.[8] Such a view hardly

---

[7] See *Pravda*, January 27, 1958, and November 4, 1958.

[8] This was argued, for instance by Dr. E. Kux, writing in the *Neue Zürcher Zeitung* (December 16, 1958), in tones suggesting that the reform was practically a fraud.

seems justifiable. It is obvious, in the first place, that a shorter working week requires greater work intensity and higher productivity not only in Russia but in the United States or any other country. If output per hour remained the same while hours were reduced by 15 percent, then — other things being equal — total output would go down by 15 percent and everyone would be correspondingly poorer, a situation which no one could possibly want. Nor is it true that the Soviet Union intends to increase productivity solely, or even mainly, by imposing heavier physical burdens on labor. This is quite evident from the great attention being paid to the mechanization of labor-intensive processes, especially in auxiliary occupations (loading, moving of materials, etc.).

The charge that weekly wages are being cut as part of the reduction in working hours is equally untenable. The fact that a major reform of the Soviet wage system has coincided with the reduction of the working week makes it difficult to determine the precise effect of either change, but average wages appear in any event to be displaying their usual tendency to rise slowly. Thus, the cut in the working week is as genuine as these things can be in an imperfect world. Those who assert the contrary are guilty of using against the Soviet Union the very same — quite unfounded — arguments by which Soviet propagandists seek to explain away the reduction of the working week in the United States.

Other Employment Reforms. Brief mention should also be made of recent steps extending the special privileges of juvenile workers. Since May 1956 workers between the ages of 16 and 18 have enjoyed a working day shortened to six hours, with extra piecework pay to make up any loss in earnings. In addition they are allowed a full month's vacation each year and special facilities for study.[9] These privileges have, indeed, caused many managers to try to avoid employing juveniles — a tendency which has aroused official criticism and contributed to the difficulties experienced by high school graduates in seeking employment.[10] The compulsory drafting of young people into labor reserve schools, introduced in October 1940, had already been terminated by a decree of March 18, 1955, and has been replaced by voluntary recruitment.

For another thing, the worker's right to change his occupation, while not explicitly recognized, has been made more real by the present regime's abolition, in 1957, of criminal penalties for leaving one's job without

permission. These penalties, as well as others for worker absenteeism and unpunctuality, had been instituted by decree in 1940. Although the decree gradually became a dead letter under Stalin's successors and was no longer mentioned in Soviet legal textbooks from 1954 on, it apparently survived on the statute books until 1957.

In still another reversal of Stalinist policy, the 1936 decree which required the rural population to give six days' unpaid labor per year for working on roads was repealed by the present leadership in November 1958. Instead, responsibility for building and repairing local roads has been placed on the "collective farms, state farms, industrial, transport, building and other enterprises and organizations." Of course, the job still has to be done, but presumably the individual is now entitled to be paid for doing it.

Wage Questions. Although wages as such are outside the province of this discussion, it may be useful to refer briefly to changes in this field insofar as they are indicative of political attitudes. The practice of the Stalin period was to maximize wage differentials, which indeed reached record dimensions; on the contrary, the trend in recent years has been in the opposite direction. In 1956, a minimum wage law was adopted, fixing a floor of 300-350 rubles per month in urban areas and 270 rubles in the country. The measure particularly benefited the appallingly underpaid groups of auxiliary personnel (janitors, cleaners, messengers, etc.) and the lowest grades of shop assistants, railroad workers, and others. This process of raising the level of the lowest-paid workers is to continue. The decree on the Seven-Year Plan provides for increasing the minimum wage to 400-450 rubles monthly during 1959-62, and to 500-600 rubles during 1963-65, as well as for a consequential (but smaller) upward revision of the pay of middle-grade workers. Since the average increase in all money wages is to be only 26 percent, it is evident that the spread between top and bottom will be sharply reduced.

This policy is reflected in other aspects of wage reform now in progress. Apart from introducing smaller differentials in basic rates, the reforms are tending to eliminate the more exaggerated forms of progressive piecework bonuses, which will cut down disparities in actual earnings. The gap between skilled and unskilled workers' pay on collective farms is also being significantly reduced.[11] There have apparently been cuts in very high salaries, such as those of government ministers and university professors. (Though no statement to this effect

---

[9] A. I. Denisov (ed.), *Trudovoe Pravo* (Labor Law), Moscow, 1959, p. 441.

[10] A decree to combat this was issued by the party Central Committee and the government on September 12, 1957.

[11] Some farms are adopting a pay ratio for unskilled as against skilled labor of 1:3 instead of the previously "recommended" 1:5. See *Voprosy Ekonomiki*, No. 2, 1959, p. 114.

seems to have appeared in print, the cuts are apparently a matter of general knowledge in the Soviet Union and have been confirmed to the writer several times.) The relative position of the lowest-paid has also been improved as a result of a decree of March 23, 1957, reducing direct taxation on incomes below 450 rubles per month. All this certainly does not indicate that the Soviets are embracing hitherto-condemned "petty-bourgeois egalitarianism," but it does show that the *excessive* inequalities of the Stalin era are being corrected.

Housing. Something must also be said about housing, since the fact that rents in the Soviet Union are far too low to bear any relation to housing costs justifies treating it as a social service rather than as a species of commercial transaction. At 1.32 rubles per square meter per month (somewhat higher for new apartments in some cities), rents are generally insufficient even to cover bare maintenance, which may explain why this is so often neglected.[12] At the same time, the miseries caused by

the shortage of housing and consequent overcrowding are too well known to require comment here. Khrushchev has declared that his aim is eventually to provide a separate apartment for every Soviet family instead of the single room which is the usual situation today. It is evident from the housing provisions of the Seven-Year Plan, however, that the separate apartments will be very small by Western standards: the plan calls for the construction of 15 million apartment units with a total floor space (including corridors, bathroom and kitchen) of 650-60 million square meters—or, at most, 44 square meters (430 square feet) per apartment. A British working-class family would be shocked at having to live in so little space. Still, no one can doubt that Soviet citizens will be much happier if and when each family can have its own front door and no longer have to share the kitchen with several neighbors.

There is no question about the sharp acceleration of housing construction under the post-Stalin leadership. This is fully evident from the following figures showing housing space (excluding private rural housing) completed in four different years from 1950 to 1958, and the Seven-Year Plan goals:

Year	Total	State	Urban Private
	(in million sq. meters of total space)		
1950	24.2	17.8	6.4
1953	30.8	23.2	7.6
1957	52.0	38.5	13.5(a)
1958	70.1	45.6	24.5(a)
1959 (plan)	80.0	—	—
1960 (plan)	101.0	—	—
1959-65 plan, total	650-60.0	—	—
do., annual average	93.0	—	—

(Source: *Vestnik Statistiki*, No. 5, 1959, p. 94). (a) These figures include private house-building by state-employed persons engaged in agriculture and forestry.

Despite the sharply-increased effort since Stalin's death, it is clear that there is still a very long way to go before tolerable housing conditions will be achieved, since a large part of new construction is necessary merely to keep pace with urban population growth. It has been pointed out that the Soviet *per capita* rate of house-building, even allowing generously for peasant construction, remains below that of the (West) German Federal Republic.[13] Nonetheless, the facts reveal considerable progress in the USSR. The ambitious plans for rebuild-

[12] In Moscow, for example, the average revenue from tenants for rent and "other items" is 1.75 rubles per square meter, while running costs, inclusive of capital repairs, average 4.31 rubles per square meter. See *Novyi Mir*, No. 10, 1959, p. 211.
[13] S. Wolk, in *Bulletin* (of the Munich Institute for the Study of the USSR), No. 5, 1959.

ing villages in connection with Khrushchev's contemplated revival of the *agrogorod* necessarily call for a still greater expansion of housing construction in rural areas, although the financial burden involved is to be shouldered by the collective farms.

Services. Finally, brief mention must be made of improvements in badly needed consumer services—restaurants, cafes, shops, repair facilities and the like. This is a very backward sector of Soviet life. To cite just one example, an article in *Pravda* (March 14, 1959) estimated the total capacity of shoe-repair establishments in the Russian republic (RSFSR) at 15 million pairs annually, although 100 million pairs of new shoes are sold each year and may be presumed to require repair at least once annually. A recent decree embodied plans for increasing the turnover of service and repair shops of all kinds to 10.3 billion rubles in 1961, as against 6.2 million rubles in 1958.[14] There have also been measures to increase the number of shops and restaurants.

Motivations of Recent Policy

This, then, is the actual Soviet record in social welfare. It suggests, first of all, that even under Stalin's rule much attention was paid to the expansion and improvement of health services and education, and fairly generous rules adopted in regard to such things as sickness benefits and paid vacations. In the late 1930's, however, some steps backward were taken, particularly affecting hours of labor, maternity leave, and the worker's right to change his occupation, and it was only after Stalin's death that moves got underway to restore the conditions which had prevailed until the mid-1930's. In the last few years, the record shows, much more has been or is being done to improve old-age pensions and disability pay, to reduce working hours, to build more housing, and to provide more consumer services, even though the Soviet citizen certainly still has—and probably will continue to have—much to complain about.

Only the willfully blind will refuse to take all this seriously. But more than *what* has been done, the vital question is *why* has it been done, and what significance, if any, do these developments have from the standpoint of assessing the nature of the Soviet system? No single, definitive answer is possible of course, but here, for what they may be worth, are a few thoughts on the subject.

While it is arguable that the Soviet rulers do as little as possible for the citizen in order to devote the largest possible share of national resources to heavy industry

---

[14] *Pravda*, March 13, 1959.

and weapons, such a formulation begs the question. One could reverse it and say that they devote as much as possible to improving the citizen's lot, subject to the necessary investment in heavy industry and weapons—which would sound better from the Soviet point of view, but mean equally little. Is the glass half-full or half-empty? In any case, neither formulation explains why more is being done for the Soviet citizen today than in the past.

One relevant factor may simply be that the USSR is now powerful enough economically to permit the diversion of an increasing amount of resources to the satisfaction of the needs of its citizens, without curtailing ambitious plans for the expansion of heavy industry. To carry out the first Five-Year Plan (1928-32), Stalin found it necessary to reduce living standards drastically, but it would be foolish to take this to be what lawyers term "evidence of system." It is obviously no part of Communist ideology to make people poorer; on the contrary, communism lays great stress on abundance. The "abundance" of communism may well be—in the author's opinion it definitely is—a meaningless, even nonsensical concept, but it surely was the intention of all Soviet leaders, including even Stalin, to raise living standards at some future date, once the painful sacrifices of "primitive accumulation" were no longer necessary. The Soviet citizen was, and still is, denied adequate housing, but it would be a mistake to conclude that the leadership believes in bad housing in the same sense that it believes in the undesirability of private peasant enterprise. Soviet leaders have been willing to sacrifice a generation, to neglect urgent needs for years, but it would be patently foolish to represent them as favoring poverty and hardship as such. They surely would concede, and even advocate, improvements in popular welfare if doing so would not interfere with the pursuit of their basic aims.

Before leaving the subject of ideology, two other points are worth making. One is the enormous attention which Communists always pay to education: however they may twist its content to suit their purposes, they have invariably lavished resources on its development, whether under Stalin or under his successors. It is true that this effort is due, in part, to the urgent need of developing technical skills, but this is far from the whole explanation. Indeed, the promise made at the 20th Congress to extend full-time secondary education to all went far beyond practical necessities, and its implementation even tended to aggravate social tensions, which was one reason for Khrushchev's subsequent counter reforms.

The second point is the great importance, from the standpoint of Communist ideology, of appearing to be doing something to improve the lot of the working masses. Even when nothing or little is actually being done, the party leaders must of necessity claim to be acting in that direction. Too great a contrast between words and deeds, however, can lead to general cynicism, as in fact it did under Stalin. Khrushchev is now engaged in an evident effort to revive the fervor of the party and to replace passive bureaucratism with initiative. It is reasonable to suppose, therefore, that with this aim in view he wants to show that the party is genuinely doing something to carry out its promises to the people.

One example of this ideological influence is the regime's insistence, for political reasons, on cheap bread and low rents even when these are economically irrational and administratively inconvenient. Thus, Khrushchev recently reasserted the *political impossibility* of raising bread prices despite the fact that, at these prices, it pays to feed bread rather than regular cattle feed to private livestock. In short, cheap bread is essential to the party's outward picture of itself.[15]

The Role of Incentives

Other factors, too, have a bearing on the regime's attitude in regard to welfare. For a number of reasons too complex to be analyzed here, the functioning of the Soviet economy is coming to depend more on incentives and less on compulsion. Prisoners can be kept working even when forced to live in overcrowded barracks on a minimum diet, but unless there is some emergency to spur them free men work better when they can expect to live better by greater effort. To achieve the leadership's ambitious plans, better work, more efficient organization, more initiative at the grass roots are all objective necessities. To some extent, of course, this was also true under Stalin and was acted upon, as evidenced by the lavish rewards given to Stakhanovites. But few analysts question that there has been a shift toward much *greater* reliance on incentives in recent years, paralleled by a scaling down of the number and powers of the police. To give but one of many examples of how this works in practice, the author, during a tour of the Soviet Union, was shown a new apartment block in Kiev, which he was told was being erected by the building industry for its own workers because, now that they could change

employment without incurring criminal penalties, they would not remain in the industry "unless we replaced the barracks and hostels with decent housing."

Of course, people's attitudes and expectations are relevant to the efficacy of incentives as well as to political stability. The more the Soviet Union boasts of its great technical progress, of its Sputniks and moon rockets, of its equality with or superiority over the United States in weapons, the more impatient its citizens become with their backward living conditions, and the less reasonable it seems to them that nothing drastic is done to improve them. Confronted by such a popular state of mind, an intelligent leadership is likely to see the wisdom of taking some action to satisfy it.

The increasing range of contacts betwen Soviet citizens and foreigners plays a dual role in this process. Many more Soviet citizens are now learning at first or second hand how the other side lives, and this affects their own expectations. Then, too, with the increasing flow of foreign visitors to Russia, it must certainly appear politically advantageous to the leadership to impress them with higher standards of living. This is much more than a matter of impressing unsophisticated tourists from the West, who can if necessary be fobbed off with Potemkin villages. Much more important are the thousands of students and others from underdeveloped countries, as well as from the Soviet Union's own allies, who actually spend some time living among the Russians and cannot help learning the truth. Khrushchev is well aware that relative living standards will play an important role in the world impact of the two opposed systems.

Some Points of Logic

For all its simplicity, one should not overlook still another point: Khrushchev wants to be popular. He may genuinely care to reduce poverty, or he may be acting on the basis of cold political calculation—it does not matter which. He may even aspire to go down in history as the man who brought prosperity to the Soviet people—on the foundations laid by his grim predecessor. There are some Western observers who seem to shy away from even considering such motives possible, as if to do so would label them as pro-Soviet. This is clearly an illogical attitude. What is primarily objectionable about the Soviet system is its totalitarian character, its lack of intellectual and political freedom; and this character is not directly affected by the shortening of working hours or the provision of a separate apartment for every family.

It is indeed true that certain features of the Soviet economy are inconsistent with the proper satisfaction

---

[15] This picture has been obscured in the West by denunciations of an allegedly huge Soviet turnover tax on bread. Although it is true that the tax was for years the major constituent of the price of bread, the reason for this was that the tax was calculated on the basis of a ridiculously low procurement price for grain. The real economic incidence of the tax was not on consumers, but on the producers—the peasants.

of consumer demand. It may also be true that the ultimate logic of a better-educated and materially more satisfied citizenry is incompatible with the totalitarian one-party state. Let us hope that it will prove so. But that is no reason for closing one's eyes to the realities: much is being done on the Soviet "welfare" front, and there is no sign that Khrushchev's consolidation of his political power will cause any change in this respect, especially since the policies being followed must, in his judgment, appear rational, right and necessary.

THE SOVIET LABOR MARKET

EMILY CLARK BROWN

ALTHOUGH the concept of the "labor market" is foreign to the philosophy of Soviet "socialist planning," the problems of distribution of the labor force and its remuneration must be dealt with both theoretically and practically by the Soviet planners. "Planned distribution of the labor force" is frequently discussed in Soviet literature, but the planning and control are far from complete. In practice, the system involves a combination of planning and reliance on market forces—including central planning, planned training and recruitment, direction of labor and control of turnover, social pressure, and self-direction under the influence of wage and other incentives, advertisements, and local and all-union recruiting machinery.

No systematic treatment of labor market problems is found in the Soviet literature, although parts of the theory and practice are discussed at length.[1] The present study seeks to analyze how the desired distribution of the labor force is brought about in a system largely planned but relying in part on forces of the market.[2] Evidence is not available to answer all questions, but it is believed that the outlines of the system in existence in the winter of 1955–1956 can be given with some assurance. It must always be remembered that what was true in 1940 is not necessarily true of 1950 or 1956. Historical perspective and identification of the period to which the data relate are essential, although these are sometimes lacking in discussions of the Soviet economy.[3] The important decree of April 25, 1956,[4] repealing the 1940 laws on labor discipline, provides a convenient cut-off date for the present study.

Sources for this study include Soviet professional journals, newspapers, the invaluable *Current Digest of the Soviet Press,*[5] Soviet books and pamphlets (many of them found in searches of Soviet bookshops), and interviews and observation in a thirty-day stay in the Soviet Union in November and December 1955.[6]

The labor market in the USSR long has constituted a source of interest to Westerners. Information on its organization and actual operation has been sparse and often confusing. In this article, based on observations and interviews during a thirty-day stay in the Soviet Union and on intensive perusal of Soviet publications, Professor Brown supplies an original and much-desired description and appraisal of the Russian labor market today.

Emily Clark Brown is professor of economics, Vassar College. She is joint author of *From the Wagner Act to Taft-Hartley* and author of other studies in labor relations law and collective bargaining.—EDITOR

[1] For example, by A. E. Pasherstnik, *Pravo na Trud* [*The Right to Work*] (Moscow, 1951). Among other experts in this field are N. G. Aleksandrov, E. L. Manevich, and N. S. Maslova.

[2] The question of forced penal labor is outside the scope of the inquiry.

[3] See, for example, the discussion of labor discipline under the 1940 laws in W. W. Kulski, *The Soviet Régime* (Syracuse, 1954), pp. 367–380.

[4] *New York Times,* May 12, 1956.

[5] Published by Joint Committee on Slavic Studies, New York.

[6] The visit was limited to Leningrad, Moscow, Kharkov, and Kiev. Through Intourist (the offi-

CENTRAL PLANNING
AND THE LABOR FORCE

Central planning of the economy establishes the framework within which the development and distribution of the labor force take place. Under the program of nationalization and industrialization, the direction of a large percentage of the gross national product into investment in heavy industry was largely responsible for the extremely rapid growth of industrial production and national income.[7] It created a large demand for labor, quickly absorbed the unemployed, led to the shift of millions of workers from agriculture to industry, pulled women into the labor market, and created a continuing labor shortage in industry.[8] The decision in 1954 to develop agriculture on a large scale in

Kazakhstan and the decision in the Sixth Five-Year Plan to concentrate on the development of industry in Siberia and the Far East[9] called for further shifts of hundreds of thousands, if not millions, of people to new areas and new industries. Central planning thus basically determines the number of jobs and their location.

The central plans formally adopted by the USSR Council of Ministers and the Supreme Soviet are based on policy decisions of the Communist party. They are worked out by Gosplan[10] in consultation with the ministries and their subordinate organizations and enterprises and the finance agencies. The work of the planners in the field of labor involves the following problems: determination of the total supply of labor and its existing and planned distribution between regions and branches of the economy; qualifications of the workers and plans for training the needed kinds of skills; incentives for the full and effective utilization of labor by employers of labor and for the full use of his capacities by each individual;[11] the recruitment and attachment on a stable basis of individual members of the working force to enterprises, offices, farms, in the areas and fields where they are needed.

The planning agencies work out first

cial travel agency) and the Society for Cultural Relations with Foreign Countries, arrangements were made for visits to five large plants in the shoe, food, textile, machine-tool, and tractor industries, with long talks in each with the director or others in plant administration and in some cases with trade union officials; for extensive conferences with officers of the Leningrad Central Council of Trade Unions, the All-Union Central Council of Trade Unions in Moscow, and a Central Committee of one union; a group conference with eight economists and others, including Mr. E. L. Manevich of the Institute of Economics, Mr. M. I. Rubenstein of the Academy of Sciences, Professor A. E. Pasherstnik of the Institute of Law, and others, and a later interview with Professor N. G. Aleksandrov of the University of Moscow; for interviews with representatives of the Chief Administration of Labor Reserves and of the Administration for the Organized Recruitment of Workers; and for visits to a People's Court, with an interview with the judge, to three ten-year schools, and to one collective farm.

The author is indebted for encouragement and aid at various stages of the study, especially to Professor Alexander Baykov and Mr. G. R. Barker of the University of Birmingham, Dr. Solomon M. Schwarz, and Mr. Jerzy Gliksman.

[7] Norman M. Kaplan, in Abram Bergson, ed., *Soviet Economic Growth* (Evanston, 1953), pp. 77–80.

[8] W. W. Eason, in Bergson, *op. cit.*, pp. 112, 114.

[9] Speech of N. S. Khrushchev to Twentieth Congress, Communist party of the Soviet Union, Feb. 14, 1956, *Current Digest of the Soviet Press*, Vol. 8, No. 4 (March 7, 1956), p. 15; Vol. 8, No. 20 (June 27, 1956), pp. 32–33.

[10] In May 1955, this agency was divided into the State Commission for Long-Range Planning of the National Economy (Gosplan) and the State Commission for Current Planning of the National Economy. *Current Digest of the Soviet Press*, Vol. 8, No. 1 (Feb. 15, 1956), p. 4. For a description of the planning process, see Harry Schwartz, *Russia's Soviet Economy* (New York, 1954), Ch. 5.

[11] See any current number of *Sotsialisticheski Trud* (journal of the State Committee on Labor and Wages) for discussion of the problem of labor productivity.

the number of workers and the total wage fund, in annual and quarterly plans. The "balances" thus established aim for "the planned utilization of all labor reserves, planned distribution of labor by branches and regions, planned preparation of skilled personnel."[12] The planners consider the demands of different branches, the desired relations between numbers in production and in "non-productive work," and the reserves of able-bodied persons, both rural and urban, who can be enlisted by various means. These balances of workers and wage funds, when approved by the USSR Council of Ministers, act as limits on the ministries and departments for major enterprises and government institutions, and limits on the ministries and departments of the republics for the republican and local economies. In turn, the various balances are distributed by the ministries to their subordinate administrations, and by these to the enterprises.[13] Thus each enterprise, state farm, or other agency receives planned limits for its wage fund and number of workers.[14]

Difficulties in the planning on these points are frequently discussed. M. Z. Saburov, chairman of Gosplan, has complained that some ministries display "bureaucratic tendencies" in their efforts to obtain excessive wage funds and numbers of workers.[15] According to reports on the budget, many enterprise directors "with the connivance of the ministries, have carried excessive numbers of workers and paid out money for wages uneconomically,"[16] and many enterprises are overexpending wage funds, "a most flagrant breach of state discipline."[17] In many years in the past, total wage expenditures ran higher than planned, and there is much evidence of evasion of wage controls by enterprises in competition to get workers.[18]

Soviet authorities speak frequently, also, of the need to improve planning for the rational distribution of manpower.[19] Western observers frequently notice wasteful use of labor, in an economy where there is evidence of great

---

[12]M. S. Urinson, *Planirovanie Narodnovo Khozyaistva po Soyuznym Respublikam i Ekonomicheskim Raionam* (Moscow, 1955), p. 93.

[13]*Ibid.*, pp. 93–96; I. N. Chigvintsev, *Zarabotnaya Plata pri Sotsializme* (Moscow, 1955), pp. 29–32.

[14]*Current Digest of the Soviet Press*, Vol. 7, No. 32 (Sept. 21, 1955), p. 21; Vol. 8, No. 3 (Feb. 29, 1956), p. 28.
Evidence is not adequate for a conclusion as to how and to what extent, if at all, these planning decisions are influenced by the trade unions. National officers of the union organizations, it must be remembered, are "more nearly civil servants than representatives of the workers," (Walter Galenson in A. Kornhauser, R. Dubin and A. M. Ross, eds., *Industrial Conflict* [New York, 1954], pp. 479, 486), but it may be that at top levels they exert some influence toward protecting the interests of workers. The work of the unions on planning was described by an official of the All-Union Central Council of Trade Unions in these terms: The Council has a very important role in the planning of wages. Annually, when Gosplan prepares proposals for consideration by the Council of Ministers, AUCCTU takes part in the preliminary work. It is apprised of the proposals of the ministries and the central committees of the appropriate unions, which have been worked up in consultation. The Council presents its independent conclusions to the government at the same time that Gosplan presents its draft proposal. The possibility of contradiction of interests is denied, but there may be differences of opinion as to wise policy; the AUCCTU however always takes into consideration "the real possibilities and the needs of the state." Once the labor and wage limits are set, the central committees of the unions work with the ministries on the distribution to lower units. For another Soviet statement, see quotation from A. E. Pasherstnik in Galenson, *loc. cit.*, p. 179.

[15]*Current Digest of the Soviet Press*, Vol. 8, No. 14 (May 16, 1956), p. 31.

[16]*Ibid.*, Vol. 7, No. 5 (March 16, 1955), p. 5.

[17]*Ibid.*, Vol. 7, No. 50 (Jan. 25, 1956), p. 8.

[18]F. D. Holzman, *Soviet Taxation* (Cambridge, 1955), pp. 33–35, 40.

[19]For example, E. L. Manevich, "K voprosu ob izuchenii putei povusheniya proizvoditelnosti truda v promyshlennosti SSSR," *Voprosy Ekonomiki*, April 1955, pp. 80–86.

labor shortage in many fields, at the same time that manual labor is used in great numbers on the farms,[20] in factories, in primitive street-sweeping by women with brooms, hand (or foot) polishing of hotel corridor floors, and in numerous other activities.

WAGES AND DISTRIBUTION OF MANPOWER

Soviet theorists deny specifically that wages in their economy are the price of labor or labor power, resulting from buying and selling in the market.[21] According to the political economy and labor law textbooks,

The provision of manpower to enterprises takes place by plan, by means of organized recruiting, organized preparation and distribution of manpower.[22]

In view of the fact that in socialist society labor power has ceased to be a commodity, wages are not the price of labor power. They express...the relation between society as a whole in the person of the socialist government and the given worker, working for himself, for his society.[23]

The reward for work in the USSR is therefore not the price of labor power,

but represents the share of that part of the social product which is distributed among workers in proportion to the quantity and quality of labor expended.[24]

In these statements there is little, if any, suggestion that wages are expected to play a role in the distribution of the labor force. When a number of Soviet economists were asked to indicate the major principles on which this distribution operates, however, they answered, "The distribution of labor takes place by economic laws and incentives. The state sees that the major fields and areas get labor first, through higher wages and better conditions." Corroboration comes in frequent statements such as the following:

The socialist government utilizes wages as a great lever for the proper distribution of labor between branches of the national economy and regions of the country, for drawing manpower into industry, for the struggle against remnants of capitalism in the consciousness of people, for training workers in communist relations to work.[25]

A spokesman in one of the trade union central offices held, to the contrary, that wage differentials were not established chiefly as a means to attract workers to different fields. He argued that the system of pay "according to work" meant that workers were compensated by differences in wages for differences in effort, in working conditions which affected the amount of effort, for the costs of training and developing skills, and for working and living conditions in various regions which made work difficult.

Both bases are present in the wage system. Differential wages are used to influence workers to enter and remain in desired occupations, levels of skill, industries, and areas by compensating them

[20]D. Gale Johnson, "Eye-Witness Appraisal of Soviet Farming, 1955," *Journal of Farm Economics*, Vol. 38 (May 1956), p. 291. Bulganin, urging increased mechanization, reported that manual labor was still used to the amount of 68 percent of all labor in lumbering, 44 percent in coal mining, 35 percent in ferrous metallurgy, and 69 percent in building. *Current Digest of the Soviet Press*, Vol. 7, No. 28 (August 24, 1955), p. 10.

[21]Although the Labor Code of 1922, still the basis for labor relations and rights and duties of workers, uses the term "hired labor," authorities explain that this terminology is no longer appropriate to conditions under nationalization and should be replaced by "workers and employees," that is, manual workers and official, professional, and all other types of personnel. N. G. Aleksandrov, *et al.*, *Zakonodatelstvo o Trude, Kommentarii*, 2d ed. (Moscow, 1954), pp. 6–7; N. G. Aleksandrov, *Sovyetskoe Trudovoe Pravo* (Moscow, 1954), pp. 145–146.

[22]*Politicheskaya Ekonomia* (Moscow, 1955), p. 430.

[23]*Ibid.*, p. 452.

[24]Aleksandrov, *Sovyetskoe Trudovoe Pravo*, p. 53.

[25]Chigvintsev, *op. cit.*, p. 18.

for differences in training and effort and in difficulties or dangers in working or living conditions. In addition, wage differences are used to promote employment in occupations, industries, and geographic regions of special national significance, the pay being related to the estimated economic importance of the work. The opportunity to increase his earnings, by working where and as the government wants, is a major incentive to the Soviet worker, since this is the way to acquire a claim to a larger share of the still scarce consumers' goods. The "material self-interest of workers in the results of their work" is relied on as a major force for increasing and maintaining stable forces where most needed for fulfilling the plans and for increasing labor productivity. The economics textbook sums it up in this way:

The policies of the government in the field of wages are built on the basis of all-round differentiations in pay. The socialist economic system is deeply hostile to equalization of wages, ignoring the differences between skilled and unskilled, heavy and light work. Skilled work, as work of much higher quality, demands training of the worker and gives greater production than unskilled work. On the strength of this it is paid more than unskilled work. Such a system of pay stimulates increase in the qualifications of workers. For equal skill, more difficult work is paid more than less difficult....

In connection with the economic necessity of much greater reward for labor in leading branches of the national economy, higher wages are established for workers of such branches of heavy industry as metallurgy, coal, oil, machine construction, etc. Under otherwise equal conditions, also, more highly paid are the workers...in economic districts having especially great significance in the economic life of the country, and also in distant and little populated regions. Thanks to this, wages are one of the economic instruments of the planned distribution and redistribution of skilled manpower between enterprises and branches of social production in accordance with the demands of the law of planned development of the national economy.[26]

WAGE DIFFERENTIALS FOR SKILL

Wage differentials are planned first when average wages are established by the central plans which set limits on the numbers of workers and the wage fund for different industries, areas, and enterprises, as discussed above. Within these limits, the distribution to different occupations and levels of skill is mainly the function of the ministries, especially since the increase in their powers in 1954. "Tariff qualification handbooks," approved by each ministry in cooperation with the central committee of the given trade union, set up a series of labor grades to which different jobs are allocated. A "tariff network" gives the coefficients for wage differentials above the base rate for Grade I, for both time and the more approved piece work. Norms for production and piece rates, under standards set by the ministries and central committees, are worked out finally in the establishments, with agreement of the local trade unions.[27] In the past, major changes in norms and wage levels required the approval of the Council of Ministers; but now it is intended that central action be limited to a few special cases, such as a decree in 1955 on norms for building construction. Such decisions as those on increases for long service and special awards continue to be a central function.

The differentials for skill may be illus-

---

[26]*Politicheskaya Ekonomia* (1955), p. 454. See also Chigvintsev, *op. cit.*, pp. 29–31.

[27]D. M. Konakov, *Organizatsia Tekhnicheskovo Normirovania i Zarabotnoi Platy v Promyshlennosti SSSR* (Moscow, 1955), pp. 18–19; Aleksandrov, *Sovyetskoe Trudovoe Pravo* (1954), pp. 249–251.

trated from those reported from some machine-building enterprises in 1955. Six types of work were shown, each with eight labor grades by skill. Hourly time rates for "cold work," the lowest-paid type of work, ranged from 1.26 rubles for Grade I (the least skilled) to 3.08 for Grade VIII (the highest skilled). Piece-rate "hot work" in certain shops was paid the most for each grade of skill, with a range from 1.64 rubles in Grade I to 4.35 in Grade VIII.[28] It is said, however, that in most industries the differentials for skill (also for piece work in comparison with time work, and for "hot work" in comparison with "cold") have decreased since 1946 and are now unduly low. In machine building, for example, the rate for the highest skill grade was said to be only 2.5 or 2.4 times that of the least skilled.[29] Actual earnings depend not only on these base rates but also upon the elaborate system of piece rates and premia for overfulfilling norms.[30] All this is said to have a great influence in stimulating workers to study to increase their skills, to transfer to higher ranks, and to increase their productivity to the highest degree possible.

INDUSTRY AND AREA DIFFERENTIALS

Interindustry planning even before the war had brought the level of wages in the petroleum, coal, metal-working, and iron and steel industries to first place.[31] In these and other industries important for war production, and also in regions

of great significance and distant regions "where harsh climatic conditions make additional hardships for workers occupied in heavy industry," additional increases were given during the war.[32] In 1946, a major decree gave a 20 percent further increase in leading industries in the Urals, Siberia, and the far north.[33] Most industries now have wage zones, with differences in the base rates for different regions. Soviet theorists are critical, however, of the way this has worked out and have asked for reforms. There are said to be many erratic differences in wage levels in the same industry and for the same types of work in particular regions, contrary to the principle of "equal pay for equal work." Zones have been established by ministries at different times and on a variety of principles.[34] It has been urged that a single system of wage zones, based on living conditions, be established in order to provide the necessary stimulus to induce transfers to the new industrial areas. One writer concludes:

Questions of the regulation of wages between industries and regions of the country acquire great significance in the Sixth Five-Year Plan in view of the tasks set by the Twentieth Congress of the Communist Party to provide manpower to enterprises and construction sites located

[28]Konakov, op. cit., p. 19. The ruble, according to the unrealistic official rate of exchange, is worth twenty-five cents.

[29]N. Maslova, "O nekhotorykh voprosakh organizatsii zarabotnoi platy v promyshlennosti," Voprosy Ekonomiki, August 1955, p. 4.

[30]For a description, see G. R. Barker, Some Problems of Incentives and Labour Productivity in Soviet Industry (Oxford, 1955), pp. 106–110.

[31]E. L. Manevich, Zarabotnaya Plata i ee Formy v Promyshlennosti SSSR (Moscow, 1951), p. 80.

[32]Ibid., pp. 98–100; N. S. Maslova, Proizvoditelnost Truda v Promyshlennosti SSSR (1953), pp. 288–289.

[33]Maslova, idem., pp. 290–291. No comprehensive wage statistics have been made available, but average earnings of production workers reported to the author in five large plants visited ranged from 750 rubles a month in the shoe, food, and textile plants, to 800 in the tractor plant and 1,000 in the machine-tool plant. Earnings were reported as varying from 450 rubles up to 1,300, 1,500, or even 2,000 or more for the most skilled. A trade union spokesman cited earnings of 2,000 to 2,500 rubles per month in coal mining as not uncommon.

[34]Manevich, Voprosy Ekonomiki, April 1955, pp. 84–85; A. Kursky, "Voprosy truda v shestoi pyatletke," Sotsialisticheskii Trud, March 1956, pp. 23–24.

in the eastern and northern regions of the country, by means of organized recruitment on a voluntary basis of workers and migrants for these areas from other regions of the country. It is necessary to increase the role of wages for the rational distribution of manpower among branches of the national economy and regions of the country.[35]

Additional incentives are set up to encourage transfer to industries and areas where increased manpower is needed and to reduce turnover in these places. These include assurance of housing and opportunity for education; higher pensions and disability payments in leading industries and in the north and other distant areas; rates of pension and disability payments varying with length of continuous service in an enterprise; and additional pay for long service, in annual or monthly percentages of base rates, in many branches of industry. For example, for underground workers in coal mining, annual bonuses for long service range from 10 percent of base rates after more than one year of steady work to 30 percent after fifteen years. Workers who enter upon labor contracts for not less than three years in the far north receive additional pay of 10 percent after six months.[36] According to one authority, "such differentiations in the conditions

of labor exert great influence on the choice by citizens of the place and type of their work."[37]

A State Committee on Labor and Wages of the USSR Council of Ministers was established on May 24, 1955 "to intensify state control over the work of ministries and departments and improve their work in the sphere of labor and wages."[38] Many Soviet leaders, speaking at the Twentieth Congress of the Communist party in Moscow in February 1956, pointed to "disorganization and muddle" in the wage system and the need for reforms to ensure that wages would provide the needed incentives. Indications were that the reforms would increase the pay of the lowest-paid workers, widen differentials for skill, establish more uniformity in regional differentials, and raise base rates to a larger share in total earnings, at the same time simplifying bonus systems and increasing their effectiveness as incentives to increase productivity. The basic principles of the system of wages, however, were reaffirmed as sound.[39]

PLANNED TRAINING OF MANPOWER

After a group of Soviet economists in Moscow had discussed differential wages as a major influence in the distribution

---

[35]Kursky, loc. cit.

[36]Aleksandrov, et al., Zakonodatelstvo o Trude (1954), pp. 100–102; Sovyetskoe Trudovoe Pravo (1954), pp. 247–248, 336–338. The new social security law provides higher pensions for underground and otherwise difficult work, and an addition to pensions of 10 percent for more than 15 years of uninterrupted work. Current Digest of the Soviet Press, Vol. 8, No. 19 (June 20, 1956), pp. 3–6. There are also honors and medals for "long and irreproachable work" in the coal industry and others and in machine tractor stations. Thus awards are provided for tractor experts after eight years, culminating in the Order of Lenin after twenty-five years of work. A. Smirnov and V. Bescherevnykh, Zakonodatelstvo o Lgotakh dla Rabotnikov MTS (Moscow, 1955), pp. 51–52; Aleksandrov, Sovyetskoe Trudovoe Pravo (1954), pp. 292–295.

[37]Pasherstnik, op. cit., p. 167.

[38]Current Digest of the Soviet Press, Vol. 7, No. 21 (July 6, 1955), p. 14.

[39]See especially N. S. Khrushchev, Current Digest of the Soviet Press, Vol. 8, No. 5 (March 14, 1956), p. 8; L. M. Kaganovich, chairman of State Committee on Labor and Wages, ibid., Vol. 8, No. 10 (April 18, 1956), pp. 17–18; N. M. Shvernik, ibid., Vol. 8, No. 14 (May 16, 1956), p. 13; N. A. Bulganin, ibid., Vol. 8, No. 12 (May 2, 1956), pp. 24–25; also Maslova, Voprosy Ekonomiki, August 1955, p. 13; Manevich, ibid., April 1955, pp. 84–85. A decree of Sept. 8, 1956 established a minimum wage system, with an average increase of 33 percent for the lowest paid workers. Current Digest of the Soviet Press, Vol. 8, No. 36 (Oct. 17, 1956), p. 3.

of the labor force, one of them protested that the planned training of skilled workers for different fields was far more important.

Central planning to ensure the needed qualifications and skills in the labor force starts with decisions on the curriculum of primary and secondary schools and continues through plans for the numbers and training of semiskilled workers and the skilled groups. Finally, it establishes the numbers and plans for the training of engineers and other technicians, and for the study of language, physics, economics, and other fields in institutes and universities at both undergraduate and graduate levels. Such educational programming is closely related to the plans for expanding industry and agriculture. After enterprises and agencies estimate their future needs, their requests are consolidated at local and district levels and go on up through republic organizations to the central planners. The Ministry of Higher Education and Gosplan work out the final "balances" which are incorporated in the state plan. The Ministry of Higher Education and the Central Administration of Labor Reserves then fix the numbers for different schools and provide the needed facilities.[40]

The system of training in relation to the supply of labor can best be seen from the production level. It includes in-plant individual and group training, full-time factory schools at the plants for young workers preparing for mass production jobs, and Labor Reserve schools for skilled trades. For secondary and advanced technical training, both full time and in night and correspondence courses, there are secondary technical schools and middle and higher institutes as well as the universities.[41]

Examples are available from five large plants visited in four major cities. In all but the machine-tool plant, factory schools were a major, if not *the* major source of new workers. In all of them, a large number of other workers—as well as foremen, engineers, and other technical personnel—were studying, both in general education programs and in technical courses of great variety, at the plant and outside, in order to qualify for better jobs or further education.[42] Many technical men and women had begun their study in these plants, continued at institutes, and returned as engineers. In two of the plants visited, the director had begun as an ordinary worker, in one case at the factory school, continued his education by correspondence and at the institute, and worked up through the plant; one director was still studying at the institute.

LABOR RESERVE SYSTEM

Labor Reserve trade schools played little part in the plants discussed above, but in other parts of industry they have been of major importance. The Chief Administration of Labor Reserves, attached to the USSR Council of Ministers, reported that in the past fifteen

---

[40]Based on interviews with Soviet experts. See also A. P. Karpenko, *Sistema Podgotovki i Povyshenia Kvalifikatsii Kadrov v Narodnom Khozyaistve SSSR* (Moscow, 1954), pp. 11–17.

[41]A recent detailed description is available in this journal. See Walter Galenson, "Industrial Training in the Soviet Union," *Industrial and Labor Relations Review*, Vol. 9, No. 4 (July 1956), pp. 562–576. See also Nicholas DeWitt, *Soviet Professional Manpower* (Washington, 1955), Chs. 1–3.

[42]For example, in a shoe plant with 11,000 workers there were 340 in factory school for a one-and-a-half or two-year course; 320 in the plant's middle technical school, which offered two years' work; and 250 in third and fourth years in a nearby institute. One hundred and fifty were in university or other higher education, 40 of them at the Institute of Light Industry; and 900 were busy in general education at the plant's night school.

years more than eight million skilled workers were trained in Labor Reserve schools and academies, mainly for leading branches of industry. Coal mining had been sent 1,200,000 workers, metallurgy 650,000, machine building 1,700,-000, construction 770,000, and rail transport 800,000. In the Magnitogorsk Metallurgical Combine 80 percent of the workers in leading production jobs were said to be Labor Reserve graduates.[43]

The Labor Reserve system was established in October 1940, as one of a series of measures which tightened control of labor in the drive for increased production in that last prewar year. It provided for a draft of urban and rural youth for two-year trade schools and railroad schools and for six-month factory schools.[44] Young graduates were obliged to work where sent, for a period of four years. Labor Reserve officials state that the draft was ended after the war, and that enrollments now are entirely by choice. To what extent the earlier quotas given collective farms and cities were filled by volunteers is not known, although officials now describe the compulsion as upon the village to let their youth go, rather than upon the individuals. It was reported in 1947 that only boys were drafted, that about half of the places were filled by volunteers, and that draftees were usually war orphans or homeless children.[45] The 1951 trade school enrollments were said to be entirely made up of volunteers.[46] Recruiting now is carried on, in the same manner as for other schools and institutes, through ads and notices in the newspapers.. Factory and trade schools are still serving as a route by which rural children and others can get a start towards industrial jobs and opportunities for further education.

Changes have occurred in recent years in the Labor Reserve system under the influences of the increased mechanization of industry, which has called for more skilled workers with broad training; the greater mechanization of agriculture; and the rising level of general education as the country moves toward universal ten-year schooling.[47] Special two-year mining-industry schools have been set up to train operators of the new coal-cutting machines, along with ten-month schools for the general run of miners. For agriculture, six-month courses for combine drivers, established in 1953–1954, were extended in 1955 to full-year schools for training in the operation of all types of agricultural machinery. Finally, since 1954 technical academies have been set up for graduates of secondary schools, to prepare highly qualified personnel and junior technicians. In addition, the curriculum of factory and trade schools has been revised to include academic subjects and to provide general as well as occupational education, in line with the new standard of universal secondary education.

The network of schools in December 1955 was reported to include more than 3,000, distributed as follows: factory schools, under 1,000; agricultural mecha-

---

[43]*Current Digest of the Soviet Press*, Vol. 7, No. 38 (Nov. 2, 1955), p. 15. See also Galenson, "Industrial Training in the Soviet Union." pp. 564–565, 573–576.

[44]In 1947 the ages subject to call were set at 14 to 17 for boys and 15 to 16 for girls for trade schools and 16 to 18 for both boys and girls for factory schools. Desertion was a criminal offense. *Osnovnye Zakonodatelnye Akty o Trude Rabochikh i Sluzhashchikh* (Moscow, 1955), pp. 8–10.

[45]Sergei Kournakoff, "Building the Builders," *Soviet Russia Today*, Vol. 15 (January 1947), pp. 19–20. See also DeWitt, *op. cit.*, pp. 13–14.

[46]Pasherstnik, *op. cit.*, p. 132.

[47]In 1954 the Central Administration of Labor Reserves was directly attached to the USSR Council of Ministers, an indication of the increased importance attached to this system of training.

nization schools, 940; trade, railroad, construction, mining schools, about 700; and the new technical academies, 450. In all, 570 "professions" were being trained.[48]

SECONDARY EDUCATION

Expansion of secondary education is providing a stronger base on which to develop the expert personnel needed by a modern industry and agriculture. At the same time, it appears to have created a problem in getting the needed recruits at lower levels.[49] All fees in secondary and higher schools and universities were abolished as of the start of the new school year in 1956, and secondary education is to be universal at an early date. In the past, the secondary schools were preparing chiefly for higher education. Now they are to include more emphasis on science and mathematics, and there is to be "polytechnical training," with practical work in industry or agriculture for all primary and secondary school pupils.[50]

Competition has increased for the limited number of openings in the higher institutes and universities, since large

numbers of the youth want these opportunities. However, they are told from the highest sources that "a large number of those leaving school will immediately go to work in various branches of the national economy," and that opportunities will be provided for study which does not interrupt their work.[51] A campaign is under way against "wrong attitudes towards work." N. Khrushchev, speaking to a conference of young builders, had this to say to his youthful audience:

Incorrect views about labor in our Soviet society have recently begun to appear within a certain section of youth. ...[Some ten-year graduates say] "It isn't suitable for us, now that we are educated, to work in a factory, at a construction site, at a state farm, or a collective farm."...It is apparently not only the young people who think this way; some members of the older generation are also to blame....Such incorrect and extremely harmful views on labor must be vigorously condemned....Everyone must be proud that through his labor he is contributing his bit to the common cause of building a communist society....

You are well aware that...every worker, every collective farmer who has received secondary education will have a chance at higher education, too—either through the higher educational institutions or through self-education or through evening higher schools—without leaving their jobs. This is all to the good. But do we say that Soviet people need not work in the factories and mills, need not grow potatoes or milk cows? And yet some people who have received secondary education are unwilling to do these things, considering such labor to be beneath their dignity, This is wrong. Comrades, such backward views must be ridiculed and banished.[52]

---

[48]Interview with officials of the Chief Administration of Labor Reserves; *Current Digest of the Soviet Press*, Vol. 6, No. 47 (Jan. 5, 1955), pp. 4–5; Vol. 7, No. 33 (Sept. 28, 1955), p. 32; Vol. 7, No. 38 (Nov. 2, 1955), pp. 15, 35. The 1956 state budget provided for the training of 645,000 skilled workers in Labor Reserve schools, 100,000 skilled workers in technical schools, and 244,000 tractor drivers and other personnel for machine tractor stations and state farms, in addition to 760,000 specialists to graduate with higher or secondary education. *Ibid.*, Vol. 7, No. 50 (Jan. 25, 1956), pp. 5–6.

[49]The number of ten-year secondary schools increased by nearly 13,000 during the Fifth Five-Year Plan, and the number of pupils in the eighth to tenth grades was more than four million higher in 1955 than in 1950. The number graduating increased 23 percent from 1954 to 1955. *Current Digest of the Soviet Press*, Vol. 7, No. 41 (Nov. 23, 1955), p. 27; Vol. 8, No. 5 (March 14, 1956), p. 27; Vol. 8, No. 17 (June 6, 1956), p. 10.

[50]*Ibid.*, Vol. 7, No. 33 (Sept. 28, 1955), p. 32.

[51]N. Khrushchev, speaking to the Twentieth Congress of the Communist party, *Current Digest of the Soviet Press*, Vol. 8, No. 5 (March 14, 1956), pp. 10–11. Admission to all middle and higher schools is by examination.

[52]*Pravda*, April 13, 1956. Translation from *Current Digest of the Soviet Press*, Vol. 8, No. 15 (May 23, 1956), p. 11. In connection with this

ADVANCED EDUCATION

Economists and others with whom these questions were discussed in the Soviet Union were unanimous in denying that there is any danger of training too many experts, since the needs are so great. Evidence from the plants visited supports the claim that the doors are open to those who wish to study, at least at night and by correspondence, and that many succeed in passing examinations and going on to institutes and universities from production work. According to a member of the admissions board of the University of Moscow, when there are several applicants of equal ability for one place, preference is given to those with work experience. Rules adopted by the Ministry of Higher Education for admission to higher correspondence and evening schools also give preference to those already working in related fields.[53] It is considered desirable that young people should have work experience before going on for further study. According to one economist, it is expected that the best engineers will come from children who start in factory or Labor Reserve schools or the technical schools, rather than going directly to the institutes.

Evidence on the experience of the 1955 graduates from two secondary schools suggests that young people in large numbers want higher education and to become intellectuals, but that their aspirations are subject at least temporarily to downgrading, as they take the places they can get in other institutes or schools or go to work, when university places are not open.[54]

In the distribution of the labor force, the crucial point for most Soviet citizens is the act of taking the first job or accepting a place in an educational institution upon leaving secondary school or primary school. At this point the citizen is free to choose within the economic and educational framework set up by the state. Educational opportunities are planned and limited by estimates of manpower needs as well as by the resources which the planners have found it possible so far to provide for education. Incentives to influence choices are provided by the differential stipends which the state pays to students in middle and higher education. Such stipends are much higher for the study of engineering than for the humanities, for example. The incentive of expected higher earnings in certain fields also influences these first crucial choices. Once at work, the worker again has a strong incentive to increase his earnings and living standard by study and advancement.[55]

---

them went to work, but these were studying at institutes and evening schools; 14 went to technical school, and 127 to higher education, including over 60 to the polytechnical institute, 15 to the local institute of economics, and 15 to the university, the rest to pedagogical, medical and other institutes. Many got in where they wanted, or, if not, went to others of the numerous institutes in the city. In another city, in a working-class neighborhood, there were 56 graduates, all boys, from one school. Fifteen went to jobs; 9 to secondary technical school; 32 to higher education, of whom 10 went to engineering institutes; several to a railroad institute; others to other technical institutes; and only one to the university for study in the humanities. The principal of another secondary school in Moscow is reported in the *New York Times*, April 15, 1956, to have said, "Last year only three fourths of our 201 graduating students went on to higher education. The rest went directly to factories or farms."

[55] The question of the success of the training itself cannot be discussed here. See Galenson, "Industrial Training in the Soviet Union," pp. 575–576. Mistakes in the planning of numbers are sometimes indicated. Khrushchev spoke of "a surplus of experts in one section of the economy

---

problem, one of the economists interviewed spoke of "the importance of the task of liquidating the difference between physical and intellectual work."

[53] *Current Digest of the Soviet Press*, Vol. 8, No. 9 (April 11, 1956), pp. 37–38.

[54] In a ten-year school in one of the large cities, there were 180 graduates in 1955. Only 29 of

PLANNED RECRUITMENT
AND JOB CHOICE

The placement of individual workers in jobs within the framework of the planned economy has occurred throughout the Soviet period in different proportions at different times, by a combination of compulsion and individual choice. Since the late 1920's, there has been, officially, no unemployment, and in fact, a great shortage has existed, especially of skilled labor, for rapidly developing industries and areas, and more recently, for the highly mechanized agriculture of the "new lands" in the east. This inevitably has strengthened the hand of the skilled worker, whatever the law. The trend in recent years has been unmistakably toward increased reliance on individual choice of employment, influenced by all the incentives set up and public opinion mobilized to support recruiting drives. It is impossible to judge the extent to which this in effect may have involved compulsion under the forms of free choice.

Soviet citizens under the Constitution have both the "right to work" and the duty to work. Current doctrine is that "under usual conditions, Soviet legislation leaves to the citizens themselves, with some exceptions, to choose for themselves the place of their employment and the nature of their work,"[56] and that ordinarily people enter into employment by voluntary agreement with the enterprise or as members of collective farms or cooperatives. In addition, there are voluntary agreements for employment made through agencies for "organized recruitment" and cases of direction to work, especially of young graduates.

COMPULSORY LABOR

Compulsory labor of ordinary citizens, apart from forced penal labor, has a long history. Under the Labor Code of 1918, industrial conscription was extensively used in 1919 and 1920.[57] The 1922 Labor Code also provided for compulsory labor service, but limited to exceptional circumstances, "fighting the elements or lack of workers to carry out important state work."[58] During World War II, workers in war plants were frozen to their jobs, and conscription was used both for industry and for harvesting.[59] Of greater long-range importance was the system of directing young graduates to jobs, starting in 1928 for graduates of technical schools and now including the entire labor reserve system and middle and higher education.[60] Finally, a decree of June 26, 1940 prohibited leaving any job without permission of the director, and another of October 19, 1940 provided for the compulsory transfer of specialists.[61]

Significantly, since the late 1940's, successive editions of the textbooks in labor law have put decreasing emphasis on the compulsory aspects of employment rela-

---

and culture, a shortage in others. A great defect is that the experts for industry and agriculture are trained without regard to the zonal peculiarities of the country, without consideration of where they will work, in which areas and at which enterprises." Translation in *Current Digest of the Soviet Press*, Vol. 8, No. 5 (March 14, 1956), p. 12.

[56]Pasherstnik, *op. cit.*, pp. 165, 173–175: Aleksandrov, *Sovyetskoe Trudovoe Pravo* (1954), pp. 143–144, 155–165.

[57]Margaret Dewar, *Labour Policy in the USSR 1917–1928* (London, 1956), pp. 43–52.

[58]Aleksandrov, *et al.*, *Zakonodatelstvo o Trude* (1954), pp. 15–16. Pasherstnik reports that this provision had "a comparatively insignificant place" before 1940 and postwar. *Op. cit.*, pp. 180, 184.

[59]Solomon M. Schwarz, *Labor in the Soviet Union* (New York, 1951), pp. 119–129.

[60]Dewar, *op. cit.*, pp. 272–273: Aleksandrov, *et al.*, *Zakonodatelstvo o Trude* (1954), pp. 12–14.

[61]*Ibid.*, pp. 44–45, 159–160.

tions.[62] A case in point is the discussion of compulsory transfers. In general, workers may not be transferred to other enterprises or other places of employment without their consent. By the decree of October 19, 1940, however, engineers, technicians, skilled workers, and certain other groups—including economists, accountants, and planning experts—could be compulsorily transferred, with provisions for payment of the costs of transfer, guaranteed housing, and increases in pay and other privileges. A 1949 textbook listed industries to which this decree was applied and said that some subordinate ministries and directors had been given the power to issue transfer orders; refusals to accept transfer on order made the worker criminally liable. The 1954 edition omitted any mention of penalties and emphasized that compulsory transfers could be made only by the USSR Council of Ministers and only of certain groups of workers. It reported also that since the war this decree has had "almost no place" and that the "high understanding" of the Soviet people has brought about redistribution of skilled personnel according to the needs of the economy.[63] To what extent the power of transfer was used in the interest of providing the needed expert personnel to new enterprises is not known. The law was finally repealed on April 25, 1956.[64] Reports of the difficulties met when the government tried in 1954 to reduce its administrative personnel and transfer those released into

production imply that its powers of compulsory transfer were not being utilized.[65]

PLACEMENT OF GRADUATES

Placement by the state of all young "specialist" graduates plays a major role in the case of new entrants to the labor force. Those completing factory schools and Labor Reserve trade schools are required by law to work at their specialties where placed for four years, those from middle and higher education for three, and from agricultural mechanization schools for two years.[66] Authorities explain that young people thus are guaranteed jobs in their specialties at the established standards of pay and conditions. They justify the compulsion by saying that students educated at state expense accepted the obligation when they entered the schools.[67]

State commissions visit the schools to make the assignments. Young people report talking over their future work with their own teachers and the commission members. Sometimes they are offered a choice of jobs, sometimes only one. They may be sent to distant jobs—young doctors, for example, usually being sent to rural areas. The commissions receive requests for personnel from enterprises, state farms, schools, and other units. In case of hardship, the young graduate may appeal his assignment, but considerable social pressure is applied by the Young Communist League and by public opinion in general.

A refusal to take the job finally assigned, wherever it may be, was subject under the 1940 laws to criminal penalties for leaving jobs without permission, but their application has not been mentioned

[62]See Aleksandrov, *Sovyetskoe Trudovoe Pravo* (1948), pp. 248–255, discussing administrative acts and the origin of employment relations, and the 1954 edition, pp. 143–144, 155–165; and similar differences between the 1947 and 1954 editions of *Zahonodatelstvo o Trude*.

[63]Aleksandrov, *Sovyetskoe Trudovoe Pravo*, 1949 edition, pp. 139–140; 1954 edition, pp. 174–175.

[64]*Current Digest of the Soviet Press*, Vol. 8, No. 16 (May 30, 1956), p 3.

[65]*Ibid.*, Vol. 7, No. 2 (Feb. 23, 1955), pp. 34–35.

[66]Aleksandrov, *Sovyetskoe Trudovoe Pravo* (1954), pp. 161–165; *Zakonodatelstvo o Trude* (1954), pp. 12–14.

[67]Pasherstnik, *op. cit.*, pp. 171, 175–176.

in recent discussions. Critical stories in the press report cases, however, where jobs are refused by young people who do not want to go into production work or to distant areas, and who remain idle or seek to continue studying in preference to working.[68]

The choice of occupation by the youngsters who are leaving secondary school each year is considered of great importance, and editorials and letters in the press urge them to consider carefully. Thus it was said, this is

a question which every boy and girl is expected to solve independently, for his own happiness and in the interests of society....
It is common knowledge that socialism is the type of society under which people work according to their abilities....And where you produce more and better is precisely where your place of work is; it is your state solution of the problem of what career to follow. So think of how you can be of most benefit to society—as an excellent weaver or a mediocre doctor.[69]

Schools invite institutes and enterprises to send representatives to talk with students about opportunities and the qualifications needed. Those who are not going on for further study generally find their own jobs. The school director ad-

vises, and the Young Communist League is supposed to help, though it has been criticized for poor work in this respect.[70] One school director said that in the fall, if any of his graduates were not studying or located in jobs, he sent them to the executive committee of the city or district soviet, where there were people to help place youngsters where needed.

EMPLOYMENT CHANNELS FOR ADULTS

The problem of finding jobs arises also for adults, such as demobilized soldiers, women who decide to return to the labor market, people whose construction jobs or other temporary work have been completed, those whose enterprises or offices have closed, persons who for family or other personal reasons have moved to a different area, peasants who have been permitted to leave their collective farm for industry, or persons released by an amnesty or after serving a sentence.

So far as can be learned, there is no system of local employment exchanges. People generally find jobs for themselves through notices at factory gates; ads in newspapers, on the radio, and on street bulletin boards; and through the general spread of job information by friends and fellow workers, a practice which operates in the Soviet labor market as much as in any American city. It is held that there are always plenty of jobs and anyone who wants can find one.[71]

It has been impossible to find out just how much help is usually available.

[68]*Current Digest of the Soviet Press*, Vol. 4, No. 16 (May 31, 1952), pp. 5–6; Vol. 5, No. 28 (August 22, 1953), p. 26; Vol. 7, No. 25 (August 3, 1955), pp. 15–16. The general rule is that graduates of factory and Labor Reserve schools and middle technical institutes may not apply to higher educational institutions until after their term of obligatory service. F. A. Artemev, *Kratkoe Posobie po Zakonodatelstvu ob Okhrane Truda* (Moscow, 1955), p. 43, n. 3. DeWitt reports, however, that 5 percent of the graduates of a technical school may apply upon graduation, and that a considerable number of graduates from higher education continue in advanced study at once. *Op. cit.*, pp. 86, 213.

[69]*Izvestia*, June 19, 1954, quoted in *Current Digest of the Soviet Press*, Vol. 6, No. 25 (August 4, 1954), p. 4; also see *Pravda*, May 24, 1955, quoted in *Current Digest of the Soviet Press*, Vol. 7, No. 21 (July 6, 1955), p. 28.

[70]*Komsomolskaya Pravda*, Dec. 19, 1954, quoted in *Current Digest of the Soviet Press*, Vol. 6, No. 50 (Jan. 26, 1955), pp. 12–14; *Pravda*, May 5, 1955, quoted in *ibid.*, Vol. 7, No. 21 (July 6, 1955), p. 28.

[71]Several Soviet spokesmen were surprised to hear that Americans consider a man unemployed if he is out of work for a week or two. They have no concept of transitional unemployment, although admitting that in some cases it may take even two or three weeks for a man with a specialty to find a job.

Trade unions help in some cases in finding new jobs for their members. City party committees are reported to have lists of people who are "not employed" and to try to place them, sometimes with difficulty from those with grandiose ideas as to appropriate work; they also assist enterprises to recruit.[72] Army bureaus have helped demobilized soldiers. There are also in major cities local committees or bureaus attached to the city or district soviets, which have information on openings, and to which people may go for suggestions. The Moscow Information Bureau, with numerous street kiosks throughout the city, sometimes has job information on hand.[73]

Evidence from observation and interviews in four large cities indicates that the initiative of enterprises* themselves has played the largest role in local recruiting. The numerous ads on bulletin boards on the streets and in farm markets in the cities give a strong impression of the great shortage of labor. They included in December 1955 notices from Orgnabor, the Central Administration for the Organized Recruitment of Workers for distant jobs, and local notices for skilled and unskilled labor.[74]

ADMINISTRATION FOR RECRUITMENT

Only for major recruitment needs in distant areas is there real recruitment machinery—the Central Administration for the Organized Recruitment of Workers.[75] The great flow of labor from the villages to industry during the 1930's was handled through contracts made by enterprises with the collective farms and individual peasants; quotas of the numbers of peasants to be released for industry were established by the planning authorities.[76] The present system was set up in 1947 to provide an orderly method of recruitment, avoiding competition of different industries in the same village. The Central Administration for Organized Recruitment makes contracts with ministries in charge of leading industries—coal, oil, iron and steel, and others —to recruit the planned numbers of workers for them. Local offices of Orgnabor receive from their republic offices quotas to be filled on request from different industries. They send out the information on openings by the means already noted, describing special advantages,

---

[72]Current Digest of the Soviet Press, Vol. 7, No. 20 (June 29, 1955), p. 23; Vol. 8, No. 5 (March 14, 1956), p. 46; David Granick, Management of the Industrial Firm in the USSR (New York, 1954), pp. 117–118.

[73]Upon inquiry, one day in December 1955, the writer's guide was told, "Today we have only drivers' jobs." For other examples of these rare references, see Current Digest of the Soviet Press, Vol. 5, No. 19 (June 20, 1953), p. 9; Vol. 7, No. 27 (August 17, 1955), pp. 31–32. Efforts to obtain interviews with these local offices were entirely without success.

[74]In Kiev the largest and most elaborate bulletin boards were seen with job information. Two, on centrally located streets, were headed "Executive Committee of Kiev District Soviet of Workers' Deputies, Department of Recruitment of Workers." Each had about twenty notices, including the usual Orgnabor ads for construction workers, coal miners, and seasonal workers in

timber, and others from local institutes, research establishments, and enterprises. Openings ranged from those for cleaners, guards, and wardrobe attendants at museums and the university through a variety of semiskilled and skilled jobs to technicians, engineers, chief of a planning department, shop foreman, engineers on norms and wages, research workers, "paymaster urgently needed," and "electrical engineer with the right to progress to a higher level."

[75]Surprising difficulty was met in getting any contact with this organization. The inability or reluctance of Intourist to make such contacts may have been due simply to the unusualness of the request, to the fact that this is a state agency carrying on important state business, or possibly to a carryover from the time when at least some degree of compulsion was involved in such recruiting, so that outside inquiry was not welcomed. Finally, a brief interview was arranged with a local representative. Information was obtained also from trade union and other spokesmen.

[76]For details, see Schwarz, op. cit., pp. 53–64.

wages and premiums, housing available, and opportunities for training. Interested workers are enlisted, by contracts signed in the name of the ministry and enterprise concerned, for a term usually of two years; or a minimum of three years for work in the Urals, Siberia, the north and far east; or for shorter periods for seasonal work. The organization, since 1951 at least, has recruited city residents, as well as peasants, for work in distant fields. *Orgnabor* arranges, at the cost of the industry, for the transportation of the worker and his family.[77]

In a city in the Ukraine in the winter of 1955 the local office, having received its orders for workers through the republic office in Kiev, was recruiting chiefly peasants for temporary winter work in forestry, petroleum, and other industries. Most of them would return to their villages in the spring, though some would decide to stay, if their collective farms gave permission. Demobilized soldiers also were recruited for permanent work, and the guarantee of housing was an incentive for them. Many were recruited for big building projects.[78]

MASS APPEALS AND VOLUNTEERS

The huge drives of recent years for workers for agriculture in the "new lands" of Kazakhstan and for construction and industry in the east and north have been conducted on the whole by mass appeals through the trade unions and party, rather than by *Orgnabor*. Unions held meetings in the plants, newspapers were filled with reports, and the YCL took special responsibility for encouraging volunteering and for clearing requests and arranging for the placements and the transfer of those chosen. "Go east, young man" has been the appeal to the sense of adventure and pioneering, as well as to loyalty. Party discipline could require volunteering if necessary, but it is not known to what extent more pressure than that of public opinion was used. Party Secretary Khrushchev reported in 1956 that 350,000 "Soviet patriots" had responded to the call of the party and gone out to reclaim the "new lands."[79] In the spring of 1955, party organizations selected 30,000 leading workers and specialists from 100,000 volunteers and "recommended them for election" as chairmen of certain backward collective farms.[80] The YCL, from its 18.5 million members, recently sent more than 50,000 members to work in building plants, power stations and railroads in distant areas.[81] The YCL was also called on to send nearly half a million more workers to new construction projects in the north and east.[82]

The Sixth Five-Year Plan continues to place emphasis on "organized recruitment and voluntary resettlement" for supplying the needs of enterprises and construction projects in these distant areas.[83] Yet an occasional note of criticism of this system of recruiting has appeared. The secretary of the Central Committee of the Young Communist League even suggested that it was time

---

[77]Aleksandrov, *Sovyetskoe Trudovoe Pravo* (1954), pp. 158–161; *Zakonodatelstvo o Trude* (1954), pp. 11–12; Pasherstnik, *op. cit.*, pp. 123–129.

[78]This office had been active in 1954 in recruiting from the city for the "new lands" in Kazakhstan. In the Ukraine, where the Central Administration had been set up in 1953, later than in the Russian Republic, its title had been changed to include "migrants" as well as workers. See a *New York Times* dispatch from Moldavia, April 19, 1956, which spoke of the Administration for Resettlement and the Organized Recruitment of Workers.

[79]*Current Digest of the Soviet Press*, Vol. 8, No. 5 (March 14, 1956), p. 3.

[80]*Ibid.*, Vol. 8, No. 2 (Feb. 22, 1956), p. 21.

[81]*Ibid.*, Vol. 8, No. 12 (May 2, 1956), p. 6.

[82]*Ibid.*, Vol. 8, No. 15 (May 23, 1956), p. 12; Vol. 8, No. 20 (June 27, 1956), pp. 32–33.

[83]*Ibid.*, Vol. 8, No. 20 (June 27, 1956), p. 14.

to abolish organized recruitment; many directors, he said, took no responsibility for the selection of personnel and did not provide proper living and cultural arrangements for young workers, "because they know beforehand that they will receive as many workers as they ask for"; as a result, there is tremendous turnover of workers in the lumber industry and at mines and construction sites.[84]

The widespread appeals and advertisements raise a question whether they may not promote uneconomic and poorly selected movement of workers. In general, it is denied by Soviet spokesmen that enterprises compete for workers and encourage turnover. They point out that wage levels are centrally determined, so that only the approved incentives are given to attract workers; the success of enterprises in providing housing and opportunities for training are, however, a major means of attracting new personnel, young and adult, and of holding stable forces.

MOBILITY AND "LABOR DISCIPLINE"

Excessive turnover of industrial workers has been a problem to the Soviet government during the entire period of rapid industrial development. Measures to combat "flitting" and to promote stability have taken a variety of forms—incentives, penalties, compulsion, and attempts to develop public opinion favorable to "self-discipline" and "responsibility." Under conditions of great labor

shortages, an inexperienced labor force, and inadequate working and housing conditions, the desire of workers to better themselves by shifting jobs could not be entirely suppressed, even if it were desired to do so. When a Soviet worker takes a job, it is considered that he has entered into a contract of indefinite duration, except when a term is definitely stated, as for work in distant areas. Under the 1922 Labor Code, employment could be terminated on seven days' notice, but efforts to limit movement culminated in 1938 in the system of permanent labor books, giving the employment record, without which no worker can be hired. A month's notice was required for leaving jobs.[85] Finally, the decree of June 26, 1940 forbad leaving any job without permission of the director and provided criminal penalties for violations. This was to be the basis for employment relations and labor discipline, supplemented during the war by special legislation, until its final repeal on April 25, 1956.[86]

Additional inducements, influential in reducing turnover, include priorities for housing and the differentials in wages and social security benefits for long service noted above.[87] Seniority is not lost when a transfer is approved, but otherwise the worker who moves by his own

---

[84]*Ibid.*, Vol. 8, No. 12 (May 2, 1956), p. 6. Manevich reported in *Voprosy Ekonomiki*, April 1955, pp. 80–81, that ministries of coal and timber production were forced to spend a hundred million rubles every year on organized recruitment of manpower. A letter in *Komsomolskaya Pravda*, March 29, 1956, brought to the writer's attention by Mr. Jerzy Gliksman, criticized the system as expensive and wasteful, and suggested that better organization of year-round work would make it unnecessary.

[85]Schwarz, *op. cit.*, pp. 94–103.

[86]The complete text is available in James H. Meisel and Edward Kozera, *Materials for the Study of the Soviet System* (Ann Arbor, 1953), pp. 356–358; *Ugolovny Kodeks, RSFSR, 1950*, pp. 157–161. For the repeal, see *Vedomosti Verkhovnovo Soveta SSSR*, No. 10, May 8, 1956, pp. 246–248; *Current Digest of the Soviet Press*, Vol. 8, No. 16 (May 30, 1956), p. 3. The penalty for leaving without permission was imprisonment for two to four months, and lesser penalties were provided for absenteeism and lateness without adequate excuse. For detailed discussion of experience under the law, see Jerzy G. Gliksman, "Recent Trends in Soviet Labor Policy," *Monthly Labor Review*, Vol. 79, No. 7 (July 1956), pp. 767–775.

[87]Pp. 182–185.

choice, or who is discharged for breach of labor discipline, loses the right to disability pay for six months.[88] In addition, there are continuous efforts through the press, the trade unions, party organizations, and older workers in the plants to censure "the minority" of people who move irresponsibly from plant to plant and to develop habits of stability and discipline.

CRIMINAL PENALTIES

No quantitative evidence is available as to the extent of enforcement of the criminal penalities for leaving jobs without permission. It is known, however, that the 1940 laws were enforced at first with considerable severity, and again for a time at the end of the war.[89]Evidence from Soviet publications shows that after 1950 the criminal penalties were no longer in general use. Books dated 1947 to 1950 included the full text of the law and extensive discussion of criminal penalties.[90] From 1952 on, in marked contrast, when the text of the law was published, the section on criminal penalties was omitted, and discussion of remedies concerned only administrative penalties for breaches of labor discipline

and education by the use of social pressure through the trade unions or the "comradely court," an informal hearing by fellow workers.[91] Aleksandrov in 1952 and again in 1954 wrote as follows:

In connection with the increase in labor discipline...the necessity passed for the application under prewar and wartime legislation of legal measures of liability for certain types of violation of labor discipline, and measures of comradely social influence or disciplinary action were substituted.[92]

Strangely, a decree of July 14, 1951, which in effect removed the criminal penalties except in extreme cases, was never published or mentioned in the textbooks.[93] In 1955, two references were made to this in Soviet Central Asian newspapers, at least one of them urging that more use be made of court action against people leaving jobs illegally.[94] Corroboration of the existence of this decree was obtained in many interviews in 1955, but its details were not available. It was said that it repealed the criminal penalties for lateness and truancy but kept the requirement of permission for leaving jobs; formally, the penalties for leaving without permission were still in

---

[88]Aleksandrov, *Sovyetskoe Trudovoe Pravo* (1954), pp. 336–338; V. V. Karavaev, *Sotsialnoe Strakhovanie* (Moscow, 1955), p. 32. Laws and court decisions give detailed rules as to situations under which directors must grant release from a job and as to the right of a worker to appeal against a refusal to joint grievance machinery, higher administrative organs, or courts. Aleksandrov, *Sovyetskoe Trudovoe Pravo* (1954), pp. 184–188.

[89]The amnesty after Stalin's death in 1953, for all with sentences of under five years, freed those then under sentence for "economic crimes," including these. *New York Times*, March 29, 1953. The decree repealing the 1940 laws on April 25, 1956 freed from sentence or from court proceedings any sentenced or charged with violations of these laws.

[90]Aleksandrov, *Sovyetskoe Trudovoe Pravo*, 1949, had some 40 pages on labor discipline, including four on criminal penalties. See also *Ugolovny Kodeks, 1950*, pp. 157–161.

[91]Aleksandrov, *Sovyetskoe Trudovoe Pravo*, 1952, pp. 101, 265; 1954, pp. 110, 299; *Zakonodatelstvo o Trude*, 1954, pp. 44–47, 69; *Ugolovny Kodeks, 1953*, omits entirely the 1940 decree; *Osnovnye Zakonodatelnye Akty o Trude Rabochikh i Sluzhashchikh* (Moscow, 1955), pp. 5–6, gives only sections 1–4 of the decree.

[92]Aleksandrov, *Sovyetskoe Trudovoe Pravo* (1954), p. 110.

[93]"On substituting disciplinary measures and public influence for responsibility in court of workers and employees for absence from work, except in cases of repeated and prolonged absence." This decree was for the first time officially mentioned in the decree of April 25, 1956, as one of the laws then repealed. See note 86 above. Its existence had been learned by G. R. Barker on a visit to the Soviet Union in 1953, but neither he, nor so far as is known, any other Western visitor had been able to obtain a copy. Barker, *op. cit.*, p. 99n.

[94]Gliksman, *loc. cit.*, p. 770.

the law, but they were not enforced. In fact, it was said that it was well known in 1951 that these were no longer actually in effect, hence there was no need to publish the new law! Two informants[95] reported that a man who left without permission might, however, suffer a deduction from his wages on the new job as a penalty imposed by the court.

One plant director described the difficult period immediately after the war, when new, inexperienced workers came into industry from villages which had been destroyed, and there was a serious problem of labor discipline. This was the time of most drastic enforcement of the 1940 law. By 1947, however, the working force was more experienced and accustomed to the needs of plant discipline, and the criminal penalties were therefore no longer used. In this plant and others visited, there was said to be presently no serious problem of labor turnover. Large numbers of the workers had long service records. In one plant, perhaps typical of the larger plants, reasons given for the decline in turnover were that wages had increased, conditions and housing were better, and most workers now had training specifically for this work. The major reasons for leaving these plants were enrollment for study in middle or higher education, finding jobs nearer home, family reasons, and in one plant, the lack of good housing. These plants had also lost workers, some of them highly skilled, in the drive for the "new lands" and for experts for collective and state farms. When a worker wished to be released, he wrote a letter to the director asking permission, and if this was refused, he sometimes obtained the permission through efforts of the trade union.

Directors said that they would try to hold a skilled man, at least until a replacement was found, but added "You can't hold a man against his will," or "In the end, it is the decision of the worker." If these plants were at all typical, a worker was permitted to go when he could make any reasonable case for the change.

The decree of April 25, 1956, which repealed not only the June 26, 1940 law but also that of October 19, 1940 on compulsory transfer, seems therefore to have done little more than to regularize what already was the fact as far as many, if not most, workers were concerned. It provided that two weeks' notice must be given of desire to leave a job. A person released from work by his own choice, however, loses as before his record of continuous service and is not eligible for disability benefits until after working six months on the new job; but this rule does not apply to a listed series of exceptions or to persons released "for other valid reasons set forth in decrees."

Evidence available, inadequate though it is, strongly suggests that in recent years, at least since 1950, there has been a surprising degree of freedom to change jobs, in spite of the fact that it has been illegal to break a three-year contract of employment, to violate the obligation to work for three or four years where directed after completing study, or to leave any job without the agreement of the director. An occasional case was sent to court, and evidently some workers were sentenced as a result;[96] but court decisions and decrees brought about a long list of circumstances under which workers had a right to be released. Even the failure of the enterprise to supply the kind

[95]A trade union representative and a judge in a People's Court. Others with whom these matters were discussed were economists, legal experts, and plant directors.

[96]See Gliksman, *loc. cit.*, pp. 769–770.

of housing promised was an acceptable excuse for workers recruited by *Orgnabor*.[97] There were still limitations upon freedom to move, but in practice the limitations were to a considerable extent those resulting from loss of the advantages of long service, rather than in the formal requirements of the law. The trend towards greater freedom of choice of job even before the 1956 decree is unmistakable.

Recent discussions continue to stress the importance of reducing turnover and maintaining stable forces. There is, however, no such urgency in the discussion, nor does this issue appear so frequently in the Soviet press as it did from 1950 to 1953, when the relaxation of criminal penalties was being accompanied by an educational drive. It is deplored that there is still a minority of irresponsible people who "flit from plant to plant" and in other ways violate labor discipline. But the major method of dealing with the problem is said to be persuasion and education, along with improvement in housing and other conditions.[98]

CONCLUSIONS

In a centrally planned economy, the methods by which the labor force is distributed are crucial both for the success of the economy in achieving its objectives and for the welfare of individual workers. Soviet experience of nearly thirty years under the Five Year Plans is of interest to western economists for its experimental, trial-and-error character and for the extent to which it came to use traditional market forces. This means a

degree of reliance upon individual choice of fields of employment and of jobs.

Marxism and Leninism, which continue as the ideological basis for the Soviet system of central planning, give no detailed blueprint and have not interfered with the experimental approach, as the planners have sought workable solutions to their problems. For instance, there is authority in these Soviet gospels both for equalization of wages and for differential wages in "the period of transition from capitalism to communism." The vast movement from agriculture into industry was engineered by a planned and, in part, controlled and compulsory system of recruitment. It was influenced also by planned wage differentials and by a system of training and assignment of graduates. Ideological motivations and enthusiasm for the great program of development without doubt had considerable influence, especially among the youth. In the intense drive for production in the late 1930's, and even more during the war, compulsion grew, direction to jobs increased, and freedom to change jobs was sharply curtailed. At the same time, incentives to enter and to remain in fields and areas of special significance were increased by differences in wages and a variety of other conditions and benefits. After the war and the immediate postwar reconstruction drive, the compulsory aspects were gradually relaxed.

In 1955–1956, even before the decree of April 1956, the distribution of the labor force depended first on centrally planned measures which determined the development programs for industry and agriculture and provided an abundance of jobs. Programs of training, both for new entrants into industry and for advanced education, were planned as to numbers enrolled, and graduates were sent where needed for their first years of

[97]Aleksandrov, *et al., Zakonodatelstvo o Trude* (1954), p. 59.

[98]For example, N. G. Aleksandrov, "Za dalneishee ukreplenie sotsialisticheskoi zakonnosti v oblasti trudovykh otnoshenii," *Sotsialisticheskii Trud,* February 1956, pp. 42–43; N. A. Bulganin, *Pravda,* July 17, 1955; *Current Digest of the Soviet Press,* Vol. 7, No. 28 (August 24, 1955), p. 12.

work. Differential earnings and other incentives were extensively relied on to cut down undesired turnover and to induce entrance into areas, fields, and jobs where more labor was needed. Compulsory limitations upon movement were still on the books, but their use had drastically decreased; and to a large extent, individuals could in the end make their own decisions, although the requirement of permission to leave, the disadvantage of breaking continuous service, and the force of public opinion slowed such movement. Recruitment was largely a matter of publicity by enterprises in local markets, with individuals finding their own jobs. Only for major activities located in distant regions, needing recruits from other urban areas as well as from agriculture, was there organized recruitment machinery. For mass movements of workers to new developments, reliance was put on huge propaganda drives and recruitment was carried on by party organizations and trade unions. Individual decision was the basis, although there must have been considerable pressure, and even compulsion, in some cases. In general, the atmosphere was unmistakably one of increased reliance upon individual choice of employment, within the framework and under the economic compulsions and inducements set by the planned development of the economy.

For individuals, the choices are greatly influenced by the differences in income offered in different industries and areas, and at different levels of skill and training, as well as by differences in prestige. The economic compulsion of need for income, with the advantage of higher income in giving more access to scarce consumer goods, is enough to keep most able-bodied citizens in the labor market and to induce efforts to get more training and to move into the better jobs available. The fact that there is scope for individual choices must give an increased feeling of freedom and opportunity to Soviet citizens. Presumably, it also increases their morale and effectiveness, in spite of the fact that satisfaction of individual preferences is to some extent limited by decisions of the planners as to the relative numbers needed, for example, of engineers and students of the humanities.

For the Soviet government, the present system reflects the facts that there is now a large labor force with experience in the traditions and discipline of the factory and that the level of general education is rapidly rising. Without giving up its essential controls based on central planning, the state has apparently found that the sorting of individuals into jobs can best be done primarily through the choices by individuals of fields of training, and after the first years of work upon graduation, by their choices of later jobs. Individual choice in the market, though the market itself is the result of planning, is evidently believed to give better results in morale and efficiency than authoritarian placement of workers. Incentives can be varied at need, and all the resources of propaganda at the command of the state and party can influence the choices.

Criticisms of the effectiveness of the system of distribution of the labor force are frequently made by Soviet spokesmen and economists, and it is to be expected that revisions will continue to be made. A turn back towards compulsion is not impossible at any time if it should be felt necessary. Present indications are, however, that there is to be a real trial of greater liberalism in this field. To the western economist, it appears that a better organized system for recruitment, both locally and for distant jobs, would facilitate the operations of the labor market and reduce waste. Nevertheless, measured by the results in economic growth, there has been a high degree of success from this combination of planning, compulsion, and reliance on individual choice in the market.

Soviet central planning, controlling economic development in chosen directions, has resulted in full employment and huge movements of labor into new areas and occupations, although apparently much underutilization of manpower still remains. It has provided very widespread educational opportunities, important for the needs of the economy. Although Soviet theorists deny the existence of a "labor market," the familiar market mechanisms, supplemented by ideological influences and a variety of other inducements, have proved useful tools, which the planners hope to make even more efficient. These comprise not only the "great lever" for the rational distribution of the labor force of which Soviet theorists speak, but also a means by which Soviet workers may expect an increase in freedom.

K. Forced Labor in the Soviet Bloc

INTRODUCTION

Notwithstanding the denials of the Soviet Government that forced labor exists within the Soviet Union and its captive countries, and despite the strict censorship of news and control of travel that has prevailed in these countries, the fact that a system of forced labor is being carried out has been attested to by students of the Soviet economy, by the investigation undertaken by an ad hoc committee on forced labor of the United Nations,[39] and by reports and testimony of those who witnessed or experienced living under conditions of involuntary

[39] United Nations. All Hoc Committee on Forced Labour Report * * * submitted to the Economic and Social Council of the United Nations and the Governing Body of the International Labour Office. Geneva, 1953. 619 p.

labor. Although censorship of news by foreign correspondents has eased somewhat since Stalin's death, it has not been lifted to the extent of allowing a discussion of prison camps or the authority in charge, the Ministry of Internal Affairs (the MVD).

The ad hoc committee's thorough and painstaking report, which covered the extent of forced labor throughout the world, concluded that, "forced-labor systems used for political coercion or in the interest of the national economy exist in the Soviet Union and four other Iron Curtain countries." This conclusion was based on a study of the laws of the countries, and on information from documents and affidavits presented by various government officials or private individuals. Countries found to have penal legislation constituting bases for forced-labor systems to be used for purposes of political coercion or economic expediency were Bulgaria, Czechoslovakia, the Soviet Union, Rumania, and Poland.

An examination by the ad hoc committee of the decrees, regulations, laws, and codes of the Soviet Union, presented by representatives of the free world, revealed that a system of forced labor has been established which had its inception in 1918.

According to the allegations, the Soviet penal system constitutes the legal basis of a system of forced labor designed to oppress and reeducate those who disagree with the ideology of the regime in power.

The Soviet representatives, on the other hand, denied that forced labor exists in the Soviet Union, and that the aim of the penal and labor codes is not to punish the offender but to reeducate him so that he might become a law-abiding citizen to a Socialist society. Such reeducation is accomplished through corrective labor performed during the period for which sentenced.

HISTORY

Forced-labor camps were established for the purpose of punishing and isolating class enemies, the elimination of which was most desired. Shortly thereafter the belief that these prisoners could be put to use to the advantage of the state began to develop. During the early 1920's a "corrective" labor policy was initiated, culminating in the issuance of the first corrective labor code in 1924. The old prison system was abolished and its place taken by a network of colonies for offenders who were put to work in factories, workshops, and on farms. Besides being subjected to compulsory labor, the prisoners were given political education. However, these two methods of reform, involuntary participation in work of benefit to the state and society and political reeducation to influence the minds of the convicted to accept the Socialist regime, were not coordinated. The code of 1924 was also found to be defective in that no clear distinction was drawn between class enemies who should be suppressed and convicted workers who needed reeducation—

to accustom them to work and live as members of the laboring community and to bring them into association with Socialist construction.

In 1933 a new corrective labor code was issued which emphasized the separation of these two types of prisoners. It appears that—

at this time the corrective labor institutions assumed an economic importance which, apparently, had hitherto been lacking, and began to play a part in the national economy.

"CORRECTIVE" LABOR

"Corrective" labor is imposed upon those who are convicted of crimes against the state as well as ordinary criminal actions. The corrective labor policy is set forth in both the corrective labor code and the penal code. Its aim is to prevent offenders from committing acts harmful to socialist construction, and from committing further crimes. Reeducation and influences are brought to bear to adapt the offenders, through organized and directed work, to conditions of a communal life in a people's state.

The penalties accompanying conviction with corrective labor depend upon the degree of the offense, and the degree of class danger which the convicted person represents. Three types of corrective labor are mentioned in the penal and corrective labor codes: (1) corrective labor without deprivation of liberty; (2) exile with corrective labor; (3) deprivation of liberty with corrective labor.

The first of these is imposed upon persons whose offenses are not considered serious and who are not a threat to "society" to such an extent as to need isolation from it. The sentence may be for a period of 1 day to 1 year, to be carried out either at a worker's normal place of work or within a specified distance from his residence. The offender may be placed in an industrial plant or a mass-production unit, or may be assigned to seasonal work in agriculture. Disciplinary measures accompanying the sentence include deduction of wages (to a maximum of 25 percent); suspension of leave; loss of recognition of time served for purposes of probation periods, grants of pensions, wage increases for length of service, and additional holidays.

Exile with corrective labor generally applies only to political enemies of the state. The importance of exile was explained by B. S. Utevski in Soviet Corrective Labor Policy (Unified State Publishing House, 1935):

> The importance of exile as a punishment increased in the reconstruction period when the accentuated opposition of class-hostile elements to socialist construction made it necessary to find new ways of countering such opposition. At the same time the possibility of organizing exile on the principle of providing persons sentenced to this penalty with a reeducation in labor on large-scale socialist construction projects in distant areas of the Soviet Union which were in need of manpower provided opportunities of so arranging exile that, while acting as a powerful repressive measure, it also served to instill a sense of discipline in workers who committed serious crimes.

Sentences imposing exile range for periods of 3 to 10 years, to be served in labor on public undertakings on a contract basis between the undertaking and the corrective labor institution; on special undertakings of the corrective labor institution; on mass work contracted for between state authorities and the corrective labor institution; and on mass work in colonies. Mass work in colonies applies also to persons sentenced to corrective labor with deprivation of liberty. However, persons serving a sentence of exile in mass labor colonies are not subject to the restrictions placed upon those deprived of liberty.

Freedom is not wholly regained upon release after serving a term in a corrective labor institution. In many cases released persons may not be allowed to go outside a certain restricted area and are under constant surveillance by the MVD. These people are numbered among the "spetsi," described by Harrison Salisbury, a former correspondent from Moscow for the New York Times. Their passports, identification papers, and labor books show that they have been inmates of a labor camp as well as the location of the camp. Such papers must be presented when seeking employment. In many cases the seeker may be considered a dangerous element, making the attainment of work a difficult matter. The only alternative is to return to work on state projects under the authority of the Ministry of Internal Affairs, the agency which has charge of the undertakings and workers of the corrective labor camps.

Mass deportations of great numbers of persons within the borders of the Soviet Union and from the captive countries to northern and eastern regions of the Soviet Union have placed in exile victims of the ruthless policy of the state to divide and weaken potentially dangerous elements. Migrations have been enforced for economic reasons also. These deportees are not persons who have committed any violations of the laws or been sentenced to punitive labor. Material presented to the ad hoc committee on forced labor gave evidence of this practice of moving whole colonies of people, but the committee did not feel that there was enough definite information to substantiate the charge that deportees were or are at present being detained in labor camps, and therefore the question of deportation and exile was not one to be considered with that of forced labor.

Nevertheless, the lack of freedom of movement beyond restricted areas under the authority of the MVD compels the deportees to seek work within a limited field of opportunities, generally limited to work for the state.

These involuntary residents are the "spetsi," mentioned above. The "spetsi" were the subject of the article (one of a series) by Harrison Salisbury which appeared in the New York Times for September 28, 1954. He commented that a great deal has been said about forced labor camps but very little attention has been paid to the "spetsi." The "spetsi," meaning, according to Salisbury, persons who live under "special residence conditions," within limited boundaries, are "the millions of citizens of the Soviet Union who, somehow or other, by their own actions or more likely by accident of geography, residence, or nationality have fallen afoul of the Soviet authorities and been sent off to live in some distant and usually unpleasant locale." They also include nationals from the Baltic States, removed from their native land as a measure of security by the MVD. They are found particularly in central Asia, Siberia, the far north, and the far east, regions where voluntary settlers will not go because of harsh living conditions. These people are not in the true sense of the word "forced laborers," for they may work wherever they can get a job and may live wherever they can find shelter within the area to which they are restricted. To all intents and purposes, however, they are prisoners of the state, subject to the authority of the MVD.

Mr. Salisbury reported that since Stalin's death, no large numbers of Soviet citizens have been sent into exile, but there has been some transfer of exiles from the captive countries. Nevertheless, Mr. Salisbury points out, the uprooting of masses of people will continue so long as the present prison system exists and so long as the MVD needs workers for the mines, mills, and farms under its authority.

Under the third type of corrective labor, punishment for crimes, political or ordinary, which calls for corrective labor with deprivation of liberty, is based on the degree of the offense committed and the extent of danger which the offender presents to the socialist society. The report of the ad hoc committtee states that, at least since the 1930's, there seems to have been two types of institutions for persons who have been sentenced to deprivation of liberty with corrective labor. Sentences of 3 years or less are served in corrective labor colonies, while those of over 3 years are served in corrective labor camps. The corrective labor code provides, however, that if the court so orders, persons sentenced to more than 3 years' labor may be received in the colonies rather than the camps. The maximum penalty with deprivation of liberty is 10 years. For cases of espionage, wreckage, and diversionary acts the period may be longer, but not to exceed 25 years.

The corrective labor colonies receive persons who have been convicted by a court or by a special decision of the MVD. It should be noted that, under the corrective labor code and by ordinance, in some instances persons may be sentenced to concentration camps solely by administrative orders of the MVD, without having been accorded a hearing and trial in a court of law. This extrajudicial power arbitrarily administered places individual freedom in jeopardy and completely annihilates the democratic principle that a person is innocent until proven guilty.

The colonies, which are considered "the basic type of place where persons are deprived of liberty," are themselves broken down into three different types: (1) Factory and agricultural colonies—organized to train people in labor habits, to educate them politically, and generally to familiarize them with life and work in an organized community; (2) mass-labor colonies in distant areas—established to receive persons who constitute a class danger necessitating more severe conditions; and (3) punitive colonies—established to receive persons who were previously in other colonies and had shown insubordination to the regime or labor discipline.

Whatever the results of corrective labor may be, insofar as influencing and reeducating the workers, it is apparent that the practice of using forced labor has been an effective means of accomplishing construction and production for the state where labor is difficult to get and at greatly reduced cost.

NUMBER OF FORCED LABORERS

The Soviet Union has closely guarded any information as to the number of persons who committed infractions of the law and were sentenced to compulsory labor. Official figures never have been published. Estimates have been made at various times by writers and by persons who have escaped from concentration camps to the Western World. A House document prepared in 1946 (Communism in Action, H. Doc. 754, 1946) reports on page 56:

The following estimates come from a variety of sources. They differ very widely because of the different sources of information of the estimators and the different years in which the estimates were made; but they all attest to the existence of the institution of forced labor and of camps conducted under harsh prison conditions and they all count the victims in the millions—not only at any one time but also year after year.

Lyons, 6 million in 1933; Dallin, 10 million in 1940; Barmine, 12 million in 1938; Souvarine, 15 million in 1937; Ciliga, 10 million in 1937; Kravchenko, 18 million in 1941; Koestler, 17 million in 1943; White, 14 million in 1945.

Other estimates have run all the way from a conservative 1,830,000 to as many as 20 million. Estimates for a single year have differed, as shown by Michael Rozanoff's claim that 11,050,000 prisoners were held by the Soviet Union in 1941 (cited in Tensions Within the Soviet Union, S. Doc. 69, 1953, p. 78) against Kravchenko's estimate of 18 million.

However, to place the number of concentration camp inmates as high as 15 million to 20 million is regarded as fantastic by at least two students of the Soviet economy. Such figures, or even only 12 million, would imply that one-third of the country's men of working age were imprisoned. It is the belief of one of these writers that there were perhaps as many as 3.5 million prisoners employed in forced labor in 1941; the other writer thinks that there were about 5 million for the period from 1947 to 1951.

Naum Jasny, after a study of the State Plan of Development of the National Economy of the U. S. S. R. for 1941, based his figures upon an interpretation of the data presented therein. He cautioned "that the compilations made with the help of these interpretations necessarily involve a great deal of estimation, partly or even largely arbitrary, and the conclusions at best will be within a rough range of approximation".[40] He summed up the number of concentration camp inmates employed in all economic activities of the NKVD (now the MVD) according to the 1941 plan to be 2,322,000. He continued:

Assuming that 20 percent of the employed concentration-camp inmates worked in enterprises other than those of the NKVD, the figures of 2,322,000 computed above for the inmates employed in the enterprises of the NKVD rises, after rounding, to 2,900,000. * * * There still remain, however, considerable numbers of concentration-camp inmates used for servicing those who are employed in gainful occupations, such as office clerks, cleaners, cooks, medical personnel, etc., and even internal policy. With those persons considered, the total number of concentration-camp victims used for work may have been as high as 3½ million. This figure does not include children, full invalids, people too old to work, etc. I have no evidence by which to estimate them.[41]

The other writer, Eugene M. Kulischer, made the following deduction:

An indirect approach to a plausible estimate of the number of forced laborers is to attempt to gage the full complement of "deportees," including those in concentration camps, by comparing election data with figures on the general population * * * From the total adult Soviet population (those 18 years of age and over) for 1947, 1950, and 1951, let us accordingly subtract voters registered in the elections of 1947, 1950, and 1951. Since registration is compulsory, this yields the number of nonvoting adults—about 13 million. In order to obtain the number of deportees (in and outside of concentration camps), three other groups of nonvoters must be excluded: Aliens * * *; persons omitted in the process of registration * * *; and the insane, ordinary criminals disfranchised for 5 years, and persons under investigation (totaling approximately 3.5 percent). The remaining nonvoting population for each of these 3 years amounts to about 9 million persons—a total which includes not only inmates of concentration camps, but also deportees who were never in concentration camps and those who have served their time or have been pardoned. * * *

How many, then, of the residual 9 million mentioned above really are forced laborers living in the notorious concentration camps? A pure guess would be 5 million; it seems the maximum compatible with the mass of deportees to be found outside of concentration camps throughout the Soviet Union and with what we otherwise know about social and demographic conditions there.[42]

---

[40] Jasny, Naum, Labor and Output in Soviet Concentration Camps. Journal of Political Economy, October 1951, p. 407.
[41] Ibid., pp. 415–416.
[42] Kulischer, E. M., Russian Manpower, Foreign Affairs, October 1952.

All these estimates deal with the number of persons sentenced to labor in concentration camps or colonies, but if the term "forced labor" is broadened to include persons sentenced to corrective labor without deprivation of liberty to be carried out at their normal place of work, the figure for victims of the system of compulsory "corrective" labor would no doubt be higher. Again, there is no way of knowing how many are in this category from day to day or month to month.

ECONOMIC IMPORTANCE

As has been stated, forced labor has been used for economic purposes in helping to increase production in all branches—in agriculture, in industry, in the mines, in forestry, in road and railroad building, and in construction of public works.

Representatives of various countries presented material to the United Nations Ad Hoc Committee alleging that forced labor in the Soviet Union is not only valuable as a means of rehabilitating the class hostile elements, but also as a factor in the economic achievements undertaken by the state, by supplying a source of cheap manpower and making possible a corps of workers to develop and exploit undeveloped areas. On the basis of the information submitted, the Committee concluded that the work of prisoners is important to the national economy of the Soviets and plays a significant part.

It is evident from several Soviet sources that, since about 1930, the work of both political and other prisoners has been used in the Soviet Union for large-scale public works (e. g., canals, railways, and roads), for the development of vast areas with abundant and hitherto unexploited resources of raw materials, and for the economic development of previously uncultivated regions. Several Soviet authors have also stressed the great importance for the national economy of the work done by the corrective labor camps and colonies. This information from Soviet sources actually relates to conditions existing before the Second World War, but nothing either in the statements made in the Economic and Social Council by the representatives of the U. S. S. R., the Byelorussian S. S. R., and Poland on the work of prisoners or in other information which the Committee has been able to obtain would seem to indicate that the situation is different today It is also clear from the most recent testimonies examined by the Committee that during the war and even after, persons sentenced to corrective labor were still used on large-scale projects or in big industrial and farming undertakings.

Mr. Salisbury's report in the New York Times shows that as recent as 1954 there has been no change in the policy of using prisoners on public works and in agriculture, mining, etc.

The Committee, however, would not attempt to estimate the extent of the value of the labor of prisoners nor to "assess its relation to the entire economic activity of the country," since definite conclusions can be made only on statistics which in this case are unobtainable.

By far the greater proportion of prisoners are located in camps or colonies under the authority of the Ministry of Internal Affairs (the MVD, formerly the NKVD). An estimate of the amount of capital construction to be performed by forced labor was made by the United States from data contained in the State Plan for the Development of the National Economy of the U. S. S. R. in 1941. This plan showed that 14 percent of the capital construction for that year was assigned to the NKVD, and that the actual percentage of capital construction by means of forced labor was even higher because indications were that some of the prisoners were farmed out to projects financed by other government agencies. A Russian refugee, formerly with the central agency in charge of the various 5-year plans (Gosplan), testified that from one-tenth to one-half of the total production in certain industries was scheduled to be produced under NKVD authority in 1941.

Although forced labor has been used extensively throughout the Soviet Union on a great number of projects, the economic value of such labor is doubted by two students of Soviet affairs.

Eugene Kulischer, in his article, Russian Manpower, expresses the belief that the Soviet Government does not expect to profit from forced labor. The productivity of a forced laborer is undoubtedly a great deal less than that of other workers. Forced labor may be economically useful in regions where free labor will not voluntarily go, but the work to be performed in these outlying districts would require only a fraction of the number of persons sentenced to concentration camps. Kulischer believes that millions have been sent to camps not because they are needed but because the Soviet would rather risk the economic and social loss of imprisoning them than to run the political risk of allowing them to be at large.

Naum Jasny gives his reasons for believing that concentration camps are a liability rather than a source of profit in his article, Labor and Output in Soviet Concentration Camps:

1. Concentration camps diminish the number of persons outside who share the burden of paying for the government's expenditures, due to low consumption levels and low wages.

2. Underuse of skills of inmates and rate of mortality in camps are losses to the economy.

3. Time is wasted in moving inmates from location to location to work on government projects.

4. Indirect loss is incurred by removing people from their normal occupations which were profitable for the state.

The only economic advantage of concentration camps that Naum Jasny sees is "the opportunity to move this labor to places and to use it for work where and for which free labor would be difficult or impossible to obtain."

Richard Carlton, in writing about the captive countries, has this to say about the economic value of forced labor:

The importance of forced labor is often questioned with the remark that it must be extremely inefficient. This is certainly true in the classical economic sense, for without initiative and cooperation no large body of workers can perform as efficiently as if they were free. Nevertheless, it must not be forgotten that the satellites use their controlled pool of forced labor wherever normal recruitment methods would have failed (a) because of the time needed to induce free laborers to move, and (b) because free laborers would not willingly work for the pay offered and under the conditions required. The essential function of forced labor is to supply manpower for the industrialization programs. This manpower can be rigidly controlled and arbitrarily assigned. Forced labor is highly productive in that it is almost invariably allotted to key segments of the development plans. It is also vitally important in the inflexible totalitarian economy in that it often provides the sole means of recruiting new labor. In a sense, the forced laborers are the shock troops of the 5-year plans.[43]

Another factor which contributes to economic waste is the fact that the policing of the whole network of camps and colonies requires a large number of MVD guards. The expense of maintaining these armed guards is considerable and an added burden to the economic structure of the country.

---

[43] Carlton, Richard. The Economic Importance of Forced Labor in Eastern Europe. New York, Mid-European Studies Center, June 28, 1954, pp. 15–16.

The pressure of the whole corrective and penal labor policy of the state upon the workers and their living standards has broad repercussions. The ever-present threat of being penalized or convicted for violating the laws or regulations, however minor, creates uncertainty for the future and tends to build up a feeling of futility and instability. With no incentive for planning ahead, the propensity to save is severely curtailed; the desire to spend income on a current basis for whatever is available places great pressure on the demand for goods. This demand, accompanied by a chronic shortage of supplies, has given rise to black markets of rather large proportions.

Whatever may be achieved economically by the use of compulsory labor of victims of the penal system, the fact remains that under Communist domination the freedom, dignity, and worth of the individual is disregarded in the drive for industrial expansion demanded by the regime.

RESTRICTION ON "FREE" LABOR

"Free" labor as it is recognized in the democratic countries does not exist in the Soviet bloc. Workers in the Communist countries are much more regimented and are subject to dictatorial rules and regulations established by the state. In the Soviet Union unjustifiable absence from work for even 1 day has been punished by corrective labor at the regular place of employment accompanied by a reduction in pay up to 25 percent. In the captive countries, absence has not been so severely dealt with. For example, in Poland 1 day's absence is reprimanded, with possibility of a fine amounting to 1 day's earnings. (See Poland: Law on Labor Discipline, in notes on labor abroad, U. S. Department of Labor, December 1950, p. 24.) Tardiness of more than 20 minutes without a valid excuse constituted an absence. The regulations governing absenteeism and tardiness have not appeared in the published laws of recent date, but there is no indication that they have been formally repealed. It would seem that presently these violations are dealt with by disciplinary action. Labor mobility on a voluntary basis is curbed by legislation placing restrictions on leaving jobs. Transfers of workers, particularly skilled and scientific workers, become mandatory upon orders from Government department heads, regardless of the desires of the workers. Trade unions exist only in name and have become an arm of the state to carry out the policies of the regime, not to represent and promote the interests of the workers.

Restrictions on the freedom of employment have been caused by governmental actions. Enforcement of regulations set forth by the Government has resulted in reducing the gap between the status of free and forced laborers. A list of restrictive regulations that effect the aims of the Government to mobilize and discipline labor shows the extent to which labor is regimented.

(a) Strikes are not forbidden by law, but are practically impossible, because of ruthless suppression as sabotage;

(b) Legislation dated December 20, 1938, introduced workbooks, in which all breaches of labor discipline committed by the holder are inscribed. This book must be produced before a worker can be hired;

(c) Under legislation dated June 26, 1940, workers are not allowed to leave their jobs without permission from the administration of their undertaking or institution;

(d) Legislation dated October 2, 1940, stipulated that every year a contingent of young persons must be drafted into the vocational-training centers and that, once their studies are completed, they must be sent for 3 or 4 years to work in undertakings or institutions. Provision is also made for persons graduating from universities and specialized schools to be assigned to jobs in a similar manner;

(e) The compulsory transfer of workers from one area to another has been authorized by legislation dated October 19, 1940; ·

(f) The labor cade and legislation dated June 8, 1946, on the fulfillment of the plan, allowed overtime to be required of workers.

Failure to comply with the provisions of these laws is considered a breach of labor discipline, punishable upon conviction. For example, appointed trainees who refuse to enter training, or who leave centers of training without permission, may be sentenced to a labor colony. Workers who refuse to transfer to other undertakings, or who leave work without authorized permission, may be imprisoned. Punishment for infractions of the laws is extended to include managers and heads of departments who fail to report cases of violation, inflict prescribed penalties, or who hire persons without authorized permission to leave former jobs.

After a study of the material submitted and the allegations made by the several free-country representatives, the ad hoc committee reached the conclusion that—

such measures, applied on a large scale and in the interests of the national economy, lead * * * to a system of forced or compulsory labor constituting an important element in the economy of the country.

The shortage of the labor supply and the utilization of manpower for industrial use were problems which were faced as far back as the 1930's. The effort to secure a greater labor force led to the policy of tightening the restrictions on the freedom of workers to accept or reject employment. Unemployment was not to be tolerated and the unemployed were not permitted to refuse any kind of work available, whether suitable or not, except for reason of illness. The labor exchanges, the Government employment agencies, were empowered to remove from their lists names of persons refusing to take jobs, thus in many cases depriving them of any chance to work. At the same time unemployment benefits were "suspended." This move was justified by the announcement that there was no more "unemployment." To date, unemployment does not exist officially and, as a result, unemployment compensation has been completely eliminated.

The suspension of unemployment benefits was a means of pressure to force the unemployed worker to accept any job offered, even if it was outside his trade, beneath his skill, and far from his place of residence.[44]

There has been evidence in recent years that these restrictive laws have been evaded, particularly in those industries where there is a heavy productivity schedule and a shortage of labor. The Soviet press in 1952 reported the censure by the Central Council of Soviet

---

[44] Schwarz, Solomon M. Labor in the Soviet Union. New York, Praeger, 1951.

Trade Unions of the housing and transport-machine-building industries for their "weakness in labor discipline." Other press reports complained of the tolerance being shown by managers toward absenteeism and tardiness, and the laxity with regard to workbooks. It was found that absentees and latecomers in many instances were not reported and turned over to the courts for trial. Workbooks were not being kept up to date, nor were they being demanded by management, thus permitting workers to leave or accept jobs without authorization. This defection of truancy and "floating" is one of the causes for concern to the Government in striving to overcome a weakening of its power to regiment workers in the effort to heighten production.

The impossibility of policing every corner of the industrial sector gives rise to the practices referred to in the complaints appearing in the press. Evasion of the laws is apparently a publicly acknowledged fact, but it must be borne in mind that the laws are still in effect and may be applied at any time the party desires to enforce them within any one area.

Further restrictions on the freedom of labor are found in the practice of drafting hundreds of thousands of youths of both sexes between the ages of 14 and 19 for industrial training. Assignments to the different training centers are made by the authorities without regard for personal preference. After the period of training, the draftees are obliged to work for Government plants for 4 years.

In similar fashion, professionals upon graduation from universities are given assignments by the ministries in charge of the schools, regardless of individual choice. These assignments are for periods of 3 to 5 years.

Collective bargaining in the Soviet Union is another example of the absence of free labor conditions. Collective agreements were reintroduced in 1947 as a matter of policy after a lapse of 14 years.[45] The agreements are not the result of negotiation between employees and employer, but are forms drawn up by the authorities, implementing the regulations governing labor and production.

The new rules positively require that "the rates of wages, of piecework, progressive piecework, and bonuses as approved by the Government must be indicated" in the agreement.

*   *   *   *   *   *   *

As before, the new regulations are based on the assumption that "the interests of the workers are the same as the interests of production in a Socialist state" and that the collective agreements are designed to be the "juridical form of expression of this unity." Accordingly, a model agreement is drafted by each ministry upon consultation with the central offices of the appropriate trade unions. Then the model agreement is sent as a fait accompli to the establishments concerned.[46]

The purpose of the collective agreements is described by Schwarz [47] as follows:

Today, collective bargaining in the Soviet Union is consciously not designed to defend the interests of wage and salary earners. As stressed by Trud, the official trade-union paper, in an editorial dedicated to the reintroduction of collective contracts: "As the guardian of workingmen's interests we have the Socialist state." Therefore the purpose of collective agreements consists not in the pro-

---

[45] Gsovski, Vladimir.   Elements of Soviet Labor Law.   (Monthly Labor Review, March, April 1951.   (U. S. Department of Labor, Bureau of Labor Statistics Bulletin No. 1026.)
[46] Gsovski, op. cit.
[47] Schwarz, op. cit.

tection of labor, but "in guaranteeing the fulfillment and overfulfillment of the state production plan for the given establishment." Hence "the main stipulation of the contracted obligation must be an increased demand from every worker. Without strengthening labor discipline and without ruthless struggle against the violators of state and labor discipline—grabbers and loafers—there can be no real fulfillment of obligations laid down in the collective agreement."

GENERAL OBSERVATIONS

The compulsory and restrictive features of the labor policy of the Soviet Union are geared to the political and economic aims of the Government. On the one hand, there has been repression of people thought to be dangerous to the Communist Party to help insure its continuance in power. By means of enforced corrective labor and indoctrination, the regime has attempted to mold the wills and minds of hundreds of thousands of victims.

On the other hand, the struggle to expand industrial production has created the demand for a large supply of labor which led to the allocation of manpower at the expense of the independence and freedom of workers. The forced labor system of the Soviets has provided a way to punish or liquidate "undesirable" elements among its ranks, but it can also be presumed that the demand for forced labor causes the use of penalties to a greater or less extent as circumstances warrant.

The vast police empire must have a natural inclination to maintain and even expand its activities. Its leaders are probably eager to lay their hands on interesting projects and the next step is to round up or retain the necessary number of prisoners. There are enough laws and decrees and their provisions are flexible enough to increase the camp population simply by insisting on a more severe and comprehensive enforcement policy. In such a case minor infractions which might otherwise have gone unnoticed will lead to long forced labor terms, and unscrupulous agents of the judicial and police systems will frame innocent people in order to curry favor in the eyes of their superiors. The dangerous combination of judicial and police power with "big business" in one single administration—the MVD—is one of the reasons for the magnitude of the Soviet forced labor system.[48]

The effect of the forced labor system and restrictive labor policies upon the economic development of the country cannot be accurately determined. Undoubtedly the productivity of forced labor is adversely affected by a number of circumstances,[49] such as the overhead cost of police administration, the time spent by prisoners in jail and being transported from camp to camp, the nonutilization of skills of camp inmates, poor administration of the camps, and work time lost through ill health and maltreatment. The forced labor system affects the productivity of nonslave labor, also, "because of the anguish it causes the relatives and friends of the prisoners and because of the ill effects on the health, morale, and training of former prisoners." The possible shortening of the lives of former inmates of camps also creates an economic loss.

Under these circumstances it is highly doubtful whether the forced laborers' net product available for investment and public consumption (such as military use) is larger than that of an equal number of free workers. But even if it should be larger, it would be simple to reduce private consumption of the nation as a whole through taxation and loans by a corresponding amount. An infinitesimal reduction in the consumption of the free population would bring about the same relation between private consumption and investment (plus public con-

---

[48] U. S. Information Service. A Red Paper on Forced Labor. U. S. Government Printing Office, 1952, p. 29.
[49] Ibid., p. 28.

sumption) that is now achieved through the starvation of several million prisoners surrounded by a large unproductive police apparatus.[50]

It is apparent that the living standards of the Soviet people have suffered because of rigid controls. Certainly the dignity and welfare of the individual have been subordinated to the intensity of the drive for large-scale industrialization.

The Soviet Government was avowedly formed on the principle of equality and the belief that the state belongs to the people who work and produce. It is hard to reconcile actual Soviet labor policies and the uncertain and oppressive conditions under which its inhabitants are compelled to live with such principles.

---

[50] Ibid., p. 28.

FOREIGN TRADE

THE SOVIET FOREIGN TRADE is and has been a smaller percentage of its GNP that that of any other nation in the world, with the possible exception of mainland China. This is, in part, a result of the fact that the U.S.S.R. possesses a large land mass and a very wide variety of resources and therefore has less need to look beyond its borders for products. It is also a result, however, of a deliberate policy of striving to achieve as high a degree of self-sufficiency as possible, thereby minimizing military and economic dependence on other nations. This does not mean that Soviet foreign trade is unimportant, however. During the First Five Year Plan the Soviets imported a significant percentage of the machinery and equipment necessary to launch their big industrialization drive. Since World War II the self-sufficiency objective has been implicitly redefined to include the other members of the Soviet bloc. Finally, since 1954, the Soviet bloc nations have begun to develop trade with and grant aid to the underdeveloped nations on an increasing scale. This has resulted in the volume of Soviet exports (and imports) rising from about 0.5 per cent of GNP in 1937 to 2.5–3 per cent in 1959.

The theory and practice of foreign trade by nations which plan and to a large extent control their economies, engage exclusively in state trading, have "irrational" internal price structures, and maintain disequilibrium exchange rates, is bound to be quite different from trade between Western capitalist nations. These differences are explored in the first two papers presented below as well as in earlier essays by A. Gerschenkron (1943), E. Ames (1953, 1954), A. Zauberman (1959), and in the symposium on "State Trading" in *Law and Contemporary Problems* (1959). Soviet bloc trade is also analyzed periodically in the publications of the U.N. Economic Commission for Europe.

The recent Soviet economic offensive in the underdeveloped areas is discussed by Professor Berliner. This paper also contains an interesting analysis of the manner in which Soviet industrialization has altered its "comparative advantage" over the past thirty years. Those who wish to read further on Soviet bloc trade with the underdeveloped nations should read H. G. Aubrey's excellent analysis (1959) and J. S. Berliner's monograph (1958).

A detailed history of pre-World War II Russian-Soviet trade can be found in A. Baykov's monograph (1946).

The Appendix contains some corrections of the article by F. D. Holzman.

THE OPERATION OF TRADE WITHIN THE SOVIET BLOC

Nicolas Spulber and Franz Gehrels

THE upheavals in Eastern Europe make it more than usually timely to examine some aspects of the postwar economic development of this area. This discussion is devoted to the mechanism of trade among the Eastern European countries and will attempt to give some evaluation of its efficiency. Section I provides some background on developments in the area since 1945; section II discusses data on the volume and pattern of trade and on current-account balances; section III describes how the volume, composition, direction, and terms of trade are determined by the state planners; and section IV evaluates the efficiency of the system as presently operated.

I

Trade of the Soviet bloc countries has undergone great changes in composition, volume, and geographic scope since 1945. The bloc now encompasses two vast areas: in Europe — Eastern Germany, Czechoslovakia, Poland, Hungary, Romania, Bulgaria, and Albania; in Asia — China, her North Vietnam satellite, and the zone of divided Sino-Soviet influence, Mongolia and North Korea. The European members of this group have undergone intensive industrial development; and, as a consequence, industrial products have become a more important part of a growing volume of trade. Finally, the restriction on trade with Western countries, together with Soviet policies toward economic integration of the area, have increased greatly the economic interdependence of members of the bloc.

For all the members of the bloc, state trading is a part of coordinated national economic planning. At the war's end all the European members of the bloc adopted comprehensive economic plans in order to speed up reconstruction, to increase the share of capital formation in national income, to promote industrialization, and to change the social structure. At first, such plans were restricted to particular indus-

tries and sectors; but by 1946 or 1947 each country had consolidated its sector plans into comprehensive national reconstruction programs. These varied in duration from one to three years. Export and import projections were included, but at first no attempt was made to reconcile the projections of different countries.

By 1949 all countries had virtually completed nationalization of the non-agricultural sectors. Economic plans were generally lengthened to five years' duration, but no attempt was made to coordinate the separate national plans. All the programs imitated Soviet emphasis on industrialization and gave special stress to the metallurgical industries and to capacity for producing machine tools. Planned domestic outputs and absorptions, together with exports and imports (which were equal to the differences between outputs and absorptions), constituted "the materials balance" plans. These plans generally aimed at providing a surplus of overall output over absorption, that is, a foreign trade surplus, despite the impossibility of achieving such an objective for all countries simultaneously.

The methodical stress on heavy industry, as well as the process of collectivization in agriculture, had led by 1953 to sharp imbalances in all of these countries, which were evidenced in a dearth of consumer goods, a catastrophic fall in agricultural output, a lack of adequate food supplies in the towns, and strong inflationary pressures. Following the East German uprising of June 1953, all the members of the bloc curtailed the share of national income devoted to investment and shifted the emphasis of investment from heavy industry to agriculture and light industry. At the same time, more attention was given to comparative advantage in foreign trade. While previously all countries had followed the same pattern of industrialization, official statements now appeared on the need to consider comparative cost in economic planning.[1] The movement away from autarkic economic development was, for a multiplicity of political and economic reasons, neither lasting nor resolute. The new five-year plans (1956–60), drawn in 1955 and the first half of 1956, concentrated as before on the development of metallurgy, machine tools, and heavy industry in general. Nevertheless, there is evidence of a greater attention to relative costs of importing versus home production on the part of planners, with an increased interchange of the products of heavy industry, including such items as heavy steel sections, machine tools, and machinery in general. For the first time, plans were to cover identical time periods for all the countries, including the Soviet Union, but excepting Bulgaria.[2] Taken together, the plans seemed to point toward the following pattern of specialization: the Soviet Union was to remain the key trading partner of each country; she was to export capital goods and basic materials, including iron ore, coal and cotton, and agricultural produce; she was to import machinery, some raw materials, including coal and a large variety of consumer goods. East Germany and Czechoslovakia were

to supply mostly machinery and manufactured goods, along with a few raw material items, such as potash and coke. Poland was to export coal, coke, railway equipment, chemicals, and manufactured consumer goods; Hungary was to supply bauxite, diesel engines, agricultural products, and consumer goods; Romania, Bulgaria, and Albania were to supply oil and ores, as well as agricultural products. At the same time, trade with the primary producing countries in Southeast Asia and the Middle East was scheduled for substantial increases.

The upheavals in Poland and Hungary in the late autumn of 1956 seriously jeopardized this scheme. Poland is now diverting some of her exports, notably coal, toward markets outside the Soviet bloc and is shifting substantially her emphasis in development from heavy to light industry. Hungary has been seriously crippled, and the reconstruction of her economy will alter her own plans for investment, output, and trade. The prospects up to 1960 consequently are now much less definite than they were at the end of 1955.

II

Magnitude of trade within the bloc. From 1948 through 1955, the share of Soviet bloc trade in the total trade of each European member increased from year to year. The Soviet share of this trade increased continuously during this period and reached remarkable levels as compared to prewar (see Table 1).

In the early postwar years the Soviet share in the trade of those countries who had been completely cut off from other trading areas loomed even larger. Thus, the Soviet share in Poland's foreign trade, which accounted for 49 per cent of the total in 1946, fell to 28 per cent in 1947, and to 17 per cent in 1948; from that year, it increased continuously, reaching 38 per cent in 1954. The increase in the Soviet Union's share of the intrabloc trade during the period 1948–55 was accompanied by a somewhat smaller, but still large, intratrade. These two developments were due: (a) to the nature of the output and investment plans, whose emphasis on heavy industry required large imports mainly from the Soviet Union; (b) to the politically determined preference of the trading companies for trade with the Soviet bloc; (c)

[1] Thus, Imre Nagy, then Hungarian premier, declared: "It is also necessary to change the one-sided nature of the development of the national economy. There is no justification for industrial autarky. In addition to the fact that autarky means economic isolation and overburdens the strength of the country, it predetermines rejection of the favourable opportunities which arise above all from the economic mutual aid and cooperation with the Soviet Union, the People's Democracies and also with People's China and from more intensive participation by the country in international trade, from trade with the capitalist countries. In their economic policy the Party and the Government will, to a greater degree, take into account these opportunities with the help of which they intend to ease the position of our national economy." "On Measures of Hungarian Working People's Party and Government Aimed at Raising the Standard of Living," in *For a Lasting Peace, for a People's Democracy* (Bucharest, July 17, 1953).

See also the statement of R. Dvorak, Minister of Foreign Trade of Czechoslovakia in *Czechoslovak Economic Bulletin*, No. 283 (Prague, 1954), 3.

For a theoretical approach to the problem, see: Tibor Liska and Antal Máriás, "A gazdaságosság és a nemzetkozi munkamegosztás" ("Optimum Returns and International Division of Labor"), *Közgazdasági Szemle* (*Economic Review*), No. 1 (Budapest, 1954), 75–94; English translation in *Economic Survey of Europe in 1954* (Geneva, 1955), 131–35.

[2] The first Bulgarian five-year plan was completed in 1952; the second was finished by the close of 1957. Bulgaria intends to fall in step with all the other countries, for the third round of long-term plans, by 1960.

TABLE I. — SHARE OF THE SOVIET UNION AND OF THE SOVIET BLOC IN THE TOTAL TRADE OF EACH
EUROPEAN MEMBER, 1937, 1948, 1954

(*In percentages*)

	1937			1948			1954		
	USSR	People's Democ- racies [a]	Rest of World	USSR	People's Democ- racies [a]	Rest of World	USSR	People's Democ- racies [a]	Rest of World
Eastern Germany	—	—	—	—75—		25	44	31	25
Czechoslovakia	1	10	89	16	15	69	36	39	25
Poland	1	6	93	23	17	60	38	32	30
Hungary	—	13	87	17	17	66	30	36	34
Romania	1	17	82	34	36	30	—72—		28
Bulgaria	—	12	88	56	27	17	45	42	13

[a] All the countries of the Soviet bloc, excluding the USSR.
SOURCES: *World Economic Survey 1955* (New York, 1956), 113, corrected with *Economic Bulletin for Europe*, Vol. VIII, No. 2 (Geneva, 1956), 82; and M. F. Kovrizhnych, A. B. Frumkin, and V. C. Pozdniakov, eds., *Vneshniaia Torgovlia Stran Narodnoi Demokratsii* ("Foreign Trade of the Countries of People's Democracy"), Moscow, 1955, 41-42.

to the embargo placed by the West on strategic goods. All of these factors are now undergoing change. Some of the output plans, e.g., in the case of Poland and Hungary, must be revised drastically. Consideration of comparative costs might modify the hitherto deliberate political preference for trading within the area. The embargo itself is undergoing a process of reappraisal. Hence, in the short run, some forces will tend to reduce the shares of both the Soviet Union and of the other members in the total trade of each. However, as specialization within the area increases, there may be a long run trend for intrabloc trade to increase both absolutely and relatively.

Trade balances and international lending. Trading procedure in the Soviet bloc has had as one objective the minimizing of unforeseen short-term capital movements. Since national output, investment, and consumption plans depend for their fulfillment in part on the timely delivery of goods by foreign suppliers, it is not surprising that trading countries should seek means of assuring such deliveries. The trade agreements have normally provided for bilateral balancing over the year, and when one partner fails to make delivery on schedule, the other may hold up shipments in order to enforce compliance with the agreement. Given the chronic shortages and sometimes over-ambitious investment and production plans, it is not surprising that countries sometimes have had difficulty in meeting export commitments. The method of settlements between exporters and importers in intrabloc transactions differs from the technique used in extrabloc trade. In the bloc, the central bank of the exporting country credits the exporter, and debits the account of the central bank of the importing country, when the goods are dispatched and the corresponding documents are presented by the exporter. The central bank of the importing country makes the opposite entries on its books upon receiving the documents from the central bank of the exporting country. The settlements in extrabloc trade are more nearly adjusted to the procedures followed in Western countries.[8]

It is interesting to compare the actual bilateral balances for the period 1946–48 with the stated objective of keeping them at zero. During that period Bulgaria, Romania, and Yugoslavia (then also in the bloc) were net lenders to Czechoslovakia, Poland, and Hungary. As the former were less developed industrially than the latter, and the demand of all countries for capital goods was great, the balances may reflect the willingness of agricultural countries to make short-term loans to their industrial partners in order to obtain scarce items of equipment. Thus, although trade agreements provided for exact balancing at the end of each three months' interval, the deliveries of industrial goods were permitted to fall behind schedule. During the same period, the Soviet Union was herself a net borrower from Czechoslovakia and a lender to Bulgaria and Yugoslavia. Details from the Soviet-Yugoslav balance of payments for the period 1948–49 indicate that the Soviet balance was due in part to the sale

[8] See Professor Witold Trampczynski, "Banking in a Planned Economy," in *A Survey of Poland*, Supplement to *The Statist*, CLXIV (November 24, 1956), 12.

of transport equipment confiscated at the end of the war, together with the sale of military equipment. In Bulgaria's case, one may surmise related causes.

Corresponding data on trade balances have not been published for the period 1949–55. However, Soviet policy toward lending has clearly changed since the early years of great general scarcity. For the period from 1949 to 1955, the Soviet Union claims to have extended credit in excess of 2.5 billion dollars (at the official exchange rate) to neighboring countries, of which the bulk has gone to Poland and China. The Soviet credits were of three types: (a) short-term credits in gold or foreign currency (representing the smallest part of the total of credits extended); (b) credits for the purchase of raw materials and other goods from the Soviet Union; and (c) long-term investment credits. The significance of these latter credits for the capital formation of the area is difficult to assess. Poland was the largest recipient of Soviet investment credits. According to the Polish premier, Wladislaw Gomulka, at the Eighth Plenum of the Polish Communist Party (October 20, 1956), a considerable part of the machines and complete installations received under the credits have not found employment in production, will not find employment for many years to come, and will have to be considered an irretrievable loss. However, it is not clear from Gomulka's speech whether the malinvestment has been due to inappropriate equipment deliveries in the first instance, or to changes in plans.

While the foregoing gives the general trade-balance picture, some at least of the Soviet countries have aimed to achieve an active balance on visible account.[4] For at least two of these cases, the purpose of the visible surplus

appears to have been to balance an invisible deficit.[5]

III

Difficulties of coordination. During the years 1945 through 1948, when individual countries were moving from sector planning to over-all planning of output, consumption, and investment, foreign trade was viewed as a means to fill specific domestic deficiencies. As national plans were not coordinated during the formulation stage, difficulties of fulfillment often arose, and these were only resolved through departures from the initial plans.

In order to cope with these difficulties two important steps were taken, in 1949 and in 1951. In 1949 the bloc countries established a Council of Economic Mutual Assistance (CEMA) with the stated objective of developing "mutual assistance" and "broader cooperation" among its members.[6] From 1951 on, the countries of the area started to conclude long-term trade agreements, with the objective of placing their own output plans on a more secure basis. The trade agreements were lengthened from one to five years to match the length of the output and allocation plans. They were drawn on a bilateral basis[7] and were not meant to determine rigidly the totality of transactions occurring in the orbit. Their purpose was to guarantee a stated minimum of key supplies so

[4] Thus, the tasks of the foreign trade plan of Hungary for 1956 were defined as follows: "The 1956 plan calls for an active balance in our foreign trade with both the friendly and the capitalist countries beginning with the first quarter of the year. This calls for the prompt delivery by industry and agriculture of goods needed for export, on schedule, in the required quantity, quality and choice; and that we reduce to the minimum the quantity of materials, equipment and other goods imported from abroad." Andor Berei, "Report on the National Economic Plan for 1956," in *Reports Delivered at the Hungarian National Assembly, November 15–16, 1955,* Supplement to *Hungarian Review,* No. 12 (1955), Corvina Publishing House, Budapest, 1956.

[5] Ibid.

See also, O. Lange: "Rozpad Jednolitego Rynku Swiatowego i Uksztaltowanie sie Dwoch Rownoleglych Rynkow w Gospodarce Swiatowej," ("Disintegration of the Single World Market and the Formation of Two Parallel Markets in the World Economy"), *Ekonomista,* Warsaw, 1953, 147–48.

[6] The Council was organized by the U.S.S.R. together with five Eastern European countries (Czechoslovakia, Poland, Hungary, Romania, and Bulgaria) half a year after the break with Yugoslavia. The official communique dated from Moscow, January 25, 1949, invited any country of Europe that shares the principles of "mutual assistance" and that "wishes to participate in broad economic cooperation with these countries" to join the Council. East Germany and Albania joined the Council later; China has an observer in the Council.

[7] E.g., Agreements of the Soviet Union with Czechoslovakia (1951–1955), with Poland (1953–1958), etc. See A. Korolenko, "Printsipi Ravenstva i Vzaimnoi Vygody v Trgvle SSSR s Evropeiskimi Stranami Narodnoi Demokratsii" ("Principles of Equality and Mutual Benefit in the Trade of the USSR with the European Countries of People's Democracy"), *Voprosy Ekonomiki (Economic Problems),* Moscow, March 3, 1952.

that a more realistic output plan could be drawn by the importing country. The need of revising these agreements by means of supplementary annual agreements was accepted by all, since production might overshoot or fall short of its target or the domestic absorptions might diverge from the allocation plan.

Throughout the period 1949–55 CEMA limited its activity primarily to the collection and dissemination of information on trade and technical assistance. The member countries continued to make their trade agreements on a bilateral basis, but with more information on their trading possibilities and with more assurance in respect to a minimum of key supplies secured through the long-term trade agreements. Since 1956, CEMA has extended its role to coordination of parts of the long-term output and trade plans of all the countries of the Soviet bloc.[8] This coordination concerns principally the development of the raw materials sectors — mining of ferrous and non-ferrous ores, coal and coking coal — which play a decisive role in the process of industrialization. Undoubtedly the role of CEMA will grow even though trade is still flowing in bilateral channels.

Price determination. Prices, as well as quantities to be traded, are fixed in the bilateral agreements, with the stated price applying for the duration of the contract. Up to February 1950, when the ruble was placed on the gold-exchange standard, the prices were stated either in currencies of the countries involved or in dollars; from that time onward, they were stated in clearing rubles. All trade agreements published before 1951 specified that world prices were the basis for the prices of the goods involved; from 1951 onward, only summaries of the trade agreements have been published, and no specific statements can be found concerning the pricing basis of these particular contracts.

Despite the provisions to use world prices it might be inferred, from some indirect evi-

dence, that price discrimination in favor of the Soviet Union existed especially in the earlier years. Data on export unit values for Czechoslovakia for 1948 suggest that her exports to the Soviet Union might have been sold at lower prices than her exports to the other East European countries.[9] In addition, according to Yugoslav sources, the Soviet Union has resold on world markets goods imported from Eastern Europe, presumably at a profit.[10] Such abuses and the Yugoslav attacks may be responsible for a joint decision of these countries, publicized in their press from 1951 on, against price discrimination with the orbit.[11] Prices in the

---

[8] At the May 1956 session of the Council, held in Berlin, "extensive work was carried out in the co-ordination of prospective plans of all main sectors of the national economies of member countries of the Council. A significant fact was the presence of the representatives of the Chinese People's Republic and the representative of the Federal People's Republic of Yugoslavia as observers." See "Economic Outline," in *Czechoslovak Economic Bulletin*, No. 312 (Prague, September 1956), 5.

[9] Thus, on the basis 1937 = 100, the unit value indexes of exports to the Soviet Union were, for footwear 605 — average 764; for cotton fabrics 316 — average 433; for iron and steel wares 137 — average 270; for electrical machinery 215 — average 300; for other power machinery 264 — average 372; for machine tools 388 — average 430. Symmetrically, the other Eastern European countries paid usually more than average, and always more than the U.S.S.R. For cotton fabrics the unit value indexes of exports to Eastern Europe was 569 — average 433; for iron and steel wares 320 — average 270; for agricultural machinery 327 — average 278; for power machines 548 — average 372; for machinery and spare parts 819 — average 458. The computations are based on: *Mesicni Prehled Zahranicniho Obchodu* ("Monthly Report on Foreign Trade") (Prague, December 1938); and *Statisticky Zpravodaj* ("Statistical Bulletin"), XII (Prague, December 1949). The categories cited are, however, aggregative, and significant differences might have existed between the goods traded with the U.S.S.R. and the goods traded generally or with the other East European countries.

[10] Thus, Bulgaria is said to have attempted to sell in the United States in 1950 a certain quantity of essence of roses at the price of $80 for seven-eighths of an ounce, whereas the Russian Amtorg is said to have offered this typical Bulgarian export product at the price of only $67 for the same quantity. Numerous other examples could be gathered in which the Soviet Union appears in the position of underselling the respective Eastern European producers; however, much of this material comes from Yugoslav sources, and is often difficult to verify. For an extensive presentation of these cases, see E. Zaleski, *Les Courants Commerciaux de l'Europe Danubienne au Cours de la Premiere Moitie du XXe Siecle* ("Commercial Trends in Danubian Europe during the First Half of the 20th Century"), Paris, 1952, 383–88.

[11] A Romanian economist formulates as follows the practice prevailing now in the bloc: "In contrast to the capitalist market, in the democratic market, there is no plurality of price for one and the same commodity. For the same commodity and for all the countries of this camp to whom this commodity is delivered, each country establishes a single price, with small differences only in the limits of differences in transportation costs." See: M. Horoviț, "Despre Decontările Internationale și Relațiile de Credit dintre Țarile Lagărului Socialist" ("On International Payments and the Credit Relations Among the Countries of the Socialist Camp"), *Probleme Economice (Economic Problems)* (Bucharest, July 1954), 107.

trade agreements are determined by the relative bargaining strengths of the trading partners. A country offering, say, scarce capital goods for export can drive the better bargain. Political strength, as in the case of the Soviet Union, is undoubtedly also a factor in the determination of prices. But the requirement against price discrimination, if enforced, limits the bargaining ability of the stronger partner; if he agrees subsequently to a lower price to another country, he must extend it retroactively to all his other trade agreements.

Differences in relative domestic unit costs (rather than wholesale prices, which contain the turnover tax) provide the economic basis for trade. However, unit costs do not give the prices (in clearing rubles) at which the exchange of goods takes place. Sometimes the trading agency will sell its exports below cost, but more commonly at a profit; and the same is true for the domestic sale of imports. In order to obtain a particularly sought-after import, it may find it desirable to sell some exports at a price below cost. In order not to affect the cost of living, or the cost calculations of industries dependent on imports or raw materials or capital goods, the trading agency will sometimes sell imports on the home market at below-cost prices.[12] Thus the connection between for-

eign trade and domestic prices is a tenuous one.

No assurance exists of complete uniformity of prices for goods exported by more than one country in the Soviet bloc to other members. However, a tendency in this direction exists, through the mobility of buyers and sellers. Buyers will seek out the low-priced suppliers, thereby tending to raise their prices toward the common level, and putting downward pressure on the high prices of other suppliers. The availability to all the countries in the bloc of price information collected by CEMA strengthens these levelling tendencies.

World prices for goods moving in trade within the bloc are likely to have some restraining influence on prices charged. Even when a buying country is unable to turn to world markets, because of lack of foreign exchange, or because of the Western embargo on strategic goods, knowledge of such outside prices is likely to exercise restraint on the seller. For the investment goods which have no close counterpart on world markets, the Soviet export prices may provide a yardstick for prices used in intra-bloc trade in general. The Soviet export price of capital goods will be above the domestic wholesale price because the latter does not always cover the cost of production. In Soviet bloc terminology, the producer goods are not treated as "commodities" in domestic trade, and are generally undervalued; however, the producer goods are, just as consumer goods, treated as "commodities" in foreign trade and are priced accordingly, with some reference to the prices prevailing in the world markets.

---

[12] According to data given by B. S. Vaganov, in Hungary each foreign trade organization had, in 1953, an established profit norm which ranged from 1–40 per cent. This profit was usually computed on the basis of the interior, *forint* prices, i.e., interior wholesale price at which the imported good is sold to an industry, and interior wholesale price, excluding the turnover tax, at which a good is sold by the interior producer to the wholesale organization. If the output price of a good is 100 *forints*, excluding the turnover tax, and the profit norm is 3.5 per cent, while the cost of transportation is 20 *forints*, the total selling price of the good by the foreign trade organization must be equal to 123.5 *forints*. If it sells the commodity abroad for 90 *forints*, the remaining 33.5 *forints* must be covered by a subsidy from the budget. If the commodity is sold for 130 *forints*, the difference of 6.5 *forints* is transferred to the budget. In the case of an imported good, the following situations might arise: the imported good has a corresponding interior wholesale price, or it has not (e.g., a new product). In the first case, if the price of the imported good plus the established profit of the foreign trade organization is lower than the domestic wholesale price, the good will be sold at the latter price and the difference will be turned over to the budget. If, on the other hand, the price of the imported good plus profit is higher than the interior wholesale price, the foreign trade organization will sell again at this latter price but will have the difference covered by

the budget. In the case of a new product, an interior price is established for the new good. Cf. B. S. Vaganov, *Voprosy Organizatsii Vneshnei Torgovli Stran Narodnoi Demokratsii* ("Problems of the Organization of Foreign Trade of the Countries of People's Democracy"), Moscow, 1954, 94.

Not having encountered specific evidence to the contrary, like that furnished above by Vaganov, Ames has erroneously assumed that each country charges in its bloc intratrade its own internal wholesale price. Thus he writes: "Although there is no indication how the 'uniform price' charged by each exporter is calculated, the payments procedures suggest that each bloc country sells to others on the general basis of its own internal wholesale prices, converted into clearing rubles at the official exchange rate. Since the price structures of the various Soviet bloc countries differ, and since the exchange rate need not reflect a purchasing power parity, each country will have its own export prices." Cf. Edward Ames, "International Trade without Markets—the Soviet Bloc Case," *American Economic Review*, XLIV (December 1954), 794.

Efficiency of the System

Assuming the limitation of trade with non-Soviet countries to be due to external causes or to political choice, can we ascertain to what extent the members of the bloc make efficient use of their remaining trading possibilities?

The rules which provide a yardstick for answering this question are three: (1) Given appropriate currency-exchange rates, each country should import all goods with a higher marginal money cost of production at home than abroad, and should export goods with a lower cost. This rule applies both when a zero balance on current account is planned, and when net lending or borrowing is provided for. The exchange rate would be adjusted downward in the case of a planned export surplus and upward in the case of a planned deficit. (2) The volume of trade in each good and service should be pushed to the point where its cost at the margin differs among all countries only by transportation cost. Where a good is not produced at all in a country because of high cost or lack of an essential resource, importation of the good should be pushed only to the point where foreign marginal cost plus cost of transportation is equal to internal price in the importing country, and where price always clears the market. (3) Investment within a country should be allocated so as to equate marginal efficiency of investment in all lines of production. Following this rule would prevent investment from taking place in import-competing industries in which marginal cost would be higher than the price of the corresponding imported good.[13]

We immediately run into difficulties when attempting to apply these efficiency rules to the Soviet economies. For the rules usually presuppose the sovereignty of consumer preference in the determination of output composition (except for the division of output between the aggregates of consumption and investment). They assume further that internal price structures are not distorted by indirect taxes or differential cost mark-ups. But in the Soviet economies consumer preferences play only a limited role in determining the composition of output

within the total allocated for consumption by the authorities. Prices on some goods are set so low that quantities available to consumers are soon exhausted; and prices are therefore not proportional to consumers' marginal preferences. Moreover, the trading agency sells some imported goods at a large mark-up and others at a loss. One is therefore tempted to stop at this point and say that resource allocation is wrong to start with because consumer preferences are suppressed. Any further evaluation thus becomes superfluous.

However, we shall go beyond this point, by asking a slightly different question: If we substitute the preferences of the authorities for those of consumers, is foreign trade carried on in such a way as to place the authorities in their most preferred positions? In order to place themselves on the highest indifference level, the authorities of each country would need to follow the first and third rules above without modification. For the principles of comparative advantage apply to a centrally planned economy as fully as they do to a liberal economy. Only the second rule requires a slight modification. Importation of each good should be pushed to the point where foreign marginal cost plus cost of transportation is equal to the domestic price less turnover tax. For domestic price less turnover tax (which equals domestic marginal cost) would reflect the relative importance placed by the authorities on each good. Price less turnover tax measures the amount of alternative output which they are willing to sacrifice for a marginal unit of a particular good.

However, for the modified rule to apply in practice, accounting costs used by the authorities must correspond to economic costs. Not only must each firm calculate its own costs correctly, but prices on all inter-firm transactions must be proportional to marginal costs. This is true even though the preferences of the authorities replace those of consumers in markets for final goods. In a limited bookkeeping sense costs are reasonably well calculated, including the prime and fixed costs and a small variable profit mark-up, but omitting interest charges (except on borrowed short-term funds).[14] The

[13] See A. P. Lerner, *The Economics of Control* (New York, 1944) ch. 26, 346–55. Our rules correspond to those formulated by Lerner.

[14] Yugoslavia is an exception to this rule in that her enterprises do include interest of all kinds in costs.

omission of interest leads to an understatement of costs in the capital-intensive industries relative to the other sectors, while the variable profit mark-up causes further distortion. Perhaps a more serious difficulty exists in the pricing of labor services and basic resources. Setting these prices to clear the market would automatically adjust economic rent for scarce resources to the appropriate level and lead to their employment in the most productive uses. But basic industries use the same costing procedure as other sectors, and their prices consequently can not cover economic rent. Similarly, at other stages of production ground rent is not included in costs, and again costs of enterprises using valuable locations are understated in relation to those requiring less valuable sites.

On the question of wages, a related argument can be used. Skill differentials appear to be adjusted roughly to relative scarcities, but there is also the question of the level of wages. As in the case of other resources, the remedy of raising wages (or lowering all product prices) until excess demand for labor is removed, would be a suitable remedy for misallocation of generally scarce labor. Doing so would not necessarily lead to an increase of consumption at the expense of capital formation; for the authorities could still limit consumption by raising prices or by restricting supplies at existing prices (just as they do at present).

We may conclude that accounting costs do not accurately reflect economic costs and that the authorities thus lack an accurate basis for determining comparative costs among countries. However, there is no particular reason why pricing could not be revised to include interest, rent, and uniform profits, and why prices of primary resources could not be adjusted to reflect their scarcities. If they chose to make these adjustments, Soviet and Eastern European planners could obtain the cost information needed for the application of the three rules above.

Within the limits of their inadequate cost data, do the Eastern European planners attempt to apply the principles of comparative cost in planning investment, output, and foreign trade? The answer is clearly negative, since uniform concentration on development of heavy indus-

try characterizes all the Soviet-bloc countries.[15] If it were possible for each country to develop the whole range of basic resources, trade might ultimately disappear completely. The present expansion of Soviet trade would then be only temporary: as a country became self-sufficient in the production of capital goods and raw materials it could dispense with outside supplies of these goods, which now come mainly from the Soviet Union. In fact, "balanced development" is unlikely to lead to complete autarky, because of the prohibitive cost or physical impossibility of developing domestic sources of all basic materials. Each country may continue to develop heavy industries, but this development is likely to cause greatly increased requirements for imported coal, iron ore, and other materials. Eastern Europe will thus become increasingly dependent on the Soviet economy, if not on sources outside the bloc. But such a form of international dependence has little to do with comparative advantage; and a further growth of trade along these lines is likely to retard, rather than to advance, the growth of real income in these countries.

Against such a distortion of international specialization, the final point of criticism is rather trivial. This relates to bilateral balancing of trade, still practiced with few exceptions in the bloc. While perhaps a natural outgrowth of the desire to enforce fulfillment of commitments by partners, it limits the possibility of selling at the highest price and buying at the cheapest, thus reducing further the gains from trade.

While Soviet bloc trade as presently carried

[15] Thus, the Romanian chief planner, M. Constantinescu, writes: "The all-round development of the machine-building industry is a major necessity for all the countries. Without this, it is impossible to achieve technical progress and greater mechanization of all branches of the economy or to insure proper care of existing equipment and its constant improvements. . . Lenin developed the Marxist tenet that accumulation in Department I (production of the means of production) is a factor making for the proportionate development of these two departments and consequently Department I must play the leading role in extended reproduction. . . Only if this condition is observed can Socialist reproduction on an extended scale be assured. From this springs the need for accelerated rates of development of heavy industry, a need that is common to all countries building Socialism." M. Constantinescu, "On the Road of Building Socialism, Some Problems of Economic Development in Romania in the Light of the Economic Tasks of the People's Democracies," in *For a Lasting Peace, for a People's Democracy* (Bucharest, September 9, 1955).

on fails to meet the efficiency criteria stated above, it may in one respect have potential superiority over the trade of capitalist economies. Trade within the bloc is carried on between state monopolies, who bargain bilaterally over volume, composition, and terms of trade. The trading agencies, as extensions of the central planning bodies, may be thought of as having trading-indifference maps which are counterparts of the allocation-indifference maps of the over-all planners. In trade between countries, the optimal trading positions lie on the "contract curve," that is, on any of an infinite number of tangency points between indifference surfaces for a pair of countries. Whenever bilateral bargaining brings about quantities and terms of trade at some point not on the contract curve, it is possible for both partners to make themselves better off by agreeing to new conditions which correspond to a point on the contract curve. The existence of bilateral monopolies makes it possible always to come to such an agreement.

On the other hand, in trade between competitive capitalist economies there is only one point on the contract curve which can be reached: the point where the reciprocal-offer curves intersect. This point can be reached only by complete freeing of trade. But if one country can affect its terms of trade more strongly than others, it generally finds it advantageous to impose tariffs or quantitative restrictions, even if other countries retaliate. There is consequently no force operating to restore the volume of trade to a point on the contract curve, because there is generally no mutual advantage in attaining this point.

Summary

1. Trading procedure in the Soviet bloc has reflected both the increased interdependence and the increased coordination of economic plans of the member countries. At the same time more systematic negotiating procedures have led toward greater uniformity of prices for trade of the bloc. However, the external price adjustments have not caused a corresponding uniformity of internal prices among the trading countries.

2. The uniform pattern of development plans has had its impact on the composition and volume of trade. On the one hand, balanced development tends to reduce general dependence on external trade; on the other hand, its increased requirements for raw materials lead to an increased need for imports, and, in the interim, development calls for an increased flow of capital goods. The future of intra-bloc trade will depend both on the nature of subsequent development plans and on the extent of trade with the outside world. Continued emphasis on heavy industrial growth, together with restriction of trade with outside countries, would intensify the dependence of Eastern Europe on trade with the Soviet economy.

3. The efficiency of bloc trade must be judged in relation to the structure of internal costs; moreover, trading efficiency can not be judged separately from the rationality of over-all economic plans. On the former question, one may say that the authorities do not at present have the cost data for planning trade on an efficient basis, for accounting costs differ to an unknown degree from economic costs. On the latter question, it appears that the authorities have so far shown only slight interest in planning economic development in consonance with comparative advantage. Thus it is doubtful that they would make proper use of cost data in planning foreign trade, even if such costs were appropriately calculated. The pattern of specialization that has developed could only be viewed as rational if one were willing to accept a certain domestic industrial pattern as an end in itself. Then the present pattern of trade could be regarded as furthering that objective, although at a sacrifice of real output for the area as a whole.

SOME FINANCIAL ASPECTS OF SOVIET FOREIGN TRADE

(By Franklyn D. Holzman,[1] University of Washington and Russian Research Center, Harvard University)

Financial factors play a less important role in the Soviet economy than they do in the economies of Western nations. This is also true of Soviet foreign trade in comparison with the foreign trade of other nations. Financial factors nevertheless have osme significance and will continue to have significance for the conduct of Soviet international transactions as long as trade is not conducted on a strictly barter basis, prices and exchange rates are quoted, and gold and foreign exchange are recognized as having value and serving as international legal tender.

The following topics are discussed below: (1) Trends in the official ruble exchange rate, (2) the disequilibrium character of the ruble exchange rate, (3) the reflection of the overvalued ruble on enterprise and budget accounts, (4) Soviet international price policy and the foreign trade accounts, (5) the impact of Soviet foreign trade on internal financial stability, (6) Soviet gold policy, and (7) payments agreements.

1. *Trends in the official ruble exchange rate* [4, pp. 292 ff.; 16, pp 198–199]

An exchange rate is the price of one currency in terms of another or in terms of gold, the common denominator of currencies. In a market in which trade flows freely and prices and exchange rates are allowed to seek their own levels, the relative prices of two currencies will reflect, roughly, the relative purchasing power of each currency in its own country, particularly of internationally tradeable goods. Neglecting the refinements,[2] it could be said that an exchange rate between two currencies which (1) more or less achieves a balance of payments without controls, and (2) roughly reflects the price differentials between countries of "tradeables," is an equilibrium exchange rate.

Since World War I, of course, the exchange rates of many Western nations have failed at one time or another to meet these specifications and have been maintained temporarily at disequilibrium levels by controls. In most cases, disequilibrium has eventually led to devaluation, as a last-resort measure, to achieve equilibrium. It is no exaggeration to say that over the past 30 years the exchange rate of no Western nation has been as far out of line from its equilibrium value as the Soviet ruble exchange rate. And no Western nation has applied such extensive controls to foreign trade, controls which are an integral part of the planning organization and which, among other

---

[1] I wish to express my appreciation to Edwin Cohn and Herbert Levine for critical comments on a draft of this paper and to the Harvard Russian Research Center for financial support.

[2] Neglecting here capital flows, levels of employment and unemployment, and income-elasticities of demand for imports.

things, make it possible for the Soviets to maintain a balance on current account with a disequilibrium exchange rate. The Soviet exchange rate has typically been so far out of line and controls have operated so successfully, that it seems fair to describe the rate as no more than an accounting device for converting foreign currency prices of Soviet exports and imports into rubles for the purpose of constructing foreign trade accounts in local currency.

While the ruble exchange rate has been a fictitious one in the sense that it has little basis in terms of relative commodity prices, the Soviets have seen fit, from time to time, to make exchange rate adjustments. First, these will be traced briefly and then their relationship to Soviet internal price trends will be indicated.

After the Revolution, the ruble was maintained at its prerevolutionary exchange rate. While the gold content of the ruble was specified at 0.774234 grams, [4, p. 297] it was typically quoted in terms of dollars as having a value of $0.5146. This nominal value of the ruble was maintained until the U.S. flight from the gold standard and devaluation of January 1, 1934. Devaluation reduced the value of the dollar from $20 to $35 an ounce of gold. Concomitantly, the ruble-dollar rate changed from $0.5146 to $0.8712 per ruble. After this date, the ruble was typically quoted in terms of francs (one of the few currencies still tied to gold) at 13.1 francs to a ruble.

The next change occurred when, in a decree of November 11, 1935, the Soviets set a special rate for tourists of 3 francs to the ruble to be effective as of January 1, 1936. On April 1, 1936, this rate was extended to cover all foreign transactions, including primarily commodity trade. The change of April 1, 1936, was, of course, a massive devaluation leaving the ruble worth less than 23 percent (1/4.38) of its previous value. It's dollar value fell from $0.8712 to $0.1992 (and franc value from 13.1 to 3.0 francs).

This situation was soon altered. In October 1936, the franc left gold and was devalued raising the franc-ruble ratio from 3 to 4.5. Ostensibly because of this devaluation, the Soviets redefined the ruble in terms of dollars on July 19, 1937. The new valuation involved a slight devaluation of the ruble from $0.1992 to $0.1887 (or 5.3 rubles to the dollar).

The ruble maintained nominal stability from 1937 until 1950. On March 1, 1950, the ruble was revalued upward by 32.5 percent and specifically defined as having a gold content of 0.222168 grams of gold and therefore worth 4 rubles to the dollar. This change was made, according to the Soviets, because of the loss in value of the dollar as a result of post-World War II inflation. (The validity of this claim will be examined below.) Only one further change has been made since 1950: The tourist rate which had been 4 rubles to the dollar along with all other transactions, was devalued to 10 rubles to the dollar in April 1957. The 4-ruble-to-the-$1 rate remains in force for all other transactions.

2. *A disequilibrium exchange rate: The overvalued ruble* [3]

As we have already noted, the exchange rate which was in force until 1936 was the same, in terms of gold, as that which prevailed

---

[3] The materials presented in this section contain some of the preliminary results of a larger study of Soviet foreign trade pricing which is nearing completion. The empirical part of this study compares Soviet export and import unit values with Soviet domestic prices and world prices, respectively, for a number of prewar and postwar years [8].

before World War I although the rates in terms of individual foreign currencies were often quite different due to the widespread revaluations in Europe after World War I and during the thirties. Under relatively stable domestic conditions, it would appear unlikely that the international value of the ruble could have remained in "equilibrium" without any change of its par value over the 25-year period. As it was, the Russian economy underwent, as is well known, a devastating war and a complete change of government and economic organization. The major consequence of these events from the point of view of the international value of the ruble was the hyperinflation, which gripped the Soviet economy after World War I. Before hyperinflation was finally eliminated by the monetary reform of 1924, the internal price level was many billions of times higher than it had been right after the Revolution [2]. It obviously makes little sense to talk of equilibrium exchange rates under such conditions.

How close to a purchasing power parity equilibrium the ruble was right after the reform in 1924 I cannot say. One observer states that "It was probably sometime in 1926 or 1927 that foreign trade became entirely divorced from the internal cost of export goods or the ruble prices of imported goods" [9, p. 170]. This was certainly the case by 1929 (and probably true for 1926–27). Comparisons of average unit values of a substantial sample of Soviet export goods with internal wholesale prices of the same commodities indicate that, on the average, Soviet exports were being sold at less than 40 percent of cost. Around this average there was a very large dispersion with, for example, manganese and iron ores selling at 50 percent above domestic wholesale price, coal and coke roughly at domestic price, and petroleum products at one-fourth domestic price. One might reasonably ask: Why, on the average, did the Soviets sell so much below domestic wholesale price? The answer is simple: With an overvalued exchange rate, the Soviets, if they were to sell abroad, had to sell at below cost in order to compete on world markets. This did not necessarily involve them in a real loss, however. For they were compensated by being able to import needed goods at a similar or greater percentage below domestic cost or price.

This type of transaction can be handled very expeditiously by a country which has nationalized its industry and foreign trade. With an overvalued exchange rate, the foreign trade monopoly is willing, for example, to export abroad for 500 rubles a commodity which costs 1,000 rubles to produce if it can use the 500 rubles of foreign currency earned to import a commodity which costs, say 1,100 rubles to produce domestically. (The difficulty in defining "dumping" under these circumstances is obvious.) A free enterprise economy, on the other hand, in which exports and imports are handled by entirely different persons and enterprises, would find this an unenviable situation (in the absence of direct controls) as profitable opportunities for imports expanded at the same time that profitable opportunities for exports contracted. Presumably under these circumstances, a capitalist nation would be forced either to devalue or to reduce the volume of trade by restricting imports to an amount which could be financed by exports (abstracting from reserves and capital flows). The foreign trade monopoly, as indicated, would be under no such constraint but could maintain the level of trade undiminished simply subsidizing

430 COMPARISONS OF UNITED STATES AND SOVIET ECONOMIES

exports out of profits from imports (the mechanics of this are described below).

The gap between export prices on the one hand and domestic wholesale prices and costs on the other increased during the first half of the thirties. This can be inferred from two sets of observations: (1) Comparison of price trends from 1929 to 1935, and (2) direct comparison of export unit values with domestic wholesale prices for 1935. Over the period 1929–35, a study published by the League of Nations [12] indicates that Soviet export prices declined to one-third of their previous level. This decline was not unique to Soviet exports, of course, but reflected the generally depressed conditions of the period. Unlike the situation in other nations where falling export prices were matched in part by falling internal prices as a result of high levels of unemployment, Soviet internal costs and prices were rising as the result of internal inflation [7]. Consumers' goods prices rose by 400–500 percent over the 6-year period. The prices of basic industrial goods rose very little—by only 6 or 7 percent.[4] These prices did not reflect costs, however. Costs had been rising very rapidly. Wage rates, the basic cost element, rose by almost 300 percent over the period. The small increase in prices of basic industrial goods reflects a deliberate Soviet policy to keep producers' goods prices stable despite rising costs by the use of liberal subsidies. To summarize: The rise in domestic prices, and especially in costs, and the fall in export prices point to an increase in the gap between domestic prices and costs and export prices.

Direct comparison of unit values of a sample of exports with domestic wholesale prices (many of which are undoubtedly below cost) supports the above results. By 1935, every group of items sampled was sold abroad at below domestic wholesale price. On an average, domestic wholesale prices were 8 times as high as export unit values[5] including petroleum products and 5½ times as high excluding petroleum products.

Without doubt, the disequilibrium character of the ruble exchange rate was at a peak in 1935. In 1936, as we have seen, the ruble underwent a 77 percent devaluation and this certainly served to bring the exchange rate closer into line with domestic costs and prices. The devaluation may have been conceived as part of the more general price reform which was accomplished in 1936. As we have seen, prices of basic industrial materials had been kept stable in the face of rising costs for a number of years. In 1936, these prices were increased by more than 50 percent in a general attempt to eliminate subsidies and thereby equalize costs and wholesale prices. This price increase had the effect, of course, of partly offsetting the effectiveness of the devaluation in bringing domestic wholesale prices and export prices into line.[6]

This, in turn, was offset, however, by the upswing in world market prices in general; the prices (measured in the currencies of the major trading nations) which the Soviets were able to obtain for their exports rose by some 50 percent over the next 2 years [12].

---

[4] This excludes petroleum. Inclusive of petroleum products, prices rose by 55 percent.
[5] Domestic cost-prices, adjusting for subsidies, must have exceeded export unit values by a factor of 12.
[6] It did not affect, of course, the relationship between domestic cost-prices and export prices.

The devaluation of 1936, then, may be viewed as an attempt to reduce the disequilibrium character of the ruble exchange rate—to bring export and domestic prices into closer alinement. Whether deliberately or not, the degree of devaluation was not extreme enough to achieve this putative objective. Despite the favorable upswing in export unit values noted above, the ratio of domestic prices to export unit values in 1937 was little less than 3 for all commodities, about 1.5 for basic industrial goods excluding petroleum, and about 2.5 including petroleum. This is considerably closer to equilibrium than the situation which prevailed in 1935 but is still far enough out of line to have necessitated the use of the most stringent controls to keep trade in balance were such controls not required in any case as part of the planning structure.

The Soviets revalued the ruble upward in 1950 by almost one-third from about $0.19 to $0.25 (or from 5.3 to 4 rubles to the dollar). As already noted, the reason given for this revaluation was the erosion of the value of the dollar due to inflation after World War II. Furthermore, the Soviets could point to the fact that their prices began a secular decline after the monetary reform of December 1947, while Western prices continued to rise. These trends notwithstanding, the critical fact is that the Soviets experienced very substantial cost and price inflation from 1936 until 1948, and an upward revaluation of the ruble would seem to have been justified only if it tended to bring Soviet costs and prices more into line with costs and prices (especially of traded goods) in other countries (as indicated by the relationship of Soviet domestic prices to export unit values). Precise comparisons for 1950 are impossible because Soviet export unit values are not available. However, rough indicators of the trends from 1937 to 1950 in domestic prices and in export prices provide sufficient clues.

Between 1938 and 1950, the world index of export prices [19, p. 28] rose from 40 to 89 (1953=100). The index of export prices of industrial nations rose from 45 to 85. Since Soviet foreign trade prices more or less follow world prices, it is probably not too far off the mark to assume that the unit values of Soviet exports (in world prices) roughly doubled from 1937 to 1950. Over the same period, the domestic prices of both basic industrial goods and consumers' goods produced in the Soviet Union roughly tripled [7]. Since domestic prices substantially exceeded export unit values in 1937, clearly the gap was increased by the relative price trends from 1937 to 1950 and the exchange rate was even more overvalued in 1950 than in 1937. We must conclude, therefore, that the upward revaluation of the ruble in 1950 increased rather than decreased the disequilibrium character of the ruble exchange rate. It is difficult to find economic justification for the 1950 revaluation. Unlike the 1936 devaluation, the motivation in this case appears to be largely political rather than economic: to boost the ruble for its forthcoming role as the "key" currency in the rapidly growing intra-Soviet bloc trade.

The trend since 1950 has been in the direction of "equilibration." However, the rate of change is slow and the distance to be covered, large. Export prices of industrial nations have risen since 1950 and in 1956 stood at a 20 percent higher level. Undoubtedly, Soviet export prices have risen to a somewhat similar extent. On the other hand, Soviet internal prices have been falling steadily. In 1956, prices of basic industrial goods and of consumers' goods were 15 and 25 percent, respectively, below 1950 levels. Clearly, the gap between domestic prices and export unit values is still far from bridged. A summing up of the trends since 1937 leads one to expect that in 1956 domestic prices should have been roughly 2½ times export prices. In the way of an independent check, direct comparison of a sample of domestic prices and export unit values for 1956 shows ratios of 2 and 2.5, respectively, for nonconsumers goods and for all goods including consumers' goods (adjusted for turnover tax).

The little information available regarding Soviet domestic price trends since 1956 indicates relative stability over the past 2½ years. Nor have world prices, and presumably Soviet export prices, changed very much. This leads to the conclusion that as of mid-1959 the ruble is still a substantially overvalued currency at the official exchange rate as it has been since at least 1929 and probably throughout the whole Soviet period.

3. *Enterprise and budget accounts and the overvalued exchange rate* [18]

The institutional use of an overvalued exchange rate has its reflection in the accounts of export and import organizations and the state budget.

Purchases and sales in international markets are conducted by Soviet export and import organizations. The export and import organizations serve as intermediaries between the domestic producers or sales organizations and the foreign buyers and sellers. There are about 25 of these organizations and they each cover either the export or import of an important group of traded commodities. [11, pp. 256–269.]

The export organizations purchase from the domestic producers, wholesalers or retailers, the commodities they are scheduled in the plan, to sell abroad. The purchase price, in the case of basic industrial goods is the normal wholesale price which any other state enterprise or organization pays for the same commodity. Consumers' goods are also procured at wholesale price. If, however, the export organization purchases consumers' goods from the retailer, this involves excusing it from having to pay the very large sales (turnover) tax levied on almost all consumers' goods sold to the population. This tax amounts, on the average, to a 100-percent markup over wholesale price on all goods sold by state and cooperative stores to the population [6, ch. 10]. The export organizations then attempt to sell their stock of goods abroad presumably at as high a price as they can obtain with certain exceptions of a political nature. (Soviet writers constantly stress that foreign trade organizations should take advantage of capitalist business cycles to buy cheap and sell dear.) In intrabloc Soviet trade, the prices of most imports and exports are determined simultaneously when the bilateral agreements are drawn up. These prices will usually bear some relationship to world prices but, since the ruble has been and is overvalued, very little relationship to domestic wholesale or retail price. The export organization is credited for export sales at the foreign price converted to rubles at the official exchange rate. Again, since the ruble is overvalued, receipts from sales will usually be below cost of purchase and will involve the export organization in a loss. The loss is financed by a subsidy to the export organization from the state budget.

For example, suppose Avtoeksport, the organization which sells motor vehicles abroad, carries out the declared Soviet intention of exporting the little Moskvich to the United States for around $1,200. Assuming transport and other costs amount to $200, the account of Avtoeksport is credited with $1,000, or 4,000 rubles at the official exchange rate. The Moskvich sells in the Soviet Union for 25,000 rubles. Assume, for sake of illustration, that this retail price includes a 100-percent sales tax markup. The wholesale price, or cost to Avtoeksport of the automobile will be 12,500 rubles. Avtoeksport sustains a loss on the transaction of 8,500 rubles (12,500 minus 4,000) which is refunded in due course by a state budget subsidy.

The situation is very much the same in the case of import organizations. Presumably, they attempt to purchase goods from abroad at a low price. The foreign price at which they consummate a transaction is converted to rubles at the official exchange rate and this constitutes the major expenditure item of the organization. In turn, they sell the commodity to domestic wholesalers or retailers at the internal price. Since the ruble is overvalued, this will usually be a much higher price than the purchase price and the organization will earn a large profit which is, after other minor expenses are deducted, paid into the State budget. This difference between the cost of purchasing a commodity abroad and internal price is, as far as I have been able to determine, often labeled by the Soviets a "tariff" and is the major form of tariff levied by them at present.[7]

The case of the import organization is also easily illustrated. Suppose that Mashino import purchases for $50,000 oil-drilling equipment which has an internal wholesale price of 500,000 rubles. Its accounts will receive a credit of 500,000 rubles and a debit of 200,000 rubles, or $50,000 converted at 4 rubles to the dollar. In due course, the 300,000 rubles (deducting minor expenses) is transferred to the budget as customs receipts.

While it is quite clear in the Soviet literature that the losses of export organizations are compensated in the form of budget subsidies and the profits of import organizations are paid into the budget as customs receipts, the actual budget accounts are not usually presented in sufficient detail to make it possible to distinguish these items directly. With respect to exports, the principal difficulty is that budget expenditures on foreign trade and domestic trade are usually not distinguished, and sometimes, apparently, only expenditures on domestic trade are reported. Fortunately, for the year 1956, the Minister of Finance, A. G. Zverev, states that expenditures on internal trade alone, were 1.1 billion rubles [15, p. 25] and another source [4, p. 347] presents a figure of 12.2 billion rubles as the measure of budget expenditures on trade. Apparently the difference, 11.1 billion rubles, was allocated to foreign trade. Now while some of this latter amount must have been devoted to investment in trading organizations, probably the bulk of it repre-

---

[7] Except for tariffs on imports by or gifts to private Soviet citizens from abroad.

NOTE.—1 was informed at Amtorg that the prewar tariff schedules are still in effect. But these are ignored in the current Soviet literature on foreign trade and probably because they tend to be absorbed by the much larger differential between the import and domestic prices.

434 COMPARISONS OF UNITED STATES AND SOVIET ECONOMIES

sented loss subsidies to export organizations.[8] The deduced figure of a little less than 11.1 billion rubles as the measure of subsidies to export organizations is unfortunately not substantiated with any precision by direct computation. Total Soviet exports amounted to 14.6 billion rubles in 1956. If domestic prices were from 2 to 2½ times export unit values, as we have estimated, then loss-subsidies should have amounted roughly to from 15 to 20 billion rubles. This is a somewhat larger figure than the estimate from budget data. However, in light of the general crudity of the estimating techniques used, the two figures may be considered to be of the same order of magnitude. Our estimate of the ratio of domestic to export prices was based on a sample of about one-third by value of total exports. If the discrepancy derives from an unrepresentative sample, the implication is that the ratio of domestic price to unit value of the remaining exports is probably somewhat less than 2.

Attempts to detect the amount of the customs receipts item in the budget are less successful. The only direct clue is provided by budgetary data for 1958. Two different breakdowns of planned budgetary receipts have been presented:

	A	B
Turnover tax	301.5	301.5
Profits tax	130.3	130.3
Income tax on co-ops and collectives	15.6	15.6
Receipts from population	72.7	72.7
Social insurance	32.1	
Income from forests	2.1	122.8
Income from other enterprises	(1)	
Income from foreign trade organizations	(1)	
Income from machine tractor stations	11.9	(1)
Unspecified residual (not listed)	76.8	0
Total	643.0	643.0

[1] Not listed.

Sources: A from [4, pp. 65–66]. B from [17].

From these two sources it can be deduced that income from foreign trade organizations and from "other enterprises" together were expected to return 76.8 billion rubles to the budget. There seems to be no way, unfortunately, of disentangling the two items. Since the ratio of domestic price to unit value is somewhat higher for imports than exports,[9] one would expect income from foreign trade organizations to amount to from 20 to 30 bilion rubles. Satisfactory reconciliation of these figures will not be possible until additional information is discovered or published. It should be noted that the budget report from which the B estimates were taken is the first to my knowledge in the past 10 years to contain any mention of receipts from foreign trade operations.

4. *Soviet international price policy and the foreign trade accounts*

Anyone engaged in a study of Soviet foreign trade sooner or later discovers that different Soviet sources often give quite widely diver-

---

[8] I have not been able to ascertain whether any part of Soviet loans to other nations is reflected in the budget and, if so, whether it would be reflected in the above-mentioned category or in miscellaneous expenditures. The same problem exists with respect to interest on and repayments of foreign loans.
[9] Imports were roughly 2.5–3.

gent figures for the exports and imports of any given year. For example, Soviet literature provides the following estimates of total Soviet trade in 1929:

[Million rubles]

	Exports (million rubles)	Imports (million rubles)	Date of publication of source
A	924	881	1933
B	4,046	3,857	1939
C	3,219	3,069	1957

In working with Soviet foreign trade data, it is extremely important to make sure one is using a consistent set of statistics and to be able to reconcile the apparent inconsistencies noted above.

The apparent inconsistencies result from the Soviet practice of revaluing all previous trade statistics every time the value of the ruble is changed in terms of foreign currencies and revaluing by the full amount of change in exchange rate. Thus, the A and B estimates differ by a factor of 4.38, the amount of the devaluation of April 1936. The B estimate is converted into the C figure by first increasing the B figure to account for the small devaluation of 1937 (divide by 0.947) and then decreasing it to allow for the 32½ percent revaluation of March 1950 (divide by 1.325). For some unstated reason, probably its small magnitude, the 1937 devaluation was not used until 1950 to adjust the value of earlier year trade returns.

This Soviet practice is quite unique and, to my knowledge, is not used by any other nation. An example may clarify the issues. Typically, when a nation devalues, the prices in foreign currency of its exports and imports at first fall whereas the prices in domestic currency remain the same.[10] Therefore, the unit value in domestic currency of the devaluing nation's trade may remain roughly the same before and after devaluation. Thus, suppose the United States were selling automobiles to Great Britain for $2,800 or £1,000 and then devalued from $2.80 to $5.60 to £1. After devaluation, the price to Great Britain in dollars would still be $2,800 though the price in sterling would have fallen to £500.

The Soviets rationalize their practice on the grounds that their foreign trade prices are fixed in accordance with world prices and, therefore (by implication) when their exchange rate changes, the world price remains the same but the value in domestic currency changes. This causes a sharp discontinuity in the unit values at which trade in domestic currency is valued (if there has been a currency revaluation). This in turn justifies their practice of revaluing earlier trade returns for comparability. Suppose, for example, the Soviets are exporting Moskvich automobiles to the United States for $1,200 or 4,800 rubles. Suppose they devalue to 8 rubles=$1. By their practice, the foreign currency price of a Moskvich remains $1,200 but increases in domestic currency, to 9,600 rubles. The Soviet trade returns (in rubles) would show, in this case, a doubling

---

[10] Actually, prices in domestic currency may rise because of the increased demand at the lower price in foreign currency; and for highly competitive products, the price in foreign currency is likely to remain unchanged.

436 COMPARISONS OF UNITED STATES AND SOVIET ECONOMIES

of the value of trade. To avoid this purely statistical illusion of an increase in the volume of trade, all trade conducted during the previous year is revalued upward for comparability with trade returns at the new exchange rate.

No attempt will be made here to evaluate the Soviet statistical practice just described. It seems clear, however, that since Soviet foreign trade prices have no reference in the domestic price-cost structure (if they did, the practice would not be necessary in the first place) changing the value of trade for comparability in world prices is certainly a step toward obtaining a consistent series of the value of Soviet trade for intertemporal comparisons.[11] Users of such series should be careful to employ them only for comparisons of Soviet trade over time and then, for many purposes, they should not be used without further adjustment. They should not be used to compare Soviet trade in some predevaluation period with the trade data of other nations in that period. Neither the revised nor the original trade figures can be used, of course, in Soviet national income accounts without an adjustment for the gap, indicated earlier, between foreign trade unit values and domestic costs and prices. Finally, it is essential to check carefully the price basis underlying any series of trade data published recently by the Soviets. In the past few years, different sources have contained historical figures some in terms of a ruble worth $0.25 and others at the earlier rates which prevailed in the years to which the figures pertain.[12]

Soviet commodity trade

[Millions of 1950 rubles]

	Exports	Imports	Balance		Exports	Imports	Balance
1913	5, 298	4, 792	506	1930	3, 612	3, 690	−78
1917	1, 698	8, 453	−6, 755	1931	2, 827	3, 851	−1, 024
1918	28	367	−339	1932	2, 004	2, 454	−450
1919	0	11	−11	1933	1, 727	1, 214	513
1920	5	100	−95	1934	1, 458	810	648
1921	70	734	−664	1935	1, 281	841	440
1922	284	940	−656	1936	1, 082	1, 077	5
1923	760	499	261	1937	1, 312	1, 016	296
1924	1, 175	906	269	1938	1, 021	1, 090	−69
1925	2, 120	2, 881	−761	1946	2, 600	3, 100	−500
1926	2, 525	2, 440	125	1950	7, 200	5, 800	1, 400
1927	2, 600	2, 642	−42	1955	13, 874	12, 242	1, 632
1928	2, 800	3, 322	−522	1956	14, 446	14, 452	−6
1929	3, 219	3, 069	150	1957	17, 526	15, 751	1, 775

Sources:
1917: "Dostizheniia Sovetskoĭ vlasti za 40 let v tsifrakh," Moscow 1957, p. 31 (converted).
1913, 1929–38: V. S. Alkhilov and others, "Vneshniaia torgovlia S.S.S.R. s kapitalisticheskimi stranami," Moscow 1957, pp. 7–11.
1918–1928: N. Liubimov and A. M. Smirnov, "Vneshniaia torgovlia S.S.S.R.," Moscow 1954, pp. 147, 165, 177.
1946, 1950: Vneshniaia torgovlia (monthly), 1958: 4, p. 21.
1955: "Vneshniaia torgovlia S.S.S.R. za 1956 god," 1958.
1956–57: "Vneshniaia torgovlia S.S.S.R. za 1957 god," Moscow, 1958.

5. *Foreign trade and internal financial stability*

As a planned economy, the Soviet economy is much more insulated from the impact of foreign trade than are the economies of other nations. It is convenient to distinguish here between three effects of

---

[11] For many purposes it would have been more useful to have revalued the trade in terms of domestic prices in those years in which domestic prices were "rational."
[12] It is worth noting that from the 1917 revolution until October 1, 1924, probably because of the hyperinflation which gripped the nation's economy, all trade data published were in 1913 prices and in terms of $0.5146 ruble [3, p. 235].

foreign trade on an economy: (*a*) The comparative advantage effect, (*b*) the employment effect, and (*c*) the financial effect (with which we are here mainly concerned).

(*a*) By the comparative advantage effect is simply meant that nations achieve a higher level of productivity and output by specializing in those activities to which their skills, resources, climate, and factor proportions are best suited and then exchanging some of the domestically produced output for goods which the country cannot produce or can produce only at high cost relative to other nations. Let it suffice to say here that both planned and unplanned economies benefit equally from the comparative advantage effects of trade. These effects constitute, of course, the basic rationale of international trade. Perhaps the one difference here between the Soviet Union and most Western nations has been that the Soviets have preferred in the past, for political and strategic reasons, to be as self-sufficient as possible and to forgo these benefits of trade. Since World War II, this policy has been reversed in trade with other Soviet bloc nations and shows signs of being relaxed slightly in trade with the West and with underdeveloped nations.

(*b*) By the employment effect of foreign trade we refer to the fact that (1) an increase in exports tends to increase the level of employment; and (2) an increase in imports, to the extent that the imports substitute for domestically produced goods, tends to reduce the level [13] of employment. The importance of this effect is dramatically attested to by the so-called beggar thy neighbor policies of the 1930's and the international rejection of such policies today. Most nations are now committed to maintaining a high level of employment through domestic fiscal and monetary policies and not by "beggaring their neighbors."

Though foreign trade has an important impact on the level of employment in Western nations, it has little or no impact on the level of Soviet employment. This is because the Soviets plan for full employment of their labor resources taking into account the foreign trade sector. In theory, should the plan schedule a rise in imports which replace domestically produced products, it should also schedule new jobs for the workers rendered unemployed by the increment to imports; should the plan call for a decline in exports, it should also call for a shift of workers from export industries to those producing for domestic consumption.[14] There is one exception to our proposition regarding the impact of trade on Soviet employment: if Soviet plans for imports of raw materials and other intermediate products are not fulfilled, and if the Soviets do not have adequate reserves on hand, then bottlenecks may develop, factories may have to reduce their activities, and labor will be temporarily underemployed or unemployed.

(*c*) By the financial effect [15] is meant the potentially inflationary or deflationary effect of foreign trade on the economy. The financial effect is virtually indistinguishable from the employment effect in the case of free enterprise economies. Thus, at full employment, an increase in exports relative to imports will create inflationary pressures

---

[13] The comparative advantage effect works through altering the "distribution" as opposed to the "level" of employment.
[14] This may require no actual physical shift, of course, since many domestic industries produce exportables.
[15] The pioneering study of this question is that of Edward Ames [1]. The analysis here differs from Ames' in several respects. A more elaborate analysis of this problem is in preparation.

and a decrease, deflationary pressures. In the Soviet economy, the financial and employment effects are quite distinct. This is because the monetary flows in the economy are not allowed to influence the employment or allocation of resources in any "substantial" way. As we have already indicated, the Soviets plan for full employment. Full employment has a very high priority in their system and they do not allow financial factors to stand long in the way of achieving this objective. While deflation has never been a problem the Soviets have had to face, they have been perennially plagued by inflationary pressures [6, ch. 2; 7]. Inflation, though it has not affected the overt level of employment directly, has had many undesirable side effects on the economy such as encouraging speculative activities; reducing work incentives; requiring, at times, rationing; and providing obstacles to planning [6, ch. 1]. The major purpose of their tax system is, in fact, the elimination of this excess purchasing power in the hands of the population and the prevention, thereby, of these undesirable side effects of inflation.[16]

The financial effect on the Soviet economy of foreign trade, while in fact not very important, in theory depends on the following factors: (i) The relative amounts of exports and imports; (ii) the relative proportions of consumers' and producers' goods in both exports and imports; (iii) the size of the sales taxes on exportables and on import substitutes, respectively; (iv) the extent of the comparative advantage effect, and related to this, the relative labor costs of producing exports and import substitutes.

(i) If exports exceed imports, whether because of long-term credits or due to a short-term imbalance, the effect is inflationary, all other things being equal. The reverse is true if imports exceed exports.

(ii) The impact of inflationary pressures is quite different in the consumers' goods and producers' goods markets, respectively. We need not be concerned here with the latter since the major interenterprise transactions are all carefully regulated by the state and the purchase and sale of important producers' goods are accomplished by direction allocation. Moreover, the state bank has been very successful, in the postwar period, in preventing enterprises from converting excess deposits into cash for the bidding up of wage rates, a practice very prevalent in the 1930's [6, ch. 2; 7]. The impact of inflationary pressures in consumers' goods markets has already been indicated. For financial stability in the consumers' goods markets, then, total exports and imports are not the crucial variables but rather the relationship of exports and imports of consumers' goods. In other words, the volume of exports might be double that of imports but if the exports consist entirely of producers' goods and the imports, of consumers' goods, the net impact on the consumers' goods markets will be deflationary. On the other hand, even if imports exceed exports, the net impact will be inflationary if the volume of consumers' goods exports exceeds the volume of consumers' goods imports.

---

[16] While taxes in the United States also serve these functions, their major purpose, when viewed in light of limitations on increasing the national debt, may be considered the procurement of resources for Government use. In the Soviet economy, resources for Government use are allocated directly and the taxes simply serve to keep the monetary flows in line with planned resource flows and thereby prevent the development of inflationary side effects just mentioned.

(iii) Consumers' goods sold in the Soviet Union almost all bear a sales tax which averages about 50 percent of price (ie., a 100-percent markup) and which varies from 1 percent on some commodities to as much as 80 percent of price on others. The export of a consumer's goods means the loss of sales tax revenue whereas the import of a consumer's goods adds sales tax revenue since imported consumers' goods are sold at the same price as equivalent domestically produced commodities. Therefore, foreign trade will be more (less) inflationary the larger (smaller) the foregone sales tax (markup) on exported goods and the smaller (larger) the markup on imported goods.

(iv) With the exception of small transfer payments, demand for consumers' goods in the Soviet economy derives exclusively from labor income (i.e., wages, salaries, income of peasants). Therefore, the inflationary effect of foreign trade will be affected by the labor cost of producing exports (both producers' and consumers' goods) compared with the labor cost of an equivalent value of import substitutes. In other words, if there have been "real" gains from trade so that the output per person available for consumption (by state and household) after trade is greater than before trade, the volume of goods will have increased relative to the size of household incomes and foreign trade will have had, on this account, a deflationary impact.

A significant fact to be noted, here, is that in discussing the financial impact of foreign trade on the economy, we have ignored both the par value of the exchange rate and the export and import unit values at which Soviet goods exchange in the international market. The reason for this is related to the fact that we are concerned here only with inflation in the consumers' goods markets. The relationship between domestic prices and foreign trade unit values arrived at via the official ruble exchange rate has important implications for enterprise accounts as we indicated in section 3, but very little for the goods-money relationship in the consumers' goods markets. As we have already indicated, since most aspects of the interenterprise markets are thoroughly administered and inflation in the labor market is under control, the inflationary effects of foreign trade in this sector can safely be ignored.

The final question to be considered is: If foreign trade has a net inflationary or deflationary effect in the consumers' goods market, is this effect likely to be very significant? My guess is that it is of no great significance for the following reasons: First, Soviet foreign trade amounts to no more than about 3 percent of gross national product and foreign trade in consumers' goods amounts to an even smaller percentage of the value of consumers' goods sold domestically. Since Soviet trade is usually close to being balanced, the net effect is smaller still.[17] Second, to the extent that exports and imports of consumers' goods are planned in advance, their net inflationary or deflationary impact on the domestic economy can be and probably is offset by adjusting other variables in the financial picture. This is not meant to imply that the Soviets have perfected the science of financial planning. Far from it. They have never succeeded in achieving an

---

[17] No attempt has been made to estimate the balance of consumers' goods in foreign trade or the relative tax rates on exports and imports of consumers' goods.

equilibrium between the money and commodity flows in their consumers' goods markets with the possible exception of 1949 [7]. It seems doubtful, however, that foreign trade has affected this problem significantly.

6. *Soviet gold policy*

The Soviets are believed to be the second largest gold producer in the world, after the Union of South Africa. The Soviets have not, however, published figures regarding either their gold stock or gold production for at least three decades. Estimates of Soviet gold production which have appeared in the League of Nations Statistical Yearbooks and in the annual reports of the Director of the U.S. Mint agree that (1) gold production fluctuated widely in the 1920's but was substantially less than 1 million fine ounces a year, and (2) increased from about 1.5 million fine ounces in 1930 to over 5 million ounces annually from 1936 to 1939. At $35 an ounce, the Soviets must have been producing close to $200 million worth of gold annually in the late thirties. Since Soviet trade deficits were small and recorded gold exports amounted to less than $700 million they may have accumulated as much as $2 billion worth of gold before World War II. This would have been an impressive stock at prewar prices.

Postwar output and stock of gold estimates are probably less firm than prewar. In its annual Bullion Review for 1955, Samuel Montague & Co. estimated that the Soviets are now producing 10 million ounces, or $350 million worth of gold a year. On the basis of this production estimate, they concluded that the Soviet gold stock is currently (1955) in the neighborhood of 200 million ounces or $7 billion.

While none of the above figures can be considered more than informed estimates, there is no question about the fact that the Soviets mine gold on a large scale and that they are one of the largest producers of gold in the world. They have admitted this much.

Why do they devote so much in the way of resources to the mining of gold? While, legally, the state bank is required to cover its note issue with 25 percent backing in gold, this probably has no significance whatsoever for Soviet practice today. Soviet economists stress that it is not gold which gives their paper currency its real value but rather the goods in circulation which the money can buy. The basic reason for mining gold, they say (postwar), is for use as a foreign exchange reserve. The gold can be used to meet planned deficits in the balance of payments; to make purchases abroad to correct maladjustments in the plan which arise during a planning period; to make payments, under bilateral clearing agreements, when indebtedness exceeds a given amount; and to extend loans to friendly nations. The existence of a reserve of gold thus gives the Soviets considerable flexibility for adjustment in foreign trade and domestic economic matters. There is no question about Soviet use of gold in the postwar period for just the reasons mentioned above. It is well known, for example, that they have made gold loans to a number of nations (e.g., Poland, Czechoslovakia, East Germany); that they have used gold to purchase sterling because of a persistent trade deficit with sterling area countries; and that gold was used to help finance the large unplanned imports of consumers' goods in 1953–54 promised by Malenkov after Stalin's death, and so forth. Gold sales, mainly through Switzerland and London, to finance these transactions have roughly amounted to:

[In millions]

	Ounces	Dollars
1953	4.3	150
1955	2.0	70
1956	4.3	151
1957	7.5	263
1958	6.0	210

Source: 10, 13.

In addition, it has been reported that the Soviets have sold abroad substantial amounts of other precious metals, notably silver and platinum.

There is some question as to whether the mining of gold is an economically profitable operation for the Soviets in terms of the imports which the gold can be used to buy. In the thirties, there is little doubt but that most of the gold was mined by forced labor. Given the institution of forced labor, and given the low world prices of goods, the mining of gold may well have been "profitable." There seems to be considerable doubt concerning its profitability today, however, what with high world commodity prices and, since the reduction in forced labor, probably a shift to use of free labor in many of the mines. Furthermore, it is generally believed that conditions for gold production in Russia are, for the most part, very high cost [5, p. 37]. It might make sense, from an economic comparative advantage point of view, for the Soviets to shift resources out of gold and into other exportables. A labor day in machine tools, for example, might earn more foreign exchange at present than a labor day in the gold mines In any event, recognition of the relatively low purchasing power of gold has led no less a luminary than Deputy Premier Mikoyan to accuse the United States of exacting a tribute from the gold-producing nations and to call for an increase in the price of gold [14].

7. Payments agreement [4, pp. 306 ff; 11, pp. 93 ff; 16, ch. 6; 20]

Before 1929, most Soviet trade was conducted on a multilateral basis. The worldwide financial crisis of that period started them on the path of bilateral agreements with the use of clearing accounts; and this form of payment agreement still characterizes most of their financial relationships with other nations today.

The Soviets argue that their use of clearing accounts in trade with capitalist nations is a result of the limitations on convertibility of many western currencies and of the trade controls used by capitalist nations; but that the use of clearing agreements among nations of the socialist camp reflects not inconvertibility or trade controls, but rather the planned nature of intrabloc trade and the long-term agreements on trade among bloc nations. Actually, the ruble is, as we have seen, the most inconvertible of currencies being greatly overvalued at its nominal exchange rate of 4 rubles to $1. For this reason the unit of account in Soviet trade with a western nation is always the currency of that nation or the currency of some other western nation, usually the United States or Great Britain. (Since 1950, trade among bloc nations has been in tems of the ruble.) The western currency, rather

442 COMPARISONS OF UNITED STATES AND SOVIET ECONOMIES

than the ruble, is also used to settle persistent trade inbalances and usually these currencies, even where not fully convertible, are guaranteed convertibility in trade with the U.S.S.R. It is hardly fair, therefore, for the Soviets to place the blame for bilateralism on the currencies of nonbloc nations. Furthermore, with respect to the planned nature of Soviet bloc trade, it has been shown that bloc bilateral trade (a) has been subject to wider fluctuations than unplanned trade among nonbloc nations and (b) has usually been wide of targets [20].

The clearing account usually encompasses all commodity trade but with many nations provides also for settlement of expenses on invisible account. Since trade between a pair of nations will never balance precisely at all times, even though bilateral balance may be achieved over time, the clearing accounts agreements typically provide either implicitly or explicitly for swing credits. These "technical" credits, as the Soviets call them, allow for a certain percentage of imbalance without an interest charge. The imbalance allowed varies from 5 to 20 percent of the value of trade in each direction, much less than is usual among capitalist nations. The absolute amount of "technical" credit allowed will depend on the value of trade, seasonal character of trade, and other such variables. Should the trade imbalance exceed the limit set, then the usual provision is that either party can ask for payment of the excess in gold or convertible currency. If the trade agreement should be concluded with an imbalance, then the total amount of the imbalance is usually settled in gold or convertible currency. The payments agreements with nonbloc nations usually contain a clause protecting the Soviets against losses from devaluation should they happen to have an active balance with a nation which devalues.

It should be noted that while in most payments agreements with Western nations, the clearing account technique is employed, this is not always the case. In some instances, the agreements provide simply for payment in convertible currencies; in others, the agreement is in strictly barter terms though, usually, with some provision for payment in convertible currency or gold should one or the other side fail to deliver as promised. It should also be noted that in a few instances in payments agreements with Western nations, provision has been made for settlement of bilateral imbalance in terms of mutual trade with a third nation. There are also a few instances of trilateral settlement in intrabloc trade. Multilateral settlement of imbalances based on the ruble seems to be a goal of the Soviets in intrabloc trade. In June 1957 the members of the bloc actually signed an agreement for multilateral settlement as a supplement to the bilateral agreements now in force. There is some question as to whether this agreement has ever been put into operation. In fact, there is considerable doubt that any system of multilateral settlement could be implemented in terms of Soviet bloc currencies so long as they each maintain exchange rates which are not mutually realistic in terms of their respective cost-price structures.

APPENDIX

The most recent complete balances of payment data released by the Soviets are those for 1935 and 1936 and published by the League of Nations. These are presented below (in 1936 rubles):

Balance of payments of the U.S.S.R. for 1935 and 1936

[In million rubles]

CURRENT ITEMS

Receipts	1935	1936	Payments	1935	1936
1. Receipts from sale of export goods (f.o.b. prices)_____	1,800	1,497	1. Cash payments for imports including overhead charges (c.i.f. prices)_____	860	1,328
2. Income from marine freightage (balance)_____	48	72	2. Expenses on technical servicing and assembly_____	23	23
3. Receipts from harbor dues and for the servicing of ships (balance)_____	11	2	3. Excess of State expenditures over State receipts abroad_____	57	55
4. Other receipts from transport (balance)_____	12	16	4. Interest on loans and credits (balance)_____	89	44
5. Receipts from insurance operations (balance)_____	6	2	5. Other expenses_____	___	62
6. Receipts from noncommercial transfers (balance)_____	62	7			
7. Receipts from the tourist trade and money spent by foreigners (balance)_____	29	35			
8. Other receipts_____	165	32			
9. Sale of gold_____	52	_____			
Total (1–9)_____	2,185	1,663	Total (1–5)_____	1,029	1,512
			Excess of receipts over payments on current items_____	1,156	151

MOVEMENT OF CREDITS AND PROPERTY HELD ABROAD

Claims	1935	1936	Counterclaims	1935	1936
1. Repatriation of property held abroad (balance)_____	_____	71	1. Repayment of State and concessionary loans_____	_____	46
2. Receipts from State loans sold abroad_____	8	_____	2. Repayment of import credits granted by foreign firms_____	694	354
3. Receipts from financial credits__	_____	242	3. Reduction of indebtedness made up of short term export and bank credits_____	319	32
Inflow of credits and property held abroad (1–3), total_____	8	313	Outflow of credits and property held abroad (1–3), total_____	1,013	432
Excess of outflow over inflow in the movement of credits and property abroad_____	1,005	119	Net increase of the Soviet banks' foreign currency accounts held abroad_____	151	32

Source: Alexander M. Baykov, "Soviet Foreign Trade," Princeton 1946, p. 39.

SOURCES

1. Ames, E. "The Exchange Rate in Soviet-type Economies," *Rev. of Econ. and Stat.*, November 1953.
2. A. Z. Arnold, "Banks, Credit, and Money in Soviet Russia," New York, 1937.
3. S. N. Bakulin and D. D. Mishustin, "Statistika Vneshnei torgovli," Moscow, 1940.
4. "Finansy i sotsialisticheskoe stroitel'stvo," Moscow, 1957.
5. Alexander Gerschenkron, "Economic Relations with the U.S.S.R.," sponsored by Committee on International Economic Policy, New York, 1945.
6. Franklyn D. Holzman, "Soviet Taxation," Cambridge, 1955.
7. Franklyn D. Holzman, "Soviet Inflationary Pressures, 1928-57: Causes, Cures, Lessons," ms.
8. Franklyn D. Holzman, "Soviet Foreign Trade Price and Exchange Rate Policy," ms.
9. L. E. Hubbard, "Soviet Money and Finance," London, 1936.
10. International Monetary Fund, "International Financial News," Mar. 29, 1957.
11. G. E. Koftova, D. F. Ramzaitseva and V. B. Spandar'iana (editors), "Spravochnik po vneshnei torgovlei S.S.S.R.," Moscow, 1958.
12. League of Nations, "Review of World Trade," Geneva (annual reports).
13. The New York Times, Mar. 11, 1950, p. 59.
14. The New York Times, Aug. 3, 1958, p. 20.
15. "Planovoe Khoziaistvo," 1957:3, p. 25.
16. V. F. Popov (editor), "Gosudarstvennyi bank S.S.S.R.," Moscow, 1957.
17. Pravda, Dec. 23, 1958.
18. V. K. Shishov, "Osnovy bukhgalterskogo ucheta i analiz khoziaistvennoi deiatel'nosti vneshnetorgovykh ob'edinenii," Moscow, 1957.
19. United Nations, "U.N. Yearbook of International Trade Statistics," vol. 1, New York, 1959, p. 29.
20. R. F. Mikesell and N. N. Behrman, "Financing Free World Trade with the Sino-Soviet bloc," Princeton, 1958.

SOVIET FOREIGN ECONOMIC COMPETITION

By JOSEPH S. BERLINER

Syracuse University

The idea of economic competition is no new thing in Soviet history. During the first great burst of industrial growth in the thirties, the reader of the Soviet press was frequently reminded of the goal of "overtaking and surpassing the United States." That goal still occupies a prominent place in Soviet economic writings, but with a notable difference: twenty-five years ago it sounded a bit quixotic, but when we see it today in the new Seven Year Plan, it reads as part of the program of the not-too-distant future. The traveler in the USSR cannot fail to be impressed with the prominence of this goal in the minds of Soviet economic officials and with their confidence that the day of attainment is not far off. "Just give us ten more years without war, just ten years more," a Soviet factory manager told me last summer in a tone of dead earnestness, "and you won't be able to tell Moscow from New York or New York from Moscow."

It takes two to make a quarrel, and we should expect that it would take two to make a competition as well. The bizarre aspect of this economic contest is that only one of the parties is racing. The lagging contestant is bending every muscle to close the distance between himself and the leader. The leader is apparently aware of his involvement in a fateful race, but does not seem to be doing anything in particular about it. He strolls amiably down the path of history, dallies from time to time at a wayside recession, and conducts his business-as-usual of satisfying customers' preferences. It is a queer competition in which only one competitor is competing.

During Stalin's lifetime the economic competition remained largely a bilateral (or perhaps unilateral) race on the field of domestic economic growth. Since his death, the new Soviet leaders have expanded the contest into the field of foreign economic relations. With their dialectical eye transfixed not only on the world of today but also on that of the future, Soviet economic policy has turned toward the underdeveloped countries. My purpose is to explore the nature and implications of recent Soviet economic policy in these lands.

The most dramatic component of the new policy is the series of long-term credit agreements under which the USSR and her allies have undertaken a variety of construction and technical assistance projects in underdeveloped countries. After a slow start in 1953 and 1954, in 1955 a number of nonmilitary credit agreements were signed totaling about 190 million dollars. Then in 1956 the figure quintupled to about

960 million dollars. This rapid build-up was the cause of the great consternation felt in the West at that time. Certainly, if one projected this sudden rate of increase into the future, as some observers were prone to do, the prospect was rather alarming. As it turned out, however, the rate of new credits extended in 1957 fell sharply to about 235 million dollars, or roughly one quarter of the 1956 peak, although an additional 175 million dollar loan to Egypt was under negotiation at the year's end. In view of the momentous events in Poland and Hungary in 1956, the fall in new lending in 1957 cannot be attributed entirely to deliberate Soviet policy, nor to increasing reluctance on the part of potential new borrowers. But the indications are that in 1958 new lending has continued at a level below the 1956 peak. Highly tentative estimates place the volume of new loans in 1958 in the range of 500 to 600 million dollars, of which 275 million has been extended to Egypt alone. However, in May, 1958, the USSR unilaterally postponed for an additional five years the outstanding portion of 285 million dollars of loans previously extended to Yugoslavia. Hence net new loans in 1958 are at roughly the 1957 level. The period is obviously too short to warrant a generalization about trend, but it is clear that the worried projections of 1956 have not been borne out in fact.

As of the beginning of this year, the total of all nonmilitary credits provided for in the agreements signed since 1953 amounted to about 1.6 billion dollars. Perhaps the outstanding characteristic of the distribution of the total is the high degree of concentration. The USSR alone accounted for 75 per cent of the credits extended, and the USSR and Czechoslovakia together accounted for 89 per cent. Among the recipients, the three largest borrowers have recieved 87 per cent of the total; they were Yugoslavia, the UAR, and India. If we exclude Yugoslavia as a special case, which we must certainly do in the light of the subsequent history of the Yugoslav loans, the two remaining large recipients still accounted for 78 per cent of the total. Thus, while some fourteen countries had entered into credit agreements, the bulk of the credits had been heavily concentrated in a few of them.

It should be stated forthrightly at this point that the figures I have presented are estimates and not official data. The Soviet government publishes no official accounting of the aid program, although the major agreements have appeared in highly publicized official communiques. Many of the smaller agreements are known only through occasional newspaper or radio reports in the recipient countries and values are not always given. Since some agreements may have escaped public attention entirely, these estimates are probably on the low side, though not by a substantial percentage.

One and six-tenths billion dollars is a large figure, but its significance has sometimes been rather exaggerated in public discussion by failure to point out (*a*) that it is a cumulative total covering several years and therefore not comparable with U.S. annual foreign aid figures and (*b*) that the total consists of what are essentially promises to deliver sometime in the future. It includes, for instance, the 100 million dollar credit to Indonesia, which will not be fully drawn upon for a number of years. While the 1.6 billion dollar figure is relevant for some purposes, it would be of great interest to know what the rate of actual deliveries has been.

In the absence of an official Soviet accounting, it is impossible to provide any precise figures on deliveries. But if we are content with orders of magnitude, it is possible to provide some estimates. My method was to estimate the time-phasing of deliveries under each separate credit agreement, employing whatever bits of information happened to be available. In some cases actual or anticipated completion dates were known. The experience of the International Bank in the rate at which funds are disbursed under its loans also provided a rough guide.[1] The results are highly suggestive. By the beginning of 1957, when the cumulative total of agreements signed had reached 1.2 billion dollars, actual deliveries had been somewhere between 130 million dollars and 200 million dollars, or between 11 and 17 per cent of the total of agreements. During 1957, as noted earlier, new credits fell and deliveries under old credits rose, so that by the beginning of 1958 deliveries had amounted to 20-25 per cent of the total of agreements signed. This considerable delay between agreements and deliveries is perfectly normal and in no way reflects on Soviet willingness to honor its commitments, but it does suggest several observations. First, the USSR has been able to reap a propaganda bonus for a large volume of aid promises without having to "pay up" for many years. And second, the Soviet economy has not yet felt the full impact of the aid program, for 75-80 per cent of all the aid promised as of the beginning of this year had still to be delivered.

Since the subject of this paper is economic competition, it would be well to provide some guideposts in what might be termed comparative philanthropics. Looking, first, only at the fourteen countries that had signed credit agreements with the USSR and her allies, in 1956 actual Soviet bloc deliveries to these countries amounted to roughly one-third of U.S. government nonmilitary aid deliveries. In 1957, however, U.S. aid deliveries actually declined while Soviet deliveries increased, and Soviet deliveries rose to about 60 per cent of U.S. deliveries. With the momentum generated from past aid agreements, Soviet deliveries have probably continued to climb relative to the U.S. in 1958 and have un-

[1] The details of the estimates may be found in Joseph S. Berliner, *Soviet Economic Aid* (New York: Praeger, 1958).

doubtedly surpassed the U.S. in a number of countries.

Now for the inevitable and vital caveats. It is important to note that roughly 80 per cent of the U.S. deliveries consist of nonrepayable grants and the balance of long-term credits. The aid provided by the USSR and her allies, in contrast, consists almost entirely of credits. Of the many implications of this difference in the two aid programs, the following may be noted. First, acceptance of Soviet aid places a greater burden on the recipient's balance of payments than an equivalent value of U.S. aid. Second, by relying on long-term credits, the Soviet aid pro-gram establishes a long-run economic tie with the recipient, involving an increase in trade for many years. Third is the perverse observation that by stressing credits the Soviet leaders have represented their program as a businesslike contractual assignment among sovereign equals, devoid of political strings, whereas the large proportion of free grants in the U.S. program has been represented as evidence of the political domina-tion of weaker nations by a more powerful one. There is considerable evidence that the acceptance of credits does less violence to the dignity of the recipient than the acceptance of grants.

We have compared thus far only long-term nonmilitary governmental aid. If we should ask what is the total value of aid flowing to these fourteen countries from the two sources, the U.S. side of the ledger would begin to mount rapidly compared to the Soviet. For instance, U.S. assistance in the form of the sale of agricultural commodities for local currencies amounted in 1957 to over twice the total value of Soviet aid deliveries. For some purposes, it would be appropriate to point out that while the underdeveloped countries receive only governmental credits from the USSR and her allies, the credits they receive from the U.S. come not only from the government but from private sources as well. We should therefore add the credits extended to the International Bank from loans floated in the U.S. and perhaps the direct and port-folio investment by U.S. firms in those countries. These additions raise the volume of U.S. aid far above that of Soviet aid. The comparison in these terms is useful for some economic purposes: if one were interested in total foreign sources of new capital formation, for instance. But this kind of comparison obscures some vital differences which from a politi-cal point of view are more important than a simple numerical compari-son. A dollar's worth of our surplus wheat does not at all have the same psychological impact as a dollar's worth of Aswan Dam or Bhilai steel mill: the wheat quickly disappears in the process of consumption, while the structure lives on as an enduring monument. Nor does a dollar's worth of private U.S. direct investment have the same political effect as a dollar's worth of Soviet: a U.S. petroleum refinery remains a symbol of foreign economic domination, a perpetual and inviting target for the next wave of nationalism, whereas when the Soviet engineers finish their steel mill, they turn it over to the Indian people and go back home. Least of all ought the global preponderance of U.S. aid in all forms be a source of complacency, for Soviet aid is heavily concentrated in a few countries and may well have a crucial political impact there. Perhaps all that can be said about the over-all preponderance of U.S. aid is that talk of Soviet aid replacing that of the U.S. in the foreseeable future is nonsense. It is in the relatively few countries where the Soviet program is concentrated that the problem lies.

The Soviet credit program has been accompanied by an increase in the volume of normal commercial trade with the underdeveloped program. Unlike the credit program, in the trade expansion program, the East European countries have assumed the major role. While the volume of Soviet trade with the underdeveloped countries has been rising steadily since 1953, Soviet trade with the whole non-Communist world has also been rising. Soviet trade with the underdeveloped countries, as a proportion of trade with the whole non-Communist world, has shown a very modest increase. In 1956 it rose by about two percentage points, an increase which was more than offset by a fall of about four percentage points in the corresponding ratio for East European trade. In 1957, Soviet trade with the underdeveloped countries as a proportion of total trade with the non-Communist world rose by another three percentage points. The pattern of trade in 1957 shows the sharp effect of rising deliveries under the credit program. According to Soviet data (*Vneshniaia torgovlia*, 1958, No. 8, pages 14-18) total trade with eleven major underdeveloped countries (including Yugoslavia) rose by 35 per cent in 1957 compared to 1956. Almost half the volume of trade is accounted for by the same three countries that are the largest recipients of Soviet credits: Yugoslavia, the UAR, and India. Soviet trade with these three countries alone increased 75 per cent. Trade with the other eight countries decreased by 3 per cent. It is evident that the expansion of trade is due in large measure to Soviet willingness to grant credits.

The future of the Soviet credit program depends among other things on the ability of the Soviet economy to support the program. If one looks first at the size of the Soviet gross national product, it is clear that the aid program constitutes an extremely small percentage. The estimated volume of deliveries under the credit program in 1957 is equivalent to about 0.1 per cent of total consumption expenditures and about one-half of one per cent of defense expenditures. Even if the credit program expanded to the absolute size of the present U.S. aid program to all underdeveloped countries, it would still be equivalent to about 1 per cent of total consumption expenditures, though it would amount to almost 5 per cent of defense expenditures. The 1957 rate of deliveries is equivalent to about 1-2 per cent of the annual increase in Soviet national product. An aid program designed to match the size of current U.S. economic aid would be equivalent to about 12 per cent of the annual increase in Soviet national product.

While these global magnitudes are of some interest, they obviously do not tell the whole story of Soviet capability. For one thing, in the short-run at least, a program which may look small compared with the GNP may nevertheless pinch badly in certain sectors of the economy. The commodities exported under the credit agreements are heavily concentrated in the machinery industries. Rough estimates indicate that the 1957 machinery exports on credit were equivalent to about 1-4 per cent of total Soviet machinery production; a credit program designed to equal the U.S. aid program would require something like 17-35 per cent of the annual increase in Soviet machinery production. The problem grows keener if we examine individual branches of the machinery industry. For instance, in Gardner Clark's study of the Soviet iron and steel industry it is reported that a Soviet steel mill, roughly equivalent to that currently being built by the USSR in India, requires 46 thousand tons of metallurgical equipment. This amounts to over one-quarter of total Soviet production of metallurgical equipment in 1957. The annual increase in the production of metallurgical equipment has been about 20 thousand tons. It is clear that if a number of underdeveloped countries simultaneously line up for new steel mills, they will not all be accommodated.

But if the global GNP estimates gave too sanguine a picture of Soviet capabilities, these individual industry ruminations perhaps understate Soviet capabilities. For one thing, there is no evidence that the aid deliveries have indeed concentrated on a few industries. But more important is the fact that in the longer run, short-run inelasticities may be modified. The exports on credit are not a gross loss, but will eventually be repaid in imports. These imports can conceivably release domestic Soviet resources that may then be reallocated toward the industries that are providing most of the exports. The course of the argument thus confronts us directly with one of the more interesting theses that have been advanced in the interpretation of the Soviet aid program. That thesis is the application of the doctrine of comparative advantage to the pattern of Soviet trade with the underdeveloped countries. The argument is as follows: In the thirty years since the inception of the five year plans, the productivity of Soviet industry in processing the mineral and agricultural products of the land has increased greatly. During the same period, the USSR has encountered diminishing returns in the extraction of the mineral and agricultural products of the land. Thus the costs of producing finished industrial products have declined substantially relative to the cost of primary agricultural and mineral production. The application of the doctrine of comparative advantage suggests that today it may be cheaper for the USSR to obtain its primary products by import rather than by domestic production and to pay for the imports by exporting the products of her more advanced industries.

The argument may be evaluated on two levels: First, do the data support the contention that Soviet comparative advantage has indeed changed in the indicated direction? And, second, if the indicated change has occurred, is there evidence that the USSR is reallocating its resources in such direction as to take advantage of the gains from the new pattern of trade?

There is abundant evidence that the average quality of coals and iron ores mined today is poorer than those mined in the twenties, before the industrialization drive began. The mines are being sunk deeper, the seams are thinner, gas and coal bursts seem to have increased, the proportion of low-grade lignite has been increasing as a percentage of total coal production, and production plans provide for larger quantities of iron ores to be charged to the blast furnace per ton of pig iron produced. In agriculture, the major push of grain production into the marginal lands of Kazakhstan and Western Siberia and the effort to expand corn production in areas which seem ill-suited to it are a classical illustration of Ricardian rent theory, with an expanding population pushing into more marginal lands.

While evidence of this kind is persuasive, it is by no means conclusive. It is quite conceivable that technological improvements have offset the mounting niggardliness of nature. What we should wish to know is not simply how the costs of primary production have moved but how they have moved relative to the costs of industrial production. For lack of data on Soviet production costs, we can do nothing but rely on relative prices, for which a good deal of information is available. The question of the adequacy with which Soviet wholesale prices reflect relative costs is one of the thorniest in the field, but recent price studies suggest that at least in certain bench-mark years—the years in which major price reforms were introduced—relative prices did bear some sort of rough correspondence to production costs.[2] The years 1928 and 1950 are two of those bench-mark years, and an examination of the 1950 price indexes of a wide variety of commodities shows the following: among the commodities whose prices rose to an index of over 1,000 (with

[2] Lynn Turgeon, "Cost-Price Relationships in Basic Industries During the Soviet Planning Era," *Soviet Studies,* Oct., 1957. Abram Bergson, Roman Bernaut, and Lynn Turgeon, "Prices of Basic Industrial Products in the U.S.S.R., 1928-1950," *J.P.E.,* Aug., 1956. Richard Moorsteen, *Prices of Railroad Rolling Stock, U.S.S.R., 1927-28—1949* (Santa Monica: RAND, 1954), RM-1258.

1928 = 100) are coke, coal, and nonferrous alloys; the indexes of blast furnace products and iron ore were 670 and 602 in 1950; and at the lower end we find trucks and automobiles (88), roadbuilding and construction machinery (116), tractors (173), diesels (258), and steam turbines (360). What does it all add up to? Certainly the minimal statement that one can make is that the data are not inconsistent with the proposition that relative costs in the fabricating industries have fallen sharply compared to the costs of primary production.

If world terms of trade had remained unchanged over the period, the changes in relative production costs within the USSR would have moved the USSR closer to the position of a capital-goods exporter, if not all the way. In fact, the world terms of trade have moved in precisely the opposite direction. Exports of manufactured products from the developed countries in the present decade exchange for a substantially greater quantity of raw material imports from the underdeveloped countries than they did in the twenties. History has been on the side of the USSR in this respect. During the period in which it was becoming relatively more costly for the USSR to produce its own primary products, it was also becoming relatively cheaper to import them from the underdeveloped countries. The change in the world terms of trade thus accelerated the movement of the USSR toward the position of an exporter of manufactured goods.

But has the USSR moved all the way over to a relative cost position at which exports of manufactured goods are now advantageous? The kind of evidence presented above cannot provide an answer to this question. All we can say is that the Soviet comparative advantage in primary product production in 1928 has been considerably reduced in the course of thirty years. The data are not inconsistent with the possibility, for example, that the progress of thirty years has done no more than bring relative costs within the USSR to a level approximately equal to prices in world trade. If this were so, the trade and aid program would involve neither a gain nor a loss.

It should be noted in passing that these arguments do not apply to the more highly industrialized countries of Eastern Europe, particularly Czechoslovakia and East Germany. To these countries, which stand on a higher plane of industrialization than the USSR, the potential gains from trade with the underdeveloped countries are undoubtedly substantial. Moreover, with lesser endowments of natural resources than the continental USSR, the expansion of trade is of greater economic benefit for them than for the USSR. It is likely that such economic pressures for trade as exist in the Communist world are generated more among the East European allies than within the USSR itself.

While there is no conclusive evidence that the USSR has swung far into the position of an exporter of manufactures on the basis of comparative cost considerations, it is probably true that, with respect to specific commodities, there are substantial gains to be enjoyed from trade. If we array all commodities in a column such that at the top appear those in which the ratio of ruble cost to world price is lowest and at the bottom are those in which the ratio of ruble cost to world price is highest, then we should probably find a number of commodities at the top that could most advantageously be exported in exchange for those at the bottom. If the present aid and trade program were based on economic considerations, these are the commodities that the USSR should be most interested in exchanging. Has Soviet foreign economic competition been conducted in such terms as to indicate a concern for the precise commodities that are to be exchanged?

If anything, the opposite is true. The typical Soviet approach to the underdeveloped countries, both in proposals of credits and trade, is "just tell us what you want and we will sell it to you; and we will accept repayment in whatever commodities you normally export." The character of the negotiations suggests that whatever economic motivations may exist for this trade, they are submerged beneath the political objectives. But more to the point is the following: If there is a strong economic motivation based on comparative advantage, there must be taking place within the Soviet economy a reallocation of resources, involving a planned reduction in domestic production of the commodities to be imported, and an expansion of capacity in the industries intended to generate surpluses for export. Is there evidence that such a reallocation is taking place?

No definitive answer to this question can be given. Our statistical information on the Soviet economy is not so detailed, nor are the magnitudes of the commodities involved so large, as to warrant great confidence in the results. But a few observations may be made. The Seven Year Plan announced last month sketches out the direction of growth of the national economy over the period 1959-65. If one examines it for indications of the role of credits and trade with the underdeveloped countries, one finds very few. The plan does contain a target figure for 1965 trade with the other Communist countries, but not for trade with non-Communist countries. This in itself is significant: the old predisposition for autarky has been somewhat relaxed in recent years, but not to the extent of permitting the kind of dependence on non-Communist countries that would be required by a full commitment to trade according to comparative advantage.

Looking further, cotton and wool are two raw materials that loom large in Soviet imports from the Middle East and some countries of Asia. Does the plan indicate that Soviet industry is being geared to a greater dependence on imported cotton and wool? In fact, the Seven Year Plan provides for a more-or-less *pari passu* growth of fiber and textile production. Cotton textile production is to increase 38-43 per cent, while raw cotton production is to increase 35-45 per cent. Wool textiles are to increase 77 per cent, while raw wool is to increase about 70 per cent. The planners show no intention of letting their textile industry become dependent on imports of wool and cotton.

Thus, consideration of the USSR's comparative advantage does suggest that the credit and trade program probably involves no great net loss and perhaps brings some net economic gains. But there is little to suggest that economic gains are an important motive underlying the new policy. The economic competition we are talking about is clearly not that of two powers competing for the rice of Burma or the jute of India. It is a political competition waged with the new weapon of economic aid.

SELECTED BIBLIOGRAPHY

The bibliography which follows is subdivided into the same sections as the readings. The following abbreviations are used:

AER—*American Economic Review*
Comparisons—Comparisons of the United States and Soviet Economies, Subcommittee on Economic Statistics, Joint Economic Committee, Congress of the United States, Washington 1959.
EJ—*Economic Journal*
JPE—*Journal of Political Economy*
Proc. AEA—*Annual Proceedings American Economic Association*
QJE—*Quarterly Journal of Economics*
RES—*Review of Economics and Statistics*
Sov. Stud.—*Soviet Studies*

At the end of the regular bibliography some general sources of information on the Soviet economy are listed.

It should be stressed that this bibliography *is selective,* based on a fairly comprehensive but far from exhaustive survey of the literature.

I. Statistics and Measurement

The first group of readings is concerned primarily with the problem of reliability; the second group with methodological problems relating to Soviet statistics and measurement.

Grossman, Gregory. *Soviet Statistics of Physical Output of Industrial Commodities: Their Compilation and Quality,* Princeton: National Bureau of Economic Research, 1960.

Jasny, Naum. *The Soviet 1956 Statistical Handbook, A Commentary.* East Lansing, 1958.

Jasny, Naum. "Intricacies of Russian National Income Indexes," *JPE,* August, 1957.

Jasny, Naum. "Soviet Statistics," *RES,* February, 1950.

Ostrovitianov, K. V. "The Discussion on Statistics Summed Up," *Sov. Stud.*, January, 1955 (trans. J. Miller).

Rice, S. A., and others. "Reliability and Usability of Soviet Statistics," *The American Statistician*, April–May, June–July, 1953.

Turgeon, L. "On the Reliability of Soviet Statistics," *RES*, February, 1953.

Becker, A. S. "Comparisons of United States and USSR National Output: Some Rules of the Game," *World Politics*, October, 1960.

Bergson, A. "A Problem in Soviet Statistics," *RES*, November, 1947. Cf. also "Comments," by Dobb and Schwartz, February, 1948.

Clark, Colin. *A Critique of Russian Statistics*. London, 1939.

Gerschenkron, Alexander. *A Dollar Index of Soviet Machinery Output*. R-197 Santa Monica, RAND, 1951.

Gerschenkron, Alexander. "Soviet Indices of Industrial Production," *RES*, November, 1947. Cf. also "Comments," by Dobb, February, 1948.

Grossman, Gregory. "A Note on the Fulfillment of the Five-Year Plan in Industry," *Sov. Stud.*, April, 1957.

Heymann, Hans, Jr. "Problems of Soviet–United States Comparisons," *Comparisons*, Vol. I, Washington, 1959.

Hodgman, Donald R. *Soviet Industrial Production, 1928–1951*, Cambridge, 1954. Ch. I.

Kasdan, S. "Relationship between Machinery and Steel Production in Russia and U.S.," *RES*, February, 1952.

Nove, A. "Some Notes on Soviet National Income Statistics," *Sov. Stud.*, January, 1955.

Nove, A. "The United States National Income à la Russe," *Economica*, August, 1956.

Nutter, Warren. "On Measuring Economic Growth," *JPE*, February, 1957. Cf. also the "Comment," by Levine, and "Rejoinder," by Nutter, August, 1958.

II. The Price System

This section contains, in addition to references on the Soviet price system, the various studies of Soviet national income.

Baran, P. "Soviet National Income in 1940," *RES*, November, 1947.

Bergson, A., R. Bernaut, and L. Turgeon. "Prices of Basic Industrial Products in the U.S.S.R., 1928–1950," *JPE*, August, 1956

Bergson, A., H. Heymann, Jr., and O. Hoeffding. *Soviet National Income and Product, 1928–1948: Revised Data*, RAND, RM 2544, November, 1960.

Campbell, Robert W. "Accounting for Depreciation in the Soviet Economy," *QJE*, November, 1956.

Campbell, R. "Accounting for Cost Control in the Soviet Economy," *RES*, February, 1958.

Dobb, M. "Notes on Recent Economic Discussion," *Sov. Stud.*, April, 1961.

Grossman, G. "Review" of *Soviet National Income and Product in 1937*, *JPE*. October, 1953.

Hoeffding, O. *Soviet National Income and Product in 1928*. New York, 1954.

Hoeffding, O., and N. Nimitz. *Soviet National Income and Product, 1949–1955*, RAND, RM 2101, 1959.

Jasny, Naum. "A Note on Rationality and Efficiency in the Soviet Economy: I," *Sov. Stud.*, April, 1961.

Jasny, Naum. *Soviet Prices of Producers' Goods*. Stanford, 1952.

Jasny, Naum. *The Soviet Price System*. Stanford, 1951.

Kaser, M. C. "Soviet Planning and the Price Mechanism," *EJ*, March, 1950.

Montias, J. M. "Rational Prices and Marginal Costs in Soviet-type Economies," *Sov. Stud.*, April, 1957.

Nimitz, Nancy. "Soviet Agricultural Prices and Costs," *Comparisons*, Vol. I.

Schlesinger, R. "Strumilin and Others on the Theory of a New Price Structure," *Sov. Stud.*, July, 1957.

Seton, Francis. "The Social Accounts of the Soviet Union in 1934," *RES*, August, 1954.

Turgeon, L. "Cost-Price Relationships in Basic Industries during the Planning Era," *Sov. Stud.*, October, 1957.

Wiles, P. J. D. "Are Adjusted Rubles Rational?" *Sov. Stud.*, October, 1955. This article was discussed in subsequent issues of *Sov. Stud.* by Joan Robinson (January, 1956), D. Hodgman and D. Granick (July, 1956), Wiles (October, 1956), F. D. Holzman and K. W. Rothschild (July, 1957).

Wyler, J. "The National Income of the Soviet Union," *Social Research*, December, 1946.

Zauberman, A. "The Soviet Debate on the Law of Value and Price Formation," in *Value and Plan*, ed. Gregory Grossman. Berkeley, 1960. Cf. also "Comment," by A. Bergson.

III. Aspects of the Soviet Industrialization Model

Dobb, Maurice. *Soviet Economic Development since 1917*. London, 1948. Ch. 8.

Erlich, Alexander. "Preobrazhensky and the Economics of Soviet Industrialization," *QJE*, February, 1950.

Erlich, Alexander. *The Soviet Industrialization Debate, 1924–1928*. Cambridge, 1960.

Jasny, Naum. *Soviet Industrialization, 1928–1952.* Chicago, 1961.

Kaufman, A. "Origin of 'The Political Economy of Socialism,' " *Sov. Stud.,* January, 1953.

Seton, Francis. "Planning and Economic Growth: Asia, Africa, and the Soviet Model," *Soviet Survey,* January–March, 1960.

Wilhelm, W. "Soviet Central Asia; Development of a Backward Area," *Foreign Policy Reports,* February, 1950.

IV. Economic Growth

A. Over-all View

Bergson, Abram (ed.). *Soviet Economic Growth.* White Plains, 1953.

Campbell, Robert. *Soviet Economic Power.* Cambridge, 1960. Ch. 3, 4, 8.

Dobb, Maurice. *Soviet Economic Development since 1917.* London, 1948. Ch. 2–7, 9.

Gerschenkron, Alexander. "The Problem of Economic Development in Russian Intellectual History of the Nineteenth Century," in *Continuity and Change in Russian and Soviet Thought,* ed. Ernest J. Simmons. Cambridge, 1955.

Gerschenkron, Alexander. "Problems and Patterns of Russian Economic Development," in *The Transformation of Russian Society,* ed. Cyril Black. Cambridge, 1960.

Jasny, Naum. *Soviet Industrialization, 1928–1952.* Chicago, 1961.

Goldsmith, Raymond. "The Economic Growth of Tsarist Russia, 1860–1913", *Economic Development and Cultural Change,* April, 1961.

Library of Congress, Legislative Reference Service. *Trends in Economic Growth: A Comparison of the Western Powers and the Soviet Bloc.* A study prepared for the Joint Committee on the Economic Report. Washington: U.S. Government Printing Office, 1955.

Library of Congress, Legislative Reference Service. *Soviet Economic Growth: A Comparison with the United States.* A study prepared for the Subcommittee on Foreign Economic Policy of the Joint Economic Committee of the United States Congress. Washington: U.S. Government Printing Office, 1957.

Rostow, W. W. "Summary and Policy Implications," *Comparisons,* Vol. III.

Schwartz, Harry. "Reflections on the Economic Race," *Comparisons,* Vol. III.

B. National Income

Bergson, Abram. *The Real National Income of Soviet Russia since 1928.* To be published by Harvard University Press.

Grossman, Gregory. "National Income," in *Soviet Economic Growth,* ed. Abram Bergson. White Plains, 1953.

Jasny, Naum. *The Soviet Economy during the Plan Era.* Stanford, 1951.

C.   Industrial Growth

Dobb, Maurice. "Rates of Growth under the Five Year Plans," *Sov. Stud.*, April, 1953.

Gerschenkron, A. "Rate of Industrial Growth in Russia since 1885," *Journal of Economic History*, Suppl. No. 7, 1947.

Gerschenkron, Alexander. "Soviet Heavy Industry. A Dollar Index of Output, 1927/8–37, *RES*, May, 1955.

Greenslade, R., and P. Wallace, "Industrial Growth in the Soviet Union: Comment, *AER*, September, 1959. Cf. also "Comment," by Nutter.

Grossman, Gregory. "Thirty Years of Soviet Industrialization," *Soviet Survey*, October–December, 1958.

Hodgman, Donald R. *Soviet Industrial Production, 1928–51*. Cambridge, 1954.

Jasny, Naum. *The Soviet Economy during the Plan Era*. Stanford, 1954.

Nutter, Warren. "Industrial Growth in the Soviet Union," *Proc. AEA*, May, 1958. Cf. "Comments," by Hans Heymann, Jr.

Nutter, Warren. "Notes on Soviet Economic Growth," *Proc. AEA*, May, 1957. Cf. "Comments, by G. Grossman.

Nutter, Warren. "Some Observations on the Soviet Economic Growth," National Bureau of Economic Research, *Occasional Paper* No. 55.

Nutter, Warren. "The Structure and Growth of Soviet Industry: A Comparison with the United States," *Journal of Law and Economics*, II, 147–74.

Powell, R. P. "An Index of Soviet Construction, 1927/28 to 1955," *RES*, May, 1959.

Seton, Francis. "Soviet Progress in Western Perspective," *Sov. Stud.*, October, 1960.

Seton, Francis. "The Tempo of Soviet Industrial Expansion," *Bulletin of the Oxford Institute of Statistics*, February, 1958.

Seton, Francis. "An Estimate of Soviet Industrial Expansion," *Sov. Stud.*, October, 1955. See "Comment," by Hodgman (July, 1956) and "Reply," by Seton (October, 1956).

Shimkin, D. B., and others. "Soviet Industrial Growth—Its Cost, Extent and Prospects," *Automotive Industries*, January 1, 1958.

D.   Agricultural Growth

Frank, A. G. "Labor Requirements in Soviet Agriculture," *RES*, May, 1959.

Frank, A. G. "General Productivity in Soviet Agriculture and Industry," *JPE*, December, 1958.

Jasny, Naum. *The Socialized Agriculture of the USSR*, Stanford, 1949.

Kahan, A. "Changes in Labor Inputs in Soviet Agriculture," *JPE*, October, 1959.

Kershaw, J. "Review" of Jasny's *Socialized Agriculture of the USSR*, *AER*, March, 1950.

E. Population and Labor Force

De Witt, Nicholas. *Soviet Professional Manpower.* Washington, D.C., 1954.

Eason, Warren. "Population Changes," in *The Transformation of Russian Society,* ed. Cyril Black. Cambridge, 1960.

Eason, Warren. "Population and Labor Force," in *Soviet Economic Growth,* ed. A. Bergson. Evanston, Ill., 1953.

Eason, Warren. "The Soviet Population Today," *Foreign Affairs,* July, 1959.

Eason, Warren. "Comparison of the United States and Soviet Economies: The Labor Force," *Comparisons,* Vol. I.

Galenson, Walter. *Labor Productivity in Soviet and American Industry.* New York, 1955.

Korol, Alexander G. *Soviet Education for Science and Technology.* Cambridge, 1957.

Lorimer, Frank. *The Population of the Soviet Union: History and Prospects.* Geneva: League of Nations, 1946.

Newth, J. A. "The Soviet Labour Force in the Fifties," *Sov. Stud.,* April, 1960.

Redding, A. David. "Comparison of Volume and Distribution of Non-Agricultural Employment in the USSR, 1928–55, with the US, 1870–1952," *RES,* November, 1954.

Siegel, Irving H. "Labor Productivity in the Soviet Union," *Journal of the American Statistical Association,* March, 1953.

F. Development Strategies: Capital Formation

Berliner, Joseph. "Capital Formation and Productivity in the USSR," Special Publication Series of the *National Academy of Economics and Political Science,* No. 14, June, 1958.

Eckstein, Alexander, and Peter Gutmann. "Capital and Output in the Soviet Union, 1928–1937," *RES,* November, 1956.

Frank, A. G. "General Productivity in Soviet Agriculture and Industry," *JPE,* December, 1958.

Granick, David. "Economic Development and Productivity Analysis: The Case of Soviet Metalworking," *QJE,* May, 1957.

Granick, David. "Organization and Technology in Soviet Metalworking: Some Conditioning Factors," *Proc. AEA,* May, 1957.

Grossman, Gregory. "Soviet Growth: Routine, Inertia, and Pressure," *Proc. AEA,* May, 1960.

Grossman, Gregory. "Some Trends in Soviet Capital Formation," in *Conference on Capital Formation and Economic Growth,* Princeton: National Bureau of Economic Research, 1955.

Hardt, John. "Industrial Investment in the U.S.S.R.," *Comparisons,* Vol. I.

Holzman, F. D. "Comments on Eckstein's 'Strategy of Economic Development in Communist China,'" *Proc. AEA,* May, 1961.

Kaplan, Norman M. "Capital Formation and Allocation," *Soviet Economic Growth,* ed. A. Bergson. Evanston, Ill., 1953.

Seton, Francis. "Production Functions in Soviet Industry," *Proc. AEA,* May, 1959. Cf. also "Comments," by R. Powell and "Reply," by Seton.

V. *Planning*

Balassa, Bela. *The Hungarian Experience in Economic Planning: A Theoretical and Empirical Study.* New Haven, 1959.

Baran, Paul. "National Economic Planning," in *Survey of Contemporary Economics, II,* ed. B. Haley. Homewood, Ill., 1952.

Bergson, A. "Socialist Economics," in *Survey of Contemporary Economics,* ed. H. Ellis. Philadelphia, 1948.

Bettelheim, Charles. *Studies in the Theory of Planning,* London, 1959.

Brutzkus, B. *Economic Planning in Soviet Russia.* London, 1935.

Campbell, Robert. "Soviet Accounting and Economic Decisions," in *Value and Plan,* ed. Gregory Grossman. Berkeley, 1960. Cf. also "Comment," by Herbert Levine.

Campbell, Robert. "Soviet and American Inventory-Output Ratios," *AER,* September, 1958.

Campbell, Robert. *Soviet Economic Power.* Cambridge, 1960, Ch. 5, 7.

Chossudowsky, M. "The Soviet Concept of Economic Equilibrium," *Review of Economic Studies,* February, 1939.

Dobb, Maurice. *On Economic Theory and Socialism.* London, 1955.

Dobb, Maurice. *Economic Growth and Planning.* London, 1960.

Dobb, Maurice. "Notes on Recent Economic Discussion," *Sov. Stud.,* April, 1961.

Dobb, Maurice. *Soviet Economic Development since 1917.* London, 1948. Ch. 1, 8, 10–14.

Grossman, Gregory. "Communism in a Hurry: The 'Time Factor' in Soviet Economics," *Problems of Communism,* May–June, 1959.

Grossman, Gregory. "Suggestions for a Theory of Soviet Investment Planning," in *Investment Criteria and Economic Growth.* Cambridge: MIT Center for International Studies, 1955.

Hayek, F. (ed.). *Collectivist Economic Planning.* London, 1935.

Holzman, F. "The Soviet Ural-Kuznetsk Combine: A Study in Investment Criteria and Industrialization Policies," *QJE,* August, 1957.

Hunter, Holland. "Optimum Tautness in Developmental Planning," *Economic Development and Cultural Change,* July, 1961.

Hunter, Holland. "Planning of Investments in the Soviet Union," *RES,* February, 1949.

Hurwicz, Leo. "Conditions for Economic Efficiency of Centralized and Decentralized Structures," in *Value and Plan,* ed. G. Grossman. Berkeley, 1960. Cf. also "Comment," by J. Berliner.

Jasny, Naum. "A Note on Rationality and Efficiency in the Soviet Economy," *Sov. Stud.*, April, 1961.

Kaplan, N. "Investment Alternatives in Soviet Economic Theory," *JPE*, April, 1952.

Khachaturov, T. S. "Criteria for Capital Investment Decisions in the U.S.S.R.," *Proc. AEA*, May, 1958.

Kornai, J. *Overcentralization in Economic Administration: A Critical Analysis Based on Experience in Hungarian Light Industry.* New York, 1959.

Lange, Oscar, and Fred M. Taylor. *On the Economic Theory of Socialism* (ed. B. E. Lippincott). Minneapolis, 1938.

Lange, Oscar. *Working Principles of the Soviet Economy.* New York, 1943.

Leontief, Wassily. "The Decline and Rise of Soviet Economic Science," *Foreign Affairs*, January, 1960.

Lerner, Abba P. *The Economics of Control.* New York, 1946.

Montias, J. M. "Planning with Material Balances," *AER*, December, 1959.

Oxenfeldt, A., and E. Van den Haag. "Unemployment in Planned and Capitalist Economies," QJE, February, 1954. Cf. also "Comment," by Holzman and "Reply," by Oxenfeldt and Van den Haag (August, 1955).

Novozhilov, V. V. "On Choosing Between Investment Projects," *International Economic Papers*, No. 6.

Schwartz, Harry. *Russia's Soviet Economy,* New York, 1954. Ch. V.

Ward, Benjamin. "The Planners' Choice Variables," in *Value and Plan*, ed. G. Grossman. Berkeley, 1960. Cf. also "Comment," by J. Berliner.

Wiles, Peter. "Rationality, the Market, Decentralization and the Territorial Principle," in *Value and Plan*, ed. G. Grossman. Berkeley, 1960. Cf. also "Comment," by N. Kaplan.

Wiles, P. J. D. "Scarcity, Marxism and Gosplan," *Oxford Economic Papers*, October, 1953.

Zauberman, A. "A Note on the Soviet Capital Controversy," *QJE*, August, 1955.

VI. Enterprise and the Organization of Industry

Berliner, Joseph. *Factory and Manager in the U.S.S.R.* Cambridge, 1957.

Bienstock, G., S. Schwartz, and A. Yugow. *Management in Russian Industry and Agriculture.* London and New York, 1944. Part I.

Gerschenkron, Alexander. "Industrial Enterprise in Russia," in *The Corporation in Modern Society*, ed. E. Mason. Cambridge, 1959.

Granick, D. *Management in the Industrial Firm in the U.S.S.R.* New York, 1954.

Granick, David. "Soviet-American Management Comparisons," *Comparisons*, Vol. I.

Granick, David. "Initiative and Independence of Soviet Plant Managers," *American Slavic and East European Review*, October, 1951.

James, R. "Management in the Soviet Union," in *Management in the Industrial World*, ed. F. Harbison and C. A. Myers, New York, 1959.

Kaser, Michael. "The Reorganization of Soviet Industry and its Effects on Decision Making" in *Value and Plan*, ed. G. Grossman. Berkeley, 1960. Cf. also "Comment," by G. Grossman.

Nove, Alec. "The Soviet Industrial Reorganization," *Problems of Communism*, Vol. VI, No. 6 (1957).

VII. Agricultural Organization and Policies

Bienstock, G., S. Schwartz, and A. Yugow. *Management in Russian Industry and Agriculture*. London and New York, 1944. Part II.

Gerschenkron, A. "Review of Jasny's Socialized Agriculture...," *Journal of Economic History*, Winter, 1951.

Grossman, Gregory. "Soviet Agriculture since Stalin," *The Annals*, January, 1956.

Jasny, Naum. *The Socialized Agriculture of the USSR*. Stanford, 1949.

Johnson, D. Gale. "Soviet Agricultural Resources Reappraised," *Journal of Farm Economics*, May, 1956.

Kershaw, J. A. "Productivity and Welfare in Soviet Agriculture," *AER*, March, 1950.

Maynard, Sir John. *Russia in Flux*. New York, 1948.

Timoshenko, V. P. "Agricultural Resources," in *Soviet Economic Growth*, ed. A. Bergson, Evanston, Ill., 1953.

Volin, Lazar. *A Survey of Soviet Russian Agriculture*, U.S. Dept. of Agriculture, Monograph No. 5, Washington, 1951.

Volin Lazar. "Agriculture under Krushchev," *Proc. AEA*, May, 1959.

VIII. Finance

Ames, E. "Banking in the Soviet Union," *Federal Reserve Bulletin*, April, 1952.

Ames, E. "Soviet Block Currency Conversions," *AER*, June, 1954.

Arnold, A. Z. *Banks, Credit and Money in Russia*. New York, 1937.

Baran, P. "Currency Reform in the USSR," *Harvard Business Review*, March, 1948.

Davies, R. W. *The Development of the Soviet Budgetary System*, Cambridge, England, 1958.

Grossman, Gregory. "Soviet Banking System," in *Banking Systems*, ed. B. H. Beckhardt. New York, 1954.

Holzman, F. D. "The Soviet Budget, 1928–1952," *National Tax Journal,* September, 1953.

Holzman, Franklyn D. "An Estimate of the Tax Element in Soviet Bonds," *AER,* June, 1957. Cf. also "Comment," by Bornstein and "Reply," (September, 1958).

Holzman, Franklyn D. "Income Taxation in the Soviet Union: A Comparative View," *National Tax Journal,* June, 1958.

Holzman, Franklyn D. *Soviet Taxation: The Fiscal and Monetary Problems of a Planned Economy.* Cambridge, 1955.

Mieczkowski, B. "The Operation of Soviet Banks," *Current Economic Comment,* November, 1954.

Powell, Raymond. *Soviet Monetary Policy.* Ph.D. dissertation, University of California, Berkeley, 1952.

Reddaway, W. B. *The Russian Financial System.* London, 1935.

Sokolnikov, G. Y., and others. *Soviet Policy in Public Finance, 1917–28.* Stanford, 1931.

IX. The Consumer and Worker

A. Consumer

Chapman, Janet G. "Real Wages in the Soviet Union, 1928–1952," *RES,* May, 1954.

Chapman, Janet. *Real Wages in Soviet Russia since 1928.* To be published by Harvard University Press.

Goldman, Marshall. "Product Differentiation and Advertising: Some Lessons from Soviet Experience," *JPE,* August, 1960.

Goldman, Marshall. "The Soviet Standard of Living, and Ours," *Foreign Affairs,* July, 1960.

Goldman, Marshall. "Retailing in the Soviet Union," *Journal of Marketing,* April, 1960.

Goldman, Marshall. "Marketing—A Lesson for Marx," *Harvard Business Review,* January–February, 1960.

Holzman, Franklyn D. "Taxes and the Standard of Living in the USSR: Postwar Developments," *National Tax Journal,* June, 1957.

Jasny, N. "Peasant-Worker Income Relationships: A Neglected Subject," *Sov. Stud.,* July, 1960.

Kaplan, N., and E. Wainstein. "A Comparison of Soviet and American Retail Prices in 1950," *JPE,* December, 1956. See also additional note *loc. cit.,* December, 1957.

Kaser, M. C. "Soviet Statistics of Wages and Prices," *Sov. Stud.,* July, 1955.

Nove, A. "The Purchasing Power of the Soviet Ruble," *Bulletin of Oxford Institute of Statistics,* May, 1958.

Sosnovy, Timothy. *The Housing Problem in the Soviet Union.* New York, 1954.

U. S. Dept. of Health, Education, and Welfare, *A Report on Social Security Programs in the Soviet Union.* Washington: U. S. Government Printing Office, September, 1960.

Wiles, Peter. "Retail Trade, Prices and Real Wages," *Bulletin of Oxford Institute of Statistics,* December, 1954.

B. Worker

Bergson, A. *The Structure of Soviet Wages: A Study in Socialist Economics.* Cambridge, 1944.

Bergson, A. "On Inequality of Incomes in the USSR," *American Slavic and East European Review,* February, 1951.

Brown, Emily Clark. "Labor Relations in Soviet Factories," *Industrial and Labor Relations Review,* January, 1958.

Brown, Emily Clark. "The Local Union in Soviet Industry: Its Relations with Members, Party, and Management," *Industrial and Labor Relations Review,* January, 1960.

Deutscher, Isaac. *Soviet Trade Unions.* New York and London, 1950.

Feldsmesser, R. A. "The Persistence of Status Advantages in Soviet Russia," *American Journal of Sociology,* July, 1953.

Gliksman, Jerzy. "Soviet Labor and the Question of Productivity," *Monthly Labor Review,* June, 1957.

Gliksman, Jerzy. "Recent Trends in Soviet Labor Policy," *Monthly Labor Review,* July, 1956. Also in *Problems of Communism,* July–August, 1956.

Inkeles. A. "Social Stratification and Mobility in the Soviet Union," *American Sociological Review,* August, 1950.

Jasny, Naum. "Labor and Output in Soviet Concentration Camps," *JPE,* October, 1951. Cf. also "Comment," by Redding and "Reply," by Jasny (August, 1952).

Newth, J. A. "Income Distribution in the USSR," *Sov. Stud.,* October, 1960.

Nove, Alec. "The State and the Wage-Earner," *Soviet Survey,* October–December, 1958.

Schwartz, Solomon. *Labor in the Soviet Union.* New York, 1953.

Yanowitch, Murray. "Trends in Soviet Occupational Wage Differentials," *Industrial and Labor Relations Review,* January, 1960.

Yanowitch, Murray. "Trends in Differentials between Salaried Personnel and Wage Workers in Soviet Industry," *Sov. Stud.,* January, 1960.

Yanowitch, Murray. "Changes in the Soviet Money Wage Level since 1940," *American Slavic and East European Review,* April, 1955.

Department of State, *Forced Labor in the Soviet Union.* Publication No. 4716, 1952.

Volin, Lazar. "The Russian Peasant: From Emancipation to Kolkhoz," in *The Transformation of Russian Society,* ed. Cyril Black. Cambridge, 1960.

X. Foreign Trade

Allen, R. L. "Economic Motives in Soviet Foreign Trade Policy," *Southern Economic Journal,* October, 1958.

Allen, Robert L. "An Interpretation of East-West Trade," *Comparisons,* Vol. II.

Ames, E. "International Trade without Markets—the Soviet Bloc," *AER,* December, 1954.

Ames, E. "Integration of European Satellite Economies with the Russian Economy," *Proc. AEA,* May, 1959. Cf. also "Comments," by Spulber.

Ames, E. "The Exchange Rate in Soviet-Type Economies," *RES,* November, 1953.

Aubrey, Henry G. "Sino-Soviet Activities in Less Developed Countries," *Comparisons,* Vol. II.

Baran, P. "The USSR, in the World Economy," in *Foreign Economic Policy for the U. S.,* ed. S. Harris. Cambridge, 1948.

Baykov, Alexander. *Soviet Foreign Trade.* Princeton, 1946.

Berliner, Joseph S. *Soviet Economic Aid.* New York, 1958.

Bornstein, Morris. "The Reform and Revaluation of the Ruble," *AER,* March, 1961.

Dewar, M. *Soviet Trade with Eastern Europe.* New York, 1951.

Gerschenkron, A. *Economic Relations with the USSR.* New York: The Committee on International Economic Policy in Cooperation with the Carnegie Endowment for International Peace, 1943.

Granick, D. "Economic Relations with the U.S.S.R.," in *Resources and Planning in Eastern Europe,* ed. N. J. G. Pounds and N. Spulber. Bloomington, Ind., 1957.

Granick, D. "The Pattern of Foreign Trade in Eastern Europe and its Relation to Economic Development Policy," *QJE,* August, 1954.

Herman, Leon M. "The Recent Economic Foreign Policy of the U.S.S.R.," *Special Publication Series No. 14,* The National Academy of Economics and Political Science.

Hodgman, Donald R. "Soviet Foreign Economic and Technical Assistance," *Soviet Trends,* October 11–12, 1956.

Hoeffding, Oleg. "Recent Trends in Soviet Foreign Trade," *The Annals,* January, 1956.

Mendershausen, Horst. "Terms of Trade Between the Soviet Union and Smaller Communist Countries," *RES,* May, 1959. Cf. also follow-up paper (May, 1960).

Mikesell, Raymond F., and Jack N. Behrman. *Financing Free World Trade with the Sino-Soviet Bloc.* Princeton, 1958.

"State Trading," in *Law and Contemporary Problems,* Spring and Summer 1959. (A symposium on state trading.)

Wycalkowski, Marcin R. "The Soviet Price System and the Ruble Exchange Rate," *IMF Staff Papers*, September, 1950.

Zauberman, A. "Economic Integration: Problems and Prospects," *Problems of Communism*, July–August, 1959.

Zauberman, Alfred. *Economic Imperialism: The Lesson of Eastern Europe*. London, 1955.

XI. Miscellaneous

Blackman, J. H. "Transportation," in *Soviet Economic Growth*, ed. A. Bergson. Evanston, Ill., 1953.

Hunter, Holland. *Soviet Transportation Policy*. Cambridge, 1957.

Hunter, Holland. "Soviet Transportation Policies—A Current Review," *Comparisons*, Vol. I.

Williams, Ernest. "Some Aspects of the Structure and Growth of Soviet Transportation," *Comparisons*, Vol. I.

Williams, Ernest W. "Freight Transportation in the Soviet Union," *Proc. AEA*, May, 1958.

Baykov, Alexander. "The Economic Development of Russia," *Economic History Review*, Vol. VII, No. 2.

Clark, M. Gardner. *The Economics of Soviet Steel*. Cambridge, 1956.

Clark, M. Gardner. "Soviet Iron and Steel Industry: Recent Developments and Prospects," *The Annals*, January, 1956.

Field, Neil. "The Amu Darya: A Study in Resource Geography," *The Geographical Review*, Vol. XLIV, No. 4, 1954.

Shimkin, Demitri. *Minerals: A Key to Soviet Power*. Cambridge, 1953.

XII. Major General Sources

American Bibliography of Slavic and East European Studies, published annually at Indiana University.

Baykov, Alexander. *The Development of the Soviet Economic System*. Cambridge, 1948. The first postwar monograph on the Soviet economy, now largely dated.

Bergson, Abram (ed.), *Soviet Economic Growth*. New York, 1953. The proceedings of a major conference on Soviet growth.

Bergson, A., and S. Kuznets. *Economics of Soviet Industrialization*. Proceedings of a conference held under SSRC sponsorship at Princeton in May, 1961, to be published. This conference emphasized the comparative (with U.S.) approach and contained papers on national income (Bergson), capital formation (Kaplan), industrial production (Powell), agricultural production (Johnson), labor force (Eason), consumption standards (Chapman), foreign trade (Holzman), summary appraisal (Kuznets).

Campbell, Robert. *Soviet Economic Power: Its Organization, Growth and Challenge*. Cambridge, 1960. An excellent and up-to-date one-semester textbook.

Current Digest of the Soviet Press, New York. A weekly culling and translating of important articles from the Soviet press.

Dobb, Maurice. *Soviet Economic Development since 1917*. London, 1948. The second postwar monograph on the Soviet economy, now largely dated, but containing some early historical material still well worth looking at as well as an interesting analytical approach to some Soviet problems.

Economic Survey of Europe, United Nations Economic Commission for Europe, Geneva, published annually. Always contains important and interesting material on recent developments in the Soviet bloc.

Economic Bulletin for Europe, United Nations Economic Commission for Europe, Geneva, published quarterly. Almost always contains important and interesting material on recent developments in the Soviet bloc.

Jasny, Naum. *Soviet Industrialization, 1928–1952*. Chicago, 1961. A newly published study which constitutes the best available economic history of the Soviet Union from 1928 until the death of Stalin.

Joint Economic Committee, Congress of the United States, *Comparisons of the United States and Soviet Economies* (3 vols.). Washington, 1959. This large collection of essays on the Soviet economy comprises the most comprehensive and up-to-date source presently available. The three volumes are purchasable from the Superintendent of Documents of the U. S. Government Printing Office for $1.75.

Problems of Communism, U. S. Dept. of State, Washington, D. C. A quarterly, interdisciplinary journal devoted to Soviet bloc affairs with many excellent nontechnical articles on the Soviet economy.

Problems of Economics, International Arts and Sciences Press, New York. A quarterly journal of translated articles from current Soviet economic journals.

RAND Corporation, Santa Monica, California. A research organization which, among other things, sponsors research on the Soviet economy. These studies are available at major libraries.

Schwartz, Harry. *Russia's Soviet Economy*, New York, 1954. A textbook rapidly becoming dated, but still useful.

Soviet Studies, Glasgow, Scotland. An interdisciplinary quarterly on Soviet affairs with heavy emphasis on economics. The best single journal for current articles on the Soviet economy.

Soviet Survey, London. An interdisciplinary quarterly journal of Soviet bloc affairs containing some good nontechnical articles on the Soviet economy.

World Economic Survey, United Nations Economic Commission for Europe, Geneva, published annually. Always contains recent information on Soviet bloc nations.

APPENDIX:

ERRATA, ADDITIONS,

AND OTHER QUALIFICATIONS[1]

R. CAMPBELL, SECTION I.1
Page 18, line 15 from top for attempt at qualification, *read* attempt at quantification.

M. DOBB, SECTION II.4
Referring to the sentence which ends at the top of page 139, Professor Dobb appends the following footnote:
"I have modified this opinion (as well as some other statements in the same paragraph) and would like to substitute for it the view that, in order to make it profitable for enterprises to take decisions about methods of production that were conducive to maximizing growth, it was desirable: (a) that price-levels in the two sectors should be built according to a uniform principle; (b) that in *both* cases a rate of profit should be included and be derived from the rate of profit or surplus which in the consumer goods sector is a function of the rate of investment; (c) that a profits-tax should be substituted for a turnover tax (in the case both of capital goods and consumer goods) as the means of diverting into the Budget that part of the surplus which is attributable to investment (though *not* that part of it which is attributable to 'social consumption'). See Chapter VI of the writer's *Essay on Economic Growth and Planning* (London and New York, 1960), esp. pp. 95–97."

A. ERLICH, SECTION III.1
Page 85, fn. 4. for vosstanovleniiu, *read* vosproizvodstvu.
Page 85, fn. 5: Professor Erlich's unpublished Ph.D. thesis referred to has since been published and is listed in the Bibliography in Section III.

A. NOVE, SECTION IV.A.1
Professor Nove writes.
"This article was written late in 1955, and naturally could not take

[1] All page numbers refer to original publications.

into account the many developments in structure, ideas, and statistical publication which have occurred since that date. In particular, the figures cited, for illustrative purposes, on the relative magnitudes of the American and Soviet output certainly overstated the latter."

D. G. Johnson and A. Kahan, Section IV.D.1

Page 214, Table 10; Data for 1937 are for collective farms.

Page 214, footnote 16, first line: Table 10 should be Table 11.

Page 215, Table 11; Data for state farms for 1957 are in man-hours, not man-days.

Page 225, Table 15; Headings should be:

| Hogs | Milk[2] | Other livestock | Inventory | Total | Horses | Total |

(million tons of feeds units)

F. D. Holzman, Section VIII.1

A better framework for discussing the data in Table 2 is contained in my article on Soviet inflation reprinted in Section VIII. See pages 177 (bottom line) –79.

L. Turgeon, Section IX.1

Page 324, paragraph 3, line 11: for more proportionately read more than proportionately.

Page 325, line 1: for any read many.

Page 336, Table IV, col. 4: for price of postage, $10.00 read .10.

E. C. Brown, Section IX.4

Professor Brown writes:

"The principles of the Soviet labor market remain essentially the same in 1960–61 as they were in 1955–56, although administration was changed by the replacement of ministries by regional economic councils in 1957, and by broad authority given the State Committee on Labor and Wages for the wage systems. (pp. 181–85). A country-wide wage reform,[2] begun in 1956 and not entirely completed in 1961, has attempted to make wage differentials more rational and more effective as a means of distributing the labor force, between areas, industries, and levels of skill. Freedom to choose and to change jobs has been further extended since the repeal of the 1940 laws (pp. 197–98). Since January 1, 1960, workers who change jobs no longer lose the right to temporary disability benefits for a period, and they retain their record of uninterrupted service if they take a new job within one month.[3] There is apparently less pressure upon young graduates to take the jobs offered them by the state and work there for a given number of years (pp. 191–92), and the law now authorizes enterprises to hire a young specialist without an order directing him to work, when he has a certificate granting him the opportunity to find his own job.[4] A problem of the necessary redistribution of workers

[2] Discussed by Walter Galenson and E. C. Brown in *Proceedings of the Industrial Relations Research Association,* December, 1960.

[3] *Vedemosti Verkhovnovo Soveta SSSR,* No. 4 (998), January 28, 1960, as translated in *Current Digest of the Soviet Press,* February 24, 1960, p. 24.

[4] N. G. Aleksandrov, *Sovetskoe Trudovoe Pravo,* 1959, p. 190.

displaced by mechanization and automation is receiving attention. Calls for improved planning for the 'balance of labor' and for finding jobs for displaced workers have been frequent in recent years, and a number of writers have argued for more legal guaranties for the protection of 'the right to work' of such workers.["]

F. D. HOLZMAN, SECTION X.2.

Page 431, top paragraph: A later and more comprehensive estimate of the value of the ruble in 1937 leads me to believe that the 1936 devaluation eliminated overvaluation of producers' goods as a whole with the exception of petroleum and products. Consumers' goods, of course, were still overvalued.

Page 431, bottom paragraph: A recent source makes it possible to estimate that Soviet export prices rose between 1950 and 1956 by 8 per cent rather than 20 per cent.

Pages 433–34: My attempt to compare the export subsidy to foreign trade combines with the budgeted subsidy figure failed to take account of the fact that some combines both export and import and in their dealings with the budget net out the profits on imports against subsidies on exports.

Page 439, last paragraph: It is stated that imports of consumers' goods amount to less than 3 per cent of the value of consumers' goods sold domestically. A Soviet source claims that in 1957 imports amounted to more than 10 per cent of domestic sales of consumers' goods.

[5] See E. C. Brown, "A Note on Employment and Unemployment in the Soviet Union in the Light of Technical Progress," *Soviet Studies*, XII (January, 1961), 231–40.

PRINTED IN U.S.A.